darina allen's ballymaloe cooking school cookbook

with photographs by ray main

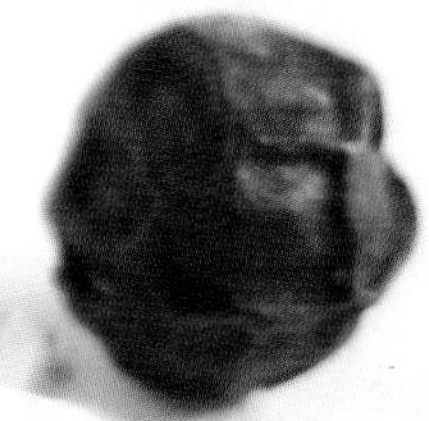

pelican publishing company

Gretna 2002

for Myrtle Allen

acknowledgements

Running the cooking school has been a wonderful voyage of discovery during which many, many people, including my students, have contributed to my culinary knowledge. The school started with the inspiration of my parents-in-law, Ivan and Myrtle Allen, and the support of many friends, including my brother Rory O'Connell, Pauline and Neil O'Kennedy, and of course my own dear mother, Elizabeth O'Connell.

When students do a 12-week Certificate course here at the Cookery School, they leave with 7 or 8 3-inch binders full of recipes, notes, and information on food-related subjects. This book is an attempt to condense this under the covers of one book – an impossible task given that if it was the size it should be, one would need a wheelbarrow to get it into the kitchen.

Despite the fact that I have written eleven cookbooks, I still cannot type or use a word processor so I am deeply indebted to Adrienne Forbes who has labored tirelessly to decipher my writing, and corrected and recorrected each draft. A special thanks also to Anne Morrissey and Rosalie Dunne who have kept the show on the road while Adrienne and I struggled to finish. We are enormously grateful for the help of Margot Heskin, Truss Boelhouwer-Grifhorst, and Marianne Jongma, who supported us particularly in the final weeks when the pressure was really on. We are also grateful to my team of teachers and assistants who tested the recipes and regularly suggested a tweak here and there as they listened to students' questions or observed their pitfalls in the kitchen due to insufficient explanation on my part. A heartfelt thank you to my garden angels and my farm manager, who are responsible for the farm and gardens and the abundance of wonderful fresh produce throughout the seasons.

A very special thank you to the many guest chefs who have delighted us over the years. Each one has added to our repertoire and shared their knowledge and passion with us. Some of their recipes have been reproduced in this book; I am deeply grateful for their generosity. Influences have come from many people and we have tried to attribute wherever possible; please forgive us for those we have inadvertently overlooked.

My greatest debt of gratitude must surely go to my mother-in-law, Myrtle Allen, who pioneered the style of cooking for which Ballymaloe is now famous.

A special thank you also to Mary Dowey who contributed to the excellent wine section and for her stoic editorial help in the early days of this book. Huge thanks to my dear and special friend, Julia Wight, who conspired with my publisher, Kyle Cathie, to lock me into the drawing room of her London home so that this book would eventually be "finished". She lavished me with lots of T.L.C., rich dark coffee, verbena tea, and her delicious food, for which I am truly grateful. And to my agent, Jacqueline Korn, who has encouraged me at every turn.

A big hug for Janie Suthering, who cooked the food for Ray Main's delicious photographs. My editors Helen Woodhall, Sheila Davies, Stephanie Horner, Elaine Koster, and James Bridgeman, along with Esme West, Sarah Epton, and the Americanizer Delora Jones, have literally worked from dawn till dusk to lick this manuscript into shape. With quite inspirational dedication and forbearance my publisher, Kyle Cathie, has had to use all her physical endurance and psychology to keep each and every one of us on track – most authors I know endlessly moan about their publishers – I am full of admiration for my publisher – she is truly heroic.

Last but not least my thanks go to my family and my long-suffering husband, Tim, who not only runs the school with me but continues to support me every step of the way, for which I am truly grateful.

contents

introduction

Ballymaloe Cookery School was founded in 1983, and our philosophy has always been to cook fresh, locally produced food in season. We cook it simply, to enhance the natural flavors so that it looks and tastes delicious.

Myrtle Allen was my inspiration; she is a woman with no time for cans and packaged food, and I feel deeply fortunate that our paths have crossed in life. When I graduated from hotel school in Dublin in the late sixties, you could just about count the number of good restaurants in Ireland on one hand, with a finger or two left over. The top restaurants didn't want a woman in the kitchens. Most of the really good restaurants wrote the menu when they opened, and it was the same 10 years later. Myrtle was different; she wrote the menu for Ballymaloe House Hotel everyday, which was seen as an amateurish thing to do. It seemed logical to her to use what was best and freshest in the garden, as well as the fresh fish that came in on the boats at Ballycotton. I was impressed by what I heard about this farmer's wife who cooked with the seasons in the wilds of East Cork. I sent off a letter and was offered a job in Myrtle's kitchens. The first person I met when I arrived was Timmy, her son, to whom I am now married.

When I came to Ballymaloe I was excited going into work each day. I was like a sponge, soaking up all the new information. Myrtle made me realize the importance of good quality produce. I could see quite clearly that to cook good produce by simple techniques made great dishes. Myrtle continues to be an inspiration and, if I have a problem or if there's an issue I want advice about, I will still to this day go and chat to Myrtle and get her reaction. She is a pioneer, and I often think that I have got some of the credit for many of the things she has achieved. Myrtle has always been delighted with the opportunities offered to me and her support and encouragement have meant that I

have been able to go on and do other things. We now work together to champion the cause of the small artisan-producers. We try to stimulate debate about food policies that we see as unsustainable, or hygiene regulations that are out of proportion to the risks involved – these threaten the very existence of some of the food producers on whom we totally depend for the quality of produce that we need to produce the food for which Ballymaloe has now become famous. Many of the recipes in this book are recipes that Myrtle originally taught me in Ballymaloe kitchen and we now pass them on to our students at the school.

The original purpose of Ballymaloe Cookery School was to keep the roof over our heads. When we married, Tim was a horticulturalist with a mushroom farm, orchards, and acres of heated greenhouses growing tomatoes, cucumbers, and lettuces. In the late seventies and early eighties, farming was becoming more difficult, there was the oil crisis and 25% inflation. We needed to find a different way to earn a living. We decided to open a cooking school in our farm buildings. I loved cooking and developed a real passion for sharing my knowledge and taking the mystery out of cooking.

There are two 12-week courses each year, from January to March and September to December, and a whole range of short courses from 1 day to a week on all types of topics. We teach an extensive range of cooking techniques: butchery, fish filleting, preserving, freezing, ethnic cooking, and so on. There are lectures on menu-planning, food costing, food hygiene, and career advice. We have olive oil and wine tastings, teaching how to serve and appreciate wines, and to choose wines to go with a meal. We cover breads, pub grub, entertaining, barbecuing, food for celiacs, new trends, buffets, vegetarian... In recent years we have extended our repertoire to include organic gardening and seed saving as well as basket-making, flower painting, and even aromatherapy and the Alexander Technique. In the autumn we teach the students to forage and hunt mushrooms. We also do courses on catering management, courses for Dads and daughters and Mums and sons – the list goes on...

Students now come from the four corners of the earth. We welcome all students who have a passion for food and really want to learn, who are prepared to work hard for three busy months, during which we will take them from "this is a wooden spoon" to being able to earn their living from cooking. On the first day we introduce them to our gardeners, Susan, Eileen, and Haulie, who will produce much of what they will cook during their 12-week stay. I show them a barrow full of rich soil and run my hands through the soil saying, "Remember, this is where it all starts, in the good earth, and if you don't have clean fertile soil you won't have good food or pure water." Some of them look askance at this eccentric gray-haired hippy woman with a mission, as I tell them about the millions of organisms and bacteria all working away underground to enrich the soil; denatured soil doesn't have the essential minerals and trace elements we need in our food.

We walk through the gardens, past the herbs, vegetables, and fruits, down to the compost heap, close to the hen house. Here they get their first recipe – how to make compost. I want them to see it all as part of a cycle starting in the good earth. Susan, our head gardener, who trained at the Henry Doubleday Research Association's organic center, talks them through the theory of making compost. Later they will go harvesting with the gardeners – a valuable way of learning how and when to harvest food. Trimmings and scraps from their cooking go either into the stock pot or to the hens or else into the composting bin. The scraps that go to the hens come back as eggs a few days later; what goes to the compost bin is returned to enrich the soil, and the stock pot creates the basis for many wonderful soups, stews, and sauces. We teach them to respect and value the work of the gardeners and to appreciate how long it takes to grow good food – they won't dare to boil the hell out of a carrot when they realize it's taken three months to grow. They begin to see everything is inter-connected and part of a holistic cycle, and to think about how things can be recycled beneficially. After we've had our composting lesson, we walk from there to the reed bed, past the gardens and the pastures where the Kerry cows, Herefords, and Shorthorn cattle graze contentedly. We come around the corner to see the Saddleback pigs foraging, and from there to the greenhouses, where Susan and Eileen show them how to sow seeds. For me this is a very important initiation to the course – I know of no better way to give people a respect for food than for them to plant a seed and to watch it grow. Each and every student gets a broccoli or lettuce plant which they

'Remember this is where it all starts, in the good earth, and if you don't have clean fertile soil you won't have good food or pure water.'

label and sow in the greenhouse, and during the next twelve weeks they watch it grow. Farmers and people who grow their food get disheartened when people don't respect their efforts; they understandably want people to appreciate the energy, passion, and hard work that have gone into growing the food. And suddenly the students realize why...

Different cooking schools have different philosophies, and because ours is residential, it seemed logical to teach in meals. Instead of doing a whole lesson on boiling techniques or making soufflés, each day we cook through a menu and incorporate the techniques, working from basic principles to advanced professional techniques – people learn to cook almost without realizing it. We aim to take people from how to boil water to how to give a dinner party in a one-week introductory course. There is a demonstration every afternoon after which the students taste what's been cooked so that, when they cook it themselves the following morning, they know what they're aiming for. At lunchtime students and teachers all sit down together to enjoy the fruits of the morning's labor. It may come as a surprise that many students lose weight rather than gaining it, though you can put it on, particularly if you visit the pub every night!

Since I started the cooking school 18 years ago, I've become increasingly concerned about how our food is produced and where it comes from. Whether we like it or not, we are going to be forced to think about the disastrous consequences of pushing animals and plants further and further beyond their natural limits. There is an indisputable link between disease and excessively intensive factory farming. BSE (bovine spongiform encephalopathy) is the obvious example, as well as stronger and stronger strains of salmonella, camphylobacter, e-coli, and so on. I welcome the fact that these issues have stimulated many strong debates among the students about how our food is produced, and increased in them the demand for a new way forward.

One of the great joys for me through the years has been to pick up the phone and invite some of the people I've admired most to come and teach at the school as guest chefs: John Ash, Rick Bayless, Wasinee Beech, Frances Bissell, John Desmond, Ursula Ferrigno, Rose Gray, Jane Grigson, Sophie Grigson, Marcella Hazan, Deh-ta Hsiung, Madhur Jaffrey, Alastair Little, Naranjan McCormack, Kevin Orbell McSean, Rory O'Connell, Seamus O'Connell, Sri Owen, Ada Parasiliti, Paul and Jeanne Rankin, Alicia Rios-Ivars, Claudia Roden, Ruth Rogers, Nina Simonds, Rick Stein, Julia Wight, Anne Willan and Antony Worrall-Thompson have all inspired us with their enormous dedication and enthusiasm, and contributed to our repertoire.

Many people have influenced me and contributed to my culinary knowledge thus far. My own mother, Elizabeth O'Connell, taught me how to cook as I pulled at her apron strings. I thought everybody's mother cooked every day but not until I got to Dublin did I realize that was not so. Aunt Florence pedalled down on her bike before electricity came to our village, with a block of ice-cream wrapped in wet newspaper and wafers, and etched in my mind is the first lesson she gave me in how to make raspberry buns, crumpets, or drop scones. My brother Rory O'Connell, now head chef at Ballymaloe House, worked with me in the school in the early days. He has always been tremendously supportive and generous with ideas and suggestions. Myrtle, of course, has been the biggest influence. And then there are the books of Elizabeth David, Jane Grigson, Margaret Costa, and of course, Alice Waters, with whose whole philosophy I completely identify; she's had the courage to motivate and inspire a whole generation of cooks, and worked with farmers and food producers to bond producers and chefs. Over the years people have been so generous – cooking schools the world over have opened their doors to me. I have been able to keep abreast of international food trends through my travel and meeting my colleagues at the conferences of the organizations of which I am a member – Slow Food, I.A.C.P., and Euro Toque. Through the years I have forged strong friendships with colleagues who share my commitment to culinary education.

On the twelve-week course, students can go into the kitchens at Ballymaloe House in the evenings to watch the chefs; some do, some don't. Often they are amazed to see the chefs using exactly the same recipes as we use in the school. We pool knowledge and share ideas. Ballymaloe is unique because their chefs have always followed recipes there – other chefs may think that's not macho. Years ago chefs did apprenticeships for five to six years and honed their palates; nowadays staff move about so quickly that it's essential to have a repertoire of tried and tested recipes so that trainees can get consistent results. Trainee chefs and cooks start off by following the recipes faithfully and, when they become more skilled and confident, they use their own creativity to introduce their own twists. One of the great mysteries of life is that every day all the students see the same demonstration. The following morning they all have the same ingredients and yet each day all the dishes taste different.

Having the school right in the middle of a farm close to the sea is a huge bonus. We have our own gardens so we can grow a lot of our own food and what we don't produce ourselves we source locally. The gardens and the farm are organic because I am passionately interested in healthy wholesome food. We get wonderful fresh fish from the boats at Ballycotton, and local farmers' wives rear for us chickens, ducks, geese, and turkeys, all free-range. The farm across the road produces wonderful soft fruit and rhubarb when ours run out, and delicious potatoes. Local fishsmokers and farmhouse cheesemakers add to the bounty. When Nora Ahearne delivers her free-range ducks, we introduce her to the students and say this is the person who reared those wonderful ducks for you – getting the students to focus on who produces the food and the quality. When our local butcher, Michael Cuddigan, comes, he shares his knowledge and long expertise as a third-generation butcher.

shopping

It sounds extraordinary but in reality about 80% of good food is about shopping, so the fundamental message we need to get across to our students is the importance of putting time and effort into sourcing good-quality ingredients. If one starts off with good, fresh, naturally-produced food in season, one needs to do so little to make it taste good. If, on the other hand, the basis of the meal is mass-produced denatured food, which has travelled hundreds or even thousands of miles, one needs to be a magician to make it taste good. This is where the chefs need to use all their wizardry to camouflage the original lack of flavor.

People who want their food wrapped in plastic or on styrofoam trays are very well catered for; they can find everything they want in our shops or supermarkets. Sourcing fresh local food in season though can be much more of a challenge. In fact, the problem has been exacerbated in recent years as supermarkets have adopted a central distribution system for food as well as dry goods.

Not everyone, of course, has a vegetable garden although more and more people seem to be getting hooked on the magic of planting even a few tomato plants or herbs. The next best thing is to head for your local farmers' market. At last the market culture is spreading across the UK and Ireland. I started a farmers' market in our local town of Midleton last year and it has continued to gather momentum. At these markets one can buy fresh local seasonal food directly from the producer. Farmers' markets, though gathering momentum, are still few and far between so for most people the option is the local store or supermarket.

- Note the variety and source when buying vegetables and fruit.
- Ask questions about the breed and name of the producers of meat and poultry.
- Seek out free-range organic produce wherever possible.
- Demand traceability.
- Look carefully for signs of deterioration, remember that perfectly shaped does not necessarily mean best flavor.

• Buy with the seasons.
• Taste whenever possible, be observant and uncompromising in your pursuit of quality.
• Demand that irradiated food is identified and labeled clearly

Remember top-quality, health-giving food comes at a price – at present much of the food we buy is unrealistically cheap because of the demands of the supermarket and our unreasonable assumption that cheap food is our right. The repercussions of this situation have forced many farmers and food producers to either go out of business or intensify further. We are all losers in this situation. Research clearly shows that an ever more intensive production system contributes to the spread of diseases and often results in less good-quality food.

local food

It makes no kind of sense to buy expensive imported food that has traveled for thousands of miles. Buy fresh local food, which tastes better and is often less expensive. Think *local*, the buzzword for the future. In some countries local produce is not as valued as it should be; there even seems to be an idea that imported food is superior whereas local food is looked on as something to be sold off cheaply. As far as I am concerned, local food wins hands down over food that's traveled thousands of miles. Nag all the local shops to identify the local produce on their shelves, to encourage people to buy it just as they do in the markets in Italy, where local produce is marked "nostrano". Italians really have their priorities right – they are prepared to pay more for local food because they know it will be fresher and better and, of course, seasonal.

Occasionally people in the school say to me: "Darina, get real, where are people going to get food of this quality again? Shouldn't you just be using normal food from the supermarket?" My response is that it's really important to cook with the best-quality produce so that students can build up a taste memory against which to measure flavors when they leave the school – something to aim for when they're cooking in the future. When the students are with us for twelve weeks they quickly appreciate this fundamental point – when they leave the school they not only make a determined effort to find the same quality of produce but also, many of them at least, start to grow their own herbs and vegetables. Some even keep their own hens because they can't imagine life without fresh eggs and feeding the hens. For those who are going into the restaurant or catering business, we encourage them to set up a network of small local producers just as we have done here so that they can get locally grown food with real traceablility. This has a double benefit – not only do they know where the food comes from and how it is produced but they are also supporting their local community and thereby generating goodwill for their own business.

After 12 weeks at the cookery school, the students shop in a different way; not as robots throwing something into the basket, walking zombie-like through the aisles. They start to look for ingredients and note varieties, think in seasons, buy fresh and local produce. They learn which varieties of apples, plums, and cherries to buy again. Don't bother to buy tasteless irradiated strawberries or French beans flown from the other side of the world in winter. At the beginning of this century we realized how important this was, but with the advent of the supermarket we have taken to buying out of season. Chinese herbal medicine has shown us how valuable it is to eat warming foods in winter and cooling foods in summer; they advise us not to eat tomatoes and cucumbers, with their chilling qualities, in mid-winter.

Food for the future

Ballymaloe food is only special because of the quality of the ingredients we have from the farmers and producers around us. If we were working with denatured food there wouldn't be any point of difference. My message to our Government and those who have the power to determine future policy, is to realize that the future of Irish agriculture and tourism will depend on us producing top-quality, naturally-produced food. After all, Ireland with its clean, green image seems to be the obvious country to lead the way in Europe in organic production. Already our image leads people to expect naturally-produced, clean, safe food from the country which Bord Bia (the Irish Food Board) so proudly promotes as "Ireland – Food Island". What is needed at this point is a visionary in government who can see sustainable agriculture as the way forward for Ireland. Take for example the Irish farmhouse cheese industry. It's a tiny industry that has had an impact far out of proportion to its size; the quality of its cheese has helped in no small way to change the image of Irish food abroad.We also need to appreciate and support and protect and cherish the small artisan-producers who labor with passion and very often not much financial reward. We also need to encourage and support farmers who want to farm in a less intensive way and then we, as consumers, need to pay the price that they need to produce the quality of food that we say we want.

why cook?

It's cool to cook

One of the exciting things for me at the moment is realizing how many young people are seeing it as cool to cook. Isaac, our son, says some of his friends who wouldn't have been "caught dead" in a kitchen until recently are now desperate to learn how to cook. It's hip to entertain casually and whip up a little feast. No need for matching cutlery or fancy place settings – cooking is a social occasion. Get your friends involved in shelling the fava beans, cooking together, and having fun. This trend owes a lot to young British TV stars, such as Nigella Lawson and Jamie Oliver, who've made it cool to cook. An interesting phenomenon, the most hip thing of all is growing your own food, and then sharing and cooking it with your friends.

Why is it so important to be able to cook?

To many people cooking is an unimportant skill: why would you bother to take time out to learn to cook when you could be furthering your career or having fun in the pub? Not surprisingly, I would argue that it's hugely important to learn how to cook, for lots of different reasons. Not least because so much depends on the food we eat – our health, our energy, our vitality, our ability to concentrate... We can't do much about our genes but we can take responsibility for our own health by controlling the food we eat. Health goes in through our mouths, and my father in law, Ivan, always used to say, our brains, too.

If you can't cook you are at the mercy of other people for what you eat, and if you are fortunate enough to have delicious, healthy, wholesome food cooked for you, you're one in a million. Otherwise, the only alternative is to drop into the local deli, buy ready-prepared meals, or make regular trips to restaurants which will prove to be an expensive business. When you can cook, it doesn't matter where you are in the world, you can gather a few ingredients together and whip up a little meal for yourself and your friends. It's certainly the easiest way to win friends and influence people. I remember once when I was staying with friends in America; I made them a loaf of soda bread, and while it was cooking, whipped up a little raspberry jam from a punnet of raspberries in the fridge – they thought I was a complete magician. In the end, the way to everyone's heart is through their tummy – no matter how beautiful you are they soon get fed up with burnt sausages and leathery hamburgers. I always tell doctors, pilots, priests, and anyone who'll listen, how important it is to take time out to learn how to cook, because no matter what else you do, every day we all need to eat. Learn some cooking skills and take control of your life.

taste, taste, and taste again

I can't stress enough the importance of tasting continually as you cook. It doesn't matter if you've been cooking all your life, remember the ingredients literally change every day. You need to taste at the beginning, in the middle, and at the end. When cooking, think about flavor and, as you cook, imagine yourself eating it and that will help you get the proportions right. Always season with your fingers and never with a spoon, because then you are in touch, and you are more likely to get the quantity right. Here I stress, taste, taste, taste. Carrots taste hugely different at different times of the year – in early spring they need more seasoning. In early summer when just pulled from the ground, they are meltingly delicious, just boiled for a very few minutes and tossed in a little butter and freshly ground black pepper and salt. Here at the school one of the experiments we do to illustrate the importance of sourcing is to cook two pans of carrots side by side, by exactly the same method. One pan contains freshly pulled carrots which arrived with the soil still on, and the other contains pre-washed carrots that came in a plastic bag. Try this yourself – taste and learn from the flavor.

Tasting helps to develop your palate and build up your taste memory. Take every opportunity when you eat out or when you travel abroad to taste foods at source. Taste the ingredients as they are meant to be and then, when you find them at home, you will be able to judge whether they are of good quality. One of the most difficult things for a beginner in the kitchen is to judge whether more seasoning is needed or not. If in doubt, follow the advice that Myrtle gave me years ago, when I was in doubt about a soup, to take out a little bit in a cup, add some seasoning, and if that improves the flavor, season the whole pot.

herbs & spices

Fresh herbs add magic to your cooking. In fact, now that I think about it, they are absolutely essential to the flavor of Ballymaloe food. If you don't have access to fresh herbs in your garden or local store, it's time to think about a little gardening. You don't even need a garden – a window box on the windowsill or a wooden tub on the balcony is all you need. Get started with parsley, either flat-leaf or curly or both, add chives, then perennial mint. French tarragon, lemon balm, annual marjoram, dill, fennel, the list is endless... Herbs have been used both as food and medicine since man first walked on this earth. More recently, the interest in herbs has gathered momentum not only among cooks and chefs but also among those who are interested in pursuing a healthier lifestyle and exploring herbal remedies and alternative medicines.

Spices too are essential. Having a few jars of fresh spices on your shelves is like having a Pandora's box to dip into when the fancy takes you. As a general rule, buy spices whole, with the possible exception of turmeric and ginger when making things such as gingerbread. Whole spices have infinitely more flavor than ground. As soon as spices are ground, the flavor starts to tick away, so use them as quickly as possible.

proportion

Proportion is important yet it is one of the most difficult things to get right. There's a little trick that helps – imagine yourself eating it and you are more likely to get it right. Don't drown a dish with too much sauce or skimp with too little. It's strange how rare it is to get a sandwich with the right amount of filling.

There are many reasons to get the portion size right:

1 Many of us dislike getting too much to eat on our plates. It causes the dilemma of being rude leaving food behind and, in my case, I have real problems if I leave food, because my host immediately thinks that it wasn't good. There's the eternal dilemma of trying to slip it into my handbag or eating more than I want.

2 People leave it behind and it's wasted.

3 It makes no sense for restaurants to give over-large helpings because their guests will be too full to order a dessert. Serve reasonable-sized helpings; at Ballymaloe we serve slightly on the small side, with a table d'hôte menu with five courses, plus cheese and coffee with petit fours.

4 In America, the helpings have become obscenely enormous; what used to be large a couple of years ago has been doubled into super-helpings. Obesity is growing – over 50 per cent of the American population is classified as obese and in Ireland, it's 10 per cent and rising. Consequently, our portions are slightly on the small side, but every diner is offered seconds.

I've generally tried to give the amounts for average portions throughout this book. In general we multiply up quite faithfully when taking a recipe for 4 and cooking it for a party of 24, except for the butter. For 48 people, use a recipe and multiply by 5 rather than 8 and reduce the butter and cream a bit.

family meals

Changes in lifestyle have led to an inevitable loss of family meals. As the grab, gobble, and go culture gathers momentum, we have more dashboard dining, TV meals, and now we're promised microwaves in cars in no time. If we stop to think about it, many of our happiest childhood recollections are connected with sharing food around the kitchen table. This is what memories are made of. Nowadays, with everybody's busy lifestyle it takes a real effort, but it is vital to understand how important it is to hang on to the tradition of eating together. It might not be possible every day but make a pledge to sit down together at least twice a week. Even if there are arguments, everyone is still communicating which has to be good! Cooking together is fun, get everyone involved in the chopping, peeling, grating – bonding over the cooker. Many people find cooking relaxing after a busy day. Keep it simple. It doesn't have to be a feast, maybe just a boiled egg and fresh soda bread – and get the damn TV out of the kitchen!

at the table

Students lay the table for lunch at the school each day. The place setting depends on the menu and the number of courses. The basic setting is a fork and two knives. Add a dessert spoon – and for pie you'll need a fork, too. If the main course is meat or steak you may want to lay a serrated knife. For fish, the more traditional fish knives and forks have now been largely dropped from modern place settings.

For dessert, the spoon and fork can go above the place setting with the fork underneath and its handle to the left, and the spoon on top with its handle to the right.

The soup spoon goes on the outside right-hand side. The butter knife should be laid either on the place setting or directly on to the side plate. In more formal place settings, the fork and spoon are usually laid as part of the place setting because, as our moms always told us, "always work from the outside in". In that case, the bread knife will be on the outside. Don't get too bothered about all this but at least try to have a fork and two knives. Glasses – normally the water glass is laid closest to the knife tip, then the white wine glass, then the red wine glass either in a triangle or a line. If there is a whole line of glasses laid in front of your place, you know you're in for a good night!

Table manners – a few guidelines

Break bread rolls rather than cutting them. Tilt the bowl away from you when eating soup from an old-fashioned, wide soup plate. Leaving your fork and knife crossed in the center of your plate indicates that you haven't finished – when placed together in the center of the plate, this indicates you've finished. Don't pick up your potato on a fork and peel it obviously; do this discreetly. Once upon a time, instead of being allowed to ask for salt and pepper, one had to offer it to one's neighbor and hopefully they would realize that you actually needed it yourself. And then of course there's afternoon tea manners, but that's more for history books. Always try to be considerate and anticipate your neighbors' needs.

Serve a finger bowl with foods that need to be eaten with the fingers, for example corn on the cob, quail, whole shrimp or artichokes. Fill a small bowl with warm water and add a segment of lemon, and rose petals if you want. When you have finished nibbling the delicious morsels, dip your fingers into the bowl and dry discreetly on your napkin. And of course don't speak with your mouth full. Many a sophisticated elegantly-dressed person lets themselves down with bad manners. And don't put your elbows on the table until you're an auntie! Be restrained and don't pile one food on top of another – it's an insult to the cook to be overly greedy and then leave food on the plate.

Clearing the table

Don't clear the table until everyone's finished eating. Clear from the left and serve from the right. Clear discreetly. Hold the plate on your hand resting on the three middle fingers, secured by the thumb and little finger; place the fork upside down and slide the knife underneath. Place the next plate on your wrist where palm meets arm, and stack plates there. Clear debris discreetly to the lower plate. Stack up to 3 or 4 plates.

store cupboard basics

Busy people who want to be able to whizz up meals in minutes will need to ensure that their store cupboard is always well stocked. The following are some suggestions for items that we find invaluable.

Store Cupboard

Onions
Garlic
Potatoes
Eggs, from free-range hens, if possible
Carrots
Flour: all-purpose, self-rising, wholewheat bread, white bread, stone-ground wholewheat
Oatmeal
Pasta: noodles, macaroni, shells, penne
Grains: couscous, bulgar, quinoa
Rice: basmati, Thai fragrant
Canned fish: sardines, tuna fish, anchovies
Canned corn
Canned tomatoes
Olives
Canned beans: chickpeas, flageolets, kidney beans, black-eyed peas
Butter
Sharp Cheddar Cheese, Parmesan cheese
Chicken stock/cube
Extra-virgin olive oil
Peanut and sunflower oil
Red and white wine vinegar
English mustard powder
French mustard
Maldon Sea Salt or kosher salt
Harissa or Chili sauce
Some whole spices, e.g., coriander, cardamom, nutmeg, cumin, cloves
Good-quality chocolate
Nuts: hazelnuts, walnuts, almonds
Dried fruit, especially apricots
Homemade jam
Good-quality honey
Marmalade
Tortillas (in the freezer)
Pita bread (in the freezer)
Crackers or Carr's Water Biscuits
Ballymaloe Tomato Relish
Ballymaloe Jalapeño Relish
Soy sauce (preferably Kikkoman)
Nam pla (fish sauce)
Oyster sauce
Plum sauce
Sesame oil
Pesto
Tapenade
Salami
Chorizo

A Few Treats

Patum Peperium (Gentleman's Relish)
Panneforte di Sienna
Truffle Oil
Salted Capers

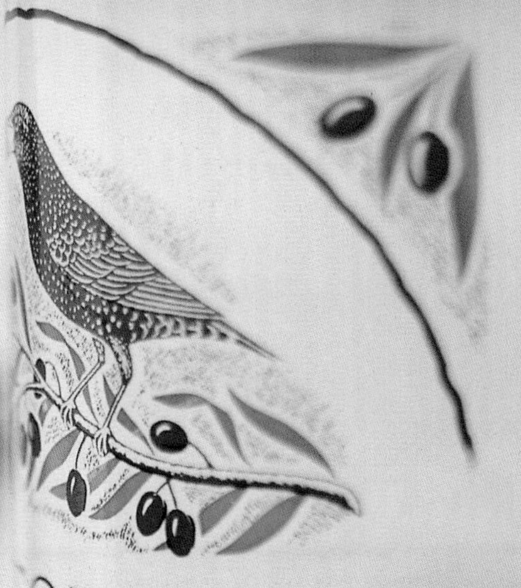
ORNEI
RGIN OLIVE
IC FARMING
System
organically grown
Olives
VEA S.A.
SPAIN
ML. (25.3 FL.OZ.)

essential kitchen equipment

Knives

1 set of knives: buy the best you can afford
1 chopping knife (cook's or chef's knife)
1 filleting knife
1 vegetable or fruit paring knife
1 serrated vegetable or fruit knife
1 carving knife and 1 carving fork
1 large and 1 small pastry spatula

Tools

1 swivel-top peeler
1 butcher's steel
1 melon baller (not essential but handy)
1 zester (not essential but handy)
1 meat thermometer (not essential but handy)
1 skewer
1 stainless steel grater
2 mesh strainers (1 tin or stainless steel, 1 plastic)
1 bottle opener
1 cork screw
1 perforated spoon
4 wooden spoons (2 large, 1 small, 1 straight ended to get into corners of pans)
2 plastic spatulas to use in food preparation (1 large, 1 small)
1 metal spatula and 1 heat-proof plastic spatula to use in stovetop cooking
2 whisks (1 coil, 1 balloon)
2 flat pastry brushes
1 pastry bag and set of nozzles (not essential but handy)
1 potato masher
1 ladle
1 rolling pin
1 pepper mill
1 salt crock (not essential but handy)

Measuring spoons

1 teaspoon
1 tablespoon

We measure with ordinary spoons that most people have in their kitchen drawers. Unless otherwise stated we measure in rounded spoonfuls – a rounded spoonful has exactly the same amount on top as underneath. A heaped teaspoon has as much of the ingredient as the spoon will hold. A level teaspoon is just that and is the equivalent of a half rounded teaspoon. If you are using standard measuring spoons, always use level measurements. Our rounded measurements are the exact equivalent of a level measuring spoon. Also note that our tablespoon is the equivalent of four teaspoons whereas a standard measuring spoon holds just three teaspoons.

Boards

2 heavy wooden cutting boards
1 small garlic board (not essential but handy)

Mark the boards so that you know which surface to use. Of the first board, mark one side for raw meat and the other side for onions. Of the second board, mark one side for cooked food and the other side for fruit.

If you have just one chopping board, mark one side R for raw and O for onion and garlic, and the other side C for cooked food, and F for fruit.

Saucepans

Buy the best heavy stainless steel saucepans you can afford. Some have a 50-year guarantee and you will be able to pass them onto your grandchildren. They don't burn or stick and do wonders for your cooking and your temper!

1 large saucepan and lid
1 medium saucepan and lid
1 small saucepan and lid
1 large sauté pan
1 small sauté pan
1 small saucepan (for boiling eggs, not essential but handy)
1 large casserole dish with lid
1 oval casserole dish with lid
1 small oval casserole dish with lid
1 non-stick frying pan
1 cast-iron pan
1 grill-pan

Pans

1 quiche pan with removable bottom (size to fit requirements)
1 tart pan (size to fit requirements)
1 jelly roll pan

Bowls

1 set 5 stainless steel mixing bowls, graded sizes
1 set of 3 Pyrex bowls, graded sizes
3–4 plastic bowls
1 Pyrex plate for tarts (not essential but handy)
1 pie dish
2 Pyrex measuring cups

Machines

1 juicer (electric, if possible, for large quantities)
1 food processor
1 food mixer or hand-held mixer
1 blender
1 coffee grinder
1 spice grinder

Luxury but great!

Dishwasher
Pasta rolling machine

using the freezer

Freezing can be a very successful method of preserving food. It retains more of the quality, character, and nutritive value of the food than methods such as bottling, canning, and drying. Nonetheless, as a guiding principle you should only freeze food when essential – it does not *improve* its quality.

Buy the smallest freezer possible. If you buy a larger freezer than you need, you will inevitably be tempted to fill it to capacity and, unless you are supremely well organized, much of the food you put in it will be forgotten about and eventually thrown away.

A full freezer costs less to run than a half-empty one. The faster the food is frozen, the smaller the ice crystals will be; large ice crystals that result from slow freezing damage the cell walls of the food and so, juice and soluble nutrients are lost when the food is thawed.

A home freezer is normally kept at 0°F (-18°C). At this temperature, both pathogenic and food spoilage micro organisms are dormant. However, over time an enzyme action takes place that results in the gradual deterioration of the quality, flavor, and color of the food. For that reason it is wise to get food in and out of the freezer as fast as is practical.

Guidelines for freezing food

1 Food must be in perfect condition before it is frozen; food that is stale or contaminated in any way will not be improved by freezing.

2 Do not freeze more than one-tenth of the capacity of your freezer in 24 hours.

3 Food should be packed in small rather than large packages and should be separated while freezing in order to allow the cold air to circulate around them.

4 For best results, the freezer should be set at the lowest temperature or "super freeze" for 8–12 hours before freezing, particularly meat and vegetables. The packs should be put into the coldest compartment of the freezer. When the packs are frozen, pack them tightly together in an appropriate part of the freezer.

5 Do not put anything slightly warm into the freezer as it will bring up the temperature and may cause other foods to deteriorate slightly.

6 Vegetables freeze very well but should be cooked immediately after they are thawed. They may be frozen without blanching but their storage time will be much less; for that reason it is worth blanching and refreshing green vegetables to prevent enzyme activity.

7 If at all possible "tray freeze" vegetables and fruit to keep them separate. This is done by spreading the fruit, or blanched and refreshed vegetables, in a single layer on a tray. They will then freeze individually and can be packed into bags or boxes. If food is "tray frozen" first, it will be less damaged and will thaw more quickly later.

Foods that benefit from being tray frozen include home-made sausages or sausage rolls, cheese croquettes, stuffed crêpes, phyllo dough, hamburgers, and bread rolls. Cakes should be frozen until the decoration is hard, and then wrapped.

Foods that do not freeze well:

Some foods cannot be successfully frozen because their texture can be spoiled by freezing, e.g., foods with a high water content. However, in some cases they may be used in soups, purées, or jams.

1 Eggs cannot be frozen in the shell.
Egg whites freeze very well.
1 ounce = 1 egg white when using them later. They will keep for up to 6 months in the freezer. Egg yolks are not so successful.
Hard boiled eggs become tough and the white turns gray.
Lightly-whisked whole egg freezes well also. Egg custard will separate in a freezer.

2 Cheese: Hard cheese or blue-veined cheese freezes well, either grated or in a piece.
Cottage and cream cheese are not very satisfactory frozen.
Camembert or Brie can be frozen but they should be ripened first.

3 Cream will separate if frozen unless it has been slightly whipped first.

4 Mayonnaise, Hollandaise, Béarnaise Sauce do not freeze well; they tend to separate when thawed.

5 Roux-based sauces freeze fairly well. Whisk slightly during reheating if possible. It's also a good idea to err on the side of having the sauce a little too thin rather than too thick, then a little roux can be whisked in during reheating.

6 Gelatin-based desserts, e.g., mousses, souffles, cheesecakes, may be frozen but become slightly rubbery. They should be used within a month. Jello, both sweet and savory, loses texture when frozen.

7 Melon has too high a water content for successful freezing.

8 Strawberries keep their color and flavor well, but collapse when thawed. However, the good varieties are worth freezing to make jams, sorbets, and fruit coulis.

9 Tomatoes may be frozen whole but again lose their structure when thawed. However, they are very useful for soups and stews and have the great advantage that they peel easily if dropped in cold or hot water for a few seconds. We freeze large quantities of tomato paste and find it invaluable.

10 Mashed potato may be piped around pre-prepared meat and fish dishes and frozen quite successfully.
Potatoes cooked whole go leathery.

11 Foods with a very high fat content go rancid after several months in the freezer.

Wrapping

All food should be carefully wrapped before freezing. If food is not properly wrapped it will dry out and get "freezer burn". This looks dry and unattractive but the food may still be safe to eat.

1 Good-quality plastic bags or plastic boxes should be used.

2 Recycled food containers, e.g., ice cream, yogurt, milk, or margarine cartons, can be used but must be thoroughly cleaned first.
Liquids, e.g., stock, can be poured into plastic bags and put into square plastic containers and frozen, later removed and easily stacked. We use half-gallon plastic milk cartons for stock; they are "free" and, if you are in a hurry, you can just cut the container without too many guilt pangs. Allow 1–2 inches of space for expansion when freezing liquids.

Labeling

1 Label all packs going into the freezer with name, date, and where appropriate, weight.

2 Keep a record of the content of the freezer in a book or on a chart. We use a large chart divided into sections roughly corresponding to where the food is kept in the freezer. Headings will vary according to your life style. Ours are:

Soups
Meat – cooked
Vegetables – cooked
Fish – cooked
Stocks
Dough
Cakes and cookies
Ice creams and sorbets
Miscellaneous – e.g., breadcrumbs, pine nuts, coffee beans

Food we find convenient to have in the freezer:
Soups and stocks
Puff and phyllo pastry dough
Fresh nuts, coffee beans, and breadcrumbs
Ice creams and sorbets
Cooked dishes with piped potatoes, e.g., Ham Morvandelle, Sole with mussels and shrimps, Scallops Mornay, Spiced Lamb Pies
Stews, Vegetable Stews, Piperonata, Tomato Fondue, etc.
Pie shells
A cake or two and maybe cookies
A loaf or two of white yeast bread
Cheese biscuits

Thawing and re-freezing food

The safest way to thaw frozen food is in a fridge. Some foods may be cooked from frozen, but it is essential, particularly for meat, to ensure that it is fully cooked. All poultry must be completely thawed before being cooked. A 3-pound (1.3-kg) chicken will take approx. 9 hours to thaw, whereas a 13½-pound. (6-kg) turkey will take 24 hours. It is now recommended to thaw poultry at room temperature. I still feel that a fridge is safer.

People worry about re-freezing food and indeed it is good to err on the side of being over-cautious. However, partially frozen food may be re-frozen provided it still has ice crystals in it. Thawed stocks should be reboiled for 5 minutes and allowed to get quite cold before re-freezing. Meat can be defrosted and then cooked, e.g., in a stew, and then refrozen without any danger. Breadcrumbs may be re-frozen without ill effect.

Emergencies

1 Power cuts

In the event of a power cut, do nothing. Provided your freezer is fairly full, food should stay frozen for at least 12 hours. At all costs, resist the temptation to keep peeping in to check because you will allow warm air into the freezer and so speed up the defrosting.

It is well worth the effort to put a note on the freezer plug to make sure that no one turns it off by accident. Put masking tape over the plug.

2 Electrical faults

In the case of an electrical fault, telephone the service engineer.

3 Moving house

Ask the furniture movers to transport the locked freezer fully loaded to your new house. Check that there is an appropriate socket to plug it into when it arrives. The freezer should be last on and first off the moving truck. Contents of the freezer should keep in perfectly good condition for 9–10 hours.

wine essentials

by Mary Dowey

Ten years ago, perhaps even five, it would have been easy to contemplate the possibility of a comprehensive new cookbook with no reference to wine. Not any more. In a remarkably short space of time, wine has abandoned its rather grand, formal air, shrugging off its Sunday suit to don a pair of jeans. With a rising proportion of retail sales now being handled by supermarkets, it has become an everyday pleasure rather than a weekend treat.

For cooks, the implications are obvious. Whereas, in the past, it might have been easy enough to get by with advice from a trusted wine merchant on what to choose for a special meal, these days anybody capable of rustling up the most casual supper needs to know the basics about wine. It's important to understand how to buy wisely, how to store wine in the best conditions, and how to serve it with confidence and style. More rewarding still is the process of learning about food-and-wine matching. Through a strange but thrilling alchemy, even the simplest food and a humble wine, when carefully paired, can create a sensational harmony of tastes.

First, a few words about buying wine. Avoid the very cheapest. Think of the costs that find their way into a bottle of wine: taxes, transportation, packaging, marketing, trade margins. In an extremely inexpensive bottle, the value of the wine itself will account for only a fraction of the total. That is why so many so-called "bargains" are bad buys. By paying just a little bit more, you may well end up with a bottle in which the wine itself is worth twice as much – simply because so many of those ancillary costs are fixed.

At the other end of the spectrum, expensive wines aren't always as memorable as their hefty price tag might suggest. The law of supply and demand exerts a grim influence on the upper end of the market. Fashionable wines, produced in limited quantities, can be exorbitant even in poor vintages. In price terms, the middle ground is often the most fruitful. When you do find a wine that you really like, consider buying it by the case. Most wine merchants offer a case discount.

Although recent international research indicates that over 90 per cent of wine is purchased to be consumed within two-and-a-half hours – an astonishing state of affairs – let's assume that prudent cooks will plan a little further ahead. Even though you may not have a cellar, nor any interest in buying bottles to lay down, it's important to store wine carefully even in the short term. Wine needs a cool, even temperature – between 50–60°F (10–15°C) is ideal, but a slightly higher temperature should do no harm provided there are no fluctuations. Light and vibration also damage wine – so put it somewhere not just cool but dark, well away from the hum of the central heating system.

Glasses play a key role in the enjoyment of wine, as any oenophile will attest. Wine lovers like to be able to see the color of their wine clearly – so that they can admire its depth or ponder the clues it gives to the wine's age. For this reason, plain, clear glass is preferable to cut crystal; colored glass gets an emphatic thumbs-down. Glass shape is equally crucial. Since more of the sensory pleasure of wine comes from its smell than its taste (try drinking with a clothes peg on your nose if you doubt that), the drinker should be able to release the precious aromas by swirling the wine around. This is only possible with a glass that comes in a little at the top, holding both the swirling wine and its evanescent perfume in place. Pick tulips, in other words, rather than lilies! The glasses made by the specialist Austrian manufacturer Riedel – now available from leading wine merchants the world over – are considered the ultimate in terms of shape, weight, and style.

It's also worth investing in a good corkscrew. Begin by removing just the top of the foil from the metal capsule –

either with a foil cutter or a pen-knife. When the cork has been drawn, pour a little wine into your own glass first and have a serious sniff at it before serving anybody else. If it is corked (which an estimated 5 per cent of wines currently are), it will smell slightly musty – like damp cardboard or wet cement. Next, have a good sip, because any mustiness will usually be even more pronounced in the taste.

If the wine seems fine, it's time to start pouring – taking care not to fill glasses more than half-full, despite any generous impulse you may have. The pleasurable sniffing and swirling ritual mentioned above (and practiced, you'll notice, by more and more people) is simply impossible with a well-filled glass. Remember to hold the bottle with the label uppermost, so that your guests can easily see what they are about to drink. Drips can easily be prevented by giving the bottle a quick little turn to the right, just as you stop pouring.

I have left decanting to the end of this brief gallop through the main points about serving wine because fewer and fewer wines need to be decanted. Only the very oldest and, occasionally, the very youngest, call for this procedure – which fortunately isn't half as complicated as it sounds. You don't even need a decanter! A clean, empty bottle and a funnel, or just a pitcher, will do.

Very mature red wines and vintage ports are decanted in order to separate the wine from the sediment which will have accumulated at the bottom of the bottle; but as old wines tend to be fragile, it's best not to decant them until just before they are to be drunk. Simply pour the wine very slowly into the decanter or substitute decanter, stopping the second you see that sediment is about to come out. (Purists hold a candle or light beneath the bottle as they pour, so that they can see the sediment as it reaches the bottle neck.)

Young wines that still taste astringent because of their extreme youth also benefit from decanting. Exposing them to the air during pouring helps to soften them and open them up. All you have to do is empty the bottle into a pitcher, then pour the wine back into its bottle. This achieves far more, by the way, than the standard practice of opening a wine a few hours before use and leaving the bottle "to breathe". Most experts now agree that, since the area of wine exposed to the air in this way is no bigger than a coin, not much breathing is done!

It goes almost without saying that too much exposure to air does wine no favors. Leftovers deteriorate fairly quickly. Any white wine remaining in a half-consumed (but re-corked) bottle will usually taste decidedly less appealing after a single day; red wines are rather more robust, and may even taste better after a day, before gradually losing their charms over the next two or three. For best results, decant leftovers into a clean half-bottle or quarter-bottle, filling it to the neck to reduce air contact. Otherwise, use a wine vacuum pump and rubber bung to remove the air from the half-empty bottle. Although perhaps not foolproof, it should be better than nothing. Another useful tip is to freeze leftover wine in ice cube trays. Wine cubes, stored in plastic bags in the freezer, can be terrifically useful when you need to add a drop of wine to a sauce.

Now to the most fascinating aspect of wine – its potential to enhance the flavors of food. The principle sounds devastatingly simple. Pair the right bottle with the right dish and you have instant magic – a blissful fusion of complementary flavors. Choose the wrong wine – one that just doesn't go with the food – and the opposite happens: the dish and the drink taste lackluster. With the growth of interest in wine and food, matching the two with skill is beginning to be viewed as an exciting new science.

With so many wine grapes and wine styles, all with their distinctive flavors – not to mention the infinite variety of tastes coming our way from the global kitchen – picking successful partnerships can seem a complicated business. Books and articles have been written, seeking to explain at painful length all the factors that should be borne in mind when attempting this mating game – sweetness, acidity, tannin, and so on. My view is that, rather than get bogged down in theory, it's best to try to follow a few basic principles, along with the instincts that your tastebuds will soon help you to develop. That way, the process of discovering sensational combinations will be enormous fun.

The first thing to think about is weight – light wines with light foods, heavier wines with heavier foods. Lobster, for instance, will suit a much richer white wine than would a delicate fish like sole – something like a buttery, oaked Chardonnay rather than a crisp and elegant Chablis.

Depending on how they are cooked, meaty fish like salmon and tuna may taste better with a light red wine (a young Pinot Noir, perhaps) than with a white of any kind. (This is especially true if, for instance, the salmon is seared in pungent spices, or the tuna served with a robust Mediterranean sauce.) The more substantial a dish, the greater the need will be for a substantial wine. Take venison, for example. Those intense, gamey flavors, which would overpower a light or medium-bodied red, meet their match in the blockbusters of the wine world – a strapping Australian Shiraz or a gloriously rich Amarone.

After you have thought about weight, consider the main flavors on the plate and try to choose a wine that will complement them. The herbaceous tang of Sauvignon Blanc brilliantly echoes the grassy character of young goat cheese, for instance. The touch of sweetness in a generously fruity white wine like Viognier perfectly parallels the element of sweetness in crab; it may even surprise you (pleasantly!) with duck in a honey glaze. Peppery red Zinfandel picks up on the punchy flavors in spicy sausages, with all the roundness and lusciousness that spice needs to slip down comfortably with wine.

Although examples of winning combinations are far too numerous to list here, it may be worth mentioning just a few more, relating to foods that are widely regarded as tricky from a wine point of view. Asparagus, which makes some wines taste metallic, seems to me to go very well indeed with Sauvignon Blanc – especially if it's from New Zealand, whose Sauvignons exude asparagus aromas. Eggs can be difficult, particularly when still slightly runny, because they tend to coat the tongue. A good excuse to splash out on champagne, or a good sparkling wine: both have wonderful palate-cleansing properties. Chinese food is often accused of a similar tongue-coating effect. The same painless remedy works!

Indian and Thai dishes, often laden with chiles, ginger, spices, cilantro, lemon grass, or other pungent ingredients, go best with wines that are fruitier and just a touch sweeter than you might normally choose. On the whole, white wines work better than reds, particularly with Thai food. New World blends of Semillon and Sauvignon, the richer Australian Rieslings, Alsace Pinot Blanc and Pinot Gris and ample southern French versions of Marsanne, Roussanne, or Viognier are all worth trying. The hottest Indian dishes, especially those involving meat, taste best with round, fruity, New World reds. Indeed, it's worth remembering that New World wines are generally more spice- and fusion-friendly than their European counterparts.

At the sweet end of the menu, chocolate is sometimes viewed as problematic – but usually only by people who haven't yet sampled it with sweet red wines! Try a wickedly rich, dark chocolate pudding with Banyuls or Maury, the exotic Grenache-based sweet reds from Roussillon, or with an Amarone Recioto, or a glass of tawny port, and see how much more divine it tastes than with a sweet white wine like Sauternes.

At least, that's what I think – but there are no rights and wrongs, no absolutes, when it comes to food and wine combinations – just as there are none with wine itself. Personal taste has a bigger role to play than any set of rules or pointers, so never be afraid to trust your own opinion. The really important thing is to sample every unfamiliar wine that comes your way and think about its character – which foods it might flatter, which it might destroy. Keep tasting, keep experimenting. You will have embarked on an endlessly fascinating journey of discovery.

stocks & soups

Making stock is really just an attitude of mind. Instead of absent-mindedly flinging things into the trashcan, keep your carcasses, giblets, and vegetable trimmings, and use them for your stock pot. Nowadays, some supermarkets and butchers are happy to give you chicken carcasses and often giblets as well, just for the asking, because there is so little demand.

General Stock Making Techniques

Stock will keep for several days in the refrigerator. If you need to keep it for longer, boil it up again for 5–6 minutes every couple of days; let it get cold, and refrigerate again. Stock also freezes perfectly. Use large yogurt cartons or plastic milk bottles – you can cut them off from the frozen stock without a conscience if you need to defrost it in a hurry!

In restaurants, the stock is usually allowed to simmer uncovered so it will be as clear as possible, but we usually advise people making stock at home to cover the pot, otherwise the whole house is likely to smell of stock and that may put you off making it on a regular basis.

Chicken livers shouldn't go into the stock pot because they cause bitterness, so save them to make wonderful smooth pâté which can be served in lots of exciting ways. Unsuitable vegetables include potatoes (they soak up flavor and make the stock cloudy); parsnips (too strong); beets (too strong also, and the dye would turn the stock red, so save for beet soup); cabbage or other brassicas (they give an off-taste when cooked for a long time). A little white turnip is sometimes an asset, but it is very easy to overdo. I also ban bay leaves from my chicken stocks because I find that the flavor can predominate and make different soups made from the stock all taste the same. Salt is another ingredient that you will find in most stock recipes, but not in mine. Why? Because, if I want to reduce the stock later to make a sauce, it can easily taste too salty.

Vegetable Stock

Makes about 2 quarts (1.75 liters)

This is just a rough guide – you can make a vegetable stock from whatever vegetables you have available, but don't use too much of any one vegetable unless you want that flavor to predominate.

1 small white turnip
2 onions, roughly sliced
green parts of 2–3 leeks
3 stalks celery, washed and roughly chopped
3 large carrots, scrubbed and roughly chopped
½ fennel bulb, roughly chopped
1 cup mushrooms or mushroom stalks
4–6 parsley stalks
bouquet garni
a few peppercorns
2½ quarts (2.3 liters) cold water

Put all the ingredients into a large pot, add the cold water, bring to a boil, then reduce the heat, cover, and let simmer for 1–2 hours. Pour through a cheesecloth.

Master Recipe

Chicken Stock

Makes about 3 quarts (3 liters)

2–3 raw or cooked chicken carcasses (or both)
giblets from the chicken, i.e., neck, heart, gizzard (save the liver for another dish)
1 onion, sliced
1 leek, split in two
1 outside stalk of celery or 1 lovage leaf
1 carrot, sliced
a few parsley stalks
sprig of thyme
6 peppercorns
1 gallon (3.6 liters) cold water

Chop up the carcasses as much as possible. Put all the ingredients into a pot and cover with cold water. Bring to a boil and skim off any surface fat with a tablespoon. Simmer for 3–5 hours. Strain, and remove any remaining fat. If you need a stronger flavor, boil down the liquid in an open pan to reduce by one-third to one-half the volume. Do not add salt.

Tip: If you have just one carcass and do not want to make a small quantity of stock, freeze it and when you have saved up 6–7 carcasses plus giblets, you can make a really big pot of stock and get good value from your fuel.

Turkey Stock

Make in the same way as chicken stock, and use the finished stock in turkey or chicken recipes.

Game Stock

Make in the same way as chicken stock; use the finished stock appropriately.

Goose and Duck Stock

Make in the same way as chicken stock. Some chefs like to brown the carcasses first to produce darker stock with a richer flavor. Use the stock in goose and duck recipes.

Master Recipe

Brown Beef Stock

Makes about 4½ quarts (4 liters)

5–6 lbs. (2.3–2.75kg) beef bones, preferably with some scraps of meat on, cut into small pieces
2 large onions, quartered
2 large carrots, quartered
2 stalks celery, cut into 1-inch (2.5-cm) pieces
large bouquet garni, including parsley stalks, sprigs of thyme, a bay leaf, and sprig of tarragon
10 peppercorns
2 cloves
4 garlic cloves, unpeeled
1 teaspoon tomato paste
5 quarts (5 liters) water

Preheat the oven to 450°F (230°C). Put the bones into a roasting pan and roast for 30 minutes or until well browned. Add the onions, carrots, and celery, and return to the oven until the vegetables are also browned. Transfer the bones and vegetables to the stock pot using a metal spoon. Add the bouquet garni, peppercorns, cloves, garlic, and tomato paste. De-grease the roasting pan and de-glaze with some water, bring to a boil and pour over the bones and vegetables in the stock pot. Add the rest of the water and bring slowly to a boil. Skim the fat off the stock and simmer gently for 5–6 hours. Strain, let cool, and skim any remaining fat off before using.

Veal Stock

Make the same way as Brown Beef Stock. Use the stock in dishes such as Osso Buco.

Lamb Stock

Make in the same way as Brown Beef Stock. Use the stock in lamb dishes such as Irish Stew.

Master Recipe
Basic Fish Stock

Makes about 2 quarts (1.75 liters)

Takes only 20 minutes to make. If you can get lots of nice fresh fish bones from your fishmarket, it's well worth making two or three times this stock recipe, because it freezes perfectly. You will then have fish stock at the ready.

2 lbs. (900g) fish bones, preferably sole, turbot, or brill
1/2–1 tablespoon butter
1 cup finely sliced onions
1/2–1 cup dry white wine
2 1/2 quarts (2.3 liters) cold water
4 peppercorns
large bouquet garni containing sprig of thyme, 4–5 parsley stalks, small piece of celery, and a tiny scrap of bay leaf

Wash the fish bones thoroughly under cold running water until no traces of blood remain, and chop into pieces. In a large stainless steel pot, melt the butter, add the onions, toss and sweat over a gentle heat until soft, but not colored. Add the bones to the pan, stir, and cook very briefly with the onions. Add the dry white wine and boil until nearly all the wine has evaporated. Cover with cold water, add the peppercorns and bouquet garni. Bring to a boil and simmer for 20 minutes, skimming often. Strain. Let cool, de-grease if necessary, and refrigerate.

Household Fish Stock

Fish heads with the gills removed, fish skin, and shellfish or mollusc shells, if available, may be added to the fish stock. It will be slightly darker in color and less delicate in flavor. Cook for 30 minutes.

Shellfish Stock

A selection of crustacean and mollusc shells, e.g., shrimp, mussels, crab, or lobster may be used. Cook for 30 minutes.

Demi-glaze

Reduce the strained fish stock by half to intensify the flavor, chill, and refrigerate or freeze.

Glace de Poisson

Reduce the stock until it becomes thick and syrupy, then chill. It will set into a firm jelly which has a very concentrated fish flavor – excellent for adding to fish sauces or soups to enhance the flavor.

Master Recipe
Light Dashi

Dashi (bonito fish stock) is essential in many Japanese dishes. It provides a savory flavor that cannot be attained by using seasoning only, and it is much easier to make than meat or fish stock. The two main ingredients are the bonito flakes and konbu, a member of the kelp family that grows to amazing heights – some of 1,500 feet (450m) have been known. There is a really distinctive smell of the sea to this stock. Bonito flakes are sold dried. Konbu is also available in dried form.

2 cups water
4-inch (10-cm) piece konbu (dried kelp)
1 teaspoon (or slightly heaped teaspoon) dried bonito flakes

Wipe and clean konbu with a dry cloth. Do not wipe off the white powder on the surface, as that is the one element that provides a unique savory flavor.

Put the water in a saucepan and soak the konbu for 30 minutes before turning on the heat. Remove any scum that forms on the surface. When the water begins to bubble, just before boiling, take out the konbu. Do not overcook or it will become slimy and the flavor of the stock too strong. Add the bonito flakes, bring back to a boil, turn off the heat, and set aside until the bonito flakes sink to the bottom. Strain through very fine cheesecloth and discard the bonito flakes. Use fresh, or freeze immediately.

Heavy Dashi

Follow the Master Recipe but increase the quantity of bonito flakes to 1–2 tablespoons and the water to 6 cups. Add two-thirds of the bonito flakes and simmer the mixture, uncovered, for 20 minutes. Add the remaining bonito flakes and proceed as above. Keeps in the fridge for 3 days.

Instant Dashi

Instant dashi is available as liquid extract and powder. Just dissolve a liquid dashi or powdered dashi in boiling water. But the flavor is far from that of homemade dashi.

Ballymaloe Basic Vegetable Soup Technique

Well over half the soups we make at Ballymaloe are made to this simple ratio: 1:1:3:4.

1 part onion
1 part potato
3 parts any vegetable, or a mixture of vegetables
4 parts stock, a mixture of stock and milk, or water
seasoning

You can use chicken or vegetable stock, and season simply with salt and freshly ground pepper. Complementary fresh herbs or spices may also be added. Don't weigh the ingredients; it is their volume that is important rather than their weight – we use an 8 fl. oz. (225ml) cup to measure out all the ingredients. The great advantage is that you can make an enormous repertoire of different soups depending on what's fresh, in season, and available. If potatoes and onions are the only option, it's still possible to make two delicious soups by increasing one or the other, and then adding one or several herbs. We have even used fava bean tops, radish leaves, and nettles in season.

Example

Serves 6

1/2 stick (1/4 cup) butter
1 cup potatoes, peeled and cut into 1/2-inch (1-cm) cubes
1 cup onions, cut into 1/2-inch (1-cm) cubes
salt and freshly ground pepper
3 cups vegetables of your choice, cut into 1/2-inch (1-cm) cubes
4 cups homemade Chicken Stock (see page 36), or stock and creamy milk

Melt the butter in a heavy saucepan. When it foams, add the potatoes and onions, and turn them until well coated. Sprinkle with salt and pepper. Cover and sweat on a gentle heat for 10 minutes. Add the vegetables and stock. Boil until soft, then blend it, strain it, or put it through a mouli. Do not overcook or the vegetables will lose their flavor. Adjust seasoning.

Chopping fresh herbs

Use a very sharp chef's knife or chopping knife. The herbs should be dry, otherwise they will bruise as they are chopped.

Strip the herbs from the stalks, saving the stalks for the stock pot.

Gather the herbs into a little ball on the cutting board with your fingers. Using your knuckles as a guide, keep the tip of the chef's knife on the board and slide the knife forward to chop the herbs roughly.

Then change the angle of the knife to a horizontal position. Hold the tip and continue to move the blade backwards and forwards until the herbs are chopped to the required texture. Use the blade of the knife to lift the freshly chopped herbs off the board.

A Chinese chopper or a mezzaluna is also excellent for chopping. This two-handled Italian blade is used in a rocking movement backwards and forwards across the board.

Master Recipe
Potato and Fresh Herb Soup

Serves 6

Most people have potatoes and onions in the house even when the cupboard is otherwise bare, so this delicious soup can be made at a moment's notice. While the vegetables are sweating, pop a few White Soda Scones or Cheddar Cheese Scones (page 476) into the oven and wow – won't everybody be impressed.

1/2 stick (1/4 cup) butter
1 lb. (450g) potatoes, peeled and cut into 1/2-inch (1-cm) cubes (about 3 cups)
1 medium onion, cut into 1/2-inch (1-cm) cubes (about 1 cup)
1 teaspoon salt
freshly ground pepper
2–3 tablespoons in total of the following: parsley, thyme, lemon, chives, all chopped
4 cups homemade Chicken or Vegetable Stock (see page 36)
1/2 cup creamy milk

Garnish
herbs, freshly chopped, and some chive or thyme flowers in season

Melt the butter in a heavy saucepan. When it foams, add the potatoes and onions, and toss them in the butter until well coated. Sprinkle with salt and a few grinds of pepper. Cover with a butter wrapper or paper lid, and the lid of the saucepan. Sweat over a gentle heat for about 10 minutes. Meanwhile, bring the stock to a boil. When the vegetables are soft but not colored, add the freshly chopped herbs and stock, and continue to cook until the vegetables are soft. Purée the soup in a blender or food processor. Taste and adjust the seasoning. Thin with creamy milk to the required consistency. Garnish and serve.

Variations

Potato and Parsley Soup

Follow the Master Recipe, omitting the herbs and adding 3–4 tablespoons of freshly chopped parsley just before blending.

Potato Soup with Parsley Pesto

My chef brother, Rory O'Connell, embellishes potato soup by drizzling a little Parsley Pesto (see page 589) over the top of each bowl just as it goes to the table.

Potato and Mint Soup

Follow the Master Recipe, omitting the herbs and adding 3–4 tablespoons chopped spearmint or Bowles' mint just before blending. Sprinkle in a little mint and cream.

Potato and Tarragon Soup

Follow the Master Recipe, omitting the herbs and instead adding 2 tablespoons of tarragon to the soup with the stock. Purée and finish as in the Master Recipe. Sprinkle a little fresh tarragon over the soup. A zig zag of soft cream is also delicious.

Potato, Chorizo, and Parsley Soup

We love Fingal Ferguson's Gubbeen chorizo so much that we dream up all sorts of ways of using it. The strong, hot, spicy taste add lots of oomph to the silky potato soup. Follow the Master Recipe, omitting the herbs. Just before serving, cook about 18 slices of chorizo for a minute or two on each side on a non-stick pan. Serve 3 slices of chorizo on top of each bowl, with sprigs of flat-leaf parsley and a few drops of chorizo oil. Serve immediately.

Potato and Melted Leek Soup

Follow the Master Recipe, but serve a teaspoonful of Melted Leeks (see page 173) on top of each helping. Scatter with snipped chives and chive flowers in season.

Potato and Lovage Soup

Follow the Master Recipe, using just lovage, and garnish with freshly snipped lovage.

Potato and Smoky Bacon Soup

Follow the Master Recipe, omitting the herbs, and add 5 ounces (150g) smoky bacon, cut into lardons, and fried until crisp.

Potato and Roast Red Pepper Soup

Potato and Fresh Herb Soup (see Master Recipe)
4 red peppers

Garnish
sprigs of flat-leaf parsley

Follow the Master Recipe, omitting the herbs.

Roast or chargrill the peppers, then peel and seed them, saving the sweet juices carefully. Purée the flesh with the juices. Taste and adjust the seasoning if necessary. Just before serving, swirl the red pepper purée through the soup or simply drizzle on top of each bowl. Top with some parsley. You might try adding one or two roast chiles to the pepper for a little extra buzz – Serrano or Jalapeño are good.

Winter Leek and Potato Soup

Serves 6–8

1/2 stick (1/4 cup) butter
1 lb. (450g) potatoes, peeled and finely diced
1 medium onion, finely diced (about 1 cup)
12 ounces (350g) white parts of the leeks, sliced (about 3 1/2 cups) – save the green tops for another soup or stock
salt and freshly ground pepper
4 cups light homemade Chicken Stock (see page 36)
1/2 cup cream
1/2 cup milk

Garnish
chives, finely chopped
cream

Melt the butter in a heavy saucepan. When it foams, add the potatoes, onions, and leeks, turning them in the butter until well coated. Sprinkle with salt and pepper. Cover with a paper lid (to keep in the steam) and the saucepan lid. Sweat on a gentle heat for 10 minutes or until the vegetables are soft but not colored. Discard the paper lid. Add the stock, bring to a boil, and simmer until the vegetables are just cooked. Do not overcook or the vegetables will lose their flavor. Blend until smooth and silky, then taste and adjust the seasoning. Add cream or creamy milk to taste. Garnish with swirls of cream and chives.

Below: Potato and Roast Red Pepper Soup

Chopping an onion

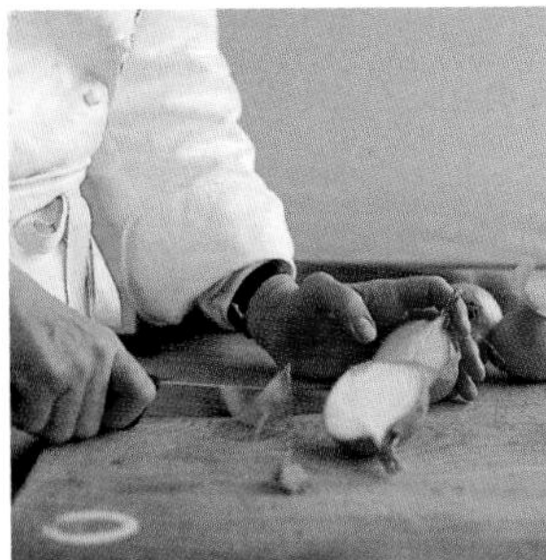

Cut the onion in half from top to bottom.

Peel back the skin and trim the base but leave the root intact to hold the onion together as it is chopped.

Lay one half of the onion cut side down on a cutting board.

With a sharp knife, make a series of horizontal cuts towards but not through the root. (The thickness of the slices will determine the size of the dice.)

Then with the tip of the knife just in front of the root, cut the onion lengthwise, almost to the root but not through it.

Finally, using your knuckles as a guide, cut the onion crosswise into dice.

Note: If the chopped onion is not to be cooked immediately, put the dice into a strainer and run under cold water to halt the enzyme action that gradually turns a cut onion sour. Otherwise the flavor of the dish you plan to cook may be spoiled.

Irish Colcannon Soup

Serves 6

Colcannon is one of Ireland's best loved traditional dishes – made from fluffy mashed potato flecked with cooked cabbage or kale. Here the same ingredients are used to make a delicious soup.

1/2 stick (1/4 cup) butter
1 lb. (450g) potatoes, peeled and cut into 1/2-inch (1-cm) cubes (about 3 cups)
1 medium onion, diced (about 1 cup)
1 teaspoon salt
freshly ground pepper
5 cups homemade Chicken or Vegetable Stock (see page 36)
1 lb. (450g) cabbage
2 tablespoons butter plus a pat of butter
salt and freshly ground pepper
1/2 cup creamy milk

Melt the butter in a heavy saucepan. When it foams, add the potatoes and onions and toss them in the butter until well coated. Sprinkle with salt and pepper. Cover and sweat over a gentle heat for 10 minutes, add the stock, bring to a boil, and simmer until the vegetables are soft.

Meanwhile make the buttered cabbage. Remove the tough outer leaves. Divide the cabbage into 4, cut out the stalks, and finely shred across the grain. Put 3–4 tablespoons of water into a wide pot with the second quantity of butter and a pinch of salt. Bring to a boil, add the cabbage, and toss constantly over a high heat, then cover for a few minutes. Toss again, add some more salt, freshly ground pepper, and a pat of butter. Add the cabbage to the soup, then purée in a blender or food processor with the freshly chopped herbs. Taste and adjust seasoning.

Thin with creamy milk to the required consistency.

Onion and Thyme Leaf Soup

Serves 6

3½ tablespoons butter
1 lb. (450g) onions, cut into ½-inch (1-cm) cubes
8 ounces (225g) potatoes, peeled and cut into ½-inch (1-cm) cubes (about 1½ cups)
1–2 teaspoons fresh thyme leaves
salt and freshly ground pepper
4 cups homemade Chicken Stock or Vegetable Stock (see page 36)
⅔ cup cream or cream and milk mixed

Garnish
a little whipped cream, optional
fresh thyme leaves and thyme or chive flowers

Melt the butter in a heavy saucepan. As soon as it foams, add the onions and potatoes, and stir until they are well coated with butter. Add the thyme leaves, season with salt and freshly ground pepper. Place a paper lid directly on top of the vegetables to keep in the steam, cover the saucepan with a tight-fitting lid, and sweat on a low heat for about 10 minutes. The potatoes and onions should be soft but not colored. Add the stock, bring to a boil, and simmer until the potatoes are cooked (5–8 minutes). Blend the soup and add a little cream or creamy milk. Taste and correct the seasoning if necessary. Serve garnished with a blob of whipped cream and sprinkled with thyme leaves and thyme or chive flowers.

Master Recipe
Carrot Soup

Serves 6

This soup may be served either hot or cold. Don't hesitate to put in a good pinch of sugar – it brings out the flavor.

3 tablespoons butter
1¼ lbs. (600g) carrots, chopped
1 medium onion, cut into ½-inch (1-cm) cubes (about 1 cup)
5 ounces (150g) potatoes, peeled and cut into ½-inch (1-cm) cubes (about 1 cup)
salt and freshly ground pepper
pinch of sugar
5 cups homemade light Chicken or Vegetable Stock (see page 36)
a little creamy milk (optional)

Garnish
a little lightly whipped cream or crème fraîche
sprigs of mint (optional)

Melt the butter. When it foams, add the chopped vegetables, season with salt, pepper, and sugar. Cover with a butter paper lid (to retain the steam) and a tight fitting lid. Let it sweat gently on a low heat for about 10 minutes. Remove the lid, add the stock, and boil until the vegetables are soft (5–8 minutes). Pour the soup into the blender and purée until smooth. Add a little creamy milk if necessary. Taste and adjust seasoning. Garnish with a swirl of cream or crème fraîche and sprigs of fresh mint if desired.

Tip: Buy unwashed, local, organic carrots whenever possible. They have immeasurably better flavor than pre-washed ones and keep longer, too. Heirloom seeds are said to have more vitality and food value than F1 hybrids.

Variations

Carrot and Mint Soup

Add a sprig of spearmint to the Master Recipe when sweating the vegetables. Remove it and add 1 tablespoon of freshly chopped mint before puréeing the soup. A few crispy croûtons are good scattered over the soup. Serve with freshly whipped cream with a little mint chopped into it.

Carrot and Cumin Soup

Make the soup as in the Master Recipe. Garnish each bowl of soup with a swirl of crème fraîche or yogurt, a little freshly roasted and ground cumin, and some cilantro. Breadsticks (see page 487) are delicious dunked in this soup.

Carrot and Coriander Soup

Substitute coriander seed for cumin in the recipe above.

Carrot and Orange Soup

Add the freshly grated rind of 2 unwaxed oranges just before the soup is puréed. If unwaxed oranges aren't available, scrub the oranges well before grating to remove the wax from the skin.

Carrot and Parsnip Soup

Follow the Master Recipe, replacing ⅓ of the quantity of chopped carrots with chopped parsnips. It can be fun to serve some Saratoga Crisps (see page 174) as a garnish. Add at the last minute or they'll go soggy.

How to chop root vegetables (carrots, parsnips, potatoes)

Wash and peel the vegetables, preferably using a swivel-top peeler. Cut a slice off one side or all four sides if a perfectly even dice is required. Cut the vegetable into slices. (The thickness of these will determine the size of the dice.) Flip over onto the flat side and then cut downwards into slices. Finally cut across to produce dice of the required size, ¼ inch (5mm), ⅛ inch (3mm), or 1/16 inch (2mm) for Brunoise.

Curried Parsnip Soup

Serves 6–8

This delicious soup was adapted from Jane Grigson's recipe in her book Good Things**. Flour may be omitted for celiacs.**

1/2 stick (1/4 cup) butter
1 medium onion, chopped (about 1 cup)
1 garlic clove, crushed
2 medium parsnips, peeled and chopped (about 3 1/2 cups)
salt and freshly ground pepper
4 teaspoons flour
1 teaspoon curry powder
5 cups Chicken or Vegetable Stock (see page 36)
2/3 cup creamy milk

Garnish
Crispy Croûtons (see page 226)
chives or parsley, finely chopped

Melt the butter in a heavy saucepan, add the onion, garlic, and parsnip, season with salt and pepper, and toss until well coated. Cover and cook over a gentle heat until soft and tender, about 10 minutes. Stir in the flour and curry powder and gradually incorporate the hot stock. Simmer until the parsnip is fully cooked, strain and purée. Correct the seasoning and add the creamy milk. Serve with crispy croûtons and sprinkle with chives or parsley.

Fennel and Parsnip Soup

Serves 8

This unexpectedly delicious combination of winter flavors is guaranteed to convert even the most ardent parsnip hater!

1/2 stick (1/4 cup) butter
6 ounces (175g) onion, diced (about 1 1/2 cups)
1 lb. (450g) parsnips, washed, peeled and diced
1 lb. (450g) fennel bulb, finely diced
salt and freshly ground pepper
5 cups homemade Chicken or Vegetable Stock (see page 36)
1/2 cup milk
1/2 cup cream

Garnish
herb fennel or bulb fennel tops, finely chopped

Melt the butter and toss the onion, parsnips, and fennel in it. Season with salt and pepper. Cover with a butter wrapper or paper lid and the lid of the saucepan. Cook on a gentle heat for 10–15 minutes or until soft but not colored. Heat the stock and add, simmering for about 20 minutes or until the vegetables are completely tender. Add the milk and cream. Purée and taste for seasoning. Serve in bowls or a soup tureen, sprinkled with the fennel.

White Turnip and Marjoram Soup

Serves 6

White turnip and marjoram is a wonderful flavor combination. Kohlrabi could also be used here.

1/2 stick (1/4 cup) butter
5 ounces (150g) potatoes, peeled and chopped (about 1 cup)
1 medium onion, finely diced (about 1 cup)
12 ounces (350g) white turnips, peeled and finely diced
salt and freshly ground pepper
5 cups homemade Chicken Stock (see page 36)
3 tablespoons annual marjoram, chopped
2/3 cup creamy milk

Melt the butter in a heavy saucepan. When it foams, add the potatoes, onions, and white turnips. Turn them until well coated. Sprinkle with salt and pepper. Cover and sweat on a gentle heat for 10 minutes. Add the stock and half of the marjoram. Bring to a boil and cook until soft. Add the remainder of the marjoram. Purée until smooth and silky, adding some creamy milk and perhaps a little more stock if necessary. Do not overcook or the soup will lose its fresh flavor. Taste and adjust seasoning.

Spiced Pumpkin Soup

Serves 6–8

2 lbs. (900g) pumpkin or winter squash, peeled, seeded and cut into 1/2-inch (1-cm) cubes
6 ounces (175g) onion, peeled and chopped (about 1 1/2 cups)
2 garlic cloves, crushed
2 tablespoons butter
1 sprig thyme
1 lb. (450g) very ripe tomatoes, skinned and chopped, or 1 x 14-ounce (400-g) can tomatoes, seeded and roughly chopped
4 teaspoons tomato paste
5 cups homemade Chicken Stock (see page 36)
salt and freshly ground pepper
pinch of nutmeg
3 tablespoons butter
1/2 teaspoon cumin seeds
1/2 teaspoon coriander seeds
1/2 teaspoon black peppercorns
1 teaspoon white mustard seeds
2-inch (5-cm) piece of cinnamon stick

Put the pumpkin or squash into a pot with the onion, garlic, butter, and thyme. Cover and sweat over a low heat for 10 minutes, stirring once or twice. Add the chopped tomatoes (plus 1/2–1 teaspoon sugar if using canned tomatoes) and tomato paste, and cook until dissolved into a thick sauce. Stir in the stock, salt, pepper, and a little nutmeg, and simmer until the squash is very tender. Discard the thyme stalk, then purée the soup in several batches and return to the pot. You may need to add a little more stock or water if the soup is too thick. Taste and adjust the seasoning. Just before serving, gently reheat the soup and pour into a warm serving bowl. Heat the coriander, cumin, and peppercorns, and crush coarsely. Melt the butter in a small saucepan and, when foaming, add the crushed spices, mustard seeds, and cinnamon. Stir for a few seconds until the mustard seeds start to pop. Remove the cinnamon and quickly pour the spiced butter over the soup. Serve, mixing in the spiced butter as you ladle it out.

Right: Spiced Pumpkin Soup

Butternut Squash Soup

Serves 8

Butternut squash is possibly the tastiest of all the squashes, but you could substitute several others such as Acorn squash.

1/2 stick (1/4 cup) butter
1 1/4 lbs. (600g) onions, chopped
1 1/3 cups chopped celery
1 1/2 cups chopped carrots
1 1/2 ounces (35g) fresh ginger root, peeled and chopped or grated
4 large garlic cloves, peeled and crushed
1 1/2 lbs. (750g) squash, peeled and cut into 1/2-inch (1-cm) cubes (weighed after peeling)
salt and white pepper to taste
2 1/2 cups homemade Chicken Stock (see page 36)
2 1/2 cups water
1/2 cup milk
1/2 cup cream

Garnish
flat-leaf parsley, freshly chopped

Melt the butter in a heavy saucepan. When it foams, add the onions, celery, carrots, ginger, garlic, and squash, and toss until well coated. Sprinkle with salt and pepper. Cover and sweat on a gentle heat for 10 minutes. Add the stock and water. Bring to a boil and cook until the vegetables are soft. Do not overcook or the vegetables will lose their flavor. Purée, adding the milk and cream as required. Taste and correct the seasoning. Sprinkle with the parsley.

Master Recipe
Jerusalem Artichoke Soup

Serves 8–10

Jerusalem artichokes are a sadly neglected winter vegetable. They look like knobbly potatoes and are a nuisance to peel but, if fresh, all they need is a good scrub. Delicious in soups and gratins, they are also a real gem from the gardener's point of view because their foliage grows into a hedge, providing shelter for compost heaps and pheasants!

1/2 stick (1/4 cup) butter
1 1/4 lbs. (600g) onions, chopped
1 1/4 lbs. (600g) potatoes, peeled and chopped
2 1/2 lbs. (1.1kg) artichokes, peeled and chopped
salt and freshly ground pepper
5 cups light Chicken Stock (see page 36)
2 1/2 cups creamy milk

Garnish
parsley, freshly chopped
crisp, golden croûtons

Melt the butter in a heavy saucepan, add the onions, potatoes, and artichokes. Season with salt and pepper, cover, and sweat gently for about 10 minutes. Add the stock and cook until the vegetables are soft. Purée and return to the heat. Thin to the required consistency with creamy milk, and adjust the seasoning. Garnish with parsley and crisp, golden croûtons.

Note: This soup may need more stock depending on how thick you like it.

Variations
Jerusalem Artichoke Soup with Crispy Bacon Croûtons

Cut 4–5 strips bacon into lardons. Fry in a little oil until crisp and golden. Drain on paper towels. Mix with the croûtons and add to the Master Recipe just before serving.

Jerusalem Artichoke Soup with Mussels

Garnish the Master Recipe with 30 or so cooked mussels (see page 254) and some snipped fennel leaves. Mussels and artichokes have a wonderful affinity.

How to string spinach

Fold the leaf in half lengthwise with the stalk pointing upwards and the ridge facing outwards.

Pull the stalk from top to bottom so that it tears off the leaf.

The stalks of spinach and similar vegetables may be cut into short lengths, cooked in boiling salted water and tossed with a little butter or olive oil – very nutritious and delicious! Kale stalks can be a little tough, however.

Green soups

There is an extra dimension to green soups. It's worth taking care to preserve the bright green color as well as the lively fresh taste.

First, remember not to overcook the green vegetables. Many greens – lettuce, kale, cabbage, spinach, watercress, for instance, cook very quickly, so they should not be added until the base vegetables are fully cooked in the stock. Then boil the soup rapidly without the lid on for only a few minutes until the greens are just cooked. Whizz in a blender and serve immediately or cool quickly and reheat just before serving. Green soups lose their fresh color if they are kept hot indefinitely.

Beet and chard tops, turnip greens, pea and fava bean shoots, and radish leaves all make delicious green soups.

Spinach and Rosemary Soup

Serves 6–8

For a simple spinach soup, omit the rosemary and add a little freshly grated nutmeg with the seasoning. Instead of spinach, you can also use mustard greens or a combination of mustard greens and red Russian kale.

1/2 stick (1/4 cup) butter
1 medium onion, chopped (about 1 cup)
5 ounces (150g) potatoes, peeled and chopped (about 1 cup)
salt and freshly ground pepper
2 1/2 cups homemade Chicken or Vegetable Stock (see page 36) or water
2–2 1/2 cups creamy milk
8–12 ounces (225–350g) spinach, de-stalked and chopped
1 tablespoon fresh rosemary, chopped

Garnish
2 tablespoons whipped cream (optional)
sprig of rosemary or rosemary flowers

Accompaniments
Cheddar Cheese Scones (see page 476)

Melt the butter in a heavy saucepan. When it foams, add the onions and potatoes, and turn them until coated. Sprinkle with salt and pepper. Cover and sweat over a gentle heat for 10 minutes. In separate saucepans, bring the stock and milk to a boil, and add to the vegetables. Bring back to a boil and simmer until the potatoes and onions are fully cooked. Add the spinach and boil with the lid off for 3–5 minutes, until the spinach is tender. Do not overcook. Add the rosemary. Purée and taste. Serve garnished with a blob of cream and rosemary. If you have a pretty rosemary bush in bloom, sprinkle a few flowers over the top for extra pizzazz.

Tip: Freshly chopped dill is also great with lettuce soup.

Tip: The trick with green soups is not to add the greens until the last minute, otherwise they will overcook, and the soup will lose its fresh taste and bright green color. Also, if you need to reheat, do so at the last minute. If the soup sits in a bain-marie or hostess trolley, its color will go.

Lettuce, Pea, and Mint Soup

Serves 6–8 approx.

Fresh mint is more fragrant at the height of summer than towards autumn, so it may be necessary to use more at the end of the season. Use outside lettuce leaves for soup and the tender inside for green salads.

1/2 stick (1/4 cup) butter
6 ounces (175g) potatoes, peeled and diced (a slightly heaped cup)
1 medium to large onion, peeled (about 1 1/3 cups)
1 teaspoon salt
freshly ground pepper
4–5 cups homemade Chicken or Vegetable Stock (see page 36)
2 cups peas
6 ounces (175g) lettuce leaves, chopped and stalks removed (about 2–2 1/2 cups)
1 tablespoon cream (optional)
2 teaspoons mint, freshly chopped

Garnish
1/4 cup cream, softly whipped
sprigs of mint

Melt the butter in a heavy saucepan. When it foams, add the potatoes and onions, and turn them until well coated. Sprinkle with the salt and pepper. Cover and sweat over a gentle heat for 10 minutes. Add the stock, bring to a boil, and cook until the potatoes and onions are softened. Add the peas and cook for 4–5 minutes. Add the lettuce, and boil with the lid off until the lettuce is cooked (2–3 minutes). Do not overcook or the soup will lose its fresh green color. Add the cream and mint, and purée. Serve garnished with a blob of whipped cream and a little mint.

Watercress Soup

Serves 6–8

There are references to watercress in many early Irish manuscripts. It formed part of the diet of hermits and holy men, who valued its special properties. Legend has it that it was watercress that enabled St. Brendan to live to the ripe old age of 180! In Birr Castle in Co. Offaly, Lord and Lady Rosse still serve soup of watercress gathered from around St. Brendan's well, just below the castle walls.

3 1/2 tablespoons butter
5 ounces (150g) potatoes, peeled and chopped (about 1 cup)
1 medium onion, peeled and chopped (about 1 cup)
salt and freshly ground pepper
2 1/2 cups water or homemade Chicken or Vegetable Stock (see page 36)
2 1/2 cups creamy milk
8 ounces (225g) chopped watercress (coarse stalks removed)

Melt the butter in heavy saucepan and, when it foams, add the potatoes and onions and toss them until well coated. Sprinkle with salt and pepper. Cover and sweat over a gentle heat for 10 minutes. Meanwhile prepare the watercress. When the vegetables are almost soft but not colored, add the stock and milk, bring to a boil and cook until the potatoes and onions are tender. Add the watercress and boil with the lid off for about 4–5 minutes until the watercress is cooked. Do not overcook or the soup will lose its fresh green color. Purée the soup in a blender or food processor. Taste and correct the seasoning; serve immediately.

Irish Nettle Soup

Serves 6

In Season: Spring, while nettles are still young and tender.

Stinging nettles grow in great profusion. With their high iron content, they were used in folk medicine. Many older people still like to eat nettles several times during Spring to purify the blood and prevent arthritis over the coming year. Don't forget to use gloves when gathering them!

3 tablespoons butter
10 ounces (275g) potatoes, peeled and cut into 1/2-inch (1-cm) cubes (about 2 cups)
1 medium onion, chopped (about 1 cup)
1 medium leek, chopped (a slightly heaped cup)
salt and freshly ground pepper
1 quart (960ml) homemade Chicken Stock (see page 36)
5 ounces (150g) young nettle leaves, washed and chopped
2/3 cup cream

Melt the butter in a heavy saucepan. When it foams, add the potatoes, onion, and leek, tossing them in the butter until well coated. Sprinkle with salt and pepper. Cover with a paper lid (to keep in the steam) and the saucepan lid, and sweat on a gentle heat for 10 minutes, or until the vegetables are soft but not colored. Discard the paper lid, add the stock, and boil until the vegetables are just cooked. Add the nettle leaves. Simmer uncovered for just 2–3 minutes. Do not overcook or the vegetables will lose their flavor. Add the cream or creamy milk and purée. Taste and correct seasoning if necessary. Serve hot.

Variation

Wild Garlic Soup

Substitute wild garlic leaves for nettles in the recipe above. Garnish with wild garlic flowers.

Spiced Cabbage Soup

Serves 6

Another winter soup from Rory O'Connell.

1/2 stick (1/4 cup) butter
5 ounces (150g) potatoes, chopped (about 1 cup)
1 medium onion, chopped (about 1 cup)
salt and freshly ground pepper
1 quart (960ml) homemade Chicken Stock (see page 36)
9 ounces (250g) spring cabbage leaves, chopped and stalks removed
1/4–1/2 cup cream or creamy milk

Spice Mixture
1/4 cup vegetable oil
1 generous tablespoon whole black mustard seeds
4 garlic cloves, peeled and very finely chopped
1/2–1 hot, dried red chile, coarsely crushed
1/2 teaspoon sugar
freshly ground pepper

Garnish
softly whipped cream
fresh cilantro leaves

Melt the butter in a heavy saucepan. When it foams, add the potatoes and onions and turn them in the butter until well coated. Sprinkle with salt and pepper. Cover and sweat over a gentle heat for 10 minutes. Add the stock (pre-heat it if you want to speed things up) and boil until the potatoes are soft. Add the cabbage and cook, uncovered, until the cabbage is just cooked, 4–5 minutes. Keeping the lid off retains the green color. Purée immediately and add the creamy milk.

Now heat the oil in a large frying pan over a medium flame. When hot, add the mustard seeds. As soon as they begin to pop, add the garlic. Stir the garlic pieces around until they turn light brown (be careful not to let it burn or it will spoil the flavor). Add the crushed red chile and stir for a few seconds. Add this spice mixture to the puréed soup along with the seasoning. Taste and correct as necessary. Serve piping hot with a blob of whipped cream and a few cilantro leaves.

Master Recipe

Savoy Cabbage Soup

Serves 6

Chinese seaweed (see page 167) can be fun to serve with this soup but in many ways it's also perfect unadorned.

1/2 stick (1/4 cup) butter
5 ounces (150g) potatoes, peeled and cut into 1/2-inch (1-cm) cubes (about 1 cup)
1 medium onion, cut into 1/2-inch (1-cm) cubes (about 1 cup)
salt and freshly ground pepper
5 cups light Chicken Stock or Vegetable Stock (see page 36)
9 ounces (250g) chopped Savoy cabbage leaves, stalks removed (about 4–4 1/2 cups)
1/4–1/2 cup cream or creamy milk

Melt the butter in a heavy saucepan. When it foams, add the potatoes and onions, and turn them in the butter until well coated. Sprinkle with salt and pepper. Cover, and sweat on a gentle heat for 10 minutes. Add the stock and boil until the potatoes are soft, then add the cabbage and cook with the lid off until the cabbage is tender. Keep the lid off to retain the green color. Do not overcook or the vegetables will lose their fresh flavor and color. Purée the soup in a blender, taste and adjust the seasoning. Add the cream or creamy milk before serving.

Variation

Cabbage and Caraway Soup

Follow the Master Recipe, adding 1–2 teaspoons of freshly crushed caraway to the potato and onion base.

Tip: If this soup is to be reheated, just bring it to a boil and serve. Prolonged boiling will spoil both color and flavor.

Cauliflower and Cheddar Cheese Soup

Serves 6

Broccoli, Romanesco, or calabrese can be used in place of cauliflower to make this soup.

1 handsome head of cauliflower, about 2 lbs. (900g), weighed with green outer leaves still on
2½ cups Cheddar Cheese Sauce (see page 581)
salt and freshly ground pepper

Garnish
½–¾ cup shredded Cheddar cheese
3 tablespoons parsley, chopped
Crispy Croûtons (see page 226)

Chop up all the outer green leaves of the cauliflower, put them in a saucepan, and barely cover with cold water. Bring to a boil and simmer for about 45 minutes until you have a well-flavored cauliflower stock. Chop up the cauliflower head, place in a saucepan, and cover with the cauliflower stock, reserving any leftover liquid for later. Bring to a boil and cook, covered, until the cauliflower is tender (5–8 minutes). Blend the cauliflower to get a smooth purée. Mix the cauliflower purée and cheese sauce together, adding enough cauliflower or chicken stock to obtain a nice consistency. Taste and season. Serve with croûtons, cheese, and parsley.

Tip: Don't keep this soup in a bain-marie or boil it for ages, or the fresh taste will be spoiled.

Rutabaga and Bacon Soup

Serves 6–8

1 tablespoon sunflower or peanut oil
5 ounces (150g) bacon, cut into ½-inch (1-cm) dice
12 ounces (350g) rutabagas, diced (about 2 cups)
1 medium onion, chopped (about 1 cup)
5 ounces (150g) potatoes, diced (about 1 cup)
salt and freshly ground pepper
1 quart (960ml) homemade Chicken Stock (see page 36)
cream or creamy milk to taste

Garnish
fried diced bacon
tiny croûtons
chopped parsley

Heat the oil in a saucepan, add the bacon, and cook on a gentle heat until crisp and golden. Remove to a plate with a slotted spoon. Toss the rutabaga, onion, and potato in the bacon fat and season. Cover with a paper lid and sweat over a gentle heat until soft but not colored, about 10 minutes. Add the stock, bring to a boil, and simmer until the vegetables are fully cooked. Purée, taste, add a little cream or creamy milk and extra seasoning if necessary. Serve with a mixture of crispy bacon, tiny croûtons, and chopped parsley sprinkled on top.

Above: French Onion Soup with Gruyère Toasts (see page 48)

French Onion Soup with Gruyère Toasts

Serves 6

French onion soup is probably the best known and loved of all French soups. It was a favorite for breakfast in the cafés beside the old markets at Les Halles in Paris and is still a favorite on bistro menus at Rungis market. In France this soup is served in special white porcelain tureens. Enjoy it with a glass of gutsy French vin de table.

½ stick (¼ cup) butter
3 lbs. (1.3kg) onions, thinly sliced
2 quarts (1.8 liters) good homemade Beef, Chicken or Vegetable Stock (see page 36)
salt and freshly ground pepper

To Finish
6 slices French bread (baguette), ½ inch (1cm) thick, toasted
¾ cup shredded Gruyère cheese

Melt the butter in a saucepan. Add the onions and cook over a low heat for about 40–60 minutes with the lid off, stirring frequently – the onions should be dark and well caramelized but not burnt. Add the stock, season with salt and freshly ground pepper, bring to a boil, and cook for a further 10 minutes. Ladle into deep soup bowls, and put a piece of toasted baguette covered with grated cheese on top of each one. Pop under the broiler until the cheese melts and turns golden. Serve immediately but beware – it will be very hot. Bon appetit!

Tip: Hold your nerve: the onions must be very well caramelized, otherwise the soup will be too weak and sweet.

How to peel tomatoes

Choose tomatoes that are very ripe but still firm. Prick the base of each one. Put them into a deep bowl and completely cover with boiling water. Count to 10 slowly before pouring off the water. The skins will then peel off easily.

How to seed tomatoes

Halve the tomatoes crosswise and, holding the halves over a bowl with the cut side down, squeeze them gently. Most of the seeds will fall out. If any remain, remove them with a teaspoon.

How to make tomato concassé

Peel the tomatoes (see above), cut into quarters, then remove the seeds and divisions with a small knife or sharp spoon. Cut the flesh into small, even-sized dice. Don't forget to season with salt, pepper, and perhaps a little sugar before using.

Master Recipe

Vine-ripened Tomato and Spearmint Soup

Serves 5

Tomato is to soup what apple tart is to desserts – top of the list of all-time favorites. And the marvelous thing about this recipe is that you can easily vary it in so many different ways, making it almost seem like a different soup each time. Of course it's best to use a purée made from vine-ripened tomatoes in season. Good quality canned tomatoes (a must for your store cupboard) also produce a really good result but, because they are rather more acidic than fresh tomatoes, you need to add extra sugar.

1 tablespoon butter
1 small onion, finely chopped
3 cups homemade tomato purée (see next page) or 2 x 14-ounce (400g) canned tomatoes, puréed and strained
1 cup Béchamel sauce (see page 580)
1 cup homemade Chicken Stock or Vegetable Stock (see page 36)
2 tablespoons spearmint, freshly chopped
salt and freshly ground pepper
1–2 slightly heaped tablespoons sugar
½ cup cream (optional)

Garnish
whipped cream
spearmint, freshly chopped

Melt the butter over a gentle heat. Add the onion, cover, and cook until soft but not colored. Add the homemade tomato purée or the puréed and strained canned tomatoes, the Béchamel sauce and stock, the mint, salt and pepper, plus sugar if you are using canned tomatoes – otherwise just a pinch. Bring to a boil and simmer for a few minutes. Purée and, if necessary, dilute with extra chicken stock. Bring back to a boil, correct the seasoning, and serve with the addition of a little cream, if you choose. Garnish with spearmint and a blob of whipped cream.

Tip: This soup needs to be tasted carefully. You may need to adjust the seasoning depending on the intensity of the tomato puree and the stock.

Tip: Like most soups, this one re-heats very well and can, of course, be frozen.

Vine-ripened Tomato Purée

2 lbs. (900g) vine-ripened tomatoes
1 small onion, chopped
good pinch of salt
a few twists of freshly ground black pepper
good pinch of sugar (optional)

Cut the very ripe tomatoes into quarters and put into a stainless steel saucepan with the onion, salt, pepper, and sugar. Cook on a gentle heat until the tomatoes are soft (no water is needed). Put through the fine blade of the mouli-legume or a nylon strainer. Let cool, and refrigerate or freeze.

Tip: This is one of the very best ways of preserving the flavor of ripe summer tomatoes for the winter. Use for soups, stews, casseroles, etc.

Variations

Tomato and Basil Soup

Add 2 tablespoons freshly torn basil leaves instead of mint.

Tomato and Cilantro Soup

Add 2 tablespoons freshly chopped cilantro instead of mint.

Tomato and Orange Soup

Add the finely grated rind of one unwaxed orange instead of mint.

Tomato and Rosemary Soup

Add 1 tablespoon freshly chopped rosemary instead of mint.

Tomato Soup with Pesto

Replace the garnish with a drizzle of lightly whipped cream and pesto over each bowl before serving. Serve with an accompaniment, either of croûtons cut into square, star, or tiny heart shapes, and fried in olive oil, or of Tapenade Toasts (see page 74).

Mushroom Soup

Serves 8–9

Mushroom soup is the fastest of all soups to make and one of the all-time favorites. It is best made with flat mushrooms or button mushrooms which are a few days old and have developed a slightly stronger flavor. Wild mushrooms appear every few years after a good warm summer – it's either a feast or a famine! Surpluses can be used to make the base of the soup and then freeze the purée (to take less room in the freezer). Add stock and milk to reconstitute just before serving.

2 tablespoons butter
1 medium onion, rinsed under cold, running water, and finely chopped (about 1/2 cup)
1 lb. (450g) mushrooms
2 1/2 cups homemade Chicken or Vegetable Stock (see page 36)
2 1/2 cups milk
1/4 cup flour
salt and freshly ground pepper

Melt the butter in a saucepan over a gentle heat and toss the onions in it. Cover and sweat until soft and completely cooked. Meanwhile, chop up the mushrooms very finely. Add to the saucepan and cook over a high heat for 4 or 5 minutes. In separate pans, bring the stock and milk to a boil (this is important: the milk may curdle if added to the soup cold). Stir the flour into the mushroom mixture, cook over a low heat for 2–3 minutes. Season with salt and freshly ground pepper, then add the hot stock and milk gradually, stirring all the time. Increase the heat and bring to the boil. Taste, and add a dash of cream if necessary. Serve immediately or cool and reheat later.

Tip: When chopping mushrooms, put the cutting board on a tray and chop a few at a time until very fine; the tray catches all the pieces that scatter as you chop fast.

Spiced Eggplant Soup with Roast Pepper and Cilantro Cream

Serves 8–10

We grow several different varieties of eggplant. The Slim Jim is our favorite for this recipe, but any type will do. Rory O'Connell taught this recipe to the students on his course here at Ballymaloe Cookery School.

2 tablespoons olive oil
6 ounces (175g) onion, chopped (about 1 1/2 cups)
8 garlic cloves, chopped
1 tablespoon cumin seeds, roasted and ground
1 tablespoon fennel seeds, roasted and ground
2 lbs. (900g) eggplant, cut into 3/4-inch (2-cm) cubes
salt and freshly ground pepper
1 1/2 quarts (1.5 liters) homemade Chicken Stock (see page 36)
freshly squeezed lemon or lime juice to taste
creamy milk if necessary

Garnish
1–2 roast red peppers, peeled, seeded, and diced (see page 80)
2 tablespoons cilantro, coarsely chopped
2/3 cup whipped cream
cilantro leaves

Gently sweat the onions with the garlic and spices in the olive oil until soft, about 10 minutes. Add the eggplant, season with salt and freshly ground pepper, and sweat until wilted, about 30 minutes. Pour in the chicken stock, bring to a boil, and cook until tender, approximately 5 minutes. Purée, taste, and correct the seasoning. You may need to add a little lemon or lime juice or a little creamy milk. Just before serving, fold the red peppers and cilantro into the cream, reserving some to garnish each bowl with the cilantro leaves.

Spiced Zucchini and Green Pepper Soup with Roast Red Pepper Cream

Serves 9

2 tablespoons butter
1 medium onion, diced (about 1 cup)
5 ounces (150g) potatoes, peeled and diced (about 1 cup)
9 ounces (250g) zucchini, diced (about 2 cups)
7 ounces (200g) green pepper, diced
1/2 chile, seeded and chopped
5 1/2 cups homemade Chicken Stock (see page 36)
1 level teaspoon each of cumin seed, cardamom seed, and ground ginger
a little creamy milk

Heat the butter in a saucepan, and sweat the onions and potatoes over a low heat for 10 minutes, covered with a buttered paper and a tight-fitting lid. Add the zucchini, green pepper, and chile. Cover with chicken stock and simmer until soft. Meanwhile, warm the spices in the oven to develop the flavor, then grind them. When the vegetables are soft, purée them, adding the spices and seasoning. Let infuse for a little while. Finish the soup by adding more chicken stock or creamy milk to achieve the required consistency. Serve hot with a garnish of Roast Red Pepper Cream.

Roast Red Pepper Cream

1 large red pepper
1/2 cup softly whipped cream or crème fraîche
pinch of salt

Roast the red pepper in a moderate oven (350°F/180°C) with a drizzle of olive oil over them, until tender and collapsed, about 25 minutes. Remove and place in a sealed plastic bag. When cool, peel and seed the pepper. Chop the pepper flesh finely and mix into the softly whipped cream with the salt.

Red Pepper Soup with Avocado and Cilantro Salsa

Serves 4–6

Rory O'Connell serves this salsa as an embellishment to this soup. A spoonful of Tomato and Chile Sauce (see page 590) is also terrific with it.

2 tablespoons butter
2 tablespoons olive oil
2 medium onions, about 10 ounces (275g)
2 star anise
4 red or yellow peppers, seeded and chopped
salt, freshly ground pepper, and sugar
2 1/2 cups homemade Chicken Stock (see page 36), enough to cover

Melt butter, add oil, and sweat onions until they start to soften. Add the star anise together with the peppers. Season with salt, pepper, and sugar, and sweat until the peppers become "oily" and start to soften. Barely cover with chicken stock and simmer until peppers are tender. Discard the star anise. Purée until smooth and let cool. Serve chilled in small bowls with a spoonful of Avocado and Cilantro Salsa on top.

Avocado and Cilantro Salsa

2 avocados, diced
4 scallions, finely chopped
1 garlic clove, crushed
a drizzle of extra-virgin olive oil
2–3 tablespoons cilantro, coarsely chopped
squeeze of lemon juice
salt, freshly ground pepper, and sugar to taste

Put all the ingredients into a bowl. Season with salt, pepper, and sugar. Mix gently.

Henny's Curried Banana Soup

Serves 6

Students occasionally give us a favorite recipe. This one, given to us by Henny Wardell, sounds rather bizarre but it got a terrific reaction.

2 tablespoons butter
1 onion, chopped
2 teaspoons curry powder
1 quart (960ml) Chicken Stock (see page 36)
12 ounces (350g) sliced bananas (about 1 1/2 cups)
2/3 cup whipping cream
pinch of salt

Melt the butter in a stainless steel saucepan and sweat the onions until soft but not colored, approximately 5 minutes. Stir in the curry powder and cook for 1 minute. Add the stock, sliced bananas, and salt. Simmer for 15 minutes uncovered. Blend well, stir in cream, and season to taste. Reheat and serve.

Tojo's Lentil Soup

Serves 8–10

Tojo cooked in the Garden Café at the Ballymaloe Cookery School one summer, and he created some memorable dishes. He uses no stock for his soups since many of his guests are vegan or vegetarian. This soup is incredibly simple to make.

1/2 cup extra-virgin olive oil
6 large onions, chopped
1/2 cup soy sauce
4 garlic cloves
salt and pepper to taste
2 1/2 cups Puy lentils
2 1/2 quarts (2.4 liters) water

Garnish
flat-leaf parsley
extra-virgin olive oil

Heat the extra-virgin olive oil in a medium-sized pot, add the onions, soy sauce, garlic, salt, and pepper. Place over a fairly high flame for about 10 minutes, then lower the heat and simmer until the onions have a slightly sweet taste. Add the water and lentils and simmer for about 45 minutes. When the lentils are cooked, taste and correct the seasoning. Be careful not to let the lentils get mushy – it's nice if there is a slight bite to them. Serve in wide soup bowls with parsley and drizzled with your best extra-virgin olive oil.

Spiced Chickpea Soup with Cilantro Cream and Pita Crisps

Serves 4–6

A speedier version of this delicious soup can be made with a can of chickpeas.

1½ cups chickpeas, soaked overnight in plenty of cold water
1½ quarts (1.5 liters) homemade Chicken or Vegetable Stock (see page 36)
2–3 teaspoons coriander seeds
2–3 teaspoons cumin seeds
½ stick (¼ cup) butter
6 ounces (175g) onions, finely chopped (about 1½ cups)
5 large garlic cloves, peeled and finely chopped
1–2 small red chiles, halved, seeded and chopped
½ teaspoon ground turmeric
⅓ cup cream
salt and freshly ground black pepper
freshly squeezed lemon juice

Garnish
crème fraîche
fresh cilantro leaves
Pita Crisps (see right)

Drain the chickpeas and put them in a saucepan, cover with the stock, and bring to a boil. Cover and simmer gently for 45–60 minutes, or until soft and tender. Strain, reserving the liquid. Meanwhile, dry-roast the coriander and cumin seeds in a frying-pan over medium heat for 2–3 minutes, then crush in a mortar and pestle or spice grinder. Melt the butter in a saucepan, add the onion, spices, garlic, and chile. Cook gently for 4–5 minutes, add the turmeric, stir, and cook for another 1–2 minutes.

Remove from the heat, add the chickpeas, and mix well. Season with salt and pepper. Now purée the chickpeas with the cooking liquid and cream. Place in a saucepan and simmer for 10–20 minutes. If the soup is a little too thick, thin out with extra stock. Taste and, if necessary, sharpen with freshly squeezed lemon juice. Serve with a blob of crême fraîche, cilantro leaves, and Pita Crisps.

Pita Crisps

3 mini pita breads, about 3 inches (8cm) in diameter, halved crosswise
4 teaspoons extra-virgin olive oil
1 teaspoon cumin, freshly ground
½ teaspoon salt

Preheat the oven to 400°F (200°C). Cut the pieces of pita into triangles. Brush evenly with olive oil and sprinkle with cumin and salt. Spread pita pieces in a single layer on a baking tray and bake in the middle of the oven for 3 minutes or until crisp and golden. Serve immediately.

Fasolatha (Greek Bean Soup)

Serves 6

This staple winter soup, which is wonderfully filling and easy to make, has nourished generations of Greeks. It is a rustic soup that re-heats well and improves with keeping.

2 cups navy or cannellini beans, soaked in plenty of cold water overnight, or 1 x 14-ounce (400-g) can cooked beans
5 cups water or homemade Chicken Stock (see page 36)
1 large onion, thinly sliced
1 leek, thinly sliced
2 carrots, finely diced
2 stalks of celery with leaves, finely chopped
1 x 14-ounce (400-g) can of tomatoes
1 slightly rounded tablespoon tomato paste
2 garlic cloves, chopped
⅔ cup olive oil
salt, freshly ground pepper, and sugar
1 tablespoon marjoram, chopped
1 tablespoon thyme leaves, chopped

Garnish
2 tablespoons parsley, chopped

Rinse the beans and drain them. Cover with fresh cold water, bring to a boil, and simmer for 5 minutes. Drain, then add all other ingredients except the parsley. Cook for 40–50 minutes or until the beans are just soft and the vegetables cooked. Taste and correct seasoning. Garnish with the parsley and serve drizzled with a little extra-virgin olive oil.

Mediterranean Fish Soup with Rouille

Serves 6–8

This gutsy fish soup is a labor of love and worth every minute. Fish soups can be made with all sorts and combinations of fish. Don't worry if you lack the exact ingredients I suggest – use a combination of whole fish and shellfish. The crab does add an almost essential richness in my opinion.

5½ lbs. (2.45kg) mixed fish, e.g., 1 whole sole, ½ cod, 2 small whiting, 3 swimming crab or 1 common crab, 6–8 mussels, 8–10 shrimp, 2 fish heads
⅔ cup olive oil
1 large garlic clove, crushed
10 ounces (275g) onions, chopped (about 2 cups)
5 large, very ripe tomatoes or 1 x 14-ounce (400-g) can of chopped tomatoes

5 sprigs of fennel
2 sprigs of thyme
1 bay leaf
fish stock or water barely to cover
1/4 teaspoon saffron
salt and freshly ground pepper
pinch of cayenne

Rouille
1 piece of French bread (baguette), 2 inches (5cm) long
6 tablespoons hot fish soup
4 garlic cloves
1 egg yolk, preferably from free-range hen
pinch of whole saffron stamens
salt and freshly ground pepper
6 tablespoons extra-virgin olive oil

Croûtons
8 slices French bread (baguette), 1/2 inch (1cm) thick
3/4–1 cup shredded Gruyère cheese

Garnish
chopped parsley

Cut the fish into chunks: bones, head, and all (remove gills first). Heat the olive oil until smoking, add the garlic and onions, toss for a minute or two, add the tomatoes, herbs, and fish, including shells. Cook for 10 minutes, then add enough fish stock or water to barely cover. Bring to a fast boil and cook for a further 10 minutes. Add more liquid if it reduces too much. Soak the saffron strands in a little fish stock. Pick out and discard the mussel shells. Taste, add salt, pepper, cayenne, saffron, and the soaking liquid. Push the soup through a food mill (this may seem like an impossible task but you'll be surprised how effective it will be – there will be just a mass of dry bones left, which you discard).

Next make the rouille. Cut the bread into cubes and soak in some hot fish soup. Squeeze out the excess liquid and mix to a mush in a bowl. Crush the garlic to a fine paste in a mortar and pestle, add the egg yolk, the saffron, and the soggy bread. Season with salt and freshly ground pepper.

Mix well and add in the oil drip by drip as in making mayonnaise. If the mixture looks too thick or oily, add 2 tablespoons of hot fish soup and continue to stir.

Toast slices of French bread slowly until they are dry and crisp. Bring the soup back to a boil. Spread the slices with rouille and sprinkle with Gruyère cheese, float a croûton in each plate of Mediterranean fish soup. Garnish with parsley and serve.

Vietnamese Shrimp Soup

Serves 4

The fresh clean taste of Asian soups like this one is soothing and addictive.

1/2 lb. (225g) shrimp or tiger shrimp, unpeeled
1 stick lemon grass
2 x 1-inch(2.5-cm) pieces fresh ginger root, peeled
1 quart (960ml) light Chicken Stock (see page 36)
1 tablespoon lime juice, freshly squeezed
1/2 teaspoon crushed dried chile or 1/4 teaspoon red chile paste
1 tablespoon fish sauce (nam pla)
3–4 ounces (75–110g) Napa cabbage or butterhead lettuce, shredded (about 1 1/2–2 cups)

Garnish
cilantro leaves

Peel the tiger shrimp or regular shrimp, put the shells into the saucepan with the lemon grass, ginger, and stock, bring to a boil, and simmer for 10 minutes. Strain, return the liquid to the saucepan. Add the lime juice, dried chile or chile paste, and nam pla, and simmer for 2 minutes. Add the tiger shrimp or regular shrimp and simmer for 4 or 5 minutes. Divide the Napa cabbage between the bowls. Ladle in the boiling soup. Garnish and serve at once.

Ballymaloe Mussel Soup

Serves 8

Because stale shellfish can cause illness, it is vital to sort the mussels carefully, discarding any that refuse to close tightly after they have been gently tapped. The maxim is, if in doubt, throw it out.

8–10 lbs. (3.6–4.5kg) mussels, scrubbed under cold running water
2 cups dry white wine
2/3 cup chopped shallots
1 garlic clove, mashed
8 parsley sprigs, 1/2 bay leaf, 1/4 teaspoon fresh thyme leaves, a sprig of fresh fennel
lots of freshly ground pepper
1/4 teaspoon curry powder (optional)
Roux made from 3/4 stick (1/3 cup) butter and 3/4 cup flour (see page 580)
3–5 cups boiling milk
a little cream if necessary

Garnish
chopped parsley or chervil
croûtons

Clean the mussels (see page 254). Put the wine, shallots, garlic, fresh herbs, and curry powder into a stainless steel saucepan, add the mussels, cover, and simmer gently. Remove the mussels as they open. Shell the mussels, saving a few in the shell for a garnish. Remove the beards, open, and place them in a bowl, discarding the shells. Strain the mussel cooking liquid into a stainless steel saucepan and boil rapidly over a high heat to concentrate the flavor. Taste frequently as it boils; if it reduces too much, the salt content will be overpowering. Whisk the roux into the mussel liquid to thicken. Add the boiling milk to thin out the soup to a light consistency. Just before serving, add the mussels and a little cream. Decorate with chopped parsley or chervil, and mussels in their shells. Serve croûtons separately.

Variation
Cockle and Mussel Soup
Use half cockles and mussels and proceed as before.

Tip: The milk must be boiling when added to the soup, otherwise it may curdle because of the acidity in the wine.

Aki Ishibashi's Miso Soup
Serves 4

Students now come from the four corners of the world to our little cooking school in Shanagarry. Aki, who came from Japan, was already a brilliant cook when she arrived.

2 1/2 cups Dashi (see page 37)
4–5 generous tablespoons miso paste
1 1/2 x 4-ounce (110-g) cakes tofu, cut into 1/2-inch (1-cm) cubes
2 teaspoons wakame (dried seaweed)

Garnish
1 scallion, thinly sliced

Heat the dashi, and dissolve the miso paste by stirring it into the dashi. When it has dissolved completely, add the tofu cubes and wakame. Bring it to a boil. As soon as it starts to boil, turn off the heat. Ladle miso soup into warmed individual soup bowls and garnish with the scallion.

Additions

Add any of the following to the basic soup:
Daikon (white radish) and wakame
Clams and scallion
Potato and scallion
Japanese shiitake mushrooms and scallion
Daikon (white radish) and radish leaves

Beef Consommé
Serves 4

A chef is always proud of a sparklingly clear, well flavored consommé. It needs to be made with great care and attention. In Ballymaloe we buy a well aged shin of beef from our butcher, Mr Cuddigan. We use the bones to make a rich beef stock and then use the meat to flavor the consommé.

3/4 lb. (350g) boneless beef shank free of any fat, finely chopped
1 small carrot, very finely chopped
green tops of 2 leeks, finely chopped
2 stalks of celery, very finely chopped
2 ripe tomatoes, quartered and seeded
3 egg whites
2 quarts (1.8 liters) well-flavored Beef Stock (see page 36)
salt and freshly ground pepper
1–2 tablespoons medium or dry sherry (optional)

Mix the chopped beef, carrots, leeks, celery, tomatoes, and egg whites in a bowl. Pour in the cold stock, whisk well, and season. Pour into a stainless steel saucepan. Bring slowly to a boil over a low heat, whisking constantly (should take about 10 minutes). As soon as the mixture looks cloudy and slightly milky, stop whisking. Let the filter of egg whites rise slowly to the top of the saucepan. DO NOT STIR. Let simmer gently for 45–60 minutes to extract all the flavor from the beef and vegetables. Add sherry if desired. Put a filter or a jelly bag into a strainer, then gently ladle the consommé into it, being careful not to disturb the filter. Do not press the sediment in the filter or the consommé will not be sparkling clear. Strain it through the cloth or filter a second time if necessary. If serving the consommé hot, bring it almost to a boil and add any flavorings, and garnish just before serving. Do not cook the garnish in the consommé as it will become cloudy. Do not let it boil.

Consommé en Gelée
This cool refreshing appetizer is perfect for a summer meal. If consommé is allowed to go cold it should become jellied. Chill and just before serving, spoon into chilled bowls. Garnish with chives or wild garlic flowers if available; sometimes we use marigold petals and chervil – pretty and delicious. Serve with freshly made Melba Toast (see page 78).

Aztec Soup

Serves 6

2 chiles, roasted, peeled, and torn into strips
1 tablespoon oil
1 onion, chopped
2 cloves garlic, finely chopped
5 cups homemade Chicken Stock (see page 36)
3–4 dashes Tabasco sauce
1 chicken breast
salt and freshly ground pepper
1 avocado
2 tomatoes, skinned, seeded, and diced
1/4 cup cilantro leaves, chopped

Garnish
fresh cilantro leaves
strips of corn Tortilla Chips (see page 494)

First roast the chiles: put either over an open flame, or under a broiler until quite black and bubbly. Put in a bowl and cover with plastic wrap for 5 minutes. Peel off the black skins with your fingers. Pull into little strips for garnish.

Heat the oil in a stainless steel pan and sweat the onion until soft. Add the garlic and cook for another 1–2 minutes. Add the chicken stock and Tabasco and simmer for 5 minutes. Meanwhile, remove the skin from the chicken if necessary. Cut it into 1/2-inch (1.25-cm) strips. Season well with salt and pepper. Add the chicken to the simmering broth and simmer for 3–4 minutes until white all the way through. Add the avocado and tomato, the cilantro and the strips of roasted chiles. Do not overcook or the avocado will dissolve. Garnish with fresh cilantro leaves and strips of corn Tortilla Chips (see page 494).

Rosemary Kearney's Chicken and Coconut Laksa (see page 160)

Thai Chicken, Galangal, and Cilantro Soup

Serves 8

This is a particularly delicious example of how fast and easy a Thai soup can be – and it looks great dished up in Chinese porcelain bowls. The kaffir lime leaves and galangal are served for dramatic effect but not eaten. The chile may, of course, be nibbled!

1 quart (960ml) homemade Chicken Stock (see page 36)
4 fresh kaffir lime leaves
2-inch (5-cm) piece of galangal, peeled and sliced, or less of fresh ginger
1/4 cup fish sauce (nam pla)
6 tablespoons lemon juice, freshly squeezed
8 ounces (225g) free-range organic chicken breast, finely sliced
1 cup coconut milk
1–3 Thai red chiles
a scant 1/2 cup fresh cilantro leaves

Put the chicken stock, lime leaves, galangal, fish sauce, and lemon juice into a saucepan. Bring to a boil, stirring all the time, then add the finely shredded chicken and coconut milk. Continue to cook over a high heat until the chicken is just cooked, about 1–2 minutes. Crush the chiles with a knife or Chinese chopper and add to the soup, with the cilantro leaves. Cook for just a few seconds and serve immediately.

Note: We usually use just one red Thai chile. The quantity will depend on your taste and how hot the chiles are.

Tip: Blanched and refreshed rice noodles are also great added to this soup.

Avgolemono

Serves 4–6

Avgolemono may be served hot or cold.

5 cups homemade Chicken Stock (see page 36)
4 eggs
juice of 1–2 small lemons
1–2 generous tablespoons freshly chopped dill

Bring the chicken stock to a boil. Whisk the eggs in a bowl with the lemon juice. Gradually add the boiling stock, whisking all the time, return to the saucepan and put back on the heat, stir, and cook until it thickens to a light coating consistency. It must not boil or it will curdle. Add the dill, taste and correct the seasoning.

You can simmer 3–5 tablespoons of rice in the stock, but you will need to allow extra stock because the rice soaks up quite a lot.

Portuguese Chicken Soup with Mint and Lemon

Serves 6

A great little soup, food for the soul!

2 quarts (1.8 liters) well-flavored homemade Chicken Stock (see page 36)
2 chicken breasts
1 unwaxed lemon
1–2 generous tablespoons freshly chopped mint
1 cup rice or orzo
salt and freshly ground pepper

Put the stock into a saucepan, add the chicken and finely pared strips of lemon peel (no pith). Bring slowly to a boil and simmer for 5 minutes. Remove the chicken, cool, and slice into thin shreds. Add the rice (or orzo), the juice from the lemon, and the mint. Season with salt and pepper. Bring back to a boil and simmer until the rice or orzo is cooked. Add the shredded chicken again. Taste and correct the seasoning; add more lemon juice if necessary. Serve immediately.

Right: Thai Chicken, Galangal, and Cilantro Soup

Chinese Fish Soup with Chile and Cilantro

Serves 6

We adore these light fish soups. Consider this recipe as a formula and vary the fish and shellfish depending on what you have available – mussels and crabmeat are particularly delicious. Lemon grass and a dice of cucumber also work well.

8 ounces (225g) lemon sole fillets, skinned
iceberg lettuce heart, finely shredded
5 cups very well-flavored Chinese Stock (see right)
salt and lots of freshly ground white pepper
½–1 red or green chile, thinly sliced
30 shrimp (we use Atlantic shrimp; if using the larger Pacific ones use less), cooked and peeled

Garnish
6 teaspoons scallion, finely sliced at an angle
freshly chopped cilantro or flat-leaf parsley
shrimp roe if available

Cut the fish fillets into pieces at an angle, each about 1½ inches (4cm). Shred the lettuce heart very finely: you will need about ¾–1 cup

When ready to eat, bring the stock to a boil, add the salt, sliced chile, and fish. Simmer for 1 minute. Add the shrimp and let them heat through. Put 2 generous tablespoons of the shredded lettuce into each soup bowl. Season generously with white pepper, and immediately ladle the boiling soup over it. Garnish with scallions, shrimp roe, and lots of fresh cilantro. Serve very hot.

Basic Chinese Stock

Makes about 2 quarts (2 liters)

This delicious stock forms the essential basis of many delicious light fish or meat soups. For the best flavor use free-range chickens.

2 lbs. (900g) chicken giblets, wings, necks, hearts, gizzards, etc. from free-range chickens
2 lbs. (900g) meaty pork spare ribs (or a total of 4 lbs. (1.8kg) any combination of chicken pieces, carcasses, giblets, or pork ribs)
1½-inch (4-cm) piece of fresh ginger root, unpeeled and thinly sliced
6 large scallions
5–7 quarts (4.8–6 liters) light Chicken Stock (see page 36)
¼ cup Shao Hsing rice wine

Put all the ingredients except the rice wine in a large saucepan and cover with cold water. Bring to a boil and skim off any scum. Reduce the heat and simmer, uncovered, gently for 4 hours approx., skimming regularly. Add the rice wine 5 minutes before the end of the cooking time. Strain the stock, cool, then refrigerate.

Remove the solidified fat from the top of the stock before use. The stock will keep in the refrigerator for several days; thereafter boil it every 2 or 3 days. It also freezes perfectly.

Green Pea Soup with Fresh Mint Cream

Serves 6–8

This soup tastes of summer. If you are using fresh peas, use the pods to make a vegetable stock as the basis for your soup. Having said that, best-quality frozen peas also make a delicious soup. Either way, be careful not to overcook them.

1 quart (960ml) homemade Chicken Stock (see page 36) or water
¼ cup sliced lean ham or 2 strips bacon
1 tablespoon butter
2 medium scallions, chopped
1½ lbs. (700g) shelled peas, fresh or frozen
outside leaves of a head of lettuce, shredded
sprig of mint
salt, freshly ground pepper, and sugar
2 tablespoons thick cream

Garnish
softly whipped cream
freshly chopped mint leaves

Heat the stock.

Cut the bacon into very fine shreds. Melt the butter and sweat the bacon for about 5 minutes, add the scallions and cook for a further 1–2 minutes. Then add the peas, lettuce, mint, and the hot stock or water. Season with salt, pepper, and sugar. Bring to a boil with the lid off and cook for about 5 minutes until the peas are just tender.

Purée and add a little cream to taste. Serve hot or chilled with a blob of whipped cream mixed with the mint.

If the soup is made ahead, reheat uncovered then serve immediately. It will lose its fresh taste and bright lively color if it sits in a bain-marie or simmers at length in a pan.

Pea and Cilantro Soup

Serves 6

This utterly delicious soup has a perky zing with the addition of fresh chile. It can also be served cold.

1 quart (960ml) homemade Chicken Stock (see page 36)
½ stick (¼ cup) butter
5 ounces (150g) onion, finely chopped (about 1⅓ cups)
2 garlic cloves, peeled and chopped
1 green chile, seeded and finely chopped
1 lb. (450g) peas (good-quality frozen ones are fine)
2 tablespoons freshly chopped cilantro
salt, freshly ground pepper, and sugar

Garnish
softly whipped cream
fresh cilantro leaves

Heat the stock.

Melt the butter on a gentle heat and add the onion, garlic, and chile. Season with salt and pepper and sweat for 3–4 minutes. Add the peas and cover with hot stock. Bring to a boil and simmer for 5–8 minutes. Add the cilantro and purée. Check the seasoning and add a pinch of sugar which enhances the flavor.

Serve with a swirl of cream and a few fresh cilantro leaves over the top.

Variation

Fava Bean and Savory Soup

Substitute peeled fava beans and savory for the peas and cilantro and proceed as above.

Potato and Corn Chowder

Serves 4–6

A satisfying and filling soup made in a short time. This could become a supper dish if eaten with a few scones and followed by a salad.

2 tablespoons butter
2–3 medium potatoes, parboiled for 10 minutes, drained, peeled, and finely chopped
6 ounces (175g) onion, finely chopped (about 1½ cups)
1¼ cups homemade Chicken Stock (see page 36)
1¼ cups milk
1 lb. (450g) corn kernels
salt and freshly ground pepper
1 cup light cream or creamy milk

Garnish
roasted red pepper dice or crispy bacon dice
sprigs of flat-leaf parsley

Melt the butter in a heavy-bottomed saucepan, add the onion and potato and sweat until soft but not colored. Gradually add in the stock and milk, stirring all the time, and bring to a boil. Simmer for a few minutes, add the corn, season with salt and freshly ground pepper, cover, and cook gently for 10–15 minutes or until the potatoes are cooked. Add the cream and heat through gently without boiling. Serve in hot bowls with a little dice of roasted red pepper or crispy bacon, and parsley on top.

Note: If the soup is too thick, thin it out with a little extra chicken or vegetable stock.

Seafood Chowder

See page 264

French Peasant Soup

Serves 6

Here is another very substantial soup – it has "eating and drinking" in it and would certainly be a meal in itself particularly if you grate some Cheddar cheese over the top. Myrtle Allen called this soup Connemara Broth when she served it at La Ferme Irlandaise in Paris.

6 ounces (175g) unsmoked slab bacon
olive or sunflower oil
5 ounces (150g) potatoes, peeled and cut into ¼-inch (5-mm) dice (about 1 cup)
¼ cup finely chopped onions
1 small garlic clove, optional
1 lb. (450g) very ripe tomatoes, peeled and diced, or 1 x 14-ounce (400-g) can of tomatoes and juice
salt and freshly ground pepper
½–1 teaspoon sugar
1 quart (960ml) homemade Chicken or Vegetable Stock (see page 36)
2 ounces (50g) cabbage (Savoy is best), finely chopped (about 1 cup)

Garnish
freshly chopped flat-leaf parsley

Remove the rind from the bacon if necessary. Prepare the vegetables and cut the bacon into ¼-inch (5-mm) cubes.

Blanch the cubes in cold water to remove some of the salt, drain, and dry on paper towels, then sauté in a little olive or sunflower oil until the fat runs and the bacon is crisp and golden. Add potatoes, onions, and crushed garlic, sweat for 10 minutes, and then add diced tomatoes and any juice.

Season with salt, pepper, and sugar. Cover with stock and cook for 5 minutes. Add the finely chopped cabbage and continue to simmer just until the cabbage is cooked. Taste and adjust seasoning.

Sprinkle with lots of chopped parsley and serve.

Variation

Mediterranean Peasant Soup

Add half a thinly sliced Kabanossi sausage to the soup with the potato. For a more robust soup, add ¾ cup cooked navy beans with the cabbage.

Lima Bean, Chorizo, and Cabbage Soup

Serves 6

2 tablespoons extra-virgin olive oil
6 ounces (175g) onion, chopped (about 1½ cups)
6 ounces (175g) chorizo or Kabanossi sausage, sliced
1 x 14-ounce (400-g) can of Italian tomatoes
salt, freshly ground pepper, and sugar
5 cups homemade Chicken Stock (see page 36)
1 x 14-ounce (400-g) can lima beans, navy beans or black-eyed peas
½ Savoy cabbage
¼ cup freshly chopped flat-leaf parsley

Heat the oil in a sauté pan over a medium heat, add the onion, cover, and sweat until soft but not colored. Slice the chorizo or Kabanossi and toss for 2–3 minutes or until it begins to crisp slightly – the fat should run. Chop the tomatoes fairly finely and add with all the juice to the pan, season with salt, freshly ground pepper, and sugar.

Bring to a boil and cook on a high heat for 5–6 minutes, add the boiling stock and lima beans. Bring back to a boil, thinly slice the cabbage, and add. Cook for another 2–3 minutes, add the chopped parsley. Taste and correct the seasoning and serve with lots of crusty bread.

Winter Vegetable and Bean Soup with Spicy Sausage

Serves 8–9

We make huge pots of this in the winter, and I usually keep some in the freezer. Kabanossi is a thin sausage, about 5–6 inches (12.5–15cm) long, and gives a gutsy slightly smoky flavor to the soup which, although satisfying, is by no means essential.

8 ounces (225g) bacon, cut into 1/4-inch (5-mm) dice
2 tablespoons olive oil
8 ounces (225g) onions, chopped (about 2 cups)
10 ounces (275g) carrot, cut into 1/4-inch (5-mm) dice (about 2 1/2 cups)
7 ounces (200g) celery, chopped into 1/4-inch (5-mm) dice (about 2 cups)
5 ounces (150g) parsnips, chopped into 1/4-inch (5-mm) dice (about 1 1/3 cups)
7 ounces (200g) white part of 1 leek, cut into 1/4-inch (5-mm) slices (about 2 cups)
1 Kabanossi (or chorizo) sausage (optional), cut into 1/4-inch (5-mm) slices
1 x 14-ounce (400-g) can of Italian tomatoes
1 1/4 cups navy beans, soaked and cooked (see below)
salt, freshly ground pepper, and sugar
2 quarts (1.8 liters) homemade Chicken Stock (see page 36)

Garnish
2 tablespoons freshly chopped flat-leaf parsley

Blanch the bacon, refresh, and dry well. Prepare the vegetables. Put the olive oil in a saucepan, add bacon, and sauté over a medium heat until it becomes crisp and golden, then add the chopped onion, carrots and celery. Cover and sweat for 5 minutes, then add the parsnip and finely sliced leeks. Cover and sweat for a further 5 minutes.

Slice the Kabanossi sausage thinly, if using, and add. Chop the tomatoes and add to the rest of the vegetables along with the beans. Season with salt, freshly ground pepper, and sugar, add the chicken stock. Let cook until all the vegetables are tender, which takes about 20 minutes. Taste and correct the seasoning. Sprinkle with chopped parsley and serve with lots of crusty brown bread.

To prepare the navy beans
Soak overnight in plenty of cold water. The next day, strain the beans and cover with fresh cold water, add a bouquet garni, carrot, and onion, cover, and simmer until the beans are soft but not mushy – this can take 30–60 minutes. Just before the end of cooking, add salt. Remove the bouquet garni and vegetables, and discard.

Master Recipe

Beet Soup with Chive Cream

Serves 8–10

2 lbs. (900g) beets
2 tablespoons butter
8 ounces (225g) onions, chopped (about 2 cups)
salt and freshly ground pepper
5 cups homemade Chicken or Vegetable Stock (see page 36)
1/2 cup creamy milk
Chive Cream
1/2 cup sour cream or crème fraîche
chives, finely chopped

Wash the beets carefully under a cold tap. Do not scrub them – simply rub off the clay with your fingers. You do not want to damage the skin or cut off the tops or tails, otherwise the beets will "bleed" while cooking. Put into cold water, bring to a boil, and simmer, covered, for anything from 20 minutes to 2 hours depending on the size and age of your beets. They are cooked when their skins rub off easily. Remove these, and top and tail the beets.

Meanwhile heat the butter in a saucepan and gently sweat the onions. Chop the cooked beets and add to the onions. Season with salt and pepper. In a separate saucepan, bring the stock to simmering point. Pour into a blender, along with the vegetables, and blend until quite smooth. Reheat, add some creamy milk, taste and adjust the seasoning; it may be necessary to add a little more stock or creamy milk. Serve garnished with swirls of sour cream and a sprinkling of chives.

Variations

Golden Beet Soup

Follow the Master Recipe using golden Chioggio beets.

Chilled Beet Soup

Follow the Master Recipe up the point where you season it. Purée it, with just enough stock to cover, until smooth and silky. Season with salt and pepper. Fold in some cream and yogurt. Serve well chilled with little swirls of yogurt and finely chopped chives.

Cold soups

So refreshing are cold soups as an introduction to summer meals that the number of possibilities keeps increasing. Spanish gaspacho – perhaps the best known of them all – is especially cooling with the addition of ice or iced water before serving. Chilled, jellied consommé served with melba toast is also a classic. Lebanese cold cucumber soup is one of the yogurt-based cold soups that has long been a favorite in Ballymaloe.

Some soups like Pea and Mint or Beet can taste equally delicious served hot or cold, but you may have to make some minor

adjustments if you choose the latter option. Remember, cold dulls flavor, so taste and correct the seasoning just before serving. You may also want to add some fresh herbs. Many soups are served rather thicker when cold than when hot. (Most thicken naturally as they cool.) Fresh vegetable juices or tomato water are served thin and chilled.

Gaspacho

Serves 4–6

1½ lbs. (700g) very ripe tomatoes, peeled and finely chopped
1 tablespoon red wine vinegar
3 thick slices good-quality stale bread made into breadcrumbs
2–3 garlic cloves, crushed
2 cups Fresh Tomato Juice (see page 576)
2 roast and peeled red peppers
1 medium onion, peeled and chopped (about 1 cup)
1 medium cucumber, chopped
¼ cup extra-virgin olive oil
2 tablespoons Homemade Mayonnaise (see page 584), optional
1 teaspoon salt
freshly ground black pepper and sugar

Garnish
2 red peppers, finely diced
1 small cucumber, finely diced
4 very ripe tomatoes, finely diced
4 slices bread made into tiny croûtons and fried in olive oil
2 heaped tablespoons diced black olives or small whole olives
1 small onion, diced
salt and freshly ground pepper
1 generous tablespoon freshly chopped mint

Put the tomatoes, vinegar, breadcrumbs, crushed garlic, tomato juice, roasted red pepper, chopped onion, cucumber, olive oil, and mayonnaise into a food processor or blender. Season with salt and freshly ground pepper and sugar. Whizz until smooth. Dilute with water and chill, taste and correct the seasoning.

Mix all the ingredients for the garnish together in a separate bowl. Each guest helps themselves; the soup should be thick with garnish. Drizzle with extra-virgin olive oil; on a very hot day you can add an ice cube or two if you wish.

Chilled Avocado Soup with Tomato and Pepper Salsa

Serves 4

This tasty soup is best made with fresh tomato juice. However, if you have any juices left from a tomato salad, tomato fondue, or a ratatouille, you could use those. Alternatively, simply purée a few tomatoes, seasoned nicely with salt, pepper, and sugar.

1 very ripe avocado
½ small onion
½ teaspoon freshly squeezed lemon juice
⅔ cup homemade Chicken Stock (see page 36)
¼ cup very good French Dressing (see page 225)
⅔ cup Fresh Tomato Juice (see page 576)

Fresh Tomato and Pepper Salsa (see page 592)

Peel the avocado. Grate the onion on a very fine grater and scrape up enough pulp to measure ½ teaspoon. Put with the remaining ingredients in a blender. Blend to a purée, taste. Salt and pepper should not be needed. Fill 4 small serving bowls and chill. Put a spoonful of salsa into each small bowl and serve.

Vichyssoise

Serves 8–10

In 1917 this cold soup was developed by Louis Diat, chef of the Ritz Carlton in New York. It is based on the potage bonne femme recipe. You need a garden to get good leeks in late summer and perhaps it is worth using a few baby leeks for this tasty soup. This soup is very rich and needs to be served in small portions.

1/2 stick (1/4 cup) butter
1 onion, finely chopped
whites of 4 leeks, cleaned and finely sliced
1 1/4 lbs. (600g) potatoes, peeled and finely diced
salt and freshly ground pepper
5 cups homemade Chicken Stock (see page 36)
1 cup cream
1 tablespoon chives, finely snipped

Melt the butter in a heavy saucepan, and as soon as it foams add the onion, leeks, and potatoes. Season with salt and pepper. Cover with a butter wrapper and tightly fitting lid and sweat until soft but not colored – about 5–8 minutes over a medium heat.

Meanwhile heat the stock and add it to the pan. Bring back to a boil and simmer, covered, for 8–10 minutes, until the vegetables are cooked. Pour into a blender and add a quarter of the cream. Whizz until very smooth and set aside to cool. This soup should be absolutely silky smooth; if it is not pour it through a strainer.

When cold, stir in the rest of the cream and refrigerate until well-chilled. Stir in the chives just before serving.

Note: taste the soup and add the cream judiciously; it may not be necessary to add it all.

Left: Beet Soup with Chive Cream (page 58)

Lebanese Cold Cucumber Soup

Serves 8

This is a cooling summer soup which can be made in almost the time it takes to grate the cucumber. If you haven't got time to chill the soup, pop the bowls into the freezer while you make it. Serve small portions because this soup is rich.

2 large crisp cucumbers
3/4 cup light cream
3/4 cup plain yogurt (preferably organic)
2 tablespoons tarragon or white wine vinegar
1/2–1 garlic clove, crushed
2 tablespoons fresh mint, finely chopped
salt and freshly ground pepper
24–32 shrimp, peeled and freshly cooked (optional)

Garnish
sprigs of mint

Seed and coarsely grate the cucumber. Stir in all other ingredients and season well. Serve chilled in small bowls garnished with mint. A few freshly cooked shrimp are a delicious addition, if available, but the soup is quite wonderful served without any embellishment. It can even be made a day ahead and kept covered in the fridge.

Tip: If this soup tastes a bit flat, a little pinch of salt works wonders.

appetizers

appetizers

Appetizers
The purpose of an appetizer is to whet the palate and set the mood for the rest of the meal. Above all, the appetizer should be light, and not so substantial as to blunt the appetite before the main course.

Menu Planning
In many ways menu planning is just common sense, but it is better to follow a few guiding principles in order to avoid potential pitfalls. In general, it is easiest to select a main course first, then choose an appetizer and dessert to complement.

The Occasion
The occasion is an important factor when choosing a menu and laying the table. For anniversaries or romantic evenings one might incorporate Coeurs à la crème or heart-shaped tarts. For a welcome party for foreign guests it's a good idea to cook a traditional meal. Christmas, Hallowe'en, and birthdays will also, of course, influence the choice. It can be fun to plan a meal on a particular color scheme – green and red for Christmas or even the colors of your favorite sports team at a victory dinner.

Pleasing Your Guests
Do some research to avoid serving dishes that your guests are unable or unwilling to eat, whether for religious, moral, or health reasons. Similarly, it is not usually wise to present anything too challenging or unusual. The golden rule is to be considerate: if you are unsure of your guests' tastes, or think that they might be unfamiliar with certain foods, it may be better to avoid them. Many people find offal awful, and very hot curries and spicy food are not always appreciated. Corn on the cob might present problems for older people and squid, sea urchins, shrimp in the shell, and artichokes can all be a challenge to tackle.

Season and Weather
People need and can digest much heartier meals in winter than in summer, so keep rich soups, stews, and cassoulets for chilly days. Serve cold soups and sunny Mediterranean salads in summer.

Availability of Fresh Ingredients
It makes sense to use fresh food in season when it is at its cheapest and best – and very little sense to incorporate a dish that includes an expensive imported ingredient that may well be past its best by the time you get it.

Don't forget about simple, everyday foods that are seldom found on restaurant menus, but which people often love to eat. My examples include cabbage, parsnips, rutabaga, whiting, rhubarb, and carrigeen.

Budget
It is perfectly possible to prepare exciting meals on a small budget. Plan meals around beans and legumes, cheaper cuts of meat, or less well-known fish. Egg-based dishes such as frittatas are economical, too.

Food Value and Nutrition
More than ever, people are aware of the importance of eating fresh and nutritious food. Include a green salad in your meal and keep cream, butter, and alcohol to the minimum. Use all fresh food if at all possible and eliminate processed foods entirely from your menu and your diet.

Number of Dishes
The number of dishes served will depend on various factors. The first is the skill of the cook: don't be over ambitious, and certainly don't cook anything new and complicated for guests. The second is the time available – make sure the menu is realistic, and write down a running order if necessary. Run through the menu to work

out whether any special equipment is needed. If you are cooking in an unfamiliar kitchen, check that all the equipment you will need is available, before you start. Consider the help available: if entertaining single-handed or with little help, plan the menu so that as much as possible can be prepared ahead, particularly any complex dishes. The number of dishes will also depend on the type of service available – whether silver service, plate service, or a self-service buffet.

Balance

In the menu itself there should be contrasts in ingredients, color, texture, and flavor.

Ingredients: It's all too easy to repeat ingredients in your menu, particularly with an ingredient such as eggs. On the face of it, the menu below looks balanced enough:

Cheese Soufflé
French Onion Tart
Tomato and Mint Salad, Green Salad
Crème Caramel with Caramel Shards

but your guest may be consuming about 5 eggs in this meal.

Color: Try not to repeat colors unless you are working to a color scheme. In particular, guard against an all-white plate – for example, Cod with Cream and Bay leaves, Buttered Cucumber and Scallion Potatoes, sounds delicious but it needs some color. The addition of Tomato Fondue, for example, or at least a sprig of chervil, fennel, or watercress would make all the difference.

Texture: Contrast crisp with creamy, for example:

Buttered crumbs on fish pie, or croûtons, with creamy soup

Flavor: Contrasts of flavor are important, for example:

Mild with Spicy – Cucumber raita with curry
Sharp with Bland – Blue cheese sauce on pasta or salad.
Sweet with Sour – Carrot and apple crudités with sweet sour dressing

In the same way, think about balancing light with heavy. Serve a green salad with lunch and dinner. It has magical properties – it certainly makes me feel less full so I have room for dessert.

Cooking Methods: Use different cooking methods – avoid all grills or sautés, for example:

Grilled mackerel with Maitre d'hotel butter
Steak with Béarnaise sauce
Apple fritters

Sauces: Don't fall into the trap of serving similar sauces, by choosing mother and daughter sauces which seem to be different but have the same basis.

Garnishes: To a great extent we "eat" with our eyes so garnishing is immensely important. Vary garnishes as far as possible. If you have an herb garden you will have access not only to herbs, but to herb flowers which are edible and make pretty garnishes. Remember the golden rule – flavor is of paramount importance and garnishes should be relevant and edible.

Seasonings: Confine strong flavoring or spices to one dish in the menu unless you are cooking a specifically Indian or Chinese meal, in which case make sure not to repeat the same spices in each course.

Master Recipe

Bruschetta with Chargrilled Peppers and Prosciutto

Serves 2

This toasted or chargrilled bread rubbed with garlic and drizzled with olive oil is found right down through Italy from Tuscany to Apulia. Once the traditional lunch of shepherds and peasants, it has now become a fashionable appetizer. That's not surprising, because made with really good bread and extra-virgin olive oil, it becomes addictive. In Tuscany it is called Fett'unta meaning "oiled slice", and in the south, very ripe tomato is also rubbed into the chargrilled bread.

2 slices country bread or good quality baguette about 1/2 inch (1cm) thick
1 garlic clove, peeled and cut in half
extra-virgin olive oil
a little Tapenade (see page 588)
arugula leaves
a few strips roast red and yellow pepper, peeled, seeded, and chargrilled
1–2 slices prosciutto

Garnish
basil leaves

Chargrill the slices of bread. Rub both sides of the bread with the cut sides of the garlic and drizzle with best quality extra-virgin olive oil.

Arrange on warm plates and spread with a little Tapenade.

Put a few leaves of arugula and some red and yellow pepper on top. Drizzle with olive oil. Lay 1 or 2 pieces of prosciutto on top.

Garnish with a leaf or two of basil and serve immediately.

Variations

Garden Café Bruschetta with Mushrooms and Slivers of Parmesan

Serves 1

This was Katie's speciality at the Garden Café beside the Ballymaloe Cookery School.

2 flat mushrooms
sea salt and freshly cracked pepper
a little extra-virgin olive oil
a little fresh marjoram
1 slice country bread
1 garlic clove, peeled and cut in two
Pesto (see page 589)
4–5 arugula leaves
shavings of Parmesan cheese (Parmigiano Reggiano)

Garnish
5 olives, chopped finely
marigold petals (optional)

Season the mushrooms with salt, pepper, olive oil, and a few leaves of marjoram, and cook in a frying pan with a little olive oil over a medium heat. Cover with a lid and cook for 3–4 minutes, turning them half way through.

Meanwhile chargrill or toast the bread. Rub with the cut sides of the garlic. Spread a little pesto on the bread and cover with a few arugula leaves. Lay the sizzling mushrooms on top. Season with sea salt and pepper and some fresh marjoram. Put a few slivers of Parmesan on top.

Garnish the plate with a circle of chopped olives and marigold petals.

Serve immediately.

Goat Cheese and Arugula Bruschetta with Tomato and Chile Jam

Serves 1

1 slice Italian bread or 1 thick 3/4-inch (2-cm) slice good quality French baguette
1 garlic clove, peeled and cut in half
a little extra-virgin olive oil
a few arugula leaves
a few slices of fresh goat cheese
Tomato and Chile Jam (see page 512)

Garnish
a few olives
freshly cracked pepper

Chargrill or toast the bread. Rub the surface with the cut sides of the garlic, then drizzle with olive oil. Put a few arugula leaves on the bruschetta and top generously with the goat cheese. Drizzle with Tomato and Chile Jam.

Pop on to a large plate, add a few olives and some freshly cracked pepper. Serve immediately.

Some other good toppings:

Tapenade (see page 588) is great with this bruschetta also.

Spicy roast peppers

Olives, chiles, and capers

Rosemary and Parsley Pesto (see page 589)

Spiced eggplant

White beans with rosemary

Zucchini with Tomato and Cumin (see page 69)

Right: Crostini with Potatoes, Goat Cheese, and Arugula Leaves

Crostini with Potatoes, Goat Cheese, and Arugula Leaves

Serves 4

Crostini come from the same derivation as croûtons. We use Ardsallagh goat cheese. Fresh kale pesto is also worth trying with this recipe.

4 potatoes
extra-virgin olive oil for deep frying
4 slices of homemade white country bread
salt and freshly ground black pepper
Ballymaloe French Dressing (see page 225)
4 slices goat cheese
Tapenade (see page 588)
Parsley Pesto (see page 589)

Garnish
a few arugula leaves

Scrub the potatoes but do not peel. Cook in boiling salted water in their skins until almost cooked. Pour off most of the water, cover the saucepan and steam over a low heat until fully cooked.

Meanwhile heat 1–1½ inches (2.5–4cm) olive oil in a small sauté pan. When the oil is very hot but not smoking, add the bread and cook for just a few seconds until golden on 1 side. Quickly flip over with tongs and cook the other side. Drain and put on to paper towels. Keep warm.

Just before eating, peel the potatoes and slice thickly into scant ½-inch (1-cm) slices. Season with salt and pepper, and gently toss in a little Ballymaloe French Dressing.

Pop a warm crostini on a plate, top with overlapping slices of warm potato, and lay 1 or 2 slices of goat cheese on top.

Put a few little dollops of Tapenade oil around the edge. Drizzle Parsley Pesto here and there. Scatter 3 or 4 arugula leaves over the crostini and serve immediately.

A Plate of Mezzes

Mezze means appetizer in Arabic. These little hors d'oeuvres are a traditional feature of Middle Eastern food and are often served with an anise-flavored drink like arak or raki, or the Moroccan mahia made with dates or figs. There is an infinite number from which to choose. You may want to prepare an assortment for a communal appetizer, or simply choose a selection to offer on individual plates. Choose from among the following:

Claudia Roden's Hummus bi Tahina (Chickpea and Tahini Dip)
Dukkah
Taramasalata
Tzatsiki
Dolmades
Eggplant Purée
Roast Red Pepper, Caper, and Preserved Lemon Salad
Zucchini with Tomato and Cumin
Carrot and Mint Salad

Claudia Roden's Hummus bi Tahina

Serves 6–10 (depending on how it is served)

Hummus bi Tahina, with its rich earthy taste, has quite a cult following. Strange to the palate when first encountered, it soon becomes addictive. It makes an excellent appetizer served as a dip with pita bread. It is also delicious with kebabs or as a salad with a main dish. Claudia showed us how to make this when she taught at the school in October 1985.

3/4–1 cup chickpeas, cooked or tinned
juice of 2–3 lemons, or to taste, freshly squeezed
2–3 garlic cloves, crushed
2/3 cup tahini paste (available from health food shops and delicatessens)
2 1/2 tablespoons extra-virgin olive oil
salt

Garnish
4 teaspoons olive oil
1 teaspoon paprika
1 generous tablespoon parsley, finely chopped
cumin (optional)
a few cooked chickpeas

Drain the chickpeas and keep a few whole ones aside to garnish the dish. Whizz up the remainder in an electric mixer or blender or food processor with a little of the cooking liquid to make a smooth paste. Add the lemon, garlic, tahini paste, olive oil, and salt to taste. Blend to a soft creamy texture. Taste and continue to add lemon juice and salt until you are happy with the flavor. Pour into a serving dish, mix the paprika with a little olive oil, and dribble over the surface in a cross. Do the same with the parsley. Cumin is also a delicious addition; use 1–1 1/2 teaspoons. Sprinkle with a few cooked chickpeas,

Serve with pita bread or any crusty white bread.

Hummus with Spicy Lamb and Toasted Pine Nuts

Serves 6–10

Hummus Bi Tahina (see left)
1 lb. (450g) lean leg or shoulder of lamb
1/2 cup pine nuts
1 1/2–2 1/2 tablespoons olive oil
salt and freshly ground pepper
1/2–1 teaspoon freshly roasted cumin seed
fresh cilantro leaves

Trim the lamb of all the fat. Cut the meat into 1/4-inch (5-mm) cubes. Toast the pine nuts in a moderate oven, 350°F (180°C), for about 5 minutes, turning regularly.

Heat the olive oil in a hot pan, toss in the meat, season well with salt, freshly ground pepper. and cumin. Cook for 3–4 minutes and add the pine nuts. Put the hummus into a bowl, pile the meat and pine nuts on top. Sprinkle with a few shredded fresh cilantro leaves.

Serve with pita or other flat breads. A little sumac is delicious sprinkled over the lamb, and gives the dish a Lebanese flavor.

Dukkah

Serves 50 depending on use

Dukkah is an Egyptian spice mix that's much loved and even used for breakfast. The mixture of spices varies from family to family. It's all the rage in Australia at present. Serve as a dip with raw vegetables, or as a spice rub for chicken breast or lamb.

Also good served with Lebanese flat bread and olive oil. It keeps for weeks or even months in a screw-top jar.

1/2 cup hazelnuts
2 1/4 cups sesame seeds
1 1/3 cups coriander seeds

1/2 cup cumin seeds
salt and freshly ground pepper

Preheat the oven to 400°F (200°C).

Roast the hazelnuts in the oven for 8–10 minutes or until the skins loosen. Rub them off.

Put the sesame seeds into a dry frying pan over a medium heat, stir until they change to a slighter darker shade and start to pop. Transfer to a plate to cool.

Next add the coriander seeds, stir and toast for a few minutes until they begin to smell more aromatic, and add to the sesame seeds.

Toast the cumin seeds next, taking care because they burn more easily than the other spices. Add to the other spices to cool.

Put the cool spices and hazelnuts into a spice grinder or food processor, and add salt and pepper. Whizz for a few seconds or better still, pulse. It's important not to over-blend or a paste will form. Dukkah should be a loose, grainy, spice mixture.

Taramasalata

Serves 4–8
In season: Winter

"Tarama" is Greek and Turkish for fish roe. Traditionally, the Greek specialty taramasalata is made with the roe of gray mullet, but today smoked cod roe is more commonly used. It is available in winter for a few months. Taramasalata is really easy to make and paler in color than the disconcertingly bright pink ready-made equivalent.

3–4 slices good quality white bread
9 ounces (250g) smoked cod roe
juice of 1–2 lemons, or to taste
1/4 cup sunflower oil
1/4 cup extra-virgin olive oil

Cut the crusts off the bread and soak the bread in water. Squeeze dry. Skin the cod roe and put it into the food processor with the bread and the freshly squeezed lemon juice. Flick on the motor. Trickle in the oil gradually as though you are making mayonnaise. Transfer to a bowl, cover, and refrigerate. The mixture will firm up as it cools.

Smoked Cod Roe

Serves 4
Serve as part of a mezze.

2–3 ounces (50–75g) smoked cod roe
olive oil
segments of lemon

Slice the chilled cod roe into 1/8-inch (3-mm) slices. Arrange on a serving plate. Pop a few segments of lemon on the side. Serve soon with lots of flat bread or freshly made toast.

Botargo (the dried roe of the gray mullet) is also delicious served in this way.

Master Recipe

Tzatziki

In season: best in Summer

This Greek speciality is a delicious cucumber and yogurt mixture which can be served as part of a mezze, as an accompanying salad, or as a sauce to serve with grilled fish or meat. Greek yogurt is usually made with sheep's milk and is wonderfully thick and creamy.

2 crisp cucumbers, peeled and diced into 1/8–1/4-inch (3–5-mm) dice
salt
1–2 garlic cloves, crushed
a dash of white wine vinegar or lemon juice
2 cups Greek yogurt or best quality whole-milk plain yogurt
1/4 cup cream (optional)
1 heaped tablespoon mint, freshly chopped
sugar, salt, and freshly ground pepper

Put the cucumber dice into a strainer, sprinkle with salt, and let drain for about 30 minutes. Dry the cucumber on paper towels, put into a bowl, and mix with the garlic, vinegar or lemon juice, yogurt, and cream. Stir in the mint and taste. It may need seasoning with salt, pepper, and a little sugar.

Variation

Follow the Master Recipe but substitute dill for the mint.

Zucchini with Tomato and Cumin

Serves 6–8
In season: best in Summer and early Autumn

1/4 cup extra-virgin olive oil
2 garlic cloves, crushed
2 large onions, finely chopped
1 teaspoon freshly chopped cumin
1 lb. (450g) zucchini, sliced 1/2 inch (1cm) thick
salt and freshly ground pepper
2 1/2 tablespoons white wine vinegar
chili powder
1 lb. (450g) very ripe tomatoes, peeled and chopped
a little sugar

Heat the olive oil in a large heavy pan, add the crushed garlic, onions, and cumin. Sweat for 4–5 minutes, add the zucchini, salt, pepper, vinegar, and chili powder.

Toss gently in the oil, add the chopped tomatoes, season with a little sugar. Cover and cook for 8–10 minutes or until the zucchini and tomato are soft.

Taste, correct the seasoning, and serve at room temperature as part of a selection of mezzes or with lamb.

Dolmades (Stuffed Vine Leaves)

Makes 30–36

In season: summer if using fresh vine leaves. Vine leaves preserved in brine are always available.

No Greek mezze is complete without a dish of dolmades. The olive stall in Cork market sells stuffed vine leaves all year round. But if you grow a vine – easier than you think – everyone can have fun making stuffed vine leaves!

36 fresh vine leaves or 8 ounces (225g) preserved vine leaves
1⅓ cups basmati rice
6 ounces (175g) onion, finely chopped (about 1½ cups)
2 generous tablespoons parsley, freshly chopped
2 generous tablespoons mint, freshly chopped
2 generous tablespoons dill, freshly chopped
¼ cup raisins
½ cup pine nuts, toasted
¼ teaspoon cinnamon
pinch of allspice
salt and freshly ground pepper

⅔ cup olive oil
⅔ cup water
pinch saffron or turmeric, optional
1 teaspoon sugar
juice of 1 freshly squeezed lemon

Plunge a few fresh vine leaves at a time into boiling water for about 30 seconds. They will become limp and pliable. Spread on a clean lint-free towel. If using preserved vine leaves, drain off the brine, put the leaves into a bowl, cover with boiling water, and let soak for about 15 minutes. Drain, then cover with cold water. Repeat this procedure once or twice more depending on how salty they are.

Pour boiling water over the rice, stir, then drain; wash it in cold water and drain again. Mix the rice with the onion, parsley, mint, dill, raisins, and pine nuts. Add the cinnamon and allspice. Season with salt and pepper.

To stuff the leaves: place a leaf on a clean work top or cutting board, vein side upwards and stem end towards you (trim off the stem if necessary). Put a heaped teaspoon of filling in the center of the leaf at the base end. Fold the stem end over the filling, then fold in both sides neatly and roll up tightly like a cigar, tucking the seam underneath. Stuff the remaining leaves in the same way. Line a saucepan with vine leaves, arrange the dolmades tightly in a circle in the pot.

Mix the olive oil with the water, add the saffron or turmeric if using, then add the sugar and lemon juice and pour over the arranged vine leaves. Put a small inverted plate on top to keep them in place and to prevent them from unravelling. Cover the saucepan and simmer gently for 50–60 minutes or until the dolmades are thoroughly cooked. Add a little more water, if necessary, during cooking. Cool in the saucepan and serve cold.

Note: Dolmades may be refrigerated for several days. Vine leaves that are stuffed with minced lamb as well as rice are often served with Avgolemono Soup (page 54).

Master Recipe

Eggplant Purée with Olive Oil and Lemon

Serves 6

This is one of my absolute favorite ways to eat eggplant. It is served all through the southern Mediterranean, and there are many delicious variations.

4 large eggplants
5–6 tablespoons extra-virgin olive oil
juice of 1–2 lemons, or to taste
salt and freshly ground pepper

Roast or broil the eggplants depending on the flavor you like (see below). Let cool. Peel thinly, taking care to save every little morsel of flesh. Discard the skins and drain the flesh in a strainer or colander.

Transfer to a bowl, mash the purée with a fork or chop with a knife, depending on the texture you like.

Add the olive oil and lemon juice, salt and pepper to taste.

How to Chargrill Eggplants

There are several ways to do this. Each method produces a slightly different taste.

1. Prick the eggplants in a few places. Roast whole in a hot oven for about 30 minutes, turning over from time to time – they will collapse and soften.

2. Prick the eggplants as above. Put them on a wire rack under the broiler and turn them regularly until the skin is black and charred.

3. Chargrill the eggplants over an open fire or barbecue – delicious.

4. For almost the most delicious flavor of all, chargrill the eggplants over an open gas flame, turning regularly until blistered, charred, and soft and miserable looking. Let cool, peel, and use as desired.

Variations

1. Freshly crushed garlic may be added.

2. In Turkey some thick Greek yogurt is often added. For this quantity of eggplant purée, allow 7–8 tablespoons yogurt, and reduce the olive oil by half.

3. Mixed with ricotta and freshly chopped herbs, e.g., marjoram; this makes a delicious "sauce" for pasta.

4. A spicier version from Morocco includes 1 teaspoon harissa, 1 teaspoon freshly ground cumin, and 2½ tablespoons coarsely chopped cilantro leaves.

5. Add some pomegranate molasses, as they do in Syria. This is our new flavor of the month! About 4–5 tablespoons could be substituted for the fresh lemon juice.

Julia Wight's Eggplant Purée

Follow the Master Recipe, adding:

2 small garlic cloves, finely chopped
½–1 teaspoon cumin, freshly ground and roasted
1½–2½ tablespoons chiffonade of mint
juice of ½–1 lemon, freshly squeezed
freshly ground pepper or Chile Pepper Oil (see page 227)

Mix well together and season to taste.

Roast Red Pepper, Caper, and Preserved Lemon Salad

Serves 6

This is a delicious way to use preserved lemons (see page 515).

6 red peppers, ripe and fleshy
sea salt and freshly ground pepper
peel of ½–1 preserved lemon, very finely diced
1½–2½ tablespoons tiny capers, diced
flat-leaf parsley sprigs
5 tablespoons extra-virgin olive oil

Roast and peel the peppers (see page 80). Cut into strips about 1 inch (2.5cm) wide. Season with salt and pepper. Sprinkle on the preserved lemon peel, a little caper dice, and some sprigs of flat-leaf parsley. Drizzle with extra-virgin olive oil.

Master Recipe

Asparagus on Toast with Hollandaise Sauce

Serves 4
In season: late spring

This is a simple and gorgeous way to serve fresh asparagus during its short season. We feast on it in every possible way for those precious weeks – roast, chargrilled, in soups, frittatas, quiches... Don't forget to dip some freshly cooked spears in a soft boiled egg for a simple luxury! This was my father-in-law's favorite way to eat Irish asparagus.

One can buy a special, tall asparagus cooking pot – a real luxury but certainly worth the money if you cook asparagus regularly – however you can survive quite well with an oval flameproof casserole dish.

16–20 spears fresh green asparagus
4 slices homemade White Yeast Bread (see page 481)
butter
a little Hollandaise Sauce (see page 581)

Garnish
sprigs of chervil

Hold each spear of asparagus over your index finger down near the root end. It will snap at the point where it begins to get tough. Some people like to peel asparagus but we rarely do. Cook in about 1 inch (2.5cm) of boiling salted water in an oval cast iron casserole dish for 4–8 minutes or until a knife tip will pierce the root end easily.

Meanwhile toast the bread, spread with butter and remove the crusts. Place a piece of toast on a hot plate, put the asparagus on top, and spoon a little Hollandaise sauce over. Garnish with a sprig of chervil and serve immediately.

Sauce Maltaise (see page 582) is also a classic accompaniment to asparagus.

Seakale on Toast with Hollandaise Sauce

Serves 4–6
In season: late spring

Seakale is an "old-fashioned" perennial vegetable, often found in country house gardens. We look forward with great anticipation to its delicate flavor in Spring. Quite apart from its gastronomic value, it is altogether a beautiful plant with its profusion of white flowers in Summer and bobbly seed heads in Autumn. Seek it out – it deserves to be better-known. Seakale tastes divine with wild salmon or Dublin bay prawns (scampi), and is delicious on toast with Hollandaise Sauce.

Follow the Master Recipe, but use:
1 lb. (450g) seakale
2½ cups water
1 teaspoon salt
½–¾ stick (¼–⅓ cup) butter
toast
Hollandaise Sauce (see page 581) or melted butter

Wash the seakale gently and trim into manageable lengths – say 4 inches (10cm). Bring the water to a fast boil and add the salt. Add the seakale, cover, and boil until tender – about 15 minutes.

Just as soon as a knife will pierce the seakale easily, drain and serve on hot plates with a little Hollandaise Sauce (see page 581) or melted butter and lots of toast.

Pink Grapefruit and Pomegranate Sorbet

Serves 4–5
In season: Winter

The jewel-like seeds of pomegranates look like glistening rubies, so appear festive. This sorbet is very versatile and may be served at the beginning, middle, or end of a meal.

1 quart (960ml) pink grapefruit juice (about 10 grapefruit)
1 cup superfine sugar
1 egg white (optional)
1–2 pomegranates

Garnish
2 pink grapefruit cut into segments
pomegranate seeds
a little sugar
fresh mint leaves

8 chilled white side plates

Put the freshly squeezed grapefruit into a bowl, add the sugar and dissolve by stirring it into the juice. Taste. The juice should seem rather too sweet to drink: it will taste less sweet in the freezing. Cut the pomegranates in half around the "equator". Open out and carefully flick the seeds into a bowl, discard the skin and all the yellow membrane.

Make the sorbet in one of the following ways.

Method 1
Pour into the drum of an ice-cream maker or sorbetiere and freeze for 20–25 minutes. Fold in the pomegranate seeds. Scoop out and serve immediately or store in a covered bowl in the freezer until needed.

Method 2
Pour the juice into a stainless steel or plastic container and put into the freezer. After about 4–5 hours, when the sorbet is semi-frozen, remove and whisk until granular. Return to freezer. Repeat several times. When almost frozen, fold in the pomegranate seeds. Keep covered in the freezer until needed.

Method 3
If you have a food processor, simply freeze the sorbet completely in a covered stainless steel or plastic bowl, then break into large pieces and whizz for a few seconds. Add one slightly beaten egg white, whizz again for another few seconds, then return to the bowl. Fold in the pomegranate seeds. Freeze again until needed.

Before serving, chill the plates in a refrigerator or freezer. Then, put 1–2 scoops of sorbet on each chilled plate, and garnish with a few segments of pink grapefruit. Sprinkle with pomegranate seeds, spoon a little grapefruit juice over the segments, decorate with fresh mint leaves, and serve immediately.

Note: For straight Pink Grapefruit Sorbet, simply omit the pomegranate seeds.

Segmenting Citrus Fruit

1. With a sharp, preferably serrated knife, cut a slice off the top and bottom of the fruit in as far as the flesh.

2. Remove the skin and pith either in a spiral as though peeling an apple, or from the top to bottom in four or five pieces (easier, but more wasteful: holding the knife perpendicular, you need to follow the line of the pith).

When every scrap of pith is removed hold the citrus fruit crosswise in the palm of your hand over a bowl.

3. With a small fruit knife, cut in front of the membrane to but not through the center. Then push the knife forward to remove the segment cleanly from the membrane. Cut in front of the next membrane, hold back the membrane with your thumb to give more leverage, then push the knife forward toward the outer edge of the fruit to remove the segment; it will drop into the bowl.

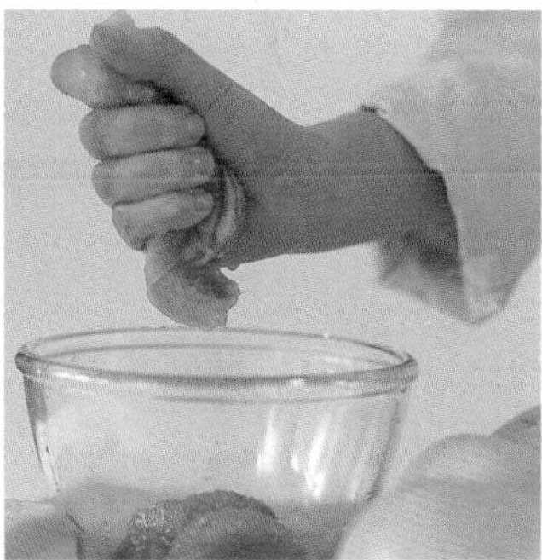

4. When all the segments have been removed, squeeze the membrane tightly in your hand over the bowl to catch the final drops of juice. If the segments are not needed immediately, store in a bowl just large enough to hold them. Cover with plastic wrap and refrigerate, otherwise those exposed to the air will oxidize and become bitter.

Left: Pink Grapefruit and Pomegranate Sorbet

Master Recipe
Carrot and Mint Salad
Serves 4

Serve as part of a plate of salads or mezze.

1 lb. (450g) carrots, peeled and coarsely grated
1/4 cup olive oil
1 tablespoon plus 1 teaspoon lemon juice or white wine vinegar
salt, freshly ground pepper, and sugar
1 1/2–2 1/2 tablespoons mint, freshly chopped
8 black olives (optional)

Put the coarsely grated carrot into a bowl. Whisk the oil and lemon juice or vinegar together, pour over the grated carrot, season with salt, pepper, and sugar. Sprinkle on 1 tablespoon of chopped mint. Mix well. Turn into a serving dish and garnish with the remainder of the mint and some black olives.

Variations
Carrot, Cumin, and Currant Salad
Follow the Master Recipe, omitting the mint and olives, and instead add 1–2 teaspoons ground, freshly roasted cumin and 3 tablespoons currants. Taste and correct seasoning.

Moroccan Carrot Salad
Sprinkle the grated carrot with some freshly squeezed lemon juice and a few drops of orange flower water. Season with salt and sugar, and marinate for 1 hour. For a more robust salad, peel 4 oranges, cut them into chunks, and mix with the carrots.

Red Pepper Mousse with Tapenade Toasts
Serves 8–10

Choose fat, ripe, fleshy peppers.

2 lbs. (900g) firm, red peppers
1 1/2–2 1/2 tablespoons water
salt, pepper, and sugar
2 rounded teaspoons gelatin
2 1/2 tablespoons cold water
1/2 cup cream
1 teaspoon brandy

Tapenade (a simple and very good version!)
a heaped cup Kalamata olives
2 large garlic cloves, peeled and chopped
2 anchovies
1/4 cup extra-virgin olive oil

Olive Oil Toasts
8–10 slices baguette bread, cut diagonally 1/4 inch (5mm) thick
olive oil

Garnish
arugula leaves
8–10 molds 2 1/2-inch (6-cm) diameter or 1 x loaf pan 5 x 8 inches (13 x 20cm)
oil such as sunflower or grapeseed, for brushing

Cut the peppers in half, remove the seeds, and cut into slices. Put into a saucepan with 1 1/2–2 1/2 tablespoons of water, season with salt, pepper, and sugar, cover with a paper lid and then with a tight-fitting lid. Cook on a low heat, stirring every now and then until soft – about 30 minutes. Purée in a food processor or blender. The mixture should be quite thick. Strain and measure it; it should yield about 2 cups.

Sponge the gelatin in 2 1/2 tablespoons of water, in a small bowl, for a few minutes. Put the bowl into a saucepan of simmering water until the gelatin is completely dissolved. Meanwhile whip the cream. Add a little pepper purée to the gelatin, stir, and mix well with the remainder of the purée. Fold in the whipped cream and brandy, taste for seasoning and add salt, pepper, and a pinch of sugar, if necessary.

Brush the molds with oil and fill with red pepper mousse. Alternatively line a terrine or small loaf pan with plastic wrap (or brush with a non-scented oil) and fill with red pepper mousse. Cover and chill in the fridge for 4–5 hours.

Meanwhile make the tapenade: put the olives, garlic, anchovies, and olive oil into a food processor and whizz for a few seconds – just long enough to chop the olives fairly coarsely: it shouldn't be a purée.

To make the olive oil toasts: fry the bread in the olive oil in a frying pan, turn over once, and drain on paper towels. Keep warm.

To serve: put a red pepper mousse on each plate. Spread a little tapenade on a warm olive oil toast. Arrange beside the mousse and garnish with fresh arugula leaves and serve immediately.

Variation
Serve Guacamole (see page 91) or Parsley and Chile Salsa (see page 592) on the olive oil toasts instead.

Warm Salads (Salades Tièdes)

Salades tièdes, or warm salads, are a legacy of the Nouvelle Cuisine movement which began in the early 1970s in France, led by Michel Guérard. Even though they are called warm salads, salades tièdes have a base of lettuces and salad greens that are tossed in a chosen dressing and topped with some morsels of something hot and delicious, e.g., a few fat shrimp, some scallops, goat cheese, roast vegetables, chicken or duck livers, bacon lardons, thinly sliced duck breast or duck confit, lamb's kidney... the variety is endless. Roast vegetables or crispy potatoes or vegetable chips may be added for contrast of texture and flavor.

Choose a selection of lettuces and salad greens as a base; these will vary from season to season and can include finely shredded red cabbage in the winter. Some fresh herbs and herb flowers will enliven the flavor. Wash and dry and keep fresh in the fridge. The dressing can be made with olive, hazelnut, walnut, or sesame oil, and the vinegars may vary, too – red or white wine, sherry, balsamic, rice vinegar – depending on the flavors in the salad.

The salad and dressings may be prepared ahead, as of course may vegetable chips or caramelized shallots. However, they need to be tossed and assembled just before serving and the hot toppings cooked and added at the last minute.

Some good combinations:

Spicy chicken, rustic roast potatoes, and mango relish
Lamb kidney tossed in marjoram, with oyster mushrooms and pink peppercorns
Chicken livers with julienne of apple and toasted hazelnuts
Shrimp
Salt and pepper squid with matchstick potatoes and sweet chile sauce

Warm Salad of Lamb Kidneys, Glazed Shallots, and Straw Potatoes

Serves 4
In season: best late spring, early summer

Kidneys from spring lamb are best because they are mild and tender. They are also inexpensive and cook in a few minutes. They will keep better if you buy them in their jackets of white fat as this seals them against the air.

Caramelized Shallots
1 lb. (450g) shallots, peeled
1/2 stick (1/4 cup) butter
1/2 cup water
1 1/2–2 1/2 tablespoons sugar
salt and pepper
sprig of thyme or rosemary

Hazelnut Oil Dressing
4 tablespoons hazelnut oil
4 tablespoons sunflower oil
2 1/2 tablespoons white wine vinegar
1/4 teaspoon Dijon mustard
salt, freshly ground pepper, and a pinch of sugar

Selection of lettuces (e.g., butterhead, lollo rosso, curly endive (sometimes mistakenly called chicory), arugula, winter purslane, watercress, etc.) – allow a generous handful per person for an appetizer portion

oil for deep frying
1 large potato, 4–6 ounces (110–175g)

2 1/2 tablespoons olive oil
4 lamb kidneys trimmed of all fat and gristle and cut into 3/4-inch (2-cm) dice
salt and freshly ground pepper
1 tablespoon marjoram or thyme leaves

First prepare the shallots: put them with the butter, water, sugar, salt, pepper, and herb into a small saucepan. Bring to a boil and simmer, covered, until the shallots are nearly tender. Remove the lid and let the juices evaporate and caramelize, taking care they don't burn.

Whisk together the ingredients for the dressing and set aside. Wash and dry the lettuces and salad greens and, if necessary, break into bite-sized pieces and place into a deep salad bowl.

Heat good-quality oil in a deep fryer to 400°F (200°C). Peel the potato and cut into fine julienne strips on a mandoline, in a food processor, or by hand. Wash off the excess starch with cold water, drain, and pat dry. Deep fry the potato strips until they are golden brown, then keep warm to serve with the salad.

Finally, heat the olive oil in a frying pan and when hot, add the kidneys.

Season with salt and pepper, add the marjoram or thyme, and cook over a medium heat until just cooked (some people like them slightly pink). Don't over-cook the kidneys or they will become tough.

While the kidneys are cooking, toss the lettuces with the dressing and divide between 4 plates. Put the warm shallots around each pile of salad, arrange the fried potato carefully on top of each shallot in a little pile. Finally sprinkle on the cooked kidneys straight from the pan. Serve immediately.

Variation
Warm Salad of Chicken Livers

We sometimes toss chicken livers in a little foaming butter and grated ginger. Spoon over a mixture of salad greens. Garnish with Game Chips, wild garlic flowers, and marigold petals.

Master Recipe

Warm Salad with Duck Livers and Marigold Petals

Serves 4

a selection of lettuce and salad greens, e.g., butterhead, iceberg, oakleaf, lollo rosso, curly endive and mysticana
1 dessert apple, peeled, cored, and diced
1 tablespoon butter
4–6 fresh duck livers or, if unavailable, chicken livers
salt and freshly ground pepper
1 tablespoon butter

Dressing
4 tablespoons extra-virgin olive oil
1½ tablespoons red wine vinegar
a little Dijon mustard
salt and freshly ground pepper

Garnish
1 generous tablespoon chopped chives
chive flowers
marigold petals

Wash and dry the salad greens and tear into bite-sized pieces. Whisk together the ingredients for the dressing. Fry the apple in a little butter until just soft and almost golden, and taste – it may need a pinch of sugar. Keep warm. Wash and dry the livers and divide each into 2 pieces.

Just before serving, melt the second quantity of butter in a sauté pan, season the livers with salt and pepper and cook over a gentle heat, turning to cook on all sides – 5 minutes in all. While the livers are cooking, toss the salad greens in just enough dressing to make them glisten.

Divide the salad between 4 large plates, sprinkle with the apple dice, divide the hot livers evenly between each salad. (They are very good slightly pink in the center, but only if you like them that way!) Sprinkle with chives, chive flowers, and marigold petals, and serve immediately.

Variations

You can do lots of variations on this appetizer. You could also cook the fillet pieces from duck breasts quickly on a pan, and slice them on to this salad.

Duck Confit Salad

Serves 4

Ingredients as above but substitute 2 preserved duck legs (Confit de Canard, see page 291) for the livers.

Remove the duck legs from the fat (it may be necessary to melt some of it). Preheat the oven to 350°F (180°C). Roast the duck for 15–20 minutes and then cook for 4–5 minutes on a hot grill pan to crisp the skin.

Strip the crispy duck from the bones and divide between the 4 plates of salad. Sprinkle with chopped chives, chive flowers, and marigold petals as described above. Serve immediately.

A Plate of Smoked Fish with Horseradish Sauce and Dill Mayonnaise

Serves 4
In season: most smoked fish is available all year round but sprats and herring are winter treats.

Occasionally we serve 3 different types of smoked fish – for example, salmon, mussels, and trout – on tiny rounds of Ballymaloe Brown Yeast Bread (see page 478), topped with a little frill of fresh lollo rosso. A little dollop of Sweet Cucumber Pickle goes with the smoked salmon, a dollop of homemade Mayonnaise is delicious with marinated smoked mussels, and a blob of Horseradish Sauce and a sprig of watercress complements the pink smoked trout. These 3 delicious morsels make a perfect light appetizer.

a selection of smoked fish, e.g., smoked salmon, smoked mussels, smoked mackerel, smoked trout, smoked eel, smoked tuna, smoked hake, smoked sprats.

Horseradish Sauce (see page 586)
Dill Mayonnaise (see page 585)
Sweet Cucumber Pickle (see page 514)

Garnish
segments of lemon
sprigs of watercress or arugula leaves

First make the Horseradish Sauce and Sweet Dill Mayonnaise and Sweet Cucumber Pickle.

Slice the salmon into thin slices down onto the skin, allowing 1 slice per person. Cut the mackerel into diamond-shaped pieces, divide the trout into large flakes. Skin and slice the eel. Thinly slice the tuna and hake.

To serve: choose 4 large white plates. Drizzle each with Sweet Dill Mayonnaise, then divide the smoked fish between the plates. Put a teaspoonful of Horseradish Sauce and Sweet Cucumber Pickle on each plate. Garnish with a lemon wedge and sprigs of watercress or arugula.

Smoked Mackerel Salad with Beet and Horseradish Sauce on Baby Salad Greens

Serve some 1-inch (2.5-cm) pieces of smoked mackerel on a mixture of baby salad greens, with ½-inch (1-cm) dice of pickled beet and a few little blobs of horseradish sauce – a delicious combination dreamed up by Rory O'Connell at Ballymaloe.

Ballymaloe Cookery School

Pâté de Campagne with Celeriac Rémoulade and Redcurrant Sauce

Serves 10

Every charcuterie in France proudly sells its own version of Pâté de Campagne. They vary enormously in content and makeup – some are made with rabbit, game, and even sweetbreads. A certain proportion of fat is essential, otherwise the terrine will be dry and dull. It is meant to be rough textured so the mixture should not be too finely minced. Resist cutting the terrine for a few days to let the flavors mature. Pâté de Campagne keeps very well, certainly for up to a week. Do try to find free range organic pork.

8 ounces (225g) fresh chicken livers
2½ tablespoons brandy
½ teaspoon ground white pepper (yes, all of it!)
*8 ounces (225g) very thinly sliced bacon (you may need more if they are not very thinly sliced) or better still, barding fat**
1 medium onion, finely chopped
1 tablespoon butter
1 lb. (450g) rindless streaky pork, ground
½ lb. (225g) veal or chicken meat, ground
2 garlic cloves, finely chopped
¼–½ teaspoon ground allspice (pimento)
a good pinch of ground cloves
1–2 teaspoons annual marjoram (optional), freshly chopped
2 small eggs, beaten
salt, freshly ground pepper and nutmeg
½ cup pistachios, shelled
6–8 ounces (175–225g) piece of cooked ham, cut in thick strips (about 1½–2 cups)
a bay leaf
a couple of sprigs of thyme
Luting Paste (see page 79) or tin foil
2-quart (1.8-liter) terrine or casserole dish with a tight fitting lid

Celeriac Rémoulade (see page 178)
Red Currant Sauce (see page 598)

**A pork butcher will supply barding fat and caul fat to order. Both can be frozen. Barding fat is the name for the very thinly sliced pork or bacon used to line terrines and pâtés and to enclose food for cooking. The caul of pigs is used by butchers to encase minced offal, such as haggis and faggots.*

Wash the chicken livers, separate the lobes, and remove any trace of green. Marinate in the brandy and freshly ground white pepper for 2 hours. Line a terrine or casserole dish with very thinly sliced stretched bacon or barding fat, keeping a few slices for the top.

Preheat the oven to 350°F (180°C).

Sweat the onion gently in the butter until soft but not colored. Mix the onion with the pork, veal, garlic, allspice, cloves, marjoram, eggs, and the brandy from the chicken liver marinade. Season with salt, freshly ground pepper, and lots of grated nutmeg, and the marinade. Mix very thoroughly. Fry a little piece and taste for seasoning – it should taste quite spicy and highly seasoned. Add the pistachios and beat until the mixture holds together.

Spread a third of the farce (stuffing) in the lined terrine, add a layer of ham strips (roughly half the quantity) interspersed with half the chicken livers, then cover with another third of the pork mixture. Add the remaining ham and livers and cover with the last third of pork. Lay the reserved barding fat or bacon slices on top, trimming the edges if necessary. Set the bay leaf and the sprigs of thyme on top and cover with the lid. Seal the lid and the steam hole with luting paste (see right) or else place a sheet of tin foil under the lid.

Cook in a bain-marie in the oven for 1¼–1½ hours or until a skewer inserted for ½ minute into the mixture is hot to the touch when taken out. If you are still in doubt, remove the lid and check: the pâté should also have shrunk in from the sides of the terrine and the juices should be clear.

Cool until tepid, remove the luting paste or tin foil and lid, and press the terrine with a board and a 2 lbs. (900g) weight until cold. This helps to compact the layers so that it will cut more easily. Keep for 2–3 days before serving to let the terrine mature. It may be frozen for up to 2 months.

To serve: unmold the terrine, cut into thick slices as needed, and serve with Celeriac Rémoulade and Red Currant Sauce and a good green salad. Gherkins and olives are often served as an accompaniment also, and don't forget some crusty white bread and a glass of red wine!

Making Melba Toast

Preheat the broiler to maximum. White bread, sliced about ¼ inch (5mm) thick, is best for melba toast. Slide an oven rack under the broiler as close to the element as possible.

Toast the bread on both sides. Lower the oven rack, it should be about 5 inches (12.5cm) from the element. Work quickly and while the toast is still hot, cut off the crusts and split the bread in half horizontally. Cut each slice into 2 or 4 triangles. Replace under the broiler on the rack or oven tray. It will curl up within seconds, be careful not to let it burn.

The second stage may also be done in a low oven 300°F (150°C). Melba toast will keep in an airtight tin for a day or two but it is much the best if served immediately.

Luting Paste

2 cups flour
2/3–3/4 cup water

Mix the flour and water into a dough firm enough to handle, roll into a rope, and use to seal the lid onto the casserole dish to prevent the steam from escaping during cooking.

Little Pots of Pâté

A fun way to serve pâté is to offer 3 or even 5 tiny pots of different pâtés as an appetizer or summer lunch. We often include potted shrimp (see page 84) or a potted meat, depending on what's available. Simply fill each little pot with a different pâté and decorate each with a different herb or herb flower – e.g., thyme leaves and flowers on the chicken liver pâté, a little fennel or dill plus the flowers, if available, on the fish pâtés. Flat-leaf parsley or chervil are decorative, while knotty marjoram would complement many potted meats. Serve with lots of crusty bread, hot thin toast, or Melba toast.

Tiny Rosettes of Pâté

All the smooth pâtés, e.g., chicken liver, smoked salmon, mackerel, herring, or potted crab, can be piped in rosettes onto 1/4-inch (5-mm) thick slices of cucumber, triangles of Melba toast, crisp croûtons, savory biscuits, or tiny tartlets. Garnish each with a little sprig of relevant fresh herb or flower, e.g., chervil and perhaps tomato concassé.

Ballymaloe Chicken Liver Pâté with Melba Toast

Serves 10–12 depending on how it is served.

This recipe has certainly stood the test of time. It has been our pâté maison at Ballymaloe since the opening of the restaurant in 1965. It is served in many different ways: its success depends upon being generous with the butter.

8 ounces (225g) fresh organic chicken livers
butter for frying
2 1/2 tablespoons brandy
2–3 sticks (1–1 1/2 cups) butter (depending on how strong the chicken livers are)
1 teaspoon fresh thyme leaves
1 large garlic clove, crushed
salt and freshly ground pepper
clarified butter (see page 103) to seal the top

Wash the livers and remove any membrane or green-tinged bits. Melt a little butter in a frying pan. When it foams, add in the livers and cook over a gentle heat. Be careful not to overcook them or the outsides will get crusty – but all trace of pink should be gone. Put the livers through a food mill or into a food processor. De-glaze the pan with brandy, let it flame, add the garlic and thyme leaves, and then scrape off with a spatula and add to the livers. Purée for a few seconds. Let cool.

Add 2 sticks of butter. Purée until smooth. Season carefully, taste, and add more butter, cut into cubes, if necessary. This pâté should taste fairly mild* and be quite smooth in texture. Put into pots or into one large terrine. Knock out any air bubbles. Run a little clarified butter over the top of the pâté to seal.

Serve with Melba toast (see page 78) or hot white bread. This pâté will keep for 4–5 days in a refrigerator.

* It should taste milder than you feel it should, just after it is made. The flavor will intensify on keeping.

Serving suggestions:

1. In little ramekins accompanied by hot, crusty white bread.

2. In tiny pottery pots as part of a second course called "Little pots of pâté" (see left).

3. We fill the pâté into a loaf pan lined with plastic wrap. When it is set, slices are arranged on individual plates with a little dice of well-seasoned tomato concassé and then garnished with chervil or lemon balm.

4. For a buffet, the loaf-shaped pâté may be covered with a thin layer of soft butter, then decorated with tiny rosettes of butter, and thyme leaves and flowers. The whole pâté is arranged on a bed of lettuces and salad greens and garnished with herbs in flower.

5. Rosettes of pâté may be piped onto tiny triangles of melba toast, Ballymaloe cheese biscuits, or slices of cucumber. These rosettes are very pretty but must be served within an hour of being prepared, otherwise they oxidize and become bitter (see tip). Garnish with a spot of tomato concassé and a little chervil.

6. Pâté may be formed into a roll, wrapped in plastic wrap or wax paper, and refrigerated. Later the paper is removed and the roll of pâté decorated. It can be coated in finely chopped herbs and decorated with herb flowers.

Tip: It is essential to cover chicken liver pâté with a layer of clarified or even just melted butter, otherwise it will oxidize and become bitter in taste and gray in color.

How to Roast Peppers

There are three alternative methods:

1. Preheat the broiler or, better still, use a charcoal grill or barbecue. Broil the peppers on all sides, turning them when necessary – they can be quite charred.

2. Preheat the oven to 475°F (250°C). Put the peppers on a baking tray and bake for 20–30 minutes until the skin blisters and the flesh is soft.

3. Put a wire rack over a mild gas jet, roast the peppers on all sides. When they are charred, remove.

Whichever way you cook them, the next step is to put them into a bowl and cover tightly with plastic wrap for a few minutes; this will make them much easier to peel. Pull the skin off the peppers, remove the stalks and seeds. Do not wash or you will lose the precious sweet juices. Divide each into 2 or 3 pieces along the natural division. Use as desired.

Slicing Raw Peppers

Insert the knife under the stalk. Cut around the sides and the base of the pepper.

Open out from the bottom. The core may then be removed intact, so there is virtually no waste. Shake out any remaining seeds. Depending on the recipe, you may want to remove the paler protruding flesh.

Cut the pepper into quarters and slice at an angle so that the slices are not too long.

Terrine of Chicken

Serves 10–20

A recipe taught to my mother-in-law, Myrtle Allen, by Simone Beck. She passed it on to me.

8 ounces (225g) chicken livers
1/2 cup brandy or madeira
salt to taste and 2 teaspoons ground white pepper (yes, use all of it)
2 1/2–3 lbs. (1.1–1.3kg) chicken
8 ounces (225g) bacon
8 ounces (225g) cooked ham, thickly sliced (about 2 cups)
marjoram, thyme, bay leaves
1 farm fresh egg, beaten
a "crepine" or sheet of bacon fat to cover the terrine, or chicken skin all in one piece

You will need: a flameproof and ovenproof terrine dish or small oval casserole dish roughly 7 x 5 x 3 inches (18 x 12.5 x 8cm)

Wash the livers, pat dry on paper towels, then put them in a flat dish along with the brandy or madeira. Pepper generously with ground white pepper. Let marinate for 2 hours if possible.

Clean the chicken in the normal way. Place the chicken, breast side down, on a board. Skin the chicken, beginning by making an incision down the back, lifting the skin with your fingers in order to separate it from the limbs. Detach limbs in order to debone them, keeping the breasts intact. Scrape all the meat from the bones and put through a meat grinder or food processor to produce a fine purée. Do the same thing with the bacon.

Preheat the oven to 375°F (190°C).

Cut the ham into long strips the length of the terrine. Use your hands to mix the meats well in a large bowl, add herbs, beaten egg, and marinade from the livers. This mixture is called the *farce* in France. Line the terrine with chicken skin or a bard of bacon (see page 378).

Spread one-third of the farce on the bottom of the terrine. Then arrange in the middle, half the well-seasoned breasts, interspersed with strips of ham and chicken livers on top of it. Repeat by covering with another layer of farce, chicken breasts, ham, and livers. Cover with the rest of the farce and then with the ends of the chicken skin or bard of bacon.

Add a sprig of thyme and bay leaf. Cover the terrine and seal with the flour and water luting paste (see page 79)

Place the terrine in a bain-marie of hot water that comes up to a third of the height of the terrine. Bring to a boil on the top of the stove, then transfer to the oven and cook for about 2 hours. Watch that it does not boil dry. Top up the water as necessary to prevent it from boiling dry.

Cooking time varies according to the constituents of the terrine. If you examine the fat coming to the surface during cooking, it will show exactly what point the cooking has reached. If the fat appears cloudy, it is not yet cooked; if the fat is clear, the terrine is fully cooked. Any juices should also be clear. Remove from the pan, let cool, then press with a board and leave for at least 3 days to mature.

Serve with green salad, lots of crusty bread, and a glass of red wine.

Pork, Spinach, and Herb Terrine

Serves about 20 – makes two loaves of terrine
In season: spring and summer

This terrine tastes different every time we make it, depending on the variety of herbs used. It should be highly seasoned before it is cooked, otherwise it may taste bland when cold. Use organically produced spinach, meat, and herbs, if possible.

1½ lbs. (700g) spinach
2 lbs. (900g) pork belly
8 ounces (225g) pig liver
6 ounces (175g) gammon or smoked lean bacon
6 ounces (175g) regular bacon
2 medium onions, finely chopped
1 tablespoon butter
2 medium cloves garlic, peeled and chopped
2 beaten eggs, preferably farm fresh
salt, freshly ground black pepper, and grated nutmeg to taste
5 tablespoons, approximately, freshly chopped mixed herbs – rosemary, thyme, basil, marjoram, parsley, and chives

2 terrines or two 8 x 4-inch (20 x 10-cm) loaf pans

Preheat the oven to 350°F (180°C).

String and cook the spinach (see page 44) until soft, drain very well, then chop it up. Grind the meat and sweat the onions in the butter. Mix together all the remaining ingredients thoroughly, and add the beaten egg, seasoning, and herbs. Fry a tiny piece of the mixture in a pan, and taste. It should taste highly seasoned at this stage. Correct seasoning if necessary.

Divide evenly between the terrines, cover with a lid or tin foil, and bake for about 1 hour. The terrine is cooked when it shrinks in from the sides of the dish, and the juices are clear. Remove the cover 15 minutes before the end of cooking time to let the top brown slightly. Serve warm or cold.

Roast Red Pepper Tart

Serves 4–6

A very delicious tart, perfect for an appetizer or a summer lunch.

Pastry Dough
Use half the amount in the recipe on page 110

3 red peppers
1½–2½ tablespoons sunflower oil
salt and freshly ground pepper
1 egg and 2 egg yolks
1 cup heavy cream
fresh basil leaves (optional)

Quiche dish with removable bottom, 8-inch (20-cm) diameter x 1½ inches (4cm) high

Preheat the oven to 475°F (250°C). Roast the oiled red pepper in the hot oven for 20–30 minutes. Put in a bowl, cover with plastic wrap and leave until cool enough to handle. Peel and seed but do not wash. Cut the flesh into ½-inch (1-cm) dice. Season with salt and freshly ground pepper. Let cool.

Reduce the oven temperature to 350°F (180°C). Make the pastry dough (see page 415). Chill for 15 minutes, then roll out to line the quiche dish. Line with wax paper and fill to the top with dried beans. Rest for 15 minutes, then bake for 20–25 minutes. Remove the beans and paper, brush a little of the egg over the base to seal it, and return to the oven for 1–2 minutes.

Whisk the egg and egg yolks with the cream, add the cooled peppers and a few leaves of torn basil, if using. Pour into the pie shell and bake in a moderate oven for 30–35 minutes or until just set and slightly golden on top. Serve with a salad of arugula leaves or a good green salad.

Goat Cheese, Roast Red Pepper, and Eggplant Tart

Serves 8–10

1½ cups all-purpose white flour
¾ stick (⅓ cup) cold butter
pinch of salt
1½ tablespoons poppy seeds (optional)
2 egg yolks
2½ tablespoons olive oil
2 red peppers
1 large eggplant
olive oil for frying
6–8 ounces (175–225g) goat cheese (we use our local cheese, Ardsallagh)
salt and freshly ground pepper
½ quantity Tomato Fondue (see page 188)
Pesto (see page 589) or basil oil

Tart pan or quiche dish, 10-inch (25-cm) diameter x 1½ inches (4cm) high

Preheat the oven to 475°F (250°C).

Put the flour, butter, and a pinch of salt into the food processor, whizz for a few seconds until butter is roughly blended in. Add the poppy seeds, if using, and then the egg yolks and oil. Whizz for a few seconds again until the dough comes together. Flatten into a circle, wrap in plastic wrap, and chill.

Meanwhile, roast the peppers in the hot oven for 20–30 minutes. Put in a bowl, cover with plastic wrap, and leave until cool enough to handle. Peel and seed but do not wash.

Slice the eggplants into ¼-inch (5-mm) slices, sprinkle with salt, and stack on a wire rack. Heat the olive oil in a frying pan, wash and dry the eggplant slices, and fry until golden on both sides; drain.

Lower the oven temperature to 350F° (180°C). Roll out the dough and line the quiche dish, then proceed to bake blind. Line with wax paper and fill with dried beans. Rest for 15 minutes, then bake for 20–25 minutes. Remove the beans and paper, brush a little egg over the base to seal it, and return to the oven for 1–2 minutes.

Cover the base of the pie shell with slices of goat cheese, and arrange a layer of roasted red pepper on top. Season with salt and freshly ground pepper. Spread a layer of eggplant slices on top, then cover with Tomato Fondue.

Return to the oven for 10–15 minutes or until hot and bubbly. Drizzle generously with Pesto or basil oil and serve immediately with a good green salad.

Tomato Tarte Tatin

Serves 8

Mary-Jo Wendel served this recipe in her superb neighborhood restaurant in Oxford, Ohio.

Paté Brisée
1½ cups all-purpose white flour
pinch of salt
¾–1 stick (⅓–½ cup) butter
1 egg yolk
3–5 tablespoons water

½ stick (¼ cup) butter
12 ounces (350g) chopped onion (about 3 cups)
½–1 red chile
2 garlic cloves, crushed
2 lbs. (900g) very ripe tomatoes peeled, seeded, and chopped
salt and freshly ground pepper
torn fresh basil, about 6 leaves

1–1½ lbs. (450–700g) tomatoes, peeled, seeded, salted, and drained, then sliced
salt
2 ounces (50g) goat cheese or 1 cup grated Parmesan (Parmigiano Reggiano is best)

9-inch (23-cm) diameter ceramic tart dish
melted butter for greasing

Preheat the oven to 375°F (190°C).

Make the dough. Sift the flour with the salt, then rub in the butter. Beat the egg yolk with 2½ tablespoons of water and bind the mixture with just enough liquid to bring the dough together. You may need a little more water, but do not make the dough too wet – it should come away cleanly from the bowl. Flatten into a circle, wrap in plastic wrap, and rest for 15 minutes.

Meanwhile melt the butter, and add the onion, chile, and garlic. Cook until soft and slightly caramelized. Add the chopped tomatoes. Add salt and pepper to taste. Simmer until reduced almost to a paste. Stir in some torn fresh basil leaves.

Line the bottom of a ceramic tart or quiche dish with a circle of wax paper. Brush generously with melted butter. Pack in a layer of tomato slices. Spread the cooked filling evenly over the tomato slices. Crumble the goat cheese over the tart or sprinkle with Parmesan. Roll out the dough to the size of the dish and cover the tomato and cheese with it.

Bake in a hot oven, until the crust is browned and cooked through. Cool a little before carefully turning out onto a warm plate, and peel away the wax paper.
The tart may be cooked ahead and reheated before serving.

Aileen Murphy's Tomato and Spinach Tart with Goat Cheese and Tapenade

Serves 4

8–10 ounces (225–275g) Puff Pastry (see page 456)
⅔ cup Tomato Fondue (see page 188)
4 teaspoons Tapenade (see page 588)
8 ounces (225g) fresh spinach leaves, stringed, blanched and refreshed
⅓ cup freshly grated Parmesan (Parmigiano Reggiano is best)
4 ounces (110g) mature goat cheese
freshly ground pepper
olive oil
few black olives

Preheat the oven to 350°F (180°C). Roll out the pastry dough to the thickness of a coin. Cut out 4 circles (7–8 inches/18–20.5cm) and perforate the surface all over with a fork. Spread each tart base with 2 to 3 tablespoons of Tomato Fondue and 1 teaspoon of tapenade. Divide the spinach between the tarts. Sprinkle Parmesan on top and place thin slices of goat cheese, overlapping, on top of the tarts. Season each layer with pepper. Place on wax paper discs. Cook for 10–15 minutes. Serve immediately, with a drizzle of olive oil and some olives.

Smoked Mackerel Tart

Serves 4

Pastry Dough (see page 110)

Filling
1 small onion, finely chopped
2 tablespoons butter
2–3 large smoked mackerel, filleted and skinned (smoked salmon can be substituted)
2 eggs
1¼ cups heavy cream
1 egg yolk
3 ripe firm tomatoes made into concassé
1 generous tablespoon of chives
2 teaspoons of tarragon
salt and pepper

8-inch (20-cm) diameter quiche pan

Preheat the oven to 350°F (180°C).

Make the pastry dough. Chill for 15 minutes, then roll out to line the tart pan or quiche dish. Line with wax paper and fill to the top with dried beans. Rest for 15 minutes, then bake for 20–25 minutes. Remove the beans and paper, brush a little egg over the base to seal it, and return to the oven for 1–2 minutes.

Meanwhile make the filling. Sweat the onion in the butter, then let cool. Flake the mackerel, but don't break it up too much. Mix together all the tart ingredients and check the seasoning. Fill the tart shell and return it to the oven for 20–25 minutes, until just set.

Smoked Salmon Tart

Substitute smoked salmon for mackerel in the above recipe.

Gravlax with Mustard and Dill Mayonnaise

Serves 24–30

In season: wild salmon season (varies yearly)

The Swedish way of pickling raw salmon, using salt, sugar, and herbs, may also be used for trout or sea trout. The Finns make many exciting variations on the basic technique, and flavor their Gravlax with beets, and black and even pink peppercorns. The Norwegians use beer. We've also used the basic mixture to pickle cod, hake, and mackerel with tremendous success. Fillets of mackerel only take 2 or 3 hours to pickle and are absolutely delicious served with Mustard and Dill Mayonnaise. Pickled salmon keeps for up to a week. Fresh dill is essential in this recipe.

2 fillets fresh wild salmon
a heaped 1/4 cup sea salt or kosher salt
a heaped 1/4 cup sugar
2 teaspoons freshly ground black pepper
5 tablespoons fresh dill, finely chopped

Double quantity of Mustard and Dill Mayonnaise (see below)

If necessary, fillet the salmon and remove all the pin bones with tweezers. Do not skin.

Mix the salt, sugar, pepper, and dill together in a bowl. Place 1 fillet of fish, skin side down, on a piece of plastic wrap on a long dish. Scatter the mixture over the surface of the fish. Lay the second fillet on top, skin side up. Wrap tightly with the plastic wrap and refrigerate for 24–36 hours. We usually turn it over every 12 hours.

To serve: wipe the dill mixture off the salmon and slice thinly down to the skin. Arrange on a plate, barely overlapping the slices. Zigzag with Mustard and Dill Mayonnaise. Alternatively, arrange the salmon slices in a rosette shape. Fill the center of the rosette with Mustard and Dill Mayonnaise. Garnish with fresh dill. Serve with brown bread and butter.

Mustard and Dill Mayonnaise

Serves 8–10

1 large egg yolk
2 1/2 tablespoons French mustard
1 tablespoon plus 1 teaspoon white sugar
2/3 cup peanut or sunflower oil
1 tablespoon plus 1 teaspoon white wine vinegar
1 generous tablespoon fresh dill, finely chopped
salt and white pepper

Whisk the egg yolk with the mustard and sugar in a medium-sized glass bowl, drip in the oil, drop by drop, whisking all the time until the mixture has emulsifed, then add the vinegar and dill and season with salt and white pepper.

Tip: Gravlax is also great served with Sweet Cucumber Pickle (see page 514) and Egg Mayonnaise (see page 101).

Salting and Brining

Salt is one of the oldest preservatives. There are two basic methods of preserving with salt – dry-salting and brining. Both can be used for fish, meat, and vegetables. Use sea salt or kosher salt – do not use salt that has chemicals or anti-caking agent. Fresh food gives best results. Salting not only preserves but also enhances flavor. Food writers in the U.S. are urging their readers to brine chicken and pork to improve the eating quality of what is invariably intensively reared meat. Dry-salting involves rubbing salt into the food. This draws out moisture which produces a brine. In the second method – brining – the food is immersed in a salt solution which must be strong enough to penetrate the food and extract the juices. A 20% salt solution is recommended. This can be measured with a salometer but the traditional method was to add salt to the water until a fresh egg will float on the solution. Use pure fresh water, the chemicals in tap water may interfere with the curing. Use these proportions:

7 lbs. (3.1kg) salt
2 1/2–4 1/2 quarts (2.4–4.2 liters) water
2 lbs. (900g) sugar (4 cups)

Traditional stoneware crocks are best for brining, but plastic is also fine. Metal or timber may affect the flavor of the food. Injecting the brine into meat speeds up the process. Particular care needs to be taken close to the bone where the meat starts to decay first.

Above: Carpaccio of Smoked Salmon or Tuna with Avocado, Red Onion, Dill, and Horseradish Cream

Carpaccio of Smoked Salmon or Tuna with Avocado, Red Onion, Dill, and Horseradish Cream

Serves 8

In season: all year for smoked salmon, summer for tuna

Arrigo Cipriani of Harry's Bar in Venice created Filetto al Carpaccio in 1961, naming it after the painter, whose work was being exhibited at the time. It is cooked and sliced fillet. The name "carpaccio" has been purloined to apply to sliced and raw meats, and fish as here. Tuna is wonderful for sushi and delicious quickly pan-grilled, but do also try it this way.

6–8 ounces (175–225g) smoked salmon or very fresh blue or yellow fin tuna, very thinly sliced
1–2 avocados
1 small red onion, finely diced
1 generous tablespoon chives, finely snipped
1 generous tablespoon fresh dill, finely chopped
1 generous tablespoon chervil or flat-leaf parsley sprigs
freshly cracked pepper
Horseradish Sauce (see page 586)

First make the Horseradish Sauce.

To serve: arrange the smoked salmon or tuna in a single layer on 4 large chilled plates. Peel and cut the avocado into ¼-inch (5-mm) dice. Drizzle some Horseradish Cream over the salmon or tuna, then sprinkle with avocado and red onion dice. Garnish with snipped chives, chopped dill and chervil, or flat-leaf parsley sprigs.

Finally add a little freshly cracked pepper. Serve with crusty brown yeast bread.

Salt Cod Buñuelos

Serves 8 – makes about 40

8 ounces (225g) skinned, boned, and dried salt cod
1 lb. (450g) small potatoes, well scrubbed
2 garlic cloves, crushed
1 generous tablespoon parsley, chopped
a little freshly ground pepper
2 egg yolks
oil for deep frying

Soak the cod in several changes of cold water for 24–36 hours, depending on how salty it is. Drain. Put the potatoes and cod into a saucepan, cover with water, bring to a boil, cover, and simmer for 30 minutes or until the potatoes are cooked. Drain, peel, and push the potatoes through a ricer into a bowl. Remove the skin from the cod, flake the flesh, and mix with the potatoes. Add the garlic, parsley, pepper, and egg yolks. Mix well. Taste and add salt if necessary.

To cook the buñuelos: drop teaspoons of the mixture into hot oil. They will puff up crisp on all sides. Drain on paper towels. Keep them warm while you cook the remainder. Serve with hot Aïoli (see page 584) and Tomato Sauce (see page 590) or Tomato Fondue (see page 188).

Three-minute Fish

Serves 4

This is the fastest fish recipe I know and certainly one of the most delicious. It's fun to mix pink- and white-fleshed fish on the same plate (like salmon and sea bass).

1 lb. (450g) very fresh fish (wild Irish salmon, cod, turbot, large sole, sea bass, or gray sea mullet)
olive oil or melted butter
finely chopped parsley, thyme, chives
salt and freshly ground pepper

4 ovenproof main course plates

Season the fish about half an hour before cutting. Chill in the fridge to stiffen it.

Preheat the oven to 450°F (230°C).

While the oven is heating, brush the plates with oil or melted butter. Put the fillet of fish on a cutting board skin-side down; cut the flesh into scant 1/4-inch (5-mm) thin slices down onto the skin. Arrange the slices on the plates but don't let them overlap or they will cook unevenly. Brush the fish with more oil or melted butter, season with salt and pepper, and sprinkle each plate with a little freshly chopped herbs. Put the plates in the preheated oven and cook for 3 minutes; you might like to check after 2 minutes if the slices are very thin. The fish is cooked when it looks opaque.

Rush it to the table and serve with crusty white bread, a green salad, and white wine.

Crab Phyllos with Thai Dipping Sauce

Serves 4
In season: spring to autumn

Another multi-purpose recipe! This makes a terrific appetizer and delicious canapes.

8 ounces (225g) cooked white crab meat (a heaped cup)
1 teaspoon fresh ginger, grated
1 garlic clove, crushed
1 tablespoon fresh cilantro, chopped
1/2 Thai chile, finely chopped
1 teaspoon Thai fish sauce (nam pla)
salt and freshly ground pepper
3–4 sheets phyllo pastry dough, depending on size
a little melted butter
egg wash: 1 egg beaten with a pinch of salt

Thai Dipping Sauce
1/4 cup Thai fish sauce (nam pla)
1/4 cup lime or lemon juice, freshly squeezed
2 1/2 tablespoons sugar, or more to taste
1/4 cup warm water
1 garlic clove, crushed
3–4 fresh hot red or green chiles

Garnish
fresh cilantro

Put the crab meat into a bowl, checking that there are no pieces of shell included. Add the ginger, garlic, cilantro, chile, and nam pla. Mix well, taste and add seasoning, going easy with the salt – nam pla is very salty.

Unwrap the phyllo pastry dough. Lay 1 sheet down on the worktop, brush with melted butter. Lay a 1-inch (2.5-cm) strip of the crab meat mixture about 1 1/2 inches (4cm) in from the edge of the longer side. Roll over and over to form a sausage. Brush with melted butter and chill. Repeat this exercise until all the filling has been used up.

Preheat the oven to 425°F (220°C). Now make the Thai Dipping Sauce.

Combine the nam pla, lime or lemon juice, sugar, and warm water in a jar, then add the crushed garlic. Mix well and pour into 4 little, individual bowls. Cut the chiles crosswise into very thin rings and divide them between the bowls. Egg wash the rolls of phyllo and cut them with a sharp knife into pieces roughly 1 1/4 inches (3cm). Bake in the preheated oven for about 10 minutes until crispy and golden. Garnish with fresh cilantro and serve warm with Thai Dipping Sauce.

Vietnamese Spring Rolls with Peanut Dipping Sauce

Serves 4 (makes about 8)

These are fun to make and yummy to eat! Nina Simonds, author of many wonderful books on Asian food, gave me this version when she came to teach at the school. Banh Trang (rice papers) break easily so handle them carefully. You can buy circular or triangular ones; here I use the circular. They come in 3 sizes and this is the medium one.

Spring Rolls
2 ounces (50g) thin rice vermicelli noodles
1 large carrot or cucumber, peeled and cut into julienne strips or coarsely grated
salt
1 teaspoon sugar
8 lettuce leaves (preferably butterhead)
5 tablespoons fresh mint leaves
16 Chinese garlic chives (optional)
2½ tablespoons fresh cilantro leaves
8 large cooked jumbo shrimp or tiger shrimp or 32 shrimp, cooked and shelled
8 rice paper wrappers (banh trang), 8 inches (20.5cm) in diameter

Peanut Dipping Sauce*
1 teaspoon sugar
1 tablespoon plus 1 teaspoon rice wine vinegar
1 teaspoon carrot, finely grated
5 tablespoons hoisin sauce
2½ tablespoons water
1 tablespoon plus 1 teaspoon peanut butter
1 red chile, seeded and finely chopped

First make the dipping sauce. Mix the sugar with the rice wine vinegar in a bowl, add the carrot, and marinate for 15 minutes. Drain, and squeeze the moisture from the carrot. Put the hoisin sauce into a small saucepan with the water and heat for a few minutes until thick and reduced; add the peanut butter, stir, and simmer for a second or two. Cool. Stir in the chile and carrot, then transfer to little serving bowls.

For the spring rolls, soak the noodles in warm water for 15–20 minutes. Drain.

Put the carrot into a bowl and sprinkle with salt and sugar. Put the lettuce, mint leaves, Chinese chives, and cilantro leaves on a plate. If the shrimp are large, cut them in half. Make spring rolls as described right. Have the dipping sauce ready in bowls. Assemble all other ingredients on the table.

* *Also try traditional Thai dipping sauce (see left).*

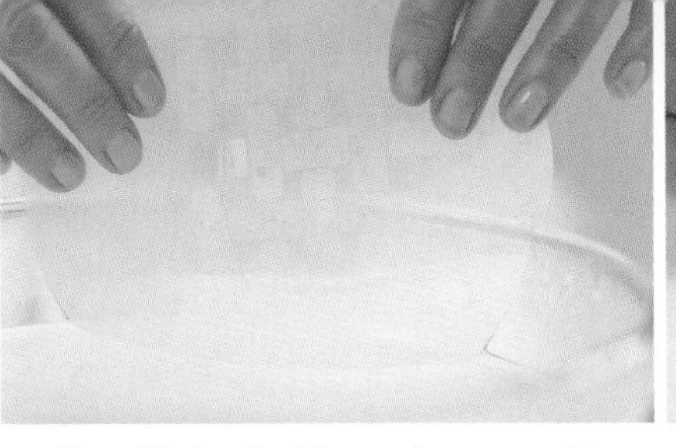

1. Fill a wide bowl with very hot water. Dip a banh trang (rice paper) into the hot water; it will soften in a second or two.

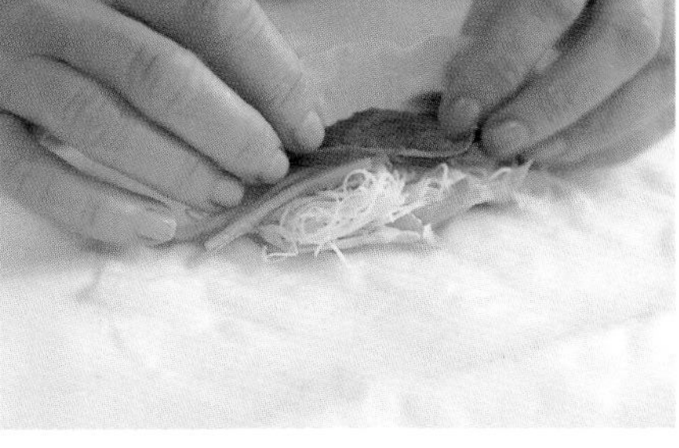

2. Remove, shake off excess moisture, and put onto a clean lint-free towel. Lay a piece of lettuce over the bottom third of the rice paper, add a tablespoon of noodles, some shredded carrot, and several mint leaves.

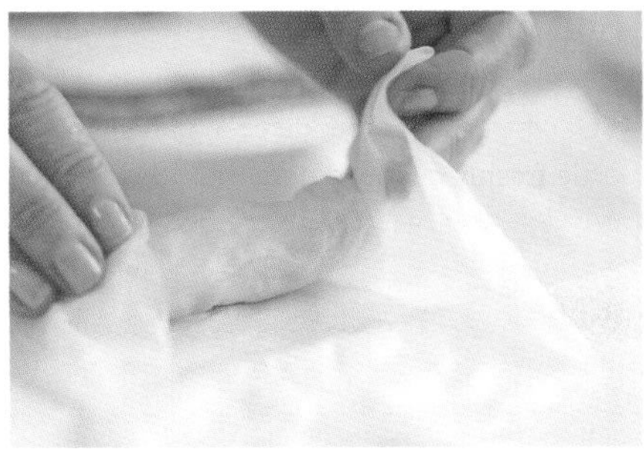

3. Roll the rice paper over halfway into a cylinder, then fold in the sides.

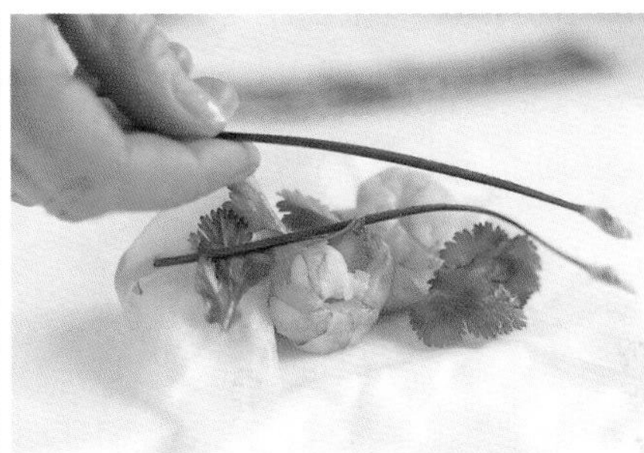

4. Arrange 2 half shrimp or 3 or 4 small shrimp along the top along with a few cilantro leaves, add a couple of garlic chives, letting them peep out from one end. Continue to roll up and press to seal.

Spring rolls may be made several hours ahead and kept covered. The general idea is that people dip their rolls in the sauce as they eat. Serve with lettuce leaves and sprig of fresh mint. Some people like to wrap the spring rolls in lettuce leaves before dipping.

Nachos with Melted Cheese

Serves 4 as an appetizer

Nachos are fried tortilla chips, and in their native Mexico, are served with melted cheese. For more substantial dishes, serve them with frijoles refritos (refried beans, see page 134) and other toppings.

8 tortillas (corn tortillas are more authentic but wheat flour ones are also delicious)
oil for frying
salt
2–3 green chiles, finely sliced
4 ounces (110g) buffalo Mozzarella cheese, shredded, or half Mozzarella, half Cheddar cheese (about 1 cup)

Tomato and Cilantro Salsa (see page 591)

Cut the tortillas into sixths or eighths, depending on size. Heat some oil – a deep fat fryer is easiest but you can manage in a frying pan. The oil should be hot – 400°F (200°C). Fry the tortilla pieces until pale golden, remove with a slotted spoon, drain on paper towels, and sprinkle with salt.

Just before serving, arrange on heatproof plates, allowing about eight nachos per person as an appetizer. Add some sliced chile to each and top with a little shredded cheese. Flash under a broiler or pop into a hot oven (450°F/230°C) until the cheese melts. Serve with Tomato and Cilantro Salsa.

Tostadas

Serves 8

Tostadas are a favorite snack in Mexico; the filling varies according to the area: it can be beef, chicken, pork, turkey, crab or just vegetables. They are quite a challenge to eat elegantly but, what the heck, they taste delicious!

8 tortillas, they ought to be corn but wheat flour tortillas can be substituted
8 ounces (225g) refried beans (see page 134), optional (about 1 cup)
1/3 iceberg lettuce, shredded
4–6 ounces (110–150g) cooked chicken breast, shredded (about 2/3–1 cup)
1 sliced chile (optional)
4 very ripe tomatoes, sliced
1 avocado or Guacamole (see page 91)
5 tablespoons scallion
1/4 cup sour cream
2–4 ounces (50–110g) shredded Cheddar cheese (about 1/2–1 cup)

Deep-fry the tortillas in hot oil until crisp and golden, drain on paper towels. Put each tortilla on a hot plate, spread with a little warm refried beans, and then top with some crunchy lettuce, shredded chicken breast, guacamole, and so on. Finish off with a blob of sour cream and a sprinkling of Cheddar cheese and chives. Serve immediately. In Mexico, Tostadas are considered to be finger food – you'll need both hands!

Above: Sweet Pea Guacamole on Warm Tortillas

Sweet Pea Guacamole on Warm Tortillas

Makes about 16, depending on size

Guacamole (see page 91) is a Mexican dip made from very ripe avocados. I came across this fresh-tasting variation in California, served on tiny warm tortillas (see page 493). Little crêpes are also very good, however, and easier to make! Allow about 3 per person as an appetizer or simply serve as finger food.

16 warm tortillas, about 2 1/2 inches (6cm)
1 lb. (450g) fresh or frozen peas, shelled (about 4 cups)
2 1/2 tablespoons extra-virgin olive oil
2 1/2 tablespoons lime juice, freshly squeezed
3 tablespoons fresh cilantro, finely chopped
1/2–1 fresh chile, seeded and finely chopped
1/4–1/2 teaspoon freshly ground cumin
3 tablespoons parsley, chopped

1/2–1 teaspoon salt
1/2 teaspoon coriander, ground

Garnish
crème fraîche or thick plain yogurt
fresh cilantro leaves

If you are using fresh peas, cook them in boiling, salted water for 3–4 minutes. Refresh under cold water and drain. Whizz the olive oil with the lime juice, cilantro, and chile in a food processor for 1 minute. Add the peas, cumin, parsley, ground coriander, and salt, and blend until almost smooth. Taste, correct seasoning, put into a bowl, and cover until needed.

Serve on tiny hot tortillas or crêpes with a blob of crème fraîche or thick whole-milk yogurt, if you like. Garnish with a sprig of cilantro.

Master Recipe
Quesadillas with Tomatilla Salsa

Serves 4

Quesadillas are massively popular in Mexico. On Sundays in Oaxaca there are little stalls on the streets and squares with women making and selling these delicious stuffed tortillas. They cooked them on a comal (a type of griddle pan) over a charcoal brazier. One of my favorites was flavored with an aromatic leaf called hoja santa**, then filled with shredded cornfed chicken and fiery tomato sauce.**

8 corn or wheat flour tortillas
4–8 ounces (110–225g) Queso fresca or mild Cheddar cheese, shredded, or a mixture of Cheddar and mozzarella (about 1–2 cups)
4 scallions, sliced
2 green chiles, cut in strips or slices (optional)

Tomatilla Salsa (see page 592)

First make the Tomatilla Salsa.
Next heat a cast-iron pan or griddle and proceed with the quesadillas. There are two ways of making them. One resembles a sandwich, the other a turnover. To make the sandwich type, lay a tortilla on the hot pan, spread about 1/4 cup of cheese over the top, keeping it a little from the edge. Sprinkle a few scallions and some chile strips on top. Cover with another tortilla. Cook for a minute or two, then carefully turn over. Serve, just as it is or cut into quarters, with the Tomatilla Salsa.

If you want to make the turnover-style quesadillas, lay a tortilla on the worktop, put a little filling onto 1 half, again keeping it in slightly from the edges, fold over, and press gently to seal. Cook for 3 or 4 minutes on each side on a preheated pan or griddle. (It should be medium–hot, otherwise the outside will burn before the inside is cooked.) Then stand it upright so that the fold is also cooked. Serve as soon as possible with the Salsa.

Variations
Quesadillas with Tomato and Cilantro Salsa and Guacamole

Follow the Master Recipe. Serve the quesadillas with Tomato and Cilantro Salsa (see page 591) and Guacamole (see right) instead of Tomatilla Salsa.

Quesadillas with Cheese and Zucchini Blossoms

A favorite filling for quesadillas in Oaxaca is simply shredded Oaxacan string cheese (mozzarella is our nearest equivalent) and fresh squash or zucchini blossoms. Thinly sliced green chile is sometimes added for extra excitement! Accompany with Guacamole (see right) and Tomato and Cilantro Salsa (see page 591).

Tortilla Chips with Guacamole and Salsa

Serves 4–6 as an appetizer

For me, Mexican food is utterly irresistible – as indeed, are all things Mexican. Tortilla chips can now be found even in local stores and gas stations. However, most are rather too highly flavored.

4–6 tortillas
salt

First use the tortillas to make tortilla chips (see page 494). Sprinkle with a little salt. Next make the Guacamole.

Guacamole

1 ripe avocado
1 garlic clove, crushed, optional
1 1/2–2 1/2 tablespoons lime or lemon juice, freshly squeezed
1 1/2 tablespoon extra-virgin olive oil (optional)
1 generous tablespoon cilantro or parsley, freshly chopped
sea salt and freshly ground pepper

Scoop out the avocado flesh. Mash with a fork, then add the garlic, lime or lemon juice, oil, cilantro or parsley, and salt and pepper to taste. Place a sheet of plastic on the surface of the guacamole to cover, otherwise it may discolor. Refrigerate until needed. Next make the Tomato and Cilantro Salsa (see page 591).

To serve, put a generous tablespoonful of Tomato and Cilantro Salsa into one bowl and a good blob of Guacamole into another. Put onto a plate, add lots of crisp tortilla chips for dipping, and serve immediately. Quite simple and addictive.

Indian Spiced Vegetable Pakoras

Serves 4–6

These crispy vegetables in a spicy batter are also good served with Mango Relish (see right) and a Yogurt Raita (see page 595).

1 thin eggplant, cut into 1/4-inch (5-mm) slices
salt
2 medium zucchini, cut into 1-inch (2.5-cm) slices (if they are very large, then cut the slices into quarters or batons)
12 cauliflower flowerets
6 large or 12 small flat mushrooms, cut in half
scallions, cut into 3–4-inch (8–10-cm) lengths

Batter
1 1/2 cups chick pea (besan) or all-purpose flour
1 generous tablespoon fresh cilantro, chopped
1 scant teaspoon salt
2 teaspoons curry powder
1 tablespoon plus 1 teaspoon olive oil
1 tablespoon plus 1 teaspoon lemon juice, freshly squeezed
3/4–1 cup iced water
vegetable oil for deep frying

Garnish
lemon wedges
cilantro or parsley
Mango Relish (see right)

Put the eggplant slices into a colander, sprinkle with the salt, and let drain while preparing the other vegetables. Blanch the zucchini and cauliflower separately in boiling, salted water for 2 minutes. Drain, refresh under cold water, and dry well. Halve the mushrooms, if necessary. Rinse the eggplant slices and pat dry.

Next make the batter: put the flour, cilantro, salt, and curry powder into a large bowl. Gradually whisk in the oil, lemon juice, and water until the batter is the consistency of thick cream.

Heat good quality oil to 350°F (180°C) in a deep fryer. Lightly whisk the batter and dip the vegetables in batches of 5 or 6. Slip them carefully into the hot oil. Fry the pakoras for 2–3 minutes on each side, turning them with a slotted spoon. Drain on paper towels and keep warm in a moderate oven (uncovered) while you cook the remainder. Let the oil come back to 350°F (180°C) between batches. When all the vegetable fritters are ready, garnish with lemon wedges and fresh or deep fried cilantro or parsley. Serve at once with Mango Relish.

Mango Relish

Relish, usually involving vinegar, is a piquant or spicy preparation eaten with plainer food to enhance flavor.

1/4 cup medium sherry
1/4 cup water
1/4 cup white wine vinegar
2 1/2 tablespoons sugar
1/2 cinnamon stick
2 star anise
1/2 teaspoon salt
pinch ground mace
1 mango, peeled and diced
1 small red pepper, seeded and diced
1 tablespoon plus 1 teaspoon lemon juice

Put the sherry, water, vinegar, sugar, cinnamon, star anise, salt, and mace into a small, heavy saucepan. Bring to a boil and simmer over medium heat for 5 minutes. Add the mango, pepper, and lemon juice, lower the heat, and simmer for 5 minutes more. Remove from the heat and let cool completely. Spoon into a screw-top jar and refrigerate until needed (it will keep for up to 10 days).

Onion Chrysanthemums

Serves 6

6 medium onions
milk
flour, well seasoned with salt
cayenne pepper or smoked paprika

Orly Sauce (see page 585) or Tomato and Chile Sauce (see page 590)

Place the onions upright on a cutting board and peel. Cut in half, then quarters, eighths, sixteenths, down to the root but not through it. By now the onion will vaguely resemble a chrysanthemum. Put the onions into a large bowl of iced water to open further. Drain well.

Heat the oil in a deep-fryer to 350°F (180°C). Dip the onion in milk, then in flour seasoned with salt and cayenne or smoked paprika. Sprinkle more flour over the top and in between the "petals". Deep-fry until crisp and golden. Serve with Orly Sauce or Tomato and Chile Sauce.

Grape, Grapefruit, and Lovage or Mint Soup

Serves 6

Fruit and fresh herb appetizers are popular at Ballymaloe. Pomelo, sweeties, ugli fruit, or ordinary grapefruit can also be used.

3 pink grapefruit
30 grapes
1 tablespoon mint, finely chopped or 1 tablespoon lovage, finely chopped
about 1 tablespoon superfine sugar

Peel and carefully segment the grapefruit, peel and seed the grapes and add to the grapefruit in a bowl. Sprinkle with mint or lovage, and sugar. Taste, and add more sugar if necessary. Chill before serving in a pretty white bowl with a sprig of mint on top.

eggs

eggs

I love hens, and there are few things better in life than getting up and going out to the hen house to collect some lovely freshly laid eggs for breakfast. Ever since I was a child we've always had our own hens – happy lazy hens that strut around freely, having dust baths in the sun. They are part of our way of life, part of a holistic system....

The food scraps go to the hens and come back as eggs a few days later – a very satisfactory arrangement. Here at the cooking school it is yet another way for the students to learn about how food is produced. The quality of the eggs laid by free-range hens fed on food scraps and organic feed, with access to lots of grass, is fantastic. They make wonderful unctuous mayonnaise, silky Hollandaise Sauce, and gorgeous scones and cakes.

There is no difference in the nutritional value between a white and a brown egg. The color of the shells is determined by the breed of the hens. The Hepden Blacks and Speckledys we have at the school are bred specially for free-range production and both lay brown and speckledy eggs. Occasionally one gets a double-yolk egg. This happens when hens are coming to the end of their laying careers, but it is not something to worry about – rather, something to celebrate.

We also have a collection of rare and rareish breeds, what we call "hens with attitude" – Silver Wyandotte, Light Sussex, Buff Orpington, Old English Game, Marrans, Leghorns, Silkies, Bantams, Poland, Minorcas, and Araucana. They lay a variety of eggs, some white, some brown and speckled. The Araucanas occasionally lay beautiful blue eggs, when the fancy takes them! The Bantams and older breeds make very good mothers and teach the chicks how to scratch and forage (in addition to laying the most wonderfully tasty, tiny eggs which are perfect for children's breakfast). All are beautiful birds that strut around looking haughty and decorative near the Palais des Poulets.

On Easter Sunday our hens lay eggs with names on them – much to the delight of our grandson Joshua and other children staying in the cottages over Easter. Several times a year a hen will arrive in from the wood with a little clutch of chicks. Sometimes they sit patiently on their eggs in the hen house but often they will hide away to hatch and then arrive proudly to show off their new clutch. It doesn't matter whether you come from Tipperary or Tokyo, baby chicks, like puppies and kittens, delight everyone.

Organic Eggs from Free-range Hens
Roughly 80 per cent of commercially produced eggs are from intensively-reared chickens (see page 268).

Those of us who are fortunate enough to have some space to keep hens are blessed indeed. The eggs have white curdy albumen and rich yellow yolks. Simply boiled eggs from such happy, lazy, free-range hens are a real treat, and a forgotten flavor for most people nowadays. Many students at the school become so attached to the hens and are so impressed by the quality of their eggs that they decide to keep a few hens when they leave.

While I cannot emphasise too strongly the virtues of eggs from free-range hens, do remember that these eggs are produced in smaller quantities than intensively-reared hens' eggs, so be prepared to pay more. Believe me – they're worth every penny. If we want better quality eggs we must be prepared to pay the producer enough to make it worth their while.

Uses

Eggs are incredibly versatile and great value for money. Two farm-fresh organic eggs for supper still represents better value than the equivalent amount of meat. So I would encourage you to always seek out the best quality eggs available, and don't begrudge the price.

Other Types of Eggs and Relative Weights

Hens' eggs, though the most common, are not the only option. Quail eggs can be fried or poached in the same way a hen's eggs can. Quail eggs have beautiful, speckled shells and are delightful for canapés, appetizers, or for children's breakfasts. Duck eggs work very well in sponge cakes.

While pheasants and other wild birds' eggs can also be eaten, people are nowadays very reluctant to do so (and it is, in some cases, illegal), when many bird populations are threatened and in decline.

Quail	3/4 ounce (20g)
Guinea fowl	1 ounce (25g)
Hen	2 ounces (50g) for small eggs, with extra-large ones weighing in at over 2 1/4–2 1/2 ounces (55–60g)
Duck	2 ounces (50g) – wash these well
Turkey	3 ounces (75g) – very similar in flavor to hens' eggs
Goose	7 ounces (200g)
Ostrich	18–20 ounces (500–550g) – equal to 10 or 11 small hens' eggs

Buying and Storage

Never buy cracked eggs. The official advice is that eggs should be consumed within 21 days of being laid, but I suggest seven days – the quality deteriorates rapidly. Boiled eggs should not be more than a day or two old; 4–5 day-old eggs are fine for baking, and week-old egg whites are still good for whipping, as fresh ones don't whip up well.

Store your eggs in a fridge as chilling slows deterioration, but do let them return to room temperature before use. If you are unsure about the freshness of your eggs, put them in a bowl of water. If they sink to the bottom, then they are fresh; if not, the gas in them will cause them to rise to the surface. When you crack really fresh eggs onto a plate, you should be able to see three, distinct layers – as they deteriorate, the albumen becomes more watery, and you will only see two.

Buttered Eggs

If you do have your own hens, you can extend the shelf life of your eggs by rubbing the newly laid, warm shells with a tiny scrap of butter to seal the pores. This old-fashioned way of preserving eggs is traditional in my part of the country and they can still be bought in the Cork market. Stored in a cool place, the eggs will keep for several weeks and have a wonderful curdy texture, reminiscent of a newly laid egg.

Nutrition and Health

Eggs are one of the most complete, naturally produced foods. They are an excellent source or protein and are rich in vitamins (A, D, E, B12) and essential minerals including calcium, zinc, and iron. They are also relatively low in calories. But despite this, they are still regarded with suspicion, because we associate them with high cholesterol and salmonella.

The good news about cholesterol is that recent American studies have demonstrated that it is saturated fat in the diet (in which eggs are relatively low) rather than dietary cholesterol, that is the major contributor to raised blood cholesterol. As a result, it is now accepted that eating an egg a day is unlikely to have an overall impact on the risk of coronary heart disease in most healthy people.

Salmonella continues to make headlines, despite the fact that since 1998, cases of salmonella poisoning have dropped by half. This drop is due in part to recommendations made by the British Government's Advisory Committee on the Microbiological Safety of Food (in particular, that eggs should be maintained at a temperature below 68°F/20°C and consumed within 21 days). Many countries have also devised symbols of quality – a shamrock in Ireland and a red lion in the UK – which are stamped on eggs, along with a "best before" date, to indicate that they are fresh and from vaccinated hens. As a precaution, do not eat raw eggs, and do not give lightly-cooked eggs to infants, the elderly, or to pregnant women. You should also follow the guidelines in Buying and Storing. Unfortunately, buying organic does not necessarily guarantee disease-free eggs, although studies do suggest that salmonella is less common in organic chickens than conventional birds.

As chefs and cooks, we deeply resent being forced to use pasturized eggs and prevented from using lightly-cooked eggs in our dishes. The onus should be on the primary producer to produce eggs that are safe to eat. And the government should ensure that all eggs that are sold to the public are guaranteed salmonella-free.

We have our own hens at Ballymaloe, living in luxury in the Palais des Poulets. They roam outside, scratch in the vegetable patch and in the fields around the school, genuine free-rangers. Their eggs taste exceedingly good. Buying good eggs is altogether a more tricky business. Look for "organic free-range" if at all possible – these are produced by birds under strict regulations: continual access to the great outdoors, in flocks of not more than 500, fed on a diet at least 80 per cent organic, and with de-beaking banned.

The color of the shell has to do with the breed of chicken that produced it. The color of the yolk depends on diet and time of year, becoming a richer yellow in the summer months when the hens have access to lots of grass. Always store eggs in a cool place, or the fridge. Remember egg shells are porous, so strong smells can be absorbed. The air pocket expands inside the egg the older it gets. If you put an egg in water and it floats instantly to the surface you will know it is not fresh!

The recipes all call for medium eggs, unless otherwise stated. Small eggs are $1\frac{1}{2}$ ounces (35g), medium ones are $1\frac{3}{4}$–2 ounces (45–50g), large ones 2–$2\frac{1}{4}$ ounces (50–55g), extra large are $2\frac{1}{4}$–$2\frac{1}{2}$ (55–60g) and jumbo are $2\frac{1}{2}$ ounces (60g) at least.

Master Recipe

Scrambled Eggs

Serves 2

Perfectly scrambled eggs are rare indeed. I've had positively horrendous concoctions served up for breakfast in some posh hotels. On one particularly memorable occasion they arrived in a solid mound garnished with a sprig of red currants! For a perfect result, really fresh eggs from free-range hens are essential. Perfectly scrambled, these need no further embellishment, except perhaps a slice of hot thin toast – but it's fun to experiment with variations, all the same.

4 eggs
5 tablespoons creamy milk
salt and freshly ground pepper
a pat of butter

Break the eggs into a bowl, add the milk, and season with salt and pepper. Whisk until the whites and yolks are well mixed. Put a blob of butter into a cold saucepan, pour in the egg mixture, and stir continuously, preferably with a flat-bottomed wooden spatula over a low heat, until the butter melts and eggs have scrambled into soft creamy curds. Serve immediately on warm plates with lots of hot buttered toast or fresh soda bread.

Tip: If the plates are too hot, the scrambled eggs will actually overcook between the stove and the table.

Variations

Scrambled Eggs with Smoked Salmon

Some hotels serve this for breakfast but I rather prefer it for supper on a tray beside the fire.

Follow the Master Recipe. A few seconds before the scrambled egg is fully cooked, add 3–4 tablespoons diced smoked salmon trimmings, stir once or twice, sprinkle with a little chopped parsley, and serve immediately.

Scrambled Eggs with Smoked Bacon

Follow the Master Recipe. Cook 3–4 tablespoons of bacon dice in 4 teaspoons olive oil until crisp and golden. Add to the scrambled eggs along with 2 teaspoons chopped parsley a few seconds before the end of cooking, and serve immediately.

Scrambled Eggs with Chorizo

Follow the Master Recipe. Cook 3 or 4 slices of chorizo in a little hot oil in the pan. Cut into slivers and scatter over the scrambled eggs just before serving along with some flat-leaf parsley.

Scrambled Eggs with Tomato

Follow the Master Recipe. A few seconds before the scrambled eggs are fully cooked, add 1 very ripe, peeled tomato that has been finely chopped and seasoned with salt, pepper, and a pinch of sugar. Stir once or twice and serve immediately.

Scrambled Eggs with Tarragon and Basil

Follow the Master Recipe. Add 1 teaspoon freshly chopped tarragon and basil a few seconds before the end of cooking time. Serve immediately.

Scrambled Eggs with Chives

Follow the Master Recipe. Add 1–2 teaspoons freshly chopped chives a few seconds before the end of cooking time.

Cold scrambled egg with chives makes the best egg sandwiches.

Scrambled Eggs with Asparagus

Follow the Master Recipe. Add 2–4 stalks freshly cooked asparagus, cut into cubes, a few seconds before the end of the cooking time.

Cholita's Mexican Scrambled Eggs

Serves 4

Cholita Diaz, a wonderful Oaxacan cook, showed me how to make this favorite Mexican breakfast dish. One mouthful transports me back to Oaxaca, one of the most magical places in the entire world.

3 tablespoons butter (in Mexico they use lard)
1 small onion, finely chopped
1–2 chiles (serrano or jalapeño), seeded and finely chopped (the amount depends on how much excitement you would like in your life!)
1–2 very ripe tomatoes, finely chopped
8 eggs
1 teaspoon salt

Melt the butter in a heavy saucepan over a medium heat, and cook the onion and chiles until the onion is soft but not colored. Add the tomato and cook gently for a few more minutes. Meanwhile whisk the eggs and salt together well, add them to the saucepan, and scramble, stirring all the time until cooked to your taste. Serve immediately on warm plates, preferably with tortillas.

Master Recipe
Baked Eggs
Serves 4

Oeufs en cocotte **sounds so much more exotic than baked eggs – or shirred eggs, as they are known in the United States. Whatever the name, they make a tasty appetizer or snack and there are countless variations. Timing is critical and, once again, the quality and freshness of the eggs really matter.**

½–⅔ cup cream
4 eggs
salt and freshly ground pepper

4 small ramekins
1 tablespoon butter, for greasing

Lightly butter the 4 ramekins. Heat the cream, then spoon about 1 tablespoon into each ramekin and break an egg into each, too. Season with salt and freshly ground pepper. Spoon the remainder of the cream over the top of the eggs.

Place the ramekins in a flameproof bain-marie (see glossary) of hot water, cover with tin foil or a lid, and bring to simmering point on top of the stove. Continue to cook either gently on top of the stove, or in a moderate oven, 350°F (180°C), for about 12 minutes for a soft egg, 15 minutes for a medium egg, and 18–20 minutes for a hard egg. Serve immediately.

Variations
Baked Eggs with Cheese
Follow the Master Recipe, sprinkling 2–4 teaspoons finely shredded cheese – Parmesan, Gruyère, or Cheddar on top of each egg. Bake uncovered in a bain-marie in the oven, if you prefer.

Baked Eggs with Tomato and Chile Fondue
Follow the Master Recipe. Put 1 generous tablespoon Tomato Fondue with Chile (see page 190) underneath each egg in the ramekins. Proceed with or without the addition of cheese. Omit the chile from the tomato fondue if you'd prefer your baked eggs less perky.

Baked Eggs with Piperonata
Follow the Master Recipe. Put 1 generous tablespoon of Piperonata (see page 190) underneath each egg in the ramekins. Spoon 1 tablespoon cream over each egg. Sprinkle 2–4 teaspoons finely shredded cheese on top of each egg; a little cooked bacon may also be added. Bake uncovered in a bain-marie in the oven, if you prefer.

Baked Eggs with Fresh Herbs and Dijon Mustard
Follow the Master Recipe. Use a total of ¼ cup freshly chopped parsley, tarragon, chives, and chervil. Mix the herbs and 2 teaspoons mustard into the cream and proceed as in the basic recipe.

Baked Eggs with Smoked Salmon, Smoked Mackerel, or Smoked Haddock
Follow the Master Recipe. Put 1 generous tablespoon chopped smoked salmon, flaked smoked mackerel, or smoked haddock in the bottom of each ramekin. (If you are using smoked haddock, it should be gently cooked in milk first – this is because the haddock is cold-smoked and as a result, still semi-raw). Add 1½–2½ tablespoons chopped parsley to the cream and proceed as in the basic recipe.

Baked Egg with Chorizo
Follow the Master Recipe. Add some diced chorizo to the ramekin with or without the tomato fondue.

Eggs Benedict
Serves 4

Rich and gorgeous, this is often eaten for breakfast but is even better as a favorite American brunch. Again, the quality of all the components can lift it from the mundane to the extraordinary. You can use smoked salmon instead, or Serrano or Pata negra ham.

½ quantity Hollandaise sauce (see page 581)
4–8 slices crispy bacon or 4 slices cooked ham, slightly smoked, is good too
4 eggs
2 English muffins, toasted, or 4 slices of toast made from good bread (preferably not sliced pan – "plastic", sliced white bread)

First make the Hollandaise sauce. If using bacon, heat a very little sunflower oil in a hot frying pan. Cook the bacon until crisp. Drain on paper towels. Meanwhile poach the eggs (see page 115) and make the toast or split and toast the muffins. Butter the hot toast or muffins. Put 2 slices of bacon or 1 slice of ham on each piece. Gently place the poached egg on top and coat with Hollandaise sauce. Serve extra hot toast and sauce separately.

How to Hard-Boil Eggs

Eggs that have been laid a few days ago are ideal for hard-boiling. Very fresh eggs tend to be more difficult to peel. Eggs in the average store or supermarket tend to be about a week old so there will be no need to worry about them being too fresh! Lower the eggs gently into boiling salted water, bring the water back to a boil and cook the eggs for 10 minutes (or 7–8 for a slightly soft center). Drain and put immediately into a bowl of cold water. (Eggs with a black ring around the yolk have been overcooked.)

Master Recipe

Egg Mayonnaise

Makes 8

Egg mayonnaise has a ring of the 1950s and 1960s about it, since it used to be such a staple on country hotel menus. The usual offering was an overcooked, hardboiled egg, cut in half lengthwise, smothered in commercial mayonnaise, and sprinkled with a little parsley and paprika. This lighter, more labor-intensive version is one of the favorites on the buffet at Ballymaloe House. We also serve it in combination with smoked salmon and cucumber pickle as an appetizer.

4 hardboiled eggs
4–5 tablespoons Mayonnaise (see page 584)
1/2 teaspoon chives, finely chopped
salt and freshly ground pepper
salad greens

Garnish
parsley or chervil

When the eggs are cold, shell them and slice in half lengthwise. Remove the yolks and press through a strainer into a bowl, mix with mayonnaise, add the chives and salt and pepper to taste. Fill into a pastry bag fitted with a large star-shaped decorating nozzle, and pipe into the whites. Garnish with a sprig of parsley or chervil and serve on a bed of lettuce.

Variations

Egg Mayonnaise with Black Olives

Follow the Master Recipe. Chop 4–6 pitted Kalamata olives into a fine dice, add to the egg yolk and mayonnaise mixture. Omit the chives if you wish. Garnish each with a sprig of chervil.

Anchovy Egg Mayonnaise

Follow the Master Recipe. Mash 4–6 salted anchovies in a bowl, add to the egg yolk and mayonnaise mixture, and continue as in the basic recipe. Omit the chives.

Ballymaloe Chutney Eggs

Serves 6

6 hardboiled eggs
1/2 stick (1/4 cup) soft butter
1 generous tablespoon Apple and Tomato Chutney (see page 511) or Ballymaloe Country Relish
salt and freshly ground pepper

Garnish
tiny sprigs of watercress or chervil

Cut the eggs in half lengthwise. Press the yolks through a strainer into a bowl, add the soft butter and chutney, and mix well. Taste the mixture, it may need a little seasoning. Fill into a pastry bag fitted with a 1-inch (2.5-cm) star-shaped decorating nozzle. Pipe a rosette of the mixture into each egg white. Garnish with the watercress or chervil. Serve as an appetizer on a little bed of salad greens. Alternatively, serve one as part of a selection of stuffed eggs.

Oeufs Mimosa

Serves 4

In this very superior version of stuffed eggs, each one has a fat shrimp or a few small shrimp hiding inside. Be sure to tell people that there is shellfish involved, in case anyone has a seafood allergy. Oeufs Mimosa is great as an appetizer, or as part of a plate of stuffed eggs, or on a cold buffet. The sprinkled sieved egg yolk on top, resembles the mimosa flower, hence the name.

4 hardboiled eggs
8 cooked shrimp or 16 small shrimp
2/3 cup homemade mayonnaise
a few lettuce leaves
salt and freshly ground pepper

Garnish
sprigs of watercress
a few whole shrimp

When the eggs are cold, shell them and cut in half lengthwise. Press the yolks through a strainer, reserve a little for the mimosa garnish, and mix the remainder with 4–5 tablespoons of the mayonnaise.

Add salt and pepper, and taste to check the seasoning. Put 1 or 2 small cooked shrimp or a fat shrimp into each egg white and spoon some egg mayonnaise mixture into each one. Round off the top, so that the shape resembles a whole egg. Thin the remaining mayonnaise with cold water to coating consistency, and coat the eggs carefully.

Sprinkle with the reserved egg yolk. Serve on a bed of lettuce and garnish with sprigs of watercress and a few whole shrimp.

Omelettes

Omelettes appear in different guises all around the world. There are three main types – folded French omelettes, flat omelettes, and soufflé omelettes, both sweet and savory. The folded omelette may be made simply with a seasoning of salt and freshly ground pepper or a sprinkling of fresh herbs or freshly shredded cheese. Alternatively, a filling such as hot Mushroom à la Crème, Piperonata, Tomato Fondue, or seafood may be added just before the omelette is folded.

Flat omelettes are quite different, however. The eggs often help to bind other ingredients – such things as potatoes, leeks, or peppers. Cheese is often added, as are freshly chopped herbs. Flat omelettes are found all over the world from Provence to the tortillas of Spain, the kuku of the Middle East, and the frittatas of Italy. The fluffy Danish omelette is a variation on this theme. It is usually cooked in a deep frying pan over a very low heat without stirring until just set and slightly puffed. Some people favor starting a frittata on top of the stove and then transferring it into a preheated oven 300°F (150°C), until just set.

Asian omelettes are usually cooked in a wok and include shrimp and fresh herbs. They are often folded in half and may be served with a volcanic chile sauce. In Japan, cooks use special rectangular pans to make omelettes that are shaped into neat rolls to slice for sushi or into thin shreds for garnishing soups. In China, thin omelettes are used as wrappers for other ingredients but are also occasionally filled with vegetables. Soufflé omelettes may be sweet or savory. The eggs are separated and the fluffy, beaten egg whites are folded into the beaten egg yolks and sugar (in the case of a sweet omelette). Don't cook on too high a heat, otherwise the outside will be burnt before the inside is set.

French Omelette

Serves 1

An omelette is the quintessential fast food but many a travesty is served in its name. The whole secret is to have the pan hot enough and to use clarified butter if at all possible. Ordinary butter will burn if your pan is as hot as it ought to be. The omelette should be made in half the time it takes to read this recipe! Your first omelette may not be a joy to behold, but persevere. Practice makes perfect. The best tender golden omelette takes no more than 30 seconds to cook – or 45 seconds if you are adding a filling. If it is cooked too slowly, it will be tough and leathery and may be pale in color rather than lightly browned. Time yourself. You'll be amazed! Note that the size of pan suggested below is just right for a two-egg omelette. If you use more eggs, the proportions of the omelette and the timing will be altered.

2 eggs
2 teaspoons water or milk
2 teaspoons clarified butter (page 103) or olive oil
filling of your choice
salt and freshly ground pepper

9-inch (23-cm) omelette pan, preferably non-stick

Warm a plate in the oven. Whisk the eggs with the water or milk in a bowl until thoroughly mixed but not too fluffy. (You can use either a fork or a hand whisk.) Season with salt and pepper. Put the warm plate beside the stove. Have the filling also at hand, hot if necessary, with a spoon at the ready.

Heat the omelette pan over a high heat. When it is very hot, add the clarified butter; it should sizzle immediately. Pour in the egg mixture. It will start to cook instantly so quickly pull the edges of the omelette towards the center with a plastic spatula, tilting the pan so that the uncooked egg runs to the sides 4 or 5 times. Continue until most of the egg is set and will not run easily any more. The center will still be soft and uncooked at this point but will continue to cook on the plate. If you are using a filling, spoon the hot mixture in a line across the center at this point.

To fold the omelette: flip the edge that is just below the handle of the pan into the center, then hold the pan almost perpendicular over the plate so that the omelette flips over again. Half roll, half slide the omelette onto the plate so that it lands folded in 3. Serve immediately.

Suggested Fillings

Fines herbes:

Add 1 teaspoon each of freshly chopped parsley, chives, chervil, and tarragon to the eggs just before cooking, or scatter them over the omelette just before folding.

Smoked salmon or smoked mackerel

Add about 2 tablespoons diced or flaked fish and perhaps a little finely chopped parsley or dill.

Kidney

Cook one cleaned and diced lamb kidney gently in a little butter, add 1 teaspoon freshly chopped parsley, and keep warm.

Tomato Fondue, with or without pesto (see page 188)

Piperonata (see page 190)

Mushroom à la Crème (see page 197)

Crispy bacon, diced cooked ham or chorizo sausage

Goat cheese, Shredded Cheddar, Gruyère, Parmesan, or a mixture

How to Clarify Butter

Clarified butter is butter with the salt and milk particles removed. It is excellent for cooking because, when the salt and milk particles are removed, it can withstand a higher temperature than normal butter. It will keep, covered in a refrigerator, for several weeks. Melt 2 sticks (1 cup) butter gently in a saucepan or in the oven. Let it stand for a few minutes, then spoon the crusty white layer of salt particles off the top. Underneath is the clear liquid butter known as clarified butter. The milky liquid at the bottom can be discarded or used in a white sauce. Cover and store.

Omelette Sambo

Serves 1

Needless to say, this technique can be applied to a whole host of different fillings, so let your imagination run riot – but don't use it as a trashcan for leftovers.

1/2 baguette
French omelette, made with 2 eggs, salt and pepper, and 1 tablespoon freshly chopped herbs, e.g., basil, annual marjoram, chives, chervil, and parsley
2 1/2 tablespoons Tomato Fondue (see page 188) or Mushroom à la Crème (see page 197)
pesto, herb-flavored oil, or chili oil

To serve
flat-leaf parsley, arugula leaves, tiny spinach, or ruby chard leaves
red and yellow cherry tomatoes

Crisp the baguette in a hot oven if necessary and, meanwhile, make a well-seasoned herb omelette. Fill with Mushroom à la Crème or Tomato Fondue. Split open the baguette and smear with pesto, herb-flavored oil, or chili oil. Pop the rolled omelette inside the baguette and close up again. Leave the baguette whole, cut it in half, or into slices. Serve immediately with a nice mixture of salad greens, a few cherry tomatoes, and a drizzle of herb-flavored oil.

Cheese Soufflé Omelette

Serves 1–2

A perfect soufflé omelette is a special treat. It takes a few minutes longer to make than a French omelette but it is well worth the effort. Irish farmhouse cheeses such as Coolea, Desmond, or Gabriel from West Cork are utterly delicious in this recipe. If you can't get these, use Gruyère or Parmesan.

3 eggs, separated
3–5 tablespoons cheese, Gruyère or Parmesan or a mixture of both, finely shredded
1 teaspoon chives or scallion tops (optional), finely chopped
2 tablespoons butter
a little more shredded cheese (optional)
salt and freshly ground pepper

9-inch (23-cm) omelette pan, preferably non-stick

Whisk the egg yolks until light, season well, and add the cheese and chives. Whisk the egg whites until they hold a stiff peak, stir a little of the whites into the yolks, then very lightly and carefully fold in the rest with a metal spoon. Melt the butter in the frying pan, shaking it gently so that the sides are covered with butter, too. As it foams, turn in the egg mixture and level it off with a spatula.

Cook very gently for 3–4 minutes. When you lift the omelette with the spatula, the bottom should be golden, and it should have started to rise. Then put the pan under the broiler, about 4 inches (10cm) from the element, and cook very gently for 3–4 minutes longer until the omelette is well risen and just set. Remove at once, loosen the edges with the spatula and, if you want to fold it over, score lightly across the center. Turn out on to a hot plate and sprinkle with a little more cheese. Serve immediately with a green salad.

Fluffy Danish Omelette

Serves 1–2

This delicious omelette is also very good with smoked salmon or smoked mackerel. A vegetarian version can be made with red or green peppers, tomatoes, and eggplant.

8 eggs
1/4 cup plus 1 tablespoon water
salt and freshly ground pepper
1 tablespoon butter
4–6 strips of bacon (smoked or unsmoked)
a little oil
6 very ripe tomatoes or 12 cherry tomatoes
2 generous tablespoons chives or tarragon, freshly chopped
2 generous tablespoons parsley, freshly chopped

9-inch (23-cm) omelette pan, preferably non-stick

Put the eggs, water, and seasoning into a bowl. Whisk until really fluffy and light – they should froth up to 3 or 4 times their original volume. Meanwhile put the pan on to heat and melt the butter. Just as it foams, add the egg mixture and turn down the heat to the minimum. You may want to use a heat-diffusing mat.

Meanwhile, in another pan, fry the bacon until crisp and golden in a little oil. Drain on paper towels, cut into 3/4-inch (2-cm) pieces and keep warm.

Cut the tomatoes into quarters, and then quarters again (halve, if using cherry tomatoes). Season with salt and pepper.

When the bottom of the omelette is set, scatter the tomatoes and hot crispy bacon on top. They will lightly sink into the fluffy top. Sprinkle with fresh herbs and serve immediately, cut into segments or whole.

Provençal Terrine with Tomato Sauce

Serves 10–12
In season: all year, depending on ingredients used

One of my favorite vegetarian terrines is really a multi-layered omelette. It makes a sensational appetizer or main course for a summer lunch party, and you can vary the flavoring if you wish. The whole secret is to prepare all the ingredients first, then cook one layer after the other very quickly.

Below: Provençal Terrine with Tomato Sauce

Zucchini Layer

2½ tablespoons extra-virgin olive oil
12 ounces (350g) zucchini, grated on the coarsest part of a grater and sprinkled lightly with sea salt (about 2–2½ cups)
3 eggs
1 tablespoon plus 1 teaspoon cream or milk
salt and freshly ground pepper
2 teaspoons freshly chopped annual marjoram

Tomato Layer

2½ tablespoons extra-virgin olive oil
14 ounces (400g) very ripe tomatoes, peeled, seeded and chopped (about 1⅓ cups)
salt, freshly ground pepper, and a pinch of sugar
pinch of fresh thyme leaves
3 eggs
1 tablespoon plus 1 teaspoon cream or milk
1 tablespoon plus 1 teaspoon extra-virgin olive oil

Olive Layer

3 eggs
1 tablespoon plus 1 teaspoon cream or milk
2½ tablespoons black olives, pitted and chopped
2 teaspoons parsley, finely chopped
salt and freshly ground pepper

Spinach Layer

1 tablespoon plus 1 teaspoon melted butter
4 ounces (110g) cooked spinach, or 7 ounces (200g) raw spinach (about 3 large handfuls of raw)
salt, freshly ground pepper, and freshly grated nutmeg
3 eggs
1 tablespoon plus 1 teaspoon cream or milk
1 tablespoon plus 1 teaspoon extra-virgin olive oil
2 tablespoons shredded Gruyère cheese

Accompaniments

fresh Tomato Sauce (see page 590) or Tomato Fondue (see page 188)

loaf pan 9 x 5 x 2 inches (23 x 12.5 x 5cm), lined with wax paper

First, prepare all the ingredients, and preheat the oven to 350°F (180°C).

Make the zucchini layer: heat 2½ tablespoons of oil in a frying pan and cook the zucchini until soft but still bright green; drain. Whisk the eggs, add the cream or milk, salt, pepper, marjoram, and zucchini. Set aside.

Make the tomato layer: heat 2½ tablespoons of oil in a pan, add the tomato, season with salt, pepper, sugar, and thyme. Cook until it becomes a soft, very thick and concentrated paste. Whisk the eggs with the cream or milk, add the concentrated tomato paste, taste, and correct seasoning. Set aside. Make the olive layer: whisk the eggs, add the cream or milk, olive, and parsley, season with pepper and a very little salt. Set aside.

Make the spinach layer: cook the spinach if raw in the melted butter in a frying pan until soft and wilted. Season with salt and pepper and a generous grating of nutmeg. Drain, press out every single drop of liquid, and chop finely. Whisk the eggs, add the cream or milk, stir in the spinach, taste, and add more salt and pepper if necessary.

To assemble: when all the preparation is done, cook the layers one after the other. Heat 1 tablespoon plus 1 teaspoon of olive oil in a non-stick pan, 8 inches (20.5cm) wide. Pour in the zucchini mixture, stir around for about 30–60 seconds until the texture is just like a softly scrambled egg, pour immediately into the lined loaf pan. Continue with the other layers, cooking each in 1 tablespoon plus 1 teaspoon of olive oil in a similar way. Sprinkle the spinach layer with Gruyère cheese and cover the top with a piece of wax paper. Cook in a bain-marie in the oven for 10–15 minutes or until set – it should feel firm in the center and a skewer should come out clean. Let cool. Serve lukewarm or cold, with hot or cold Tomato Sauce, lots of crusty bread, and a green salad.

Note: Sweet little individual "terrines" can be made in small ramekins – they take about 10 minutes to cook.

Seek out organic eggs from free-range hens whenever possible.

How to Whisk Egg Whites

Choose a large bowl, preferably with a round bottom. Unlined copper is best, but stainless steel, glass, or delph are also fine (although the whites tend to detach from the sides of glass or delph bowls). Plastic is least successful because it is difficult to remove all traces of grease and detergent residue – and these prevent the whites from fluffing up. Make sure that it is spotlessly clean and dry. Similarly, the egg whites must be free of any egg yolk, oil, grease, or water.

If there is a spot of egg yolk in the white, the easiest way to remove it is with the edge of the egg shell (it has an affinity to the shell). A pinch of salt or cream of tartar (Bextartar) added to the egg whites at the beginning will help to increase the volume. Superfine sugar added at the end of whisking will help to stabilize the foam. This is called "meringuing" the egg whites.

To whisk: put the egg whites into the bowl. Using a light balloon whisk or a coil whisk, turn the bowl onto its side and start to whisk, slowly at first and then faster until the egg whites are stiffly beaten. They will form a stiff peak on the end of the whisk when lifted out of the bowl. At this point change the angle of the whisk and stir in a full circular movement to tighten the egg white and make it more stable. If using sugar in a sweet soufflé, add a little just before this stage and then "tighten" the egg whites. It should be possible to turn the bowl upside down at this stage without the egg whites falling out. Over-whisked egg white will become granular. If egg whites separate and become grainy, add 1 unbeaten egg white for every 4 whites in the bowl and continue to whisk for 30 seconds. This should re-emulsify the problem egg whites.

Egg whites may, of course, be whisked with an electric beater but this method does not result in as great a volume as those hand-whisked in a copper bowl. These can achieve up to eight times their own volume. Stiffly beaten egg whites should be used immediately as they deflate very quickly. Note: slightly stale egg whites whip up better than very fresh ones. Egg whites that have been frozen whisk well. (1 egg white = 2 tablespoons.)

To prepare a copper bowl: before whisking egg whites, the bowl needs to be carefully cleaned to remove any toxic copper carbonate. Put about 2 generous tablespoons of salt into the bowl, then add a few tablespoons of plain white vinegar. Alternatively, use a cut lemon. Clean the entire inside of the bowl very well; it will turn a bright pinkish copper color. Rinse and dry well. Clean again in two hours if necessary.

Folding egg whites

The technique of folding egg whites into a base mixture is a crucially important one for many dishes. Whisked egg whites are the lightest of all ingredients. When sugar is added, as in meringue, they tend to be firmer. The lighter the base mixture, the easier it is to fold in the egg whites. Stir about a quarter of the whites into a firmer mixture to lighten it before folding in the remainder of the egg whites. Then gently pour this mixture on to the top of the stiffly beaten egg whites in the bowl. Using a long-handled spatula or a metal spoon, cut down into the center of the bowl and lift the mixture up and over, turning the bowl counter-clockwise at the same time as you repeat the motion. Stop as soon as all the egg whites are incorporated.

Master Recipe
Basic Frittata

Serves 2–4

Frittata is an Italian omelette. Kuku and Tortilla all sound much more exciting than a flat omelette although that's basically what they are. Unlike their soft and creamy French cousin, these omelettes are cooked slowly over a very low heat during which time you can be whipping up a delicious salad to accompany it! A frittata is cooked gently on both sides and cut into wedges like a piece of cake. The basic recipe, flavored with shredded cheese and a generous sprinkling of herbs, is delicious. As with omelettes, though, you may add almost anything that takes your fancy.

8 large eggs, preferably farm-fresh organic
2 teaspoons parsley, chopped
2 teaspoons basil or marjoram
1 teaspoon thyme leaves
3/4 cup shredded Gruyère cheese
1/2 cup grated Parmesan cheese
2 tablespoons butter
1 teaspoon salt
lots of freshly ground black pepper

All the frittate here can be cooked in a non-stick frying pan, 7-inch (18-cm) base and sloping sides with 9-inch (23-cm) rim

Whisk the eggs in a bowl, add the fresh herbs, salt, pepper, and shredded cheese into the eggs. Melt the butter in the frying pan. When it starts to foam, tip in the eggs. Turn down the heat, as low as it will go. Let the eggs cook gently for 12 minutes on a heat diffuser mat, or until the underneath is set. The top should still be slightly runny.

Preheat a broiler. Pop the pan under the broiler for a minute to set, but not brown, the top.

Slide a spatula under the frittata to free it from the pan. Slide onto a warm plate. Serve, cut in wedges, with a good green salad and perhaps a tomato salad.

Mushroom Frittata

Clean, slice, and quickly fry 1 pound (450g) flat mushrooms in a little olive oil, cooking until they are slightly golden. Season with salt and pepper. Add to the basic frittata mixture and proceed as in the Master Recipe. A mixture of wild mushrooms is divine.

Tip: Slice the mushroom stalks into thin rounds up to the cap, then lay the mushroom, gills down, on the cutting board and slice. Use both stalk and caps for extra flavor and less waste. Alternatively, put the stalks into a vegetable stock.

Asparagus, Arugula, and Wild Garlic Frittata

Serves 6

This is an example of how we incorporate seasonal ingredients into a frittata.

8 ounces (225g) thin asparagus
8 eggs
1 cup freshly grated Parmesan (Parmigiano Reggiano if possible)
3–4 tablespoons wild garlic and arugula leaves, roughly chopped
2 1/2 tablespoons olive oil
1 teaspoon salt
lots of freshly ground pepper

Garnish
wild garlic and arugula leaves and flowers

Bring about 1 inch (2.5cm) water to a boil in an ovenproof and flameproof oval casserole dish. Trim the tough ends of the asparagus, add salt to the water, and blanch the spears until just tender, for 3 or 4 minutes. Drain. Slice the end of the spears evenly at an angle, keeping 1 1/2 inches (4cm) of the heads intact. Save for later. Whisk the eggs together in a bowl. Add the asparagus, most of the Parmesan, and wild garlic leaves. Season with salt and pepper.

Preheat the broiler. Heat the oil in the pan, add egg mixture, and reduce the heat to the bare minimum, using a heat diffuser mat if necessary. Continue to cook over a gentle heat until just set, about 15 minutes. Arrange the asparagus over the top. Sprinkle with the remaining Parmesan. Pop under the broiler for a few minutes, making sure the pan is at least 5 inches (12cm) from the element. The frittata should be set and slightly golden. Turn out on a warm plate, cut into wedges, and garnish with wild garlic and arugula leaves and flowers. Serve immediately with a green salad.

Isaac's Frittata

Serves 1

Isaac, my eldest son, makes individual frittatas that are light and fluffy. He says the secret is to add lots of milk and to whisk the eggs very well.

pat of butter
2 eggs
salt and freshly ground pepper
1/4 cup milk
1/3 cup shredded Gruyère cheese
2 teaspoons chives or parsley, freshly chopped

8-inch (20.5-cm) heavy frying pan

Melt a pat of butter in the frying pan. Break the eggs into a mixing bowl and season. (1 pinch of salt and 2 twists of pepper per egg is a good guide line if you are a little wary of tasting raw eggs.) Now add the milk, whisk thoroughly until the whites and yolk have completely blended together, add the shredded cheese, chopped herbs, and mix in gently.

Preheat the broiler. When the butter is foaming, pour all of the mixture into the hot pan. Using a wooden spoon, scrape the cooked mixture from the bottom, filling its space with liquid. Do this just 5 or 6 times, then let the mixture cook on a high flame for a further minute.

Take the pan off the heat and place under the broiler. Continue cooking until the mixture has fluffed up nicely and is beginning to turn golden brown on top.

Using a metal spatula, loosen the edges and slide on to a plate. Serve on its own with a green salad or with a little drizzle of pesto.

Once the basic mixture and cooking technique are mastered, one can experiment with many variations on the theme:

Irish Breakfast Frittata

Follow the Basic Frittata recipe, adding the following to the basic egg mixture just before cooking:
1/4 cup sliced mushrooms, fried in a little butter and seasoned with salt and pepper, and 2 strips of bacon, cut into 1/2-inch (1-cm) pieces and fried until crispy.

Frittata Ranchero

Add to the Master Recipe egg mixture just before cooking:

1/4 cup onion, chopped and sweated in a little oil or butter
1 small tomato, cut into 1/2-inch (5-mm) dice
1 teaspoon chopped chile, or more to taste
2 teaspoons cilantro (instead of parsley or chives), chopped

Smoked Salmon and Goat Cheese Frittata

Follow the Master Recipe, adding to the basic egg mixture 3 slices smoked salmon, diced, and substituting a mild goat cheese for half the Gruyère, crumbling it into the mixture just before cooking.

Zucchini and Herb Frittata

Follow the Master Recipe, adding the following to the egg mixture just before cooking:
4 green or golden zucchini (or a mixture), 1 crushed garlic clove and 2 1/2–3 1/2 tablespoons of freshly chopped herbs (mint, marjoram, or torn basil leaves), fried in a little olive oil for 3 or 4 minutes.

Tortilla de Patatas (Spanish Potato Omelette)

Serves 6

In Spain, you must understand, tortilla is not just a dish. It is a way of life. Tortillas or flat omelettes, not to be confused with Mexican tortilla which is a flat bread, are beloved by Spaniards and tourists alike. You'll be offered them in every home, in the most elegant restaurants, and the most run-down establishments. No Spanish picnic would be complete without a tortilla, and every tapas bar will have them on display. People even eat them at the cinema! Tortilla de Patatas **sounds deceptively simple but it's not as easy to make to perfection as you might think. The secret of success is to use enough oil.**

Spanish olive oil, such as Lerida
8 ounces (225g) potatoes, peeled and thinly sliced (about 1 1/2 cups)
5 ounces (150g) onions, thinly sliced (about 1 1/3 cups)
8 eggs
1 teaspoon sea salt or kosher salt
freshly ground pepper

frying pan, 7–8-inch (18–20.5-cm) diameter, non-stick if possible

Put a generous 1 inch (2.5cm) of olive oil into the pan, then cook the onions and potatoes over a medium heat until crisp and golden. This can take up to 20 minutes. Drain off the oil and reserve.

Whisk the eggs in a bowl, season with salt and pepper, add the potato and onion. Put 2 1/2 tablespoons oil back into the pan. When it begins to sizzle, pour in the egg mixture, then lower the heat. When the egg begins to cook, loosen around the edge and continue to cook, shaking the pan occasionally.

When the tortilla is well set and golden underneath, cover the pan with an oiled plate and turn the tortilla upside-down on to it, taking care not to burn your hand. Add a little more oil to the frying pan, if necessary. Slide the tortilla back in. Cook until the lower side is golden and the whole of it is firm but still slightly moist in the center. Serve hot or at room temperature, cut into wedges or squares.

Tip: The quality of the eggs really matters here. Keep the heat low or the tortilla will be tough.

Omelette Arnold Bennett

Serves 1–2 as a main course

Theatre critic, playwright, and author, Arnold Bennett, was staying at the Savoy Hotel to write his novel, The Imperial Palace, when he asked the chefs to make this dish for him. It is another flat omelette, but this time the egg white is

folded in to give a light, fluffy texture. This delicious omelette is also very good made with smoked salmon, smoked mackerel, or chorizo sausage. Roast red and yellow pepper, blanched and refreshed broccoli flowerets or asparagus are lovely, too.

2–3 ounces (50–75g) smoked haddock
a little milk
2 tablespoons butter
2/3 cup cream
3 eggs
2 1/2–3 1/2 tablespoons Parmesan cheese (preferably Parmigiano Reggiano), grated
salt and freshly ground pepper

Garnish
parsley, freshly chopped

non-stick omelette pan, 8-inch (20.5-cm) base and slopping sides with 10-inch (25-cm) rim.

Put the smoked haddock into a small saucepan. Cover with milk, and simmer gently until it is cooked enough to separate into flakes (about 10 minutes). Drain and remove any bones. Toss the flaked haddock over a moderate heat along with half the butter and 2 tablespoons of the cream and set aside. Separate the eggs, beat the yolks with a tablespoon of the cream and season with salt and freshly ground pepper. Whip the egg whites stiffly. Fold the yolks into the haddock mixture and add half the grated Parmesan cheese. Fold in the egg whites, the haddock, and egg yolk mixture.

Preheat the broiler. Melt the remaining butter in the omelette pan. Pour the mixture in gently and cook over a medium heat until the base of the omelette is golden. Spoon the remaining cream over the top and sprinkle with the rest of the finely grated Parmesan. Pop under a hot broiler for a minute or so until golden and bubbly. Slide on to a hot dish, sprinkle with parsley, and serve immediately with a good green salad.

Tip: Avoid smoked haddock which is bright orange. The color has much more to do with dye than smoke.

How to Make a Hot Soufflé

Even for a seasoned chef, a perfect, well-risen soufflé, puffed and golden, is a source of considerable pride and satisfaction – the ultimate triumph of the chef's art. But don't be intimidated. Essentially, it is simply a well-seasoned sauce or purée, enriched with egg yolks and lightened with stiffly beaten egg whites. When cooked, the mixture expands in the hot oven, hence the impressive height.

11 key points about soufflés:

1. The egg whites should be stiffly whisked (see page 105) in a bowl which is dry, spotlessly clean, and free of grease. A copper bowl is best; glass and porcelain are satisfactory; plastic is less successful.

2. Use a thin, flat-bladed spoon or long-handled spatula to fold the egg whites carefully into the base mixture. A thick wooden spoon may knock out some of the precious air that you have so carefully incorporated as you whisked the egg whites.

3. The base for savory soufflés is usually Béchamel or Velouté sauce (see pages 580 and 581), flavored with vegetable or fish purée. The base mixture must be highly flavored or seasoned because egg white tends to dull flavor. The soufflé base must be the correct consistency – soft enough to fold in the egg whites easily. If it is too firm, stir a little stiffly beaten egg white in to lighten it, then fold in the remainder, gently but firmly.

4. To increase the volume, 1 or 2 extra egg whites are added to many soufflés. The final volume should be at least double the base mixture.

5. The volume will decrease in varying degrees when the egg whites are folded in, depending on the content of the base mixture. The oil in chocolate tends to deflate egg whites dramatically, so it is essential to work fast and get the soufflé into the oven without delay. The cooked soufflé will increase by at least 50 per cent in volume and may even increase by 100 per cent.

6. A classic soufflé is best baked in a straight-sided soufflé dish or dishes. For a professional result, fill the dish to within 1/2 inch (1cm) of the top. Individual soufflés are best filled right to the top and smoothed with a palette knife. Chefs often run a clean thumb around the inner edge of the filled soufflé mold to make a groove. This creates a "top hat" effect in the oven. Most soufflés, except chocolate, may be refrigerated at this stage for an hour or two, but must be served as soon as they are baked.

7. When baking a large soufflé, place the mold low in the oven to allow space for expansion. Some chefs like to bake savory soufflés, particularly cheese soufflés, in a bain-marie.

8. Try to avoid opening the oven door while the soufflé is cooking. Whereas a soufflé will probably not sink if you do this halfway through the cooking time (to turn it so that it cooks evenly), it is best to avoid draughts.

9. The soufflé is ready when the top is brown and puffed and the center is slightly soft and creamy when shaken gently. Serve on a hot plate, immediately. The cool air will cause the soufflé to shrink within 3–5 minutes.

10. Soufflés that are cooked at a higher temperature rise faster and fall faster.

11. A soufflé mixture may also be cooked on a jelly roll pan and rolled up like a roulade.

A cold soufflé is not a real soufflé at all, but a mousse-like mixture lightened with egg whites and set in a soufflé dish with a high collar to give the impression of a risen soufflé.

Parmesan and Gruyère Cheese Soufflé

Serves 8–10

Well-risen soufflés always produce a gasp of admiration when brought to the table. Don't imagine for one moment that you can't master the technique – soufflés are much more good-humored than you may think and can even be frozen when they are ready for the oven. The French create infinite variations on the theme, both sweet and savory.

For the molds

pat of butter, melted

1/2 ounces (10g) Parmesan cheese (Parmigiano Reggiano is best), optional

3 tablespoons butter

1/4 cup flour

1 1/4 cups milk

4 eggs

1/2 cup finely shredded Gruyère cheese

1 cup freshly grated Parmesan (Parmigiano Reggiano if possible)

pinch of cayenne pepper

freshly grated nutmeg

salt and freshly ground pepper

8–10 individual soufflé dishes, 2 3/4-inch (7.5-cm) diameter x 1 1/2 inches (4cm) deep, or one large dish, 6-inch (15-cm) diameter x 2 1/2 inches (6cm) high

First prepare the soufflé dish or dishes: brush evenly with melted butter and, if you like, dust with a little Parmesan. Then preheat the oven to 400°F (200°C) and heat a baking sheet.

Melt the butter in a heavy saucepan, stir in the flour, and cook over a gentle heat for 1–2 minutes. Draw off the heat and whisk in the milk. Return to the heat, whisk as it comes to a boil, cover, and simmer gently for 4–5 minutes. Remove from the heat. Separate the eggs and put the whites into a large copper, glass, or stainless steel bowl, making sure it is spotlessly clean and dry. Whisk the yolks one by one into the white sauce and add the cheese. Season with salt, pepper, cayenne, and freshly grated nutmeg, and stir, over a gentle heat for a few seconds until the cheese melts. Remove from the heat. *

Whisk the egg whites with a little pinch of salt, slowly at first and then faster until they are light and hold a stiff peak when you lift up the whisk. Stir a few tablespoons into the cheese mixture to lighten it and then carefully fold in the rest with a spatula or tablespoon. Fill the mixture into the soufflé dishes (if you fill them 3/4 full you will get about 10, but if you smooth the tops you will have about 8). Bake in the oven for 8–9 minutes for the individual soufflés or 20–25 minutes for the large one. For the latter, you will need to reduce the temperature to 350°F (180°C), after 15 minutes. Serve immediately.

* Can be made ahead up to this point. Individual frozen soufflés may be baked from frozen but will take a few minutes longer to cook.

Tip: To get the "top hat" effect, fill the soufflé dishes to the top, smooth off with a butter knife, and run a washed thumb around the edge of the dishes before they go into the oven. Don't open the oven halfway through as the soufflé may collapse. If this does happen, the best course of action is to turn it out into a dish, pour some cream over it, sprinkle with grated parmesan, and pop it back into the oven for 5–10 minutes, depending on whether it's hot or cold. It will puff up amazingly. Call it a twice-baked Soufflé, and serve!

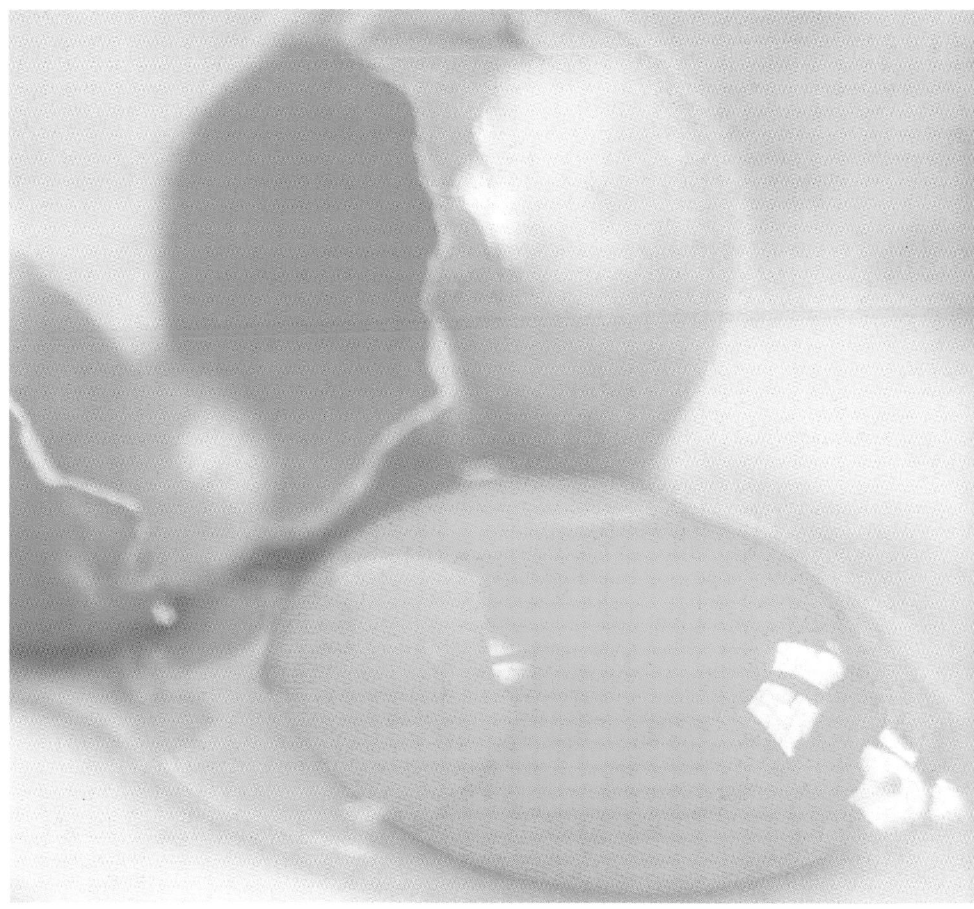

Goat Cheese and Thyme Leaf Soufflé

Serves 6

We bake this soufflé golden and puffy in a shallow, oval dish instead of the traditional soufflé bowl. It makes a perfect lunch or supper dish.

1¼ cups cream
1¼ cups milk
a few slices of carrot
1 small onion, quartered
sprig of thyme, a few parsley stalks, and a little piece of bay leaf
4–5 black peppercorns
¾ stick (⅓ cup) butter
¼ cup plus 2 tablespoons flour
5 eggs, separated
1 cup crumbled goat cheese (we use St. Tola or Ardsallagh)
¾ cup shredded Gruyère cheese
½ cup shredded sharp Cheddar cheese (Coolea, Desmond, Parmesan, or Regato may also be used)
a good pinch of salt, freshly ground pepper, cayenne, and nutmeg
2 teaspoons fresh thyme leaves

Garnish
thyme flowers, if available

12-inch (32-cm) shallow oval dish (not a soufflé dish) or 6 individual wide soup bowls with a rim
melted butter, for greasing

Preheat the oven to 450°F (230°C).

Brush the bottom and sides of the dish with melted butter. Put the cream and milk into a saucepan, add the carrot, onion, herbs, and peppercorns. Bring slowly to a boil and let infuse for 10 minutes. Strain and discard the flavorings (we rinse them off and throw them into the stockpot if there is one on the go).

Melt the butter, add the flour, and cook for 1–2 minutes. Whisk in the strained cream and milk, bring to a boil, and continue whisking until it thickens. Cool slightly. Add the egg yolks, goat cheese, Gruyère, and most of the Cheddar (or Parmesan, if using). Season with salt, pepper, cayenne, and nutmeg. Taste and correct the seasoning. Whisk the egg whites stiffly and fold them gently into the mixture with a flat spatula to make a loose consistency. Put the mixture into the prepared dish, scatter the thyme leaves on top, and sprinkle with the remaining cheese.

Cook in the oven for 12–15 minutes, or until sides and top are nicely puffed up and golden. The center should still be creamy. Garnish with thyme flowers. Serve immediately on warm plates with a good green salad.

Pastry Dough for Savory Tarts and Quiches

Water gives a perfectly good texture but egg makes the dough a little richer.

2 cups all-purpose white flour, spelt, or sifted whole wheat flour
*1 stick (½ cup) butter**
water or beaten egg mixed with a little water

Keep everything as cool as possible; if the fat is allowed to melt, the finished dough may be tough. Sift the flour into a large bowl along with the salt. Cut the butter into cubes and rub into the flour with your fingertips. When the mixture looks like coarse breadcrumbs, stop. Whisk the egg, if using, and add a little water. Take a fork or knife – whichever you feel most comfortable with – and add just enough liquid to bring the dough together, then discard the fork and collect the dough into a ball with your hands. This way you can judge more accurately whether you need a few more drops of liquid. Although rather damp pastry dough is easier to handle and roll out, the resulting crust can be tough and may well shrink out of shape as the water evaporates in the oven. Drier and slightly more difficult-to-handle pastry dough will give a crispier, "shorter" crust.

Cover the dough with plastic wrap and let rest in the fridge for a minimum of 15 minutes. This will make the dough much less elastic and easier to roll.

** 1¼–1½ sticks butter will produce a richer dough, but beginners would be wiser to use half butter to flour for ease of handling.*

How to Line a Flan Ring

Use either a flan ring or a fluted tart pan with a removable bottom. It should be at least 2 inches (5cm) deep.

Pastry dough made with:
1 cup flour will line a 6–7-inch (15–18-cm) tart pan
1½ cups flour will line a 9-inch (23-cm) tart pan
2 cups flour will line a 10–11-inch (25.5–30.5-cm) tart pan

Sprinkle the worktop and rolling pin lightly with flour and roll out the dough quite thinly, making sure to keep it in a circular shape. The dough should be 1½–2 inches (4–5cm) wider than the flan ring.

Sprinkle the dough with flour, fold in half and then into quarters and then lift on to the ring. Alternatively, roll the dough over the pin and unroll into the ring. Gently press the dough on to the bottom of the pan and right into the edges or, if you are using a flan ring, onto the baking sheet. Next, press some of the overhanging pastry dough forward and cut off the rim by pressing it down on to the edge of the pan with your thumb. Tuck the cut edge in against the sides of the pan or flan ring, and decorate the resulting rounded edge with a knife or pastry crimpers. Make sure that no dough sticks to the outer edge or it will be difficult to remove the pan later. Prick the base of the dough lightly with a fork.

How to Bake Blind

Line the empty pie shell with wax paper and fill it to the top with dried beans (keep them in a screw top jar for the purpose) to hold the dough in place while the pie shell is being baked. Bake for 15–20 minutes at 350°F (180°C).

Gruyère and Dill Tart

Serves 8

Mervyn Mark from Just Desserts in San Francisco gave me this recipe after I waxed lyrical about its flavor and texture.

Pastry dough
1 1/2 cups all-purpose white flour
3/4 stick (1/3 cup) butter (if using unsalted butter, add a pinch of salt)
1/4 cup water, approx.

Filling
4 eggs
1 1/2 cups cream
*3/4 cup freshly shredded Gruyère or Emmenthal cheese**
1/2 cup freshly grated Parmesan cheese (Parmigiano Reggiano if possible)
2–3 generous tablespoons fresh dill, chopped
1 teaspoon salt
lots of freshly ground pepper
freshly grated nutmeg

9-inch (23-cm) tart pan

Preheat the oven to 350°F (180°C).

First make the dough in the usual way (see page 110). Flatten into a small circle, cover with wax paper and let rest in the fridge for a minimum of 15 minutes. Roll it out on a lightly floured board until 1/16 inch (2 mm) thick, then fit into the pan, bringing the pastry dough just a little above the rim. Rest in the fridge for a further 15 minutes.

Bake the pie shell blind (see left) for 20 minutes. Take out of the oven, then remove the beans and paper. Brush the tart shell with a little beaten egg and pop back into the oven for 1–2 minutes to seal the base. Set aside to cool.

Meanwhile whisk the eggs and the cream together in a bowl, add the Gruyère and Parmesan cheese and the dill. Season with salt, pepper, and nutmeg. Pour the filling into the tart shell, bake in the preheated oven for 30 minutes, or until the filling is slightly puffy and golden brown.
Serve with a tomato salad (see page 220) and a good green salad.

Tip: Buy a chunk of cheese, wrap it well, store in the fridge, and grate when needed. Ready-grated cheese does not taste nearly as good.

French Onion Tart

Serves 6

Here the dough is richer than in the previous recipe. Organic onions are not sprayed with an anti-sprouting mixture. Seek them out if you can.

Pastry dough
1 cup flour
pinch of salt
3/4 stick (1/3 cup) cold butter
1 egg yolk
2 teaspoons cold water

Filling
1 1/2 tablespoons butter
2 teaspoons olive oil
14 ounces (400g) onions, finely chopped (about 3 1/2 cups)
2 whole eggs and 1 egg yolk
1 cup cream
salt, freshly ground pepper, and nutmeg

7-inch (18-cm) tart pan, or small individual tart pans

Preheat the oven to 350°F (180°C).

First make the dough: sift the flour with the salt into a large bowl. Cut the butter into cubes, toss into the flour, then rub in with the fingertips until the mixture resembles coarse breadcrumbs. Whisk the egg yolk with 2 teaspoons of cold water and bind the mixture with this. You may need a little more water, but do not make the dough too wet – it should come away cleanly from the bowl. Flatten into a circle, wrap in plastic wrap, and rest in the fridge for 15 minutes.

Roll the pastry out thinly on a lightly floured board and line the tart pan with it. Then line the pie shell with wax paper and fill to the top with dried beans. Rest for 15 minutes in the fridge. Bake the tart base blind (see above left) for about 15 minutes or until pale and golden. Remove the beans and paper. Brush the tart shell with a little beaten egg and pop back into the oven for a minute or two to seal the base. Set aside to cool.

Now make the filling: melt the butter with the oil in a heavy saucepan. Put in the onions, cover, and cook over a low heat until they are quite soft, transparent, and pale golden color, about 10 minutes. Cool. Whisk the eggs and egg yolk with the cream and mix thoroughly into the onions. Season

How to Line Tartlets

Roll the pastry dough thinly: the smaller the pan, the thinner the dough needs to be. If the tartlets are 4 inches (10cm) in diameter, it's worth lining each individually with dough, then wax paper, filling with baking beans and baking blind if necessary (see page 111). However, smaller pans can be lined by laying a single sheet of dough over them.

Press the pastry gently into each pan and then run a rolling pin over the lot to cut off the unwanted dough.

Instead of filling each one with paper and a few beans, you can pile the pans up in groups of two or three, placing an empty pan on top. This helps the tartlets to keep their shape. Remember to chill for at least 10 minutes before baking, to avoid shrinkage. Tarts or tartlets may be frozen either cooked or uncooked, and kept for up to 4 weeks.

with salt, pepper, and a little nutmeg. Taste. Pour the filling into the tart shell, bake in the preheated oven for about 20 minutes. Serve with tomato and basil salad and a good green salad.

Variation:

Add 1½–2½ tablespoons of chopped marjoram or thyme leaves to the onions with the eggs and cream.

Tip: If you want a wonderfully rich flavor, cook the onions until they are a rich golden color, almost caramelized.

Mushroom and Thyme Leaf Tart

Serves 6

This really flavorsome tart is one of the few that tastes super, warm or cold. Buy your Parmesan cheese (preferably Parmigiano Reggiano) in a piece if at all possible, because ready-grated cheese is frequently rancid and may spoil the recipe. May I also respectfully suggest that you use cream. Both the flavor and texture are quite different if milk is substituted.

Rich pastry dough
1 cup all-purpose white flour
½–¾ stick (¼–⅓ cup) butter
a little water or a mixture of water and beaten egg to bind

1 tablespoon butter
8 ounces (225g) mushrooms, flat if possible, finely chopped (about 2⅓ cups)
1 teaspoon fresh thyme leaves
sea salt
freshly ground black pepper
1 cup cream
2 eggs and 1 egg yolk
1 cup freshly grated Parmesan cheese (preferably Parmigiano Reggiano)
a good pinch of cayenne
7-inch (18-cm) flan ring or pan with removable bottom

Make the pastry dough in the usual way, let it rest, line the flan ring and bake blind (see page 111). Meanwhile, melt the butter in a pan and fry the mushrooms over a very high heat. Add thyme leaves and season with salt and pepper. Cook until all the juice has been absorbed, then let cool.

Preheat the oven to 350°F (180°C).

Whisk the cream in a bowl with the eggs and egg yolk, then stir in the mushrooms and most of the Parmesan cheese. Taste, add the pinch of cayenne and more seasoning if necessary. Pour into the pie shell. Sprinkle with the remainder of the cheese. Bake in the oven for about 30–40 minutes or until the filling is set and the top delicately brown. Serve with a good green salad (see page 225).

Note: Tiny mushroom quiches may be served straight from the oven as appetizers before dinner or for a drinks party.

Ballymaloe Quiche Lorraine

Serves 6

½ quantity Pastry Dough (see page 110)

Filling
4–6 ounces (110–175g) bacon strips (green or slightly smoked)
1 tablespoon plus 1 teaspoon olive or sunflower oil
1 cup chopped onion
2 large eggs and 1 egg yolk
1¼ cups heavy cream or half milk, half cream
1 teaspoon freshly chopped parsley
½ teaspoon freshly chopped chives
¾ cup freshly shredded Cheddar or ½ cup shredded grated mature Gruyère
salt and freshly ground pepper

Flan ring or deep quiche pan, 7½-inch (19-cm) diameter x 1¼ inches (3cm) high

Preheat the oven to 350°F (180°C).

Make the pastry dough. Chill for 15 minutes, then roll out to line the flan ring or quiche pan. Line with wax paper and fill to the top with dried beans. Rest for 15 minutes, then bake for 20–25 minutes. Remove the beans and paper, brush a little egg over the base to seal it, and return to the oven for 1–2 minutes.

Cut the bacon into 1/2-inch (1-cm) lardons, blanch and refresh if necessary. Dry on paper towels. Heat the oil and crisp off the bacon, remove and sweat the onions gently in the oil and bacon fat for about 10 minutes. Cool.

Meanwhile, whisk the eggs, add the cream (or cream and milk), herbs, cheese, and cooled bacon and onions. Season and taste. Pour the filling into the par-baked pie shell and return to the oven for 30–40 minutes, or until the center is just set and the top golden (don't over-cook or the filling will be slightly scrambled).

Serve warm with a green salad.

Variations

Smoky Bacon, Flat Mushroom, and Chive Quiche

Follow the Master Recipe, using 4 ounces (110g) bacon and a heaped cup sliced and sautéed flat mushrooms. Cool before adding to the egg mix. Increase the amount of chives to 1 tablespoon.

Tomato Tart

10 ounces (275g) Tomato Fondue, strained and sieved (see page 188)
2 teaspoons chopped marjoram or 1 generous tablespoon chopped basil
2 eggs and 1 egg yolk
1 cup cream

Follow the Master Recipe.

Piperonata Quiche

10 ounces (275g) concentrated Piperonata, drained (see page 190)
2 eggs and 1 egg yolk
1 cup cream

Follow the Master Recipe.

Asparagus and Scallion Tart

Serves 6
In season: early summer

My children and their friends reckon that Tim makes the best quiches in the whole world. They're not biased – he does. Try this one.

1/2 quantity Pastry Dough (see page 110)

Filling
2 tablespoons butter
1 tablespoon plus 1 teaspoon olive oil
9 ounces (250g) onion, finely chopped (about 2 cups) – we use about half scallions, complete with green tops, and half ordinary onion)
5 ounces (150g) fresh asparagus, trimmed and with ends peeled
3 eggs
1/2 cup heavy cream
1 cup shredded Cheddar cheese
salt and freshly ground pepper

1 x 7-inch (18-cm) quiche pan or flan ring

Preheat the oven to 350°F (180°C).

First make the dough. Chill for 15 minutes, then roll out to line the tart pan or flan ring to a thickness of about 1/8 inch (3mm). Line with wax paper and fill to the top with dried beans. Rest for 15 minutes and bake for 20 minutes. Remove the beans and paper, and wash a little of the egg over the bottom then return the pie shell to the oven for 1–2 minutes. This seals the pastry and helps to avoid a "soggy bottom".

Melt the butter in a pan, add the olive oil and onions; sweat the onions with a good pinch of salt until soft but not colored. Cook the asparagus in boiling salted water until "al dente" (4–5 minutes, depending on the thickness of the asparagus), then drain. When it is cool enough to handle, cut into 1/2-inch (1-cm) pieces.

Whisk the eggs in a bowl, add the cream, almost all the cheese, the onion, and cooked asparagus. Season. Pour into the pie shell, sprinkle the remaining cheese on top, and return to the oven for 40–45 minutes.

Crab, Tomato, and Ginger Tart

Serves 6

This recipe comes from my brother, Rory O'Connell, the chef at Ballymaloe House.

1/2 quantity Pastry Dough (see page 110)

8 ounces (225g) fresh cooked crab meat, brown and white (about 1 cup)
5 ripe tomatoes, peeled, quartered, and made into concassé (see page 48)
2 eggs and 1 egg yolk, beaten
1 cup cream
2 1/2 tablespoons finely chopped chives
1 teaspoon freshly grated ginger
salt and freshly ground pepper

1 x 7-inch (18-cm) quiche pan or flan ring

Preheat the oven to 350°F (180°C).

Make the pastry dough (see page 415). Chill for 15 minutes, then roll out to line the quiche pan or flan ring to a thickness of about 1/8 inch (3mm). Line with wax paper and fill to the top with dried beans. Rest for 15 minutes, then bake blind for 20 minutes. Remove the beans and paper, and brush a little of the egg over the bottom and return to the oven for 1–2 minutes. The egg wash dries and seals the pastry dough and helps to avoid a "soggy bottom".

Gently combine all the ingredients for the filling in a bowl, and season to taste. Fill the pie shell with the filling and return it to the oven. Cook until the top is golden colored and the filling is just set – about 30–40 minutes. It is delicious served warm with a tossed green salad and perhaps a little Hollandaise Sauce (see page 581).

Khai Loog Kheoy (Son-in-Law's Eggs)

Serves 6

This delicious version of Son-in-Law's Eggs was given to us by Wasinee Beech who was born in Thailand but now lives in Clonakilty in Co. Cork. Her food is absolutely delicious.

6 eggs, cooked and shelled
2 dried red chiles
1/4 cup plus 2 1/2 tablespoons cooking oil
8 shallots, sliced thinly
5 fresh or dried Chinese or shiitake mushrooms
3 garlic cloves, crushed and chopped finely
4 ounces (110g) free-range pork, ground

3 tablespoons palm sugar (jaggery)
2 1/2 tablespoons fish sauce (nam pla)
2 1/2 tablespoons tamarind water (see right)
1 tablespoon plus 1 teaspoon lemon juice, freshly squeezed
3 scallions, sliced in 1/2-inch (1-cm) slices

Garnish
fresh cilantro leaves

Boil the eggs gently for 7 minutes in salted water. Cool and remove the shells. Roast the chiles until fragrant but not burnt. Heat the oil in a pan, fry the shallots until crispy, drain on paper towels, and reserve the oil.

If you are using dried Chinese mushrooms, soak them for 20 minutes, slice them, and reserve the soaking water for use later.

Heat 1/4 cup of the oil in a wok, add the eggs, and fry until all sides are golden brown and slightly crispy. Cut each egg in half and arrange nicely on a serving dish. Clean the wok and add the rest of the oil. Stir-fry the garlic until golden. Add the pork and mushrooms and stir until the pork is cooked (about 5 minutes). Add the palm sugar, nam pla, tamarind water, and lemon juice. If more liquid is required, add a little bit of water from the soaked mushrooms.

Taste and correct the seasoning, add the scallions, give a quick stir, and spoon the sauce over the eggs along with the crispy shallots and chiles. Garnish with fresh cilantro and serve with plain boiled rice (see page 124).

How to make Tamarind Water

Tamarind is a souring agent used extensively in Indian and Asian cooking. It is very easy to use and gives dishes a special bitter-sweet flavor. The most common form of tamarind found in the West comes in a block of dark, sticky pulp, which can be kept without refrigeration. Tamarind water keeps in a jar in the fridge for up to a week.

a piece of tamarind pulp the size of a table tennis ball
2/3 cup hot water

Put the pulp and hot water together into a small bowl. Let soak for 30 minutes. Squeeze the softened pulp between your fingers and when you feel the pips, remove and discard them. Pour the tamarind pulp and the liquid into a wire mesh strainer, press to extract as much flavor as possible, then discard the fibrous remains. Use the tamarind water as required

Swiss Bacon and Egg Salad

Serves 4

A favorite lunch salad during skiing holidays in Verbier.

enough frisée lettuce for 4 portions (no other lettuce will do)
4 eggs
1 tablespoon plus 1 teaspoon sunflower or peanut oil
6 ounces (175g) lightly smoked bacon, cut into lardons
Ballymaloe French Dressing (see page 225)
2 hardboiled eggs

Garnish
1 generous tablespoon parsley, chopped
1 generous tablespoon chives, chopped

Wash and dry the frisée lettuce leaves. Just before serving, poach the eggs in barely simmering water for 4 minutes or until "mollet", still soft in the center.

Meanwhile heat a little oil in a pan over a high heat. Add the bacon and fry until crisp and golden. Drain on paper towels.

In a deep bowl, toss the salad with the dressing and divide between 4 plates. Chop the hardboiled egg coarsely and sprinkle between the 4 plates. Next, sprinkle on the hot bacon. Top each salad with a poached egg. Garnish with parsley and chives and serve immediately.

How to Boil an Egg

Far be it for me to sound too dramatic but there's absolutely no point in serving either a boiled or poached egg unless you can get really fresh organic eggs from free-range hens. First, boiled eggs. Let the eggs reach room temperature if they have been in the fridge. Bring a small saucepan of water to a boil, add a little salt, then lower the eggs gently into the water on a spoon. The eggs must be covered with water. Bring the water back to a boil and simmer gently for 6 minutes, according to your taste. A 4-minute egg will be still quite soft. 5 minutes will almost set the white while the yolk will still be runny. Six minutes will produce a boiled egg with a soft yolk and solid white.

Ouefs Mollet, or Molly Eggs as they are affectionately known in Ballymaloe kitchen, are soft boiled eggs that are carefully peeled and served often on a croûton with a complimentary sauce spooned over the top.

How to Poach Eggs

No fancy egg poachers or molds are required to produce a perfect result. All you need is a really fresh egg from a happy, lazy hen. Bring a small saucepan of water to a boil, add a little salt, reduce the heat, swirl the water, crack the egg, and slip gently into the whirlpool in the center. For perfection, the water should not boil again but bubble very gently just below boiling point. Continue to cook for 3–4 minutes until the white is set and the yolk still soft and runny. Lift out gently on a slotted spoon, and drain thoroughly. Serve on hot toast.

Alternatively, slip the poached egg into a bowl of cold water. Unlikely though it may sound, poached eggs reheat very well when popped back into barely simmering water (to compensate, slightly undercook them in the initial stage).

Warm Salad of Bacon with Poached Egg and Cheese

Serves 4

This gorgeous little salad depends totally on good ingredients. Make it with battery-produced eggs and indifferent bacon and you'll wonder why you bothered. We use Gubbeen bacon, which is cured and smoked by a brilliant young Irish artisan producer called Fingal Ferguson – the son of Tom and Giana Ferguson, from West Cork, who make the famous Gubbeen farmhouse cheese. If you can't lay your hands on this, look out for the best-quality smoked bacon you can find. We also use Gabriel cheese, a hard cheese made by the Fergusons' neighbour, Bill Hogan. A good nutty Parmesan may be used instead.

Caesar Salad dressing (see page 214)
4 eggs, poached
6 ounces (175g) smoked bacon lardons
a mixture of salad greens
1/2 cup freshly grated hard cheese (such as Gabriel or a good Parmesan like Parmigiano Reggiano)
parsley, freshly chopped

First, make the dressing – you will have more than you need for this recipe but it keeps for several weeks so save it in the refrigerator for another time.

Meanwhile, heat a frying pan, add a little olive or sunflower oil, and cook the bacon until crispy. Poach the eggs (see left).

To assemble, put a little dressing on the plates. Arrange a selection of lettuce and salad greens on top (we also add freshly cooked asparagus or chicory in season, or some chard or beet greens). Sprinkle the sizzling bacon over the salad and top with a poached egg. Drizzle more dressing over the eggs and salad greens. Sprinkle with the cheese and parsley and serve immediately.

How to Fry an Egg

Choose very fresh eggs, organic and from free-range hens if possible. Never buy cracked eggs. Put a frying pan on a low heat, melt a little butter, and break the egg into the pan, then cover with a Pyrex plate. After a few minutes the egg yolk will film over. Serve immediately.

Basted Fried Eggs

Melt quite a large pat of butter or a few tablespoons of bacon fat in a pan, turn the heat to medium, let the egg cook for about a minute, then baste with the hot fat or butter. Serve as soon as the gold has filmed over.

Easy Over

Fry the egg for 1–2 minutes and as soon as it is firm enough, slide a spatula underneath and gently flip it over. Cook for a minute or two more. Serve immediately.

Sunny Side Up

Fry the eggs in a little melted butter for 4–5 minutes on a low heat without flipping over. Serve immediately.

Deep-fried Eggs

Heat 1 inch (2.5cm) of oil (sunflower or pure olive) in a frying pan, or use a deep fryer. The oil should be hot enough to brown a cube of bread in 30 seconds. Crack the egg and drop gently into the oil. Alternatively crack the egg into a cup first and then slide gently into the oil.

Immediately, using 2 wooden spatulas or perforated spoons, fold the egg white over the yolk to cover it. When the egg yolk is completely covered, let the egg cook for a minute or so until the white is firm and crisp and the yolk is still soft. Lift out with a perforated spoon. Drain on paper towels and serve immediately.

Deep-fried eggs are delicious with a spicy tomato sauce, or on top of a mixture of salad greens as in Warm Salad of Bacon.

How to Cook Crêpes

Choose an iron or non-stick crêpe pan. Heat on a brisk flame. Batter made from half milk and half water produces a lighter, lacier crêpe. Be sure to whisk melted butter into the batter. This will help to prevent the crêpes from sticking to the pan and will save you the trouble of greasing the pan between each one. Choose a small ladle that holds just enough batter to cover the bottom of the pan with a thin film. Alternatively, put the batter into a pitcher with a good pouring lip. When the pan is really hot, pour just enough batter in to cover the bottom when the pan is tilted from side to side. If the pan is as hot as it ought to be, the crêpe should be ready to turn almost immediately. Loosen the crêpe around the edge. (A flexible plastic spatula is best for this.) Turn over quickly – a few seconds will be enough to cook the other side. (The crêpe should be just flecked with brown spots.) Slide on to a plate and continue to cook the remainder of the batter. The crêpes may be stacked on top of each other and peeled apart later. Crêpes stored in this way may be kept in the fridge and used hours or even days later. They will peel off each other easily.

Ballymaloe Crêpes Suzette

Serves about 4

Crêpes Suzette are the aristocrats of the pancake family, served in smart restaurants by the head waiter from a trolley. We serve them in Ballymaloe House on Shrove Tuesday. Myrtle Allen flambés them at the table. She once caused considerable consternation by setting her hair ablaze as she did this a little too enthusiastically! This recipe comes from The Ballymaloe Cookbook with her permission.

For the Batter:
makes 8 crêpes
1/2 cup all-purpose flour
1 tablespoon plus 1 teaspoon oil
1 egg
1 egg yolk
2 teaspoons Orange curaçao liquer
2/3 cup milk

For the Sauce:
1/2 lb. (225g) large ripe oranges
3/4 stick (1/3 cup) softened butter
1/4 cup superfine sugar
generous tablespoon each of brandy and curaçao
superfine sugar for sprinkling

First, make the batter: put the flour in a bowl and make a well in the center. Into this, pour the oil, egg, egg yolk, and orange curaçao. Stir, gradually drawing in the flour from the sides. Add the milk slowly until it is the consistency of thin cream. Set aside in the refrigerator for 30 minutes. Then make the crêpes by putting a small ladleful of batter at a time into a hot non-stick frying pan; as soon as bubbles rise to the surface, flip it over and cook the other side. Keep the crêpes ready for use later.

For the sauce, grate the rind of the oranges very carefully so as not to penetrate the pith. Add to the butter and sugar, and cream vigorously until smooth.

To finish: put the pan over a high heat. Melt about 1 tablespoon orange butter in it. When bubbling, put a cooked crêpe in and heat through, turning so that both sides get warm. Fold it into a fan shape and rest it against the side of the pan. Continue in the same way with the remaining crêpes. Sprinkle them with superfine sugar. Pour brandy and curaçao over them. Ignite it, to burn off the alcohol, keeping your face away from the flames. Tilt the pan and spoon the juices over the crêpes until the flame subsides. Serve immediately on hot plates.

Crawford Café Spinach and Mushroom Crêpes

Serves 6–7
In season: all year, depending on filling

The Crawford Café in Cork, run by my sister-in-law, Fern Little, cannot take these crêpes off the lunch menu or there would be a riot! There are lots of variations, but this is a particularly delicious version.

1 lb. (450g) spinach (weighed after stalks have been removed)
1 x Mushroom à la Crème recipe (see page 197)

Soda Water Crêpes (see page 118)

Hollandaise Sauce (see page 581), full quantity

10-inch (25.5-cm) non-stick pan

To make the filling: remove the stalks from the spinach and cook as for Buttered Spinach (see page 170). Mix the Mushroom à la Crème with the spinach. Taste and correct the seasoning.

Make the crêpes, following the instructions overleaf.

Lay a crêpe on a clean worktop. Put 2 generous tablespoons of filling in the middle, fold in the sides, and fold over the ends to make a parcel. Repeat with the others. If the components are cold, reheat on a baking tray in a moderate oven 350°F (180°C) for approximately 10 minutes. Serve with a little light Hollandaise Sauce and a good green salad.

Some other good fillings

Cooked chicken or ham; mussels or shrimp; or some chunks of cooked salmon or scallops are delicious added to the mushroom mixture.

Left: Ballymaloe Crêpes Suzette

Soda Water Crêpe Batter

Makes 12–14 crêpes

2¾ cups flour
pinch of salt
6 eggs
3 cups milk
1 small bottle soda water
1 tablespoon plus 1 teaspoon oil

To make the batter: sift the flour and salt into a bowl, make a well in the center, and drop in the lightly beaten eggs. With a whisk or wooden spoon, starting in the center, mix the egg and gradually bring in the flour. Add the liquid (milk and soda water) and beat until the batter is covered with bubbles, then add the oil. Let the batter stand in a cold place for an hour or so – longer will do no harm. Alternatively, put all the ingredients into a blender or food processor and whizz for a minute or so. Cook small ladlefuls of the batter on a hot, non-stick pan. Stack the crêpes one on top of another, ready for use.

Almspurses with Tomato Sauce

This is a fun way to serve savory crêpes. Serve 1 as an appetizer or 3, each with a different filling, for a substantial main course. The filling can include meat, fish, or just a juicy vegetable mixture.

Savory or Herb crêpes (see right)

Suggested fillings
Piperonata (see page 190)
Mushroom à la Crème (see page 197)
Tomato Fondue (see page 188)
Creamed Spinach (see page 171)
seafood
chicken and ham

long chives for tying
Tomato Sauce (see page 590)

Lay a crêpe on the worktop. Put two heaped teaspoons of hot chosen filling into the center. Gather the edges together and then tie into a purse with a blanched and refreshed chive. Serve on a hot plate surrounded by homemade Tomato Sauce.

Savory or Herb Crêpe Batter

Makes 12 crêpes

1½ cups white flour, preferably unbleached
good pinch of salt
2 large eggs and 1–2 egg yolks
2 cups milk or, for very light and crisp crêpes, milk and water mixed
2 generous tablespoons freshly chopped herbs (parsley, thyme, chives…), (optional)
2–3 tablespoons melted butter

11-inch (30.5-cm) pan

Sift the flour and salt into a bowl, make a well in the center, and drop in the lightly beaten eggs. With a whisk or wooden spoon, starting in the center, mix the egg and gradually bring in the flour. Add the liquid slowly and beat until the batter is covered with bubbles. Stir in the herbs, if using.

Let the batter stand in a cold place for an hour or so – longer will do no harm. Just before you cook the crêpes, stir in the melted butter. This will make all the difference to the flavor and texture of the crêpes and will make it possible to cook them without greasing the pan each time.

Heat a heavy cast-iron crêpe pan or non-stick pan to very hot. Pour in just enough batter to cover the bottom of the pan thinly. Loosen the crêpe around the edge, flip it over with a spatula, cook for a second or two on the other side, and slide off the pan on to a plate. The crêpes may be stacked on top of each other and peeled apart later.

They will keep in the fridge for several days and also freeze perfectly. For freezing, place wax paper between each crêpe.

Rory's 'Blinis'

Makes about 30
In season: all year

These are really cheat blinis (sometimes called crumpets or pikelets), but they are really quick to make and you can choose from a whole array of yummy toppings. Serve an assortment as an appetizer or just nibble them with drinks.

2 cups white flour
¼ teaspoon salt
½ teaspoon baking soda
1 teaspoon cream of tartar (bextartar)
2 tablespoons butter
2 eggs
¾–1 cup milk
1 generous tablespoon chopped parsley

11-inch (30.5-cm) non-stick pan

Sift the dry ingredients into a bowl and rub in the butter. Drop the eggs into the center, add a little of the milk, and stir rapidly with a whisk allowing the flour to drop gradually in from the sides. When half the milk is added, beat until air bubbles rise. Add the remainder of the milk and let stand for 1 hour if possible. Then add the parsley.

Drop a good teaspoonful of the batter into a hottish pan and cook until bubbles appear and start to burst on the top. (It usually takes a bit of trial and error to get the temperature right.) Flip it over and cook until golden on the other side. Cool on a wire rack and serve as soon as possible, with a mixture of toppings.

Suggested toppings

Smoked salmon, crème fraîche, and dill or chives
Smoked mussels, crème fraîche, and cucumber pickle
Roast red and yellow pepper and pesto or basil leaves
Chopped hardboiled egg, mayonnaise, and chives

Cream cheese with Chile and Red Pepper Relish (see page 514)
Salami and Guacamole (see page 91)
Spiced beef, avocado, and arugula leaves

Bread Pudding with Asparagus and Fontina

Serves 8
In season: late spring

Mary Risley from Tante Marie's Cooking School in San Francisco shared this delicious recipe with us. The technique can be used with many ingredients – mushrooms, tomatoes, roast peppers, and so on.

12–16 thick slices of best quality white bread, buttered
4 eggs
2½ cups milk or 2 cups milk plus ½ cup buttermilk
1 lb. (450g) asparagus, trimmed
1 teaspoon salt
1 teaspoon pepper, freshly ground
⅓ cup freshly grated Parmesan cheese (Parmigiano Reggiano if possible)
8 ounces (225g) Fontina cheese, Swiss cheese, or other white cheese, roughly shredded (about 2 cups)
1 tablespoon butter

lasagne dish, 8 inches x 10 inches (25cm x 20.5cm), buttered

Preheat the oven to 350°F (180°C).

Butter the bread. Whisk the eggs with the milk. Bring a little water to a boil in an oval heavy flameproof and ovenproof casserole dish and add salt. Add asparagus and cook for 3–4 minutes or until al dente. Drain and refresh under cold water. Cut the asparagus in thin diagonal slivers.

Pour a little of the egg and milk mixture into the bottom of the lasagne dish. Arrange a layer of bread on top. Sprinkle half the asparagus over the bread. Season well with salt and pepper. Strew one third of each of the cheeses on top. Pour some of the egg mixture on this layer, then repeat the layers and seasoning and finish with a layer of bread. Pour the remainder of the liquid evenly over the top. Sprinkle with the remaining cheese. Bake in a bain-marie in the oven for about 45 minutes or until crisp and golden on top. Serve with a good green salad (see page 225).

rice, other grains, and legumes

rice, other grains, & legumes

Grains and legumes have been an important staple food for thousands of years. When fully ripe, harvested and dried, they can be stored for several months, providing reliable winter food. Grains, wheat, corn, rice, and legumes, as well as dried peas and beans, provide an alternative and relatively inexpensive source of protein.

Rice

Rice has to be one of the world's greatest staples, and one of the most versatile cooking ingredients. With around 2,500 different varieties of rice (including long, medium, or short grain, refined or whole), there's plenty of scope for choice. All varieties of rice have their own unique characteristics. The trick is to use the right type of rice for the dish you are making.

White or Brown?

Buy organic rice whenever possible. White and brown rice are both delicious but differ in terms of flavor and texture. Nutritionally speaking, brown rice is superior – lots of good B vitamins come with its rich, earthy flavor. It is unrefined, so it's got a shelf life of around 6 months only. White rice, on the other hand, is refined – meaning that the outer bran layers and the germ have been removed – and as a result it has a longer shelf life of between 2 and 3 years. White rice is best eaten when fresh and fragrant, though, and it has a more delicate and aromatic flavor than brown rice.

Short grain rice

Pearl rice is used for risottos, rice pudding, and paellas. The grains are short and fat and the amylopectin within them causes them to stick together when cooked, forming a soft, creamy pudding. They absorb more liquid than long grain rice – between 2–4 times their volume, depending on the variety.

Calasparra is my absolute favorite for paella. It is a short grain rice grown in Spain.

Japanese Rice, another short grain rice, is perfect for making sushi. It's naturally sticky, so you can roll it into little balls and wrap it in nori seaweed or top it with a sliver of tuna.

Long Grain Rice

Use long grain rice for savory dishes, pilâvs, pullaos, salads, and stuffings. Properly cooked, the grains will stay separate and fluffy; if overcooked, they will stick together and become mush.

Basmati is the aristocrat of long grain rice, and tilda is one of the finest basmati. It is delicious in Indian pullaos, pilâvs, and biryanis. It's definitely worth the extra price one pays for its fine flavor. Brown and white basmati are both available. Brown basmati takes less time to cook than other brown rice.

Thai fragrant/Jasmine Rice, is deliciously aromatic and slightly sticky when cooked. It's wonderful hot or cold.

Glutinous Rice, sometimes called sweet, sticky, or Japanese-style rice, is used in Southeast Asia for sweet and savory dishes. Ironically, it doesn't contain gluten. The grains are flat and rounded and should be soaked before steaming. When cooked, the little round grains stay separate, but they can be pressed together into little balls or rolls. Eat it with your fingers and with Thai or Chinese food.

Black Glutinous Rice is unrefined and the grains are long and wide. It cooks like glutinous rice and can be used for both sweet and savory dishes.

Wild Rice is not actually a rice but is a long-grain marsh grass. It is sometimes sold as a mixture of white wild rice and brown rice, which baffles me because wild rice takes longer to cook than brown rice! The full flavor emerges when the grains burst after 50–60 minutes of nice slow cooking by the absorption method (boiled rather than steamed).

Red Rice is unrefined and grown in small quantities in France. It is very popular and tastes similar to brown rice.

Cooking Rice

1/3 cup of rice per person is usually about right, but if your guests are hungry they will easily polish off 1/2–2/3 cup each. Of course you can boil rice in a pot of water or cook it in a steamer, but many respected chefs, including Sri Owen, Madhur Jaffrey, and Deh-Ta Hsiung, swear by electric rice cookers and say they're foolproof.

Storage and Reusing Cooked Rice

Buy rice little and often from a store with a quick turnover. Keep it in glass jars in a cool, dry place. Eat it within a year. And no, it doesn't improve with age!

Cooked rice is excellent for fried rice, salads, and stuffings. Of course it is best to use freshly cooked rice, but if you have leftover rice, pop it in the fridge as soon as it's cooled down. Eat within 2 or 3 days as cooked rice is susceptible to *Bascillus cereus*, which causes severe stomach cramps and diarrhea. If you need it hot, reheat cooked rice very thoroughly: *Bascillus cereus* cannot survive temperatures lower than 39°F (4°C) or higher than 140°F (60°C). Some use a microwave, but I prefer to throw the rice in some boiling water for 1 minute only, or to steam it over boiling water. Serve it in a nice hot dish and no one will be any the wiser!

Other Grains

Botanically, grains are the fruit of cereal plants in the grass family. There are about 8,000 species of grain, but only a few are commonly used in the kitchen. Harvested grains are significantly dehydrated and are only palatable after they have absorbed water and been cooked. Water is usually used for cooking, but stock or milk is also used in some cases. Many of the grains are cooked in the form of pilâvs, and some need soaking.

Wheat is perhaps the most important and widely used grain. It is most commonly processed into flour. **Wheat berries or kernels** are grains that have had the husks removed. These are cooked as pilâv and are excellent in salads with other grains. **Cracked wheat** (including **bulgur** which is the basis of tabouleh) comes in fine, medium, and coarse grain. The finer grains can be used for bread and batter, the coarser for pilâv. Semolina is made from a hard durum wheat and its flour is used in pasta, gnocchi, and milk puddings. **Couscous** is not actually a grain, but a pasta made from durum wheat. It appears in this chapter because it is always cooked like a grain.

Corn is another important staple. There are two main types, field corn and sweet corn. Field corn is harder and has more starch. It is used for animal feed and is also processed into cornstarch and cornmeal for breads, pancakes, and **Polenta**. Some types of sweet corn are used for popcorn and others (such as **blue corn**), when ground, are used in bread or corn chips.

Other Grains include **buckwheat** (again not a grain, but treated as one, ground into a flour and used for blinis), **barley** (used for brewing beer) and **pearl barley** (the hulled grain of which is used in stews and soups). **Oats** are sold in various forms (pinhead, rolled, or flaked) and are used for porridge, breakfast cereals, biscuits, and oatcakes. **Rye** is mostly grown for flour and is used in dark breads. The whole grains may be cooked as a pilâv and are sometimes used in soups and casseroles. Two "supergrains", **quinoa** (a rice substitute, also used in breads and pasta) and **amaranth** (good in casseroles or cooked like polenta), are packed with essential nutrients.

Legumes

Legumes, the dried seeds of different varieties of peas and beans, have been a staple for thousands of years – they were even found beside the graves in the pyramids, meant as food for the pharaohs in the afterlife. It's easy to see why they are still so popular: they're cheap, earthy, and versatile. They're great for salads, but are also good for absorbing gutsy flavors like tangy sausage, fresh herbs and spices, and also go well with a piece of salt pork or lamb. They are an important source of protein and roughage, and are a vital part of a vegetarian or vegan diet.

Larder

We're all hooked on beans and pulses, and every larder could benefit from a few packets of navy, lima, or kidney beans or black-eye peas, chickpeas, and lentils. A few cans are also a brilliant standby for those days when we need to whip up a meal in a matter of minutes. Each variety has its own flavor and different cooking time, so you can't just throw a load of different legumes together and hope for the best.

Chickpeas are the main ingredient in hummus and are also used in stews and casseroles. **Lentils**, or dahl, come in a range of colors and are used in numerous Indian dishes. **Mung beans** and **alfalfa** are most well-known in the form of bean sprouts. **Split peas** are usually puréed (as in pease pudding) and can also be used in soups. Dried **marrowfat peas** with their slightly minty taste, were the bane of my life when I was a child, but now that they're harder to come by, I love them! They're used in soups and stocks and are often served with fish and chips in the form of mushy peas. **Red kidney beans** are one of the most popular beans, valued for their flavor and color. They are an essential ingredient in chili con carne. Other dried beans, such as **borlotti**, **flageolets**, **navy**, **lima**, **pinto**, and **dried fava beans**, are used in stews and salads.

Storage and Preparation of Legumes

Though very long-lasting, legumes will not last forever, and the older they are the longer they will take to cook; so, as with rice, buy a little and often, and make sure they are stored in a cool, dry place.

Legumes should be rinsed and soaked before cooking. Place them in a large bowl of fresh water and let them soak for about 6–8 hours, or overnight. Soaking more or less doubles their size. Allow 5 cups of water per 1 pound (450g). If any beans float to the surface during soaking, they should be thrown away, as they are not good. Once they have been soaked, they are ready to be simmered slowly until cooked. It is imperative that red kidney beans, in addition to soaking, are boiled vigorously for 10 minutes at the start of their cooking time, in order to destroy toxins.

If you get really stuck and haven't had time to soak them, pop the beans in cold water and bring to a boil as slowly as you can, as they will need to cook for longer. Do not add salt until the end of the cooking time.

When you're cooking peas and beans, soak twice the amount you need and, once cooked, pop half of them in a plastic box in the freezer for when you next need them. They will last for months. Keep the water you cooked them in as well – it's ideal for stocks and stews.

Master Recipe
Plain Boiled Rice

Serves 8

I find this way of cooking rice in what we call "unlimited water" to be very satisfactory for plain boiled rice even, dare I say, foolproof. The grains stay separate and it will keep happily covered in the oven for up to half an hour.

5 quarts (4.8 liters) cold water
2 teaspoons salt
2 2/3 cups best quality long-grain rice, preferably basmati rice
a few little pats of butter (optional)

Bring the water to a fast boil in a very large pot. Add the salt. Sprinkle in the rice and stir at once to ensure that the grains don't stick. Boil rapidly, uncovered.

After 4 or 5 minutes (depending on the type of rice), test by biting a few grains between your teeth – they should still have a slightly resistant core. If the rice overcooks at this stage, the grains will stick together later. Strain well through a fine strainer.

Put into a warm serving dish, dot with a few pats of butter, cover with tin foil or a lid, and leave in a low oven, 275°F (140°C), for a minimum of 15 minutes. Remove the lid, fluff up with a fork, and serve.

Variation
Basmati Rice with Parsley

Follow the Master Recipe, tossing in 3–5 tablespoons freshly chopped parsley when the rice is cooked.

Pilâv Rice

Serves 8

Pilâv is the national dish of Turkey. It is more commonly known as pilaf or pilau on our restaurant menus, and many versions are found in the Middle East.

A pilâv looks after itself once the initial cooking is underway. It is versatile – serve it on its own or with meat, fish, and herbs. Beware, however, of using pilâv as a leftovers dumping ground – all additions should be carefully seasoned and balanced.

2 tablespoons butter or ghee
2 1/2 tablespoons onion or shallot, finely chopped
2 1/3 cups long-grain rice, preferably basmati
scant 1 quart (960ml) homemade Chicken Stock (see page 36)
2 1/2 tablespoons herbs (parsley, thyme, chives), freshly chopped, optional
salt and freshly ground pepper

Melt the butter or ghee in a flameproof casserole dish or other flameproof and ovenproof pan, add the onion, and sweat for 2–3 minutes. Add the rice and toss for 1–2 minutes, just long enough for the grains to change color.

Season with salt and pepper, add the stock, cover and bring to a boil. Reduce the heat to a minimum and then simmer on top of the stove or in the oven 325°F (170°C) for about 10 minutes. By then the rice should be just cooked and all the liquid absorbed. Just before serving, stir in the fresh herbs, if using.

Note: Basmati rice cooks quite quickly; other types of rice may take up to 15 minutes.

Master Recipe
Chicken Pilâv

Serves 8

This recipe may sound dull but in fact it is a delicious and economical way to serve large numbers for a party. Serve with a Pilâv Rice and Tomato Fondue and garnish with sprigs of parsley or watercress. It may be prepared ahead of time, and reheats well. Add the liaison just before serving, otherwise the sauce will curdle if heated over 355°F (180°C).

1 x 4–4 1/2 lbs. (1.8–2kg) boiling fowl or good free-range and organic chicken
1 large carrot, sliced
1 large onion, sliced
5 peppercorns
a bouquet garni made up of a sprig of thyme, parsley stalks, a tiny bay leaf, a stalk of celery
2–2 1/2 cups water and white wine mixed or light Chicken Stock (see page 36)
2 tablespoons, roughly, Roux (see page 580)
1–1 1/4 cups cream or creamy milk
salt and freshly ground pepper

Liaison
1 egg yolk
1/4 cup cream

Pilâv Rice (see left), full quantity

Season the chicken with salt and pepper; put into a heavy flameproof and ovenproof casserole dish along with the carrot, onion, bouquet garni, and peppercorns. Pour in water, water and wine, or stock. Cover, bring to a boil, and simmer either on top of the stove or in the oven for 1 1/2–3 hours, depending on the age of the bird. When the bird is cooked, remove from the casserole dish. Strain and de-grease the cooking liquid and return it to the casserole dish. Discard the vegetables and the bouquet garni: they have already given their flavor to the cooking liquid. Over medium-high heat, reduce the liquid in an uncovered flameproof casserole dish or large frying pan for a few minutes. If it tastes a little weak, add cream and reduce again; thicken to a light coating consistency with Roux. Taste, add salt, correct the seasoning.

Skin the chicken and carve the flesh into 2-inch (5-cm) pieces; add the meat to the sauce and let it heat through and bubble (the dish may be prepared ahead to this point).

Finally, just before serving, mix the egg yolk and cream to make a liaison. Add some of the hot sauce to the liaison, then carefully stir into the chicken mixture. Taste, correct the seasoning, and stir well but do not let it boil further or the sauce will curdle. Serve with Pilâv Rice.

Above: Chicken Pilâv with Tomato Fondue

Variations

Chicken and Mushroom Pilâv

Follow the Master Recipe, but add 1 lb. (450g) sautéed sliced mushroom to the chicken pilâv just before serving.

Chicken and Bacon Pilâv

Follow the Master Recipe and add cubes of cooked bacon to either the original Chicken Pilâv, or the Chicken and Mushroom Pilâv, just before serving.

Note: Any of the above may be served as a pie, covered with pastry dough, mashed potatoes, or champ (mashed potatoes and scallions). They can also be used as a filling for pies or pastries.

Chicken Pilâv with Herb Crust

Adding an herb soda bread topping turns this dish into a chicken cobbler.

half-quantity White Soda dough with herbs (see page 474)
egg wash (1 egg beaten with about 1 tablespoon of milk)
grated Cheddar cheese (optional)

Preheat the oven 350°F (180°C).

Roll out the dough into a 3/4-inch (2-cm) thick circle, stamp out 2-inch (5-cm) circles with a cookie or pastry cutter. Keep refrigerated until needed.

Follow the Master Variation until the chicken is almost cooked, remove the lid from the casserole dish, and cover the top of the stew with slightly overlapping herb scones, brush with egg wash, and sprinkle with a little cheese, if you wish. Increase the heat to 450°F (230°C) for 10 minutes, then reduce the heat to 400°F (200°C) for a further 20 minutes or until the crust is baked.

Fried Rice

Serves 6

Fried rice is a terrific and very nutritious way of using up leftovers. It can be ready to eat in just a few minutes. There are dozens of variations of fried rice in China. Some cooks like to add the eggs to the wok first, followed by the rice. My family favor adding the egg at the later stage for a moister result. Other tasty bits, such as bamboo shoots, bean sprouts, and Chinese mushrooms may be added.

2 eggs, lightly beaten
2½ tablespoons chopped scallions, green and white parts
1 teaspoon salt
¼ cup sunflower or olive oil
a heaped cup mushrooms, chopped
1 cup cooked meat, cooked chicken, pork, ham, or spicy sausage, cut into small dice or 1 cup peeled shrimp
1 cup cooked green peas or green pepper
3½ cups boiled rice (see page 124)
1½–2½ tablespoons light soy sauce

Whisk the eggs with the scallions and lots of salt. Heat the oil in a very hot wok, add the mushrooms, and stir-fry for 1–2 minutes; then add the meat or shrimp, and peas. Continue to stir-fry for another minute or so. Add the rice and soy sauce, continue to stir-fry, add the eggs and stir-fry for about 2 minutes until the eggs are set. Stir to make sure that each grain of rice is separate. Taste, correct seasoning, and serve immediately.

Persian Rice

Serves 8

Serve with pan-grilled chicken (see page 271) and harissa.

½ teaspoon saffron
1½ tablespoons boiling water
2½ tablespoons salt
1⅔ cups Basmati rice
¼ cup olive oil
6 ounces (175g) onion, peeled and chopped (about 1⅓ cups)
¼ teaspoon freshly ground cardamom
½ teaspoon freshly ground coriander seed
¼ cup dried cranberries
2 tablespoons dried cherries
½ cup raisins
½ cup pistachio nuts, roughly chopped
2½ tablespoons freshly chopped cilantro leaves
salt and freshly ground pepper

Put the saffron in a little bowl and cover with the boiling water. Bring 5 quarts (4.5 liters) cold water to a boil, add the salt. Sprinkle in the Basmati rice, stirring all the time. Bring back to a boil and cook for 6–7 minutes by which time the grain should have doubled in size and be slightly "al dente". Drain, put into a bowl, add the saffron and the soaking liquid. Mix well and let cool.

Meanwhile, heat the oil in a frying pan, add the onions and cook until crisp and golden, then add the freshly ground spices. Cook for 3–4 minutes, add the dried cranberries, dried cherries, and raisins. Cook for a further 1–2 minutes. Then add the rice. Season, add the pistachio nuts, and toss well. Taste and correct the seasoning. Sprinkle with the freshly chopped cilantro

Thai Jasmine Rice

Serves 4–6

Thai fragrant rice, a plain long-grain variety, has a slight jasmine scent and is perfect for south-east Asian meals. When cooked, it is shiny with just a slight hint of stickiness.

2 cups Thai fragrant rice
2 cups water

Put the rice and water into a heavy saucepan, bring to a boil, stir once, cover with a tight fitting lid, and lower the heat to the absolute minimum – use a heat diffuser mat if possible. Continue to cook on the lowest heat for 15 minutes. Do not uncover during cooking. Remove from the heat, keep covered, and let sit for 5 minutes before serving. The rice will stay warm for several hours if necessary.

Note: Cover with tin foil if the saucepan lid is really not tight fitting.

Coconut Rice

Serves 4–6

A delicious way to cook rice which we enjoyed in Asia.

2⅔ cups Thai fragrant or Basmati rice
2 tablespoons butter
4 cups coconut milk (Chaokoh)
1 teaspoon salt
1 pandanus leaf or, if unavailable, use a bay leaf

Soak the rice for 1 hour, drain well. Melt the butter in a flameproof casserole dish or other heavy pan over a medium heat, add the rice, toss and cook for 2–3 minutes. Add the coconut milk, salt, and the pandanus leaf or bay leaf. Bring to a boil and cook until all the coconut milk has been absorbed. Cover, reduce the heat to absolute minimum. Cook for a further 10 minutes. Serve hot.

Kunie's Sushi Plate

For appetizer serves 4

Occasionally we have 1 or 2 Japanese students on the 12 week course. Kunie Akita taught us how to make this delicious sushi. The texture and stickiness of Japanese rice is essential. There are 2 main kinds of sushi – nigiri which is hand-formed, and maki which is rolled. Here we have both. Fresh tuna makes an excellent filling too.

Sushi Rice
2⅔ cups Japanese rice (short-grain)
2½ cups water
½ cup rice vinegar
½ teaspoon salt
2–3 tablespoons sugar, to taste
3 sheets nori seaweed

Filling
7–8 slices smoked salmon
2 avocado slices, finely diced
cucumber, seeded and cut into ¼-inch (5-mm) strips
2 tablespoons cream cheese
3–4 basil leaves

Garnish
fennel leaves

Sauce and accompaniment
wasabi paste
Kikkoman soy sauce
pickled ginger

Special equipment
Bamboo sudari mat for rolling
(These mats are available from Japanese or Asian stores, many health food stores, and now even some supermakets. If you can't find one, just use a clean lint-free towel as though you were making a jelly roll.)

Wash the rice and soak in the water in a heavy pot for at least 1 hour before you cook. Bring to a boil over a high heat, cover, then reduce the heat to minimum. Cook for 15 minutes. Before turning off the heat, turn to high heat again for just 10 seconds. Remove and let sit for 10 minutes. Do not open the lid at any stage.

Meanwhile mix the vinegar, sugar, and salt in a bowl until it is dissolved. Turn the rice out onto a big flat plate (preferably wooden). While it is hot, pour the vinegar over the rice. Mix together as if slicing the rice with a wooden rice spoon. Don't stir. You must do it quickly, preferably fanning the rice with the wooden rice spoon. This is much easier if you have a helper. Let it cool on the plate and cover with paper towels or a lint-free towel. The rice will soak up the liquid.

To make Maki sushi: lay a sheet of nori on the bamboo mat and spread a layer of rice over it. Make a shallow indentation and put in the filling. Fold over the bottom end of the nori and, using the mat, gently but firmly roll up the nori. Press to seal.

To make Nigiri sushi: make a little long ball with rice. Put a slice of fresh or smoked salmon on top. Garnish with fennel leaves or tie with a strip of nori.

Cut the maki sushi into 6–8 pieces. Arrange 6 pieces of maki or nigiri sushi in total on a plate. Put a little blob of wasabi paste about the size of a small pea on the plate, a little dish of Kikkoman soy sauce, and a few slivers of pickled ginger.

Sticky Rice

Serves 4–6

Sticky rice, sometimes called glutinous rice or sweet rice, is the daily staple of Laos and the millions of Thais of Laotian heritage who live in northern and north-eastern Thailand. This chewy, satisfying, long-grain rice is soaked for several hours or overnight, and then steamed until it is sticky and soft. It is eaten with the fingers, starting with a fist-sized portion and pinching off a walnut-sized lump, which is rolled into a small ball with 1 hand. It is paired with meat or vegetables, dipped into a pungent sauce, or eaten as it is.

Sticky rice is presented in beautiful hand woven baskets for special occasions; family meals are served on a large plate along with accompanying dishes. Since sticky rice can be served hot, warm or at room temperature; it's particularly great for picnics and outdoor meals. This recipe comes from Nancie McDermott's Real Thai.

2⅓ cups sticky rice (such as mochi)

Put the rice into a bowl. Cover with cold water by 2 inches (5cm) and soak for at least 3 hours, or overnight. Fill the bottom of a steamer pan or wok or saucepan with water. Place a steamer rack or tray about an inch (2.5cm) or more above the water, cover the steamer, and bring the water to a rolling boil over high heat.

Drain the rice and transfer to a traditional bamboo sticky rice-steaming basket, or use something like a colander or strainer suspended above boiling water.

Uncover the pan and place the rice-filled steaming basket on the rack over the steam, taking care not to burn your hands. Reduce the heat to maintain a steady flow of steam through the rice, and cook until the grains swell and glisten and are sticky enough to be squeezed into small lumps, 30–45 minutes. Add boiling water to the steamer pan as needed to maintain original level.

As soon as the rice is cooked, turn it out onto a baking sheet and gently spread it into a shallow layer with a wet wooden spoon. This will release some of the steam and moisture. As soon as it cools enough to touch, gather the rice gently into a large lump and serve it in a basket or on a plate. Serve hot, warm, or at room temperature.

Note: The cooking time for sticky rice varies according to how long the rice soaks. The longer you soak it, the faster it will cook.

Rice Cakes with Palm Sugar

Makes 24–36

This sweet snack, called nahng let **in central Thailand, came to the south from Laos, but today it's popular all over the kingdom. Rice cakes are made by shaping warm, freshly steamed, sticky rice into discs, drying them in the sun or in a warm oven, and then frying them crisp in hot oil. The dried rice cakes swell and bloom into puffy blossoms and are crowned with a delectable swirl of caramelized palm sugar.**

You'll need to plan ahead for this dish. If you soak the rice overnight and then steam it and shape the cakes the next morning, you can fry the kao taen **in the afternoon or evening. The dried, unfried cakes, sealed airtight in a tin, will keep well for a month. Another gem from Nancie McDermott's** Real Thai**.**

3 cups hot, cooked Sticky Rice (see recipe, page 127)
vegetable oil for deep-frying
1 cup palm sugar (jaggery)

Cook the rice and spread while still hot onto a large tray or baking sheet. Wet a wooden spoon and quickly and gently spread the rice into a shallow layer to release some of the steam and moisture.

As soon as the rice cools enough to touch, shape it into small, thin discs, 2–3 inches (5–8cm) in diameter, and 3 or 4 grains thick. Make them as thin as you can, but resist the urge to press them into submission or they will be very hard. Work fast – the cakes needn't be perfectly round; a ragged edge is fine. Wet your fingers a little now and then if the rice sticks to your hands.

Place the shaped discs on cooling racks or trays to air-dry as you work. When all the discs are formed, set them in the full sun until brittle and very dry, turning them over several times to dry them evenly, 6–8 hours. Or place them in a warm oven, on the lowest setting, and with the door open (see below).

To fry the cakes, pour the oil into a wok or large, deep frying pan to a depth of 3 inches (8cm). Place over medium heat and heat to 325–350°F (170–180°C). Meanwhile, line a platter or bowl with paper towels and place a large, long-handled mesh scoop or slotted spoon by the pan for turning the discs in the oil and for removing them when cooked.

Drop a small piece of rice cake into the pan. If it sinks to the bottom and then immediately floats to the top, blooms, and puffs, the oil is ready. Gently slide 3 cakes along the side of the pan into the oil and tend them as they float and swell into thick, white crackers. Turn them when they stop swelling on the first side and let them cook on the other side just until they're fully puffed.

Before they begin to brown, transfer them to the towel-lined platter to drain. Continue frying in batches of 3 until all are cooked.

Place the palm sugar in a small, heavy saucepan and bring to a gentle boil over medium heat. Simmer, stirring occasionally, until all the sugar melts into a syrup and darkens to a rich caramel color, somewhere between honey and maple syrup, 5–10 minutes. The sugar should form a shiny ribbon when it is dribbled from a spoon. Quickly drizzle some of the syrup onto each rice cake in a spiral design, starting at the center and twirling out to the edge. Let the rice cakes dry at room temperature until the sugar sets. They can be stored in an airtight container for up to 1 week.

Note: You can also dry the rice cakes in a warm oven 225°F (110°C) for about 3 hours. The oven will be faster than a sunbath, so check them every hour and remove them as soon as they're dry. They shouldn't brown at all. You could also leave them out on a counter to air dry for 1 or 2 days, turning them occasionally.

Thai cooks decorate *kao taen* by shaping a simple cone, with a small opening at the point, from a piece of banana leaf. The caramelized palm sugar is poured into the cone and allowed to drip out the opening onto the rice cakes.

Rice and Lentils with Crispy Onions

Serves 6

The Lebanese restaurant Le Mignon in Camden Town, London, makes what they call Mudarara – delicious comfort food. There are versions of this from Syria to Egypt and it was traditionally eaten by the Jewish people on Thursday evenings. Serve it alone or as part of a mezze.

1½ lbs. (700g) onions (about 4 onions), finely sliced
1½ cups olive oil
1 quart (960ml) water
1⅓ cups brown lentils
1½ cups long-grain rice
salt and freshly ground pepper

Heat the oil in a frying pan, add the onions, toss and cook until richly golden.

Bring the water to a boil, add the lentils, and cook for 20 minutes. Add half the fried onions and the rice. Season with salt and pepper. Stir well. Cover and cook on a very low heat for about 20 minutes or until both rice and lentils are cooked. Taste and correct seasoning if necessary.

Meanwhile, continue to cook the remaining onions in the frying pan until crisp and caramelized. Serve the rice and lentils at room temperature, decorated with the crispy onions.

Right: Rice and Lentils with Crispy Onions

Moroccan Couscous

Serves 4–6

This is the basic Moroccan Couscous recipe which Claudia Roden made for us at the school, and around which you can improvise. Claudia explained: "This dish can be varied indefinitely. Fry the meat and chopped onions in oil on top before adding the other ingredients, if you like. Add baby onions, sliced green peppers, and a slice of pumpkin, small shredded white cabbage, a few pitted dates, or, as Algerians sometimes do, pole beans and peas. Color the stew with tomato paste and paprika, and make it fiery with cayenne or harissa. Or add a little cinnamon and rose water to the butter when you melt it into the couscous."

In Morocco, the untreated couscous would be steamed over the stove. I've always had a huge complex about my couscous – I simply can't get it anything like as light and fluffy gorgeous as the couscous I've seen in Morocco. Claudia cheered me up by explaining that it is virtually impossible to get untreated couscous over here and that even in Morocco, many people settle for the pre-cooked couscous. I have to tell you, though, its not a patch on the real thing... I suppose I will just have to go to Morocco to taste at source.

2 lbs. (900g) lean stewing lamb or 1 lb. (450g) lamb and 1/2 lb. (225g) each beef and chicken
2 onions, chopped
a heaped 1/4 cup chickpeas, soaked overnight
2 turnips, quartered
2 large carrots, sliced
2 1/2 tablespoons olive oil
salt and freshly ground black pepper

1/4 teaspoon ground ginger (optional)
1/4 teaspoon saffron (optional)
1/4–1/3 cup raisins
3 zucchini, sliced, or 1/2 marrow, cut in pieces
3/4 cup fresh shelled or frozen fava beans
2 tomatoes
a bunch of parsley, finely chopped
a bunch of cilantro, finely chopped
cayenne or chile pepper
1 teaspoon paprika
2 2/3 cups couscous (see below)

Put the meat, chicken if using, onions, chickpeas, turnips, and carrots – all the ingredients that require longer cooking – in the bottom part of the pan. Cover with water, add the oil, pepper, ginger, and saffron if you like, bring to a boil and simmer for about one hour. Add salt only when the chickpeas have softened. Add raisins, zucchini or marrow, fava beans, tomatoes, parsley, and cilantro to the simmering stew. Cook for a further 1/2 hour. Take a good cupful of sauce from the stew and stir in cayenne or chile pepper, and a little paprika – enough to make it very fiery.

Pile the couscous on to a large dish, preferably wooden or earthenware. Arrange the meat and vegetables over the couscous and pour the broth over it. Pass the hot, peppery sauce around separately in a little bowl. Alternatively, serve the couscous, the meat and vegetables, the broth, and the peppery sauce in separate bowls.

How to Cook Couscous

The commercial varieties of couscous we get here are pre-cooked and instant. You do not need to steam it in the traditional way, in fact it's no advantage to do so. Once the grain has absorbed an equal volume of water, all you need to do is heat it through. Claudia Roden's advice is:

For 6 people, put 3 cups of medium-ground couscous in a Pyrex or pottery bowl. Add 3 cups of warm salted water (with 1/2–1 teaspoon salt added) gradually, stirring so that it gets absorbed evenly. After about 10 minutes, when the grain has become a little plump and tender, add 1/4 cup of sunflower oil and rub the grain between your hands to air it and break up any lumps. Heat it through in the oven, covered with foil. A small quantity for 2 or 3 can be heated in a saucepan, stirring so as not to burn the bottom, or in the microwave. Before serving, break up any lumps very thoroughly and work in 2 1/2 tablespoons of butter or sunflower oil.

Israeli Couscous with Shiitake Mushrooms and Parmesan Cheese

Serves 6

Israeli couscous is made from the same toasted semolina as regular couscous but comes in little round balls about the size of whole peppercorns.

2 1/2 tablespoons olive oil
1 medium onion, chopped
2 shallots, chopped
1 garlic clove, crushed
4 ounces (110g) shiitake mushrooms or white mushrooms, sliced (about 1 heaped cup)
2 2/3 cups Israeli couscous
1/2 cup dry white wine
1 quart (960ml) homemade Chicken or Vegetable stock (see page 36)
finely grated unwaxed lemon zest
3–4 firm ripe tomatoes, seeded and diced or 2 roast red peppers, peeled, seeded and cut into strips
2 1/2 tablespoons chives, chopped
1 generous tablespoon parsley
1 cup freshly grated Parmesan cheese

Topping
sautéed fresh shiitake or ordinary mushrooms
roast scallions (see page 187)
a few drops of truffle oil (optional)

Garnish
sprigs of flat-leaf parsley

Heat the oil in a medium saucepan, add the onion, shallots, garlic, and mushrooms, and sauté until lightly colored. Add the couscous and cook for 1 minute. Add the wine and 1 cup of stock, and cook, stirring occasionally until the liquid is absorbed. Add the remaining stock by the ladle and continue to cook and stir occasionally until the stock is almost absorbed (about 10 minutes). Stir in the lemon zest, tomatoes or roast peppers, herbs and cheese, and serve immediately in warm bowls, topped with sautéed mushrooms and grilled scallions. If you have a bottle of truffle oil, drizzle some over the top for extra zizz. Garnish with some sprigs of flat-leaf parsley on top.

Couscous with Vegetables and Coriander

Serves 8

1 1/3–2 cups couscous
3/4 cup olive oil
12 ounces (350g) onions, chopped (about 2 1/2–3 cups)
12 ounces (350g) carrots, cut into 1/4-inch (5-mm) dice
2 garlic cloves, mashed
1/2 –1 tablespoon coriander seeds, freshly ground
1 lb. (450g) very ripe tomatoes, peeled and chopped or 1 x 14-ounce (400-g) can tomatoes including the juice
1–2 fresh chiles, cut into thin slices
12 ounces (350g) zucchini, sliced into 1/4-inch (5-mm) rounds
salt and freshly ground pepper
2/3 cup Vegetable Stock (see page 36) or water
1–1 1/2 cups peas
2 1/2 tablespoons parsley, freshly chopped
4–5 tablespoons fresh cilantro leaves
1/3 cup black olives (optional)

Preheat the oven to 350°F (180°C). Measure the volume of couscous and soak in an equal volume of warm water for about 15 minutes, or until all the water has been absorbed.

Heat 1/4 cup of olive oil in a saucepan, add the onions, carrots, garlic, and coriander, cover, and sweat over a gentle heat until soft but not colored. Add the tomatoes and the chiles, season with salt and freshly ground pepper, and cook, uncovered, for a further 10–15 minutes. Meanwhile toss the zucchini in 2 tablespoons of olive oil, add to the vegetable mixture, and remove from the heat.

Season the couscous with salt and pepper and stir in about 1/4 cup of olive oil or 1/2 stick (1/4 cup) of melted butter. Put into an ovenproof dish and cover with foil and a tight fitting lid. Put into the oven for about 20 minutes or until heated through. Cook the peas in about 2/3 cup of boiling salted water or vegetable stock and add both peas and liquid to the vegetables, along with a tablespoon of parsley. Taste and correct seasoning. Taste the vegetables and add a tablespoon of fresh cilantro.

Spread the couscous on a hot serving dish and make a well in the center. Add 2 tablespoons of fresh cilantro to the hot vegetables and fill into the center. Sprinkle with the remainder of the cilantro, parsley, and the olives. Serve immediately.

Couscous Salad with Capers, Olives, Pine Nuts, and Currants

Serves 6–8

2 cups water
1/3 cup currants or raisins
3/4 teaspoon salt
1/4 cup plus 1 tablespoon extra-virgin olive oil
1 1/2 cups couscous
2 large garlic cloves, minced
1 medium onion, finely chopped (about 1/2 cup)
2 1/2 tablespoons red wine vinegar
1/2 cup green olives, drained and sliced thinly
2 1/2 tablespoons capers, drained
3/4 cup pine nuts, toasted lightly
2 1/2 tablespoons flat-leaf parsley, finely chopped
2 1/2 tablespoons mint, finely chopped
salt and freshly ground pepper

Put the water with the currants or raisins, salt, and 1 tablespoon of oil into a saucepan and bring to a boil. Stir in the couscous, cover, and let stand, off the heat, for 5 minutes. Fluff up the couscous with a fork and transfer to a bowl.

Sweat the onion and garlic in 2 tablespoons of olive oil until soft and golden. Stir the onion mixture into couscous with the vinegar, olives, capers, toasted pine nuts, parsley, mint, and the remaining oil. Season with salt and pepper to taste.

This salad may be made a day ahead. Cover and refrigerate but let it return to room temperature before serving.

Master Recipe

Navy or Flageolet Beans with Tomato and Rosemary

Serves 4–6

Serve as an accompaniment to roast lamb.

1 1/4 cups dried navy beans or flageolet beans
bouquet garni
1 carrot, chopped
1 onion, chopped
1/4 cup olive oil
6 ounces (175g) onions, chopped (about 1 1/2 cups)
4 large garlic cloves, crushed
1 x 14-ounce (400-g) can tomatoes
1 large sprig rosemary, chopped
salt, freshly ground pepper, and sugar

Soak the beans overnight in plenty of cold water. Next day, drain the beans, put them in a large saucepan, and cover with fresh cold water. Add the bouquet garni, carrot, and onion, bring to a boil over high heat, cover, and simmer until the beans are soft but not mushy – anything from 30–60 minutes. Just before the end of cooking, add 1 teaspoon salt. Remove the bouquet garni and vegetables and discard.

Meanwhile, heat the oil in a wide saucepan and sweat the onions gently until soft but not colored; add the garlic and cook for 1–2 minutes. Add the tomatoes and their juice, the beans, and rosemary. Simmer for 10–15 minutes, using some of the bean liquid if necessary, and season well.

Note: The mixture should be juicy but not swimming in liquid.

Variations

Gratin of Navy Beans with Tomato and Rosemary

Follow the Master Recipe, and put the mixture into a shallow ovenproof dish. Scatter a mixture of Buttered Crumbs (see page 248) and grated cheese over the top and put into a hot oven 450°F (230°C) or flash under a broiler until crisp and golden on top.

Bean Stew with Spicy Sausage

Follow the Master Recipe, but add 2 sliced Kabannosi or chorizo sausages to the stew with the beans. Then proceed as before.

Soaking and Cooking Legumes

Soak legumes overnight in plenty of cold water. Next day, drain the legumes and cover with fresh water. Add a carrot, an onion, and a bouquet garni. Cover and cook for ½–¾ hour or until the legumes are soft but not mushy. Add salt. Drain, and discard the vegetables and bouquet garni. Save the cooking water for vegetable stock.

Below: Cassoulet (French Bean Stew)

Cassoulet (French Bean Stew)

Serves 8

I am one of Elizabeth David's greatest fans, but it took me years to gather up the courage to try cassoulet after I had read and reread the descriptions of different types in French Provincial Cooking**. My mouth watered – I longed to try this most comforting of winter stews – but I felt I would never manage to get all those ingredients together at one time. Eventually I realized that it's really just a bean stew. At its most basic it can consist simply of sausage and beans and everything else is a bonus. It also reheats very well and, unless it's my imagination, it gets better and better. Use Polish sausage, Italian Zampone or Cotechino, or Saucisson de Toulouse.**

3²/₃ cups navy beans
1 carrot
1 onion studded with 2 cloves
2 x bouquet garni
1/2 lb. (225g) bacon or pickled pork
1/4 cup olive oil
3 onions, sliced
5 garlic cloves, crushed
6–8 very ripe tomatoes, peeled and sliced
salt and freshly ground pepper
5 cups homemade Chicken Stock (see page 36)
4 legs of confit de canard (duck) or 2 pieces of confit d'oie (goose) or 4 fresh duck legs
1 lb. (450g) shoulder of lamb, cut into 4 thick chops
3/4–1 lb. (350–450g) coarse pork sausages
1 1/4 cups fresh breadcrumbs

Garnish
parsley, chopped

Preheat the oven to 300°F (150°C).

Soak the beans overnight in plenty of cold water. Next day cover with fresh water, add the carrot, the clove-studded onion, and one of the bouquet garni. Cover and cook for 1/2–3/4 hour or until the beans are three-quarters cooked. Drain and discard the vegetables and bouquet garni.

Meanwhile, cut the bacon into 1-inch (2.5-cm) squares. Heat the olive oil in a flameproof casserole dish or other flameproof and ovenproof pot, add the bacon and fry until beginning to turn golden, add the onions, garlic, tomatoes, salt, pepper, and a new bouquet garni. Cook for 1–2 minutes, add the stock, and let simmer for 15 minutes.

Discard the bouquet garni, then add the duck or goose confit, lamb, sausage, and finally, put the beans on top. Bring the cassoulet to a boil, then spread a layer of breadcrumbs over the top. Put the pot into the slow oven, and continue to cook for 1–1 1/2 hours or so, until the beans and meat are fully cooked. By this time a crust will have formed and the beans will have absorbed most of the stock; if they haven't, remove the lid from the pot and cook uncovered for a further 15 minutes or so.

Sprinkle with chopped parsley and serve from the casserole dish (if you have cooked it in an earthenware pot, all the better). Serve with a good green salad (see page 225).

Master Recipe

Mediterranean Bean Stew

This is a delicious rustic bean stew, cheap to make yet wonderfully filling and nutritious, and a particularly good dish for vegetarians. Do not add the salt to the beans until near the end of the cooking time, otherwise they seem to harden.

2 cups dried navy or kidney beans or black-eyed peas, or a mixture of all 3 – but cook separately as they all cook at different rates
1–3 carrots
1–3 onions
1–3 bouquet garni
2 1/2 tablespoons virgin olive oil

8 ounces (225g) onions, sliced (about 2 cups)
1 chile, seeded and diced (optional)
1 large red pepper, cored, seeded, and sliced
1 large green pepper, cored, seeded, and sliced
2 garlic cloves, crushed
1 x 14-ounce (400-g) can of tomatoes, or 1 lb. (450g) peeled, very ripe tomatoes, chopped
2 1/2 tablespoons tomato paste
1 generous tablespoon marjoram, thyme, or basil, chopped
1 bouquet garni (see page 140)
salt, freshly ground pepper, and sugar
1/3 cup black olives
2 1/2 tablespoons parsley, chopped

Prepare and cook the beans separately (see page 132). When tender but not mushy, strain and reserve 1 1/4 cups of the liquid and discard the vegetables and bouquet garni.

Heat the oil in a flameproof casserole dish or other flameproof and ovenproof pot, and sweat the onions and chile on a low heat for about 5 minutes. Add the peppers and garlic, cover, and continue to sweat gently for 10 minutes. Stir in the tomatoes along with their juice, tomato paste, herbs, beans, bouquet garni, reserved cooking liquid, salt, pepper, and a pinch of sugar. Cover and simmer for about 20 minutes, or until the beans and peppers are cooked.

Five minutes before the end of cooking time, add the olives and freshly chopped parsley. Remove the bouquet garni, taste, and correct the seasoning.

Note: 1 lb. (450g) bacon, blanched and cut into 1/2-inch (1-cm) cubes may be added. Brown the cubes in olive oil before adding the peppers. If this bean stew is being eaten without meat, then eat rice in the same meal to get maximum food value from the beans.

Variation

Mediterranean Bean and Chorizo Stew

Follow the Master Recipe, but add 4 ounces (110g) sliced chorizo with the beans and proceed as above.

Black Bean, Avocado, Tomato, and Corn Salad with Chile and Cilantro

Serves 4

Serve either as a course on its own or as an accompaniment to a piece of pan-grilled steak, chicken breast, or fish.

1 cup black beans
1 teaspoon salt

Dressing
3/4 cup extra-virgin olive oil
5–6 tablespoons lime or lemon juice
2 1/2 tablespoons parsley, chopped

4 vine-ripened tomatoes
2 avocados, peeled and diced
1 red onion, sliced into rings
2 chiles, Jalapeño or Serrano, sliced
3/4 cup cooked, fresh or frozen corn or corn niblets
5 tablespoons cilantro, freshly chopped
salt, freshly ground pepper, and sugar

Prepare and cook the beans (see page 132).

To make the dressing: mix the olive oil with the lime or lemon juice and parsley, and season well with salt and pepper. When the beans are fully cooked, drain and toss immediately in half of the dressing.

Cut the tomatoes into quarters and then each quarter in half crosswise. Sprinkle with salt, freshly ground pepper, and sugar. Combine the tomatoes, avocados, red onion, and chile in a bowl, season gently, toss with the corn and the remainder of the dressing in a bowl, add the beans and cilantro. Taste, correct the seasoning, and serve immediately.

Frijoles de Olla

Serves 6–8

Beans cooked simply like this and the Frijoles Refritos that are made from them are virtually a staple in Mexico, served at almost every meal including breakfast. In Mexico, the markets are often divided into two sections, the regular stalls serving all manner of things, and the eating side where people eat simply and cheaply at large tables covered in colorful oil cloth. Hundreds of people eat these beans every day in simple market fondas with some coarse salt, some hot green chiles, and a stack of tortillas, and maybe a few small pieces of creamy cheese melting over them. They keep well and taste even better the next day or the day after.

2 1/2 cups dried black beans or red kidney or pinto beans
1 1/2–2 1/2 tablespoons good quality lard or butter
1 small onion, chopped
1 teaspoon salt, approximately
1–2 sprigs of epazote or Mexican tea – a green herb used in Mexican cooking (optional)

The day before
Cover the beans generously with cold water and soak overnight. Alternatively, if you are in a hurry, bring the beans to a boil, cook for 3–4 minutes, then remove from the heat and set aside for an hour or so.

Either way, drain the beans, cover with fresh water (about 1 1/2 quarts/ 1 1/2 liters), add the lard or butter, and onion, but not the salt. Bring to a boil and simmer gently for 1–2 hours, depending on the beans. About 1/2 hour before the end of the cooking, add the salt and the sprig of epazote, if you have it.

Ensure that the beans are always covered while they cook; top up with boiling water to cover them by about 1/2 inch (1cm). When cooked, the beans should be completely soft and the liquid slightly thickish and soupy.

Frijoles Refritos (Refried Beans)

1/2–3/4 stick (1/4–1/3 cup) best-quality pork lard or butter
1 medium onion, finely chopped
1 1/2 cups Frijoles de Olla (see page 133)

Heat the lard or butter in a heavy frying pan and cook the onion until soft and brown. Increase the heat and add about a third of the beans and their broth to the pan and cook over a high heat, mashing them as you stir. Gradually add in the rest of the beans until you have a thick, coarse purée. Taste, and season if necessary. This process takes less than 10 minutes. The beans are ready when the purée begins to dry out and sizzle at the edges.

Frijoles Refritos keep well and may be reheated many times in a saucepan over a medium heat. They accompany many snacks, including Mexican scrambled eggs.

Borlotti or Cannellini Beans

Serves 8

Serve with slow-roasted or grilled meals.

2 1/2 cups borlotti or cannellini beans
1/4 cup plus 1 tablespoon extra-virgin olive oil
6 cloves garlic, cut in half
1 red chile (optional)
2 very ripe tomatoes
10 sage leaves or 4–6 sprigs of thyme
salt and freshly ground pepper

Cover the beans generously with cold water and let soak overnight.

Next day, discard water. Put the beans into a saucepan. Cover with fresh water and add 5 tablespoons olive oil, the garlic, chile, tomatoes, and sage or thyme. Bring to a boil and skim, and then simmer for 1–1 1/2 hours or until the beans are tender.

Remove the chile, tomatoes, herbs, and garlic. Drain the beans and save the water. Season with salt and freshly ground pepper. Drizzle with best extra-virgin olive oil. Taste, and correct seasoning.

Note: If not using the beans immediately, it's best to leave them sitting in the water until ready to use. Season with salt and pepper.

Tuscan Bean Purée

We sometimes purée the beans coarsely and then drizzle with extra-virgin olive oil or alternatively, purée a ladle full with the cooking liquid and mix that with the remainder of the beans to give a creamy soupy texture. Drizzle with extra-virgin olive oil or chili oil, and decorate with freshly snipped flat-leaf parsley.

Salad of Fresh and Dried Beans

Serves 8

2/3 cup navy beans
2/3 cup red kidney beans
2/3 cup flageolet beans
2/3 cup black-eyed peas
1 lb. (450g) freshly cooked green beans
1/4 cup plus 1 tablespoon well seasoned French dressing (see page 225)
2 1/2 tablespoons chopped parsley
2 1/2 tablespoons chopped fresh cilantro
3/4–1 cup toasted hazelnuts, roughly chopped

Garnish
coarsely chopped fresh cilantro

Prepare and cook the beans (see page 132), remembering to soak the different varieties separately. Drain, and reserve the cooking water for soup. Cook the green beans (see recipe, page 196) and drain them. Toss the beans in well-flavored dressing while still warm. Add the parsley and cilantro and season well. Scatter with hazelnuts and garnish with cilantro.

Chickpeas with Fresh Spices

Serves 8–10

A few little jars of fresh spices are a must for your store cupboard, they add zest and lots of exotic flavor to your food.

3 cups chickpeas, covered and soaked overnight in cold water
2 fresh green chiles
2-inch (5-cm) piece fresh ginger, peeled and roughly chopped
4 garlic cloves
1/4 cup plus 1 tablespoon olive oil
8 ounces (225g) onion, finely chopped (about 2 cups)
1 teaspoon whole cumin seeds, crushed
2 teaspoons whole coriander seeds, crushed
1–2 teaspoons chili powder
8 very ripe tomatoes, peeled and chopped
salt and freshly ground pepper

Garnish
2 1/2 tablespoons cilantro leaves, freshly chopped
1 generous tablespoon fresh mint leaves

Drain the chickpeas, cover with fresh water, and cook until tender; anything from 30–60 minutes depending on the quality. Drain and reserve the cooking liquid.

Meanwhile discard the seeds from the chiles and grind to a paste in a mortar and pestle or food processor, along with the ginger and garlic.

Heat the oil in a heavy frying pan, sweat the onions until soft but not colored, add the chile paste together with the cumin, coriander seeds, and the chili powder. Cook for 1–2 minutes, then add the tomatoes, chickpeas, and a little of the liquid (save the rest for soup), and simmer gently for about 10 minutes until the flavors have mingled. Taste, season with salt and pepper. Sprinkle with the cilantro and mint and serve immediately. This is quite delicious served either hot or cold.

Right: My lovely daughter – Lydia

ICING
SUGAR

Master Recipe
Supplì
Serves 6, makes about 24

I've only recently discovered these delicious little Roman specialities: little crispy balls of rice with a melting center of molten mozzarella (the name comes from supplì al telefono**, because the cheese becomes stringy like the telephone wires). It's worth making twice the basic risotto just to make sure you have enough left over to make** supplì.

1 quantity risotto recipe (see page 138)
1 egg, beaten
salt and freshly ground pepper
1½ cups diced mozzarella cheese
1 cup grated Parmesan cheese
egg wash – 2 eggs beaten with a pinch of salt
dried bread crumbs
olive oil or sunflower oil for frying
arugula leaves

Mix the cold risotto with the egg, taste, and correct seasoning if necessary. Mix the mozzarella with the Parmesan. Take about 1 tablespoon of rice and flatten it on the palm of your hand, put a generous teaspoon of cheese into the center and gather the rice around the filling to shape into a ball or an oval about 2 inches (5cm) long.

The rice should be a thin shell, not more than ½ inch (1cm) thick. Put onto a baking tray lined with wax paper.

When all the supplì have been shaped, dip in beaten egg and then in crisp bread crumbs (see page 318). Just before serving: heat the oil to 375°F (190°C) in a deep fryer.

Cook the supplì a few at a time until crisp and golden. Drain on paper towels. Serve immediately on a bed of arugula leaves.

Variation
Follow the Master Recipe mixing 1 cup diced mozzarella, 4 ounces (110g) prosciutto (about 7 slices) or crumbled crispy bacon, 2 tablespoons of chopped flat-leaf parsley (or half parsley/half chives), and ½–1 finely chopped chile to make the filling.

Sprouting Seeds for Bean Sprouts

Use approximately 2 tablespoons of seeds or 4 tablespoons of legumes (such as alfalfa, mung beans, or soy beans). Put the seeds in a large jar, cover with warm water, and soak for 8 hours. Drain off the liquid, rinse the seeds, and drain again. Now lay the jar on its side. Rinse the sprouts 2–3 times a day and replace the jar on its side. Do not let the sprouts sit too long in water or dry out, or this will spoil the crop. Within 3–4 days the sprouts will have developed completely and will be ready to eat and/or refrigerate.

Keep the sprout jar in a dark place for the first 2–3 days and bring it out in the light on the last day when the chlorophyll develops. This process generally produces nice green sprouts.

Buy legumes and seeds for sprouting from natural food stores and health food stores. We particularly recommend using alfalfa seeds because of their delicate taste. But you can also use mung or soy beans.

Bouquet Garni

A small bunch of fresh herbs used to flavor stews, casseroles, stocks, or soups, usually consisting of parsley stalks, a sprig of thyme, perhaps a bay-leaf, and an outside stalk of celery, tied together with a little string. Remove before serving.

Phad Thai Mae Sawad (Fried Noodles Thai-Style)

Wasinee Beech was born and brought up in Thailand. She moved to Clonakilty in West Cork seven years ago with her family. She teaches our students many wonderful Thai recipes. This is one of them.

2½ tablespoons of cooking oil
10 shallots, thinly sliced
½–1 teaspoon freshly roasted ground chiles
7 ounces (200g) uncooked shrimp (about 2 cups), shell and de-vein, quickly stir fry or deep fry, put aside for later
¼ cup dried shrimp
1 tablespoon chopped dry radish (optional)
¼ cup plus 1 tablespoon palm sugar (jaggery)
2½ tablespoons lemon juice
2½ tablespoons tamarind juice
2½–3½ tablespoons of Thai fish sauce (nam pla), depending on how salty the dry shrimp is
9 ounces (250g) Thai rice noodles, soak until soft (approximately 2 hours), then drain
1–2 eggs (optional)
8 ounces (225g) bean sprouts (3½–4 cups)
4 scallions or 5 Chinese chives, cut into 1-inch (2.5-cm) long pieces
4–5 tablespoons freshly crushed roasted peanuts

Heat the oil in a wok. Add the shallots and stir-fry until they are golden brown. Add the chiles and stir quickly. Stirring all the time, add the dry shrimp, radish, palm sugar, lemon, tamarind juice, and fish sauce. Add the noodles and stir in well. Add the shrimp and mix really well but being careful not to break up the noodles. Add the eggs, toss around gently. Finally add the bean sprouts and scallions. Sprinkle with peanuts. Serve hot.

Tabouleh

Serves 6–12, served as an appetizer or main course
In season: best in summer

This refreshing and highly nutritious Middle Eastern salad is usually served on its own but we also love it with chargrilled lamb or lamb kebabs. We use Mani Greek organic olive oil for this salad.

3/4 cup bulgur (cracked wheat)
1/3 cup extra-virgin olive oil
juice of 2 organic lemons or more if you need it, freshly squeezed
salt and freshly ground pepper
1/2–1 cup freshly chopped parsley
1/2–1 cup freshly chopped mint
2–4 ounces (50–110g) scallions, green and white parts, chopped (about 3/4–1 1/2 cups)

Garnish
small crisp lettuce leaves (romaine or iceberg)
6 very ripe firm tomatoes, (a selection of red and yellow looks great), seeded, diced, and sprinkled with a little salt, pepper, and sugar
2 firm crisp cucumbers, cut into 1/4-inch (5-mm) dice
arugula leaves or flat-leaf parsley
black olives (optional)

Soak the bulgur in cold water for about 30 minutes, drain, and squeeze to remove any excess water. Stir in the olive oil and some of the lemon juice. Season with salt and pepper and set aside to absorb the dressing. Just before serving, mix the herbs with the bulgur, taste, and add more lemon juice if necessary. It should taste fresh and lively.

To serve: arrange on a serving plate surrounded by lettuce leaves and little mounds of well seasoned tomato and cucumber dice. Garnish with arugula or sprigs of flat-leaf parsley. A few black olives wouldn't go amiss either if you enjoy them. Warm pita or Middle Eastern flatbread is the perfect accompaniment.

Right: Tabouleh

Master Recipe
Creamy Polenta

Serves 6–8

2 quarts (1.8 liters) water
2 teaspoons salt
1½ cups coarse polenta flour (cornmeal)
1 stick (½ cup) butter
1½–2 cups freshly grated Parmesan
sea salt or kosher salt, and freshly ground pepper

Put the water into a deep heavy pot and bring to a boil, add salt, then sprinkle the polenta flour in very slowly, letting it slip gradually through your fingers, whisking all the time (this should take 3–4 minutes). Bring to a boil and when it starts to "erupt like a volcano", turn the heat down to the absolute minimum – use a heat diffuser mat if you have one.

Cook for about 40 minutes stirring regularly.* (I use a whisk at the beginning but as soon as the polenta comes to a boil, I change to a flat-bottomed wooden spoon.) The polenta is cooked when it is very thick but not solid, and comes away from the sides of the pot as you stir.

As soon as the polenta is cooked, stir in the butter, Parmesan, and lots of pepper. Taste, and add a little more sea salt if necessary. It should be soft and flowing; if it is a little too stiff, add a little boiling water.

*If you stir constantly on a slightly higher heat, the cooking time can be reduced to about 20 minutes but it is more digestible if cooked more slowly over a longer period.

Variations
Polenta with Fresh Herbs

Follow the Master Recipe, but add 2–4 tablespoons of freshly chopped herbs, e.g., parsley, chives, thyme leaves, sage, rosemary, etc. into the polenta when it is cooked.

Left: Chargrilled Polenta with Roasted Red and Yellow Peppers, Arugula Leaves, and Olives

Chargrilled Polenta

Polenta can be served the moment it's ready or it can be turned into a wet dish and allowed to get cold. It can then be sliced and chargrilled, pan-grilled, toasted, or fried, and served with all sorts of toppings. It can even be cut into thin slices and layered with a sauce, just like lasagne.

Follow the Master Recipe but omit the butter and Parmesan cheese. Pour the cooked polenta into a wet dish (I use a lasagne dish: 9 x 7 x 2 inches (23 x 18 x 5cm) which is just perfect for this quantity, but you could use a jelly roll pan and cut it into squares or diamonds when it is cold). Let it get completely cold. Polenta can be stored like this, covered in the fridge, for several days. It makes the most delicious snack or you can make a sophisticated appetizer for a dinner party in just a few minutes.

To serve: cut into slices ½–¾ inch (1–2cm) thick, and chargrill, pan-grill, or fry. Put it directly on to the bars of the grill on the highest heat without oil, and cook until it is hot through and grill marked on each side. If the polenta is to be sautéed, use a little olive oil or butter. Serve the slices of grilled polenta as an accompaniment to meat or fish dishes. There are countless other possibilities. Just use your imagination and a little restraint.

Chargrilled Polenta with Caramelized Onions and Pesto

Follow the Chargrilled Polenta recipe, then spread a slice of grilled polenta with Warm Caramelized Onions (see page 188) and top with a teaspoonful of Pesto (see page 589).

Chargrilled Polenta with Arugula and Olives or Roasted Red and Yellow Peppers

Follow the Chargrilled Polenta recipe, arranging some fresh arugula leaves on the grilled polenta, and topping with olive paste (see olive stuffing recipe) and/or roasted red and yellow peppers (see page 80). A slice or two of prosciutto is also delicious.

Chargrilled Polenta with Tomato Fondue and Pesto

Follow the Chargrilled Polenta recipe, spreading 1 tablespoon of hot Tomato Fondue (see page 188) on the grilled polenta and topping with a teaspoonful of pesto.

Chargrilled Polenta with Gorgonzola, Cashel Blue, or Goat Cheese

Follow the Chargrilled Polenta recipe, spreading the hot grilled polenta with Gorgonzola, Cashel Blue, or goat cheese and serve immediately.

pasta and noodles

pasta and noodles

My first tentative attempt at homemade pasta was in 1970. I had just come across a recipe in the American food and travel magazine, *Gourmet*, and was so excited, I couldn't wait to try it. Soon the kitchen was festooned with sheets of pasta drying on the front of the Aga. It was so delicious that we were immediately hooked.

Homemade Pasta

Making homemade pasta is surprisingly easy, but the rolling is unquestionably laborious. It's definitely worth considering investing in a pasta machine – even the most basic ones will simplify the process, and a motorized model makes all the difference between fun and actual hard work. Pasta machines with a zillion attachments that promise to make lots of different shapes are rarely worth the money. The flour is different in every country so the results from these machines often disappoint. Crafting your own shapes can be fun, once you've rolled out some sheets of pasta. Then all you have to do is decide what you fancy – from simple noodles to lasagne or pappardelle, plump ravioli, cappelletti or tortellini...

Dried Pasta

Tender homemade pasta is one of life's little luxuries, but it's certainly not the only option. If you don't feel you have the time or the inclination to make your own, don't be disheartened. Many delis and speciality food stores produce a variety of homemade pasta, so you can cheat a little. There's also an ever-increasing range of dried pasta which is perfectly acceptable. The Italians have never been sniffy about dried pasta. They believe that while homemade pasta is best for some dishes, dried is better for others. Although it is faster to cook fresh pasta, no pasta takes very long. Good dried pasta is better than fresh, poor quality pasta; however, do try to buy brands made to Italian specifications.

In the early 1980s, I longed to learn more about Italian food, so I went to Marcella Hazan's classes in Bologna. I wanted to learn at source, as I've always believed that if you want to learn the cuisine of a particular country, you need to go there and immerse yourself in the culture, visit its markets, and taste the ingredients. You can't begin to reproduce the flavors, or even think of teaching it to others, before you know what the food is meant to taste like.

"Pasta" is an Italian word that means "paste". Wheat grows in northern Italy, so in Tuscany, pasta is made with wheat flour, eggs, and no salt. Further south it is made with durum semolina. Pasta is usually served as a first course in Italy, so be careful not to over-indulge, or you won't have room for the main course.

Cooking and Serving

Pasta is the ultimate fast food. Low in fat and high in carbohydrates, it's certainly much better for you than running down to the local burger bar, and it can be prepared in less time than it would take for the speediest of take-out meals to arrive. Everyone should have a few boxes of pasta stashed in their store cupboard. Combined with even the simplest of tomato sauces, you can whip up a delicious little supper in a few minutes. Pasta's brilliant for casual entertaining – there's nothing quite like it for feeding a crowd of friends in the minimum of time with little fuss and virtually no washing up. Most of the dishes in this chapter are quick and easy to make.

Of course, some pasta recipes will take a little more time to prepare (ragu sauce can take several hours to cook down to a luscious, juicy taste sensation), but they're certainly worth it for a special treat. Remember that with dishes like lasagne, although it's great to stick to the traditional recipe, it should be viewed as a formula. Experiment with different combinations of flavors – fish or vegetable lasagnes are equally delicious, made all the nicer by the fact that they're a little unusual. The same applies to stuffed pastas like raviolli, capaletti, and tortellini. Once you've made the classic version once or twice, you can move on to experiment and have fun with all sorts of fillings.

There are hundreds of different pasta shapes to choose from, so be sure to choose a shape and sauce that complement each other. As a general rule, serve light, thin sauces with delicate pastas (like capellini or spaghetti), and heavier sauces with thicker shapes (like penne). Pasta shapes with holes or ridges, like Rigatoni, are perfect for chunky sauces.

Cooking Pasta

Pasta, whether fresh or dried, needs to be cooked in a large pot of salted boiling water.

If cooking ahead, take it off the heat while it still has a slight bite ("al dente"). Drain, but not too meticulously. Toss immediately with olive oil. This, combined with the few remaining tablespoons of cooking water, will prevent the pasta from sticking together. Serve immediately, or reheat the pasta later in the sauce, and serve. Leftover pasta can be reheated. The Italians would be appalled but one can, in fact, fry off cooked pasta and add it to an omelette. Cooked noodles are yummy fried like a cake in a frying pan until they are crispy on the bottom.

Freshly grated Parmesan, though wonderful, is hardly essential with every pasta dish. In Italy, cheese is never served with shellfish pasta.

For best flavor in **pasta salads** it's crucial to toss the freshly cooked pasta in a well-flavored dressing while still warm.

Storage and Freezing

Dry, uncooked pasta can be stored for a year or two if kept in a cool, dry place in a sealed package or covered container. Fresh pasta will keep for 3–4 days if refrigerated, and can be frozen for up to a month.

In an ideal world, it should not be necessary to refrigerate pasta, but if needs be, cooked pasta can be refrigerated in an airtight container for 2–3 days. Add a little olive oil to prevent the pasta from sticking.

Pasta dishes like lasagne, canelloni, and ravioli freeze well. For the best results, prepare the recipe and freeze it before baking. Defrost, and bake when needed.

Nutrition

Pasta is high in fiber, low in fat, and is sodium- and cholesterol-free. It is full of complex carbohydrates which give a slow and steady release of energy. Most bought pasta is now enriched with folic acid (which helps to prevent some birth defects and may protect against heart disease and some types of cancer), iron, thiamin, riboflavin, and niacin.

Celiacs, who have a gluten intolerance (the protein found in wheat, rye, and barley) and who, therefore, need to maintain a gluten-free diet, need not avoid pasta. Although the majority of pasta is made from durum wheat flour or semolina, non-wheat options do exist. Alternatives include rice, corn, soy, and buckwheat pasta, and noodles made from peas, lentils, and mung beans. Rice and soy pasta is wheat- and gluten-free, and is one of the most complete protein foods.

Unrefined wholewheat pasta provides the same quantity of energy as processed white pasta but contains more fiber and much more magnesium.

Noodles

Asian noodles are becoming increasingly popular. Many of them are sold dried, and they are made from four different types of flour: wheat flour (Japanese somen, udon, and Chinese wheat flour noodles – including flavored noodles and egg noodles), rice flour (vermicelli), mung-bean flour (cellophane noodles), and buckwheat flour (Japanese soba).

Cellophane noodles have little or no taste and absorb the flavors of the ingredients they are cooked with. They are prized for their texture. **Chinese wheat flour noodles** are the oldest form of noodles. They vary in thickness and may be round or flat. The thinnest are used in light soups, whereas the thicker varieties stand up to heartier soups and casseroles. **Vermicelli** are thin and delicate noodles used in soups, salads, and stir-fries. The dried noodles are also deep-fried and used as "nests" for stir-fried foods. **Soba noodles** have a nutty flavor and are rich in protein and fiber. They are most commonly served cold with a dipping sauce, or hot in soups. Soba may also be flavored with green tea, lemon zest, or black sesame seeds. **Somen** are the most delicate Japanese noodles. Like soba, they are served cold with a dipping sauce, but they also make a light and delicate garnish for hot soups. **Udon** are fat, white, slippery noodles, used for hearty soups and casseroles.

Master Recipe
Homemade Pasta

Makes 1 lb., 5 oz. (600g)

In Tuscany pasta is made just with flour and eggs – no water and usually no salt.

3½ cups all-purpose white flour
3–4 eggs
1 teaspoon salt (optional)

Sift the flour into a bowl and add the salt, if using. Whisk the eggs together, make a well in the center of the flour, and add in most of the egg. Mix into a dough with your hand, adding the remainder of the egg only if you need it. If it is much too wet it is very difficult to get it right; the pasta should just come together but shouldn't stick to your hand – if it does add a little more flour.

Knead for a few minutes until smooth and then put on a plate covered with an upturned bowl for 1 hour to relax. Divide the dough in half and roll out one piece at a time as thinly as possible, keeping the other piece covered. You ought to be able to read the print on a matchbox through the pasta. A long thin rolling pin is a great advantage but you can manage perfectly well with an ordinary domestic rolling pin.

Pasta can be flavored and colored in all sorts of ways. Add anything from tomato paste for orange pasta to squid ink for black designer pasta (the latter is not worth the trouble, I assure you!).

Variations
Pasta Verde

2 cups all-purpose white flour
2 eggs
5 ounces (150g) cooked spinach – about ¾ cup (8 ounces/225g raw spinach, stalks removed, should yield the cooked amount)

Use a potato masher to squeeze every single drop of water out of the spinach, chop well or purée, add the spinach to the flour with the eggs and continue as for basic pasta dough. (you may not need all the egg). Rest for just 10 minutes and then roll out and proceed as in Master Recipe.

Pasta with Fresh Herbs

Mix ¼ cup finely chopped fresh herbs (parsley, chives, thyme, marjoram, or a mixture) with the flour, and continue as in the Master Recipe

Tomato Pasta

Add 2½ tablespoons of tomato paste with most of the beaten eggs and continue as in the Master Recipe.

Black Pepper Pasta

Add 2½ tablespoons of freshly ground black pepper to the flour and proceed as above.

How to cook pasta

Fresh pasta cooks very quickly indeed. It should take only 1–2 minutes to be perfectly cooked but still have bite – "al dente", as the Italians say.

For dried pasta, be guided by the instructions on the package but start to test about 2–3 minutes before the suggested time.

Choose a large deep pot; two handles are an advantage for ease of lifting. To cook 1 lb., 2oz. (500g) pasta, use 2½ tablespoons of kosher salt or sea salt to 5 quarts (4.8 liters) of water. Bring the water to a boil before adding the salt. Tip the pasta in all at once and stir well to ensure the strands are separate, then cover the pan just long enough to bring the water back to a boil. Cook, uncovered, until "al dente".

Drain the pasta as soon as it is cooked. Don't overdrain. Fresh pasta, and all long pasta, should still be still wet and slippery: toss the sauce in immediately. Pasta shapes need to be thoroughly drained, otherwise the water they contain may dilute the sauce too much. It is a good idea to keep aside a few tablespoons of the pasta water to adjust the consistency of the sauce.

Tomato, Mint, and Caper Sauce

Serves 4: sufficient for 1 lb. (450g) fettucini, spaghetti, or penne.

2½ cups prepared Tomato Fondue (see page 188)
2 garlic cloves, crushed
2½ tablespoons capers, roughly chopped
1½–2½ tablespoons freshly chopped mint
½–1 cup freshly grated Parmesan

While the pasta is cooking, heat the Tomato Fondue, add the garlic, capers, and mint, and simmer for 4–5 minutes. Drain the pasta, toss with the sauce, add a little Parmesan, and serve immediately with the rest of the pasta.

Variation

Chorizo or Kabanossi sausage can be substituted for capers.

Gorgonzola Sauce

Serves 4 as a main course
Sufficient for 1 lb. (450g) fettucini, spaghetti, or penne

Flowerets of cooked broccoli (about 4 cups) are delicious added to this dish.

1 tablespoon butter
7 ounces (200g) Gorgonzola (Cashel Blue would also be good)
a scant cup cream or ½ cup cream and ⅓ cup milk
freshly ground pepper
freshly grated nutmeg

While the pasta is cooking, melt the butter in a little saucepan, add the crumbled cheese, and cream or the cream and milk. Stir over a low heat until smooth and creamy, season with freshly ground pepper and a little nutmeg. Toss with the cooked pasta and serve immediately.

Tapenade Cream Sauce

Mix Tapenade (see page 588) with thick rich cream – about equal quantities. Toss with freshly cooked pasta and lots of chopped parsley.

Roast Red Pepper Sauce

Makes sufficient for 1 lb. (450g) of pasta

4 red peppers
1 cup freshly grated Parmesan
salt and freshly ground pepper
1 teaspoon balsamic vinegar
⅓ cup ground almonds
½ garlic clove, crushed
¼–½ teaspoon lemon zest

Preheat the oven to 400°F (200°C). Rub a little oil onto the skins of the peppers, and roast for about 18 minutes or until the skin is wrinkly and the peppers are slightly soft. Put into a bowl, cover with plastic wrap or a lint-free towel for about 5 minutes. Then peel and seed but do not wash.

Whizz the peeled peppers, Parmesan, salt, pepper, almonds, garlic, lemon zest, and balsamic vinegar in a food processor. Taste and correct seasoning. The sauce can be stored in a fridge under a film of oil. To serve: toss freshly cooked pasta in sauce, serve with plenty of basil and shavings of Parmesan.

Pasta with Chanterelles, Tapenade, and Flat-leaf Parsley

Serves 4–6

8 ounces (225g) penne, conchiglie, or farfalle (about 3 cups)
½–1 lb. (225–450g) fresh chanterelles
2 tablespoons butter
salt and freshly ground pepper
½ cup cream
2½–3½ tablespoons Tapenade (see page 588)
2 generous tablespoons freshly chopped flat-leaf parsley

Cook the pasta until "al dente". Meanwhile, quickly but gently wash the chanterelles under cold running water. Trim the base of the stalks and discard. Slice the chanterelles thickly.

Melt the butter in a frying pan on a high heat. When it foams, add the chanterelles. Season with salt and pepper. Cook on a high heat, letting the juices exude at first and then cook until the chanterelles re-absorb them. Add the cream and bubble for a minute or two. Stir in the Tapenade. Strain the pasta and drain well, put back into the saucepan and add the sauce. Sprinkle with parsley, toss gently, then put into a hot bowl and serve immediately.

How to make long pasta

Let the rolled out pasta dry for about 30 minutes, or until just dry to the touch. Roll up from one end like a jelly roll and slice with a chopping knife into whatever thickness you need (see below). You can use the rolling pin as a guide for your knife. Open out and let it run through your fingers to separate the strands. Use immediately or let dry on a lightly floured tray.

Tagliatelle or Noodles:	¼ inch (5mm) wide
Fettuccine:	⅛ inch (3mm) wide
Pappardelle:	⅝ inch (1.5cm) wide – cut with a pasta wheel

Penne with Tomatoes, Spicy Sausage, and Cream

Serves 6

This makes a tasty Autumn or Winter supper or lunch dish, but you can serve it at any time of year.

1 lb. (450g) penne
2 tablespoons butter
1 teaspoon finely chopped rosemary
1½ lbs. (700g) fresh ripe tomatoes, peeled, seeded and cut into ½-inch (1-cm) dice or 1½ x 14-ounce (400-g) cans tomatoes, chopped
salt, freshly ground pepper, and sugar
6–8 ounces (175–225g) Chorizo or Kabanossi sausage
pinch of crushed chiles
½–¾ cup cream
2 generous tablespoons flat-leaf parsley, finely chopped
a heaped ¼ cup freshly grated Parmesan
extra flat-leaf parsley, snipped

Tip: Although freshly grated Parmesan is wonderful with every type of pasta, in Italy cheese is never served with shellfish pasta.

Melt the butter in a large frying pan, add the chopped rosemary and diced tomatoes.

Season with salt, freshly ground pepper, and sugar. Cook until the tomatoes have just begun to soften into a sauce, which takes about 5 minutes.

Slice the sausage into ¼-inch (5-mm) rounds, add to the pan with the crushed chiles, season lightly with salt (not too much as the sausage may be somewhat salty). Add the cream and chopped parsley, let them bubble for 3–4 minutes, stirring frequently until the cream has reduced by about half. Remove the pan from the heat and set aside. Cook the pasta until it is "al dente", drain, and toss with the sauce, add the grated Parmesan. Toss again, check the seasoning. Sprinkle with the snipped flat-leaf parsley, and serve at once.

Master Recipe
Spaghetti with Mussels

Serves 6

1 lb. (450g) spaghetti
6 lbs. (2.6kg) cleaned mussels (weight in shells)
¼ cup plus 1 tablespoon olive oil
3 large garlic cloves, finely chopped
1 red chile, chopped, or 1 teaspoon chili flakes
½ cup dry white wine
2 lbs. (900g) very ripe tomatoes, peeled, seeded and chopped
2 generous tablespoons freshly chopped marjoram, oregano, or basil leaves
salt and freshly ground pepper
pinch of sugar if necessary

2½ tablespoons freshly chopped flat-leaf parsley
extra-virgin olive oil

Heat 2 tablespoons of the olive oil in a wide frying pan, add the washed mussels. Cover and cook for a few minutes or until just opened. Scoop out the mussels onto a tray to cool. Strain the liquid and return to the pan to reduce by half. When the mussels are cool, remove from the shells (discard the beard and shells) and add the mussels to the concentrated liquid.

Heat the remaining olive oil in another pan, add the garlic and chile and cook for a couple of minutes. Add the wine and cook to reduce by half. Then add the tomatoes, season with salt, freshly ground pepper, and a pinch of sugar. Add the marjoram (or oregano or basil) and cook for 10–15 minutes or until the sauce is reduced. Add mussels and the cooking liquid.

Cook the pasta until almost "al dente". Drain. Add the pasta to the bubbling sauce, continue to cook for a couple of minutes. Serve on hot plates, sprinkled with chopped parsley and drizzled with extra-virgin olive oil.

Variations

Spaghetti with Clams

Substitute clams for mussels in the Master Recipe. The tomatoes may also be omitted and the amount of chile increased. Serve with wedges of lemon.

Spaghetti with Mussels and Zucchini

Add 1 lb. (450g) sliced zucchini, softened in olive oil, to the Master Recipe.

Spaghetti with Squid

Substitute 4 medium squid (about 1¼–1½ lbs. / 600–700g, after cleaning) for the mussels. Slice the body and wings into ½-inch (1-cm) strips, separate the tentacles. Be careful not to overcook the squid.

Spaghetti with Chili Flakes, Shrimp, and Flat-leaf Parsley

Serves 4

½–1 lb. (225–450g) spaghetti
2 fleshy red peppers
1 garlic clove

1/4 cup extra-virgin olive oil
8 ounces (225g) cooked peeled shrimp
salt and freshly ground pepper
red pepper flakes (optional)
3/4 cup cream
2–4 tablespoons chopped flat-leaf parsley

Quarter the peppers, remove the seeds, and cut into dice.

Heat the olive oil in a frying pan, add the garlic and peppers, season with salt and freshly ground pepper, and cover and sweat on a gentle heat until tender but not colored.

Cook the pasta; when it is almost "al dente" add the shrimp to the pepper, toss around for a minute of two to heat through, add the cream and parsley. Let it bubble up and taste for seasoning. As soon as the pasta is "al dente", drain well, add to the pan, and toss in the sauce over the heat until well coated. Turn into a hot pasta dish, sprinkle with chopped parsley, and serve immediately on hot plates.

Variation

Chunks of tuna or salmon may be substituted for shrimp in this recipe. Crispy bacon, Kabanossi or Chorizo sausage is also good.

What pasta?

Spaghetti – thin strands
Spaghettini – thinner strands
Tagliatelle – medium egg noodles
Fettuccini – plain egg noodles
Pappardelle – broad egg noodles
Bucatini – thick hollow strands
Macaroni – thicker hollow strands
Penne – pasta cut diagonally into quills, smooth or ridged
Cannelloni – thick tubes
Rigatoni – large ridged tubes
Orecchiette – little ears, medium saucer-shaped shells
Conchiglie – little shells
Gnocchetti – ridged shell-shaped pasta

Below: Spaghetti with Chili Flakes, Shrimp, and Flat-leaf Parsley

Pasta Portion Size

Depends on appetite! As a rough guideline we use:

Dry pasta
2½ ounces (60g) for an appetizer
4 ounces (110g) for a main course

Fresh pasta
4 ounces (110g) for an appetizer
5 ounces (150g) for a main course

Master Recipe
Ragu Sauce (Bolognese Sauce)

Serves 6

I've been told that if you want to make your way to an Italian man's heart it is essential to be able to make a good ragu. This is a wonderfully versatile sauce – the classic Bolognese sauce for Tagliatelle alla Bolognese, indispensable for lasagne and also delicious with polenta and gnocchi. I have been making Marcella Hazan's version for many years from her Classic Italian Cookbook**. Marcella says it should be cooked for at least 3½ hours at the merest simmer and that 5 hours would be better, but I find you get a very good result with even 1½ hours' cooking on a diffuser mat. Ragu can be made ahead and freezes very well.**

3 tablespoons butter
¼ cup extra-virgin olive oil
2½ tablespoons onion, finely chopped
2½ tablespoons celery, finely chopped
2½ tablespoons carrot, finely chopped
¾ lb. (350g) ground lean beef, preferably chuck or neck meat
salt
1¼ cups dry white wine
½ cup milk
⅛ teaspoon freshly grated nutmeg
1 x 14-ounce (400-g) can Italian tomatoes, roughly chopped with their own juice

In Italy, they sometimes use an earthenware pot for making ragu, but I find that a heavy enamelled cast-iron pot with high sides works very well. Heat the butter with the oil and sauté the onion briefly over medium heat until just translucent. Add the celery and carrot and cook gently for 2 minutes. Next add the ground beef, crumbling it in the pot with a fork. Add salt to taste, stir, and cook only until the meat has lost its raw red color (Marcella says that if it browns it will lose its delicacy).

Add the wine, turn the heat up to medium-high and cook, stirring occasionally, until all the wine has evaporated, stirring every now and then. Turn the heat down to medium, add in the milk and the nutmeg, and cook until the milk has evaporated, stirring every now and then. Next add the chopped tomatoes and stir well. When the tomatoes have started to bubble, turn the heat down to the very lowest so that the sauce cooks at the gentlest simmer – just an occasional bubble. I use a heat diffuser mat for this.

Cook uncovered for a minimum of 1½ hours (better still 2 or even 3 depending on how concentrated you like it), stirring occasionally. If it reduces too much, add a little water and continue to cook. When it is finally cooked, taste and correct seasoning. Because of the length of cooking time, it would be worthwhile to make at least twice the recipe.

Tagliatelle alla Bolognese

Serves 6

Italians wince when we talk about Spaghetti Bolognese. They say there's no such thing – that Bolognese sauce should not be served with spaghetti but with tagliatelle instead!

1 lb. (450g) Homemade pasta cut into tagliatelle or noodles
Ragu recipe (see above)

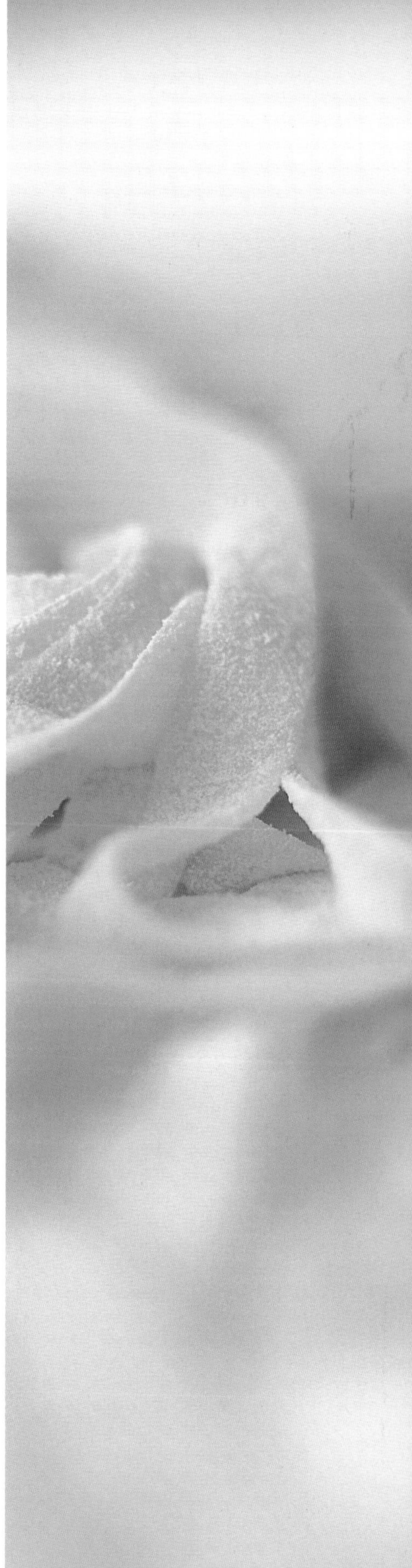

2 tablespoons butter
3/4–1 cup freshly grated Parmesan cheese

Heat the ragu, adding a little water if it is too thick. Cook the pasta until it is "al dente" and strain immediately. Put a little sauce in a warm serving dish, top with the hot tagliatelle or noodles, and pour the remainder of the sauce on top. Dot with butter, sprinkle with Parmesan cheese, toss well, and serve immediately with an extra bowl of Parmesan.

Pappardelle with Fava Beans and Arugula Leaves

Serves 4

1 lb. (450g) pappardelle
8 ounces (225g) fava beans, shelled (about 1 2/3 cups)
2/3 cup Fava Bean Purée (see page 196)
fistful of arugula leaves
1/4 cup extra-virgin olive oil, approximately
lots of freshly ground pepper and sea salt

First make the Fava Bean Purée, and cook and keep warm the shelled fava beans.

Cook the pappardelle until "al dente". Drain quickly. Add a little extra-virgin olive oil to the pan, add the fava beans, pasta, and arugula leaves and toss well. Season with lots of pepper and some sea salt. Put two tablespoons of Fava Bean Purée onto each plate. Put a portion of pasta on top and serve immediately.

Master Recipe
Tagliatelle with Cream and Parmesan

Serves 4 as a main course

We use this recipe as the basis for dozens of delicious sauces – add whatever takes your fancy, depending on the season.

8 ounces (225g) tagliatelle, preferably fresh and homemade
2 tablespoons butter
3/4 cup best quality cream
1 cup freshly grated Parmesan
freshly ground pepper, sea salt or kosher salt, and nutmeg

Cook the tagliatelle until barely "al dente", (remember it will cook a little more in the pan).

Melt the butter in a wide saucepan, add half the cream, simmer for a couple of minutes until the cream thickens slightly, then add the hot drained tagliatelle, the rest of the cream, and the freshly grated cheese. Season with freshly ground pepper, nutmeg, and sea salt. Toss briefly to coat the pasta, taste, and add a little more seasoning if necessary. Serve immediately on hot plates.

Variations

Tagliatelle with Smoked Salmon and Parsley

Omit the Parmesan from the Master Recipe. Add 2–4 ounces (50–110g) smoked salmon, cut into cubes, and 2 1/2 tablespoons of freshly chopped flat-leaf parsley.

Tagliatelle with Roasted Pumpkin

Follow the Master Recipe, adding 8 ounces (225g) of roasted pumpkin (about 1 cup cut up) and a few toasted pine nuts with the hot drained tagliatelle.

Tagliatelle with Red Pepper and Arugula

Follow the Master Recipe, adding some strips of roasted red pepper and a few arugula leaves with the hot drained tagliatelle.

Tagliatelle with Fava Beans or Peas

Follow the Master Recipe, adding shelled and cooked fava beans or peas with the hot drained tagliatelle. Arugula is also good here.

Which Sauce?

Spaghettini and spaghetti are best served with olive oil sauces, but the flatter ribbon noodles of varying widths may also be served with butter, cream, egg, and cheese, and meat-based sauces.

When serving pasta shapes and tubes, the chunkier the sauce, the larger the pasta shapes need to be.

Marcella Hazan's Pappardelle or Noodles with Chicken Liver Sauce

Serves 4

It was Marcella Hazan who first introduced me to classic Italian cooking and she has become a legend in her lifetime. This recipe is one of my favorites from her Classic Italian Cookbook.

10 ounces (275g) pappardelle or noodles
1/2 lb. (225g) fresh chicken livers
1/4 cup extra-virgin olive oil
2 tablespoons butter
1 1/2 ounces (35g) diced pancetta or prosciutto (about 3 slices) – I use unsmoked bacon
2 1/2 tablespoons shallot or onion, chopped
1/4 garlic clove, peeled and finely chopped
1 1/2 teaspoons fresh sage leaves
1/4 lb. (110g) ground lean beef
salt and 6–8 twists freshly ground pepper
1 teaspoon tomato paste dissolved in 4 tablespoons dry white vermouth

freshly grated Parmesan

Wash the chicken livers, trim off any fat or traces of green and cut them into 3 or 4 pieces. Dry thoroughly on paper towels.

Heat the oil and half the butter in a small saucepan, add the diced bacon and fry gently until it begins to crisp, then remove to a plate. Add the rest of the butter and sauté the onions over a medium heat until translucent. Add the garlic, stir 2 or 3 times, add the cooked bacon and the sage leaves, then add the ground meat, crumbling it with a fork, and cook until it has lost its raw red color.

Season with salt and freshly ground pepper, turn the heat up to medium high and add the chicken livers. Stir and cook until they have lost their raw color; add the tomato paste and vermouth and cook for 9–10 minutes. Taste.

Meanwhile, cook the pappardelle or noodles until "al dente". The moment the pasta is drained, transfer to a warm dish, add the sauce, toss thoroughly, and serve immediately with grated Parmesan, if desired. This sauce is also delicious served with Risotto (see page 138).

Master Recipe

Lasagne Verde (Green Lasagne)

Serves 12

As a recipe, lasagne has all the virtues – it is mildly exotic, suitable for large numbers, not too expensive, and it can be made ahead and reheated very successfully. It's best made with home-made pasta verde but can also be made with good-quality dried pasta. You can use the lasagne technique with all sorts of fillings (see variations).

In my experience, the "no-cook" lasagne benefits from being blanched and refreshed first, but whichever type you use, be particularly careful not to overcook it. Mushy lasagne is all too common.

1 lb. (450g) Spinach Pasta or Egg Pasta
2½ cups Ragu (see page 152) or chosen filling
5 cups well-flavored Béchamel Sauce (see page 580)
1½–2 cups freshly grated Parmesan
a few pats of butter

2 dishes, 8 x 10 inches (20.5 x 25.5cm), or 1 large rectangular one, 10 x 12 inches (25.5 x 30cm)

First prepare the Ragu and Béchamel sauces and set aside.

If using homemade pasta, make it and let it rest. Roll it out and cut into rectangular strips about 4 x 9 inches (10 x 23cm).

Preheat the oven to 450°F (230°C).

Cook 3 or 4 strips of pasta at a time, stir and cook for just 30 seconds after the water comes back to a boil. Remove the pasta and put into a bowl of cold water, then drain on a lint-free towel.

Taste each sauce; they should be well seasoned. Grease the lasagne dishes, spread a little béchamel on the bottom, cover with a layer of barely overlapping sheets of pasta. Spread a little of the chosen filling on the pasta, just enough to dot it with meat (remember ragu is a very rich and concentrated sauce). Spread a layer of béchamel over the ragu, sprinkle lightly with freshly grated Parmesan, then continue with another layer of pasta and so on up to within 1 inch (2.5cm) of the top of the dish (don't make more than 6 layers). Finish with a layer of pasta coated with béchamel, sprinkle with the remainder of the cheese, and dot with a few little pats of butter.*

Wipe the edges clean. Bake in the preheated oven for 10–15 minutes or for 30 minutes if using dried bought pasta – don't overcook. Let it rest for about 10 minutes so that the layers compact slightly. Serve from the dish – it should be bubbly and golden on top.

*May be prepared ahead to this point and kept in the fridge for several days or frozen for up to 3 months.

Variations

Lasagne with Ragu and Piperonata

We make a variation on the above by substituting Piperonata (see page 190) for Ragu in one or two of the layers.

Chicken Pilâv and Spinach Lasagne

Alternate Chicken Pilâv and cooked spinach in the layers.

Green Chicken Curry Lasagne

Also makes delicious lasagne. Experiment with other fillings.

Vegetarian Lasagne

Serves 12

1 lb. (450g) fresh Homemade Lasagne Verde or 13 ounces (375g) dried plain or spinach lasagne
Piperonata (see page 190)
2 quantities Mushroom à la Crème (see page 197)
2 quarts (1.8 liters) milk made into well-seasoned Béchamel Sauce (see page 580)
4 cups freshly grated Parmesan or 2 cups sharp Cheddar, or a mixture
salt and freshly ground pepper

2 dishes, 8 x 10 inches (20.5 x 25.5cm), or 1 large rectangular one, 10 x 12 inches (25.5 x 30cm)

First, taste each component, make sure it is delicious and well-seasoned. Ensure the Béchamel is not too thick for good coverage. Blanch the lasagne pasta. Spread a little Béchamel sauce on the bottom of each dish, cover with strips of pasta, and a layer of Piperonata. Add another layer of pasta. Spread with Béchamel sauce and sprinkle with grated cheese. Add the Mushroom à la crème next, then more pasta, Béchamel sauce, cheese, and so on, ending with a layer of sauce and a good sprinkling of Parmesan cheese. (Make sure all the pasta is under the sauce.) Cook as above. Serve with a good green salad.

Lasagne with Zucchini

Serves 6

If yellow crookneck squash or golden zucchini are available, this looks pretty made with half green and half yellow.

Homemade pasta dough made with 2 eggs (see page 148) or bought lasagne, blanched
3 lbs. (1.3kg) zucchini
2½ tablespoons extra-virgin olive oil
2 tablespoons butter
1 teaspoon finely chopped garlic
1½ tablespoon finely chopped flat-leaf parsley
3–4 tablespoons marjoram, chopped
salt and freshly ground black pepper
Béchamel Sauce (see page 580; you need 1½ times the recipe)
⅛ teaspoon freshly grated nutmeg
1½ cups freshly grated Parmesan (Parmigiano Reggiano is best)

Trim the zucchini and cut them in half lengthwise. Lay the halves cut side down, and slice crosswise into ¼-inch (5-mm) semi-circles. Put the olive oil, butter, and garlic in a large frying pan over a medium heat. When the garlic begins to change color, add the parsley and marjoram and stir well. Mix in the zucchini, season with salt and black pepper, and continue cooking, stirring from time to time until tender. Remove the zucchini and herb mixture using a slotted spoon and set it aside.

Make the Béchamel Sauce. Pour about four-fifths of it into a bowl, add the zucchini mixture, freshly grated nutmeg, and 1 cup of the Parmesan and stir.

Preheat the oven to 400°F (200°C). Smear the bottom of the baking dish with half of the remaining Béchamel sauce and cover with a layer of pasta. Cover the pasta with a thin layer of the Béchamel and zucchini sauce. Continue layering the pasta and the sauce until there are at least 5 layers. Spread the remaining Béchamel and the zucchini mixture over the final layer of pasta so that it is dotted with zucchini. Sprinkle the remaining Parmesan on top.

Above: Lasagne with Zucchini

Place on the upper shelf of the oven. Bake for 15–20 minutes or until a light golden crust forms on top. Remove from the oven and let rest for 10 minutes before serving.

Variations

You can make vegetarian lasagne with many different layers. Here are a few to try:
Tomato Fondue (see page 188)
Buttered or Creamed Spinach (see page 170–171)
Eggplant, Roast Red Pepper, and Pesto
Mushroom à la Crème (see page 197)

Ravioli

Makes about 36, serves 6 as an appetizer, 4 as a main course

Ravioli, those tiny stuffed pockets of pasta, may be made ahead and kept covered for up to 3 days in the refrigerator, depending on the filling, or may be frozen. Make sure you defrost it thoroughly before cooking.

8 ounces (225g) fresh Homemade pasta dough
chosen filling
2 cups freshly grated Parmesan

fluted pastry wheel or ravioli cutter

Make the pasta dough as for the Master Recipe. Cover with an inverted bowl and let it relax for ½–1 hour, so that the dough loses its elasticity. Roll out until paper thin and divide in half. Brush one piece of dough lightly with water and put teaspoons of filling at 1½-inch (4-cm) intervals. Cover with the remaining sheet of dough, press the top piece down gently to seal each mound of filling, making sure that all the air is released. Cut into squares with a fluted pastry wheel or stamp out squares with a ravioli cutter. If they are not being cooked the same day, transfer to floured wax paper and leave for 5–6 hours to dry, depending on the filling.

Poach the ravioli for 8–10 minutes, or until "al dente" and drain. Serve the grated Parmesan separately.

Fillings

Chicken and Fresh Herb

Mix ½ lb. (225g) cooked chicken or a mixture of chicken and cooked ham with ¼ cup thick Béchamel Sauce (see page 580), Tomato Sauce (see page 590) or cream, and 2½ tablespoons of freshly chopped flat-leaf parsley or other herbs, e.g., tarragon or marjoram. Bind with a lightly beaten egg and season to taste. Basil would be good with Tomato Sauce.

Spinach Ravioli

Wash 8 ounces (225g) fresh spinach without stems (about 4 large handfuls), and cook in a covered pot on a low heat until the leaves wilt. Drain the spinach thoroughly and squeeze it dry. Let it cool, then chop it and mix with 1/2 cup fresh ricotta cheese, 1/2 teaspoon freshly grated nutmeg, and salt and pepper to taste.

Cheese Ravioli

Mix together 1 cup freshly grated Parmesan, 1/2 cup fresh ricotta, 1 lightly beaten egg or 2 egg yolks, 1 tablespoon chopped fresh basil or parsley, and salt and freshly ground black pepper to taste.

Variations

Ravioli in Sage Butter

Serve with Sage Butter (see page 588)

Baked Ravioli in Cream Sauce

Make a Béchamel Sauce in the usual way with 3 cups milk. Add 2/3 cup heavy cream, taste for seasoning and keep warm.

Cook the ravioli in a large pot of boiling salted water until "al dente," drain well and arrange in layers, in a shallow buttered baking dish, with the sauce and ending with a layer of sauce.

Sprinkle with 1 cup freshly grated Parmesan. Bake in a preheated oven, 350°F (180°C) for 20–25 minutes until bubbling and golden brown on top. Make sure it is thoroughly heated, especially if the ravioli has been frozen.

Ravioli in Tomato Sauce

Make a Tomato Sauce (see page 590). Cook the ravioli in plenty of boiling salted water until "al dente", drain and layer with the Tomato Sauce in a shallow, buttered baking dish, ending with a layer of sauce. Sprinkle with 1 cup freshly grated Parmesan and cook as above.

Fresh or dried?

A recent myth that needs to be de-bunked once and for all is that fresh pasta is better or preferable to dried pasta. Neither is superior, they are quite simply different. There are two types of dried pasta, plain pasta made from egg, durum semolina flour and water, and egg pasta made from durum wheat and eggs.

Oil-based sauces are usually served with plain pasta, while butter or cream-based sauces are usually served with egg pasta.

Cappelletti and Tortellini

Serves 10–12 people: makes about 300

Cappelletti and tortellini are little stuffed pasta, very much a labor of love to make but quite delicious. I was interested to discover that it is tradition to serve cappelletti in broth on Christmas and New Year's Day in parts of Emilia Romagna. On Christmas Eve the entire family, from children to grannies, become involved – everyone sits around the kitchen table and shapes the little dumplings. In fact, children are often best at this because their fingers are so small and nimble. By the time several hundred have been made, everyone has had lots of fun and the skill has unwittingly been passed from one generation to the next. This recipe, one of my great favorites, is adapted from The Classic Italian Cookbook by Marcella Hazan.

Homemade pasta dough (see page 148)

Filling

2 tablespoons butter
1/4 lb. (110g) pork tenderloin, cut into 1/2-inch (1-cm) dice
6 ounces (175g) chicken breast, cut into 1/2-inch (1-cm) dice (about 3/4 cup)
1 1/2 ounces (35g) garlic salami
a heaped cup ricotta or strained cottage cheese
1 egg yolk
1 3/4 cups freshly grated Parmesan
1/2 teaspoon nutmeg, freshly grated
salt and freshly ground pepper

First make the pasta dough, cover, and let rest while you make the filling.

Melt the butter in a heavy saucepan, add the diced pork, season with salt and pepper, and cook gently until nicely browned and cooked through. Remove to a plate, then add the diced chicken breasts to the saucepan, season again, and cook – they won't take so long: about 2–3 minutes. Add to the pork. Let cook while you prepare the other ingredients.

Chop the garlic salami very finely and mix with the cottage cheese, Parmesan, and egg yolk. Chop the cooked pork and chicken very finely (you can do this in a food processor if you are very careful, using the pulse button, but don't let it reach a purée).

Add to the other ingredients, grate in the nutmeg, season with salt and pepper, mix well, taste, and add more seasoning, if necessary. Cover and keep in the fridge until you are ready to make the cappelletti.

Divide the dough in half, cover one piece, and roll the other piece into a very thin sheet. Repeat with the other half. Then cut the pasta into 1 3/4-inch (4.5-cm) squares for cappelletti or 2-inch (5-cm) circles for tortellini. (You will probably have to trim the edges quite a bit to get even strips and squares, but keep the trimmings. Cut them into noodles and you can cook them another time.)

The dough for stuffed pasta should not be dried, so gather your helpers around you and set to work right away. Put the equivalent of 1/4 teaspoon of filling in the center of each square (do this with your fingers – it's so much faster). Then fold the square in half diagonally to make a triangle, press down firmly to seal the sides, pick up the triangle by one end of its long base, hold it between your thumb and index fingers with tip of the triangle pointing towards your knuckle, catch the other end of the base with your other hand, and wrap it around your index finger, and press the two ends firmly together to seal. Then slide the cappelletti off your finger and push the little peak ends upwards so they resemble those wondrous bonnets worn by nuns years ago.

Tortellini are made in a similar way, starting with a circle of pasta rather than a square. Fill as for the capelletti, fold up the edges so the little parcel looks like a plump belly button. Both cappelletti and tortellini can, of course, be made slightly larger depending on how you plan to serve them.

At this point I reckon it's worth the effort to pause and cook two or three in a little boiling salted water to check the flavor. Although it's great fun, this is not exactly fast food and nothing is more disappointing than to discover that they could have done with a little more seasoning when it's too late.

As you make the cappelletti or tortellini, put them out on clean dry lint-free towels. You can cook them right away, but otherwise turn them every couple of hours until they are uniformly dry (in Restaurant Diana in Bologna they have a wooden frame with perforated zinc specially for drying the cappelletti). When they are dry they will keep for up to a week.

Tip: When making pasta salads, pasta should be tossed in a well-flavored dressing while still warm.

Cappelletti or Tortellini with Butter and Cream

Serves 8

150 cappelletti or tortellini (see page 156)
3 tablespoons butter
2/3 cup cream
1 cup freshly grated Parmesan
extra Parmesan for sprinkling

First cook the pasta in boiling salted water: drop in the cappelletti, stir gently, and as soon as the water comes back to a boil, time them: fresh cappelletti will take 4–5 minutes but dry cappelletti may take up to 20 minutes. Have a colander or large slotted spoon ready.

Meanwhile, melt the butter and cream in a wide frying pan. As soon as the cappelletti are cooked, scoop up and drain, add to the butter and cream, put on a low heat, and toss gently in the sauce. Add the grated Parmesan and continue to toss until they are evenly coated. Turn into a hot serving dish and serve immediately on warmed plates with an extra sprinkling of Parmesan cheese.

Orzo Salad with Pesto, Cherry Tomatoes, and Knockalara Cheese

Serves 4–6

Orzo is one of my best discoveries in recent years. Essentially, it is pasta grain, which may be used in a whole variety of dishes, hot and cold. For this salad we use Knockalara cheese, made from ewe's milk in Cappoquin, County Waterford – but you could use Feta cheese instead.

8 ounces (225g) Orzo
2 1/2 tablespoons Pesto (see page 589)
12 cherry tomatoes, red and yellow mixed, if possible
balsamic vinegar or red wine vinegar
a pinch of sugar
salt and freshly ground pepper
1/4 cup toasted pine nuts
3 ounces (75g) Knockalara or Feta cheese cut into 3/4-inch (2-cm) cubes (about 3/4 cup)

Garnish
arugula leaves if available
sprigs of basil

Cook the orzo for 10–12 minutes or until "al dente". Drain, rinse quickly under the tap, and let cool. Put into a large bowl and toss with the Pesto. Quarter the tomatoes, season with salt and freshly ground pepper. Sprinkle with balsamic or red wine vinegar and sugar, and toss well. Toast the pine nuts until golden.

Add the tomatoes and pine nuts to the orzo which should by now be cool. Toss gently. Add the cubes of cheese and toss one more time. Turn on to a serving dish, and garnish the top with arugula leaves and perhaps a sprig or two of basil. Eat immediately.

Cheat's Method of Cooking Dried Pasta

We developed this method of cooking pasta when we taught a survival course for students who live in small apartments with limited cooking facilities. Italians are usually shocked but it works perfectly.

Bring a large pot of salted water to a boil, add the pasta, stir, put the lid on the pot, and bring back to a boil. Cook for 2 minutes for spaghetti and tagliatelli, or 4 minutes for penne, small shells, etc. Keep the pot covered. Then turn off the heat and let the pasta continue to cook for the time indicated on the package. Test, drain, and proceed as usual.

Pasta made by this method is good, and does not overcook as easily as pasta made by the conventional method.

Cannelloni

Makes 8

Serves 4 as an appetizer, 2 as a main course

Cannelloni are rolls of pasta with a delectable filling – the same filling may be used for Lasagne or indeed Cappelletti or Tortellini. Like ravioli, cannelloni may be prepared ahead and reheated, provided each component is cold when it is put together, so keep them in the fridge. They can also be frozen and will keep for 2 months. You can also adapt the components of the recipe to make Lasagne. This is a recipe I enjoy very much, based on one from the French Cookery School Book **by Anne Willan and Jane Grigson.**

4 ounces (110g) Homemade Pasta dough (see page 148)

Sauce

3 tablespoons butter
6 tablespoons flour
2 cups milk
salt, freshly ground pepper, and nutmeg
1¼ cups cream
¼ cup freshly grated Parmesan

Filling

6 ounces (175g) stewing veal or chicken, ground
6 ounces (175g) lean pork, ground
2 small egg yolks
good pinch ground mace or freshly grated nutmeg
salt and freshly ground pepper

Topping

½ cup freshly grated Parmesan
1 tablespoon butter

lasagne dish, 10 x 8 inches (25.5 x 20.5cm)

To make the pasta dough, follow the Master Recipe and let it rest for 30 minutes. Roll it out as thinly as possible with a rolling pin. Cut it into 4-inch (10-cm) squares, spread it on paper towels and let dry while you prepare the other ingredients. If making ahead, pack the squares between sheets of wax paper and store in a plastic bag in the refrigerator for up to 4 days.

Next make the sauce. Melt the butter in a heavy-bottomed saucepan, stir in the flour, and cook for 2 minutes, then pour in the milk, bring to a boil, whisking all the time, season with salt, freshly ground pepper, and grated nutmeg, and cook for 2 minutes. Add enough cream to make a fairly thick sauce and remove from the heat.

Mix the minced veal or chicken and pork together, add the egg yolks and 1¼ cups of the sauce, season well with salt, freshly ground pepper, and ground mace or nutmeg.

Put 4½ quarts of water in a large pot and bring to a boil. Add 2½ tablespoons of salt. Cook the cannelloni squares for 1–2 minutes if very fresh or for longer if dried, until "al dente". Drain and refresh in a bowl of cold water.

Preheat the oven to 350F° (180°C).

To assemble: butter the lasagne dish lightly, drain the squares on paper towels, and fill each one with 1–2 tablespoons of the filling, roll them up and place side by side in the dish. Reheat the sauce, stir in the remaining cream, stir in half the freshly grated Parmesan, and taste for seasoning. Spoon the sauce over the cannelloni – it should cover them completely. Sprinkle the remaining Parmesan over the top, dot with butter, and bake in the oven, 350F° (180°C), for 40–45 minutes. Ten minutes before the end of cooking, remove the lid so that the cheese browns.

Below: Cannelloni

Pasta with Sardines, Pine Nuts, and Raisins

Serves 6

Purists would be very sniffy about my use of canned rather than fresh sardines in this classic Sicilian dish. However, I make no apologies: it tastes delicious – and anyway, fresh sardines are thin on the ground in Ballycotton, not to speak of Cullohill! Dried toasted breadcrumbs, incidentally, were once the poor man's Parmesan in Sicily.

12 ounces (350g) spaghetti or tagliatelle
2½ tablespoons olive oil
1 medium onion, chopped (about 1 cup)
½ cup pine nuts, lightly toasted
¼ cup raisins, plumped up in hot water
3–5 tablespoons chopped fennel leaves
2 cans best-quality sardines preserved in olive oil
½ cup fine dried breadcrumbs or ¼ cup freshly grated Parmesan

Cook the pasta in plenty of boiling salted water.

Heat the olive oil in a frying pan, add the onion, and cook on a gentle heat until soft and golden, add the toasted pine nuts, raisins, and fennel, toss well. When the pasta is almost cooked, add the sardines to the sauce. Drain the pasta, drizzle with a little extra-virgin olive oil, add the sardine mixture, toss gently. Taste and correct the seasoning.

Turn into a hot serving dish and serve immediately, sprinkled with fine dried breadcrumbs or grated Parmesan.

Variation

Pasta with Mackerel

Substitute pan-grilled mackerel for the sardines in the recipe above.

Taglierini al Profumo di Limone (Fresh Noodles with Lemon)

Serves 6

This recipe was given to me by Mimmo Baldi, the chef-owner of Il Vescovino in Panzano. His restaurant, overlooking many of the best vineyards in Chianti, serves some of the most inspired food I have tasted in Italy – certainly worth a detour.

7 ounces (200g) fresh or dried taglierini (thin noodles)
2 lemons, preferably unwaxed
⅔ cup very fresh cream
salt and freshly ground pepper to taste
pat of butter

If the lemons are not unwaxed, scrub gently to remove any wax, then grate the lemon zest on the finest part of a stainless-steel grater, add it to the cream, cover the bowl, and leave to infuse in the fridge for 5–6 hours.

Cook the pasta in plenty of boiling salted water until "al dente", drain well, and put into a hot pasta dish, adding the cream and lemon mixture. Season with salt and freshly ground pepper, add a pat of butter, and toss well. Serve instantly. This sauce should not be thick.

Spicy Korean Beef with Crispy Noodles

Serves 6

When Nina Simonds came to teach at the school in the summer of 1998, she charmed us all with her delicious recipes. This was one of our favorites, which I have adapted slightly for our ingredients.

1 lb. (450g) firm tofu (4 x 4-ounce cakes)
1 lb. (450g) freshly ground beef
3 tablespoons finely chopped scallions, white parts only
1½ tablespoons grated fresh ginger
2–3 cloves crushed garlic
1½ teaspoons toasted sesame oil
2 ounces (50g) thin rice noodles
2½ tablespoons sunflower oil

oil for deep-frying

Sauce
¼ cup Chinese ground bean sauce or sweet bean paste
3 tablespoons sugar
2 tablespoons toasted sesame oil
1½ teaspoons hot chili paste

leaves of 1 butterhead lettuce, washed, gently dried, and arranged in a bowl on the table
fresh cilantro leaves

Put the tofu into a dish, cover with a plate, and weight it gently for about 30 minutes. Put the ground beef in a bowl, add the scallions, ginger, garlic, and sesame oil. Heat the oil in a deep-fryer or wok. Put in a few rice noodles at a time – they puff up instantly. Remove immediately and drain on paper towels. Arrange on 6 serving plates.

Cut the pressed tofu into ¼-inch (5-mm) cubes. Mix all the ingredients for the sauce together. Heat the sunflower oil in a wok or pan until very hot, add the beef, and stir-fry until it changes color, then turn into a strainer over a bowl to drain.

Wipe out the wok or pan. Heat the wok again, add the sauce mixture. Stir until it thickens, add the beef and tofu cubes and toss gently to coat with the sauce. Spoon over the noodles.

Garnish with some fresh cilantro leaves. Each diner puts some of the noodles and sauce into a lettuce leaf, rolls it up, and enjoys.

Indian Spicy Noodles with Tomato

Serves 4–6

A filling vegetarian noodle dish where you wouldn't miss the meat! Whip up this addictive dish from a package of those crispy noodles in your cupboard.

4 ounces (110g) egg noodles, cooked
1/4 cup sunflower oil
1/2 teaspoon cumin seeds
5 garlic cloves, finely chopped
1 green chile, finely chopped
1 teaspoon freshly grated ginger
a good pinch ground asafetida, optional
1/4 teaspoon ground turmeric
1/4–1/2 teaspoon cayenne pepper
6 ripe tomatoes, peeled and coarsely chopped
1 medium onion, finely chopped (about 1 cup)
salt, freshly ground pepper, and sugar
1/4 cup fresh cilantro leaves, finely chopped

Cook the noodles according to the instructions on the package. Drain and reserve.

Heat the oil in a wok or large, preferably non-stick, frying pan over a medium-high heat.

When hot, add the cumin seeds, stir for a few seconds. Add the garlic, chile, and ginger. Stir and fry for 2–3 minutes until the garlic begins to color. Add the asafetida, if using, turmeric, and cayenne pepper. Stir very quickly and then, add the onions and cook for 3 or 4 minutes on a medium heat. Then toss in the chopped tomatoes, season with salt, pepper, and sugar, and cook for 5–6 minutes, stirring frequently. Add the cilantro, taste, and correct seasoning.

Simmer for 2–3 minutes or until the tomatoes are tender. Stir the noodles into the tomato mixture. Let it bubble for a minute or two to heat the noodles through. Serve immediately with lots of fresh cilantro.

Below: Indian Spicy Noodles with Tomato

Rosemary Kearney's Chicken and Coconut Laksa

Serves 6–8

Rosemary taught us this on her one-day course for celiacs – it's now one of our favorite soups.

6 ounces (175g) fine rice noodles
2 chicken breasts
2 red chiles, chopped with seeds
4 garlic cloves, finely chopped
1-inch (2.5-cm) piece of ginger, peeled and finely chopped
6 ounces (175g) fresh cilantro, leaves and stalks, coarsely chopped (about 3/4–1 bunch)
juice of 1–2 limes
1/4 cup toasted sesame oil
2 x 14-ounce (400-ml) cans coconut milk
generous 3 cups homemade Chicken Stock (see page 36)
1 tablespoon plus 1 teaspoon fish sauce (nam pla)
salt and freshly ground black pepper
8 scallions, peeled, trimmed and finely sliced at an angle

Pour boiling water over the bowl of rice noodles and let soak until soft. Drain and cut into 2-inch (5-cm) lengths. Thinly slice the chicken breasts at an angle and set aside. Put the chiles, garlic, ginger, cilantro, and the juice of one lime into a food processor and pulse to a coarse paste. Heat the sesame oil in a large saucepan and fry the chile paste for 3 minutes. Add the coconut milk and chicken stock.

Bring to a boil, reduce heat, and simmer for 5 minutes. Add the thinly sliced chicken and simmer for a further 5 minutes or until the chicken is cooked through. Add the fish sauce, taste, and add more lime juice, salt, and pepper, if necessary.

Divide the noodles into serving bowls, ladle in the hot soup, and garnish with scallions and cilantro leaves.

Asian Chicken and Noodle Salad

Serves 6–8

Dressing

1½ tablespoons peanut butter
1 clove garlic crushed
¼ teaspoon Chinese or English mustard
¼ cup soy sauce
½ teaspoon sugar
¼ cup rice wine vinegar
2 tablespoons Chile Pepper Oil (see page 227)

¼ cup sesame oil
⅔ cup homemade Chicken Stock (see page 36)
1 teaspoon salt
2 lbs. (900g) chicken breasts
8 ounces (225g) Chinese noodles or fettuccini, cooked
1½ tablespoons toasted sesame seeds
1½ cucumbers
2–3 stalks of celery
2 scallions
2½ tablespoons freshly chopped cilantro leaves

Mix all the dressing ingredients except the oil in a bowl, then gradually whisk in the oil. Bring the chicken stock to a boil, add the salt and chicken breasts, cover, and simmer gently for 10–12 minutes. Alternatively, simmer for 4 minutes, turn off heat, cover, and let it finish cooking in the hot stock for about 10–12 minutes.

Drain, then let cool for a few minutes. Shred into long strips along the grain of the chicken breast, put into a large bowl. Add the cooked noodles.

Toast the sesame seeds in a dry pan over a medium heat for 2–3 minutes, stirring regularly, then let cool on a plate.

Cut the cucumbers in half, remove the seeds, and cut into 1½-inch (4-cm) julienne or ¼-inch (5-mm) slices cut at an angle, add to the bowl. Cut celery into ¼-inch (5-mm) dice. Slice the scallions at an angle and add these to the bowl.

Above: Crispy Noodle Pancake

Add the cilantro. Toss in the dressing. Taste and correct the seasoning. Serve sprinkled with toasted sesame seeds and more fresh cilantro leaves.

Crispy Noodle Pancake

Serves 4

8 ounces (225g) Chinese noodles or fettuccini
water
salt
¼ cup extra-virgin olive oil, or 2 tablespoons chili oil plus 2 tablespoons olive oil, or 2½ tablespoons soy sauce and 1½ tablespoons sesame oil or sunflower oil
2½ tablespoons sunflower oil for frying

Bring a pot of water to a boil, add salt, add the noodles, and stir. Cook for 3 or 4 minutes or until "al dente," drain. Transfer to a bowl. Sprinkle with olive oil or chili oil or a mixture of soy sauce and sesame oil.

Heat the 2½ tablespoons of sunflower oil in a frying pan, add the noodles, flatten into a "cake" ½ inch (1cm) thick. Cook for 4 or 5 minutes on one side or until crisp and golden. Flip over onto a plate and slide back into the pan to cook the other side. Drain on paper towels.

Note: The crispy noodle pancake can be reheated in a moderate oven.

vegetables

vegetables

The Ballymaloe Cookery School is in the midst of a 100-acre farm in East Cork, Ireland. Both the farm and gardens are certified organic with the Irish Organic Trust. We still have an acre of greenhouses, a legacy of days when we were horticulturalists, growing 6 acres of tomatoes and cucumbers, and 65 acres of apples. Originally the greenhouses were heated with oil but the oil crisis in the early seventies, which resulted in 25 per cent inflation, finished all that.

Now, even though they are no longer heated, we grow a wide range of crops year round. The extra protection of the glass makes it possible to grow early potatoes and carrots, a wonderful variety of kales, early beets, herbs, Swiss chard, and leeks. Later in the year, we have 20 or 30 different types of tomatoes including many heirloom varieties, cucumber, corn, beans, calabrese, spinach, tomatillas, eggplant, peppers, chiles, a variety of lettuces and salad greens, cilantro, arugula, and a selection of tender herbs.

The potager (kitchen garden) in the old haggard, close to the school, is designed to be decorative as well as functional. The vegetables are planted in patterns to provide a contrast of texture, color, and flavor, and are carefully rotated each year. The old herringbone brick paths bisect the garden and the vegetables are interplanted with edible flowers, which encourage beneficial insects to help with pollination.

The edible flowers: nasturtiums, marigolds, violas, and even bachelor's buttons, are used in salads with chive flowers, pea shoots, purslane, mustard greens, and oriental greens like mizuna and mibuna. We allow the seed heads of poppies and nigella to dry so we can collect the seeds to scatter over breads and biscuits. When the fava beans reach the height of a couple of feet we pinch out the tops, this discourages black fly and we have the extra bonus of being able to use the tender shoots in salad and to make a delicious soup.

Even though the vegetable garden is very small, probably less than half an acre, we grow a wide range of vegetables with many old and unusual varieties. We've got a particularly good strain of artichokes which came from Myrtle Allen's family garden in Rushbrooke, cut-and-come kale (*Brassica oleracea*) from the gardens at Glin Castle, Jerusalem artichokes from the walled garden at Ballymaloe, and Chinese artichokes.

Students on our 12-week course meet the gardeners at 8am on a rota basis. They go out with them to bring in the vegetables and herbs for the morning cooking. On short courses, it's a matter of choice. Some students understandably choose to roll over and sleep for another hour, while others find that the experience enhances their overall enjoyment of the course.

The gardeners, Susan, Eileen and Haulie, are deeply knowledgeable and enormously generous with their information so students who are interested in growing their own produce can get valuable tips and practical advice. This experience is an intrinsic part of the 12-week course at the Ballymaloe Cookery School. It gives the student a unique understanding of how food is produced and a respect for food and those who produce it, which in my opinion, is vital for all good cooks and chefs. It also establishes a dialogue and understanding between the farmer and the chef, which is so often lacking. Considering that we are all interdependent, it is extraordinary how rare this logical situation is. What we don't produce ourselves we buy from a network of local farmers, particularly our neighboring farm owned by the Walsh family, who grow a wide range of vegetables and fruit. Hopefully when the students leave, their experience at the school will encourage them to establish a network of small food producers to provide them with fresh, naturally produced, seasonal ingredients for their own businesses.

Buying Vegetables

Not surprisingly, my advice is: buy fresh, local food in season whenever possible. Faced with a decision whether to buy organic carrots from abroad or local food in season grown with the minimum of sprays, I would always opt for the latter. I see little point in buying vegetables (even if they are organic) that may be several weeks old and have travelled several thousand miles before getting to us. Choose the freshest and liveliest looking vegetables. Note the source and name of the producer and seek out local produce.

Doctors and nutritionists urge us to eat more vegetables and fruit for a healthier diet, so understandably the demand is growing for information to be made available to the consumer about the level of pesticides and herbicides in fresh produce. Seek out local, organically produced vegetables wherever possible and ask your store or supermarket to highlight local, and to identify goods that have been irradiated – then the choice is yours.

One sure-fire way of knowing exactly where your vegetables have come from, and how they were grown, is by shopping at your local farmers' market. There, the producers will be able to answer all of your questions and will also be glad to have your feedback on their produce.

Vegetables – an Alternative to Meat

Vegetables add flavor, interest, and color to all meat and fish dishes. But whereas once they were viewed as purely optional side dishes, they are now celebrated in their own right as an alternative, often inexpensive, meat substitute and an essential part of a balanced diet.

The variety of vegetables continues to grow as more and more people adopt a vegetarian or semi-vegetarian diet. Don't just stick to what you know – experiment with less-known varieties and the many "exotic" vegetables, such as okra, bok choi, white cucumbers, and sweet chiles, that are now available over here. Choose the freshest and liveliest-looking vegetables, note the varieties you buy, and compare flavors when you cook.

Health Benefits

Vegetables are high in vitamins, minerals, and fiber, and have a low fat and sodium content. There are strong links between increased consumption of fruit and vegetables and the decreased risk of chronic diseases such as heart disease, some types of cancer (such as cancer of the stomach, esophagus, and lung) and strokes – all of which are diet-related due to diets high in fat and too low in fruit and vegetables. Numerous studies have shown how "lesser" illnesses (like obesity) also benefit from a vegetable-enriched diet. As a result of these studies, there have been campaigns to raise awareness of the benefits of eating fruit and vegetables, and to encourage people to eat at least five servings a day. (The National Cancer Institute in America claim that people who eat five portions of fruit and vegetables a day have half the risk of developing cancer as those who eat only one or two servings.)

Remember that the darker colored vegetables tend to have more nutrients, so seek out things like beets and kale. Spinach, carrots, sweet potatoes, sweet red peppers, and cabbages are particularly nutritious and are packed with beta-carotene, which boosts immunity and is said to lower the risk of cancer and heart disease.

How to Cook Vegetables

There are three principal ways to cook vegetables simply:

1. In abundant salted water in an uncovered pot. E.g., green beans, broccoli, and sugar snap peas. Use 1 tablespoon of salt for every 5 cups of water.
2. In a little water in a covered pot. E.g., cauliflower, carrots, Swiss chard, and celery.
3. Using no water except the drops that adhere after the vegetables have been washed. Use a heavy pot for cucumber, Jerusalem artichokes, white turnips, and leeks.

Master Recipe

Green Broccoli, Calabrese, or Romanesco

Serves 4

The secret of real flavor in broccoli, as in many other green vegetables, is not just freshness; it needs to be cooked in well-salted water. If you grow your own broccoli, cut out the central head but leave the plant intact and very soon you'll have lots of smaller flowerets. Romanesco is a variety of calabrese and is in season from summer to autumn.

1 lb. (450g) calabrese or romanesco
2½ cups water
1½ teaspoons salt
2–3 tablespoons butter
lots of freshly ground pepper

Peel the stems of calabrese or romanesco with a knife or potato peeler to remove the tough outer parts and cut the stalk close to the head into ¼–½-inch (½–1-cm) pieces. If the heads are large, divide the flowerets into small clusters.

Add the salt to the water and bring it to a fast boil. First add the stalks and then the flowerets, and cook, uncovered, at a rolling boil for 5–6 minutes. Drain off the water while the broccoli still has a bite. * Melt 2 tablespoons butter in a saucepan until it foams, and toss the broccoli in it gently. Taste, season with pepper, and serve immediately.

* Broccoli can be blanched and refreshed earlier in the day and then reheated in a saucepan of boiling salted water just before serving.

Variations

Broccoli or Calabrese with Sugar Snaps and Green Beans

Follow the Master Recipe. Cook the vegetables in separate pans. Sugar snap peas and green beans are cooked in exactly the same way. They are delicious mixed together – toss them all in a little melted butter, taste, and correct seasoning before serving.

Broccoli or Calabrese with Oyster Sauce

Follow the Master Recipe omitting the butter, cooking the calabrese until al dente. Douse with oyster sauce to taste and serve immediately.

Broccoli or Calabrese with Chile and Garlic

Follow the Master Recipe, cooking the broccoli until "al dente". Heat ¼ cup olive oil in a saucepan, add 1 or 2 chopped garlic cloves, and 1 chopped and seeded chile. Let sizzle for 1–2 minutes, pour over the hot broccoli, and toss gently. Serve immediately.

Broccoli or Calabrese with Butter and Lemon

Follow the Master Recipe, cooking the broccoli until al dente. If you like lemon, add the juice of ½ a lemon to the foaming butter.

Sprouting Broccoli (green, purple, or white)

Follow the Master Recipe. There is no need to peel the stalks.

Master Recipe

Buttered Cabbage

Serves 4

Irish people usually boil cabbage for ages, so when I cooked it this way on my TV program some years ago, it caused a sensation. This method takes only a few minutes to cook but first the cabbage must be carefully sliced into fine shreds. It should be served the moment it is cooked.

1 lb. (450g) fresh Savoy cabbage
2–4 tablespoons butter
salt and freshly ground pepper
a pat of butter

Remove the tough outer leaves from the cabbage. Divide into 4, cut out the core, and then cut into fine shreds across the grain. Put 3–4 tablespoons of water into a wide pot with the butter and a pinch of salt. Bring to a boil, add the cabbage, and toss constantly over a high heat, then cover for a few minutes. Take care it doesn't boil dry. Toss again and add some more salt, freshly ground pepper, and a pat of butter. Serve immediately.

Variation

Buttered Cabbage with Caraway Seeds

Add ½–1 tablespoon of lightly crushed caraway seeds to the cabbage, toss constantly as above.

Creamed Savoy Cabbage

Serves 4

1 head Savoy cabbage
1 cup of water or bacon water
½ stick (¼ cup) butter
1½ cups cream
salt and freshly ground pepper

Remove the tough outer leaves from the cabbage. Divide into 4, cut out the core, and then cut into fine shreds across the grain.

Bring the water to a boil in a wide pot, add the cabbage, and season it well. Cover with a wax paper lid and the saucepan lid and cook briskly until the cabbage is just tender. Drain off any excess water. Add the cream to the cabbage and return to a boil to let the cream thicken slightly.

Now remove from the pot and purée to a coarse consistency. Check the seasoning and add the butter if you think it needs it. Reheat in a non-stick pan.

Chinese Seaweed (Deep-fried cabbage)

Surprisingly, the "crispy dried seaweed" served in many Chinese restaurants is no such thing – merely deep-fried cabbage shreds. This original way of cooking cabbage tastes absolutely delicious and once you start to eat it, just like peanuts or popcorn, it is quite addictive.

Savoy cabbage or spring green cabbage
salt
sugar

Remove the stalks from the outer leaves. Roll the dry leaves into a cigar shape and slice with a very sharp knife into the finest possible shreds.

Heat the oil in a deep-fryer to 350°F (180°C). Toss in some of the cabbage and cook for a few seconds. As soon as it starts to crisp, remove and drain on paper towels.

Sprinkle with salt and sugar, toss, and serve cold.

Red Cabbage with Apples

Serves 6–8

This recipe, the simplest and best I've tasted, was given to us by a German neighbor, Elsa Schiller. She explained how she would first buy a red cabbage at a stall in their local farmers' market and then move onto another stall to buy the weight of the cabbage in cooking apples. Red cabbage is particularly good with duck, goose, venison, or pork. Add a few plump golden raisins occasionally to ring the changes.

1 lb. (450g) red cabbage
about 1 tablespoon wine vinegar
1/2 cup water
1 level teaspoon salt
about 2 heaped tablespoons sugar
1 lb. (450g) Bramley Seedling cooking apples or, if unavailable, Granny Smiths

Remove any damaged outer leaves from the cabbage. Cut into quarters, remove the core, and slice the cabbage finely across the grain. Put the wine vinegar, water, salt, and sugar into a cast iron casserole dish or stainless steel pot. Add the cabbage and bring it to a boil.

Meanwhile, peel and core the apples and cut into quarters (no smaller). Lay them on top of the cabbage, cover, and continue to cook gently until the cabbage is tender, 30–50 minutes. Do not overcook or the color and flavor will be ruined. Taste for seasoning and add more sugar if necessary. Serve in a warm serving dish.

Note: Some varieties of red cabbage are quite tough and don't seem to soften much, even with prolonged cooking. Our favorite variety, Red Drummond, gives best results.

Master Recipe

Cauliflower Cheese

Serves 6–8

1 medium cauliflower with green leaves
salt

Mornay Sauce
2 1/2 cups milk with a dash of cream
a sliced onion
3–4 slices of carrot
6 peppercorns
thyme or parsley
Roux (see page 580)
salt and freshly ground pepper
1 1/4 cups shredded cheese, Cheddar or a mixture of Gruyère, Parmesan, and Cheddar
1/2 teaspoon English mustard powder

Garnish
parsley, chopped

Preheat the oven to 450°F (230°C).

Prepare and cook the cauliflower (see page 169).

Meanwhile make the Mornay Sauce. Put the cold milk into a saucepan along with the onion, carrot, peppercorns, and herb. Bring to a boil, simmer for 3–4 minutes, remove from the heat and let infuse for 10 minutes.

Strain out the vegetables, bring the milk back to a boil, and thicken with roux to a light coating consistency. Add most of the shredded cheese, reserving enough to sprinkle over the dish, and a little mustard. Season with salt and pepper, taste, and correct the seasoning if necessary. Spoon the sauce over the cauliflower and sprinkle with the remaining cheese. The dish may be prepared ahead to this point.

Put into the oven or under the broiler to brown. If allowed to get completely cold, it will take 20–25 minutes in the oven. Serve sprinkled with chopped parsley.

Variation

Cauliflower Cheese Soup

Follow the Master Recipe but, instead of browning in the oven or under the broiler, purée the lot with any leftover cauliflower cooking water and enough light chicken stock, about 1 quart (960ml) to make a nice consistency. Taste and correct the seasoning. Serve with croûtons, cubes of diced Cheddar cheese, and parsley.

Leeks au Gratin

Leeks are also delicious served in this way. For a more substantial meal, wrap each cooked leek in a slice of cooked ham before coating them with the sauce.

Seek out organic vegetables in your local area. Why not buy a few packets of seeds and grow your own?

Sicilian Green Cauliflower with Black Olives

Serves 8

Anna Tasca from Regaleali in Sicily gave me this recipe. We used Romanesco but in Sicily they use the wonderful green cauliflowers in season in the autumn.

2 heads green cauliflower or Calabrese, about 2 lbs. (900g)
1 medium onion, finely chopped (about 1 cup)
1/2 cup extra-virgin olive oil
1/3 cup black olives, pitted and sliced
salt and freshly ground black pepper
1/2 cup freshly grated Parmesan or Pecorino cheese
2 cups shredded Mozzarella cheese (optional)

Preheat the oven to 400°F (200°C). Cut the cauliflower or calabrese into 2-inch (5-cm) flowerets and boil in well-salted water until "al dente", about 5 minutes. Drain. Meanwhile, sauté the onion in half the olive oil until tender and slightly golden, about 3–4 minutes. Remove from the heat and add the olives. Set aside.

Spread out the cauliflower or calabrese in a large, flat dish and mix in the onion-olive mixture. Add the remaining olive oil, salt and pepper to taste, (remembering that the Parmesan may be salty). Toss the cauliflower or calabrese with about half of the Parmesan and top with the mozzarella, if desired. Sprinkle the remaining Parmesan over the top and bake for 20–30 minutes or until the top is nice and golden. Serve warm or at room temperature.

Cauliflower with Anchovy and Chille

Serves 4–6

1 medium cauliflower
1 medium onion, finely chopped (about 1 cup)
1/4 cup olive oil
1/2–1 red chile, seeded and finely chopped
4 anchovy fillets, chopped
2 generous tablespoons parsley, freshly chopped
1 tablespoon red wine vinegar

Cook the cauliflower. Meanwhile, sweat the onion in the olive oil over a gentle heat for a few minutes. Add the chile and continue to cook until the onion is soft but not colored. Add the anchovies, parsley, and vinegar, stir to heat through, pour over the hot cauliflower, and serve them immediately.

Crunchy Cauliflower with Garlic Butter

Serves 4–6

1 medium cauliflower
1/4 cup Garlic Butter (see page 588)
1 3/4 cups white breadcrumbs
3 1/2 tablespoons butter
2 1/2 tablespoons olive oil

Prepare and cook the cauliflower. Melt the garlic butter in a frying pan and toss the cauliflower flowerets and chopped stalks in it. Put in a hot serving dish. Melt the butter and oil in the frying pan, toss in the crumbs and cook, tossing all the time until golden. Sprinkle them over the cauliflower and serve them immediately.

Italian Cauliflower Fritters

Serves 6–8

A quick and easy way to perk up cauliflower which, let's face it, can be a pretty tasteless vegetable without some help from a perky cheese sauce or some spices.

1 medium cauliflower (in flowerets, steamed)
well-seasoned flour
2 eggs, beaten
1 cup freshly grated Parmesan cheese (Parmigiano Reggiano if possible)
olive oil for deep frying

Dip the steamed cauliflower flowerets into the seasoned flour one by one. Next, dip in beaten egg and then in Parmesan cheese. Fry the cauliflower flowerets in hot oil in a deep-fryer at 400°F (200°C) until golden and crisp. Serve immediately.

To Cook Cauliflower

Remove the outer leaves and wash both the cauliflower and the leaves well. Put no more than 1 inch (2.5cm) of water in a pot just large enough to take the cauliflower; add a little salt. Chop the leaves into small pieces and cut the cauliflower into quarters. Place the cauliflower on top of the green leaves in the pot, cover, and simmer until the cauliflower is cooked, about 15 minutes. Test by piercing the stalk with a knife; there should be just a little resistance. Remove the cauliflower and the leaves to an ovenproof serving dish, depending on how it is being served.

Master Recipe

Brussels Sprouts

Serves 4–6

Not surprisingly many people hate Brussels sprouts because they are all too often overcooked.

The traditional way to cook sprouts was to cut a cross in the stalk so that they would, hopefully, cook more evenly. Fortunately I discovered quite by accident when I was in a mad rush one day, that if you cut the sprouts in half lengthwise, they cook much faster and taste infinitely more delicious so with this recipe I've managed to convert many ardent Brussels sprout haters!

1 lb. (450g) Brussels sprouts, cut lengthwise top to bottom
2½ cups water
1½ teaspoons salt
2–4 tablespoons butter
salt and freshly ground pepper

Choose even, medium-sized sprouts. Trim the outer leaves if necessary and cut them in half lengthwise. Salt the water and bring to a fast rolling boil. Toss in the sprouts, cover the pot just for 1 minute until the water returns to a boil, then uncover and cook for 5–6 minutes or until the sprouts are tender but still have a slight bite. Pour off the water.*

Melt the butter in a saucepan, roll the sprouts gently in the butter, season with lots of pepper and salt. Taste and serve immediately in a hot serving dish.

* If the sprouts are not to be served immediately, refresh them under cold water just as soon as they are cooked. Just before serving, drop them into boiling salted water for a few seconds to heat through. Drain, and toss in the butter, season and serve. This way they will taste almost as good as if they were freshly cooked: certainly much more delicious than sprouts kept warm for half an hour in an oven or a hostess trolley.

Variations

Brussels Sprouts with Buttered Almonds

Follow the Master Recipe. Meanwhile melt 1 tablespoon butter in a frying pan, toss in about ¼ cup nibbed or sliced almonds and cook for a few minutes or until golden. As soon as the sprouts are cooked, drain and toss with the buttered almonds. Serve immediately in a hot dish.

Brussels Sprouts with Buttered Almonds and Bacon

Follow the Master Recipe. Add 2–4 ounces (50–110g) of crispy bacon to the almonds in the recipe above, and serve immediately.

Pixie's Yummy Brussels

Follow the Master Recipe. Heat 2½ tablespoons of oil in a wok over a high heat, add 1 tablespoon butter, add ½ cup slivered almonds, toss for 1–2 minutes and add the sprouts, 1 teaspoon of garam masala, and ⅔ cup of cream. Season with freshly ground pepper, and let it bubble. Taste and serve immediately.

Purée of Brussels Sprouts

1¼ lbs. (600g) Brussels Sprouts
⅔–1 cup cream
2 tablespoons butter
salt and freshly ground pepper

Cook the sprouts, then drain and put them in a blender along with the cream and butter, and purée until smooth. Season with salt and pepper to taste. Reheat in a non-stick saucepan or sauté pan.

Master Recipe
Bok Choi

Serves 4–6

1 lb. (450g) bok choi (pak choi)
5 cups water
2 teaspoons salt
freshly ground pepper
2 tablespoons butter

Cut the bok choi into about ¾-inch (2-cm) squares. Steam or cook in boiling, salted water until tender – 3–5 minutes. Drain well. Melt the butter in the pan and toss the bok choi in it. Serve immediately.

Variations

Bok Choi with Oyster Sauce

Follow the Master Recipe, omitting the butter. Douse in 3–4 tablespoons of oyster sauce and serve immediately.

Bok Choi with Ginger, Garlic, and Chile

Follow the Master Recipe, omitting the butter. Heat 3–4 tablespoons of sunflower oil in a hot wok, add 1 teaspoon of grated ginger, 1 teaspoon of chopped garlic, and ½–1 sliced green chile. Cook for 1–2 minutes in the hot oil, add the bok choi, toss gently to coat, taste, and correct seasoning – a few tablespoons sliced scallion greens is a good addition.

Bok Choi with Tomato and Ginger

Follow the Master Recipe, omitting the butter. Just before serving, toss in a hot wok with ¼–½ of the recipe for Tomato Fondue (see page 188) and 1 teaspoon of freshly grated ginger. Finish with a few drops of toasted sesame oil.

Master Recipe
Buttered Spinach

Serves 4–6

Here are 3 different basic methods of cooking fresh spinach – all of them a huge improvement on the watery mush that frozen spinach often ends up as.

2 lbs. (900g) fresh spinach, weighed without stalks
salt, freshly ground pepper, and a little freshly grated nutmeg
½–1 stick (¼–½ cup) butter

Method 1

Melt a scrap of butter in a wide frying pan or pot, toss in as much spinach as will fit easily, season with salt and freshly ground pepper. As soon as the spinach wilts and becomes tender, strain off all the liquid, increase the heat and add some butter and freshly grated nutmeg. Serve immediately.

Method 2

Wash the prepared spinach and drain. Put into a heavy pot on a very low heat, season, and cover tightly. After a few minutes, stir and replace the lid. As soon as the spinach is cooked, about 5–8 minutes, strain off the copious amount of liquid that spinach releases and press the spinach between two plates until almost dry. Chop, or purée in a food processor if you like a smooth texture, and return to the pot. Increase the heat, add butter, correct the seasoning, and add a little freshly grated nutmeg to taste.

Method 3

Cook the spinach uncovered in a large pot of boiling salted water until soft, about 4–5 minutes. Drain and press out all the water. Continue as in method 2. Method 3 produces a brighter colored spinach.

Variations

Caribbean Spinach with Dill

The little island of St. Barths is a French-owned colony in the Caribbean. Just opposite the tiny airport building, Gucci, Versace, Cartier, Hermès, all have shops to tempt the well-heeled tourists who frequent the island. Virtually no food is produced there; it's all imported from France or neighboring islands and even the milk and yogurt is French. In general, the food was expensive and bad. The last straw was when I asked for local fish in one of the restaurants and the waiter told me excitedly that there was no local fish but they had Dover Sole which had just arrived in from France. This spinach was almost the best thing we ate. Add half the recipe of Tomato Fondue (see page 188) to Buttered Spinach cooked by Method 1 in the Master Recipe. Just before serving, add 3–5 tablespoons of freshly chopped dill. Taste, and correct the seasoning. Serve with lamb or pan-grilled local fish.

Spinach with Raisins and Pine nuts

Cook the spinach as in the Master Recipe. Soak 2–3 tablespoons seedless raisins in boiling water for 10 minutes until they are plump and juicy. Toast 1/4–1/3 cup of pine nuts until they are golden brown. Add the raisins and pine nuts to the spinach. Season well and let bubble for 4–5 minutes. Add a splash of balsamic vinegar and serve.

Creamed Spinach

Follow the Master Recipe, cooking the spinach by method 2 or 3; drain very well. Add 1–1½ cups of cream to the spinach and bring to a boil, stir well, and thicken with a little Roux (see page 580) if desired, otherwise stir over the heat until the spinach has absorbed most of the cream. Season with salt, pepper, and freshly grated nutmeg to taste. Creamed spinach may be cooked ahead of time and reheated.

Oeufs Florentine

A classic dish and one of the most delicious combinations, this is one of our favorite lunch or supper dishes. Serve freshly poached fresh organic eggs on top of creamed spinach.

Saag

Serves 4–6

4 ounces (110g) sliced onion (about 1 cup)
3 cloves garlic, crushed (optional)
1–2 chopped fresh Jalapeño chiles (or less of Thai)
2½ tablespoons olive oil
1 lb. (450g) very ripe tomatoes
3 lbs. (1.3kg) spinach, destalked and sliced
1 teaspoon garam masala

Sweat the sliced onions and garlic and chile (if used) in oil on a gentle heat. It is vital for the success of this dish that the onions are completely soft before the tomatoes are added. Remove the hard core from the tomatoes. Put them into a deep bowl and cover them with boiling water. Count to 10 and then pour off the water immediately; peel off the skins, chop, and add to the onions. Season with salt, freshly ground pepper, and sugar. Add the spinach, toss on a high heat, cover for a few minutes. Add the garam masala and continue to cook for 20–25 minutes or until virtually no liquid remains. Cook for just 10 minutes, or until the tomato softens. Taste, correct seasoning. May be served immediately or reheated later.

Wilted Greens

Serves 4

Allow about 1 fistful of greens per person: a mixture of young vegetable leaves (young beet greens, Swiss chard, spinach, sorrel, arugula)
2½ tablespoons olive oil
1/4–1/2 red chile, seeded and chopped
1 garlic clove, chopped
salt and freshly ground pepper

Heat the olive oil in a pan, add in the garlic and chile, then the greens, and toss well, season with salt and freshly ground pepper. Taste and serve as soon as they have just wilted.

Master Recipe

Ruby Chard or Swiss Chard with Butter

Serves 4

There are several ways of using chard stalks including tossing them in vinaigrette or olive oil and lemon juice. Cook the green leaves as you would spinach (see left).

1 lb. (450g) Swiss chard stalks (weigh after leaves are removed)
butter or olive oil
salt and freshly ground pepper

Pull the green leaves off the chard stalks and wash and drain. Cut the chard stalks into pieces about 2 inches (5cm) long. Cook in boiling, salted water until they feel tender when pierced with the tip of a knife. Drain very well. Toss in a little melted butter or olive oil and serve immediately.

Variation

Ruby Chard or Swiss Chard with Parmesan

Follow the Master Recipe, until the draining stage. Grease an earthenware dish – 10 x 8 inches (25 x 20cm) with a little butter, arrange some of the chard stalks in

a single layer, and season with salt and pepper. Sprinkle with about 1½ cups of freshly grated Parmesan cheese and dot with a little butter. Repeat until the dish is full, finally sprinkle the top layer generously with the freshly grated Parmesan cheese. Dot with a little butter. Bake in a preheated oven, 400°F (200°C), for 15–20 minutes or until crisp and golden. This also works well with fennel.

Master Recipe
Grilled Belgian Endive or Radicchio
Serves 6

Marcella and Victor Hazan told me about this delicious way to cook Belgian endive while we ate huge pizzas in a trattoria in Venice. Serve hot or lukewarm, as an accompanying vegetable or as part of an appetizer. A plate of Italian antipasto might include some char-grilled peppers with basil, a slice or two of bresaola or prosciutto, sun-dried tomatoes sprinkled with parsley and garlic and drizzled with olive oil, a few black olives, and a slice of bruschetta.

6 perfect plump heads of Belgian endive or radicchio trevisano
extra-virgin olive oil
sea salt or kosher salt
freshly ground pepper

Preheat the broiler.

Discard any discolored or wilted leaves from the Belgian endive or radicchio, trim the base, and wash if necessary. Cut them in half lengthwise and then make little cuts in the root part so that the heat and oil can penetrate. Arrange the endive halves, cut side up, in the broiler pan and paint with olive oil. Sprinkle with sea salt and pepper and put under the hot broiler about 4 inches (10cm) from the flame.

After 7–8 minutes, turn the endive over and paint again with olive oil. Cook for a further 7–8 minutes and then turn again, basting with the oil in the broiler pan and adding more if necessary. Cook for another 5–8 minutes, depending on size. The Belgian endive or radicchio is cooked when the root end can be pierced easily with the tip of a knife. At this stage it will look slightly sad and blackened but will taste quite delicious.

Variation
Mimmo's Grilled Belgian Endive with Gorgonzola and Walnuts
Follow the Master Recipe and just before serving put some gorgonzola and a very little finely chopped walnut on top of each piece. Exquisite hot or lukewarm!

Master Recipe
Braised Belgian Endive
Serves 6

6 heads of Belgian endive, tightly closed with no trace of green
5 cups water
1 teaspoon sugar
2 teaspoons salt
good squeeze of lemon juice
1–2 tablespoons butter
freshly chopped flat-leaf parsley

Remove a thin slice from the root end of each endive. Remove the center root with the tip of a sharp knife if you find it too bitter. Bring the water to a boil, add the salt, sugar, a good squeeze of lemon juice, and the Belgian endive. Cook for about 45 minutes to 1 hour or until almost or completely tender, depending on how you intend to finish the cooking (when it is completely tender, a knife tip will pierce the root end without resistance). Remove the endive, drain well, then squeeze out all excess water (I do this in a clean lint-free towel).

Melt the butter in a wide sauté pan, put in the endive in a single layer and cook over a *very* low heat turning occasionally until golden on all sides. This takes about 30–40 minutes. Serve in a hot serving dish sprinkled with a little parsley.

Variation
Chicory à la Crème
As above but add ½ cup of cream to the endive when it is golden, increase the heat, and let it bubble for a few minutes.

Master Recipe
Melted Leeks
Serves 6–8

8 medium leeks
½ stick (¼ cup) butter
2 tablespoons water, if necessary
salt and freshly ground pepper
parsley or chervil, chopped

Cut off the dark green leaves from the top of the leeks. Slit the leeks about half way down the center and wash well under cold running water. Slice into ¼-inch (5-mm) rings.

Melt the butter in a heavy saucepan; we use an oval Le Creuset casserole; when it foams, add the sliced leeks and toss gently to coat with butter. Season with salt and pepper. Cover with a wax paper lid and a close-fitting saucepan lid. Reduce the heat and cook very gently for about 10–20 minutes, or until soft and moist.*

Check and stir every now and then. Serve on a warm dish either plain or sprinkled with parsley or chervil.

Note: The leeks may be cooked in the oven preheated to 325°F (170°C) if that is more convenient.

*Frequently, we turn off the heat after 5–8 minutes and let the leeks finish cooking in the saucepan.

Leeks with Yellow Peppers and Marjoram
Serves 6

This mixture is also irresistible served in crispy shortcrust pastry tartlets or phyllo triangles.

Melted Leeks (see above)
3 yellow peppers
1½ tablespoons water
1½–2½ tablespoons fresh annual marjoram or a mixture of parsley, basil, and marjoram, chopped

Add the peppers to the Melted Leeks in the pan, toss, and add a drop more water if necessary, and half the herbs. Cover, and continue to cook until the peppers are soft. Taste, add the remainder of the herbs, correct the seasoning, and serve.

Variation
Leeks with Yellow Peppers and Marjoram Tart
Fill a fully-baked savory tart shell with the cooked vegetable mixture and serve immediately.

Master Recipe
Leek Vinaigrette
Serves 8

The secret of this recipe is to toss the leeks in vinaigrette while they are still warm.

8 medium leeks
4–5 tablespoons Ballymaloe French Dressing (see page 225)

Trim the leeks down to the pale end (save the trimmings for the stock pot). Clean them thoroughly under running water, and poach them gently in a little boiling salted water until just tender.

Alternatively cut the leeks into ½-inch (1-cm) rings at an angle. Poach in a covered saucepan in just a very little boiling salted water.

Remove the leeks from the water with a perforated spoon and let cool for a few minutes. Coat with French dressing while still warm and let them marinate. The leeks may be served as a first course or an accompanying salad.

Variations
Leek Vinaigrette Terrine with Beet Sauce
Follow the Master Recipe. When the warm leeks have been tossed in vinaigrette, arrange in layers in a lined terrine, cover, and gently press with a board and light weight. Next day, turn out and cut into thick slices with the utmost care. Serve with lots of crusty white bread, and a beet sauce made from Pickled Beets (see page 514), from which the onion has been omitted.

Coolea Cheese and Leek Fritters
Makes 25 approx. depending on size.

Helene Willems cooked these little fritters over a camp stove in the open air at the Slow Food Convivium at Bill Hogan's in Schull, Co. Cork. They smelled tantalizing and tasted delicious. Gouda can be used if you can't find Coolea.

14 ounces (400g) leeks, trimmed and thinly sliced
2 tablespoons butter
1¾ cups flour
2 eggs
1 cup milk
1¾ cups freshly shredded mature Coolea farmhouse cheese or Gouda
salt and freshly ground pepper
chile pepper
freshly grated nutmeg

Melt the butter in a large pan, add the sliced leeks, cover, and sweat on a gentle heat until soft but not colored. This will take about 5 minutes. Cool.

Sift the flour into a bowl, make a well in the center, add the eggs, and break up with a whisk. Add the milk gradually, whisking all the time in a circular movement from the center to the outside of the bowl. Add the cooled leeks and the shredded cheese. Season with the salt, pepper, chile pepper, and nutmeg to taste.

Heat a frying pan, preferably non-stick, on a medium heat. Drop a small spoonful of the batter onto the pan, let cook until golden, flip over onto the other side and cook for 1–2 minutes. Taste, and correct the seasoning if necessary.

Cook the remainder in the same way. Serve hot on their own or with a little Tomato and Chile Sauce (see page 590) or Tomato Fondue (see page 188).

Oven-roasted Winter Root Vegetables

about equal volumes of:
parsnips
rutabagas
celeriac (celery root)
carrot
salt and freshly ground pepper
olive oil
winter herbs (thyme, rosemary, chives, and parsley), freshly chopped

Preheat the oven to 400°F (200°C).

Peel the vegetables and cut into similar-sized pieces – 3/4-inch (2-cm) cubes are a good size. Put all the vegetables into a large bowl. Drizzle generously with olive oil and season well with salt and pepper.

Spread them in a single layer on 1 or several roasting pans. Roast, uncovered, stirring occasionally until they are fully cooked and just beginning to caramelize. Be careful, a little color makes them sweeter, but there is a narrow line between caramelizing and burning. If they become too dark, they will be bitter.

Serve sprinkled with the herbs.

Note: some freshly roasted and ground cumin or coriander is also a delicious addition just before the end of cooking.

Mashed Parsnips

Serves 4

In their valiant efforts to help the poor during the potato famines of 1845 and 1846, The Society of Friends encouraged the cultivation of parsnips which had been grown in Ireland since early Christian times. In early writings, there are many references to meacan, which scholars believe to be parsnips. Originally they would have been boiled and mashed with country butter. They are also delicious mixed with carrots, or cut into chunks and roast, alone or around a joint of beef. Crispy parsnip cakes also make an irresistible and inexpensive treat.

1 1/2 lbs. (700g) parsnips
salt and freshly ground pepper
chopped parsley
1/2–3/4 stick (1/4–1/3 cup) butter

Peel the parsnips thinly. Cut off the tops and tails and cut them into wedges. Remove the inner core if it seems to be at all woody, and divide the wedges into 3/4-inch (2-cm) approx. cubes. Cook them in boiling salted water for 15–20 minutes. They should be quite soft. Drain. Mash with a potato masher, add a nice bit of butter, and season well with salt and freshly ground pepper. The texture should not be too smooth.

Variation

Parsnip Cakes with Crispy Bacon

Follow the Master Recipe, let cool, then wet your hands and shape the mixture into 6 cakes. Dip each in flour, beaten egg, and breadcrumbs. Heat a little olive oil with some butter in a wide frying pan, fry the cakes on a gentle heat until golden on both sides. Serve hot with lardons of crispy bacon or as an accompaniment to a main course.

Pan-roasted Parsnips

Serves 6–8

I have a real passion for pan-roasted parsnips – we eat them 3 or 4 times a week during the parsnip season.

4 parsnips
olive oil
salt and freshly ground pepper

Preheat the oven to 450°F (230°C).

Peel the parsnips and cut them into quarters – the chunks should be quite large. Roast in olive oil in the hot oven for 30 minutes, turning them frequently so that they do not become too crusty. We often roast them in the same pan as Rustic Roast Potatoes (see page 181). Cooked this way they will be crisp outside and soft in the center.

Saratoga Fries

Parsnips also make very good fries. Cook them in a deep-fryer using good quality oil at 350°F (180°C).

Parsnip Chips (see page 287)

Soy-Glazed Parsnips with Sesame Seeds

Serves 4–6

Naranjan McCormack from Malaysia but now living in Fermoy, Co Cork teaches this recipe to our students at an Asian class. Palm sugar, also known as "Gula Melaka" and, in the U.S., as "jaggery." This is a hard brown sugar made from the sap of the Aaren palm. If not available, substitute with light soft brown sugar with a touch of maple syrup. The natural sweetness of parsnips, the intense savoriness of the soy sauce, and the crisp nuttiness of the sesame seeds make an excellent combination in this inexpensive vegetable recipe.

1 lb. (450g) smallish parsnips, peeled and sliced into strips
1½ tablespoons peanut oil
2 ounces (50g) palm sugar (jaggery) (about ¼ cup)
4–5 tablespoons light soy sauce
2½ tablespoons toasted sesame seeds

Put the parsnips in a heavy saucepan with the peanut oil and cook them until halfway tender. Add the palm sugar and cook over a medium heat until the sugar has dissolved. Stir in the soy sauce and continue cooking until the parsnips are tender. Transfer to a hot serving dish and sprinkle with the toasted sesame seeds.

Note: Carrots, turnips, yams, mooli, sweet potato, and other root vegetables can be cooked this way. Add a splash of rice vinegar or coconut vinegar for a sweet and sour tang.

Master Recipe
Glazed Carrots

Serves 4–6

Unwashed carrots keep better and have infinitely more flavor than ready washed carrots. If you don't believe me, experiment. Early Nantes and Autumn King carrots have particularly good flavor. Cook some of each in exactly the same way in different saucepans and the difference in flavor is a revelation.

This method of cooking carrots takes a little vigilance but the resulting flavor is delicious.

1 lb. (450g) carrots, topped, tailed, and cleaned
1 tablespoon butter
½ cup cold water
pinch of salt
a good pinch of sugar

Garnish
parsley or mint, freshly chopped

Cut the carrots into slices ¼ inch (5mm) thick, either straight across or at an angle. Leave very young carrots whole.

Put them in a saucepan with the butter, water, salt, and sugar. Bring to a boil, cover, and cook over a gentle heat until tender, by which time the liquid should have all been absorbed into the carrots, but if not, remove the lid and increase the heat until all the water has evaporated. Taste and correct the seasoning.

Shake the saucepan so the carrots become coated with the buttery glaze. Serve sprinkled with parsley or mint.

Variation
Glazed Carrots with Cumin Seeds

Follow the Master Recipe, adding ½–1 teaspoon cumin seeds just before all the water has evaporated. Garnish with freshly chopped parsley. Freshly roasted coriander seeds are equally delicious.

Carrot Croquettes with Apricots and Pine nuts

Makes about 24 croquettes

Another delicious recipe from Antony Worrall-Thompson.

10 medium carrots, peeled and cooked until soft
2 slices white bread, made into crumbs
6 dried apricots, finely diced
4 scallions, finely diced
2½ tablespoons toasted pine nuts
3 garlic cloves, finely chopped
1 teaspoon dried chili flakes
1 egg
1 bunch parsley, finely chopped
½ bunch mint, finely chopped
½ bunch dill, finely chopped
salt and ground black pepper
flour for coating
sunflower oil for frying

Yogurt Dip
1 cup Greek yogurt or thick wholemilk yogurt
1½ tablespoons lemon juice
1½ tablespoons crushed garlic
1½ tablespoons fresh mint, chopped

Mash the carrots, add remaining ingredients, and knead well. If too wet, add more breadcrumbs – the mixture should be moist and sticky.

Mold the purée into 2 x 1-inch (5 x 2.5-cm) oblongs, coating hands with flour to stop the mixture sticking to you. Roll each oblong in flour. Refrigerate until ready to use.

Prepare the Yogurt Dip by mixing all the ingredients in a small bowl and seasoning with salt and pepper (can be prepared 1 day ahead, covered, and refrigerated). Fry the carrot rolls in oil in a sauté pan until brown all over. Serve immediately as an appetizer with the Yogurt Dip.

Carrot and Potato with Cream and Fresh Spices

Serves 6

Fresh spices can add magic to your cooking – here they give an altogether new dimension to carrots and potatoes. Cardamom is a member of the ginger family and also known as "grains of paradise". Often used in Indian curries, in Scandinavia it is used to flavor cakes and breads. Sophie Grigson introduced us to this dish when she was guest chef at the school.

2 lbs. (900g) medium potatoes
1 lb. (450g) carrots
2½ teaspoons cumin seeds
1 tablespoon coriander seeds
1-inch (2.5-cm) piece of cinnamon stick
1 teaspoon cardamom seeds
8 cloves
¼ teaspoon black peppercorns
1 tablespoon butter
1 large red onion, roughly diced

1 garlic clove, finely chopped
1 ounce (25g) fresh ginger (about the size of 2 large marbles), peeled and grated
1/4 teaspoon freshly grated nutmeg
1/2 teaspoon turmeric
1 teaspoon sugar
1/2 teaspoon salt
1 1/2 lbs. (700g) very ripe tomatoes, peeled and chopped
3/4 cup yogurt
1/2–1 cup creamy milk
2–3 tablespoons fresh cilantro, chopped

Garnish
sprigs of fresh cilantro
Ballymaloe Tomato Relish

Cook the potatoes, unpeeled, in boiling, salted water until just cooked. Scrape or thinly peel the carrots and cut into 1/2-inch (1-cm) thick slices; cook in a little boiling, salted water until just tender.

Put the whole spices into a spice grinder or mortar and pestle and grind finely. Melt the butter in a saucepan and cook the onion until golden. Add the garlic, ginger, ground spices, nutmeg, turmeric, sugar, and salt. Cook for 1–2 minutes, then add the tomato, and finally the yogurt, bit by bit, stirring well.

Peel the cooked potatoes and cut into 1/2-inch (1-cm) slices. Add with the carrots to the sauce, stir in the milk, simmer until they have warmed through. Stir in the cilantro, taste and correct the seasoning, and serve immediately with a good green salad.

Carrot, Parsnip, and Cabbage with Mustard Seed

Serves 6

8 ounces (225g) carrots, coarsely grated (about 2 cups)
8 ounces (225g) parsnips, coarsely grated (about 2 cups)
8 ounces (225g) cabbage, finely shredded against the grain (about 3 3/4 cups)
1/4 cup sunflower oil
1 1/2 tablespoons black mustard seeds
1 chile, seeded and chopped
2 1/2 tablespoons parsley, chopped
2 1/2 tablespoons mint, freshly chopped
salt, freshly ground pepper, and sugar
freshly squeezed lemon juice, to taste

Heat the oil in a sauté pan and add the mustard seeds. They will start to pop almost instantly. Add the chopped chile and stir and cook for a minute or so. Add the carrots, parsnips, and cabbage. Toss over a medium heat for 2 or 3 minutes, then add the parsley and mint and toss again. Season with salt, freshly ground pepper, and a little sugar. Add the lemon juice, taste, and correct seasoning. Serve immediately.

Master Recipe
Buttered Celery

Serves 4–6

When you arrive at the delicious tender leaves at the center, do not cut off the base, simply break off, nibble, or save for crudités. A little block of root remains. Trim this and taste; it resembles celeriac and is delicious, eaten raw or diced and cooked with the celery.

1 head of celery
2 tablespoons butter
salt and freshly ground pepper

Garnish
chopped parsley

Pull the stalks off the head of celery. If the outer stalks seems a bit tough, peel the strings off with a swivel-top peeler or simply save these tougher stalks for the stock pot. Cut the celery into 1/2-inch (1-cm) chunks, preferably at an angle.

Bring 2/3 cup water to a boil in a saucepan. Add a little salt and the chopped celery. Cover and cook for 15–20 minutes or until a knife will go through the celery with ease. Drain, add the butter, and season with salt and pepper. Serve garnished with parsley. A little snipped lovage is also a delicious addition.

Variation
Celery with Cream and Parsley

as above plus
1/2–3/4 cup cream
Roux (see page 580)
freshly chopped parsley

Follow the Master Recipe until the celery is cooked then remove it, pour off most of the water, and add the cream. Thicken with a little roux, add the celery back in and let it bubble for a few minutes. Put into a hot serving dish, sprinkle with parsley, and serve.

Celeriac and Apple Purée

Serves 4

Particularly delicious with game, celeriac is a knobbly root vegetable that can be dug from the ground all through the winter months when needed.

1 lb. (450g) celeriac, after peeling
4 cups lightly salted water
12 ounces (350g) dessert apples, e.g., Cox's orange pippin (about 2 medium-sized apples)
1/4 cup cream
salt and freshly ground pepper

Peel the celeriac and cut it into large chunks. Simmer them in the water until soft and tender, about 15 minutes.

Meanwhile, peel and core the apples, cut them into quarters, and cook with a teaspoon of sugar and a very little water (about 2 teaspoons) in a covered saucepan until soft. When the celeriac is cooked, drain and add it to the apple. Purée them in a food processor until smooth and add the cream. Taste, and season with salt and pepper.

Right: Carrot, Parsnip, and Cabbage with Mustard Seed

This purée can be prepared ahead and reheated in a moderate oven (350°C/180°C).

Celeriac Rémoulade

Serves 12–15

A favorite winter salad when I was an au pair in France. Use it in combination with other winter salads as an appetizer.

1½ lbs. (700g) celeriac
1½ cups Homemade Mayonnaise (see page 584)
freshly ground pepper
lemon juice, freshly squeezed
1 tablespoon plus 1 teaspoon Dijon mustard

Trim with a knife and peel the celeriac thickly. Grate it coarsely. Stir the Dijon mustard into the mayonnaise and add some to the celeriac (keep back a little in case not all is needed). It should be saucy but not too sloppy. Add lemon juice to taste and a little more seasoning if necessary.

Celeriac Crisps

Serve with game or sprinkled over salades tièdes.

1 celeriac root
acidulated water
oil for deep-frying
salt

Peel the celeriac. Leave whole or cut into quarters and drop into acidulated water until ready to cook.

Heat the oil in deep fryer to 330°F (150°C). Dry the celeriac and slice into paper thin slices on a mandoline. Fry a few at a time until pale golden. Drain on paper towels and sprinkle with a little salt.

How to Cook Beets

Leave 2 inches (5cm) of leaf stalks on top and the whole root on the beet. Hold it under a running faucet and wash off the mud with the palms of your hands, so that you don't damage the skin; otherwise the beets will bleed during cooking. Cover with cold water and add a little salt and sugar. Cover the pot, bring to a boil, and simmer on top, or in an oven, for 1–2 hours depending on size. Beets are ready if they dent when pressed with a finger. If in doubt, test with a skewer or the tip of a knife.

Hot Beets

Serves 6

We all adore beets. In summer we eat them from the time they are walnut sized, when they cook in just 10 or 15 minutes and are sweet and tender. Serve with duck, beef, or lamb. Hot beets are also divine with fish, particularly cod.

1½ lbs. (700g) beets, cooked (see above)
1 tablespoon butter
½–¾ cup cream
salt and freshly ground pepper
a sprinkling of sugar (may not be necessary)
1½–2½ teaspoons chives, finely chopped

Peel the cooked beets, using rubber gloves for this operation if you are vain. Chop the beet flesh into cubes. Melt the butter in a sauté pan, add the beets, toss, add the cream, and let bubble for a few minutes. Season with salt, pepper, and sugar, if necessary. Sprinkle over the chives and serve immediately.

Roast Beets with Goat Cheese and Balsamic Vinegar

Serves 4

6–12 baby beets, a mixture of red, golden, and Clioggia would be wonderful
sea salt or kosher salt, and freshly cracked pepper
extra-virgin olive oil
balsamic vinegar
6 ounces (175g) goat cheese
arugula and beet greens
wild garlic leaves (if available)

Preheat the oven to 450°F (230°C).

Wrap the beets in tin foil and roast in the oven until soft and cooked through – between ½ and 1 hour, depending on size.

To serve: rub the skins off the beets and keep whole or cut into quarters. Toss in the extra-virgin olive oil. Scatter a few arugula and tiny beet leaves on each serving plate. Arrange a selection of warm beets on top. Drizzle with more olive oil and balsamic vinegar. Put 2 teaspoons of goat cheese beside the beets. Sprinkle with sea salt and pepper and garnish with tiny beet greens or wild garlic flowers, and serve.

Beet Tops

Beet tops are full of vitamins and minerals. They are often unnecessarily discarded – if you grow your own, remember to cook them as well as the beets. When the leaves are tiny, they make a really worthwhile addition to the salad bowl, both in terms of nutrition and flavor.

1 lb. (450g) fresh beet tops
butter or olive oil
salt and freshly ground pepper

Cut the stalks and leaves into approx. 2-inch (5-cm) pieces. Cook in boiling salted water (2 quarts [1.8 liters] water to 1½ teaspoons salt) for 6–8 minutes or until tender. Drain, season, and toss in a little butter or olive oil. Serve immediately.

Right: Roast Beets with Goat Cheese and Balsamic Vinegar

Rutabagas with Caramelized Onions

Serves 6

The humble rutabaga is wonderfully perked up by being served with soft sweet onions.

2 lbs. (900g) rutabagas
salt and freshly ground pepper
1/2–1 stick (1/4–1/2 cup) butter

Garnish
finely chopped parsley
Caramelized Onions (page 188)

Peel the rutabaga thickly in order to remove the thick outer skin. Cut into 3/4-inch (2-cm) cubes. Cover with water. Add a good pinch of salt, bring to a boil, and cook until soft. Strain off the excess water, mash the rutabagas well and beat in the butter. Taste and season with plenty of freshly ground pepper and extra salt if necessary. Garnish with the parsley and serve piping hot with the Caramelized Onions.

Braised White Turnips with Marjoram

Serves 4–6

This recipe is sensational on its own but particularly delicious with duck.

1 lb. (450g) small white turnips
2 tablespoons butter
1 1/2–2 1/2 tablespoons oregano or annual marjoram

sprigs of annual marjoram
salt and freshly ground pepper

Wash and peel the white turnips and cut into 1/2-inch (1-cm) slices. Melt the butter in a heavy flameproof casserole dish. Add the sliced turnips and season with salt and freshly ground pepper. Add 1 1/2 tablespoons water and 2 teaspoons chopped marjoram. Cover and cook on a gentle heat until tender, 8–10 minutes, until the turnip is just tender. Taste and correct seasoning, and add a little more freshly chopped marjoram and serve immediately.

Variation

Kohl Rabi with Marjoram

Substitute Kohl Rabi for white turnips in the recipe above, using less marjoram so as not to overpower the delectable but delicate flavor.

Radishes with Butter, Crusty Bread, and Sea Salt

When I was just 19, alone and frightened in Besançon in eastern France, a French girl took pity on me and invited me to have lunch with her in a café. We had a plate of charcuterie and radishes. I watched in fascination as she buttered her radishes, dipped them in sea salt, and ate them greedily. I followed suit – I've never forgotten the flavor.

fresh radishes complete with leaves
butter pats
sea salt or kosher salt
crusty bread

Gently wash the radishes, trim the tail and the top of the leaves if they are large. Cut a chunk of butter into 1/2-inch (1-cm) cubes. If you have butter pats, soak them in cold water and then roll each cube into a butter ball; drop them into a bowl of iced water.

To serve: put 7 or 8 chilled radishes on each plate, add 2 or 3 butter balls and a little mound of sea salt. Serve fresh crusty bread as an accompaniment.

Roasted Jerusalem Artichokes

Serves 4–6

Just delectable, roast Jerusalem artichokes are high on my list of favorite winter vegetables – if you have any space at all, pop a few into the ground; they grow and multiply really easily. The foliage grows to a height of 7–8 feet (2.1–2.5m) in the summer; ideal to provide privacy from prying neighbors or to make a maze for children to play in. There are "dwarf" varieties, too. The season finishes about mid-March.

1 lb. (450g) Jerusalem artichokes, well scrubbed and sliced into 1/2-inch (1-cm) rounds
2 1/2 tablespoons sunflower or olive oil
salt and freshly ground pepper
a few rosemary or thyme sprigs (optional)

Preheat the oven to 400°F (200°C).
Toss the Jerusalem artichokes with the oil in a roasting pan. Season well with salt. Bake for 15–30 minutes depending on size. Test with the tip of a knife – they should be mostly tender but offer some resistance. Sprinkle with thyme or rosemary. Season with pepper and serve.

Braised Jerusalem Artichokes

Serves 4

The flavor of Jerusalem artichokes is particularly good with game, beef, or shellfish.

1 1/2 lbs. (700g) Jerusalem artichokes
2 tablespoons butter
2 teaspoons water
salt and freshly ground pepper
parsley, chopped

Peel the artichokes thinly and slice them into 1/4-inch (5-mm) rounds. Melt the butter in a cast-iron pot or flameproof casserole dish, toss the artichokes and season with salt and pepper. Add the water and cover with a wax paper lid (to keep in the steam) and the saucepan lid. Cook on a low heat* or put in a moderate oven, 350°F (180°C), until the artichokes are soft but still keep their shape; about 15–20 minutes. Toss every now and then during cooking. Serve sprinkled with parsley.

* If cooking on the stove top rather than in the oven, turn off the heat after about 10 minutes – the artichokes will continue to cook in the heat and will hold their shape.

Master Recipe
Roast Potatoes

Everybody loves roast potatoes, yet people ask over and over again for the secret of golden crispy roast potatoes. Duck or goose fat gives a delicious flavor to roast potatoes. Good-quality pork fat or lard from free-range pigs is also worth saving carefully for roast or sauté potatoes. All three fats will keep for months in a cold larder or fridge. Good chicken fat and olive oil are also good for browning roast potatoes.

Buy good quality "floury" potatoes such as russets. Waxy potatoes are not very good for roasting. Cut the potatoes into similar sizes. For perfection, peel them just before roasting. Do not leave them soaking in water or they will be soggy inside because of the water they absorb. This always applies, no matter how you cook potatoes. Unfortunately, many people have got into the habit of peeling and soaking potatoes even if they are just going to boil and mash them.

Dry the potatoes carefully, otherwise they will stick to the roasting pan, and when you turn them over you will lose the crispy bit underneath. If you have a fan oven, it is best to blanch and refresh the potatoes first, then proceed as below.

Heat olive oil or fat in a roasting pan and toss the potatoes to make sure they are well coated. Roast in a hot oven (400°F/200°C), basting occasionally, for 30–60 minutes depending on size.

Rustic Roast Potatoes

Serves 4–6

These are my children's favorite kind of roast spuds. They particularly love all the crusty skin.

6 large potatoes
olive oil or duck or goose fat or beef dripping (unless for Vegetarians)
sea salt or kosher salt

Preheat the oven to 450°F (230°C).
Scrub the potatoes well, cut them into quarters lengthwise or cut into thick rounds 3/4 inches (2cm) approximately. Put into a roasting pan, drizzle them with olive oil, and toss so they are barely coated. Roast in the oven for 30–40 minutes depending on size. Sprinkle with sea salt and serve.

Variations

Rustic Roast Potatoes with Rosemary

Follow the Master Recipe, adding a few sprigs of rosemary or some coarsely chopped rosemary with the olive oil and proceed as above. Serve garnished with a fresh sprig of rosemary.

Rustic Roast Potatoes with Thyme

Follow the Master Recipe, substituting thyme for rosemary; marjoram is also gorgeous.

Rustic Roast Potatoes with Garlic Cloves

Follow the Master Recipe, adding 18 or more unpeeled garlic cloves after the potatoes have been cooking for 10–15 minutes. Toss in the oil. Keep an eye on the garlic cloves; they will probably be cooked before the potatoes and, if so, remove and keep them warm in a serving dish. Press the soft sweet garlic out of the skins and eat it with the crispy potatoes.

Below: Rustic Roast Potatoes with Garlic Cloves

Master Recipe
Fluffy Mashed Potato
Serves 4

Duchesse is the rather posh French name for mashed potato enriched with boiling milk and egg.

2 lbs. (900g) unpeeled potatoes
1¼ cups creamy milk
1–2 egg yolks or 1 whole egg and 1 egg yolk
2–4 tablespoons butter
salt and freshly ground pepper

Scrub the potatoes well. Put them into a pot of cold water, add a good pinch of salt, and bring to a boil. When the potatoes are about half-cooked, 15 minutes approx. for floury potatoes, strain off two-thirds of the water, replace the lid on the pot, put on to a gentle heat and let the potatoes steam until they are cooked. Peel immediately by just pulling off the skins, so you have as little waste as possible, mash while hot. (If you have a large quantity, put the potatoes into the bowl of a food mixer [not a food processor] and beat with the spade).

While the potatoes are being peeled, bring the milk to a boil, add enough boiling creamy milk into the hot mashed potatoes, mix to get a soft light consistency suitable for piping, add the eggs, then beat in the butter, the amount depending on how rich you like your potatoes. Season with salt and freshly ground pepper. Taste, and add more butter and seasoning if necessary.

Note: If the potatoes are not peeled and mashed while hot and if the boiling milk is not added immediately, the Duchesse potato will be lumpy and gluey. If you only have egg whites, they will be fine and will make a deliciously light mashed potato also. Do not use a food processor or you will have gluey mashed potatoes.

Mashed Potatoes may be put aside and reheated later in a moderate oven, 350°F (180°C). Cover with tin foil while it reheats so that it doesn't get a skin.

Master Recipe
Scallion Champ or Scallion Mash
Serves 4

3 lbs. (1.3kg) large potatoes
1¼–1½ cups milk
4 ounces (110g) scallions, chopped (about 1½ cups)
½–1 stick (¼–½ cup) butter
salt and freshly ground white pepper

Scrub the potatoes and boil them in their skins. Drain off the water and return the potatoes to the pan. Cover with cold milk and bring slowly to a boil. Simmer for about 3–4 minutes, turn off the heat, and let infuse. Drain the potatoes, reserving the milk. Peel and mash the freshly boiled potatoes and, while hot, mix with the scallions and the boiling milk, and beat in the butter. Season with salt and pepper.

Variations
Scallion and Horseradish Mash
Follow the Master Recipe, adding 5 tablespoons of grated horseradish with the scallions.

Scallion and Potato Cakes
Shape leftover Scallion Mash into potato cakes and fry until golden on both sides in clarified butter or a mixture of butter and oil. Serve piping hot.

Wild Garlic Mash
Follow the Master Recipe, adding 2–3 ounces (50–75g) of roughly chopped wild garlic leaves (about 1¾–2¾ cups) to the milk just as it comes to a boil.

Master Recipe
Parmesan and Olive Oil Mash
Serves 4

Fresh chicken livers cooked in a little butter with some fresh sage leaves are delicious served on top of olive oil mash.

2 lbs. (900g) potatoes
⅓ cup extra-virgin olive oil
1 cup boiling milk
1 cup freshly grated Parmesan (Parmigiano Reggiano is best)
salt and freshly ground pepper

Scrub the potatoes but do not peel them. Cook in boiling salted water until they are about three-quarters cooked. Pour off most of the water, cover, and steam for the rest of the cooking.

Meanwhile bring the milk to a boil. Skin the potatoes as soon as they are cooked and mash or purée through a "potato ricer." Beat in half the hot milk, most of the olive oil, and the Parmesan.

Finally add the remainder of the milk if necessary. The amount will depend on the variety of potato – some absorb more than others. It should be light and fluffy. Season with salt and freshly ground pepper and drizzle with a little extra-virgin olive oil. Taste and serve immediately.

Variation
Olive Oil Mash
Utterly delicious and frightfully fashionable. Follow the Master Recipe, but omit the Parmesan cheese. Garnish with a few chopped olives for extra pizzazz.

Master Recipe
Mustard Mash
Serves 4–6

3 lbs. (1.3kg) potatoes
2/3 cup milk
2/3 cup cream
3/4 stick (1/3 cup) unsalted (sweet) butter
2 teaspoons dry English mustard powder or 2 1/2 tablespoons Dijon mustard
salt and freshly cracked black pepper

Scrub the potatoes and cook them in their skins in boiling, salted water until cooked through. Drain, skin, and mash immediately. Put the milk and cream into a saucepan and bring to boiling point, then add to the hot mashed potatoes, together with the butter and mustard. Season with salt and pepper. Taste and correct seasoning.

Variations
Mustard and Parsley Mash
Follow the Master Recipe, and add 1 1/2–2 1/2 tablespoons of chopped parsley to the mash.

Master Recipe
Ulster Champ
Serves 8

Traditionally in this northern Irish dish, homemade country butter would have been used. Young nettle tops or leeks were also used instead of peas. This recipe was given to me by Deborah Shorley from Claragh.

4 lbs. (1.8kg) potatoes
1/2–1 stick (1/4–1/2 cup) butter
2 1/2 cups milk
1 lb. (450g) young peas, weight after shelling
2/3 cup parsley, chopped
salt and freshly ground pepper

Cook the potatoes in boiling salted water until tender and drain well. Dry over the heat in the pan for a few minutes, then peel and mash with most of the butter while hot. Meanwhile bring the milk to a boil and simmer the peas in it until just cooked, about 8–10 minutes. Add the parsley for the final 2 minutes of cooking. Add the hot milk mixture to the potatoes. Season well, beat until creamy and smooth, and serve piping hot with the remaining pat of butter melting in the center.

West Cork Mash
Serves 6

West Cork Farmhouse cheese maker, Giana Ferguson makes this delicious rustic mash. It's been a favorite in her family for several generations and she calls it broken potatoes. Giana replaces the butter with lashings of Spanish extra-virgin olive oil in the Summer.

3 lbs. (1.3kg) potatoes
milk
salt and freshly ground pepper
butter

Scrub the potatoes, so that no trace of soil remains. Put into a pot, cover with salted water, bring to a boil, cover. When the potatoes are almost cooked, pour off most of the water, replace the lid, and continue to boil/steam until they are cooked through.

Bring the milk to a boil. Mash the potatoes while hot with a hand masher. Add enough milk to soften. Season with salt and freshly ground pepper and heat a nice big blob of butter. Taste – this rustic mash will be flecked with the potato skins and taste quite delicious.

Colcannon
Serves 8 approx.

Songs have been sung and poems have been written about Colcannon, a traditional Irish dish associated particularly with Halloween. Kale was used at first but now cabbage is more common. This comfort food at its very best has now been "discovered" and is often on smart restaurant menus in London and New York.

Did you ever eat colcannon
When 'twas made with yellow cream
And the kale and praties blended
Like a picture in a dream?
Did you ever scoop a hole on top
To hold the melting lake
Of the clover-flavored butter
Which your mother used to make?

1 lb. (450g) Savoy or spring cabbage
2–3 lbs. (900g–1.3kg) potatoes
1 cup plus 2 tablespoons milk
1–2 scallions (optional)
salt and freshly ground pepper
1/2 stick (1/4 cup) butter

Scrub the potatoes and put them in a pot of cold water. Add a good pinch of salt and bring them to a boil. When the potatoes are half-cooked, about 15 minutes, strain off two-thirds of the water, put the lid back on the pot, and cook over a gentle heat so that the potatoes steam until they are tender.

Remove the dark outer leaves from the cabbage. Wash the rest and cut into quarters, removing the core. Cut the cabbage finely across the grain. Boil in a little boiling water or bacon cooking water until soft. Drain and season with salt, pepper, and a little butter.

When the potatoes are just cooked, put the milk and scallions into a saucepan and bring to a boil. Skin the potatoes and mash them quickly while still warm, beating in

The Perfect French Fry

1 Straw potatoes: finest possible strips about $2^1/_2$ inches (6cm) long.

2 Matchstick or Shoestring: similar length but slightly thicker.

3 Mignonette: $^1/_4$ inch (5mm) thick and $2^1/_2$ inches (6cm) long.

4 Pont Neuf: about $^1/_2$ inch (1cm) thick and $2^1/_2$ inches (6cm) long.

5 Jumbo: about 1 inch (2.5cm) thick and $2^1/_2$ inches (6cm) long.

6 Buffalo: similar size to Jumbo but unpeeled.

Sales of frozen and pre-prepared chips have rocketed in a relatively short time – so much so that I feel many people have forgotten how easy it is to make chips at home. Here are the simple secrets of really sensational chips:

1 Good quality floury potatoes, e.g., russet, Yukon Gold.

2 Best quality oil, lard, or beef fat for frying. We frequently use olive oil because its flavor is so good and because when properly looked after, it can be used over and over again. Avoid poor quality oils that have an unpleasant taste and a pervasive smell.

3 Scrub the potatoes well and peel, or leave unpeeled, according to taste.

Cut into similar size chips so they will cook evenly.

4 Rinse quickly in cold water but do not soak. Dry meticulously with a damp lint-free towel or paper towel before cooking – otherwise the water will boil on contact with the oil in the deep fryer, possibly making it overflow. Do not overload the basket, otherwise the temperature of the oil will be lowered, making for greasy rather than crisp chips. Shake the pan once or twice to separate the chips while cooking.

To cook the first three types: Fry quickly in oil at 385°F (195°C) until crisp.

To cook the last three sizes: Fry first at 310°F (160°C) until they are soft and just beginning to brown (the time will vary from 4–10 minutes depending on size). Drain, increase the heat to 375°F (190°C) and cook for a further 1–2 minutes or until crisp and golden.

To serve: Shake the basket, drain well, toss onto paper towels, sprinkle with a little salt, turn onto a hot serving dish, and serve immediately.

enough boiling milk and scallions to make a fluffy purée. (If you have a large quantity, put the potatoes in the bowl of a food mixer and beat with the spade.) Then stir in the cooked cabbage and taste for seasoning. For perfection, serve immediately in a hot dish with a lump of butter melting in the center. Colcannon may be prepared ahead and reheated in a moderate oven (350°F/180°C), for about 20–25 minutes. Cover while reheating so it doesn't get too crusty on top.

Master Recipe

Potato Chips or Game Chips

A mandoline slicer is useful though not essential for slicing. Potato chips are sliced on a plain cutter and game chips on a crinkled cutter.

These are paper-thin slices of potato which are deep-fried in extra-virgin olive oil at 350°F (180°C) until absolutely crisp, drained on paper towels and sprinkled with salt. Serve hot or cold.

Provided they are properly cooked, they will keep perfectly in a tin box for several days. These chips or game chips are the traditional accompaniment to roast pheasant or guinea fowl.

Variations

Garlic Chips

Follow the Master Recipe, putting the chips into a warmed serving dish. Melt some Garlic Butter (see page 588) and drizzle it over the chips. Serve immediately as a snack or as an accompaniment to hamburgers or steaks or on a salade tiede.

Volcanic Chips

Follow the recipe above, adding 1–2 tablespoons of chili flakes to the butter along with the garlic and parsley.

Pommes Gaufrette

Follow the Master Recipe. A mandoline is essential for slicing these potatoes. Rotate the potatoes 90° between each cut so the slices are latticed. Deep-fry for 2–3 minutes at 375°F (190°C) or until crisp and golden.

Soufflé Potatoes

Slice potatoes very thinly (1/16 inch/2mm) on a mandoline. Deep-fry at 350°F (180°C) for 4–5 minutes or until just beginning to brown. Drain and cool. Just before serving fry again at 385°F (195°C); they will puff up immediately. Cook for 1–2 minutes more until crisp and golden.

Sauté Potatoes

Serves 4–6

2 lbs. (900g) potatoes
2–4 tablespoons clarified butter
2½ tablespoons olive oil
salt and pepper

Scrub the potatoes and boil or steam them until just cooked. When they are cool, peel and cut into ½-inch (1-cm) slices. Heat the butter and oil in a frying pan until foaming, put the potatoes in a single layer, and season with salt and freshly ground pepper. Fry on a medium heat until golden on one side and then turn over to brown on the other side. Serve in a hot dish sprinkled with chopped parsley.

Peppered Pops

Add 1½–2½ tablespoons of freshly cracked pepper to the foaming butter and proceed as above.

Pommes Julienne

Serves 4–6

2 lbs. (900g) potatoes, peeled
2–4 tablespoons butter
salt and freshly ground pepper

shallow flameproof baking pan, 10-inch (25.5-cm) diameter

Cut the peeled potatoes into julienne strips and dry well. Rub a thick even coating of butter over the bottom and sides of the pan. Press a thick layer of potatoes into the bottom of the pan. Season. Cover with a butter wrapper and a close fitting lid. Cook on a gentle heat for about 20–30 minutes. Loosen the sides with a spatula. Turn out onto a plate when the bottom is golden brown and crisp.

Variation

Julienne Tart with Smoked Salmon, Crème Fraîche, and Crispy Capers

Follow the recipe above. When the potatoes are cooked, invert the cake onto a hot serving plate and top with crème fraîche and chives. Place slices of smoked salmon on top, sprinkle with Deep-fried Capers (see page 199), and serve immediately.

Baked Potatoes

Serves 8

Do not wrap baked potatoes in tin foil, as this softens the skins and spoils the flavor; it can even make them wet and soapy.

8 x 8-ounce (225-g) potatoes
sea salt or kosher salt, and butter

Preheat the oven to 400°F (200°C).
Choose large potatoes. Scrub the skins well. Prick each potato 3 or 4 times so the skins don't burst while cooking and bake in the oven for about 1 hour, depending on size. Serve immediately, while skins are still crisp, and be sure to eat the skins with lots of butter and sea salt.

There are so many good things to eat with baked potatoes; here are a few suggestions:

Garlic mayonnaise with tuna fish
Garlic butter with crispy strips of bacon
Crème fraîche with chopped smoked salmon and chives
Crème fraîche with roast peppers and a drizzle of pesto

Master Recipe
Gratin Dauphinois

Serves 4–6

There are many wonderful French potato gratins that I love, but if I were forced to choose one I think it would have to be this sinfully rich Gratin Dauphinois. This is a particularly good version of the classic recipe because it can be made ahead and reheated with great success.

2 lbs. (900g) even-sized potatoes
salt and freshly ground pepper
1 cup plus 2 tablespoons milk
1 cup plus 2 tablespoons heavy cream
small garlic clove, crushed
freshly grated nutmeg

Preheat the oven to 400°F (200°C).

Peel the potatoes and slice them into very thin rounds 1/8 inch (3mm) thick. Do not wash them but dab them dry with a cloth. Spread them out on the worktop and season with salt and freshly ground pepper, mixing it in with your hands.

Pour the milk into a saucepan, add the potatoes, and bring to a boil. Cover, reduce the heat, and simmer gently for 10 minutes.

Add the cream, garlic, and a generous grating of nutmeg and continue to simmer for 20 minutes, stirring occasionally so that the potatoes do not stick to the saucepan. Just as soon as the potatoes are cooked, take them out with a slotted spoon and put them into 1 large or 6 small ovenproof dishes. Pour the creamy liquid over them.* Cook in a bain-marie in the oven, for 10–20 minutes or until they are bubbly and golden on top.

*Can be prepared ahead to this point.

Right: Onion Bhajis with Tomato and Chile Sauce

Variations
Smoked Mackerel and Potato Gratin

Follow the Master Recipe. Remove the skin and bones from 8 ounces (225g) smoked mackerel and divide into chunky bits. Put a layer of smoked mackerel and a sprinkling of chopped parsley in the center as you put it into the dishes.

Smoked Salmon and Dill Gratin

Follow the Master Recipe. Add 6 ounces (175g) smoked salmon, cut in small cubes, and 1 generous tablespoon of dill in between the layers of potato.

Potato and Chorizo Gratin

Follow the Master Recipe. Add 6–8 ounces (175–225g) of chorizo or Kabannossi sausage in between the layers of potato.

Crispy bacon, mussels, shrimp, etc., may also be used.

Gratin of Potato and Mushroom

Serves 6

If you have a few wild mushrooms, chanterelles or field mushrooms, mix them with cultivated mushrooms for this gratin. If all you can find are flat mushrooms, all the better; one way or the other the gratin will still be delectable. This gratin is terrifically good with a pan-grilled lamb chop or a piece of steak.

1 lb. (450g) potatoes, peeled and thinly sliced
butter
1/2 lb. (225g) wild or cultivated mushrooms, or a mixture of cultivated, brown, oyster, and shiitake, sliced (about 2 1/3 cups)
1 garlic clove, finely chopped
salt and freshly ground pepper
1 1/4 cups light cream
1/4 cup grated Parmesan cheese
ovenproof gratin dish, 10 x 8 inches (25.5 x 20.5cm)

Preheat the oven to 350°F (180°C).

Blanch and refresh the potato slices. Grease a shallow gratin dish generously with butter and sprinkle the garlic over it. Arrange half the potatoes in the bottom of the dish, season with salt and pepper, and put in the mushrooms. Season again and finish off with a final layer of overlapping potatoes. Bring the cream almost to boiling point and pour over the potatoes. Sprinkle the cheese on top and bake for about 1 hour in the oven, until the gratin becomes crisp and golden brown with the cream bubbling up around the edges.

Gratin of Potato and Celeriac

Serves 4–6

2 lbs. (900g) waxy potatoes, thinly sliced
1 large celeriac, thinly sliced
1¼ cups cream
1 teaspoon tarragon or marjoram, chopped
salt and freshly ground pepper

Preheat the oven to 375°F (190°C).

Peel the celeriac, cut into quarters, and slice thinly. Put the slices into acidulated water to prevent it discoloring. Blanch and refresh both the potatoes and celeriac. Drain the slices and dry them thoroughly on paper towels. In a gratin dish, arrange alternate layers of potatoes and celeriac, ending with a layer of potato. Season each layer with salt and freshly ground pepper. Add the chopped tarragon and pour the cream over the top. Bake the gratin for about an hour until bubbly and golden.

Variations

Gratin of Potato and Vegetables

Experiment with parsnips, white turnips, Jerusalem artichokes...

Roast Onions

I'm always surprised that so few people cook onions in this ultra simple way. We call them roast onions but I suppose, strictly speaking, they are baked. One way or the other, they are absolutely delicious and my children adore them. Choose small or medium onions.

Preheat the oven to 400°F (200°C).

Roast Whole Onions

Bake the unpeeled onions until soft; this can take anything from 10–30 minutes, depending on size. Serve in their skins. The diner can pull off the root end, squeeze out the onion, and eat it with butter and sea salt.

Roast Onion Halves

Split the unpeeled onions in half lengthwise. Put a little olive oil on the bottom of a roasting pan, sprinkle with sea salt, put the onions cut side down into the pan and roast until golden on the cut side. Turn off the oven and continue to cook until soft – great with steak, lamb, etc.

Roast Onion Slices

Choose large onions, cut into thick slices around the equator, spear each side with a soaked kebab stick or a skewer. Roast in a little olive oil and sea salt as above. Turn half-way through cooking.

Roast Scallions

Peel the outer layer from the scallions. Toss in extra-virgin olive oil, then roast in a preheated oven, 400°F (200°C), until tender, 8–20 minutes, depending on size. Turn them regularly.

Onion Bhajis with Tomato and Chile Sauce

Serves 4 as an appetizer

Cheap, cheerful, and delicious – ideal pub grub!

1 cup all-purpose flour
2 teaspoons baking powder
1 teaspoon chili powder
2 eggs, beaten
⅔ cup water
4 onions, thinly sliced
2½ tablespoons fresh chives, snipped
oil, for deep frying

Tomato and Chile Sauce *(see page 590)*

First make the Tomato and Chile Sauce.

Sift the flour, baking powder, and chili powder into a bowl. Make a well in the center, add the eggs, gradually add in the water, and mix to make a smooth batter. Stir in the onions and chives. Season well with salt and pepper.

Just before serving, heat the oil to about 170°C (325°F). Fry spoonfuls of the batter for 5 minutes on each side until crisp and golden, and drain on paper towels. Serve hot or cold with the Tomato and Chile Sauce.

Aigre-doux Onions with Thyme Leaves

Serves 4–6

A basket of baby onions is a real treasure to have in the pantry. We save the small onions of the crop carefully; gorgeous for roasting, sweet and melting cooked whole in stews, or in an onion "Tarte Tatin" and irresistible with a shiny sweet-sour glaze. Aigre-doux means sweet and sour, as does agrodolce in Italian.

1 lb. (450g) pearl onions
2 tablespoons butter
2 teaspoons thyme leaves
2 tablespoons sugar
1/4 cup vinegar or 2 1/2 tablespoons white wine vinegar
salt and freshly ground pepper

Peel and trim the onions leaving root base intact. Melt the butter in a heavy saucepan and toss the onions in it. Add the thyme. Cover with a butter wrapper and a tight fitting lid. Cook over a low heat until almost soft. Add the sugar and vinegar, increase the heat, and cook until the salt, vinegar, and onion juices make a syrupy glaze. Spoon into a hot serving dish and serve immediately.

Oignons à la Monégasque

Serves 6–8

This gutsy French salad keeps for not just days but weeks, and is delicious with cold meat or game or as part of a salad.

1 lb. (450g) pearl onions, scallions, young summer onions, or leeks
1 1/2 cups water
1/2 cup white vinegar
1 tablespoon plus 1 teaspoon olive oil
2 1/2 tablespoons sugar
1 cup plus 2 tablespoons homemade Tomato Purée (see page 49) or 2 1/2 tablespoons tomato paste mixed with 1 cup plus 2 tablespoons water
1/2 bay leaf
1/2 teaspoon thyme
sprig of parsley
6 tablespoons seedless raisins
salt and freshly ground pepper

This can also be made with larger onions if they are cut lengthwise so that each segment has a piece of root left on, which will hold the onion together. Simply put all the ingredients into a saucepan, cover, and stew gently until the onions are soft, anything from 20 minutes to 2 hours. Pearl onions take about 2 hours. Remove the lid after the first hour.

Note: We also use young Japanese onions in the spring for this recipe, and cook them whole with 3–4 inches (7.5–10cm) of the green shoot left on.

Caramelized Onions

1 lb. (450g) onions, sliced
2 1/2–3 1/2 tablespoons olive oil

Caramelized onions take a long time to cook. Heat the olive oil in a heavy saucepan, toss in the onions, and cook over a low heat for as long as it takes for the onions to soften and caramelize to a golden brown. Allow about 30–45 minutes.

French Fried Onions

Serves 6

1 large onion
milk
seasoned flour
good quality oil or beef dripping for deep-frying

Slice the onion into 1/4-inch (5-mm) rings around the middle. Separate the rings and cover with milk until needed. Just before serving, heat the oil to 350°F (180°C). Toss the rings, a few at a time, in seasoned flour. Deep fry until golden in the hot oil. Drain on paper towels and serve hot with steaks, hamburgers, etc.

Sun-dried Tomatoes

Sun-dried tomatoes can be bought at enormous expense preserved in olive oil but you can make your own quite easily. I find this method of drying them in the coolest oven of my 4-door Aga quite successful. A fan oven works well also.

very ripe tomatoes
sea salt or kosher salt
sugar
olive oil

Cut the tomatoes in half crosswise, place on a wire rack, season with sea salt and sugar, and drizzle with olive oil. Leave in the coolest part of a 4-door Aga, or in a fan oven at the minimum temperature, until they are totally dried out and wizened. I leave them in for 24 hours, depending on size (after about 1 hour, turn upside down). Store in sterilized jars covered with olive oil. A few basil leaves or a couple of sprigs of rosemary, thyme, or annual marjoram added to the oil make them especially delicious. Cover and keep in a cool, dry, preferably dark place. Use on salads, with pasta, etc.

Oven-roasted Tomatoes

Proceed as above but remove and use tomatoes while they are still plump but have reduced in size by half.

Tomato Fondue

Serves 6

Tomato fondue is one of our great convertibles, it has a number of uses, we serve it as a vegetable, sauce, filling for omelettes, topping for pizza, stuffing, etc... Make this in the summer, when tomatoes are at their juicy best, or use canned ones the rest of the year.

1 tablespoon plus 1 teaspoon extra-virgin olive oil
1 medium onion, sliced (about 1 cup)
1 garlic clove, crushed
2 lbs. (900g) very ripe tomatoes, peeled, or 2 1/2 x 14-ounce (400-g) cans tomatoes
1 generous tablespoon of any of the following, freshly chopped, or a mixture: thyme, parsley, mint, basil, lemon balm, marjoram
salt, freshly ground pepper, and sugar to taste

Right: Oven-roasted Tomatoes

earthenware dish, 12 x 10 inches (32 x 25.5cm)

Preheat the oven to 400°F (200°C).

Slice the eggplants into 1/4-inch (5-mm) thick rounds or lengths. Put into a colander. Sprinkle with salt and leave for 15 minutes to de-gorge.

Meanwhile, make the tomato sauce: heat the olive oil in a saucepan and sweat the onion until soft but not colored. Add the tomatoes. Season with salt, pepper, and sugar. Bring to a boil and simmer gently with the lid on at first, until rich tasting.

When the eggplants have de-gorged for 15 minutes, rinse in cold water and pat dry.

Brush a baking tray generously with olive oil and place the eggplants in a single layer on the tray. Sprinkle with rosemary, drizzle with oil, and bake for about 10 minutes in the oven or until golden.

Grate the zest of the lemon; add it to the tomato sauce, and mix well. Taste the sauce and adjust the seasonings as desired. Arrange a layer of eggplants in an earthenware or gratin dish, sprinkle with torn basil leaves and slivers of Parmesan. Cover with a layer of tomato sauce followed by more eggplant, basil, and Parmesan.

Continue layering in this way and finish with a sprinkle of Parmesan on top. Bake for 10 minutes or until bubbling and golden.

Okra in Batter

Serves 4

Look for unblemished and deep green okra or Lady's fingers. Only add salt to okra dishes after cooking, as it causes the vegetable to sweat. Don't cook okra with water either, as it makes it slimy. There are 2 types of pod – the oblong gomba, essential to New Orleans gumbo, to which it has given its name, and the round bamya.

8 ounces (225g) fresh okra or lady's fingers
1 cup flour
2 tablespoons ground rice or rice flour
1 tablespoon plus 1 teaspoon cayenne pepper
1/2 teaspoon ground cumin
1/2 teaspoon ground turmeric
1 teaspoon salt
1 teaspoon thyme leaves
olive oil for frying

Slice the caps off the okra and discard the rest. Cut into 1/2-inch (1-cm) thick rounds. Sift the flour, rice flour, cayenne, cumin, turmeric, and salt into a bowl. Add the thyme leaves, mix thoroughly, and make a well in the center. Add about 1/2 cup water and whisk in a little at a time to make a light batter about the consistency of thick cream.

Heat the oil in a deep fryer over a medium-low heat. Fold the slices of okra gently into the batter. Drop tablespoons of the okra gently into the oil. Fry, turning now and then, until the fritters are crisp and golden. This will take about 6–7 minutes. Serve immediately.

Baba Ganouj

Serves 4

This Lebanese dish has a rich, smoky flavor and is delicious as an appetizer with pita bread. This recipe comes from The Bathers Pavilion by Victoria Alexander and Genevieve Harris.

6 medium purple eggplants
3 garlic cloves, crushed
2/3 cup tahini
2 teaspoons cumin, roasted and ground
1 tablespoon plus 1 teaspoon lemon juice
sea salt or kosher salt

The eggplants must be roasted. If you have gas burners you can rest the eggplants on a metal mesh over the flames. If not, roast them in the oven at 400°F (200°C) by placing them whole in a roasting pan and baking for about 30 minutes. The eggplants are cooked when the skin is blackened and the flesh is soft.

Let the cooked eggplants cool a little, then peel off the charred skin and let the flesh drain in a colander for 30 minutes. Place the eggplant flesh in a food processor or blender (in batches) with the garlic, and mix to a smooth paste.

Add the tahini and cumin and mix in, then add the lemon juice and salt to taste. The proportions of cumin, garlic, tahini, and lemon juice can be adjusted to suit your taste.

Chargrilled Red and Yellow Peppers

Serves 8

The sweet, slightly smoky flavor of roast or char-grilled peppers makes this summery appetizer one of my absolute favorites. In fact, every now and then I roast lots of peppers and store them peeled and seeded in a glass Kilner jar, with a few fresh basil leaves and lots of extra-virgin olive oil. Then I can dip in whenever I fancy and eat them as they are, or use them in a salad or as an accompaniment to pan-grilled fish or meat, or with lentils and goat cheese.

8 red and 8 yellow peppers
2 garlic cloves, cut in very fine slivers (optional)
8 fresh basil leaves
extra-virgin olive oil
10–12 black Kalamata olives (optional)
sea salt or kosher salt, and freshly cracked pepper

Preheat the broiler or better still use a charcoal grill. Grill the peppers on all sides, turning them when necessary, until they are quite charred. Alternatively preheat the oven to 475°F (250°C); put the peppers on a baking tray, and bake for 20–30 minutes until they are soft and the skin blistered.

Put them into a plastic bag to cool and seal the end – this will make them much easier to peel.

Peel the peppers and remove stalks and seeds – don't wash. Choose a wide, shallow serving dish. Arrange the peeled peppers and what juices you can, add the garlic, basil, and a good drizzle of olive oil. Scatter a few black olives over the top, if you like.

Serve with Bruschetta as a first course.

Fresh Corn with Marjoram

Serves 6

6 ears of corn, freshly picked if possible
2–4 tablespoons butter
salt and freshly ground pepper
1½–2½ tablespoons freshly chopped annual marjoram

Bring a large pot of water to a boil, add salt.

Peel the ears of corn, trim both ends, drop into the water. Cover the saucepan and bring back to a boil, cook for just 3 minutes.

Drain, let cool, then slice the kernels vertically off the cob. Melt a little butter in a saucepan and add the corn. Season, add the marjoram, stir once or twice. Taste, correct the seasoning. Serve immediately.

Right: Baba Ganouj

Char-grilled Fennel

Fennel is very good baked, grilled, or roasted. Grilling is a very quick way of preparing it.

1–2 fennel bulbs, trimmed and cut into diagonal slices
extra-virgin olive oil
salt and freshly ground pepper

Drizzle the fennel with oil and turn gently to coat. Season with salt and pepper. Cook for 1–2 minutes on both sides on a chargrill or grill. Garnish with a little of the trimmed feathery leaves and serve immediately.

Master Recipe

Artichokes with Melted Butter

Serves 6 as an appetizer

Whole artichokes are quite fiddly to eat. First you pull off each leaf separately and dip in the sauce. Have plenty of bowls for the discarded part of the leaves. Eventually you are rewarded for your patience when you come to the heart. Don't forget to scrape off the tickly "choke;" then cut the heart into manageable pieces, sprinkle it with a little sea salt before you dip it into the remainder of your sauce. Simply delicious!

Trim the base of the artichoke just before cooking so it will sit steadily on the plate and rub the cut end with lemon juice or vinegar to prevent it from discoloring.

6 artichokes
5 cups water
2 teaspoons salt
about 2 teaspoons white wine vinegar

1½ sticks (¾ cup) butter
juice of ¼ lemon, freshly squeezed

Have a large pot of boiling water ready and add 2 teaspoons of vinegar and 2 teaspoons of salt to every 5 cups of water. Pop in the artichokes and bring the water back to a boil. Simmer steadily for about 25 minutes. After about 20 minutes you could try testing to see if they are done. I do this by raising the artichoke out of the water and tugging off one of the larger leaves at the base; if cooked, it should come away easily; if not continue to cook for another 5–10 minutes. Remove and drain upside down on a plate.

While they are cooking, melt the butter and add lemon juice to taste.

To serve: put each warm artichoke onto a hot serving plate and serve the sauce or melted butter in a little bowl beside it. Artichokes are eaten with your fingers, so you might like to provide a finger bowl of warm water with a slice of lemon.

Variations

Artichokes with Vinaigrette Dressing

Follow the Master Recipe to cook the artichokes. Serve them with Vinaigrette (see page 226).

Artichokes with Hollandaise Sauce

Follow the Master Recipe to cook the artichokes. Serve them with Hollandaise Sauce (see page 581).

Artichoke Hearts Braised in Olive Oil

Serves 4

1 quart (960ml) water
1 lemon
6 artichokes
1/2 cup extra-virgin olive oil
1 onion, coarsely diced
2 garlic cloves, chopped
5 tablespoons parsley, coarsely chopped
salt and freshly ground black pepper

Preparing the artichokes is the fiddliest part of this recipe. Acidulate the water with the juice of the lemon. Drop in the squeezed lemon halves too. Cut a ring around the stalk where it meets the base of the artichoke. Break off the stalk and the toughest fibers will come with it. Then, with a sharp knife, starting from the base, ruthlessly cut off all the leaves and trim the top down as far as the heart. Scrape out the hairy choke, either with the tip of a knife or a sharp-edged spoon. Work quickly and drop the trimmed hearts into the acidulated water immediately, or they will discolor.

Heat the oil in a wide frying pan, add the onion and garlic, and sweat for a few minutes. Cut the artichoke hearts into quarters or eighths, add to the pan along with the parsley. Season with salt and pepper and toss well. Add 1/4 cup water, cover, and cook for 10–15 minutes, until the artichokes are tender. Serve hot or at room temperature.

Cardoons with Cream and Parmesan

Serves 6

Cardoon plants look very like their cousins the artichokes but unlike the latter, the cardoon is cultivated for its stalks, not its thistle-like flowers. We've been growing them for about a decade now, but only have about 8 or 10 plants so we tend to eat them in the same way every year – raw, cut into strips, and dipped in a Bagna Cauda Sauce, or cooked and then stewed in butter with some cream and lots of Parmesan.

4 lbs. (1.8kg) cardoon ribs, trimmed
acidulated water
salt
butter
cream
Parmesan cheese (Parmigiano Reggiano), freshly grated

Preheat the oven to 400°F (200°C).

Separate the stalks and heart. Use the tender heart for eating raw with Bagna Cauda if you like. Cut the stalks into manageable lengths, 3–4 inches (8–10cm), cook in acidulated water for 30–35 minutes. Drain and refresh in cold water and remove the strings from the outer stalks.

Smear a large, shallow dish with butter, arrange a layer of cardoons in the bottom, dot with butter, season with salt and pepper. Sprinkle with Parmesan, another layer of cardoons, butter, seasoning, Parmesan, and continue until the dish is full, finishing with a layer of cardoons. Pour on a little cream and sprinkle the top with Parmesan cheese. Bake in the oven for 15–20 minutes or until the cardoons are tender and the top is bubbling and golden.

Asparagus with Sauce Maltaise

Serves 4–6 as an appetizer

16–20 spears of very fresh green asparagus
Sauce Maltaise (see page 582)

Garnish
chervil

Trim the root end of the asparagus, and peel if you wish (save the trimmings for soup). Cut into uniform lengths. Just before serving, cook the asparagus in boiling salted water. Depending on the thickness of the spears it may take from 4–8 minutes to cook. Test by putting the tip of a sharp knife through the thicker end. The knife should go through easily. Remove from the water and drain.

Put a spoonful of Sauce Maltaise on each warmed serving plate and place a few spears of asparagus beside it.

Master Recipe
French Beans (Haricot Verts)

Serves 8

I find that French beans need a lot of salt in the cooking water to bring up the flavor. They don't benefit from being kept warm, so if you need to cook them ahead, try the method I suggest below. I think it works very well.

2 lbs. (900g) French beans (or green beans)
5 cups water
2 teaspoons sea salt or kosher salt
2–4 tablespoons butter
salt and freshly ground pepper

Top and tail the beans. If they are small and thin, leave them whole; if they are larger, cut them into $1–1\frac{1}{2}$-inch (2.5–4-cm) pieces at an angle. Bring the water to a fast rolling boil, add 2 teaspoons of salt, then toss in the beans. Continue to boil very fast for 5–6 minutes or until just cooked (they should still retain a little bite). Drain immediately.* Melt the butter in the saucepan, toss the beans in it, taste, season with pepper and a little sea salt, if necessary.

* The beans may be refreshed under cold water at this point and kept aside for several hours.

Tip: To reheat precooked beans: Just before serving, plunge into boiling salted water for $\frac{1}{2}$–1 minute, drain, and toss in butter. Season and serve immediately.

Variations
French Beans with Fresh Chile

Follow the Master Recipe until the beans are well drained. Heat $2\frac{1}{2}$ tablespoons of olive oil in a wide frying pan, and add 1 chopped garlic clove, $1\frac{1}{2}$ tablespoons coarsely chopped parsley, and 1–2 chopped chiles. Toss over a medium heat for a few seconds, season well with salt and pepper, add the beans, taste, and serve.

French Beans with Tomato Fondue

Follow the Master Recipe until the beans are well drained. Mix with 1 quantity of the recipe for Tomato Fondue (see page 188). Heat through and serve.

Fava Beans with Summer Savory

Serves 8

Summer savory is an herb that has an extraordinary affinity with beans, seeming to make them taste more "beany". If you don't have it, simply leave it out!

$\frac{2}{3}$ cup water
1 teaspoon salt
1 lb. (450g) shelled fava beans
sprig of summer savory
about 2 tablespoons butter
sea salt or kosher salt, and freshly ground pepper
1–2 teaspoons summer savory, freshly chopped

Bring the water to a rolling boil, add the sea salt, fava beans, and a sprig of savory. Boil very fast for 3–4 minutes or until just cooked. Drain immediately.

Melt a little butter in a saucepan, toss in the fava beans and season with freshly ground pepper. Taste, add some more savory and a little sea salt, if necessary.

Variation
Fava Bean Purée

Follow the recipe above, then slip the beans out of their skins. Add 3–4 tablespoons of cream, then purée, check the seasoning, and serve.

Fava Beans with Olive Oil and Thyme Leaves

Serves 6

$2\frac{1}{2}$ cups water
1 teaspoon salt
$1\frac{1}{2}$ lbs. (700g) shelled fava beans
$\frac{1}{2}$ cup olive oil
1 teaspoon thyme leaves

Bring the water to a boil, add the salt and beans, and cook for 6–8 minutes or until tender. Refresh in cold water. Drain the beans and peel off the outer skin. Pour the oil into a saucepan, toss in the beans and thyme leaves.

Cook for 2–3 minutes on a gentle heat – just long enough for the beans to heat through. Taste, add more salt if necessary, and serve immediately.

Fava Bean & Mint Dip

Serves 4

A fresh-tasting dip best made with fresh young fava beans, but frozen ones will do at a push. Serve with crudités or bread.

1 lb. (450g) fresh fava beans, shelled
leaves from 6–8 mint sprigs
4–5 tablespoons extra-virgin olive oil
about $2\frac{1}{2}$ tablespoons lemon juice, freshly squeezed
salt and freshly ground pepper

Garnish
sprigs of mint

Cook the fava beans in boiling water until tender (just a few minutes). Drain, reserving the cooking liquid. Rinse to refresh under running cold water.

Put the beans into a food processor or blender. Add the mint, olive oil, and lemon juice and mix to a purée, adding enough of the reserved cooking liquid to give a soft consistency. Season to taste with salt and pepper.

Taste, and adjust the levels of lemon and oil if necessary.

Transfer the dip to a small serving dish. Serve at room temperature, garnished with sprigs of mint.

Runner Beans

Runner beans need topping and tailing; they also need the strings removed. Cook as for French beans; though the flavor is different, some people just love runner beans with their colorful flowers.

Garden Peas with Fresh Mint

Serves 8

Really fresh peas from the garden are exquisite; it is difficult to resist eating them all raw as you pod them!

2/3 cup water
1 teaspoon salt
1 teaspoon sugar
1 sprig mint
1 lb. (450g) garden peas or petit pois, freshly shelled
2 tablespoons butter
1–2 teaspoons mint, freshly chopped

Bring the fresh cold water to a boil, add the salt, sugar, mint, and the peas. Return to a boil over a high heat and simmer until the peas are cooked, 4–5 minutes at most. Strain, reserving the water for soup or gravy. Add some butter and the mint and a little extra seasoning if necessary. Eat immediately.

Tip: Frozen peas can be extraordinarily good. The cheaper brands tend to lack flavor so buy the best you can afford.

Sugar Peas or Snow Peas or Sugar Snap Peas

Serves 6

Beware–these can go on cooking after they've been drained so err on the side of undercooking.

5 cups water
1 1/2 teaspoons salt
1 lb. (450g) sugar peas, sugar snap peas, or snow peas
2–4 tablespoons butter
freshly ground pepper

String the sugar peas. Bring the water to a good rolling boil, add the salt and the peas and continue to boil furiously with the lid off until just cooked: this will take about 4–6 minutes. They should still have a slight crunch. Drain immediately.*

Toss in a little melted butter, taste, and correct seasoning. Serve immediately in a hot serving dish.

* As with many green vegetables, sugar peas or snow peas or sugar snap peas can be refreshed with cold water at this point and reheated just before serving in boiling salted water.

Mushroom à la Crème

Serves 4

Mushroom à la crème may be served as a vegetable, or as a filling for vol au vents, bouchées, or crêpes. It may be used as an enrichment for casseroles and stews or, by adding a little more cream or stock, may be served as a sauce with beef, lamb, chicken, or veal. A crushed clove of garlic may be added while the onions are sweating. Flat mushrooms are even better than white mushrooms for this recipe.

1–2 tablespoons butter
3 ounces (75g) onion, finely chopped (about 2/3 cup)
8 ounces (225g) mushrooms, sliced (about 2 1/3 cups)
salt and freshly ground pepper
squeeze of lemon juice
1/2 cup cream
freshly chopped parsley
1/2 tablespoon freshly chopped chives, optional

Melt the butter in a heavy saucepan until it foams.

Add the chopped onions, cover, and sweat on a gentle heat for 5–10 minutes or until quite soft but not colored; remove the onions to a bowl. Meanwhile cook the sliced mushrooms in a hot frying pan, in batches if necessary. Season each batch with salt, pepper, and a tiny squeeze of lemon juice. Add the mushrooms to the onions in the saucepan, then add the cream and let bubble for a few minutes.

Taste and correct the seasoning, and add parsley and chives, if using.

Mushroom à la Crème keeps well in the fridge for 4–5 days and freezes perfectly.

Variation

Wild Mushroom à la Crème

Substitute wild field mushrooms or a mixture of mushrooms, e.g., oyster, enoki, shiitake, nameko, girolles, or chanterelles for the mushrooms in the recipe above.

Portobella Mushrooms with Parsley Pesto and Balsamic Vinegar

Serves 6

6 Portobella mushrooms or large meaty flat mushrooms
salt and freshly ground pepper
2 large garlic cloves, crushed
olive oil
4 ounces (110g) cooked beets (about 1/2 cup)
1/4 cup homemade Chicken or Vegetable Stock (see page 36)
2 1/2 tablespoons cream
1/4 cup balsamic vinegar

Parsley or Basil Pesto (see page 589)

Garnish
Fresh thyme leaves and flowers or wild garlic flowers

Preheat the oven to 475°F (250°C).

If you are using Portobella mushrooms, split them in half widthwise and arrange on a baking tray in a single layer. Flats should be kept whole. Sprinkle with salt, a few grinds of pepper, and the garlic. Drizzle with olive oil and roast in a fully preheated hot oven for 10–15 minutes or until cooked through. Purée the beets with a little chicken or vegetable stock, and the cream. Taste and correct seasoning.

When the mushrooms are almost cooked, put the balsamic vinegar in a small saucepan and boil to reduce until slightly syrupy. Sandwich the 2 pieces of each mushroom or 2 flats together with a dollop of Parsley or Basil Pesto. Arrange each in the center of a hot plate. Drizzle balsamic vinegar and beet purée around the edge. Garnish with thyme leaves and flowers or wild garlic flowers.

Portobella Mushroom Burger

Cook a large flat mushroom on a pan-grill or in the oven, drizzled with olive oil. Season with salt, freshly ground pepper, a little crushed garlic, and some thyme leaves. Toast 2 hamburger buns, spread with goat cheese and pesto or garlic butter. Top with the juicy portobella and the other half of the bun. Serve immediately.

Mushroom Crostini with Arugula and Parmesan

Serves 2

This is a poshed-up version of mushrooms on toast. Virtually all fungi are delicious on toast so this can be very humble or very exotic, depending on the variety chosen.

2 slices large good-quality baguette
extra-virgin olive oil
4–6 flat mushrooms or large oyster mushrooms
marjoram, thyme, or rosemary
1 garlic clove (optional)
arugula leaves
Parmesan cheese, freshly grated

Heat 1 inch (2.5cm) of olive oil in a frying pan until just below smoking point. Fry the pieces of bread 1 at a time, whip them out just as soon as they become golden, drain on paper towels, and keep warm. (The oil may be strained and used again for another purpose.)

Heat a little olive oil or half olive oil and half butter in a frying pan. Remove the stalks from the mushrooms and place the mushroom caps skin side down on the pan in a single layer. Put a little dot of butter into each or better still, use garlic or marjoram butter, made quite simply by mixing some chopped garlic and parsley or some annual marjoram into a little butter. Alternatively, sprinkle with marjoram and some crushed garlic if you like. Season with salt and pepper.

Cook first on 1 side (the length of time will depend on the size of the mushroom: it could be anything from 3–6 minutes), then turn over as soon as you notice that the gills are covered with droplets of juice. Cook on the other side until tender. Meanwhile, rub the surface of the warm crostini with a cut clove of garlic, put on 2 hot plates.

Arrange a few fresh arugula leaves on each one, top with overlapping mushrooms. Sprinkle with Parmesan cheese and serve immediately. If there are any buttery juices in the pan, spoon every drop over the mushrooms for extra deliciousness.

Roast Pumpkin

a slice of pumpkin with seeds and cottony fibers removed
olive oil or beef dripping
salt and freshly ground pepper
parsley or grated Gruyère cheese

Preheat the oven to 350°F (180°C).

Cut the pumpkin into chunks with a bit of skin on each piece. Season with salt and pepper. Toss in olive oil or melted dripping and roast in the oven for 3/4–1 hour depending on size, turn occasionally during cooking.

Serve either sprinkled with parsley or arrange in a dish, scatter with shredded Gruyère cheese and flash under a broiler until the cheese becomes bubbly and brown. If you then scatter it with crispy bacon and lots of chopped parsley you have a supper dish rather than just an accompanying vegetable.

Deep-fried Capers

If the capers have been packed in salt, wash in cold water, and if packed in brine, drain; either way, dry well.

1/3 cup capers
olive oil for frying

Heat the oil in a deep fryer to 350°F (180°C). Fry the capers for 1–2 minutes until they puff up. Drain on paper towel and serve immediately.

Zucchini or Marrow in Cheddar Cheese Sauce

Serves 4–6

Most people who grow zucchini find it difficult to eat them fast enough; when they turn into marrows, try this – it is unexpectedly good.

3 lbs. (1.3kg) large zucchini or small marrows (should yield about 2 lbs. [900g] prepared)
3 1/2 tablespoons butter
salt and freshly ground pepper
about 1 cup creamy milk
Roux (see page 580)
1/2 cup shredded sharp Cheddar cheese
1 generous tablespoon parsley, chopped

Peel and seed the zucchini or marrow and cut the flesh into 1-inch (2.5-cm) chunks. Melt the butter in a heavy pan, toss in the zucchini or marrow and season with salt and pepper. Cover with a butter wrapper and the lid of the saucepan. Cook over a low heat until soft and juicy, about 20 minutes.

Remove the marrow or zucchini with a slotted spoon to a warm serving dish. Add the creamy milk to the juices in the pan and bring to a boil. Whisk in enough roux to thicken the sauce. Add the cheese, taste, and correct the seasoning. Pour the sauce over the zucchini and serve sprinkled with a little parsley.

Variations

1 Sprinkle a little extra grated cheese or a mixture of grated cheese and Buttered Crumbs (see page 248) on top and flash under the broiler until crispy and golden.

2 Put a layer of shepherd's pie mixture in a deep ovenproof dish, top with marrow and cheese sauce, and bake in a preheated oven (375°F/190°C) for 30 minutes.

3 A layer of Tomato Fondue (see page 188) under the zucchini is also delicious.

Master Recipe

Tian of Mediterranean Vegetables Baked with Olive Oil and Herbs

Serves 8–10

A tian is a large, heavy earthenware pot made in Provence. You will need one (or a large shallow ovenproof dish) 14 x 12 inches (36 x 32cm). Provençal tian is strictly made of green vegetables – marrow, spinach, chard, and perhaps peas. This is a more colorful version.

3 small eggplants (about 1 1/2 lbs. [700g])
2 lbs. (900g) very ripe tomatoes, peeled
1 1/4 lbs. (600g) zucchini
1/2–3/4 cup extra-virgin olive oil
4 scallions, thinly sliced or 1 onion, very thinly sliced
2–4 teaspoons herbs (rosemary, thyme, or annual marjoram), chopped
salt and freshly ground pepper

Garnish
1 1/2–2 1/2 tablespoons parsley, freshly chopped

Preheat the oven to 400°F (200°C).

Prepare the vegetables: cut the eggplants into 1/2-inch (1-cm) slices, sprinkle them with salt, and let drain for 15–20 minutes. Rinse to remove the excess salt and pat dry with paper towels. Peel the tomatoes and cut in thick slices. Slice the zucchini at an angle in 1/2-inch (1-cm) slices.

Drizzle a tian or shallow baking dish with half the olive oil, sprinkle in the scallions and some chopped herbs, arrange the eggplant slices alternately with tomatoes and zucchini. Season with salt and pepper, drizzle with the remaining oil and sprinkle over a little more marjoram.

Bake for 25–30 minutes or until vegetables are cooked through. (Keep an eye on them: you may need to cover with tin foil if they are getting too charred.) Sprinkle with parsley and serve.

Variation

Gratin of Vegetables

Sprinkle Buttered Crumbs (see page 248) mixed with grated Parmesan, Cheddar, or Gruyère cheese on top, and brown under the broiler before serving.

Chargrilled Summer Vegetables with Tapenade Toasts

Serves 8 as an appetizer or 4 as a main course

2–3 eggplants, sliced 1/4 inch (5mm) thick
4 medium green zucchini, sliced 1/8 inch (3mm) lengthwise
sea salt or kosher salt
2–3 fleshy red peppers
2–3 fleshy yellow peppers
4–6 pieces of green asparagus
1 head fennel, sliced 1/8 inch (3mm) lengthwise
salt and freshly ground pepper

Dressing
1/3 cup best Italian extra-virgin olive oil
juice of 1/2 lemon, freshly squeezed or 2 1/2 tablespoons balsamic vinegar
10–12 whole basil leaves or annual marjoram
sea salt or kosher salt, and freshly cracked pepper

Slice the eggplants and zucchini, sprinkle with pure salt, let drain in a colander to get rid of excess liquid – 30 minutes at least. If the zucchini are small, home grown, and very fresh, this step is scarcely necessary.

Chargrill the peppers, turning them so they become completely black on all sides (see page 80). Remove and place in a bowl. Cover and leave in the fridge for 5 or 10 minutes. They will be easier to peel.

Blanch the asparagus in boiling, salted water for no more than 30 seconds, then plunge into iced water to refresh. Drain. Lay out the eggplants and zucchini on clean cloths or paper towels to dry off all the excess liquid. Brush each piece sparingly with olive oil. Grill the eggplants first using a chargrill or hot grill pan – they should be soft when pressed, and scorched by the grill but not blackened. Put each vegetable into a large bowl as you grill.

Next chargrill or pan-grill the zucchini and fennel slices, just giving them a few seconds – sufficient time to brown where they touch the grill. Finally season the blanched asparagus with salt and pepper. Grill for about 1/2 minute on each side.

The peppers should now be cool. Peel off the charred skin, remove the stalk and seeds with your hands, divide the peppers into 4 (they will divide naturally) and add to the other chargrilled vegetables. Don't wash them or you'll loose some of their sweet flavor. Mix the extra-virgin olive oil with lemon juice or vinegar.

Toss the vegetables in the dressing, taste, and season with salt and black pepper (we crush ours in a mortar and pestle for this recipe). Arrange on a large white platter. Drizzle with olive oil, scatter with basil or marjoram leaves and a few black olives. Serve with Bruschetta (see page 66), Tapenade Toasts (see page 74), or whole roasted garlic cloves.

Vegetarian Moussaka

Serves 8

This is a vegetarian version of a Greek peasant recipe served in almost every taverna in Greece. There are many variations on the theme, some of which include cooked potato and raisins.

12 ounces (350g) eggplant (1 medium)
12 ounces (350g) zucchini (about 2 x 6-inch long zucchini)
1 x 14-ounce (400-g) can tomatoes or very ripe tomatoes in summer
1 onion, finely chopped (include some green part of scallion if you have it)
4 garlic cloves, crushed
olive oil for frying
1 lb. (450g) mushrooms, sliced (about 4 1/2–5 cups) and sautéed
2 teaspoons chopped fresh marjoram or fresh thyme
2 teaspoons chopped fresh parsley
pinch of grated nutmeg
2 teaspoons flour
2 boiled potatoes
salt and freshly ground pepper

For the topping:
3 tablespoons butter
1/4 cup plus 2 tablespoons flour
2 1/2 cups milk
2 egg yolks
2 1/2 tablespoons cream
1 cup shredded Gruyère or sharp Cheddar cheese
1 bay leaf
salt and freshly ground pepper

earthenware dish, 10 x 8 1/2 inches (25.5 x 21.5cm)

Preheat the oven to 375°F (190°C).

Slice the eggplants and zucchini into 1/2 inch (1cm) slices, score the flesh with a sharp knife, and sprinkle with salt. Leave for half an hour. Roughly chop or cut up the canned tomatoes, peel and chop the fresh tomatoes if using. Keep the juices.

Meanwhile, in a heavy saucepan over a gentle heat, soften the onions and garlic in one tablespoon of olive oil. Add the sautéed mushrooms, freshly chopped herbs, and nutmeg to the onions. Stir in the flour and cook for a minute or two, then pour in the tomatoes and their juice. Bring to a boil, stirring, and simmer for 2–3 minutes. Season well.

Rinse and wipe the eggplants dry. Heat 1/2 inch (1cm) of olive oil in a frying pan. Fry first the eggplants on both sides, then the zucchini until light golden color, heating up more oil if necessary. As the zucchini are done, put them into the bottom of a shallow casserole dish. Add a layer of sliced potato. Season with salt and freshly ground pepper. Tip the mushroom mixture onto the zucchini and potato, then lay the fried eggplant on top of that. Keep the top as flat as possible. Set the oven to 350°F (180°C).

Melt the butter in a saucepan. Stir in the flour. Cook, stirring for 1 minute, then draw off the heat. Add the milk slowly, whisking out the lumps as you go. Add the bay leaf. Return the pan to the heat and stir until boiling. Season with salt and pepper and simmer for 2 minutes. Mix the egg yolk with the cream in a large bowl. Pour the sauce on to this mixture, stirring all the time. Add half the cheese and pour the sauce over the casserole. Sprinkle the rest of the cheese on top and bake for 30–35 minutes until completely reheated and well browned.

Moussaka can be made up in large quantities ahead of time, cooled quickly, and frozen after it has been closely covered with plastic wrap.

Spiced Vegetable Pie

Serves 6

9 ounces (250g) chopped onions (about 2 cups)
8 ounces (225g) peeled and chopped potatoes (about 1 1/2 cups)
9 ounces (250g) chopped carrots (about 2–2 1/4 cups)
8 ounces (225g) peeled and chopped celeriac (about 2 cups)
1 cup peeled and chopped parsnip or/and 1 cup sliced and sautéed mushrooms
1 1/2 tablespoons olive oil
2 teaspoons cumin seeds
1 tablespoon coriander seeds
1/2 teaspoon cardamom seeds
1 teaspoon turmeric
2 1/2 tablespoons flour
salt, freshly ground pepper, and sugar
1 1/4 cups vegetable stock

Pastry Dough
4 cups flour
salt
2 1/4 sticks (1 cup plus 2 tablespoons) butter
3/4 cup water

Egg Wash
1 egg, preferably from a free-range hen
a pinch of salt

1 pan, 8 inches (20.5cm) in diameter, 1 1/2 inches (4cm) high

Cut the vegetables into uniform-sized cubes of about 1 inch (2.5cm). Heat 2 1/2 tablespoons olive oil in a wide frying pan, add the onions, potatoes, carrots, celeriac, and parsnips. Season with salt and freshly ground pepper, toss in the oil, cover the pot, and sweat on a gentle heat for 4 or 5 minutes. Meanwhile heat the cumin, coriander, and cardamom seeds on a pan until they smell aromatic – just a few seconds. Crush lightly, add to the vegetables. Cook for 1–2 minutes. Remove from the heat – sprinkle the flour, turmeric, and a pinch of sugar over it, and stir well. Return to the heat and add the vegetable stock gradually, stirring all the time. Cover the pot and simmer for 20–30 minutes or until the vegetables are almost tender but not mushy.

Meanwhile, make the pastry dough. Sift the flour and salt into a mixing bowl and make a well in the center. Dice the butter, put it into a saucepan with water, and bring to a boil. Pour the liquid all at once into the flour and mix together quickly; beat until smooth. At first the dough will be too soft to handle but as it cools, it may be rolled out 1/8–1/4 inch (3–5mm) thick, to fit the pan. The dough may be made into individual pies or one large pie. Keep back one-third of the pastry dough for lids.

Preheat the oven to 450°F (230°C).

Fill the pastry-lined pans with the vegetable mixture which should be almost, but not quite, cooked and cooled a little. Brush the edges of the pastry dough with the water and egg wash and put on the pastry dough lids, pinching them tightly together. Roll out the trimmings to make pastry leaves or twirls to decorate the tops of the pies; make a hole in the center, egg-wash the lid, and then egg-wash the decoration also. Bake the pies for 30 minutes.

Patty Pan Squash with Basil or Marjoram

Serves 6

12–18 patty pan squash or a mixture of patty pan squash and small green zucchini
olive oil
2 1/2 tablespoons freshly chopped marjoram or torn basil leaves
lemon juice, optional
salt and freshly ground pepper

Trim the squash and cut each one into 6 or 8 pie-shaped pieces depending on size. Slice the zucchini on the diagonal into one-third inch slices. Heat a few tablespoons of olive oil in an iron pan or wok, add the patty pan squash and zucchini, if using. Season with salt and freshly ground pepper, toss rapidly over the heat, add the chopped or torn herbs. Toss for another minute or so. Taste and correct seasoning. Maybe a few drops of lemon juice might be good, serve immediately.

Stir-fried Vegetables

Serves 2–4

You can stir fry a number of different vegetables but think about texture, color, and flavor before you make your choice. A wok is by far the most useful bit of kitchen equipment but useless unless you have a powerful gas cooker, and a good heavy frying pan will suffice for this recipe.

2 1/2 tablespoons scallions, cut into thin slices at an angle
1 generous tablespoon grated or finely chopped fresh ginger
2–3 cloves garlic, chopped
2 ounces (50g) mushrooms, cut into quarters and sliced thinly (about 1/2 cup)
1/2 cup French beans (or green beans), cut into 1 1/4-inch (3-cm) slices, at an angle
2/3 cup yellow or green zucchini, cut in half lengthwise and sliced thinly
a handful of snow peas, cut into small pieces approx. 1/2 inch (1cm) at an angle
1 cup broccoli, cut into tiny flowerets
1/4 cup peanuts or cashew nuts, optional
salt, freshly ground pepper
a pinch of sugar
1 generous tablespoon freshly chopped parsley
1 generous tablespoon freshly chopped mixed herbs – mint, chives, thyme, or basil

First prepare the vegetables. Heat the wok until it smokes, add the oil and heat again. Add the scallions, ginger, and garlic, toss around, then add the vegetables one after the other in the following order, tossing between each addition – mushrooms, French beans, zucchini, snow peas, broccoli, and nuts. Season with salt, freshly ground pepper, and sugar. Sprinkle with freshly chopped herbs, taste, correct the seasoning. Serve immediately in a hot serving dish.

salads

salads

Doctors and nutritionists have been urging us to eat more fruit and vegetables as part of a healthy diet. Lots of yummy salads full of vitamins and minerals sound like a good idea, but there seems to be little point in following this advice if most fresh produce contains harmful residues of pesticides and herbicides. Understandably, consumers feel that they have a right to know which chemicals have been used during production and there is, as a result, a growing demand for more information on the labels of fresh produce. Given that a jar of jam has to be labeled with a detailed list of its contents and additives, the fact that fruit and vegetables do not, currently, require the same, seems to many a double standard. Where possible, seek out organically grown lettuces and salad greens.

Grow Your Own

It is such fun to grow your own salads – buy a couple of seeds and get started. Get the kids involved too, they'll love it. You'll be surprised at how productive even a few containers on a small balcony or window sill can be. Some lettuces, salad greens and fresh herbs need very little space and one really gets a huge buzz from eating homegrown produce. The freshness and flavor will also be far superior to anything you can buy from a supermarket. Rather than harvesting the whole lettuce, just pick off the outside leaves as you need them and the plant will continue to flourish.

When buying lettuce and salad greens, seek out produce that has grown in rich, fertile soil full of complex nutrients, rather than hydroponically grown plants.

In the greenhouses here at the Ballymaloe Cookery School, we grow many different salad greens, including claytonia, corn salad, mibuna, mizuna, mysticana, garland chrysanthemum, red orach, chickweed, and purslane – a big thank you to Joy Larkcom for introducing us to many of these. Quite a few weeds are edible, too. Chickweed, the bane of many gardeners' lives, is one such plant. I even saw it for sale in New York City's Union Square farmers' market for several dollars a bunch! Ground elder (another garden pest) has quite a pungent taste, made all the sweeter for knowing it is a weed.

Treat Your Salad Gently

Well-known chef Shaun Hill, of the Merchant House in Ludlow, told me some years ago that when he was interviewing young chefs he would invite them to spend a day or two in his kitchen. At some point he would ask them to wash lettuce for the green salad. Watching from across the kitchen, he would know very quickly whether they had a real interest in food and a respect for ingredients, simply by they way they handled the lettuce.

At Ballymaloe, one of the first things the students are taught is how to wash lettuce. They fill a sink to the top with cold water, take the lettuce in their hands and break off its leaves, one by one, until they reach the tender little heart. After gentle washing, they use a salad spinner to dry the leaves a few at a time (this step is important as water dilutes the dressing). When washing organic lettuce and salad greens, if you are concerned about the possibility of slugs or green fly, add a little salt to the washing water. When drying lettuce and salad greens, be aware that you do need to handle the leaves carefully. Don't give in to the temptation to put the washed lettuce in a kitchen towel and swing it around your head, like I used to do when I was a child. You will only bruise the leaves.

Salads All Year Round

At Ballymaloe, we serve green salad with every lunch and dinner throughout the year. At the Cookery School, we fill our huge Irish beech salad bowl, made by Keith Mosse from

Bennetsbridge, with leaves and edible flowers that vary through the seasons: marigolds, daisies, bachelor's buttons, zucchini and chive flowers in summer; and in winter more robust lettuces, a little chard, beet leaves, shredded green and red cabbage, wild and garden sorrel, purslane and corn salad – which survives even in snow. In winter, dressings are often more robust than in summer, using red wine vinegar, honey, and whole-grain mustard.

Warm Salad
Warm salads or salades tièdes, the legacy of nouvelle cuisine (the 1980s French food trend), have stood the test of time. They are an interesting combination of lettuce, salad greens and herb leaves topped with a few delicious hot morsels. Warm salads give us the freedom to experiment with a wider range of tastes and textures.

The Basic Ingredients
Making a good salad is, as ever, totally dependent on using good ingredients. Always use local, seasonal produce – avoid out of season, lackluster fruit and vegetables that have been transported halfway across the world. Celebrate the seasons in your salads; each season provides us with a whole new palate of tastes to choose from. In winter, salads can include apples, beets, fennel, cabbage, root vegetables, cauliflower, broccoli, citrus fruit, and pomegranate seeds. In summer, artichokes, fava beans, snow peas, cherry tomatoes, zucchini, asparagus, and peas.

Salads aren't just about iceberg lettuce and slices of cucumber. Use your imagination. Be creative and spontaneous, using everything from fruit and seeds, to vegetables and pasta. Think carefully about how the flavors and textures will combine together, and choose a complementary dressing.

Green Salads
A green salad should be a mixture of lettuces and salad greens with a contrast of color, texture, and flavor. For color, add radicchio, copper oak leaf lettuces, and orach leaves. A burst of flavor can be introduced with peppery hot arugula leaves, mustard greens and pungent golden marjoram. Including romaine or a good iceberg will add a welcome crunch to your salad.

Salad Dressings
Many people seem to imagine that there is a mystery to making salad dressing. Well, let me demystify it for you. All you need is the finest quality oil and some good vinegar, a little freshly ground pepper and sea salt or kosher salt. Whisk 3 parts extra-virgin olive oil with 1 part wine vinegar, add a little freshly ground pepper and some sea salt. One could also add a little crushed garlic and a spot of Dijon or grainy mustard, a few chopped herbs, maybe even a little honey to ring the changes. But provided that the oil and vinegar are top quality, even a basic dressing will be delicious.

I first tasted authentic balsamic vinegar in Italy in 1981. The making of traditional balsamic vinegar is a lengthy process that stretches over many generations. This precious vinegar made from the concentrated juice of the trebbiano grape is used sparingly and respectfully. Originally it was given as part of a bride's dowry. Nowadays, however, because it has become so fashionable, it is largely produced through the solera system of tiered barrels in a process similar to the making of sherry. The best wine vinegars are wood-aged, for example Spanish Forum Vinegar. Also look out for Chinese red vinegar which is delicious. Verjuice is another super product to experiment with.

The best oils are cold-pressed – a natural, chemical-free process that produces a low acidity level. Extra-virgin olive oil is the result of the first pressing of olives and has the lowest acidity. A good cold-pressed extra-virgin olive oil is better for you than most other oils, and has even been shown to reduce harmful cholesterol.

Other types of oils, such as nut and seed oils, are also suitable for dressings. Try hazelnut, walnut, pistachio, sunflower, peanut, rapeseed (canola), grapeseed, sesame, pumpkin seed and even macadamia nut oil. Some of these are rich and aromatic and their distinctive flavors tend to dominate. They are best used in moderation and with a specific purpose in mind. Olive oils infused with herbs, chiles or truffles are also fun to experiment with.

Dressing a Salad
Be careful not to use too much dressing – use just enough to make the leaves glisten. Dress at the last moment in a deep bowl and toss the salad gently. The opposite is true for tomato salad; dress as soon as the tomatoes are cut, to seal in the flavor. Whether for eight or eighty, the sliced tomatoes are best spread in a single layer. They can then be seasoned evenly. If they are in a deep bowl they are difficult to season properly and even gentle tossing can cause the seeds to fall out. Once the tomatoes have been seasoned with salt, freshly ground pepper, and a little sugar, and then dressed with extra-virgin olive oil and freshly squeezed lemon juice (or a few drops of vinegar), they can be transferred to a serving bowl, if you wish.

Ballymaloe Buffet
Every Sunday night at Ballymaloe House, we have a special buffet dinner. The joints of meat are cooked and the fish is poached in the afternoon. Salads are freshly made and kept cool, but not refrigerated. (If you *have* to put a salad in the fridge, always allow it to return to room temperature before serving.) When making salads for a buffet, think carefully about combinations, and try not to use a mumbo jumbo of ingredients. Make single ingredient salads, such as eggplant, mushroom, and caramelized onion, cucumber, or potato. Most people will mix the salads on their plates anyway, so their flavors should complement each other.

A Little Secret
Serve a salad of lettuces and salad greens with, or just after, the main course as it has a miraculous effect – you will suddenly feel less full and have room for dessert after all!

Coleslaw

Serves 16–24

Coleslaw is an American salad, the "cole" being a general word for all true cabbages, Brassica oleracea.

1 lb. (450g) green cabbage (we use Drumhead), thinly sliced
1 large carrot, cleaned and roughly grated
1 onion, thinly sliced into rings
2/3–1 1/4 cups homemade Mayonnaise (see page 584) or mayonnaise and yogurt mixed
1 generous tablespoon parsley, chopped
salt and freshly ground pepper

Mix the cabbage, carrot, and onion together and season. Fold in the mayonnaise, or mayonnaise and yogurt mix. Taste, and correct the seasoning. Sprinkle with parsley and serve immediately or keep refrigerated.

Variations

Add some diced or finely sliced celery stalks
or 1 crisp eating apple tossed in 2 1/2 tablespoons lemon juice
or 1/4 cup golden raisins and 1 1/2 tablespoons freshly chopped mint.

Broadway Coleslaw

Serves 10

12 ounces (350g) red cabbage, cut into 1/4-inch (5-mm) dice (about 6 cups)
12 ounces (350g) green cabbage, cut into 1/4-inch (5-mm) dice (about 6 cups)
2/3 cup red onion, cut into 1/4-inch (5-mm) dice, rinsed under cold water
1 cucumber, cut into 1/4-inch (5-mm) dice
1–2 apples, finely diced
1 1/2 tablespoons parsley, freshly chopped
1 1/2 tablespoons mint, freshly chopped
1/2 cup Ballymaloe French Dressing (see page 225)
salt, freshly ground pepper, and sugar

Mix all the ingredients in a large bowl. Toss in the dressing. Taste, and correct seasoning. This salad often needs a good pinch of sugar.

Cabbage, Pineapple, and Onion Salad

Serves 6

Make this salad with the canned pineapple left over after you have used the juice for glazing bacon. It is quite delicious with cold meat, particularly ham, bacon, or pork.

1/2 small Savoy cabbage (12 ounces/350g)
1/2 15-ounce (425-g) can pineapple, cut into chunks if in rings
1 small onion (3 ounces/75g), very finely sliced into onion rings
2 1/2 tablespoons parsley, finely chopped
salt, freshly ground pepper, and sugar

French Dressing
1/4 cup sunflower oil
1/4 cup olive oil
2 1/2 tablespoons white wine vinegar
1 garlic clove
1/3 teaspoon mustard
salt and freshly ground pepper

First make the French dressing by putting all the ingredients into a screw-top jar and shaking thoroughly.

Rinse the cabbage under cold water. Cut into quarters, cut out the hard core, and slice into very thin shreds across the grain. Put into a salad bowl and add the pineapple chunks, onion rings, and half the parsley. Toss in the dressing and season with salt, pepper, and sugar. Sprinkle the remaining parsley on top and serve.

Cabbage Salad with Raisins and Mint

Serves 8
In season: autumn and winter

If you are tiring of the ubiquitous coleslaw, then you might like to try this fresh-tasting cabbage salad.

1/2 green cabbage with a good heart
2–3 large dessert apples, grated
2 1/2 tablespoons raisins
2 1/2 tablespoons mint, freshly chopped
1 tablespoon chives, freshly chopped
1/4 cup plus 1 tablespoon runny honey
1 1/2 tablespoons white wine vinegar
salt and freshly ground pepper

Cut the cabbage into quarters, discarding any coarse outer leaves. Cut away the core and shred the heart very finely. Put it into a bowl with the apples, raisins, mint, and chives.

Mix the honey and vinegar together. Toss the salad in the dressing until well coated. Taste, and correct the seasoning and serve immediately.

Master Recipe

Apple, Celery, Walnut, and Chicken Salad

Serves 6

2 heads of celery
1 large green dessert apple (about 8 ounces/225g)
1 large red dessert apple (about 8 ounces/225g)
about 2 1/2 tablespoons lemon juice, freshly squeezed
1 level teaspoon superfine sugar
3/4 cup homemade Mayonnaise (see page 584)
2 ounces (50g) fresh walnuts, shelled (1/2 cup)
1 head of crisp lettuce, washed

Garnish
sprigs of watercress
2 pan-grilled spicy Chicken Breasts or plain Pan-Grilled Chicken Breasts (see page 271)
parsley, freshly chopped

Separate the celery and remove the strings from the outer stalks with a potato peeler. Chop or julienne the stalks into 1 1/2-inch (4-cm) lengths. Put them into a bowl of iced water for 15–30 minutes. Wash and core the apples, cut into 1/2-inch (1-cm) dice.

Make a dressing by mixing the lemon juice, sugar, and 1 tablespoon of mayonnaise (reserve a little lemon juice and sugar). Toss the diced apple in the dressing and let it stand while you prepare the remainder of the ingredients.

Chop the walnuts coarsely. Drain the celery and add it, and most of the walnuts, to the diced apple along with the rest of the mayonnaise, and mix thoroughly. Slice the cold pan-grilled chicken breasts crosswise and toss lightly through the salad.

Line a serving dish with the lettuce leaves and pile the salad into the center. Garnish with sprigs of watercress and scatter some chopped parsley and the remainder of the chopped walnuts over the center.

Variation

Apple, Celery, and Walnut Salad

Follow the Master Recipe, but omit the pan-grilled chicken breasts. Serve as a main course.

Above: Black Bean, Corn, and Roasted Red Pepper Salad

Black Bean, Corn, and Roasted Red Pepper Salad

Serves 6–8

1½ cups dried black beans
1 garlic clove
dried chipotle chiles
1 large onion, halved
*1 cup long grain rice**
1 tablespoon plus 1 teaspoon olive oil
8 ounces (225g) cooked corn (about 4 ears)
2 sweet red peppers, roasted, peeled, seeded, and diced (see page 80)
2½ tablespoons fresh cilantro or mint
2½ tablespoons fresh parsley
6 scallions, chopped

Dressing
¼ cup red wine vinegar
2½ tablespoons lemon juice, freshly squeezed
1 clove garlic, crushed
1½ teaspoons toasted and ground cumin seed
½ teaspoon toasted and ground coriander
¾ cup olive oil

Cover the beans with plenty of cold water and soak for at least 3 hours or overnight. Next day, drain them. Place the beans in a large pot with the garlic, chiles, and onion. Cover with plenty of fresh water and bring to a boil. Continue to simmer for 1–1½ hours or until the beans are tender.

Meanwhile, make the dressing by whisking all the ingredients together in a jar. When the beans are tender but still intact, remove the onion, garlic, and chiles. Drain, and toss in the dressing while still warm. While the beans are cooking, cook the rice also: bring a large pot of water to a boil, add salt and the rice and return to a boil for 5–10 minutes or until the rice is tender. Drain, and toss in the olive oil.

In a large bowl, mix the beans with the rice, corn, red peppers, cilantro or mint, parsley, and scallions, and more dressing. Taste, and correct seasoning if necessary.

**Substitute 4–8 ounces (110–225g) penne or orso for rice in the above recipe, if you prefer a pasta salad.*

Arizona Rice and Black Bean Salad

Serves 4–6

2½ cups black beans
2⅔ cups basmati rice
*3 lbs. (1.3kg) medium salsa**
2 bunches of scallions
1 lb. (450g) vine-ripened tomatoes, diced
1 tablespoon salt
¼ teaspoon cayenne pepper
2 tablespoons cumin, roasted and freshly cracked
2 ounces (50g) cilantro (a good ¼-bunch), chopped
¼ cup lime juice, freshly squeezed

* *If you don't have medium salsa, use 1 lb. (450g) hot and 1 lb. (450g) canned tomatoes instead – omit the cayenne.*

Wash beans thoroughly. Cook the beans in boiling, salted water for 2–3 hours or until tender. Top up with boiling water if necessary. Drain and rinse with cold water. Cook the rice in boiling, salted water until tender. Drain well. Combine all ingredients in a large bowl and toss together gently. Mix well and check seasonings.

Salad of Quail with Grapes

Serves 4

4 quail
4 generous teaspoons honey
sea salt, or kosher salt, and freshly ground pepper
20 grapes, black or green
⅓ cup lardons of bacon
1 tablespoon plus 1 teaspoon olive oil
selection of lettuces and salad greens (about 4 cups)

Hazelnut Oil Dressing
¼ cup hazelnut oil
1 tablespoon plus 1 teaspoon sunflower oil
1 tablespoon plus 1 teaspoon vinegar
¼ teaspoon mustard
salt, pepper, and sugar

Preheat the oven to 350°F (180°C). Brush each quail with 1 teaspoon of honey and season with sea salt and pepper. Place in a roasting pan in the oven and cook for 10–20 minutes, depending on the size of the quail. Baste while cooking. The birds are done when the juices run clear if you pierce the meat on the leg.

Meanwhile, halve the black grapes or peel and seed green ones. Make up the dressing and toss the grapes in 1 tablespoon of it. Blanch the lardons of bacon, pat dry, and reserve. When the quail are cooked, joint them by removing the drumstick and thigh in one portion and the breasts in one portion each. Keep the quail warm.

Sauté the blanched lardons in olive oil and keep warm.

Arrange the grapes around each plate and toss the lettuces carefully in the hazelnut oil dressing and place in the center of the plates. Sprinkle on the warm lardons of bacon and finally put the warm quail on top of the lettuces and serve immediately.

Bulgar Wheat and Pecan Nut Salad

Serves 8

1 quart (960ml) homemade Chicken or Vegetable Stock (see page 36)
2¼ cups bulgur wheat
1 cup pecans, coarsely chopped
a generous ½ cup currants
¼ cup flat-leaf parsley, freshly chopped
1 tablespoon plus 1 teaspoon olive oil
grated zest of 1 orange
salt and freshly ground pepper

Bring the stock to a boil. Put the bulgur into a bowl and pour the boiling stock over it. Let sit until the stock is absorbed and the bulgar is cool.

Add the pecans, currants, parsley, olive oil, and orange zest. Season with salt and freshly ground pepper. Toss well and serve at room temperature.

Fattoush

Serves 6

There are many delicious ways of using up bread, particularly in the Mediterranean countries. Fattoush is a good example, as is Panzanella, or Tuscan bread salad, which you may see on menus in Italy. Marjoram or basil may be included or substituted for cilantro. Sumac flakes give this salad a characteristic, slightly sour taste. If you can't get it, the salad will still taste delicious but not so authentic.

2 stale pita breads or 2–3 thick slices of stale sour dough or good country bread
a little bunch of arugula or purslane
1 mild sweet red pepper (optional)
2–3 teaspoons sumac, if available
4 vine-ripened tomatoes, cut into quarters and then into halves crosswise
1 cucumber, coarsely chopped
3 scallions, sliced at an angle
3–4 tablespoons freshly chopped parsley
2½ tablespoons fresh cilantro leaves
3–4 tablespoons fresh mint
salt and freshly ground pepper

Dressing
¼ cup freshly squeezed lemon juice
½ cup extra-virgin olive oil
2 garlic cloves, crushed
salt and freshly ground pepper, maybe even a pinch of sugar or a dash of balsamic vinegar

If the bread isn't stale, toast it until crisp. Cut into uneven-sized pieces. Chop the arugula or purslane coarsely. Cut the sweet red pepper into rounds or dice. Put into a salad bowl with the sumac flakes, if using, the tomato, cucumber, and scallions, herbs, and bread. Season.

Whisk the dressing ingredients together. Spoon over the salad, toss gently, taste. Let the salad sit for at least 30 minutes, better still, 1 hour before serving, so the bread soaks up lots of yummy dressing and juice.

Blood Orange, Beet, and Arugula Salad

Serves 6
In season: Late winter–early spring

Pickled Beets (see page 514), preferably still warm

3–4 blood oranges

Dressing
zest of 1 orange, finely grated
juice of ½ orange
1 small shallot, very finely diced
¼ cup extra-virgin olive oil
1 teaspoon balsamic vinegar
sea salt, or kosher salt, and freshly ground pepper
4 small fistfuls of arugula leaves
24 fresh walnut halves, slightly toasted

To make the dressing, put the finely grated orange zest in a bowl along with the shallot and juice of ½ orange. Whisk in the oil and vinegar. Season with salt and pepper. It should taste nice and perky. Peel all the oranges and cut into thin slices.

Divide the arugula between the plates. Top with sliced beets and blood orange slices and scatter with walnut halves. Drizzle a little dressing over and serve at once.

Old-fashioned Salad with Shanagarry Cream Dressing

Serves 2–4

This simple old-fashioned salad, which is the sort of thing you might have had for tea on a visit to your Gran on a Sunday evening – perhaps with a slice of meat from the Sunday roast – is one of my absolute favorites. It can be quite delicious when it is made with crisp lettuce, good home-grown tomatoes and cucumbers, eggs from free-range hens, and home-preserved beets. If, on the other hand, you make it with pale eggs from intensively-reared hens, watery tomatoes, tired lettuce and cucumbers, and worst of all, vinegary beets from a jar, you'll wonder why you bothered. We serve this traditional salad at Ballymaloe as an appetizer, with an old-fashioned dressing which would have been popular before the days of mass-produced mayonnaise. Our recipe came from Lydia Strangman, a Quaker lady who was the previous occupant of our house.

lettuce leaves
2 hard boiled eggs, quartered
2–4 tomatoes, quartered
16 slices of cucumber
2–4 sliced radishes
4 slices of Pickled Beets (see page 514)

4 tiny scallions
sprigs of watercress
chopped parsley

Shanagarry Cream Dressing (see below)

Arrange a few lettuce leaves on each plate. Then scatter a few tomatoes, egg quarters, slices of cucumber, 1 radish, and 2 slices of beet on top. Garnish with scallion, sprigs of watercress, and the remaining egg white from the dressing. Sprinkle some chopped parsley over the top and serve with a tiny bowl of dressing in the center of each plate. Serve immediately while the salad is crisp and before the beet starts to run.

Shanagarry Cream Dressing

2 hard boiled eggs
1 level teaspoon dry mustard
pinch of salt
1½ tablespoons dark, soft brown sugar
1½ tablespoons brown malt vinegar
¼–½ cup cream

Cut the eggs in half, sieve the yolks into a bowl, add the sugar, salt, and mustard. Blend in the vinegar and cream. Chop the egg whites and add some to the sauce. Keep the rest to scatter over the salad.

Cellophane Noodle Salad with Chicken and Shrimp

Serves 8 as an appetizer or 4 as a main course

Mooli is the south-east Asian white radish, also known as daikon. A root vegetable, it is served raw in salads and has a cool sharp tang, which is lost when cooked. Now widely available in Asian stores. A delicious recipe inspired by Sri Owen.

¼ ounce (7g) Chinese mushrooms (wood ears)
2½ cups homemade Chicken Stock (see page 36)
2 skinless chicken breasts
7 ounces (200g) cellophane noodles
3 ounces (75g) mooli or French radishes
¼ cup fish sauce (nam pla)
¼ cup lime juice, freshly squeezed
1 tablespoon superfine sugar
2–4 Thai red chiles, seeded and finely chopped
1 red onion, thinly sliced
2 scallions, thinly sliced at an angle
a few tender celery leaves if available
32 cooked scampi or 48 smaller shrimp
4 ounces (110g) cilantro leaves (a good ½-bunch)
salt and freshly ground pepper

Garnish
sprigs of cilantro and a couple of red and green chiles

Put the mushrooms into a bowl, cover with warm water, and allow to reconstitute for about 15 minutes. Drain, rinse, and trim off any hard bits. Slice into thin strips.

Bring the chicken stock to a boil, add salt, and slip in the chicken breasts; return to a boil and simmer gently for 8 minutes. Remove from the heat, cover, and let cool. Then shred the chicken.

Put the noodles into another bowl, cover with boiling water, and let stand for 5 minutes. Drain, cut into 3 to 4-inch (8 to 10-cm) lengths with a knife or clean scissors. Peel the mooli and slice very thinly. Put in a bowl of iced water to crisp up.

Mix the fish sauce, lime juice, sugar, and chopped chiles in a large bowl. Add the onions, scallions, celery leaves, and wood ears, and mix well.

Drain the mooli well and add along with the noodles, shrimp, chicken, and cilantro to the other ingredients. Toss gently. Taste, and correct seasoning. Serve garnished with cilantro sprigs and a few slices of red and green chiles.

Seared Beef Salad with Horseradish Mayonnaise and French Fried Onions

Serves 6 as an appetizer or light lunch

The crispy onions are best cooked at the last minute, but they may be cooked ahead and reheated just before serving. Strips of roast red pepper and crumbled blue cheese are also great on this salad.

6–18 slices of beef fillet, ¼ inch (5mm) thick (use 1 slice per person from the mid-fillet or 3 slices from the tapered end)
salt and freshly ground pepper
olive oil
selection of lettuce and salad greens
Horseradish Mayonnaise (see page 586)
French Fried Onions (see page 188)
a few fresh arugula leaves
freshly cracked pepper

Dressing
5 tablespoons extra-virgin olive oil
1½ tablespoons white wine vinegar
¼ teaspoon whole-grain mustard (we use Lakeshore)
1 teaspoon freshly chopped herbs; thyme, parsley, tarragon would be good
salt and freshly cracked pepper

First make the dressing by whisking all the ingredients together in a bowl. Season well. Wash and dry the salad greens. Prepare and cook the French Fried onions.

Heat a grill-pan on a high heat, season the beef on both sides with salt and freshly ground pepper and a drizzle of olive oil. Sear the beef on the hot grill-pan, first in one direction and then the other to give a criss-cross effect.

Toss the salad greens in just enough dressing to make the leaves glisten. Divide between six warm plates, piling them up in the center. Arrange the seared beef around the salad. Dribble a little Horseradish Mayonnaise over each slice of beef. Put a clump of hot crispy onions on top of the salad. Serve immediately with an arugula leaf or two on each plate and a little sprinkling of freshly cracked pepper.

Barossa Valley Cucumber Salad

Serves 6–10

3 cucumbers
salt
1 small onion, finely chopped
1 tablespoon plus 1 teaspoon white wine vinegar
freshly ground pepper and sugar
1½–2½ tablespoons heavy cream or crème fraîche

Right: Cellophane Noodle Salad with Chicken and Shrimp

Peel and slice the cucumber into paper-thin slices. Spread on a large plate and sprinkle with salt. Let them degorge for 30 minutes. Drain, and put into a bowl. Add the finely chopped onion and sprinkle with the white wine vinegar. Season with freshly ground pepper and sugar. Cover and refrigerate. Just before serving, stir in the cream. Taste for seasoning, and serve.

Spicy Beef Salad with Thai Chile Dressing

Serves 8 for light lunch or 16 as an appetizer

This is a great recipe from a recent trip to Australia.

1 red pepper
1 small red onion
2 scallions
24 red cherry tomatoes or a mixture of red and yellow
2 handfuls each fresh mint and cilantro leaves
2/3 cup peanuts, roasted
1 1/2–2 lbs. (700–900g) beef fillet or sirloin
1 1/2 tablespoons extra-virgin olive oil
salt and freshly ground pepper

Chile Dressing
2 garlic cloves, peeled and crushed
1–2 fresh red Thai chiles, seeded and roughly chopped
2 1/2 tablespoons light soy sauce
2 1/2 tablespoons lime juice, freshly squeezed
1 1/2 tablespoons fish sauce (nam pla)
2 tablespoons palm sugar or light soft brown sugar

First make the dressing: pound the garlic and chiles together in a mortar and pestle, if available. Put into a bowl and add the soy sauce, lime juice, fish sauce, and palm sugar, and mix well until dissolved.

Cut the pepper into quarters, seed and cut into thin slices at an angle. Slice the red onion thinly, slice the green and white parts of the scallions at an angle, halve or quarter the cherry tomatoes. Put into a bowl with the mint, cilantro and peanuts. Toss gently and cover with plastic wrap until ready to use.

Preheat a grill-pan. Cut the beef into thick slices; season. Sprinkle with a little olive oil and cook until medium rare or medium. Let rest on an upturned plate for 5–10 minutes.

Slice the beef thinly and add to the other ingredients. Taste the dressing and correct the balance if necessary. Spoon the dressing over the salad and toss gently. Serve immediately.

Tuna Fish, Bean, and Pasta Salad

Serves 8

The cooked pasta is soaked in French dressing while it is still warm so that it absorbs extra flavor.

3 ounces (75g) pasta shells (conchiglie, orecchiette or fusilli), about 1–1 1/3 cups
oil and lemon for cooking
2/3 cup Ballymaloe French Dressing (see page 225)
*1 x 7-ounce (200-g) can each of flageolet beans, borlotti beans and red kidney beans, rinsed and drained**
1 bunch scallions, chopped diagonally
*1 box mustard and cress,** or alfalfa sprouts*
1 1/2 tablespoons chives, freshly chopped
1 1/2 tablespoons parsley, finely chopped
lemon juice, freshly squeezed
7-ounce (200-g) can tuna fish, drained
15 small black Niçoise olives
salt and freshly ground black pepper

Cook the pasta in plenty of boiling, salted water with 1 tablespoon of oil and a slice of lemon, until tender. This will take about 10 minutes. Drain thoroughly and rinse the pasta well under cold running water. Soak the pasta in French Dressing for about 30 minutes, seasoning well. Mix it with the cooked beans, scallions, half the mustard and cress, half the chives and parsley, and some lemon juice. Add the tuna and mix gently so as not to break up the flesh too much.

Pile into a serving dish and scatter the remaining herbs, the black olives, and the mustard and cress over them.

** We also use 1/2 cup dried black-eyed peas, 1/2 cup dried navy beans and 1/2 cup red kidney beans. Soak them separately overnight in cold water. Next day cook each type in fresh water with a few slices of onion and carrot and a bouquet garni. They take about 30 minutes to cook.*
*** If you don't have mustard and cress or alfalfasprouts at hand, omit them – the salad is still delicious, although it is more nutritious if they're included.*

Italian Seafood Salad

Serves 8

Seafood salad is possibly the most popular cold seafood dish around the coast of Italy. Every port has its own version and even though the content varies, they are all tossed simply in a mixture of olive oil and fresh lemon juice. Tiny squid or calamare are also a favorite addition. In this recipe, I've included some grilled red pepper, a dice of cucumber, and a few black olives which are delicious if not very traditional.

1 lb. (450g) cooked salmon or monkfish (or a mixture of both), cut into 1/2-inch (1-cm) flakes or chunks
1 lb. (450g) cooked shrimp, or a mixture of shrimp and scallops
4 lbs. (1.8kg) mussels, steamed, opened, and removed from the shells or 2 lbs. (900g) mussels and 2 lbs. (900g) cockles or clams
1 roasted red pepper, peeled and diced, optional
3 cucumbers, seeded and cut into 1/4-inch (5-mm) dice, optional
8 black olives, pitted (optional)
1 1/2 tablespoons freshly chopped parsley
salt and freshly ground pepper

Dressing
1/3 cup extra-virgin olive oil
3 tablespoons freshly squeezed lemon juice
1/2 garlic clove
1 1/2 tablespoons freshly chopped mixed herbs, e.g., parsley, chives, and annual marjoram
salt and freshly ground pepper

Garnish
sprigs of flat-leaf parsley
lemon segments
a few whole shrimp

Mix together all the ingredients for the dressing, adding salt and freshly ground pepper to taste. Shake well to emulsify. Put the fish and shellfish into a wide serving bowl, add the cucumber dice, roasted red pepper, and pitted olives, if using, and season with salt and pepper.

Very gently toss the fish in a few tablespoons of dressing – just enough to coat lightly, and sprinkle with chopped parsley. Marinate for 1 hour.

Just before serving, garnish with large sprigs of fresh parsley, segments of lemon, and a few whole cooked shrimp.

Master Recipe

Salade Niçoise with Seared Tuna

Serves 6
In season: best in Summer and early Autumn

In Provence there are many versions of this colorful salad, which makes a wonderful summer lunch. Some include crisp red and green peppers and some omit the potato. Now that we can get fresh tuna occasionally we sear it quickly and serve warm on the salad. Alternatively, use good-quality canned tuna.

8 medium waxy potatoes, cooked but still warm
salt, freshly ground pepper, and sugar
3–4 ripe tomatoes, peeled and quartered
4 ounces (110g) cooked young green beans, topped and tailed and cut into 2-inch (5-cm) lengths, blanched and refreshed (about 1 cup)
2½ teaspoons chives
2½ teaspoons parsley, chopped
2½ teaspoons annual marjoram or thyme
*12 ounces (350g) fresh tuna or 14-ounce (400-g) can of tuna**
1 crisp lettuce
3 hardboiled eggs, shelled and quartered
12 black olives
1 teaspoon capers (optional)
1 can anchovies
8 tiny scallions
salt and freshly ground pepper
French dressing
¼ cup white wine vinegar
¾ cup extra-virgin olive oil
2 large garlic cloves, mashed
2 teaspoons Dijon mustard
good pinch of salt and freshly ground pepper
1½ tablespoons parsley, chopped
1½ tablespoons basil or annual marjoram

Mix all the ingredients for the dressing together in a screw-top jar – it must be very well-seasoned otherwise the salad will be bland.

Slice the potatoes into ¼-inch (5-mm) thick slices and toss in some dressing while still warm. Season with salt and pepper.

Toss the tomatoes and beans in some more dressing, season with salt, pepper, and sugar, and sprinkle with some chopped herbs. Heat a grill-pan or frying pan. Cut the tuna into ¾-inch (2-cm) thick steaks. Season with salt and freshly ground pepper, and cook quickly on both sides; it should still be rare in the center. Beware: tuna overcooks very easily and becomes dry and boring.

Line a shallow bowl with lettuce leaves. Arrange the potatoes on top and then the rest of the ingredients, finishing off with olives, capers, and chunks of tuna and/or the anchovies. Drizzle some more dressing over the top. Sprinkle the remainder of the herbs and the scallions on top, and serve.

* *Pan-grilled mackerel is a delicious alternative*

Variation

Vegetarian Salade Niçoise

Follow the Master Recipe but omit the tuna and anchovies. Add strips of roasted red and yellow peppers and char-grilled onions.

Caesar Salad

Serves 4

This legendary salad, first made in Mexico by Caesar Cardini in the 1920s, has become all the rage. It takes only a few minutes to make at home. Serve it in deep bowls as they do in Australia or on chilled white plates or deep, wide soup bowls.

1 large romaine lettuce
2½ tablespoons extra-virgin olive oil
1 tablespoon butter
2 slices white bread, diced into 1-inch (2.5-cm) cubes
1 cup freshly and coarsely grated Parmesan cheese (Parmigiano Reggiano if possible)

Dressing
2-ounce (50-g) can anchovies
2 egg yolks
1 garlic clove, crushed
2½ tablespoons lemon juice, freshly squeezed
a generous pinch of English mustard powder
½ teaspoon salt
½–1 tablespoon Worcestershire sauce
½–1 tablespoon Tabasco sauce
¾ cup sunflower oil
¼ cup extra-virgin olive oil
¼ cup cold water

Wash the lettuce leaves, dry really thoroughly, lightly wrap in a lint-free towel and chill in a bowl in the fridge while you make the dressing.

The dressing can be made in a food processor but is also quick to make by hand. Drain the anchovies and crush lightly with a fork. Put into a bowl with the egg yolks, garlic, lemon juice, mustard powder, salt, Worcestershire and Tabasco sauces. Whisk all the ingredients together. As you whisk, add the oils slowly at first, then a little faster as the emulsion forms. Finally whisk in water to make a spreadable consistency. Taste and season: this dressing should be highly flavored.
Heat the olive oil and butter in a frying pan over a medium heat. When the butter is melted, toss in the cubes of bread and cook for a few seconds on all sides until golden. Drain through a metal strainer and spread out on paper towels.

To serve, put 1 tablespoon of dressing per person in a big bowl, add in the chilled whole lettuce leaves, about half the croûtons and half the Parmesan. Toss the leaves gently but thoroughly in the dressing. (This is done most effectively using your hands, or use salad servers.) Add more dressing if necessary to coat the leaves. Arrange the dressed leaves on individual chilled plates. Add a few croûtons and sprinkle the remaining Parmesan on top. Serve immediately.

Note: The remaining dressing will keep covered in a fridge for several days.

Traditional Greek Salad with Marinated Feta Cheese

Serves 6
In season: summer

This salad is served in virtually every taverna in Greece and is delicious when made with really fresh ingredients and eaten immediately. Buying good-quality feta can be difficult; try sourcing it in Cypriot delicatessens. Don't bother to make this salad unless the tomatoes are sweet and ripe, and the cucumbers are crisp and juicy. We use Mani, organic Greek extra-virgin olive oil.

¾–1 cup fresh feta, cubed (we sometimes use local Knockalara ewe's milk cheese)
1½–2½ tablespoons extra-virgin olive oil
1½ tablespoons marjoram
1–1½ crisp cucumbers
1–2 red onions or 6 scallions
6 very ripe tomatoes
12–18 Kalamata olives
2½ tablespoons fresh annual marjoram, chopped
¼ cup extra-virgin olive oil
1½ tablespoons lemon juice, freshly squeezed
salt, freshly cracked pepper, and sugar

Garnish
sprigs of flat-leaf parsley

Cut the cheese into 1-inch (2.5-cm) cubes. Drizzle with extra-virgin olive oil and some marjoram.

Just before serving, halve the cucumber lengthwise and cut it into chunks. Slice the red onions or chop coarsely the green and white parts of the scallions. Core the tomatoes and cut into wedges. Mix the tomatoes, cucumber, scallions, olives and marjoram in a bowl. Sprinkle with olive oil and lemon juice. Season with salt, pepper, and sugar, and toss well. Sprinkle with cubes of cheese and parsley. Serve at once.

Greek Salad in Pita Bread

Split a pita bread in half across or lengthwise. Fill with Greek salad drained of dressing, and shredded lettuce. Serve immediately. The filling should be spooned into the pita bread just before it is to be eaten, otherwise the bread will go soggy.

Greek Green Salad

romaine or similar crisp lettuce, washed
sprigs of fresh dill, about 3–4 tablespoons
3–4 scallions, sliced
1½–2½ tablespoons freshly squeezed lemon juice
5 tablespoons extra-virgin olive oil
salt and freshly ground pepper

Slice the lettuce across the grain, about 1/4 inch (5mm) thick. Put into a bowl, sprinkle with scallion and sprigs of dill. Just before serving, mix the oil and lemon juice. Sprinkle it over the salad, season, toss and serve immediately.

Warm Salad of Goat Cheese with Walnut Oil Dressing

Serves 4

This is a perfect supper dish but you can equally serve it as an appetizer, main, or cheese course. Include a few cherry tomatoes or a few strips of roast red pepper if you want to make it more substantial.

A selection of lettuces, herbs, and salad greens, e.g., butterhead, chicory, oakleaf, radicchio treviano, arugula, salad burnet, golden marjoram
12 slices French bread, toasted
1 fresh soft goat cheese (our favorites are Ardsallagh, Croghan, St Tola, Lough Caum, or St Macha), 6–8 ounces (175–225g)
16–20 fresh walnut halves

Dressing
5 tablespoons walnut oil plus 2½ tablespoons sunflower or peanut oil, or ½ cup extra-virgin olive oil
2½ tablespoons white wine vinegar
dash of Dijon mustard

Garnish
Chive or wild garlic flowers or marigold petals (Calendula officinalis) *in season*

Wash and dry the salad greens, tear the larger ones into bite-sized pieces. Make the dressing by whisking all the ingredients together. Cover each piece of toasted French bread with a ¾-inch (2-cm) slice of goat cheese. Just before serving, preheat the broiler. Place the slices of bread and cheese under the broiler and toast for 5–6 minutes or until the cheese is soft and slightly golden.

Meanwhile, toss the salad greens lightly in just enough dressing to make the leaves glisten, then put a small handful onto each plate. Place 1 or 3 hot goat cheese croûtons onto each portion. Scatter with a few walnut pieces and decorative chive or wild garlic flowers. Serve immediately.

Salad of Goat Cheese and Sun-dried Tomatoes

Serves 6

6–12 Sun-dried Tomatoes (see page 188)
4–6 ounces (110–175g) goat cheese (for example, St Maur, Valençay, St Tola or Cais Cleire)

Green Salad
a mixture of green lettuces, herbs, and salad greens (oakleaf, arugula, butterhead, mysticana, watercress, iceberg, golden marjoram, and tiny scallions…)

Dressing
2½ tablespoons white wine vinegar or white wine vinegar and balsamic vinegar mixed, or freshly squeezed lemon juice
½ cup extra-virgin olive oil
1 garlic clove, crushed
2 teaspoons grain mustard such as Moutarde de Meaux or Lakeshore wholegrain and honey mustard
salt and freshly ground pepper

fresh basil leaves

Whisk all the ingredients together for the dressing. Wash and dry the salad greens and tear into small pieces. Toss the greens in just enough dressing to make them glisten. Arrange in a wide serving dish, crumble the goat cheese and scatter over the top. Cut the tomatoes into quarters and scatter over the salad too. Garnish with basil and serve.

Ballymaloe Cauliflower, Broccoli, or Romanesco, Salad

Serves 6

Cauliflower or broccoli salad is not an obvious choice but it is surprisingly delicious. The secret is to dip the flowerets in a good dressing while still warm so they really absorb the flavors.

1 head cauliflower
½ Ballymaloe French Dressing (see page 225)

Ideally this should be made with a slightly shot head (one that is starting to go to seed) at the end of season. Take a head with the leaves on and trim off the damaged leaves. Wash and shred the remaining leaves and stalk. Split the cauliflower into about 8 pieces so it will cook evenly.

Take a saucepan that fits the cauliflower exactly and boil 1 inch (2.5cm) of water in it. Add a little salt, put in the shredded leaves, and sit the cauliflower on top, stems down, and cover closely. Control the heat so that the pan does not boil dry. Remove from the pan when the stalks are barely tender.

Divide into flowerets and dip each into dressing while still warm. Arrange like a wheel on a round plate. Build up layer upon layer to reform the cauliflower head. This looks and tastes delicious on a cold buffet.

Note: Purple, white sprouting, and green broccoli (calabrese) can also be cooked this way. A mixture of all three looks and tastes delicious.

Broccoli, Feta, and Cherry Tomato Salad

Serves 4–6
In season: summer–winter

1 lb. (450g) broccoli flowerets
1 1/3 cups feta cut into 1/2-inch (1-cm) cubes
10 ounces (275g) cherry tomatoes, halved (about 1 1/2–2 cups)
Ballymaloe French Dressing (see page 225)
1 1/2 tablespoons freshly chopped mint
sugar and freshly ground pepper

Blanch the broccoli for 2–3 minutes, drain, refresh, and put in a bowl along with the feta and tomatoes. Sprinkle with dressing. Season, add the mint, and toss gently. It is unlikely the salad will need salt because of the feta.

Leek Vinaigrette with Red Onion, Egg Mimosa, and Parsley

Serves 4
In season: summer–winter

4 handsome leeks
2 large eggs
2 1/2 tablespoons chopped flat-leaf parsley
sea salt, or kosher salt, and freshly ground black pepper

Vinaigrette
1 red onion, chopped
2 1/2 tablespoons champagne vinegar or white wine vinegar
5–6 tablespoons olive oil
salt, freshly ground pepper, and sugar

Trim the leeks of roots and green leaves. Leave 1 inch (2.5cm) of green at top of each for color and flavor. Slice the leeks lengthwise and holding the layers together, rinse under cold running water. Fold the sliced leeks inwards to form a u shape and tie with cotton string. Poach the leek bundles in barely simmering, salted water until just tender. Remove and place on a wire rack to drain.

Make the vinaigrette: put all the ingredients into a screw-top jar and shake well. When the leeks are slightly cooled, put them in a dish and drizzle the vinaigrette over them; set aside to marinate until later.

Hardboil the eggs. Set the yolks aside, chop the whites.

To serve, arrange 2 pieces of leek on each of 4 plates. Dress generously with the vinaigrette. Sprinkle the egg whites around the leeks. Sieve the egg yolks and sprinkle over the top, together with the parsley.

Moroccan Chickpea Salad

Serves 4

Chickpeas have been grown since Roman times all over the Middle East and southern Europe. The white species (garbanzos), said to be the finest, is grown in Spain. Keep a few canned chickpeas in your larder.

6 tablespoons extra-virgin olive oil
1 cup finely chopped onion
2 garlic cloves, finely crushed
1 1/2-inch (4-cm) piece fresh ginger, peeled and grated
2 x 14-ounce (400-g) cans chickpeas, drained
pinch of dried chile flakes
juice and finely grated rind of 1 1/2 lemons
leaves from a bunch of cilantro, chopped
salt and freshly ground pepper

mixed ground cumin and paprika, for serving

Heat 1 tablespoon of the oil in a frying pan, add the onion, garlic, and ginger, and cook gently for 5–7 minutes, until soft and transparent.

Add the chickpeas, chile flakes, and lemon rind and stir for about 30 seconds, then add the lemon juice and let the mixture bubble until it is almost dry. Add the cilantro and season to taste with salt and pepper.

Turn the chickpea mixture into a warm serving bowl and pour over it the remaining oil. Sprinkle a little ground cumin and paprika over the top.

Note: For dried chickpeas, use 1 1/2 cups of chickpeas. Cover with cold water overnight. Next day discard the water. Cover with fresh water, bring to the boil and cook until tender – about 45 minutes.

Salad with Pomegranates, Persimmons, and Pecans

Serves 8

A delicious salad that I came across in California with Mary Risley.

*3 ripe Fuyu persimmons (*Diospyros kaki *– little firm persimmons)*
3 ripe pears (Choose d'Anjou pears if you can find them)
1 lime, freshly squeezed
seeds from 1/2 pomegranate
a selection of chicory, watercress, and arugula leaves
1 cup pecans, freshly toasted

Vinaigrette
2 1/2 tablespoons balsamic or sherry vinegar
2 teaspoons Dijon mustard
2 shallots, finely chopped
6 tablespoons extra-virgin olive oil
salt and freshly ground pepper

Preheat the oven to 350°F (180°C). To make the vinaigrette, mix the vinegar, mustard, shallots, salt and pepper in a screw-top jar along with the oil, until emulsified.

Slice the persimmons and pears into slices about 1/2 inch (1cm) thick. Put into a bowl and sprinkle with the lime juice. Add the pomegranate seeds and toss gently.

Right: Salad with Pomegranates, Persimmons, and Pecans

Wash and dry the lettuces and store in a clean towel in the fridge until ready to use. Put the nuts on a baking sheet in the oven for 5–6 minutes, tossing gently from time to time. Alternatively toast under a broiler.

When ready to serve: toss the lettuce in some of the vinaigrette and arrange on eight plates. Toss the fruit mixture lightly in the remaining vinaigrette. Arrange on top of the greens and sprinkle with the toasted pecans. Serve immediately.

Cucumber Mousse with Tomato and Cilantro Salsa

Serves 6–8 as an appetizer

2½ cups Lebanese Cold Cucumber Soup, (see page 61)
¼ ounce (7g) gelatin
2½ tablespoons water

Tomato and Cilantro Salsa (see page 591)

6–8 little demi tasse cups and saucers, preferably white

Garnish
sprigs of mint or cilantro, chive or garlic flowers in season

First make the cold cucumber soup and measure the quantity required.

Put the water into a small bowl, and sprinkle the gelatin over the water. Let it sponge, then dissolve in a saucepan of simmering water until all the granules are melted. Mix some of the cold soup with the gelatin and then stir into the remainder of the mixture, stirring very well.

Pour into small cups or little bowls. Cover and chill in the fridge until set.

Next make the Tomato and Cilantro Salsa. Put a little salsa on top of each mousse. Garnish with a sprig of mint or cilantro and sprinkle with chive or garlic flowers if in season.

Potato and Scallion Salad

Serves 4–6

The secret of delectable potato salad is simple, use good quality potatoes, peel and toss in French Dressing while still warm. Mayonnaise may be omitted if a less rich potato salad is your choice. Allow about 2½ lbs. (1.1kg) raw potatoes. Use Yukon Gold or long whites, but many people prefer to use a waxy potato like round reds or round whites.

2 lbs. (900g) freshly cooked potatoes, diced
2½ tablespoons chives or scallions, chopped or 2 teaspoons onion, chopped
2½ tablespoons parsley, chopped
½ cup Ballymaloe French Dressing (see page 225)
½ cup homemade Mayonnaise (see page 584)
salt and freshly ground pepper to taste

Boil the potatoes in their skins until tender; drain, cool, and peel. Dice them while still hot. Mix immediately with onion, parsley, salt and pepper. Stir in the French dressing, and let cool. Finally add the mayonnaise. Keeps well for about 2 days.

Note: Potato salad may be used as a base for other salads; for example, add cubes of garlic salami, cooked Kabanossi sausages, or cooked mussels.

Soft Piped Potato Salad with Fresh Herbs

The first time we made this salad, it was out of necessity because we overcooked the potatoes. It was a great success and now we make it regularly by choice!

4½ cups freshly mashed potato (see page 182)

Add Ballymaloe French Dressing, finely chopped parsley, chives, mayonnaise, and seasoning to the stiff potato to taste. Pipe onto individual leaves of lettuce or use to garnish an appetizer salad or hors d'oeuvres.

Lime and Pepper Salad

Serves 4 as an appetizer

Tim and I adore being invited to dinner by our students. Kelley Ryan-Bourgoise and her husband Don cooked a wonderful meal for us at their house overlooking the sea. This fresh tasting salad was our first course. It would also be delicious served as an accompaniment to a pan-grilled chicken breast or a piece of salmon.

1 red pepper
1 yellow pepper
1 orange pepper
3 ripe tomatoes, sliced
1 green jalapeño chile pepper, finely chopped
3–4 tablespoons coarsely chopped fresh cilantro
2 avocados, peeled and sliced

Vinaigrette
¼ cup freshly squeezed lime juice
2 teaspoons grated lime zest
1½ tablespoons honey
a few drops of Tabasco sauce (or any hot pepper sauce you like)
5 tablespoons olive oil
2 small garlic cloves, crushed
salt and freshly ground pepper

First make the dressing. Put the freshly squeezed lime juice and half the zest in a bowl. Whisk in the honey, oil, and Tabasco sauce, add the crushed garlic, and season with salt and freshly ground pepper.

Slice the peppers into thin julienne strips and add the sliced tomatoes. Toss together with the chopped jalapeño chile, coarsely chopped cilantro and rest of the lime zest. Add the vinaigrette and gently fold in the avocado. Taste and correct the seasoning. Serve on individual plates with crusty bread

White Turnip and Oregano Salad

Serves 4

Use very small turnips; they taste sweeter and fresher than those left to grow to fairy-tale size. It is delicious with most meats.

1 lb. (450g) white turnips
French dressing (see page 226)
3–4 tablespoons oregano or annual marjoram, chopped
salt and freshly ground pepper

Wash and peel the turnips if necessary and top and tail them. Cut into 1/4-inch (5-mm) slices and cook in boiling salted water until tender, this will take just a few minutes. Drain. Toss in dressing while still hot and sprinkle with oregano or marjoram. Correct the seasoning and eat warm. Delicious with most meats.

Shanagarry Summer Tomato Salad

Tomatoes have been grown in the greenhouses here in Shanagarry since my father-in-law, Ivan Allen, built his first timber house in the winter of 1934. For years the crops were grown commercially but for the past 8–10 years we have concentrated on growing as many varieties as we have space for, with the emphasis totally on flavor – yield is not a high priority and every tomato is vine-ripened on the plant. We even grow the tiny Tumbler variety in hanging baskets interspersed with herbs outside the cottages and around the school. Freshly picked, sweet-tasting tomatoes, piled high in baskets, are part of every day, and tomato salads made from a mixture of colors, shapes, and varieties are part of almost every menu in late summer and early autumn.

Left: Red and Yellow Tomato Salad with Basil (see page 220)

Heirloom Tomato Salad

Use a mixture of vine-ripened heirloom tomatoes in the recipe above, a mixture of freshly squeezed lemon juice and extra-virgin olive oil enhances the flavor in a delicious way. Don't forget the seasoning. We grow a lot of heirloom varieties every year, all shapes, sizes and colors: red, green, black, orange, and several streaky varieties. They make a divine salad in later summer and early autumn. This year we plan to grow 35 different tomatoes and will carefully taste, compare, and eliminate the ones we feel are not justified on grounds of flavor.

Tip: Never store tomatoes in the fridge as this will have a detrimental effect on both the flavor and texture.

Tomato Salad

In the late summer when we have intensively sweet, vine-ripened tomatoes, we often serve a tomato salad as a first course. The flavor is so wonderful; it is a revelation to many people who have forgotten what a tomato should taste like.

8–12 tomatoes: use one variety, or a mixture, of very ripe red or yellow vine-ripened tomatoes. (We enjoy Sweet 100's, Green Zebra, Ox Heart, Valencia, Golden Jubilee, etc. Try to include some cherry tomatoes, pear-shaped, and if you can get them – the pretty striped Green Zebra, they look and taste particularly stunning.)

Ballymaloe French dressing (see page 225) or *balsamic vinegar* or *at least white wine vinegar*
extra-virgin olive oil
2–4 teaspoons basil leaves or *mint leaves*
sea salt, or kosher salt, freshly ground pepper, and sugar

Cut the tomatoes in half or lengthwise or into wedges, or simply into ½-inch (1-cm) thick slices depending on shape and size. Spread out in a single layer on a large flat plate, season with salt, pepper, and a sprinkling of sugar. Sprinkle with dressing or sparingly with balsamic vinegar and generously with extra-virgin olive oil. Scatter with torn basil or mint leaves. Toss gently, just to coat the tomatoes. Serve soon either as a first course or as an accompanying salad.

Tip: Tomatoes must be dressed as soon as they are cut to seal in their flavor.

Tomato Salad with Mozzarella and Tapenade Toasts

Serves 4

4 small hand-rolled Mozzarella cheeses
Tomato Salad for 4 (see above)
Tapenade (see page 588)
4 crostini, freshly cooked in extra-virgin olive oil (see page 67)
extra-virgin olive oil
freshly cracked pepper
basil leaves

Put a fresh, milky, hand-rolled Mozzarella on each of 4 white plates, and arrange a helping of tomato salad beside it. Spoon tapenade onto a freshly cooked crostini and pop it decoratively on the side. Drizzle with your best extra-virgin olive oil and a sprinkling of pepper. Put a fresh basil leaf on top and serve immediately.

Arugula and Cherry or Sun-dried Tomato Salad

Serves 6

Serve with pan-grilled chicken breasts.

2 large handfuls fresh arugula leaves or a mixture of mysticana and arugula leaves
Sun-dried Tomatoes (see page 188) or red and yellow cherry tomatoes

Dressing
2½ tablespoons white wine vinegar or white wine vinegar and balsamic vinegar mixed or freshly squeezed lemon juice
½ cup extra-virgin olive oil
1 garlic clove, crushed
½ teaspoon Moutarde de Meaux or Lakeshore wholegrain and honey mustard
salt and freshly ground pepper

Whisk all the ingredients together for the dressing. Wash and dry the salad greens and tear into small pieces.

Just before serving, toss the salad greens in just enough dressing to make the leaves glisten. Arrange in a wide serving dish. Cut the sun-dried tomatoes into quarters and scatter over the salad.

Eggplant Salad with Olives, Sun-dried Tomatoes, and Arugula Leaves

Serves 8
In season: Summer and Autumn

We now grow several varieties of eggplant. Choose firm medium-sized eggplants and seek out the slim Indian varieties for extra flavor. If the eggplants are cooked in extra-virgin olive oil, they are also divine served as a simple salad with no embellishment.

4–8 eggplants, depending on size
olive oil for frying
1/3 cup Sun-dried Tomatoes (see page 188)
1/4 cup extra-virgin olive oil
2 1/2 tablespoons parsley, chopped
1 1/2 tablespoons annual marjoram, chopped
salt and freshly ground pepper
handful of arugula leaves
1/3–1/2 cup tiny Tunisian black or picholine olives, pitted and chopped

Slice the eggplants into 1/2-inch (1-cm) thick rounds. Sprinkle with salt and de-gorge for 15–20 minutes on a rack over a baking tray. Heat 3/4–1 inch (2–2.5cm) of olive oil in a frying pan until very hot. Fry the eggplant slices in batches until golden brown on both sides. Drain on a wire rack.

While the eggplants are cooling, chop the sun-dried tomatoes, add the olive oil, parsley, marjoram and season to taste. Arrange the eggplant slices on a large serving dish and decorate with the arugula leaves. At the last minute, drizzle the sun-dried tomato dressing over and around the salad and finally sprinkle with olives.

Tuscan Pepper and Pasta Salad

Serves 12–14

3/4 cup Ballymaloe French Dressing (see page 225)
2 1/2 tablespoons Pesto (see page 589)
1/2–1 lb. (225–450g) penne or pasta shells
1 yellow pepper, preferably Italian or Spanish
2 red peppers, preferably Italian or Spanish
2 large cucumbers
8–10 very ripe tomatoes
1 red onion, sliced very thinly
1 1/2 tablespoons parsley, chopped
3–5 tablespoons annual marjoram, chopped, or basil, torn
sugar
1/3–1/2 cup black olives
salt and freshly ground pepper

First make the dressing and whisk the Pesto into it. Cook the pasta until "al dente" in boiling, salted water. Cut the peppers in quarters, remove the seeds, and cut into 1 1/2-inch (4-cm) strips on the bias. Halve the cucumbers, remove the seeds, and cut into 2-inch (5-cm) batons. Cut the tomatoes into quarters or sixths, depending on the size.

Drain the pasta as soon as it is cooked. While it is still warm, toss it in a little of the dressing. Mix all the ingredients in a bowl. Add the onion with the herbs. Season with salt, pepper, and sugar to taste. (In winter, this salad needs lots of sugar.) Pour the rest of the dressing over the salad. Serve in a wide bowl, sprinkled with black olives and parsley.

Zucchini Salad with Olive Oil and Sea Salt

Serves 4 as a first course or 6–8 as an accompanying salad
In season: summer to early autumn is best

This simple salad can be perfection, when served warm with nothing more than a sprinkling of extra-virgin olive oil and a little sea salt.

8 small zucchini with flowers, if available (choose shiny, firm zucchini)
olive oil (the very best Italian oil)
sea salt, or kosher salt, and freshly ground pepper

Separate the flowers from the zucchini. Remove the stamens and little thorns from the base of the flowers. Plunge the zucchini into boiling, salted water and poach until barely tender. Remove from the pan and let cool slightly. While still warm, slice them at an angle to allow 6 slices to each zucchini. Season them with sea salt and freshly ground pepper and sprinkle them with extra-virgin olive oil. Toss gently and serve immediately, surrounded by zucchini blossoms.

Hot crusty bread is the only accompaniment needed.

Note: A few fat scampi and some homemade Mayonnaise turn this into a divine summer lunch or supper dish.

Mushroom and Caramelized Onion Salad

Serves 6–8

Great with cold meats or poached salmon. Best eaten on the day it is made, but also delicious for a day or two.

2 1/2 tablespoons olive oil
2 large onions, sliced
2–4 tablespoons butter
1 large garlic clove, crushed
lemon juice, freshly squeezed
12 ounces (350g) mushrooms, thinly sliced (about 3 1/2 cups)
salt and freshly ground pepper

Heat a little olive oil in a heavy saucepan and cook the onions gently over a low heat. Stir every few minutes so that they brown evenly. This operation may take 20–30 minutes until the onions are slightly caramelized.

Meanwhile, melt the butter in a wide pan, add the mushrooms, and sauté for 4–5 minutes. Season each batch with salt and pepper, a very little crushed garlic, and a squeeze of lemon juice. Add the onions to the mushrooms as soon as they are cooked, and taste. Correct seasoning if necessary.

Like most salads, this is best served at room temperature.

A Plate of Ballymaloe Garden Salads

We frequently serve a selection of vegetable salads on a plate as an appetizer or main course.

A Summer selection might include:
Red and Yellow Tomato Salad with Mint or Basil
Cucumber Salad
Zucchini Salad with Olive Oil and Sea Salt
a few Radishes
Mushroom and Caramelized Onion Salad
Green Salad
Egg Mayonnaise
Potato and Scallion Salad

A Winter selection might include:
Potato and Scallion Salad
Pickled Beet and Onion Salad
Cucumber Salad
Winter Green Salad
Carrot and Apple Salad
Onions or Leeks Monégasque
Egg Mayonnaise
Green Salad

Isaac's Mimosa Salad

Serves 6 as an appetizer

This light and lovely salad has egg yolk on top and gives the effect of a Mimosa flower. We vary the lettuces in this recipe according to the season and availability.

use one or a mixture of chicory, watercress, arugula or wild garlic leaves. We also use young pea shoots when available
4 eggs
24 large black olives, preferably Kalamata
1–1½ cups grated Parmesan (Parmigiano Reggiano)

Dressing
¼ cup extra-virgin olive oil
½ cup balsamic vinegar
1 garlic clove, crushed
pinch of Maldon sea salt, or kosher salt, freshly cracked pepper, and large pinch of sugar

Hard boil the eggs for 10 minutes in boiling salted water. Chill under a cold running tap. Peel the eggs and separate yolks and finely chop the whites.

Beets will bleed if they're trimmed as below. Leave the tops and tails on while cooking.

Pit the olives and chop finely. Mix the olive oil, balsamic vinegar, and crushed garlic. Season with salt, pepper, and sugar to achieve a tasty dressing.

Mix the greens in a large bowl and coat with enough dressing to make the leaves glisten.

Place a bunch of the dressed leaves on each plate. Sprinkle the chopped egg whites and olives on top and finish with the sieved egg yolk and parmesan. Serve immediately.

La Grande Anchoïade

Anchoïade (see page 594) is a Provençal and Corsican dish of anchovies, tomatoes, almonds, herbs, and olive oil pounded to a paste and seasoned with lemon juice. The Corsicans add figs and red peppers.

La Grande Anchoïade can be a meal in itself when it is served with a basket of crudités and lots of crusty bread.

The crudités might include:
tomatoes
celery
radishes
carrots
cucumbers
peppers
tiny artichoke hearts
scallions
fresh fava beans
fresh raw mushrooms
young carrots
hard boiled eggs
black olives

Crudités with Aïoli

Crudités, meaning raw vegetables, is one of my favorite French appetizers: small helpings of very crisp vegetables with a good garlicky, homemade Mayonnaise. It fulfils all my criteria for a first course: the plates look tempting, taste delicious and, provided you keep the helpings small, are not too filling. Better still it's actually good for you – so you can feel very virtuous at the same time!

Children also love crudités, they may not fancy tapenade but you can use other dips such as Garlic Mayonnaise (see page 584) or Guacamole (see page 91). Cut the vegetables into bite-sized pieces so they can be picked up easily. Use as many of the following vegetables as are in season:

very fresh button mushrooms, quartered
tomatoes quartered, or left whole with the calyx on if they are freshly picked
purple sprouting broccoli, broken (not cut) into flowerets
calabrese, broken into flowerets
cauliflower, broken into flowerets
young green beans or snow peas
baby carrots, or larger carrots cut into sticks about 2 inches (5cm) long.
cucumber, cut into sticks 2 inches (5cm) long.
tiny scallions, trimmed
celery, cut into sticks about 2 inches (5cm) long
Belgian endive, in leaves
red, green, or yellow peppers, cut into strips about 2 inches (5cm) long, and seeded
fresh fennel
very fresh Brussels sprouts, cut into halves or quarters
whole radishes, with green tops left on
parsley, finely chopped
thyme, finely chopped
chives, finely chopped
sprigs of watercress

Aïoli (see page 584)

A typical plate of crudités might include the following: 4 sticks of carrot, 2 or 3 sticks of red and green pepper, 2 or 3 sticks of celery, 2 or 3 sticks of cucumber, 1 mushroom cut in quarters, 1 whole radish with a little green leaf left on, 1 tiny tomato or 2 quarters, 1 Brussels sprout cut in quarters, and a little pile of chopped fresh herbs. Wash and prepare the vegetables. Arrange on individual plates in contrasting colors, with a little bowl of Aïoli or chosen sauce in the center. Alternatively, do a large dish or basket for the center of the table. Pretty edible sauce containers can be made from zucchini flowers, hollowed-out tomatoes, or cucumber.

Pinzimonio

A Tuscan appetizer made up of fresh, crunchy vegetables (fresh fennel, asparagus, baby carrots, celery stalks...), dipped into a bowl of the finest Tuscan extra-virgin olive oil. Simple, but delicious!

Kinoith Summer Garden Salad with Ballymaloe French Dressing

A selection of fresh lettuces, herbs, and salad greens; for example:
butterhead, oakleaf, iceberg, lollo rosso, chicory, mizuna, mibuna
Mesclun or saladisi
Red orach
arugula
edible chrysanthemum leaves
wild sorrel leaves or Buckler leaf sorrel
golden marjoram, annual marjoram
tiny sprigs of dill, tarragon, or mint
salad Burnet
borage flowers
young nasturtium leaves and flowers
marigold petals
chive or wild garlic flowers
zucchini blossom
herb leaves, e.g., lemon balm, mint, flat-leaf parsley
green pea shoots or fava bean tips
tiny chard and beet leaves

Ballymaloe French Dressing

Makes 1¼ cups

Affectionately known as Billy's French dressing after a chef who has starred in Ballymaloe kitchens for almost 30 years.

¾ cup olive oil or a mixture of olive and other oils, e.g., sunflower and peanut
¼ cup white wine vinegar
1 level teaspoon mustard (Dijon or English)
1 level teaspoon salt
few grinds of black pepper
1 large garlic clove, peeled (and mashed if not using a blender)
sprig of parsley
1 small scallion
sprig of watercress

First, make the dressing: put all the ingredients into a blender and run at medium speed for about 1 minute or mix oil and vinegar in a bowl, add mustard, salt, pepper, and garlic. Chop the parsley, scallion and watercress finely and add in. Whisk before serving.

Wash and dry the lettuces and salad greens. Tear into bite-sized bits. Sprinkle with edible flowers and petals. Just before serving, toss in a little dressing, not too much; just enough to coat the leaves lightly. Serve immediately.

Winter Green Salad with Timmy's Dressing

For this salad, use a selection of winter lettuces and salad greens (butterhead, iceberg, radicchio, endive, chicory, watercress, Buckler leaf sorrel, arugula leaves and winter purslane and mysticana). Tips of purple sprouting broccoli are also delicious and, if you feel like something more robust, use some finely shredded Savoy cabbage and maybe a few shreds of red cabbage, too.

Left: Crudités (see page 223)

Timmy's Dressing

Makes 1¼ cups

A delicious dressing – everyone's favorite at the Cookery School. Cider vinegar may be substituted for wine vinegar.

¾ cup olive oil or a mixture of olive and other oils, e.g., sunflower and peanut
¼ cup white wine vinegar
2 teaspoons runny honey
2 heaped teaspoons whole grain honey mustard
2 garlic cloves, peeled and crushed
salt and freshly ground pepper

First make the dressing: mix all the ingredients together in a screw-top jar; shake thoroughly before use.

Wash and dry the lettuces and other greens very carefully in a large sink of cold water. If large, tear into bite-sized pieces and put into a deep salad bowl. Cover with plastic wrap and refrigerate if not to be served immediately. Just before serving, toss in the dressing – just enough to make the leaves glisten. Serve immediately.

Note: green salads must not be dressed until just before serving, otherwise they will be tired and unappetizing.

Italian Green Salad

Serves 4
In season: summer and autumn

A selection of lettuces and salad greens: romaine, radicchio, lollo rosso, arugula leaves, Buckler leaf sorrel, golden marjoram, zucchini blossoms, and dark opal basil.

Italian Salad Dressing

*1½ tablespoons freshly squeezed lemon juice or balsamic vinegar**
¼ cup Italian extra-virgin olive oil
sea salt, or kosher salt, and freshly cracked pepper

Whisk all the ingredients together for the dressing.

Wash and dry the salad greens. Combine the ingredients for the dressing in a screw-top jar. Just before serving, toss the salad with the dressing in a deep bowl and serve immediately.

** If you choose to use lemon juice, remember that Italian lemons are much sweeter and juicier than the fruit we have access to, so it may be necessary to add sugar to the dressing.*

Herb Leaf Salad

We love to serve little bunches of herb sprigs tossed in an appropriate dressing as a garnish or an accompaniment.

Bits and Pieces to add to a basic Green Salad to make a meal

1 Roughly diced avocado, tomato, and cucumber, lots of parsley, mint leaves

2 Broccoli or sprouting broccoli flowerets

3 Black olives

4 Slivered Parmesan and arugula leaves. Anchovy vinaigrette is particularly good with this salad

5 Orange segments, Belgian endive leaves, and black olives, and perhaps some walnuts

6 Blue cheese: crumble a piece of Blue Cheese (Cashel Blue, Stilton, or Roquefort) over the salad and use Honey and Mustard Vinaigrette

7 Toasted pine nuts, pistachios, hazelnuts, or slivered almonds sprinkled with a little sea salt, or kosher salt

8 Crispy Croûtons (see right)

9 Lardons of crispy bacon We use Gubbeen bacon.

10 Shredded red cabbage and green Savoy cabbage, raisins, and freshly chopped mint

11 Cubes of Cheddar cheese tossed in Ballymaloe Relish or Apple and Tomato Chutney (see page 511)

12 Slivers of smoked salmon and avocado

13 Smoked trout with a dill horseradish dressing

14. Thinly shaved fennel and pomegranate seeds.

Crispy Croûtons

Makes enough for a salad for 4 people.

1 tablespoon butter
1½ tablespoons olive oil
1 slice of slightly stale loaf bread, crusts removed and cut into a ¼-inch (5-cm) dice

Melt the butter in a clean frying pan with the olive oil. Turn up the heat, add the croûtons. The pan should be quite hot at first, then reduce the heat to medium and keep tossing all the time until the croûtons are golden brown all over. Drain on paper towels.

Alternatively, cook a few croûtons at a time for a few seconds in hot olive oil in a clean frying pan. When the croûtons are pale golden, drain through a metal strainer, catching the oil in a Pyrex bowl. Turn the croûtons out onto paper towels to drain, and return the oil to the pan, reheat, and fry the remaining batches. The oil may be filtered and used again.

Dressings

The flavor of your dressing will depend on the quality of your oils and vinegars. A basic French dressing is usually 3 or 4 parts oil to 1 part vinegar. There are many variations on the theme.

Master Recipe

Basic Vinaigrette or French Dressing

Makes enough to dress a salad for 4 people

½ cup extra-virgin olive oil
2½ tablespoons white wine vinegar
sea salt, or kosher salt, and freshly ground pepper

Whisk all the ingredients together just before the salad is to be eaten.

Variations

Mustard Vinaigrette

Follow the Master Recipe, and add ½–1 teaspoon Dijon or whole grain mustard and 1 teaspoon of finely chopped parsley.

Garlic Vinaigrette

Follow the Master Recipe, and add 1 small peeled and crushed garlic clove and ½–1 teaspoon of Dijon or whole grain mustard and 1 teaspoon of finely chopped parsley.

Honey and Mustard Vinaigrette

Follow the Master Recipe, and add 2 teaspoons of runny honey, 1 small peeled and crushed garlic clove and ½–1 teaspoon of Dijon mustard.

Herb Vinaigrette

Follow the Master Recipe, and add 1 generous tablespoon of freshly chopped herbs to the basic dressing; choose from parsley, chives, thyme, and mint.

Herb and Garlic Vinaigrette

Follow the Master Recipe, and add 1 small peeled and crushed garlic clove and a spot of honey to the herb vinaigrette.

Anchovy Vinaigrette

Follow the Master Recipe, and add 2 mashed anchovy fillets, 1 teaspoon of chopped parsley, and 1 peeled and crushed garlic clove.

Cilantro and Ginger Dressing

Follow the Master Recipe, and add 1 generous tablespoon of freshly chopped cilantro leaves and 1 teaspoon of peeled and finely chopped ginger and 1 finely chopped scallion.

Tapenade Oil

Add enough extra-virgin olive oil to the Tapenade recipe (see page 588) to make a pouring consistency. Use to drizzle on plates.

Basil Dressing

Makes 1¼ cups

¾ cup extra-virgin olive oil
¼ cup white wine vinegar
salt, freshly ground pepper, and sugar
1 garlic clove
10–15 basil leaves

Blend all the ingredients and store in a screw-top jar in a cool, dark place. It will keep for 3–4 days. Shake well before use.

Blue Cheese Dressing

Serves 4

½ cup extra-virgin olive oil
4 teaspoons lemon juice
½ teaspoon runny honey
3 tablespoons Roquefort or Cashel Blue cheese, crumbled
freshly ground black pepper

Mix the oil, lemon juice, and honey together, add the crumbled cheese, season with black pepper, taste and adjust if necessary.

Chile Pepper Oil

Makes about 2 cups

A condiment to add zizz to every dish! Try a few tablespoons in your bread dough or use it as a dip to dunk your bread in.

1 ounce (25g) chile pepper flakes (a scant ½ cup)
2 cups sunflower or olive oil

Put the chile pepper into a saucepan, cover with cold oil, and gradually bring to a boil. Turn off the heat immediately. Let cool. Strain into a sterilized bottle. Store in the fridge – it lasts almost indefinitely.

fish and shellfish

fish and shellfish

Are we not thrice blessed? The Ballymaloe Cookery School is within sight and smell of the sea – just two miles from the little fishing village of Ballycotton, where we get our fish. Every time I take a bite of deliciously fresh fish or a succulent Dublin Bay prawns I bless the fishermen who labor in all kinds of weather to catch the fish for our delight. During the 12-week course, I encourage the students to go over to Ballycotton to see the boats arriving with their catch of gleaming fish, so they too will be able to recognize really fresh fish and appreciate the labors of the fishermen who risk their lives to catch it.

As a result of overfishing and ill-conceived fishing policies in the European Union in recent years, fish has gotten gradually scarcer as boats have had to go out further to find fish. At Ballymaloe, we are deeply fortunate to still be able to get a certain proportion of day-boat fish at a time when many boats have to stay out for anything from three days to a week to get to the fishing grounds and catch enough fish to make the trip worthwhile.

The availability of fresh fish depends on the weather. The type of fish that we have access to from the boats varies through the seasons – herrings, sprats, and whitebait in December and January as well as Dover sole, plaice, turbot, brill, John Dory, monkfish, squid, ling, hake, haddock, cod, and pollock. When the weather improves, the fishermen put out their pots to catch shrimp, prawns, crabs, and lobsters. The latter are becoming scarcer and, understandably, more expensive.

Every Friday Dot Haynes, another of our treasured food suppliers, arrives from Kilmackalogh Harbour on the Beara Peninsula with mussels, clams, palourdes, roghans, cockles, scallops, and sea urchins in season. For over 20 years now, Dot has been bringing us the precious "fruits de mer" which go straight onto the menu at Ballymaloe or into the school.

The wonderful fresh fish we get from the boats in Ballycotton Harbour is a far cry from my early introduction to fish. As a child I lived in a country village called Cullohill, in County Laois. On Thursday, "fresh fish" was dropped off in the village by the bus on its long journey from Dublin to Cork. At that time in Ireland, Friday was the fast-day so people would flock to the village shop to buy whiting, smoked haddock, or occasionally, plaice as a special treat. I loved plaice, fried simply in butter – that was until I tasted plaice at Ballymaloe. On the evening I arrived, a local fisherman came to the kitchen door with a bucket full of shiny stiff fresh plaice as a present. Myrtle and Tim showed me how to fillet the sparkling fish and then we cooked it "à la meunière" under Myrtle's direction. The first bite was a complete revelation, meltingly tender, sweet and delicate. I simply couldn't believe it was the same fish that I had previously eaten and even enjoyed. I now know that the fish of my youth was possibly a week old when I ate it. I also realized why so few people enjoy fish – the reality is that many of them, particularly those who live inland, never taste really fresh fish, and as a result, can't quite understand why people wax lyrical about it.

Another source of fish is the famous market in Cork city. Four fish stalls vie with each other to provide an extraordinary selection of fresh fish. Not only fish from the waters around our coast, but also from France, Spain, Ecuador, Florida, and the Caribbean. Mahi mahi, doctor fish, kelapia, ruby snapper, yellow fin tuna, snapper, orange roughy, and red emperor all jostle for space on the marble slabs beside mackerel, salt cod, and sprats from around our coast.

Fast Food

Fish and shellfish are the quintessential fast food – so many delicious recipes can be cooked in minutes, pan-grilled, baked, roasted, boiled, steamed, or cooked in a little butter in the pan. Keep it simple; there's no need to smother a piece of really fresh fish in a complicated sauce. Just enjoy its natural flavor.

Buying Fresh Fish and Shellfish

It is absolutely vital to be able to judge accurately whether fish is fresh or not, and for many people this is very difficult. For me the most important thing to remember is that fresh fish doesn't smell fishy, it just has the merest scent of the sea, reminiscent of fresh seaweed. Really fresh fish looks bright, slippery, and lively, and not at all dull, whereas stale fish looks distinctly miserable. The eyes will be sunken and the skin can be gritty and dry, with a strong fishy smell. That's all straightforward enough, but between the time fish is fresh and the time it is really stale there are several days during which it will be gradually deteriorating. It is during this period that it is most difficult to tell just what condition the fish is in, particularly if it has been cut into small pieces. You have to judge by the color and smell. Check that the flesh of white fish is white and not at all discolored. The underskin of flat fish should be quite white also and not yellowing.

It is well worthwhile building up a good relationship with your fishseller, just as you do with your butcher. Ask for help and take the opportunity to learn every time you go shopping. When you get some delicious fresh fish remember to say how much you enjoyed it, but on the other hand if you get stale fish, hand it back gently but firmly. Most fishsellers are very conscientious and do all they can to get the fish to you in perfect condition – and this is easier said than done, because they are dealing with a very perishable product.

Remember also that fish have their seasons just as other fresh foods. For example, many of the flat fish such as plaice, sole, and lemon sole are not worth eating in January and February because they are full of roe, the flesh tends to be soft and watery – look out for some delicious herrings instead.

For those of you who live far from the sea, frozen fillets can be excellent. Good firms freeze their fish in prime condition within hours of being caught, so it is far preferable to fresh fish several days old.

Shellfish should, ideally, be purchased alive (prawns and scallops are the exception to the rule; they can be dead when you buy them, but should still smell fresh). Shells of live mussels may open naturally but will close tightly when tapped, indicating that they are alive. Throw away any dead ones. Crabs and lobsters can be very lively, so be wary. Many will already have their pincers tied with rubber bands. Pick up lobsters from behind their heads with a good firm grip, and lift crabs by their small back legs, keeping your fingers well out of the way of their powerful pincers. Freshly shucked oysters and scallops have a fresh sea-breeze smell and a clear milky or light gray liquid should surround freshly shucked oysters.

Farmed Salmon versus Wild Salmon

There is indeed much debate surrounding salmon. At Ballymaloe, we only serve wild salmon in season which, in our area, only lasts a short six weeks. 90 per cent of salmon sold throughout the year is farmed. All farmed salmon are bred in small pens, and most have antibiotics and anti-parasitic medicine added to their feed to ward off disease. They are also fed pigment-fortified pellets, to improve the color of the flesh (which is not as pink as wild salmons'). Then there are other environmental concerns – many blame intensive farming off the west cost of Ireland for the virtual extinction of the sea trout... All of this is worrying, but the issue is not so cut-and-dried. It is made more confusing by the fact that wild salmon populations are in decline and some species are endangered. While most foodies would prefer wild salmon for taste and texture, if eating it contributes to their extinction, then questions need to be raised. A balance needs to be struck, and there needs to be a concerted push to clean up salmon aquaculture. When buying farmed salmon, look out for organic fish, raised to the IFOAM (International Federation of Organic Agriculture Movements) standards and fed on organic feed.

Nutrition

Fish and shellfish sales have rocketed in recent years as food scares, concerns about cholesterol and food additives have focused attention on the fact that fish is healthy. It is an excellent source of protein. Shellfish, fish, and particularly fish oil, are also high in omega-3 (unsaturated fatty acids), which help to lower blood pressure, fend off heart disease, and improve psoriasis, rheumatoid arthritis, and kidney disease. The oilier, darker-fleshed fish like anchovies, salmon, mackerel, and herring generally have more omega-3s than leaner types. Many dieticians recommend eating fish twice a week.

How to Cook a Whole Salmon or Sea Trout

A whole poached wild salmon served hot or cold is always a dish for a special occasion. Long gone are the days when the servants in great houses complained bitterly if they had to eat salmon more than twice a week. To poach a salmon or sea trout whole, with the head and tail on, then you really need a fish poacher. This is a long narrow pan that will hold a fish of 8 pounds (3.6kg) in weight. Most people do not have a fish poacher, so if you want to keep the fish whole, then the best solution is to bake it in the oven wrapped in tin-foil. Alternatively, you can cut the salmon into 3 pieces, and cook them separately in the way I describe for cooking a piece of salmon. Later, you can arrange the salmon on a board or serving dish, skin it, and do a cosmetic job with rosettes of mayonnaise and lots of fresh herbs. An 8 pound (3.6 kg) salmon will feed 16 people very generously and it could quite easily be enough for 20. Four to five ounces (110–150g) of cooked salmon is generally plenty per person, as salmon is very rich. Use any left-over bits for Salmon Pâté or Salmon Rillettes (see page 85 and 554).

Below: Salmon in a fish poacher

Poaching Fish

Most cookbooks will tell you to poach salmon in a "court-bouillon," a mixture of wine and water with perhaps some sliced carrots, onion, peppercorns, and a bouquet garni including a bayleaf, but I feel very strongly that a beautiful salmon is at its best poached gently in just boiling, salted water. The proportion of salt to water is very important. We use 1 rounded tablespoon salt to every 5 cups water. The aim is to use the minimum amount of water to preserve the maximum flavor. The fish should be just covered so use a pan that will fit the fish exactly.

Other fish such as cod, gray mullet, hake, or sea bass may be poached in the same way, but you will need to adjust the time depending on size.

To poach a piece of fish

Choose a pan that will just fit the piece of fish: an oval cast-iron pan is usually perfect. Half-fill with measured salted water (see above), bring to a boil, and put in the piece of fish. Cover the pan, return to a boil, and simmer gently for 20 minutes. Turn off the heat, let it sit in the water for 4–5 minutes, and serve within 15–20 minutes. *Never poach fish cutlets* because the maximum surface is exposed to the water giving maximum loss of flavor.

Tip: Wild salmon has a short season which varies slightly from area to area. The tails and fins of farmed salmon are often damaged or deformed slightly if there were large numbers in the cages. Depending on the production method, they tend to be fatter and slighter or much flabbier than wild salmon who have much more exercise in the wild. Look out for Organic Farmed Salmon which is reared to IFOAM standards and fed on organic feed. The color of the salmon flesh is determined mostly by what the fish feeds on. The color of farmed salmon can literally be chosen from a color card, the feed is then made up and colored to order.

Poached Whole Salmon or Sea Trout to be served cold

1 whole salmon or sea trout
water
salt

Garnish
crisp lettuce leaves
sprigs of watercress, lemon balm, fennel and fennel flowers (if available)
a segment of lemon for each person
homemade Mayonnaise (see page 584)

fish poacher

Clean and gut the salmon carefully; do not remove the head, tail, or scales. Carefully measure the water and half fill the fish poacher, adding 1 rounded tablespoon of salt to every 5 cups of water. Cover the fish poacher and bring the water to a boil. Add the fish and let the water come back to a boil. Simmer for just 2 minutes and then turn off the heat. Keep the lid on and let the fish cool completely in the water (the fish should be just barely covered by the water).

To serve: when the fish is just cold, remove from the fish poacher and drain for a few minutes. Line a large serving dish with fresh crisp lettuce leaves, top with sprigs of watercress, lemon balm, and fennel, and fennel flowers if available. Carefully slide the salmon onto the dish. Just before serving, peel off the top skin, leaving the tail and head intact. (We don't scrape off the brown flesh in the center because it tastes good.) Pipe a line of homemade mayonnaise along the center of the salmon lengthwise and garnish with tiny sprigs of fennel and fennel flowers or very thin twists of cucumber. Put some segments of lemon around the dish between the lettuce and herbs. Resist the temptation to use any tomato or, horror of horrors, to put a slice of olive over the eye. The pale pink of the salmon flesh with the crisp lettuce and fresh herbs seems just perfect. Serve with a bowl of good Homemade Mayonnaise.

Poached Whole Salmon or Sea Trout to be served hot or warm

1 whole salmon or sea trout
water
salt

Garnish
sprigs of fresh parsley, lemon balm, and fennel
Hollandaise Sauce (see page 581)
a segment of lemon for each person

fish poacher

Clean and gut the salmon carefully; do not remove the head, tail, or scales. Carefully measure the water and half-fill the fish poacher; add 1 rounded tablespoon of salt to every 5 cups of water. Cover the fish poacher and bring the water to a boil. Add the salmon or sea trout and let the water return to a boil. Cover and simmer gently for 20 minutes. Then turn off the heat and leave the salmon in the water for 4–5 minutes to settle. Then remove from water. It will keep hot for 20–30 minutes.

To serve: carefully lift the whole fish out of the fish poacher and let it drain on the rack for a few minutes. Then slide onto a large, hot serving dish. Garnish with lots of parsley, lemon balm, and fennel, and 10–12 segments of lemon. I don't remove the skin until I am serving it at the table, then peel it back gradually as I serve; however, if you prefer, remove the skin at the last second before bringing it to the table. When you have served all the fish from the top, remove the bone as delicately as possible, put it aside, and continue as before. Serve with Hollandaise Sauce – a marriage made in heaven.

Whole Salmon or Sea Trout cooked in Foil

8–9 lbs. (3.6–4.2kg) salmon or sea trout, cleaned
1 stick (1/2 cup) butter
sea salt, or kosher salt, and freshly ground pepper
sprig of fennel

Garnish
segments of lemon
sprigs of parsley or fennel

a large sheet of good quality aluminum foil

Preheat the oven to 350°F (180°C).

Put the aluminum foil on a large baking sheet, preferably with edges. Place the salmon in the center. Smear butter on both sides of the fish and put a few lumps in the cavity. Season with salt and pepper and put a sprig of fennel in the center if you have it. Be generous with the butter; it will mix with the juices to make a delicious sauce to spoon over the fish. Bring the aluminum foil together loosely and seal the edges well.

Bake for about 90 minutes (allow 10 minutes per pound/450g). Open the package, being careful of the steam. Test by lifting the flesh off the backbone just at the thickest point where the flesh meets the head. The fish should lift off the bone easily and there should be no trace of blood; if there is, seal again, and pop back in the oven for 5–10 minutes, but be careful not to overcook it.

Serve hot or cold. If you are serving it hot, spoon the juices over each helping, or use the butter and juice to make a Hollandaise-type sauce by whisking the hot, melted butter and salmon juice gradually into 2 egg yolks, and add a little lemon juice to taste. Garnish with parsley and fennel. If the fish is to be eaten cold, serve with some freshly made salads and a bowl of Homemade Mayonnaise (see page 584). Serve warm with asparagus or sea kale, or fresh green peas and waxy potatoes.

Poached Monkfish with Red Pepper Sauce

Serves 6 as a main course

A whole monkfish (also called angler fish) is quite a sight to behold – years ago fishermen were concerned that no one would want to eat this exceptionally good fish because of its ugly appearance so they took the precaution of cutting off the head before they sent the tails to the fishmongers.

Monkfish has a similar texture to Dublin Bay prawns (scampi) so it was regularly substituted for the latter before it became almost as expensive. In recent years it has become one of the most highly regarded fish. Monkfish are now becoming scarce so do not accept tiny monkfish tails, rather make your feelings known to your fishseller or supermarket.

Monkfish are brilliantly designed with a huge mouth with a double row of teeth; they come equipped with what looks like a radar and a little fishing rod. The latter has what looks like a tiny fish on the end which attracts shoals of smaller fish in the sea to swim right into the monkfish's open mouth and chomp!

1½ lbs. (700g) monkfish tails, carefully trimmed of skin and membrane, filleted
5 cups water
1 teaspoon salt

Note: *measure the ingredients above carefully, it really matters.*

Roast Red Pepper Sauce (see page 149)

Garnish
sprigs of flat-leaf parsley or chervil

Cut the monkfish into ½-inch (1-cm) slices and refrigerate until needed.

Meanwhile, make the Red Pepper Sauce.

Bring the water to a boil and add the salt. Add the monkfish and simmer for 4–5 minutes or until completely white and no longer opaque.

Drain well. Arrange in a warm serving dish or on individual plates, coat with the Red Pepper Sauce, garnish with sprigs of flat-leaf parsley or chervil, and serve immediately.

Baked Trout with Spinach Butter Sauce

Serves 4–6

We can sometimes get lovely fat pink trout about 2 years old which have wonderful taste – much better than the smaller ones. This is a horrendously rich-sounding sauce but it tastes delicious and the flavor is sublime.

2 x 2-lb. (900-g) whole rainbow trout
2–4 tablespoons butter
salt and freshly ground pepper
sprig of fennel

Spinach Butter Sauce (see page 594)

aluminum foil

Gut the trout and wash well making sure to remove the line of blood from the inside near the back bone, dry with paper towels, season inside and out with salt and freshly ground pepper.

Put a blob of butter and a sprig of fennel into the center of each trout. Take a large sheet of aluminum foil, smear a little butter on the center, put the trout onto the buttered bit and fold over the edges into a papiotte shape. Seal well to ensure that none of the juices can escape. Repeat with the other trout. Preheat the oven to 375°F (190°C). Put the two aluminum foil parcels on a baking tray but make sure they are not touching. Bake for 30 minutes approx.

Meanwhile make the Spinach Butter Sauce.

When the fish is cooked, open the foil. There will be lots of delicious juices; use some of these to thin out the sauce. Put the two parcels onto a hot serving dish and bring to the table. Skin the fish and lift the juicy pink flesh onto hot plates.

Spoon the Spinach Butter Sauce over the fish and serve immediately.

Variation

Baked Turbot or Brill with Spinach Butter Sauce

Cook whole turbot or brill as for Baked Plaice (see page 240). Skin and carefully lift the fillets off the bone. Serve on hot plates with Spinach Butter Sauce. Rich but exquisite!

Tip: Turbot and Brill are both flat fish and look very similar. Turbot is superior and more expensive, but brill can be really delicous when absolutely fresh. They are interchangeable in recipes. Turbot can be distinguished from brill by its slightly thorny or knobbly skin.

Tronçon of Turbot with an Olive Oil Sauce Vièrge

Serves 4

Rick Stein charmed us all with his scrummy fish dishes when he came to the school in the summer of 2001. He describes his food as "a bit simple" but it's just what we love – I can't wait to make another trip to his restaurant in Padstow in Cornwall.

4 x 6–8-ounce (175–225-g) tronçons (fillets) of turbot
1/3 cup extra-virgin olive oil, plus extra for brushing
1 teaspoon chopped rosemary
1 teaspoon chopped thyme
1 bay leaf, very finely chopped
1/2 teaspoon crushed fennel seeds
1 teaspoon coarsely crushed black peppercorns
1 teaspoon sea salt flakes, or kosher salt

Olive Oil Sauce Vièrge

1/3 cup extra-virgin olive oil
2 1/2 tablespoons freshly squeezed lemon juice
1 plum tomato, seeded and diced
8 black olives, pitted and cut into fine strips
2 anchovy fillets in oil, drained and diced
1 garlic clove, finely chopped
1 heaped teaspoon coarsely chopped parsley
salt and freshly ground black pepper

Pre-heat the broiler to high. Mix together the olive oil, chopped herbs, fennel seeds, crushed peppercorns, and sea salt, or kosher salt, in a shallow dish. Add the pieces of turbot and turn them over in the mixture so that they are well coated. Place on an oiled baking tray, skin-side up, and broil for 7–8 minutes.

Meanwhile, make the sauce. Put everything except the chopped parsley and seasoning into a small pan. Just as the fish is ready, place over a very low heat just to warm through.

To serve, lift the pieces of fish into the center of 4 warmed plates. Stir the parsley and seasoning in to the sauce and spoon it around the fish. Brush the top of each piece of fish with a little more oil and sprinkle with a few sea salt flakes.

Master Recipe

Roast Salmon with Teriyaki Sauce

Serves about 20

Roasting salmon is so blissfully easy. In fact it is one of the simplest dinner party dishes I know. It is also good at room temperature or even cold. Teriyaki is a Japanese sauce.

1 whole fresh salmon (about 9 lbs./4kg)
salt and freshly ground pepper
1/2 stick (1/4 cup) butter, melted
5 tablespoons extra-virgin olive oil

Odette Rocha's Teriyaki Sauce

1 cup Kikkoman soy sauce
1 cup dry white wine
2 large cloves garlic, peeled and thinly sliced
1 1/2-inch (4-cm) piece ginger root, peeled and thinly sliced
2 1/2 tablespoons wholegrain mustard with honey
2 1/2 tablespoons soft brown sugar

Preheat the oven to 475°F (250°C).

Put all the ingredients for the Teriyaki Sauce into a stainless steel saucepan. Bring to a boil and simmer for 4–5 minutes. Set aside.

Scale the salmon, fillet and remove the pin bones. Line a baking tray with aluminum foil. Put the fillets of fish on top and season with salt and pepper. Brush with melted butter and oil. Roast the salmon in the oven for 20–25 minutes or until cooked and tender. Transfer to a hot serving dish. Spoon some Teriyaki Sauce over the hot salmon and serve immediately, with the remainder of the sauce served separately.

Waxy potatoes and bok choi are good accompaniments.

Smaller quantity

Halve or quarter the amount of Teriyaki Sauce. Cut the salmon into 3-ounce (75-g) portions, cook in a smaller ovenproof dish, and serve in the same way.

Variations

Roast Salmon with Dill Butter

Melt 2 sticks (1 cup) butter, add 5 tablespoons freshly chopped dill, and spoon over the salmon as soon as it comes out of the oven. Serve with Tomato Fondue (see page 188) and waxy potatoes; divine!

Cumin-crusted Fish with Olive and Chile Salsa

Serves 6

1/4 cup cumin seeds
6 fillets very fresh fish (haddock, hake, gray mullet, turbot, cod or salmon, approximately 3 ounces/75g each)
salt and freshly ground pepper

Olive and Chile Salsa

1 cup Kalamata olives, pitted and roughly chopped
3 tablespoons flat-leaf parsley, chopped
2 chiles, seeded and finely chopped
1 garlic clove, crushed
1/2 cup olive oil
sea salt, or kosher salt, and freshly ground pepper
lemon juice, freshly squeezed (optional)

Garnish
arugula leaves

First make the Olive and Chile salsa: mix all the ingredients together. Taste; it may need a squeeze of lemon juice.

Dry roast the cumin seeds in a pan over a medium heat and then grind in a mortar and pestle. Season both sides of the fish with salt and pepper. Dip the flesh side in cumin seeds. Just before serving, heat a pan-grill over a medium to high heat. Cook the fish in a very little oil until crisp and golden on both sides. Serve on hot plates with a little of the Olive and Chile Salsa sprinkled around the edge. Garnish with arugula leaves and serve immediately.

Roast Seabass with Olive Oil and Lemon

Serves 6

6 x 6-ounce (175-g) fillets of seabass, cod, or hake
extra-virgin olive oil
salt and freshly ground white pepper

Garnish
lemon-flavored olive oil (we use Colonna Granverde)
1–2 lemons
bunch of watercress

Preheat the oven to 450°F (230°C).

Score the fish quite deeply on the skin side to prevent curling. Heat a thin film of olive oil in a non-stick pan to just before smoking point. Season the fillets and place skin side down in the pan until a nice crust forms. Turn on the other side and complete cooking in the oven.

Arrange skin side up on a serving dish, drizzle a little lemon-flavored olive oil over the fish, garnish with lemon wedges and fresh watercress.

Salted Fish with Fresh Herbs

A Japanese trick is to salt fillets of whole fish (bass, bream, gray mullet, or cod) for 2–3 hours to intensify the flavor and firm the flesh. Wash off the salt and dry well, brush with olive oil, pan-grill, and sprinkle with more oil mixed with freshly snipped herbs.

Seared Fresh Salmon with Vine-ripened Tomatoes and Herbs

Serves 6

I love this simple, fresh-tasting dish which can be enjoyed as an appetizer or a main course.

3/4–1 1/2 lbs. (350–700g) fillet of wild fresh salmon, scales removed but skin on
a little olive oil or Clarified Butter (see page 103)
salt and freshly ground pepper

3–5 tablespoons basil, marjoram, mint, and flat-leaf parsley, freshly chopped
3–6 very ripe tomatoes, peeled and coarsely chopped
pinch of sugar
1/3–2/3 cup extra-virgin olive oil

Cut the salmon into strips 2 1/2–4 inches (6–10cm) wide approximately. Season well with salt and pepper. Fry or pan-grill carefully in a little olive oil or clarified butter. Transfer to a serving dish, flesh side up. Mix the herbs with the tomato dice, season with salt, pepper, and sugar, and add the olive oil. Spoon over the fish. Serve warm or cold.

Seared Tuna with Piperonata and Tapenade

Serves 6

The secret of cooking tuna is to undercook it like a rare steak, otherwise it becomes dry and dull. The sweetness of Piperonata and the gutsy taste of Tapenade are great with it.

6 x 6-ounce (175-g) pieces of tuna
2 1/2 tablespoons olive oil
salt and freshly ground pepper
Piperonata (see page 190)
Tapenade (see page 588)

Garnish
6–8 leaves of flat-leaf parsley or basil

First make the Piperonata and Tapenade.

Preheat the grill-pan. Brush the tuna with oil and season well with salt and freshly ground pepper. Sear the tuna on the hot grill-pan, first in one direction and then the other. Cook on both sides for 2–3 minutes. The center should still be pink.

Meanwhile reheat the Piperonata if necessary, put a few tablespoons onto each plate, place a piece of sizzling tuna on top. Put a little Tapenade on top or dot irregularly around the edge of the Piperonata. Add a few sprigs of flat-leaf parsley or basil and serve immediately.

Pan-grilled Tuna with Tomato and Basil Salsa and an Herb Salad

Serves 6

6 x 6-ounce (175-g) tuna fillets
salt and freshly ground pepper
2 1/2 tablespoons olive oil, plus extra for herb salad

Tomato and Basil Salsa

6–8 very ripe tomatoes peeled and seeded and cut into 1/4-inch (5-mm) dice
salt, freshly ground pepper, and sugar
5 tablespoons olive oil
freshly squeezed lime juice
6–8 leaves of fresh basil

a mixture of fresh herbs such as flat-leaf parsley, chervil, mint, lemon balm, tarragon, golden marjoram

Preheat the grill-pan. Make the Tomato and Basil Salsa: Season the tomato dice with salt and freshly ground pepper and sugar and add the olive oil, a squeeze of lime, and torn basil leaves. Taste and correct seasoning if necessary.

Season the tuna well with salt and freshly ground pepper, brush with oil, and cook on both sides for 3–6 minutes. The center should still be pink.

Meanwhile warm the tomato slightly; it will probably be enough to put the bowl into the oven while you heat the plates.

Toss the herbs in a little extra olive oil and lemon juice. Season with a few flakes of sea salt, or kosher salt.

Serve the tuna immediately on hot plates with a little of the tomato salsa on top.

How to Skin Fish Fillets

Put the fillet of fish skin side down onto the board.

Cut through the flesh down onto the skin at the tail end, with the knife at a 45° angle, hold onto the skin and half push, half saw the flesh off the skin.

If the knife is at the right angle, there should be no waste. Use the skins for a fish stock.

How to Skin Sole or Flounder

1 Lay the fish on a cutting board, dark skin uppermost. With a sharp knife, cut across the skin where the tail joins the body. Lift the edge of the skin and run your index finger between the skin and the flesh to loosen it.

2 Then grip the skin with a cloth in one hand, use your other hand to hold down the tail end. Pull the skin towards the head. Turn the fish over, repeat on the other side.

3 Alternatively, holding the fish by the head, continue to pull the skin down towards the tail.

Broiled Sole on the Bone

Serves 1

Sole on the bone, the mainstay of many fish restaurants, is still my absolute favorite way to eat this fish. Surprisingly, sole is one of the fish that can be tough if it is too fresh; a day old is perfect.

1 sole, skinned
2–4 tablespoons butter, melted
salt and freshly ground pepper

Garnish
segment of lemon

About 30 minutes before cooking, sprinkle the fish on both sides with salt and brush liberally with butter. Broil on both sides until cooked through; the length of time will depend on the size and thickness of the fish. Test by lifting a little of the flesh close to the head where it is thickest; it should lift easily from the bone and there should be no trace of blood. Transfer to a hot plate and serve immediately with the lemon and freshly ground pepper.

Grilled Salmon Tortilla with Arugula, Tapenade, and Aïoli

Serves 4
In season: early summer for wild salmon

A great recipe from Mary Risley who owns an inspirational cooking school called Tante Marie's in San Francisco.

1 lb. (450g) fresh wild salmon
extra-virgin olive oil
sea salt, or kosher salt, and freshly ground pepper
Tapenade (see page 588), made with 1 cup Niçoise or Kalamata olives, pitted
4 flour tortillas
Aïoli (see page 584)
1 bunch arugula leaves
4 very ripe tomatoes, sliced and seasoned with salt, pepper, sugar, and freshly chopped mint

To prepare the salmon, remove the pin bones, if necessary, and divide into 4 portions. Sprinkle with salt and pepper and brush with extra-virgin olive oil.

Next make the Tapenade, keeping it as a chunky paste.

Pan-grill the salmon over a moderately high heat until it is just cooked through. Remove from the heat. Quickly warm the tortillas on each side under the broiler or on a pan. Put a piece of salmon, some arugula, a spoonful of Tapenade, and some Aïoli in the bottom half of each tortilla. Top with a few sliced tomatoes. Fold over and serve immediately.

Broiled John Dory on the Bone

Serves 4

Johnny Dory, as the fisherman in our nearby port of Ballycotton call this ugly-looking flat fish, is one of the most exquisite fish in the sea. It is one of just two fish said to have the thumbprint of St. Peter clearly on the side. The other, which has two distinct black marks, is the round fish, haddock. St. Peter is supposed to have leant over the edge of his boat in the Sea of Galilee and picked them out of the water, hence they are blessed. John Dory is also very good pan-grilled or baked.

4 very fresh whole John Dory (if unavailable, use porgy or Alaskan halibut)
salt and freshly ground pepper
butter
Herb Butter (see page 240)

Remove the head from the fish. Score the skin crosswise on both sides, sprinkle with a little salt and pepper, and spread butter on both sides of the fish. Broil for 10–12 minutes at a medium heat; you will need to turn the fish once during the cooking time, which will depend on the size or thickness of the fish. Serve immediately with a little Herb Butter.

Left: Broiled John Dory on the Bone

First make the batter: sift the flour and salt into a bowl, make a well in the center and gradually whisk in the beer and water. Let stand while you make the chips.

Cut the potatoes into chips, buffaloes if you like but basically any size you fancy (see page 184). Remember, the bigger they are, the longer they take to cook.

Heat the oil in a deep-fryer with a basket to 350°F (180°C) and add the chips. Make sure they are absolutely dry (don't cook too many together). Cook for a few minutes until they are just soft, and drain.

Just before serving, dip the fish fillets in batter, allow excess to drip off and lower gently into the oil – 1 piece at a time. Cook until crisp and golden, drain on paper towels and keep warm. Increase the heat to 375°F (190°C). Put the chips back in and cook for a minute or two until really crisp. Drain on paper towels, sprinkle with salt.

Serve the fish and chips immediately, either on a plate or in a cornet of newspaper. Serve vinegar as an accompaniment if you want to have really traditional fish and chips, or offer segments of lemon.

Tip: Dip a tiny morsel of fish in batter, deep fry, and taste to check the seasoning; if necessary, add more salt to the batter. Shake the basket as the fish is lowered into the oil to prevent it sticking to the base of the pan.

Cheat's Beer Batter

I sometimes make an even faster batter just by whisking beer into flour to achieve a coating consistency. Add a pinch of salt to taste – works brilliantly.

Variations

Teeny Weeny Fish and Chips

It's fun to serve scaled-down fish and chips as canapés with drinks. Put freshly cooked goujons of plaice, sole, or monkfish, and freshly cooked fine chips in tiny cornets of plain paper and serve hot. Allow 6 ounces (175g) fish per person.

Monkfish with Tartare or Orly Sauce

Cut the monkfish tail into roughly 1½-inch (4-cm) strips. Dip in batter or in flour, egg, and breadcrumbs, and deep-fry until crisp and golden. Serve with Tartare Sauce (see page 585) or Orly Sauce (see page 585). Allow 6 ounces (175g) fish per person. Exquisite!

Fish and Chips with Tartare Sauce and Ulster Champ

Serve freshly fried fish and chips with a bowl of Tartare Sauce (see page 585) and some Ulster Champ (see page 183).

How to Deep-fry

As ever, the quality of the oil is crucially important to the flavor of the food. At Ballymaloe House we use beef fat and occasionally pure olive, peanut, or sunflower oil, depending on the food. Beef fat is high in vitamin D and gives a particularly delicious flavor to fish and chips. Lard from organically reared pigs also produces delicious results.
It is important to realize that different oils and animal fats have a different "smoking point." Animal fats: around 375°F (190°C). Vegetable fats: 400°F (200°C), or even higher. The "smoking point" of "all-purpose" oils will differ according to the blend and method of processing. Many have a low smoking point because they contain preservatives or emulsifiers. In general, these oils are poor quality and in some cases the quality is downright disgraceful.

If possible, use a thermostatically controlled deep-fryer. The temperature should not drop below 325°F (170°C), or the food will be soggy and greasy. Raw fish, poultry, meat, croquettes, fritters, and beignets are best fried at 350–375°F (180–190°C), while vegetables are best at the higher temperature. At smoking point the structure of the fat changes, giving it an unpleasant taste and smell. It should not be used again, even at a lower temperature.

To deep-fry fish, heat the oil or fat to the correct temperature, dip the fish in the coating, drop individually into the hot oil shaking the basket slightly so it doesn't stick to the bottom; this is particularly important with batter. Continue to cook until crisp on the outside and cooked through to the center. For this reason, smaller pieces of fish are more suitable than large.

Fritto Misto di Mare

Serves: depending on quantity of fish

Fritto Misto literally means "mixed fry" and certainly sounds much better in Italian than in English. Fritto Misto di Mare is a mixture of fish which is either pan-fried or deep-fried, served with an appropriate sauce or sauces.

It is delicious only if you use a variety of very fresh fish and good olive oil to fry in. Don't use the atrociously poor quality oil on general sale for deep frying. It will ruin the flavor of even superb fish and the smell will permeate your hair and clothes and, if you don't shut the doors, your whole house as well! Invite your friends to eat in the kitchen for a fritto misto party. Serve straight from the fryer – it will be memorable.

A typical Fritto Misto might include the following deep-fried fish:

shrimp, dipped in batter
mussels, dipped in batter or flour, egg and crumbs
monkfish strips dipped in batter or flour, egg and crumbs
fillets of plaice or sole dipped in batter or flour, egg and crumbs
squid rings dipped in batter, egg and crumbs, or in seasoned flour
pan-fried crab cakes
a slice of salmon pan-fried and served with Maître d'Hôtel Butter (see page 586)

C23

Sauces
Tartare Sauce (see page 585)
Orly Sauce (see page 585)
Garlic Mayonnaise (see page 584)

Garnish
sprigs of parsley or watercress
segments of lemon

Put a selection of freshly fried fish on hot plates, garnish with parsley and lemon, and serve with the selection of sauces. Some deep-fried vegetables, such as slices of zucchini or zucchini blossoms, are also delicious with the fritto and help to spin out the fish.

Spicy Goujons of Plaice or Lemon Sole with Cilantro and Red Pepper Mayonnaise

Goujon is a French term to describe small fried strips of sole or plaice, possibly derived from gudgeon, a small tasty freshwater fish.

4–6 fillets plaice or lemon sole about 1½ lbs. (700g), skinned

Spicy seasoned flour
1½ cups flour
1 teaspoon salt
¼ cup sesame seeds
2 teaspoons chili powder
1 teaspoon freshly ground pepper
2 teaspoons curry powder

Roast Red Pepper Mayonnaise (see page 585)
Tomato and Cilantro Salsa (see page 591)

oil for frying
a little milk
cilantro sprigs

Skin the fillets of fish if the fishseller won't do it for you. Cut them into ¼-inch (5-mm) thick strips lengthwise or on the diagonal if the fillet is very long. They look great if they are 4–5 inches (10–12.5cm) long.

Mix together the ingredients for the seasoned flour in a wide pie dish. Make the Aïoli and the Salsa. Just before serving, heat the oil to 400°F (200°C), toss a few pieces of fish in milk, then in the spicy flour. Deep-fry a few pieces at a time and serve immediately.

Pile up on warm plates with the Cilantro and Red Pepper Aïoli, and Tomato and Chile Salsa. Garnish with sprigs of fresh cilantro.

Deep-fried Whitebait with Chile Mayonnaise

whitebait
Red Chile Mayonnaise (see page 585)

Toss the whitebait in seasoned flour and deep-fry for a few minutes until crisp. Serve with Chile Mayonnaise.

Thai Squid Salad

Serves 4–6 as an appetizer

Young squid are best for this salad. One must be careful not to cook for more than a few minutes or they become rubbery, unless you continue to cook for about 40 minutes.

1½ lbs. (700g) small squid, cleaned
1 quart (960ml) water
½ teaspoon salt

Dressing
freshly squeezed juice of 1 lime
1½ tablespoons fish sauce (nam pla)
1½ tablespoons light soy sauce
2 teaspoons rice vinegar
1–2 small red bird chiles, finely chopped
2 shallots, very finely sliced
2 teaspoons superfine sugar
5 tablespoons warm water
1 generous tablespoon chopped cilantro leaves
1 generous tablespoon chopped basil leaves

2 cucumbers

Slice the body of the squid into ¼-inch (5-mm) circles, divide the tentacles, and slice the wings into thin strips at an angle.

Mix all the ingredients for the dressing, except the cilantro and basil leaves, in a glass or pottery bowl. Bring the water to a boil, add the salt. Put the squid pieces into the boiling water and cook, with the water just bubbling a little, for 3–4 minutes. Drain immediately.

While the squid pieces are still warm, put them into the bowl with the dressing and mix well.

Cut the cucumbers in half lengthwise, scoop out the seeds using a melon baller or teaspoon, then cut the flesh into thin half moon shapes. When the squid is cool, mix the cilantro, basil leaves, and cucumber slices into the salad. Taste, and add more salt if necessary. Serve at room temperature.

Squid with Tomato and Herbs

Serves 6

A Julia Wight recipe.

4 medium-sized squid
6 tablespoons olive oil
2 large onions, sliced
2 cloves garlic, sliced
glass red, white, or rosé wine
salt and freshly ground pepper
bouquet of herbs, including some fresh fennel
5 tomatoes, peeled, seeded, and diced
salt, pepper, and paprika

Tomato Purée (see page 49)
2 teaspoons sugar
parsley, chopped

First prepare the squid and cut into 1/4-inch (5-mm) rounds (see right).

Heat 5 tablespoons olive oil in a stew-pan, and in this melt the onion and garlic. Put in the squid, stir well around, then pour in the wine. Let it bubble a minute, season, turn down the heat, add the bouquet of herbs, and let simmer, covered, for 1–1 1/2 hours till tender. This can be done on the stove or in the oven, very slowly.

Lift out the squid and keep warm. Reduce the sauce till fairly thick.

Meanwhile melt the tomatoes in 1 1/2 tablespoons olive oil, uncovered. Season well and add about 2 teaspoons Tomato Purée, the same of sugar, and some paprika. Add the tomatoes to the wine sauce, pour it over the squid, sprinkle with parsley, and serve very hot with plain, boiled rice.

Master Recipe
Salt and Pepper Squid with Sweet Chile Sauce

Serves 6

Squid is immensely nibbleable – pile a plate high for a main course.

1 1/4 lbs (600g) whole squid
1 cup all-purpose white flour
1 tablespoon plus 1 teaspoon salt, preferably sea salt or kosher salt
1 tablespoon plus 1 teaspoon freshly ground black pepper
1 1/2–2 1/2 tablespoons chili powder (depending on whether it is mild or hot)
peanut or sunflower oil for deep-frying
8 sprigs of cilantro

Garnish
lemon segments
sweet chile sauce (available from Asian grocers)

Prepare the squid in the usual way (see right). Mix the flour, salt, pepper, and chili powder in a bowl. Heat the oil to 350°F (180°C) in a deep-fryer. Toss the squid in the seasoned flour. Shake off any excess and drop one at a time into the hot oil. Fry for 2 minutes and remove, drain on paper towels. Don't overcrowd the basket.

Put the cilantro into the oil and cook for 1 minute. This has a tendency to spit so be careful. Drain on paper towels. Divide the squid between 4 plates. Top with the fried cilantro. Garnish with a lemon wedge and serve immediately with sweet chile sauce.

Variations
Spicy Squid

Follow the Master Recipe but substitute freshly roasted cumin seed or five-spice powder for chili powder. Panko crumbs, the crispy Japanese bread crumbs, make a delicious coating for squid. Serve with Tartare Sauce (see page 585) and Hot Chile Sauce (see page 591).

Squid with Garlic Butter

Serves 4 as an appetizer, 2 as a main course

2 medium-sized squid
about 2 1/2 tablespoons Garlic Butter (see page 588)

Garnish
segments of lemon

First prepare the squid (see right). Just before serving, heat 4 plates. Melt the garlic butter in the frying pan, let foam, toss in the squid (do it in two batches if necessary). Toss around for 30–60 seconds or until the pieces turn from opaque to white. Serve instantly on hot plates with a segment of lemon on each.

How to Prepare Squid

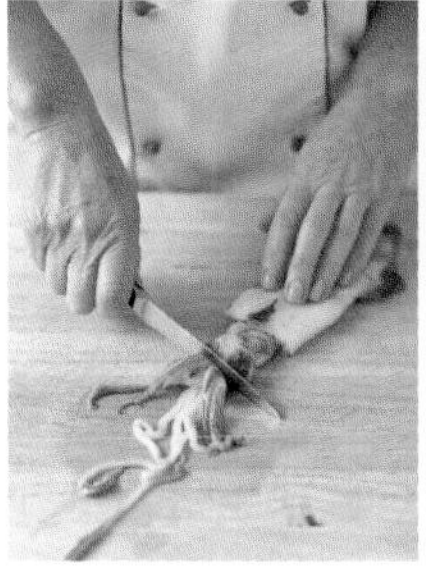

Cut off the tentacles just in front of the eyes.

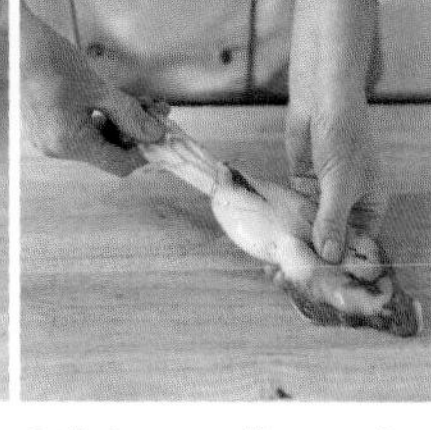

Pull the entrails out of the sac and discard.

Remove the beak.

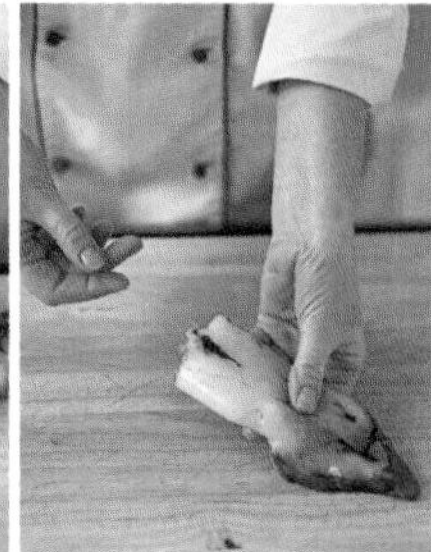

Catch the tip of the quill and pull it out of the sac.

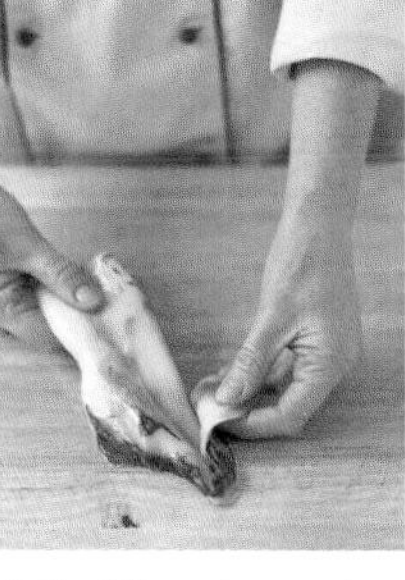

Pull off the wings and scrape the purplish membrane off them and the sac.

Wash the sac, wings, and tentacles well.

Cut into 3/4-inch (2cm) rounds or slices.

Master Recipe

Cod with Buttered Crumbs

Serves 6–8

Cod with Buttered Crumbs may be served in individual dishes. Scallop shells are also attractive, completely ovenproof, and may be used over and over again.

Haddock, hake, pollock, ling, gray sea mullet, or in fact any of the round fish may be used for this delicious recipe; it's a simple formula but so good, with lots of variations. Very basic or quite elaborate, made with really fresh fish, this recipe is always a winner.

2 lbs. (900g) fillets of cod, hake, ling, haddock, gray sea mullet, or pollock
salt and freshly ground pepper

Mornay Sauce (see page 581)
1 cup shredded cheese

Buttered Crumbs
2 tablespoons butter
a heaped cup soft, white breadcrumbs

4 cups Fluffy Mashed Potato (see page 182)

First make the Mornay Sauce, and mix in two-thirds of the shredded cheese. Next make the Buttered Crumbs: melt the butter in a pan and stir in breadcrumbs. Remove from the heat immediately and let cool.

Skin the fish and cut into portions: 6 ounces (175g) for a main course, 3 ounces (75g) for an appetizer. Season with salt and pepper. Coat the bottom of an ovenproof dish or individual dishes with the Mornay Sauce. Lay the pieces of fish on top. Top with another layer of sauce.

Mix the remaining grated cheese with the buttered crumbs and sprinkle over the top. Pipe a ruff of fluffy Mashed Potato around the edge if you want to have a whole meal in one dish.

The dish can be prepared ahead to this point and cooked later, but because the fish is raw it should be cooked on the same day.

Cook in a moderate oven, 350°F (180°C), for 25–30 minutes or until the fish is cooked through and the top is golden brown and crispy. If necessary, flash under the broiler for a minute or two before you serve, to brown the edges of the potato.

Note: Buttered Crumbs are worth knowing about: keep a batch of them in your fridge to scatter over gratins or creamy dishes. The crumbs crisp up in the oven and make a yummy crust. Mix with grated cheese or fresh herbs as a coating for fish or meat. Buttered Crumbs keep for a week or more in a covered box in the fridge.

Tip: When assembling this dish, particularly in individual portions, be generous with the sauce and more sparing with the fish, the result will be juicy and delicious. If the cheese is sprinkled on top of the buttered crumbs it makes a tough crust, so mix together before sprinkling on top.

Variation

For pubs, cafés, restaurants, or delicatessens, or anyone who would like to prepare this fish dish and refrigerate or freeze it. Use the same ingredients as above but go by the following alternative method.

Skin the fish and cut into portions: 6 ounces (175g) for a main course, 3 ounces (75g) for an appetizer. Season with salt and freshly ground pepper. Lay the pieces of fish in a lightly buttered sauté pan, cover with cold milk. Bring to a boil, simmer for 4–5 minutes, or until the fish has changed color.

Remove the fish to a serving dish or dishes using a perforated spoon.

Bring the milk back to a boil and thicken with Roux to a light coating consistency. Add the mustard and two-thirds of the grated cheese; keep the remainder of the cheese for sprinkling over the top. Season with salt and freshly ground pepper, taste, and correct the seasoning if necessary. Add parsley if you like.

Next make the Buttered Crumbs. Coat the fish with the sauce. Mix the remaining grated cheese with the buttered crumbs and sprinkle over the top. Pipe a ruff of Fluffy Mashed Potato or Champ around the edge for a more substantial dish.

Cool and freeze, or refrigerate and reheat later in a moderate oven for 15–20 minutes, as above.

Variations

Cod with Buttered Leeks

Sweat 1 pound (450g) finely sliced leeks in 2 tablespoons butter in a covered flameproof casserole dish (or other heavy flameproof pan) over a gentle heat until tender, and add in layers to the fish dish. Proceed as in the Master Recipe.

Cod with Cucumber and Dill or Fennel

Peel and sweat 2 small cucumbers cut into ½-inch (1-cm) dice in a little butter. Add 1–2 teaspoons dill or fennel. Proceed as in the Master Recipe.

Cod with Tomato Fondue

Put a layer of Tomato Fondue (see page 188) under or over the fish, and proceed as in the Master Recipe.

Cod with Piperonata

Put a layer of Piperonata (see page 190) under or over the fish, and proceed as in the Master Recipe.

Cod with Mussels or Shrimp and Buttered Crumbs

Add 16–24 cooked mussels or shrimp to the dish before saucing, and proceed as in the Master Recipe.

Cod with Mushrooms

$2^1/_3$ cups mushrooms, sliced
1 tablespoon butter
salt and freshly ground pepper
1 generous tablespoon parsley, freshly chopped (optional)

Sauté the mushrooms in the foaming butter, season with salt and pepper, and add the parsley. Put a layer under the fish and proceed as in the Master Recipe.

Baked Cod Niçoise

Serves 6 as main course

This is an extremely simple fish dish with a rich, robust flavor. Virtually any round fish may be used, and it is just as suitable for an appetizer as for a main course, but remember to halve the quantities!

$1^1/_2$ lbs. (700g) cod or haddock fillet, cut into 6 portions
salt and freshly ground pepper
1 lb. (450g) very ripe tomatoes, skinned, seeded, chopped, and sprinkled with a little sugar (about $2^1/_2$-3 cups)
1–2 cloves garlic, crushed
$1^1/_2$ tablespoons capers, rinsed
12 black olives, pitted and sliced
$2^1/_2$ tablespoons parsley, chopped
1 teaspoon fresh thyme leaves
$^1/_4$ cup extra-virgin olive oil

Preheat the oven to 400°F (200°C). Season the fish with the salt and pepper. Prepare and mix all the remaining ingredients. Place the fish in a single layer in an oiled ovenproof dish. Spoon the tomato mixture over it. Bake until just cooked through – about 15 minutes. Serve with a good green salad and tiny waxy potatoes.

Ceviche

In Latin America, raw fish is marinated in lime or lemon juice, often with some sliced vegetables, peppers, chile, or sliced onion. The fish may be sliced in thin strips or cut into dice and then left in the marinade for anything from 4 to 24 hours. The acid in the lime or lemon juice "cooks" the fish by acting on the albumen so the flesh turns whiter and firmer in texture – it has a clean fresh taste. The fish should always be very fresh and from unpolluted water. Extra freshly sliced vegetables are often added before serving for their texture and color. Keep refrigerated until served.

Susie Noriega's Peruvian Ceviche

Serves 10–12 as an appetizer

2 lbs. (900g) fillets of monkfish, cod, plaice, lemon sole, or scallops
4 limes
2 lemons
2 garlic cloves, finely chopped
salt and freshly ground pepper
fresh cilantro, chopped
1–2 fresh chiles
2/3 cup onions, finely sliced
1 green pepper, finely diced
1 red pepper, finely diced

Garnish
crisp lettuce leaves
5–6 scallions
corn, optional
2 avocados
diced peppers

Skin the fish; slice or cube into 1/2-inch (1-cm) pieces and put it into a deep stainless steel or china bowl. Squeeze the juice from the lemons and limes and pour over the fish. Sprinkle with salt, pepper, and garlic. Cover and let marinate for 2–3 hours in a fridge.

Next add the fresh cilantro, onions, chiles, and the red and green peppers. Cover and leave for 2 1/2 hours in the fridge. Then serve or keep covered until later.

To serve: arrange a few crisp lettuce leaves on a plate and place a tablespoon of Ceviche in the center. Decorate with slices of avocado, diced peppers, corn, and scallions. Serve it with crusty white bread or tortillas.

Left: Susie Noriega's Peruvian Ceviche

Finnish Beet-marinated Salmon

Serves 15–20

In the Scandinavian countries they do many variations on the basic Gravadlax. I came across this version in Finland.

2 sides of salmon
1/4 cup Maldon sea salt, or kosher salt
1/4 cup sugar
freshly ground black pepper
1 3/4 cups grated raw beets
2 tablespoons grated horseradish, optional
1/2 cup sunflower oil
1/4 cup vodka

Beet Sauce
1 3/4 cups cooked beets, chopped
2 teaspoons Dijon mustard
2 1/2 tablespoons sugar
2/3 cup red wine vinegar
1 cup oil
pinch of salt
freshly ground black pepper

Garnish
sprigs of dill

Place one fillet of fish skin side down in a dish, sprinkle with salt, sugar, and freshly ground pepper. Place the other fillet on top. Wrap tightly in plastic wrap. Marinate the salmon for 24 hours. Mix the grated beet and horseradish together and add the oil and vodka.

Spread the mixture evenly over the fish, sandwich together again, and marinate in the fridge for one more day.

Next make the Beet Sauce: whizz the chopped beet, mustard, and sugar in a blender. Add the vinegar and oil alternately. Season with salt and pepper. Wipe the vegetable mixture off the salmon and slice the salmon thinly. Arrange on a plate and drizzle sauce around them. Garnish with sprigs of dill.

Soused Mackerel and Mustard and Dill Mayonaise

Serves 8 as a main course, 16 as an appetizer

Sousing is a form of pickling – steeping or cooking in vinegar or white wine. It is particularly suited to oily fish. Treat herrings this way, too.

8 mackerel, about 6 ounces (175g) each, cleaned
1 onion, thinly sliced
1 teaspoon whole black peppercorns
6 whole cloves
1 teaspoon salt
1 teaspoon sugar
1 1/4 cups white wine vinegar
1 bay leaf
Mustard and Dill Mayonnaise *(see page 585)*

Preheat the oven to 250°F (130°C).
Fillet the mackerel, ensuring there are no bones, a tall order – but do your best. Roll up the fillets, skin side out, and pack tightly into a cast-iron casserole dish. Sprinkle with onion, peppercorns, cloves, salt, sugar, vinegar, and bay leaf. Bring to a boil on top of the stove and then put into the oven, for 30–45 minutes. Let the mackerel get quite cold. It keeps for 7–10 days in the fridge.

To serve: put 1–2 fillets of soused mackerel on a plate and zig-zag Sweet Mustard and Dill Mayonnaise over the fish. Serve with fresh crusty bread.

Scallops with Jerusalem Artichokes and Beurre Blanc Sauce

Serves 2 as a main course

Jerusalem artichokes have a wonderful affinity with shellfish, particularly scallops and mussels. This is an exquisite dish, worth the little extra effort.

8 scallops
Beurre Blanc Sauce (see page 583)
2–4 Jerusalem artichokes depending on size
2 tablespoons butter
freshly squeezed lemon juice
salt and freshly ground pepper

Garnish:
chervil or fennel sprigs

First prepare the scallops: wash and slice the nuggets in half horizontally, keep the corals whole. Keep chilled.

Next make the Beurre Blanc Sauce and keep warm.

Wash and peel the artichokes and cut into 1/2-inch (1-cm) rounds. Put them into a casserole dish along with the butter and a squeeze of lemon juice (to prevent discoloration). Season with salt and freshly ground pepper, cover, and cook gently until just tender.

To assemble: season the scallops and cook in a non-stick pan until golden on each side. Put 2–3 tablespoons of Beurre Blanc Sauce onto each plate. Put 4 artichoke rounds on top of the sauce on each plate. Divide the cooked scallops between the 2 plates, placing them on top of the artichoke rounds. Put the coral in the center and garnish with chervil or fennel, and serve immediately.

Char-grilled Scallops with Eggplant and Pesto

Serves 4

12 scallops
1–2 eggplants
Pesto (see page 589) or a jar of good-quality store-bought pesto
salt and freshly ground pepper
olive oil

Garnish
sprigs of basil

Slice the eggplant lengthwise into thin slices, sprinkle with salt, and let it degorge for 15–20 minutes. Meanwhile make the Pesto.

Wash the eggplant slices and pat dry with paper towels. Brush with a little olive oil and char-grill quickly on both sides either on a char-grill or on a very hot grill-pan.

Just before serving, season the scallops with salt and pepper. Cook on the char-grill or grill-pan (a non-stick pan also gives a very good result). Let them brown well on one side before turning over onto the other.

To serve, cover the base of the plate with eggplant slices, arrange 3 or 4 scallops and their coral on top, put a blob of soft Pesto between the scallops. Garnish with a sprig of fresh basil and serve immediately.

Scallops in Mornay Sauce

Serves 12-14 as an appetizer, 6-7 as a main course

12 scallops
dry white wine and water to cover
1/4 cup chopped shallots or onion
1/4 stick (2 tablespoons) butter
scant 3 cups chopped mushrooms
5 tablespoons flour
about 1 cup creamy milk
Salt and freshly ground pepper
1/2–3/4 cup shredded Cheddar cheese
2 American tablespoons chopped parsley
Duchesse potato, optional

Put the scallops in a medium-sized stainless steel pan and cover in half white wine and half water. Poach for 3-5 minutes (be careful to simmer and not to overcook). Remove the scalops and reduce the cooking liquid to about 1 1/4–1 1/2 cups.

Sweat the shallots gently in butter until soft (about 5–6 minutes). Add the mushrooms and cook for another 3–4 minutes. Stir in the flour and cook for a further minute. Add creamy milk to the scallop cooking liquid to make up to 2 1/2 cups and add to the pan. Taste the sauce, reduce until the flavor is really good, and season.

Cut the scallops into quaters and add the sauce along with some of the cheese and parsley. Decorate individual scallop shells or a serving dish with Duchesse potato, fill the center with the scallop mixture and sprinkle the top with the remaining cheese. Just before serving, reheat in a medium-hot oven (350F/180C) until just bubbling (about 20 minutes).

Note: This mixture also makes a delicious filling for crepes or vol au vents.

Prawns Bretonne

Serves 8–10

1 lb. (450g) fresh prawns or shrimp
1 stick (1/2 cup) butter
Bretonne Sauce (see page 582)

Toss cooked shelled prawns or shrimp in sizzling butter until hot. Serve with Bretonne Sauce. Divine.

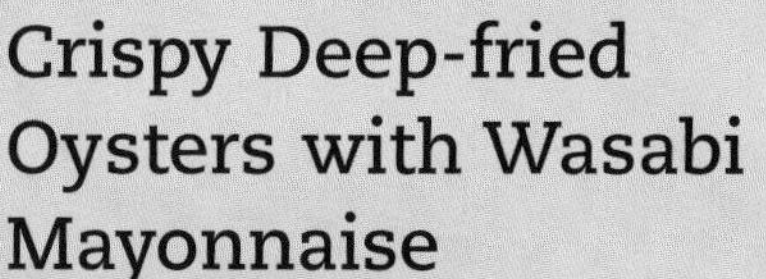

Crispy Deep-fried Oysters with Wasabi Mayonnaise

Serves 4

12 Pacific oysters
Beer Batter (see page 243)
Wasabi Mayonnaise (see page 585)
oil for deep frying

Garnish
4 segments of lime or lemon

First make the Wasabi Mayonnaise. Next make the Batter.

Heat good-quality oil in a deep-fryer.

Dip the oysters individually in batter and deep-fry until crisp and golden. Drain on absorbent paper. Serve immediately – three per person with a blob of Wasabi Mayonnaise and a segment of lime or lemon.

How to Cook Shrimp

The secret of ensuring flavor in shrimp is to cook them in well-salted water, so carefully measure the salt to water (use 1 tablespoon salt to every 5 cups of water). Bring a large pot of water to a boil and add correct amount of salt. Put the shrimp into the fast-boiling, salted water. As soon as the water returns to a boil, test a shrimp to see if it is cooked. A cooked shrimp should be firm and white, not opaque or mushy. Cooked shrimp should rise to the top. When cooked, remove shrimp immediately. Very large ones may take ½ to 1 minute more.

Let cool on a tray in a single layer and then remove the shells. (Shrimp yield about one-sixth of their original volume.)

Note: Do not cook too many shrimp together, or they may overcook before the water comes back to a boil – better to cook them in batches.

How to Remove the Intestine from Scampi (Dublin Bay Prawns)

Remove the head of the raw scampi and discard or use for making fish stock. With the underside of the scampi uppermost, tug the little fan-shaped tail at either side and carefully draw out the trail (the trail is the intestine, so it is very important to remove it before cooking, regardless of whether the scampi are to be shelled or not).

Scampi with Tartare Sauce

Serves 8–10

Scampi (Nephrops norvegicus) is the Venetian name for this crustacean. They are what we commonly call Dublin Bay Prawns, although those fished from the Adriatic are twice the size. Scampi was the "must have" appetizer of the '60s and '70s. It is utterly delicious when made with fresh scampi; sadly nowadays it is more often a travesty made with inferior, soggy, frozen ones. Pieces of fresh monkfish are also delectable.

1 lb. (450g) very fresh scampi, peeled
Tartare Sauce (see page 585)

Batter
2½ cups all-purpose white flour
¼ cup olive oil
2–3 egg whites
sea salt, or kosher salt

Garnish
lemon segments

Preheat oil to 350°F (180°C) in a deep fryer. Then make the batter: sift flour into a bowl, make a well in the center, pour in the olive oil, stir, and add enough water to make a batter about the consistency of sour cream. Let stand for at least 1 hour.

Just before serving, whisk the egg whites to a stiff peak and fold into the batter, adding a good pinch of salt.

Dip the scampi individually in the batter and deep-fry until crisp and golden. Drain on paper towels. Serve immediately with a little bowl of Tartare Sauce and a slice of lemon.

Ballycotton Prawns or Shrimp with Homemade Mayonnaise

Serves 4

We eat Dublin Bay prawns (scampi) in several ways but they are almost best just freshly cooked and served with Homemade Mayonnaise.

32 large very fresh scampi or 64 shrimp
¼–½ cup Homemade Mayonnaise (see page 584)

Garnish
watercress leaves
4 segments lemon

First cook the scampi or shrimp (see left). Put 8 cooked whole scampi on each plate. Spoon a tablespoon or two of Homemade Mayonnaise into a little bowl or oyster shell. Pop a segment of lemon on the plate. Garnish with some fresh watercress. Serve with crusty brown soda bread.

Variation

Scampi or Shrimp with Brown Bread and Homemade Mayonnaise

Stamp out a large round of thinly sliced Ballymaloe Brown Yeast Bread (see page 478) per person, spread with a little butter, and add a frill of lollo rosso lettuce.

Peel the scampi or shrimp and arrange 6–8 in a circle on each piece of bread. Pipe a rosette of Homemade Mayonnaise in the center, garnish with sprigs of chervil and fennel and perhaps a few fennel flowers. They are also delicious with a little Sweet Cucumber Pickle or Dill Mayonnaise. Do individual ones for finger food.

How to Cook Mussels

Check that all the mussels are tightly shut. If open, tap the mussel on the work top; if it does not close within a few seconds, discard it. (The rule with shellfish is always, "If in doubt, throw it out.") Wild mussels occasionally have barnacles attached to the shells. Scrape them off the shells with the back of a knife. Wash the mussels well in several changes of cold water. Spread them in a single layer in a pan, covered with a folded lint-free towel or a lid, and cook over a gentle heat. This usually takes 2–3 minutes, and the mussels are cooked just as soon as the shells open. Remove them from the pan immediately or they will shrink in size and become tough. Remove the beard (the little tuft of tough "hair" which attached the mussel to the rock or rope it grew on). Discard one shell. Loosen the mussel from the other shell but leave it in the shell. Let them get cold.

Mussels with Thai Flavors

Serves 4

4½ lbs. (2kg) mussels
2½ tablespoons peanut or sunflower oil
6 cloves garlic, crushed
1–2 red chiles, finely chopped
1 stalk lemongrass, finely chopped
2½ tablespoons fish sauce (nam pla)
2½–3½ tablespoons mint or cilantro, chopped

Check the mussels carefully, discarding any broken or open shells. Wash well, drain. Heat the oil on a medium heat, add the garlic and chiles, and fry for a minute or two. Add the lemongrass and fish sauce and then the mussels. Cover with a folded lint-free towel or the lid of the pan. The mussels will open in just a few minutes.

Discard one shell from each mussel, and remove the beards. Add the chopped mint or cilantro to the mussel juices. Divide the mussels between four deep, wide bowls, pour the hot juices over, and serve immediately.

Moules Provençales

Serves 6–8

Mussels are a perennial favorite; don't skimp on the garlic in butter for this recipe.

48 mussels, approx. 3¼–4 lbs. (1.5–1.8kg)
Provençale Butter (see page 588)
1¼–1¾ cups fresh, white breadcrumbs

Cook and cool the mussels (see left). Meanwhile make the Provençale Butter. If you have it made in advance, you will need it to be soft enough to spread evenly over the mussels in their shells. Dip each one into the breadcrumbs. They may be prepared ahead to this point and frozen in a covered box lined with plastic wrap or aluminum foil.

Arrange in individual serving dishes. Brown under the broiler and serve with crusty white bread to mop up the delicious juices.

Isaac's Shellfish Paella

Serves 8–10

5 tablespoons olive oil
1 stick (½ cup) butter
⅔ cup sliced shallot
2⅓ cups Paella rice
5 tablespoons dry white wine
2½ cups light fish stock (see page 37)
2½ cups vegetable cooking water
8 garlic cloves, mashed
24 each of mussels, clams, and large prawns or shrimp
1 lb. (450g) squid, cleaned and cut into rings plus whole tentacles
1 lb. (450g) baby zucchini, sliced
1 lb. (450g) fresh peas or snow peas
20 asparagus tips
4 large tomatoes
juice of 1 lime
5 tablespoons freshly chopped parsley and chives
a good few strands of saffron
Salt, freshly ground pepper, sugar

18-inch (46-cm) paella pan

Melt the butter and olive oil in a paella pan, and sweat the shallot and garlic slowly until they are soft. Add the shelled shrimp and raw squid and cook until they stiffen, remove and set to one side.

Then add the rice and wine. Stir until the rice is completely coated with the wine and butter. Continue to cook until nearly all the liquid has been absorbed, then add half the fish stock. Stir gently and occasionally (you can over-stir this).

The temperature is critical; the mixture should be just barely bubbling and should continue this way until the dish is fully cooked. If it cooks too quickly or too slowly, the rice will become stodgy and heavy. Allow the liquid to be absorbed before adding more stock, and repeat until all the stock has been used.

Meanwhile, cook the asparagus and peas in a little boiling salted water. Use the same water for both but cook them separately. When they are cooked, rinse under cold water and set to one side. Keep the cooking water.

Cook the zucchini in a frying pan over a high flame with some olive oil, salt, and pepper; again keep to one side.

Steam the mussels and clams in a covered pot until they open. Put aside and keep the juices. Strain the mussel and clam juice, add the saffron, the lime juice, and the vegetable cooking water. When all the fish stock has been used up, continue to add the vegetable water and shellfish and saffron liquid. The rice may not take all the liquid. You will know by the texture of the rice when it is cooked – there shouldn't be any bite.

When the paella is fully cooked, gently fold the vegetables and shellfish through the rice. Sprinkle with chopped tomato, parsley, and chives, and serve from the paella dish.

Ballycotton Seafood Lasagne

Serves 8

10–12 sheets of homemade Lasagne (see page 148 and 154) or very thin commercial lasagne
1 teaspoon salt
2½ tablespoons olive oil
1 cup finely chopped onion
1 large clove garlic, finely chopped
1¾ cups sliced mushrooms
2½ tablespoons chopped parsley
1 glass white wine
6 ounces (175g) scallops (out of shells)
4–6 ounces (110–175g) cooked prawns or shrimp, shelled
12 mussels
8–10 ounces (225–275g) monkfish, cut into collops
salt and freshly ground pepper

creamy milk
Roux (see page 580)
Parmesan cheese

Bring a large pot of water to a fast rolling boil and add salt. Cook the sheets of pasta a few at a time until al dente, about 1 minute for homemade pasta, about 5–8 minutes for store-bought pasta. Drop immediately into a bowl of cold water, drain, and lay out on lint-free towels in a single layer. Heat the olive oil in a sauté pan, add the onions, and sweat until soft and just beginning to color. Add the garlic and stir. Increase the heat, add the sliced mushrooms, and toss for a minute or two. Remove from the pan and set aside.

Put the scallops into a small saucepan, cover with water and wine, and poach gently for 4–5 minutes until just cooked. Remove with a slotted spoon and drain. Bring the liquid back to a boil, add the monkfish pieces, and poach for 3–5 minutes until they change color to white rather than opaque. Add to the rest. Next put the scrubbed mussels into the liquid and remove just as soon as the shells open. Remove the beard and discard the shells. Add to the scallops.

If the shrimp are raw, cook in a little butter until they turn pink, cut in half, and add to the rest of the fish. If using cooked peeled shrimp, just add to the fish. Mix the fish with the mushroom mixture and add 2½ tablespoons parsley. Season with salt and pepper.

Make a sauce by measuring the cooking liquid and make up to 5 cups with whole milk. Bring to a boil, thicken with Roux (see page 580), and let simmer gently for 5–6 minutes until the flavor is mellow and delicious.

Preheat the oven to 350°F (180°C).

To assemble: spread a little of the sauce on the bottom of an ovenproof dish, keep back a little for the top of the lasagne, and mix the rest with the fish and mushrooms. Lay lasagne over the sauce in the bottom of the dish, spread some of the seafood sauce over the pasta, and sprinkle with Parmesan. Continue until there are least 4 layers, finishing with a layer of pasta. Spread the reserved sauce over the top layer. Sprinkle with grated cheese and bake for 15–20 minutes until bubbly and golden on top. Let rest for 10 minutes before serving.

Lobster or Crayfish

Serves 2–4

The method described here is considered by the RSPCA to be the most humane way to cook lobster and certainly results in deliciously tender and juicy flesh. When we are cooking lobster we judge by color, or allow 15 minutes for the first pound (450g) and 10 minutes per pound (450g) after that.

2 x 2-lb. (900-g) live lobsters

Court Bouillon
1 carrot
1 onion
2½ cups water
2½ cups dry white wine
bouquet garni: parsley stalks, sprig of thyme, celery stalks, and a small bay leaf
6 peppercorns

Cover the lobsters with lukewarm salted water (¼ cup of salt to every 2½ quarts[2.4 liters]. Put the pot over a low heat and bring slowly to simmering point: lobster and crab die at about 112°F (44°C). By this stage the lobsters will be changing color so remove them and discard all the cooking water.

Slice the carrot and onion and put with the water, wine, bouquet garni, and peppercorns into a stainless steel pot and bring to a boil. Put in the lobsters and cover with a tight-fitting lid. Steam them until they change color to bright red, or follow the time given for weight, and remove them from the pot. Strain the cooking liquid and reserve for a sauce.

Lobster:

A 2½-lb. (1.1-kg) lobster will yield about 12 ounces (350g) meat, depending on the time of year.

Crayfish (Spiny Lobster):

A 5-lb. (2.2-kg) crayfish will yield about 2½ lbs. (1.1kg) meat. Crayfish is therefore less expensive in the long run.

Ballymaloe Hot Buttered Lobster

Serves 4 as a main course

Ballymaloe is famous for this dish. One of the most exquisite ways to eat fresh lobster, but for perfection the lobster must come straight from the sea, not from a holding tank. Sadly lobsters are becoming more scarce so enjoy while you can. When buying lobster, do not buy undersized or female ones. Bord Iascaigh Mhara (the Irish Fisheries Board) introduced a system whereby the fishermen cut a V-shaped notch in the tail of female lobster so they can be identified easily even when they do not have eggs – do not accept female lobster in a restaurant; we all have a responsibility to conserve the stocks.

4 lbs. (1.8kg) live lobster
Court Bouillon (see recipe left)
1 stick (½ cup) butter
lemon juice, freshly squeezed

Garnish
sprigs of watercress, flat-leaf parsley, or fennel
lemon segments

Cook the lobsters in Court Bouillon (see recipe left).

As soon as they are cool enough to handle, split them in half and extract all the meat from the body, tail, and large and small claws. Scrape out all the soft, greenish tomalley (liver) from the part of the shell nearest the head and put it with the firmer meat into a warm bowl wrapped in a lint-free towel. Cut the meat into chunks.

Heat the lobster shells. Melt half the butter and, when it is foaming, toss the meat in it until it is cooked through and the juices turn pink. Spoon the meat into the hot shells. Put the remaining butter into the pan, heat, and scrape up any bits. Add a squeeze of lemon juice. Pour the buttery juices into small, heated ramekins and serve beside the lobster on hot plates. Garnish with sprigs of watercress, flat-leaf parsley, or fennel, and lemon segments. Hot buttered lobster should be eaten immediately.

Ballymaloe Lobster with Cream and Fresh Herbs

Serves 4 as a main course, 8 as an appetizer

The filling may also be served in the lobster shells, or in a vol au vent case, or as a chunky lobster sauce for baked plaice, sole, or turbot. Crawfish may be used in this recipe also.

12 ounces (350g) cooked lobster meat
1/2 stick (1/4 cup) butter
2 1/3 cups sliced button mushrooms
salt and freshly ground pepper
a little lemon juice, freshly squeezed
4 teaspoons shallot, finely chopped
1/4 cup dry white wine
1 cup Court Bouillon (see left)
1–1 1/2 cups cream
Roux (see page 580)
1 teaspoon thyme leaves
2 teaspoons parsley, chopped
1–2 1/2 tablespoons Hollandaise Sauce (see page 581)

Garnish
sprigs of watercress and fennel

Melt the butter in a wide sauté pan and toss the mushrooms on a high heat for a minute or two. Season and add a little lemon juice. Set aside.

Add a little more butter to the pan and toss the lobster meat and green juices in the foaming butter until the meat is cooked through and juices turn pink. Remove the lobster meat and add to the mushrooms. Then cook the shallots gently in the sauté pan. After approx. 2 minutes add the white wine and reduce by half. Now add the court bouillon and reduce again. Add cream, whisk in some Roux, add the mushrooms and lobster meat. Boil up the sauce again for the last time, stir in the herbs and Hollandaise, taste, and correct seasoning.

Reheat the lobster shells, fill with the lobster mixture. Garnish with the sprigs of watercress and fennel. Serve immediately.

Above: Lobster and Mango Salad

Variation
Lobster Vol au Vent

Pile the creamy lobster mixture into buttery vol au vents – this is often served on the Sunday night buffet in Ballymaloe. Individual vol au vents made with puff pastry make a sensational appetizer.

Master Recipe

Lobster and Mango Salad

Serves 6

Choose a ripe, juicy, perfumed mango to partner an exquisite lobster.

A selection of lettuces and salad greens e.g., butterhead, iceberg, oakleaf, lollo rosso, watercress, and arugula leaves
1 ripe mango
12 ounces (350g) lobster tail and claw meat – a 2–2½-lb. (900–1.1-kg) lobster should yield this quantity

Dressing
½ cup extra-virgin olive oil
2½ tablespoons lemon juice, freshly squeezed
salt and freshly ground pepper
pinch of sugar
2 teaspoons parsley, freshly chopped

Garnish
sprigs of fennel, chervil, and borage flowers

Wash and dry the salad greens. Combine all the ingredients for the dressing. Peel the mango and cut into slices or dice depending on presentation; sprinkle with lemon juice.

To assemble: toss the salad greens in just enough dressing to make the leaves glisten. Arrange a little mound on each plate, intersperse with slices or the dice of mango. Garnish with a few slices of lobster tail and perhaps a lobster claw. Brush a very little dressing over the lobster and garnish with sprigs of fennel, chervil, and a few borage flowers, if available.

Variation

Lobster and Avocado Salad

Follow the Master Recipe and substitute avocado for the mango. Add some diced unpeeled cucumber to the salad. Serve with homemade mayonnaise. The soft meat mixed with Homemade Mayonnaise (see page 584) is delicious served underneath the salad greens.

How to Cook Crab

First catch your crab! Choose heavy, lively ones. Female crabs tend to yield more meat. They are easy to recognize because they have a broader flap of shell than the male. Meat yield varies, depending on the type and size of the crab and the time of year. Crabs should either be live or ready-cooked from your fish market. If a fresh crab shows no sign of life, do not risk using it.
Put the crab into a saucepan, cover with cold or barely lukewarm water (use ⅔ cup) salt to every 2½ quarts (2.4 liters) water. This sounds like an incredible amount of salt but try it; the crab will taste deliciously sweet.

Cover, bring to a boil and then simmer, allowing 15 minutes for first pound (450g) and 10 minutes for the second and third (I've never come across a crab bigger than that!). Pour off two-thirds of the water half-way through cooking, cover, and steam the crab for the remainder of the time. As soon as it is cooked remove it from the saucepan and let it get cold.

To Extract the Crab Meat

First remove the large claws. Hold the crab with the underside upper-most and lever out the center portion – I do this by catching the little lip of the projecting center shell against the edge of the table and pressing down firmly. The Dead Man's Fingers (gills) usually stay attached and come out with this central piece, so check occasionally; if 1 or 2 remain in the body shell, remove and discard them.

Press your thumb down over the light shell just behind the eyes so that the shell cracks slightly, and then the sac which is underneath can be removed easily and discarded. Everything else inside the body of the crab is edible. The soft meat varies in color from cream to coffee to dark tan, and towards the end of the season it can contain quite a bit of bright orange coral which is stronger in flavor than the rest. Scoop it all out and put it into a bowl. There will also be 1 or 2 teaspoonsful of soft meat in the center portion attached to the small claws – add that to the bowl also.

Scrub the shell and keep it aside if you need it for dressed crab. Crack the large claws with a hammer and extract every bit of white meat from them. Poke out the meat from the small claws, using a lobster pick, skewer, or even the handle of a teaspoon. Mix the brown and white meat together or use separately, depending on the recipe.

Crab Claws

At Ballymaloe we buy whole crabs only, rather than claws, for fear of encouraging fishermen to pull off the claws and discard the bodies. If a crab loses 1 claw, it can feed itself and gradually grow another, but if both claws are removed, it will die slowly from hunger. The other consideration is that the crab meat in the body is really delicious!

Note: 1 lb. (450g) cooked crab in the shell yields about 6–8 ounces (175–225g) crab meat, depending on the time of the year.

Master Recipe

Tomatoes Stuffed with Crab Mayonnaise

Serves 6 as an appetizer

Crab Mayonnaise is versatile. It is delicious used as a filling for a cucumber or tomato ring as well as a stuffing for tomatoes.

It also marries very well with a simple tomato salad or as a first course for a dinner party.

6 very ripe but firm tomatoes
5 ounces (150g) mixed white and brown freshly cooked crab meat (1 medium-sized cooked crab should yield enough)
salt and freshly ground pepper
3/4–1 cup Homemade Mayonnaise (see page 584) or a couple of tablespoons French Dressing instead of some of the mayonnaise
2 teaspoons finely grated onion

Garnish
small lettuce leaves
garden cress or watercress
edible flowers such as chives

Cut the tops off the tomatoes, remove the seeds with a melon baller or a teaspoon, season inside with salt, and turn upside down to drain while you prepare the filling.

Mix the crab meat with the Homemade Mayonnaise, and add 1/2 teaspoon of the onion juice. Taste and season if necessary.

Fill the tomatoes with the crab mixture and replace the lids. Arrange a bed of lettuce and salad greens on a white plate.

Serve 1 large or 2 small tomatoes per person, garnished with sprigs of fresh herbs and edible flowers.

Variation

Cherry Tomatoes Stuffed with Crab Mayonnaise

Follow the Master Recipe but use cherry tomatoes. Garnish with a sprig of fennel or chervil – a fiddle to do but delicious served as a canapé

Ballymaloe Crab Salad

Serves 4–6

We serve this as an appetizer or a main course.

white and brown meat of 2–3 medium crabs, freshly cooked
Homemade Mayonnaise (see page 584)
Ballymaloe French Dressing (see page 225)

Mix the white meat with mayonnaise and the brown meat with French Dressing to taste. Set aside until you are ready to assemble your salads.

Soft Potato Salad with Fresh Herbs

2 cups mashed potato
2 1/2 tablespoons Ballymaloe French Dressing (see page 225)
2 1/2 tablespoons Homemade Mayonnaise (see page 584)
1 generous tablespoon parsley, finely chopped
1 generous tablespoon chives, finely chopped

Mix all the ingredients together, making sure there are no lumps or large pieces of herbs to stick in the pipe. Fill into a pastry bag fitted with a 1-inch (2.5-cm) star nozzle.

Tomato and Mint or Basil Salad

8–12 tomatoes, chopped
salt and freshly ground black pepper
1/2 teaspoon sugar
Ballymaloe French Dressing (see page 225)
2 teaspoons chopped basil or mint

Next make the Tomato Salad. Firm but ripe tomatoes make the best salad. Sometimes one finds rather small sweet fruit with green streaks on the skin near the calyx. They usually come from cold houses with a rather low production. Do not peel them; the skin will be crisp and pleasant to eat and the fruit deliciously sweet. Soft ripe tomatoes also make a good salad, but they must be dipped for an instant in boiling water and peeled. Do not leave them sitting in the water or the flesh will become disgustingly mushy.

Slice the tomatoes finely. Sprinkle with salt, sugar, and several grinds of black pepper. Toss immediately in just enough French dressing to coat the tomatoes and sprinkle with some fresh basil or mint.

Cucumber and Fennel Salad

2 medium cucumbers
salt
2 teaspoons wine vinegar
1–2 1/2 tablespoons sugar
1 teaspoon fennel, finely chopped

Finely slice the cucumber (leave the peel on if you like it), sprinkle with salt and vinegar and lots of sugar, stir in the snipped fennel.

To assemble the salad: pipe a line of potato salad down the center of a white plate, put a little brown crab meat on 1 side and white crab meat on the other. Then place rings of tomato salad beside the white meat and rings of cucumber salad beside the brown meat.

Garnish with fennel or chervil.

Ivan Allen's Dressed Crab

Serves 5–6 as a main course

When I first came to Shanagarry crabs were considered a nuisance by most fishermen because they found their way into the lobster pots and were much less lucrative to sell. The legendary Tommy Sliney, who sold his fish from a donkey and cart on Ballycotton pier, occasionally brought us a few, and it was always a cause for celebration. We would prepare all the other ingredients and then my father-in-law, Ivan Allen, would mix and taste the Dressed Crab.

15 ounces (425g) crab meat, brown and white mixed (2 or 3 crabs should yield this)
1 3/4–2 cups soft white breadcrumbs
2 teaspoons white wine vinegar
2 1/2 tablespoons tomato chutney or relish
2 tablespoons butter
generous pinch of dry mustard or 1 level teaspoon French mustard
salt and freshly ground pepper
3/4 cup White Sauce (see page 580)

Topping
2½ cups Buttered Crumbs (see page 248)

Preheat the oven to 350°F (180°C).

Thoroughly scrub the crab shells. Mix together all the ingredients except the buttered crumbs, taste carefully and correct the seasoning. Fill the shells and sprinkle the tops with the buttered crumbs.

Bake in the preheated oven, for about 15–20 minutes, or until heated through and brown on top. Flash under the broiler, if necessary, to crisp the crumbs.

Crab Cakes

Crab cakes can be made with the same mixture. We add finely chopped chile and lots of fresh cilantro, then flour, egg, crumb, and deep fry.

Ballymaloe Fish Terrine with Cherry Tomato Sauce

Serves 10–12 as an appetizer

A perfect appetizer for a summer lunch or wedding, it can be made several days ahead and freezes well. Most fish terrines are based on sole and, though they are delicious when served hot, they can be very dull and bland when cold. This layered fish pâté is a great favorite at Ballymaloe. Its content varies depending on the fish available to us.

Potted Shrimp (see page 84)
Smoked Mackerel Pâté (see page 85)
Smoked Salmon Pâté (see page 85)
chopped parsley and chives

5- x 8-inch (12.5- x 20.5-cm) loaf pan or, better still, a longer, thinner mold, if available.

Line the pan neatly with a double thickness of plastic wrap.

Make the potted shrimp. Let cool, pour into the pan in an even layer, sprinkle with a little chopped parsley, and chill while you prepare the next layer.

Make the smoked mackerel pâté. When the shrimp have set hard, spread an even layer of the mackerel on top. Sprinkle with a little more parsley or chopped chives. Refrigerate while you prepare the salmon layer.

Lastly, make the salmon pâté and spread this final layer onto the fish terrine. Cover with plastic wrap to compact the layers and chill until needed.

Cherry Tomato Sauce

1 lb. (450g) very ripe cherry tomatoes
1 tablespoon onion, chopped
2 teaspoons balsamic vinegar
2½ tablespoons olive oil
1 teaspoon salt
1 teaspoon sugar
freshly ground black pepper
2 basil leaves or 4 fresh mint leaves

Chop the tomatoes and whizz briefly in a blender with the other ingredients. Strain, taste and correct seasoning.

To serve the terrine, turn out onto a chilled dish and remove the plastic wrap. For a buffet, decorate with salad greens and with any fresh herbs and herb flowers you can find. Serve in slices and offer a little tomato coulis with each helping. Alternatively, pour a little cherry tomato sauce onto individual white plates, place a slice of the fish terrine on top, and garnish with tiny sprigs of fennel or alfalfa sprouts and fennel flowers, if available. Serve with Melba Toast (see page 78).

Ballymaloe Fish Mousse with Shrimp Butter Sauce

Serves 16–20

This recipe makes a large number of light fish mousses. It is a favorite on the menu at Ballymaloe and can be served with many sauces. Although the mousse is light it is also very rich, so do serve it in small ramekins. They can be done in several batches as the raw mixture keeps perfectly overnight, covered, in the fridge. The fish must be absolutely spanking fresh for this recipe, otherwise it will taste stale as there is nothing to hide a taint. A teaspoon of salt may sound excessive but it is vital to season the raw mixture well, or the mousse will be bland.

12 ounces (350g) very fresh fillets of whiting or pollock, skinned and totally free of bone or membrane
1 teaspoon salt
pinch of freshly ground white pepper
1 egg and 1 egg white
3 cups heavy cream, chilled
Beurre Blanc recipe x 2 (see page 583)
½ lb. (225g) shrimp, cooked and peeled
1 teaspoon butter

Garnish
sprigs of chervil
whole cooked shrimp (1–3 per person), optional

individual ramekins, 2½ fl. oz. (60ml) capacity, 2-inch (5-cm) diameter x 1 inch (2.5cm) deep

Chill the bowl of the food processor while you trim the fish.

Cut the fillets into small dice. Purée in the chilled bowl of the food processor. Add the salt and freshly ground pepper and then add the egg and egg white and continue to purée until it is well incorporated. Rest and chill in the fridge for 30 minutes.

Heat the oven to 400°F (200°C). Line the ramekins with plastic wrap or brush with melted butter. When the fish has rested, pour in the cream, put the bowl back on to the food processor, and whizz again until it is just incorporated. Taste and correct seasoning. (If tasting raw fish doesn't appeal, poach a little blob in a pan of simmering water.)

Fill the ramekins with mousse and put them in a bain marie. Cover with a pricked sheet of aluminum foil or wax paper. Pour boiling water into the bain marie. Put it in the oven and bake for 20–30 minutes. The mousses should feel just firm in the center and will keep perfectly for 20–30 minutes in a plate-warming oven.

Meanwhile, make the Beurre Blanc Sauce and keep warm. When the mousses are cooked, remove them to a warm place. Toss the shrimp in a sauté pan in a very little foaming butter until hot through, then add them to the sauce, taste, and correct the seasoning: the sauce should be very thin and light.

To serve: unmold each mousse onto a warm plate. Spoon a little hot sauce on top and garnish with shrimp and sprigs of fresh chervil.

Master Recipe
Fish Cakes with Olive and Anchovy Butter

Makes 8

Originally an economical way of using up leftover scraps of boiled fish, fish cakes of all kinds are now a "must have" on trendy menus. They are absolutely scrummy when carefully made and served hot with a small dollop of flavored butter melting on top.

2 tablespoons butter
1 cup onion, finely chopped
1/2 cup mashed potato
8 ounces (225g) cold leftover fish, e.g., salmon, cod, haddock, hake (a proportion of smoked fish such as haddock or mackerel is good), flaked
2 tablespoons fish sauce (nam pla), optional 1 egg yolk
1 generous tablespoon parsley, chopped
salt and freshly ground pepper
seasoned flour
1 beaten egg
fresh white breadcrumbs
Clarified Butter (see page 103) or a mixture of butter and oil for frying

Olive and Anchovy Butter (see page 588)

First make the Olive and Anchovy Butter and refrigerate.

Next make the fish cakes: melt the butter in a saucepan, toss in the onion, cover, and sweat over a gentle heat for 4–5 minutes, until soft but not colored. Scrape the contents of the pan into a bowl, add the mashed potato and the flaked cooked fish, fish sauce (if using), egg yolk, and parsley. Season well with salt and pepper. Taste. Form the mixture into fish cakes about 2 ounces (50g) each. Coat them first in flour, then in beaten egg, and finally in crumbs. Chill until needed, then cook on a medium heat in clarified butter until golden on both sides. Serve piping hot with Olive and Anchovy Butter. Accompany with Tomato Fondue (see page 188) and a good green salad (see page 225).

Variation
Spicy Fish Cakes

Follow the Master Recipe and add 1–2 seeded and chopped chiles to the onion and substitute freshly chopped cilantro for parsley in the recipe above. Serve with Tomato and Chile Sauce (see page 590) and garnish with sprigs of fresh cilantro.

Tiny Fish Cakes

Follow the Master Recipe and form into tiny fish cakes. Serve as canapés.

Thai Fish Cakes with Cucumber Relish

Serves 4

We don't have the same varieties of fish (redfish or red snapper) as they have in Bangkok, where we ate these delicious morsels, but they do taste similar and are nonetheless addictive when made with cod or hake. Green beans may be used instead of the yard-long beans used in Thailand.

10 ounces (275g) cod or hake
Chile Paste (see right)
1 egg
1/4 cup fish sauce (nam pla)
1 teaspoon sugar
5 kaffir lime leaves, stem removed and shredded very, very finely
7 or 8 green beans, finely sliced across

Thai Cucumber Relish
2 cucumbers
5 tablespoons rice vinegar
2–4 teaspoons sugar
1 teaspoon salt
1 small red bird chile, chopped
1 shallot, very thinly sliced
2 1/2 tablespoons hot water

Chile Paste
3 dried long red chiles, seeded and chopped
2 garlic cloves, crushed
1 stalk lemongrass, finely chopped
1 teaspoon galangal, peeled and chopped
1 cilantro root
1 teaspoon lime zest (best to use kaffir lime if you can find it)
1 teaspoon kapi shrimp paste, roasted
10 white peppercorns, ground

sunflower or peanut oil for deep-frying

Garnish
fresh cilantro leaves
finely sliced chile

First make the Thai Cucumber Relish. Peel the cucumber and cut in half lengthwise. Seed it with a melon baller or teaspoon and then slice the cucumber into thin slices at an angle. Mix the remainder of the ingredients in a bowl and stir to dissolve the sugar and salt. Add the cucumber slices, stir, and let the relish stand for at least 1 hour before serving.

Meanwhile make the Chile Paste by pounding all the ingredients in a mortar and pestle. Alternatively use a food processor to purée all the ingredients together using as little water as possible.

Next make the fish cakes: put the fish, Chile Paste, egg, fish sauce, and sugar into a food processor and blend well. Transfer to a bowl. Add the lime leaves and beans and mix well until sticky in texture. Shape the mixture into little disks 2 inches (5cm) in diameter and 1/4-inch (5mm) thick. Deep-fry the fish cakes in hot oil for about 4–5 minutes or until golden.

Serve with Cucumber Relish and garnish with fresh cilantro leaves and chile.

Smoked Eel with Brown Bread and Lemon

Good smoked eel needs no embellishment.

freshly smoked eel
segments of lemon
green salad
brown bread

Skin the eel and cut into 3–4-inch (8–10-cm) lengths. Serve 2 or 3 pieces per person either on or off the bone. Garnish with a segment of lemon and a little green salad. Serve with fresh brown bread.

Deh-ta Hsiung's Shrimp Satay

Serves 4–6

Shrimp, or cubes of monkfish are marinated in spices, then threaded onto bamboo satay sticks and cooked on the barbecue or under the broiler. Satays are terrifically versatile. They may be served as an appetizer with drinks, or as a light meal when served with rice and salad. The marinade is also good for pork or chicken.

1 lb. (450g) raw shrimp
1 garlic clove, finely chopped
2 shallots, or 1 small onion, finely chopped
2 1/2 tablespoons light soy sauce
1 tablespoon plus 1 teaspoon sugar
1 tablespoon plus 1 teaspoon freshly ground coriander
1 tablespoon plus 1 teaspoon lemon juice or red wine vinegar

1–2 tablespoons vegetable oil (for brushing)
1 cup Peanut Sauce (see page 275)

24–26 bamboo satay sticks (soak satay sticks in cold water for at least 30 minutes)

Peel and drain the shrimp, marinate with all the remaining ingredients for at least 1 hour. Thread the shrimp onto bamboo satay sticks. Be careful to keep the shrimp down to one end. Brush each satay with a little oil and char-grill until just cooked, turning frequently. Serve hot with Peanut Sauce.

Monkfish Spiedino with Summer Marjoram Sauce

Serves 4

There are lots of variations you can do on the kebab theme. This Italian spiedino is quick, easy, and irresistible. Use unsmoked bacon and leave out the peppercorns or vary the herbs, if you like.

1 lb. (450g) monkfish, cut into 1-inch (2.5-cm) cubes
4–6 smoked bacon strips, cut into 1-inch (2.5-cm) squares
1 small red pepper, cut into 1-inch (2.5-cm) squares
bulbs of tiny scallions (optional)
1 level teaspoon whole black peppercorns
1 level teaspoon sea salt, or kosher salt
2 1/2 tablespoons herb fennel, freshly chopped
olive oil

Summer Marjoram Sauce

2 heaped tablespoons annual marjoram leaves (with stalks removed)
1 scant level teaspoon sea salt, or kosher salt
1 teaspoon sugar
1 tablespoon plus 1 teaspoon lemon juice
1/3–1/2 cup extra-virgin olive oil

Garnish
segments of lemon

First make the Summer Marjoram Sauce: pound the marjoram with the sea salt and sugar in a mortar and pestle until completely crushed. Slowly add the lemon juice and olive oil as for mayonnaise. Set aside.

Thread the monkfish, bacon, pepper, and scallions alternately on 4 skewers. Crack the black peppercorns in a mortar and pestle, add the sea salt and fennel.

Spread this mixture out onto a work surface or plate. Roll the filled skewers in it, then cover with plastic wrap and refrigerate until the barbecue or char-grill is hot enough for cooking. Brush the spiedini with a little olive oil – they usually take about 4–5 minutes on each side. Serve drizzled with Summer Marjoram Sauce and garnished with lemon segments.

Note: The spiedino can be cooked under a radiant broiler also. Serve with Beurre Blanc (see page 583) for a change.

Ballycotton Fish Pie

Serves 6–8

Many different types of really fresh fish may be used for a fish pie, so feel free to adapt this recipe a little to suit your needs. Periwinkles are a good and cheap addition and a little smoked haddock is tasty also, but use sparingly unless you want the smoky flavor to predominate. A little left-over Hollandaise Sauce will enrich the pie.

2½ lbs. (1.1kg) fillets of cod, haddock, ling, hake, salmon, pollock, or monkfish, or a mixture (use up to ½ lb./225g smoked haddock)
18 mussels, optional
salt and freshly ground pepper
Béchamel Sauce made with 2½ cups (600ml) whole milk and a very little cream, optional, (see page 580)
1 small onion, finely chopped
2 tablespoons butter
2 cups mushrooms, preferably flat, sliced
2½ cups milk
Roux made with 2 tablespoons butter and ¼ cup flour (see page 580)
1–2 tablespoons heavy cream (optional)
2½ tablespoons parsley, chopped
1 generous tablespoon dill, chopped
4 hard-boiled eggs, shelled and chopped (optional)
4 cups Fluffy Mashed Potato or Scallion Champ (see page 182)

Cut the fish into 5-ounce (150-g) chunks. Season with salt and freshly ground pepper. Check that all the mussels are tightly shut. Wash them, put into a shallow pan in a single layer, cover, and cook over a medium heat just until the shells open – 3 or 4 minutes will do. Cool.

Make the Béchamel Sauce (see page 580).

Meanwhile, sweat the onion in a little melted butter over a gentle heat until soft but not colored, and remove to a plate. Increase the heat, sauté the sliced mushrooms in the hot pan, season with salt and freshly ground pepper and add to the onions. Put the fish into a wide sauté or frying pan, in a single layer, cover with the milk, season with salt and pepper. Cover and simmer gently until the fish is just cooked – no more than 3–4 minutes. Remove the fish with a slotted spoon, carefully removing any bones or skin. Bring the liquid to a boil and thicken with Roux, add a little cream and the parsley, dill, eggs, mushrooms, fish, and mussels. Stir gently, taste, and correct the seasoning. Spoon into 1 large or 6–8 small dishes and pipe potato or Scallion Champ on top. The pie may be prepared ahead to this point.

To cook or reheat, put into a moderate oven, preheated to 350°F (180°C), for about 10–15 minutes if filling and potato are warm, or 30 minutes if reheating from cold. Flash under the broiler if necessary, to brown the top. Serve with Garlic Butter (see page 588) or Parsley Butter (see page 586) if you want.

Seafood Okra Gumbo

Serves 6 as a main course

Say Gumbo and you immediately think of New Orleans. Summer is the time when all the main ingredients are at their best, though you can enjoy it all year round. As with most stews, gumbo is best prepared in advance, to the point before the shrimp are added, to let the flavors marry. When reheating, stir frequently and take care not to overcook the shrimp.

2 lbs. (900g) fresh or frozen shrimp, heads on
2 small fresh crabs
4 quarts (3.6 liters) water
2½ tablespoons vegetable oil for frying
18 ounces (500g) fresh okra, sliced into 1-inch (2.5-cm) rounds
¾ cup vegetable oil
1 cup flour
2 cups onion, chopped
1 medium green pepper, chopped
⅔ cup celery, chopped
1 garlic clove, peeled and finely chopped
1 x 14-ounce (400-g) can Italian tomatoes, chopped
2 bay leaves
2 teaspoons salt (to taste)
½ teaspoon black pepper
½ teaspoon white pepper
¼ teaspoon cayenne pepper

Peel and de-vein the shrimp (see page 254) and set aside, covered, in the fridge. Rinse the shells and heads and place in a large stainless-steel pot with 2½ quarts (2.4 liters) of cold water. Bring to a boil, reduce the heat, and simmer for 30–45 minutes. Strain, discard the shells and heads, and set the stock aside.

Meanwhile, wash the crabs under running water, drop into a pan of 5 cups of boiling water and simmer for 20–30 minutes. Strain, reserving the stock, and let the crabs cool. When you can handle the shells, snap off both claws then break open the shell and extract all the meat. Set aside.

In a heavy-bottomed skillet or large frying pan, heat the oil and add the sliced okra. Sauté over a medium heat for 10–15 minutes or until soft but not soggy. Heat the remaining vegetable oil in a deep-sided, heavy metal flameproof casserole dish and add the flour to make a Roux (see page 580). Add the onions, pepper, celery, and garlic, and sauté, stirring occasionally, until tender. Don't be concerned if some of the vegetables stick to the bottom; their caramelized juices add flavor to the dish.

Add the tomatoes, bay leaves, and the seasonings, and cook for about 10 minutes before adding the okra slices. Cook gently for a further 10 minutes.

Add the reserved crab stock and half the shrimp stock. Bring to a boil, stirring constantly, then lower the heat, partially cover, and simmer for 30 minutes. If the gumbo becomes too thick, adjust with more shrimp stock. Check the seasoning. Add the crab meat and simmer for 10 minutes, then add the peeled shrimp, return to a boil, then simmer for a further 5 minutes, until the shrimp are firm and pink. Serve in large bowls with plain boiled rice.

Cod, Sweet Potato, and Coconut Stew

Serves 4–6

This one-pot stew, adapted from a recipe sourced by Philippa Davenport, comes from the Solomon Islands. Omit the brazil nuts if you wish, but they add a delicious crunch. You can use white- or orange-fleshed potatoes. It is very quick to prepare, making a great supper dish for mid-week.

1 lb. (450g) cod (steaks or fillets)
1 lb. (450g) sweet potatoes, peeled and cut into 1-inch (2.5-cm) chunks
2½ tablespoons extra-virgin olive oil
1 medium onion, peeled and chopped
3 garlic cloves, peeled and finely chopped
1-inch (2.5-cm) cube ginger, peeled and finely chopped
2½ cups homemade Fish Stock (see page 37)
⅔ cup creamed coconut
1 x 14-ounce (400-g) can Italian tomatoes, chopped
⅓ cup shelled brazil nuts
2 tablespoons freshly chopped cilantro
salt and freshly ground pepper

Cut the fish into large chunks, removing any bones, and set aside on a plate at room temperature. Put the peeled chunks of sweet potato into cold water, to prevent discoloration. Heat the oil in a deep-sided, cast-iron flameproof casserole dish and sweat the onion for 3 minutes until it is soft but not brown. Add the garlic and ginger and cook gently for a further 4–5 minutes.

Drain the sweet potato, add to the casserole dish, and stir well to coat. Cook for about 3 minutes, then add the hot fish stock and creamed coconut. Cook over a low heat, covered, until the coconut has melted, stirring from time to time. Then add the tomatoes and simmer, uncovered, for 7–10 minutes, or until the sweet potato is just cooked.
Add the fish pieces and cook gently, covered, for a further 5 minutes, or until the fish is done. Taste and season. Meanwhile, roughly chop the brazil nuts (you may also toast them under a preheated broiler for 3–5 minutes for extra flavor).

To serve: sprinkle the chopped brazil nuts and cilantro over the stew. This makes a meal in itself, but you can serve with fresh warm hunks of bread.

Seafood Chowder

Serves 6

A chowder is a wonderfully substantial fish soup; in fact it could almost be classified as a stew. It is certainly a meal in itself and there are plenty of variations on the theme. Firm-fleshed fish works best. The base of the chowder can be prepared in advance.

1½ lbs. (700g) haddock, monkfish, cod, or other firm white fish (or a mixture), free of bones and skin
1 lb. (450g) mixed, cooked shellfish – mussels, clams, scallops, shrimp, and the cooking liquor
1½ tablespoons olive or sunflower oil
8–10 strips bacon, cut into ¼-inch (5-mm) dice
1½–2 cups onions, chopped
¼ cup flour
1 quart (960ml) homemade Fish Stock (see page 37) or, as a last resort, water
2 cups milk
bouquet garni made up of 6 parsley stalks, 2 sprigs of thyme, and 1 bay leaf
6 medium-sized potatoes, cut into ¼-inch (5-mm) dice
salt and freshly ground pepper
pinch of mace
pinch of cayenne pepper
⅔ cup light cream

Garnish
freshly chopped parsley and chives

Heat the oil in a stainless-steel pot and brown the bacon well until it is crisp and golden. Add the onion, cover, and sweat for a few minutes over a low heat. Stir in the flour and cook for 1–2 minutes. Add the fish stock or water gradually, then the milk, bouquet garni, and potatoes. Season well with salt, pepper, mace, and cayenne. Cover, and simmer until the potatoes are almost cooked – this takes 5–6 minutes. The chowder may be prepared ahead up to this point.

Cut the fish into 1-inch (2.5-cm) cubes. Add to the pot as soon as the tip of a knife will go through the potato. Simmer gently for 3–4 minutes, stir in the cream, and add the shellfish and any liquor obtained from opening the mussels or clams. When the soup returns to a boil, remove from the heat.

Remember that the fish will continue to cook in the heat of the chowder, so make sure it is not overcooked. Taste, correct the seasoning, and sprinkle with freshly chopped parsley and chives.

Crusty hot white bread or hot crackers are usually served with a chowder.

Tip Stir the chowder as little as possible once the fish has been added to avoid it breaking up. Be careful not to overcook the fish, particularly if using softer varieties like cod.

poultry

poultry

Although we have lots of free-range hens in the fields around the cookery school, we do not rear our own poultry for the table. Locally produced free-range and organic chicken is now available at the farmers' market in Midleton. This market, which I started with a group of producers in June 2000, has been warmly welcomed by producers and consumers alike – local food for local people.

Nora Ahearne sells us wonderful, free-range ducks, geese, and turkeys, and when she delivers them to the school I introduce her to the students so they can meet the person who rears this delicious poultry. The quality and taste are, for many people, a forgotten flavor, and for those brought up on mass-produced supermarket chickens, it is a revelation.

Another local farmer rears us plump guinea fowl. The flavor of these birds is deliciously gamey. They are much sought after by local restauranteurs and are a favorite on our menu at Ballymaloe House.

Free-range versus Intensively-reared Chickens

Consumers are becoming more and more concerned as they learn about the conditions under which most of the poultry on the supermarket shelves have been raised – of intensively-reared birds fed on a cocktail of meal, which can include antibiotics, hormones, anti-depressants, muscle strengtheners, and growth promoters. Not to mention the over-crowding in the sheds where they are stacked with no natural light....

A large proportion of the poultry available nowadays is intensively reared. Don't be misled by the labels. The term "free-range" does not always guarantee that the chicken has led a contented life pecking around a farmyard. There are varying degrees of "free-range", so ask lots of questions and keep looking until you find a good source. The description "maize fed" can also be misleading. Unless specifically stated, they are simply intensively-reared birds that have been partly fed on corn meal, and are not necessarily superior to other chickens.

To add to the confusion, a large percentage of the chicken sold at present in the European Union is imported from Thailand and Brazil. Once it arrives in the EU at a registered abattoir, it can then be re-labeled and miraculously turned into an "Irish" or "English" chicken. This causes resentment among producers and consumers who wish to be able to source and buy poultry that is reared in their own country.

A true free-range chicken must have access to grass and be able to range freely. Organic birds will, in addition, be fed on specially compounded meal made from organically grown grain. No poultry or fish protein supplements or growth stimulants are added to their diet and they are allowed to grow to full size naturally.

Poussins (squab chickens) are intensively-reared baby chickens – about 4 weeks old. Although they are tender, they often have little flavor, and even less meat. Having said that, I have tasted excellent French poussins.

Buying

Seek out free-range, certified organic poultry where you can be sure that the birds were fed an additive-free diet, had access to open air, and were free to range. It takes 37–41 days to produce a conventional chicken in an intensive system. It takes more than twice that long to rear an organic chicken. Consequently the feed and production cost is much higher. So, if you want this kind of bird, find a good local supplier and pay them what they need to produce the quality you seek. This might be double the price (or more) of a conventional supermarket chicken. The choice is yours.

Duck, guinea fowl, quail, and turkey, are also intensively reared. Geese, on the other hand, are difficult to breed in this way and tend to be reared more extensively. You may want to ask questions about the content of their feed.

When choosing poultry, look for meaty birds with skin that's creamy-white to yellow and that are free of bruises, feathers, and torn or dry skin.

Quite often nowadays, poultry is sold without their giblets – this is mostly because people don't know how to cope with them. This is a shame, as they're invaluable for making a flavorsome stock. The hearts and gizzards are also excellent, added to a salade tiède.

Free-range poultry needs to hang for slightly longer than intensively-reared birds, as they've had more exercise because of the outdoors life and can, therefore, be a little tougher.

Salmonella and Campylobacter

Besides being economical, poultry offers high-quality protein. It has also, however, been blamed for almost 25 per cent of food poisoning outbreaks in recent years – more than any other type of food.

Although salmonella has had more prominent press coverage, three times as many cases of campylobacter infection have been reported.

Unfortunately, buying organic does not necessarily mean that your meat will be disease-free. In a recent study, while salmonella was found to be less common in organic chicken than intensively-reared birds, there was little difference in the occurrence of campylobacter.

Both campylobacter and salmonella bacteria cause infection, although the symptoms are different. Neither is usually fatal, but they can cause serious complications in the very young, old, and pregnant – whose immune systems are unable to successfully fight off infection.

Infection is usually contracted by eating food that has been contaminated by the bacterium and has not been properly stored or cooked. The best way to kill the bacteria is to ensure that poultry is cooked through thoroughly, and to wash your hands after touching uncooked meat. It is perfectly possible to avoid infection by taking sensible preventative precautions. These are outlined in the Storing and Cooking sections below. Countries, such as Sweden and Norway, have also shown that it is possible to completely eliminate salmonella from their flocks. We can only hope that the government here makes it a priority to learn from their example.

Storing

Poultry, particularly chicken, should be used while it's fresh (certainly within a day or two of purchase) – or frozen right away.

If you've bought your poultry from a supermarket, take it out of the plastic wrapping as soon as you get home, put it on a plate, cover with plastic wrap, and store in the fridge. Try not to let poultry sit at room temperature for more than 15 minutes. Always store raw meat at the bottom of the refrigerator, to ensure that it cannot drip down and cross-contaminate cooked meat and other foods.

Cooking

Make sure that frozen poultry is fully defrosted before cooking it. Never leave it to thaw on a counter. Ideally it should be allowed to defrost in the refrigerator, but a quicker method is to submerge it (inside a water-proof freezer bag) in cold running water. If you use a microwave for defrosting, the bird should be cooked immediately after thawing as microwaving might well have already started the cooking process.

Scrub, wash, and dry the cutting board and any utensils that you've used to prepare raw chicken before using them again. Try to keep one side of your cutting board for raw poultry only, and stick to the other side for any other food. In catering, separate boards are obligatory.

It is essential that chicken is cooked through properly, in order to safe-guard against salmonella or campylobacter poisoning. To ensure that a roast is thoroughly cooked, roast it at 350°F (180°C), to an internal temperature of 185°F (85°C). Let it cook without interruption. Many chefs now use a meat thermometer to check for readiness, but home cooks can judge by the color of the juices, which should run clear when a skewer is inserted into the thickest part of the thigh. If you stuff your chicken, pack it loosely and ensure that the center of the stuffing reaches 165°F (75°C). Never cook stuffed poultry in a microwave, and ensure that leftover poultry and stuffing are refrigerated separately.

Poultry is remarkably versatile, and every part of it can be used. Be sure to keep the giblets, wing tips, and carcasses to make stock for soups, stews, casseroles, and sauces. On the European continent, chickens come with their head and feet still on. When added to soups and stews, these bits give extra flavor and depth.

Many of the recipes for chicken, turkey, and guinea fowl and, indeed, pheasant are interchangeable – although you'll need to adjust the cooking time and quantities.

Duck and goose are brown meat throughout. They're naturally fatty and some chefs suggest pricking the bird with a skewer before cooking, to let some of the fat run out. We don't do that. I would simply recommend that you find a good-quality bird to begin with, then all you will need to do is rub a little salt over the breast before roasting it. Save the fat for roast or sauté potatoes and confit (it'll keep for months in your fridge). Many cooks value duck and goose fat so highly that they buy it in cans.

Master Recipe

Pan-grilled Chicken Breasts with Cardamom

Serves 8

A spice crust improves the flavor of chicken breasts immeasurably – a single spice or a combination of spices may be used. The chicken breasts can be marinated as in this recipe or simply applied as a crust.

8 chicken breasts
1 teaspoon cardamom seeds
1 teaspoon black peppercorns
a good pinch cayenne pepper
5 tablespoons olive oil

Lemon Butter (see page 588)

Flatten the chicken breasts slightly. Pound the cardamom and peppercorns together in a mortar and add the cayenne and olive oil. Dip the chicken breasts in this marinade, cover, and let marinate for about 2 hours.

Pan-grill the chicken breasts (see Technique right) or barbecue them on an oiled rack about 5 inches (12.5cm) from the coals, cook for several minutes each side, brushing with extra marinade while cooking. Serve with Lemon Butter, a good green salad, and a Red Chile Mayonnaise (see page 585).

Variations

Pan-grilled Chicken Breasts with Persian Rice

Follow the Master Recipe and serve it with Persian Rice (see page 126).

Tip: Seek out free-range and organic poultry, whenever possible.

Left: Pan-grilled Chicken Breasts with Parsley Salad and Sun-dried Tomatoes (see page 272)

Pan-grilled Chicken Breasts with Tomato and Basil Sauce

Follow the Master Recipe and serve with Tomato and Basil Sauce (see page 594).

Pan-grilled Chicken with Rosemary

Follow the Master Recipe and substitute 1–2 tablespoons of freshly chopped rosemary for the cardamom, peppercorns, and cayenne. If time permits, marinate for 10–30 minutes. Thyme and marjoram also greatly enhance the flavor of chicken breasts.

Serve with any of the following: Tomato and Chile Jam (see page 512), Sweet Chile Sauce (available in Asian groceries and many supermarkets), Chile and Cilantro Butter (see page 588) or Char-grilled Summer Vegetables (see page 199).

Cajun Chicken with Spicy Mayonnaise

For six chicken breasts, substitute the following Cajun Spice mix for the cardamom and peppercorns in the Master Recipe.

1 teaspoon each salt, dried oregano, and dried thyme leaves.
1/2 teaspoon each freshly ground black pepper, white pepper, onion powder, garlic powder, paprika, and cayenne

Mix the spices. Brush the chicken breasts with oil and dip into the spices. Cook on a hot grill-pan. Serve with Red Chile Mayonnaise (see page 585) or Tomato and Chile Jam (see page 512).

Cumin and Coriander-crusted Chicken with Cucumber and Mint Raita, and Ballymaloe Tomato Relish

Follow the Master Recipe and substitute 1/4 cup freshly roasted and ground cumin seeds and 1/4 cup freshly roasted and ground coriander seeds for the cardamom, peppercorns, and cayenne. Serve with Cucumber and Mint Raita, and Ballymaloe Tomato Relish.

Pan-grilled Chicken Breasts with Fire and Brimstone Sauce and Rustic Roast Potatoes

Follow the Master Recipe, and substitute Fire and Brimstone Sauce (see page 596) for the cardamoms, peppercorns, and cayenne.

Fill a little bowl of sauce and put it on each plate for dipping. Add a few sprigs of fresh cilantro or flat-leaf parsley.

Note: Chicken fingers (the little inside fillet of the chicken breast), may be used as a substitute in any of the above recipes.

How to Pan-grill Chicken Breasts

Use skinless chicken breasts, remove the fillet, refrigerate, and save for another dish.

Heat a cast-iron grill-pan until quite hot. Brush each chicken breast with olive oil, season with salt and freshly ground pepper. Place the chicken breasts on the hot grill-pan for about 1 minute, change to the opposite direction to get criss-cross markings on the chicken breast. Repeat on the other side. If the chicken breasts are very large, the grill-pan may now be transferred to a preheated moderate oven 350°F (180°C). They can take from 8–15 minutes to cook, depending on size.

Pan-grilled Chicken Breasts with Parsley Salad and Sun-dried Tomatoes

Serves 8

Separate the fillet from the underneath side of the meat, cook separately or slice thinly at an angle and quickly stir-fry. The chicken breast cooks more evenly when the fillet is removed.

8 chicken breasts
olive oil
salt and freshly ground pepper

Basil Dressing (makes a large quantity)
1 good handful fresh basil
2 1/2 cups olive oil
2/3 cup rice wine vinegar
1 shallot, finely chopped
2 garlic cloves crushed
salt and freshly ground pepper

Parsley Salad
4 handfuls Italian and curly parsley, de-stalked
Worcestershire sauce
8 chopped Sun-Dried Tomatoes (see page 188)
slivers of Parmesan cheese (Parmigiano Reggiano)

First make the basil dressing: whizz the basil with the oil, vinegar, shallot, garlic, and seasoning in a blender or food processor. Keep aside.

Just before serving, brush the chicken breasts with olive oil and cook on a preheated grill-pan until just cooked through and golden on both sides and criss-crossed with markings from the grill-pan. Season with salt and pepper.

To serve: put a pan-grilled chicken breast on each plate. Toss the parsley in a little of the basil dressing, and sprinkle with a little Worcestershire sauce. Put a portion of parsley salad on each plate, sprinkle with a few pieces of sun-dried tomato and slivers of parmesan cheese. Serve immediately with Rustic Roast Potatoes (see page 181) or Buffalo Chips (see page 184).

Pan-grilled Chicken Breasts with Couscous, Raisins, and Pistachio Nuts

Serves 8

Hot peppery harissa smeared over the pan-grilled chicken breasts adds even more excitement. Harissa can be bought ready-made in tubes and jars; this North African spice mixture is best made from hot dried red chile peppers, garlic, coriander and cumin seeds.

2 cups couscous
1–2 tablespoons olive oil
2 1/2 cups well-flavored homemade Chicken Stock (see page 36)
1/2 cup raisins
1/2 cup pistachio nuts, or toasted pine nuts
3/4 cup split almonds, toasted
salt and freshly ground pepper
8 chicken breasts
5 tablespoons extra-virgin olive oil
a little butter or extra-virgin olive oil, optional
harissa, optional

Garnish
sprigs of fresh cilantro

Preheat the oven to 350°F (180°C).

Put the couscous into a bowl. Sprinkle with a few drops of olive oil, and rub with fingers to coat the grains. Cover the couscous in its own volume of chicken stock or water (2 cups) and let soak for 15 minutes, stirring every now and then. When the liquid has been absorbed, add the raisins, and pistachio or pine nuts, and almonds, and season with salt and pepper. Put into a heavy covered dish and heat through in the oven for about 20 minutes.

To cook the chicken (see Technique on page 271): brush the chicken breasts with the olive oil and cook on a preheated grill-pan until just cooked through and golden on both sides, and criss-crossed with markings from the grill-pan. Season with salt and pepper.

How to prepare a Chicken Paillarde

An excellent way to prepare chicken breasts particularly for the barbecue – they cook faster and more evenly.

Remove the fillet from each chicken breast and save for another dish. Slice each chicken breast from top to bottom, so that you can open it out like a book.

Flatten with the palm of your hand to ensure a good, flat shape.

Add butter or olive oil to the couscous to taste. Season with salt and freshly ground pepper. Spread a little harissa (if using) on the pan-grilled chicken breasts.

To serve, divide the couscous into hot deep plates. Put a chicken breast on top, de-grease the grill-pan, and de-glaze with a little well-flavored chicken stock. Garnish with sprigs of cilantro and serve immediately.

Char-grilled Chicken Paillarde with a Smoked Chile Butter

Serves 8

A favorite recipe inspired by Belfast's super-chefs, Paul and Jeanne Rankin.

8 chicken breasts
5 tablespoons olive oil
2 1/2 tablespoons freshly chopped herbs (parsley, marjoram, rosemary, thyme)
salt and freshly cracked pepper

Smoked Chile Butter
1 stick (1/2 cup) soft butter at room temperature
2 teaspoons lemon juice, freshly squeezed
1 generous tablespoon cilantro, freshly chopped
2 anchovies, chopped
2 teaspoons shallots, chopped
2 1/2 tablespoons smoked barbecue sauce (or smoked ketchup)
2 smoked jalepeño (chipotle) chiles or fresh chiles, sliced
salt and freshly ground pepper
Char-grilled Vegetables (see page 199)

Garnish
fresh cilantro leaves

First prepare the Chicken Paillarde (see left).

Mix the olive oil and herbs together in a shallow dish. Season each chicken paillarde with salt and pepper and coat both sides in the herbed oil.

Then make the Chile Butter: put all the ingredients into a food processor and whizz for a few seconds until almost smooth.

Next, char-grill the vegetables and keep them warm. Cook the chicken on the char-grill or grill-pan for approx. 4 minutes on each side, turning each after a few minutes to give a nice criss-cross effect.

Place a mixture of grilled vegetables in the middle of a warm plate, put a chicken paillarde on top and a blob of Smoked Chile Butter. Garnish with fresh cilantro leaves.

Master Recipe

Chicken Breasts with Mushrooms and Marjoram

Serves 4

Soaking the chicken breasts in milk gives them a tender and moist texture but it is not essential for this dish. We often serve this recipe with orzo, a pasta which looks like grains of rice and is all the rage in our house nowadays.

4 chicken breasts
milk (optional)
salt and freshly ground pepper
2 tablespoons butter
2 tablespoons shallot or scallion, chopped
1 cup sliced mushrooms
2/3 cup homemade Chicken Stock (see page 36)
2/3 cup cream
1 tablespoon parsley or marjoram, chopped

Garnish
sprigs of flat-leaf parsley

Soak the chicken breasts in milk, just enough to cover them, for about 1 hour. Discard the milk and dry with paper towels. Season with salt and pepper (this step is not essential).

Choose a sauté pan just large enough to take the chicken breasts in a single layer. Heat half the butter in the sauté pan until foaming, put in the chicken breasts and turn them in the butter; do not brown. Cover with a piece of wax paper and the lid. Cook on a gentle heat for 5–7 minutes or until just barely cooked.

Meanwhile, sweat the shallots gently in a pan in the remaining butter. Increase the heat, add the mushrooms, season with salt and pepper, and cook for 3–4 minutes. They should be slightly golden. Set aside. When the chicken breasts are cooked, remove to a warmed serving plate and keep hot. Add the chicken stock and cream to the saucepan.

Reduce the liquid by one-third over a medium heat; this will thicken the sauce slightly and intensify the flavor. When you are happy with the flavor and texture of the sauce, add the chicken breasts and mushroom mixture, together with the parsley or marjoram. Simmer for 1–2 minutes, taste, and correct the seasoning. * Scatter some sprigs of parsley over the top. Serve with freshly cooked orzo.

* May be prepared ahead to this point. Cool quickly, cover, refrigerate, and reheat later.

Variations

Chicken with Mushrooms and Ginger

Add 1–2 teaspoons of freshly grated ginger to the mushrooms in the pan.

Chicken with Mushrooms and Rosemary

Tuck a sprig of rosemary in between the chicken breasts as they cook; discard later. Substitute 1 teaspoon of chopped rosemary for ginger in the above recipe. Garnish with sprigs of rosemary. Serve with penne or orzo.

Tojo's Chicken Khorma with Basmati Rice and Poppadums

Serves 8–12

2¼ lbs. (1kg) chicken fillets
1¼ cups plain yogurt
2 tablespoons garlic cloves, crushed
2 tablespoons fresh ginger, peeled and grated
2 tablespoons fresh chile, finely chopped

2 teaspoons freshly ground black pepper
2 teaspoons whole cumin seeds
2 teaspoons whole coriander seeds
1 teaspoon cloves
1 teaspoon ground cinnamon
1 teaspoon turmeric
½ stick (¼ cup) butter
1 lb. (450g) onions, sliced
1¼ cups coconut milk
1 lb. (450g) very ripe tomatoes, half peeled and puréed, the other half peeled and diced
1 tablespoon freshly chopped cilantro
1 teaspoon salt

lime juice (optional)
cream

Cut the chicken fillets into 1-inch (2.5-cm) cubes. Mix the yogurt, garlic, ginger, and chile in a bowl, then add the chicken. Season, mix well, cover, and let marinate in the fridge for at least 6 hours or overnight.

Later or the following day, preheat the oven to 475°F (250°C). Warm all the spices except the cinnamon in a pan for 1–2 minutes, and grind to a fine powder. Soften the onions in butter, add the freshly ground spices, and cook for 5 minutes. Add the coconut milk little by little and continue to cook until the onions are completely softened, then add the puréed tomatoes.

Spread the chicken cubes on an oiled oven tray and cook for 10–15 minutes in the hot oven, then keep warm. Purée the onion and coconut milk mixture and return to the pot. Add the cooked chicken, diced tomatoes, and cilantro. Reheat.

Taste, correct the seasoning, adding a little lime juice if necessary. The curry should be mild and have a creamy consistency; add a little cream if needed.

Serve with Basmati Rice (see page 124) and Poppadoms (see page 492).

Crispy Chicken Sandwich

Serves 4

4 chicken breasts
salt and freshly ground pepper
French mustard
4 slices Gruyère cheese or sharp Cheddar
2–3 teaspoons parsley, freshly chopped
4 slices cooked ham or 4 cooked bacon strips
seasoned white flour, preferably unbleached
beaten egg
fine dry breadcrumbs
Clarified Butter for frying (see page 103)

Detach the fillet from the chicken breasts and set aside for another recipe. Carefully slit the chicken breast down the side and open out. Season with salt and pepper. Smear with a little French mustard, put a thin slice of Gruyère cheese or sharp Cheddar cheese lengthwise on one side of the chicken breast, sprinkle with a little parsley, and top with a slice of cooked ham or bacon strip. Fold over the other side of each chicken breast, and press well to seal. Dip each one first in seasoned flour, then into beaten egg, and then breadcrumbs. Press them in well again.

Fry until golden and cooked all the way through, in some clarified butter in a shallow pan, or deep-fry in good quality oil at 325°F (170°C) for 10–15 minutes, depending on the size of the chicken breasts. Serve whole or cut lengthwise at an angle so the melted cheese begins to ooze out irresistibly. Serve immediately with an Arugula and Cherry Tomato Salad or Parsley Salad (see pages 220 and 272)

Alternative Fillings

Salami, Mozzarella, and thyme leaves
Mozzarella, pesto, and sun-dried tomato
Crushed garlic and chopped parsley
Prosciutto and Taleggio

Mexican Chilaquiles

Serves 4

We grow tomatillas and epazote in the greenhouse but if you can't find the pretty green tomatillas with their papery husk, use a Tomato and Chile sauce.

6–8 corn tortillas (stale is fine)
1 large chicken breast, cooked and shredded
salt and freshly ground pepper
1½ cups Tomato and Chile Sauce (see page 590) or Tomatilla Salsa (see page 592)
1 cup chicken broth
1 large sprig epazote (optional)
⅓–⅔ cup crumbled queso fresco or Mozzarella and Cheddar mixed

To serve
2–5 tablespoons sour cream
1 onion, thinly sliced (optional)
fresh cilantro leaves

8- x 5-inch (20.5- x 12.5-cm) ovenproof dish

Preheat the oven 450°F (230°C).

Cut the tortillas into eighths. Dry them out in a moderate oven if they are moist; they are best stale and leathery for this dish. Heat oil in a deep-fryer and cook the tortilla pieces in batches until crisp and light golden. Drain on paper. Just before serving, spread half the tortillas over the bottom of a deep-sided serving dish. Cover with the chicken, and season with salt and pepper.

Thin out the sauce with a little chicken broth if too thick. Put another layer of tortillas on top. Cover with the hot sauce and a sprinkling of cheese.

Heat through in the oven for 5–10 minutes or until hot and bubbly. Serve immediately with sour cream, more grated cheese for sprinkling, a little onion if you like, and cilantro.

Malaysian Chicken Satay

Serves 8–12

Naranjan Kaur McCormack comes from Malaysia and fell in love with an Irishman, hence the surname. She now lives in Fermoy, County Cork, and delights our students with tastes of her native food on every 12 week course. This is her recipe.

Satay is the Southeast Asian Kabob – seafood or meat cooked on a skewer. There are endless "satay" variations, using different meat and marinade combinations. Try to include a little fat with each piece of meat, or the satay will become dry when cooked. For the most authentic and optimum flavor, cook the satay on a charcoal barbecue. Satay is usually eaten as a snack with drinks or served with cucumber salad and "longtong" (compressed rice). This is a very popular "hawker" food. Street traders selling from kiosk-like stalls are a very popular feature in Malaysia.

This is an all time favorite summertime barbecue dish with my family and friends. And I have found that the chicken satay is by far the most popular of meat satays. The marinade helps to tenderize the meat – hence the chicken seems to simply melt in your mouth!

1 lb. (450g) chicken meat, skinned and boned

Marinade

2 teaspoons ground turmeric
½ teaspoon garam masala
1 teaspoon freshly ground cumin
1 teaspoon salt
1 tablespoon plus 1 teaspoon brown sugar
juice of 1 lemon

Above: Malaysian Chicken Satay

Peanut Sauce

a heaped cup unsalted peanuts
½ cup chopped onion
2 garlic cloves
¼ teaspoon chili powder
1 rounded teaspoon salt
1 tablespoon plus 1 teaspoon peanut oil
2½ tablespoons tamarind water (saved after a piece of tamarind the size of a golf ball has been dissolved into this amount of water and the liquid strained off)
juice of 1 lemon
¼ cup raw sugar
1 tablespoon plus 1 teaspoon cornstarch mixed into 1¼ cups water
20 bamboo skewers (soaked in cold water for a few hours or overnight to prevent them burning on the barbecue)

First mix all the marinade ingredients. Cut the chicken into 1-inch (2.5-cm) cubes. Place in a bowl with the marinade. Marinate for about 6–8 hours or preferably overnight.

Heat the broiler on a high heat for a few minutes. Thread pieces of chicken onto the bamboo skewers until each skewer holds about 3 inches (8cm) of meat at its pointed end. Broil the chicken for about 15–20 minutes, turning to ensure even cooking. Next make the Peanut Sauce. Fry the peanuts in a dry pan till lightly brown. Spread them on a tray, and when cool, rub the peanut skins between your thumbs and fingers and "blow away" the loose skins. Be careful, peanuts retain heat for quite a long time. Purée the peanuts in a food processor until they are just slightly gritty, add the onion, garlic, chili powder, and salt. Whizz together for a few seconds.

Heat the peanut oil in a shallow frying pan. Add the peanut mixture and fry over a medium heat. Add the tamarind water, lemon juice, and sugar, and mix well. Then add the cornstarch mixture and simmer until the sauce thickens. Serve hot or cold with Peanut Sauce, a side salad, and the "longtong" (compressed rice).

Chicken Satay Deh-Ta Hsiung

Serves 6–8 depending on course

Cubes of tender meat, pork, beef, lamb, or shrimp may also be marinated in spices, then threaded onto bamboo satay sticks and cooked on the barbecue or under the broiler. Satays are terrifically versatile – they can be served as an appetizer with drinks or as a light meal when served with rice and salad.

Marinade
1 garlic clove, crushed
2 shallots or 1 small onion, finely chopped
2½ tablespoons light soy sauce
1 generous tablespoon sugar
1 generous tablespoon coriander, freshly ground
1 tablespoon plus 1 teaspoon lemon juice or red wine vinegar

1 lb. (450g) chicken breast or thigh meat, boned and skinned
crispy lettuce leaves
cilantro leaves
1–2½ tablespoons vegetable oil
1 cup Peanut Sauce (see page 275)
24–36 bamboo skewers (soaked in cold water for a few hours or overnight to prevent them burning on the barbecue)

Mix all the ingredients for the marinade in a bowl. Cut the chicken into 1-inch (2.5-cm) cubes and toss into the bowl, marinating chicken for at least 1 hour.

Thread the meat cubes onto 1 end of the bamboo satay sticks. Brush each satay with a little oil and char-grill on a barbecue until just cooked, turning frequently.

Arrange some crispy lettuce and cilantro leaves on plates, add the skewers, and serve with a small bowl of peanut sauce.

Note: chicken breast may be cut into strips instead of cubes. Thread onto the soaked satay sticks.

Bang Bang Chicken

Serves 6

This explosive-sounding chicken dish was made popular in restaurants like the Ivy and Le Caprice in London. There are lots of versions.

5 chicken breasts
4 ounces (110g) cellophane noodles
3 cucumbers cut into thin strips

Poaching Stock
5 cups Chicken Stock (see page 36)
2 scallions
1 chile
4 garlic cloves
3 slices fresh ginger

Sauce
4 large garlic cloves, crushed
⅓ cup freshly chopped cilantro
¾ cup smooth peanut butter
⅓ cup light soy sauce
2½ tablespoons honey
1 teaspoon chili oil
1 tablespoon plus 1 teaspoon Japanese rice vinegar
1 teaspoon dry sherry

Garnish
fresh cilantro leaves
6 red chiles (optional)

Put all the ingredients for the poaching stock in a saucepan and add the chicken breasts. Bring slowly to a boil, simmer for 5 minutes, and turn off the heat. Cover, and let sit in the poaching liquid until fully cooked.

Put the noodles in a bowl and cover with hot water. Leave for about 5 minutes and then drain. They are served lukewarm.

Whizz all the ingredients for the sauce in a food processor or mix well in a bowl. If it appears very thick, thin to a coating consistency with water.

Peel the cucumbers, seed them, and cut into 2-inch (5-cm) julienne strips. Wash your hands, then shred the chicken with your fingers or with two forks.

To serve: divide the noodles between the plates, top each one with cucumber julienne, then shredded chicken, and drizzle the sauce over the chicken and garnish with cilantro and a whole chile pepper.

Thai Green Chicken Curry with Thai Fragrant Rice

Serves 4

4 chicken breasts or thighs (1 lb./450g after bones are removed)
1 cup coconut milk (we use Chaokoh)
¼ cup sunflower or peanut oil
2 garlic cloves, finely chopped,
1–2½ tablespoons Green Curry Paste (see right) – or use the ready-made Amoy brand
¼ cup fish sauce (nam pla)
1 teaspoon sugar
1 cup homemade Chicken Stock (see page 36)
4 fresh kaffir lime leaves (use more if they are frozen)
20 pea eggplants (if available) or ⅓ of 1 eggplant, cut into 20 pea-sized pieces
15 Thai basil leaves

First make the Green Curry Paste (see right).

Slice the chicken finely and set aside. Heat the coconut milk gently in a small saucepan but don't let it boil. Heat the oil in a wok or frying pan until almost smoking. Add the garlic and toss over once or twice (watch out – the garlic can burn very easily) for a few seconds until golden. Add the curry paste and stir-fry for a few seconds, then add the warm coconut milk and stir until it curdles and thickens in the oil. Add the fish sauce and sugar. Next mix in the chicken, stir well, and cook until it changes color (thighs will take longer to cook). Add the stock and bring to a boil and cook for

2–3 minutes, add the kaffir lime leaves, eggplants and basil. Cook for 1 minute, turn into a hot dish, and serve immediately with Thai Jasmine Rice (see page 126).

Green Curry Paste

This is my favorite recipe for Green Curry Paste. It comes from The Taste of Thailand by Vatcharin Bhumichitr.

2 long green chiles, chopped
10 small green chiles, chopped
1 generous tablespoon lemon grass, chopped
3 shallots, chopped
2 tablespoons chopped garlic (about 4 cloves)
1-inch (2.5-cm) piece galangal, chopped
3 cilantro roots, chopped
1 generous tablespoon coriander seed, ground
1/2 teaspoon cumin, ground
1/2 teaspoon white pepper, ground
1 teaspoon chopped kaffir lime juice or finely chopped lime leaves
2 teaspoons shrimp paste
1 teaspoon salt

Grind the whole spices, first in a spice grinder or coffee grinder, then proceed using a mortar and pestle.

Crunchy Chicken and Mushroom Phyllo Pies

Serves 6 as a main course – but these pastries can be made in different sizes and used as a canapé or appetizer also.

Mushroom à La Crème (see page 197)
12 ounces (350g) chicken, poached and diced
8 ounces (225g) ham or bacon, cooked and diced
1 package phyllo pastry – use what you need and carefully freeze the remainder
Clarified Butter (see page 103)
egg wash

Preheat the oven 400°F (200°C).

First make the Mushroom à la Crème. Add the coarsely chopped cooked ham or bacon, and cooked chicken to it. Taste and correct the seasoning of the filling. Defrost the phyllo dough, if necessary, and unfold to make the pastry shapes.

Brush the top sheet of phyllo with melted butter. Put 1–2 tablespoons of the filling in the center of the sheet, in about 2 1/2 inches (6cm) from the narrow end. Fold the dough over the filling twice and then fold in one of the edges, roll over and then fold in the other side so there is even thickness of pastry at both sides. Continue to roll over to enclose the filling. Brush with egg wash and melted butter.

Bake in the oven for 15–20 minutes depending on size.

To make triangles: cut each sheet in 4 lengthwise, brush each strip with melted butter, put a heaped teaspoon of filling near the end of the strip. Fold over and over from side to side to form a triangle. Brush with melted butter and egg wash.

Serve with a good green salad and some spicy greens.

Chicken Goujons with Garlic Mayonnaise

Serves 4

2–3 chicken breasts, skinned
good-quality oil, for deep frying
salt and freshly ground pepper

Olive Oil Batter
1 1/4 cups all-purpose white flour
2 1/2 tablespoons extra-virgin olive oil
water
1–1 1/2 egg whites
sea salt, or kosher salt

Garlic Mayonnaise (see page 584)

First make the batter. Sift the flour into a bowl, make a well in the center, pour in the olive oil, stir, and add enough water to make a batter about the consistency of sour cream. Let it stand. Just before cooking, whisk the egg whites until stiff and fold into the batter with sea salt to taste.

Heat the oil in a deep-fryer. Cut the chicken breasts into 1/2-inch (1-cm) strips on the bias, and season. Drop individually into the batter and fry for 2–3 minutes or until crisp.

Drain on paper towels and serve immediately on a hot plate with a blob or bowl of well-seasoned garlic mayonnaise.

Preparing Buffalo Wings or Mini-drumsticks

With a small knife, cut through the skin just above the bone at the less fleshy end. Push the flesh upwards and turn inside out, pulling it up over the end of the bone so that it resembles a drumstick. Marinate the chicken wings, Chinese drumsticks, or Buffalo wings in a chosen marinade.

How to Poach Chicken or Turkey Breasts

Bring a saucepan of chicken stock to a boil, add the chicken breasts, simmer gently for 5–7 minutes, depending on size. Turn off the heat, cover, and let the chicken breasts cool in the liquid. Remove with a slotted spoon. Use for chicken salads. Turkey breasts will take longer, depending on size.

Master Recipe
Chicken Tonnata Salad

Serves 8

Baby beets can be used instead of beans.

8 chicken breasts, skinned
salt and freshly ground black pepper
8 ounces (225g) French beans (about 1½ cups)
a little olive oil for brushing

Tonnata Sauce
a heaped ⅓ cup homemade Mayonnaise (see page 584)
3 ounces (75g) canned tuna in oil, plus 2½ tablespoons of the oil
2 salted anchovies
1 rounded tablespoon salted capers
1 tablespoon plus 1 teaspoon lemon juice

Garnish
16–24 black olives
16 salted anchovies
16 salted capers
flat-leaf parsley sprigs

First make the Tonnata Sauce. Wash the capers and anchovies and pat dry. Put all the ingredients for the sauce in a food processor, along with a little pepper, whizz until smooth, and then put into a bowl. Cover, and set aside.

Season the chicken breasts with salt and pepper, then brush with oil. Heat a grill-pan and cook the chicken for 8–10 minutes on each side. Set aside to cool.

Top and tail the beans and cut in half at an angle if large. Bring a saucepan of water to a boil, add salt, and cook the beans for 3–4 minutes or until tender but al dente. Drain, refresh under cold water, and spread on a plate to dry. Put a little green salad on each plate and scatter some beans on top. Slice each chicken breast into 5 or 6 pieces, place on top of the leaves, drizzle with the sauce. Garnish with capers and anchovies, a few olives, and sprigs of parsley.

Variation
Turkey Tonnata Salad

Follow the Master Recipe, but substitute poached turkey breast for chicken.

Curried Chicken Salad with Mango and Roasted Cashew Nuts

Serves 8–10

If you are fortunate enough to find really ripe, perfumed mango, this is an excellent salad – typical of a New York deli.

3 lbs. (1.3kg) chicken breasts
salt and freshly ground black pepper
5 cups homemade Chicken Stock (see page 36)
2 tablespoons lemon juice, freshly squeezed
2 ripe mangoes, peeled, pitted and cut into ½-inch (1-cm) pieces
1⅓–1⅔ cups chopped celery
4 scallions, chopped, including green part
½ cup plain yogurt
½ cup homemade Mayonnaise (see page 584)
1½ teaspoons curry powder
½ teaspoon cumin seed, freshly ground
1¼ cups roasted cashew nuts

Garnish
2 generous tablespoons cilantro, freshly chopped

Season the chicken with salt and pepper and poach it in the stock for 5–7 minutes, until cooked (see above left). Drain using a slotted spoon, and cut into a medium dice. Mix the chicken with the lemon juice in a large bowl, and season well with salt and pepper. Add the mango, celery, and scallions. Whisk the yogurt into the mayonnaise. Toast the cumin seeds in a hot frying pan for a few seconds, add the curry powder and cook for a futher 1–2 seconds. Grind, cool, and add to the yogurt and mayonnaise. Mix and pour over the other ingredients. Toss gently. Taste and correct seasoning.

Just before serving, add the roasted cashew nuts, scatter with cilantro and serve.

Thai Chicken and Coconut Salad

Serves 4–6

1 x 14-ounce (400-g) can coconut milk (we use the Chaokoh brand)
¼ cup fish sauce (nam pla)
¼ cup palm sugar or light brown sugar
1¾ lbs. (800g) chicken thighs, boned
4 kaffir lime leaves
2 red shallots or 1 small red onion, very finely sliced
1 red pepper, seeded and very finely sliced
2 medium Thai chiles, seeded and very thinly sliced
1–2 cucumbers, seeded and cut in fine julienne strips
2 handfuls fresh cilantro leaves
1 heaped tablespoon peanuts, unsalted and freshly roasted (see right)

1 banana leaf or some vine or lettuce leaves (optional)
a little sunflower oil

Garnish
fresh mint
cilantro leaves
a few whole chiles

Put the coconut milk, fish sauce, and palm sugar into a saucepan over a medium heat. Stir until the sugar dissolves. Add the chicken and bring slowly to a boil. Simmer, covered, for 4–5 minutes, then remove from the heat and let cool in the covered saucepan. The chicken will continue to cook but will be moist and tender.

Remove the center rib from the kaffir lime leaves. Roll the leaves into a cigarette shape and slice as finely as humanly possible. Mix the sliced vegetables, shredded lime leaves, fresh cilantro, and peanuts in a bowl.

Drain the chicken and pour a generous amount of the coconut milk poaching liquid over the vegetables and toss gently. Cut the chicken into 1/2-inch (1-cm) thick strips and toss gently again. Taste for seasoning

If you happen to have a banana leaf, cut it into 4–6 large squares and polish with a little sunflower oil. Put on a plate and pile high with chicken salad, alternatively use vine leaves or a bed of lettuce. Drizzle with extra poaching liquid. Garnish with little sprigs of mint and cilantro and perhaps a few whole chiles. Serve.

How to Roast Peanuts

Crushed, roasted peanuts are a common seasoning throughout most of south-east Asia. They add a nutty taste, a crunchy texture, and protein to a dish. Raw peanuts are sold in every market in this region, usually still covered with their red inner skins.

To roast them at home, put them into an ungreased, well-heated, cast-iron frying pan or wok over a medium heat. Stir the peanuts around until they are roasted, reducing the heat if necessary. The red skins will turn crisp and papery. When the peanuts have cooled, rub them with both hands and blow the skins away.

To crush them, lightly or finely as required, either whizz them for a few seconds in a clean coffee grinder or, if only a few tablespoons are needed, chop them up with a large knife.

How to cut up a chicken (4 pieces)

1 Remove the wishbone (keep for the stock pot).

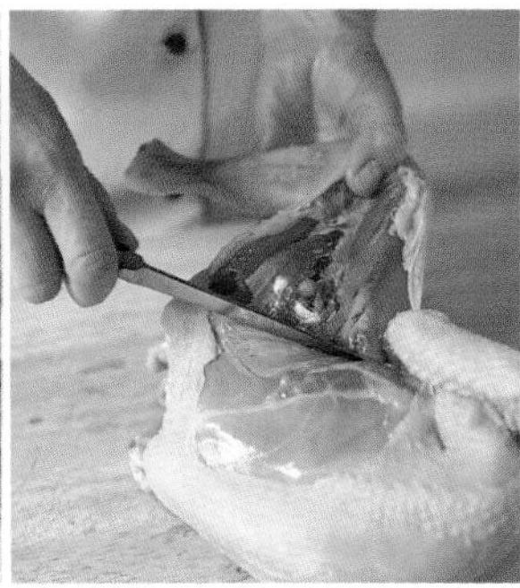

2 Cut through the loose skin between the leg and the breast.

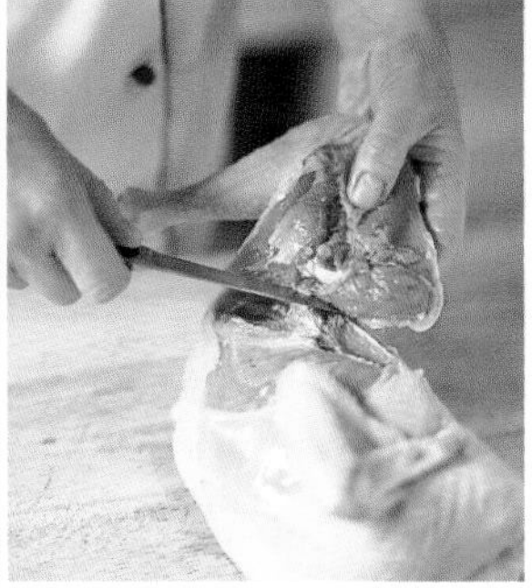

3 Turn the bird onto its side, break the ball and socket joint and carefully cut around the oyster piece so that it remains attached to the leg. Ideally remove the drumstick and thigh and oyster in 1 piece.

4 Chop off the wing tips and add to the stockpot.

5 Cut off the pinion at the first joint (and use for a chicken wing recipe or keep for the stock pot).

6 Place the chicken on the board, neck end away from you, then cut along the edge of the breastbone to loosen the white meat, using long sweeping movements, and remove the breast in one piece with the wing attached. Alternatively use poultry shears to cut through the breast bone and ribs. This adds extra flavor particularly for a casserole. Repeat on the other side.

How to cut up a chicken (8 pieces)

Cut the bird into four pieces as above.
Cut the leg in half by cutting through the line of fat at the knuckle between the thigh and drumstick.
Cut the breast in half using either a knife or poultry shears and leaving 1 piece attached to the wing.
Repeat on the other side.

Master Recipe

Shanagarry Chicken Casserole

Serves 4–6

A good chicken casserole, even though it may sound "old hat," always gets a hearty welcome from my family and friends. Sometimes I make an entire meal in a pot by covering the top with whole peeled potatoes just before it goes into the oven. Pheasant or rabbit may also be used.

1 chicken, about 4 lbs. (1.8kg)
a little butter or oil for sautéeing
12 ounces (350g) fresh bacon (blanch it if salty)
1 lb. (450g) onions (baby onions are nicest)
12 ounces (350g) carrot, peeled and thickly sliced – if the carrots are small, leave whole, if large, cut in chunks (about 1½–2 cups)
sprig of thyme
3 cups homemade Chicken Stock (see page 36)
Roux (see page 580), optional
Mushroom à la Crème (see page 197), optional

Garnish
1 generous tablespoon parsley, freshly chopped

Preheat the oven to 350°F (180C°).

Cut up the chicken into 8 pieces (see page 279), season well with salt and pepper. Cut the bacon into roughly ½-inch (1-cm) cubes. Heat a little butter or oil in a frying pan and cook the bacon until crisp, remove, and transfer to a flameproof casserole dish or other heavy flameproof and ovenproof pot.

Add the chicken pieces to the pan, 2 or 3 at a time, and sauté until golden, and then remove to the casserole dish. Then toss the onion and carrot in the pan to coat them well, adding a little butter if necessary. Remove to the casserole dish.

Tip: Heat control is crucial here, the pan mustn't burn yet it must be hot enough to sauté the chicken. If it is too cool, the chicken pieces will stew rather than sauté and, as a result, the meat may be tough.

De-grease the frying pan and de-glaze with stock, bring it to a boil, and pour into the casserole dish. Season well and add thyme. Put the casserole dish over a medium heat and bring to a simmering point on top of the stove, then put into the oven for 30–45 minutes. When the chicken is just cooked, pour the whole casserole contents into a clean pan. Strain off the cooking liquid, de-grease, return the de-greased liquid to the casserole dish and bring to a boil over a high heat. Thicken with a little Roux if necessary. Add the meat, carrots, and onions back into the casserole and bring to a boil. Taste and correct the seasoning. The casserole is very good served at this point, but it's even more delicious if some Mushroom à la Crème is stirred in as an enrichment. Serve sprinkled with parsley and bubbling hot.

Variations

Shanagarry Chicken Casserole with Herb Crust

Casserole recipe as above
½ Soda Bread recipe with herbs (see page 474)
egg wash
1–2½ tablespoons grated Cheddar cheese

Roll out the dough into ¾-inch (2-cm) thick circle, and stamp out circles with a 2-inch (5-cm) cookie cutter. When the casserole is almost cooked, remove the lid and cover the top of the stew with these herb scones, slightly overlapping them, and then brush them with egg wash and sprinkle with a little cheese if you wish. Increase the heat to 450°F (230°C) for 10 minutes, then reduce the heat to 400°F (200°C) for a further 20 minutes or until the crust is baked.

How to Stuff a Bird

A complementary stuffing not only adds flavor and interest to a roast bird but helps to make it go a little further and keeps the breast meat moist.

Stuffing is usually based on breadcrumbs, potato, or rice, flavored with herbs and perhaps dried fruit such as apricots or prunes. A little chopped onion is often added but it needs to be sweated first in butter otherwise it may still be slightly raw when the bird is cooked. Chestnut stuffings are much loved, particularly in the UK and in the US. Oysters are added to the Thanksgiving stuffing for the turkey. Turkeys may be stuffed both in the cavity and at the neck (crop) end. Tuck the wing tips underneath the bird to keep the flap of skin in place to enclose the stuffing.

Potato-based stuffing is traditional with goose or duck in Ireland. Apple is sometimes added to cut the richness.

Watchpoint

Many cookery writers caution against putting the stuffing into a bird and suggest that it is safer to cook the stuffing separately, wrapped in aluminum foil or placed in an ovenproof dish. There is, in fact, no problem about stuffing a bird provided you follow a few basic food safety rules:

1 Do not over-fill the cavity with stuffing; leave a space between the top of the stuffing and the breast bone to allow the heat to penetrate, so that the bird can cook fully.

2 If a frozen bird is being used, it should be fully defrosted before being stuffed.

3 Do not put warm stuffing into poultry or a joint of meat unless you plan to cook it immediately. If it is left uncooked, particularly at room temperature, even for a short time, you can provide perfect incubating conditions for bacteria to grow. The Food Safety Authority tell us to assume that poultry, particularly intensively-reared birds, will be infected with salmonella so ensure that the birds and the stuffing are fully cooked and there will be no problem.

How to Carve a Chicken or Turkey

Let the chicken rest for 10 minutes in a warm place before carving. Put the chicken on a small cutting board, sitting on a tray in order to catch any juices; these may be added to the sauce or gravy later. Each portion of chicken should have some white and dark meat.

A 3½ pound (1.6kg) chicken will yield 4 portions

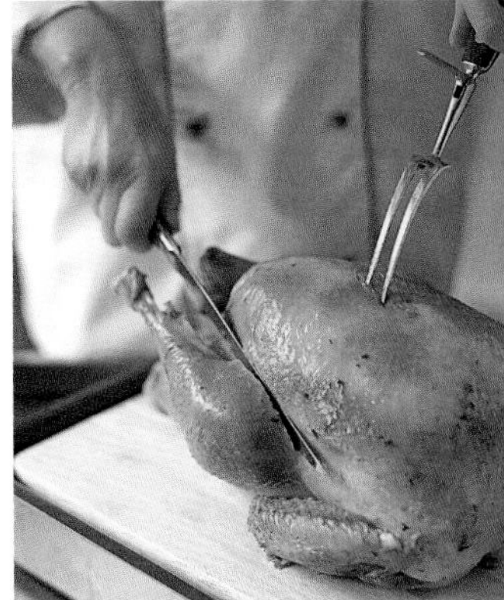

1 Cut through the skin between the leg and the breast.

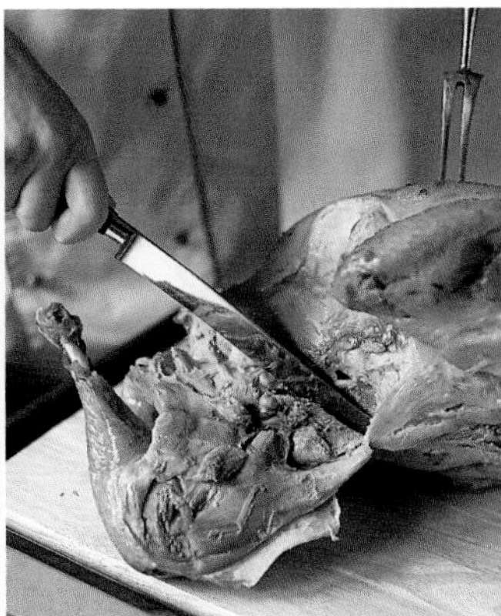

2 Turn the bird onto its side, break the ball and socket joint, and carefully cut around the oyster piece so that it remains attached to the leg. Ideally, remove the drumstick and thigh and oyster in 1 piece.

3 Cut the leg in half by cutting through the line of fat at the knuckle between the thigh and drumstick. Put the 2 pieces of dark meat on a warm serving dish or on individual hot plates.
Carve off a generous piece of white meat with the wing still attached and serve with the thigh.

4 Carve the remainder of the white meat into slices and put with the drumstick

Repeat on the other side.

A 4½ 5-pound (2–2.2kg) chicken will yield 6 portions

Cut off the leg as above. Separate the drumstick and thigh by cutting through the line of fat at the knuckle.

Then further divide the thigh into two pieces by cutting in half along the bone.

Put these three pieces of brown meat on a warm serving dish or separate plates. Carve a generous piece of white meat with the wing attached, and combine with the piece of dark meat that has no bone.

Carve the remainder of the white meat into slices and divide between the drumstick and the thigh piece with the bone.

Now each portion has both dark and white meat plus some bone.

Larger Casserole roasting

An excellent cooking method for turkey, chickens, pheasant, or even a leg of pork. The joint of meat is cooked whole in the covered casserole dish with no added liquid. During the cooking process, some of the juices escape into the casserole dish and are flavored with the herbs or spices. This liquid forms the basis of the sauce.

Master Recipe

Casserole – Roast Chicken with Tarragon

Serves 4–6
In season: summer

There are two kinds of tarragon, French and Russian; we use French because it has the better flavor. Unfortunately this is more difficult to grow because it is propagated by root cuttings; you can't just grow it from seed as you can the Russian tarragon. French tarragon grows to a height of about 9 inches (23cm) whereas the Russian will grow to about 4 feet (1.25m) in summer.

chicken, about 3½ lbs. (1.6kg)
1 generous tablespoon French tarragon, freshly chopped, and 1 sprig of tarragon
2 tablespoons butter
⅔ cup cream
salt and freshly ground pepper
½-1 tablespoon French tarragon, freshly chopped (for sauce)
⅔ cup homemade Chicken Stock (see page 36), optional
Roux (see page 580), optional

Garnish
sprigs of fresh tarragon

Preheat the oven to 350°F (180°C).

Remove the wishbone and keep for the stock. Season the cavity of the chicken with salt and pepper and stuff a sprig of tarragon inside. Mix the chopped tarragon with two-thirds of the butter. Smear the remaining butter over the breast of the chicken, place breast side down in a flameproof casserole dish or other heavy flameproof and ovenproof pot, and let it brown slowly over a gentle heat. Turn the chicken breast-side up, and smear the tarragon butter over the breast and legs. Season with salt and pepper. Cover the casserole and cook in the oven for 1¼-1½ hours.

Tip: To test if whole birds are cooked, pierce the flesh between the breast and the base of the thigh. This is the last place to cook so, if there is no trace of pink here and if the juices are clear, the chicken is certainly cooked.

Remove and place on a carving dish, set it in a warm oven, and let it rest for 10–15 minutes before carving.

Meanwhile, spoon the surplus fat from the juices, add a little freshly chopped tarragon, and cream (or just stock, if you prefer*) and boil up the sauce until it thickens slightly. Alternatively bring the liquid to a boil, whisk in just enough Roux to thicken the sauce to a light coating consistency. Taste, and correct the seasoning.

Carve the chicken, arrange on a serving dish, nap with the sauce and serve.

Note: Some chickens yield less juice than others. If you need more sauce, add a little more homemade Chicken Stock with the cream. If the sauce is thickened with Roux, this dish can be reheated.

*This dish is also delicious without cream, just using chicken juices, stock, and fresh herbs.

Variations

Casserole – Roast Chicken with Marjoram

Substitute annual marjoram for tarragon in the recipe above.

Casserole – Roast Chicken with Summer Garden Herbs

Substitute 4–6 teaspoons of freshly chopped summer herbs, e.g., parsley, thyme, tarragon, chervil, chives, etc., for the tarragon in the recipe above.

Casserole – Roast Turkey with Marjoram and Piperonata

Serves 10–12
In season: all year, best in summer

Provided you have a large enough pot, this is a fantastic way to cook turkey – vary the herbs or mixture of herbs to the season. Ideal for entertaining. There are several varieties of marjoram, the one we use for this recipe is the annual sweet marjoram (Origanum marjorana).

1 turkey, 10–12 lbs. (4.4–5.3kg)
1 stick (½ cup) butter
2–3 sprigs marjoram
⅓ cup marjoram, finely chopped
4 cups light cream
salt and freshly ground pepper
Roux (see page 580), optional

Piperonata (see page 190)

Garnish
sprigs of marjoram

Follow the Master Recipe smearing the breast of the turkey with half the butter. Cook in the oven for about 2–2½ hours. Meanwhile, make the Piperonata.

Serve with Piperonata and garnish with sprigs of fresh marjoram.

Note: Use the turkey carcass to make stock on exactly the same principle as the Chicken Stock (see page 36). Use for soups.

Master Recipe

Old-fashioned Roast Turkey with Fresh Herb Stuffing

Serves 10–12

This is my favorite roast stuffed turkey recipe. You may think the stuffing seems dull because it doesn't include exotic-sounding ingredients like chestnuts and spiced bulk sausage, but in fact it is moist and full of the flavor of fresh herbs and the turkey juices. Cook a chicken in exactly the same way but use one-quarter of the stuffing quantity given.

1 turkey, with neck and giblets 10–12 lbs. (4.4–5.3kg)
2 sticks (1 cup) butter
large square of cheesecloth (optional)

Garnish
large sprigs of fresh parsley or watercress

Fresh Herb Stuffing
12 ounces (350g) onions, chopped (about 3 cups)
1½ sticks (¾ cup) butter
14–16 ounces (400–450g) soft breadcrumbs, blitzed in a blender (about 8–10 cups)
2 handfuls freshly chopped herbs such as parsley, thyme, chives, marjoram, savory, lemon balm
salt and freshly ground pepper

Preheat the oven to 350°F (180°C).

Remove the wishbone from the neck end of the turkey, for ease of carving later. Make a Turkey Stock (see page 36).

Next make the stuffing: sweat the onions gently in the butter until soft, remove from the heat, then stir in the crumbs, herbs, and a little salt and pepper to taste. Let it get quite cold. If necessary, wash and dry the cavity of the bird, then season and half-fill with cold stuffing. Put the remainder of the stuffing into the crop at the neck end.

Weigh the turkey and calculate the cooking time (15 minutes per pound/450g and 15 minutes over).

Melt 4 teaspoons of butter and soak a large piece of good-quality cheesecloth in the melted butter; cover the turkey completely with the cheesecloth and roast in the oven for 3–3½ hours. There is no need to baste it because of the butter-soaked cheesecloth. The turkey browns beautifully, but if you like it even browner, remove the cheesecloth 10 minutes before the end of the cooking time.

The turkey is cooked when the juices run clear (see page 283). Remove the turkey to a carving dish, keep warm, and let it rest.

Note: Alternatively, smear the breast, legs, and crop well with soft butter, and season with salt and freshly ground pepper. If the turkey is not covered with butter-soaked cheesecloth then it is a good idea to cover the whole dish with aluminum foil. However, your turkey will then be semi-steamed, not roasted in the traditional sense of the word.

To make the gravy: spoon off the surplus fat from the roasting pan. De-glaze the pan juices with fat-free stock from the giblets and bones. Using a whisk, stir and scrape well to dissolve the caramelized meat juices from the roasting pan. Boil it up well, season, and thicken with a little roux if you like. Taste, and correct the seasoning. Serve in a hot gravy boat.

Present the turkey on your largest serving dish, surrounded by crispy roast potatoes, and garnished with large sprigs of parsley or watercress, and maybe a sprig of holly. Make sure no one eats the berries.

Serve with Cranberry Sauce (see page 597) and Bread Sauce (see page 594).

Traditional Roast Chicken with Herb Stuffing and Gravy

Serves 4–6

1 chicken, 3½-5 lbs. (1.6–2.2kg)

Stock
giblets, wing tips, and wishbone (keep the liver for a pâté)
1 sliced carrot
1 sliced onion
1 stalk celery
a few parsley stalks and a sprig of thyme

Stuffing
3½ tablespoons butter
⅔ cup chopped onion
2 cups soft white breadcrumbs
2 generous tablespoons finely chopped fresh herbs, e.g., parsley, lemon thyme, chives, and annual marjoram
salt and freshly ground pepper
a little soft butter

sprigs of flat-leaf parsley

Follow the Master Recipe.

For the gravy, spoon off the surplus fat from the roasting pan. De-glaze the pan juices with the fat-free stock from the giblets and bones. Using a whisk, stir and scrape well to dissolve the caramelized meat juices from the roasting pan. Boil it up well, season, and thicken with a little roux if you like. Taste and correct seasoning.

Boning Birds

All birds have a similar anatomy so they are boned in the same way. Sometimes they are partially boned, leaving the leg and wing bones intact to add shape when stuffing is added – this is more usual for small birds. For galantines or ballotines, the bird is boned completely. Choose a bird with the skin intact, so it can be kept whole to use for wrapping.

How to Bone a Bird

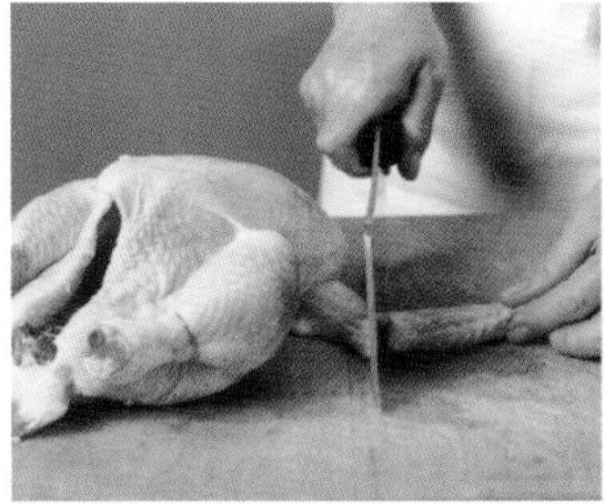
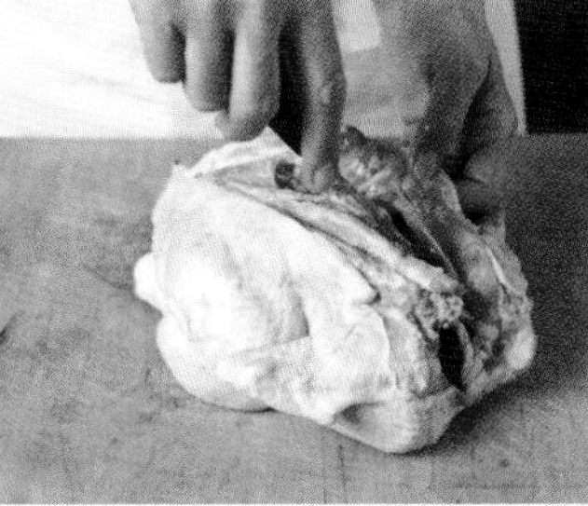
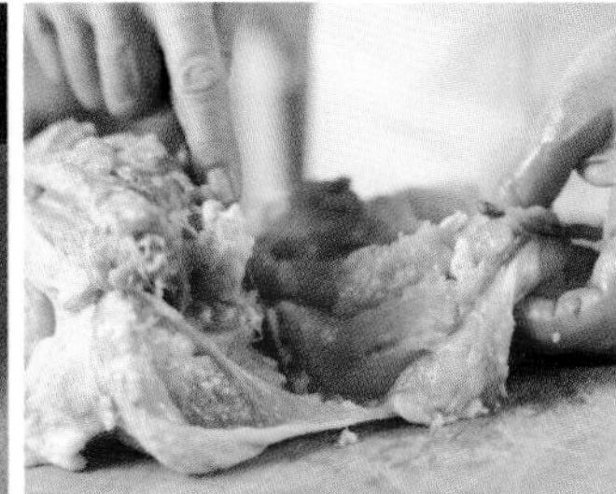
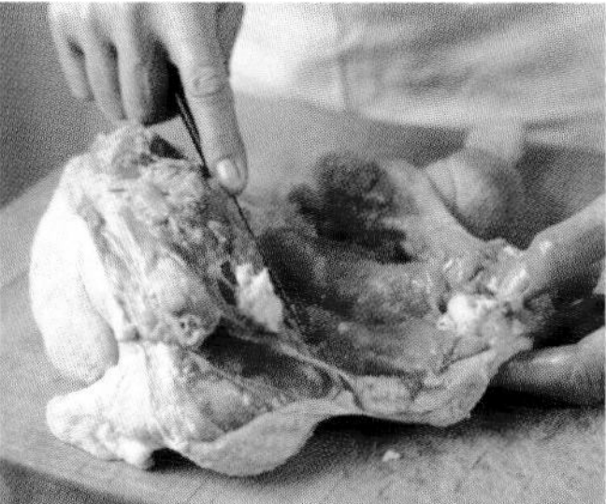

1 Using poultry shears or a Chinese chopper, cut off the wing tip and middle section leaving the largest wing bone.

2 Put the bird, breast side down, on the cutting board. Using a small knife with a point, slit the skin in a line down the backbone from neck to tail, exposing the backbone.

3 Cut the flesh and skin away from the carcass, working evenly with short sharp strokes of the knife. After each stroke, carefully ease the flesh and skin away from the carcass, using the fingers of your left hand.

4 Cut the flesh from the saber-shaped bone near the wing. As you reach the ball and socket joints connecting the wing and thigh bones to carcass, sever them, the wing and thigh are thus separated from the carcass but are still attached to the skin.

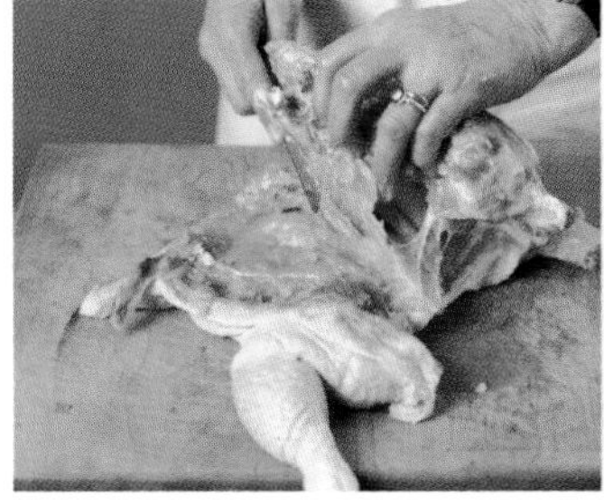

5 Using longer strokes of the knife, continue cutting the breast meat away from the bone until you reach the ridge of the breastbone where skin and bones meet. Take great care not to sever the skin here as it is very thin and close to the tip of the bone.

6 When the skin and meat have been freed from the carcass on both sides of the bird, they will remain attached to the carcass only along the breastbone. Lift up the carcass of the bird in one hand so that the skin and meat hang loosely from the breastbone. Cut against the ridge of the breastbone to free the skin and pull to remove the breastbone and the carcass from the flesh. Be careful – the skin here is easily pierced or torn.

7 Spread the chicken, skin-side down, on the cutting board. The bird is partially boned at this point, the wing and leg bones are still in place.

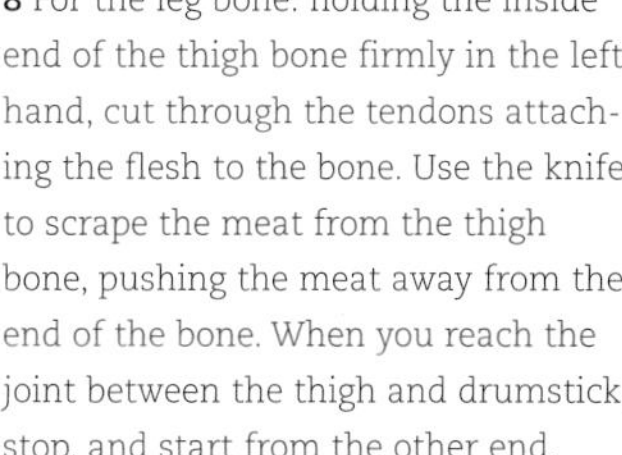

8 For the leg bone: holding the inside end of the thigh bone firmly in the left hand, cut through the tendons attaching the flesh to the bone. Use the knife to scrape the meat from the thigh bone, pushing the meat away from the end of the bone. When you reach the joint between the thigh and drumstick, stop, and start from the other end.

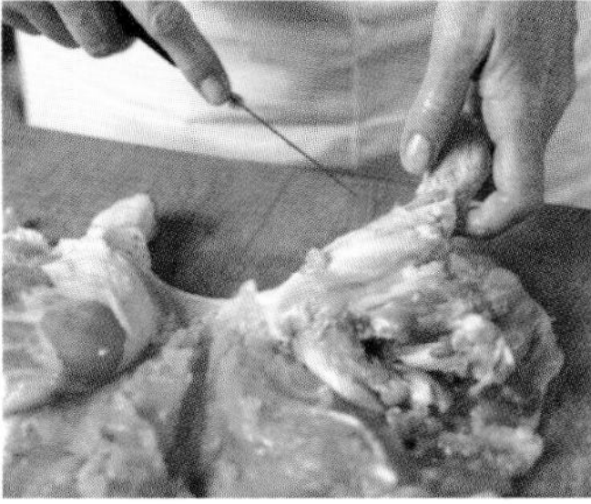
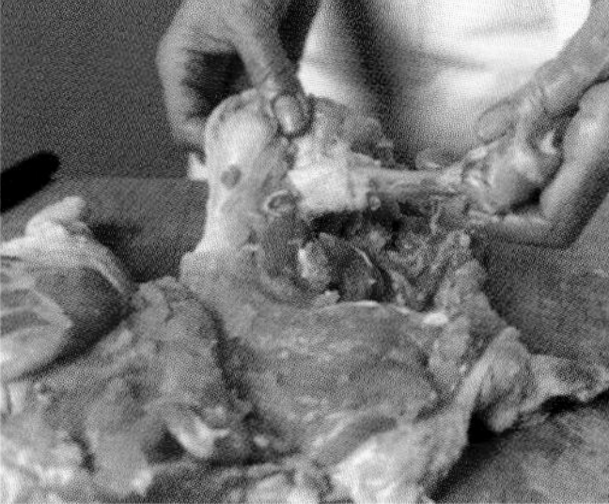
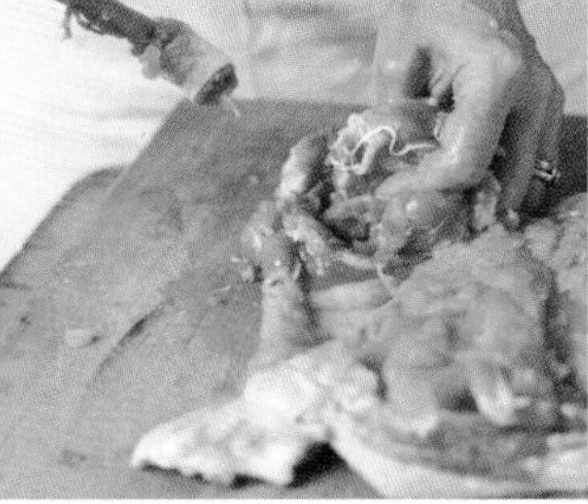
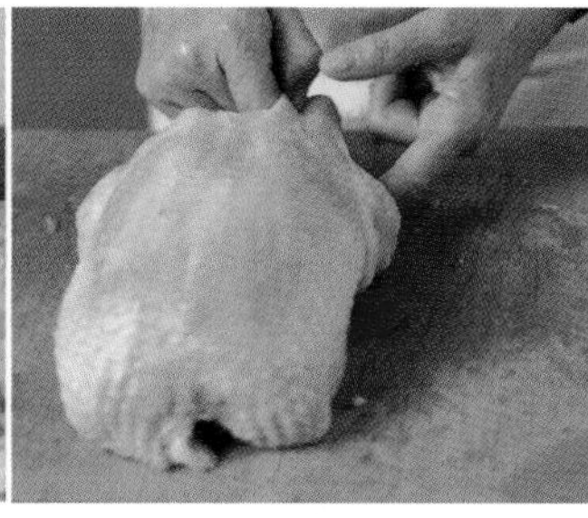

9 Cut through the skin around the claw end of the drumstick, then push the meat up towards the knuckle, loosening inside with your thumb. Be careful of the splinter bone, which runs downwards close to the bone. Then, with the tip of a small sharp knife, cut the meat from around the knuckle joint; using your fingers as a guide, feel whether it is free.

10 Tug the thigh bone and drumstick and they should come out in 1 piece, drawing the skin inside out. Repeat on the other side.

11 Push the skin from the legs and wings right side out. The completely boned bird will now be flat.

Arlene Hogan's Boned Chicken

Serves 8–10

These two methods for cooking a boned chicken – roasting and casserole-roasting – are both from Arlene Hogan.

1 chicken, 3½–4 lbs. (1.6–1.8kg), boned (see page 285)

Stuffing
1 onion, chopped
1 garlic clove, crushed
2 tablespoons butter
1 chicken liver, chopped
6 ounces (175g) bulk sausage
finely grated rind of 2 unwaxed lemons
2 generous tablespoons herbs, chopped (parsley, tarragon, thyme, chives, marjoram, lemon balm)
1½ cups breadcrumbs
2 beaten eggs
2 teaspoons brandy (optional)
freshly ground pepper and salt to taste

Gravy
1 quart (960ml) homemade Chicken Stock (see page 36)

Preheat the oven to 400°F (200°C).

Make the stuffing: sauté the onion and garlic in the butter, add the chicken liver, and toss for 2–3 minutes. Cool. Mix with the other ingredients and bind with half a beaten egg. Fry a little ball of stuffing to test for seasoning.

Stuff the chicken, reshape, and roast in the oven for 1¼–1½ hours. Reduce the temperature to 350°F (180°C) if it is getting too brown. Let it rest in a warm place for 10 minutes before carving.

Meanwhile, make some gravy (see page 594).Carefully slice the chicken into ¼-inch (5-mm) thick slices. Serve with Char-grilled Summer Vegetables (see page 199) and some gravy. Serve immediately.

Variation

Use half the recipe of Duxelle Stuffing (see page 306) instead of the bulk sausage stuffing. Add a heaped cup of breadcrumbs, and a beaten egg to the Duxelle.

Boned Chicken, Casserole-Roasted, with Port and Cream

1 chicken, 3¼–4 lbs. (1.5–1.8kg)
2 teaspoons herbs, chopped
2 tablespoons butter

Port and Cream
2½ tablespoons port
⅔ cup homemade Chicken Stock (see page 36)
⅔ cup cream
2 generous tablespoons herbs, freshly chopped (tarragon, thyme, chives, lemon balm)
salt and freshly ground pepper

Preheat the oven to 350°C (180°C).

Smear the breast with a 1 tablespoon of the butter and place the chicken, breast side down, in a heavy flameproof casserole dish or other flameproof and ovenproof pot. Let it brown over a gentle heat. Mix the herbs with the rest of the softened butter. When the breast is nicely golden, turn the chicken right side up again and smear the herb butter over the breast. Cover the casserole dish with a tight fitting lid. Cook for about 1¼ hours in the oven. Remove the chicken to a warmed serving dish and keep warm while it rests.

Next make the sauce: de-grease the juices in the casserole dish, de-glaze with the port and chicken stock, and reduce to half the volume. Add the cream and herbs, correct the seasoning.

Carve the chicken and serve with sauce. Serve with green beans or Char-grilled Summer Vegetables (see page 199).

Roast Guinea Fowl with Parsnip Crisps and Red Currant Sauce

Serves 4
In season: autumn and winter

The tart bittersweet flavor of the red currants is great with guinea fowl. I also love bread sauce (see page 594) with guinea fowl.

1 guinea fowl, 3½–4 lbs. (1.5–1.8kg)
⅔ cup homemade Game or Chicken Stock (see page 36)

Stuffing
3 tablespoons butter
⅔ cup chopped onions
1½ cups white breadcrumbs
1 generous tablespoon herbs, freshly chopped (parsley, thyme, chives, marjoram)
salt and freshly ground pepper

Parsnip Crisps (see right)
Red Currant Sauce (see page 598)

4 large sprigs of watercress

How to prepare a chicken, pheasant, turkey, or guinea fowl for roasting

First, remove the wishbone from the neck end of the chicken; this isn't at all essential but it does make carving much easier later on. Tuck the wing tips underneath the chicken to make a neat shape.

If necessary, wash and dry the cavity of the bird, then season and half-fill with cold stuffing.

Tie a knot around the "pope's nose" or "parson's nose" and secure the legs with a bow. Season the breast and legs, and smear with a little soft butter or olive oil.

Preheat the oven to 375°F (190°C).

Eviscerate the guinea fowl if necessary and remove the "crop" which is at the neck end; wash and dry well.

To make the stuffing: melt the butter and sweat the onions until soft but not colored, then remove from the heat. Stir in the breadcrumbs and herbs, season with salt and pepper, and taste. Unless you are about to cook the bird right away, let the stuffing get quite cold before putting it into the bird. Season the cavity with salt and freshly ground pepper, and stuff the guinea fowl loosely. Smear the breast and legs with soft or melted butter. Roast in the oven, for about 1¼ hours. Test by pricking the leg at the thickest point: the juices should just run clear (see tip on page 283).

Meanwhile, make the Sauce and the Crisps. Put the chicken on a warmed serving dish and keep hot. Spoon off any surplus fat from the pan (keep it for roasting or sautéeing potatoes). De-glaze the pan with stock. Bring it to a boil and use a whisk to dislodge the caramelized juices so they can dissolve into the gravy. Season, taste, and boil until you are happy with the flavor. Carve the guinea fowl into four portions giving each person some brown and white meat. Spoon gravy over the meat. Pile some Parsnip Crisps over the top and garnish with watercress. Serve with Red Currant Sauce.

Above: Roast Guinea Fowl with Parsnip Crisps and Red Currant Sauce

Parsnip Crisps

Serves 6–8

We serve these delicious crisps on warm salads, as a garnish for roast pheasant or guinea fowl, and as a topping for parsnip or root vegetable pie.

1 large parsnip
sunflower or peanut oil for deep frying
salt

Heat the oil in a deep fryer to 300°F (150°C). Scrub and peel the parsnips. Either slice into wafer-thin rounds or peel off long slivers lengthwise with a swivel-top peeler. Let them dry on paper towels.

Drop a few at a time into the hot oil. They color and crisp up very quickly. Drain on paper towels and sprinkle with salt.

Roast Goose with Potato Stuffing and Bramley Apple Sauce

Serves 8–10
In season: autumn and winter

This is almost my favorite winter meal. However, a word of warning! A goose looks enormous because it has a large carcass. Many people have been caught out by imagining that it will serve more people than it does. Allow 1 pound (450g) cooked weight per person. This stuffing is also delicious with duck but use one-quarter of the quantity given below.

1 goose, about 10 lbs. (4.5kg)

Stock
neck, giblets, and wishbone of goose
1 onion, sliced
1 carrot, sliced
Bouquet Garni (see page 140)

Potato Stuffing
2 tablespoons butter
1 lb. (450g) onions, chopped
1 lb. (450g) cooking apples, peeled and chopped
1 teaspoon each thyme and lemon balm
3–4 tablespoons fresh orange juice
2 lbs. (900g) potatoes
1/4 teaspoon finely grated orange rind
salt and freshly ground pepper

Bramley Apple Sauce (see page 597)

Preheat oven to 350°F (180°C).

Combine the stock ingredients in a saucepan, cover with cold water, and simmer for 1 1/2–2 hours

For the stuffing, melt the butter in a heavy saucepan. Add the onions, cover, and sweat over a gentle heat for about 5 minutes; add the apples, herbs, and orange juice. Cook, covered, until the apples are soft and fluffy. Meanwhile, boil the potatoes in their skins until cooked, peel, mash, and add to the fruit and onion mixture. Add the orange rind and seasoning. Let it get quite cold before stuffing the goose.

Season the cavity of the goose with salt and freshly ground pepper; rub a little salt into the skin also. Stuff the goose loosely and roast for about 2 hours in the moderate oven. Prick the thigh at the thickest part; the juices that run out should be clear. If they are still pink, the goose needs a little longer. When cooked, remove the goose to a serving dish and put it in a very low oven while you make the gravy.

To make the gravy, spoon off the surplus fat from the roasting pan (save for sautéing or roasting potatoes – it keeps for months in a fridge). Add about 2 1/2 cups of the strained giblet stock to the roasting pan and bring to a boil. Using a small whisk, scrape the pan well to dissolve the meaty deposits which are full of flavor. Taste for seasoning and thicken with a little Roux, if you like. If the gravy is weak, boil it for a few minutes to concentrate the flavor; if it's too strong, add a little water or stock. Strain and serve in a hot gravy boat.

Carve the goose and serve the Bramley Apple Sauce and gravy separately.

Roast Duck with Sage and Onion Stuffing and Red Cabbage

Serves 4
In season: autumn and winter

1 duck, 4 lbs. (1.8kg)

Sage and Onion Stuffing
3 tablespoons butter
2/3 cup onion, finely chopped
1 generous tablespoon sage, freshly chopped
2 cups soft white breadcrumbs
salt and freshly ground pepper

Stock
neck and giblets from duck
1 carrot, sliced
1 onion, quartered
Bouquet Garni (see page 140)
2–3 peppercorns

Red Cabbage (see page 167)
Bramley Apple Sauce (see page 597)

Preheat oven to 350°F (180°C).

To make the stock, put the neck, gizzard, heart, and any other trimmings into a saucepan along with the sliced carrot and quartered onion. Add the bouquet garni, cover with cold water, and add the peppercorns but no salt. Bring slowly to a boil and simmer for 2–3 hours. This will make a delicious stock, which will be the basis of the gravy.

Meanwhile, make the stuffing: heat the butter in a heavy pan, sweat the onion over a gentle heat for 5–10 minutes until soft but not colored, and add the breadcrumbs and sage. Season with salt and pepper to taste. Unless you plan to cook the duck immediately, let the stuffing get cold.

When the stuffing is quite cold, season the cavity of the duck and spoon in the stuffing. Truss the duck loosely and roast in a moderate oven for about 1 1/2 hours.

Then cook the Red Cabbage and Bramley Apple Sauce.

When the duck is cooked, remove to a serving dish, and let it rest while you make the gravy. De-grease the cooking juices in the pan (keep the duck fat for roast or sauté potatoes). Add stock to the juices, bring to a boil, taste, and season if necessary. Strain gravy into a sauceboat and serve, accompanied by the Red Cabbage and Bramley Apple Sauce.

Duck Roast with Honey and Rosemary and Salade Composée

Serves 4

We are very fortunate to have Nora Ahearne in the area. She rears the most wonderful free-range duck, geese, and turkeys with the most incredible flavor.

1 duck, about 3–4 lbs. (1.3–1.8kg)
2½ tablespoons honey
2 teaspoons thyme leaves
2 teaspoons rosemary sprigs
2½ tablespoons shallot or onion, chopped
2 garlic cloves, finely chopped
¾ cup homemade Chicken Stock (see page 36)
2 tablespoons butter
sea salt, or kosher salt, and coarsely ground pepper

Salade Composée (see right)
Hazelnut or Walnut Vinaigrette (see right)

Garnish
2 oranges, segmented
sprigs of flat-leaf parsley

Preheat the oven to 350°F (180°C).

Brush the duck with the honey. Season generously with sea salt and pepper. Sprinkle on the herbs, shallot, and garlic. Roast in the oven for about 1 hour. Baste the duck regularly during cooking; it should develop a rich glaze. Remove the duck to another roasting pan for the remainder of the cooking time, reduce the heat to 325°F (170°C) if it's browning a little too much.

Meanwhile, make the gravy in the original roasting pan: de-grease the roasting pan and de-glaze the caramelized juices with chicken stock. Let the stock boil and simmer gently to dissolve the caramelized juices and to reduce slightly. When the duck is fully cooked, let it rest in a warm oven for 10–15 minutes.

Carve into 4 portions, arrange on a hot serving dish, add the de-greased juices from the carving dish to the gravy. Return it to a boil, whisk in the butter, and spoon over the duck. Garnish with orange segments and sprigs of flat-leaf parsley or watercress, and serve with a Salade Composée.

Salade Composée

8 croûtons of bread (small french stick if possible)
⅓ cup lardons of bacon
Selection of salad greens: butterhead, raddichio, romaine or Napa cabbage, corn salad, chicory, watercress, arugula leaves, beet or Swiss chard leaves.
2 ounces (50g) young green beans, blanched and refreshed (about ½ cup)
1–2 oranges, carefully segmented
a little duck fat

Preheat the oven to 350°F (180°C).

Brush the croûtons with duck fat and place on a baking tray and cook until golden brown. Blanch the lardons of bacon for 15–20 minutes to remove the excess salt. Dry them and fry in a little sunflower oil until golden and crispy. Remove from pan and keep warm.

Carefully tear the lettuces into bite-sized pieces and toss with the beans in the dressing, until the leaves just glisten. Carve the duck and arrange on individual plates. Arrange some salad next to the duck, and the croûtons and orange segments around the salad. Sprinkle the warm lardons of bacon over the salad and serve immediately.

Hazelnut or Walnut Vinaigrette

2 tablespoons white wine vinegar
2 tablespoons sunflower or peanut oil
½ cup hazelnut or walnut oil
pinch of mustard, salt, pepper, and sugar

To make the dressing, combine all the ingredients in a screwtop jar and shake well.

Duck Legs with Onions and Thyme Leaves

Serves 2

This delicious recipe was described to me by John Desmond late one night after a delicious meal in his restaurant on Hare Island just off Baltimore on the south coast of Ireland.

2 duck legs
very little oil
1¼ lbs. (600g) medium-sized onions, peeled and cut into quarters
¼ teaspoon fresh thyme leaves
sea salt, or kosher salt, and freshly ground pepper

Garnish
sprigs of fresh thyme

Preheat the oven to 475°F (250°C).

Season the duck legs all over with crushed sea salt. Heat a tiny drop of oil in a heavy flameproof casserole dish or other ovenproof pot, cook the duck, skin side down, over a medium heat until well-browned, then turn, and brown on the other side.

Remove the duck legs to a plate, increase the heat, and toss the quartered onions in the duck fat until slightly golden, pouring off some of the fat if there is an excessive amount. Sprinkle with a few thyme leaves, season with salt and freshly ground pepper, put the duck legs back in on top of the onions, cover, and cook in the oven for one hour or until the duck is cooked through and the onions are soft and juicy. Check every now and then.

Serve the duck legs on the bed of onions. Garnish with sprigs of fresh thyme.

Variation:
Duck Legs With Turnips

Substitute 2 pounds (900g) white turnips, peeled and cut into chunks, for the onions in the above recipe. The white turnips will soften and absorb the duck juices. Delicious.

How to cut up a duck

(and make the most of every little morsel)

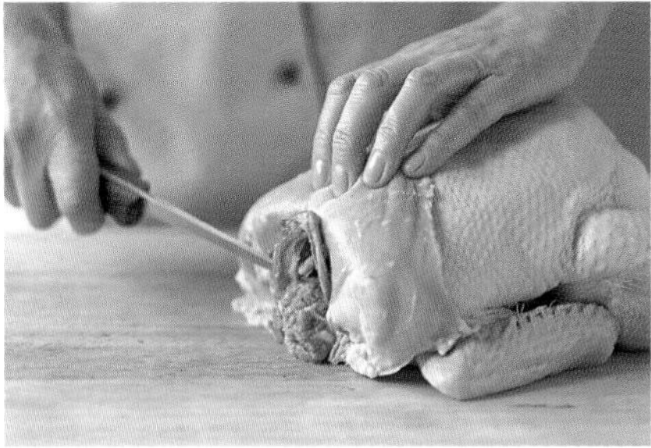

1 First remove the wishbone from the neck end.

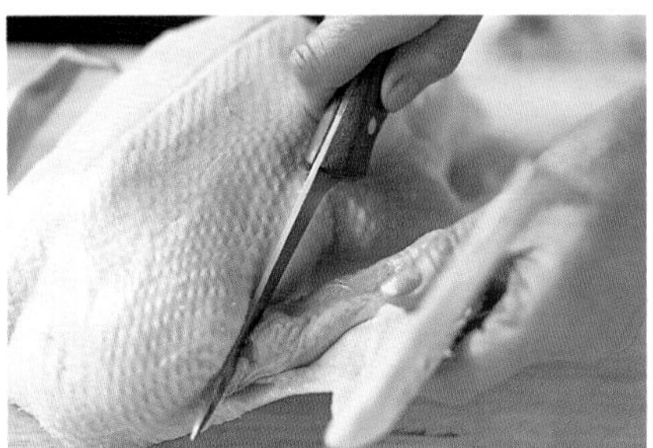

2 Remove the wings – use these for the stockpot.

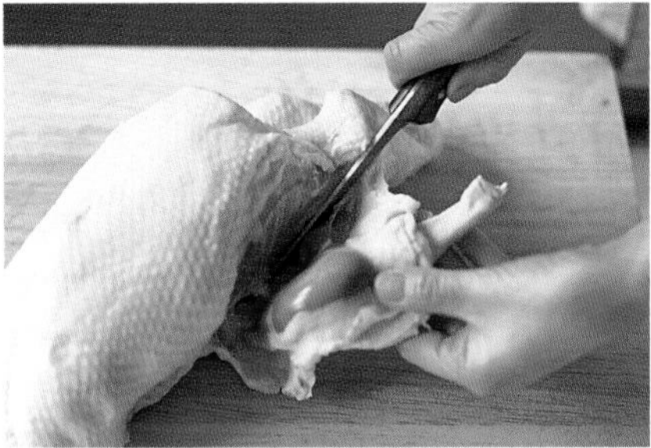

3 Remove the legs – roast, or use for duck confit.

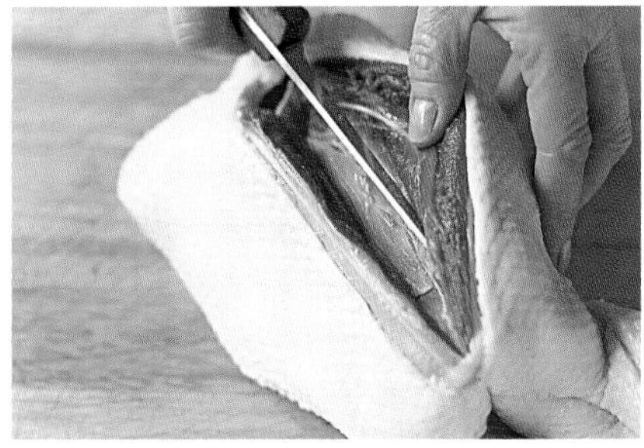

4 Remove the duck breasts. Tear off the inside fillet and use on a salade tiède.

Trim excess fat off the duck breasts and save to render down for duck fat.

Remove all the rest of the duck fat from the carcass – particularly the pieces near the tail end inside the carcass. Cut into small pieces and put into a roasting pan in a low oven 200°F (100°C). The liquid fat will render out slowly, the skin will gradually become crisp and golden. Pour the fat into a stainless steel saucepan or Pyrex bowl.

Save the crispy "grillons" – in France these delicious morsels are sprinkled over a salad.

Finally, there is the duck carcass; if you have a cleaver, chop into smaller pieces and use for duck stock. Add the duck wings and giblets except the liver, and lots of aromatic vegetables and seasoning. Save the duck liver for pâté or for a salade tiède.

In France, I once ate delicious duck rillettes in a restaurant called La Treille in the Dordogne. The chef explained that he used the little pieces of meat from the duck and carcass, which had cooked in the stock. The shredded meat was seasoned with salt and freshly ground pepper and quatre èpices, and mixed with duck fat and served with hot thin toast. It was absolutely delicious. In this way every scrap of the duck is utilized and the stock may be used for duck gravy or beet soup.

How to Pan-grill Duck Breasts – Magret de Canard

Score the fat of the duck breast. Heat a cast-iron grill-pan on a low heat, for a few minutes, and put the duck breasts in breast side down. Cook over a low heat for 15–20 minutes on the fat side, when the fat is thin and crisp, turn over onto the flesh side. The duck breast should be about half cooked by then. Sprinkle with a little salt and continue to cook until it reaches the required degree of doneness – medium to well done is many people's preference. I personally find that rare duck, which was very fashionable when nouvelle cuisine was all the rage, can be unpleasant and tough.

How to prepare a duck or goose for roasting

First gut the bird if necessary, and clean well.

Singe carefully over a gas jet.

Remove the wishbone from the neck end.

Goose Tuck the wings in close to the body.

Duck Use a sharp chopper to trim the wings just above the first joint, nearest the body.

Goose Legs leave intact.

Duck Chop off the knuckle just above the knee.

Season the cavity. Stuff with cold stuffing just before the bird goes into the oven. Truss loosely with cotton string.

Note

It is not absolutely essential to chop off the wings and legs of a duck unless you want a more formal restaurant presentation.

Confit de Canard (Preserved Duck Legs)

Makes 4

Confit is an almost exclusively French way of preserving. First, the meat is salted and then it is cooked, long and slowly, in fat. Originally confit was made to preserve meat, particularly goose and duck, for the winter but nowadays this essentially peasant dish has become very fashionable.

4 duck legs (or 2 legs and 2 breasts, or the equivalent amount of goose)
1 garlic clove
1 generous tablespoon sea salt, or kosher salt
1 teaspoon freshly cracked black peppercorns
a few gratings fresh nutmeg
1 teaspoon thyme leaves
1 crumbled bay leaf

2 lbs. (900g) duck or goose fat
1 bay leaf
2 sprigs thyme
parsley sprigs
6 garlic cloves, unpeeled

Rub the duck legs all over with a cut clove of garlic. Mix the salt, pepper, nutmeg, thyme, and bay leaf together and rub the duck legs with the mixture. Put into an earthenware dish, cover, and leave overnight in a cold pantry or fridge.

Cut every scrap of fat off the duck carcasses – you will need about 2 pounds (900g). Render the fat in a low oven, 200°F (100°C), strain, and set aside.

Next day, melt the fat over a low heat in a wide saucepan. Clean the salt cure off the duck legs and put them into the fat – there should be enough to cover the duck pieces. Bring to a boil, add the herbs and garlic, and simmer over a low heat until the duck is very tender (about 1–1½ hours – a bamboo skewer should go through the thickest part of the leg with no resistance). Remove the duck legs from the fat. Strain it, let it rest for a few minutes, and then pour the fat off the meat juices. When the duck is cold, pack it into a sterilized earthenware crock or jar, pour the cool fat over so that the pieces are completely submerged, and store in the fridge until needed. (Leave for at least a week to mature. When needed, melt the fat to remove the confit.)

Serve hot and crisp on a salad or add to cassoulet (see page 132) or serve simply with thickly sliced potatoes sautéed in duck fat and some Puy Lentils (see below).

Confit of Duck Legs with Puy Lentils

Serves 6 as a main course
In season: winter

6 large duck legs made into confit (see left)

2¼ cups Puy lentils
1 carrot
1 onion, stuck with 2 cloves
bouquet garni
butter or extra-virgin olive oil
lots of freshly squeezed lemon juice
2½–3½ tablespoons herbs, freshly chopped (annual marjoram or parsley)
sea salt, or kosher salt, and freshly ground pepper

Garnish
whole garlic cloves and a sprig of rosemary

Preheat the oven to 450°F (230°C).

Cook the lentils: put them into a saucepan and cover with cold water. Add the carrot, onion, and bouquet garni, bring slowly to a boil, reduce the heat, and simmer very gently for 10 minutes, testing regularly. The lentils should be "al dente" but not hard. Drain, remove and discard the carrot, onion, and bouquet garni. Season the lentils while warm with a good pat of butter or some olive oil, then add lots of lemon juice and the herbs. Season with sea salt and pepper.

Meanwhile, as the lentils are cooking, melt the duck fat and remove the duck confit. Roast the duck confit in the oven until hot and crisp (15 minutes approximately).

Put a portion of lentils on individual, warmed plates, top with a piece of duck confit. Serve with crispy Pan-roasted Parsnips (see page 174) and coarsely-diced Rustic Roast Potatoes (see page 181). Garnish with whole garlic cloves and a sprig of rosemary.

Pan-grilled Duck Breast with Kumquat Compôte

Serves 6
In season: winter

4 duck breasts
salt and freshly ground pepper
Kumquat Compôte (see page 391)

Garnish
sprigs of fresh rosemary or flat-leaf parsley

First make the compôte.

Score the fat of the duck breasts. Pan-grill over a low heat (see page 290). When cooked, season with salt and pepper and transfer to an upturned plate resting on a larger plate. This will catch any juices that may escape and will ensure that the meat is not sitting in a pool of liquid.

Reheat enough kumquat compôte to accompany the duck. Add the duck juices to the kumquat compôte. Cut the duck breasts into slices crosswise, arrange on individual plates with 1–2 tablespoons of kumquat compôte. Garnish each with a sprig of rosemary or flat-leaf parsley.

Duck with Orange

Serves 4

1 duck, 4 lbs. (1.8kg) in weight
3 brightly colored oranges
1/4 cup granulated sugar
1/4 cup red wine vinegar
1 1/4 cups Duck or Chicken Stock (see page 36)
1/4 cup red wine
1/2 cup Port
1/2–1 tablespoon Grand Marnier
salt, pepper, and a few drops of lemon juice

Garnish
sprigs of parsley or watercress

Preheat the oven to 425°F (220°C).

Scrub the oranges. Peel the zest from two, and cut two-thirds into fine julienne strips, blanch, and refresh. Season the duck cavity and skin with salt and pepper. Put the remaining one-third of the orange peel into the cavity, and transfer the duck to the hot oven. After 30 minutes, reduce the temperature to 350°F (180°C). Continue to roast for a further 30–45 minutes.

Meanwhile, make a sweet and sour caramel. Boil the sugar and vinegar over a moderately high heat for several minutes until the mixture has turned into a chestnut-brown colored syrup. Remove from the heat immediately and pour in 2/3 cup of the stock. Simmer for a minute, stirring to dissolve the caramel. Then add the rest of the stock, port, wine, and juice of one orange. Simmer until the sauce is clear and lightly thickened; add the liqueur little by little. Add the remainder of the orange julienne. Taste, correct the seasoning, and sharpen with lemon juice if necessary; set aside. Cut the remaining 2 oranges into neat segments and reserve for garnishing.

When the duck is cooked, let it rest in a warm oven for at least 10 minutes before carving. Spoon sauce over the top, and garnish with orange segments and herbs.

Left: Duck Breast with Spiced Lentils and Caramelized Apples

Duck Breast with Spiced Lentils and Caramelized Apples

Serves 4

4 duck breasts
salt and freshly ground pepper
a heaped cup Puy lentils
1 large or 2 small chiles, finely chopped
2 generous tablespoons fresh cilantro
lemon juice, freshly squeezed
extra-virgin olive oil

Caramelized Apples
2 eating apples (Cox's Orange Pippin or Golden Delicious)
2 tablespoons butter
1 tablespoon plus 1 teaspoon sugar
juice of 1/2 lemon
1 tablespoon Calvados (optional)

Garnish
sprigs of cilantro or flat-leaf parsley

Season the duck breasts and score the fat with a sharp knife. Heat a grill-pan over a high heat, put the duck into the pan, fat side down. Cook for 15–20 minutes, depending on thickness. Turn over and continue until fully cooked but still tender and juicy. Reduce the heat and cook on a low heat for 10–15 minutes until the fat is crisp and fully cooked. A lot of fat will run out and it may be necessary to pour some off.

Cook the lentils (see page 136), and prepare the apples. Peel, core, and cut into 1/4-inch (5-mm) slices. Melt the butter in a non-stick frying pan, toss in the apple, and cook gently for 5 minutes, add the sugar and let it caramelize slightly. Add the lemon juice and Calvados. Let it become syrupy, then remove from the pan and keep warm.

Heat the lentils, stir in the chile, cilantro, and a squeeze of lemon juice. Season with salt and pepper and some olive oil to taste. Divide the lentils between hot plates, arrange a crispy duck breast on top, and garnish with caramelized apple, sprigs of cilantro or flat-leaf parsley.

lamb

lamb

Easter Sunday at Ballymaloe would never be complete without a succulent roast leg of Spring lamb, served with a mint sauce made from the very first tender leaves of the new season's mint.

Michael Cuddigan, our local butcher, provides us with the most delicious lamb. He buys his animals on the hoof from local farmers and keeps them on his own pasture until he deems them ready for slaughter. He hangs his lamb for a week or more and then brings it out to Ballymaloe. We usually buy the whole carcass and use every scrap in a variety of dishes.

Lamb, Hogget, and Mutton

Spring lamb is approximately five months old and is in season for just a few weeks over Easter. From then on up until Christmas, it is referred to as lamb. After Christmas, until the following Easter, it's called hogget (or yearling in the U.S.). Mutton is two years old and has a distinctive flavor. Ballymaloe is one of the few places where one finds hogget identified on a menu. It has a more pronounced flavor than lamb and, although you can roast it in the normal way, we find it responds particularly well to slow roasting or braising with the first of the wild garlic or winter vegetables. Mutton is stronger in flavor than hogget or lamb. It can be marginally tougher than lamb, if not cooked with care, but it has a wonderful if slightly more mature flavor. It is becoming increasingly rare to find mutton as most farmers can not afford to keep their lambs out at pasture for so long.

Breeds to Look For

Most sheep are grass fed; and the fine quality of Ireland's sweet, green grass is reflected in the excellent flavor of our lamb.

Mountain lamb is at long last getting the recognition that it deserves. It tends to be leaner than some of the other lowland breeds, and living on hilly pastures, they have access to a variety of grasses, heather, wild herbs and flowers on the hills, which gives the meat a unique and delicious flavor. Lamb from the hills of Connemara, Wicklow, West Cork, Kerry and Donegal is now particularly sought after in Ireland.

Nowadays there is also a growing interest in rare breeds of lamb among chefs and other discerning consumers. In the U.K., in the upland areas and the fells, there are superb Swaledale and Herdwick sheep. Many rare breed farmers have realized that there is a growing market for this type of lamb and now target the public directly and sell their meat through farmers' markets. They also understand the value of highlighting the name of the breeds, so look out for them – and if you've never tasted a rare breed, you really should. The meat might not be as lean as other breeds, but the flavor is distinctive and full of character.

Traceability

Supermarkets and independent butchers have responded to recent health scares and customer concerns by putting traceability schemes into operation and by identifying the source of their meat.

When I buy a cut of meat, I like to know where it's come from and how the animal has been reared. Fortunately for us, we have a very good and trustworthy local butcher, who has all the answers to my questions. Butchers who build up a bond of trust with their consumers by knowing the provenance of their meat, and by guaranteeing that it is both hormone- and antibiotic-free, are at a distinct advantage – they soon build up a loyal customer base.

Uses and Cooking

Unlike beef, every part of the lamb carcass can be roasted – from the shoulder down to the leg.

The **neck** has lots of bone and is normally added to a stew together with what we call here in Ireland rack chops. These chops from the shoulder are known in the U.S. as blade chops. Ask your butcher to cut them at least 1 inch (2.5cm) thick because if they are too thin there's a tendency for the meat to toughen a little bit during cooking.

The **shoulder** is less expensive than the leg or loin. It is most often used for stews or curries, but is absolutely delicious slow roasted. It's a bit more difficult to carve but the bone in the shoulder gives it extra sweetness and flavor. It has a little more fat but this merely enhances the flavor and adds succulence. Scrape up all the little juicy bits of caramelized sediment in the roasting pan to make delicious gravy. Slow-roasted shoulder of lamb with rosemary or cilantro, with a sprinkling of sea salt or kosher salt is, without a doubt, one of my favorite meals.

One can also bone the shoulder and roll it up with your favorite stuffing or some gutsy tapenade. Or simply tie it up, pop a spot of rosemary and garlic on top, and then roast it.

All of the loin – both the **center loin** (where the chops have a T-bone) and the **side loin** (the cutlets) – can be roasted, pan-grilled, fried, or sautéed. The end part, or "breast of lamb", can be cut into pieces, dipped in flour, egg, and crumbs, and made into little epigrams which are then roasted until beautifully plump and crispy. Alternatively, make lamb riblets by cutting the breast into thin slices with the bone still in. These can be marinated using one of the marinades in the barbecue chapter (see page 538), or bought ready-marinated from many butchers, and simply roasted at home with no further fuss.

To prepare a **rack of lamb**, you'll need to buy the side loin – the part of the loin with the cutlet bones in it. Two prepared racks can be interlinked to create a "Guard of Honor" (see page 299) which is guaranteed to impress your guests. Even though it looks quite elaborate, it's easy to carve. Don't get too carried away when trimming the end of the cutlets. Nowadays posh restaurants seem to leave just the bare eye of the cutlet, and cut off the lovely streaky bit along the bone. Ironically, the more they trim off, the more they charge for it. It's a pity to lose all of that because it is sweet, juicy, and good.

For a simple dinner, you can cut between the bones for lamb cutlets, but for an extra special dinner party, it's worth making a **crown roast of lamb**. When you're preparing the rack of lamb, follow the images on page 298 carefully. Saw along the top of the ribs where they meet the chine bone, then run your knife underneath the bone and lift it off. When it is cooked, you'll be able to carve through between the cutlets unimpeded.

The **leg** can, of course, be roasted whole, or cut into two joints. One can also barbecue or char-grill big thick, juicy steaks from the leg or use chunks of it in stews and curries – we like to use it in our Mild Madras Curry. Lamb shanks, cut from the front leg, are very fashionable today as people have discovered how succulent they are. Shanks are less expensive than many other cuts and are great for gutsy stews. They become meltingly tender with long, slow cooking. The meat

Saddle of Lamb and how to prepare it

A saddle of lamb consists of both loins of the lamb, attached at the backbone, in the same way as a baron of beef (a double sirloin).

First remove the papery outer skin with a small sharp knife. If the meat is well-chilled, it should be possible to lift a corner of the skin and tug sharply to peel off. Trim off any excess fat from the edges of the saddle, but leave the back fat. Tuck the flaps underneath the saddle. Cut off the kidneys but keep them (they can be attached to the end of the saddle with wooden skewers 30 minutes before the end of the roasting time and roasted). With a sharp knife, score the back fat all over in a fine criss-cross pattern.

To prepare a rack of lamb or lamb cutlets

Chill the meat well first. Skin the side loin or rack, lift a corner of the skin from the neck end with a small knife, hold it firmly, and peel it off (use a cloth to get a good grip). Chine if the butcher has not already done so; this means to saw carefully through the chine bone (or spine) just where it meets the rib bones. Take care not to saw right through into the eye of the meat. Now remove the chine bone completely. Chop off the cutlet bones so that the length of the remaining bones is not more than twice the length of the eye of the meat. Remove the half-moon shaped piece of flexible cartilage found between the layers of fat and meat at the thinner end of the rack. This is the tip of the shoulder blade. It is simple to work out with a knife and your fingers.

For lamb cutlets

Cut off half the streaky meat at the end in one piece.

For epigrams

Clean all the fat and scraps of meat off the bones, score the fat. If thin small cutlets are required, cut between each bone as evenly as possible, splitting the rack into six or seven small cutlets. If thicker cutlets are required, carefully ease out every other rib bone, then cut between the remaining bones into thick cutlets. Now trim the fat from the thick end of each cutlet, and scrape the rib bones free of any flesh or skin.

Noisettes of Lamb

These are boneless cutlets, tied into a neat round shape with a string. They are made from the loin of rack. Skin the meat: lift a corner of the skin with a small knife, holding it firmly (using a cloth to get a good grip), and pull it off or else trim off neatly with the knife. Now remove first the chine bone and then all the rib bones, easing them out with a short sharp knife.

Trim off most of the fat from the meat and roll it up tightly, starting at the meaty thick side and working towards the thin flap. Tie the roll neatly with separate pieces of cotton string tied at $1\frac{1}{2}$-inch (4-cm) intervals. Trim the ragged ends of the roll to neaten them. Now slice the roll into pieces, cutting accurately between each string. The average rack will give 6 good noisettes. The string from each noisette is removed after cooking. Noisettes are often served on a croûton of fried bread or a potato galette.

Crown Roast

Two racks (side loin) are needed. For a more impressive roast use 3. Each side loin is prepared in the same way as for roast rack of lamb but the bones are left slightly longer. It is skinned, chined, and the shoulder cartilage is removed. All fat is removed and the top 1–2 inches (2.5–5cm) of the bones are scraped in the same way.

Bend each rack into a semi-circle, with the fatty side of the ribs inside. To facilitate this, it may be necessary to cut through the membrane about 1 inch (2.5cm), between each cutlet, from the thick end. Be careful not to cut into the fleshy part of the meat.

With fine cotton string, sew the end of the racks together to make a circle with the meaty part, forming the base of the crown. Tie a piece of string around the waist of the crown. Traditionally, crown roast is stuffed, but this can result in undercooked inside fat unless it is completely trimmed before cooking.

Guard of Honor

Prepare 2 racks or side loins exactly as for the crown roast. Score the fat in a criss-cross pattern.

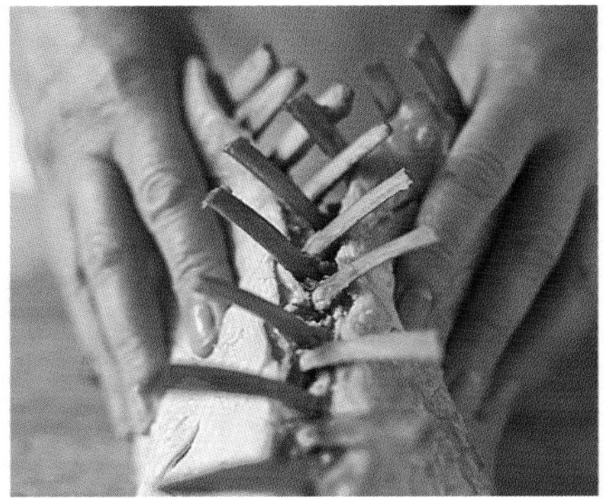

Hold the 2 racks, one in each hand, facing each other with the meaty part of the racks on the board, and the fatty sides on the outside. Adjust them so the rib bones interlock and cross at the top.

Tie with cotton string in several places. Stuff the arch if required. Serve with cutlet frills on top of each bone for extra class.

Master Recipe

Lamb Roast with Rosemary and Garlic

Serves 8–10

Rosemary survives year round even in colder gardens. Spike your leg of lamb with this pungent herb and garlic – delicious hot, warm, or at room temperature on a buffet. Loin of lamb, shoulder, or rump may be cooked in the same way.

1 leg of lamb, 6–7 lbs. (2.6–3.1kg)
4–5 garlic cloves
2 sprigs of rosemary
salt and freshly ground pepper
Gravy (see overleaf)
2 1/2 cups stock, preferably homemade Lamb Stock (see page 37)
Roux (see page 580) (optional)

Preheat the oven to 400°F (200°C).

Choose a good leg of lamb with a thin layer of fat. Ask the butcher to trim the knuckle and remove the aitch bone for ease of carving later, otherwise prepare it as on page 300. With the point of a sharp knife or skewer, make deep holes all over the lamb, about 1 inch (2.5cm) apart. It is a good idea not to do this on the underside of the joint, in case somebody insists on eating their lamb unflavored.

Divide the rosemary sprigs into tufts of 3 or 4 leaves together. Peel the garlic cloves and cut them into little spikes about the same size as a matchstick broken into 3.

Stick a spike of garlic with a tuft of rosemary into each hole in the lamb. Cover, and refrigerate for 1–2 hours if you have time. Alternatively, cook immediately.

Sprinkle the joint with salt and pepper and put it into a roasting pan in the oven. Reduce the heat to 350°F (180°C) after 20 minutes.

Cook for 1 hour more for very rare lamb, 1 1/2 hours if it is to be well done. Remove the joint to a serving dish and let it rest while you make the gravy.

Gravy

Spoon the fat out of the roasting pan. Pour the stock into the cooking juices remaining in the pan. Boil for a few minutes, stirring and scraping the pan well, to dissolve the caramelized meat juices (I find a small whisk ideal for this). Thicken with a very little Roux if you like (see page 580).

Taste, and add salt and pepper if necessary. Strain and serve the gravy separately in a gravy boat. Serve with Roast Potatoes (see page 181).

Variations

Roast Leg of Lamb with Marjoram and Garlic

Follow the Master Recipe but substitute little tufts of marjoram for rosemary.

Lamb Roast with Thyme and Garlic

Follow the Master Recipe but substitute little sprigs of thyme for rosemary.

Lamb Roast with Coriander Seeds

Follow the Master Recipe but omit the rosemary and substitute 2½ tablespoons of coriander seeds. Insert garlic with a few seeds warmed in a pan and then crushed in a mortar and pestle. Drizzle the lamb with olive oil before roasting. Add 1 tablespoon freshly ground coriander to the gravy.

Lamb Roast with Cumin

Follow as for Lamb Roast with Coriander Seeds but substitute freshly ground cumin for coriander. Alternatively mix cumin and coriander.

How to Prepare a Leg of Lamb for Roasting

Trimming the shank end of the leg is merely for appearance but the removal of the pelvic bone is essential because it makes carving so much easier. Your butcher may well do it for you but, armed with a sharp knife, it only takes a few minutes to do at home.

The pelvic bone is made up of the aitch-bone and the hip bone. Because it is an irregular shaped bone at an angle to the leg bone, it makes carving difficult. It is attached by a ball and socket joint.

Place the leg of lamb on a cutting board, skin side down. Trace the outline of the bone with a sharp knife; cut deeper around the pelvic bone, keeping the knife as close to the bone as possible. Free all the bones and then loosen and separate the ball and socket joint. Use this bone and the shank end to make a little stock for gravy.

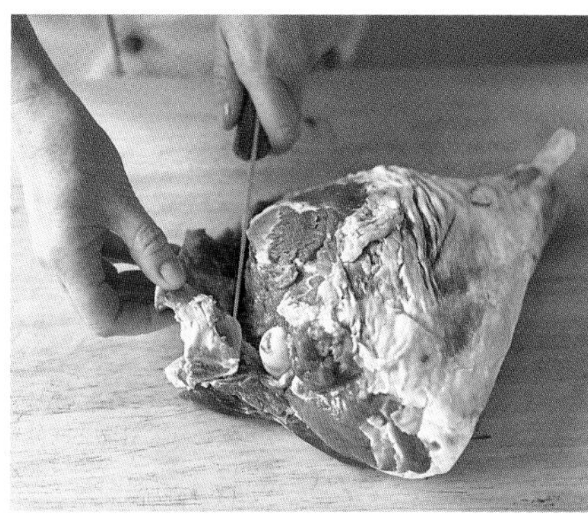

Removing the aitch-bone for ease of carving.

To trim the shank end

Saw through the bone just above the knuckle. Trim the meat off the end of the bone. Add to the stockpot and cook for about 1½ minutes. In cooking, the meat will shrink a little further and leave the end of the bone exposed. A paper frill may be slipped over the end of the bone for extra class when serving.

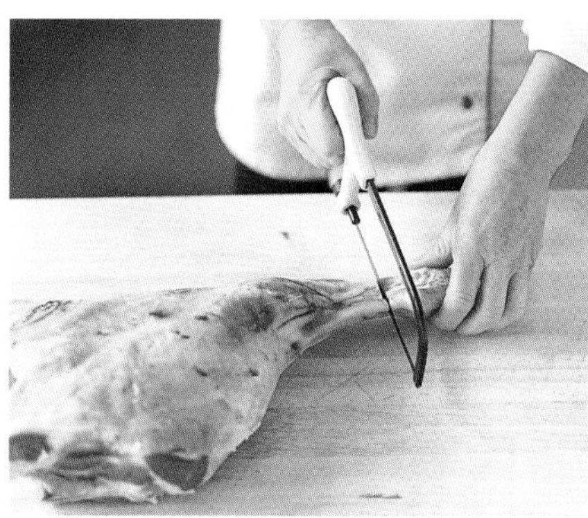

Trimming the shank end of the leg with a saw.

Lamb shanks come from the foreleg or shoulder.

Lamb Roast with Garden Herbs

Serves: an average-weight leg of lamb 7–8 lbs. (3.1–3.6kg) will serve 8–10 people. Allow about 6 ounces (175g) per person.
In season: best late spring to autumn

I like to tie a little bunch of herbs onto the end of the bone just before I bring the roast to the table for carving.

1 leg of lamb, 6–7 lbs. (2.6–3.1kg)

Herb Marinade
3 large garlic cloves
1–2 handfuls herbs (parsley, thyme, lemon balm, mint, tarragon, chives, rosemary, and marjoram), chopped*
1/2–1 cup olive oil
salt and freshly ground pepper

Gravy
2 1/2 cups Lamb or Chicken Stock (see page 36–37)
2 teaspoons herbs as above, freshly chopped
Roux (see page 580)
2 tablespoons butter (optional)
salt and freshly ground pepper

**If you don't have access to such variety, use whatever fresh herbs you have, e.g., parsley, chives, thyme, and mint.*

First make the herb relish: peel and crush the garlic cloves. Put them, along with the olive oil, salt and pepper, and fresh herbs, into a food processor and whizz them for about 1 minute or until it becomes a soft green paste, otherwise just mix them in a little bowl.

If possible, remove the aitch bone from the top of the leg of lamb so that it will be easier to carve later, then trim the end of the leg. Score the fat lightly, rub in the herb mixture, and let it marinate for several hours if possible.

Roast for a good 1 hour for rare, 1 1/2 hours for medium, and 1 3/4 hours for well done meat. When the lamb is cooked, remove the joint to a carving dish. Rest the lamb for 10 minutes before carving.

To make the gravy: de-grease the juices in the roasting pan, add the stock, bring to a boil, and thicken with a little roux if desired. Just before serving, whisk in some pats of butter to enrich the gravy. Taste for seasoning and add salt and pepper if necessary.

Serve with Ulster Champ (see page 183) and Oven-roasted Tomatoes (see page 188). Or serve with Char-grilled Peppers (see page 192) and Gratin Dauphinois (see page 186).

Roast Shoulder of Lamb Stuffed with Tapenade

Serves 16–20

Monique Avril (wife of the vigneron Paul Avril) showed me how to make this delicious Provençal recipe on a sunny afternoon in Châteauneuf du Pape. You will need cotton string.

1 shoulder of lamb, 8 lbs. (3.6kg) with bones or 7 lbs. (3.1kg) without bones. Two small shoulders are even better.

Tapenade stuffing
1 1/4 cups black olives, pitted
2 large garlic cloves, peeled and chopped
2 anchovies
2 1/2 tablespoons extra-virgin olive oil

Gravy
1 quart (960ml) homemade Lamb or Chicken Stock (see page 36–37)

Preheat the oven to 350°F (180°C).

Ask your butcher to bone the shoulder of lamb for you or do it yourself. Use the bones to make stock for the gravy.

To make the tapenade: put the olives, garlic, anchovies, and olive oil into a food processor and whizz for a few seconds – just long enough to chop the olives fairly coarsely – it shouldn't be a pureé.

Score the skin of the lamb lightly then put the meat skin side down on your worktop. Remove surplus fat from the inside, spread the olive mixture over the lamb, and roll lengthwise, tying at regular intervals with string. Sprinkle lightly with salt and roast in the oven, for about 1 1/4 hours. This will produce lamb with a faint pink tinge. Remove to a carving dish and let rest while you make the gravy in the usual way (see page 594). Carve at the table and serve with a little gravy, some char-grilled vegetables, and Rustic Roast Potatoes (see page 181).

Butterflied Leg of Lamb with Spices

Serves 8–10

1 leg of lamb, 5–6 lbs. (2.2–2.6kg)

Marinade

2 teaspoons cumin seeds
1 teaspoon black peppercorns
1 teaspoon cardamom seeds
1/2 teaspoon chili powder, optional
1 teaspoon salt
a scant 1/2 cup extra-virgin olive oil
1 1/2 tablespoons balsamic or wine vinegar or sherry
3 garlic cloves, peeled and crushed

Follow the instructions right to butterfly the lamb.

Thick pieces of meat may be slightly opened out by slitting part of the way with a sharp knife. It is not necessary to get the meat all the same thickness – one of the attractions of this dish is that it provides a mixture of well done and underdone pieces of meat. Remove any excess fat.

Roast the cumin seeds in a pan over a medium heat for 1–2 minutes and add the peppercorns and cardamom seeds. Remove from the heat and crush coarsely in a mortar and pestle. Mix the other marinade ingredients together in a bowl and add the ground spices. Put the lamb inside a large plastic bag and pour the marinade over it; knot the end tightly. Leave in the fridge for 24 hours, turning from time to time.

Preheat the oven to 400°F (200°C) and cook the lamb for 1–1 1/2 hours, basting with marinade every 10 minutes. Rest the meat for 15–20 minutes before carving.

If you prefer to barbecue the lamb, light the barbecue and let it reach full heat. It's difficult to give a time for this, barbecues vary so much. Drain the lamb, arrange the rack at least 10 inches (25.5cm) from the coals, otherwise the inside will be raw while the outside is charred. It will take about 45 minutes to cook. Baste the lamb with marinade regularly during cooking.

Rest the meat for 15–20 minutes before carving.

Serve with crusty potatoes and a good green salad and maybe Apple and Mint Jelly (see page 507), Ballymaloe Country Relish, or Apple and Tomato Chutney (see page 511).

How to Butterfly a Leg of Lamb

If the leg has already been boned, simply cut open from top to bottom and lay flat – it will roughly resemble the shape of a butterfly, hence the name. Alternatively cut down along the leg and shank bone on the underside and carefully remove.

Open out the lamb as above. You will need to make a few further cuts to let the lamb lie flat on the board.

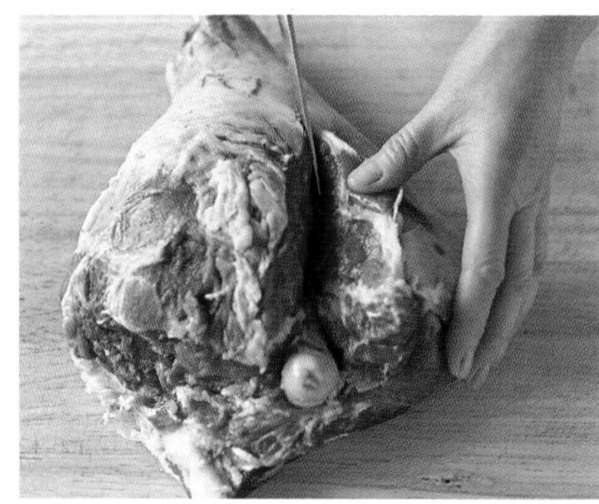

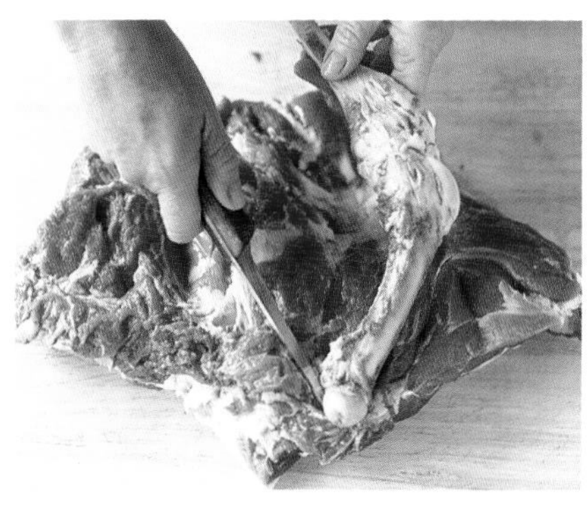

Boiled Mutton or Hogget with Caper Sauce

Serves 6–8

My butcher, Michael Cuddigan, explained to me the correct terms for lamb: spring lamb from Easter, then from Easter until Christmas it is lamb, and from Christmas until the following Easter it should be known as hogget. Mutton is from an older animal, and difficult to find these days.

This is a wonderful dish for a cold winter's evening. Ballymaloe House is one of the few places where hogget is on the menu – often braised with winter vegetables or wild garlic.

1 x 6 1/2-lb. (3-kg) leg of mutton or hogget
3 onions, peeled and halved
4–5 carrots, halved if large
2 stalks of celery, halved
6 peppercorns
1 sprig thyme
1 bay leaf
salt and freshly ground pepper

Caper Sauce

2 tablespoons butter
1 tablespoon plus 1 teaspoon all-purpose white flour
2 1/2 cups milk
2 1/2 tablespoons chopped capers
1 generous tablespoon parsley, chopped (optional)

Ask your butcher to cut the leg at the shank end. Put the meat into a saucepan just large enough to fit it nicely. Cover with water, add a good sprinkle of salt, and bring to a boil. Remove any scum that rises to the surface.

Add the vegetables and bay leaves. Cover the pan and simmer very gently, depending on the weight of the meat; allow 30 minutes for every pound (450g) plus 25 minutes.

Meanwhile, make the Caper Sauce. Melt the butter in a saucepan, stir in the flour, and cook for a minute or two.

Gradually mix in the milk, bring to a boil, and simmer for 4 or 5 minutes. Season with salt and freshly ground pepper and set aside.

Just before serving, add 2/3 cup of de-greased broth from the saucepan. Bring back to a boil, add the roughly chopped capers and parsley. Taste, and correct the seasoning.

Carve the meat into slices at the table and serve with Caper Sauce.

Below: Butterflied Leg of Lamb with Spices

Tagine of Lamb with Preserved Lemon

Serves 6

The word tagine refers both to the distinctive earthenware cooking pot with shallow base and conical top, and to a multitude of stew-like dishes cooked in it. These can be based on meat, fish, poultry, or vegetables. I lugged my precious tagine, plus the brazier that goes underneath it, all the way from Morocco. Without question it is the most expensive tagine in the whole of Ireland because even though I got a bargain in Medina, I had to pay excess baggage at the airport and the Moroccans would not settle for my leftover diarhams – they wanted sterling or dollars and would not part with the tagine until they got them!

1 shoulder of lamb, 3 lbs. (1.3kg)
2 teaspoons ground cinnamon
1 teaspoon ground ginger
1 teaspoon black pepper, freshly ground
generous pinch saffron
1/2 stick (1/4 cup) unsalted butter
2 onions, chopped
2 garlic cloves, finely chopped
salt
3/4 cup raisins, soaked in water and drained
2 1/2 tablespoons honey
1/4 cup fresh cilantro, chopped
1 1/2 tablespoons sunflower oil
1/3 cup sliced almonds
1 Preserved Lemon (see page 515), half if large

Couscous (see page 130)

Trim the lamb, discarding excess fat. Cut it into 1 1/2-inch (4-cm) cubes. Mix the cinnamon, ginger, pepper, and saffron with 5 tablespoons of water. Toss the lamb in this mixture. If you have time, let it marinate for up to 24 hours in the fridge.

Melt the butter in a tagine or wide pan. Add the lamb, onions, garlic, salt, and enough water to come half way up the meat. Bring up to a boil, cover, and reduce heat to a gentle simmer. Cook for about 1 hour, turning the lamb occasionally, until the meat is meltingly tender. Add the drained raisins, honey, and half the cilantro. Continue simmering for a further 30 minutes or so, uncovered, until the sauce is thick and unctuous. Taste, and adjust seasoning.

While the tagine is cooking, scoop the soft flesh out of the preserved lemon and chop up the peel. Fry the almonds gently in the oil until almost golden brown, then add the diced lemon and toss 2 or 3 times. Drain on paper towels. Sprinkle preserved lemon, almonds, and the remaining cilantro leaves over the lamb just before serving.

Serve with Couscous (see page 130).

Preserved Lemons

Preserved lemons are one of the indispensable flavors in Moroccan cooking. Buy them loose in the souks or make them easily at home. You probably won't be able to source the Doqq or Boussers lemons used in Morocco but do try to use unwaxed lemon. Several presentation methods are used. The Moroccan Jews use olive oil; in the Safi area, some spices and herbs are added. Use plain salt with no chemicals (e.g. sea salt or kosher salt). It is important to ensure that the salted lemons are completely covered with lemon juice, otherwise they won't keep. The pickling liquid may be reused several times. See page 515 for recipe.

Braised Lamb Shanks with Garlic, Rosemary, and Flageolet Beans

Serves 4

Antony Worrall-Thompson cooked me lamb shanks when he came to teach at the school – a really gutsy, comforting dish.

4 lamb shanks, about 2 1/2 lbs. (1.1kg)
8 small sprigs of rosemary
8 slivers garlic
4 anchovy fillets, halved
salt and freshly ground black pepper

Braising ingredients
2 tablespoons goose or duck fat or olive oil
2 carrots, roughly chopped
2 celery stalks, roughly chopped
1 leek, roughly chopped
1 onion, roughly chopped
1 head garlic, halved horizontally
1/2 bottle good red wine
2/3 cup homemade Chicken or Lamb Stock (see page 36–37)
1 sprig of thyme
2 sprigs of rosemary
2 bay leaves
2 strips of dried orange peel

Sauce
2 1/2 tablespoons extra-virgin olive oil
4 ounces (110g) bacon, cut into lardons and blanched
4 ounces (110g) carrot, finely diced (about 1 cup)
4 ounces (110g) celery stalk, finely diced (about 1 cup)
4 ounces (110g) onion, finely diced (about 1 cup)
6 garlic cloves
4 very ripe tomatoes, peeled and diced or 7 ounces (200g) canned tomatoes plus juice
2 sprigs of thyme
leaves from 2 sprigs of rosemary, chopped
1 x 14-ounce (400-g) can flageolet beans, drained, or 2/3–1 cup dried flageolet beans, soaked overnight and then boiled rapidly for 20 minutes
2/3 cup homemade Chicken or Lamb Stock (see page 36–37)

Garnish
sprigs of rosemary and thyme

Preheat the oven to 300°F (150°C). Remove most of the fat from each shank, then scrape the meat away from the bone to loosen it. Make 2 deep incisions in each joint and insert a sprig of rosemary and a sliver of garlic wrapped in half an anchovy fillet into each incision. Season the meat with salt and

Above: Braised Lamb Shanks with Garlic, Rosemary, and Flageolet Beans

pepper. Heat the goose fat or olive oil in a heavy ovenproof sauté pan or flameproof casserole dish and sauté the meat in it until well-browned on all sides. Remove the meat from the pan. Add the carrots, celery, leek, onion, and garlic, and cook over a high heat until well-browned. Add the red wine and bring to a boil and stir for 1–2 minutes. Add the stock, herbs, and orange peel, then place the lamb shanks on top. Cover, and cook in the oven for 2¼ hours.

Meanwhile, make the sauce: heat the olive oil in a saucepan and brown the bacon in it. Then reduce the heat and add the carrot, celery, onion, and garlic, and cook for about 8 minutes or until the vegetables have softened. Add the tomatoes, herbs, flageolets, and enough stock to half-cover the beans. Cover, and simmer for ½–1 hour.

When the lamb has finished cooking, remove the thyme, bay leaves, and orange peel. Taste, and correct seasoning. Serve in a hot, deep dish with the beans and vegetables poured over and around the lamb. Garnish with sprigs of fresh rosemary and thyme. Serve with Fluffy Mashed Potato (see page 182).

Master Recipe

Roast Rack of Spring Lamb with Three Sauces

Serves 4–6
In season: late spring

We use grass-fed lamb from our butcher, who buys his animals directly from local farmers. He is our vital link with safe food because he knows on what the animals are fed and how they are reared.

2 racks of spring lamb (6 cutlets each, most butchers will prepare it for you)
salt and freshly ground pepper

Accompaniment
Fresh Mint Chutney (see page 595)
Onion Sauce (see page 581)
Red Currant Sauce (see page 598)

Garnish
little sprigs of fresh mint

Preheat the oven to 425°F (220°C).

Prepare the racks of lamb (see page 298). Remove the skin and score the fat. Refrigerate until needed.

Sprinkle the racks of lamb with salt and freshly ground pepper. Roast fat side upwards for 25–30 minutes depending on the age of the lamb and how well done you want it to be. When cooked, remove to a warm serving dish. Turn off the oven and let the lamb rest for 5–10 minutes before carving so that the juices re-distribute evenly through the meat.

Carve the lamb into cutlets, allowing 2–3 per person depending on size. Serve with fresh Mint Chutney, Onion Sauce, and Red Currant Sauce and lots of Rustic Roast Potatoes (see page 181).

Variation
Saddle of Lamb Chops with Three Sauces

Pan-grill the saddle lamb chops and serve with three sauces. Choose from Ballymaloe Mint Sauce (see page 595), Onion Sauce (see page 581), and Red Currant Jelly or Sauce (see page 508 or 598).

Epigrams

Cheap and absolutely delicious. Remove the streaky part of the loin of lamb in one piece. Score the fat side and cut into strips about 3 inches (8cm) wide. Dip into flour, then beaten egg, and then breadcrumbs. Roast in a hot oven, 400°F (200°C), for 40–45 minutes.

Master Recipe
Roast Loin of Lamb with Duxelle Stuffing and Mint Sauce

Serves 10–12
In season: late spring – autumn

Irish lamb is still remarkably sweet and for the most part naturally reared. No lamb I've tasted on any of the starred restaurant menus on the continent could equal the flavor of the lamb I buy from my local butcher, Michael Cuddigan, who rears his animals on rich old pastures full of wild flowers and herbs. There are still many conscientious butchers like Michael around the country so search them out and support them.

1 whole loin of lamb, about 6½ lbs. (2.8kg). Allow 6–8 ounces (175–225g) boned loin per person
salt and freshly ground pepper

Duxelle Stuffing
1 stick (½ cup) butter
2 cups chopped onion
1 lb. (450g) mushrooms, chopped (about 4–5 cups)
1 lb. (450g) cooked ham or bacon, chopped
2 tablespoons parsley, chives, and fresh thyme leaves, mixed
salt and freshly ground pepper

Gravy
2½ cups homemade Lamb or Chicken Stock (see page 36–37)
Roux (see page 580)
1 generous tablespoon herbs (chives, thyme, and parsley), freshly chopped

Preheat the oven to 350°F (180°C).

First make the stuffing: melt the butter in a heavy saucepan on a low heat and add the onions. Sweat on a gentle heat until soft, about 6–8 minutes. Increase the heat, add the mushrooms, season with salt and pepper, cook for 2–3 minutes until just tender. Add the ham and herbs, taste, and check seasoning. Let the mixture cool before stuffing the loin of lamb.

Bone the loin of lamb, put the bones into a saucepan with a few aromatic vegetables and a bouquet garni, bring to a boil and simmer for a few hours, to make a little stock for the gravy. Lightly score the fat side of the meat, turn over, and trim off the excess flap, keep to make Epigrams (see left). Sprinkle the joint with salt and pepper. Spread the stuffing on the boned side and roll up like a jelly roll and tie with cotton string.

Roast in a moderate oven for about 1½ hours. When the loin is cooked, remove from the roasting pan, place on a serving dish, and keep warm.

To make the gravy: de-grease the roasting pan and de-glaze with the stock. Let the stock boil for a few minutes. Whisk in a little roux if a slightly thick gravy is preferred. Season with salt and pepper and, if you have them, add perhaps a sprinkling of freshly chopped herbs.

Serve with Mint Sauce (see page 595) or Apple and Mint Jelly (see page 507).

Lamb Chops Duxelle

Even a few simple lamb chops can be made into a feast with the duxelle stuffing from the Master Recipe.

Cut a pocket in the eye of the chops, fill with a generous teaspoonful of duxelle stuffing. Dip the chops first in seasoned flour, then in beaten egg, and then in breadcrumbs. Bake on an oiled baking sheet in a preheated oven 400°F (200°C) for 25–30 minutes.

Lamb Poitivine

Serves 8–10

This was one of the winter lamb dishes that I learned when I first came to Ballymaloe. I was flabbergasted when I saw half a bottle of brandy going into a casserole – it really is good.

1 leg of lamb, 6–7 lbs. (2.6–3.1kg)
2–4 tablespoons Clarified Butter (see page 103)
salt and freshly ground pepper
2 cups brandy
2 cups (425ml) water or light homemade Chicken or Lamb Stock (see page 36–37)
24 garlic cloves, peeled
Roux (see page 580)

Preheat the oven to 300°F (150°C).

Cut thick slices from the leg of lamb and season them with salt and pepper. Melt the butter in a heavy pan, and brown the meat on both sides. Transfer to a flameproof casserole dish, or other flameproof and ovenproof pot, and layer with the garlic cloves. Add the brandy and water or stock, bring to a boil, cover with a butter wrapper and the lid of the casserole dish. Simmer gently on top or transfer to the oven for 1½–2 hours. De-grease the juices and thicken slightly with Roux. Serve with boiled potatoes and seasonal vegetables – green beans are good.

Stewing

Stewing involves long, slow, gentle cooking in a covered, heavy pot or casserole dish. It's worth remembering the old saying "a stew boiled is a stew spoiled". If a stew is allowed to boil fast for even a short time, the protein and gelatin in the meat harden and so the meat becomes tough and chewy rather than meltingly tender.

Less prime cuts are best for stewing. Meat should be well-trimmed of all fat and gristle. Cut into cubes up to 2 inches (5cm) in size, but certainly not smaller than 1 inch (2.5cm). Stewing beef, particularly, should be cut into larger cubes because it needs long, slow cooking. The meat is often tossed in well-seasoned flour and then quickly sealed in a hot pan; this adds another layer of flavor and helps to thicken and enhance the color of the gravy.

Vegetables (such as onions and carrots) are cooked with the stew. Celery and cubes of root vegetables help to flavor and bulk up the stew. Fresh herbs, chiles, and spices add excitement to the flavor.

The liquid can be water or stock and occasionally canned tomatoes and their juices are added. A proportion of red or white wine may also be added. White stews or blanquettes may be made from veal or pork – onions, leeks, or mushrooms are added but no carrots. A blanquette of veal would be enriched with a liaison of egg yolk and cream at the end of cooking.

Every country has its stews – France has its ragoûts, and navarins and daubes; Hungary has its famous goulash; Morocco its tagines; and Greece the estoufado. Some cooks add freshly cooked vegetables at the end of cooking, such as green beans or broccoli. In our experience it is best not to add mushrooms to the stew at the beginning – they can become bitter and dark with long, slow cooking. Add them to the stew close to the end of cooking in the form of sautéed, sliced mushrooms or Mushroom à la Crème (see page 197).

Stews may be cooked on a very gentle heat on top of the stove. Use a heat diffuser mat or cook in a low oven. Bring to boiling point on top of the stove before transferring to the oven. Stews usually improve in flavor if kept for a day or two.

Ballymaloe Irish Stew

Serves 4–6

In season: Best in early summer, made with young lamb and new season's carrots and onions.

3 lbs. (1.3kg) lamb chops not less than 1 inch (2.5cm) thick
6 medium or 12 baby onions
6 medium or 12 baby carrots
8–12 potatoes or more if you like
1 quart (960ml) stock (Lamb Stock if possible, see page 37) or water
1 sprig of thyme
about 1 tablespoon Roux (see page 580), optional

Garnish

1 generous tablespoon parsley, freshly chopped
1 generous tablespoon chives, freshly chopped

Preheat the oven to 350°F (180°C).

Cut the chops in half and trim off some of the excess fat. Set aside. Render down the fat on a gentle heat in a heavy pan (discard the rendered down pieces).

Peel the onions and scrape or thinly peel the carrots (if they are young, you could leave some of the green stalks on the onions and carrots). Cut the carrots into large chunks, or if young, leave them whole. If the onions are large, roughly chop them; if they are small, they are best left whole.

Toss the meat in the hot fat until it is slightly brown. Set aside. Quickly toss the onions and carrots in the fat. Build the meat, carrots, and onions up in layers in the casserole dish, carefully season each layer with salt and pepper.

Using lamb stock, de-glaze the pan the meat was cooked in, and pour the liquid into the casserole dish. Peel the potatoes and lay them whole on top of the stew,

so they will steam while the stew cooks. Season the potatoes. Add a sprig of thyme, bring to a boil on top of the stove, cover, and transfer to the oven or let it simmer on top of the stove until the stew is cooked, about 1–2 hours, depending on meat.

When the stew is cooked, pour off the cooking liquid. Transfer the meat and vegetables to a clean pan. De-grease the juices and pour over the meat. Reheat and slightly thicken with a little Roux if you like. Check the seasoning. Bring back up to boiling point, sprinkle with parsley and chives, and serve from the pan. Or transfer to a large pottery dish and then garnish.

Mild Madras Curry with Fresh Spices

Serves 8

This is a korma curry made with nut milk and no chiles: it is deliciously spiced but not hot. Measure the spices meticulously because these proportions really work.

2 lbs. (900g) boneless lamb or mutton (leg or shoulder is perfect)
1 generous tablespoon pounded fresh ginger
salt

1/4 cup ghee or Clarified Butter (see page 103)
4 onions, sliced in rings
4 garlic cloves
2 teaspoons coriander seeds
1/2 teaspoon black peppercorns
1 teaspoon cardamom seeds (from whole green cardamom pods if possible)
8 cloves

Nut milk
1 cup almonds
2 cups cream

1 tablespoon plus 1 teaspoon turmeric powder
1/2 teaspoon sugar
freshly squeezed lime juice

First make the nut milk. Blanch, peel, and chop up the almonds until they're reduced to 1/8-inch (3-mm) pieces. Put them into a small saucepan along with the cream, and simmer for 4–5 minutes. Turn off the heat and let infuse for 15 minutes.

Meanwhile, peel the ginger thinly with a vegetable peeler, and pound into a paste in a mortar and pestle, or chop or grate finely. Cut the meat into 1½-inch (4-cm) cubes and mix it with the ginger and a sprinkling of salt.

Melt the butter in a large saucepan and cook the onion rings and crushed garlic over a gentle heat for 5 minutes. Remove the seeds from the cardamom pods and measure 1 teaspoon. Discard the pods. Grind the fresh spices, coriander, pepper, cardamom, and cloves in a clean spice or coffee grinder. Add the spices to the onions and cook over a medium heat for 2–3 minutes. Remove onions and then add the meat to the saucepan. Stir over a high heat until the meat browns, return onion and spices to the pot. Add in the nut milk, turmeric, and sugar. Stir well. Cover and simmer gently on top of the stove or better still in a low oven 325°F (170°C) until the meat is cooked (about 1 hour).

Add lime juice to taste.

Serve with plain boiled rice and other accompaniments which might include:

Apple and Tomato Chutney (see page 511)
Hot Chile Sauce (see page 591)
Banana and Yogurt Raita (see page 595)
sliced bananas, chopped apples, and of course some Indian breads – Poppadoms or Nan

You can substitute 2 cups coconut milk for nut milk in this recipe.

For a hotter curry, add 1–2 chopped chiles along with the onions and garlic.

Raan (Marinated Roast Lamb)

Serves 8

Another delicious recipe from Alison Henderson.

5-lb. (2.2-kg) leg of lamb, fat mostly removed
2 medium onions, coarsely chopped
6 large garlic cloves
2-inch (5-cm) piece ginger root, peeled and chopped
1/4 cup slivered almonds
2½ cups plain yogurt
4 teaspoons ground cumin seeds
4 teaspoons ground coriander seeds
1 teaspoon cayenne pepper
4 teaspoons ground paprika
1 teaspoon whole black peppercorns
4 cardamom pods
1 cinnamon stick
1 teaspoon whole cloves
5 tablespoons vegetable oil
salt and freshly ground black pepper

Put the onions, garlic, ginger, almonds, and 2 tablespoons of the yogurt into the bowl of a food processor and blend until they form a paste. Remove, and whisk into the rest of the yogurt. Add the cumin, coriander, cayenne, paprika, and a little salt, and mix well.

Put the leg of lamb into a roasting pan and make some deep incisions with a knife, then pour the marinade over it. Cover, and refrigerate overnight.

The next day, remove the dish from the refrigerator and bring the lamb to room temperature. Preheat the oven to 400°F (200°C). Heat the oil in a frying pan and tip in the whole spices. Pour the hot oil and spices over the lamb, cover tightly with aluminum foil, and bake for 1½ hours. Remove the foil, baste with the marinade, and bake uncovered for a further 15–30 minutes until the meat is done.

Place on a serving dish and spoon the remaining sauce around the leg.

Asian Lamb Stew

Serves 8

3 lbs. (1.3kg) lean leg or shoulder meat (trimmed of all fat)
4 fat leeks
2 cups homemade Lamb or Chicken Stock (see page 36-37) or water
2½ tablespoons sunflower oil
¼ cup soy sauce
¼ cup dry sherry
1 tablespoon red wine vinegar
2 tablespoons soft brown sugar
4 garlic cloves, crushed
5 star anise
½–1 teaspoon crushed red pepper flakes
3 strips of dried orange zest (from unwaxed oranges)
Roux (see page 580) or cornstarch

Cut the meat into 2-inch (5-cm) cubes. Trim and wash the leeks and cut into 2-inch (5-cm) lengths at an angle. Heat a little sunflower oil in a sauté pan over a high heat. Brown the meat on all sides and transfer to a flameproof casserole dish or other heavy pot. Add a little more oil if necessary, and toss in the leeks. Cook for 5 minutes and add to the meat in the casserole dish.

De-glaze the pan with the stock or water, bring it to a boil, and add to the meat and leeks. Add the soy sauce, sherry, vinegar, brown sugar, and garlic. Tie the star anise, pepper flakes, and orange zest in a piece of cheesecloth and add to the stew. Bring to a boil, cover, and simmer for 1 hour, or until the lamb is melting and tender. When cooked, discard the cheesecloth bag and thicken the juices with a little Roux or cornstarch mixed with 2 tablespoons of water.

Serve with a bowl of Plain Boiled Rice (see page 124).

Spicy Indian Meatballs with Banana and Yogurt Raita

Serves 6

These spicy meat balls have a secret center.

1 lb. (450g) shoulder of lamb, ground
4 cardamom pods
1 teaspoon coriander seeds
1 clove
½–¾ teaspoon chili powder
2 garlic cloves, crushed
salt and freshly ground pepper
1 egg

about 2 tablespoons curd cheese (or ricotta or paneer) mixed with 1 teaspoon parsley, chopped

pork (caul) fat, optional

Banana and Yogurt Raita (see page 595)

Remove the seeds from the cardamom and discard the pods. Grind the cardamom seeds with the coriander and clove. In a large bowl, mix the ground lamb with the spices, chili powder, and garlic, and add the beaten egg. Season with salt and pepper. Fry a tiny bit of the meat to check the seasoning. Divide the mixture into 6, shape each portion into a circle, about 4 inches (10cm) in diameter. Put a full teaspoon of curd cheese and parsley into the center, and gather up the edges so that the filling is completely enclosed. Repeat with the remainder of the mixture.* Cover and chill until required, or barbecue or fry immediately on a medium heat in a barely oiled frying pan. They will take about 5 minutes on each side. Serve immediately, with a green salad and Banana and Yoghurt Raita.

* Wrap loosely in caul fat if the lamb patties are to be barbecued.

Greek Moussaka

Serves 8

This is a Greek peasant recipe served in almost every taverna in Greece. There are many variations on the theme, some of which include a layer of cooked potato slices and raisins. I'm not sure if it is my imagination but I sometimes feel that moussaka is even better on the second day.

12 ounces (350g) zucchini (1 medium-to-large)
12 ounces (350g) eggplant (about 1 medium)
1 x 14-ounce (400-g) can tomatoes, or very ripe fresh tomatoes in summer
olive oil for frying
1 onion, finely chopped (include some green part of scallion if you have it)
1 garlic clove, crushed
1 lb. (450g) ground lamb, cooked
1 generous tablespoon marjoram or thyme, freshly chopped
2 teaspoons parsley, freshly chopped
1 bay leaf
pinch of grated nutmeg
2 teaspoons flour
salt and freshly ground pepper

For the topping
3 tablespoons butter
¼ cup plus 2 tablespoons flour
2½ cups milk
1 bay leaf
2 egg yolks
2½ tablespoons cream
1 cup shredded Gruyère or sharp Cheddar cheese
salt and freshly ground pepper

earthenware dish 10 x 8 inches (25.5 x 20.5cm)

Preheat the oven to 350°F (180°C).

Slice the eggplant and zucchini into ½-inch (1-cm) slices, score the flesh with a sharp knife, and sprinkle with salt. Leave for half an hour. Roughly chop or cut up the canned tomatoes, or peel and chop the fresh tomatoes finely, if using. Keep the juices. Heat 1 tablespoon of olive oil in a heavy saucepan over a gentle heat, add the onion and garlic, and cover and sweat for 4 minutes. Add the meat, herbs, and nutmeg to the onions. Stir in the flour and cook for 2 minutes. Pour in the tomatoes and their juice. Bring to a boil, stirring, and simmer for 2–3 minutes. Season well.

Rinse and wipe the eggplant dry. Heat a generous amount of olive oil in a grill-pan until hot. Cook the eggplant on both sides until golden. Brush the zucchini with olive oil, pan-grill until light golden on each side. As the zucchini are done, put them into the bottom of a shallow casserole dish. Tip the meat mixture on top of the zucchini and add a layer of the eggplant. See that the top is as flat as possible, and set aside.

Make the topping: melt the butter in a saucepan. Stir in the flour. Cook, stirring, for 1 minute, then draw off the heat and add the milk slowly, whisking out the lumps as you go. Add the bay leaf. Return the pan to the heat and stir until boiling. Season with salt and pepper and simmer for 2 minutes. Mix the egg yolks with the cream in a large bowl. Pour the sauce onto this mixture, stirring all the time. Add half the cheese and pour over the casserole. Sprinkle the rest of the cheese on top and bake for 30-35 minutes in the oven until completely reheated and well-browned on top.

Moussaka can be made up in large quantities ahead of time, cooled quickly, and frozen after it has been closely covered with plastic wrap.

Lamb Kebabs with Tzatziki

Serves 8

Choose kebab skewers carefully. They need to be flat and at least 1/8-inch (3mm) wide, better still 1/4-inch (5mm). If they are round, the meat will swivel as you try to turn it. Kebabs are best barbecued but may also be pan-grilled or cooked under a salamander or broiler.

2 lbs. (900g) lean shoulder or leg of lamb

Marinade 1

1 1/4 cups plain yogurt
1 teaspoon ground coriander
1 teaspoon ground cumin
1/4 teaspoon freshly ground pepper
juice of 1/2 lemon
OR

Marinade 2

1/2 cup olive oil
juice of 1 lemon
1 generous tablespoon annual marjoram, rosemary, or thyme leaves
2 large garlic cloves, crushed
salt and freshly ground pepper

Accompaniment

Tzatziki (see page 69)

metal skewers or kebab sticks

Mix either or both marinades and set each aside. Cut the meat into 1-inch (2.5-cm) cubes, season with salt and pepper, and put into the marinades for 1 hour at least. Drain the meat and thread onto metal skewers or kebab sticks. Grill for 7–10 minutes over a barbecue, turning and basting with the marinade 2 or 3 times. Serve with a green salad and Tzatziki.

Right: Lamb Kebabs with Tzatziki

Babotie

Serves 8–10

This South African recipe was given to us by Alicia Wilkinson from Silwood Kitchens in Capetown.

1 1/2 teaspoons butter
generous 2 tablespoons oil
2 onions, chopped
2 garlic cloves, crushed
1 lb. (450g) lamb, freshly ground
1 cup carrot, grated
2 teaspoons curry powder
1 teaspoon ground coriander
2 1/2 teaspoons ground ginger
1 tablespoon mixed herbs, finely chopped
1 teaspoon turmeric
1/2 teaspoon cinnamon
sugar to taste – about 1 teaspoon
a piece of red chile
1 teaspoon salt
1 teaspoon pepper
1 1/2 tablespoons almonds, chopped
some lemon leaves or 1/2 teaspoon lemon rind, finely grated
2 slices of white bread, 1 inch (2.5cm) thick, soaked in water, drained, and squeezed dry
generous tablespoon wine vinegar

Topping
1 cup plus 2 tablespoons buttermilk
2 large eggs
salt and freshly ground pepper
2 1/2 teaspoons turmeric
seasoning

Preheat the oven to 350°F (180°C).

Heat the butter and oil in a heavy pan over a medium heat, add onions and garlic and cook until soft. Add the lamb and stir well, then the carrot, spices, herbs, sugar, chile, seasoning, almonds, and lemon rind. Stir well and continue to cook until the flavors mingle. Stir in the bread and wine vinegar. Mix well, taste, and correct seasoning.

Put the meat into a shallow, rectangular baking dish and smooth over.
Make the topping by whisking all the ingredients together, check the seasoning, and strain over the meat through a coarse strainer. Bake at once in the oven until the topping is set and golden.

Left: Babotie

Master Recipe

Shepherd's Pie with Garlic or Parsley Butter

Serves 6

I adore Shepherd's Pie. It is best made with leftover cooked roast lamb. Nowadays, however, people rarely cook large enough joints of meat to have much left over, so raw ground lamb is frequently used – nothing like as delicious.

2 tablespoons butter
1 cup chopped onion
1/4 cup flour
2 cups stock and leftover gravy
1 teaspoon tomato paste
2 teaspoons mushroom ketchup, optional
2 teaspoons freshly chopped flat-leaf parsley
1 teaspoon thyme leaves
salt and freshly ground pepper
1 lb. (450g) cooked lamb, minced
4 cups Fluffy Mashed Potatoes (see page 182) or Mashed Parsnips (see page 174)
Garlic or Parsley Butter (see page 588 or 586)

Preheat the oven to 350°F (180°C).

Melt the butter in a small saucepan, add the onion, cover with a sheet of greased or wax paper, and cook over a slow heat for 5 minutes. Add the flour and cook until brown but take care not to burn it. Pour in the stock and gravy, bring to a boil and skim if necessary. Add the tomato paste, mushroom ketchup, parsley, thyme, salt and pepper, and simmer for 5 minutes. Stir the minced meat into the sauce and bring to a boil. Taste and correct the seasoning.

Put in a pie dish. Cover with the mashed potatoes and score with a fork. Reheat in the oven for about 30 minutes until the potato is nicely browned. Serve with Garlic and Parsley Butter, melting in the center.

Cottage Pie

Follow the Master Recipe but substitute beef for the lamb.

Lamb Cutlets with Tarragon Vinegar

Serves 4

A delicious simple dish, sherry vinegar may be substituted for tarragon vinegar here.

8 lamb cutlets
salt and freshly ground pepper
2 tablespoons butter
2 ounces (50g) shallots, finely chopped (about 2 medium)
2 1/2 tablespoons tarragon vinegar
2/3 cup cream
sprigs of fresh tarragon

Ask your butcher to prepare the cutlets for you, leaving only the eye of the meat on the bone or just a little of the streaky part. Season them with salt and pepper.

Heat a cast-iron pan over a high heat. Add the butter and when foaming, add the cutlets and cook until brown on both sides but still pink in the center – you may need to cook them in 2 batches depending on the size of the frying pan. Put the lamb to rest on a plate and keep warm.

Add the shallots to the pan and toss for 1–2 minutes. Add the vinegar carefully; it will probably flame. Allow the fumes to burn off and then pour in the cream, letting it bubble for 1–2 minutes; taste, and correct the seasoning. Spoon the sauce over the cutlets and serve immediately with sprigs of fresh tarragon. Young green beans or young fava beans go well.

pork & bacon

Master Recipe

Glazed Ham with Pickled Kumquats

Serves 20–25

A perfectly glazed ham always looks stunning. Buy ham made from pigs that have ranged freely and have been fed organic feed so the ham has a nice covering of fat. You will need to order well ahead – this is crucially important to the success of this recipe. Ultra-lean hams are much less flavorful and juicy. A layer of fat is essential for glazing the ham. You don't have to eat it although it will be difficult to resist the sweet caramelized bits. A really sweet ham is irresistible hot or cold and works well with many accompaniments. Loin of bacon may be glazed in the same way and is easier to carve – both are perfect for effortless entertaining.

10–12 lbs. (4.4–5.2kg) fresh or lightly smoked ham
1/3–1/2 cup of the juice from 1 small can of pineapple
2 1/4 cups light brown sugar
60–80 whole cloves, depending on the size of the diamonds

Pickled Kumquats (see page 512)

If the ham is salty, soak it in cold water overnight; next day, discard the water. Cover the ham with fresh cold water and bring it slowly to a boil. If the meat is still salty, there will be a white froth on top of the water. Discard the water, cover the ham with fresh cold water again, and repeat the process. Finally, cover the ham with hot water and simmer until it is almost cooked. Allow 20 minutes to the pound (45 minutes to the kg).

Meanwhile make the Pickled Kumquats.

When the ham is fully cooked, a skewer will come out effortlessly and the skin will peel off easily. Glaze the ham (see right) and serve hot or cold with Pickled Kumquats.

Left: Glazed Ham with Pickled Kumquats

Suggested accompaniments to hot Glazed Ham or Loin of Bacon

Tomato Fondue (see page 188)

Piperonata (see page 190)

Mushroom à la Crème (see page 197)

Ulster Champ (see page 183)

Colcannon (see page 183)

Fluffy Mashed Potato (see page 182).

Pickled Kumquats (see page 512).

Cumberland Sauce (see page 595)

Tomato and Chile Sauce (see page 590)

Mango Relish (see page 92)

Variation

Glazed Loin of Bacon

Follow the Master Recipe, but use 4–5 pound (1.8–2.2kg) loin of bacon, either smoked or green (unsmoked). Cook for 15 minutes to the pound.

How to glaze Ham or Bacon

Peel off the rind, cut the fat into a diamond pattern, and stud each diamond with a whole clove. Blend the brown sugar to a thick paste with a little pineapple juice. Be careful not to make it too liquid. Spread this over the ham. Bake it in a very hot oven, 475°F (250°C), for 20 minutes or until the top has caramelized. While it is glazing, baste regularly with the syrup and juices.

Portuguese Pork, Bean, and Chorizo Stew

Serves about 10

3 cups cannellini beans, navy beans, lima beans or black beans
5 tablespoons olive oil
2½ lbs. (1.1kg) pork belly
1½ lbs. (700g) bacon or pancetta
1 lb. (450g) ham hocks
4 garlic cloves, sliced
1 lb. (450g) onions, roughly chopped
1 lb. (450g) carrots, cut into ⅜-inch (7mm) slices
2 green peppers, seeded and chopped
sprig thyme
bay leaf
1 lb. (450g) very ripe tomatoes, peeled and chopped or 1 x 14-ounce (400g) can Italian tomatoes
1 lb. (450g) chorizo, cut into ¼-inch (5mm) slices
freshly ground pepper
1 teaspoon hot or smoked paprika
bunch of parsley stalks as bouquet garni
fistful of fresh cilantro or parsley leaves

Soak the beans overnight in plenty of cold water. Remove the pork rind. Cut the pork, bacon, and ham into 1½-2 inch (4-5cm) chunks.

Heat a little oil in a frying pan, brown on all sides the pork, bacon, and ham hocks, a few at a time. Transfer to a large flameproof casserole dish or other flameproof and ovenproof pot. Pour the excess fat out of the frying pan but leave enough to fry the garlic, onions, carrots, and pepper, along with the thyme and bay leaf. Cook on a gentle heat, stirring occasionally.

Transfer to the casserole dish, add the chopped tomatoes, chorizo, pepper, and paprika. De-grease and de-glaze the pan with a little water. When all the caramelized meat and vegetable juices have dissolved, pour them into the casserole dish, then add just enough water to almost cover the meat. Bring to a boil, add the parsley stalks if using, and cover. Simmer gently on a low heat for 2–2½ hours, or transfer to a moderate oven, 325°F (170°C).

Meanwhile, drain the soaked beans, cover with fresh cold water, bring to a boil and simmer until cooked. This takes about 40 minutes to 1½ hours, depending on the type of bean. Add to the stew 15–20 minutes before the end of cooking. Check the seasoning; it is unlikely to need salt.

Serve in deep wide soup bowls sprinkled with lots of coarsely chopped cilantro or parsley. Mop up the juices with crusty bread.

Loin of Pork cooked in Milk

Serves 6–8

At the Cookery School we rear free-range organic saddleback pigs. Happy lazy pigs who play in the field and eat windfall apples in the orchard in autumn. When Rose Grey and Ruth Rodgers came to the School as guest chefs they cooked many of their trademark dishes, including this one. The meat we have now is even better than what we had access to then: succulent juicy pork – quite divine.

4–5 lbs. (1.8–2.2kg) pork, rindless
sea salt or Kosher salt, and freshly ground pepper
dash of olive oil
1½ quarts (1.5 liters) whole milk
½ stick (¼ cup) butter
6 garlic cloves, peeled and split in half
2 unwaxed lemons

Season the pork well on all sides with salt and freshly ground pepper. Heat the oil in a large round flameproof casserole dish or other flameproof and ovenproof pot over a medium heat. Slowly brown the meat on all sides, then remove to a plate. Pour out any excess fat and save it for roast or sauté potatoes. Do not wash the pan.

In a separate pan, bring the milk almost to boiling point. Melt the butter in the casserole dish and then add the halved garlic cloves and toss. Replace the meat and add enough hot milk to come half way up the pork. Bring to a boil. Use a swivel-top peeler to take off the peel from the lemon without removing any pith, and add to the milk.

Lower the heat to reduce the casserole to the merest simmer. Leave the pot partly uncovered and barely simmering for 1½–2 hours, by which time the milk will have curdled into a golden curd.

Carve the meat carefully and spoon some of the delicious curd over each slice.

Carbonnade of Pork with Mushrooms

Serves 6–8

A quick and delicious recipe. If you haven't got any wine at hand, just add a little more stock. The same formula can be used for fillet steak or chicken breast but be careful not to overcook the meat.

2 lbs. (900g) pork fillet
1–2 tablespoons olive or sunflower oil or a little butter
1 cup finely chopped onion
¼ cup dry white wine
⅔ cup homemade Chicken Stock (see page 36)
8 ounces (225g) mushrooms, sliced (about 2⅓ cups)
1¼ cups sour cream or light cream
Roux (see page 580)
fresh lemon juice
salt and freshly ground pepper
2½ tablespoons freshly chopped flat-leaf parsley

Garnish
6–8 heart-shaped croûtons made with white bread fried in clarified butter or olive oil

Cut the pork into slices about 3/8-inch (7mm) thick. Pour a little oil into a very hot frying pan, sauté the pork pieces a few at a time, until brown on both sides. Remove to a plate and keep warm.

Add a little more oil or butter and cook the onions gently until soft and golden. Deglaze the pan with wine and bring to a boil, add the stock, and boil again to reduce by a quarter.

Meanwhile, sauté the sliced mushrooms in batches in a little butter and oil in a very hot pan, then remove and add to the pork. Add the cream to the sauce, bring back to a boil, and thicken with a little Roux. Add the cooked pork and mushrooms to the sauce, along with all their juices.

Taste, add a little lemon juice, and simmer gently for a couple of minutes. Dip the tip of the croutons in the sauce and then into the chopped parsley, add the remainder of the parsley to the sauce, taste again and correct seasoning if necessary. Pour into a hot serving dish and garnish with the crisp croûtons.

Ham Morvandelle

Serves approx. 20

This is a terrific recipe for a party. It freezes well and reheats perfectly. The recipe comes from the Burgundy area of France and takes its name from the Morvan forests. Loin or oyster cut of bacon may be used for this recipe.

an 8–10 lb. (3.6–4.4kg) whole ham
2 tablespoons butter
1 tablespoon oil
8 ounces (225g) carrots, sliced (about 2 cups)
8 ounces (225g) onions, sliced (about 2 cups)
12 parsley sprigs
1 bay leaf
12 peppercorns
sprig thyme
4 cloves
1/2 bottle of white Burgundy, Chablis (we use a Petit Chablis), or Pouilly Fuissé
4 cups homemade Chicken Stock (see page 36)

Sauce
1/3 cup chopped onion or shallot
2 lbs. (900g) mushrooms, sliced
salt and freshly ground pepper
2 1/4 cups cream
Roux (see page 580)

Liaison
3 egg yolks
1/4 cup cream

Soak the ham in cold water overnight and discard the water the next day. Place the ham in a large pot and cover with fresh cold water. Bring it slowly to a boil and discard the water. Repeat the process once or twice more, depending on how salty the ham is. (This is particularly important if the dish is to be frozen because freezing seems to intensify the salty taste.)

Preheat the oven to 350°F (180°C) if you are going to cook the ham in the oven.

Meanwhile, melt the butter and oil in a flameproof casserole dish or other flameproof and ovenproof pot, large enough to take the ham. Toss the sliced carrots and onions in the fat and sweat for about 10 minutes. Place the ham on top of the vegetables and add the parsley, bay leaf, peppercorns, thyme, and cloves. Pour the wine and stock over them, cover with the lid, bring to a boil, and simmer on top of the stove or in the moderate oven, until the ham is cooked. Allow about 2 1/2–3 hours for this weight, or 15 minutes per pound plus 15 minutes. You can test when the ham is cooked by lifting the skin: if it peels off easily, the ham is cooked. Check very carefully to make sure the ham is fully cooked before proceeding with the sauce.

To make the sauce, cook the onion or shallot in a little butter on a low heat until soft. Remove from the pan. Sauté the mushrooms over a high heat and add to the onion. When the ham is cooked, remove it from the casserole dish, and strain and degrease the cooking liquid. Return the liquid to the casserole dish, along with the cream, and bring to a boil. Thicken with prepared Roux to a light coating consistency and simmer for 5 minutes. Add the mushrooms and onions and taste for seasoning. Skin the ham and slice carefully; arrange in one or more serving dishes.

To make the liaison, mix the egg yolks with the cream and add a ladleful of the simmering sauce to the liaison, mix well and add back into the remaining sauce. Do not let it boil again or it may curdle.

Spoon the sauce over the slices of ham in the serving dish. (The recipe may be prepared ahead to this point.) Reheat in a moderate oven, 350°F (180°C), for 20–30 minutes. It should be bubbling and slightly golden on top.

For a dinner party, you may want to pipe a border of Fluffy Mashed Potatoes (see page 182) around the outside of the serving dish. Tomato Fondue (see page 188), Piperonata (see page 190), and a good green salad make excellent accompaniments.

Roast Kassler

Serves 10–12

The delicious German specialty, Kassler, is actually fresh loin of pork marinated with pepper, cloves, and juniper berries for 12–24 hours and then oak-smoked for a further 12 hours. It used to be quite difficult to find but is now becoming more widely available as many pork butchers produce their own. It is best roasted rather than boiled. It may be served hot, warm, or cold.

5 lbs. (2.2kg) Kassler

Preheat the oven to 350°F (180°C).

Put the piece of Kassler into a roasting pan and cook for about 1¾ hours or for 20 minutes per pound. During cooking, baste once or twice with the fat which will render out. Test the meat: the juices should run clear when cooked. Turn off the oven or set to a very low heat; let the meat relax for about 20 minutes before carving. De-grease the pan and serve the sweet juices with the Kassler. Keep the pork fat to roast or sauté potatoes.

Casserole-Roast Pork with Normandy Mustard Sauce

Serves 12–15

Leg of pork can often be very dry, particularly if it is too lean, but casserole-roasting gives a much more juicy result. This recipe is perfect for a dinner party because it can be made ahead and reheats perfectly. It is even better made with shoulder meat, which is less expensive.

6 lbs. (2.6kg) boneless joint of pork, rindless but with the fat intact (leg, shoulder, or loin)
2 tablespoons olive or sunflower oil
mirepoix of vegetables:
2 onions, sliced
2 carrots, sliced
1 outside stalk of celery, sliced
2 garlic cloves
1 bouquet garni (see page 140)
1¼ cups dry white wine or light Chicken Stock (see page 36) or a mixture of both
salt and freshly ground pepper

Sauce
⅔ cup cider vinegar
12 crushed peppercorns
2½ cups cream or creamy milk
salt and freshly ground pepper
4 teaspoons English mustard powder, mixed with 1 tablespoon water
salt
Roux, optional (see page 580)

Garnish
freshly chopped flat-leaf parsley

Preheat the oven to 325°F (170°C).

Remove the rind from the pork, if necessary, and discard. Tie the joint into a neat shape using cotton string. Select a flameproof casserole dish or other flameproof and ovenproof pot, large enough to take the piece of meat without too much waste of space. Heat the oil in the casserole dish and brown the joint on all sides over a medium heat. Remove the pork to a plate and pour off all but a couple of tablespoons of fat from the casserole dish.

Toss the vegetables and unpeeled garlic in the remaining fat, season, add the bouquet garni, and place the joint of pork on top. Add the stock and/or dry white wine, cover, and bring to a boil on top of the stove. Transfer to the preheated oven for about 2–2½ hours, basting a couple of times during cooking.

To make the sauce, remove the meat to a warm serving dish, strain the cooking juices and vegetables through a strainer, and de-grease the casserole dish.

Add the cider vinegar and peppercorns to the casserole dish and reduce to about 2–3 tablespoons. Add the de-greased juices and a few tablespoons of the strained mirepoix. Add the cream and simmer for 5 minutes. Taste, and add salt if necessary. Whisk in the mustard and simmer for a few more minutes. The sauce should be a light coating consistency – if it is too thin, thicken slightly by whisking in a little Roux.

Taste again and correct seasoning. Strain into a sauce boat and serve with the pork. Alternatively, the pork may be carved onto a serving dish, coated with the sauce, and reheated later. In this case, pipe a border of Fluffy Mashed Potato (see page 182) around the dish. Serve sprinkled with the chopped parsley.

Pork en Croûte with Duxelle Stuffing and Bramley Apple Sauce

Serves 6

2 fresh pork steaks

Marinade
¼ cup olive oil
¼ cup lemon juice
3 sprigs parsley
sprig thyme or fennel
1 bay leaf
1 garlic clove, crushed
pinch of salt and freshly ground pepper

Duxelle Stuffing (see page 306); use a quarter of the recipe
8–10 ounces (225–275g) Homemade Flaky or Puff Pastry Dough (see page 413 or 456)
egg-wash made with 1 egg and a pinch of salt

Bramley Apple Sauce (see page 597)

Trim the pork steaks of all fat and trim the chain (the long thin strip of meat on the edge of the tenderloin). Mix all the ingredients for the marinade in a bowl and marinate the pork steaks for 3–4 hours.

Meanwhile make the Duxelle Stuffing.

To assemble: split the pork steaks down one side and open out flat. Season with salt and pepper, divide stuffing between both steaks, fold the meat over.

Divide the pastry dough in two, roll out each piece, and cover the pork with it, as though it was a parcel, and decorate with cut-out pastry leaves. Egg-wash, and bake in a hot oven 425°F (220°C) for 10 minutes, turn down heat to 350°F (180°C) and cook for 20 minutes. Serve with Bramley Apple Sauce.

Note: If the "chain" has not already been removed by the butcher, you can chop it up, cook it in a little butter, and add it to the stuffing.

Filipino Pork with Peppers and Fresh Ginger

Serves 6

Oriental meat recipes make the most of a little meat. This delicious pork dish was cooked for me by Susie Noriega. Serve with Plain Boiled Rice (see page 124).

1 lb. (150g) pork fillet (tenderloin)
2½ tablespoons light soy sauce
freshly ground pepper
¼ cup unsalted peanuts, shelled
1 fresh red or green chile
1½ ounces (85g) bamboo shoots (about ¼ cup)
2 small green peppers
1 inch (2.5cm) fresh ginger root
large garlic clove
4 large scallions
2½ tablespoons peanut oil
1 teaspoon tapioca
¼ cup water, approx
1 generous tablespoon Tabasco or oyster sauce
pinch of sugar

Cut the pork into ¼-inch (5mm) strips, marinate in light soy sauce, season with freshly ground pepper, and set aside. Put the peanuts on a baking sheet and roast for about 20 minutes in a moderate oven, 350°F (180°C), until golden. Rub off the loose skins.
Cut the chile in half and remove the seeds. Cut into small dice. Cut the bamboo shoots in pieces the same size as the pork. Halve and quarter the green pepper, remove the seeds, and cut into similar-sized pieces.

Peel the ginger root and garlic, and chop finely. Also chop the scallions finely, at an angle.

Heat a wok, add half the oil, and fry the garlic, ginger, and scallions for a few seconds. Remove to a plate. Heat the wok to very hot, add the other tablespoon of oil, toss the pork for 2 minutes maximum and then add in the rest of the vegetables.

Season with salt and freshly ground pepper, add a drop of water, cover, and cook for 3-4 minutes until the vegetables are cooked but still crunchy. Then add the chile and roasted peanuts.

Dissolve the tapioca in about ¼ cup of water, add a dash of Tabasco or oyster sauce and a pinch of sugar. Add to the wok, bubble up again, and serve immediately in a hot serving dish.

Roast Suckling Pig with Apple and Jalapeño Jelly

Serves 10–12

1 suckling pig
salt and freshly ground pepper
3–4 tablespoons freshly chopped rosemary, optional
olive oil
Sage and Onion Stuffing (see page 288 and use double the recipe)
rosemary and watercress sprigs

Apple and Jalapeño Jelly (see page 507) or Bramley Apple Sauce (see page 597)

Rub salt, pepper, and rosemary over the skin and into the cavity of the pig. Let it marinate overnight.

The next day, make the stuffing. Fill the cavity loosely with stuffing. Truss with skewers and lace over the skewers with cotton string to close the cavity. Truss the front and back legs loosely to keep a neat shape.

Use a sharp knife to make an incision along the backbone, then score the back diagonally at 1-inch (2.5-cm) intervals from head to tail.

Preheat the oven to 350°F (180°C).

Roast the suckling pig on its belly in a large roasting pan, sprinkle a little more salt over the meat, and drizzle with olive oil. Wrap the ears with tin foil to protect them from the direct heat – they burn easily.

Roast in the preheated oven, basting every 30 minutes. It will take 2½–3½ hours, depending on size. A 10–pound (1.4–kg) pig will be cooked in about 2½ hours. Allow 3 hours for 13 pounds (5.8kg) and 3½ hours for an 18–pound (8–kg) pig.

The pig is ready to eat when the skin has turned to crisp golden crackling.

To serve: make gravy from the juices in the pan. Remove the skewers and trussing strings. Arrange on a large serving platter surrounded by crispy Roast Potatoes (see page 181) and sprigs of rosemary and watercress. Please, don't put an apple in its mouth! Serve with gravy, Apple and Jalapeño Jelly, or Bramley Apple Sauce.

Master Recipe

Roast Pork with Crackling and Green Gooseberry Sauce

Serves 10–12

Pork has suffered more than almost any other meat from modern intensive rearing methods. For years I longed and searched in vain for the sweet juicy pork we ate as children. In despair, much to the great consternation of my husband and family, I bought two saddleback pigs from West Cork and a black Berkshire boar from the Comeragh mountains. They live happily and completely naturally in our orchard and are fed on organic feed. They have produced several large litters of Bonhams, which delight us all. The boar would appear to be a descendant of the early Irish pig as he, too, can clear a fence with the greatest of ease – I've spent many hours chasing him around the immediate countryside. The pork is sweet and delicious! The acidity in green gooseberries cuts the richness of the pork deliciously.

1 loin of pork with the rind still on, 5 lbs. (2.2kg)
salt and freshly ground pepper
sprigs of rosemary, optional

Gravy
2½ cups homemade Chicken Stock (see page 36)
Roux (see page 580), optional
Green Gooseberry Sauce (see page 598)

Preheat the oven to 375°F (190°C).
Skin side up on the work top, rub salt over the rind and into the fat. Turn the pork over, skin side down on the work top, season the meat well with salt and pepper and perhaps a little chopped rosemary, roll up tightly and tie with cotton string. Cook in a roasting pan on a trivet, allowing 25–28 minutes to the pound. Baste every now and then.

Just before the end of cooking time, remove the pork to another roasting pan, replace in the oven and turn up the temperature to 450°F (230°C), to get crisp crackling. When the joint is cooked, the juices should run clear. One shouldn't eat pork pink. Put the pork onto a hot carving dish and let it rest in a very cool oven while you make the gravy in the original roasting pan.

To make the gravy, de-grease the roasting pan (keep the delicious pork fat for sautéing potatoes), put on a medium heat, add the chicken stock, and whisk to dissolve the caramelized pork juices. Bring to a boil. Season and thicken with a little Roux, if desired. Freshly chopped herbs may be added to the gravy. Serve with crispy roast potatoes and Green Gooseberry Sauce.

Variation

Roast Stuffed Pork with Sage and Onion Stuffing and Bramley Apple Sauce

Follow the Master Recipe. Make the Sage and Onion Stuffing (see page 288), spread it over the flesh side. Roll up tightly and tie with cotton string. Serve with Bramley Apple Sauce (see page 597).

Tip: For really good crackling, score the skin at ¼-inch (5-mm) intervals running with the grain – you may want to ask your butcher to do this because the skin can be quite tough. (This will also make it easier to carve later.) Use a Stanley knife to score the rind at home.

Pork Tenderloin with Gentle Spices

Serves 4–6

An excellent dish for entertaining; serve with a green vegetable and a bowl of orzo or Pilâv Rice. You can also use chicken breasts.

2 pork tenderloins or 1½ lbs. (700g) pork leg or shoulder
1–2 teaspoons whole cardamom pods
1 teaspoon whole coriander seeds
1 teaspoon whole cumin seeds
2 tablespoons butter
1 cup chopped onion
salt and freshly ground pepper
⅔ cup homemade Chicken Stock (see page 36)
⅔ cup cream
Roux (see page 580), optional

Garnish
flat-leaf parsley or cilantro

Press the cardamom pods and extract the seeds; grind to a fine powder along with the coriander and cumin seeds in a mortar and pestle or in a spice grinder.

Melt the butter in a large sauté pan, add the onions, and sweat over a gentle heat until soft. Remove from the heat. Slice the pork tenderloin into ¾-inch (2-cm) slices. If using pork leg or shoulder, cut into ¾-inch (2-cm) cubes and trim off the fat. Season with salt and pepper, toss the meat in the ground spices, add to the onion, and sauté gently for a few minutes. Cover the pan tightly and cook for 10–15 minutes for pork tenderloin. If leg or shoulder is being used, transfer the sauté pan to a preheated oven, 300°F (150°C) for 20–40 minutes or until the pork pieces are cooked but still nice and juicy. Remove the pork to a serving dish and keep warm. * Put the sauté pan back on the heat, add the stock and cream, and let bubble for 3 or 4 minutes. Taste and adjust the seasoning, add the pork pieces back into the sauce, let reheat for 2 or more minutes. Serve on a hot dish, garnished with flat-leaf parsley or cilantro.

* May be prepared ahead to this point. Reheat in a saucepan over a gentle heat until piping hot.

Right: Pork Tenderloin with Gentle Spices

Master Recipe

Home-made Sausages with Scallion Mash

Serves 6–8 (makes about 12–16)

Homemade sausages are just as easy to make as hamburgers, and make a cheap and comforting meal. Use organic free range pork, and at least 1/4-inch (5-mm) fat to lean, better still 3/8-inch (7-mm), otherwise the sausages will be dry rather than juicy.

1 lb. (150g) good, fat, belly pork
2–4 teaspoons mixed fresh herbs – parsley, thyme, chives, marjoram, and rosemary or sage
1 large garlic clove, crushed
1 egg
1 1/2 cups soft white breadcrumbs
salt and freshly ground pepper
a little oil

Grind the pork – once for coarse sausages, twice for a finer texture. Chop the herbs finely. Crush the garlic to a paste with a little salt. Whisk the egg, then mix all the ingredients together thoroughly in a bowl and season well.

Heat a frying pan, fry off a little ball of the mixture to check the seasoning, and correct it if necessary. Divide into 16 pieces and roll into sausages. Fry gently on a barely oiled pan until golden on all sides. These sausages are particularly delicious served with Bramley Apple Sauce (see page 597) and a big bowl of buttery Scallion Mash (see page 182).

Tip: Resist the temptation to make them too large, otherwise they are difficult to cook properly into the center without burning the outside.

Variations

Home-made Sausages with Cilantro and Thai Dipping Sauce

For a change I recently substituted 2 tablespoons of fresh cilantro for the mixed herbs in the sausage mixture and found it completely delicious. I also added a good pinch of sugar to enhance the sweetness in the oriental way. If you want to continue in that vein, serve the sausages with Thai Dipping Sauce (see page 88), instead of the more traditional mash and apple sauce.

Chile Bangers

Add 1–2 chopped chiles to the pork for extra excitement. Chili flakes can be used if you have no chiles.

Thai Stir-fried Pork with Ginger and Cilantro

Serves 4–6

The quantity of fresh ginger may seem extraordinary here but it tastes great, so don't be tempted to reduce it.

1 lb. (150g) pork tenderloin
2 teaspoons cornstarch
a good pinch of salt
2 1/2 tablespoons sesame oil
1/4 cup sunflower or peanut oil
1/3 cup fresh ginger, peeled and finely chopped
2 1/2 tablespoons fish sauce (nam pla)
2 1/2 tablespoons soy sauce
1 teaspoon sugar
freshly ground pepper

Garnish
fresh cilantro leaves

Trim the pork and cut into 1/4-inch (5-mm) thick slices. Cut each slice into 4 chips. Put them into a bowl and toss well with the cornstarch, salt, and sesame oil. Let marinate for 20–30 minutes.

Just before eating, heat the sunflower oil in a wok, add the ginger and stir-fry in the hot oil until just beginning to crisp, (this may take 2–3 minutes but it's worth persevering). Add the pork and toss until it changes color, then add the fish sauce, soy sauce, sugar, and lots of freshly ground pepper. Taste and correct the seasoning if necessary.

Turn into a hot serving dish, garnish with fresh cilantro leaves, and serve with rice and perhaps some snow peas.

Spare Ribs with Ginger

Serves 4–6

2 lbs. (900g) nice meaty spare ribs
2-inch (5-cm) piece fresh ginger, peeled and crushed
1/2 cup less 1 tablespoon dark soy sauce
1/2 cup less 1 tablespoon sugar
4 spring onions or scallions
1/4 cup Chinese rice wine or dry sherry

Unless you are adept with a chopper, give your butcher a big smile and ask him to separate the spare ribs and chop each into 3-inch (8-cm) lengths.

Choose a wide sauté pan or frying pan, and add the ginger, soy sauce, sugar, spring onions, rice wine, and water. Stir and add the spare ribs. Bring to a boil, cover, and simmer over a medium heat. Stir every now and then. After about 35 minutes, increase the heat. Remove and discard the spring onions and ginger.

Cook for another 20–25 minutes until the liquid is thick and syrupy. Turn the spare ribs in the glaze until they are evenly coated. Serve hot.

Vietnamese Pork and Lemongrass Patties

Serves 4–6 (makes 16 approx.)

1 lb. (150g) lean, ground pork
1 ounce (25g) shallots, chopped (about 1 medium)
2 stalks lemongrass, trimmed and very finely chopped
1/2 teaspoon salt
lots of freshly ground black pepper

Put everything into a food processor, season well with salt and pepper, and whizz for just a few seconds. Heat a frying pan and cook a tiny piece to check the seasoning, adjusting if necessary.

Make the meat mixture into patties up to 3 inches (8cm) in diameter and pan-grill for 5 minutes on each side. Or you can make the meat into small balls about 2 inches (5cm) in diameter and thread them onto well-soaked bamboo skewers and barbecue them for 10–15 minutes, turning on all sides. Serve with a Dipping Sauce (see page 88).

Sweet Sour Pork with Prunes, Raisins, and Pine Nuts

Serves 6

Jo Bettoja, whose food I adore, served us this rich sweet sour stew in her home in Rome. It's an old family recipe for wild boar that has been passed down through the generations. Tim and I loved the rich gutsy flavor so she kindly shared her recipe.

4 lbs. (1.8kg) boneless shoulder or leg of pork, cubed

Marinade
6 juniper berries
10 black peppercorns
2 bay leaves
1/2 teaspoon thyme leaves.
1 carrot, chopped
1 onion, chopped
1 stalk celery, chopped
3 or more cups dry red wine
1/4 cup red wine vinegar

1/2 cup less 1 tablespoon olive oil
sea salt or Kosher salt
3/4 cup red wine vinegar
freshly ground pepper
36 prunes soaked in water
1/4 cup raisins, plumped in hot water
1/4 cup pine nuts, toasted
2 1/2 tablespoons sugar
1/2 cup grated dark chocolate

Accompaniment
Creamy Polenta (see page 143)

Mix all the ingredients for the marinade together in a bowl. Add the cubes of pork, stir well. Cover and marinate for 48 hours in the fridge. Stir every now and then during this period.

Drain the meat, reserving both the marinade and vegetables. Dry the meat on paper towels.

Preheat the oven to 325°F (170°C).

Heat 5 tablespoons of olive oil in a frying pan on a high heat. Brown the meat on all sides and then transfer to a flameproof casserole dish or other flameproof and ovenproof pot, season with salt. Add a little more oil to the frying pan, cook the marinated vegetables for 5–8 minutes or until the onion is soft; add a few tablespoons of the marinade to prevent the vegetables from burning, if necessary. Add to the meat in the casserole dish. De-glaze the frying pan with the rest of the marinade, plus 1/4 cup of red wine vinegar, and bring to a boil and scrape into the casserole dish.

Add 1/2 teaspoon freshly ground pepper to the casserole, and bring to a boil, cover, and cook in the oven for approximately 1 1/2 hours until the meat is tender.

Remove the meat to a bowl and strain the sauce into a saucepan (one large enough to fit the meat). Press the vegetables through a strainer to get the last of the juices, and discard the vegetables. Add the prunes, raisins, and pine nuts to the sauce.

In a small saucepan, simmer 1/2 cup of red wine vinegar with 2 tablespoons sugar for 4 minutes, then pour into the larger saucepan and add the grated chocolate and the meat. Bring slowly to a boil and simmer for 15 minutes. Taste, and adjust the seasoning if necessary.

Serve with soft Polenta and follow with a good green salad.

Pork Chops with Pineapple Chile and Cilantro Salsa

Serves 8

8 pork chops, free range if possible

Chile and Rosemary Marinade
1/3 cup finely chopped rosemary
4 cloves garlic, crushed
1 tablespoon black peppercorns, freshly cracked
1 teaspoon fennel seeds, crushed
1/4–1/2 chili flakes
1/2 cup olive oil

Pineapple Chile and Cilantro Salsa
1/2–1 fresh pineapple, diced
1–2 red chiles, seeded and diced
1 medium red onion, finely diced
2 1/2 tablespoons cilantro or mint, finely chopped
grated zest of 1 lime
3–4 tablespoons freshly squeezed lime juice
salt
pinch of sugar, optional

Mix all the ingredients for the marinade together. Snip the fat off the chops. Dip both sides of the meat in the marinade, cover, and leave to absorb the flavors for an hour or more.

Meanwhile make the salsa. Mix all the ingredients in a ceramic or stainless steel bowl. Taste, and correct seasoning. Let the flavors mingle for 15–30 minutes, if possible.

Just before serving, season the pork chops with salt. Grill over a barbecue or on a pan-grill until cooked through. Serve with the salsa.

Right: Vietnamese Pork and Lemongrass Patties

beef

beef

At Ballymaloe we are deeply fortunate to have a local butcher, who also owns a farm. Michael Cuddigan, a third generation butcher, buys his meat on the hoof (alive) and keeps them on his own land until he judges that they are ready for slaughter. This really is the best of all scenarios. Michael's farm is almost unique with both old and new pastures. Some of his land is "virgin soil" and has never been turned in living memory, so it has dozens of species of grass, herbs, and wild flowers. It stands to reason that an animal grazed on mixed pasture will have far more flavor than one fed on only two or three rye grasses.

Butchers like Michael represent real traceability since they know exactly where their meat comes from. Michael has been buying from the same farmers for generations and knows how all the animals are reared. As far as I'm concerned, he's my vital link with safe meat, and I would trust him implicitly.

Butchers

The art of a butcher does not merely involve killing and cutting up meat. The skill starts when he sees an animal in a field and judges whether it will kill out into good meat or not. Then there is the ability to keep the animals relaxed, to slaughter humanely, and the judgement involved in knowing how long to hang the meat (this is, of course, vitally important, but is only one of many factors). Finally there is the practical skill involved in cutting up the meat. These craft butchers have in some cases learned the trade from their fathers and grandfathers, or they have been apprenticed to a good butcher. They understand and know every part of the process. In an abattoir, on the other hand, there may be hundreds of people each having knowledge of only one or two parts of the production line. It seems completely incredible to me that we do not appreciate and value these small, conscientious local butchers more – they have a wealth of knowledge and experience. It is these butchers who are virtually being hassled out of existence by EU (European Union) and government regulations, which would prefer to have only eight or ten abattoirs across the country, to make regulation easier.

Breeds

Apart from the pasture the animals graze on, the flavor of the meat is determined by the breed. The breeds that I prefer for flavor are what I call the traditional breeds: Aberdeen Angus, or Aberdeen Angus crossed with Shorthorn; Hereford; and Pole Angus. There are also a lot of delicious U.K. rare breeds, such as Devons, Longhorn, and Ayrshires.

Here on the farm I have some Aberdeen Angus, Herefords, and some crosses. I also have a small herd of beautiful, black Kerry cattle. Kerry is not really a beef breed (they are very good for dairy), but I've been rearing them because they were an endangered species and I wanted to help to preserve the breed. They are the oldest Irish breed – possibly even the oldest in Europe. Timmy gave me my first Kerry cow about ten years ago as a birthday present. She came from an organic farmer called Ivan Ward from County Wexford. Ivan didn't realize when he sold me a cow that he would have to provide an after-sales service for evermore, but he has been really wonderful and continues to give me advice.

The breeds that I'm not so fond of are European breeds such as Limousin, Charolais, and Belgium Blues. I think they're wonderful on the European continent (they have very big carcasses and are usually very lean), but I find that they don't have nearly the same flavor as the Irish breeds. The traditional Irish breeds can thrive and fatten on our fine grass, whereas the continental breeds need lots of meal.

In recent years, the principal emphasis in agriculture has been on producing food as cheaply as possible through maximum yields, and farmers have been encouraged and pressured in this direction. The unfortunate consequence of this policy is that animals and plants are consistently pushed beyond their natural limit. In an effort to satisfy the unrealistic demands of supermarkets and consumers, farmers have sourced cheaper and cheaper protein for animal feeds, resulting in meal that contained not only meat and bone meal, but also wood pulp and even on occasion, feces. The end result has been BSE in animals and CJD (Creutzfeldt-Jakob disease) in humans. At present it is still very difficult to source animal feed that can be guaranteed GM free – a considerable concern for a growing number of farmers and consumers.

Buying

In Ireland we can grow grass like virtually nowhere else. In fact many of our best foods, meat and dairy, are grass based. Although most cattle are fed a little grain, I prefer the flavor of grass-fed to exclusively grain-fed beef. Good grass-fed beef has rich golden fat and a really delicious beefy flavor.

When buying your meat, choose meat with a little layer of fat. Fat gives flavor. While a joint of meat is roasting, fat renders out and bastes the meat, giving it an extra sweetness and succulence. One doesn't have to eat the fat, but it does need to be on the meat originally for flavor. Both the color of the fat and the amount of marbling in the flesh is determined by the breed, age, and diet of the animal.

Dieticians are perfectly correct to caution us against eating too much fat, but don't get caught up in the low-fat mania. It is not only how much fat you eat, but the kind of fat it is, that is important – a little quality fat is good for us. The main reason to be careful is that toxins from an animal's feed collect in its fat. If we eat too much of it, it can in turn be absorbed into our own fat tissue.

A T-bone steak should consist of the T-bone, sirloin, tenderloin, and sometimes a little streaky piece on the end. Steak should be cut at least 3/4-inch (2-cm) thick, better still 1-inch (2.5-cm) thick – unless they are medallions of tenderloin or minute steaks.

Cooking

The majority of the prime cuts are from the hind quarter, with most of the stewing and braising meat in the fore-quarter. Remember that the parts of the animal that are exercised the most tend to be the toughest, but they are also the cuts that have the best flavor. For example, a stew made from shin of beef will have a much stronger beefy flavor than a more expensive cut, but it needs longer, slower cooking.

Prime ribs, sirloin, and tenderloin steaks, which are suitable for roasting, pan-grilling, or sautéing, are found along the loin. Tenderloin steaks are always tender, but not necessarily full of beefy flavor. The shoulder and neck meat (chuck) is lean, good for mincing and casseroles. Prime rib is excellent for roasting while the rump, round, tip, and short plate are best in pot roasts. Parts that are a little tougher, such as round steak, flank, and shins, have excellent flavor and benefit from being stewed or braised.

With any meat, and not just beef, much of the flavor comes from the bones. It is therefore very important, particularly for stews, casseroles, and roasting, to include the bones when cooking. A prime rib of beef roasted on the bone is superb.

Roasting time (see page 336) can only be a guideline, since it depends not only on the weight, but also on the thickness of the cut. When you calculate cooking time, be sure to incorporate some resting time. Remember that the internal temperature of the meat will continue to rise by a degree or two as it rests in a warm oven.

At Ballymaloe we occasionally serve baby beef, but we do not serve intensively-reared veal. Veal is the meat from calves slaughtered at four or five months. In some systems, the calves are kept indoors all their lives and light is excluded, so the flesh is pale. They are milk-fed and their feed includes antibiotics. Baby beef are also milk-fed, but the flesh is not so pale and the flavor not so delicate. We find it sweet and delicious and our guests enjoy it very much.

Corned and Spiced Beef

Corned beef has always been associated with Ireland; in fact many people (particularly in the U.S.) think that we live almost exclusively on corned beef and cabbage. I am glad to say this is not the case, even though it can be truly delicious. Meat was originally corned (brined) to preserve it in the days before refrigeration. Beef was also spiced for the same reason. Many spices have preservative and antiseptic properties, so spiced beef lasts as long, if not longer, than corned beef. Enormous quantities of corned and spiced beef were exported from Cork and one can still buy both in the Cork market, all year round. Our butcher, Michael Cuddigan, does a very good corned beef which we serve for lunch at Ballymaloe occasionally.

Hanging

Hanging meat is important because it both tenderizes the flesh and develops its flavor. The hanging time depends on several factors including breed and age. Mr. Cuddigan hangs our beef for ten days before he delivers it to Ballymaloe. We then hang it in a cold room for a further week or ten days. That might sound quite short, but Mr. Cuddigan kills mostly maiden heifer (females that have never calved), which are about 18 months old, so they do not need to be hung as long as older carcasses, which in some cases would take about three weeks' hanging, or occasionally longer.

Traditional Roast Rib of Beef with Horseradish Sauce, Gravy, and Yorkshire Pudding

Serves 8–10

Few people can resist a roast rib of beef with horseradish sauce, Yorkshire pudding, lots of gravy, and crusty roast potatoes. Choose the meat carefully. Always buy beef on the bone for roasting; it will have much more flavor and it isn't difficult to carve. Ask your butcher for a traditional breed as these have the best flavor.

6–8 lbs. (2.6–3.6kg) prime rib of beef on the bone
salt and freshly cracked pepper
Yorkshire Pudding (see page 338)
Horseradish Sauce (see page 586)

Gravy
2½ cups cold homemade Beef or Chicken Stock (see page 36)
Roux (see page 580), optional

Ask your butcher to saw through the upper chine bone so that the "feather bones" will be easy to remove before carving. Weigh the joint and calculate the cooking time (see right).

Preheat the oven to 475°F (250°C). Score the fat and season with salt and pepper. Place the meat in a flameproof roasting pan with the fat side uppermost. As the fat renders in the heat of the oven, it will baste the meat. The bones provide a natural rack to hold the meat clear of the fat in the roasting pan. Put the meat into a fully preheated oven; after 15 minutes turn down the heat to moderate, 350°F (180°C), until the meat is cooked to your taste.

Meanwhile make the batter for the Yorkshire pudding and let it rest. Make the Horseradish Sauce, cover, and refrigerate.

When the meat is cooked, it should be allowed to rest on a plate in a cool oven for 15–30 minutes before carving, depending on the size of the roast. A plate-warming oven would be perfect. The internal temperature of the meat will continue to rise by as much as 5°F (2–3°C), so remove the roast from the oven while it is still slightly underdone.

Put the Yorkshire pudding into a hot oven (about 450°F [230°C]) to cook; it will take about 20 minutes.

Meanwhile make the Gravy: tilt the roasting pan to the side and spoon off as much of the fat as possible. Pour the cold stock into the cooking juices remaining in the pan. The last globules of fat will solidify. Quickly remove them with a spoon, bring to a boil, stirring and scraping the pan well to dissolve the caramelized meat juices (I find a small whisk ideal for this). Thicken very slightly with a little Roux if you like. Taste, and add salt and pepper if necessary. Strain and serve in a warm gravy boat.

Carve the beef at the table and serve with Horseradish Sauce, Yorkshire pudding, gravy, and lots of crusty Roast Potatoes (see page 181).

Roast Rib of Beef with Three Sauces

At Ballymaloe House we serve prime Rib of Beef with Horseradish Sauce (see page 586), Béarnaise Sauce (see page 586), and Garlic Mayonnaise (see page 584), and lots of crusty Roast Potatoes (see page 181) – a delicious combination.

Roasting Times

Since ovens vary enormously in efficiency, thermostats are not always accurate and some joints of meat are much thicker than others, these figures must be treated as guidelines rather than rules. The times below include the 15 minute searing time at a high heat.

Beef on the bone
Rare 10–12 minutes per pound (450g)
Medium 12–15 minutes per pound (450g)
Well-done 18–20 minutes per pound (450g)

Beef off the bone
Rare 8–10 minutes per pound (450g)
Medium 10–12 minutes per pound (450g)
Well-done 15–18 minutes per pound (450g)

How do I know when the meat is cooked?
There are various ways of checking. I usually put a skewer into the thickest part of the joint, leave it there for about 30–45 seconds, and then put it against the back of my hand: if it still feels cool, the meat is rare; if it is warm, it is medium rare; if it's hotter, it's medium; and if you can't keep the skewer against your hand for more than a second, then you can bet it is well done. Also, if you check the color of the juices, you will find they are clear as opposed to red or pink for rare or medium.

If you own a meat thermometer, that will eliminate guesswork altogether but make sure the thermometer is not touching a bone when you are testing.

Beef is rare at an internal temperature of 140°F (60°C), medium at 145°F (70°C), and well-done at 165°F (75°C).

Boning and Carving a Rib of Beef

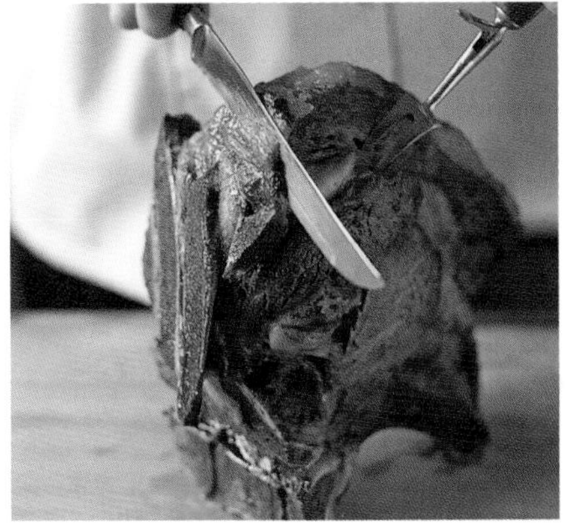

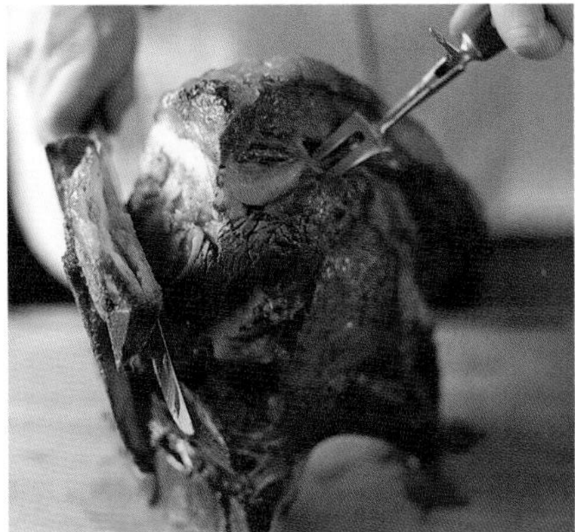

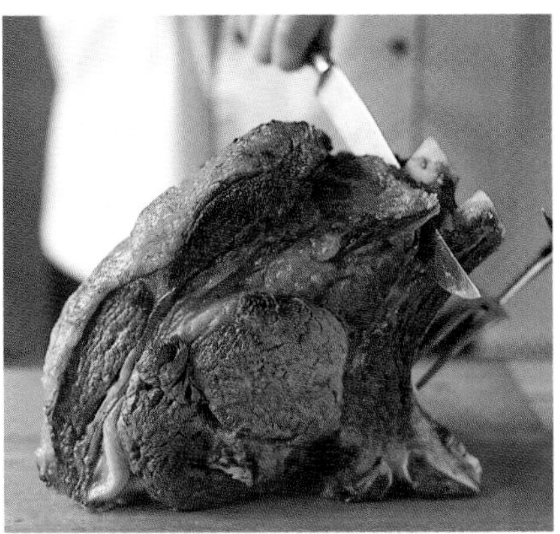

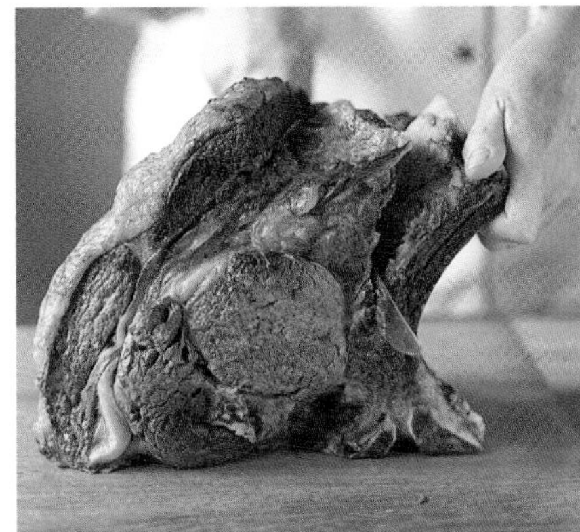

For maximum flavor, cook the rib of beef with the chine bone still attached, and remove it before carving. You can also remove the meat from the ribs to facilitate carving. We prefer, however, to carve the meat while it is still on the bone. Be sure to have a really sharp carving knife.

Master Recipe
Yorkshire Pudding

Serves 8–10

Simply irresistible with lots of gravy! I cook individual ones which I'm sure would be very much frowned on in Yorkshire but, if you want to be more traditional, cook 1 large pudding in a roasting pan and cut it into squares.

1 cup white flour, preferably unbleached
pinch of salt
2 eggs
1¼ cups milk
1 tablespoon butter, melted
olive oil or pure beef dripping (unless for vegetarians) for greasing pans
deep muffin pan

Sift the flour and salt into a bowl, make a well in the center, and drop in the eggs.

Using a small whisk or wooden spoon, stir continuously, gradually drawing in flour from the sides, adding half the milk in a steady stream at the same time. When all the flour has been mixed in, whisk in the remainder of the milk and the cool melted butter. Let stand for 1 hour.

Grease a hot deep muffin pan with beef dripping or olive oil and fill half to two-thirds full with the batter. Bake in a hot oven (about 450°F [230°C])for about 20 minutes. Remove from the pans and serve warm.

How to Cook Steak

The approximate cooking times for each side of the steaks are:

	sirloin	fillet (tenderloin)
rare	2 minutes	5 minutes
medium rare	3 minutes	6 minutes
medium	4 minutes	7 minutes
well done	5 minutes	8–9 minutes

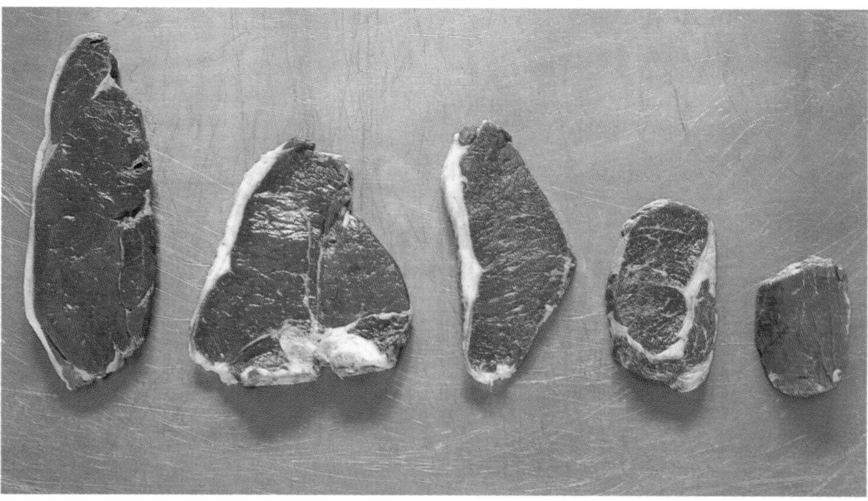

From left to right: sirloin steak, T-bone steak, minute steak, fillet steak (tenderloin) and medallion.

Variations

Olive Yorkshire Puddings

Follow the Master Recipe and grease the pans with olive oil. Drop 2 or 3 pitted olives into each pudding.

Mustard and Thyme Leaf Yorkshire Pudding

Follow the Master Recipe and add some thyme leaves to the mixture, and English or French mustard to each pudding.

Sirloin of Beef Roast with Cracked Peppercorns served with Olive Yorkshire Puddings

Serves 1

4 lbs. (1.8kg) sirloin of beef, well aged
extra-virgin olive oil
⅓–⅔ cup black peppercorns, cracked
sea salt or Kosher salt

Olive Yorkshire Puddings (see above)
Gravy (see page 594)

Garnish
sprigs of rosemary, watercress, or flat-leaf parsley

Preheat the oven to 475°F (250°C).

An hour or so before you plan to cook the meat, score the fat lightly, brush the surface of the meat with olive oil, coat with freshly cracked black pepper.

Place the meat in a roasting pan, fat side up. Sprinkle with sea salt and put into the fully preheated oven. Reduce the heat to moderate, 350°F (180°C), after 15 minutes. As the fat renders down, it will baste the meat. Roast until the beef is cooked to your taste. Transfer to a carving dish. Keep it warm while you make the gravy. Taste the gravy and strain into a sauce boat.

Serve with a little Gravy and an Olive Yorkshire Pudding.

Serve Horseradish Sauce (see page 586) and Béarnaise Sauce (see page 586) separately. Salsa Verde (see page 592) makes a good accompaniment in summer; in winter, Roast Parsnips (see page 174) go well.

Pan-Grilled Steak with Béarnaise Sauce, French Fried Onions, and Chips

Serves 6

Of all the sauces to serve with steak, Béarnaise is my absolute favorite. We find a heavy-ridged cast-iron grill pan best for cooking steaks when you don't need to make a sauce in the pan.

6 x 6–ounce (175g) sirloin or fillet steaks
1 garlic clove
a little olive oil
salt and freshly ground pepper

Béarnaise Sauce (see page 586)
French Fried Onions (see page 188)
Chips (see page 184)

Garnish
fresh watercress (optional)

Prepare the steaks about 1 hour before cooking. Cut a garlic clove in half; rub both sides of each steak with the cut face of the garlic. Grind some black pepper over the steaks and sprinkle on a few drops of olive oil. Turn the steaks in the oil and set aside. If using sirloin steaks, score the fat at 1 inch (2.5cm) intervals.

Prepare the French Fried Onions and make the Béarnaise Sauce and keep them warm. Just before serving, heat the grill-pan, season the steaks with a little salt, and place them on the hot pan. Turn a sirloin steak over onto the fat and cook for 1–2 minutes or until the fat becomes crisp.

Put the steaks on a plate and let rest for a few minutes in a warm place while you cook the Chips. Garnish with watercress and serve.

Steak with Irish Whiskey Sauce

Serves 4

4 well-aged sirloin or fillet steaks
1 clove of garlic
lots of freshly ground pepper
olive oil
salt
4–8 ounces (110–225g) mushrooms (about 1½–3 cups)
3–5 tablespoons Irish whiskey
½ cup homemade Beef Stock (see page 36)
½ cup cream
1 generous tablespoon freshly chopped parsley

Cut the clove of garlic in half and rub the cut side over the steaks. Crush the garlic and reserve for the sauce. Season the steaks with freshly ground pepper and drizzle a little olive oil over them.

Just before serving, sauté the mushrooms in a hot pan, season with salt and pepper, and keep warm. Wash out the pan. Season the steaks with salt and cook to your taste. Remove to a plate. De-glaze the pan with whiskey and let it flame; as the flames die away, add the crushed garlic, stock, cream, and parsley. Bring to a boil and simmer for a few minutes, add the mushrooms, and continue to cook until the sauce tastes really good and lightly coats the back of a spoon. Put the steaks on to 4 warm plates. Pour any escaped juices into the sauce, taste, and correct the seasoning. Spoon the sauce over the steaks and serve immediately.

Sirloin Steak Sandwich with Bonnie Stern's Barbecued Onion Sauce

Serves 8

An extraordinary sounding sauce, it really takes an act of faith to make it but it tastes delicious. Bonnie Stern is a fellow cook from Toronto whose Heart Smart books are full of little gems.

1½ lbs. (700g) sirloin, cut into generous 1-inch (2.5-cm) thick steaks
2½ tablespoons balsamic vinegar
1 generous tablespoon Dijon mustard
½ teaspoon freshly ground pepper
2 garlic cloves, crushed
2 thin French sticks (baguettes)
handful of fresh parsley, chopped

Bonnie Stern's Barbecued Onion Sauce
2½ tablespoons olive oil
3 large onions, sliced
3 garlic cloves, chopped
⅔ cup canned tomatoes
½ cup less 1 tablespoon brown sugar
½ cup rice vinegar or cider vinegar
½ cup strong coffee
1 tablespoon plus 1 teaspoon Worcestershire sauce

Pat the steak dry. Mix the balsamic vinegar, mustard, pepper, and garlic in a small bowl. Rub all over the meat. Cover and refrigerate.

Make the onion sauce: heat the olive oil in a saucepan. Add the onions and garlic and cook until soft but not colored. Add the tomatoes, sugar, rice vinegar, coffee, and Worcestershire sauce. Bring to a boil and simmer gently for 15 minutes.

Just before serving, barbecue or pan-grill the steak, 4–6 minutes on each side for sirloin steak depending on the thickness. Let it rest for 5 minutes. Slice thinly. Cut the crusty French sticks into 8 equal lengths, slit each in half, and make hot, juicy sandwiches with the steak and barbecued onion sauce. Sprinkle with lots of parsley and eat immediately.

Seared Beef with Gorgonzola, Polenta, and Red Onion Marmalade

Serves 6

6 x 6–ounce (175g) fillet steaks

Red Onion Marmalade (see page 512)

Gorgonzola Polenta
6 cups homemade Chicken Stock (see page 36)
a heaped cup cornmeal
salt and freshly ground pepper
6 ounces (175g) Gorgonzola or Dolcelatte

Garnish
arugula leaves

First make the Red Onion Marmalade.

Next make the polenta: bring the chicken stock to a boil and whisk in the cornmeal. Turn the heat down to a minimum and cook for 30–35 minutes, stirring regularly. Remove from heat and stir in the cheese. Season to taste.

To serve, barbecue or pan-grill the steaks to your taste. Spoon a little soft polenta onto the center of each plate.

Arrange a steak and top with a small spoon of Red Onion Marmalade. Garnish with some arugula leaves.

Sirloin Steak with Chimichurri Sauce

Serves 6–8
Makes 1 cup or a little over that

Chimichurri is a hot perky sauce from Argentina.

6 x 6–ounce (175g) sirloin steaks

Chimichurri Sauce
1 cup flat-leaf parsley
4 large garlic cloves, peeled and crushed
1/2 cup extra-virgin olive oil
1/4 cup red wine vinegar
2 1/2 tablespoons water
salt
1 red onion, finely chopped
1/2 chile, seeded and chopped, or 1/4 teaspoon chili flakes

Chop the parsley finely with the garlic. (Alternatively, pulse in a food processor, scraping down the sides of the bowl, until well mixed.) Transfer to a bowl. Whisk in the oil, vinegar, and water gradually. Add the red onion, chile, and salt. Taste and add more seasoning if necessary. Pan-grill the steak, transfer to hot plates, spoon some chimichurri over the top, and serve immediately with some crusty fried potatoes or Rustic Roasts (see page 181).

Other sauces for steaks

Salsa Verde (see page 592)
Mushroom à la Crème (see page 197)
Sauce Beurre Rouge (see page 583)
Tapenade (see page 588)
Anchoïade (see page 594)
Olive and Anchovy Butter (see page 588)
Provençale Butter (see page 588)
Barbecue Sauce (see page 591)

Rib Eye Steak with Roquefort Cheese, Glazed Onions, Roast Red Peppers, and Rosemary on Soft Polenta

Serves 6

6 rib eye steaks
cut clove of garlic
lots of freshly ground pepper
salt
4 roast red peppers, skinned and peeled
4–6 onions
3 ounces (75g) Roquefort cheese or Gorgonzola or Cashel Blue Cheese

Garnish
sprigs of flat-leaf parsley
rosemary sprigs
tarragon sprigs

Creamy Polenta (see page 143)

Rub the steaks with a cut clove of garlic. Season with lots of freshly ground pepper. Next make the Polenta.

Peel and slice the onion. Melt some butter and oil in a sauté pan and cook over a medium heat, stirring occasionally until soft and slightly caramelized. Keep both the onions and the thick strips of roasted red pepper warm.

Preheat a heavy grill pan. Season the steaks with salt and cook to perfection on the hot pan. Meanwhile, reheat the Polenta if necessary. Taste and correct seasoning. Spoon some polenta onto each hot plate. Put a steak on top. Divide the hot caramelized onions and the pepper strips between each steak. Crumble some chunks of Roquefort, Gorgonzola, or Cashel Blue cheese on top. Garnish with rosemary sprigs, tarragon, and flat-leaf parsley.

Peppered Beef with Scallion and Horseradish Mash

Serves 4

4 x 6–ounce (175g) fillet steaks
freshly cracked black peppercorns
salt
1–2 tablespoons olive oil
1/4 cup brandy
1/2 cup homemade Beef Stock (see page 36)
3/4 cup cream
2 tablespoons green peppercorns
arugula leaves
Scallion and Horseradish Mash (see page 182).

Cook the Scallion and Horseradish Mash.

Roll the fillet steaks in cracked peppercorns. Season with salt. Heat a heavy pan, add a little oil, and seal the steaks on all sides. Reduce the heat and cook to the desired stage. Remove from the pan and let them rest in a warm place while you make the sauce: pour off any excess fat, de-glaze the pan with brandy, add the beef stock, cream, and whole peppercorns. Reduce to a light pouring consistency. Put a large spoonful of Scallion and Horseradish Mash on the plate, arrange the arugula leaves beside it, and lay the steak on top. Spoon over some sauce.

Variation

Pan-grilled Steak with Grainy Mustard Butter, Scallion, and Horseradish Mash

Pan-grill the steak, serve with Scallion and Horseradish Mash (see page 182) and a slice of Grainy Mustard Butter (see page 588) melting on top.

Chili con Carne with Sour Cream, Cheddar Cheese, and Tortillas

Serves 4–6

In the US every year there are huge chili "cook offs" with passionate rivalry between the contestants, all of whom are determined that they make the best chili. Even though it is usually associated with beef, chili can be made from lamb, pork, or veal also. Use stewing cuts; leftover cooked meat may be used but it's best to avoid ground meat. Cubed meat produces a far more appealing texture.

1–1½ lbs. (450–700g) meat
2–3 tablespoons olive oil
1 large onion, chopped
2–3 garlic cloves, peeled and crushed
1 small green pepper, seeded and sliced

Hot Chile Sauce (see page 591)
1½ tablespoon tomato paste
1 teaspoon ground cumin
1¼ cups red kidney beans, soaked and cooked
salt and brown sugar

Garnish
sour cream
fresh cilantro sprigs
Cheddar cheese, freshly grated

Trim the meat where necessary and cut into ½–¾ inch (1–2cm) cubes. Heat a little olive oil in a frying pan and brown the meat. Transfer to a flameproof casserole dish or other flameproof and ovenproof pot. Brown the onion and garlic lightly in the same oil, and scrape out onto the meat. Add the peppers, Chile Sauce, and enough water to almost cover the ingredients in the casserole dish. Cover tightly, bring to a boil, and simmer gently until cooked. Check the liquid occasionally. By the end of the cooking time it should have reduced to a thick sauce. If it reduces too soon, add a little water.

Finally add the tomato paste, cumin, kidney beans, salt, and brown sugar to taste. Simmer for a further 15 minutes. Serve in deep, wide soup bowls with a blob of sour cream each.

Garnish with cilantro and some cheese on top, and serve with tacos, Guacamole (see page 91), and Tomato and Cilantro Salsa (see page 591) .

Stewing

The tougher cuts of meat are perfect for long, slow stewing which tenderizes the meat. Cuts of meat suitable for stewing:

Lamb: neck, shoulder, breast.
Beef: neck, fore shank, brisket, short plate, chuck, blade, flank, tip
Veal: shank, flank, neck
Pork: neck, leg, shoulder

Master Recipe
Winter Beef Stew

Serves 6–8

A stew like this is great for family meals or perfect for a shooting lunch; robust and filling, it will even stand up to being reheated several times.

2 lbs. (900g) good stewing beef (rump, fore shank or flank), well aged
2 tablespoons butter
4–5 tablespoons olive oil
2 cups sliced onions
8 ounces (225g) celery, chopped into ½-inch (1-cm) dice (about 2 cups)
1 large carrot, sliced into ½-inch (1-cm) pieces
4 ounces (110g) parsnip, or rutabaga
6 ounces (175g) streaky bacon, cut into ½-inch (1-cm) dice
2½ tablespoons seasoned flour
2–2½ cups Homemade Beef Stock (see page 36)
bouquet garni
8 ounces (225g) mushrooms, sliced (about 2⅓ cups)
salt and freshly ground pepper
Roux (see page 580), optional

Garnish
3–4 tablespoons flat-leaf parsley, freshly snipped

Preheat the oven to 275–300°F (140–150°C).

Trim the beef and cut it into 1-inch (2.5-cm) cubes. Melt half the butter and olive oil in a pan and lightly brown the onion. Then add in all the other vegetables except the mushrooms, toss them in the oil, and transfer to a casserole dish.

Turn up the heat and add a little more olive oil. Fry the bacon until crisp and add to the casserole dish. Toss the meat lightly in seasoned flour and cook in the pan in batches until lightly brown on all sides. Transfer to the casserole dish.

Pour the stock into the pan, bring to a boil, and scrape the pan to dissolve the bits of sediment and caramelized juices. Pour this over the meat, and add the bouquet garni and season the casserole with salt and pepper. Cover with the lid and simmer in the oven for about 1 1/2-2 1/2 hours, depending on the cut of meat.

Sauté the mushrooms in the remainder of the butter, and add them to the casserole about 20 minutes before the end of cooking. When the meat is cooked, taste the juice; if it is a little weak, strain it off into another saucepan and reduce to concentrate the flavor or, if it is too liquid, whisk in a little roux. Remove the bouquet garni. Correct the seasoning and sprinkle with parsley. Serve with potatoes and a winter green salad.

Variations

Winter Beef Stew with Herb Crust

1/2 White Soda Bread recipe with herbs (see page 474)
egg wash
grated Cheddar cheese

Follow the Master Recipe. Roll out the White Soda Bread dough into a 3/4-inch (2-cm) thick shape. Stamp out round scones with a 2-inch (5-cm) cutter. When the stew is almost cooked, remove the lid from the casserole dish and cover the top of the stew with slightly overlapping herb scones, brush with egg wash, and sprinkle with a little cheese if you wish. Increase the heat to 450°F (230°C) for 10 minutes, then reduce the heat to 400°F (200°C) for a further 20 minutes or until the crust is baked.

Winter Beef Stew with Olives

Follow the Master Recipe. Add 1/3–1/2 cup of pitted black or green olives to the stew about 10 minutes before the end of cooking.

Master Recipe
Boeuf Bourguignonne

Serves 6

In Ireland, stew is generally regarded as something you feed the family, not your guests. Not so in France, where this most famous of all beef stews might be served for a special Sunday lunch or dinner with friends. After all, it is not cheap to make: you need top-quality well-aged beef and the best part of a good bottle of red wine. As the name suggests, it used to be made with Burgundy, but with current Burgundy prices, I might settle for a good Beaujolais or a full-bodied Côtes du Rhône.

3 lbs. (1.3kg) best stewing beef, cut into 2-inch (5-cm) cubes
6 ounces (175g) salt pork or bacon
1–2 tablespoons extra-virgin olive oil
1 medium carrot, sliced
1 medium onion, sliced
2 tablespoons brandy, optional
2–2 1/2 cups full-bodied red wine
1 1/4–2 cups homemade Brown Beef Stock (see page 36)
1 1/2 tablespoons tomato paste
2-inch (5-cm) piece of dried orange peel, see below
1 sprig thyme
1 bay leaf
2–3 garlic cloves, peeled but left whole
salt and freshly ground pepper
Roux (see page 580), optional
18–24 small onions, depending on size
1 lb. (450g) fresh white or field mushrooms, cleaned and quartered
2 generous tablespoons parsley, chopped

Trim off the rind and cut the bacon into 1/2-inch (1-cm) cubes. Blanch and refresh if salty, then dry well on paper towels. Heat the olive oil in a frying pan, sauté the bacon until crisp and golden, and transfer it to a flameproof casserole dish or other flameproof and ovenproof pot. Turn up the heat so that the oil and fat from the bacon are almost smoking. Dry off the cubes of

meat. Sauté a few pieces at a time until nicely browned on all sides, then add to the casserole dish, along with the bacon. Toss the sliced carrot and onion in the remaining fat and add these, too.

If there is any fat left in the pan at this stage, pour it off. Add the brandy, if using, and flame it to burn off the alcohol. Then de-glaze the pan with the wine, scraping the little bits of sediment from the bottom of the pan until they dissolve. Bring to a boil and pour over the beef.

The casserole may be prepared ahead to this point. Let it get cold, cover, and refrigerate overnight, or at least for a few hours. The wine will have a tenderizing effect on the meat, and the other ingredients will add extra flavor as the meat marinates.

After marinating, bring the casserole to a boil, add enough stock to cover the meat, and add the tomato paste, orange peel, thyme, bay leaf, and the cloves of garlic. Season with salt and freshly ground pepper. Bring to a boil, cover, and simmer very gently either on top of the stove or in a low oven, 325°F (170°C), for 1 1/2–2 1/2 hours, depending on the cut of meat used. The meat should not fall apart but it should be tender enough to eat without too much chewing.

Meanwhile, cook the onions and mushrooms. Peel the onions (see tip, right). Simmer gently in a covered pan with about 1/2-inch (1-cm) of water or beef stock – they will take about 30–35 minutes, depending on size. When cooked, a knife should pierce them easily. Toss the quartered mushrooms, a few at a time, in a little olive oil in a hot pan, and season with salt and freshly ground pepper.

When the meat is tender, pour everything into a strainer placed over a saucepan. Discard the herbs, carrot, onion, and orange peel. Return the meat to the casserole dish along with the onions and mushrooms. Remove the fat from the strained liquid. There should be about 2½ cups sauce. Taste, bring back to a boil, and simmer. If the sauce is too thin or too weak, reduce for a few minutes, otherwise thicken slightly by whisking in a little roux. Pour over the meat, mushrooms and onions, bring back to a boil, simmer for a few minutes until heated through, and correct seasoning if necessary. Sprinkle with parsley, and serve

Tip: Peeling Small Onions
This task is made easier if you drop the onions in boiling water for 1 minute, then drain, run them under the cold tap, "top and tail" them, and then slip off the skins.

Variation

Ostrich Stew

Follow the Master Recipe, substituting stewing ostrich meat for beef in the above recipe – it takes approx. 1½ hours to cook.

Dried Orange Peel

A strip of dried orange peel is often added to stews in France and can really enhance the flavor. Use an unwaxed organic orange, if possible. Otherwise scrub the skin well and remove thin strips of peel, using a swivel-top peeler, without the pith. Allow to dry overnight close to a radiator or an Aga. Dried orange peel may be stored in a screw-top jar and keeps for weeks.

Daube de Boeuf Provençale (Beef Provençale)

Serves 8

This gutsy winter stew has a rich robust flavor. It reheats perfectly and can also be made ahead and frozen.

3 lbs. (1.3kg) lean stewing beef – use rump or chuck

Marinade
2½ tablespoons olive oil
1¼ cups dry white or red wine
1 teaspoon salt
½ teaspoon pepper
½ teaspoon thyme, sage, or annual marjoram
1 bay leaf
2 garlic cloves, peeled and crushed
1 cup thinly sliced carrots
1 cup thinly sliced onions

1 lb. (450g) bacon cut into ½-inch (1-cm) lardons
1 x 14-ounce (400g) can Italian tomatoes, chopped
⅔ cup homemade Beef Stock (see page 36)
1¾ cups sliced mushrooms
10 anchovy fillets
2½ tablespoons capers
¼ cup white or red wine vinegar
2 generous tablespoons freshly chopped flat-leaf parsley
2 cloves garlic, mashed
Roux (see page 580), optional

Garnish
freshly chopped flat-leaf parsley

You will need a flameproof casserole dish or other flameproof and ovenproof pot

Cut the beef into large chunks, about 3 inches (8cm). Mix the marinade ingredients in a bowl or large casserole dish. Add the meat, cover, and marinate overnight in a fridge or cool pantry. Remove the meat to a plate. Strain the marinade, reserve the vegetables and the marinade separately.

Heat the oil in a frying pan, cook the bacon lardons until crisp, add to the casserole dish. Dry the meat with paper towels. Seal the meat on the hot pan, and add to the bacon along with the marinated vegetables and canned tomatoes.

De-grease the frying pan and de-glaze with the marinade and ⅔ cup good Beef Stock, then add to the casserole dish. Bring to a boil and either simmer very gently on top of the stove or transfer to a preheated oven 325°F (170°C) for about 1½–2 hours.

Meanwhile sauté the sliced mushroom in a hot pan and set aside.

When the meat is soft and tender, purée the anchovies along with the capers, parsley, wine vinegar, and garlic. Add to the casserole along with the mushrooms. Simmer gently for 8–10 minutes. Taste and correct the seasoning. De-grease and if necessary, thicken the boiling liquid by whisking in a little roux.

Sprinkle with chopped parsley and serve with Fluffy Mashed Potatoes or Ulster Champ (see page 183).

Osso Buco

Serves 4

In this classic Italian recipe, each piece of veal should include a piece of bone, with the delicious marrow intact. Traditionally the dish would be served with a Risotto Milanese.

5 lbs. (2.2kg) foreshank of veal (baby beef), cut into 2-inch (5-cm) thick pieces.
½ stick (¼ cup) butter
⅔ cup dry white wine
⅔ cup homemade Veal Stock (see page 37)
12 ounces (350g) ripe tomatoes
pinch of sugar, optional
salt and freshly ground pepper

Gremolata
2 generous tablespoons chopped flat-leaf parsley

1 unwaxed lemon
1 garlic clove, peeled

Melt the butter in a heavy flameproof casserole dish or other flameproof and ovenproof pot, brown the veal on both sides, a few at a time. Remove to a plate and continue until all the pieces have been browned, adding a little extra butter if necessary. Return all the meat to the casserole dish, arranging the pieces side by side so that they remain upright. This way, the precious marrow doesn't fall out during cooking.

Add the white wine and cook for 10 minutes. Meanwhile, skin, chop, and seed the tomatoes, add to the casserole along with a pinch of sugar, depending on their sweetness. Add the stock, season, and cook for 1½–2 hours.

Shortly before serving, prepare the gremolata. Chop a handful of parsley with the garlic and the grated rind of half the lemon. Sprinkle the gremolata over the osso bucco just before serving.

Ballymaloe Spiced Beef

Serves 12–16

Although spiced beef is traditionally associated with Christmas, in Cork we eat it all year round! It may be served hot or cold and is a marvellous stand-by. This delicious recipe for spiced beef has been handed down through Myrtle Allen's family and, though I have tried several others, it is still my favorite. It includes saltpeter, nowadays regarded as a health hazard, so perhaps you should not live exclusively on it! Certainly people have lived on occasional meals of meats preserved in this way for generations.

The recipe below makes enough spice to cure 5 flanks of beef, each about 4 pounds (1.8kg) in size. Leftover spice mixture will keep for weeks or even months in a screwtop jar. If it is properly spiced and cooked, spiced beef will keep for 3–4 weeks in the fridge.

3–4 lbs. (1.3–1.8kg) lean flank of beef or round

Ballymaloe Spice for Beef
1 cup turbinade or light brown sugar
12 ounces (350g) salt (about 1⅓ cups)
½ ounce (10g) saltpeter (available from pharmacists)
¾ cup whole black peppercorns
¾ cup whole allspice (pimento or Jamaican pepper)
¾ cup whole juniper berries

Grind all the ingredients, preferably in a food processor, until fairly fine.

To prepare the beef: if you are using flank of beef, remove the bones and trim away any unnecessary fat. Rub some of the spice well into every crevice of the beef. Put it into an earthenware dish and leave in a fridge or cold pantry for 3–7 days, depending on the thickness of the meat. Turn it occasionally. (This is a dry spice, but after 1–2 days some liquid will come out of the meat.) The longer the meat is left in the spice, the longer it will last and the greater will be the spicy flavor.

Just before cooking the meat, roll and tie the joint neatly with cotton string into a compact shape, cover with cold water, and simmer for 2–3 hours or until soft and cooked. Or if the beef is to be eaten cold, remove it from the liquid, press by putting it on a flat pan or into an appropriate sized bread pan; cover it with a board and weight, and leave for 12 hours.

Serving suggestions
Serve cut into thin slices with some freshly-made salads and home-made chutneys, or use in sandwiches.

Spiced beef is delicious cold in paper-thin slices with a Potato and Scallion Salad (see page 218) and avocado and salad greens including arugula.

Spiced beef is also excellent with Sweet Cucumber Pickle (see page 514) and Ballymaloe Country Relish or Apple and Tomato Chutney (see page 511).

Stir-fried Beef with Oyster Sauce

Serves 6-8

Deh-Ta Hsiung has come to teach a Chinese cooking course at the Ballymaloe Cookery School several times. This is one of his favorite beef recipes, which we have been making ever since. A stir-fry is a terrific way to make a little beef go a long way.

12–14 ounces (350–400g) beef steak (sirloin for preference)
4 ounces (110g) bamboo shoots (about 1 cup)
4 ounces (110g) carrots (about 1 cup, cut up)
4 ounces (110g) broccoli, snow peas, zucchini or a mixture (about 1 cup, cut up)
4 ounces (110g) baby corn cobs, optional (about 10)
5–6 tablespoons sunflower or peanut oil
1–2 scallions, cut into short lengths
1 teaspoon ginger, peeled and freshly grated
1 scant teaspoon salt
1 teaspoon sugar
stock or water
2–3 tablespoons oyster sauce

Marinade
1 teaspoon sugar
1 tablespoon plus 1 teaspoon light soy sauce
2½ tablespoons rice wine or dry sherry
2 teaspoons cornstarch, mixed with 1 tablespoon water

Garnish
1 generous tablespoon flat-leaf parsley or cilantro leaves, freshly chopped

Cut the beef into thin slices across the grain about the size of a large postage stamp. Mix the marinade ingredients in a bowl; add the beef slices, toss, and let marinate for 25–30 minutes.

Meanwhile prepare the vegetables: cut the bamboo shoots and carrots into roughly the same size as the beef; slice the broccoli or zucchini and corn cobs, if using. Top and tail the snow peas (cut lengthwise at an angle if large).

Heat the oil in a preheated wok. Stir-fry the beef for about 30–40 seconds or until the color changes and then quickly remove with a slotted spoon. In the same oil, add the scallions, ginger, and the vegetables; stir-fry for about 2–3 minutes, then add the salt, sugar, and a little stock or water if necessary. Add the beef and oyster sauce, blend well. Stir for 1 more minute. Turn into a hot serving dish and sprinkle with parsley or cilantro.

Using Ground Meat

Ground meat, inexpensive and incredibly versatile. Used in a wide variety of dishes all over the world, from meat balls to hamburgers to Bolognaise sauce, to Middle Eastern kibbeh.

Pork, lamb, veal, and chicken can be ground as well as the most familiar beef. Because grinding bruises the meat, it is crucially important that it is used when very fresh – I personally will only use meat that has been ground on the same day, as I find that it sours quickly even when refrigerated.

The cuts of meat affect the quality of the ground meat, for ground beef it's useful to know that very lean cuts from the leg, such as round, can dry out in cooking. Flank, chuck, and other cuts from the shoulder are fatter and have a sweeter flavor and juicier texture. Flank is also excellent but ensure that the connective tissue is removed otherwise the end result will be tough. The difference is not so noticeable in other meats.

If possible, buy a whole piece of meat and ask your butcher to grind it or, if you own a grinder, do it at home. Keep ground meat refrigerated; it keeps up to 2 days but the flavor deteriorates. Fresh ground meat may be frozen for 1–2 months. Freeze in shallow blocks so it defrosts quickly, and use immediately.

Basic Hamburgers

Serves 4-6

The hamburger is the universal fast food, immortalized by the Americans and enjoyed by the rich and famous, the down and outs, and all the rest of the world as well. It can be a feast or a travesty, simply a burger in a bun or an elaborate creation with lots of sauces and pickles. Hamburgers, love them or hate them, they're here to stay and with a bit of effort they can be simply delicious. The secret of really good hamburgers is the quality of the meat. It doesn't need to be an expensive cut but it is essential to use the beef on the day it is ground. A very small percentage of fat in the beef will make the hamburgers sweet and juicy. The egg is not essential, although it helps to bind the burgers and increases the food value.

1 tablespoon butter
1/2 cup finely chopped onion
1 lb. (450g) beef (flank, chuck or foreshank would be perfect), freshly ground
1/2 teaspoon fresh thyme leaves
1/2 teaspoon parsley, finely chopped
1 small egg, beaten
salt and freshly ground pepper
pork caul fat (optional)
oil or dripping

Melt the butter in a saucepan and toss in the onion, sweating until soft but not colored. Let it get cold. Meanwhile mix the ground beef with the herbs and beaten egg, season with salt and pepper, add the onions, and mix well. Fry off a tiny bit in the pan to check the seasoning, and correct if necessary. Then shape into hamburgers, 4–6 depending on the size you want. Wrap each in caul fat if using. Cook to your taste in a medium-hot pan or grill pan, in a little oil, turning once.

Variations

Homemade hamburgers are a vast improvement on most mass-produced burgers. There are endless ways to serve them – with cheese, bacon, chili, blue cheese, and mushroom. The following are a few of our favorites, always served with lots of crispy Chips (see page 184).

Hamburgers with Caramelized Onions (see page 188) **and Pesto** (see page 589)

Hamburgers with Guacamole (see page 91) **and French Fried Onions** (see page 188)

Hamburgers with Mushroom à la Crème (see page 197)

Hamburgers with Bonnie Stern's Barbecued Onion Sauce (see page 339)

The Great American Hamburger, served in a bun with lettuce, sliced onions and tomato, gherkins, a dill pickle, mayonnaise, and ketchup and of course lots of crispy chips.

Tip: If the hamburgers are to be wrapped in caul fat, wrap loosely to allow for contraction during cooking.

If the hamburgers are being cooked in batches, make sure to wash and dry the pan between batches.

Mexican Ground Beef with Tacos and Tomato Salsa

Serves 6

Ground beef cooked in this Mexican way is absolutely addictive – I adore all the accompaniments. Serve with freshly cooked tortilla chips – Totopos.

1 lb. (450g) beef, freshly ground
2 1/2 tablespoons sunflower oil
1 1/2 cups chopped onions
2 garlic cloves, crushed
1 teaspoon cumin, freshly ground
2 teaspoons annual marjoram or oregano, chopped
1 fresh chile, seeded and chopped or a pinch of chili powder or 1 teaspoon chile sauce
good dash of soy sauce
salt, freshly ground black pepper, and a pinch of sugar

Heat the oil in a frying pan, add the chopped onion and garlic, and cook over a medium heat until soft and slightly golden. Increase the heat, add the ground beef, and stir until brown. Add the cumin, marjoram or oregano, and chile. Then shake in the soy sauce and season well with salt, freshly ground pepper, and sugar. Taste, this mixture needs a surprising amount of salt. Serve with Tomato and Cilantro Salsa (see page 591), Guacamole (see page 91), shredded, crispy lettuce, sour cream, grated Cheddar cheese, and tortillas (see page 493). Put them together in whatever combination you fancy, and enjoy!

Sri Owen's Sumatran Rendang

Serves 10–12

Rendang is nothing like curry. A well-cooked one is brown, sometimes almost black. It should be chunky and dry, yet succulent, with the dryness of meat that has absorbed its juices and its sauce during a long period of cooking. The cooking process is, according to Sri, unique, for it is the only dish that passes from boiling to frying without any interruption. The cooking time is therefore very long.

Sri learnt the traditional Rendang from her grandmother in Padang Panjang, West Sumatra; used buffalo meat, and it was almost always cooked in large quantities. We loved this recipe when Sri was guest chef at the school in 1993.

3 lbs. (1.3kg) brisket, round, or good stewing steak
6 shallots, thinly sliced
4 cloves garlic
1 inch (2.5cm) ginger root, roughly chopped
6 red chiles, seeded and roughly chopped, or 3 teaspoons chili powder
2 quarts (1.8 litres) coconut milk
1 teaspoon turmeric
1/2 teaspoon galangal
1 salam leaf or bay leaf
1 stalk fresh lemongrass, bruised
2 teaspoons salt

Cut the meat into biggish cubes. Put the shallots, garlic, ginger, and chiles in a blender or a food processor, and reduce to a purée. Put all these ingredients and the coconut milk in a large pot, along with the salam or bay leaf, lemon grass, salt, and meat, which must be completely covered by the coconut milk. Stir, and start cooking on a medium heat, uncovered. Let this bubble for 1 1/2 hours, stirring from time to time. By this time the coconut milk will be quite thick.

Transfer the whole dish into a wok. Again let this bubble for half an hour, stirring occasionally. You'll notice by now the coconut milk is already starting to become oily. The dish now needs to be stirred frequently. Taste and add more salt if necessary.

When it becomes thick and brown, stir all the time for about 15 minutes, until the oil has all but disappeared, absorbed by the meat. Now the dish is ready. Serve hot with plenty of rice.

Rendang will keep for more than 1 week in the fridge, and can be reheated as often as you like. It can be frozen successfully, and kept frozen for 5–6 months. Thaw completely before you reheat it in an ovenproof dish in a moderate oven for 10–15 minutes.

Spicy Koftas

Serves 4–6

This is a great way to use up leftovers.

2 lbs. (900g) beef or lamb, finely ground
1 1/2 cups finely chopped onions
1/2 teaspoon ginger, freshly grated
2 teaspoons cumin seeds, freshly roasted and ground
1 teaspoon coriander seeds, freshly roasted
a good pinch cayenne
1 teaspoon paprika
1 egg
1/4 cup parsley, freshly chopped
1/4 cup cilantro or marjoram, freshly chopped
salt and freshly ground pepper

Mix the ground meat with the spices, season well, cook a morsel on a frying pan, taste for seasoning. Correct, if necessary. Let it sit for an hour or so if possible. Shape the ground meat into sausage shapes around a flat skewer, not too large or they will break. Brush with a little oil, then cook on a barbecue or a grill-pan, turning on all sides until crisp and golden. Serve with a green salad and tzatziki.

Beef Stroganoff

Serves 6–8

Margot Heskin's delicious version of this much-loved recipe.

1 3/4 lbs. (775g) fillet of beef (tenderloin), cut into very thin strips
1/2 stick (1/4 cup) butter
2 1/2 tablespoons olive oil
1 large onion, chopped finely
8 ounces (225g) mushrooms, sliced (about 2 1/3 cups)
freshly grated nutmeg
1 teaspoon Dijon mustard
1 cup sour cream
1 teaspoon paprika, optional
salt and freshly ground pepper

Melt half the butter in a sauté pan with 1 tablespoon of the oil, add the chopped onions. Season well with salt and pepper. Cook on a medium heat for about 10 minutes, until the onions are soft but not colored.

While the onions are cooking, heat the remaining oil in another pan over a high heat. Add the mushrooms, season with salt, pepper, and grated nutmeg.

When the onions and mushrooms are cooked, remove from the pans. Melt the remaining butter in one of the pans. When it starts to foam, add the beef and stir-fry over a high heat until just cooked. Return the onions and mushrooms to the pan. Check the seasoning. Stir in the mustard, paprika, and, finally, the sour cream. Continue to cook until the stroganoff is just bubbling. Serve with Plain Boiled Rice (see page 124).

Fondue Bourguignonne

Serves 4

This meat fondue is fun for a small dinner party. Only cut up the beef just before you are about to cook, otherwise it will dry out. This is one of the national dishes of Switzerland and it is eaten communally, often on long double-pronged spiky forks. The cooking is done on an alcohol burner, and the main cooking vessel is known as a caquelon, which is filled with oil in which to cook the meat. Fondue sets are available at a reasonable price and usually cook for up to 6 people. Many are the stories of fines raised on those who lose their meat in the fondue pot!

2 lbs. (900g) fillet or sirloin of beef, trimmed and cut into 1-inch (2.5-cm) cubes
extra-virgin olive oil

Sauces
Garlic Mayonnaise (see page 584)
Horseradish Sauce (see page 586)
Béarnaise Sauce (see page 586)

Half-fill the fondue pot with olive oil. Divide the cubes of meat between 4 bowls. Place the fondue lamp on the table, light it, and put the saucepan of hot olive oil on top.

Provide each guest with a bowl of meat cubes and a plate and 1 or preferably 2 fondue forks, in addition to their other cutlery. Pass around the 3 sauces separately. Each guest spears 1 cube of meat at a time on their fondue fork and cooks it to their taste – rare, medium, or well-done. Accompany with a good green salad and plenty of crusty, home baked bread or Chips (see page 184).

Baby Beef Scallopini with Spinach, Raisins, and Pine Nuts

Serves 6

We do not serve intensively reared veal either at Ballymaloe House or at the Cookery School but once or twice a year we have a naturally reared milk-fed calf from Sibylle Knoble or one of my own Kerry bull calves. The meat is not so pale as conventional veal but is wonderfully sweet and delicious. This is one of Tim's favorite meals, reminding him of the Jersey baby beef of his childhood when his father was a Jersey breeder.

1½ lbs. (700g) lean Baby Beef from the top round
salt and freshly ground pepper
seasoned flour
beaten egg
fresh white breadcrumbs
Clarified Butter (see page 103)
lemon segments

Spinach with Raisins and Pine Nuts (see page 171)

With a very sharp knife, cut the top round into ¼-inch (5-mm) thick slices across the grain. Trim off any fat or sinews. Put between 2 sheets of plastic wrap and flatten a little more with a meat pounder or rolling pin.

Dip each piece in well seasoned flour, beaten egg, and soft white breadcrumbs. Pat off the excess. Melt 3 or 4 tablespoons of clarified butter in a wide frying pan. Fry the scallopini a few at a time until crisp and golden on one side, then flip over onto the other. Drain briefly on paper towels. Serve hot with segments of lemon, and Spinach with Raisins and Pine Nuts.

Thai Beef Salad

Serves 4

14-ounce (400g) sirloin steak, cut into 2 steaks if more convenient
¼ cup soy sauce
2 garlic cloves, crushed
2½ tablespoons lime juice, freshly squeezed
assorted lettuce leaves and salad greens
½ cup fresh mint leaves
½ cup fresh basil leaves
½ cup fresh cilantro leaves
½–1 English cucumber, peeled, seeded and sliced

Dressing
2 red chiles, chopped
¼ cup soy sauce
2½ tablespoons lime juice
2 teaspoons palm or brown sugar
2 kaffir lime leaves, finely shredded

Preheat a chargrill. Cook the steak (or steaks) for 2–3 minutes on each side or until cooked to your liking. They shouldn't be cooked more than medium rare. Cover the steak and let rest on a plate.

Mix the soy sauce, garlic, and lime juice in a bowl and add the steak; let marinate for 10 minutes. Toss lettuce, mint, basil, cilantro, and cucumber in a bowl. Arrange on serving plates.

To making dressing: combine the chiles, soy sauce, lime juice, palm sugar, and lime leaves. Taste, and balance if necessary. Just before serving, sprinkle some dressing over the salad greens, and toss. Slice the beef thinly and place on top of salad. Serve at once.

Carpaccio with Slivers of Desmond, Arugula, and Chopped Olive

Serves 12

We use the wonderful Desmond cheese made by Bill Hogan in West Cork, but a nutty Parmesan or Grana Padana would also be superb.

1 lb. (450g) fillet of beef (tenderloin), preferably Aberdeen Angus (fresh not frozen)
arugula leaves, about 5 per person
4–5 very thin slivers of Desmond or Parmesan cheese
sea salt or Kosher salt and freshly ground pepper
24–36 olives (we use Kalamata)
extra-virgin olive oil or truffle oil

Chill the meat, and pit and chop the olives. Just before serving, slice the beef as thinly as possible with a very sharp knife. Place each slice on a piece of oiled plastic wrap and cover with another piece of oiled plastic wrap. Roll gently with a rolling pin until it is almost transparent and has doubled in size. Peel the plastic off the top, invert the meat onto a chilled plate, and gently peel away the other piece of plastic. Put the arugula leaves of top of the beef and scatter very thin slivers of cheese over the top of the arugula. Put a little chopped olives around the edge. Sprinkle with flakes of sea salt and freshly cracked pepper. Drizzle with your best extra-virgin olive oil or truffle oil, and serve immediately with crusty bread.

variety meats

variety meats

Cork city has been a trading port since the time of the Phoenecians. The market in the center of Cork is unique in Ireland. You can buy everything from sun-dried tomatoes, native and exotic fish, and artisanal breads, to offal (or variety meats, as the Americans call it). Side by side with nam pla, bok choi, and mooli radishes are pigs' heads, tails, skirts, salted pigs' trotters (crubeens), offal bones and bodice (the ribs) which can be either salted or fresh.

It is fascinating to wander through the labyrinth of market stalls and see third and fourth generation stall holders trading alongside new age arrivals, each passionate about the food they are selling. Historically, Cork was the last port of call for ships and liners before they crossed the Atlantic. Thousands of Cork people were employed in the provisioning trade, and part of their weekly wage was paid in offal, so to this day, Cork people eat more offal than in any other part of the country.

Offal or variety meats are defined as every part of a dead animal – excluding the skin, hide and meat. Cuts such as liver, kidney, tongue, heart and sweetbreads (the pancreatic and thymus glands) are most regularly eaten, although brain, trotters, tripe, cheeks, ears and pig's head are also consumed. Ironically, despite the fact that in Ireland and Britain, offal is now harder to come by (butchers are often forbidden to sell the innards because of concerns over BSE and foot and mouth), it has suddenly become enormously popular in our posh restaurants.

The best time of the year for lamb's liver is in spring when it's really delicious, tender, and mild. Calves liver and good veal liver are marvellous. I often long for liver around Easter – I think it is my body telling me that it is craving iron after the long winter. At that time of year I also often crave rhubarb and cabbage, spinach or kale. I am sure that we are really meant to eat with the seasons. After all, it is logical that at certain times of the year our bodies needs specific nutrients.

Nutrition

Variety meats, and most particularly liver, is extremely nutritious and is rich in vitamins B12, A, C and D, folic acid, riboflavin, and iron (which is needed to make red blood cells and helps to prevent fatigue and anemia).

Buying and Cooking

Many people are squeamish about eating variety meats, or any part of an animal that is too recognizable. Others have been turned off variety meats remembering, with a shudder, the overcooked slabs of shoe-leather liver served in their schooldays. But really, the rules about buying and cooking variety meats are the same for any other cut of meat – as long as you seek out top-quality fresh meat and treat it with respect, you can make a feast out of the most unlikely ingredients. Beef or Pigs' cheek and Oxtail Stew make some of the most satisfyingly rich stews.

Of course an added advantage of most variety meats is that, because demand for it tends to be lower, it's usually quite cheap. So you can rustle up an inexpensive family meal with little effort.

Uses

Haggis is the most traditional of all Scottish dishes, eaten on Burns Night (25th January) and at Hogmanay (New Year's Eve). It consists of a sheep or lambs' stomach, stuffed with oatmeal and liver. The finest haggis is made with deer liver, but most are made with lambs' liver.

Pigs' intestines are used for homemade sausages, salamis, and chorizo. Pigs' blood is a key ingredient in **black puddings**, for which Ireland is famous. White puddings contain no animal blood, hence the color, and are a blend of pork, pigs' liver, bacon, grains, eggs, cornstarch, and spices. The old Irish blood pudding, **drisheen**, is still sold in the Cork market.

Tripe is made from the muscular lining of a cows' stomach. There are four types of tripe. Three come from different parts of the honeycomb (or second stomach) and one from the first stomach. Honeycomb tripe is the finest, but still very tough and needs to be cooked for at least 12 hours. It is glutinous but delectable. So is **spleen**. I remember, much to Timmy's disgust, eating yummy spleen sandwiches in soft rolls with grated Parmegiano Reggiano in Palermo in Sicily some years ago.

Giblets, from chicken, turkey, duck, and geese are often used to flavor stocks and gravies. Chicken livers are used whole or in paté. One of my favorite salades tièdes includes hearts and gizzards – not for the faint-hearted! **Foie gras** and paté de canard is made from the livers of geese and ducks that have been force-fed on a special diet – the subject of much controversy.

Storage

Fresh variety meats can be stored in the refrigerator for 1 or 2 days. They should be covered and kept in the coldest part of the fridge (usually near the bottom). Put it on a plate and make sure that it cannot drip onto, and cross-contaminate, raw products such as vegetables. Variety meats can also be stored for up to 1 month in the freezer.

Oxtail Stew

Serves 4

Oxtail makes an extraordinarily rich and flavorsome winter stew. This is a humble dish which has recently been resurrected by trendy chefs who are capitalizing on their customers' nostalgic craving for their gran's cooking. All the flavor comes if the meat melts off the bone, so allow plenty of cooking time for a hearty stew.

4 ounces (110g) bacon
2 oxtails
2 tablespoons beef dripping or olive oil
2 cups finely chopped onions
8 ounces (225g) carrots, cut into 3/4-inch (2-cm) cubes (about 2 cups)
1/2 cup chopped celery
1 bay leaf, 1 sprig of thyme, and parsley stalks
salt and freshly ground pepper
2/3 cup red wine and 2 cups homemade Beef Stock (see page 36) **or** *2 1/2 cups Beef Stock*
1 tablespoon homemade Tomato Purée (see page 49)
6 ounces (175g) mushrooms, sliced (about 1 3/4 cups)
1 teaspoon Roux (see page 580)
2 generous tablespoons parsley, chopped

Preheat the oven to 325°F (160°C). Cut the bacon into cubes and cut the oxtail into joints. Heat the dripping or oil, add the bacon, and sauté for 1–2 minutes. Then add the vegetables and cook for 2–3 minutes, stirring occasionally. Remove and set aside. Add the oxtail pieces and brown lightly all over.

Return the bacon and vegetables to the pan. Add the herbs, salt and pepper, wine, stock, and tomato purée. Cover and cook very gently, either on top of the stove or in the oven, for 2–3 hours, or until the oxtail and vegetables are very tender.

Cook the mushrooms in a hot pan in the butter for 2–3 minutes. Stir into the oxtail stew and cook for about 5 minutes. Transfer the oxtail joints to a hot serving dish and keep warm. Remove the bay leaves, thyme, and parsley stalks. Bring the liquid back to a boil, whisk in a little Roux, and cook until slightly thickened. Add back in the oxtail along with the parsley and bring to a boil. Taste and correct the seasoning and serve in the hot serving dish with lots of Champ (see page 182) or Colcannon (see page 183).

Scalloped Potato with Steak and Kidney

Serves 4–6

1 lb. (450g) well-aged stewing beef
1 beef kidney
salt and freshly ground pepper
2 1/2–3 lbs. (1.1–1.35kg) "old" potatoes
12 ounces (350g) onion, chopped (about 3 cups)
1/2 stick (1/4 cup or a little more) butter
1 1/2 cups water or homemade Stock (see page 36)

Garnish
freshly chopped parsley

2 1/2-quart (2.4 liter) capacity flameproof gratin or casserole dish

Preheat the oven to 300°F (150°C). Remove the skin and white core from the kidney and discard; cut the flesh into 1/2-inch (1-cm) cubes, put them into the bowl, cover with cold water, and sprinkle with a good pinch of salt. Cut the beef into 1/2-inch (1-cm) cubes also. Peel the potatoes and cut them into 1/4-inch (5-mm) thick slices.

Put a layer of potato slices on the base of the casserole dish. Drain the kidney and mix with the beef, then scatter some of the meat and chopped onion over the layer of potato. Season well with salt and freshly ground pepper, dot with butter, add another layer of potato, more meat, onions, and seasoning, and continue right up to the top of the casserole dish. Finish with an overlapping layer of potato.

Pour in the stock, bring to a boil, and cover and cook in a preheated oven for 2–2 1/2 hours or until the meat and potatoes are cooked. Sprinkle with chopped parsley and serve from the casserole dish.

Pickled Ox Tongue with Oignons à la Monégasque

Serves 8–10 approx.

There's a great saying around the Cork area when someone is about to venture home after a night of liquid socializing: "Ah, there'll be nothin' for you for dinner but hot tongue and cold shoulder." Order a pickled ox tongue a week or so ahead from your butcher, unless you live near Cork Market where pickled ox and lamb's tongues are available all year round.

1 pickled ox tongue
cold water
Oignons à la Monégasque (see page 188)

In a narrow saucepan with high sides, cover the tongue with cold water, bring to a boil, cover the saucepan, and simmer for 4–4 1/2 hours until the tongue is tender and the skin will easily peel off the tip. Do not use salt; the tongue will be salty enough.

Remove from the pot and reserve the liquid. As soon as the tongue is cool enough to handle, peel off the skin and remove all the little bones at the neck end. Sometimes I use a skewer to prod the meat to make sure no bones are left behind. Curl the tongue and press into a small plastic bowl. Pour a little of the cooking liquid over it.

Nowadays the butcher often removes all the little bones. If this is the case, the liquid may not set into a jelly without the help of gelatin – use 2 teaspoons or 2 leaves to 2 1/2 cups of liquid. Put a side plate or saucer on top and weigh down. Cool, and refrigerate. Serve thinly sliced, with Oignons à la Monégasque and a green salad.

Tip: pickled ox tongue, cooked and pressed, will keep for 5–6 days in the fridge.

Other Accompaniments

Sweet Cucumber Pickle (see page 514)
Red Currant Jelly (see page 508)
Horseradish Sauce (see page 586)
Pickled Beets (see page 514)
Salsa Verde (see page 592)

Variations

Spiced Ox Tongue

"Spiced Tongue" was a common nineteenth century dish on the tables of the middle classes. It was spiced with cloves and flavored with onion, thyme, parsley, salt, and pepper. In Cork, spiced ox tongue is also seasonally available just before Christmas, when a few tongues are thrown into the spice barrel. Mr. Breslin in Cork Market spices tongues for me occasionally and they have been much enjoyed, not just at Christmas but for summer picnics also. Cook as for Pickled Ox Tongue (see page 353).

Sweetbreads

Sweetbreads are the thymus or pancreatic glands of young milk-fed animals, that is to say, those of calves or lambs. Calves' sweetbreads are best. The sweetbreads tend to shrink and toughen when the animals' diet changes to grass and meal.

Sweetbreads come in pairs. The compact heart sweetbread is more highly prized because it slices more evenly than the looser, more elongated throat sweetbread. Choose sweetbreads that are white or pale pink in color, not bruised and compact in texture. They are extremely perishable when raw, so should be prepared and pre-cooked immediately.

Put the sweetbreads into a bowl and cover with cold water. Soak for 2 hours and discard the water. Cut away any discolored parts. Cover in fresh, cold water or chicken stock, bring to a boil, and simmer for 3 minutes (lamb) and 5 minutes (calf), and then drain. Cool. Gently pull away any gristly bits. Be careful that the sweetbreads don't come apart because some of the connective tissue will have dissolved during cooking. The sweetbreads need to be pressed between 2 plates with a weight not more than 2 pounds (900g) for 3–4 hours in the refrigerator before being sliced for further cooking.

Left: Warm Salad with Sweetbreads and Walnuts

Warm Salad with Sweetbreads and Walnuts

Serves 4

4 lamb sweetbreads
2 tablespoons butter
1 small carrot, diced
1 onion, diced
2 stalks celery, diced
bouquet garni
2½ cups homemade Chicken Stock (see page 36)

French beans or young green beans, cut in julienne, blanched and refreshed, optional
8 walnuts, freshly shelled
selection of salad greens (iceberg, oakleaf, butterhead, radicchio, sorrel, escarole, arugula, watercress)

seasoned flour
beaten egg
butter and oil for sautéeing

Walnut Dressing
1 tablespoon white wine vinegar
1 tablespoon peanut or sunflower oil
2 tablespoons walnut oil
¼ teaspoon Dijon mustard
salt and freshly ground pepper

Garnish
chive flowers

Soak the sweetbreads in a bowl of cold water for 2 hours. Discard the water. Poach the sweetbreads in fresh water, gently, for about 20 minutes. Cool, remove the gelatinous membranes and any fatty bits carefully.

Melt the butter in a pan, add the vegetables, and sweat to soften. Add the bouquet garni. Bring the chicken stock to a boil and add the vegetables.

Prepare the salad: wash and dry the lettuce leaves, and prepare the French beans, if using.

Slice the sweetbreads into escalopes and dip in seasoned flour and then in beaten egg. Heat a little butter and oil in a heavy pan so it foams, and sauté the sweetbreads until golden on both sides.

Shake together the ingredients for the dressing in a screw-top jar. Toss the salad leaves and walnuts in the walnut dressing, divide between 4 plates, and lay the hot sweetbreads on top of the salad. Sprinkle with chive flowers and serve immediately.

Lamb Kidneys in their Jackets

Serves 2

Lamb kidneys cooked in their suet are one of our favorite naughty treats. Lamb kidneys are also delicious wrapped in caul fat and roasted.

2 kidneys
sea salt or Kosher salt

Preheat the oven to 450°F (230°C).
If there is an excessive amount of suet on the kidneys, trim them a little. Sprinkle with sea salt. Cook in a roasting pan for 10–12 minutes, depending on size. The fat should be crispy on the outside and soft within and, when the kidneys are almost cooked, let them rest for a few minutes. Serve with boiled potatoes and a green salad.

Butterflied Lamb Kidneys with Rosemary

Serves 4 as an appetizer, 2–3 as a main course

8 lamb kidneys
8–16 tough rosemary sprigs, stripped of most of the leaves but leave the tip intact
salt and freshly ground pepper
8 flat mushrooms
1–2 tablespoons olive oil
1 tablespoon rosemary, chopped
4 slices country bread

Remove the skin from the kidneys just before cooking and season the kidneys.

Cut the kidneys from the base, open them out, but keep them attached at the top so they are butterflied. Remove all the core. Skewer each kidney with 1 or, if necessary, 2 rosemary sprigs. Season both kidneys and mushrooms with salt and pepper. Brush with olive oil and sprinkle with chopped rosemary. Grill or pan-grill the kidneys and mushrooms on both sides until cooked through, 3–5 minutes. Serve on toasted country bread.

Tip: Overcooking toughens kidneys so don't cook for more than a few minutes.

Lamb or Veal Kidneys in Grainy Mustard Sauce

Serves 4 as an appetizer, 2–3 as a main course

Lamb kidneys are very under-appreciated – we absolutely love them, so tender and so fast to cook. Veal kidneys are mild and delicate in flavor but less easy to come by.

8 lamb or 2 veal kidneys (buy fresh lamb kidneys still in the suet)
little butter
3 tablespoons of whole-grain mustard
1 cup cream
salt and freshly ground pepper

Garnish
flat-leaf parsley, freshly snipped

How to prepare beef or veal kidneys

Choose fresh kidneys that have no strong smell of ammonia. Richer tasting beef kidney is wonderful in stews and soup, whereas the more delicate veal kidneys are sautéed or grilled. If your butcher has not already done so, remove the suet and peel off the outer membrane.

Beef suet, when trimmed of all traces of blood or meat, may be used in mince pies, plum puddings, suet pastries or suet puddings. Suet keeps for months in the fridge.

Cut in half lengthwise and remove the membrane.

Remove the kidneys from the suet.

Remove suet and peel off the outer membrane.

Cut into cubes or slices depending on the dish.

Remove the ducting from the kidneys with scissors.

Remove the skin, membrane, and core from the kidneys and cut into bite-sized pieces. Sauté in a little butter in a pan, turn occasionally until nicely cooked, about 5 minutes over a medium heat. Season with salt and pepper. Add the cream and mustard, bring to a boil, and simmer for 3 or 4 minutes until the sauce thickens slightly. Taste, and correct the seasoning.

Serve immediately on hot plates, scattered with parsley. Homemade noodles, rice, or orzo are delicious with this dish for a main course. Serve too with a good green salad.

Calves' or Lambs' Liver with Onions

Serves 4

1/4 cup olive oil
4 large onions, thinly sliced
1 lb. (450g) calves' or lambs' liver
salt and freshly ground pepper

Garnish
flat-leaf parsley, snipped

Heat the oil in a frying pan, add the onions, and continue stirring regularly until crisp and golden. Remove from the pan and keep warm.

Just before serving, prepare the liver: cut into thin slices, and season with salt and freshly ground pepper.

Reheat the pan with the onion-flavored oil, so it is very hot. Cook the liver quickly on both sides and transfer to warm plates. Add the onions back into the pan. Fry for a minute or two to heat all through, and spoon over the liver, scatter with parsley, and serve immediately.

Above: Lamb or Veal Kidneys in Grainy Mustard Sauce

How to prepare liver

Unless you plan to cook it immediately, buy the liver in a larger piece and slice just before cooking. Peel off the outer membrane. Cut the liver diagonally into slices and cook very quickly and eat immediately. Overcooking toughens the liver.

Lambs' Liver with Freshly Cracked Pepper

Serves 4 as an appetizer or 2 as a main course

1 lb. (450g) lambs' liver
flour seasoned with salt
freshly cracked pepper
2–4 tablespoons butter, clarified
arugula leaf salad

Slice the lambs' liver into 1/2-inch (1-cm) thick slices. Dip the slices of liver in well-seasoned flour and lots of freshly cracked pepper, and shake off the excess.

Melt the butter in a frying pan. Cook gently in the foaming butter for 1–2 minutes on each side. It should still be slightly pink in the center.

Serve immediately with an arugula leaf salad, and perhaps some toasted or chargrilled country bread.

Warm Salad of Chicken Livers with Ginger and Borage

Serves 4

selection of salad greens (Lollo Rosso, oakleaf, iceberg, butterhead, arugula)
4 very fresh chicken livers
1 tablespoon olive oil
1 tablespoon butter
2 garlic cloves, peeled and chopped finely
1 teaspoon ginger, freshly grated
sea salt or Kosher salt and freshly ground pepper

Dressing
2 tablespoons olive oil
2 tablespoons walnut oil
1 tablespoon red wine vinegar
2 teaspoons Dijon mustard

Garnish
borage flowers (or chives or marigolds)

Wash and dry the salad greens and tear into bite-sized bits. Combine the ingredients for the dressing and mix well in a screw-top jar. Wash the livers and carefully remove any traces of green gall. Cut each into 4 pieces, dry, and season with salt and pepper.

Melt the oil and butter in a frying pan over a medium heat, add the garlic and ginger, and cook for 30 seconds. Add the livers and cook until nicely brown on the outsides but still vaguely pink in the center (or to your taste). Meanwhile toss the salad in the dressing, just enough to lightly coat the greens.

Put a little handful of salad into the center of a large white plate. Arrange chicken livers on top and sprinkle with borage flowers.

Crostini di Fegatini

Serves 10–20

Crostini comes from the same root as croûtons; in Italy they are served with various toppings. Chicken liver crostini are the best loved in Tuscany. Recipes vary but I particularly loved this version which was given to me by Mimmo Baldi and is served at his restaurant "Il Vescovino" in Panzano in Chianti. He likes to add a small tablespoon of chicken stock to each crostino just as soon as it is fried in olive oil. Mimmo then sprinkles them with a little freshly grated Parmesan cheese, a generous amount of fegatini, and serves them immediately – you always know when they have been served to a table because conversation stops and all one can hear is mmm, mmm!

8 ounces (225g) fresh chicken livers
salt and freshly ground pepper
1/4 cup extra-virgin olive oil
1 carrot, finely chopped
1 onion, finely chopped
1 stalk celery, finely chopped
3 anchovy fillets
2 tablespoons capers
1 medium gherkin, about 2 1/4 inches 5.5cm
1 stalk flat-leaf parsley
1/2 cup port or marsala
1/2 cup good homemade Chicken Stock (see page 36)
1/2–1 cup freshly grated Parmesan
15–20 slices of French bread, about 2 3/4 inches (7cm), chargrilled, toasted, or fried in olive oil until golden brown on each side.

Season the chicken livers with salt and pepper. Sauté the chicken livers in 1 tablespoon of the olive oil in a small sauté pan over a medium heat until they are just firm. Remove from the pan and drain in a strainer or colander for 10 minutes.

Meanwhile, prepare the vegetables. Heat the rest of the olive oil in the same saucepan, and add the carrot, onion, and celery. Cover, and cook until soft – about 5–6 minutes. Add the chicken livers and cook for about 10 minutes more, then let this mixture cool for 30 minutes.

Add the anchovies, capers, gherkins, and parsley to the livers, and either mash with a fork or roughly blend in a food processor. Reheat this mixture, add the port or marsala, and reduce until all the liquid has been absorbed, then add the chicken stock. The mixture should have a moist creamy consistency. Taste, and correct seasoning. Use the French bread to make the crostini, and just as soon as they are fried or toasted, sprinkle with Parmesan, spread with a generous amount of the fegatini mixture and serve immediately.

Serving suggestion: To make a more substantial plate, add a few ruffles of freshly sliced prosciutto and some arugula leaves – one of my favorite appetizers.

Salad of Duck or Chicken Livers with Apples, Hazelnuts, and Wild Garlic Flowers

Serves 4

1 dessert apple
4 duck or chicken livers
2 tablespoons hazelnuts, crushed
1 teaspoon butter
1 tablespoon olive oil

selection of lettuce greens (butterhead, frisée, oakleaf, radicchio, arugula, salad burnet)
wild garlic flowers

Hazelnut Oil Dressing
1/4 cup hazelnut oil
2 tablespoons sunflower oil
2 tablespoons white wine vinegar
2 teaspoons mustard
salt, pepper, and sugar

First make the Hazelnut Oil Dressing by shaking all the ingredients together in a screw-top jar. Season with salt and freshly ground pepper.

Cut the apple into thin julienne strips, and mix with the hazelnuts and 1 tablespoon hazelnut oil dressing.

Melt the butter and oil in a frying pan and cook the livers gently until just tender. While the livers are cooking, toss the lettuces in enough dressing to make them just glisten and divide between 4 serving plates. Place a quarter of the apple julienne on top of each salad, and finally the warm duck or chicken livers on top. Sprinkle with wild garlic flowers and serve immediately.

Head Cheese

Serves 16–20

My eldest son reckons to be very cool; like many of his generation nothing seems to faze him. However one day when he lifted the lid off a pot on the Aga, he shrieked and uttered some quite unprintable expletives when he caught sight of the pig's head bubbling in the pot. My daughters continually count my happy bonhams in the orchard to make sure that none of them end up as head cheese.

half a salted pig's head
1 boiling fowl or a free-range chicken
2 carrots, sliced
2 onions, sliced
1 stalk celery (optional)
a sprig of thyme and a few parsley stalks
4 or 5 peppercorns
1 generous tablespoon chopped fresh parsley and thyme

2 x 2 1/2-pint (1.2-liter) pudding basins or ovenproof bowls

Wash the pig's head, remove the brain and discard. Put the head into a pot and cover with cold water. Bring to a boil, then discard the water. Bring to a boil in fresh water and cook for 3 or 4 hours or until the meat is soft and tender and parting from the bones. Meanwhile, put the boiling fowl or chicken into another pot. Add the carrots and onions, celery if you have it to spare, parsley stalks, and a sprig of thyme. Add about 2 1/2 inches (6cm) of cold water and a few peppercorns Cover, bring to a boil, and cook until the bird is tender.

When both meats are cooked, remove them from the cooking liquid and take the meat from the bones. Skin the chicken and chop it, and the pig's head, into pieces. Mix the meats together and add the chopped parsley and thyme leaves. Taste, and correct the seasoning.

Pack the meat into one large or two small pudding basins and add a little of the cooking liquid from each pot. Press with a weight. When cold, turn out and serve in slices with a salad. Brawn will keep for several weeks in the fridge.

Collared Head

Serves 15 (approximately)

Sister Bernadette from the Presentation Convent in Crosshaven, County Cork, sent me her favorite recipe for collared head.

1 whole pig's head (or 2 half-heads)
1 ox tongue
2 medium-sized onions, finely chopped
1 level tablespoon plus 1 teaspoon salt
2 level teaspoons pepper
1 level tablespoon plus 1 teaspoon allspice

Soak the heads for 24 hours. Cook until very tender and let it cool in the water. They should be so well cooked that you will need to take them up with both hands. Leave overnight. Next day gather the pig's jelly around them and on the dish. You will need 2/3 cup (150ml), so if not sufficient, get the remainder from the pot in which they were cooked. Skin and remove the meat from the bone. Cut into 1/4-inch (5-mm) pieces, fat and lean as it comes.

On the same day as the pig's heads, cook the ox tongue until very tender and let it cool in the water. Next day, skin and cut up in small pieces (do not use the fat) and mix with the pig's head meat. Get a large pot and par-cook the finely chopped onions in the pig's jelly. Mix the salt, pepper, and spice with the meat and add to the pot. Bring to blood heat (do not boil). Stir to prevent burning, but do no over-stir.

As collared head containers are no longer sold, I got a handyman to prepare a large empty bean can, 6 pounds (2.6kg) in capacity, for me. He bored a circular row of holes around the bottom, plus two rows of holes lengthwise on sides. I kept the cover of the can.

Put the mixture into the can, cover, and press with a half brick or old iron until all the fat has oozed through the holes. Put the can on a dry dish and leave until the next day.

To turn out, place on the stove on a very gentle heat for about five minutes and insert a flat knife around the sides of the can. It will keep in the fridge for around 10 days.

game

Rabbit with Mustard and Sage Leaves

Serves 6

Many French peasants rear their own rabbits in hutches either beside or in their farmhouses. This recipe brings back memories of delicious rabbit stews I ate with Mamie and Papie Viénot in Lille-sur-le-Doube. I have a feeling that many of you may be a bit squeamish about eating rabbit, but this recipe is also very good made with chicken.

1 rabbit about 2½–3 lbs. (1–1.3kg) or 1 chicken, the same weight
6 fresh sage leaves
2 teaspoons English mustard powder
2 teaspoons grainy mustard, e.g., Moutarde de Meaux
½ cup dry white wine
1 tablespoon butter
2 teaspoons olive oil
1 tablespoon wine vinegar
18 baby onions, peeled
1 cup crème fraîche or fresh cream and lemon juice
a little Roux (see page 580), optional
salt and freshly ground pepper

Garnish
fresh sage leaves

Cut the rabbit into 6 portions. Put it into a terrine with the chopped sage leaves. Mix half the mustard powder and half the grainy mustard with ¼ cup water. Pour this and the wine over the rabbit and let marinate for about 1 hour. Drain the rabbit pieces and dry them well on paper towels. Season well.

Put the butter and oil into a wide sauté pan over a medium heat and lightly brown the rabbit on all sides, then remove to a flameproof casserole dish or other heavy pot. De-grease the pan, de-glaze with the vinegar, and pour this and the marinade on to the rabbit. Add the onions and the rest of the mustard. Add another ¼ cup water, season, and stir well. Cover, and let cook gently for about 1 hour.

When the rabbit is tender, take out the pieces and arrange them on a hot plate along with the onions (making sure the onions are fully cooked). De-grease the juices, add the cream to the pot, and reduce over a high heat until it thickens, whisking in a little roux if necessary. Taste, and sharpen with lemon juice if necessary. Pour the sauce over the rabbit pieces – through a strainer if you prefer a smoother sauce. Decorate with some sage leaves and serve immediately.

West Cork Rabbit Casserole

Serves about 6

Rabbits and hare run wild all over Ireland. They are extremely prolific and though sweet and cuddly, are considered to be a pest by the farmers, so don't feel guilty – tuck in!

12 ounces (350g) unsmoked bacon
a 3½–4 lb. (1.6–1.8kg) rabbit, wild if possible
a little butter and oil
1 lb. (450g) onions (baby ones are nicest)
12 ounces (350g) carrot, peeled and thickly sliced (about 3 cups)
sprig of thyme
3 cups homemade Chicken Stock (see page 36)
a little Roux (see page 580), optional

Mushroom à la Crème (see page 197), optional

Garnish
2 teaspoons freshly chopped parsley

Cut the bacon into cubes roughly 1 inch (2.5cm) square (blanch if salty). Dry in paper towels. Cut the rabbit into 8 pieces.

Heat a little oil in a sauté pan and sauté the bacon until crisp; remove, and put in a flameproof casserole dish or other heavy flameproof and ovenproof pot. Add the rabbit pieces to the pan and sauté until golden, then add to the bacon in the casserole dish. Heat control is crucial here: the pan mustn't burn, yet it must be hot enough to sauté the rabbit. If it is too cool, the rabbit pieces will stew rather than brown and as a result the meat may be tough.

Then sauté the onion and carrot, adding a little butter if necessary. Add to the casserole dish, de-grease the pan and de-glaze with stock, bring to a boil, and pour over the rabbit mixture.

Season well, add a sprig of thyme, and bring to simmering point on top of the stove, then put into the oven for 30–45 minutes at 350°F (180°C). The cooking time depends on how long the rabbit pieces were sautéed. When the casserole is just cooked, strain off the cooking liquid, de-grease, and return the de-greased liquid to the casserole dish and bring to a boil.

Thicken with a little Roux if necessary. Add back the meat, carrots, and onions, and bring to a boil. The casserole is very good served at this point, but even more delicious if some Mushroom à la crème are stirred in as an enrichment. Serve bubbling hot, sprinkled with chopped parsley.

Jugged Hare

Serves 6

Jugged hare is the English equivalent of the famous French civet de lièvre. This is one of Jane Grigson's recipes from her splendid book English Food**. The method was the obvious way of cooking game slowly, in the days when most cooking was done over the hearth fire. More usually today the dish is cooked in a casserole dish. The blood of the hare is added, so this robust and comforting dish is not for the faint-hearted! Rabbit can be substituted for the hare.**

1 hare, prepared and jointed
strips of pork or bacon fat for larding, optional
salt, freshly ground pepper, and ground mace
bouquet garni
1 onion, stuck with 3 cloves
1 stick (about 1/2 cup) butter
2/3 cup white wine
1 anchovy, chopped
pinch cayenne pepper
1 tablespoon butter
1 tablespoon flour
blood of the hare or rabbit, optional
lemon juice, optional

Garnish
triangles of fried bread

Unless your hare or rabbit is young and tender, you will be wise to lard it. Put the pieces into a large jug (the unlipped stoneware jugs still made in France, and widely sold in England are ideal) after rubbing them with salt, pepper, and mace. Add the bouquet garni, onion, and butter.

Cover the jug tightly and securely with kitchen foil tied with string to make sure it keeps in place. Stand the jug in a pan of boiling water and keep it simmering until the hare is cooked – about 3 hours, but the time depends on the age and toughness of the creature. This can either be done on top of the stove (a solution to the problems of slow cooking without an oven) or in the oven, if this is more convenient.

Remove the cooked pieces to a serving dish. Strain the juices into a pan. Add the wine, anchovy, and pepper to taste. Thicken either with the flour and butter mashed together, and added in little pats, or with the blood of the hare – in the latter case, mix a little of the sauce with the blood, then return it to the pan and stir over a low heat until thick. The sauce must not boil again once the blood has been added or it will curdle.

Sharpen with a little lemon juice if you like, and serve with the fried bread.

Stewed Hare, Rabbit, Wood Pigeons, or Venison with Forcemeat Balls

Serves 6

Another delicious recipe from George Gossip.

1 hare or rabbit, jointed, or six whole pigeons, or 3 lbs. (1.5kg) stewing venison, cut in pieces
a little seasoned flour
1/3 cup lard
8 ounces (225g) bacon, cut in strips
2 cups chopped onion
1 heaped teaspoon fresh thyme
1 heaped tablespoon freshly chopped parsley
1/2 bay leaf
homemade Game or Beef Stock (see page 36)
1/3 cup port
Red Currant Jelly (see page 508)
salt and freshly ground pepper

Forcemeat balls
2 1/2 cups fresh white breadcrumbs
1/4 cup chopped suet
1 tablespoon freshly chopped parsley
1 teaspoon fresh thyme
grated rind 1/2 lemon
4–5 strips finely chopped bacon
salt and freshly ground pepper
1 large egg

Turn the joints, pigeons, or pieces of venison in seasoned flour (in the case of hare or rabbit, keep the brains, liver, and blood for the final thickening), then brown them in the lard with the bacon and onion. Transfer to a flameproof casserole dish or other heavy pot.

Put in the herbs and just enough stock to cover them. Simmer gently until the meat is tender and parts easily from the bone. Add the port, jelly, and seasoning to taste.

To thicken the sauce, either mix some of the liquid with a little of the remaining seasoned flour (about a tablespoon) and return it to the pot, or mash the brains, liver, and blood together. Pour on a little hot liquid and then return this mixture to the pot and cook without boiling for a few minutes until the sauce is thickened.

The second method produces the better flavor – a good game butcher will give you the blood of a hare or wild rabbit.

Meanwhile mix the ingredients for the forcemeat balls, and shape them into balls about 1 inch (2.5cm) diameter. Fry them in lard until brown and add to the stew. They are also good in game soups, but in this case make them smaller. If you do not want to make forcemeat balls, serve the stew with triangles of fried bread.

Roast Pheasant with Game Chips, Cranberry Sauce, and Bread Sauce

Serves 2–3

A roast pheasant makes the perfect Christmas dinner for 2 and you'll probably have a little left over for a cold snack or lunch. This slightly unorthodox way of cooking the pheasant produces a moist, juicy bird. Guinea fowl is also wonderful cooked and served in this way. You will need a piece of cheesecloth.

1 plump young pheasant

Stuffing
3 tablespoons butter
3/4 cup chopped onions
1 1/2 cups soft white breadcrumbs
1 tablespoon freshly chopped herbs (parsley, thyme, chives, marjoram)

1/2 stick (1/4 cup) butter
salt and freshly ground pepper

Gravy
1 1/4 cups Game or Chicken Stock (see page 36)
1/2 stick (1/4 cup) butter
Game Chips (see page 185)
Cranberry Sauce (see page 597)
Bread Sauce (see page 594)

Preheat the oven to 375°F (190°C).

Gut the pheasant, if necessary, and remove the crop, which is at the neck end; wash all over and dry well.

To make the stuffing: melt the butter and sweat the onions until soft but not colored, then remove from the heat. Stir in the breadcrumbs and herbs, season with salt and pepper, and taste.

Unless you are about to cook the bird right away, let the stuffing get quite cold before you use it.

Season the cavity of the pheasant with salt and pepper and fill it loosely with the stuffing. Sprinkle the breast with salt and pepper. Melt the butter and soak a piece of cheesecloth or handiwipe in it. Wrap the pheasant completely in the cheesecloth.

Roast in the preheated oven, for about 1 1/4 hours. Test by pricking the leg at the highest point: the juices should just run clear. Remove the cheesecloth and keep the pheasant warm on a serving dish while you make the gravy.

Spoon off any surplus fat from the roasting pan (keep it for roasting or sautéeing potatoes). De-glaze the pan with the Game or Chicken Stock. Bring it to a boil, and use a whisk to dislodge the crusty caramelized juices so they can dissolve into the gravy. Season with salt and pepper, taste, and boil until you are happy with the flavor. Pour into a hot gravy boat.

Carve the pheasant and serve with stuffing, gravy, Game Chips, Cranberry Sauce, and Bread Sauce.

Casserole-roast Pheasant with Apple and Calvados

Serves 2–3

This recipe comes from the Vallé d'Auge in Normandy in France, where they have wonderfully rich cream and delicious apples. Chicken or guinea fowl may also be used in this recipe.

1 plump young pheasant, about 1¾–2 lbs. (725–900g)
½ ounce (10g) butter
5–6 tablespoons Calvados (or apple brandy)
1 cup cream or ½ cup cream and ½ cup homemade Chicken Stock (see page 36)
Roux (see page 580), optional
salt and freshly ground pepper
2 tablespoons butter
2 dessert apples

Garnish
sprigs of watercress or chervil

Preheat the oven to 350°F (180°C).

Heat a flameproof casserole dish or other heavy flameproof and ovenproof pot, preferably oval, just large enough to fit the bird. Season the cavity, spread the butter over the breast and legs of the pheasant, and place breast-side down into the casserole dish. Let it brown over a gentle heat, turn over, and sprinkle with salt and pepper. Cover with a tight-fitting lid and cook in the oven for 40–45 minutes. Check to see that the pheasant is cooked (there should be no trace of pink juices coming out from a fork poked between the leg and the breast). Transfer the pheasant to a serving dish and keep warm.

Carefully strain and de-grease the juices in the casserole dish. Bring to a boil, add the Calvados, and ignite it with a match. Shake the pan and when the flames have gone out, add the cream (or stock and cream). Reduce by boiling until the sauce thickens, stirring occasionally; taste for seasoning. Fry the peeled, cored, and diced apple in butter until golden. Carve the pheasant and arrange on a hot serving dish or individual plates. Cover with the sauce. Put a little of the apple in the center and garnish with watercress or chervil.

Note: Although many game recipes are very traditional, feel free to be creative with accompaniments. Roast pheasant or quail are wonderful with Spicy Chickpeas, Caribbean Spinach (see page 171), Spiced Eggplant, or Roast Vegetables.

Pheasant with Wild Mushrooms and Colcannon

Serves 6–8.

2 plump pheasants about 1¾ lbs. (800g) each
1 tablespoon olive oil
4 ounces (110g) bacon, diced
¼–½ cup brandy
4 juniper berries, crushed
1¼ cups dry white wine

2 lbs. (900g) Wild Mushroom à la Crème (see page 197)
Colcannon (see page 183)

Garnish
flat-leaf parsley

Preheat the oven to 350°F (180°C).

Season the pheasants inside and out with salt and pepper.

Heat the oil in an oval flameproof casserole dish or other heavy flameproof and ovenproof pot, just large enough to take the birds. Toss in the bacon and cook for a few minutes until it begins to get crisp, remove the bacon, and let the pheasants brown on the breast side. Turn them the other way up, add the bacon back in, pour in the brandy, flambé by lighting the brandy juices with a taper or match, and boil for a few minutes to cook off the alcohol. Add the juniper berries. Cover the casserole dish, put in the oven, and cook for about 40–45 minutes.

Meanwhile, make the Colcannon and Wild Mushroom à la Crème.

Remove the pheasants to a serving dish and keep them warm. De-grease the cooking juices and add the white wine. Bring to a boil and reduce until slightly thickened.

Meanwhile, joint the pheasant and arrange it on a warmed serving plate, spoon the sauce over it and garnish with flat-leaf parsley sprigs.

Serve with Colcannon and Wild Mushroom à la Crème.

Pheasant with Jerusalem Artichokes

Serves 4

Pheasants adore Jerusalem artichokes, and many of the large estates specially plant a patch as a treat for them. It seemed logical to cook them together and indeed, it turns out to be a very good marriage of flavors. Casserole-roasting, the cooking method used here, is a particularly good way to cook pheasant, especially if it is not in the first flush of youth. Chicken or guinea fowl may also be cooked in this way.

1 plump pheasant
2 tablespoons butter
salt and freshly ground pepper
2 lbs. (900g) Jerusalem artichokes

Garnish
freshly chopped parsley or flat-leaf parsley sprigs

Preheat the oven to 350°F (180°C).

Smear a little butter on the breast of the pheasant and brown it in a flameproof casserole dish, or other heavy flameproof and ovenproof pot, over a gentle heat. Meanwhile, peel and slice the artichokes into ½-inch (1-cm) pieces. Remove the pheasant, add a little butter to the casserole and toss the Jerusalem artichoke slices in the butter. Season, and sprinkle 1 tablespoon of water over the top. Return the pheasant, tucking it right down into the sliced artichokes so that they come up around the sides of the bird. Cover with a butter wrapper and the lid of the casserole dish.

Cook for a further 1–1¼ hours.

Remove the pheasant as soon as it is cooked, strain and de-grease the cooking liquid if there is need, but usually there is virtually no fat on it. The juices of the pheasant will have flavored the artichokes deliciously. Arrange the artichokes on a hot serving dish, carve the pheasant into 4 portions and arrange on top.

The artichokes always break up a little – that is their nature. Spoon some juices over the pheasant and artichokes and serve scattered with chopped parsley or flat-leafed parsley sprigs.

Below: Faisinjan

Faisinjan

Serves 4

The Grigsons have delicious ways of serving game. This recipe is from Sophie Grigson's Ingredients Book**.**

1 plump pheasant, cut into 8 portions
2 tablespoons oil
1 onion, chopped
2 cups shelled walnuts, coarsely ground or very finely chopped
1 cinnamon stick
3 tablespoons pomegranate syrup
2 cups water
salt and pepper
sugar
1 tablespoon freshly chopped parsley
fresh pomegranate seeds, optional

Brown the pheasant pieces in the oil. Set aside, and fry the onion in the same oil until browned, stirring to prevent burning. Turn down the heat, add the walnuts and cinnamon and cook gently for a few minutes, stirring.

Mix in the pomegranate syrup, water, and a little salt and pepper. Bring up to a boil, stirring occasionally, then add the pheasant pieces. Cover, and simmer gently for 30 minutes.

Uncover and continue simmering for another 15–30 minutes until the meat is very tender and the sauce is thick. Taste, and add more salt or pepper, or a little sugar to give a sweet and sour sauce. Sprinkle with the chopped parsley and with fresh pomegranate seeds, if using, before serving.

Pheasant and Potato Pie

Serves 6–8

This was another of my favorite winter dishes at the Arbutus Lodge restaurant in Cork when the Ryan family were there.

12 ounces (350g) of raw meat using a combination of pheasant and chicken, or pheasant, chicken, and veal – for example, 6 ounces (175g) pheasant, 3 ounces (75g) chicken, 3 ounces (75g) veal
2 ounces (50g) shallots (2 medium), finely chopped and sweated in 2 tablespoons butter
1 tablespoon chopped parsley
1 teaspoon thyme leaves
salt and freshly ground pepper
5 tablespoons white wine
8 ounces (225g) potatoes (about 2 medium), peeled, very thinly sliced and left under a cold running tap to wash off all their starch
1 lb. (450g) Puff or Flaky Pastry (see pages 456 and 413)
egg wash
3/4 cup cream, reduced to thicken slightly

Preheat the oven to 350°F (180°C).

Chop up the meat into small pieces. Season the meat with the shallot, herbs, salt and pepper, and white wine – it should be highly seasoned. Dry the washed sliced potatoes and add to the meat.

Roll out 2 circles of pastry dough – one 10 inches (25.5cm) round, and one 12 inches (32cm) round. Place the larger one on a baking sheet and put the filling on it. Egg-wash the edge of the pastry dough and then place the smaller piece of dough on top to cover the filling. Fold the bottom piece of dough up, to enclose the pie and seal well. Scallop the edges of the crust and egg-wash the whole pie. Make a small hole in the center to let the steam escape.

Place in the oven and cook for approximately 45 minutes. Five minutes from the end of the cooking time, cut a 4-inch (10-cm) lid in the top of the pie and pour in the reduced cream. Replace the lid and finish cooking. Serve the pie as soon as possible after it is cooked.

We serve a little Beurre Blanc sauce (see page 583) with it – decadent but delicious!

Quail Véronique

Serves 2 as a main course or 4 as an appetizer

4 quail
a little butter and oil
20 green grapes (peeled and seeded, being careful to reserve any juices)
5 tablespoons heavy cream
salt and freshly ground pepper

Preheat the oven to 350°F (180°C).

Split the quail in half by cutting lengthwise through the breastbone with a strong sharp knife. Season each bird. Heat butter and oil in a heavy flameproof and ovenproof pan just big enough to fit the quail. Sauté until golden brown on the breast side; quail needs to be well-browned and almost crispy to enhance the flavor.

Cover the pan tightly with a lid and tin foil. It is important that the steam does not escape otherwise the juices from the cooking birds will evaporate. Put the quail into the oven for about 10 minutes.

Remove the quail from the oven as soon as they are cooked, and keep them in a warm place. Remove any excess fat from the juices and put the pan on a low heat. Add the cream, peeled grapes, and any grape juice. Simmer the sauce for 2–3 minutes. Finally check for seasoning.

To serve: spoon a little sauce and some grapes over and around the spatchcock quail on 2 or 4 plates.

Pigeon Breasts with Juniper Berries

George Gossip is unquestionably the best game cook I know – and this is another of his recipes.

Pluck the breasts of the pigeon, then cut the breast, still attached to the breast bone, off the carcass. Discard the remainder of the carcass. Pack the breasts into a plastic box, cover with red wine, add a sliced onion, some thyme and a bay leaf. Cover and leave in the fridge for a couple of days (they will keep several weeks if necessary).

When you want to cook the pigeon breasts, take out the number you need and slice the meat thinly.

Sauté a few lardons of fat, unsmoked bacon in a hot pan (blanch and refresh the bacon if very salty, and sauté in a little oil). Remove when crisp, add a little butter if necessary, add and quickly toss the pigeon breast slices. They should be still pink. Add a good few crushed juniper berries and flambé in gin, add back in the bacon. Pour in some Game, Beef, or Chicken stock, and let simmer for a couple of minutes, taste and correct seasoning. Enrich the pan juices with some pats of butter.

Serve on very hot plates. Sprinkle with chervil or parsley. Serve as a first course with heart-shaped croûtons, or as a main course with a baked potato and a good green salad.

Pigeon Stew and Pie

Serves 10–12

This was a favorite recipe for winter house parties at Ballymaloe. Tim and his brother Rory would bag a few dozen pigeons, doubly welcome because pigeons tend to breed at an incredible rate and damage crops on the farm.

4–6 pigeon breasts
their weight in lean beef
half their weight in bacon
bacon fat or olive oil for frying
8 baby carrots or sticks of carrot
10–12 pearl onions
1 clove garlic
1–2 teaspoons flour
1 cup red wine
1 cup good stock
2/3 cup homemade Tomato Purée (see page 49) or smaller quantity of tinned purée or tomato paste: use according to concentration and make up with extra stock
Roux (see page 580), optional
2 teaspoons chopped thyme and parsley
salt and freshly ground pepper

1 cup Mushroom à la Crème (see page 197)

For the pie topping
8 ounces (225g) Puff or Flaky Pastry (pages 456 or 413)

Preheat the oven to 300°F (150°C).

Cut the bacon into "lardons" about 1 inch (2.5cm) wide, cut the beef and pigeon into similar sized pieces.
Heat some bacon fat or olive oil in a pan and fry until crisp and golden, then remove to a 2½-quart (2.4 liter) flameproof casserole dish (or other heavy flameproof and ovenproof pot). Add beef and pigeon a little at a time to the pan and toss until it changes color. Put into the casserole dish.

In the pan, turn the carrots, onions, and crushed garlic in the fat, and add them to the meat in the casserole dish. Stir the flour into the fat in the pan, cook for a minute or so, and then stir or whisk in the wine, stock, and tomato purée.
Bring to a boil, and thicken with Roux if necessary. Pour over the meat and vegetables in the casserole dish.

Season the stew with salt and pepper, add thyme and parsley, return to a boil, cover, and cook in the oven for 1–2 hours, depending on the age of the pigeons. When it is cooked, add the Mushroom à la Crème. Check seasoning.* Let it get quite cold: flavor will improve overnight.

* The pigeon stew can be eaten at this point, served with fluffy mashed potatoes and a green vegetable, such as Buttered Cabbage (see page 166).

To assemble and bake the Pigeon Pie:
As soon as the pigeon stew is cold, or the next day, fill into a pie dish, cover with Puff or Flaky Pastry lid, and bake for 10 minutes at 450°F (230°C), then for about 20 minutes at 375°F (190°C).

Serve with a good green salad.

Roast Wild Mallard

Serves 2

1 mallard
3–4 juniper berries
1 sprig of thyme
1 sprig of marjoram
4–5 strips bacon or butter
salt and freshly ground pepper
2/3 cup homemade Game or Chicken Stock (see *page 36)*
a splash of red or white wine, or juice of 1 orange

Preheat the oven to 450°F (230°C).

Trim the end off the wing tips at the first joint. Chop the ends off the legs just above the "knee". Remove the wish bone (make sure the crop has been removed). Season the cavity and add a few crushed juniper berries along with the herbs.

Smear the breast with butter or bard with bacon, then truss with string. Roast for about 20 minutes if you like it fairly rare, or 30 minutes if you prefer it better done. Careful not to overcook or it will be dry. Note that duck which has been barded with bacon will take longer to cook – up to 10 minutes.

As soon as the duck is cooked, remove to a warm serving dish. De-grease the roasting pan and add some stock and a splash of wine or the juice of an orange. Boil well, taste, correct seasoning, and strain. Carve the duck and serve the hot gravy with it.

Widgeon, Pintail, or Shoveller can also be roasted in this way, cooking temperature as above, for 13–20 minutes. Teal takes about 12–15 minutes.

Terrine of Wild Duck with Golden Raisins

Serves 8–10

A smooth and very rich game pâté as made by the inspirational chef, Michel Guérard. It should be made at least a day in advance. Chicken livers can successfully be substituted for duck livers in this terrine. We cooked individual ones in the smallest ramekins and they took 10 minutes. Individual soufflé dishes take 15–20 minutes. If you make it in a terrine, use a very sharp knife for slicing it to keep its shape. Alternatively, serve direct from the terrine with a spoon.

2 young mallards weighing about 2 1/4 lbs. (1kg) each
1/4 cup best-quality golden raisins
3 tablespoons of Armagnac or best-quality brandy
salt and freshly ground pepper
1 tablespoon sunflower or peanut oil

For the forcemeat
7 ounces (190g) very fatty bacon, and with no lean meat if possible
12 ounces (325g) wild duck or chicken livers (threads and any traces of green removed)
2 heaped teaspoons salt
3/4 teaspoon pepper
*pinch of quatre épices**
1 cup heavy cream
4 egg yolks

You only need the breasts or "supremes" of the ducks in this recipe, so remove the legs before cooking the ducks but leave the breasts on the carcass. The legs can be used for other recipes.

Wash the raisins, pat dry, and soak in the armagnac for about 1 hour. Set aside to add later.

Preheat the oven to 475°F (250°C).
Put the ducks, legs removed, into a small roasting pan, season with salt and pepper, sprinkle with oil, and roast for 15–20 minutes in the very hot oven. The flesh should still be pink.

Meanwhile, prepare the forcemeat. Cut the bacon into small chunks, put with the duck livers, salt, pepper, and quatre épices in a blender or food processor and blend to a smooth creamy consistency. Add the cream, egg yolks, and strained armagnac, and continue to blend until the mixture becomes liquid, perhaps 30 seconds. Push the mixture through a strainer into a bowl with the help of a spoon. Any small fibers from the bacon or livers will be caught in the mesh.

Remove the four breasts from the cooked ducks by sliding a flexible knife along the breast bone on either side and lifting the flesh away. Skin the fillets and cut them into dice, 1/4-inch (5-mm) across. Add the diced duck fillet and the raisins to the liver mixture and mix thoroughly.

To cook the terrine, lower the oven heat to 400°F (200°C). Pour the forcemeat mixture into an earthenware terrine. The pâté should be about 2 inches (5cm) deep. Cover with a lid or aluminum foil and cook in a bain-marie for 45–60 minutes. Leave in a cool place overnight.

The following day, serve the pâté with crusty white bread or thick slices of toast and a glass of red wine!

***Note:** Quatre épices is a French spice blend used mainly in pork products. It can occasionally be found in shops outside France, but can easily be made up at home with:

1/2 cup freshly ground black pepper
4 teaspoons cloves, ground
6 tablespoons ground ginger
1/2 cup plus 1 tablespoon freshly ground nutmeg

Right: Terrine of Wild Duck with Golden Raisins

Roast Woodcock or Snipe

Serves 4

Woodcock and snipe are highly regarded not only for their delicious flesh but also for their innards, with the exception of the gizzard, which is removed before the livers are roasted.

2 woodcock, or 4 snipe, gizzards removed
bacon (optional)
2–4 tablespoons melted butter
4 croûtons, large enough for the birds to sit on
salt and freshly ground pepper

Garnish
sprigs of watercress or fresh herbs

Preheat the oven to 450°F (230°C). Remove the gizzard from the birds by making a small insertion in the thin abdominal skin, slightly to the right of the center. Locate the hard lump of the gizzard with a skewer or trussing needle, remove, and detach from the innards which should remain in the bird. Brush the birds with melted butter and season, or wrap in bacon and truss with string.

Toast and butter 1 side of the bread, put the toast buttered side down on a baking tray, with the snipe or woodcock on top. Roast in the preheated oven for 18–22 minutes for woodcock, depending on size, and half that time for snipe. The birds are usually cooked when the bacon is crispy! Remove the trussing string and serve the woodcock or snipe on the croûtons. Garnish with sprigs of watercress or fresh herbs.

Note: If you want to make a sauce to serve with the birds, add a tablespoon of brandy to the juices in the roasting pan, along with the cooked mashed innards, and season. Warm through but don't boil. Arrange the croûtons on a hot serving dish, spoon the sauce over them and sit the birds on top; garnish and serve immediately. Medlar jelly is very good with this dish.

Medallions of Ostrich with Celeriac and Red Currant Sauce

Serves 6

This dish can also be made with loin of venison.

1½–2 lbs. (700–900g) loin of ostrich
salt and freshly ground pepper
extra-virgin olive oil

Celeriac Purée (see page 377, right) or Gratin of Potato and Celeriac (see page 187)
Red Currant Sauce (see page 598)
watercress salad

First make the Celeriac Purée or Gratin and the Red Currant Sauce. Trim any gristle or membrane from the eye of the loin. Just before serving, slice the meat into ½-inch (1-cm) thick medallions, season with salt and freshly ground pepper.

Heat a grill-pan or cast-iron frying pan. Drizzle the meat with a little olive oil. Sauté over a high heat for 1–2 minutes each side. The center of the medallions should still be rare.

Serve with the creamy gratin and a little Red Currant Sauce. A peppery Watercress Salad is a perfect accompaniment.

Medallions of Venison with Blackberry Sauce

Serves 4

4 medallions of venison
butter to fry
2 cups blackberries, fresh or frozen
2 cups homemade Chicken Stock (see page 36)
⅓ cup port
5 tablespoons sloe gin or brandy
lemon juice, to taste
salt and freshly ground pepper

Garnish
fresh blackberries
sprigs of fresh herbs

Purée and strain the blackberries. If you are using frozen ones, they may need a little sugar. Put the stock and port into a stainless-steel saucepan and boil and reduce for a few minutes. Add the gin (or brandy) and fruit, and boil until the sauce coats the back of a spoon.

Meanwhile, season the medallions of venison, and fry in a very little butter on a hot pan for 2 minutes each side.

Sharpen the sauce with a little freshly squeezed lemon juice, taste, and correct the seasoning. Put the medallions on a hot plate, spoon over a little sauce, and garnish with a few fresh blackberries, if available, and a few sprigs of fresh herbs.

Serve immediately with Gratin Dauphinois (see page 186) and a good green salad.

Venison with Celeriac Purée

Serves 4

This recipe was a favorite of Canice Sharkey's when he was chef at the much-loved Arbutus Lodge restaurant in Cork. As ever, it is important not to marinate the venison for too long, nor to overcook it, or it will be dry and dull. A little Red Currant Jelly may be added to the sauce at the end, or served separately.

1 lb. (450g) loin of venison (makes 12 noisettes)
butter and oil to pan-fry

Marinade
½ cup olive oil
½ cup white wine
dash of sherry vinegar
1 garlic clove
4 juniper berries
1 small onion, sliced

1 small carrot, sliced
bay leaf and thyme
a few pats of butter

Sauce
$1^{1}/_{2}$ tablespoons chopped shallot
dash white wine
2 cups homemade Beef Stock (see page 36)

Celeriac Purée
1 head celeriac, peeled and chopped
milk
cream and a pat of butter
salt and freshly ground pepper
mashed potato

Garnish
sprigs of rosemary

Preheat the oven to 350°F (180°C).

Begin by making the celeriac purée. Cook the celeriac in milk and when cooked, drain and purée. Season with salt and freshly ground pepper, a little cream or butter may be added. Cut the purée with about $^{1}/_{3}$ the quantity of mashed potato and keep it warm in the oven.

Meanwhile, place the whole loin of venison in the marinade for about 10–15 minutes. Take out and cut into noisettes about $^{3}/_{4}$-inch (2-cm) thick. Pan-fry in butter and oil, until well-sealed. Place on a tray and put into a moderate oven to keep warm while you make the sauce.

Meanwhile, de-glaze the pan with a little white wine; add the shallots. Add the stock and reduce by half. Add about a tablespoon of the marinade and whisk in a little butter. Place three noisettes on each plate with 3 quenelles of celeriac purée.

Place some sauce over the quenelles and garnish with rosemary.

Right: Venison with Celeriac Purée

Larding and Barding

Very lean meat is larded or barded to introduce fat, to baste the meat during cooking.

Larding: You will need 8 ounces (225g) fatback or very fatty streaky pork or pork caul fat, cut into 1/4-inch (5-mm) wide strips (or lardons).

Insert a larding needle into a strip, draw a lardon through the meat to make a stitch; trim the end.

Repeat the stitches at 1 inch (2.5cm) intervals to make horizontal rows, positioning each row about 1/2 inch (1cm) away from the previous row; repeat with the remainder of the fat.

Barding: Wrap the entire joint in caul fat or in a very thin sheet, or sheets, of pork fatback. Thin strips of bacon may also be used.

Master Recipe
Roast Haunch of Venison with Potato and Mushroom Gratin

Serves about 16–20 people

A haunch of venison makes a splendid party dish. Calculate the cooking time carefully, as it is easy to overcook venison. We like our venison slightly pink and still very juicy, so I usually turn off the oven at the end of the cooking time and let the meat relax for 20–30 minutes.

1 haunch venison, about 6–7 lbs. (2.6–3.1kg)

To lard or bard the venison
8 ounces (225g) fatback or very streaky pork or pork caul fat, cut into 1/4-inch (5-mm) wide strips

Marinade
2 teaspoons mixed fresh herbs (thyme, savory, marjoram, sage)
5 tablespoons olive oil
1/2 cup (125ml) dry white wine

Gravy
5 cups homemade Beef or Venison Stock (see page 36)
dry white wine, to taste, optional
Roux (see page 580), optional

Gratin of Potato and Mushroom (see page 186)

Preheat the oven to 350°F (180°C).

First lard the venison (see left).
Put the haunch into a shallow stainless-steel or cast-iron dish (not tin or aluminum). Sprinkle it with the herbs. Pour the olive oil and wine over the meat.

Cover the dish and marinate the meat for about 4 hours at room temperature or in a refrigerator overnight, turning the meat occasionally. The marinade liquid will be used to baste the meat during cooking.

To cook: Weigh the venison and calculate 10 minutes for every pound (450g). During the cooking time, baste every 10 minutes with the oil and wine marinade, and turn the joint over halfway through. When the venison is cooked, remove it to a warmed serving dish while you make the gravy.

De-grease the roasting pan, add the stock and perhaps a dash of wine. Bring to a boil, scraping and dissolving the sediment and crusty bits from the pan. Thicken slightly with a little Roux, taste, and correct the seasoning, and pour into a warm gravy boat. Serve with Gratin of Potato and Mushroom.

Other accompaniment suggestions:
Gratin Dauphinois (see page 186)
Roast Potatoes (see page 181)
Red Cabbage with Apples (see page 167)
Celeriac Purée (see page 377)
Brussels Sprouts (see page 169)

Note: It is very easy to overcook venison mainly because it goes on cooking after the oven has been turned off.

Variation
Roast Haunch of Venison with Plum or Francatelli Sauce

Follow the Master Recipe.

Serve the haunch of venison on a large serving dish surrounded by roast potatoes, red cabbage, celeriac purée, or Brussels sprouts.

Carve on to very hot plates. Serve with Plum Sauce or Francatelli sauce (see below).

Plum or Damson Sauce

Serves 10–15

Also delicious with duck.

1 lb. (450g) blood plums or damsons
1 cup sugar
2 cloves
1 inch (2.5cm) piece cinnamon stick
2 tablespoons butter
2 1/2 tablespoons Red Currant Jelly (see page 508)
1/2 cup port

Put the plums into a stainless steel saucepan along with the sugar, cloves, cinnamon, one tablespoon of water, and the butter. Cook slowly until reduced to a pulp. Push the fruit through a fine strainer and return the purée to a clean saucepan.

Add the Red Currant Jelly and port, bring to a boil, and simmer for a few minutes. The sauce may be served either hot or cold.

Tip: Venison medallions cook in minutes and marry well with any of the sauces used for Haunch of Venison.

Francatelli Sauce

This delicious sauce was invented by Queen Victoria's chef, Francatelli. It is very easy to make. You may need to double the quantity for 20 hungry people.

2 1/2 tablespoons port
1 cup Red Currant Jelly (see page 508)
small stick of cinnamon, bruised
thinly pared rind of a lemon

Simmer together for 5 minutes, stirring. Strain into a hot sauceboat.

Venison Stew with Melted Leeks

Serves 8

When you buy venison, allow time for marinating, and remember that an ingredient like fat salt pork or fat unsmoked bacon is essential, either for cooking with the meat (stew) or for larding (roasting or braising), unless the meat has been well aged.

3 lbs. (1.3kg) shoulder of venison, trimmed and diced into 1 1/2-inch (4-cm) cubes
seasoned flour

Marinade
1 1/4-1 1/2 cups red wine
1 medium onion, sliced
1/4 cup brandy
1/4 cup olive oil
salt, lightly crushed black pepper
bouquet garni

Sauce
8 ounces (225g) fat salt pork or unsmoked bacon, diced
2 1/2 tablespoons olive oil
2 large onions, chopped
1 large carrot, diced
1 large garlic clove, crushed
2 cups homemade Beef or Game Stock (see page 36)
bouquet garni (see page 140)
24 small mushrooms, preferably wild ones
2 teaspoons lemon juice or Red Currant Jelly (see page 508)
salt, freshly ground pepper, sugar
Melted Leeks (see page 173)

Season the venison well and soak in the marinade ingredients for 24–48 hours. Drain the meat well (reserving the marinade), pat it dry on paper towels, and turn in a little seasoned flour.

Preheat the oven to 300°F (150°C). Brown the pork or bacon in olive oil in a frying pan, cooking it slowly at first to make the fat run, then raising the heat. Transfer to a flameproof casserole dish (or other heavy flameproof and ovenproof pot).

Brown the venison in the fat, then sauté the onion, carrot, and garlic. Do all this in batches, transferring each one to the casserole dish when cooked. Do not overheat or the fat will burn. Pour off any surplus fat, de-glaze the pan with the strained marinade, and pour this over the venison. Heat up enough stock to cover the ingredients in the casserole dish and pour it over the venison. Add the bouquet garni to the stew, bring to a gentle simmer, then transfer to the preheated oven. Cover closely and leave until the venison is tender.

Test after 1 1/2 hours, but allow 2 1/2 hours cooking time. For best results, it is wise to cook this kind of dish one day in advance and then reheat it. This improves the flavor and gives you a chance to make sure that the venison is tender.

Sauté the sliced mushrooms in butter. Season with salt and pepper and add to the stew.

Finally, taste the venison sauce. It will need seasoning and perhaps a little lemon juice. It also sometimes benefits from a pinch of sugar or just a little Red Currant Jelly.

Serve with Melted Leeks, baked potatoes, and perhaps a green vegetable: Brussels sprouts, broccoli, or cabbage.

Variation
Venison Pie

Serves 8
In season: late Autumn and Winter

Venison Stew (see recipe left)

Pastry Dough
12 ounces (350g) Puff or Flaky Pastry (see pages 456 or 413), rolled out thinly
egg-wash

Preheat the oven to 475°F (250°C).

Pour the stew into one large or several small, greased pie dishes and cover with pastry dough. Flute the edges, egg-wash, and decorate with pastry dough leaves. Bake in the oven for 10 minutes and then reduce heat to 350°F (180°C) for 25–30 minutes or until the crust is crisp and golden and the pie is bubbling.

desserts

desserts

The sweet trolley at Ballymaloe House is legendary. It has been a highlight of dinner ever since the restaurant opened in 1963. There's always a homemade ice-cream served in an ice bowl, and a meringue gâteau filled with a complementary filling. The yolks of freshly laid eggs from our free range hens are used to make the ice-cream, and the whites are used for the meringues. There will also be a compôte of fruit in season: perhaps a mousse, a soufflé of Carrigeen moss, or a fruit tart made with buttery homemade flaky or puff pastry. The choice changes with the seasons. Coming up to Christmas there is Myrtle Allen's Plum Pudding with brandy butter and mince pies, and if you are there in Winter, you may catch a steamed pudding or a blood orange tart. On Shrove Tuesday, Myrtle or Hazel make crêpes Suzettes at your table, and in Autumn, there will be crushed blueberries, wild berries, and maybe some hazelnuts from the wood....

The art of the pastry chef is becoming ever more exciting. Using specialist pastry, chocolate and sugar techniques, skilled chefs can create amazing confections, some so elaborate that one almost feels reluctant to eat them. Most of the desserts in this book are simple to master and won't make you feel guilty for digging in.

Choosing Your Dessert

Of course dessert isn't obligatory, but many people have a sweet tooth so this could be the part of the meal that they most look forward to. Particularly nowadays, where many people only allow themselves dessert as a special treat (either because they're too busy, health- or weight-conscious), it's worth putting some extra thought into creating something special.

The choice of dessert depends on the meal. Follow a rich main course with a compôte of fruit or perfectly ripe fresh fruit, local summer berries, or citrus fruits in season. A tart, luscious meringue or ice-cream will be enjoyable after a piece of simple pan-grilled fish or meat. Try to provide a contrast in terms of texture. Chocolate always seems to be a hit – regardless of what came before or how full one is!

Presentation

Many desserts need very little embellishment to look mouth-wateringly delicious – maybe just a sprig of mint or a light dusting of confectioners sugar. Others benefit from elaborate decorations and presentation. Dramatic results can be achieved relatively easily with simple techniques using chocolate leaves and curls, caramel shards, crystalized flowers, candied orange or julienne zest, brandy snap baskets, chocolate coffee beans, and lashings of cream.

In Ireland we have wonderful rich cream but remember, cream tastes different depending on how you serve it. Choose runny cream to serve with a silky chocolate mousse, but softly whipped cream, which barely holds the print of the whisk, is best served with most puddings. Stiffly whipped cream has the least flavor of all, and don't even think about cream that comes squishing out of a can!

The Ballymaloe Ice Bowl

The ice bowl was Myrtle Allen's brilliant solution to keeping the ice-cream cold during the evening on the sweet trolley in the restaurant. I quote from *The Ballymaloe Cookbook*, published by Gill and Macmillan.

"It took me twelve years to find the solution

to keeping ice-cream cold on the sweet trolley in my restaurant. At first we used to unmold and decorate our ices on to a plate. This was alright on a busy night when they got eaten before melting. On quieter occasions, the waitresses performed relay races from the dining-room to the deep freeze. I dreamed about nineteenth-century ice boxes filled from ice houses, to my husband's increasing scorn, and then I thought I had a solution. A young Irish glass blower produced beautiful hand-blown glass cylinders which I filled with ice-cream and fitted into beautiful tulip shaped glass bowls. These I filled with ice cubes. Six months later, however, due to either the stress of the ice or the stress of the waitresses, my bowls were gone and so was my money.

In desperation I produced an ice bowl. It turned out to be a stunning and practical presentation for a restaurant trolley or a party buffet."

To make a Ballymaloe Ice Bowl

Take two bowls, one about double the capacity of the other. Half fill the big bowl with cold water. Float the second bowl inside the first. Weight the small bowl down with water or ice cubes until the rims are level. Place a square of fabric on top, covering both bowls, and secure it with a strong rubber band or string under the rim of the larger bowl, as one would tie on a jam jar cover. Adjust the small bowl through the cloth to a central position. The cloth will hold it in place.

Put the bowls on a jelly roll pan and place in a deep freeze – re-adjusting the position of the small bowl, if necessary, as you put it in. After 24 hours or more take it out of the deep freeze.

Remove the cloth and leave for 15–20 minutes, by which time the small bowl should lift out easily. Then try to lift out the ice-bowl. It should be starting to melt slightly from the outside bowl, in which case it will slip out easily. If it isn't, then just leave for 5–10 minutes more: don't attempt to run it under the hot or even cold tap, or it may crack. If you are in a great rush, the best solution is to wring out a dish towel in hot water and wrap that around the large bowl for a few minutes. Altogether the best course of action is to perform this operation early in the day and then fill the ice bowl with scoops of ice-cream, so that all you have to do when it comes to serving the ice-cream is to pick up the ice bowl from the freezer and place it on the serving dish. Put a folded napkin under the ice bowl on the serving dish to catch any drips.

At Ballymaloe, Myrtle Allen surrounds the ice bowl with vine leaves in Summer, scarlet Virginia creeper in Autumn, and red-berried holly at Christmas. However, as I'm a bit less restrained, I can't resist surrounding it with flowers. Whatever way you present it, ice-cream served in a bowl of ice like this usually draws gasps of admiration when you bring it to the table.

In the restaurant, we make a new ice-bowl every night, but at home when the dessert would be on the table for barely half an hour, it should be possible to use the ice bowl several times. As soon as you have finished serving, give the bowl a quick wash under the cold tap and get it back into the freezer again. This way you can often get two or three turns from a single ice bowl. One more point: don't leave a serving spoon resting against the side of the bowl or it will melt a notch in the rim.

Fresh Figs with Fresh Raspberry Sauce

Serves 8

8 fresh figs
Fresh Raspberry Sauce (see page 599)
whipped cream

Decoration
mint or lemon balm sprigs
fig leaves, optional

Trim the stalk and cut a cross in each fig, cutting down almost to the base. Gently open out the fruit to resemble a flower unfurling. Make a nick just under the stalk, peel off the skin in strips. If you can find any, put a fig leaf on each plate, a fig on top, then a dollop of cream in the center.

Spoon a little Fresh Raspberry Sauce over the top and serve the remainder in a bowl. Decorate with a sprig of mint or lemon balm. Eat immediately.

Agen Stuffed Prunes with Rosewater Cream

Serves 6

This ancient recipe from the Middle East will change your opinion of prunes. Claudia Roden introduced us to this pretty and delicious dish when she was guest chef at the school. Agen prunes are a variety from the southwest of France.

1 lb. (450g) Agen prunes, pitted
same number of fresh walnut halves
2/3 cup each water and red wine, or more, or 1 1/4 cups water
1 1/4 cups cream
2 1/2 tablespoons superfine sugar
1 tablespoon rose blossom water

Decoration
a few chopped walnuts
rose petals, optional

We've experimented with removing the pits from both soaked and dry prunes – unsoaked works best. Use a small knife to cut out the pits and then stuff each prune with half a walnut. Arrange in a single layer in a sauté pan. Cover with a mixture of water and wine, if using. Put the lid on the pan and simmer for about 30 minutes. Add more liquid if they become a little dry. The prunes should be plump and soft.

Lift them gently onto a serving plate in a single layer and let them cool.
Whip the cream to soft peaks, add the sugar and rose blossom water. Spoon dollops over the prunes and chill well.

Just before serving, scatter a few chopped walnuts over each dollop of cream, sprinkle with rose petals and serve well chilled. This dessert tastes even better the next day.

Mangoes in Lime Syrup

Serves 2

This simple recipe must be made with a perfectly ripe mango; if the fruit you buy is under-ripe, wrap it in newspaper and keep it in your kitchen for a few days. Papayas are also delicious served in exactly the same way.

1 ripe mango
1/2 cup sugar
1/2 cup water
1 lime

Put the sugar and water into a saucepan, stir over a gentle heat until the sugar dissolves, bring to a boil, and simmer for 2 minutes; let cool.

Peel the mango and slice quite thinly down to the seed. Put the slices into a bowl and cover with the cold syrup.
Remove the zest from the lime either with a

zester or a fine stainless-steel grater and add to the syrup along with the juice of the lime. Let it macerate for at least an hour. Serve chilled.

Variation

Bananas in Lime Syrup

Substitute 4 bananas for the mango in the above recipe – a brilliant little gem, made in minutes. Peaches, nectarines, and papayas respond well to this recipe, too.

Bananas in Coconut Milk

Serves 4–6

A favorite quick and easy Asian dessert. Delicious served warm or cold.

1/2 cup white sugar
1/4 teaspoon salt
1 teaspoon freshly squeezed lime juice
3 cups coconut milk
8 ripe bananas

Put the sugar, salt, and lime juice into a saucepan along with the coconut milk. Bring it to a boil over a low heat. Keep the heat low, otherwise the coconut milk will curdle and separate. Cut each banana into 4 pieces, add to the pan. Remove from the heat once the bananas are soft and tender.

A Simple Fresh Fruit Salad

Serves 6–8

Don't fall into the trap of using too much apple. Also, it is surprisingly important to cut the fruit into nicely shaped pieces, otherwise it can look a mess. The sugar and lemon juice draw out the juice from the fruit and give a very fresh-tasting fruit salad.

1 ripe pear
1 ripe apple
2 ripe oranges
2 tablespoons superfine sugar
freshly squeezed juice of 1 lemon
1 ripe banana

Optional extras
1 kiwi fruit
3/4 cup peeled and pitted grapes
1 cup fresh strawberries
1 peach or nectarine

Garnish
mint leaves
chopped chile

Peel the pear and apple, cut into quarters, core, and cut across the grain into slices less than 1/4-inch (5-mm) thick. Peel the oranges with a stainless-steel serrated knife as though you were peeling an apple, making sure to remove all the pith, then cut each segment individually and add to the apple and pear. Sprinkle with sugar and lemon juice. About 15 minutes before serving, add the sliced bananas, taste, and add more juice or sugar if necessary. If using kiwi fruit, grapes, or strawberries, add them along with the orange. Serve garnished with mint leaves and a little chopped chile and pass a bowl of lightly whipped cream.

Citrus Fruit Salad

Serves 6

In the winter when many fruits have abysmal flavor, the citrus fruits are at their best. This delicious, fresh-tasting salad uses a wide variety of the ever-expanding citrus family. It's particularly good when a few blood oranges are included. Ugli fruit, pomelos, tangelos and sweeties all add excitement and zing. A great palate-cleanser after a heavy winter meal.

8 ounces (225g) kumquats
1 1/2 cups water
3/4 cup plus 2 tablespoons sugar
1 lime
3 medium clementines
2–3 medium tangerines or mandarins
1 pink grapefruit
2 blood oranges
lemon juice, if necessary

Slice the kumquats into 1/4-inch (5-mm) rounds, remove seeds. Dissolve the sugar in the water over a low heat, and add the sliced kumquats. Cover and simmer for about 30 minutes or until tender. Remove from the heat. Let cool.

Remove the zest from the lime with a zester and add, along with the juice, to the kumquats. Meanwhile, peel the clementines and tangerines (or mandarins) and remove as much of the white pith and strings as possible. Slice into rounds 1/4-inch (5-mm) thick, and add to the syrup. Segment the grapefruit and blood oranges and add to the syrup also. Let macerate for at least 1 hour. Taste, and add a squeeze of lemon juice if necessary. Serve chilled.

Fruit Chat (North Indian-style fruit salad)

Serves 8

Use a combination of fresh fruit such as mango, papaya, bananas, peaches, melon, kiwi, guava, strawberries, raspberries, blackberries, and blueberries for this recipe. Jaggery is a raw cane sugar with a very special taste. If you can't find it, substitute soft brown or golden granulated sugar instead.

1–1 1/2 lbs. (450–700g) prepared fruit
juice of 1–2 lemons
salt to taste
2 teaspoons chat masala (black salt)
2 teaspoons roasted cumin seeds, ground
1/2 teaspoon freshly ground black pepper
3/4 cup freshly chopped mint leaves
2 tablespoons fresh ginger, peeled and finely grated
8–12 hot green chiles, sliced (if that terrifies you – use much less)

Decoration
fresh mint and cilantro
whole chiles
crushed jaggery

Prepare the fruit in generous-sized pieces and mix in a large platter, add lemon juice, salt, and chat masala, toss gently to mix, sprinkle over them the other ingredients, and toss again.

Serve the fruit salad over lettuce leaves, decorate with mint and chiles, and sprinkle cumin and jaggery over as needed.

Orange Salad

Serves 4

6 juicy oranges, Navel or Valencia, organic or unwaxed
1–2 tablespoons orangeflower water
a little sugar

Scrub the oranges. Grate the zest carefully from 1 of the oranges using the finest side of the grater. Peel and remove all pith, leaving 6 clean oranges. Slice them thinly into a large bowl containing the zest. Sprinkle the orangeflower water onto the orange slices.

Sprinkle with sugar, arrange in overlapping slices on a wide platter. Chill for as long as possible.

Summer Fruit Salad with Sweet Geranium Leaves

Serves 8–10

Sweet geranium (Pelargonium graveolens) and many other varieties of scented geraniums are ever present on our window sills at Ballymaloe. We use the delicious lemon-scented leaves in all sorts of ways, and occasionally we use the pretty purple flowers to enliven and add magic to otherwise simple dishes. The crystalized leaves, all frosty and crinkly, are wonderful with fresh cream cheese and fat juicy blackberries. I discovered this recipe which has now become a perennial favorite quite by accident, a few summers ago as I raced to make a pudding in a hurry with the ingredients I had at that moment.

1 cup raspberries
1 cup loganberries
1 cup redcurrants
1 cup blackcurrants
1 cup small strawberries
1 cup blueberries
1 cup fraises des bois or tiny strawberries

Syrup
1¾ cups sugar
2 cups water
6–8 large sweet geranium leaves

Put all the freshly picked berries into a white china or glass bowl. Put the sugar, water, and sweet geranium leaves into a stainless-steel saucepan and bring slowly to a boil, stirring until the sugar dissolves. Boil for just 2 minutes. Cool for 4–5 minutes, then pour the hot syrup over the fruit and let macerate for several hours.

Remove the geranium leaves. Serve chilled, with softly whipped cream or Vanilla Ice Cream (see page 398), or just as it is, decorated with a few fresh sweet geranium leaves.

For a winter version, follow the Summer Fruit Salad recipe but substitute best-quality frozen berries and currants – pour the boiling syrup over the frozen berries in the bowl.

Tip: The geranium syrup can be stored in the fridge or even frozen.

A Jelly Dessert of Fresh Raspberries with Fresh Mint Cream

Makes 10 ramekins

4 cups fresh raspberries

Syrup
1 cup sugar
1 cup water
4 sprigs fresh mint
2 teaspoons framboise (raspberry) liqueur
1 tablespoon plus 1 teaspoon freshly squeezed lemon juice
3 rounded teaspoons gelatin
¼ cup water

Fresh Mint Cream
15 mint leaves
1 tablespoon plus 1 teaspoon freshly squeezed lemon juice
¾ cup cream

10 ramekins or individual molds, lined with plastic wrap

Make a syrup by bringing sugar, water, and mint sprigs slowly to a boil. Simmer for a few minutes, let cool, then add the framboise and lemon juice.

Sponge the gelatin in the water in a small bowl or heatproof measuring cup, then place the bowl in a pan of simmering water until the gelatin completely dissolves. Remove the mint leaves from the syrup, then pour the syrup onto the gelatin and then add to the raspberries. Fill the lined molds. Put into the fridge and let set for 3–4 hours.

Meanwhile, make the Fresh Mint Cream. Crush the mint leaves in a mortar and pestle along with the lemon juice, add the cream, and stir (the lemon juice will thicken the cream, if the cream becomes too thick, add a little water).

To assemble, spread a little Fresh Mint Cream on a white plate, turn out a raspberry jelly, and place in the center. Place five mint leaves on the cream around the jelly. Decorate with a few perfect raspberries. Serve chilled.

Variation

Blueberry Jelly with a Fresh Mint Cream

Follow the recipe above, substituting 4 cups blueberries for the raspberries, and add 2 teaspoons of myrtle liqueur or other blueberry brandy to the syrup instead of the framboise.

Right: Summer Fruit Salad with Sweet Geranium Leaves

Agar Agar

Agar Agar is derived from seaweed. This vegetarian product works exactly like gelatin, but needs to be boiled with some or all of the liquid ingredients in the recipe before it will set. Use 2 teaspoons for 2½ cups of liquid.

Agar Agar is available at health food shops.

Summer Fruit Gelatin with Sweet Geranium Cream

Serves 10

4 cups summer fruit, perhaps:
2 cups fresh raspberries
1 cup fraises des bois or tiny strawberries
1 cup blueberries or black currants

Syrup
1 cup sugar
1 cup water
4 sweet geranium leaves
1 tablespoon plus 1 teaspoon freshly squeezed lemon juice

3 rounded teaspoons gelatin
¼ cup water

Sweet Geranium Cream
4–5 sweet geranium leaves
1 tablespoon plus 1 teaspoon lemon juice
¾ cup cream
sugar to taste, optional

10 individual ramekin dishes or molds, lined with plastic wrap or brushed lightly with non-scented vegetable oil.

Make a syrup by bringing sugar, water, and sweet geranium leaves slowly to a boil. Simmer for a few minutes, let cool, then add lemon juice.

Sponge the gelatin in ¼ cup of water, then place the bowl over a pan of simmering water until the gelatin is completely dissolved.

Remove the sweet geranium leaves from the syrup, then pour the syrup onto the gelatin and then add to the fruit, stir gently. Fill the lined molds. Put into the fridge and let set for 3–4 hours.

Meanwhile make the Sweet Geranium Cream. Crush the leaves in a mortar and pestle along with the lemon juice, add the cream and stir. (The lemon juice will thicken the cream, so if it becomes too thick, add a little water.) Taste, and add a little sugar if it is too bitter, but remember the sauce should be tart.

To serve: spread a little Sweet Geranium Cream onto a white plate, turn out a jelly, and place in the center. Place 3–5 tiny sweet geranium leaves on the cream. Decorate with a few perfect raspberries, serve chilled.

Tip: You will need to use 1 tablespoon of gelatin to each pint (600ml) of fruit and liquid.

Fresh Orange Gelatin with Mint

Serves 6–8

This is best during the winter when citrus fruits are in their prime.

6 oranges, organic or unwaxed
juice of 1 freshly squeezed lemon
1 cup syrup, made with ¾ cup water and ¾ cup sugar
1 teaspoon Grand Marnier
2 rounded teaspoons gelatin
2½ tablespoons water

Sauce
1 cup fresh orange juice, sweetened to taste with sugar
2 generous tablespoons freshly chopped mint

Decoration
sprigs of mint or lemon balm

1 terrine, 1 quart capacity, or 6–8 oval or round molds, ½-cup capacity, lined with plastic wrap or brushed with non-scented vegetable oil

Grate the rind from 2 of the oranges very carefully on a stainless-steel grater. Segment all six oranges and add the syrup, orange zest, lemon juice, and Grand Marnier. Mix well. Then strain the liquid off the oranges again and measure 1¼ cups. Set the remainder aside for the sauce.

Sponge the gelatin in 2½ tablespoons of cold water in a small bowl for a few minutes. Put the bowl into a saucepan of simmering water until all the gelatin crystals are dissolved. Mix with the orange liquid, stirring carefully. Add the orange segments and fill into the individual molds or terrine. Put in the fridge and allow 3–4 hours to set.

To make the sauce, measure the remaining orange liquid and make up to 1 cup with more freshly squeezed orange juice. Taste and sweeten if necessary, then add the freshly chopped mint.

To serve: turn out the jellies onto individual plates. Pour a little sauce around each jelly and decorate with mint leaves or lemon balm.

Variations

Blood Orange Gelatin

Substitute 6–8 blood oranges and follow the above recipe.

Citrus Fruit Gelatin with Mint

2 pink grapefruit
2 blood oranges or mandarins
2 oranges, organic or unwaxed
juice of ½ lemon
1 cup syrup, made with ¾ cup water and ¾ cup sugar

2 rounded teaspoons gelatin
2½ tablespoons water

Sauce
½ cup pink grapefruit juice
½ cup fresh orange juice, sweetened to taste with sugar

Decoration
sprigs of fresh mint

Follow the recipe for Fresh Orange Gelatin, omitting the Grand Marnier. Make the sauce in the same way, but using freshly squeezed orange and grapefruit juice to make 1 cup.

Summer Pudding

Serves 12–16

Everyone seems to become wistful when you mention Summer Pudding. Bursting with soft fruit and served with lots of softly whipped cream, it's one of the very best desserts of summer. We make our Summer Pudding with cake, although many people use slices of white bread to line the bowl. Summer fruit salad with sweet geranium leaves (see page 386) also makes a successful filling, but you need to cook the black currants and red currants until they burst before adding the soft fruit. Make sure the fruit and syrup is boiling when you pour it into the spongecake-lined bowl, otherwise the syrup won't soak through the spongecake properly.

2 x 7-inch (18-cm) Great Grandmother's Cake (see page 447)
2 cups black currants
2 cups red currants
4 cups raspberries or 2 cups raspberries and 2 cups strawberries
2½ cups granulated sugar
4 cups water
6–8 sweet geranium leaves, optional

2 quart (1.8 liter) pudding basin

First make the spongecake. Cut each round of spongecake in half, horizontally. Line the bowl with the cake, crusty side inwards. It doesn't matter if it looks quite patched, as it will blend later.

Dissolve the sugar in the water, add the sweet geranium leaves (if using) and boil for 2 minutes. Add the black currants and red currants and cook until the fruit bursts – about 3–4 minutes – then add the raspberries (and strawberries, if using).

Taste, and remove the sweet geranium leaves and discard. Immediately, ladle some of the hot liquid and fruit into the cake-lined bowl. When about half full, if you have remaining scraps of cake, put them in the center. Then fill to the top with fruit. Cover with a layer of spongecake. Put a plate on top and press down with a heavy weight. Let it get cold. Store in the refrigerator for a minimum of 24 hours before serving, but it will keep for 4–5 days.

To serve: Unmold onto a deep serving dish and pour any leftover fruit and syrup over the top and around the side. Serve with lots of softly whipped cream.

Variation

Black Currant Summer Pudding

In winter, you can follow the recipe above, but use 2 pounds frozen black currants, 2½ cups granulated sugar and 3 cups water in place of the fresh summer fruits.

Poached Black Currants with Icy Cold Cream

Serves 4

3 cups black currants
Stock Syrup (see recipe page 568)
icy cold cream

warm Shortbread Cookies (see page 465)

Cover the black currants with stock syrup. Bring to a boil and cook until the fruit bursts – this takes about 4–5 minutes. Serve with warm shortbread cookies and icy cold cream.

Poached Plums

(see page 523) are delicious served with Mascarpone cream, or just on their own for breakfast.

Poached Quince with Cloves

Serves 6

The Greeks adore quince and all kinds of compôte, jams, and pastes are made with them, but they also cook quince with meat. I, too, adore this compôte as it was cooked for me by Maria Katsiou-Maroulaki in Thessaloniki.

6 ripe quince
2 1/2 cups water
1–1 1/2 cups sugar
6–8 cloves
freshly squeezed lemon juice

To make the syrup, dissolve the sugar in the water and boil together for 2 minutes. Peel the quinces and cut into quarters or eighths depending on size, put immediately into the hot syrup (otherwise they will go brown), along with the cloves.

Cover and simmer for about 1 hour or until the fruit is tender, tasting about halfway through and adding more sugar or lemon juice as necessary. They will become a glorious deep red color. Let them get cold, and serve chilled with some pouring cream.

Note: a vanilla bean could be substituted for cloves in this recipe.

Variations

Poached Quince with Vanilla

Substitute a vanilla bean for the cloves in the above recipe.

Poached Guava with Cinnamon

Poach 8 guava with a small cinnamon stick and follow the recipe above but simmer for only 20 minutes approximately.

Apricot and Cardamom Compôte

Serves 4

1 lb. (450g) fresh apricots (about 8–12) or 8 ounces (225g) best-quality dried apricots (about 1 1/4–1 1/2 cups)
12 cardamom pods
5 cups water
3/4–1 3/4 cups sugar
2 1/2 tablespoons freshly squeezed lemon juice

If you are using dried apricots, soak them overnight in plenty of cold water. Crush the cardamom pods slightly. Put them with the water, sugar, and lemon juice into a saucepan, bring to a boil, add the apricots, and simmer until tender. The time varies depending on whether they are fresh or dried – between 15 and 30 minutes. Pour into a bowl, chill, and serve. Alternatively, remove the apricots and continue to simmer until the syrup is more reduced.

Serve chilled with Pannacotta (see page 407) or crème fraîche.

Kumquat Compôte

Serves 6–8

Kumquats are the baby of the citrus family. This compôte keeps for weeks in the fridge. You can serve it with Pannacotta (see page 407), but it is equally delicious with a duck breast, roast pork, or gammon steak. Serve warm or cold.

3 1/4 lbs. (1.5kg) kumquats
1 quart (960ml) water
2 1/4 cups sugar

Cut the kumquats into four lengthwise and remove the seeds. Put the kumquats in a saucepan along with the water and sugar and let them cook very gently, uncovered, for half an hour until tender.

Pears Poached in Saffron Syrup

Serves 4

Most exotic of the fruit compôtes, pears cooked in this way turn a wonderful deep golden color and are delicately infused with the flavors of saffron and cardamom, two of the world's most precious spices. We use Conference (similar to Bosc) and Doyenne de Comice pears. This compôte is rich, intensely sweet, and best served well-chilled.

a scant cup sugar
2 cups water
6 whole cardamom pods, lightly crushed
1/4 teaspoon good quality saffron threads
1/4 cup freshly squeezed lemon juice
4 firm pears

Put the sugar, water, cardamom pods, saffron, and lemon juice into a shallow wide pan: we use a stainless-steel sauté pan. Stir to dissolve the sugar and bring to a simmer. Meanwhile, peel the pears, halve and core them, and immediately put them into the simmering syrup, cut side uppermost.

Cover with a paper lid and the lid of the pan and cook gently for 20–30 minutes, spooning the syrup over them every now and then. Carefully remove the pears and arrange in a single layer in a serving dish, cut side down. Pour the syrup over them and let cool. This compôte keeps for several weeks, covered, in the fridge.

Rhubarb Compôte or Rhubarb and Strawberry Compôte

(see page 523)

Green Gooseberry and Elderflower Compôte

Serves 6–8

When I'm driving through country lanes in late May or early June, suddenly I spy the elderflower coming into bloom. Then I know it's time to go and search the gooseberry bushes for the hard, green fruit, far too under-ripe at that stage to eat raw, but wonderful cooked in tarts or fools or in this delicious compôte. Elderflowers have an extraordinary affinity with green gooseberries and, by a happy arrangement of nature, they are both in season at the same time.

3–4 elderflower heads
2 cups sugar
2 1/2 cups cold water
2 lbs. (900g) green gooseberries, topped and tailed

Tie the elderflower heads in a little square of cheesecloth. Put into a stainless-steel saucepan, add the sugar, and cover with cold water. Bring slowly to a boil and continue to boil for 2 minutes. Add the gooseberries and simmer just until the fruit bursts. It is essential to cook the fruit until it actually bursts, otherwise the compôte will be too bitter. Let it get cold. Serve in a pretty bowl and decorate with fresh elderflowers.

Below: Green Gooseberry and Elderflower Compôte with Elderflower fritters (see page 391)

Fruit Fools

Fools are old-fashioned and gorgeous and so quick to make. We serve fruit fools right through the seasons at Ballymaloe. They are essentially purées of sweetened fruit into which softly whipped cream is swirled. Soft fruits, such as raspberries, loganberries and strawberries, are usually left raw, whereas black currants, gooseberries or apples, are usually cooked in a stock syrup, and rhubarb may need a little gelatin or it may otherwise be too runny. The amount of cream used depends on your own taste. A little stiffly beaten egg white may be added to lighten the fool. It should be the texture of softly whipped cream. If it is too stiff, stir in a little milk rather than more cream.

Fools may be served immediately or chilled for several hours. Serve with Shortbread (see page 465) or Jane's Biscuits (see page 461). Leftover fool may

be frozen into a simple parfait; some will be more crystalline than others, depending on the water content of the fruit. Serve in slices with a complementary sauce or compôte.

Green Gooseberry Fool

Serves 6

Tart green gooseberries picked in May make the best gooseberry fool. It will keep for several days covered in a fridge.

1 lb. (450g) hard green gooseberries
Stock Syrup (see page 568), made with 1¼ cups cold water and 1 cup sugar
heavy cream

Barely cover the green gooseberries with stock syrup. Bring to a boil and cook until the fruit bursts – about 5–6 minutes. Blend or purée the fruit and syrup, and measure. When the purée has cooled completely, add half its volume of softly whipped cream, or according to taste.

Variation

Green Gooseberry and Elderflower Fool

Add 3–4 elderflower heads tied in cheesecloth with the gooseberries and proceed as above.

Rhubarb Fool

Serves 6

1 lb. (450g) red rhubarb, cut into chunks
¾–1 cup sugar
2½ tablespoons water
1¼ cups cream, whipped

Put the rhubarb into a stainless-steel saucepan along with the sugar and water, stir, cover, bring to a boil and simmer until soft, which takes about 20 minutes. Stir with a wooden spoon until the rhubarb dissolves into a mush. Let it get quite cold. Fold in the softly whipped cream to taste.

Variation

Rhubarb and Strawberry Fool

Serves 6–8

A divine combination.

1 lb. (450g) red rhubarb, cut into chunks
1 cup sugar
2½ tablespoons water
2 cups strawberries
1¼ cups cream, whipped

Follow the recipe above for cooking the rhubarb, and let it get quite cold. Mash the strawberries and add to the rhubarb. Fold in the softly whipped cream to taste.

Strawberry, Raspberry, Loganberry, Tayberry, or Boysenberry Fool

1 lb. (450g) fruit
sugar to taste
2–2½ cups whipped cream

Simply crush the fruit, and add sugar to taste. Swirl in softly whipped cream. Taste, and add more cream as necessary. Serve immediately.

Black Currant Fool

Serves 6

3 cups black currants, fresh or frozen
Stock Syrup (see page 568)
whipped cream

Cover the black currants with Stock Syrup. Bring to a boil and cook until the fruit bursts – about 4–5 minutes. Blend or purée the fruit and syrup, strain through a nylon sieve, and measure. When the purée has cooled, add up to equal quantity of softly whipped cream, according to taste.

An alternative presentation is to layer black currant purée and softly whipped cream in tall sundae glasses. Finish your layers with one of cream, drizzle a little thinned purée on top, and serve chilled with shortbread cookies.

Variation

Black Currant Ice-cream

Leftover black currant fool makes a delicious ice-cream. Make a black currant coulis by thinning the black currant purée with a little more water or syrup. We set ours in loaf pans lined with plastic wrap – a great recipe for a party and amazingly good for so little effort.

Blackberry and Apple Fool

Serves 4–5

2–4 heaped cups blackberries
cooking apples to make a heaped cup apple purée (see Bramley Apple Sauce, page 597)
½ cup sugar
1 cup softly whipped cream

Pick over the blackberries and wash if necessary. Make a dry purée by cooking the apples in 1–2 tablespoons of water on a low heat. Blend or sieve and sweeten to taste while still hot. Let cool. Purée the raw blackberries and add them, along with the softly whipped cream, to the apple purée.

Apricot and Sweet Geranium Fool

Apricot and Cardamom Compôte (page 391)
softly whipped cream

Purée the apricots with a little of the syrup. Fold in softly whipped cream into the thick purée to taste. Serve with scones and cookies.

Meringues

There are few desserts that are as easy and impressive as meringues. The meringue bases will keep for several weeks in a tin, so you can assemble an impromptu filling with whatever you have at hand. There is no magic to making meringue, provided your mixing bowl is dry, free of grease, and spotlessly clean, and that when you separate the eggs, not a drop of yolk gets into the whites. If it does, no amount of whisking will get you fluffy white clouds of egg white – you'll have to start again. A copper bowl is best, stainless-steel and glass are also fine, but a plastic one should only be used as a last resort because it tends to hold grease and detergent residue unless meticulously washed and rinsed.

Tip: The proportion of filling to meringue really matters. Too much and it will be too luscious; too little and it will appear dry. As a rough guide, the filling should be about the thickness of one disc of meringue.

Master Recipe

Ballymaloe Break all the Rules Meringue

Serves 6–8

Unlike other meringue recipes, we just put everything into the same bowl rather than folding it in carefully. We think it's foolproof – as long as the bowl is spotlessly clean. Make double this amount if using a food mixer, otherwise the whisk won't reach the egg white in the bottom of the bowl.

2 egg whites
1/2 cup superfine sugar or 1 cup (125g) confectioners sugar

2 baking sheets
wax paper

Preheat the oven to 300°F (150°C), or according to the individual recipe. Line 2 baking sheets with wax paper. Draw 2 x 7 1/2-inch (19-cm) circles or heart shapes on the wax paper and set aside.

Check that your bowl is dry, free of grease, and spotlessly clean. Break up the egg whites with the whisk and then add all the sugar in one go. Whisk at full speed until the mixture forms stiff dry peaks.

Divide the mixture between the circles or heart shapes and spread evenly with a spatula. Bake immediately for 45–60 minutes or until crisp. The meringues should peel off the paper easily. Turn off the oven and let cool.

Tip: Do not put hot meringues straight from the oven on to a cold surface as they will crack, or at least craze, if you do.

Variations

Meringue Gâteau with Fruit

Follow the Master Recipe. Sandwich the meringues together with 1 1/4 cups of whipped cream and 2 cups fruit such as strawberries, kiwi fruit, peaches, or nectarines. Chill for several hours before serving. Decorate with rosettes of whipped cream stuck with little pieces of fruit.

Strawberry Meringue Blobs

Serves 8

4 egg whites
1 cup superfine sugar
1–2 tablespoons slivered almonds
1 1/4 cups whipped cream
4 cups strawberries

Decoration
sprigs of mint, lemon balm, or sweet cicely

Follow the Master Recipe until the meringue mixture forms stiff dry peaks. Put 8 blobs of meringue on a prepared baking sheet, and scatter a few flaked almonds over each one. Bake in the preheated oven for 10–15 minutes. Let the meringue cool on the trays.

To assemble: pipe or spoon some whipped cream into each meringue. Top with sliced strawberries, and decorate with a mint, lemon balm, or sweet cicely leaf if you have one at hand. Eat immediately!

Lemon Curd Meringue Blobs

Follow the recipe above and serve with whipped cream and homemade Lemon Curd (see page 510) and Crystallized Lemon Peel (see page 515).

Heart-shaped Lemon and Elderflower Curd Meringue

Follow the recipe above and divide the mixture between two heart shapes drawn on wax paper. Bake immediately for about 45 minutes or until crisp. Let cool, in the oven if possible. When completely cold, sandwich the meringue discs together with Lemon and Elderflower Curd (see page 511) and whipped cream. Decorate with rosettes of cream and lemon balm or sweet geranium leaves.

Meringue Nests with Kiwi and Lime

Serves 6

Meringue
2 egg whites
1 cup confectioners sugar

Filling
8 ounces (225g) kiwi fruit
1 cup whipped cream
juice of 1 lime

Decoration
whipped cream
fresh mint or lemon balm leaves

pastry bag

Preheat the oven 300°F (150°C). Draw out four 3½-inch (9-cm) circles on wax paper on a baking sheet. Follow the Master Recipe until the mixture forms stiff peaks. Put the meringue mixture into a pastry bag with a number 5 rosette nozzle. Pipe a few blobs onto each circle and spread thinly with a butter knife or spatula. The meringue should not be more than ¼-inch (5-mm) thick. Then carefully pipe a wall of meringue rosettes around the edge of each circle.

Bake for 45 minutes or until the meringue nests lift easily off the paper. Turn off the oven and let them cool in the oven. To assemble: peel the kiwi and cut them into wedges lengthwise. Toss in freshly squeezed lime juice. Pipe some whipped cream into each nest and arrange the slices of kiwi on top. Top with tiny rosettes of cream and decorate with fresh mint or lemon balm leaves.

Almond Meringue with Chocolate and Rum Cream

Serves 6

We use this all-in-one meringue recipe for birthdays, anniversaries, Valentine's Day, or simply for a special dessert. If you chill the assembled dessert for an hour before serving, it will be easier to cut. Almond meringue is particularly delicious with soft berry fruits, but peaches, nectarines, or kiwi fruit are also very good. Mango and passion fruit is irresistible.

Meringue
As for the Master Recipe
6 tablespoons whole unskinned almonds

Filling
1 ounce (25g) (about 1 square) good-quality dark chocolate
½ ounce (10g) (½ square) unsweetened baking chocolate
1 tablespoon rum
1 tablespoon light cream
1¼ cups whipped cream

Decoration
5 toasted almonds

Blanch and skin the almonds. Grind or chop them, not to a fine powder but until slightly coarse and gritty. Follow the Master Recipe until your mixture forms stiff dry peaks. Fold in the almonds. Divide the mixture between the circles or heart shapes and spread evenly with a butter knife or spatula. Bake immediately for 45 minutes or until crisp. The meringues should peel off the paper easily. Turn off the oven and let cool.

To make the filling, melt the chocolate with the rum and light cream very gently, either in a very cool oven, or over hot water. Cool, and then fold the mixture into the whipped cream.

To assemble, sandwich the meringues together with the filling. Decorate with rosettes of chocolate and rum cream stuck with halved toasted almonds.

Almond Meringue with Strawberries and Cream

Follow the recipe above, then sandwich together the two meringues with 1¼ cups cream, whipped, and 2 cups sliced strawberries. Decorate with rosettes of whipped cream and strawberries, or with little sprigs of mint or lemon balm.

Almond Meringue with Loganberries or Raspberries

Follow the recipe above, using 2 cups loganberries or raspberries.

Hazelnut Meringue with Raspberries and Cream

Substitute 6 tablespoons hazelnuts for the almonds, then follow the recipe above.

Walnut or Brazil Nut Meringue with Pears

Serves 6

Meringue
As for the Master Recipe
12 walnut or brazil nuts, chopped

Filling
1–2 ripe dessert pears
1 cup unsweetened whipped cream

Decoration
5 walnut halves

Follow the Master Recipe until your mixture forms stiff dry peaks. Gently fold in the chopped nuts. Bake in a very low oven 200°F (100°C) for 3–4 hours. Turn off the oven and let them get quite cold.

To assemble: put one of the meringue discs on a serving plate. Peel the pears, core, and slice. Spread most of the cream over the meringue, arrange the pears on top of the cream, and put the second disc of meringue on top of this. Decorate with rosettes of cream and walnut halves.

Ballymaloe Irish Coffee Meringue with Chocolate Coffee Beans

Serves 8

Meringue
2 egg whites
1 cup confectioners sugar
2 teaspoons instant coffee powder (not granules)

Filling
1¼ cups whipped cream
1 generous tablespoon Irish whiskey

pastry bag

Line 2 baking trays with wax paper. Follow the Master Recipe, but keep back 2 tablespoons of confectioners sugar. Whisk until mixture stands in firm dry peaks – this may take 10–15 minutes. Sift the coffee and the remaining confectioners sugar together and fold in carefully.

Use approximately half the meringue mixture to pipe 8 small rosettes onto the wax paper. Spread the remainder of the mixture carefully with a tablespoon or a butter knife into 8 circles on the wax paper.

Bake in a low oven 300°F (150°C) for approximately 1 hour or until crisp. The meringue discs should peel easily from the paper. Let them get quite cold.

To serve: add the whiskey to the whipped cream. Put a meringue disc onto a serving plate, pipe or spoon a blob of whiskey-flavored cream on top. Decorate with a meringue rosette and Chocolate Coffee Beans if available. Dust with a little sifted coffee or cocoa.

Toffee Meringue with Caramel Shards

Serves 6

Meringue
2 egg whites
1/2 cup soft brown sugar

Toffee Filling
2 teaspoons butter
1 1/2 tablespoons soft brown sugar
1 tablespoon sugar
2 tablespoons golden syrup or, if unavailable, corn syrup
2 tablespoons cream
a drop of pure vanilla extract

Decoration
2/3 cup cream, softly whipped
Caramel Shards (see right)

Preheat the oven to 300°F (150°C).

Follow the Master Recipe until the mixture makes stiff peaks. Divide the meringue between the 2 circles and spread evenly with a butter knife. Bake for 45–60 minutes, or until crisp and firm. Peel off the paper. Cool on a wire rack.

To make the filling, melt the butter with the sugars and golden syrup, simmer for about 2 minutes. Stir in the cream and a drop of vanilla extract. Continue to stir on a low heat until smooth. Let it get cold.

To assemble, spread a generous layer of whipped cream over the base of the meringue. Spoon an even layer of toffee filling on top. Cover with the second meringue disc. Decorate with a few rosettes of whipped cream and shards of caramel.

Caramel Shards
Put a layer of wax paper onto a baking sheet. Put 1/2 cup sugar into a saucepan, stir over a medium heat until melted. Let it caramelize to a pale chestnut color. Take the pan off the heat, let cool for 4–5 minutes, then drizzle the caramel over the paper in squiggles, pyramids, or latticed triangles. Let harden, peel off, and use as needed.

Variation

Toffee Meringue with Caramel Shards and Banana

Put one or two sliced bananas (tossed in a little freshly squeezed lemon juice) on top of the toffee filling.

Coffee Marjolaine Cake

Serves 8–10

If you make the cake several days in advance, it will have softened and be much easier to cut. It should be kept in the fridge, covered, at least overnight.

Meringue
3/4 cup almonds
4 egg whites
2 cups confectioners sugar

Coffee Butter Cream
1/2 cup granulated sugar
2/3 cup water
4 egg yolks
2 1/2 sticks (1 1/4 cups) butter
coffee extract to flavor (we use Irel)

Decoration
1 1/2–2 cups slivered almonds, toasted

Cover 4 baking sheets with wax paper. Draw out 4 circles, approx. 8 inches (21cm) in diameter, on the paper.

Preheat the oven to 300°F (150°C).

Blanch and skin the almonds. Chop or grind in a food processor so that they are slightly coarse and gritty, not ground to a fine powder. Follow the Master Recipe until the mixture forms stiff dry peaks. Fold in the almonds. Divide the meringue between the four circles on the wax paper, spread neatly, about 1/4-inch (5-mm) thick.

Bake immediately for about 1 hour or until the discs are quite crisp and will peel off the paper easily. Let them get quite cold.

Next make the coffee butter cream. Put the sugar and water into a small saucepan and stir over a gentle heat until dissolved.

Remove the spoon and bring to a boil, boil gently until 233–236°F (106–113°C) is reached or until the syrup is at "thread" stage. Whisk the egg yolks in a bowl until pale and fluffy. Gradually pour the hot syrup over the egg yolks, whisking all the time, continue until the mixture is thick and light.

Cream the butter and gradually beat into the egg mixture. Flavor with coffee essence. Set aside. Toast the flaked almonds and set aside to cool.

To assemble the Marjolaine, sandwich the four circles of meringue together with coffee butter cream. If necessary, trim the edges to neaten (if they are jagged it will be difficult to ice the cake), then spread more butter cream around the sides of the cake and press on the flaked almonds.

Cover the top of the cake with butter cream and sprinkle generously with the remainder of the toasted almonds. Cover and refrigerate until needed.

Meringue Roulade with Mango and Passion fruit Sauce

Serves 10

We also fill this roulade with sliced strawberries, fraises des bois, raspberries, loganberries, tayberries, blueberries, kiwi, and poached kumquats in season. Serve with a complementary sauce.

Meringue
4 egg whites
1 cup superfine sugar

Mango and Passion Fruit Sauce
1 large ripe mango
4 passion fruit
1–2 tablespoons freshly squeezed lime juice
1–2 tablespoons superfine sugar

Filling
1 large ripe mango, peeled and thinly sliced
2 passion fruit
2–2½ cups whipped cream

Decoration
sweet cicely
whipped cream

Jelly roll pan, 12 x 8 inches (32 x 20.5cm), lined with tin foil and brushed with non-scented vegetable oil

Preheat the oven to 350°F (180°C).

First make the roulade. Follow the Master Recipe to achieve a meringue that holds a stiff peak. Spread the meringue gently over the pan with a butter knife or spatula, it should be quite thick and bouncy. Bake in the pre-heated oven for 15–20 minutes. Put a sheet of tin foil on the work top and turn the roulade onto it. Remove the base tin foil and let the meringue cool.

Meanwhile, make the Mango and Passion Fruit Sauce. Peel the mango, chop the flesh, and purée in a food processor. Put into a bowl, add the passion fruit seeds and juice, add freshly squeezed lime juice, and sugar to taste. Cover and chill. Slice the mango for the filling into another bowl, add the passion fruit seeds and juice, toss gently. To assemble: turn the roulade out onto a sheet of wax paper dredged with confectioners sugar. Spread two-thirds of the cream over the roulade, cover with a layer of fruit (keeping some back for decoration). Hold your breath and roll up the roulade like a jelly roll.

Above: Meringue Roulade with Mango and Passion fruit Sauce

Transfer carefully onto a serving dish. Pipe some rosettes of cream onto the top, decorate with some of the reserved fruit. Garnish with sweet cicely, dredge with confectioners sugar and serve.

Coconut Meringue with Pineapple and Cream

Serves 10–12

Fresh mango and cream is another delicious filling for coconut meringue.

Meringue
4 egg whites
1 heaped cup superfine sugar
4 ounces dried coconut (about 4 cups)

Filling
1 ripe pineapple, peeled, sliced, cored, and cut into chunks
whipped cream

Follow the Master Recipe until the mixture forms stiff peaks, then fold in the dried coconut gently. Use a butter knife or spatula to spread the meringue mixture onto the circles and bake for 25–35 minutes or until crisp and dry. Let cool in the oven. Sandwich the layers together with fresh pineapple and cream.

Meringue Christmas Trees

See page 423.

Master Recipe
Frosted Meringue Cake

We started to make this recipe to use up left-over or broken meringues. It became such a favorite on the sweet trolley at Ballymaloe that we now have to make meringues to break meringues to make this cake! It is difficult to write the recipe accurately because it depends on the quantity and size of the broken meringue pieces.

We use about equal volume of lightly whipped cream and broken meringue. For best results the broken meringue should be in biggish chunks – say 1–1½ inches (2.5–4cm) at least, although you often have to use what you have. Err on the side of having too little rather than too much cream. Mix the broken meringue pieces gently into the whipped cream. Turn into a cake or loaf pan which is lined with plastic wrap, smooth over the top, and cover tightly. Freeze. To serve: remove from the freezer, put onto a chilled plate, and cut into thick slices in one of the following ways:

Variations
Frosted Meringue Cake with Summer Fruit and Coulis

Decorate with rosettes of whipped cream and summer berries – fresh strawberries, raspberries, loganberries, blueberries, or blackberries. Decorate with mint or lemon balm leaves, and serve a coulis made of the fruit as an accompaniment.

Frosted Meringue Cake with Chocolate Sauce

Decorate with rosettes of cream, chocolate wafers or caraque and crushed praline, and serve with Chocolate Sauce (see page 599).

Frosted Meringue Cake with Irish Coffee Sauce

Decorate with rosettes of cream, chocolate coffee beans, and crushed Praline (page 400), and serve with Irish Coffee Sauce (see page 599).

Brown Sugar Meringues

Serves 10–12

4 egg whites
½ cup superfine sugar
½ cup soft brown sugar

Filling:
1 cup heavy cream, whipped
5 tablespoons Lemon Curd (see page 510)

Preheat the oven to 225°F (110°C).

Line two baking trays with wax paper. Whisk the egg whites with both the sugars (except 2 tablespoons of superfine) until it is so stiff that the mixture will not flow at all when the whisk is lifted. Fold in the remaining sugar. Spoon or pipe the mixture in circles the size of a golf ball, onto baking trays. Bake for 1½–2 hours or until meringues are dry right through and can be easily removed from the paper (or cook for about 45 minutes if you like your meringues toffee-centered). Let cool.

Sandwich pairs with a mixture of whipped cream and lemon curd.

Srikhand

Serves 6–8

Another of Alison Henderson's delicious recipes.

2¼ pints (1kg) Greek-style yogurt or other thick, creamy yogurt
generous pinch saffron strands
2 cups superfine sugar
¼ teaspoon roughly crushed cardamom seeds
2 generous tablespoons pistachio nuts

Spoon the yogurt onto a large square of cheesecloth, tie the ends into a knot and hang over a bowl, letting it drip overnight. Tip the drained yogurt into a bowl. Infuse the saffron in a little warm water and then stir it into the yogurt, together with the cardamom seeds and the sugar. Mix well, cover, and chill. Scatter the pistachio nuts over the pudding and serve with a bowl of mixed berries.

Ice Creams

The Ballymaloe ice creams are very rich and very delicious, made on an Italian egg mousse base with softly whipped cream and flavorings added. Ice creams made in this way have a smooth texture and do not need further whisking during the freezing period. They should not be served frozen hard. Remove from the freezer at least 10 minutes before serving. The other method for making ice cream is a custard base (see Cinnamon Ice Cream, page 403).

Master Recipe
Ballymaloe Vanilla Ice Cream

Serves 6–8

Make twice this amount at a time if at all possible, especially if you are using a food mixer to whisk the mousse; less and you risk the blades not reaching all of the egg in the bottom of the bowl.

2 egg yolks
1/4 cup sugar
1/2 cup water
1/2 teaspoon pure vanilla extract
2 1/2 cups softly whipped cream (measure the cream whipped)

Put the egg yolks into a bowl and whisk until light and fluffy (keep the whites for meringues). Combine the sugar and water in a small heavy saucepan, stir over heat until the sugar is completely dissolved, then remove the spoon and boil the syrup until it reaches the "thread" stage, 223–236°F (106–113°C). It will look thick and syrupy and, when a metal spoon is dipped in, the last drops of syrup will form thin threads. Pour this boiling syrup in a steady stream onto the egg yolks, whisking all the time. Add vanilla extract and continue to whisk until it becomes a thick creamy white mousse. Fold the softly whipped cream into the mousse, pour into a bowl, cover, and freeze.

Variations

Ice Cream Sandwich

A layer of ice cream between 2 chocolate and hazelnut chip cookies.

Chocolate and Praline Ice Cream Wafers

Sandwich a slice of chocolate ice cream between 2 wafers of chocolate. Dip the sides in crushed Praline (see page 400), freeze, and serve as soon as possible.

Fudge Ripple Ice Cream

Swirl Butterscotch Sauce (see page 599) or Toffee Sauce (see page 599) through soft frozen ice cream.

Ice Cream Parfait

Fill a loaf pan lined with plastic wrap with 3 layers of vanilla ice cream, layered with crushed praline powder or with 1, 2, or 3 different ice creams in layers. Serve cut into slices, sprinkled with extra crushed praline and perhaps a Toffee Sauce (see page 599).

Ballymaloe Vanilla Ice Cream with Espresso (Affogato)

Put a scoop of vanilla ice cream into a cappuccino cup, pour a shot of espresso over the top, and serve immediately.

Ballymaloe Chocolate Ice Cream

Serves 30 or 15 depending on greed!

1/3 cup sugar
1 cup water
4 egg yolks
1 teaspoon vanilla extract
2 1/2 pints (1.2 liters) whipped cream
4 ounces (110g) dark chocolate (about 1 1/3 cups)
2 ounces (50g) (2 squares) unsweetened baking chocolate

Dissolve the sugar in the water, bring slowly to a boil and simmer until the syrup reaches the "thread stage" (it will look thick and syrupy and when a metal spoon is dipped in, the last drops will form thin threads). Meanwhile, whisk the egg yolks until white and fluffy, and when the syrup is at the correct stage, pour the boiling syrup gradually onto the egg yolks, whisking all the time. Continue to whisk until the mixture is a thick white mousse. Melt the two kinds of chocolate in a bowl over simmering water or in a very low oven. Cool slightly, add some of the mousse to the chocolate, and stir quickly, add more and then mix the two mixtures thoroughly, and fold in the softly whipped cream. Freeze until well set.

Ballymaloe Chocolate Ice Cream in Chocolate Cups with Rum Cream

Serves 6

12 individual Chocolate Cups (see page 559)

Ballymaloe Chocolate Ice Cream (see above)

Rum cream
1/2 cup whipped cream
1/2 teaspoon superfine sugar
2 teaspoons Jamaica rum

Chocolate Caraque (see below) or chocolate coffee beans
unsweetened cocoa powder

Remove the ice-cream from the freezer for about 10 minutes, meanwhile chill the chocolate cups. Whip the cream to a soft peak, fold in the rum and sugar, and continue to whip until stiff enough to pipe. Keep chilled. Spoon the ice-cream into the chocolate cups and smooth over the top, cover, and freeze again. To serve, pipe a large rosette of rum-flavored cream on top of each chocolate case, sprinkle with chocolate caraque or decorate with a chocolate coffee bean. Sift a dusting of unsweetened cocoa powder over the top of each. Serve immediately on chilled plates, allowing 2 per person.

Chocolate Caraque

4 ounces (110g) best-quality dark chocolate (about 1 1/3 cups)

There are three ways to make caraque:

1 Melt the chocolate and spread it thinly using a butter knife or spatula onto a marble slab. Let it set almost completely, then, using a sharp knife or a clean paint scraper, shave off long, thin scrolls. Use a slight sawing action and keep your hand upright. This is fun to do but there's quite a lot of skill involved. You'll improve with practice, and you can always eat the rejects!

2 Spread the chocolate in the same way on the back of a baking sheet. When it is almost set but still pliable, use a cheese slice to shave off curls of chocolate. Lay the curls on wax paper.

3 Take a large block of chocolate and use a clean potato peeler to shave off curls of chocolate from the edge of the block.

Use immediately or store in a covered box until needed.

Chocolate Decorations

Chocolate may be piped into ornamental shapes for garnishing. With some experience, one can pipe chocolate freehand into the desired shapes from a pastry bag. Beginners should pipe over traced outlines on wax paper. See page 561 for guidelines on melting chocolate.

Chocolate Shapes

Spread an even layer of melted chocolate about 1/16-inch (1.5-mm) thick onto a sheet of wax paper or a non-stick mat. Let cool to the point of setting. Cut into squares, diamonds, triangles, and use cutters to stamp out hearts or any fancy shapes that seem appropriate.

Curved Shapes

Curved shapes may be made by spreading melted chocolate over a strip of wax paper. Let cool to the point of setting, then wrap the chocolate-covered paper around flexible card or cut into triangles and wrap around a rolling pin. When the chocolate is completely set, peel off the triangles.

Chocolate Leaves

Choose stiff fresh leaves such as rose, lemon, or bay leaves, with the stem still attached. Brush some melted chocolate on the underside, being careful not to let it drip onto the other side (or they may break when you try to peel them). Arrange on a sheet of non-stick paper. When set, carefully peel away the leaf, holding onto the stem rather than the chocolate leaf.

Chocolate Mint Leaves

Dip spearmint leaves in chocolate and chill, there's no need to peel the leaves away. Serve chilled as a petit four with coffee.

Ballymaloe Coffee Ice Cream with Irish Coffee Sauce

Serves 6–8

ingredients for Ballymaloe Vanilla Ice Cream
1 tablespoon instant coffee
1/2 teaspoon boiling water

Irish Coffee Sauce (see page 599)

Follow the method for Vanilla Ice Cream, until the point you add in the vanilla extract to the mousse. Dissolve the instant coffee powder in just 1/2 teaspoon of boiling water. Add some mousse to the coffee paste and then fold the two together. Carefully fold in the softly whipped cream. Pour into a stainless-steel or plastic bowl, cover, and freeze.

To serve: scoop the ice cream into a serving bowl or ice bowl. Serve the Irish Coffee Sauce separately.

Cappuccino Ice Cream

Serves 8

ingredients for Coffee Ice Cream but substituting
1 tablespoon espresso coffee powder
1/2 teaspoon boiling water

2/3 cup light cream
unsweetened cocoa or drinking chocolate

Chocolate Caraque (see page 399)

Follow the method for Vanilla Ice Cream, until the point you add in the vanilla extract to the mousse. Dissolve the espresso powder in just 1/2 teaspoon of boiling water.

Add some mousse to the coffee paste and then fold the two together. Carefully fold in the softly whipped cream. Pour into a stainless-steel or plastic bowl, cover, and freeze.

Divide the ice cream between 8 cold-resistant tea or coffee cups (not more than half full). Cover and freeze for 5–6 hours or until set.

To serve, remove the ice cream from the freezer. Put the cups onto the saucers with a teaspoon for each. Whip the cream until soft and fluffy, spoon a little over each "cappuccino," dust with chocolate powder and some chocolate shavings or caraque. Serve immediately.

Ballymaloe Praline Ice Cream

Serves 6–8

ingredients for Vanilla Ice Cream

Praline
1 cup unskinned almonds
1/2 cup superfine sugar

Follow the method for Vanilla Ice Cream. To make the praline, put the unskinned almonds along with the sugar into a heavy saucepan over a low heat until the sugar gradually melts and turns a caramel color, and DO NOT STIR. When this stage is reached and not before, carefully rotate the pan until the nuts are all covered with caramel. When the nuts go "pop," pour this mixture onto a lightly oiled jelly roll pan or a marble slab and let them get cold. When the praline is quite hard, crush in a food processor or with a rolling pin – the texture should be quite coarse and gritty.

After about 1½ hours, when the ice cream is just beginning to set, fold in 4 tablespoons of praline powder and freeze again. (If you fold it in too early, it will sink to the bottom of the ice cream.)

To serve: scoop out into balls with an ice cream scoop. Serve in an ice bowl, sprinkle with the remainder of the praline powder.

Caramel Ice Cream with Caramel Sauce and Bananas

Serves 6–8

2 egg yolks, preferably from free-range hens
1/4 cup sugar
1/2 cup cold water
1/2 cup hot water
1/2 teaspoon pure vanilla extract
1 pint (600ml) softly whipped cream

Caramel Sauce (see page 598)

Decoration
2 bananas, sliced

Put the egg yolks into a bowl and whisk until light and fluffy (keep the whites for meringues). Combine the sugar and cold water in a small heavy saucepan. Stir over a gentle heat until the sugar is completely dissolved, then remove the spoon and boil until the syrup caramelizes to a chestnut brown.

Quickly pour in the hot water. Do not stir. Boil gently until it again becomes a smooth, thick syrup and reaches the "thread" stage, at 223–236°F (106–113°C). It will look thick and syrupy when a spoon is dipped in. Pour this boiling syrup onto the egg yolks. Add the vanilla extract and continue to whisk until it becomes a thick, creamy mousse. Fold the softly whipped cream into the mousse, pour into a bowl, cover, and freeze.

To serve: scoop the ice cream into a chilled bowl or ice bowl. Slice the bananas at an angle and add to the sauce. Spoon over the ice cream or serve separately.

Caramel Sauce keeps almost indefinitely in a glass jar in the fridge or any cold place. Our Caramel Ice Cream is also divine served in Brandy Snap Baskets (see page 424).

Strawberry Ice Cream with Fresh Strawberry Sauce

Serves 6–8

Italian ice creams and sorbets are legendary. If I had to choose just one, it would have to be strawberry.

2 lbs. (900g) very ripe strawberries
1 cup superfine sugar
1 1/4 cups water
juice of 1/2 lemon
juice of 1/2 orange
2/3 cup whipped cream

Fresh Strawberry Sauce (see page 599)

Decoration
fresh mint leaves
a few sugared strawberries

Dissolve the sugar in the water, boil for 7–10 minutes, let cool. Purée the strawberries in a food processor, or rub through a sieve. Add orange and lemon juice to the syrup. Stir into the purée, then fold in the whipped cream. Freeze in an ice cream machine or in a covered bowl in the freezer until slushy. Stir once or twice during the freezing to break up the crystals.

Meanwhile, make the Fresh Strawberry Sauce. Store in the fridge until ready to serve.

To serve: scoop out the ice cream into a pretty glass bowl and serve with a few sugared strawberries and fresh strawberry sauce. Decorate with fresh mint leaves.

Variation

Double Strawberry Ice Cream

Marinate diced fresh strawberries in a little fraises or cassis liqueur and stir into the ice cream.

Raspberry Parfait with Fresh Raspberry Sauce

Serves 6
In season: summer and autumn

Raspberries have a high water content so the clever trick in this recipe is to use gelatin to help to cut the ice crystals. Loganberries may also be used.

1 lb. (450g) fresh raspberries (about 4 cups)
1 1/4 cups sugar
2/3 cup water
1 teaspoon gelatin
1 tablespoon plus 1 teaspoon water
1 1/4 pints (600ml) whipped cream (2 1/2 cups)

Fresh Raspberry Sauce (see page 599)

Decoration
fresh raspberries
mint leaves

1 loaf pan, 5 x 8 inches (13 x 20cm), approximately

Line the loaf pan carefully with plastic wrap.
Purée, then sieve the raspberries. Dissolve the sugar in the water and boil for 2 minutes. Let the gelatin sponge in the water for a few minutes. Place the bowl of gelatin in a saucepan of simmering water until it melts and dissolves fully – there should be no residual granules.

Mix the raspberry purée with the syrup, add a little to the gelatin and then whisk the two together. Fold in the whipped cream, pour into the prepared loaf pan, cover, and freeze.

Meanwhile make the Fresh Raspberry Sauce and let cool.

To serve: Turn out the parfait and cut into slices. Serve on chilled plates, drizzled with the Fresh Raspberry Sauce. Decorate with fresh raspberries and mint leaves.

Summer Bombe with Fresh Strawberry Sauce

Serves 12–16

Ballymaloe Vanilla Ice Cream (see page 398)

Black currant Ice Cream
2 egg yolks
2½ tablespoons sugar
½ cup water
1¼ cups Fresh Black currant Sauce (see page 599)
2½ cups whipped cream

Strawberry Ice Cream (see page 401)

Decoration
8 ounces (225g) whole strawberries (about 2 cups)
whipped cream and fresh mint leaves

Fresh Strawberry Sauce (see page 599)

First make the vanilla ice cream, following the method on page 398. Put it into the freezer for about 10 minutes, so that it becomes icy cold. Line a bowl with the ice cream in an even layer, put it into the freezer and after about 1 hour, take it out and improve the shape if necessary.

Meanwhile make the fruit-flavored ice creams, beginning with the black currant. Follow the same method up to the mousse stage, then add the Black Currant Sauce. Alternatively, use raw fruit sweetened with Stock Syrup (see page 568) to taste. Taste for sweetness after adding to the mousse, adding more syrup if necessary. Fold in the cream. Cover the frozen vanilla ice cream with an even layer of the fruit-flavored ice cream and place in freezer to freeze.

Next make the Strawberry Ice Cream. and freeze in an ice cream machine or in the freezer until slushy. Fill the middle of the bombe with the strawberry ice-cream, cover the bowl with a plastic lid or plastic wrap, and freeze solid. Leave overnight if possible.

To serve, remove the bombe from the freezer and let it sit for 10–15 minutes. You may need to dip the bowl quickly into hot water to loosen the bombe. Decorate with fresh strawberries, rosettes of whipped cream, and fresh mint leaves. Serve with Fresh Strawberry Sauce.

Spanish Lemon Ice Cream with Crystallized Lemon Peel

Serves 4

This is a fresh, tangy, and light ice cream, made using an easy-peasy but quite different recipe. It is a delight to eat at the end of any meal, winter or summer.

1 egg
1 cup plus 2 tablespoons milk
½ cup plus 2 tablespoons superfine sugar
zest and juice of 1 good lemon

Decoration
Crystallized Lemon Peel (see page 515)
fresh mint leaves and borage flowers

Separate the egg, and set the white to one side, while you whisk the yolk with the milk in a small bowl. Gradually mix in the sugar. Carefully grate the zest from the lemon on the finest part of a stainless-steel grater. Squeeze the juice from the lemon and add this, along with the zest to the liquid. In a small bowl, whisk the egg white until quite stiff and fold into the lemon mixture. Freeze in a sorbetière following the manufacturer's instructions, or put in a freezer in a covered plastic container. When the mixture starts to freeze, remove from the freezer and whisk again, or break up the crystals in a food processor. Then put it back in the freezer until it is frozen completely. Meanwhile, chill the serving plates.

To serve: Scoop the ice cream into the curls, arrange on chilled plates or in pretty frosted glass dishes. Decorate with crystallized lemon peel, and, in summer, borage flowers and fresh mint leaves.

Cinnamon Ice Cream

Serves 12–15

1 cinnamon stick, 2–3 inches (5–7.5cm) in length
2 cups milk
2 cups cream
10 egg yolks, from free-range hens, if possible
1 cup sugar

Grind the cinnamon stick coarsely in a coffee grinder to make about two teaspoons full.

Put the milk in a saucepan, add the ground cinnamon, bring slowly to scalding point, add the cream, then let cool. Let it infuse for 10–15 minutes.

Whisk the egg yolks and sugar until white and fluffy, then whisk in the warm infusion. Pour back into the saucepan and cook over a gentle heat until the mixture just coats the back of a spoon. Strain it, then cool quickly and freeze in an ice cream maker or sorbetiere, according to the manufacturer's instructions. Or pour in a plastic box, cover, and put into the freezer, whisking once or twice during freezing.

Sorbets

Sorbets, water ices, or what the Italians call granita, are balm to the soul or palate in hot weather. They are a delicious way to end a meal, but are sometimes used to refresh the appetite between courses. If you have a sorbetière or an ice cream maker, sorbets can be frozen in about 25 minutes. However, you can use the freezer too, in which case you need to be ready to whisk the sorbet every few hours as it starts to freeze, in order to break up the ice crystals and keep it smooth. A stiffly beaten egg white, whisked in when the sorbet is almost frozen, keeps it light. Sorbets are very similar to sherbet but have a slightly softer feel, and don't contain milk as some sherbets do.

Strawberry Sorbet

Follow the ingredients for Strawberry Ice Cream (see page 401), omitting the cream.

Tip: If you do not have a sorbetière or ice cream maker, you can fold half a stiffly beaten egg white into the sorbet to lighten the texture.

Blackberry and Sweet Geranium Sorbet

Serves 6

1 lb. (450g) blackberries (about 4 cups)
½ cup sugar
½ cup water
4–6 large sweet geranium leaves

Put the sugar, water, and sweet geranium leaves into a saucepan and bring slowly to a boil, boil for 3–4 minutes. Let cool. Meanwhile, blend and sieve the blackberries through a nylon sieve. When the syrup is cold, mix with the blackberry purée and taste, it ought to taste a little too sweet at this stage, but add some fresh lemon juice if it's cloying.

Freeze in a sorbetière for about 20 minutes. Alternatively put into a freezer until almost frozen, stir to break up the crystals with a whisk or in a food processor, and return to the freezer. Repeat this once or twice more.

To serve: put a scoop of sorbet on chilled white plates, decorate with whole blackberries and sweet geranium leaves.

Black currant Leaf Sorbet

Serves 6
In season: early summer

2 large handfuls of young black currant leaves
1 cup sugar
2½ cups cold water
juice of 3 lemons
1 egg white (optional)

Crush the black currant leaves tightly in your hand, and put into a stainless-steel saucepan along with the cold water and sugar. Stir to dissolve the sugar, bring slowly to a boil. Simmer for 2–3 minutes. Let cool completely. Add the juice of 3 freshly squeezed lemons.

Strain and freeze for 20–25 minutes in an ice cream maker or sorbetière. If you do not have one, simply freeze the sorbet in a bowl in the freezer. When it is semi-frozen, whisk until smooth and return to the freezer again. Whisk again when almost frozen and fold in one stiffly beaten egg white. Keep in the freezer until needed.

Serve in chilled glasses or chilled white china bowls or on pretty plates lined with fresh black currant leaves.

Elderflower Sorbet

We also use the black currant leaf recipe to make an elderflower sorbet – in late spring, you can substitute 4–5 elderflower heads in full bloom. Try it with Green Gooseberry Compôte.

Tip: if you have a food processor, freeze the sorbet completely in a tray, then break up and whizz for a few seconds in the processor, add 1 lightly beaten egg white, whizz, and freeze again. Serve.

Winter Tangerine Sorbet

Serves 10–12

The quantity of ice below is enough to fill 10–18 tangerine shells. Clementines, mandarins, or satsumas may also be used.

Syrup
1 cup sugar
juice of 1/4 lemon
2/3 cup water

20–28 tangerines
juice of 1/2 lemon
confectioners sugar (optional)

Decoration
vine leaves or bay leaves

First make the syrup. Heat the first three ingredients over a low heat, until they are dissolved together and clear. Bring to a boil, and boil for 2–3 minutes. Cool. Grate the zest from 10 of the tangerines, and squeeze the juice from them.

Cut the remaining tangerines so that they each have a lid. Scoop out the sections with a small spoon and them press them through a nylon sieve (alternatively, blend the pulp and then strain). You need 1 quart (960ml) of juice. Add the grated zest, the lemon juice, and the syrup to taste. Taste, and add confectioners sugar or extra lemon juice, according to whether more sweetness or sharpness is required. Freeze until firm.

Chill the shells in the fridge or freezer, fill them with the frozen water ice. Replace the lids and store in the freezer. Cover with plastic wrap if not serving on the same day. Serve on a white plate decorated with vine leaves or bay leaves.

Julia Wight's Exquisite Black currant Sorbet

Serves 4
In season: summer

First grow your own black currants, then you will capture all the perfume of the fruit. You can also make our delicious sorbet flavored with black currant leaves.

1 lb. (450g) fresh black currants (about 4 cups)
3/4 cup superfine sugar

Purée the freshly picked berries in a blender or mouli-legumes. Rub through a sieve (this takes ages), and mix in the sugar. Freeze the mixture in an ice cream machine or put it in a container in the freezer, covered, whisking as it begins to freeze, to break up the ice crystals.

Serve on chilled plates. This looks very fetching decorated with the tiny bunches of berries, dipped first in iced water and then in superfine sugar.

Pear Sorbet

Serves 4

10 ounces (275g) ripe Bartlett pears (about 2 medium)
2 lemons
3/4 cup confectioners or superfine sugar

Peel the pears, cut into quarters, and core. Rub the pieces all over with half a lemon to keep them white. Put the quartered pears in a small saucepan along with the sugar and just enough cold water to cover them. Poach gently for 10–15 minutes or until a knife will pierce them easily.

Remove the pears and reduce the cooking liquid until it starts to thicken and become syrupy, but don't let it get brown. Let the pears and syrup get quite cold, then add the juice of a lemon. Purée everything together in a blender or food processor. Taste, and pour the mixture into an ice cream maker or sorbetière and freeze. Alternatively, put it in a container in the freezer, covered, whisking as it begins to freeze, to break up the ice crystals.

To serve, scoop the sorbet into balls with a tablespoon dipped in hot water, and serve on well-chilled plates.

Thai Coconut Sorbet

Serves 6–8

1 x 14-ounce (400-ml) can coconut milk (we use Chaokah)
1/2 cup sugar
2/3 cup water
juice of 1 small lemon

First make the sugar syrup. Put the sugar and water into a small saucepan, bring to a boil, and simmer for 2–3 minutes. Cool and refrigerate. When the syrup is chilled, whisk in the coconut milk and lemon juice. Taste, then pour the mixture into an ice cream maker or sorbetière, and freeze. Alternatively, put it in a container in the freezer, covered, whisking as it begins to freeze to break up the ice crystals. Serve on chilled plates with fresh pineapple.

Lemon Verbena or Lemon Balm Sorbet

Serves 8

Rory O'Connell served this deliciously fresh sorbet as an appetizer in Ballymaloe, it just flits across the tongue and scarcely needs to be swallowed. A perfect start, or end, if you prefer, to a late summer meal.

1 cup sugar
2 1/2 cups cold water
2 large handfuls of lemon verbena or lemon balm leaves, or one handful of each
freshly squeezed juice of 3 lemons
1 egg white (optional)

Put the first three ingredients into a non-reactive saucepan and bring slowly to a boil, and simmer for 2–3 minutes. Let it get quite cold. Add the lemon juice. Strain, and freeze for 20-25 minutes in an ice cream maker or sorbetière.

Alternatively, freeze the sorbet in a bowl in the freezer. When it is semi-frozen, whisk until smooth and return to the freezer again. Whisk again when almost frozen and fold in one stiffly beaten egg white. Keep in the freezer until needed. Serve in chilled glasses or chilled white china bowls. Decorate with lemon balm and verbena leaves.

Melon Sorbet with Lime Syrup

Serves 6–8 as an appetizer or a dessert

This sorbet, too, works well either as an appetizer or a dessert.

1 x 1-lb. (450-g) Charentais or Ogen Melon
1 small lemon
1/3-1/2 cup superfine or confectioners sugar
pinch of salt
1 cup Stock Syrup (see page 568)
1 lime

Decoration
1 small melon
fresh mint or lemon balm leaves

Cut the melon in half horizontally. Take out the seeds and then scoop out the flesh and purée in a blender. Strain the puréed melon into a bowl through a fine sieve or strainer. Add the lemon juice, sugar, and a tiny pinch of salt, and whisk to dissolve the sugar. Taste, and pour the mixture into an ice cream maker or sorbetière and freeze. Alternatively, put it in a container in the freezer, covered, whisking as it begins to freeze to break up the ice crystals.

Remove the zest from the lime with a zester, add to the syrup, then add the juice of half the lime.

To serve: quarter the small melon, remove the seeds, and cut into thin slices. Arrange 3 or 4 slices on chilled plates. Put a scoop of sorbet beside the melon, spoon a little syrup and zest over the slices, and decorate with fresh mint or lemon balm leaves.

Espresso Granita

Serves 6–8

2 1/2 cups Espresso coffee
2 1/2 cups (Stock Syrup (see page 568)
whipped cream

Mix the coffee and syrup together in a bowl. Put into a plastic container and freeze for a couple of hours until just beginning to freeze at the edges. Whisk the frozen mixture into a liquid. Re-freeze and repeat the whisking every few hours. Meanwhile chill some serving glasses.

Remove from the freezer 10 minutes before serving. Spoon some granita into a chilled glass. Spoon a layer of whipped cream on top, then another layer of granita, more cream, and finally granita. Serve immediately.

Black currant Parfait with Black currant Coulis

Serves 8

This exquisite black currant mousse is rich and intense. It needs softly-whipped cream as an accompaniment. Fresh black currants are bursting with vitamin C.

12 ounces (350g) black currants, fresh or frozen (about 3 cups)
1 cup sugar
4 egg yolks
1 1/2 teaspoons gelatin or 1 1/2 leaves of gelatin
2/3 cup cream
2 teaspoons crème de cassis

Fresh Black Currant Sauce (see page 599)
a little whipped cream, whole black currants, and a few lemon balm leaves for decoration

8 x individual molds or 1 x flan ring, lightly oiled or lined with plastic wrap

To make the parfait, put the black currants and sugar in a heavy stainless steel saucepan and let the sugar dissolve slowly before the mixture comes to a boil. Then boil gently for 2 minutes.

Meanwhile, whisk the egg yolks until they become a pale lemon-colored mousse. Whizz the black currants in a food processor, then push the mix through a nylon sieve to get a smooth purée. Pour directly onto the egg yolks and whisk up to a stiff mousse.

Put 2 tablespoons of cold water in a small bowl or heatproof measuring cup, sprinkle the gelatin over it, and let it sponge for a few minutes. Put the bowl into a saucepan of boiling water and let the gelatin dissolve, it should be liquid and clear with no trace of granules. (If using leaf gelatin, cover the leaves with cold water for 10 minutes or so, discard the water, and then dissolve the softened leaves in 2 tablespoons of water in the saucepan.)

Meanwhile, lightly whip the cream softly. When the gelatin has dissolved, blend carefully with the black currant mousse. (Add a little of the mousse mixture to the gelatin first, and then fold this into the remainder of the mousse.) Finally, add the crème de cassis and fold into the lightly whipped cream. Turn the mousse into 1 large mold or into 8 individual molds. Allow 2–3 hours for the small molds to set in the refrigerator, 4–5 hours for the large one.

Prepare the Black Currant Sauce. If the purée you obtain is very thin, use 1 teaspoon gelatin to set 1 cup of sauce, then let it cool before you add the water. For this dessert, we sometimes pour some of the thick black currant purée, before the water has been added, over the top of the parfait to make a shiny top.

To serve: pour a little Black Currant Sauce on each of 8 white plates, if the mousses are in individual molds. Turn out a mousse into the center of the coulis. Decorate the coulis by piping on cream and "feathering" it with the tip of a knife, if you like. Pipe a little rosette of cream on top of the mousse, put a whole black currant in the center, and decorate with lemon balm leaves. Serve with softly whipped cream.

Alternative serving suggestion:
Set in pretty cocktail glasses, spoon a little thick purée over the top, and decorate with fresh black currants and black currant leaves.

Passion Fruit Mousse with Sugared Strawberries

Serves 12

10 passion fruit
2 leaves gelatin (or 2 teaspoons powdered gelatin)
2½ tablespoons water
1¼ cups cream
¼ cup superfine sugar

Decoration
1 lb. (450g) strawberries, superfine sugar, and mint leaves
Fresh Strawberry Sauce (see page 599), optional

12 individual ramekins or soufflé dishes, brushed with non-scented vegetable oil

Cut the passion fruit in half and scoop out the pulp and seeds. Purée in a food processor (not a blender, as this will crush the seeds), then strain through a nylon sieve or cheesecloth.

Soften the leaves of gelatin or sponge the powdered gelatin in the water for a few minutes, then dissolve fully over a pan of hot water.
Add some of the passion fruit pulp to the gelatin, then stir both mixtures together thoroughly. Chill, stirring from time to time. Whip the cream until fairly stiff but not grainy, and add the sugar. Fold carefully into the passion fruit mixture, just as it begins to set. It should be a smooth creamy mixture. Spoon the mixture into the ramekins or soufflé dishes and chill for 1–2 hours before serving. Meanwhile slice the strawberries and sprinkle with superfine sugar.

To assemble: ease the mousses gently out of the molds (dip the bottoms into hot water for a few seconds if necessary to loosen them). Place each mousse in the center of a white plate, decorate with sugared strawberries and fresh mint leaves. Drizzle with Fresh Strawberry Sauce, if using.

Cold Lemon Soufflé

Serves 6–8

Mouth-wateringly light. Best made with fresh unwaxed lemons.

2½ lemons, preferably organic or unwaxed
3 large eggs
1 cup superfine sugar
1¼ cups cream
scant ½ ounce (10g) gelatin (about 1½ tablespoons)
2½ tablespoons water
¼ cup cold water
oil

Decoration
⅔ cup whipped cream
2 generous tablespoons toasted chopped almonds
sprigs of lemon balm or sweet geranium leaves
Crystallized Lemon Peel (see page 515), optional

1 x 6-inch (15-cm) soufflé bowl or 6–8 small bowls or a pretty glass bowl
wax paper

Grate the zest of the lemons on the finest part of the grater and squeeze and strain the juice. Separate the eggs and put the yolks, sugar, and grated lemon zest into a bowl. Put the whites to one side.

Using an electric food mixer if possible, whisk the egg yolk mixture until thick and fluffy. Heat the lemon juice, add to the egg yolks, and continue to whisk until the mousse reaches the "ribbon" stage, which takes about 15 minutes. If you don't have a food mixer, place a Pyrex bowl containing the yolks, sugar, grated lemon zest, and strained lemon juice, in a saucepan of barely simmering water, and whisk the mixture until quite thick. Remove from the heat and continue to whisk until the bowl is cold.

Put the cold water in a small bowl, sprinkle the gelatin over the top, stir, and let sponge until the water has absorbed the gelatin. Put the bowl into a saucepan of simmering water until the gelatin has dissolved completely.

Meanwhile, whip the cream softly and fold into the mixture. Stir a few tablespoons of the lemon mixture in the dissolved gelatin and then carefully fold both mixtures together. Set the soufflé mixture on ice or chill in the refrigerator. Fold a strip of wax paper, deep enough to come half-way up again over the top of the bowl. Brush the paper with a non-scented vegetable oil and tie it firmly around the bowl.

Just as the mixture begins to thicken, whisk the egg whites until they form a stiff peak, fold gently into the soufflé base. Pour into the prepared soufflé bowl and put in a cool place to set for several hours.

When the soufflé is set, peel off the paper. Press the toasted nuts gently around the sides. Decorate the top with rosettes of cream, crystallized lemon peel (if using), and tiny sprigs of lemon balm or sweet geranium leaves.

Variation

Lime Soufflé

Follow the above recipe but use 3 limes. Decorate with very fine slices of lime which have been simmered in a sugar syrup until they are translucent.

Carrigeen Moss Pudding

Serves 4–6

Carrigeen moss is bursting with goodness. I ate it as a child but never liked it as it was always too stiff and unpalatable. Myrtle Allen changed my opinion. Hers was always so light and fluffy. This is her recipe, it's the best and most delicious. We find that visitors to the country are fascinated by the idea of a dessert made with seaweed and they just love it. The name, carrigeen, comes from "little rock."

a scant 1/4 ounce (6g) cleaned, well dried carrigeen moss (1 semi-closed fistful)
1 quart (960ml) milk
1 egg
1 tablespoon superfine sugar
1/2 teaspoon pure vanilla extract or a vanilla bean

softly-whipped cream
soft brown (Barbados) sugar

Soak the carrigeen in tepid water for 10 minutes. Strain off the water and put the carrigeen into a saucepan with milk and vanilla bean, if using. Bring to a boil and simmer very gently with the lid on for 20 minutes.

At that point and not before, separate the egg, put the yolk into a bowl, add the sugar and vanilla extract, if using, and whisk together for a few seconds, then pour the milk and carrigeen moss through a strainer onto the egg yolk mixture, whisking all the time. The carrigeen will now be swollen and exuding jelly. Rub all this jelly through the strainer and beat it into the milk mixture. Test for a set in a saucer as one would with gelatin.

Whisk the egg white stiffly and fold or fluff it in gently. It will rise to make a fluffy top. Serve chilled with soft brown (Barbados) sugar and cream, and/or with a fruit compôte, say poached rhubarb.

Pannacotta

Serves 6–8

2 1/2 cups heavy cream
1/4 cup superfine sugar
1–2 vanilla beans, split lengthwise
scant 2 teaspoons gelatin
2 1/2 tablespoons water

6–8 1/2-cup molds, lightly brushed with non-scented vegetable oil

Put the cream into a heavy saucepan along with the split vanilla beans and sugar. Put on a low heat and bring to the "shivery" stage.

Meanwhile, sponge the gelatin in the water and put the bowl in a saucepan of simmering water until the gelatin is fully dissolved. Add a little of the cream to the gelatin, then stir both mixtures together. Remove the vanilla beans, then pour into the molds. When cold, cover and refrigerate until set, preferably overnight.

Serve with summer berries, fruit salad with sweet geranium leaves, Green Gooseberry Compôte or Apricot and Cardamom Compôte, or simply a dark, almost bitter, Caramel Sauce (see page 598).

Pannacotta with Espresso

Make the Pannacotta. Pour into cups or small bowls. Cover and chill. When ready to serve, pour a shot of espresso over the top of the pannacotta. Serve immediately.

Ballymaloe Crème Brûlée

Serves 4

The ultimate custard! It was created in Trinity College, Cambridge and is a universally favorite pudding. I like to eat it with a compôte of fruit – perhaps poached apricots with sweet geranium leaves.

Custard
2 large egg yolks, from free-range hens, and organic
1/2 tablespoon sugar
1 1/4 cups heavy cream
1/2 vanilla bean, optional

Caramel topping
1/2 cup sugar
1/3 cup water
1/2 cup whipped cream, optional

Make the custard the day before the crème brûlée is needed. Mix the egg yolks with the sugar. Heat the cream with the vanilla bean to the "shivery" stage but do not boil. Pour the cream slowly onto the egg yolks, whisking all the time. Return to the saucepan and cook on a medium heat, stirring until it is thick enough to coat the back of a spoon. It must not boil. Remove the vanilla bean, pour into a serving dish, and chill overnight. Be careful not to break the skin or the caramel may sink later.

The following day, make the caramel.

Dissolve the sugar for the caramel topping in the water. Bring to a boil and cook until it caramelizes to a chestnut brown color. Remove from the heat and immediately spoon a thin layer of caramel over the top of the custard. Let it get cold and pipe a line of whipped cream around the edge to seal the joint where the caramel meets the side of the dish. Serve within 12 hours, or the caramel will melt.

To serve, crack the top by knocking sharply with the back of a serving spoon.

Note: Two yolks only just set the cream. Be sure to use big eggs and measure your cream slightly short of 1¼ cups. The cream takes some time to thicken and usually does so just under boiling point. If the custard is not properly set, or if the skin which forms on top while cooling is broken, the caramel will sink to the bottom of the dish. If there are cracks in the custard, freeze the pudding for 1–2 hours before spooning on the hot caramel.

The alternative way to make the topping is to sprinkle the custard with a layer of white superfine sugar or pale tubinado or golden sugar, spray with a film of cold water, then caramelize with a blow torch.

Variations

Crème Brûlée with Praline Topping

Instead of the caramel topping, sprinkle finely crushed Praline (see page 400) over the chilled custard not more than 30 minutes before serving.

Star Anise Crème Brûlée

Add 6 star anise to the cream instead of the vanilla bean. Heat very slowly and infuse for 15 minutes before removing.

Due Kem Caramen (Vietnamese Crème Caramel)

Serves 6

A variation on the classic French dessert.

½ cup palm sugar (jaggery) or golden brown sugar
½ cup water
1 cup milk
1 cup coconut milk
4 eggs
¼ cup golden brown sugar
½ teaspoon pure vanilla extract

6 ramekins

Put the sugar and water into a heavy saucepan over a medium heat, stir until all the sugar is dissolved, and the mixture turns to a rich brown caramel. Pour the caramel syrup into 6 ramekins, swirling it around so that it coats the sides a little as well as the bottom. Preheat the oven to 325°F (170°C).

Put the coconut milk and the milk into a saucepan, stir, and heat until it starts to bubble around the edge. Meanwhile, whisk the eggs in a mixing bowl with the golden sugar and vanilla extract. Remove the milk from the heat and pour it steadily over the egg mixture, whisking all the time.

Divide the mixture between the ramekins, cook in a bain-marie with boiling water to halfway up the side of the ramekins. Bake in the preheated oven for 40 minutes or until just cooked.

Remove from the oven and let cool. Run a knife around the edge of each one and turn them out onto individual dessert plates.

Sue Cullinane's Banoffee Pie

Banoffee Pie is none the worse for being prepared a day in advance.

2 x 14-ounce (400-ml) cans condensed full cream sweetened milk
¾ stick (⅓ cup) butter
8 ounces (225g) digestive biscuits or graham crackers
6–8 bananas, depending on size
1 lemon
2 cups heavy cream
¼ cup coffee essence or Tia Maria
toasted slivered almonds

12-inch (32-cm) removable-bottomed pan, lightly oiled with non-scented vegetable oil

Put the unopened tins of condensed milk into a saucepan, keep covered with water, and simmer for 3 hours (it is worth doing a few extra for the next time you make this!).

Melt the butter in a pan over a gentle heat. Crush the biscuits (put them in a plastic bag and use a rolling pin) and add to the butter. Line the bottom of the pan with the biscuit mix and let it set.

Open the tins of milk and spread the toffee contents over the bottom of the biscuit crust. Slice the bananas, toss in freshly squeezed lemon juice, and arrange on top of the toffee.Whip the cream, add the coffee essence or Tia Maria. Spread over the bananas. Cover lightly and refrigerate to set. Serve sprinkled with the toasted almonds.

Variation

Mini Banoffee Pies

Make individual pies in tiny sundae glasses.

Chocolate Fudge Pudding

Serves 6–8

Chocolate puddings run neck and neck with apple tarts as people's favorite dessert. This one is wickedly rich with a melting texture. It should be moist in the center, so don't overcook or it will be dull.

5 ounces (150g) best-quality chocolate (about 1 2/3 cups)
1 1/4 sticks (2/3 cup) unsalted (sweet) butter
1 teaspoon pure vanilla extract
2/3 cup warm water
1/2 cup superfine sugar
4 eggs
1/4 cup self-rising flour
pinch of cream of tartar

2 1/2-pint (1.2-liter) capacity pie dish or 8 individual 3-inch (8-cm) ramekins, well greased with a little butter

Preheat the oven to 400°F (200°C).

Break up the chocolate into small pieces and melt, along with the butter, in a Pyrex bowl over a pan of simmering water. As soon as the chocolate has melted, removed from the heat, add the vanilla extract, then stir in the warm water and sugar. Continue to stir until the mixture is smooth. Separate the eggs, whisk the yolks into the chocolate mixture, then fold in the sifted flour. Whisk the egg whites in a clean bowl with a pinch of cream of tartar, until it reaches stiff peaks. Fold this gently into the chocolate mixture and pour into the dish or ramekins.

Put in a bain-marie of hot water and cook for 10 minutes (for the single dish), then lower the heat to 325°F (170°C) and cook for a further 20–30 minutes. If you are cooking individual ramekins, they will only need 15 minutes at the higher heat. The pudding should be firm on top but still soft and fudgy underneath. Cool a little and dredge with confectioners sugar. Serve with softly whipped cream.

Tiramisù

Serves 8

Tiramisù is now well established on the dessert menu. This luscious cake looks stunning and is very easy to serve.

2 1/2 packets of Boudoir biscuits – about 90 biscuits
2 1/2 cups strong espresso coffee (if your freshly made coffee is not strong enough, add 1 teaspoon of instant espresso powder)
1/4 cup brandy
1/4 cup Jamaica rum
5 ounces (150g) dark chocolate (about 1 2/3 cups)
5 eggs, separated
1/2 cup superfine sugar
15 ounces (425g) mascarpone cheese
unsweetened cocoa
1 cup toasted hazelnuts, chopped

9 1/2-inch (24-cm) round springform "angelfood cake" pan, lined with a double thickness of wax paper.

Mix the coffee with the brandy and rum. Roughly grate or chop the chocolate (we do it in the food processor using the pulse button). Whisk the egg yolks with the sugar until you have a mousse that has reached the "ribbon" stage and is light and fluffy. Fold in the mascarpone, a tablespoon at a time. Whisk the egg whites stiffly and fold gently into the cream cheese mixture. Now you are ready to assemble the Tiramisu.

Dip each side of the Boudoir biscuits, one at a time, into the coffee mixture, and arrange side by side upright against the walls of the pan and also line the bottom of the pan. Spread one-third of the mascarpone mixture gently over the biscuits, sprinkle a third of the grated chocolate over the top, continue with another layer of soaked biscuits, more mascarpone, a sprinkle of chocolate, more biscuit, and finally mascarpone. Cover the whole pan carefully with plastic wrap or better still, slide it into a plastic bag and secure the end. Refrigerate for at least 4 hours.

Unmold onto a serving plate and pat the toasted hazelnuts onto the sides of the cake. Sprinkle the top with chopped chocolate and sprinkle with cocoa.

The Tiramisù Cake will keep for several days in a fridge, but keep it covered so that it doesn't pick up any taints.

Variation

Tiramisù in Chocolate Cups

Fill Chocolate Cups (see page 559) with Tiramisù and dredge the top with unsweetened cocoa.

Chocolate Mousse

Serves 8–10

Rich, sinful, and really good! Make sure your chocolate has a high percentage of cocoa solids. You can use milk chocolate if you prefer the taste, or a mixture of milk and dark.

8 ounces (25g) best-quality dark chocolate (about 2 2/3 cups)
1 tablespoon unsalted (sweet) butter
2/3 cup water
1 tablespoon Jamaican rum, optional
6 small or 4 large eggs

ramekins or Chocolate Cups (see page 559)

Break the chocolate into small pieces and put in a bowl along with the butter and water, and melt over a low heat. Stir gently until melted and completely smooth. Remove from the heat, let cool, then whisk in the rum (if using). Separate the eggs, letting the whites fall into a bowl, and add the yolks to the chocolate mixture.

Whisk the egg whites and fold them in. Beat for 5–6 minutes: this makes the mousse smooth and silky and it will thicken towards the end. Turn into ramekins or fill little Chocolate Cups (see page 559). Let set for 5–6 hours or overnight. Serve with a rosette of cream and a little unsweetened cocoa powder.

Master Recipe

Darina Allen's Bread and Butter Pudding

Serves 6–8

Bread and butter pudding is the most irresistible way of using up leftover white bread – this is a particularly delicious recipe. Cinnamon or mixed spice may also be used but nutmeg is our favorite.

12 slices good-quality white bread, crusts removed
1/2 stick (1/4 cup) butter, preferably unsalted
1/2–1 teaspoon freshly grated nutmeg
a scant cup golden raisins
4 large eggs, from free-range hens, and organic, beaten lightly
1 pint (600ml) cream
1 cup milk
1 teaspoon pure vanilla extract
3/4 cup superfine sugar
pinch of salt
1 tablespoon granulated sugar for sprinkling

Garnish
softly whipped cream

1 x 8-inch (20.5-cm) square earthenware or china dish

Butter the bread and arrange 4 slices, buttered side down, in a single layer in the dish. Sprinkle the bread with freshly grated nutmeg and half the raisins. Arrange another layer of bread, buttered side down, over the fruit, and sprinkle the remaining nutmeg and raisins on top. Cover with the remaining bread, again buttered side down.

In a bowl, whisk the eggs, add the cream, milk, vanilla extract, sugar, and a pinch of salt. Pour the mixture over the bread through a fine sieve or mesh strainer. Sprinkle the sugar over the top and let the mixture stand, covered loosely, at room temperature for at least 1 hour, or chill overnight.

Preheat the oven to 350°F (180°C). Place in a bain-marie – the water should go halfway up the sides of the baking dish and bake in the middle of the oven for about 1 hour until the top is crisp and golden. Serve warm, with softly whipped cream.

Variations

Gooseberry and Elderflower Bread and Butter Pudding

Make a Gooseberry and Elderflower Compôte by putting 2 pounds (900g) of gooseberries into a saucepan with 2 cups of sugar and 3 elderflower heads tied in a cheesecloth bag. Stir over a moderate heat until the fruit bursts, and discard the elderflowers. Follow the Master Recipe, substituting gooseberries for the raisins. Reserve a little of the compôte to serve with the pudding.

Rhubarb Bread and Butter Pudding

Slice 1 pound (450g) of red rhubarb into 1/2-inch (2-cm) pieces, put into a dish and sprinkle with sugar, and let macerate for an hour. Follow the Master Recipe, substituting the rhubarb for the raisins.

Irish Barmbrack and Butter Pudding

Follow the Master Recipe, using 12 slices yeast barmbrack instead of the Panettone.

Brioche Bread and Butter Pudding

Follow the Master Recipe, spreading the brioche with apricot jam and adding a little apricot brandy to the cream.

Panettone Bread and Butter Pudding

Follow the Master Recipe, substituting Panettone for the white bread, and brandy or eau de vie in place of the vanilla extract.

Savory Bread and Butter Puddings

Try zucchini, lots of basil, and a well-seasoned cheese sauce with lots of Parmesan. Or a Tomato Sauce with lots of Parmesan. One of our favorite ideas is to add asparagus and Fontina cheese.

Below: Our garden angel – Eileen

Crêpes with Orange Butter

Serves 6 – makes about 12 crêpes

This crêpe recipe is very nearly as good as those Crêpes Suzette they used to serve with a great flourish in posh restaurants when I was a child. These are, though, only half the trouble and can be made for a fraction of the cost.

Crêpe Batter
1½ cups white flour, preferably unbleached
a good pinch of salt
2 teaspoons superfine sugar
2 large eggs plus 1 or 2 egg yolks
1¾ cups (or a smidge more) milk, or for very crisp, light delicate pancakes, milk and water mixed
2–3 tablespoons melted butter

Orange Butter
1½ sticks (¾ cup) butter
1 tablespoon finely grated orange rind
1⅔ cups confectioners sugar

freshly squeezed juice of 5–6 oranges

8-inch (20.5-cm) non-stick crêpe pan

First make the batter. Sift the flour, salt, and sugar into a bowl, make a well in the center and drop in the lightly-beaten eggs. With a whisk or wooden spoon, starting in the center, mix the egg and gradually incorporate the flour. Add the liquid slowly and beat until the batter is covered with bubbles. (If the crêpes are to be served with sugar and lemon juice, stir in an extra tablespoon of superfine sugar, and the finely grated rind of half a lemon.)

Let the batter stand in a cold place for an hour or so – longer will do no harm. Just before you cook the crêpes, stir in 2–3 tablespoons melted butter. This will make all the difference to the flavor and texture of the crêpes and will make it possible to cook them without greasing the pan each time.

Next, make the orange butter. Cream the butter with the finely grated orange rind. Then add the sifted confectioners sugar and beat until fluffy.

When you are ready to eat, heat the pan to very hot, pour in just enough batter to cover the bottom of the pan thinly, swirling the batter around to get it even. Loosen the crêpe around the edge, flip over with a spatula or quick flick of the wrist, cook for a second or two on the other side, and slide off the pan onto a hot plate. The crêpes may be stacked on top of each other and peeled apart later. If you have several crêpe pans, it is perfectly possible to keep 3 or 4 pans going in rotation, but this is only necessary if you need to feed the multitudes.

Tip: the crêpes will keep in the fridge for several days and also freeze perfectly. If they are to be frozen, put a disc of wax paper between each for ease of separation.

To serve: melt a blob of the orange butter in the pan, add some freshly squeezed orange juice, and toss the crêpes in the foaming butter. Fold in half, and then in quarters, to make fan shapes. Serve 2 per person on warm plates, spooning the buttery orange juices over the top. Repeat until all the crêpes and butter have been used.

Note: A tablespoon of orange liqueur, e.g., Grand Marnier or Orange Curaçao, is very good added to the orange butter if you are feeling extravagant!

Variations

Rosalie's Crêpes with Toffee Sauce and Bananas

Follow the Master Recipe to make the crêpes. To serve: fold 2 warms crêpes into a fan shape and arrange on a warmed plate. Top each portion with half a sliced banana and hot Toffee Sauce (see page 599). Put a dollop of cream or ice cream alongside, and serve immediately.

Crêpes with Chocolate Sauce

Follow the Master Recipe to make the crêpes. Serve with Chocolate Sauce (see page 599) and toasted hazelnuts.

Apple Crumble

Serves 6–8

Crumbles are the ultimate comfort food. Vary the fruit according to the season; use plums or apricots in autumn. In summer you can use soft fruit, such as peaches and raspberries, in which case there is no need to pre-cook the fruit base.

1½ lbs. (700g) Bramley Seedling or other tart cooking apples (e.g. Granny Smiths)
3–4 tablespoons sugar
1–2½ tablespoons water

Crumble
1 cup white flour, preferably unbleached
½ stick (¼ cup) butter
¼ cup superfine sugar

2½-pint (1.2-liter) capacity pie dish

Stew the apples gently with the sugar and water in a covered flameproof casserole dish or stainless steel saucepan until about half-cooked. Taste, and add more sugar if necessary. Turn into a pie dish. Let cool slightly while you make the crumble. Preheat the oven to 350°F (180°C).

Rub the butter into the flour just until the mixture resembles coarse bread crumbs, then add the sugar. Sprinkle this mixture over the apple in the pie dish. Bake for 30–45 minutes or until the topping is cooked and golden. Serve with whipped cream and soft brown sugar, or try stirring a little Amaretto into your cream.

Variations

Blackberry and Apple Crumble

Use three-quarters apple to one-quarter fresh or frozen blackberries, and proceed as above.

Rhubarb Crumble

Use the same weight of rhubarb as in the apple recipe, stew with just sugar – no water – until half cooked, and proceed as above.

Rhubarb and Strawberry Crumble

Stew two-thirds rhubarb with sugar, stir in one-third strawberries, and proceed as above.

Gooseberry Crumble

Stew green gooseberries with brown sugar, and proceed as above.

Gooseberry and Elderflower

Stew green gooseberries with white sugar and 2 elderflower heads tied in cheesecloth. After stewing, remove elderflowers and proceed as above.

Variations on the Crumble

Add 1/4 cup rolled oats or sliced hazelnuts or nibbed almonds could be added to the crumble. A teaspoon of ground cinnamon or pumpkin pie spice is also a delicious addition.

Peach and Raspberry Crisp

Serves 8

A few summers ago I spent some time at Zingermann's Deli in Ann Arbor, Michigan. They make sensational sandwiches, salads, and desserts. Ari Weinzweig sent me a recipe for this delicious dessert.

2 lbs. (900g) peaches
3/4 lb. (350g) raspberries (about 3 cups)
1 tablespoon cornstarch

Crisp
1 cup all-purpose white flour
a heaped cup brown sugar
3 cups rolled oat
1/4 teaspoon freshly ground nutmeg
1/4 teaspoon ground cinnamon
1 stick (1/2 cup) butter, melted

lasagne-type dish measuring 10 1/2 x 9 1/2 inches (25 x 24cm) at the base

Preheat the oven to 350°F (180°C).

Put all the dry ingredients for the Crisp into a bowl, add the melted butter, and mix until crumbly. Slice the fruit into a bowl. Sprinkle with cornstarch and mix well. If the fruit is unusually tart you may need a little sugar. Top with an even layer of crumble – a generous 1/2-inch (1-cm) thick. I use about a pound (450g) of the Crisp mixture and keep the rest for another time or to use with another fruit.

Bake in a preheated oven for 30–40 minutes or until the topping is crisp and the fruit tender. The juices should bubble up around the edges. Serve with softly whipped cream.

Sticky Toffee Pudding

Serves 6–8

8 ounces (225g) chopped dates (about 1-1 1/3 cups)
1 1/4 cups tea
1 stick (1/2 cup) unsalted (sweet) butter
3/4 cup superfine sugar
3 eggs
2 cups self-rising flour
1 teaspoon baking soda
1 teaspoon vanilla extract
1 teaspoon espresso coffee

Toffee Sauce (see page 599)

8-inch (20.5-cm) springform pan with removable bottom

Preheat the oven to 350°F (180°C). Soak the dates in hot tea for 15 minutes. Brush the cake pan with oil and line the bottom with oiled wax paper.
Cream together the butter and sugar until light and fluffy. Beat in the eggs, one at a time, and then fold in the sifted flour. Add the sifted baking soda, vanilla extract, and coffee, to the dates and tea, and stir this into the batter. Turn into the lined pan and cook in the preheated oven for 1–1 1/2 hours or until a skewer comes out clean.

About 10 minutes before the end of cooking time, make the Hot Toffee Sauce.

To serve: pour some hot sauce on to a serving plate. Put the sticky toffee pudding on top, pour more sauce over the top. Put the remainder into a bowl to serve with the pudding, as well as softly whipped cream.

Spiced Pan-Roasted Pear Cake

Serves 8–10

The incorrigible Antony Worrall-Thompson is one of our favorite guest chefs – this goodie came from him.

1 cup soft brown sugar
1 stick (1/2 cup) unsalted (sweet) butter, cut in four
1 1/2 cups all-purpose flour
a generous cup superfine sugar
2 teaspoons cinnamon
1 1/4 teaspoons baking powder
1/2 teaspoon salt
2 large eggs
2/3 cup sunflower oil
1 pear, coarsely grated
1 tablespoon peeled and grated ginger
4 pears, peeled, cored, and cut into 6

1 round pan, 9 inches (23cm) in diameter and 2 1/2 inches (6cm) high

Preheat oven to 350°F (180°C).

Sprinkle brown sugar over the bottom of the cake pan. Add the butter to the pan. Place the pan in the oven until the butter melts (about 5 minutes).
Mix the flour, sugar, cinnamon, baking powder, and salt together. Beat in the eggs and oil. Mix in the grated pear and ginger. Remove the cake pan from the oven and whisk the butter and sugar until the sugar dissolves.

Arrange the pear slices in the pan. Pour the batter over the pears and bake until the cake is springy to the touch and a skewer comes out clean – this takes about 1 hour.

Let cool slightly; loosen the edges of the cake with a knife and turn out onto a hot plate. Serve warm with softly whipped cream or Homemade Vanilla Ice Cream (see page 398).

Cullohill Apple Pie

Serves 8–12

This tart was a favorite of patrons of my family's pub, the Sportsmans Inn in Cullohill, County Laois. The dough is made by the creaming method so people who are convinced they suffer from "hot hands" don't have to worry about rubbing in the butter. Use it for a variety of fruit tarts. It can be difficult to handle when first made, and benefits from being chilled for at least an hour, or preferably overnight.

2 sticks (1 cup) butter
1/4 cup superfine sugar
2 eggs, preferably from free-range hens, and organic
3 cups white flour, preferably unbleached

1 1/2 lbs. (700g) Bramley Seedling or other tart cooking apples, e.g., Granny Smiths
2/3 cup sugar
2–3 cloves

egg wash
superfine sugar for sprinkling

1 rectangular pan, 7 x 12 x 1 inch, (18 x 32 x 2.5cm) or 1 round pan, 9 inches (23cm) in diameter

First make the dough. Cream the butter and sugar together by hand or in a food mixer. Add the eggs and beat for several minutes. Reduce the speed and mix in the flour. Turn out onto a piece of floured wax paper, flatten into a circle, wrap, and chill overnight, if possible.

Preheat the oven to 350°F (180°C).

Use a little less than two-thirds of the pastry dough to line the pan. Roll the dough to a thickness of approximately 1/8 inch (3mm). Peel and dice the apples and place into the pan. Sprinkle with sugar and add the cloves. Cover with the rolled pie dough, seal the edges, and use the leftover dough to decorate the top. Brush with egg wash and bake in the preheated oven for 45–60 minutes until the apples are tender. When cooked, cut into squares, sprinkle lightly with superfine sugar, and serve with whipped cream and Barbados sugar.

Flaky Pastry Dough

For this pastry dough, the method must be carefully followed and the dough rolled correctly. Butter is the most suitable fat. All ingredients should be chilled. Flaky pastry dough may be kept wrapped in the fridge for 1–2 days or it may be frozen. This pastry dough is more economical to make than puff pastry, and gives a very good flaky result, suitable for all dishes, both sweet and savory, where you might use puff pastry, except perhaps vol au vents or feuilletée.

3 cups all-purpose white flour
pinch of salt
2 sticks (1 cup) butter
1/2 cup cold water, approx. (if using bread flour, more water may be needed)

Sift the flour and salt into a bowl. Divide the butter into four equal parts. Rub one part of this into the flour and mix to a firm dough with the cold water. Cover with plastic wrap and let rest for 15–20 minutes in the fridge.

Roll out into a strip about 8 inches (20.5cm) wide, and dot tiny pieces of a second portion of the butter on two-thirds of the pastry dough. Fold in three, being careful to align all the edges. Turn the pastry 90 degrees (so that it looks like a book) and roll out, pressing it away from you. Fold in three again, cover, and let rest again for 15–20 minutes in the fridge.

Roll out as before, dot tiny pieces of the third portion of butter on two-thirds of the strip, again fold in three carefully, roll, fold in three, rest as before, then add the final portion of butter, roll out once more, fold in three again. If the pastry dough still appears streaky, roll it one more time. Cover, and let rest in the refrigerator for at least 20–30 minutes.

Wrap in plastic wrap or wax paper if not using immediately.

Ballymaloe Flaky Fruit Tart

Virtually every night at Ballymaloe House there's a warm fruit tart on the sweet trolley. You can use the Flaky Pastry Dough, or the pastry dough used for our Cullohill Apple Pie, to make tarts with whatever fruits are in season: some of our favorites are:

Rhubarb and Strawberry
Green Gooseberry and Elderflower
Apple and Mincemeat
Apple and Raspberry
Apple and Loganberry
Apple and Apple Spice
Peach and Raspberry
Plum
Damson
Apricot

Open French Apple Tart

Serves 8–12 (Makes about 12 tartlets or two open tarts, 8 inches (20.5cm) in diameter)

8 ounces (225g) Flaky Pastry Dough (see page 413) or puff pastry trimmings
3 or 4 cooking apples, e.g., Bramley or Granny Smith
2 tablespoons sugar, approx.
2 teaspoons butter

Preheat the oven to 425°F (220°C).

Line pie plates or patty shell tins with thinly rolled pastry dough, about as thick as a coin for tartlets, slightly thicker for tarts. Thinly peel and quarter apples, then cut them into slices 1/8-inch (3-mm) thick, keeping a good even shape. Arrange them on the pastry shells in overlapping slices. Sprinkle liberally with sugar and dot with pieces of butter. Bake for about 15 minutes in the hot oven. The juice of the apples will caramelize the sugar.

Remove from the tins immediately, otherwise they will stick fast as the caramel cools. Serve with a bowl of softly whipped cream.

Apple and Sweet Geranium Vol au Vents

Makes 12–14 individual vol au vents or 2 large ones

1 1/4 lbs. (600g) Puff Pastry Dough (see page 456)
a scant 2 cups Pastry Cream (see page 460)
egg wash
a generous cup whipped cream
4–5 tablespoons Calvados or other apple brandy
Apple and Sweet Geranium Compôte (see page 524)

Prepare the puff pastry following the recipe. Preheat the oven to 475°F (240°C).

To make individual vol au vents (patty shells), roll out puff pastry to 1/4-inch (5-mm) thick. Stamp out 3-inch (8-cm) circles, and egg wash carefully. This quantity should give you at least 12. Make the center by cutting halfway into the circles of dough with a 1 1/2-inch (4-cm) cutter. Score the pastry dough in a pattern.

To make 2 large vol au vents, roll the dough to 1/2-inch (1-cm) thickness. Use a 9-inch (23-cm) dinner plate as a guide to cut two circles. Cut the pastry at an angle all around the dinner plate. Turn the pastry upside down, miraculously it will now rise with straight sides.

Egg wash carefully and, if possible, refrigerate for 5–10 minutes. Mark an inner circle with an 8-inch (20.5-cm) cutter (we use a saucepan lid as a template) and then cut halfway into the pastry with a tip of a knife. When the vol au vent has been cooked, you will be able to remove this inner circle to use as a lid.

Decorate the edges and score around the center. Place the vol au vents on a heavy baking sheet that has been sprinkled with a few drops of water. If possible, refrigerate for 15–30 minutes, and then bake in a very hot oven 475F° (240°C) about 20 minutes for small vol au vents, 30–40 minutes for large ones. Turn down the heat to 425°F (220°C) after about 15 minutes.

When the vol au vents are risen and well-browned, remove the lids and scrape out the soft pastry from the inside. Return to the oven to dry for a few minutes. Do not fill until completely cold.

Stir the Calvados into the Pastry Cream and then fold in the whipped cream. The mixture should be fairly stiff; if it is too stiff, add a little of the juice from the cooked apples. Taste, and add a little more Calvados if you like.

Fill the vol au vent cases half to two-thirds full with this mixture, top with apple slices. Put on the pastry lid and dredge heavily with confectioners sugar.

The vol au vents will be delicious if served almost immediately with Apple and Sweet Geranium Compôte.

Pâte Sucrée or French Flan Pastry

The French make pastry dough directly on the work top. This method produces a different textured dough. Delicious for tarts, both sweet and savory.

1 cup all-purpose white flour
tiny pinch of salt
1/2 stick (1/4 cup) unsalted (sweet) butter
1/4 cup superfine sugar
2 egg yolks, preferably from free-range hens
2 drops of pure vanilla extract

Sift the flour with a pinch of salt on to the table or marble slab, make a well in the center, and in this, place the other ingredients. Using the fingertips of one hand, work the butter, sugar, and yolks together until mixed; then quickly draw in the flour. Toss up between your fingers until it becomes quite sandy. Gather up into a ball, then work with the heel of the hand, gather up again, work again, and once more, 3 times in all.

Wrap in a plastic bag or paper, and chill for at least 1 hour before using. Preheat the oven to 375°F (190°C).
Bake the pastry until it is a pale biscuit color. Be careful not to overcook because if this pastry gets too brown it will be bitter, hard, and unappetizing.

Pâte Brisée or Savory Shortcrust Pastry Dough

Follow the recipe for Pâte Sucrée, omitting the sugar.

Tarte Française

Serves 4
In season: all year

The secret of a successful Tarte Française is tightly packed, neatly over-lapping rows of fruit – be generous with both fruit and glaze. Remember, the jam is the only sweetener in the dish so do be generous. In the autumn, a tart can be made with a combination of dark fruits, which looks spectacular – blueberries, raspberries, figs, damsons, dark plums, red currants, black currants and blackberries. Use red currant jelly to glaze red and black fruits.

6 ounces (175g) Flaky Pastry Dough (see page 413) or Puff Pastry (see page 456)
egg wash

Filling
A mixture of fruit:
2 oranges
1/2 cup black grapes
2 bananas
1 kiwi fruit
1 red plum
Apricot Glaze (see page 508)

Preheat the oven to 425°F (220°C).

Roll out the dough into a rectangle about 10 x 8 inches (25.5 x 20.5cm). It should be about 1/8-inch (3-mm) thick. Prick lightly all over. Cut a border 3/4-inch (2-cm) wide from the remaining pastry dough, to exactly fit the rectangle. Brush the outside edge of the rectangle with a little beaten egg and put the border on top.

Flour the blade of a knife and use this to "knock up" the sides of the pastry dough: what you are doing is slightly separating the leaves of the pastry horizontally so that the edges will flake during cooking.

Mark a pattern on the border of the tart shell with the back of the knife. Try not to cut through the pastry.

Brush the pastry border carefully with egg wash. Don't let it drip over the side or it will prevent the pastry from rising. Bake in the preheated oven for 15–20 minutes or until golden brown, then reduce the temperature to 350°F (180°C). Let cool on a wire rack.

Segment the oranges, cut the grapes in half, and remove the seeds, peel and slice the bananas. Remove the seed from the plum and cut the plum into small neat segments; peel and slice the kiwi fruit.

Arrange the fruit in contrasting rows on the pastry as neatly as possible. Brush generously with apricot glaze. Serve with a bowl of softly whipped cream.

Tarte Tatin

Serves 6–8
In season: all year but best in late autumn

The ultimate French apple tart. The Tatin sisters ran a restaurant at Lamotte-Beuvron in Sologne at the beginning of the last century. They created this tart, some say accidentally, but however it came about it is a triumph – soft, buttery, caramelized apples (or you can use pears) with crusty golden pastry underneath. It is unquestionably my favorite French tart! One can buy a special copper tatin especially for this tart.

2 3/4 lbs. (1.25kg) approx. Golden Delicious, Cox's Orange Pippin, Bramley Seedling, or Granny Smith cooking apples
6 ounces (175g) Puff Pastry (see page 456) or rich French Flan Pastry Dough (see left)
1 stick (1/2 cup) unsalted (sweet) butter
1 cup superfine sugar

a heavy 8-inch (20.5-cm) tatin mold or copper or stainless-steel sauté pan with low sides

Preheat the oven to 425ºF (220ºC) for puff pastry or to 350ºF (180ºC) for regular pie dough.

First, roll out the pastry dough into a circle slightly larger than the mold or pan. Prick it all over with a fork and chill until needed. Peel, halve, and core the apples. Melt the butter in the ovenproof pan, add the sugar, and cook over a medium heat until it turns golden – the color of fudge. Put the apple halves in upright, peeled side down, packing them in very tightly side by side. Replace the pan on a low heat and cook until the sugar and juice are a dark caramel color. Hold your nerve otherwise it will be too pale. Put into a hot oven for about 15 minutes.

Cover the apples with the pastry dough and tuck in the edges. Put the pan back into the oven until the pastry is cooked and the apples are soft – about 25–30 minutes. For puff pastry, reduce the temperature to 400°F (200°C) after 10 minutes.

Take out of the oven and rest for 5–10 minutes or longer if you like. Put a plate over the top of the saucepan and flip the tart on to a serving plate. (Watch out – this is a rather tricky operation because the hot caramel and juice can ooze out. Do it quickly and confidently). Reshape the tart if necessary and serve warm with softly whipped cream.

Sally Clarke's Hazelnut and Chocolate Tart

Serves 8

Pastry Dough

1½ cups white flour
¾ stick (⅓ cup) butter
2 teaspoons of superfine or confectioners sugar
beaten egg to bind

Filling

1¾ cups hazelnuts
3 ounces (75g) best-quality dark chocolate (1 cup)
¾ stick (⅓ cup) butter, unsalted (sweet)
⅔ cup superfine sugar
2 beaten eggs
1 teaspoon orange zest
¼ cup all-purpose white flour
3 tablespoons freshly squeezed orange juice

1 x 9-inch (23-cm) pie plate

First make the pastry dough, following the instructions as for Pâte Sucrée on page 415. Line the pan and bake the pie shell using wax paper and baking beans to weigh it down.

Preheat the oven to 350°F (180°C).

Put the hazelnuts on a baking sheet and bake until the skins start to flake away. Rub off the skins with a cloth and chop the hazelnuts roughly.

Chop the chocolate into small pieces.

Cream the butter with the superfine sugar until light and fluffy. Add 1 egg. Lightly beat in the remaining ingredients, adding the remaining egg last.

Spread this mixture in the cooked pie shell and bake 20–25 minutes. Serve when cool. It should be slightly soft in the center.

Mary Risley's Rustic Peach Tart with Summer Berries

Serves 6–8

Pastry Dough

2 cups all-purpose white flour
1 tablespoon sugar
1 stick (½ cup) butter , cut into ½-inch (1-cm) dice
cold water or beaten egg to mix

Filling

⅓–½ cup superfine sugar
2 generous tablespoons cornstarch
1½–2 lbs. (700–900g) ripe peaches or nectarines, peeled and sliced ½-inch (1-cm) thick
1 cup fresh blueberries
1 cup fresh raspberries or loganberries
1 tablespoon, approx, superfine sugar for sprinkling

1 x 9-inch (23-cm) pie plate or tart pan

First make the pastry dough. Sift the flour into a bowl and add the sugar. Rub in the cold butter. When the mixture resembles coarse breadcrumbs, add just enough water or beaten egg to bind. Knead lightly to bring the mixture together. Cover with wax paper and rest in the fridge for at least 20 minutes.

Roll out the dough on a lightly floured surface into a 14-inch (35-cm) circle. Line the pie plate or tart pan with it but do not trim it. Put the plate over a bowl to let the edge hang down, and chill for 30 minutes in the fridge.

Just before baking, preheat the oven to 450°F (230°C) and prepare the filling. Mix the sugar with the cornstarch. Toss in the sliced peaches or nectarines. Let sit for 5 minutes and no more, tossing occasionally. Stir the blueberries and raspberries gently into the peaches. Pour the fruit and the juices onto the chilled pie shell and distribute them evenly. Fold the overhanging edge to cover the outer portion of the filling, leaving a 5 inch (12.5 cm) opening of exposed fruit in the center of the pie. Brush the pastry dough with water, sprinkle with a little sugar.

Bake in the preheated oven for 20 minutes. Reduce the temperature to 350°F (180°C) and bake for a further 30–35 minutes. Serve warm or cold with softly whipped cream.

Right: Caramelized Banana Tart

Tuscan Plum Tart

Serves 10–12
In season: autumn and winter

We ate this gorgeous tart in a little restaurant outside Chianti. It's a real wow for an autumn party and so easy to make. You need a pan that can be used in the oven as well as on the stove.

2 lbs. (900g) plums
1¼ sticks (⅔ cup) soft butter
¾ cup sugar
1¾ cups self-rising flour
3 eggs

1 x 10-inch (25-cm) ovenproof sauté pan or a cast-iron frying pan

Preheat oven to 325°F (170°C).

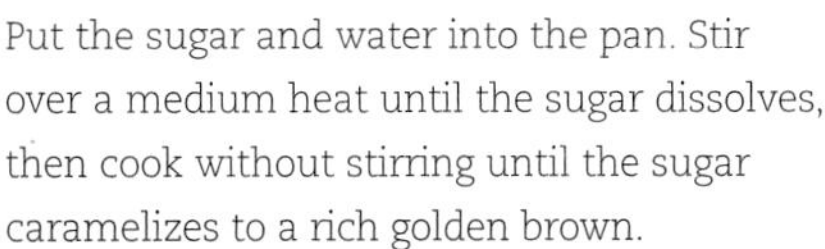

Put the sugar and water into the pan. Stir over a medium heat until the sugar dissolves, then cook without stirring until the sugar caramelizes to a rich golden brown.

Meanwhile cut the plums in half and remove their seeds, and arrange cut side down in a single layer over the caramel.

Put the butter, sugar, and flour into the bowl of a food processor. Whizz for a second or two, add the eggs, and stop as soon as the mixture comes together. Spoon over the plums, spread gently in as even a layer as possible.

Bake in the preheated oven for about one hour. The center should be firm to the touch and the edges slightly shrunk from the sides of the pan. Let rest in the pan for 4–5 minutes before turning out. Serve with crème fraîche or softly whipped cream.

Caramelized Banana Tart

Serves 6–8

Rich and sticky, another delicious dessert for chilly days. This one was inspired, as on many occasions, by a recipe from Sue Lawrence.

Base
¾ stick (⅓ cup) butter
3 tablespoons soft brown (Barbados) sugar
3 tablespoons superfine sugar
4–5 bananas
a little freshly squeezed lemon juice

Topping
1 ripe banana, mashed
2 tablespoons crème fraîche (if unavailable, use thick cream or sour cream)
1 teaspoon pure vanilla extract
¾ cup superfine sugar
¾ stick (⅓ cup) butter
2 eggs
1½ cups self rising flour

1 flameproof and ovenproof sauté pan, 10 inches across x 2 inches deep (25.5 x 5cm) deep, or a similar heavy weight pan.

Preheat the oven to 350°F (180°C).

Melt the butter in the sauté pan or heavy pan, add the sugars, and stir well to dissolve. Slice the bananas and arrange in concentric circles over the bottom. Squeeze a little freshly squeezed lemon juice over the bananas.

Next make the topping. Mash the banana, add the crème fraîche and vanilla extract. Cream the butter, add the sugar, and beat until light and fluffy. Add the eggs one at a time and continue to beat well. Gently fold in the flour and banana mixture alternately.

Spread the topping evenly and carefully over the bananas.

Bake in the pre-heated oven for 45–50 minutes or until golden brown and fully cooked.

Let rest in the dish for 5–10 minutes before turning out onto a warm serving plate, so that the bananas are uppermost. Be careful of the hot juices.
Serve warm with softly whipped cream or crème fraîche.

Winter Apple Pie

Serves 8–10

This pie, in fact, uses a scone dough, which cooks on top and is then inverted for serving.

2½ lbs. (1.1kg) apples
1 cup, or a bit more, granulated sugar
1–1½ teaspoons ground cinnamon or apple spice

Scone Dough
2¾ cups flour
1½ tablespoons sugar
1 heaped teaspoon baking powder
pinch of salt
½ stick (¼ cup) butter
1 egg
¾ cup whole milk, approx.
egg wash

9 x 2 inch (23 x 5cm) flameproof and ovenproof round pan.
(We use a heavy stainless steel sauté pan, which works very well; if you don't have a suitable flameproof and ovenproof pan, par cook the apples slightly first, and then transfer to an ovenproof pan)

Preheat the oven to 450°F (230°C).

Peel and core the apples, cut into chunks. Put into the bottom of a pan or sauté pan, sprinkle with the sugar, and cinnamon or apple spice. Put the sauté pan on a low heat while you make the scone dough.

Sift all the dry ingredients into a bowl. Cut the butter into cubes and rub into the flour until the mixture resembles coarse breadcrumbs. Whisk the egg with the milk. Make a well in the center of the dry ingredients, pour in the liquid all at once and mix to a soft dough. Turn out onto a floured board and roll into a 9-inch (23-cm) circle about an inch (2.5cm) thick. Place this circle on top of the apple and tuck in the edges neatly. Brush with a little egg wash.

Bake in the fully preheated oven for 15 minutes, then reduce the temperature to 350°F (180°C) for a further 30 minutes approx. or until the top is crusty and golden and the apples soft and juicy.

Remove from the oven and let sit for a few minutes. Put a warm plate over the top of the sauté pan, and turn upside down onto the plate but be careful of the hot juices.

Serve warm with soft brown sugar and cream.

Variations

Apple and Mincemeat Pie

Omit the cinnamon or apple spice. Put a layer – about 1 cup of mincemeat (see page 515) on top of the apples and continue as above.

Rhubarb Pie

Follow the recipe for Winter Apple Pie, substituting rhubarb, and sugar to taste, for the apples.

Elsa Schiller's Apple Strudel

Makes 2 strudels – serves 12–14

Strudel can be served cold but the pastry softens, so in my opinion apple strudel is best served fresh from the oven. The pastry dough for strudel is very similar to phyllo.

Pastry Dough
3 cups flour
pinch of salt
1 egg, preferably from a free-range hen
½ teaspoon oil, e.g., sunflower or peanut
½ teaspoon vinegar
⅔ cup lukewarm water

Filling
2 lbs. (900g) cooking apples (Bramley Seedling or Grenadier or Granny Smiths, etc.)
½ cup golden raisins
⅓–½ cup superfine sugar
1 teaspoon ground cinnamon
grated rind of 2 lemons, or 1 orange and 1 lemon
½ cup chopped walnuts
1¼ cups ground almonds
½ stick (¼ cup) butter, for brushing strudel

For serving
confectioners sugar
softly whipped cream
soft brown sugar

Sift the flour and salt into a bowl, add the egg, oil, and vinegar, and enough warm water to mix to a smooth pliable dough.

Knead for 8–10 minutes, then cover and let it rest for 30 minutes in a warm kitchen.

Meanwhile, prepare the filling. Peel the apples, cut into quarters, remove cores, and cut into thin slices. Mix the sliced apples with the raisins, sugar, cinnamon, lemon peel, and chopped walnuts.

Preheat the oven to 450°F (230°C).

Divide the dough into two, keep one piece covered. Spread a tablecloth over a work surface, large enough to roll the dough to a 3 x 2 feet (90 x 60cm) shape. Flour it well. Roll out one half of the dough as thinly as possible with a rolling pin, then stretch into an oblong shape as gently as possible using floured hands. Do not hurry – do this gradually, and eventually you should be able to see your hand through the pastry dough. Try not to have any holes if possible. When the rectangle of dough is as near as possible to 3 x 2 feet cut off the thick edges and let the pastry dough harden slightly for about 15 minutes. Brush with melted butter, sprinkle with half the ground almonds, and lay half the filling over two-thirds of the pastry dough. Roll up the narrow end so that the outside of the strudel is wrapped in several layers of pastry. Pinch the ends of the roll together and cut off any excess pastry.

Make the second strudel in the same way. Transfer the strudels to a buttered baking sheet and shape into a crescent. Brush with melted butter and cook for 10 minutes in the hot oven. Reduce the temperature to 400°F (200°C) and cook for a further 20 minutes. Brush with melted butter 3 or 4 times during cooking.

When the strudels are cooked, dust with confectioners sugar and serve immediately with a bowl of softly whipped cream and soft brown sugar.

Right: Elsa Schiller's Apple Strudel

Brandy Snap Baskets

Makes 12

Brandy snaps may be stored in an airtight tin for several days.

1 stick (1/2 cup) butter
1/4 cup superfine sugar
5 tablespoons golden syrup, or 1/4 cup corn syrup plus 1 tablespoon molasses
juice of 1/2 lemon
1 cup white flour
large pinch of ground ginger

clean small jars to use as molds

Preheat the oven to 350°F (180°C). Line a baking sheet with wax paper. Over a low heat, gently melt the butter and the sugar and golden syrup in a pan, then remove from the heat and stir in the sifted flour, lemon juice, and ginger. Let cool.
Drop generous tablespoon-sized blobs of the mixture onto the baking tray, spaced well apart. They should spread into a 5–6-inch (12.5–15-cm) circle. Bake for 5–6 minutes or until lacy and golden.

Meanwhile, have your jars upturned, ready to use as molds. Let the brandy snap baskets cool for a minute or so, then lift them quickly off the tray using a spatula. Shape them over the upturned jars to form your baskets. Cool on a wire rack. Do one tray at a time, otherwise they will harden before you have time to shape them. Fill with sliced bananas, Butterscotch Sauce, and caramel ice cream.

Brandy Snaps

Follow the recipe above and roll around the handle of a wooden spoon while the snaps are still warm. As soon as they harden and cool, slide off on to a wire rack. Fill with brandy-flavored whipped cream.

Brandy Snap Petit Fours

Drop 1/2 level teaspoonfuls of the mixture onto the baking sheet and cook as above. As soon as they are cooked, roll around a pencil or skewer.

Above: Brandy Snaps. Right: Brandy Snap Baskets

Myrtle Allen's Plum Pudding with Brandy Butter

Serves 8–10

Making the Christmas Puddings (from *The Ballymaloe Cook Book* by Myrtle Allen)

The tradition that every member of the household could have a wish, which was likely (note, never a firm promise) to come true, was, of course, a ruse to get all the children to help with heavy work of stirring the pudding. I only discovered this after I was married and had to do the job myself. This recipe, multiplied many times, was made all at once. In a machineless age, mixing all those expensive ingredients properly was a formidable task. Our puddings were mixed in an enormous china crock which held the bread for the household for the rest of the year. My mother, nanny, and the cook, took it in turns to stir, falling back with much panting and laughing after a few minutes' work. I don't think I was really much help to them.

Christmas puddings should be given at least 6 weeks to mature. They will keep for a year. They become richer and firmer with age, but one loses the lightness of the fruit flavor. We always eat our last plum pudding at Easter. If possible, prepare your own fresh beef suet – it is better than the pre-packed product.

3/4 cup shredded beef suet (or use the vegetarian substitute)
3/4 cup sugar
4 cups soft breadcrumbs
1 cup currants
1 cup raisins
3/4 cup candied peel or citrons
1–2 teaspoons apple spice
pinch of salt
21/2 tablespoons flour
1/4 cup flesh of a baked apple

3 eggs
1/4 cup Irish whiskey
4-pint (1.8-liter) capacity pudding basin or ovenproof bowl, greased

Mix the dry ingredients thoroughly. Whisk the eggs and add them, along with the apple and whiskey. Stir very well indeed. Fill the pudding bowl. Cover with a circle of wax paper or a butter-paper pressed down on top of the pudding. Put a large circle of wax or brown paper over the top of the bowl, tying it firmly under the rim. Place in a saucepan, one-third full of boiling water, and simmer for 10 hours. Do not let the water boil over the top, and do not let it boil dry either. Store in a cool place until needed.

On Christmas Day: Boil for 1½–2 hours before serving. Leftover pudding may be fried in butter. Serve with brandy butter.

Brandy Butter

3/4 stick (1/3 cup) butter
3/4 cup confectioners sugar
3–8 tablespoons brandy

Cream the butter until very light, add the icing sugar and beat again. Then beat in the brandy, drop by drop. If you have a food processor, use it: you will get a wonderfully light and fluffy butter.

Christmas Fruit Salad

Serves 10

a generous 3/4 cup sugar
1 cup water
juice of 2–3 limes
1 large or 2 small melons
1½ cups green grapes
4 small juicy pears, if under-ripe, poach for a few minutes in a light syrup (see page 568)
1 star fruit (carambola), optional
4 passion fruit
4 bananas
1 pomegranate or 4 ounces (110g) kumquats

Put the sugar and water into a saucepan, bring to a boil, cook for 2 minutes, (if using carambola, slice into 1/8-inch (3-mm) thick slices, and poach in the hot syrup for approximately 10 minutes), let cool. Remove the lime zest with a zester, add to the syrup, along with the freshly squeezed lime juice.

Cut the melon in 2, remove the seeds, scoop the flesh into balls using a melon baller, and then scrape the remainder into the bowl also. Discard the rind. If you have the energy, peel and seed the grapes, otherwise just cut in half and remove the seeds; either way, add to the melon in the bowl.

Peel the pears, cut in quarters, remove the core, and slice lengthwise, and add to the rest. Cut the passion fruit in half, scoop out the seeds, add to the fruit along with the sliced banana. Cut the pomegranate in half around the equator and carefully remove the jewel like seeds from the membrane, and add the seeds to the fruit salad. Let it macerate for at least 1 hour. Serve chilled.

Christmas Fruit Salad with Kumquats and Star Fruit

Slice the kumquats and star fruit in thin rounds. Divide the syrup* in half, and poach each fruit individually. Star fruit will take about 10 minutes, kumquats about 15–20 minutes. Chill, add lime zest and juice, and then add the remainder of the fruit.

* Do not add the lime syrup and zest until later.

Lemon Meringue Pie

Serves 6

1 cup white flour
1/2–3/4 stick (1/4–1/3 cup) butter
pinch of salt
1 egg yolk (keep the white aside for meringue)
about 2 tablespoons cold water

Lemon Curd (see page 510)

Meringue
2 egg whites, preferably from free-range hens
1/2 cup superfine sugar
7-inch (18-cm) round pie or tart pan with a removable bottom

First make the dough. Sift the flour with the salt, cut the butter into cubes, and rub into the flour using your fingertips. Keep everything as cool as possible; if the fat is allowed to melt, the finished pastry dough may be tough. When the mixture looks like coarse breadcrumbs, stop. Whisk the egg and add the water. Take a fork or knife (whichever you feel most comfortable with), and add just enough liquid to bring the pastry dough together, then set the fork down and use your hands to collect it into a ball, this way you can judge more accurately if you need a few more drops of liquid. Cover with plastic wrap and chill for half an hour, if possible. Roll out the pastry dough, line the tart pan, and chill again for 15–20 minutes. Line the pie shell with wax paper, and fill with dried beans. Bake blind for 25 minutes, 350°F (180°C). The pie shell must be almost fully cooked. Remove paper and beans, paint the shell with a little lightly beaten egg white, and put back into the oven for 5 minutes approx.

Meanwhile, make the Lemon Curd and pour into the pie shell. Next, make the Meringue – whisk the egg whites in a perfectly clean dry bowl, until they begin to get fluffy, then add half the sugar and continue to whisk until they form stiff peaks. Fold in the remaining sugar and either pipe or spread the meringue over the lemon mixture, using a spoon. Turn the oven down to 250°F (130°C) and bake for about 1 hour, until the mixture is crisp on the outside. Serve warm or cold.

Variation

Mile High Lemon Meringue Pie

Double the quantity of meringue in recipe and pile into a cone or pyramid on top of the tart.

Left: Myrtle Allen's Plum Pudding with Brandy Butter

cheese

cheese

One of the most exciting developments on the Irish food scene over the past 20 years has been the emergence of an Irish farmhouse cheese industry. Prior to that, we were a nation of Calvita eaters (a hugely processed cheese wrapped in tin foil). This farmhouse cheese industry, made up of passionate, spirited, and deeply dedicated people, has had an impact far out of proportion to its size, and has helped in no small way to change the image of Irish food, both at home and abroad.

At Ballymaloe House, we have a cheese trolley every night. We proudly serve five, six, and sometimes more, Irish farmhouse cheeses for our guests to taste. It is part of our menu so they do not have to choose between cheese and dessert, and they seem to love to hear about the local cheesemakers who now make prize-winning cheeses.

Just as all wine: red, white, rosé, or bubbly; dry, medium, or sweet, starts with a bunch of grapes, so all cheese starts with milk. It can be cow's milk, goat's milk, sheep's milk, buffalo milk or even camel's milk. The diversity is truly amazing. Milk sours and curdles naturally, so cheese, like many other things, will have been discovered by accident originally. There are various theories, some say it was Arab nomads who made the discovery when carrying milk in a bag made from a calf stomach – who knows?

Most cheese is now made from pasteurized milk – a controversial subject. Connoisseurs of good cheese believe that a truly great cheese can only be made from un-pasteurized milk since it still contains the natural bacteria, which contributes to the cheese's unique character and flavor. Food technologists argue that when milk is pasteurized, it is then sterile so cheesemakers are in control of the quality and can introduce exactly the starters they choose. The issue is certainly not black and white – a skilled cheesemaker can make superb cheese starting with pasteurized milk, whereas a less skilled or knowledgeable operator can manage to make a poor quality product with raw milk. In Europe the farmhouse cheesemakers are under continuous pressure to pasteurize their milk. Several organizations, including the Slow Food Movement and the Euro Toque Association of Chefs, are battling to save the raw milk cheeses and to safeguard our right as consumers to have the choice.

We teach each batch of 12-week certificate students at the school the rudiments of cheese making and how to make a cottage cheese. Each day, one of the students looks after the cheeseboard for lunch. They learn how to care for cheese and label it, so that the other students can become familiar with their names. Most Irish cheeses are called after the townland where it is made or after an Irish saint, as in St. Tola and St. Killian. They are made from cow, goat, or ewe's milk – Milleens, Gubbeen, Durrus, Baylough, Cashel Blue, Desmond, Croghan, Min gabhair, Ardsallagh, Kerry, Knockalara, Cooleney, Coolea, Abbey Blue, Killorglin, Ardrahan, Lavistown, Ring, Boilie… there are over 80 to choose from.

One of the highlights of the term is when we take the students to visit a farmhouse cheesemaker's. They meet the cheesemakers themselves and see the process from beginning to end. As with harvesting the vegetables, this gives them a greater understanding and appreciation, not only of the passion and dedication, but of the sheer hard work that goes into making a farmhouse cheese.

A Plate of Irish Farmhouse Cheeses
The Irish farmhouse cheesemakers are a charismatic lot – mostly women with just a few exceptional men. I feel truly grateful to these artisans who spend long hours making and nurturing their cheese, which is what it takes to ensure that each cheese develops to its full peak of perfection, as the season changes. It is sheer joy to talk to them about their produce. Many speak of their cheese fondly, as though they were their children – sometimes behaving well, sometimes naughty. Veronica Steele, who is considered to be the matriarch of the farmhouse cheese-makers, refers to her small Milleens as her "little dotes."

Many of the Irish farmhouse cheeses are available outside Ireland in specialist cheese shops. Some, however, are not exported, so when you come to Ireland, seek them out and taste these wonderful cheeses that are sweeping the boards at all the top cheese-shows worldwide.

Types of Cheese
Every cheese is different. The nature of the paste, rind, veins, and the size of the holes are all clues to the condition of the cheese. Many cheeses now carry an Appellation d'Origine, so read the label carefully. Sometimes the rind of the cheese itself is stamped, for example Parmigiano Reggiano, Gruyère, and Emmenthal. If it is a French cheese, the label will also tell you if the cheese is made in a farmhouse (*fermier*) or a factory (*laitier*), and whether it is made from pasteurized or unpasteurized milk (*lait cru*). It will also indicate the type of milk used and the fat content.

Soft Cheeses
Very soft cheeses must be kept refrigerated and should be eaten within two days. These cheese are uncooked and unripened – e.g., cottage cheese, curd cheese, fromage frais, fromage blanc, quark, Petit Suisse, and Camargue and Puzol. Cream cheese such as Mascarpone is, as the name implies, made from cream rather than milk.

Soft spreadable cheeses include Coulommiers, Explorateur, Taleggio, Brie, and Camembert. These cheeses are sprayed with a mold (*Penicillium candidum*), which develops into a bloomy white rind.

Semi-soft cheeses are slightly firmer, often crumbly, springy in texture, but still moist – e.g., Gorgonzola, Cashel Blue, St. Paulin, Reblochon, Munster, Gubbeen, and Durrus. The distinctive rind of the latter cheese comes from a culture of *Breyibacterium linens*.

Semi-hard cheeses form the largest cheese family. They can be sliced easily. Cheddar types include Cheddar, Cheshire, Caerphilly, Wensleydale, Double Gloucester and Stilton, and Raclette. Gouda types include Gouda and Edam. Gruyère types are Gruyère, Comté, Fontina, Jarlsberg, and Appenzell.

Hard Cheeses
These are pressed to produce a dense cheese which may be sliced when young but needs to be grated when old. Grana-type cheese, Parmesan (Parmigiano Reggiano), Grana Padana, Pecorino Romano, mature Gruyère and Emmenthal, mature English Cheddar, aged Gouda, Desmond and Gabriel.

Buying Cheese
Wherever feasible, buy a whole cheese in perfect condition. Alternatively, buy a freshly cut piece of cheese rather than a prepacked section. Cheese should be cut cleanly with a wire or a special cheese knife, and wrapped in cheese paper, greaseproof paper or tin foil – not in plastic. Unless you can trust your cheesemonger implicitly, it is vital that you know a little about the character of the cheeses – as with wine. This knowledge comes from lots of tasting and accumulated experience. Meanwhile, find a reputable shop that has a wide selection of cheese in good condition. This is not always easy because many shops either have a very poor selection, or else they stock far too many cheeses without having the turnover to justify it, and so many of the cheeses are past their best.

Storing Cheese
For perfection, cheese (other than very fresh soft cheese) should be stored in a cool pantry or cheese cupboard. If you do store cheese in a fridge, keep it in the warmest part, and remove it a few hours before serving to let it come back to room temperature. Hard or semi-hard cheese needs high humidity or they will dry out. All other cheese should be wrapped individually in its own wrapping or in greaseproof paper or tin foil. Plastic wrap is not good for wrapping cheese. Blue cheese, particularly those without a thick rind, should be wrapped closely in silver or gold foil, otherwise the blue mold (*Penicillium roquerfortii*), which is very prolific, will spread into other cheese in the fridge

Do not keep any cheese in a warm kitchen for long – soft cheese tends to liquefy, and harder cheese sweats and become oily. Despite the fact that some manufacturers recommend freezing, it is better not to freeze cheese unless it is a stop gap measure.

Serving Cheese
A single cheese in perfect condition, or a selection of cheeses, may be served. Ask your guests whether they would like cheese before or after dessert. Traditionally the French eat theirs after the main course so they can finish their red wine, which is delicious with cheese, before they eat dessert. Others tend to favor cheese after dessert. Don't automatically assume that a red wine is best with cheese, many whites complement cheese exquisitely.

Raclette

Serves 6

Raclette cheese is produced throughout Switzerland, and this way of cooking it originated in the canton of Valais; the 13½-pound (6-kg) wheels of cheese were cut in half and melted over an open wood fire, and then scraped onto the plates. If you own a raclette stove with little invidual pans, and have a chunk of delicious raclette cheese, this is one of the easiest and most delicious ways to entertain, and is great fun for a dinner party.

18–24 ounces (500–700g) raclette cheese

6–12 freshly boiled potatoes
lettuce
pickled onions and gherkins (optional)
sea salt or Kosher salt, and freshly ground pepper

Put the raclette stove in the center of the table and turn on the heat.

Cut the cheese into very thin slices (about ¼-inch [5-mm]), and put a slice on each little pan. Place on the stove.

Meanwhile, serve freshly boiled and seasoned potatoes, and crisp lettuce leaves on hot plates. Just as soon as the cheese melts, each guest spoons the melting cheese over the potatoes, and puts another piece on to melt.

Master Recipe

Swiss Cheese Fondue

Serves 4

The 2 cheeses that make this great Swiss dish are Emmenthal and Gruyère. Emmenthal comprises nearly 45% of Swiss cheese production, and wheels can average 180 pounds (80kg) or more. It is thought to have been made since the thirteenth century, and the holes are caused by a second fermentation process (which other cheeses don't go through), which gives it a nutty and distinctive flavor. Gruyère, named after Count de Gruyère of the medieval town of Gruyère in western Switzerland, has an entirely different taste and texture and is a great cooking cheese, with its sharp, honest flavor. The holes are few and small.

A fondue set is obviously an advantage but not essential. The fondue pot is called a coque, and the stove called a réchaud.

10 ounces (275g) Gruyère
10 ounces (275g) Emmenthal
1 garlic clove, cut in 2
1¼–1¾ cups white wine
1 generous tablespoon Kirsch
1 tablespoon plus 1 teaspoon cornstarch
freshly ground pepper
pinch nutmeg
1¼ lbs. (600g) good crusty white bread, cubed

Rub the cut faces of the garlic clove around an earthenware fondue dish. Pour in the wine and heat to just simmering point, then add the cheese, and stir constantly with a wooden spoon.

When the mixture is bubbly but not burning, stir in the cornstarch blended with the Kirsch. Add the pepper and nutmeg and continue stirring.

Transfer to a fondue stove on the table. Serve with the bread. Take care not to let the fondue burn. Make sure it is always being stirred.

Ballymaloe Cheese Fondue

Serves 2

Myrtle Allen's Cheese Fondue recipe made from Irish Cheddar cheese can be made any time. It's a great favorite at Ballymaloe and, even though it's a meal in itself, it may be made in minutes and is loved by adults and children alike. It is great fun for a party because you must kiss the gentleman or lady on your right if you drop your bread into the pot, so choose your spot carefully!

2½ tablespoons dry white wine
2 small garlic cloves, crushed
2 teaspoons Ballymaloe Country Relish or Apple and Tomato Chutney *(see page 511)*
2 teaspoons parsley, freshly chopped
6 ounces (175g) sharp Cheddar cheese, grated (1½ cups)
crusty white bread

Put all the ingredients, except the bread, into a small saucepan or fondue pot and stir. Just before serving, put over a low heat until the cheese melts and begins to bubble.

Put the pot over the fondue stove and serve immediately with fresh French bread or cubes of ordinary white bread, crisped up in a hot oven.

Reblochon en Croûte

Serves 4

Reblochon is a cheese with an orange rind from Haute-Savoie in France; in the Middle Ages the peasants of the region asked the Carthusian monks of La Combe du Reposoir monastery to bless their chalets and offered cheese as the reward. Since the Revolution, Reblochon has been marketed throughout France. This cow's milk cheese is renneted and put into cloth-lined molds, then brine-washed. The chip-board discs prevent the cheese from becoming soggy. Gubbeen cheese also works well in this recipe.

1 whole Reblochon cheese, ripe and ready to eat
a couple of sprigs of thyme
freshly cracked black pepper
4 ounces (110g) Puff Pastry *(see page 456)*
egg wash

Preheat the oven to 450°F (230°C).

Remove the timber disc from the base of the cheese. Make small slashes in the cheese and push a little sprig of thyme into each cut. Sprinkle the cheese with black pepper.

Roll out the puff pastry to sufficient size to wrap the cheese completely. Seal the edges and lightly brush with the egg wash on top. Decorate with a few pastry leaves if you want to make it look a little fancier.

Place on a baking tray and cook in the oven for 10 minutes. Reduce the temperature to 350°F (180°C) for a further 15–20 minutes or until the pastry is crisp and golden.

To serve: cut into 4 wedges and serve immediately, with warm crusty bread and a green salad.

Melted Vacherin Mont d'Or

Serves 4–8

Made in France, near the border with Switzerland, Vacherin can be made from 15th August until 31st March from cow's milk, and is one of the most succulent of cheeses. Bark and cheese are sealed together by bathing in brine, and the resinous perfume permeates the cheese as it ripens. Scrape any residue of cheese from the bark when you slice it.

This gorgeous winter cheese comes from the Massif du Mont d'Or in France near the Swiss border. The French and Swiss battled over the origin for years and years, but the Swiss have now conceded. We look forward to the arrival of the first Vacherin in Iago in the Cork Market in late autumn. The cheese comes in a wooden box bound by a band of spruce bark. It is wonderful served with crusty bread or with a green salad and charcuterie, gutsy salamis, prosciutto, or smoked duck.

Preheat the oven to 450°F (230°C).

Put the covered box in the oven for 20–30 minutes or until warm and melting. Serve hot in the box with boiled potatoes and a green salad.

Melted Gubbeen or Reblochon Cheese with Winter Herbs

Serves 6-8

Giana Ferguson tells me that this is also irresistible with Cooleeney Camembert cheese.

1 baby Gubbeen or Reblochon
freshly chopped thyme
1 large or 2 small garlic cloves finely chopped
freshly ground pepper
tin foil

Preheat the oven to 350°F (180°C).

Cut a square of tin foil, approximately 12 inches (30.5cm). Split the cheese in half around the equator. Put the bottom half onto the center of the tin foil, sprinkle the cut surface generously with freshly chopped herbs, chopped garlic, and some freshly ground black pepper.

Top with the other half of the cheese. Gather up the edges but allow a little vent for the steam to escape. Bake in a moderate oven for 20-30 minutes or until soft and melting. Cooleeney would be perfect in about 10 minutes.

Open the parcel. Lift off the rind and serve the soft herby melting cheese on slices of hot crusty bread

Lady Elizabeth's Cheddar Cheese Muffins

Makes 24

A little gem of a recipe given to me by Lady Elizabeth Rose from Hardwicke House, Pangbourne. They are made in minutes – perfect for spontaneous bread making.

We ate them from the oven with a delicious chunky beet soup, with slices of Polish sausage floating on top. You will need 24 muffin cups in a muffin pan.

2½ cups of white flour, or half and half white flour and wholewheat flour
1 tablespoon baking powder
1 generous tablespoon sugar
½ teaspoon salt
1 egg
½ cup milk
4 ounces (110g) sharp Cheddar cheese, grated (1 cup)
¼ cup melted butter
Parmesan cheese, grated

Preheat the oven to 375°F (190°C).

Put the dry ingredients, except the Parmesan, into a bowl. Whisk the egg and milk together and add the cheese and the melted butter. Mix into the dry ingredients, stirring it in a few quick strokes; do not beat, and don't worry about lumps.

Divide the mixture between 24 paper-lined muffin cups. Sprinkle with finely grated Parmesan and cook for 25–30 minutes. Cool on a wire tray and eat at once.

Ballymaloe Cheese Biscuits

Makes 25–30 biscuits

We serve these biscuits with our Irish farmhouse cheeses in the restaurant. They keep for several weeks in an airtight tin and also freeze well.

1 cup brown wholewheat flour
1 cup white flour, preferably unbleached
1/2 teaspoon salt
1/2 teaspoon baking powder
2 tablespoons butter
1 tablespoon cream
water as needed, about 5 tablespoons

Preheat the oven to 300°F (150°C). Mix the brown and white flour together and add the salt and baking powder. Rub in the butter and moisten with cream and enough water to make a firm dough. Roll out very thinly to 1/16-inch (2-mm). Prick with a fork. Cut with a 2 1/2–3-inch (6–8-cm) round cookie cutter. Put onto a lightly greased baking sheet and bake in the oven for about 45 minutes or until lightly browned and quite crisp. Cool on a wire rack.

Homemade Butter

Butter may be salted or unsalted (also known as "sweet".) Most American and Continental butter is unsalted, while English and Irish butter tends to be salted. Ghee is a clarified butter widely used in India and some Arab countries, where it is called samna. The butter is first melted, then simmered until the moisture evaporates and the butter caramelizes, producing a sweet nutty flavor.

When I was a little girl, my great-aunt Lil made butter in an electric churn almost every day from the rich ripened cream that was separated from the milk in the Alfa-Laval separator. When the butter was made, we washed it, sprinkled on salt, and patted it into little butter pats and butter balls with wooden butter hands. Nowadays, one usually makes butter by accident when one overwhips cream.

2 1/2 cups cream
salt to taste, optional

Put the cream into the spotlessly clean stainless steel bowl of a food mixer. Whisk as fast as possible until the cream whips to a soft peak. Continue, and quite soon there will be a sloshing sound and when you look into the mixing bowl, you will see little globules of butter and lots of watery milk. Strain through a cold sterilized sieve. Save the buttermilk for soda bread, and wash the butter under a cold tap. Using chilled wooden butter hands, pat the butter and continue to wash to ensure that no milk remains trapped in the butter, as this would sour and taint the butter. Sprinkle with salt, and mix evenly through. Form into slabs of 4 ounces (110g) [1 stick], 8 ounces (225g) [equal to 2 sticks] or 1 pound (450g) [equal to 4 sticks]. Alternatively, make into little balls.

Master Recipe

Homemade Cottage Cheese

Yields 1 lb. (450g) of cheese

Rennet is a natural extract from the lining membrane of a calf's stomach; it was first produced in bottled form by a chemist in Denmark in 1876. It is used in cheese-making and is also essential to junket, rennet custard. Seek out non-GM rennet. This cottage cheese is very different from the pasty white cottage cheese made commercially.

2 1/2 quarts (2.4 liters) whole milk
1 teaspoon liquid rennet

good quality muslin or cheesecloth

Put the milk into a spotlessly clean stainless steel saucepan. Heat it very gently until it is barely tepid. Add the rennet, stirring it well into the milk (not more than 1 teaspoon, as too much will result in a tough acid curd). Cover the saucepan with a clean dish towel and the lid. The dish towel prevents the steam from condensing on the lid of the pan and falling back onto the curd. Set it aside and leave undisturbed for 2–4 hours, by which time the milk should have coagulated and will be solid.

Cut the curd with a long sterilized knife, first in 1 direction, then the other, until the curd is cut into squares. Heat gently until the whey starts to run out of the curds. It must not get hot or the curd will tighten and toughen too much.

Ladle into a muslin-lined colander over a bowl. Tie the corners of the cloth and let it drip overnight. Next day, the curd may be used in whatever recipe you choose.

Variation

Cottage Cheese with Herbs

Follow the Master Recipe and add some chopped dill or a mixture of freshly chopped herbs to the cheese. Season, and add a little cream, if you like.

Coeurs à la Crème with Summer Fruits

Serves 4

A most exquisite summer pudding. Also delicious with a Kumquat Compôte (see page 391), or Green Gooseberry Sauce (see page 598). You may use 1 large mold or individual molds. In France, they are traditionally heart-shaped. The molds must be well-perforated to let the cheese drain.

8 ounces (225g) unsalted cream cheese or Homemade Cottage Cheese (see left)
1 1/4 cups softly whipped heavy cream
2 tablespoons superfine sugar

Right: Coeurs à la Crème with Summer Fruits

Above: Blue Cheese and Honey

2 egg whites, stiffly beaten
summer berries: fraises des bois, strawberries, raspberries, loganberries, blackberries, red currants, blueberries
$1\frac{1}{4}$ cups cream, softly whipped
superfine sugar

Garnish
mint leaves

Press the cheese through a fine nylon sieve and blend it gently with the heavy cream. Stir in the sugar and, lightly but thoroughly, fold in the stiffly beaten egg whites. Turn the mixture into muslin-lined, heart-shaped, perforated molds. Stand them on a wide plate, cover with a large plastic bag, and leave in the refrigerator overnight to drain.

Just before serving, turn the cheese hearts out on to white plates, top with mint leaves, and scatter summer fruits around the cheese hearts. Serve with softly whipped cream and superfine sugar, and a Fresh Strawberry Sauce (see page 599), Fresh Raspberry Sauce (see page 599), or Fresh Black Currant Sauce (see page 599).

Note: If you have not got the traditional heart-shaped molds, make Coeurs à la Crème in a cheesecloth-lined bread basket or even a strainer.

Blue Cheese and Honey

Serve each guest a section of good quality blue cheese such as Cashel Blue. Pass around a bowl of pure Irish honey, drizzle a little over each helping.

Homemade Crème Fraîche

Crème fraîche, with its ripened flavor, is easy to make at home and keeps well.

1 pint (450ml) rich cream
1 cup cultured buttermilk

Put the cream and the buttermilk into a stainless steel saucepan. Warm gently to 85°F (30°C). Pour into a Pyrex bowl and cover with plastic wrap, pierced in several places.

Leave at room temperature for 6–8 hours until it thickens and tastes characteristically acidic. Cover, and refrigerate.

Soft Yogurt Cheese with Chives and Parsley

Makes enough for 4–6

Be sure that the chives and parsley are thoroughly dry before chopping them.

2 cups whole milk yogurt
pinch salt
$\frac{1}{2}$ teaspoon chives, very finely sliced
1 teaspoon parsley, finely chopped
lemon balm or chervil and a little garlic (optional)
sugar to taste

good-quality muslin or cheesecloth

Follow directions for making soft yogurt cheese on the opposite page. Let the cheese drip overnight. Mix the yogurt cheese with all the other ingredients in a stainless steel or Pyrex bowl. Mix well. Taste for seasoning and add a little sugar if necessary. Cover, and refrigerate for at least 1 hour. If some liquid accumulates, just discard it before you serve.

Alternatively, add freshly chopped mint, dill, or marjoram, and a drizzle of olive oil. A little sea salt or Kosher salt and some smoked paprika is also good.

Homemade Mascarpone

$2\frac{1}{2}$ pints (1.2 liters) rich cream
$\frac{1}{4}$ teaspoon cream of tartar

Heat the cream gently to 350°F (180°C) stirring every now and then. Remove from the heat, add the cream of tartar, and stir for 30 seconds, then pour it in to a Pyrex bowl. Stir for 2 minutes.

Line a small colander or a strainer with cheesecloth or muslin and let drip in a cold place overnight, or covered in the refrigerator. Use as required, or keep in the refrigerator in a tightly-covered clean container for up to a week.

How to make Yogurt

Yogurt can be made from unpasteurized milk if it is thoroughly boiled and cooled to lukewarm before using. Skimmed or lowfat milk may be used but the resulting yogurt lacks flavor. The boiling is to destroy unwanted bacteria in the milk which could interfere with the bacterial action of the yogurt bacilli (*Lactobacillus bulgaricus*** and ***Streptococcus thermophilus***). Use unflavored yogurt for the starter culture.**

2½ cups whole milk (boiled or sterilized)
2 teaspoons live unflavored yogurt

Warm the milk until lukewarm (or cool it to lukewarm, if it has been boiled). It should be around 108°F (42°C). Stir in the yogurt. Pour it into a Pyrex bowl, cover with plastic wrap, and put into a warm, draft-free place until set. This usually takes about 14 hours at 78–85°F (24–29°C). Wrap the bowl in a towel to keep it warm. The cooler the temperature, the longer the yogurt will take, but too high a temperature will kill the bacillus and yogurt will not form. The yogurt will become slightly sour if left for too long in the warmth. Refrigerate the yogurt once it is ready.

Yogurt can be set in a warm draft-free place, e.g., near a radiator or warm stove, and can also be set in a vacuum flask with a wide neck or in an insulated ice bucket. Or it can be made in a bowl, set in a larger bowl of warm water, standing in the sink with the hot tap dripping steadily into the outer bowl to keep the water warm. An earthenware pot with a lid, wrapped up in a warm blanket and put near a radiator, will also do the job. The aim is to provide steady, even warmth to allow the bacillus to grow.

Remember to keep back 2 teaspoons of your bowl of yogurt as the starter of the next batch. Yogurt keeps for up to a week refrigerated.

Yogurt with Honey and Toasted Hazelnuts

Serve a portion of chilled unflavored yoghurt per person. Just before serving, drizzle generously with really good honey and sprinkle with toasted hazelnuts.

How to make Soft Yogurt Cheese called Labna in the Arab world

Whole milk yogurt makes a rich, creamy cheese. You may, if you prefer, substitute skimmed milk yogurt but I never would! This cheese keeps for up to a week in the refrigerator.

Line a strainer with a triple thickness of cheesecloth. Place it over a bowl. Spoon in the yogurt.

Now tie the 4 corners of the cheesecloth to make a loose bundle.

Suspend the bundle or bag of yogurt over a bowl so that it can drip for 3–8 hours, as your recipe requires.

Remove the cheesecloth. Refrigerate the yoghurt cheese until needed, in a covered plastic container. Add fresh herbs or spices – do this before you refrigerate it.

Marinated Mozzarella on Arugula Leaves

Serves 4

We can't hope to get the wonderful, fresh, tender, hand-rolled mozzarella that one finds in Italy; however, we now get buffalo mozzarella in plastic pouches still in a pool of whey, hugely different from the blocks of Danish mozzarella used for the mass pizza market. But of course there are far fewer buffaloes in Italy than there used to be, and a lot of the milk is being replaced by cow's milk. Smoked mozzarella has a golden skin and is fun for a change.

Mozzarella can be greatly improved by marinating in good extra-virgin olive oil and perhaps some fresh herbs and chile or even chile flakes. This makes a lovely appetizer or light supper dish.

1/2 cup extra-virgin olive oil
1 fresh chile, diced, or pinch red pepper flakes
crushed garlic (optional)
2 balls mozzarella
marjoram or torn basil leaves
salt and freshly ground pepper

arugula leaves
focaccia
cherry tomatoes

Put the olive oil into a small saucepan, add the chile flakes and garlic, and warm gently for a few minutes, then let cool. Slice the cheese thickly or dice into 1-inch (2.5-cm) cubes. Put into a shallow dish, scatter some herbs over the cheese, and season with salt and pepper. Pour the chile oil over the top and let marinate for several hours, or cover and keep in the fridge for several days.

To serve: put a bed of arugula leaves on a plate, top with a few slices of marinated mozzarella. Serve with char-grilled focaccia and maybe a few tiny cherry tomatoes, fresh, or roasted quickly on the branch.

Saganaki – Greek Fried Cheese

Serves 6–8

Cheese is cooked in a little round aluminum frying pan called a saganaki; it can be made with various hard cheeses, such as Haloumi, Kefalotiri, Parmesan, even Gruyère. It must be served piping hot; Greek waiters occasionally run to get it to the customer while it is still bubbling.

8 ounces (225g) hard cheese
butter or olive oil
lemon juice, freshly squeezed
freshly ground pepper
crusty white bread

Cut the cheese into slices, about 1/2-inch (1-cm) thick. Have some white crusty bread ready on the table. Melt a little butter or olive oil in a small frying pan, put in a few slices of cheese, reduce the heat, and let the cheese cook for 1–2 minutes until it begins to bubble. It should not brown. Sprinkle with a few drops of lemon juice and some freshly cracked pepper, rush to the table, and eat with crusty white bread.

Note: the cheese can also be dipped in beaten egg and breadcrumbs before frying.

Paneer with Tomato and Chile Sauce

Serves 4

A fresh curd cheese made in India, paneer is a prime source of protein for Buddhists, Jains, and Hindu Brahmins. It is found extensively in the north but less often in the south where cows are not so prevalent. Paneer can be kept for up to 4 days in the refrigerator. The most common vegetable dish on our Indian restaurant menus is Matar Paneer, peas and cheese in tomato sauce.

2 quarts (1.8 liters) milk (not lowfat)
4–5 tablespoons lemon juice or white wine vinegar

Tomato and Chile Sauce (page 590)
chopped fresh cilantro
Nan Bread

Bring the milk to a boil in a large pot; just as it begins to rise in the pot, add 4 tablespoons of lemon juice or vinegar. Stir, and turn off the heat; the milk should start to curdle immediately. If it doesn't, bring to a boil again and add another tablespoon of lemon juice or vinegar, and stir, and turn off the heat as before.

Put a large strainer over a deep bowl, line it with a double thickness of muslin or cheesecloth, pour the curds and whey into the muslin-lined strainer, letting the whey drain away. Gather up the ends of the muslin. Then put it into a mold with holes, cover with a plate, and weight it down.

Alternatively, just put the cheese onto a board, cover with another board, and weight it down for about 3–4 minutes. It is then ready to be used or served.

Meanwhile make a little Tomato and Chile Sauce. Add a little chopped fresh cilantro as well.

To serve: slice the cheese into 1/4-inch (5-mm) slices and spoon a little sauce on top. Serve with hot crispy Indian flatbread.

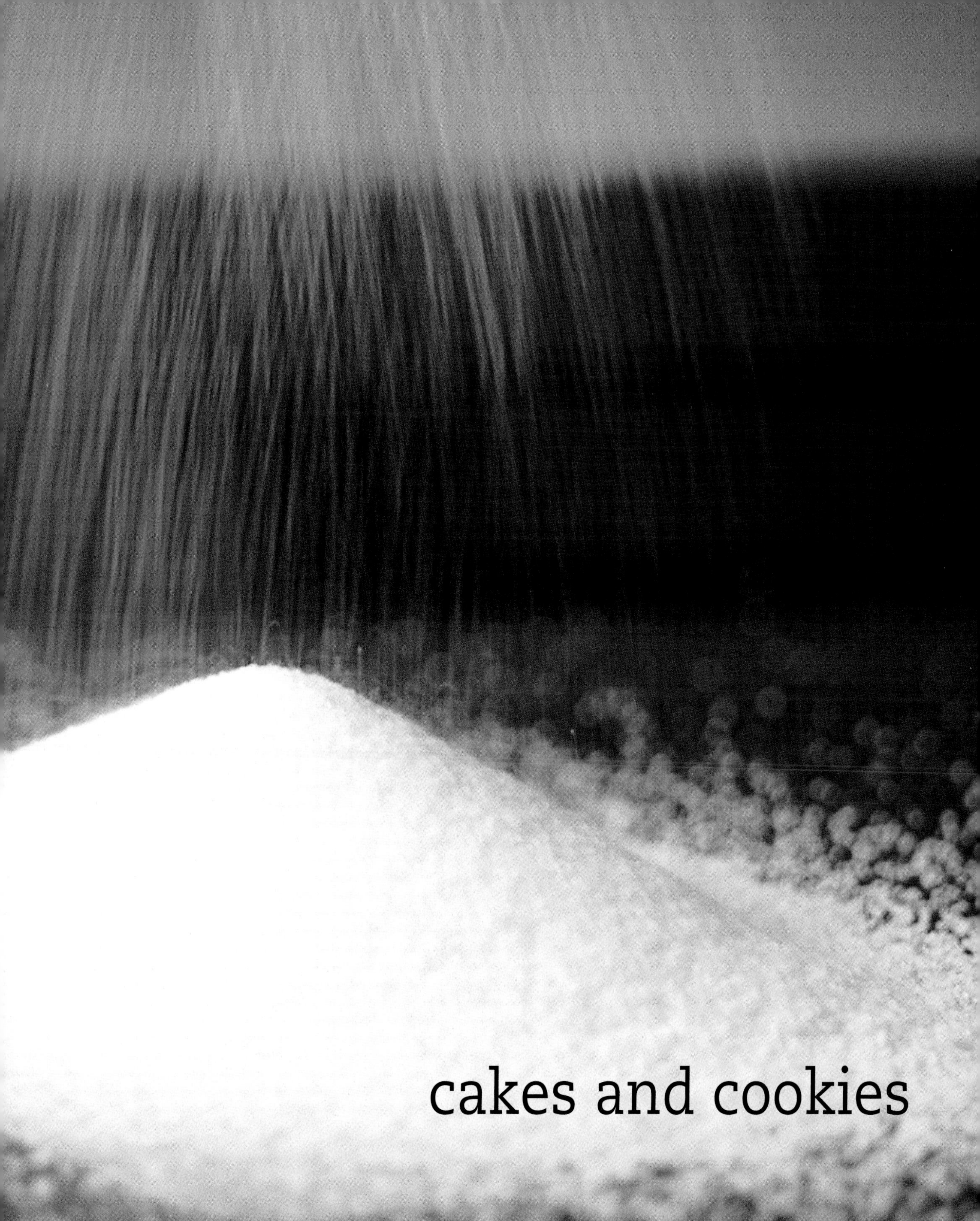

cakes and cookies

cakes and cookies

All cooks seem to divide naturally into those who enjoy savory cooking best, and bakers and pastry chefs. Forced to choose, I would plump for the latter. Decoration is an important part of the art of cake making, and baking is an exact science – you can't just throw in a tablespoon of this or a fist of that at random; for success and consistency you need to measure accurately and follow a recipe precisely. The basic ingredients for cakes are few – butter, sugar, eggs, and flour – and with them, skilled pastry chefs create an art form.

There are three basic types of cake: **whisked cakes** (fatless sponge cakes such as génoise and angel food cake); **creamed cakes** (madeira, sponge cakes which include fat, pound cakes, and most fruit cakes) and **molten method cakes** (such as gingerbread, porter cake, pain d'épices, and panforte). Some cake recipes are made by a mixture of two methods, such as whisked up sponge, which may have melted butter folded in at the end. Cookies also fall into three categories: those made by the rubbing in (shortbread), creaming (lemon squares) and molten methods (brandy snaps). Once again, many (like toffee squares) use a combination of two or three techniques.

Ingredients

As ever, always choose the finest ingredients for the most delicious end result.

Fat adds moistness and improves the shelf life of cakes and cookies. **Butter** gives the best results and you should use unsalted (sweet) or salted butter as the recipe indicates. Although there is no substitute for butter in terms of flavor, margarine can also be used, with a similar result. Shortening produces a light texture but very little flavor, and olive oil is used in some Tunisian, Greek, and Moroccan recipes. Use large-sized **eggs, from free-range hens** (organic, if possible). Eggs should be stored at room temperature. Duck eggs are particularly good for sponge cakes. **Granulated and superfine sugar** is most commonly used in cakes. Golden brown sugar gives color and a slightly richer flavor. Confectioners sugar is used for icings. Most cake recipes use all-purpose **flour**. Self-rising flour contains raising agents and should only be used where specified – do not substitute it for all-purpose flour. Sift the flour to increase the lightness of your cakes. **Nuts** and coconut add moistness and improve the keeping quality of cakes and cookies.

Preparation and Baking

When choosing pans, always buy good quality, heavy gauge pans. Use the exact size of pan stated in a recipe, otherwise the cooking time will need to be adjusted. If pans are very light, tie a layer of brown paper around the outside to protect heavy cakes, such as fruit cakes, that require a long cooking time. It is well worth taking the time to grease and line a cake pan so that the cake will unmold easily – use butter or oil to do this, as poor-quality fat or oil can ruin the flavor. Use a brush to apply the melted butter evenly to the bottom and sides of the pan. Dust with flour and shake off any excess. For whisked and creamed cakes, the bottom of the pan should also be lined with wax paper. Loaf pans need to be lined for cakes and gingerbread.

I prefer to use a conventional oven for most cakes and cookies, as those cooked in a fan-assisted oven become stale more quickly.

To test for doneness

All cakes shrink in slightly from the side of the pan when cooked. To test if a cake is ready, press the center gently with your fingertips – when fully cooked, it should be the same texture as the outer edge. Alternatively, insert a skewer or toothpick into its center. If it comes out clean with no trace of stickiness, then the cake is done. Most cakes benefit from standing for a few minutes before being turned out. Cool cakes and cookies on a wire rack so they don't get soggy underneath. Let heavy fruit cakes cool in the pan first.

Darina Allen's Christmas Cake with Toasted Almond Paste

This makes a moist cake, which keeps very well. I have a passion for almond paste so I "ice" the cake with almond icing and decorate it with heart shapes made from the almond paste. Then I brush it with beaten egg yolk and toast it in the oven – simply delicious!

3/4–1 cup candied cherries
1/3 cup whole almonds
1 1/2 cups best quality golden raisins
1 1/2 cups best quality currants
1 1/2 cups best quality raisins
2/3 cup ground almonds
3/4–1 cup homemade Candied Peel (see page 515)
zest of 1 orange
zest of 1 lemon
a generous 1/3 cup Irish whiskey
2 sticks (1 cup) butter
1 cup pale brown sugar
6 eggs
2 1/2 cups all-purpose white flour
1 level teaspoon apple spice
1 large or 2 small Bramley apples or Granny Smiths, peeled, cored, and grated

9-inch (23-cm) round, or 8-inch (20-cm) square pan, lined with brown paper and wax paper, with an outer collar of brown paper to come half as high again as the height of the pan.

Preheat the oven to 350°F (180°C).

Wash and dry the cherries. Cut them into 2 or 4 pieces, as desired. Blanch the almonds in boiling water for 1–2 minutes, rub off the skins, and chop them finely. Mix the dried fruit, whole almonds, ground almonds, candied peel, and grated orange and lemon zest. Add about half of the whiskey and leave for 1 hour to macerate.

Cream the butter until very soft, add the sugar, and beat until light and fluffy. Whisk the eggs and add them in, bit by bit, beating well between each addition so that the mixture doesn't curdle. Mix the spice with the flour and stir in gently. Add the grated apple to the fruit and mix in gently but thoroughly (don't beat the mixture again or you will toughen the cake). Put the mixture into the prepared cake pan. Make a slight hollow in the center, dip your hand in water, and pat it over the surface of the cake: this will ensure that the top is smooth when cooked. Lay a sheet of brown paper over the top of the pan. Put into the oven; reduce the heat to 325°F (170°C) after 1 hour. Bake for 3–3 1/2 hours; test in the center with a skewer – it should come out completely clean when the cake is cooked. Pour the rest of the whiskey over the cake and let it cool in the pan.

Next day, remove from the pan. Do not remove the lining paper but wrap in extra wax paper and tin foil until needed. The cake keeps for weeks or even months at this stage.

Almond Paste

2 cups superfine sugar
1 lb. (450g) ground almonds (5 cups)
2 small eggs
drop of pure almond extract
2 generous tablespoons Irish whiskey

Sift the sugar, and mix with the ground almonds. Beat the eggs, add the whiskey and almond extract, then add to the other ingredients and mix to a stiff paste. (You may not need all of the egg.) Sprinkle the worktop with confectioners sugar, turn out the almond paste, and work lightly until smooth.

To brush on the cake
1 egg white, lightly beaten

Glaze
2 egg yolks

Remove the paper from the cake. To make life easier, put a sheet of wax paper on the worktop; dust with some confectioners sugar. Take about half the almond paste and roll it out on the paper: it should be a little less than 1/2-inch (1-cm) thick. Paint the top of the cake with the lightly beaten egg white and put the cake, sticky side down, onto the almond paste.

Give the cake a "thump" to make sure it sticks, and then cut around the edge but, if the cake is a little "round shouldered," cut the almond paste a little larger. Pull away the extra bits and keep for later to make hearts or holly leaves. With a palette knife or spatula, press the extra almond paste in against the top of the cake to fill any gaps. Then slide a knife underneath the wax paper and turn the cake right way up. Peel off the paper.

Preheat the oven to 425°F (220°C).
Next, measure the circumference of the cake with a piece of string. Roll out 2 long strips of almond paste to half that length, and trim them so their width is equal to the height of the cake. Paint both the cake and the almond paste lightly with egg white. Press the almond paste strips against the sides of the cake: do not overlap or there will be a bulge. Use a straight-sided water glass to even the edges and smooth the join. Rub the cake well with your hand to ensure a nice flat surface. Roll out the remainder of the almond paste to about 1/4-inch (5-mm) thick. Cut out heart shapes, paint the whole surface of the cake with some beaten egg yolk, and stick the heart shapes at intervals around the sides of the cake and on the top. Brush these with egg yolk also.

Carefully lift the cake onto a baking sheet and bake in the oven for 15–20 minutes or until just slightly toasted. Remove from the oven, let cool, and then transfer onto a cake board.

Note: As I'm an incurable romantic, my Christmas Cake is always decorated with hearts, but you may feel that holly leaves and berries made of almond paste would be more appropriate for Christmas. You can, of course, decorate it any way that takes your fancy.

Porter Cake

Porter cake made with the black stout of Ireland is now an established Irish cake, rich and moist with "plenty of cutting." Guinness, Murphy, or Beamish stouts can be used, depending on where your loyalties are.

4 cups all-purpose white flour
pinch of salt
1 level teaspoon baking powder
1 cup superfine sugar
1 level teaspoon nutmeg, freshly grated
1 level teaspoon apple spice
2 sticks (1 cup) butter
2 cups golden raisins
1/2 cup Candied Peel (see page 515)
1/2 cup candied cherries
1 1/4 cups porter or stout
2 eggs

round cake pan, 8 x 3 inches (20 x 7cm), lined with wax paper

Preheat the oven to 350°F (180°C).

Sift the flour, salt, and baking powder into a bowl, then add the sugar, nutmeg, and spice, and rub in the butter. Add the fruit. Then, in a separate bowl, mix the porter with the beaten eggs, and pour into the other ingredients and mix well. Turn into the lined pan and bake for about 2 hours in the oven. Let cool in the pan, wrap in wax paper, and keep for several days before cutting, to let the cake mature.

Below: Porter Cake

Myrtle Allen's White Christmas Cake

This cake, with its layer of crisp frosting, is a delicious alternative for those who do not like the traditional heavy fruit cake. It is best made not more than a week before Christmas. Good for those of us who leave things until the last moment!

1¼ sticks (⅔ cup) butter
1¾ cups flour
pinch of salt
¼ level teaspoon baking powder
1 teaspoon lemon juice
1 teaspoon Irish whiskey
1 cup ground almonds
6 egg whites
1 cup superfine sugar
¾–1 cup green or yellow candied cherries
½ cup finely-chopped homemade Candied Peel (see page 515)

American Frosting (see page 450)
Crystallized Flowers (see page 447), angelica, or Christmas decorations

round pan with 3-inch (8-cm) sides and 7-inch (18-cm) diameter

Preheat the oven to 325°F (170°C).

Line the pan with wax paper. Cream the butter until very soft, sift in the flour, salt, and baking powder, then add the lemon juice, whiskey, and ground almonds. Whisk the egg whites until quite stiff; add the sugar gradually and whisk again until stiff and smooth. Stir some of the egg white into the butter mixture and then carefully fold in the rest. Lastly, add the chopped peel and the cherries. Pour into the prepared pan and bake for about 1½ hours. Let cool, cover, and frost the next day.

Frost the cake with the American Frosting. Decorate with Christmas decorations or crystallized violets and rose petals, and angelica.

Simnel Cake

Simnel was originally a spiced bread, probably introduced to Ireland by Elizabethan settlers in the sixteenth century. In and around the Dublin Pale, there was a tradition that the mistress of the house provided the ingredients for the maid-servants to bake a plum cake, iced with almond paste, to take home on Mothering Sunday, the Sunday before Lent begins. In the funeral scene in Ulysses, **James Joyce describes hawkers selling simnel cakes outside Glasnevin Cemetery in Dublin. Were they smaller then or was he merely using poetic licence?**

Use the same ingredients for Christmas Cake (page 443). Follow the method until the mixture is prepared. The first difference from the Christmas cake recipe is that you should put ½ of the cake mixture into the prepared pan, roll out about half of the almond paste into an 8½-inch (22-cm) circle, place this on top of the cake mixture, and cover with the remaining mixture. Cook as for the Christmas Cake.

When you are ready to finish the cake, roll out two-thirds of the remainder of the almond paste into a 9-inch (23-cm) circle. Brush the cake with a little lightly beaten egg white and top with the almond paste. Roll the remainder of the paste into 11 little balls.

Score the top of the cake in 1½-inch (4-cm) squares, brush with beaten egg or egg yolk, stick the 11 "apostles" around the outer edge of the top, brush with beaten egg. Toast in a preheated oven 425°F (220°C), for 15–20 minutes or until slightly golden. Decorate with an Easter chicken, if you like.

Remember to use organic eggs from free-range hens whenever possible.

Rum and Raisin Walnut Cake

One of our favorite cakes – it keeps for ages, and goes well with coffee.

¾ cup raisins
½ cup rum
2½ sticks (1¼ cups) butter
¾ cup superfine sugar
4 eggs
¼ cup milk
1½ teaspoons pure vanilla extract
2½ cups all-purpose white flour
1 tablespoon plus 1 teaspoon baking powder
½ cup walnuts, shelled

removable-bottomed round 9-inch (23-cm) pan, lined with wax paper

Preheat the oven to 350°F (180°C).

Soak the raisins in the rum for 30 minutes. Drain and save the rum. Cream the butter, add the sugar, and beat until light and fluffy. Separate the eggs, and add the egg yolks, one by one. Beat well between each addition. Add the rum, milk, and vanilla. Mix the flour and baking powder together and fold into the batter bit by bit. Whisk the egg whites in a spotlessly clean bowl until stiff and fluffy.

Fold into the cake mixture one third at a time, adding the raisins and chopped nuts with the last addition of egg white.

Pour into the prepared pan and cook in the oven for 45 minutes to 1 hour, or until the top is golden and the center is set and firm. Let the cake cool in the pan, tip it upside down and remove from the pan, then turn it right side up and cool on a wire rack.

Aunt Florence's Orange Cake

When my Aunt Florence brings a present of this delicious cake in a tin, lots of people suddenly emerge out of the woodwork pleading for a slice. Without question, it is the best orange cake any of us has ever eaten.

2 sticks (1 cup) butter
1 cup superfine sugar
zest of 1 orange, finely grated
4 eggs
2 cups all-purpose white flour
1 level teaspoon baking powder
1 tablespoon orange juice, freshly squeezed

Orange Butter Filling
1 stick (1/2 cup) butter
1 3/4 cups confectioners sugar
zest of 1 orange, grated
1 tablespoon orange juice, freshly squeezed

Orange Glacé Icing
2 1/2 cups confectioners sugar
orange juice, freshly squeezed

Candied Orange Peel (see recipe page 515)

2 x 8-inch (20-cm) round cake pans, or 1 x 11-inch (30.5-cm) pan

Preheat the oven to 350°F (180°C).

Grease and flour the cake pans. Line the bottom of each with wax paper.

Cream the butter and gradually add the superfine sugar. Beat until soft and light and quite pale in color. Add the orange zest. Add the eggs, one at a time, beating well between each addition. Sift the flour and baking powder and stir in gradually. Mix all together lightly; stir in the orange juice.

Divide the mixture evenly if using 2 pans, hollowing it slightly in the center. Bake in the oven for 35 minutes or until cooked. Turn out onto a wire tray and let cool. Meanwhile, make the filling. Cream the butter; add the confectioners sugar and orange zest. Beat in the orange juice bit by bit.

To make the frosting, simply squeeze the juice from an orange and add enough to the confectioners sugar to make a spreadable frosting. When the cakes are cold, split each one in 2 halves, and spread with a little filling, then sandwich the pieces together. Spread frosting over the top and sides, and decorate the top, if you like, with little diamonds of candied peel. This cake keeps very well – as long as you hide it well enough!

Tip: If the butter and sugar are not creamed properly, and if you add the eggs too fast, the mixture will curdle, resulting in a cake with a heavier texture.

Coconut Macaroon Cake

This cake has an irresistible crispy topping – the crumb is moist and rich with coconut and almonds, so it will keep well, stored in an airtight tin.

Cake
2 sticks (1 cup) butter
1 cup superfine sugar
4 eggs and 1 egg yolk
1/4 teaspoon pure vanilla extract
2 cups all-purpose white flour
1/2 level teaspoon baking powder
1/3 cup ground almonds
a scant 1/2 cup dried, unsweetened coconut

Macaroon topping
1 egg white
a scant 1/4 cup dried, unsweetened coconut
1/3 cup ground almonds
1/3 cup superfine sugar
1/4 teaspoon pure vanilla extract
2/3 cup slivered almonds

pan with sides about 2 inches (5cm) high and diameter of 8 inches (20cm), lined with wax paper

Preheat the oven to 350°F (180°C).

Cream the butter, add the sugar, and beat until light and fluffy. Whisk the eggs and egg yolk and add gradually, beating well between each addition. Add the vanilla extract. In a separate bowl, mix the dry ingredients well, and stir in to the butter gently. Turn into the prepared pan.

For the topping, whisk the egg white lightly and fold in the coconuts, ground almonds, sugar, and vanilla. Spread carefully over the cake batter in the pan. Sprinkle with slivered almonds and bake in the oven for about 1 1/2 hours. Cool in the pan, then on a wire rack.

Note: pure vanilla extract is labeled as such, and comes from the cured pods of the vanilla, a tropical plant and member of the orchid family. It is amber in color and vastly superior in flavor than imitation vanilla flavoring. It is also more expensive, but buy it if you can.

Lemon Crunch Cake

Makes 1 cake

1 1/2 sticks (3/4 cup) butter
3/4 cup superfine sugar
2 eggs
2 1/4 cups self-rising flour
grated zest of 1 unwaxed lemon
juice of 1/2–1 unwaxed lemon
1/4 cup superfine sugar

square pan, 8 1/2 x 2 3/4 inches (13 x 20cm), lined with wax paper

Preheat the oven to 350°F (180°C).

Cream the butter, add the sugar, and beat until light and fluffy. Add in eggs, one by one, and lemon zest. Fold in the flour. Turn into the prepared pan. Smooth the surface, and bake for 30–40 minutes.

Meanwhile, mix the lemon juice with the sugar. When the cake is fully cooked, remove from the oven, cool a little, prick all over with a skewer, and spoon the lemon "icing" over the top while still warm. It will crystallize and become crunchy as it cools

Lemon Bars

Follow the Lemon Crunch Cake recipe, but bake in a lined jelly roll pan for 25–30 minutes, and add the lemon rind to the icing rather than to the cake batter.

Master Recipe

Great Grandmother's Cake

Makes 1 cake

1 stick plus 1 tablespoon (1/2 cup plus 1 tablespoon) butter
3/4 cup superfine sugar
3 eggs
1 1/2 cups flour
1 teaspoon baking powder
1 tablespoon plus 1 teaspoon milk

Filling
1 cup Raspberry Jam (see page 504)
1 1/4 cups whipped cream

superfine sugar to sprinkle

2 x 7-inch (18-cm) sponge cake pans

Preheat the oven to 350°F (180°C).

Grease and flour the pans and line the bottom of each with a circle of wax paper.

Cream the butter and gradually add the sugar, beat until soft and light, and quite pale in color. Add the eggs, one at a time, and beat well between each addition.

Sift the flour and baking powder and stir in to the batter gradually. Mix all together lightly and add the milk to moisten. Divide the mixture evenly between the 2 pans, hollowing it slightly in the center. Bake for 20–25 minutes or until cooked. Turn out onto a wire tray and let cool. Sandwich together with homemade Raspberry Jam and whipped cream. Sprinkle with sifted superfine sugar. Serve on an old-fashioned plate with a paper doily under the cake.

Variations

Lemon Victoria Sponge Cake

Makes 1 cake

Follow the Master Recipe, but include the grated zest of 1 lemon when creaming the butter.

homemade Lemon Curd (see page 510)

Icing
3 cups confectioners sugar
5–6 tablespoons boiling water

2 cups confectioners sugar will be sufficient to ice the top of a 7-inch (18-cm) sponge

Decoration
crystallized Violets (see right)

Split the cakes in half horizontally, and spread on a little lemon curd to sandwich them together. Sift the confectioners sugar into a bowl, and add enough boiling water to mix to a fairly stiff coating consistency. The icing should hold a trail when dropped from a spoon. Put the rest of the lemon curd into a pastry bag fitted with a fine writing nozzle or use a paper nozzle.

Spread the icing smoothly and evenly over the top and sides of the cakes, using a warm palette knife or spatula. While it is still wet, quickly pipe lines with the lemon curd, about an inch (2.5cm) apart, across the top of the cake. Then draw the tip of a skewer or pointed knife through the colored lines, at right angles, going in opposite directions each time, this is called feathering and may be done in lines or in a circular spider web pattern. Alternatively, decorate the iced cake with crystallized flowers and leaves.

Crystallized Flowers

The art of crystallizing flowers simply takes patience and a meticulous nature – the sort of job that drives some people around the bend, but which others adore. If it appeals to you, the work will be well rewarded as they look and taste divine.

egg whites
superfine sugar

1. Use freshly picked, strong-textured leaves, and small flowers such as primroses, violets, apple blossom, and violas.

2. The superfine sugar must be absolutely dry, so to be quite sure, sift and dry it out in a jelly roll pan in a low oven, 275°F (140°C), for about 2 hours.

3. Break up an egg white slightly with a fork. Using a thin paintbrush, brush the egg white very carefully over part of the petal and into every surface. Pour the sugar over the flower or leaf with a teaspoon. Arrange carefully on wax paper to ensure a good shape. Let dry overnight in a warm

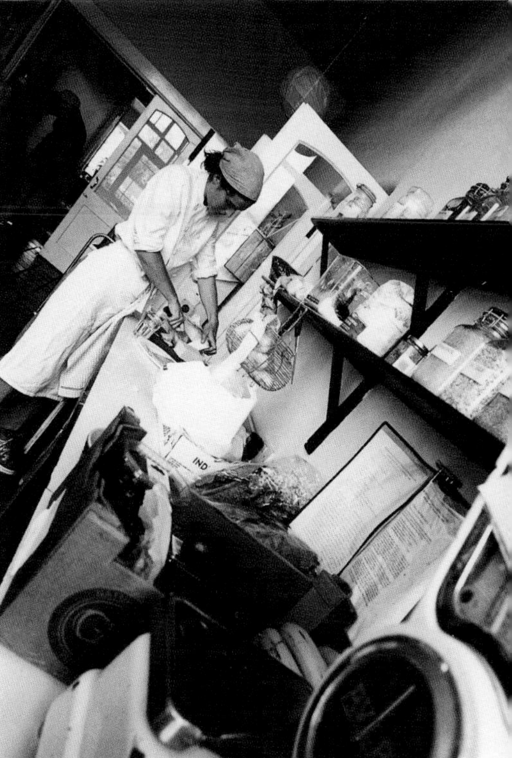

dry place, (close to an Aga or over a radiator). If properly crystallized these flowers will last for months, even years, provided they are kept dry. We store them in a covered pottery jar or a tin box.

4. Remember to do lots of leaves as well as flowers so one can make attractive arrangements – mint, lemon balm, wild strawberry, salad burnet, or marguerite and daisy leaves also work well.

Basic Genoise Sponge Cake

Serves 4

This is the type of sponge cake that is used as the base for many gâteaux in France.

1 cup flour
1/2 stick (1/4 cup) butter
4 eggs
1/2 cup sugar

For flavoring
1/2 teaspoon vanilla extract, or grated rind of 1 lemon or orange, or 1 teaspoon orange flower water
1–2 teaspoons coffee essence (we use Irel)

9-inch (23-cm) round genoise cake pan, with 2 inch high sides that slope outwards

Brush the inside of the cake pan with a little melted butter. If you like, line the bottom with a circle of wax paper that exactly fits, and butter it also. Leave it for a few minutes and then sprinkle the pan with flour, shaking out the excess.

Preheat the oven to 350°F (180°C).

Sift the flour well. Clarify the butter (see page 103). Put the eggs in a large bowl, gradually whisk in the sugar. Put the bowl over hot, but not boiling water, for 8–10 minutes, or until the mixture is light and thick enough to make a distinct figure of 8 when the whisk is lifted. Remove the bowl from the heat, add the chosen flavoring, and continue beating uncooled.
Sift the flour over the mixture in three batches, folding each batch as lightly as possible with a wooden spatula or metal spoon. Just after the last batch, pour the cooled butter around the side of the bowl and fold in gently and quickly because the whisked mixture quickly loses volume after the butter is added.

Pour the mixture into the prepared pan and bake in the oven for 35–40 minutes, or until the cake shrinks slightly from the side of the pan and the top springs back when lightly pressed. Turn it out on a rack to cool.

Coffee Cake

Serves 8–10

Another splendid cake that keeps well.

2 sticks (1 cup) butter
1 cup superfine sugar
4 eggs
2 cups white flour
1 teaspoon baking powder
5–6 tablespoons coffee essence (we use Irel)

Coffee Butter Cream (see right)
Coffee Icing (see right)

Decoration
hazelnuts or chocolate coffee beans

2 round layer cake pans, 8 inches (20.5cm) in diameter

Preheat the oven to 350°F (180°C).

Brush the pans with melted butter, dust with flour, and line the bottom of each with a circle of wax paper. Brush with melted butter.

Cream the butter until soft, add the sugar, and beat until pale and light in texture. Whisk the eggs. Add to the mixture, bit by bit, beating well between each addition. Sift the flour with the baking powder and stir gently into the cake batter, finally adding in the coffee essence, and mix thoroughly.

Spoon the batter into the prepared sandwich pans and bake for about 30 minutes in the oven. When the cakes are cooked, the center will be firm and springy, and the edges will have slightly shrunk from the sides of the pan.

Let it rest in the pan for a few minutes before turning out onto the wire rack, remove the wax paper from the bottom, then turn the cakes right side up so the top of the cakes don't get marked by the wire rack. Cool the cakes on the wire rack. When cold, sandwich the cakes together with Coffee Buttercream and ice the top with Coffee Glacé icing. Decorate with caramelized hazelnuts or chocolate coffee beans.

Coffee Butter Cream Filling

1/2 stick (1/4 cup) butter
1 cup confectioners sugar (sifted)
1–2 teaspoons coffee essence (we use Irel)

Beat the butter with the confectioners sugar and the coffee essence.

Coffee Glacé Icing

2 cups confectioners sugar
scant 1 tablespoon coffee essence (we use Irel)
about 2 tablespoons boiling water

Sift the confectioners sugar into a bowl. Add the coffee essence and enough boiling water to make it the consistency of thick cream.

Chocolate Mousse Cake

Serves 6–8

For the Genoise Sponge Cake

3/4 cup plus 2 tablespoons flour
6 tablespoons cocoa powder
1½ level teaspoons baking powder
pinch of salt
½ stick (¼ cup) unsalted (sweet) butter
4 eggs, preferably from free-range hens
2/3 cup sugar
½ teaspoon pure vanilla extract

For the Chocolate Mousse
10 ounces (275g) dark dessert chocolate, chopped (about 2 cups)
6 eggs, separated
1½ sticks (3/4 cup) unsalted (sweet) butter
1 teaspoon vanilla extract or 2 tablespoons Grand Marnier liqueur

Chantilly Cream
1 pint (425ml) heavy cream
2 tablespoons sugar
1 teaspoon vanilla extract

Chocolate Caraque (see page 399)

9-inch (23-cm) round cake pan

Preheat the oven to 350°F (180°C).

Prepare the cake pan. Sift the flour with the cocoa, baking powder, and salt, and make the genoise mixture following the basic recipe (see left). Add the vanilla extract. Pour the mixture into the prepared pan and bake in a preheated oven for 35–40 minutes or until the mixture springs back when lightly pressed with a fingertip. Cool on a wire rack. The cake can be baked ahead and kept in an airtight container for 2–3 days, or it can be frozen.

For the Chocolate Mousse, melt the chocolate in a pan over hot water or in a very cool oven, and stir until smooth. Beat the egg yolks one by one into the hot mixture so that it thickens slightly. Beat in the butter and vanilla extract or liqueur. Let cool slightly. Whip the egg whites until stiff, add a spoonful of the tepid chocolate mixture to them, and fold the two together as lightly as possible; the warm mixture will lightly cook and stiffen the whites. Let cool at room temperature, not in the fridge, otherwise the mousse will harden and become difficult to spread.

Make the Chantilly Cream: mix the sugar into the cream and add the vanilla extract.

To assemble the Gâteau, split the sponge cake into 3 layers horizontally. Spread the chocolate mousse on the bottom layer. Place the second layer of sponge cake on top and spread it with two-thirds of the Chantilly cream, reserving the remaining cream for decoration. Top with the third layer and spread the remaining mousse on the top and sides of the cake. Decorate the top and sides with chocolate caraque or curls and Chantilly cream.

Chocolate Meringue Extravaganza

Serves about 10 approx.

8 egg whites
18 ounces (500g) confectioners sugar (4–4½ cups)
2 tablespoons cocoa

Icing and Filling
2½ cups cream
1 lb. (450g) best quality dark chocolate
1–2 tablespoons rum or orange liqueur

Line 2 or 3 baking sheets with wax paper. Draw out 3 ovals, about 11 x 17 inches (30.5 x 18cm), on the paper. Check that the bowl is dry and spotlessly clean. Put the egg whites into the bowl and add 1 pound (450g) of the icing sugar all at once. Whisk until the mixture forms stiff dry peaks, this may well take 10 minutes. Sift the cocoa with the remaining half-cup of confectioners sugar, and fold it very gently into the stiff meringue mixture. Spread the meringue with a palette knife or spatula over the ovals to a thickness of about 2 inches (5cm). Put the remainder of

the meringue into a pastry bag with a 3-inch (8-cm) round nozzle, and pipe into long strips.

Bake the ovals and the strips in a preheated oven 300°F (150°C) for about 1 hour or until it lifts easily from the paper. Meanwhile make the chocolate filling.

Put the cream in a heavy, preferably stainless steel, saucepan and bring it almost to a boil. Remove from the heat and add the chopped chocolate. With a wooden spoon, stir the chocolate into the cream until it is completely melted. Transfer the chocolate cream to the bowl of a food mixer and let it cool to room temperature. Add the liqueur and whisk until it is just stiff enough to pipe. Remove the meringue from the oven as soon as it is cooked, peel off the paper, and let it get completely cold on a wire rack.

Arrange one oval on a large serving dish. Spread a layer of mousse over the meringue, top with another layer, then more mousse and the top layer of meringue. Press down gently, then cover the whole surface with the remaining mousse. Break the meringue strips into 1½-inch (4-cm) bits and cover the sides and top of the "cake" with them, they can be stuck on haphazardly or porcupine fashion, one way or the other it will look very dramatic. Refrigerate for 1 hour. Just before serving, dredge with unsweetened cocoa and confectioners sugar. Serve with softly whipped cream.

Naranjan's Lemongrass and Palm Sugar Cake

Although lemongrass is not as yet usually associated with confections and desserts, it is fairly widely used in sweet as well as savory dishes in the East. This is a recipe adapted from a Malay version. Serve it with afternoon tea, or make a lemongrass syrup, pour it over the cake while it is still hot, and cut it up into diamonds or squares.

1½ cups white, self-rising flour
a pinch of salt
2 teaspoons baking powder
3½ cups dried coconut
3 sticks (1½ cups) unsalted butter, softened
1½ cups palm sugar or golden sugar
5 large eggs, separated
2 teaspoons lemon juice
3–4 stalks fresh lemongrass – cut up very finely so that the pieces resemble grains of sugar

round cake pan, 6 inches (15cm) in diameter, greased and lined with wax paper

Preheat the oven to 325°F (170°C).

Sift together the flour, salt, and baking powder, and add the dried coconut. Cream the butter and the palm sugar together in a bowl, and beat until light and fluffy. Beat in the egg yolks, one at a time, then fold in the dry ingredients. Whisk the egg whites until stiff, then fold into the cake mixture, together with the lemon juice and the lemongrass.

Pour into the prepared baking pan and bake in the oven for about 1½ hours or until a fine skewer inserted into the middle of the cake will come out clean.

Let the cake cool in the pan before removing it.

Note: palm sugar – or jaggery as it is known in India – comes from the palmyra palm; it is sweet, crumbly, and brown, and often sold wrapped in banana leaves in local markets. Now it is quite widely available in supermarkets and ethnic shops in the West. The flavor is close to that of maple sugar, and palm sugar is used to balance the saltiness of soy or fish sauce, and the heat in chiles, as well as the acidity of lemon juice.

Walnut Cake with American Frosting

Even though it is very laborious, we quite often crack open the walnuts for this cake, to ensure that they are fresh and sweet. Shelled walnuts turn rancid easily, so taste one to be sure they are still good.

1¾ cups all-purpose white flour
a pinch of salt
2½ level teaspoons baking powder
¾ cup very fresh walnuts, shelled
¾ stick (⅓ cup) butter
1 cup superfine sugar
½ teaspoon pure vanilla extract
2 eggs
½ cup milk

Filling
½ stick (¼ cup) butter
1 cup confectioners sugar
a few drops of pure vanilla extract

American Frosting
1 egg white
1 cup granulated sugar
¼ cup plus 1 tablespoon water

Decoration
5 or 6 walnut halves

3 round 7-inch (18-cm) cake pans

Preheat the oven to 375°F (190°C).

Brush the pans with a little melted butter, and line the bottom of each with a circle of wax paper. Brush the paper with melted butter also, and dust the bottom and edges with flour.

Sift the flour with a pinch of salt and the baking powder. Chop the walnuts roughly.

Cream the butter, gradually add the superfine sugar and the vanilla extract. Separate the eggs, add in the yolks, but set the whites aside until later. Add the walnuts to the batter. Fold in the flour and milk alternately into the batter.

Whisk the egg whites until they are stiff. Stir a little into the cake batter and then fold the rest in gently. Divide between the 3 pans and smooth over the tops. Bake in the oven for about 20 minutes or until firm to the touch. Turn out of the pans onto a wire rack. Remove the wax paper and let them get completely cold.

Meanwhile for the filling, cream the butter and add the sifted confectioners sugar and vanilla extract. When the cake is cold, sandwich the 3 layers together with butter cream. The delicious frosting is a little tricky to make, so follow the instructions exactly. Quick and accurate decisions are necessary in judging when the icing is ready, and then it must be used immediately.

Bring a saucepan of water, large enough to support a Pyrex mixing bowl, to a boil and let it simmer. Meanwhile, whisk the egg white until very stiff in the Pyrex bowl. In a small saucepan, dissolve the sugar carefully in the quarter-cup of water, and boil for about 1½ minutes until the syrup reaches the "thread stage" 223–236°F (106–113°C). It will look thick and syrupy and, when a metal spoon is dipped in, the last drops of syrup to drip off will form a thin thread. Pour this boiling syrup over the stiffly-beaten egg white, whisking all the time. Sit the bowl in the saucepan of simmering water. Continue to whisk in the bowl over the water until the icing is snow white and very thick (this can take up to 10 minutes).

Spread quickly over the cake with a palette knife or spatula. It sets very quickly at this stage, so speed is essential. Decorate with 5 or 6 walnut halves.

Above: Ballymaloe Chocolate Almond Cake

Ballymaloe Chocolate Almond Cake

An incredibly rich cake, use the best chocolate you can buy: Valrhona, Menier, Suchard, or Callebaut. We use Lesmé Belgian chocolate at Ballymaloe. Enjoy a small slice with a cup of espresso. This cake keeps really well if one can resist.

4 ounces (110g) best-quality dark chocolate (about 1⅓ cups)
2½ tablespoons red Jamaica rum
1 cup whole almonds
1 stick (½ cup) butter, preferably unsalted
½ cup superfine sugar
½ cup all-purpose white flour
3 eggs, separated
1 tablespoon superfine sugar

Chocolate Icing

4 ounces (110g) best-quality dark chocolate (about 1⅓ cups)
2½ tablespoons red Jamaica rum
1 stick (½ cup) unsalted butter

Decoration

Crystallized Violets (see page 447) and toasted slivered almonds

2 x 7-inch (18-cm) cake pans

Garden Café Chocolate Mousse Cake

3 eggs
1 cup superfine sugar
1/2 cup water
1 cup white flour
1/4 cup cocoa
1 level teaspoon baking powder

Chocolate Ganâche
1 1/4 cups cream
8 ounces (225g) best-quality dark chocolate, finely chopped (about 2 2/3 cups)

Decoration
Chocolate Decorations (see page 400)

2 x 8-inch (20.5-cm) diameter cake pans

Preheat the oven to 375°F (190°C).

Line the bottoms of the pans with a circle of wax paper, then grease and flour the sides of the pans and the wax paper. Separate the eggs. Whisk the yolks and sugar for two minutes. Blend in the water. Whisk until firm and creamy, about 10 minutes. Sift in the flour, cocoa, and baking powder. Beat the egg whites in a separate bowl until they form stiff peaks. Fold them in very gently. Divide the mixture between the two pans and bake in the oven for about 30 minutes. Cool on a wire rack.

Meanwhile make the Chocolate Ganâche. Put the cream in a heavy, preferably stainless steel, saucepan and bring it almost to a boil. Remove from the heat and add the chopped chocolate. With a wooden spoon, stir the chocolate into the cream until it is completely melted.

Transfer the chocolate cream into the bowl of a food mixer, and let it cool to room temperature. Whisk until it is just stiff enough to pipe (do not over-whisk or it will curdle and separate).

Sandwich the cakes together with whipped cream or Ganâche. Spread Ganâche all over the top and sides of the cake. Pipe eight or nine rosettes of Ganâche on top of the cake and decorate with curls of chocolate. Dredge with unsweetened cocoa.

Chocolate Chestnut Cake

This is a very rich and decadent cake. The chestnuts add a unique flavor and depth to the chocolate, with a smooth-as-velvet finish. It keeps very well for several days. Super chef, Jeanne Rankin, made this cake when she came to the school – we just love it.

4 ounces (110g) dark chocolate, chopped (about 1 1/3 cups)
a scant cup unsweetened chestnut purée
4 eggs, separated
1 cup minus 2 tablespoons superfine sugar

Icing
3 ounces (75g) best-quality chocolate (about 1 cup)
1 egg yolk
1 tablespoon butter
1 tablespoon rum (optional)
1 tablespoon superfine sugar
1/3 cup heavy cream, softly whipped
extra cream for serving

loose-bottomed pan, 8 inches (20.5cm)

Preheat the oven to 350°F (180°C). Grease the pan thoroughly. Melt the chocolate in a heatproof bowl over a saucepan of hot (not boiling) water. Pass the chestnut purée through a mouli or fine mesh strainer to loosen its texture. (It tends to be very compressed straight out of the can.)

Place the 4 yolks, and two-thirds of the sugar into the bowl of a mixer, and beat at high speed for 3–5 minutes, until it is very light and fluffy. By hand, whisk the egg whites until they are firm and shiny, and whisk in the rest of the sugar. Continue to whisk for another 30–60 seconds, until they are glossy and stiff. Add the chestnut purée to the yolk mixture and mix in at low speed. Fold in the melted chocolate. Once it is well incorporated, fold in the egg whites by hand.

Pour into the greased springform pan, and place in the center of the oven for 30–40 minutes, until a toothpick inserted into the center comes out clean. Remove from the oven and let cool before removing from the pan.

To make the icing, melt the chocolate, and while it is still warm, stir in the egg yolk and butter. Whisk for one minute, and then set aside. Whisk the rum, if using, and sugar into the cream, and fold it all into the chocolate mixture, a bit at a time. With the aid of a spatula, spread the icing on the top and the sides of the cake. Let set in the fridge for at least one hour before serving. Serve with a dollop of cream.

Tunisian Orange Cake

Sophie Grigson introduced us to this cake on her course here at the school. It is a real goodie and keeps for not just days but weeks.

1 1/3 cups (50g) slightly stale white breadcrumbs
1 cup minus 2 tablespoons (200g) sugar
1 cup (100g) ground almonds
1 1/2 level teaspoons baking powder
1 cup minus 2 tablespoons (200ml) sunflower oil
4 eggs
zest of 1 large unwaxed orange, finely grated
zest of 1/2 unwaxed lemon, finely grated

Citrus syrup
juice of 1 unwaxed orange
juice of 1/2 unwaxed lemon
1/3 cup (75g) sugar
2 cloves
1 cinnamon stick

cream, Greek yogurt or crème fraîche

8-inch (20.5-cm) round pan, 2 inches (5cm) deep

Line the bottom of the pan with a circle of wax paper. Grease and flour the pan. Mix the breadcrumbs with the sugar, almonds, and baking powder. Whisk the oil with the eggs, pour into the dry ingredients, and mix well. Add the orange and lemon zest. Pour the batter into the prepared pan. Put into a cold oven, and turn on with the heat set to 350°F (180°C).

Bake for 45–60 minutes or until the cake is golden brown. A skewer inserted into the center should come out clean. Let cool for 5 minutes before turning out onto a plate.

Meanwhile make the citrus syrup. Put all the ingredients into a stainless steel saucepan, bring gently to a boil, stirring until the sugar has dissolved completely. Simmer for 3 minutes. While the cake is still warm, pierce it with a skewer. Spoon the hot syrup over the cake. Let it cool. Spoon excess syrup back over the cake every now and then until it is all soaked up. One can remove the cloves and cinnamon stick, but we leave them on top of the cake.

Serve with softly whipped cream, thick Greek yogurt, or crème fraiche.

Below: Tunisian Orange Cake

Angel Food Cake with Rosewater Cream and Summer Berries

A very delicious way of using up spare egg whites.

1 cup plus 2 tablespoons all-purpose white flour
a scant 3/4 cup superfine sugar
pinch of salt
7 large egg whites
1 level teaspoon cream of tartar
1 teaspoon rosewater

For decoration
confectioners sugar
rose petals, if available
summer berries – raspberries, strawberries, blueberries, loganberries, fraises des bois
Rosewater Cream (see right)

round cake pan, 3 inches (8cm) deep, and 9 inches (23cm) in diameter, greased and floured

Preheat the oven to 350°F (180°C).

Put 2 tablespoons of superfine sugar aside. Sift the flour with the remainder of the superfine sugar and a little pinch of salt. Put the egg whites into a large bowl, whisk slowly at first until foamy, add the cream of tartar and whisk again. Slowly add the reserved superfine sugar and beat until the egg whites hold soft peaks. Add the rosewater, then fold in the flour and sugar, a third at a time.

Pour the mixture gently into the greased pan, and bake in the oven for 30–35 minutes or until firm and slightly golden. A skewer should come out clean when inserted into the cake. Let cool for 20–30 minutes in the pan. Turn out onto a wire rack to cool.

Serve the cake, dusted with confectioners sugar and accompanied by summer berries and Rosewater Cream.

Rosewater Cream

2 cups whipped cream
1 teaspoon rosewater, or to taste
a little superfine sugar

Mix the whipped cream, rosewater, and sugar gently together.

Puff Pastry Dough

Makes about 2 3/4 pounds (1 1/4kg)

Homemade puff pastry takes a little time to make but it is more than worth the effort for the wonderful flavor that bears no relation to the commercial equivalent. It's essential to use butter. It should have 729 layers!

1 lb. (450g) chilled flour (use bread flour if possible)
pinch of salt
1 1/4–1 1/2 cups cold water
squeeze of lemon juice (optional)
4 sticks (2 cups) butter, firm but pliable

Sift the flour and salt into a bowl and mix to a firm dough with water and a squeeze of lemon juice. This dough is called détrempe. Cover with wax paper or plastic wrap and let it rest for 30 minutes in the refrigerator.

Roll the détrempe into a square about a half-inch (1-cm) thick. If the butter is very hard, beat it (still in the wrapper) with a rolling pin until pliable but not sticky.

Unwrap the butter and shape into a slab roughly three-quarter inch (2-cm) thick, place in the center of the dough and fold the dough, over the edges of the butter to make a neat package.

Make sure your chilled marble slab or pastry board is well-floured, then flatten the dough with a rolling pin, and continue to roll out into a rectangle about 18 inches (45cm) long and 6 inches (15cm) wide (this is approximate, so don't get into a fuss if it's not exactly that measurement). Fold neatly into three, with the sides aligned as accurately as possible. Seal the edges by pressing with a rolling pin.

Give the dough a one-quarter turn (90°): it should now be on your pastry board as though it was a book with the ends facing north/south. Roll out again, fold in three, and seal the edges with the rolling pin. Cover with plastic wrap or wax paper meticulously, and let it rest in the fridge for 30 minutes.

The pastry has now had two rolls or "turns." Repeat the process two more times, giving the dough six rolls altogether, with a 30 minutes rest in the fridge between every two turns. Chill for at least 30 minutes before using.

Note: Each time you start to roll the pastry dough, place it on the worktop with the ends north/south as if it were a book. In hot weather, it may be necessary to chill the dough slightly longer between rollings.

Gâteau Pithivier

Serves 8

My brother, Rory O'Connell, does a delicious Chocolate Gâteau Pithivier, adding 4 ounces (110g) of chopped chocolate to the filling.

half-quantity Puff Pastry Dough (see left)

Filling
1 cup ground almonds
1/2 cup superfine sugar
3 tablespoons melted butter
2 egg yolks
2 1/2 tablespoons cream
2 teaspoons rum (optional)
egg wash made with 1 beaten egg and a tiny pinch of salt

Glaze
confectioners sugar

Preheat the oven to 450°F (230°C).

Divide the pastry dough in half, roll out thinly, cut into two circles about 10 inches (25.5cm) in diameter. Put one onto a damp baking sheet and chill; also chill the other piece.

Mix all the filling ingredients together in a bowl until smooth. Put the filling on the dough that's on the baking sheet, leaving a rim of about an inch (2.5cm) free around the edge. Brush the rim with beaten egg or water, and put the other pastry dough circle on top; press it down well around the edges.

Make a small hole in the center, brush with egg wash, and leave for 5 minutes in the refrigerator. With the back of a knife, nick the edge of the pastry dough 12 times at regular intervals, to form a scalloped edge with a rose petal effect. Mark long curving lines from the central hole outwards, to designate formal petals. Be careful not to cut through the pastry dough, just score it.

Bake for 20 minutes in the oven, then lower the heat to 400°F (200°C) and bake for about 30 minutes. While still hot, dredge it heavily with confectioners sugar and return to a very hot oven or pop under a broiler for an instant or two and no longer – the sugar will melt and caramelize to a dark brown glaze. Serve warm or cold, with a bowl of softly whipped cream.

Note: Gâteau Pithivier is best eaten warm, but it also keeps well and may be reheated.

Mille-feuille

Serves 8

A labor of love, but so delicious...

8 ounces (225g) Puff Pastry Dough (see left)
about 1/2 cup (Red Currant Jelly (see page 508)
1 1/4 cups whipped cream
1 1/4 cups Pastry Cream (see page 460)
2–3 tablespoons Kirsch
8 ounces (225g) raspberries or strawberries (about 1 1/2 cups)
confectioners sugar

Garnish
mint or lemon balm leaves

Preheat the oven to 425°F (220°C).

Roll out the pastry dough into a very large, thin rectangle, about 16 x 34 inches (40 x 87cm). This dough should be no thicker than a coin. Transfer to a baking sheet or sheets. Prick all over with a fork. Cover the baking tray or trays with a second tray and bake – this sounds rather bizarre but it prevents the puff pastry from rising too much or unevenly. Chill for 30 minutes. Bake in the oven for about 20 minutes and then reduce the heat to 350°F (180°C) until brown.

Remove from the oven and while it is still warm, cut the pastry into 3 neat equal-sized strips, about 5 x 10 inches (12.5 x 25.5cm). Reserve the trimmings of cooked pastry for later. Dredge the 3 pieces of pastry heavily with confectioners sugar and place under a hot broiler. Let the sugar caramelize. Remove from under the broiler, flip them over, and repeat the process on the other sides of the pastry. Let cool completely.

To assemble the mille-feuille, place one of the pastry strips on a board and brush lightly with slightly warmed red currant jelly. Mix the pastry cream with the stiffly whipped cream, and flavor with kirsch. Put into a pastry bag. Pipe half of this mixture onto the first layer of pastry. Cover with a layer of raspberries or sliced strawberries, (reserve a few whole ones for decoration). Now brush the second piece of pastry with red currant jelly, put on top of the first, and pipe the remaining pastry cream mixture on top of it. Place the last piece of pastry on top. Dredge the top of the pastry with confectioners sugar. Crush the leftover pastry trimmings with your hands and push them onto the ends of the cake. They will stick to the pastry cream. Finally, score the top of the cake with a red-hot skewer in a criss-cross pattern. Decorate with rosettes of cream and fresh strawberries or raspberries. Place on a serving dish and serve. Use a serrated knife to slice.

Feuillitée of Summer or Autumn Berries

Serves 4

Puff Pastry Dough (see page 456)
Pastry Cream (see page 460)
Kirsch
cream
strawberry, raspberries, loganberries, blueberries, blackberries, or a mixture
egg wash

Garnish
mint or lemon balm leaves
confectioners sugar

Preheat the oven to 475°F (250°C).

Roll out the pastry dough to three-quarter inch (2cm) thickness, stamp out 3 1/2–4-inch (9–10-cm) circles with a cookie cutter. Sprinkle a few drops of water onto a baking sheet. Turn the circles upside-down and place on the damp sheet, brush with egg wash in both directions. Take a 2 1/2–3-inch (6–8-cm) cookie cutter, press down halfway into the pastry; the inner circle will become the lid. Lightly score the edges and the lid into a pattern with the back of a knife. Let it rest for 10–15 minutes in a fridge.

Bake the circles of dough in the oven for 10 minutes, then reduce the temperature to 400°F (200°C) until fully cooked. A few minutes before the end of cooking time, remove the pastry lid, scoop out the uncooked pastry dough in the center, and continue to cook for a few minutes more. Cool on a wire rack.
To assemble, lace the pastry cream well with kirsch, mix in some stiffly whipped cream (about half cream to half Pastry Cream).

Put the pastry shells onto 4 serving plates, and fill them two-thirds full with the pastry cream mixture. Top generously with berries, pop the lid on top, decorate with lemon balm or mint leaves, and dredge with confectioners sugar.

Master Recipe

Jalousie

Serves 4–5

8 ounces (225g) Flaky Pastry Dough (see page 413) or Puff Pastry Dough (see page 456)
7–8 tablespoons apricot jam
1 egg white beaten until frothy
granulated sugar (for sprinkling)

Preheat the oven to 425°F (220°C).

Roll out the dough into an 8 x 12-inch (20.5 x 32-cm) rectangle. Trim the edges neatly and cut in half lengthwise. Place one piece of dough on a dampened baking sheet. Fold over the other piece lengthwise and, with a sharp knife, cut across the fold at quarter-inch (5mm) intervals to within a half-inch (1cm) of the outer edge, like the teeth of a comb.

Spoon the jam filling down the center of the uncut piece of dough to within an inch (2.5cm) of the edges. Brush the edges with cold water and set the cut rectangle on top, with the fold in the center. Open out the folded dough and press the edge down onto the lower piece. Trim the edges to neaten them, and chill the Jalousie for 10–15 minutes.

Bake the pastry in the oven for 25–30 minutes or until puffed and browned. About 5–10 minutes before the end of baking, brush the Jalousie with the beaten egg white, sprinkle generously with sugar, and resume baking.

Serve the Jalousie hot, or slide it onto a rack to cool and serve at room temperature. It is best eaten the day it is baked, or it can be frozen, baked or unbaked. Alternatively, when the Jalousie is cooked, dredge heavily with confectioners sugar and put under the broiler to glaze.

Variations

Jalousie may also be filled with apple purée, frangipan, or a mixture of homemade mincemeat and apple purée; or savory fillings such as cheese, salmon, and mushrooms.

Almond Filling for Jalousie

3/4 cup whole skinned almonds
3/4 stick (1/3 cup) unsalted butter
1/3 cup superfine sugar
3/4 cup candied orange peel (see page 515)
1/4 teaspoon grated orange zest
1 large egg
1 teaspoon kirsch

Preheat the oven to 350°F (180°C).

Toast the almonds for 10 minutes, cool, and grind to a slightly gritty powder in the food processor. Cream the butter, add the almonds, sugar, orange zest and peel, beaten egg and kirsch. Mix well, fill the center of a puff pastry tart or jalousie.

Sacristains

Makes about 35

These French pastry twists can also be made as savory sacristains by replacing the sugar with grated Parmesan cheese.

Flaky Pastry Dough or Puff Pastry Dough (page 413 & 456)
1 egg, beaten to mix with a pinch of salt (for glaze)
1 cup almonds, finely chopped or sliced
1 cup minus 2 tablespoons sugar

Preheat the oven to 425°F (220°C). Make the Flaky or Puff Pastry dough and chill thoroughly. Roll out to a very thin rectangle and trim the edges. Brush the pastry dough with egg glaze. Sprinkle with half the almonds, then with half the sugar.

Turn the pastry dough over. Brush the other side with egg glaze and sprinkle with the remaining almonds and sugar. Cut the dough into 5-inch (12.5-cm) strips, then crosswise into sticks three-quarter inch (2-cm) wide. Twist them several times and place on a greased baking sheet. Press the ends down firmly so that they do not unroll during baking.

Chill for 15 minutes. Bake the pastries in the oven for 8–12 minutes or until puffed and brown.

Note: Be very careful as these burn easily. Transfer to a rack to cool. Strips can be sandwiched together with cream and raspberry jam, and served for afternoon tea.

Eccles Cakes

Makes 10

Originally Eccles cakes were filled with blackcurrants and mint leaves. Now they are similar to Banbury cakes, without the candied peel. Make them round or oval in shape.

8 ounces (225g) Flaky Pastry Dough (see page 413) or Puff Pastry Dough (see page 456)
1/2 cup currants
3/4–1 cup Candied Peel (see page 515)
1 teaspoon orange zest, grated
1/2 stick (1/4 cup) melted butter
1/4 cup granulated sugar
extra granulated sugar for tops

Preheat the oven to 425°F (220°C).

Roll out the dough to an eighth-inch (3-mm) thickness and cut with a 3-inch (8-cm) round cookie cutter. Mix the remaining ingredients together.

Place one teaspoon of the filling in the center of each circle, pinch the sides into the center, and turn over and roll out until the fruit is just coming through. Brush with cold water, dip the top in granulated sugar, and slit the tops with a knife two or three times. Bake for 15 minutes.

Moroccan Snake

Serves 10–15 people

One of the glories of Moroccan confectionery, great for a party. Keeps well.

Filling

4 cups ground almonds
1½ cups superfine sugar
1 tablespoon freshly ground cinnamon
⅓–½ cup (orange flower water

1 package best-quality phyllo pastry dough

¾–1 stick (⅓–½ cup) melted butter
egg wash
confectioners sugar for dusting

Preheat the oven to 350°F (180°C).

Put all the dry ingredients together in a bowl. Add enough orange flower water to form a paste.

To assemble: lay one sheet of phyllo on the counter and brush it with melted butter. Take a handful of the paste and form into a snake about an inch (2.5cm) thick. Lay this along the long side of the sheet of phyllo, about an inch (2.5cm) from the edge. Roll up and coil it into a "snail shell." Put a sheet of wax paper on a baking sheet and put the snail in the center of the baking sheet. Continue with the rest of the phyllo and almond paste. Press the ends of the outer coils together to seal the joints, and continue to make the snake until all the filling is used up.

Brush with egg wash and then with melted butter. Bake in the oven for about 30 minutes or until crisp and golden. Slide off the baking tray and cool on a wire rack. Dust with confectioners sugar and perhaps a little cinnamon. Wonderful, warm or cold.

Master Recipe

Choux Pastry Dough

1¼ cups white bread flour
pinch of salt
1 cup water
1 stick (½ cup) butter, cut into ½-inch (1-cm) cubes
4–5 eggs depending on size

Sift the flour with the salt onto a piece of wax paper. Heat the water and butter in a saucepan until the butter is melted. Bring to a fast rolling boil, remove from the heat. (**Note:** Prolonged boiling evaporates the water and changes the proportions of the dough.)

As soon as the pan is removed from the heat, add all the flour at once and beat vigorously with a wooden spoon for a few seconds, until the mixture is smooth and pulls away from the sides to form a ball. Put the saucepan back on a low heat and stir for a half minute or until the mixture starts to fur the bottom of the saucepan. Remove from the heat and cool for a few seconds.

Meanwhile break one egg into a bowl and whisk it. Add the remaining eggs to the dough, one by one, with a wooden spoon, beating thoroughly after each addition. Make sure the dough comes back to the same texture each time before you add another egg. When it will no longer form a ball in the center of the saucepan, add the beaten egg little by little. Use just enough to make a mixture that is very shiny and drops reluctantly from the spoon in a sheet.

Note: You may not need all of the reserved egg. If too much is added, the dough cannot be shaped. (Choux pastry dough should just hold its shape when piped.)

Although the dough puffs up better if used immediately, choux pastry can be stored for up to 8 hours before baking. Rub the surface with butter while the dough is still warm, so it doesn't form a skin. When cool, use as needed or cover tightly and keep in the fridge until needed.

Chocolate or Coffee Eclairs

Makes 20

Choux Pastry Dough (see left)

Creme Chantilly

1¼ cups whipped cream
½–1 tablespoon confectioners sugar
2–3 drops pure vanilla extract

Chocolate Icing (see page 451) or Coffee Icing (see page 448)

wax paper

Preheat the oven to 425°F (220°C).

Make the choux pastry dough in the usual way. Line a baking sheet with wax paper and sprinkle with a few drops of cold water. Fill the choux pastry into a pastry bag fitted with a ¾-inch (2-cm) round eclair nozzle. Pipe the dough into 3–4 inch (8–10cm) strips, 1½ inches (4cm) apart, to allow for expansion.

Bake immediately in the oven, for 15 minutes, then reduce the heat to 400°F (200°C), for a further 15–20 minutes or until they are crisp and golden. Remove from the oven, make a hole in the side of each éclair to let the steam escape, return to the oven, and bake for about 5 minutes more. Remove to a wire rack. Meanwhile make the chosen icing or icings. Make the Chantilly Cream by sweetening the whipped cream to taste, with confectioners sugar and a dash of vanilla extract, put into a pastry bag fitted with a small nozzle. As soon as the éclairs are cold, fill them with cream through the hole where the steam escaped (they can be split lengthwise and filled that way, too).

Dip the tops in the icing and put onto a wire rack over a tray to catch the drips. Serve within 1 or 2 hours of being made. **Note:** Sometimes instead of icing éclairs, we dip them in caramel and cool on oiled trays or wax paper.

Choux Puffs

Pipe 1–2 blobs of Choux Pastry Dough (see page 459) for each puff, onto a baking tray. Flatten the tops with a wet teaspoon, brush with egg wash, and bake for 20–25 minutes at 425°F (220°C).

Lemon Curd Eclairs or Choux Puffs

Makes 12–15

12–15 éclairs or Choux Puffs (see above)
Lemon Curd (see page 510)
1¼ cups whipped cream
Crystallized Lemon Peel (see page 515)

Split the éclairs or choux puffs in half. Mix the cream with the lemon curd to taste – you will not need all the lemon curd, save the rest for another use. Cover, and keep refrigerated. Fill the éclairs or choux puffs with lemon cream. Drizzle the remains of the lemon curd on the plate. Put an éclair or a choux puff on top. Decorate with crystallized lemon peel and a sprig of mint.

Chocolate Profiteroles

Serves 8–10

Profiteroles are simply choux puffs filled with a mixture of Pastry Cream and Chantilly Cream, or just Chantilly Cream.

Choux Puffs (see above)
Pastry Cream (see right)

Chantilly Cream
⅔ cups heavy cream, whipped with
1 level tablespoon confectioners sugar
a few drops of pure vanilla extract

Chocolate Sauce (see page 599)

Croque en Bouche

A spectacular French wedding cake consisting of a pyramid of profiteroles dipped in caramel. It is often decorated with spun sugar and silver dragees.

Crème Patissière (Pastry Cream)

Pastry Cream is the most common filling for sweet choux pastries. Be sure to cook it thoroughly – uncooked, it has an unpleasant taste of raw flour. It is also often spread in tart shells and topped with fruit, or spread between layers of sponge cake.

6 egg yolks
½ cup sugar
6 tablespoons flour
2 cups minus 2 tablespoons milk
pinch of salt
vanilla bean

Beat the egg yolks with the sugar until thick and light. Stir in the flour.

Scald the milk by bringing it just to a boil with the salt. Add the vanilla bean to the hot milk, cover the pan, and let infuse for about 10–15 minutes. Remove the vanilla bean and reheat the milk to boiling point. Whisk the boiling milk into the egg mixture, return to the pan, and whisk over a gentle heat until boiling.*

Cook the cream gently, whisking constantly for two minutes or until the cream thins slightly, showing the flour is completely cooked. Remove from the heat, transfer to a bowl, rub a piece of butter over the surface to prevent the formation of a skin, and cover with plastic wrap and let it cool. Use as directed in the recipes.

* Be sure that the Pastry Cream is smooth before letting it boil. If lumps form as it thickens, remove the pan from the heat and beat until smooth.

Important points
If the finished cream is too thick, simply thin it with a little milk.

Special care must be taken in keeping Pastry Cream, since lightly cooked egg yolks spoil fairly rapidly. Refrigerate as soon as it is cool and keep for not longer than a day or two. Thick Pastry Cream can be frozen, but thin cream made with a minimum of flour will separate on freezing.

Crème St. Honoré (Light Pastry Cream)

To make approx. 2½ cups

1¼ cups milk
vanilla bean or vanilla extract
3 small eggs
½ cup sugar
¼ cup flour

In a heavy saucepan, bring the milk just to a boil, with a small piece of vanilla bean in the pan, or add a few drops of vanilla extract afterwards.

Separate two of the eggs. Whisk the yolks and the whole egg with the sugar until light in color. Stir in the flour and then pour in the milk, return to the saucepan, and stir over gentle heat until it comes to a boil.
Let it boil for two minutes, still stirring all the time. (I find a little wire whisk better than a wooden spoon for this operation.) Whisk until the pastry cream is thick. Transfer to a bowl. Whisk the egg white stiffly in a clean bowl, fold into the pastry cream while still warm. Let cool before using.

Lapis Legit (Indonesian Cinnamon Layer Cake)

Serves 20

Sri Owen enchanted us when she came to teach at the cookery school in 1989. She explained that in Indonesia, Lapis Legit is eaten usually with afternoon tea. It also goes well with coffee, either mid-morning or after dinner. It should be sliced very thin and cut into pieces about 2 inches (5cm) long – it is very rich so the pieces must be small.

4 sticks (2 cups) unsalted butter
1 drop vanilla extract
1 cup superfine sugar
16–19 egg yolks (size 2)
¼ cup creamy milk
1¼ cups all-purpose flour
1 pinch of salt
8 egg whites
2 teaspoons ground nutmeg
4 teaspoons ground cinnamon
1 teaspoon ground cloves

Beat the butter, vanilla and half the sugar until creamy. In another bowl, beat the egg yolks with the rest of the sugar until creamy and thick. Beat these mixtures together and add the milk. Sift the flour and salt into the bowl, and fold in carefully. Beat the egg whites until stiff, and fold in. Divide this mixture between two bowls. Stir the spices into one of them, so that you have one bowl colored brown by the spices, and the other cream-colored.

Butter an 8 x 9-inch (20–25-cm) square cake pan with a loose bottom. Heat the broiler to its maximum temperature (if using a broiler inside an oven, heat the oven to 300°F (150°C), then turn it off before turning the broiler on). Pour a layer of the cream batter, about an eighth-inch (3-mm) thick, over the bottom. Broil this for a few minutes until the batter has set firm. Remove from the oven, and pour in the same thickness of the spiced, brown batter. Broil this as before. Continue this process, with alternate layers of brown and cream-colored batter, until the batter is finished. (A good Lapis Legit will consist of 12–14 layers or more.) Transfer the cake to the oven and bake at 300°F (150°C) for 10 minutes. Remove cake from the pan and cool on a wire rack.

Lapis Legit will keep moist and fresh in a cake pan or in the fridge for a week, well-wrapped in aluminum foil. It can also be frozen.

Cookies

Jane's Cookies

Makes 25

This is a great little recipe because it is quick and its formula of 2/4/6 is easy to remember. The flavor is quite different, but still delicious, if you use unsalted butter.

6 ounces (175g) white flour (1½ cups)
1 stick (½ cup) butter
2 ounces (50g) superfine sugar (¼ cup)

Preheat the oven to 350°F (180°C).

Put the flour and sugar in a bowl and rub in the butter as for shortcrust pastry. Gather the mixture together and knead it lightly. Roll out to a quarter-inch (5-mm) thick. Cut into circles with a 2½-inch (6-cm)

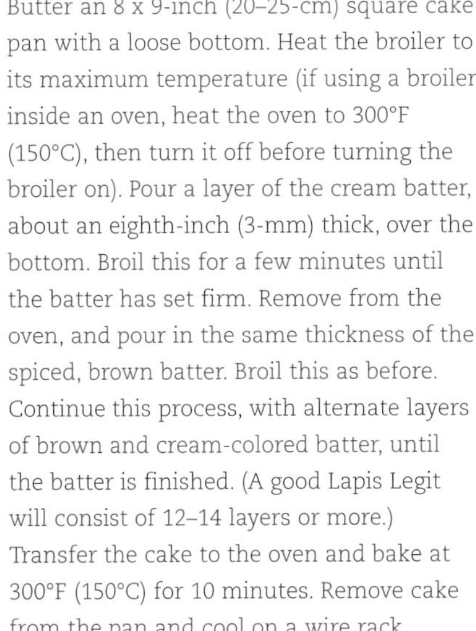

Left: Jane's Cookies

cookie cutter, or cut into heart shapes. Arrange on wax paper on a baking tray and bake in the moderate oven until pale brown, 10–15 minutes.

Remove, and cool on a rack. Serve with fruit fools, compôtes, and ice creams.

Sablé Stars

Makes about 40, depending on the size

A French biscuit, originally from Normandy, sablés can be eaten plain, with fresh berries, or simply stuck together with a little jam and cream; savory sablés are also made, using cheese.

1½ cups all-purpose white flour
¾ cup confectioners sugar
tiny pinch of salt
1¼ sticks (⅔ cup) unsalted butter
1 egg yolk

Sift the flour and confectioners sugar into a bowl and add a tiny pinch of salt. Rub in the butter and the egg yolk. Press the mixture together, wrap in plastic wrap and let it rest for 30 minutes in the refrigerator. Alternatively, combine in a food processor but stop the machine just as soon as the mixture comes together.

Preheat the oven to 300°F (150°C).
Roll out the pastry dough into an eighth-inch (3-mm) thick sheet, and stamp into stars or heart shapes with a cookie cutter. Carefully lift onto a baking sheet lined with wax paper. Bake for about 15–20 minutes, until they are pale golden in color. Cool on a wire rack.

Sprinkle with sifted confectioners sugar and serve with fruit salads, ice creams, mousses, etc.

Shortbread Stars with Strawberries and Cream

Makes about 25

These may be cut tiny or quite large. Raspberries, loganberries, fraises des bois are all delicious fillings.

Jane's Cookie mixture *(see page 461)*

strawberries
whipped cream
sugar
tiny mint or lemon balm leaves

Preheat the oven to 350°F (180°C).

Make the shortbread. Roll out to a quarter-inch (5-mm) thick on a lightly floured surface. Stamp out into star shapes. Bake in the oven until pale brown, about 8–12 minutes, depending on thickness. They should be pale golden – be careful, they burn easily. Remove and cool on a rack.

To assemble: put a star on a plate and pipe a little sweetened cream onto the cookie. Add a few slices of strawberry, then pipe another tiny blob of cream. Top with another biscuit. Pipe a little cream in the center and decorate with mint leaves or lemon balm. Dredge lightly with confectioners sugar. Repeat with the others and serve as soon as possible.

Shortbread Hearts with Strawberries and Cream

Use a heart-shaped cutter and proceed as above. Perfect for Valentine's Day or as a little surprise when you want to say "I love you" or simply to bring on a proposal!

Macaroons

Makes 24–36

These lovely old-fashioned macaroons are easy to make and keep for ages. Originally the macaroon came from Italy, but the French brought it to fame and it became the custom for French nuns to make these and offer them to visitors, along with a glass of wine. Amaretti, mandorla, and pinoccate are all forms of Italian macaroons.

1¼ cups ground almonds
¾ cup superfine sugar
2 small egg whites
¼ teaspoon pure almond extract
a little granulated sugar
24–26 blanched almonds

Preheat the oven to 350°F (180°C).

Put the almonds and sugar in a bowl. Whisk the egg whites lightly and mix into the dry ingredients, a little at a time. Add the almond extract and beat well to make a fairly smooth, stiff mixture. Line two baking trays with wax paper. Spoon the mixture onto the trays in lumps the size of a walnut.

Sprinkle with sugar and decorate each with an almond. Place in the oven and bake for 10–15 minutes, or until just firm. Cool for a few minutes, then lift off the tray and cool on a wire rack.

Carol Fields' Biscotti

Makes 60–72

Carol Fields' books are redolent with the flavors of Italy and baking is her passion. This recipe is from Italy in Small Bites.

¼ cup raisins
6 tablespoons Cointreau or Curaçao
5 eggs
2 cups sugar
1 teaspoon vanilla extract

1 3/4 cups unblanched almonds, toasted and roughly chopped
4 cups all-purpose white flour
1 1/2 teaspoons baking soda (bread soda), sifted
pinch of salt

Jelly roll pan, 12 x 18 inches (32 x 45cm)

Preheat the oven to 350°F (180°C).

Soak the raisins in the liqueur for 20 minutes and then drain, reserving the liqueur. Separate the eggs and beat the yolks with all but two heaped tablespoons of the sugar, until thick and pale. Beat in the reserved liqueur and the vanilla extract. In another bowl, beat the egg whites until they just hold stiff peaks, and slowly add the two tablespoons of sugar, beating until they hold stiff peaks.

Whisk a quarter of the egg whites into the yolk mixture to lighten it, then fold in the remaining whites delicately but thoroughly, and finally fold in the drained raisins and the nuts.

Mix together the flour, baking soda, and salt. Using a rubber spatula, fold the flour mixture into the egg mixture, a quarter at a time.

Butter the jelly roll pan. Gently spread the mixture to cover the bottom of the pan as evenly as possible. Bake for 20–22 minutes, until pale golden. Remove from the oven and let cool until comfortable to handle, about 10 minutes. Ease out of the pan onto a cutting board and use a serrated knife to cut it into 1 1/2-inch (4-cm) strips. Cut the strips into 3/4-inch (2-cm) wide slices.

Arrange them on the jelly roll pan, cut side down, and return them to the oven to bake for another 7–8 minutes on each side, until pale golden. Cool on racks.

Aunt Alice's Cookies

Serves 30

Mary Dowey, who edited several of my books, gave me this lovely recipe.

1 stick (1/2 cup) butter
1 tablespoon golden syrup (or, if unavailable, corn syrup)
1 1/4 cups white flour
a scant cup brown sugar
3/4 cup rolled oats
1/2 teaspoon baking soda (bread soda), sifted

Preheat the oven to 400°F (200°C).

Melt the butter and syrup together in a small saucepan over gentle heat. Put all the ingredients into a bowl, pour in the butter/syrup liquid, and mix well. Make into small balls and space them out on baking trays. Bake in the oven for about 10 minutes or until golden brown. Cool on a wire rack.

Anzac Cookies

Makes around 34 cookies, depending on size

These cookies commemorate the Australian and New Zealand participation in the two World Wars, and are traditionally made in my publisher's office in a competition in April around Anzac Day by the Antipodean contingent.

1 1/4 cups flour
1/2 cup rolled oats
a scant cup dried coconut
2/3 cup superfine sugar
1/2 teaspoon baking powder
1 1/4 sticks (2/3 cup) butter
2 1/2 tablespoons golden syrup (or, if unavailable, use corn syrup)

Preheat the oven to 300°F (150°C).

In a large bowl, stir together the flour, oats, coconut, sugar, and baking powder. In a small saucepan, combine the butter and syrup and cook the mixture over a moderately low heat, stirring until the butter is melted. Pour the butter mixture into the flour mixture and combine them well.

Make into small balls and put them 2 inches (5cm) apart on baking sheets, and flatten them slightly with the back of a fork dipped in water. Bake the cookies in the middle of the oven for 15 minutes or until they are golden.

Let the cookies cool slightly on the baking sheet, then, using a spatula, transfer them to a rack, and let them cool completely.

Orange Tuiles

Makes about 20

These light crisp cookies look very impressive, they are easy to make and are great with ice cream and mousses. They will soften if they are kept in a moist atmosphere so, as soon as they are cold, store in an airtight tin. They are shaped like curved tiles, hence the name (tuile is French for tile).

2 egg whites
1/2 cup superfine sugar
1/2 stick (1/4 cup) butter
1/2 cup all-purpose flour
zest of 1 unwaxed orange, grated

Preheat the oven to 375°F (190°C).

Line a baking sheet with wax paper. Whisk the egg whites until quite stiff and add the superfine sugar. Continue to whisk until smooth and glossy.

Melt the butter, add it to the egg white mixture by degrees, along with the sifted flour. Fold in the orange zest. Spread out teaspoonfuls, well apart, on the baking sheet and bake until pale brown, about 5–6 minutes. Drape the tuiles over a rolling pin to make them round. Cool on a wire rack.

Coupelles or Langues de Chats

Makes 8 "containers," 3$^1/_2$ inches (9cm) in diameter

Simple to make and charming as containers for ices, fruits, and dessert creams, these crisp little cookie cups are made from the French egg-white batter known as langues de chats, because it is usually baked in flat cat's tongue shapes. Here the batter is spread in thin discs on baking sheets and, as soon as the edges have browned in a hot oven, they are removed one by one and pressed into a teacup, where they immediately crisp into shape. This recipe is adapted from Mastering the Art of French Cooking by Beck, Bertholle, and Child.

$^1/_2$ stick ($^1/_4$ cup) butter
$^1/_3$ cup superfine sugar
zest of 1 lemon or orange, grated
2 egg whites
a scant $^1/_2$ cup all-purpose flour
tasteless salad oil

2 baking sheets about 14 x 18 inches (35 x 45cm), buttered and floured
a vol au vent cutter, pot lid, or saucer, about 5 inches (12.5cm) in diameter
a rubber spatula
2 large teacups or small bowls, about 5 inches (12.5cm) in diameter at the top and 2 inches (5cm) at the bottom, and 2$^1/_2$ inches (6cm) deep.

Preheat the oven to 425°F (220°C).

Set a rack in middle of the oven. Butter and flour the baking sheets, then, using the cutter and point of the rubber spatula, mark 4 circles on each. Lightly oil the cups or bowls, and set them at a convenient place near the oven.

Beat the butter, sugar, and lemon or orange zest in the bowl using an electric mixer or wooden spoon, until pale and fluffy. Pour in the egg whites and mix for a few seconds, only just enough to blend. Place the flour in a sieve or sifter, and shake it over the batter, rapidly folding it in with a rubber spatula. Place 2 teaspoons of the batter in the center of each of the 4 circles on the baking sheets. Using the back of the spoon, smear the batter out very thinly to fill the circles (less than a sixteenth-inch (1-mm) thick). Place in the middle of the oven, set the timer for 5 minutes, and bake until the cookies have browned lightly, nearly to the center, or in large splotches. Form more cookies on a second sheet while these are baking.

As soon as they are done, set the baking sheet on the open oven door so that the cookies stay warm and pliable – they crisp as soon as they cool and then cannot be molded. Working rapidly, slide the long side of spatula blade under one biscuit to scrape and lift it off the baking sheet, turn it upside down over one of the oiled cups or bowls, and press into the cup with your fingers.

Rapidly remove a second cookie from the sheet and press into the second cup. Immediately take the first cookie out of the first cup – they crisp in seconds – and place on a wire rack. Rapidly mold the third cookie, and finally the fourth (they will be fragile, so handle with care).

Close the oven door and wait for a few minutes for temperature to return to 425°F (220°C), and bake and mold the second sheet of cookies.

Note: If this is the first time you have done this type of cookie, experiment with one or two first so that you will understand the system of baking, removing, and molding; they are easy to do as soon as you know what to expect.

Cookies will stay crisp for several days in dry weather if stored in an airtight container; for longer storage, freeze them. Spoon sorbet, ice cream, or fruits into the cookie cups just before serving. For fruit sorbets or ice cream, such as strawberry, save some of the fruit to decorate the top of each serving.

Fork Cookies

Makes 45–50 cookies

Freshly ground cinnamon, ginger, or chocolate chips can be a delicious addition to these cookies but they're delicious just as they are, too. This is the first cookie recipe the students make.

2 sticks (1 cup) soft butter
$^1/_2$ cup superfine sugar
2$^1/_2$ cups self rising flour, sifted
grated zest of 1 lemon or orange

Vanilla Sugar

Cream the butter, add in the sugar, flour, and zest, and mix just until it all comes together. Alternatively, place all four ingredients in the bowl of a food mixer and mix slowly until all the ingredients come together. At this stage, the dough can either be used right away or put in the deep freeze, or kept in the fridge for up to a week.

Preheat the oven to 350°F (180°C) when about to cook.

Bring the dough up to room temperature and form into small balls the size of a walnut. Flatten them out onto a baking sheet using the back of a fork dipped in cold water. Allow plenty of room for expansion. Bake in a preheated oven for about 10 minutes. Sprinkle with vanilla sugar. When cold, store in an air tight container.

Vanilla Sugar

Fill a glass jar with superfine sugar and put a couple of vanilla beans into the sugar. It stops the vanilla beans drying out too much and makes a wonderful, fragrant sugar. The flavor comes through in around a week. We get fragrant vanilla beans from Mexico. You can use the vanilla bean a couple of times, if you wash and dry it.

Toffee Rice Krispies

Makes 24

These don't need baking and so are good to make with children.

1½ sticks (¾ cup) butter
1 slab toffee, 2 x 4 inches (5 x 10cm)
about regular white marshmallows or miniature marshmallows
13½ ounces (375g) Rice Krispies (about 15½ cups)

Grease 2 small jelly roll pans. Melt the butter, toffee, and marshmallows together in a saucepan, and add the rice krispies. Mix well and pour into the pans. Cool, and cut into sticks or squares.

Isobel Burnett's Ginger Cookies

Makes 20–30

When you are ready to eat these round, crackly-topped, aromatic cookies, make a wish, crack the cookie on your elbow and, if it splits into 3 pieces, your wish will come true. If it cracks in 3 more or less pieces, it's a great excuse to eat another cookie! They keep for ages in an airtight container.

3 cups all-purpose white flour
½ level teaspoon ground ginger
½ level teaspoon baking soda
1¼ sticks (⅔ cup) butter
¾ cup golden syrup (or, if unavailable, use corn syrup but include a tablespoon or 2 of molasses)
⅔ cup sugar

Preheat the oven to 350°F (180°C).

Sift the first three ingredients together into a bowl and rub the butter into them.

Meanwhile heat the syrup lightly in a small saucepan until runny. Add the sugar and mix well. Add to the dry ingredients and mix well. Roll the mixture into walnut-sized balls and arrange them on a tray lined with wax paper. Bake for 15–20 minutes. Leave on the tray for 2–3 minutes, then lift off with the long side of a spatula and cool on a rack.

Tray Bakes

Master Recipe
Shortbread

Makes 24–32, depending on size

For some reason it has become a tradition at Kinoith always to have shortbread in the Aga. Many years ago when I was attempting to hide the shortbread from the children, who seemed to devour it as fast as it was made, I discovered quite by accident that it keeps beautifully for days in the coolest oven in our 4-door Aga. Now, not only the children, but all our friends know where to look.

Shortbread is an ancient Scottish recipe, particularly associated with Christmas and Hogmanay (New Year's). It comes in all shapes and sizes, and sometimes the edges are fluted. This shortbread has a more granular texture than Jane's Cookies.

3 cups all-purpose white flour
½ cup superfine sugar
½ cup ground rice
good pinch of salt
good pinch of baking powder
2½ sticks (1¼ cups) butter
Vanilla Sugar (see page 464) or superfine sugar for sprinkling

jelly roll pan, 10 x 15 inches (25.5 x 38cm)
Preheat the oven to 275–300°F (140–150°C).

Sift the dry ingredients into a bowl. Cut the butter into cubes and rub it in until the whole mixture comes together. Spread evenly into the jelly roll pan. Bake for 1–1½ hours in the oven. The shortbread should be pale golden but fully cooked through. Cut into squares or sticks while still hot.

Sprinkle with Vanilla Sugar or superfine sugar and let cool in the pan.

Variations

Cumin Shortbread

Follow the Master Recipe, adding to the dry ingredients 2 teaspoons of freshly roasted cumin seeds, ground to a powder.

Poppyseed Shortbread

Follow the Master Recipe, adding 1–2 tablespoons of poppy seeds to the dry ingredients. Cut into 4-inch (10-cm) circles and serve sprinkled with superfine sugar.

Coconut and Walnut Bars

Makes 24–32 (depending on how you cut them)

Shortbread mixture
1½ sticks (¾ cup) butter
2¼ cups all-purpose white flour
⅓ cup superfine sugar

Nut layer
2 eggs
few drops vanilla extract
1 tablespoon all-purpose white flour
½ cup Barbados sugar and ½ cup superfine sugar or 1 slightly heaped cup soft brown sugar
a pinch salt
¼ level teaspoon baking powder
2 cups dried coconut
1 cup walnuts, chopped

jelly roll pan, 8 x 12 inches (20.5 x 32cm)

Preheat the oven to 350°F (180°C).

Prepare the shortbread mixture first by crumbling the butter into the flour. Add the sugar and turn into the greased jelly roll pan. Press flat with the back of a spoon. Then partially bake in the oven for 15–20 minutes or until pale golden

Next, prepare the nut mixture: beat the 2 eggs until light. Add the vanilla, flour, sugar, salt, baking powder, and coconut. Beat until smooth.

Lastly, stir in the nuts and pour over the partially cooked shortbread base. Continue cooking in the oven for another 20–30 minutes. Cool a little and cut into sticks.

Caramelized Almond Squares

Makes 24

1½ cups flour
2 tablespoons superfine sugar
1 stick (½ cup) butter
drop of vanilla extract
1 egg yolk or ½ a whole egg, beaten

Topping
1¼ cups slivered almonds
¾ stick (⅓ cup) butter
¼ cup light brown sugar
¼ cup set honey
1 tablespoon cream

greased jelly roll pan, 8 x 12 inches (20.5 x 32cm)

Preheat the oven to 350°F (180°C).

Put the flour and sugar into a bowl, rub in the butter, add the vanilla, and bind with the egg yolk or beaten egg. Press into the greased pan. Prick the pastry and bake for 10–15 minutes, or until golden. Remove from the oven, cool in the pan for a few minutes.

Next make the topping: put all the ingredients except the cream into a saucepan, and cook together over low heat until they are a pale straw color. Stir in the cream and cook for a few more seconds. Spread this topping over the cooked base and bake until the topping is a deep golden brown color – anything from 8–20 minutes, depending on the length of time the topping ingredients were cooked for originally.

Let cool in the pan for 10 minutes, then remove to a wire rack to cool. Cut into squares about 2 inches (5cm).

Chocolate Peanut Butter Squares

Makes about 24

Sue Lawrence is one of the most talented bakers. This recipe is inspired by one from her book, Sue Lawrence On Baking**. She, in turn, was inspired by the Village Bakery in Melmerby, Cumbria.**

1¾ cups white self rising flour
¾ cup all-purpose flour, sifted
1 slightly heaped (225g) soft dark brown sugar
1 stick (½ cup) butter, softened
½ cup peanut butter, sugar-free
2 eggs, beaten

Topping
5 ounces (150g) chocolate, milk or dark (about 1 cup)
⅓ cup peanut butter
2 ounces (50g) dried coconut

greased jelly roll pan, 8 x 12 inches (20.5 x 32cm)

Preheat the oven to 350°F (180°C).

Mix the flours, sugar, butter, peanut butter, and eggs together. Spoon into the jelly roll pan and level off the top with a spatula. Bake in the oven for about 25 minutes, or until the edges are slightly firm and the center is still slightly soft. Let cool for about 5–10 minutes.

Meanwhile prepare the topping: melt the chocolate by placing it in a bowl and setting it over a pan of simmering water. Stir in the peanut butter and coconut, and spoon it on top of the base, carefully smoothing the surface. Cut into squares and let cool in the pan for about 20 minutes. Then transfer to a wire rack and let it become completely cold before hiding it away in an airtight tin.

Apple and Raisin Squares

Makes 12–16

2 cups self rising flour
2 heaped cups rolled oats
1 teaspoon baking soda (bread soda)
2 sticks (1 cup) butter
1 cup sugar
2 tablespoons golden syrup (or, if unavailable, corn syrup)
2 dessert apples, peeled, cored, and finely chopped
1/2 cup raisins

square pan, 9-inch (23-cm), greased and lined

Preheat the oven to 350°F (180°C).

Mix the flour, oats, and baking soda together. Melt the butter, sugar, and golden syrup together in a small saucepan over a gentle heat and add to the mixture. Press half the mixture into the pan.

Mix the apple with the raisins and sprinkle on top, then spread the remaining oat mixture on top. Bake for 30 minutes, then let it cool for 5 minutes, before cutting into squares and transferring to a wire rack.

Brownies

Makes 16

A great American favorite – the relatively large amount of sugar gives brownies their delicious and characteristic crust.

2 ounces (50g) best-quality dark chocolate (about 2/3 cup)
3/4 stick plus 1 tablespoon (a generous 1/3 cup) butter
3/4 cup plus 2 tablespoons superfine sugar
2 eggs, lightly whisked
1/2 teaspoon vanilla extract
3/4 cup white flour
1/2 teaspoon baking powder
pinch salt
1 cup (110g) chopped walnuts
square pan, 8-inch (20.5-cm)

Preheat the oven to 350°F (180°C).

Melt the chocolate in a bowl over a pan of gently simmering water or in a double boiler or a low oven. Cream the butter and sugar and beat in the eggs, vanilla extract, and melted chocolate. Lastly stir in the flour, baking powder, salt, and chopped nuts. Spread the mixture in the pan and bake in the oven for about 30–35 minutes. Cut into 2-inch (5-cm) squares for serving.

Below: Brownies

LATED
BROWN SOD

Chocolate Chip Cookies

Makes about 36–40, depending on size

The quintessential American cookie, now much-loved the world over.

2 sticks (1 cup) butter
a scant cup brown sugar
3/4 cup sugar
2 eggs, beaten
1 teaspoon pure vanilla extract
3 cups all-purpose white flour
1 level teaspoon baking powder
1 level teaspoon baking soda (bread soda)
pinch of salt
1 cup chocolate chips
1 cup chopped nuts

Preheat the oven to 350°F (180°C).

Cream the butter, add the sugars, and beat until light and fluffy. Add the egg a bit at a time, and then the vanilla extract. Mix the dry ingredients together and fold them in. Lastly, add the chocolate chips and chopped nuts.

Divide the mixture into quarter-ounce (7-g) pieces for teeny weeny cookies, or one ounce (25g) for medium cookies or two ounces (50g) for American-style cookies on a baking sheet. Remember to allow lots of room for spreading. Bake for about 8–10 minutes, depending on size.

Cool for a few minutes in the tray and then transfer to wire racks. Store in an airtight container.

Master Recipe
Oatmeal Cookie Squares

Makes 24–32

These nutritious cookies keep very well in a tin. Children love to munch them with a banana. Don't compromise – make them with butter, because the flavor is immeasurably better. Oats come from the berry of a cultivated grass. Oatmeal is obtained by grinding oats after the husk has been removed, and it comes in 3 grades – fine (used mostly in oatcakes and scones), medium, and coarse (used mostly in porridge, soups, black and white puddings, haggis, and here).

3 sticks (1 1/2 cups) butter
1 tablespoon golden syrup (or corn syrup)
1 teaspoon pure vanilla extract
1 cup sugar
4 heaped cups rolled oats

jelly roll pan, 10 x 15 inches (25.5 x 38cm); use half the recipe for a 9 x 13-inch (23 x 33-cm) pan

Preheat the oven to 350°F (180°C).

Melt the butter, add the golden syrup and vanilla extract, stir in the sugar and oatmeal, and mix well. Spread into the jelly roll pan and bake in the oven until golden and slightly caramelized – about 30 minutes. Cut into 24–32 squares while still warm.

Oatmeal and Banana Crunch

For an instant dessert, cover an oatmeal cookie square with slices of banana, put a tiny dollop of cream on top, and eat. Simply delicious!

Oatmeal and Apple Crumble

Loose crumbs may be scattered over some stewed apple for an instant crumble.

Variations

Follow the Master Recipe but substitute 1/3 cup of unsweetened dried coconut for 1/3 cup of the oatmeal.

Follow the Master Recipe but add 2 tablespoons chocolate chips and/or 2 tablespoons raisins to the above recipe, and reduce the oatmeal by 1/4 cup.

Pecan Puffs

Makes about 30

1 stick (1/2 cup) butter
2 1/2 tablespoons superfine sugar
1/2 teaspoon vanilla extract
5 ounces (150g) pecans, finely ground (about 1 1/2 cups)
1 1/4 cups all-purpose white flour, sifted

confectioners sugar

Preheat the oven to 300°F (150°C).

Cream the butter, add the sugar, and beat until soft and light. Mix the nuts in with the butter and sugar, add the flour and vanilla extract. Pinch off teaspoonfuls of the mixture and roll into balls. Place well apart on greased baking sheets. Bake for 30 minutes or until pale and golden.

Remove from the oven. Handle very carefully as they will be fragile, brittle, and very hot. Cool on a wire rack, dredge with confectioners sugar and store in an airtight container.

Homemade Crackers

Makes 20–25

2 cups all-purpose white flour
1/2 teaspoon baking powder
1/2 teaspoon salt
2 tablespoons butter
1 tablespoon cream
about 6 tablespoons water

Preheat the oven to 300°F (150°C).

Put the flour, salt, and baking powder into a bowl. Rub in the butter and moisten with the cream and enough water to make a firm dough.

Roll out very thinly to one-sixteenth inch (2-mm). Prick with a fork. Cut into squares with a pastry wheel or sharp knife. Bake for 30 minutes until lightly browned and quite crisp. Cool on a wire rack.

breads, scones, and pizzas

breads, scones, & pizzas

We make all sorts of breads at the school, virtually every day – yeast, soda and sour dough breads, flat bread, pizza, and many variations on each. We all adore baking – I've baked my entire adult life and quite a bit of my childhood, yet every time I take a loaf of bread out of the oven, I still get a buzz out of it. I also love teaching people how to make bread because somehow, of all the many skills and techniques we teach at the school, the one that seems to give most satisfaction and pleasure is breadmaking.

Breads are much more adventurous nowadays. You can buy them with all sorts of interesting ingredients added (olives, sun-dried tomatoes...), and once you've learned the basics of breadmaking, you can play around with these flavors, too.

Baking Bread

In our experience, traditional soda breads and most yeast breads, with the exception of the Ballymaloe Brown Yeast Bread, are best baked in a conventional oven (i.e., electric oven with heating element at top). Wet doughs, such as the Simply Nutritious Loaf and the Ballymaloe Brown Yeast Bread benefit from the drying heat of a fan-assisted oven, but may also be baked in a conventional oven. We also have a wood-burning oven at the school (that came as a kit from an Italian firm), and it gives fantastic results.

Bread should sound hollow when cooked. Test it by tapping lightly with the finger tips over all the top and bottom. It should sound the same both in the center and at the sides. With a round loaf, the center is the last part to cook, so be quite sure that the bread sounds hollow when tapped there. Cutting a cross in soda bread enables it to open out in the center and thus cooks more evenly.

After you've made bread a few times and lost your fear of yeast, you'll be amazed how forgiving these breads are. With very little effort, one can fit them into virtually any schedule. Remember, cold doesn't kill yeast whereas heat over 105–120°F (40–50°C) does. One can decide to let the bread rise in a cooler place, or even in the fridge overnight, to slow the fermentation, and bake it next day for breakfast.

Occasionally when a dough over-rises or is forgotten about, we just feed it with a little more flour and water and let it ferment and develop into a sour dough, which is then kneaded into another dough the next day. Sour dough breads, which depend on natural yeast, take much longer to rise but are full of character and always a surprise.

Because of space restrictions in this book, I can only give a tiny taste of the bread-making possibilities – just to whet your appetite. However my husband, Tim, is also passionate about bread-making and has written *The Ballymaloe Bread Book* (Gill & Macmillan) – seek it out for more temptations.

Raising Agents

There are two basic types of raising agent: biological ones (such as yeast) and chemical ones (like baking powder).

Yeast is a living organism – a one-celled plant of the fungus family. Given the right conditions: warmth (approximately 95°F [35°C]), food and moisture, it reproduces amazingly fast, giving off bubbles of carbon dioxide which puff up the dough, giving a light and aerated result. It can be bought in three forms: fresh or compressed, dried, and fast action yeast. We prefer to use fresh yeast, but it can be difficult to obtain, especially in small quantities. If you buy a couple of pounds (a kilo) at a time, however, it can be frozen in small pieces so that you can thaw them when needed. Use as soon as the yeast has defrosted. It will keep, wrapped, in the refrigerator for at least a week. Dried yeast (often called 'active' dry yeast) is sold in granular form, in 1/4-ounce packages or a can. You need half, or less than half, the weight specified for fresh yeast. Active dry yeast keeps fresh for six months in a cool, dry place. Bread made with dried yeast tends to have a more yeasty taste and a slightly heavier texture. Fast action, or rapid-rise, yeast is a variation on dried yeast. It is finer in texture and rises the bread in approximately half the time, giving a good flavor. Stir directly into the dry ingredients. Knead and let the dough rise just once.

Baking powder consists of an acid (cream of tartar) and an alkali (bicarbonate) in correct proportion. Cornstarch or rice flour is included to create bulk and to absorb moisture. Action starts immediately when the mixture is moistened, so it is essential to add it last and get the cake or scones into the oven immediately.

Bicarbonate of soda, more commonly known as baking soda, is used for soda breads, scones and rolled biscuits, and other mixtures (e.g., gingerbread or porter cake). The lactic acid in the milk acts on the baking soda to produce CO^2, which raises the bread. Measure baking soda meticulously – a level teaspoon means just that. Use a knife to level off the spoon – too much soda will not make the bread rise more, it will simply result in a bread that has a strong flavor, the smell of soda, and a greenish-brown tinge to the crumb. Store baking soda in a screw-top jar. It keeps for years.

Cream of tartar is used in some batters and reacts with baking soda to raise the mixture. If sour milk is not available for soda bread, use ordinary milk but add one teaspoon of cream of tartar, as well as the baking soda, to each pound (450g) of flour.

Flours

In Ireland we have wonderful flours, some are roller-milled, others stoneground. The resulting flour with flakes of bran and wheatgerm is perfect for our soda breads. Flour varies enormously from country to country, so making bread is always a matter of trial and error until you find a flour to suit your needs for a particular bread recipe. It is nearly impossible to replicate exactly the taste of breads from a foreign country because the flour is different; however, they will still be delicious.

Wheat flour (rather than rye, rice, potato, or corn flour) is most commonly used because of its high gluten content. Gluten is the protein in wheat that allows the dough to become elastic. The more gluten, the more it will rise.

White flour is made from wheat that has had its outer casing of bran and the inner center of wheat germ removed. White flour is very fine and can be bought bleached or unbleached. The more refined and processed the flour, the less flavor and vitamins it will have. Some white flours are enriched with B vitamins.

Strong flour, also known as Bread flour and Baker's flour, is made from hard wheat. The best varieties come from North America and have a very high gluten content. This makes it suitable for use in puff, flaky, and choux pastry, pizza and yeast breads. It produces a light, well-risen loaf and is used by professional bakers.

All-purpose white or household flour is a general, all-purpose flour suitable for soda breads, cakes, biscuits and scones, since it does not have the high gluten content of bread flour. It is generally made from soft European wheat.

Self-rising flour is usually made from soft wheat, which has a raising agent added. It is not used in yeast cookery. Buy in small quantities and store in a dry place.

Whole wheat flour (or wholemeal flour) is milled from the whole wheat grain so it includes the bran and wheat germ. Bread made from whole wheat is more nutritious because it includes more B vitamins and fiber. Some whole wheat flour is stone-ground by the ancient method of milling between stone rollers. This flour is less processed than the flour made by modern milling methods. The texture is slightly coarser and sometimes needs more yeast to rise the bread.

Bran is the outer husk of the wheat grain. It can be added to bread and provides roughage, but has little in the way of flavor or nutrition.

Wheat germ is the "living" part of the wheat grain from which new plants can grow. It's usually extracted from the grain during flour making. Wheat germ is full of B vitamins and can be eaten on its own or added to breakfast cereals or breads. As it goes rancid easily, buy it in small quantities and keep it refrigerated.

Pizzas

Pizzas have undergone a sea-change since chefs such as Alice Waters and Wolfgang Puck in California rescued us from predictable pizzas. There are just a few pizza recipes in this book, but let your imagination run wild with different combinations of ingredients. Keep in mind, too, that pizzas are not only savory. A banana, strawberry, and chocolate spread pizza makes an unusual and delicious feast! The thing to remember is that there must be a balance between the base and topping – very often the base is too thick and heavy.

Scones and rolled biscuits

Scones and rolled biscuits can be made from most bread mixtures – crunchy- or sugar-topped, square or round, sweet or savory, seeded or plain… there are endless varieties. They are very quick to assemble and cook in almost the same amount of time that it will take to heat a bowl of soup.

Simply Nutritious Whole Wheat Bread

Makes 1 loaf

This is a more modern version of Soda Bread, and couldn't be simpler, just mix and pour into a well greased pan. It is the first bread we teach students to cook, to take the mystery out of breadmaking – even a child could cook this bread. It keeps well for several days and is also great toasted.

3½ cups stone-ground whole wheat flour
½ cup white flour, preferably unbleached
1 tablespoon bran
1 tablespoon wheat germ
1 level teaspoon baking soda (bread soda), sifted
1 teaspoon salt
1 teaspoon soft dark brown sugar
1 egg
1–2 tablespoons peanut or sunflower oil, unscented
2 cups buttermilk or sour milk
sunflower or sesame seeds, optional

loaf pan, 9 x 5 x 2 inches (23 x 12.5 x 5cm)

Preheat oven to 400°F (200°C).

Put all the dry ingredients, including the sifted baking soda, into a large bowl and mix well. In a separate bowl, whisk the egg, add the oil and most of the buttermilk. Make a well in the center of the dry ingredients and pour in the liquid, mix well, and add more buttermilk if necessary. The mixture should be soft and slightly sloppy; pour into an oiled pan and bake for 60 minutes, or until the bread is nice and crusty and sounds hollow when tapped. Cool on a wire rack.

Tip: Always use a large, wide bowl when making bread so that you can mix comfortably with big generous movements. This results in a lighter bread.

Master Recipe
White Soda Bread

Soda bread only takes 2 or 3 minutes to make and 20–30 minutes to bake. It is another of my "great convertibles." We have had the greatest fun experimenting with different variations and uses. It's also great with olives, sun-dried tomatoes, or caramelized onions added, so the possibilities are endless.

4 cups all-purpose white flour, preferably unbleached
1 level teaspoon salt
1 level teaspoon baking soda (bread soda)
1¾ cups sour milk or buttermilk (quantity varies with thickness of sour milk or buttermilk)

Preheat the oven to 475°F (250°C).

Sift the dry ingredients. Make a well in the center. Pour in all of the milk at once. Using one hand, with your fingers stiff and outstretched like a claw, stir in a full circular movement from the center to the outside of the bowl in ever-increasing circles. The dough should be softish, not too wet and sticky. When it all comes together, turn it out onto a well-floured work surface. **Wash and dry your hands.**

Tidy it up and flip over gently. Pat the dough into a circle about 1½ inches (4cm) deep. Cut a deep cross on the loaf and prick in the four corners to let the fairies out! Bake in the oven for 15 minutes, then turn down to 400°F (200°C) for 30 minutes or until cooked. If you are in doubt, tap the bottom of the bread: when it is cooked it will sound hollow. Cool on a wire rack.

Note: Soda breads are best eaten on the day they are made but are still good for a day or so more.

Tip: Seek out plain dairy, cooking, or kosher salt. Avoid free-run salt, which includes chemicals.

Variations

White Soda Bread with Herbs

Follow the Master Recipe, adding to the dry ingredients 1–2 tablespoons of freshly chopped herbs (rosemary, sage, thyme, chives, parsley, or lemon balm).

White Soda Bread with Cumin

Follow the Master Recipe, adding 1–2 tablespoons of freshly roasted cumin seeds to the flour.

Seedy Bread

If you like caraway seeds this is a must, delicious served for afternoon tea. Follow the Master Recipe, adding 1 tablespoon of sugar and 2–3 teaspoons of caraway seeds to the dry ingredients.

Tip: All soda breads should be put into a fully pre-heated oven as soon as they are made, otherwise they will be heavy and not rise fully.

Spotted Dog

Makes 1 loaf

Spotted Dog is also called railway cake in some parts of the country: "a currant for each station." This bread is one of the great homely foods of our family. It has always been a favorite with my children. Freshly made on a Sunday morning for our picnics on the cliffs at Ballyandreen. Or relished with delight when eaten with lashings of butter, jam, and steaming mugs of hot chocolate after a winter walk on Shanagarry strand. It is also a staple in our "pre-weighed repertoire"; made on our family boating trips on the Shannon and given as a parting gift to the many boats we met on the way.

4 cups all-purpose white flour, preferably unbleached
1 level teaspoon baking soda (bread soda)
1 level teaspoon salt
2 teaspoons sugar
⅓–½ cup golden raisins
1 egg

1½ cups buttermilk

Preheat the oven to 425°F (220°C).

In a large mixing bowl, sift the flour and the baking soda and add the salt, sugar, and fruit. Mix well by lifting the flour and fruit up in your hands and then letting them fall back into the bowl through your fingers. This adds more air and therefore, hopefully, more lightness to your finished bread. Now make a well in the center of the flour. Break the egg into the bottom of your measuring cup and add the buttermilk to the 14 fluid ounce (400ml) line – the egg is part of your liquid measurement. Whisk briefly to blend. Pour most of this milk and egg into the flour. Using one hand with the fingers open and stiff, mix in a full circle, drawing in the flour from the sides of the bowl, adding more milk if necessary. The dough should be softish, not too wet and sticky.

The trick with Spotted Dog, like all soda breads, is not to over-mix the dough. Mix it as quickly and as gently as possible, thus keeping it light and airy. When the dough all comes together, turn it out onto a well-floured work surface. **Wash and dry your hands**. With floured fingers, roll lightly for a few seconds – just enough to tidy it up. Pat the dough into a circle, pressing to about 2 inches (5cm) in height.

Place the dough on a baking tray dusted lightly with flour. With a sharp knife, cut a deep cross on it, letting the cuts go over the sides of the bread. Prick with a knife at the 4 angles as, according to Irish Folklore, this is to let the fairies out!

Cook in the oven for 10 minutes, then turn the oven down to 400°F (200°C), for 35 minutes or until cooked. If you are in doubt about the bread being cooked, tap the bottom: if it is cooked it will sound hollow. Serve freshly baked, cut into thick slices and smeared with butter and jam. Spotted Dog is also really good eaten with cheese.

Spotted Puppies

In the window of E.A.T. in New York on St. Patrick's weekend, I spied lots of little spotted puppies – they were selling like the proverbial hot cakes. Make the Spotted Dog as above. Divide the dough into 6 pieces, shape each piece into a little round loaf. Cut a cross on top and bake for about 20 minutes. Cool on a wire rack.

Stripy Cat

While Paul and Jeanne Rankin were teaching a class at the Cookery School, Timmy showed their daughter how to make Spotted Dog and when she had mastered that, she tried the next batch with chocolate chips and this was the delicious result. She called it Stripy Cat.

Follow the Master Recipe, adding ½ cup of roughly chopped best quality dark chocolate to Spotted Dog recipe in place of the raisins. This is good made into scones also.

Note: Careful, the chocolate's very hot when it comes out of the oven so handle very carefully.

Below: Stripy Cat

"Focaccia" with Red Onion, Olives, and Rosemary

Makes 1 loaf

Here we use White Soda Bread as a base for Focaccia; it sounds sacrilegious but tastes delicious. White Yeast Bread dough may, of course, be used instead.

1 quantity White Soda Bread dough (see page 474)

extra-virgin olive oil
10 black olives (Kalamata or Gaeta)
a heaped 1/2 cup red onion, finely chopped
about 1 tablespoon fresh rosemary, chopped
sea salt or Kosher salt

1 small jelly roll pan, 9 x 12 inches (23 x 32cm)

Preheat the oven to 475°F (250°C).

Follow the recipe for White Soda Bread. Brush the pan generously with olive oil. Roll the dough quickly into a rectangle and press gently into the pan. Brush the surface generously with olive oil, dot with pitted black olives and thin wedges of onion. Sprinkle with chopped rosemary and flakes of sea salt, and bake in the oven for about 15 minutes or until brown and crisp and golden on top. Brush with a little extra olive oil. Cool on a wire rack and serve still warm.

Gluten-free White Soda Bread

Makes 1 loaf

Celiacs can also enjoy delicious soda bread and scones if they follow Rosemary Kearney's recipes.

2 1/2 cups rice flour
1 cup tapioca flour
1/2 cup dried milk powder
1 scant level teaspoon baking soda (bread soda), sifted
1 heaped teaspoon gluten-free baking powder
1 teaspoon salt
1 heaped teaspoon xanthan gum
2 tablespoons superfine sugar
1 egg, lightly beaten
1–1 1/4 cups buttermilk

Preheat the oven to 450°F (230°C).

Sift all the dry ingredients together into a large bowl and mix well. Lightly whisk the egg and buttermilk together. Make a well in the center and pour in most of the egg and buttermilk at once.

Using one hand, mix in the flour from the sides of the bowl, adding a little more buttermilk if necessary. The dough should be softish, not too wet and sticky. When it comes together, turn it out onto a rice floured board and knead very gently for a few seconds.

Transfer to a baking sheet sprinkled with a little rice flour. Pat the dough into a circle 1 1/2 inches (4cm) deep and cut a deep cross in it. Bake in a hot oven for 5 minutes and then reduce the heat to 350°F (180°C) for a further 25 minutes or until cooked. If you are in doubt, tap the bottom of the bread: if it is cooked it will sound hollow.

Note: This soda bread is best served the day it is made. However, it is lovely served toasted the next day. If there is any bread left over, I whizz it in a food processor and keep the gluten-free bread crumbs in the freezer for a future use.

Scones (or Rolled Biscuits)

Any soda bread recipe can be made into scones of different sizes. Follow either the White Soda Recipe (see page 474) or the Gluten-free Recipe and flatten the dough a little more, to about an inch (2.5cm). Preheat the oven to 475°F (250°C) for scones made from White Soda Bread Dough, and to 450°F (230°C) for scones made from Gluten-free Soda Bread dough. Bake for 20 minutes.

White Soda Scones

Make the dough for White Soda Dough (see page 474) or Gluten-free White Soda Dough (see left). Flatten the dough to about an inch (2.5cm). Cut into scones with a knife or scone cutter. Bake at 475°F (250°C), or 450°F (230°C) for the gluten-free recipe, for 20 minutes.

Herb Scones

Add 1–2 tablespoons of freshly chopped herbs (rosemary, sage, thyme, chives, parsley, or lemon balm) to the dry ingredients.

Cheddar Cheese Scones

Make the soda bread dough. Cut or stamp into scones, brush the top of each one with egg wash, and then dip into grated Cheddar cheese. Bake as for soda scones, or use to cover the top of a casserole or stew (see Shanagarry Chicken Casserole, page 280).

Cheddar Cheese and Thyme Leaf Scones

Add 2 tablespoons of thyme leaves to the dry ingredients and proceed as above.

Tip: It is better not to put the cheese into the dough as this makes the bread heavier. Reduce the heat to 425°F (220°C) and then 350°F (180°C) or the cheese may burn on top.

Rosemary and Olive Scones

Add 1 1/2 tablespoons of chopped fresh rosemary and 2 tablespoons roughly chopped pitted black olives to the dry ingredients.

Rosemary and Raisin Scones

Substitute 3 ounces (75g) raisins for olives in the above recipe.

Rosemary and Sun-dried Tomato Scones

Add 1–2 tablespoons of chopped rosemary, and 2 tablespoons of chopped sun-dried tomatoes to the dry ingredients.

Olive Scones

Flatten soda bread dough into a 1½-inch (4-cm) square. Dot the top with whole olives. Brush generously with olive oil, sprinkle with sea salt or Kosher salt, and cut into square scones.

Chili Scones

Add ½–1 tablespoon chili powder to the flour.

Chile and Cheddar Cheese Scones

Add 1–2 chopped green chiles to the flour. Brush the top of the scones with egg wash, then dip into grated Cheddar cheese, and proceed.

Teenie Weenies

Makes about 40

Follow the Master Recipe for White Soda Bread (see page 474) or Gluten-free White Soda Bread (see page 476), and flatten the dough into a circle just less than an inch (2.5cm) thick and stamp out into teeny weeny scones using a 1½-inch (4-cm) cutter. Add chopped fresh herbs such as rosemary or thyme, or olives, to the dry ingredients to make delicious little herb scones. Brush the tops with egg wash and dip in grated Cheddar cheese for yummy Cheddar teeny weenies. Bake for 8–15 minutes at 450°F (230°C).

Above: White Soda Scones

Crunchy Tops

Makes 7 scones

These crunchy topped scones join together in the cooking to make an appetizing loaf. We've used a selection of toppings here, but use just one if that seems more appropriate to your meal.

White Soda Bread (see page 474) or Gluten-free White Soda Bread dough (see page 476)
egg wash or buttermilk
sunflower seeds, sesame seeds, cracked wheat, caraway seeds, poppy seeds, oat flakes and grated cheese
1 round pan, 9 inches (23cm) in diameter and 1½ inches (4cm) high, well greased with butter or olive oil
3-inch (7.5-cm) scone or biscuit cutter

Preheat the oven to 450°F (230°C).

Pat the dough into a circle about 1½ inches (4cm) thick and stamp out 7 scones with a 3-inch (7.5-cm) scone or biscuit cutter. Brush the top of each scone with egg wash or buttermilk, and dip in the seeds of your choice. Arrange side by side in a well-greased pan.

Bake for 15 minutes, then reduce the temperature to 400°F (200°C) and bake for a further 15 minutes. Remove from the pan and replace in the oven for a further 5–8 minutes or until fully cooked. If you are in doubt, tap the bottom of the bread. When it is cooked it will sound hollow. Let it cool on a wire tray.

Brown Soda Bread

Makes 1 loaf

Bread should always be cooked in a fully preheated oven, but ovens vary enormously so it may be necessary to adjust the temperature accordingly.

5 cups brown whole wheat flour, preferably stone-ground
5 cups all-purpose white flour, preferably unbleached
2 teaspoons salt
2 teaspoons baking soda (bread soda), sifted
about 3 cups sour milk or buttermilk

Preheat the oven to 450°F (230°C).

Mix all the dry ingredients together in a large wide bowl, make a well in the center and add all of the sour milk or buttermilk. Using one hand, stir in a full circle starting in the center of the bowl, working towards the outside of the bowl until all the flour is incorporated. The dough should be soft but not too wet and sticky. When it all comes together (a matter of seconds), turn it out onto a well-floured board. **Wash and dry your hands**. Roll the dough around gently with floury hands for a second, just enough to tidy it up. Flip over and flatten slightly to a thickness of about 2 inches (5cm). Sprinkle a little flour onto a baking sheet and place the loaf on top of the flour. Cut a deep cross on the loaf, prick in the four corners to let the fairies out, and bake in the preheated oven for 15–20 minutes, then reduce the heat to 400°F (200°C) and cook for a further 20–25 minutes or until the bread is cooked (In some ovens it is necessary to turn the bread upside-down on the baking sheet for 5–10 minutes before the end of baking.) The loaf will sound hollow when tapped. Cool on a wire rack.

Variations

Rich Brown Soda Bread

You could add 1/4 cup fine oatmeal, 1 egg, and 2 tablespoons butter to the above to make a richer soda bread dough.

Lighter Brown Soda Bread

If a lighter bread is preferred, use 5 cups white flour and 4 cups brown whole wheat flour.

Brown Soda Scones

Make the dough as above. Form it into a circle and flatten to 1½ inches (4cm) thick. Stamp out into scones with a cutter, or cut with a knife. Bake for about 30 minutes.

Tip: Use the cutter as efficiently as possible so that only the minimum amount of dough needs to be rerolled. The less the dough is handled or rolled, the lighter the scones will be.

Cracked Wheat Scones

Follow the Recipe for Brown Soda Bread. Brush the top of the scones with egg wash or buttermilk, dip in cracked wheat, and proceed.

Ballymaloe Brown Yeast Bread

Makes 1 loaf

This much loved bread is Myrtle Allen's version of the Doris Grant loaf. When making yeast breads, remember that yeast is a living organism. In order to grow, it requires warmth, moisture, and nourishment. The yeast feeds on the sugar and produces bubbles of carbon dioxide which cause the bread to rise. Too much heat (over 140°F [50°C]) will kill yeast. Keep the ingredients and equipment at a luke warm temperature. White or brown sugar, honey, golden syrup, treacle, or molasses may be used. Each will give a slightly different flavor to the bread. At Ballymaloe we use treacle. The dough rises more rapidly with 3 ounces (75g) yeast (about 6 tablespoons) than with 2 ounces (50g) yeast (about 4 tablespoons).

We use a stone-ground whole wheat flour. Different flours produce breads of different textures and flavor. The amount of natural moisture in the flour varies according to atmospheric conditions. The quantity of water should be altered accordingly. The dough should be just too wet to knead – in fact it does not require kneading. The main ingredients – whole wheat flour, treacle, and yeast – are highly nutritious.

Dried yeast may be used instead of fresh baker's yeast. Follow the same method but use only half the weight given for fresh yeast. Allow longer for it to rise. Fast-action yeast may also be used; follow the instructions on the package. From start to finish, this bread takes 1½ hours to make but the time you are working on it is only a couple of minutes.

4 cups whole wheat flour or 3½ cups whole wheat flour plus ½ cup white bread flour
1 teaspoon salt
1 teaspoon black treacle
a scant 2 cups luke warm water (mix yeast with 2/3 cup lukewarm water)
1 ounce (25g) fresh yeast (a scant 2 tablespoons)
sesame seeds, optional

5 x 8-inch (13 x 20-cm) bread pan, greased with sunflower oil

Preheat the oven to 450°F (230°C).

Mix the flour and salt. The ingredients should all be at room temperature. In a small bowl or Pyrex measuring cup, mix the treacle with 2/3 cup of water and crumble in the yeast.

Sit the bowl for a few minutes in a warm place to let the yeast start to work. After about 4 or 5 minutes it has a creamy, slightly frothy appearance.

Right: Brown Soda Bread

When ready, stir and pour it, with all the remaining water, into the flour to make a loose dough. The mixture should be too wet to knead. Put the mixture into the greased pan. Sprinkle the top of the loaves with sesame seeds if you like. Cover the pan with a dish towel to prevent a skin from forming. Let it rise. Just before the bread comes to the top of the pan, about 10–15 minutes depending on the temperature of the kitchen, remove the towel and pop the loaf in the oven for 50–60 minutes or until it looks nicely browned and sounds hollow when tapped. It will rise a little further in the oven. This is called oven spring. If, however, the bread had risen to the top of the pan before it went into the oven, it would have continued to rise and flow over the edges.

We usually remove the loaf from the pan about 10 minutes before the end of cooking and put it back into the oven to crisp all around, but if you like a softer crust, there's no need to do this.

Variations

Back to Front Bread

Follow the Master Recipe, reversing the proportion of white flour and whole wheat flour which make up the pound (450g) of flour. This makes a lighter bread, which we discovered by accident when a student with a hangover couldn't read! The result is delicious.

Tip: Dried yeast may be used instead of fresh baker's yeast. Follow the same method but use only half the weight as given for fresh yeast. Allow longer to rise.

Russian Village Bread

Tim and I enjoyed several bread courses at the Village Bakery in Cumbria with Andrew Whitley. Andrew makes many Russian breads, one with coriander seeds on the top and bottom. On our return we experimented with our Brown Yeast Bread, and although it is not as complex as Andrew's Sour Dough version, it is still very delicious.

Follow the recipe for Ballymaloe Brown Yeast Bread (page 478), substituting 3½ cups whole wheat flour, ½ cup rye flour and ½ cup white bread flour. Brush the pan with sunflower oil, sprinkle a layer of whole coriander seeds over the bottom of the pan and another layer over the top of the bread before baking.

Frank's "Pumpernickel" Bread

Makes 1 loaf

Frank McLaughlin, a student from Montreal in Québec, Canada, loved to experiment with our bread recipes. One day he majored on the treacle and produced this fantastic dark bread, reminiscent of pumpernickel but a fraction of the work.

4 cups whole wheat flour
1 teaspoon salt
1¼ cups luke warm water
½ cup black treacle
1 ounce (25g) fresh yeast (a scant 2 tablespoons)
sesame seeds (optional)

Preheat the oven to 450°F (230°C).

Mix the flour with the salt and warm it very slightly (in the cool oven of an Aga, or in a gas or electric oven when starting to heat). In a small bowl, mix the treacle with two-thirds cup water and crumble in the yeast. Put the bowl in a warm position, such as the back of the stovetop. In about 5 minutes, the mixture will have a creamy and slightly frothy appearance on top.

When ready, stir it well and pour it, with most of the remaining water, into the flour to make a wettish dough. The mixture should be too wet to knead. Put the mixture into a loaf pan and sprinkle with sesame seeds, if you like them.

Put the pan back in the warm place and put a dish towel over it. In 10–15 minutes the loaf will have risen to twice its original size. Remove the towel and bake the loaf in the oven for 45–50 minutes, or until it sounds hollow when tapped.

We usually remove the loaf from the pan about 10 minutes before the end of cooking, and put it back into the oven to crisp all around, but if you like a softer crust there's no need to do this.

Tip: brush the inside of the cup measure with oil before measuring treacle, golden syrup, corn syrup or honey; it just slides off into the pan or bowl.

Ballymaloe White Yeast Bread

Makes 2 loaves, 2 lbs. (450g)

This basic white yeast bread dough is multi-purpose. It takes about 5 hours from start to finish, but for much of that time the bread is rising or baking so it's not "your time." In reality, the time spent kneading and making is about 20 minutes. Once you've made it, shape it in loaves or use it for braids, rolls, twists, or for pizza bases.

3/4 ounce (20g) fresh yeast (about 1 1/2 tablespoons)
2 cups water, more as needed
2 tablespoons butter
2 teaspoons Kosher salt
1 tablespoon sugar
6 cups white bread flour

poppy seeds or sesame seeds for topping, optional

2 loaf pans, 5 x 8 inches (13 x 20cm), optional

Preheat the oven to 450°F (230°C).

Mix the yeast with two-thirds cup lukewarm water until dissolved. Put the butter, salt, and sugar into a bowl with two-thirds cup of very hot water, stir until the sugar and salt are dissolved and the butter melted. Add two-thirds cup of cold water. By now, the liquid should be luke warm, so combine with the yeast.

Sift the flour into a bowl, make a well in the center, and pour in most of the lukewarm liquid. Mix to a loose dough, adding the remainder of the liquid, or more flour or liquid if necessary. Turn the dough onto a floured board, cover, and let it relax for 5 minutes approximately. Then knead for about 10 minutes or until smooth, springy, and elastic (if kneading in a food mixer with a dough hook, 5 minutes is usually long enough).

Put the dough in a bowl. Cover the top tightly with plastic wrap – yeast dough rises best in a warm, moist atmosphere. If you want to speed up the rising process, put the bowl near your stove, or a radiator, or close to an Aga. Rising time depends on the temperature; however, the bread will taste better if it rises more slowly. When the dough has more than doubled in size, knead again for about 2–3 minutes or until all the air has been forced out – this is called "knocking back" or "punching down". Let it relax again for 10 minutes.

Shape the bread into loaves, braids, or rolls, transfer to a baking sheet, and cover with a light dish towel. Let rise again in a warm place, this rising will be shorter, only about 20–30 minutes. The bread is ready for baking when a small dent remains when the dough is pressed lightly with the finger. Brush with water and sprinkle with flour. Sprinkle with poppy or sesame seeds, if using.

Bake in the oven for 30–45 minutes, depending on size.

Tip: If you are using pans, brush well with oil before putting in the dough.

The bread should sound hollow when tapped underneath. Cool on a wire rack.

Ballymaloe Braids

Take one quantity of white yeast bread dough after it has been "punched down," divide into three equal pieces. With both hands, roll each one into a rope; thickness depends on how fat you want the braid.

Then pinch the three ends together at the top, bring each outside strand into the center alternately to form a braid, pinch the ends and tuck in neatly. Transfer onto a baking tray. Let it double in size. Egg wash or mist with water, and dredge with flour. This makes a very large braid. Divide the dough in 2 or 4, for smaller braids.

Rolls and Other Shapes

Makes 12–15 rolls

Though they are sometimes made with a bread dough rich with butter and eggs, rolls can be made from any bread dough. Rolls also cook faster than bread, and can be served straight out of the oven, while bread must cool before it can be sliced. You can get 12–15 rolls from the amount of dough used for one loaf.

Preheat the oven to 375°F (190°C).

General directions for rolls

Form about one loaf's worth of bread dough into a log shape; the log should be 1 1/2 to 2 inches (4–5cm) in diameter, and is formed by rolling the dough between hands and bread board. Cut the log into equal-sized pieces.

Shape into one or more of the following types of rolls or some other shape. Let rise for 20 minutes. Brush with egg wash, sprinkle with poppy or sesame seeds, and bake in the oven for about 25 minutes until nicely browned.

Plain Rolls

Take half-ounce (10-g) or one-ounce (25-g) pieces of dough, flatten, and roll into rolls; place on a greased baking sheet sprinkled with cornmeal.

Clover Leaf Rolls

Divide sections into 3 pieces. Shape each into a ball. Place three balls in a greased muffin cup.

Snail or Spiral Rolls

Roll each section into a length about 6 inches (15cm) long. Coil it up and place in greased muffin cups.

Flower Rolls

Flatten a one-ounce (25-g) piece of dough into a circle, divide into 6 but keep attached to the center.

Butterhorns or Crescents

Do not shape the dough into a log. Roll out in a circle about 1/4-inch (5-mm) thick. Brush with melted butter. Cut into 8–12 wedges. Roll up starting from the wide end. Twist to form a crescent. Place on a greased baking sheet.

Knots

Roll a 1 to 2 ounce (25g–50g) piece of dough into a rope, tie into a loose knot, and let all the rolls or shapes rise before baking.

Sunflower Bread

Makes 1 loaf

1 lb. (one-half recipe) (450g) White Yeast Bread dough or 1 lb. Soda Bread dough (see page 481 or 474)
cornmeal

Roll the dough into a circle, about 8 inches (20cm) across. Sprinkle a baking tray with cornmeal, transfer the dough onto the baking tray. Let the yeast dough rest for about 5 minutes. Brush with water and sprinkle with cornmeal.

Press a 3-inch (7.5-cm) cookie cutter or small glass into the center of the dough. With a pastry wheel or knife, divide the dough into half, quarters, eighths, sixteenths. Give each "petal" a quarter turn so part of the cut side faces upwards. Let rise to double in size.

Preheat the oven to 450°F (230°C). Bake for 10–15 minutes, then reduce heat to 350°F (180°C) until crusty and golden. Cool on a wire rack.

Rosemary and Raisin Buns

Makes 12

1 lb. (one-half recipe) (450g) White Yeast Bread dough
1/4 cup raisins
2 1/2 tablespoons extra-virgin olive oil
1 tablespoon rosemary, freshly chopped
olive oil
egg wash

Preheat the oven to 350°F (180°C). Soak the raisins in hot water for about 20 minutes.

Make the dough in the usual way, cover, and let rise to double in size. Punch down. Gently heat the olive oil in a frying pan, add the drained raisins and the finely chopped rosemary, stir-fry for 1–2 minutes. Let cool.

Roll out the dough to a rectangle about 12 x 8 inches (30 x 20.5cm). Sprinkle the rosemary, raisins, and oil over the dough. Fold in the long edges and roll into a jelly roll. Cut into 8 pieces. Let rise on a lightly oiled baking sheet. When puffy and about double in size, brush gently with egg wash. Bake in the oven for 20–25 minutes. Cool on a wire rack.

Flowerpot Bread

White yeast bread can be baked in well-seasoned flowerpots. Oil well before using.

Bean Can Breads

Bake the dough in well-greased bean cans.

Olive Oil Dough for Pizzas

Makes 6 pizzas

Substitute 2–4 tablespoons of olive oil for butter in the White Yeast Bread recipe (see page 481), and proceed as for the recipe.

Preheat the oven to 475°F (250°C).

When the dough has doubled in size, knead again for about 2–3 minutes to "punch down". Let it relax for 10 minutes. Divide the dough into 6 equal pieces or more. Roll out as thinly as possible into circles 10 to 12 inches (25–30cm) in diameter, or chosen size. Spare dough can be shaped into rolls, loaves, and braids. Sprinkle some semolina on a pizza paddle and place dough on top. Cover with chosen topping and bake for 9–11 minutes.

How to Cook Pizzas and Get a Well Browned Bottom!

I experimented a lot with different ovens to get the best result or at least the result that I'm happy with, and I found I had to cook a different way in each oven. For all types of oven, preheat well ahead to maximum temperature – 475°F (250°C).

Here at the cookery school we have a wood burning oven, which unquestionably makes the best pizzas. In just 1 1/2 minutes, the thin crust bubbles up and is ready to eat, everyone adores them. The challenge is to achieve a similar result in a domestic oven.
The faster the thin-crust pizzas cook, the more delicious they are.

In directly-heated gas ovens, or electric ovens with elements at the sides, I get best results by preheating a good heavy baking sheet in the oven on a high shelf. I slide the pizza from the paddle directly onto the baking sheet – a 10 to 12-inch (25–30cm) pizza, 1/8- to 1/4-inch (3–5-mm) thick, has a crusty base and bubbly golden top in 9–11 minutes. In a fan-assisted oven, I put a wire rack in the oven and cover it with four 8 x 8 inch (20 x 20 cm) quarry tiles, which I preheat for at least 20 minutes before sliding the pizza on top. This gives an excellent result in a similar length of time.

In my 48-year-old Aga, I preheat the baking sheet in the center of the hot oven and slide the pizza directly on to it. Heat varies from Aga to Aga so some people may find it better to cook lower down in the oven.

If you don't have a pizza paddle, use a flat baking tray with no lip, in its place. It's a bit more tricky, and if you plan to make pizzas often, I'd recommend investing in a pizza paddle.

Pizza Margherita

Makes 1; serves 1–2

Possibly the most traditional and universally popular pizza in Italy, it was apparently named in the last century in honor of Margherita, the pizza loving Queen of Italy. So there you are, now you know!

One-sixth recipe Pizza Dough (see page 482), about 7 ounces (200g) dough

*1 1/2 cups shredded mozzarella cheese**
1/4 cup olive oil
5 tablespoons Tomato Fondue (see page 188)
2 teaspoons freshly chopped annual marjoram
1 tablespoon Parmesan, freshly grated

semolina, if using a pizza paddle

Preheat the oven to 475°F (250°C).
Roll out the pizza dough in the usual way. Grate the mozzarella and sprinkle with the olive oil. Sprinkle a little semolina all over the surface of the pizza paddle and put the pizza base on top. Spread the mozzarella over the base to within 3/4 inches (2cm) of the edge. Mix the marjoram through the Tomato Fondue and spread over the top. Sprinkle with the freshly grated Parmesan. Bake in the fully preheated oven for 10–12 minutes or until the base is crisp and the top bubbly and golden. Serve immediately.

* The best mozzarella available in Italy, particularly around Naples, is made from the milk of the water buffalo. Its texture and flavor are sensational and quite different from the mozzarella made with cow's milk, Fior di latte, and either are altogether different from the mozzarella available outside Italy. However, I have had great success with Marcella Hazan's wonderful tip to improve the flavor of mozzarella for cooked dishes. She suggests grating it on the largest part of a grater and then sprinkling it with olive oil, 1 tablespoon to every half-cup; mix well, and let steep for 1 hour.

Pizza with Caramelized Onions, Blue Cheese, and Rosemary

Makes 1; serves 1–2

This is one of my great favorites, but it does take a little longer to make than some of the others.

One-sixth recipe Pizza Dough (see page 482), about 7 ounces (200g) dough
4 onions, thinly sliced
2–3 tablespoons olive oil
1/2 cup Gorgonzola or Cashel Blue cheese
1 teaspoon finely chopped fresh rosemary
semolina, if using pizza paddle

First make the caramelized onions because they take a long time to cook. (They are so delicious with steaks or even on toast that it's worth cooking 2–3 times the recipe and keeping them in the fridge.) Heat the olive oil in a heavy saucepan, toss in the onions, and cook over low heat for whatever length of time it takes for them to soften and caramelize to a golden brown – about 30–45 minutes.

Preheat the oven to 475°F (250°C). Roll out the dough as thinly as possible into a 10- to 12-inch (25–30-cm) circle in diameter.

Sprinkle some semolina on the pizza paddle and place the dough on top. Cover the surface of the dough to within 3/4 inches (2cm) of the edge with caramelized onions. Crumble the blue cheese and scatter it on top, then sprinkle with chopped rosemary. Drizzle with a little olive oil and slide off the paddle into the fully preheated oven. Bake for 10–12 minutes and serve immediately.

Pizza with Potato, Onion Marmalade, and Wild Mushrooms

Makes 4 pizzas; serves 4–8

One-half recipe Pizza Dough (see page 482), about 1 1/4 pounds (600g) dough
4 large "floury" potatoes, such as russet
1 egg yolk
1 cup creamy milk
1/2 stick (1/4 cup) butter

5 tablespoons Onion Marmalade (see page 512)
4–8 ounces (110–225g) wild mushrooms (1–2 1/2 cups)
2 tablespoons tarragon, thyme, or marjoram, finely chopped
olive oil
salt and freshly ground black pepper
arugula leaves
Parmesan
black olives

Preheat the oven to 475°F (250°C). First make the pizza bases and place on wax paper. Cook the potatoes in boiling, salted water until tender and then mash with the egg yolk, milk, and butter. Brush the edges of the pizza bases with olive oil and spread each base with the potato purée. Next spread the Onion Marmalade. Sauté the mushrooms in a little olive oil, season with salt and pepper and herbs, and divide between the pizzas. Place the pizzas on preheated baking sheets in a hot oven and bake for 8–12 minutes, until the bases are crisp and the topping is bubbling. Serve with arugula, olives, and Parmesan shavings.

Pizza with Broccoli, Mozzarella, and Garlic Slivers

Makes 1; serves 1–2

This is one of my favorite pizzas, originally made for me by an American student, Erin Thomas.

one-sixth recipe Pizza Dough (see page 482), about 7 ounces (200g) dough
2 heaped cups calabrese or green broccoli flowerets
2 1/2 tablespoons olive oil
2–3 garlic cloves, cut into thin slivers
3/4 cup mozzarella, shredded
1/4 cup Parmesan cheese, optional
sea salt or Kosher salt

Preheat the oven to 475°F (250°C).

Cook the broccoli flowerets in boiling salted water until al dente.

Roll out the dough as thinly as possible into a 10- to 12-inch (25–30-cm) circle. Sprinkle some semolina on the pizza paddle and place the dough on top. Brush the surface of the dough with olive oil. Sprinkle on the

slivers of garlic, arrange the broccoli on top, and sprinkle with mozzarella and, if you like, a little grated Parmesan. Drizzle with olive oil and season with sea salt. Slide off the paddle onto a hot baking sheet in the fully preheated oven. Bake for 10–12 minutes and serve immediately.

Suggested Toppings for Pizzas

Tuna and Tomato Pizza

Spread some Tomato Sauce on the pizza base. Sprinkle some tuna on top, followed by some grated cheese, mozzarella, and Parmesan. Crisscross the top with anchovies and dot with a few olives. Bake for 10–12 minutes in a preheated oven at 450°F (230°C). Garnish with basil leaves and serve.

Pizza Quattro Formaggio

Spread the pizza base with Tomato Sauce. Sprinkle grated Parmesan on one quarter, grated Gruyère on another, crumbled blue cheese, e.g., Gorgonzola, Stilton, Cashel Blue, or Chetwynd on the third quarter, and mozzarella on the fourth quarter, and bake in the usual way.

Pizza Variations

Try any of the toppings below for a delicious pizza.

Piperonata (see page 190), mozzarella, and marjoram

Piperonata (see page 190), mozzarella, and pepperoni

Mozzarella, Tomato Fondue (see page 188), black olives, basil oil

Mozzarella, Arugula and a drizzle of olive, truffle, or chili oil

Tomato Fondue (see page 188), anchovies, black olives, mozzarella, basil oil
Tomato Fondue (see page 188), Mushroom à la Crème (see page 197), and crispy bacon

Eggplants cooked in olive oil, roast red peppers, and marjoram

Mushroom à la Crème (see page 197), crispy bacon, marjoram

Sliced garlic, sliced fresh chile, mozzarella, marjoram, and Tomato Fondue (see page 188)

Pan-grilled eggplant and pesto

Pesto, mozzarella, and arugula

Roast tomatoes, eggplant slices, mozzarella, and fresh roughly-torn herbs.

Onion Marmalade (see page 512), Gorgonzola, rosemary, and whole cloves of garlic.

Roast tomatoes, deep-fried capers, smoked salmon, red onion rings, and a drizzle of mango chutney

Sautéed mushrooms with garlic, marjoram, and a drizzle of truffle oil.

Tomato Sauce (see page 590), red onion, chorizo, goat cheese, thyme leaves

Tomato Sauce, Mozzarella, Prosciutto, arugula

Tip: pop a few rolled-out uncooked pizza bases into the freezer. You can take one out, put the topping on, and slide it straight into the oven.

Garden Café Pizza Dough

Makes 8 x 10-inch (20 x 25cm) pizzas

This recipe is so quick and easy that by the time your tomato sauce is bubbling in the oven, your pizza base will be ready for its topping.

6 cups white bread flour
1/2 level teaspoon salt
1 tablespoon sugar
1/2 stick (1/4 cup) butter
1 package fast-action yeast
2–4 tablespoons olive oil
1 1/2–1 3/4 cups lukewarm water – more if needed

In a large wide mixing bowl, sift the flour and add in the salt and sugar, rub in the butter and fast-action yeast, mix all the ingredients thoroughly.

Make a well in the center of the dry ingredients, add the oil and most of the lukewarm water. Mix to a loose dough. You can add more water or flour if needed.

Turn the dough onto a lightly floured work top, cover, and let it relax for about five minutes. Then knead the dough for about ten minutes or until smooth and springy (if kneading in a food mixer with a dough hook, 5 minutes is usually long enough). Let the dough relax again for about ten minutes. Shape and measure into 8 equal balls of dough, each weighing approximately 5 ounces (150g). Lightly brush the balls of dough with olive oil.

If you have time, put the oiled balls of dough into a plastic bag and chill. The dough will be easier to handle when cold, but it can be used immediately. On a well floured work surface, roll each ball into a circle, about 10 inches (25cm) across.

This dough also makes delicious white yeast bread which we shape into rolls, loaves, and braids.

Left: Pizza with Caramelized Onions, Blue Cheese, and Rosemary

Focaccia

Makes 1 or 4 pieces (see recipe)

The classic Italian flat bread, great to nibble before dinner. Also good served with a selection of olives or roasted vegetables as an appetizer, and great for sandwiches.

1 quantity Pizza Dough (see page 482)
olive oil and sea salt or Kosher salt

Preheat the oven to 450°F (230°C).

Roll out your dough, you can either roll it into 1 large circle or 4 smaller circles. The circles need to be about a half-inch (1cm) thick. Place them on an oiled baking sheet and make indentations all over the surface with your fingers. Brush liberally with olive oil and sprinkle with sea salt. Let the Focaccia rise again. Put it in the oven and bake for 5 minutes, then reduce the temperature to 400°F (200°C) and bake for a further 15–20 minutes.

Variations

Focaccia with Rosemary

Follow the Master Recipe and sprinkle 2 teaspoons of finely chopped rosemary over the oil and then sprinkle with sea salt and proceed and bake as above.

Focaccia with Sage

Follow the Master Recipe and knead 2 teaspoons of finely chopped sage into the dough before rolling it out.

Focaccia with Black Olives

Follow the Master Recipe, adding 1–2 tablespoons of pitted black olives to the top of the dough. 1 teaspoon of chopped marjoram or thyme leaves is a delicious addition here also.

Calzone

Serves 1 very hungry person or 2 people who feel sharing is fun!

Calzone originated in Apulia, the high heel of Italy. Basically it is a covered pizza, baked in the shape of a turnover or half moon. Again there are many fillings one can use. Here is one we enjoy.

One-sixth recipe for White Yeast Bread dough (see page 481), about 7 ounces (200g) dough

1/2 cup goat cheese, crumbled
1/2 cup mozzarella cheese, roughly grated, soaked in 1 tablespoon olive oil if possible
1 teaspoon parsley, finely chopped
1 teaspoon annual marjoram, finely chopped
1/2 cup cooked ham or crispy bacon, optional
2 tablespoons Piperonata (see page 190), or Pesto, or Tapenade

semolina, if using pizza paddle
olive oil for brushing

Preheat the oven to 475°F (250°C).

Mix all the ingredients for the filling together. Roll the dough very thinly into a 12-inch wide (30cm) circle. Sprinkle the paddle, if using it, with semolina, put the dough on top, and spoon the filling over the bottom half to within three-quarter inch (2cm) of the edge. Brush the edge with water, fold over the rest of the dough, and seal the edge by crimping with your fingers. Brush the top with cold water and slide into the fully preheated oven.

Bake for 20–30 minutes. Brush with olive oil when baked, and serve with an Arugula and Cherry Tomato Salad (see page 220). A steak knife is a good idea for cutting it.

Ham and Cheese Sfinciuni

Serves 8–10

one-half recipe White Yeast Bread dough (see page 481)
olive oil
1 1/2–2 cups cooked ham, thinly sliced
1 1/4 cups mozzarella cheese, grated
1 cup Parmesan cheese
1–2 tablespoons parsley, chopped

jelly roll pan, 13 x 9 inches (33 x 23cm)

Preheat the oven to 475°F (250°C). Make the dough in the usual way. Punch it down and let it rest for a few minutes.

Divide the dough in half. Roll one piece into a rectangle the same size as the pan. Brush the pan with olive oil and spread the dough over the bottom. Cover with slices of ham, sprinkle with a mixture of mozzarella and Parmesan cheese, and finally the parsley. Spread the filling right out to the edges and corners. Roll out the remainder of the dough and cover the filling, pressing down gently at the edges. Brush with egg wash and bake in the oven for 15–20 minutes; then reduce the temperature to 400°F (200°C) and bake for a further 5–10 minutes. Serve warm, cut into squares.

Mediterranean Pizza Pie

Serves 1–2

We love these pizza pies. You can have lots of fun experimenting with fillings.

one-third recipe (375g) White Yeast Bread dough (see page 481)
1 eggplant, sliced, de-gorged, and chargrilled in olive oil, cut into slices
1 zucchini, chargrilled in olive oil, sliced
2 small red peppers, roasted, peeled, and sliced
salt and freshly ground pepper
extra-virgin olive oil
5 or 6 basil leaves
1 tablespoon marjoram

Preheat the oven to 450°F (230°C).

Divide the dough in half, roll both pieces into circles. Put one on a baking tray, arrange the vegetables, sprinkle with marjoram, seasoning between each layer. Brush the edge with water. Lay the other piece of dough on top and seal the edges.

Brush with water and bake for 25–30 minutes. Brush with olive oil and serve. It may be necessary to reduce the temperature to 400°F (200°C) after 20 minutes, if the pie looks like it's burning. Serve warm or cold.

Panzarotti

Makes 16

one-half recipe (450g) White Yeast Bread dough (see page 481)
4 very ripe tomatoes, peeled, seeded, and chopped
salt and freshly ground pepper
1 teaspoon sugar
4 teaspoons marjoram, freshly chopped
1/2 cup buffalo mozzarella, grated
1–2 tablespoons Parmesan cheese, freshly grated

Divide the dough into one-ounce (25g) pieces, shape into rolls, let relax for a few minutes. Roll into circles to less than a 1/4-inch (5-mm) thick. Put about 1/2 teaspoon of chopped tomato, seasoned with salt, pepper, and sugar, onto the dough. Sprinkle with a little marjoram and 1/2 teaspoon freshly grated Parmesan. Brush the edge of the circles with water, fold over into a half-moon shape. Seal with your fingers or press with the tines of a fork.

Preheat the oven to 450°F (230°C). Bake for 15–20 minutes or until they are golden brown. Alternatively, deep-fry a few at a time until golden on both sides. You will need to turn them over halfway through cooking. Drain on paper towels. Serve immediately.

Breadsticks

Makes millions

Crusty breadsticks are all the rage. The more rustic looking the better, great with soups, salads, or just to nibble.

one quantity Ballymaloe White Yeast Bread dough (see page 481)
sea salt or Kosher salt, chopped rosemary, crushed cumin seeds, sesame seeds, poppy seeds, ground black pepper, chili flakes, grated parmesan cheese

When the dough has been punched down, preheat the oven to 425°F (220°C). Sprinkle the work surface with coarse sea salt or chosen flavoring.

Pull off small pieces of dough, 1/2 to 1 ounce (10–25g) in weight, roll into very thin, medium, or fat breadsticks with your hands. Roll in chosen "sprinkle." Place on a baking sheet. Repeat this process until all the dough is used. Bake in a preheated oven for 8–15 minutes, depending on size, until golden brown and crisp. Cool on a wire rack.

Note: Breadsticks are usually baked without a final rising but for a slightly, lighter result, let the shaped dough rise for about 10 minutes before baking.

Variations

Wiggly Worms

Shape a very thin breadstick, which has been rolled in finely grated parmesan cheese, into a wiggly worm.

Tuscan Breadsticks – Sgabei

Makes 30–32 depending on size

Completely addictive – utterly irresistible

one-half recipe (450g) White Yeast Bread dough (see page 481)
sea salt or Kosher salt
olive or sunflower oil for frying

Make the dough in the usual way, knead, let it rise, punch it down and let it rest for 5-10 minutes. Keep covered. Heat the oil in a deep-fat fryer to 450°F (190°C). Pull off quarter-ounce (7g) pieces, roll into thin bread sticks with your finger tips. Cook a few at a time in the hot oil. After a minute, when they are puffed and golden on one side, turn over onto the other side and continue to cook for another 1 1/2 minutes or until cooked through. Drain on paper towels. Sprinkle with sea salt. Eat as soon as possible with hot Garlic Butter (page 588), Chile Pepper Oil (page 227) or sweet chile sauce (available from Asian shops) to dip.

Sgabei with cheese

Pull off 2-ounce (50g) pieces of bread dough. Roll into fat bread sticks. Deep fry in hot oil for 4 to 5 minutes, turning halfway through. Drain on paper towels, slit along the side, and fill with Taleggio or Stracchino cheese and eat as the cheese melts – yummy!

Anchovy Bread Sticks

Break off half-ounce (10g) pieces of bread dough, roll out, and flatten. Lay one or two anchovies along one side, pinch to cover, roll again, and deep fry as above.

Pretzels

Makes 10–12

1 Ballymaloe White Yeast Bread dough recipe (see page 481)
egg wash
sea salt or Kosher salt

poppy seeds, sesame seeds, grated cheese for sprinkling

Preheat the oven to 450°F (230°C). Mix and knead the bread dough and let it rise until doubled in size.

Punch it down. Divide the dough into pieces about 4 ounces (110g) in weight. Roll each piece into a thin rope, about 2 feet (60cm) long and a half-inch (1cm) thick. To shape the pretzels: form each piece of dough into a loose horseshoe shape with the ends pointing towards you. Take the ends, and cross them over twice, and rest both ends on the edge of the loop of dough.

Transfer each one onto a greased baking sheet. Cover and let rise in a warm place for about 10 minutes. Glaze gently with a light egg wash and sprinkle with coarse crystals of sea salt and poppy seeds, sesame seeds, or grated cheese, if using.
Bake the pretzels for about 15 minutes or until golden brown. Transfer to a wire rack and serve warm or cold.

Maldon Sea Salt Crackers

Makes about 30

one-half recipe (450g) White Yeast Bread dough (see page 481)
1–2 tablespoons extra-virgin olive oil
1–2 tablespoons Maldon sea salt (if unavailable, use Kosher sale or other coarse salt)

3 baking trays

Preheat the oven to 450°F (230°C). Divide the dough in 3 pieces and roll out as thinly as possible.

Knead, roll, and then let it rest for 1–2 minutes, and then roll again. We bake these crackers on the upturned bottoms of the baking trays so the edges don't get in the way.

Brush the tray with extra-virgin olive oil.*
Lay the sheet of paper-thin bread dough on top. Brush with olive oil and prick with a pastry picker or fork. Cut into 4 strips lengthwise with a pastry wheel or knife, and then cut into 2-inch (5-cm) diamonds (smaller if you wish). Sprinkle with flakes of sea salt. Bake for 6–10 minutes in the preheated oven. They will bubble up and shrink apart in the oven. As soon as they are crisp and golden, lift off and transfer to a wire rack to cool. Store in an airtight container.

Variation

Rosemary Crackers

Proceed as above to *. Sprinkle with a half-tablespoon finely chopped rosemary evenly over the oil. Lay the dough on top. Sprinkle with salt and more finely chopped rosemary. Cut into 3 strips lengthwise, then into 4 across to make 12 large squares (36 for 3 trays). Bake as above and cool on a wire rack. Store in an airtight container.

Master Recipe

Green or Black Olive Bread

Makes 4 loaves

Olive bread is made in many of the Mediterranean countries with many variations on the theme. In Provence, the olives are left whole, but in Greece they are pitted and then chopped.

8 cups white bread flour
1 teaspoon salt
1/2 cup olive oil
two ounces (50g) fresh yeast (about 4 tablespoons) or 1 ounce (25g) (4 1/4-ounce envelopes) dried yeast
2 teaspoons sugar
1 3/4 cups warm water approx.
2 cups green or black olives, pitted and chopped – yields about 1 1/2 cups
2 tablespoons olive oil, for greasing

Put the flour and salt in a bowl along with the olive oil. Mix the yeast with the sugar and 2/3 cup of the water. Leave it for 3–4 minutes in a warm place until the yeast starts to work. Pour this mixture into the flour, add the remaining water, and mix to a pliable dough. Knead for about 10 minutes or until the dough is smooth and elastic, then knead in the olives.

Put 1 tablespoon of oil into the bowl and turn the dough in it to grease the surface and prevent a dry crust forming. Cover the bowl with a damp cloth or plastic wrap and let the dough rise in a warm place for about 1 1/2 hours or until it doubles in bulk. Punch the dough down by kneading for 3 or 4 minutes; divide it into 4 balls. Place the balls on an oiled baking tray.

Press them down gently or shape them in any way you like. Let the dough rise again, covered with a damp cloth, for about 1 hour or until it has doubled again.

Preheat the oven to 450°F (230°C).

Brush the loaves with water to soften the crust and bake for about 30 minutes or until they sound hollow when tapped on the bottom – cooking time depends on the size of the loaves. Brush with the remaining olive oil and cool on a wire rack.

Variations

Olive and Rosemary Bread

Follow the Master Recipe, adding 2 tablespoons chopped rosemary along with the olives. Bake in pans or as round loaves.

Walnut and Raisin Bread

Follow the Master Recipe, omitting the olives and kneading in 2 cups (225g) walnuts and 1/4 cup (50g) raisins and let rise. Bake in loaf pans or as round loaves.

Herb Bread

Follow the Master Recipe, adding a quarter-cup (4 tablespoons) of finely chopped fresh mixed herbs (rosemary, sage, thyme, chives, parsley, lemon balm) to the dough along with the yeast.

Evie Lanitis' Hamburger Buns

Makes about 20 large buns

Evie Lanitis from Cyprus developed this recipe when she was with us at the School.

10 cups white bread flour
2 level teaspoons salt
3 level tablespoons sugar
3/4 stick plus 1 tablespoon (1/3 cup plus 1 tablespoon) butter
1 1/2 ounces (35g) fresh yeast (about 3 tablespoons)

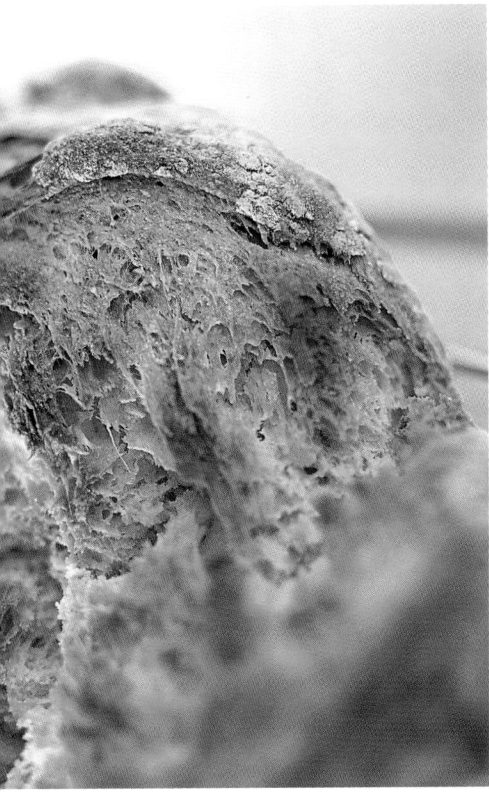

2 1/4 cups tepid milk
a scant cup plain yogurt
1 beaten egg

For glaze
1 egg, beaten with about 1/3 cup water

Sift the flour and salt into a bowl. Add the sugar. Rub in the butter. Dissolve the yeast in the tepid milk. Add the beaten egg to the yogurt. Pour the milk, then the yogurt into the flour, knead in the food mixer with the dough hook fitted, for 5–6 minutes. Cover and let rise until the dough doubles in size – this takes about 1 hour. Cut the dough into 3 pieces. Roll out the dough into a 1 1/2-inch (4-cm) thick circle.

Cut with a cookie cutter to get even sizes. Make balls out of each piece, then flatten with the heel of your hand. Put 6 rolls on a baking tray, cover, and let rise for about 1 1/2 hours (they don't rise too much). Brush them gently with egg wash.

Preheat the oven to 450°F (230°C), open quickly, and spray the inside of the oven well with water, put the tray in and close the door at once. Cook for 20–25 minutes.

Spray with water twice more during baking – around oven, bottom, sides, and over the buns. Cool on a wire rack.

Granary Loaf

Makes 1 loaf

Granary flour is a mixture of malted wheat and rye, with a proportion of whole wheat berries. Some people find the malt flavor rather strong, so you can mix a proportion of white all-purpose or white bread flour with the granary meal. Homemade granary bread stays fresh and moist for an unusually long time.

5 cups granary flour or 4 cups of granary flour and 1 cup white bread flour
1 rounded teaspoon salt
3/4 ounce (20g) yeast (about 1 1/2 tablespoons)
about 1 1/4 cups lukewarm water
1 teaspoon black treacle, optional
2 tablespoons light olive oil
1 tablespoon cracked wheat, optional

1 loaf pan, about 5 x 8 inches (12 x 20cm)

Preheat the oven to 450°F (230°C).

Mix the flours with the salt. Mix the yeast with tepid water, treacle, and oil, then add to the flour and mix to a dough; it will be very lithe and pliable. Knead for a few minutes, then form it into a ball, cover it, and let it rise in the usual way. When the dough has at least doubled in bulk and is puffy, punch it down and knead for 2 or 3 minutes.

Put the dough into the well-oiled loaf pan, cover, and leave it for about 30 minutes until it has filled the pan and is beginning to rise above the rim. Brush lightly with water and sprinkle with cracked wheat, if using. Bake in the oven for about 25 minutes, then reduce the heat to 400°F (200°C) for the remaining time: 20 minutes approximately. Remove from the pan and let it cool on a wire rack.

Note: For a crispier crust on the bottom, the bread may be removed from the pan 10 minutes before the end of cooking time, and replaced in the oven to cook on its own.

Rye and Caraway Seed Bread

Makes 1 loaf or 3 small loaves

3 cups white bread flour
1 1/4 cups dark rye flour
1 teaspoon salt
3 tablespoons caraway seeds
1/4 ounce (7g) fresh yeast (about 1/2 tablespoon)
1 1/4 cups lukewarm water
3 tablespoons butter
poppy seeds (optional)
eggwash

1 loaf pan, 5 x 8 inches (12 x 20cm)

Preheat the oven to 450°F (230°C).

Crumble and mix the yeast with the water. Mix the flours, salt, and caraway seeds in a bowl and add the yeast with extra warm water, if necessary, to make a soft but not sticky dough. Add the butter and knead until smooth, about 10 minutes. Cover and let it rise in a warm place.

Punch down and shape into 1, 2, or 3 round or oval loaves. Cover and let rise again for about 30 minutes, until well-risen. Alternatively, place in the well-oiled loaf pan to rise. Brush with egg wash, sprinkle with poppy seeds, and slash the top in a cross with a sharp knife or baker's blade. Bake for 40–45 minutes for a loaf in a pan, or until the bread sounds hollow when knocked underneath. Small loaves will take 25 minutes. Cool on a wire rack.

Handkerchief Bread

Makes about 24

When we stayed in the Leela Hotel in Mumbai in India the chefs made many wonderful flat breads. This one particularly intrigued me. We tried it with well-rested White Yeast Bread Dough.

1 x White Yeast Bread recipe (see page 481)

Make the dough in the normal way; punch it down. Heat a wok or Indian wok karhai on a hot flame. Take 2 ounces (50g) of the dough, roll it out into a very thin circle. The Indian chefs start with a rolling pin, but then spin it around their heads, pizza-style! Roll one piece as thinly as possible, let it rest for a few minutes while you start to roll out another piece. Then go back to the first and roll it so thinly that one could almost read through it.

Slap it onto the hot upturned karhai. It will bubble and blister almost immediately. Turn it over onto the other side, then fold in the sides and fold in three or four to make a little parcel like a folded handkerchief. Serve immediately.

Ciabatta

Makes 4 loaves (each about the width of a hand and the length of the arm from wrist to elbow)

The students love to make this recipe from The Italian Baker by Carol Field.

"'Ciabatta' means slipper in Italian; one look at the short stubby bread will make it clear how it was named. Ciabatta is a remarkable combination of rustic country texture, and elegant and tantalizing taste. It is much lighter than its homey shape would indicate, and the porous chewy interior is enclosed in a slightly crunchy crust that is dusted with flour.

The dough should be made in a mixer. I have made it by hand but wouldn't recommend it unless you are willing to knead the wet, sticky mass between your hands. You can't work it on the table because the natural inclination is to add lots of flour to this very sticky dough and pretty soon you wouldn't have a Ciabatta. Resist the temptation to add flour and follow the instructions. The dough will feel utterly unfamiliar and probably a bit scary. And that's not the only unusual feature – the shaped loaves are flat and look definitely unpromising; even when they are puffed after the second rise, you may feel certain you've done it all wrong. Don't give up. The loaves rise nicely in the oven."

Biga, see below (appetizer – made 12–24 hours ahead)
1/4 ounce (7g) fresh yeast (about 1/2 tablespoon)
1/4 cup warm water
1 1/2 cups warm water at room temperature
4 1/2 cups all-purpose flour

Ciabatta
1/4 ounce (7g) fresh yeast (about 1/2 tablespoon)
1/2 cup warm milk
1 1/4 cups warm water
1 tablespoon olive oil
2–2 1/2 cups Biga
4 1/2 cups all-purpose flour
1 1/2 tablespoons salt

To make the Biga: stir the yeast into 1/4 cup warm water and let stand until creamy, about 10 minutes. Stir in the remaining water and then the flour, 1 cup at a time. Remove to a lightly oiled bowl, cover with plastic wrap and let it rise at a cool room temperature for up to 24 hours. It will triple in volume and still be wet and sticky when ready. Cover and refrigerate until ready to use. When needed, scoop out desired amount.

To make the Ciabatta: Stir the yeast into the milk in the mixer bowl, let it stand until creamy, about 10 minutes. Add the water, oil, and Biga, and mix with the paddle until blended. Mix the flour and salt, add to the bowl, and mix for 10 minutes. Change to the dough hook and mix for 15–25 minutes at high speed, or until the dough is stringy and pulling away from the sides of the bowl (this stage is essential for final shaping of the dough).

Place the dough in an oiled bowl, cover with plastic wrap, and let rise until doubled in size, about 1 1/4 hours. The dough should be full of air bubbles, very supple, elastic, and sticky.

Cut the dough into 4 equal pieces on a well-floured surface. Roll up each piece into a cylinder, then stretch each into a rectangle, about 10 x 4 inches (25 x 10cm), pulling with your fingers to get it long and wide enough. Generously flour 2 baking trays. Place 2 loaves, seam side up, on a tray. Dimple the loaves vigorously with your fingertips or knuckles so that they won't rise too much. The dough will look heavily pockmarked, but it is very resilient so don't be concerned. Cover loosely with dampened towels, and let rise until puffy but not doubled: 1 1/2–2 hours. The loaves will look flat and definitely unpromising but don't give up for they will rise more in the oven.

Preheat the oven to 425°F (220°C). Bake for 20–25 minutes, dusting with flour and spraying 3 times with water in the first 10 minutes. Cool on a wire rack.

Moroccan Bread

Makes 2 loaves

In Morocco, they knead with clenched fists; I did my best to learn from the cooks in La Gazelle d'Or in Taroudant but eventually reverted to my own method! This recipe is based on one from Paula Wolfert's book Good Food from Morocco.

1 ounce (25g) fresh yeast (about 2 tablespoons) or 1 1/4-ounce (7g) envelope active dry yeast
1 teaspoon granulated sugar
lukewarm water
4 1/2 cups white flour
1 1/4 cups fine whole wheat flour
2 teaspoons salt
1 teaspoon sesame seeds
1 tablespoon aniseed
1 cup lukewarm milk
cornmeal or polenta

Preheat the oven to 400°F (200°C).

Put the yeast into a small bowl with the sugar and 2 tablespoons of lukewarm water, stir, and leave in a warm place until the yeast starts to bubble. Mix the flours with the salt and spices in a large mixing bowl. Make a well in the center. Add the yeast, pour in the milk and enough lukewarm water to form a stiff dough. Since flours differ in their ability to absorb moisture, it is difficult to give a precise amount. Turn the dough out onto a lightly floured board and knead hard. In Morocco they knead with clenched fists. It will take anywhere from 10 to 12 minutes to knead the dough thoroughly; it should be smooth and elastic.

In an electric beater with a dough hook, knead for 7 or 8 minutes at slow speed. When the dough is smooth and elastic, shape into two balls and let it rest for 5 minutes on the board.

Lightly grease a mixing bowl. Transfer the first ball of dough to the greased bowl and form into a cone shape by grasping the dough with one hand and rotating it against the sides of the bowl, held by the other hand. Turn out onto a baking sheet that has been sprinkled with cornmeal. Flatten the cone with the palm of the hand to form a circle, about 5 inches (12.5cm) in diameter, with a slightly raised center. Repeat with the second ball of dough. Cover loosely with a damp towel and let rise about 2 hours in a warm place. To see if the bread has fully risen, poke your finger gently into the dough – the bread is ready for baking if the dough does not spring back.

Using a fork, prick the bread around the sides 3 or 4 times and place on the center shelf of the oven. Bake for 12 minutes, then lower the heat to 300°F (150°C) and bake for 30–40 minutes more. When done, the bread will sound hollow when tapped on the bottom. Remove and let cool. Cut into wedges just before serving.

Note: at the Gazelle d'Or they also cooked a flattened circle of the dough on a griddle until browned on both sides. This is absolutely delicious with fresh butter and honey. They also kneaded thyme into the dough and and brushed the circles with oil and cooked them on a griddle for lunch; they called them Berber breads.

Sicilian Semolina Bread

Makes 2 loaves

This bread, which comes from the hill town of Erice in Sicily, is made from durum semolina flour and is shaped into an extravagant variety of forms. Mafalda, the most common one, looks like a snake curled back and forth with a baton laid over it. If it is made without the baton, it's called scaletta or little ladder. The shape that looks like a pair of slightly askew glasses is in homage to Santa Lucia, the patron saint of vision. All the loaves have a crunchy golden crust with a sesame seed topping.

3/4 ounce (20g) fresh yeast (about 1 1/2 tablespoons) or 2 1/2 teaspoons dried yeast
1/4 cup warm water
1 tablespoon olive oil
1 teaspoon sugar
3/4 cup water at room temperature
3 cups plus 2 tablespoons durum flour or very fine semolina as used for pasta
1 cup unbleached all-purpose flour
2 teaspoons salt
2 tablespoons sesame seeds

Dissolve the yeast in the warm water in a large mixing bowl, add the oil, sugar, and water. Mix the flours and salt in a bowl, add the liquid, and mix to a dough. Let it rest for a few minutes, then knead for 8–10 minutes by hand or 5 minutes by machine. Put the dough into a lightly oiled bowl, cover tightly with plastic wrap, and let it rise until doubled in size, about 2 1/2 hours. The dough should be springy and blistered, but still soft and velvety.

Punch the dough down, knead it briefly, and let it rest for 5 minutes. Flatten it with your forearm into a square. Roll it into a long, fairly narrow rope, about 20 to 22 inches (50–55cm) long. The dough should be very elastic. Cut the dough in half and mold into your chosen shape.

Put the loaves onto floured wax paper or oiled baking sheets. Brush the entire surface of each loaf lightly with water, and sprinkle with sesame seeds; pat the seeds very gently into the dough. Cover with a cloth and let rise until doubled in size, 1–1 1/2 hours.

Preheat the oven and a baking sheet to 425°F (220°C). Sprinkle the baking sheet with cornmeal just before sliding the loaves onto it. Bake for 10 minutes, spray the bread with water at three different times throughout the baking. Reduce the heat to 400°F (200°C) and bake 25–30 minutes longer. Cool on racks.

Arnaud's Pita Bread

Makes 8–10

1 ounce (25g) fresh yeast (about 2 tablespoons)
1 1/3 cups lukewarm water
4 cups bread flour
2 teaspoons salt

Crumble the yeast into a half-cup (125ml) of the water. Leave for 10 minutes until the yeast is dissolved. Sift the flour and salt into a bowl, add the yeast and the rest of the water. Stir by hand until well mixed. The dough should not be too dry. Knead the dough until it is very smooth and elastic. If too sticky, add flour while kneading. Transfer the dough to an oiled bowl and oil the whole surface of the dough. Cover and let rise in a warm place for 1–1 1/2 hours or until more than doubled in volume.

Knead the dough again until smooth. Roll into a thick log and cut with a floured knife into 8–10 equal-sized pieces. Roll each piece into smooth balls. Place onto a floured surface, cover, and let rise for about 30 minutes or until double again.

Preheat the oven to the highest setting.

Heat the baking sheets. Roll the balls to circles about 6 inches (15cm) wide and 1/4-inch (5mm) thick. Bake 2 at a time – 2 per baking sheet. Bake for about 3 minutes until just browning and puffed. Let cool on wire racks if not using immediately. They can be frozen but will not be as good as fresh.

Sometimes one or two will not puff enough to make a pocket – they are still fine to eat.

Timmy's Sour Dough Bread

Makes 1–2 loaves

4 cups white bread flour
2 teaspoons salt
1 teaspoon sugar
1/4 ounce (7g) fresh yeast (about 1/2 tablespoon)
2/3–3/4 cup warm water
1 1/4–1 1/2 cups sour dough starter (see below)
3 tablespoons butter
flour for dusting

Sour Dough Starter, see below (made at least 24, and better still, 48 hours ahead)
1/4 ounce (7g) fresh yeast (about 1/2 tablespoon)
1/4 cup warm water
1 1/2 cups warm water
4 1/2 cups all-purpose white flour

To make the Sour Dough Appetizer: stir the yeast into a quarter-cup warm water and let stand until creamy, about 10 minutes. Stir in the remaining water and then the flour, a cup at a time. Remove to a lightly oiled bowl, cover with plastic wrap, and let rise at room temperature for 24–48 hours or longer. It will triple in volume and still be wet and sticky when ready. Cover and refrigerate until ready to use. When needed, scoop out desired amount.

To make the bread dough: stir the yeast into a quarter-cup water in the mixer bowl and let stand for about 10 minutes. Add the remaining water, and the starter, and mix with the dough hook until blended. Mix the flour, salt, and sugar, add to the bowl, and blend for 2 to 3 minutes. Let it rest for 10 minutes, knead for 5 minutes at low speed, then 2 minutes at medium speed until smooth, or knead by hand for 10 minutes. Drop the butter into the bowl in small pieces while kneading.

Let it rest again for 10 minutes. Shape the bread into loaves, braids, or rolls, brush with water, and dust with flour again. Cover with a dish towel. Let rise in a warm place; this rising will take 1–1 1/2 hours. The bread is ready for baking if a small dent remains when pressed lightly with the finger.

Bake in a hot oven at 450°F (230°C) for 30–35 minutes for a loaf, 20–25 minutes for rolls.

How to Cook Poppadoms

Poppadoms come in a package, you'll be glad to hear! There are several flavors – from chili, to peppercorn, to garlic, but I prefer the plain ones best. I also favor the brands in the simple cellophane packages rather than those with fancy packaging. They can be cooked in various ways: deep-frying is best. Cook in sunflower oil for a few seconds, when they have expanded to almost double their size; drain well on paper towels. If your deep-fat fryer is not large enough, cook them in halves or quarters, or even strips.

Alternatively, cook under the broiler or in a microwave, but they don't expand so much when cooked this way.

Look out for mini pappads or poppadoms, which are great for canapé bases or just for nibbling.

Poppadoms with toppings

Serves 4

We were served poppadoms with various toppings in both Mumbai and Kerala. They came instead of bread but would make a perfect simple appetizer or a delicious nibble to go with drinks. You may want to go easy on the chili powder although they are, in fact, very spicy in India.

8 cooked poppadoms
2 very ripe tomatoes, peeled
3 tablespoons finely diced red or white onion
chili powder
freshly chopped cilantro

Dice the tomato flesh very finely, add the tiny onion dice, and sprinkle a little over each poppadom. Dust with a little chili powder and freshly chopped cilantro leaves. Serve immediately.

Kelley's Sweet Hot Corn Bread

One of my students, Kelley Ryan-Bourgoise from Los Angeles, gave me this terrific recipe for cornbread.

2¼ cups yellow cornmeal
3¼ cups all-purpose white flour
⅔ cup sugar
1½ teaspoons salt
1½ tablespoons baking powder

½ cup melted butter
1½ cups buttermilk
½ cup milk
2 beaten eggs
tabasco to taste

½ cup corn kernels (canned is fine)
¾ cup Cheddar cheese, grated
1 cup chopped scallion
2 tablespoons cilantro, chopped

Preheat oven the to 425°F (220°C).

Combine the cornmeal, flour, sugar, salt, and baking powder in a bowl.

In another bowl, whisk together the butter, buttermilk, milk, eggs, and add tabasco to taste. Combine both mixtures together and fold in the remaining ingredients.

Pour the mixture into a square baking pan, big enough to let the mixture come two-thirds the way up the side of the pan. Bake for 20 minutes or until golden brown and a toothpick inserted into the center comes out clean.

Cut into squares. Butter, and eat while still warm.

Master Recipe

Tortillas De Harina De Trigo (Flour Tortillas)

Makes about 25 tortillas, 9 inches (23cm) in diameter

Wheat flour tortillas are usually larger than corn tortillas and they come from northern Mexico, where maize does not grow so easily. They are made with animal fat (usually lard), salt, and all-purpose white flour (I use butter and get a very good result). Cooked on a hot griddle, they must be very pliable and soft for storage. For most purposes, flour tortillas can be used instead of corn tortillas, and many people prefer them. They can be used in the same way but are never eaten cold.

To freeze flour tortillas, put a sheet of wax paper between each one as they tend to stick together, especially when frozen. They defrost easily if left at room temperature for 30 minutes.

4 cups all-purpose white flour
2 teaspoons salt
⅓ cup lard, vegetable shortening, or butter
about 1 cup warm water (at body temperature)

Heat a heavy frying pan (without greasing it) on medium heat until a drop of water will sizzle in it.

Sift the flour and salt together in a bowl and rub in the butter as you would for pie dough. Slowly add the warm water – the amount may vary with the type of flour used. Knead the dough on a floured board with floured hands until it is no longer sticky. Keep the dough covered with a warm damp cloth.

Take about an ounce (25g) of dough at a time and knead for a few seconds, folding it back on itself to trap air. Now make it into a little ball and flatten it. Place the flattened ball on a floured board, and roll it out with a floured rolling pin until it is so thin that you can see the board through the dough. Cut into 7- to 9-inch circles (18–23cm). Slap a tortilla straight onto the pan, cook for 30 seconds on one side then turn over, and cook for 15–30 seconds on the other.

Remove, cover with a dish towel, and keep them warm or store in a tortilla basket if you have one. If you need to warm up a lot of tortillas together, wrap 6 tortillas in tin foil and reheat them in a moderate oven (350°F [180°C]) for 15 minutes.

Tortilla chips

Cut the tortilla into 6 pieces and deep-fry for a few seconds.

To shallow-fry: cover the bottom of a heavy frying pan with an inch (2.5cm) of cooking oil. When the oil is hot, fry one tortilla at a time for about 20 seconds. Remove from the oil and drain on absorbent paper towels until needed.

To deep fry: heat the oil in a deep-fat fryer to 400°F (200°C). Immerse the tortilla and fry for 1–1½ minutes. Remove from the oil when they are light gold, as they keep browning after they have been removed. Drain on paper towels.

Variations

Flavored Tortillas

In the farmer's market in St. Paul, Minnesota, a Mexican stallholder offered a whole range of flavored tortillas, even chocolate, which he insisted would be delicious with ice cream and hot chocolate sauce.

Chili Tortillas

Follow the Master Recipe, adding ½–1 tablespoon of cayenne pepper to the flour.

Fresh Herb Tortillas

Follow the Master Recipe, adding 2–3 tablespoons of freshly chopped thyme, chives, or parsley to the flour.

Rosemary Tortillas

Follow the Master Recipe, adding 2–3 tablespoons very finely chopped rosemary to the flour.

Cilantro Tortillas

Follow the Master Recipe, adding 2–3 tablespoons of very finely chopped cilantro to the flour.

Tomato Tortillas

Follow the Master Recipe, mixing 2–3 tablespoons of tomato paste with the water.

Spinach Tortillas

Follow the Master Recipe, adding ½ cup of very dry, well-seasoned spinach purée to the flour, with the water, and proceed as above.

Sun-dried Tomato Tortillas

Follow the Master Recipe, adding 2 ounces (50g) of puréed and sifted sun-dried tomato (about ⅓ cup) to the flour.

Chocolate Tortillas

Follow the Master Recipe, adding ½ cup sweetened cocoa to the flour.

Cinnamon Tortillas

Follow the Master Recipe, adding 3–4 tablespoons of ground cinnamon to the flour.

Chocolate Tortillas with Ice Cream, Bananas, and Butterscotch Sauce

Put a couple of scoops of ice cream on the tortilla, roll up, and freeze.

To serve: Pop into a hot oven for 3 or 4 minutes to crisp. Serve with Butterscotch Sauce (see page 599) and sliced banana.

Master Recipe

Mummy's Sweet White Scones

Makes 18–20 scones using a 3-inch (7.5-cm) biscuit or cookie cutter

I regularly meet people on the street who make these, having watched me make them on television in Ireland, and they love the crunchy topping.

8 cups all-purpose white flour
pinch of salt
¼ cup superfine sugar
3 heaped teaspoons baking powder
1½ sticks (¾ cup) butter
3 eggs
a scant 2 cups milk to mix

For glaze:
egg wash
granulated sugar for sprinkling

Preheat the oven to 475°F (250°C).

Sift all the dry ingredients together in a large wide bowl. Cut the butter into cubes, toss in the flour, and rub in the butter. Make a well in the center. Whisk the eggs with the milk, add to the dry ingredients, and mix to a soft dough. Turn out onto a floured board.

Knead lightly, just enough to shape into a circle. Roll out to about an inch (2.5cm) thick and cut or stamp into scones. Place on a baking sheet – no need to grease.

Brush the tops with egg wash and dip each one in granulated sugar. Bake in the oven for 10–12 minutes until golden brown on top. Cool on a wire rack.

Serve split in half with homemade jam and a blob of whipped cream, or just butter and jam.

Variations

Fruit Scones

Follow the Master Recipe, adding ½ cup plump golden raisins when the butter has been rubbed in. Continue as in the Master Recipe.

Lexia Raisin Scones

Follow the Master Recipe, adding ½ cup lexia raisins to the basic recipe and continue as in the Master Recipe.

Cherry Scones

Follow the Master Recipe, adding ½ cup quartered candied cherries to the basic mixture when the butter has been rubbed in. Continue as in the Master Recipe.

Craisin Scones or Dried Cherry Scones

Follow the Master Recipe, adding 1/2 cup craisins or dried cherries. Continue as in the Master Recipe.

Crystallized Ginger Scones

Follow the Master Recipe, adding 1/2 cup chopped crystallized or drained ginger in syrup to the dry ingredients, and continue as in the Master Recipe.

Candied Citrus Peel Scones

Follow the Master Recipe, adding 1/2 cup best-quality candied orange and lemon peel to the dry ingredients after the butter has been rubbed in; coat the citrus peel well in the flour before adding the liquid.

Cinnamon Scones

Follow the Master Recipe, adding 4 teaspoons of ground cinnamon to the dry ingredients in the basic mixture.

Mix 1 teaspoon of ground cinnamon with 1/4 cup granulated sugar. Dip the top of the scones in the sugar mixed with the cinnamon. Bake as in the Master Recipe.

Poppy Seed Scones

Follow the Master Recipe, adding a heaped quarter-cup poppy seeds to the dry ingredients after the butter has been rubbed in. Proceed as in the Master Recipe. Serve with freshly crushed strawberries and cream.

Chocolate Chip Scones

Follow the Master Recipe, adding 4 ounces (110g) best-quality dark chocolate, chopped (about 2/3 cup), to the dry ingredients after the butter has been rubbed in, and proceed as in the Master Recipe.

Lemon or Orange Scones

Add the grated rind of one lemon or orange to the flour, and proceed as in the Master Recipe. Sandwich together with Lemon Curd (see page 510) or serve with Orange or Lemon Butter (recipe follows).

Scones with Orange or Lemon Butter

Serve the freshly baked scones with orange butter.

Orange or Lemon Butter
1 1/2 sticks (3/4 cup) butter
1 tablespoon orange or lemon zest, finely grated
1 3/4 cups confectioners sugar

Cream the butter with the finely grated rind. Add the sifted confectioners sugar and beat until fluffy.

Tip: scone mixture may be weighed up ahead – even the day before. Butter may be rubbed in but do not add raising agents or liquid until just before baking.

Coffee and Walnut Scones

Makes 18–20 scones, using a 3-inch (7.5-cm) biscuit or cookie cutter

In the US, scones are rarely eaten with butter or cream so be generous with the icing.

8 cups flour
pinch of salt
1/4 cup superfine sugar
3 heaped teaspoons baking powder
1 1/2 sticks (3/4 cup) butter
3 eggs
2–3 tablespoons coffee essence
about 2 cups milk, to mix
1 1/4 cups walnuts, chopped coarsely

Coffee Icing
3 1/2 cups confectioners sugar
scant 2 tablespoons coffee essence
about 1/4 cup boiling water

First preheat the oven to 475°F (250°C).

Sift all the dry ingredients together. Rub in the butter and add the walnuts. Make a well in the center. Whisk the eggs and coffee essence with the milk, add to the dry ingredients, and mix to a soft dough. Turn out onto a floured board. Knead lightly, just enough to shape into a circle. Roll out to about an inch (2.5cm) thick and stamp into 3-inch (7.5-cm) scones. Place on a baking sheet. Bake in a hot oven for 10–15 minutes until golden brown on top. Cool on a wire rack.

Meanwhile make the coffee icing: sift the confectioners sugar into a bowl. Add coffee essence and enough boiling water to make it the consistency of thick cream. Spread each scone generously with coffee icing. Let them set.

Rosemary Kearney's Gluten-free Sweet White Scones

Makes 15 scones using a 2 1/2-inch (6-cm) biscuit or cookie cutter

Rosemary Kearney, a past student and teacher at the School, teaches an excellent one-day course on gluten-free cooking for celiacs every year. She has been a celiac all her life.

2 1/2 cups rice flour
1/2 cup tapioca flour
4 teaspoons gluten-free baking powder
2 teaspoons xanthan gum
1 level teaspoon salt
a heaped 1/4 cup superfine sugar
1 stick (1/2 cup) butter
2 eggs
1/2–3/4 cup plain yogurt
egg wash

Preheat the oven to 475°F (250°C).

Sift all the dry ingredients together into a large bowl and mix well. Rub in the butter. Lightly whisk the eggs and yogurt together.

Make a well in the center and add the eggs and yogurt to the dry ingredients. Mix to a soft dough, adding a little more yogurt if necessary.

Turn out onto a rice-floured board and knead lightly, just enough to shape into a circle. Roll out to about an inch (2.5cm) thick and stamp into scones using a 2½-inch (6-cm) biscuit or cookie cutter. Put on a rice-floured baking sheet and brush with a little egg wash.

Bake in a hot oven for 10 minutes approximately, until golden brown on top. Cool on a wire rack.

Serve split in half with homemade Raspberry Jam and a blob of whipped cream.

Walnut and Cinnamon Buns

croissant dough (see page 528)
melted butter
cinnamon
sugar
chopped walnuts
Caramelized Walnuts (see page 565)

Preheat the oven to 400°F (200°C).

Roll the dough into a rectangle. Brush with melted butter and sprinkle with sugar, cinnamon, and chopped walnuts.

Roll up, cut into 2-inch (5-cm) pieces and let rest on a baking tray. When the buns have doubled in size, brush with egg wash, put a spoonful of caramelized walnuts on top, and bake for 30–35 minutes or until fully cooked, slightly caramelized and deliciously sticky.

Left: Brioche

Brioche

Makes 15–20 individual brioches or 2 large ones

Brioche is the richest of all yeast doughs and absolutely irresistible to eat. Some recipes can be intimidating but this very easy version works well and I've designed it so that the dough can rise overnight in the fridge and be shaped and baked in the morning. In France, brioche is traditionally baked in fluted pans but it can, of course, be baked in any size or shape, either free-form or molded. The individual brioches à tête, which literally means brioches with a head, are usually eaten warm for breakfast with butter and homemade jam. The dough can also be used for all sorts of "grand" recipes – anything from Saucisson en Brioche to a whole fish encased in brioche dough – Saumon or Loup de Mer en Croûte for example. Pretty impressive!

1 ounce (25g) fresh yeast (about 2 tablespoons) (or use half-quantity of dry yeast)
¼ cup superfine sugar
¼ cup plus 1 tablespoon tepid water
4 eggs
4 cups white bread flour
large pinch of salt
2 sticks (1 cup) soft unsalted butter

egg wash
1 beaten egg, preferably from free-range hen

Dissolve the yeast and sugar in the water, add the beaten eggs, and pour into a mixing bowl. Add the flour and salt and mix to a stiff dough either by hand or with the dough hook of an electric mixer. When the mixture is smooth, beat in the butter in small pieces. The finished dough should have a silky appearance. Place it in an oiled bowl, cover, and rest it overnight in the fridge.

Next day
Preheat the oven to 350°F (180°C). Knead the dough lightly, weigh it into 2-ounce (50-g) pieces, and roll it into balls or divide in half for large brioches. With the side of your hand, make a deep indent into each ball of dough slightly off-center. Put the dough (heavy end first) into well-buttered brioche molds. With a floured index finger, push the "little hat" towards the center, leaving it just protruding above the body of the dough.* This classic technique takes practice and skill; if it seems too difficult, just form them into a roll, or cheat by pushing the floured handle of a small wooden spoon down through the hat into the base, this helps to anchor it firmly. Brush the top of each brioche with egg wash and let them rise in a warm place until doubled in size.

Gently brush the brioches once again with egg wash and cook in the oven for 20–25 minutes. Large brioches will take 40–50 minutes to cook. A skewer inserted into the center should come out clean. Serve freshly baked with butter and homemade Strawberry Jam (see page 504).

* They can be frozen at this stage.

Cheese Brioche

Makes 1 loaf

This is really scrummy, particularly when eaten warm.

half-quantity brioche dough
¾–1 cup coarsely grated Gruyère cheese
egg wash

1 loaf pan, 9 x 5 x 2 inches (23 x 12.5 x 5cm)

Make the dough as in the preceding recipe. Next day, preheat the oven to 400°F (200°C).

Knead half of the cheese into the dough after it has been punched down. Put it in a well-buttered loaf pan and brush with egg wash. Let it double in size, egg wash it again, sprinkle with the remainder of the cheese, and bake for 15 minutes. Then reduce the temperature to 350°F (180°C) for 25–30 minutes approximately. Remove from the pan and cool on a wire rack.

Basic Bun Dough

Makes about 32

Bun dough is the basis for doughnuts, Bath buns, currant buns, hot cross buns, Chelsea buns, iced whirls, etc.

8 cups white bread flour
1/3 cup superfine sugar
pinch of salt
1 1/2 sticks (3/4 cup) butter
2 eggs, preferably organic, and from free-range hens
2 ounces (50g) yeast (about 3–3 1/2 tablespoons)
1 1/4–2 cups luke warm water

Dissolve the yeast in a little luke warm water. Sift the flour, sugar, and salt into a bowl. Rub in the butter and then add the eggs. Add the yeast and enough water to obtain a fairly soft dough. Cover, and rest the dough for 10 minutes. Knead well until the dough becomes firm and springs back when pressed with a finger (5–10 minutes). Place in a deep Pyrex or ceramic bowl, cover with plastic wrap and let rise until it doubles in size. Punch down by kneading well for 2 or 3 minutes, rest briefly, and shape as desired.

Water Icing

Mix icing sugar with boiling water. It should be a reasonably thick liquid that can be brushed onto the buns.

Bun Wash

Make a syrup with 2 1/2 cups water and 2 cups sugar, and boil for 2 minutes. Bun wash keeps very well.

Bath Buns

1 lb. (450g) Bun Dough
1/2 cup golden raisins
1/3 cup candied peel
grated rind of 1 lemon
1 egg for egg wash
1/4–1/3 cup coarse sugar

Knead the raisins, peel, sugar, and lemon rind into the bun dough. Roll into a thick cylinder and break off into 16 equal pieces. Place them on a baking sheet, flatten slightly, and brush them with egg wash. Dip the tops into coarse sugar and let rise in a warm moist atmosphere until double their size.

Bake at 450°F (230°C) for 10 minutes and brush with bun wash after baking.

Chelsea Buns

1 lb. (450g) Bun Dough
1/4 cup melted butter
1/2 cup golden raisins
3/4 cup candied peel
1/4–1/3 cup brown sugar
grated rind of 1 lemon
1 teaspoon apple spice or cinnamon

Roll the bun dough into a 10 x 16-inch (25 x 40-cm) rectangle and brush with the melted butter. Sprinkle the buttered dough with the raisins, peel, brown sugar, lemon rind, and apple spice. Roll into a fairly tight cylinder, brush with melted butter, and divide into 16 pieces. Place them face down on a lightly greased, 1-inch (2.5-cm) deep, four-sided tray, fairly close together. Egg wash the tops and let rise in a warm and moist place until doubled in size. By then all the buns should be touching each other.

Bake at 400°F (200°C) for about 20–30 minutes. Remove from the oven when cooked, and while still hot, brush with bun wash and dust with confectioners or superfine sugar. Cool on a wire rack.

Variation

Easter Ring

1 lb. (450g) Bun Dough
12 diamonds of angelica
6 cherries
1/4 cup slivered almonds

Make as for Chelsea buns and roll into a cylinder, then transfer to a baking tray and form into a circle. Pinch the edges together to seal. Cut down halfway in eight places and twist so the cut surface is facing upwards. Brush with egg wash, let rise to double size. Preheat oven to 425°F (220°C). Bake for 15 minutes, then reduce temperature to 400°F (200°C), until fully cooked.

Transfer to a wire rack, brush with bun wash while still hot.

Then ice the top with white icing, it will drip down over the sides. Decorate with cherries, diamonds of angelica, and toasted slivered almonds.

Iced Whirls

Divide a pound (450g) of bun dough into eight 2-ounce (50-g) pieces. Form each piece into a roll and pull to about 10 inches (25cm) long. Roll up from one end and seal with egg wash. Place on a greased baking tray and let rise until double in size. Egg wash and bake for about 15 minutes. Brush the top with bun wash and then ice with fondant or water icing.

Hot Cross Buns

Makes about 16

Nowadays, Hot Cross Buns are traditionally eaten in Ireland on Ash Wednesday and on Good Friday. This practice would have been frowned upon in the past, when these were strict fast days and the people would scarcely have had enough to eat, let alone spicy fruit-filled buns.

1 ounce (25g) fresh yeast (about 1 3/4 tablespoons)
1/3 cup superfine sugar
1–1 1/4 cups tepid milk
4 cups white bread flour

3/4 stick (1/3 cup) butter
1/4 teaspoon cinnamon, freshly ground
1/4 teaspoon nutmeg, freshly grated
1–2 teaspoons apple spice
2 eggs
1/3 cup currants
1/4 cup golden raisins
3 tablespoons chopped peel
4 ounces (110g) shortcrust pastry dough (see page 415) or a paste made from flour and water, a little melted butter, and sugar
egg wash made with milk, sugar, and 1 egg yolk

Preheat the oven to 425°F (220°C).

Dissolve the yeast with 1 tablespoon of the sugar in a little tepid milk.

Put the flour into a bowl, rub in the butter, add the cinnamon, nutmeg, apple spice, and the remainder of the sugar.
Mix well. Whisk the eggs and add to the milk. Make a well in the center of the flour add the eggs, yeast, and most of the milk, and mix to a soft dough – add more milk if necessary.

Leave for 2 or 3 minutes, then knead until smooth. Add the currants, raisins, and candied peel and continue to knead until the dough is shiny. Cover the bowl with plastic wrap and let it rise in a warm place until it doubles in size.

Punch down by kneading for 3 or 4 minutes, rest for a few minutes, shape in one-ounce (25g) buns. Put them on a baking sheet, egg wash, and mark each with a cross. Roll out the pastry thinly; cut into narrow 2-inch (5-cm) long strips. Carefully put a cross of shortcrust pastry on each bun. Let the buns rise to double the size. Egg wash again carefully.

Bake in the oven for 5 minutes, then reduce the heat to 400°F (200°C) for a further 10–15 minutes or until golden. Cool on a wire rack.

Cinnamon Rolls

Serves 4–5

1 lb. (450g) Bun Dough
1–2 tablespoons melted butter
1/4 cup sugar
1 teaspoon ground cinnamon
egg wash
raisins (optional)

Preheat the oven to 375°F (190°C). First make the Bun Dough. Roll out into a rectangle about 1/4-inch (5-mm) thick. Brush with melted butter. Sprinkle with brown sugar and cinnamon, and raisins, if using. Roll up from the long side. Cut into 1½-inch (4-cm) pieces and place flat on a greased baking sheet. Let rise until double in size, 20–30 minutes approximately. Brush with egg wash. Bake in the oven for 20 minutes or until cooked through.

Pecan Nut Roll

Serves 4–6

Preheat the oven to 350°F (180°C). Prepare the recipe for cinnamon rolls as above (omitting the sugar in the filling). Use a 9 x 9 x 2-inch (23 x 23 x 5-cm) pan. Cover the bottom of the pan with a thick layer of honey, and sprinkle on 3/4 to 1 cup of chopped nuts (walnuts, pecans, or others). Place cut rolls next to each other on top of this mixture. Let rise until double in size, about 20–30 minutes, and bake for about 30 minutes. Turn the rolls upside-down onto a serving plate.

Hallowe'en Barmbrack

Makes 2 loaves

The word barm comes from an old English word beorma**, meaning yeasted fermented liquor. Brack comes from the Irish word brac, meaning speckled – which it is, with dried fruit and candied peel. Hallowe'en has always been associated with fortune-telling and divination, so various objects are wrapped up and hidden in the cake mixture – a wedding ring, a coin, a pea or a thimble (signifying spinsterhood), a piece of matchstick (which means that your husband will beat you!).**

4 cups (450g) white bread flour
1/2 level teaspoon ground cinnamon
1/2 level teaspoon apple spice
1/4 level teaspoon ground nutmeg
pinch of salt
2 tablespoons (25g) butter
3/4 ounce (20g) fresh yeast (1–1¼ tablespoons)
1/3 cup (75g) superfine sugar
1¼ cups (300ml) tepid milk
1 egg
1 cup (225g) golden raisins
1/2 cup (110g) currants
1/3 cup (50g) chopped candied peel
1 tablespoon sugar

Ring, matchstick, dried pea, piece of cloth, each separately wrapped in wax paper

All utensils should be warm before starting to make barmbrack. Sift the flour, spices, and salt into a bowl, rub in the butter. Mix the yeast with 1 teaspoon of sugar and 1 teaspoon of tepid milk, leave for 4–5 minutes, until it becomes creamy and slightly bubbly. Add the rest of the sugar to the flour mixture and mix well. Pour the tepid milk and the beaten egg into the yeast mixture and add to the flour. Knead well, either by hand, or in the warmed bowl of an electric mixer, set with the dough hook at high speed for 5 minutes. The batter should be stiff but elastic. Fold in the dried fruit and chopped peel, cover with a cloth, and leave in a warm place until the dough has doubled in size. Punch down again for 2–3 minutes and divide into two portions. Grease 2 x 7-inch (18-cm) loaf pans and put one portion in each pan. Add the wrapped ring, stick, pea, and piece of cloth. Cover again and let rise for about 30–60 minutes.

Preheat the oven to 350F (180°C). Bake for about one hour until golden.

Glaze the top with the tablespoon of sugar dissolved in 2 tablespoons of boiling water, and put back into the oven for 2 or 3 minutes. Turn them out to cool on a wire tray. When cool, serve cut into thick slices, buttered.

jams and preserves

Jams, jellies, and marmalades are all made by boiling fruit with sugar to setting point. Fruit contains acid, pectin, and sugar, and these need to be in the correct proportions to set. Preserves need a minimum of 60 per cent sugar to prevent mold forming after bottling. Jams or conserves are made with cut or whole fruit, marmalade with citrus fruit, and jelly is made from strained fruit juice.

Taking the Mystery out of Jam Making

As a child I lived in an Irish country village and vividly remember life before electricity. There were no fridges or freezers, so preserving was essential. In the soft fruit season (late summer), mummy made lots of jam – enough to last the family through the winter. The process of jam making was exciting but always seemed to be a huge performance. There was a great build-up to jam-making day. It seemed as though there were jam pots everywhere I looked, with vast mountains of fruit and sugar, and the inevitable sticky saucepans. We would spend our day at school eagerly looking forward to going home to taste the new season's preserve on mummy's freshly made scones. So for me, jam making was a huge task that disrupted the daily routine, and was not something to be undertaken lightly!

Years later, shortly after I arrived at Ballymaloe House from hotel school, my (now) mother-in-law Myrtle Allen announced very matter-of-factly, late one night as she went around checking the fridges: "We ought to make these strawberries into jam; they won't last till the morning". I couldn't believe my ears! It was almost midnight – was she completely mad? Memories of the mammoth jam-making sessions of my childhood came flooding back to me; but I was new and anxious to impress, so I just asked how I could help.

Myrtle asked me if I would weigh the berries on the scales. She called out rapid instructions as she looked for jam jars; and before I knew what had happened, in a few minutes there was jam. As we began to fill and cover the jam jars, I realized Myrtle's secret. It is easy to make jam, provided you make it in small quantities, and often. So I soon forgot those fruit and sugar pyramids of years ago. Whenever you have fruit left over, it can easily be made into jam – even just a carton of raspberries or strawberries.

Pectin

Pectin is a mucilaginous substance, the setting agent in jams. It is found in the skin, seeds, and core of fruit. Acidic or very slightly under-ripe fruit has a higher pectin content than fully ripe fruit. Cooking apples, red currants, black currants, plums, and damsons all have high pectin content, whereas strawberries, blackberries, and cherries have low pectin levels. For this reason, cooking apples, the reduced juice of cooking apples, red currant or lemon juice are added to some jams to help them set.

People ask me if it's necessary to use jam-making sugar (sugar with an artificial pectin). My view is that if you have good quality fruit, you won't need artificial pectin, and if the fruit is not of a good enough quality, you shouldn't bother to make jam with it at all. I find that jam sugar affects the character, flavor, and keeping quality of the jam.

Equipment

A shallow, wide, heavy, stainless steel preserving pan of 9½ quarts (9 liters) capacity is perfect for jam making but is not essential. Choose your widest saucepan with low sides for fast evaporation. A sugar thermometer is a failsafe way to discover when the jam has reached setting point 220°F (105°C). A jam funnel is very useful for avoiding drips when filling jars – they are cheap and worth seeking out if you make preserves on a regular basis. A jellybag (a conical cloth bag that can be suspended over a bowl to allow fruit juice to drip through) is also worth having for jelly-making. You could use a pillowcase or nylons, but this can be a messy operation. Treat yourself to a jellybag – they last for years.

Containers

Containers for preserves must always be sterilized. Glass jars can be placed in a moderate oven at 350°F (180°C) for 10 minutes, or put into boiling water for the same period and then dried upside-down in an oven. The lids must also be boiled. If recycling jars, remove all the labels and wash thoroughly before sterilizing.

Glass jars are sold in various sizes. 450g (1lb) used to be a standard, but now it is more common to find jars of 200g (7oz), 350g (12oz), 500g (18oz) or 750g (1lb 10oz).

Other Preserves

There are many traditional ways of preserving food using natural preservatives such as salt, sugar, vinegar, and spices. Aside from jam- and jelly-making, there is drying, salting, curing, smoking, pickling, preserving in fat or alcohol, spicing, crystallizing, candying, and cheese and butter-making. Chutneys, confit, fruit syrups, ketchup, salami, sausages, patés, and potted meats are all preserved foods.

A couple of years ago, chefs wouldn't be caught dead making chutneys (not macho enough!) – now it's all the rage. Chutneys and relishes are made from vegetables, fruit, or a combination of the two – dried fruit is often included. If you make them with white malt vinegar, you should let them mellow for two weeks before eating. We sometimes use wine vinegar instead of malt. Flavored vinegars, such as tarragon, are too strong and tend to dominate.

Average Composition of Some Fruits

Fruit	*Solids*	*Sugar*	*Acid*	*Pectin*
Gooseberries	11.1%	3.5%	2.2%	0.8%
Strawberries	11.1%	5.5%	0.9%	0.5%
Raspberries	14.1%	3.6%	1.7%	0.5%
Red currants	16.2%	4.8%	2.5%	0.6%
Black currants	19.9%	6.4%	3.5%	1.1%
Plums	13.7%	7.4%	1.6%	0.8%
Apples	14.3%	7.6%	1.1%	0.75%
Blackberries	18.7%	5.1%	0.8%	0.6%

Guidelines for Making Delicious Jam

1 For really good jam, fruit must be freshly picked, dry, and unblemished. Top quality fruit makes top quality jam.

2 If the fruit is picked slightly under-ripe, it contains more pectin and so will set better.

3 Jam made from fruit picked while wet is likely to go moldy in a short time.

4 Make jam in small quantities – no more than two pounds (900g) of raspberries at a time and four pounds (1.8kg) of strawberries; small quantities will reach setting point in a few minutes, so both the color and jam itself are perfect.

5 Ideally you should use a preserving pan for jam making. Failing that, choose a wide pan with sides at least 9 inches (22cm) deep.

6 Sugar acts as a preservative in jams, so it is important to use the correct amount: too little and the jam may ferment, too much may cause crystallization.

7 Citrus fruit peel, black currants, gooseberries, etc., must be thoroughly softened before sugar is added to the jam, otherwise they will toughen and no amount of boiling will soften them later, as sugar has a hardening effect on fruits.

8 Sugar must be completely dissolved before the jam comes to a boil (otherwise the jam will crystallize at the top of the jar). For this reason, it is better to add heated sugar, which dissolves more quickly. Stir with a wooden spoon until the "gritty feeling" disappears.

9 Fruit should be simmered until the sugar is added, but from then on, it is best to boil as fast as possible until setting point is reached.

10 If necessary, skim near to the end of cooking – or, if there is only a little scum, dissolve it by stirring in a lump of butter after the jam has reached setting point. Test for setting frequently so that the jam is not allowed to overcook. It should read 220°F (105°C) on a sugar thermometer. Alternatively, put 1 teaspoonful on a cold plate and leave in a cool place for a few minutes – if the jam wrinkles when pushed with the finger, it has reached setting point.

11 Make sure the jam jars are spotlessly clean, inside and out, and sterilize them in the oven before filling.

12 Fill the jars to within an eighth-inch (3mm) from the top, to allow for shrinkage when cooling (use a jam funnel to avoid drips).

13 Press a circle of wax paper onto the surface of the jam immediately after filling (waxed side next to the jam).

14 Wet the cellophane paper on one side and stretch over the pot, securing with an elastic band. Label the jar clearly with date and type of jam, and store in a dry airy cupboard.

Master Recipe
Raspberry Jam

Fills about 3 1-pound (450g) jars
In season: mid summer

This is the first recipe I show my students to take the mystery out of jam making. It takes just 5, maybe 6 minutes to reach setting point. In fact it is possible to make a batch of scones and, while they are baking, make some jam – remember, you can make jam with as little as even a punnet of fruit, just using equal quantities of sugar.

2 lbs. (900g) fresh raspberries
4 cups white sugar (use 1/2 cup less if the fruit is very sweet)

Wash, dry, and sterilize the jars in a moderate oven (350°F [180°C]), for 10 minutes. Heat the sugar in the same oven for 5–10 minutes. Put the raspberries into a wide stainless steel saucepan and cook for 3–4 minutes until the juice begins to run. Bring the raspberries to boiling point and add the hot sugar. Stir over gentle heat until fully dissolved. Increase the heat and boil steadily for about 5 minutes, stirring frequently.

Test for a set. Remove from the heat immediately. Skim and pour into sterilized jam jars. Cover immediately. Hide the jam in a cool place or else put on a shelf in your kitchen so you can feel great every time you look at it! Anyway, it will be so delicious it won't last long.

Variations

Raspberry and Cassis Preserve

Follow the Master Recipe, and add 1/4 cup of cassis to the jam just before potting.

Raspberry and Blackberry Jam

1 3/4 lbs. (800g) raspberries
1/2 cup fresh blackberries

Follow the Master Recipe using the above proportion of blackberries to raspberries.

Raspberry and Loganberry Jam

1 lb. (450g) raspberries
1 lb. (450g) loganberries

Follow the Master Recipe, using the above proportion of loganberies to raspberries.

Loganberry Jam

Follow the Master Recipe and substitute loganberries for raspberries.

Tayberry Jam

Follow the Master Recipe and substitute tayberries for raspberries.

Boysenberry Jam

Substitute boysenberries for the raspberries in the Master Recipe.

Strawberry Jam

Makes about 7 pints (3kg)
In season: mid summer

Homemade strawberry jam can be sensational but only if the fruit is a good variety. It is one of the most difficult jams to set because strawberries are low in pectin, so don't attempt it if your fruit is not perfect. Red currants are very high in pectin and their bitter-sweet taste greatly enhances the flavor.

4 lbs. (1.8kg) unblemished organic strawberries (El Santa or Rapella, if available)
7 1/2–8 cups granulated sugar
2/3 cup Red Currant Juice (see right) or the juice of 2 lemons

First prepare the fruit juice (see below) using about a pound (450g) of fruit to obtain two-thirds cup of juice. Put the strawberries into a wide stainless steel saucepan with the red currant juice. Use a potato masher to crush about 90% of the berries, leaving the rest intact. Bring to a boil and cook the crushed strawberries in the juice for about 2–3 minutes. Warm the sugar in a low oven, add it to the fruit, and stir over gentle heat until the sugar is dissolved. Increase the heat and boil for about 10–15 minutes, stirring frequently. Skin, test, and pour into sterilized jars.

Note: This jam sticks and burns very easily so be careful.

Red Currant Juice

Put a pound (450g) of red currants (they can be fresh or frozen) into a stainless steel saucepan with 3/4 cup of water. Bring to a boil and simmer for about 20 minutes. Strain through a fine sieve. This juice can be frozen for use another time if necessary.

Rhubarb and Ginger Jam

Fills about 8 1-pound (450g) jars
In season: late spring, early summer

This delicious jam should be made when rhubarb is in full season and not yet thick and tough.

4 lbs. (1.8kg) trimmed rhubarb
8 cups granulated sugar
grated zest and juice of 2 unwaxed lemons
1–2 ounces (25–50g) fresh ginger, peeled and bruised
1/4 cup preserved candied ginger in syrup, chopped (optional)

Wipe the rhubarb and cut into one-inch (2.5-cm) pieces. Put it in a large bowl layered with the sugar, and add the lemon zest and juice. Let stand overnight. Next day put it into a wide, stainless steel saucepan, add the bruised ginger tied in a cheesecloth bag, stirring all the time over low heat until the sugar is dissolved, then boil rapidly until the jam sets, which takes about 10 minutes. Stir in the chopped candied ginger, if using, at the end of the cooking time. Remove the bag of fresh ginger and then pour the jam into hot clean jars, cover, and store in a dry airy cupboard.

Black Currant Jam

Makes 8–9 pints (3.6–4kg) jam
In season: late summer

4 lbs. (1.8kg) fresh or frozen black currants
5 cups water
19 cups white granulated sugar

Remove the stalks from the black currants, put the fruit into a greased preserving pan, add the water, and cook until the fruit begins to break. Put the sugar into a stainless steel bowl and heat it for almost 10 minutes in a preheated oven at 300°F (150°C). (It's vital that the fruit is soft before the sugar is added, otherwise the black currants will taste hard and tough in the finished jam.) Add the sugar and stir over gentle heat until the sugar is dissolved. Boil briskly for about 20 minutes, stirring frequently. Skim, test, and pour into sterilized jars.

Elderflower and Green Gooseberry Jam

Fills 6 1-pound (450g) jars
In season: late spring

Gooseberries should be tart and green and hard as hail stones – as soon as the elderflowers are in bloom in the hedgerows, search for the gooseberries under the prickly bushes or seek them out in your local vegetable market or farmers' market. This jam should be a fresh color, so be careful not to overcook it.

3 lbs. (1.3kg) green gooseberries
2½ cups water
5–6 elderflower heads
7 cups sugar

Wash the gooseberries, if necessary. Top and tail them and put into a wide, stainless steel preserving pan, along with the water, and elderflowers tied in cheesecloth. Simmer until the gooseberries are soft and the contents of the pan are reduced by one third, about 30 minutes. Remove the elderflowers and add the warm sugar, stirring until it has completely dissolved. Boil rapidly for about 10 minutes until setting point is reached. Pour into hot sterilized jars.

Master Recipe
Victoria Plum Jam

Makes 6–7 pints (2.6-3kg)
In season: autumn

4 pounds (1.8kg) Victoria or Opal plums
6–8 cups sugar (taste the plums – if they are very sweet use minimum)
2½ cups water

Wash the plums and remove the pits. Save the pits and tie them in a cheesecloth bag. Put the sugar into a moderate oven 350°F (180°C) to heat for about 10 minutes. Grease the stainless steel preserving pan, put in the plums, bag of plum pits, and water, and cook until the plums burst. Add the hot sugar, stir until it has completely dissolved. Turn the heat to maximum and boil until the jam will set, about 15–20 minutes. Discard the bag of pits. Test, skim, and pour into hot sterilized jars.

Greengage Jam

Follow the Master Recipe and substitute greengages for plums.

Damson Jam

Makes about 9–10 pints (4–4.5kg)
In season: autumn

Damson jam has always been a great favorite of mine. As a child, my school friends and I used to collect damsons every year in a field near the old castle in Cullohill. First we ate so many we almost burst – the rest we brought home for Mummy to make into damson jam. The preserving pan is greased to prevent the fruit from sticking to the bottom.

6 lbs. (2.6kg) damsons
12 cups sugar
4 cups water

Pick over the fruit carefully, wash and drain well, discarding any damaged damsons. Put the damsons and water into a greased, stainless steel preserving pan and stew them gently until the skin breaks. Heat the sugar in a low oven, add it to the fruit, and stir over a gentle heat until the sugar is dissolved. Increase the heat and boil steadily, stirring frequently. Skim off the pits and scum as they rise to the top. Test for a set after 15 minutes boiling. Pour into hot sterilized jars and cover.

Blackberry and Apple Jam

Fills 9–10 1-pound (450g) jars

All over the countryside every year, blackberries rot on the hedgerows. Think of all the wonderful jam that could be made – so full of Vitamin C. This year, organize a blackberry-picking expedition and take a picnic. You'll find it's the greatest fun, and when you come home, one person can make a few scones while someone else is making the jam. The children could be kept out of mischief and gainfully employed drawing and painting home-made jam labels, with personal messages like "Lydia's Jam – keep off!", or "Grandma's Blackberry Jam." Then you can enjoy the results of your labors with a well-earned cup of tea. Blackberries are low in pectin, so the apples help the set as well as adding extra flavor. A few lemon-scented geranium leaves enhance the flavor of this jam.

2 lbs. (900g) cooking apples
5 lbs. (2.2kg) blackberries
8 cups sugar (use 1 cup less if blackberries are sweet)

Wash, peel, core, and slice the apples. Stew them until soft with 1¼ cups water in a stainless steel saucepan; when soft, remove from the heat and beat to a pulp.

Pick over the blackberries, cook until soft, adding about ⅔ cup water if the berries are dry. If you like, push them through a coarse sieve to remove seeds. Heat the sugar in a slow oven for 10 minutes.

Put the blackberries into a wide stainless steel saucepan or preserving pan along with the apple pulp and the heated sugar, and stir over a gentle heat until the sugar is dissolved.

Boil steadily for about 15 minutes. Skim the jam, test it for a set, and pour into warm, sterilized jars.

Peach or Nectarine and Sweet Geranium Jam

Fills 2 1-pound (450g) jars
In season: summer

2 lbs. (900g) nectarines or peaches, pitted, peeled, and sliced (the nectarines don't have to be peeled)
1½ cups sugar
juice of 1 unwaxed lemon, freshly squeezed
3–4 sweet geranium leaves

Put the fruit and sugar into a small, stainless steel saucepan, add the lemon juice and geranium leaves. Bring to a boil over medium heat, stirring constantly. Cook until the fruit is soft, which takes about 15 minutes. Test for a set. Pour in sterilized jars, cover, and store in a cool dry place.

Julia Wight's Fresh Apricot Jam

Makes about 6 pints
In season: summer

This is a lovely golden preserve that keeps well. The flavor of apricots straight from the tree comes through in Julia's simple recipe. The kernels give a delicious almond flavor to the jam. Apricot jam can also be made with dried fruits.

3½ lbs. (1.6kg) whole fresh apricots to yield 3 lbs. (1.3kg) of fresh apricots when pitted
6 cups sugar
juice of 2 unwaxed lemons, freshly squeezed

Cut the apricots in half and remove the pits, keeping a few kernels to add to the finished jam. In a large bowl, layer the apricots and sugar, finishing with a layer of sugar, and leave in a cool place overnight.

Put the lemon juice in a large saucepan and add the fruit and sugar. (If the fruit is lacking in juice, you could add about 1¼ cups water with the lemon juice.)

Bring to a boil very slowly. Make sure that all the sugar has dissolved, then simmer for 30–40 minutes, stirring occasionally. Add blanched and halved kernels, halfway through the simmering.

Test for a set and let the jam cool slightly before pouring into hot, sterilized jars.

Making Jellies

We make 2 types of jellies: with and without water.

For jelly making, the fruit must be cooked before the juice is extracted. Apples and pears, for example, should be washed, any blemishes or bruises removed, and then chopped. There is no need to peel or discard the cores, they add pectin and flavor.

Cover the fruit with water and cook over medium heat, stirring occasionally until soft and pulpy. Pour into a jelly bag and let drip over a bowl overnight or at least for a few hours. Resist the temptation to squeeze the jelly bag or the jelly will be cloudy. Jellies may be flavored with all types of herbs and spices. Quince or japonica may also be added to make up a proportion of the fruit.

Red currants are very high in pectin. Red currant Jelly may be made as above, but a more intensely delicious jelly is made by the quick method on page 508. The method may also be used for black currants, but add 2½ cups water to reduce the intensity.

Master Recipe
Crab Apple or Bramley Apple Jelly

Makes 6–7 pints (2.7-3kg)
In season: autumn

5½ lbs. (2.4kg) crab apples or windfall cooking apples or a mixture
11¼ cups (2.6 litres) water
2 unwaxed lemons
sugar

Wash the apples and cut them into quarters, do not remove either the peel or core. Windfalls may be used, but make sure to cut out the bruised parts. Put the apples into a large pot, along with the water and the thinly pared zest of the lemons. Cook until reduced to a pulp, about ½ hour. Turn the pulp into a jelly bag and let drip until all the juice has been extracted – usually overnight. Measure the juice into a preserving pan and allow 2 cups sugar to every 2½ cups of juice. Warm the sugar in a low oven.

Squeeze the lemons, strain the juice, and add it to the preserving pan. Bring to a boil and add the warm sugar. Stir over a gentle heat until the sugar is dissolved. Increase the heat and boil rapidly without stirring for about 8–10 minutes. Skim, test, and immediately pour into sterilized jars.

Variations

Apple and Lemon-scented Geranium Jelly
Follow the Master Recipe, adding 6–8 large leaves of sweet geranium while the apples are stewing, and put a fresh leaf into each jar as you pour in the jelly.

Apple and Clove Jelly
Follow the Master Recipe, adding 3–6 cloves to the apples as they stew, and put a clove in each jar. Serve on bread or scones.

Apple and Mint Jelly
Follow the Master Recipe, adding 4–6 large sprigs of fresh mint to the apples while they are stewing, and 3–4 tablespoons of finely chopped fresh mint to the jelly just before you can it. Serve with lamb as an alternative to mint sauce.

Apple and Rosemary Jelly
Follow the Master Recipe, adding 2 sprigs of rosemary to the apples as they stew, and put a tiny sprig into each jar. Serve with lamb.

Apple and Elderberry Jelly
Follow the Master Recipe, adding a fist or 2 of elderberries to the apple, and continue as above. Up to half volume of elderberries can be used. A sprig or two of mint or sweet geranium, or a cinnamon stick enhances the flavor further.

Apple and Marjoram Jelly
Follow the Master Recipe, adding 4–6 large sprigs of fresh marjoram to the apples while they are stewing, and add 3–4 tablespoons of finely chopped fresh marjoram to the jelly just before you can it.

Apple and Chili Jelly
Follow the Master Recipe, adding 2 tablespoons of chili flakes to the apples. Vary the amount according to how hot you like things.

Apple and Cranberry Jelly
Follow the Master Recipe, adding 4–8 cups cranberries to the apples.

Apple and Jalapeño Jelly
Follow the Master Recipe, adding 2–4 jalapeño chiles to the strained juice.

Apple and Sloe Jelly
Follow the Master Recipe, adding a fist or two of sloes to the apples.

Red Currant Jelly

Fills about 3 1-pound (450g) jars
In season: summer

Red currant jelly is delicious and a versatile product to have in your pantry. It has myriad uses: used like jam on bread and scones; served as an accompaniment to roast lamb, bacon, or ham; good with rough pâtés and game; and invaluable as a glaze for red fruit tarts.

This recipe is a particular favorite of mine, not only because it is fast to make and results in a delicious, intensely-flavored jelly, but because you can use the leftover pulp to make a fruit tart; double value from the red currants. Unlike most other fruit jellies, no water is needed in this recipe.

2 lbs. (900g) red currants
4 cups granulated sugar

Remove the strings from the red currants either by hand or with a fork. Put the red currants and sugar into a wide, stainless steel saucepan and stir continuously over medium heat until they come to a boil.

Boil hard for exactly 8 minutes, stirring only if they appear to be sticking to the bottom. Skim carefully. Turn into a nylon sieve and let drip through. Do not push the pulp through or the jelly will be cloudy. You can stir it gently once or twice, just to free the bottom of the sieve of pulp. Pour the jelly into hot, sterilized jars immediately.

Red currants are very high in pectin so the jelly will start to set just as soon as it begins to cool.

Fruit Glazes

Fruit glazes are essential in the pastry section of a restaurant kitchen – they are brushed over fruit tarts to enhance the flavor and to give a shiny appearance. Apricot glaze is used for yellow and green fruit such as apricots, peaches, nectarines, grapes, kiwi fruit, and orange segments. Red currant jelly, with its bitter, sweet flavor, makes a delicious glaze for red and black fruits, such as strawberries, raspberries, loganberries, boysenberries, tayberries, blackberries, blueberries, and black currants.

Fruit glazes keep for several weeks. They should be stored in sterilized jars, as for jams.

Apricot Glaze

Makes about 1¼ cups
In season: summer

Apricot glaze is used to glaze orange or green fruits such as peaches, nectarines, oranges, grapes, and kiwi, particularly in fruit tarts.

1½ cups apricot jam (see page 506)
juice of ¼ lemon or 2 tablespoons water

In a small stainless steel saucepan, melt the apricot jam with 1–2 tablespoons of juice or water. Push the hot jam through a nylon sieve and store in a sterilized airtight jar.

Melt and stir the glaze before use, if necessary.

Red Currant Glaze

Makes a generous 1¼ cups
In season: summer

This is immeasurably better if you start off with homemade red currant jelly; remember it only takes 8 minutes to make! Use it to glaze red fruits.

1½ cups Red Currant Jelly (see left)
about 1 tablespoon water (optional)

In a small stainless steel saucepan, melt the Red Currant Jelly, add the water only if necessary to thin it out. Stir gently, but do not whisk or it will become cloudy. Cook it for just 1–2 minutes. The jelly will darken if cooked for longer. Store any leftover glaze in an airtight jar, and reheat gently to melt it before use, if necessary.

Making Marmalade

When you are making marmalade, be it orange, lemon, or lime, you should always wash the fruit beforehand to remove any deposits and grime on the skin. Bitter Seville or Malaga oranges are used. Cut around the equator of the fruit, squeeze out all the juice, and save the seeds. Remove the peel carefully, and slice and chop it to the thickness you are after. Then remove the pulp (but not the pith) with a sharp spoon. Tie the seeds and the pulp up in a cheesecloth bag and boil with the peel in a mixture of water and the juice.

The peel must be soft and the liquid reduced to between a third and half its original volume before you add the sugar. If you add the sugar too soon, it will have a hardening effect upon the peel and no amount of cooking will soften it; it will, in fact, become more like candied peel. Also, if there is too much liquid, the marmalade will take far longer to set, losing its fresh taste. It will become dark and more bitter in flavor, but some people actually prefer this. You can also make a darker marmalade by adding molasses to the recipe.

Seville Orange Marmalade made with Whole Oranges

Makes 13–15 pints (5.6–6.6kg)
In season: late winter

You'll find Seville and Malaga oranges in the stores for just a few short weeks after Christmas. Buy what you need, and make the marmalade while the oranges are fresh, if possible. If not, just pop them into the freezer; this recipe works brilliantly for frozen oranges and it's not even necessary to defrost them. Some recipes slice the peel first but in this one, the whole oranges are boiled and then the peel is sliced. Use bitter oranges; marmalade demands bitterness, and the flavor of the rind is quite different from that of the sweet orange. The word "marmelade" derives from marmelo, which is the Portuguese word for quince. Mary Queen of Scots frequently demanded orange preserves, which she had tasted in France, and it is believed that "marmelade" could also be a corruption of "marie-melade."

4½ lbs. (2kg) Seville or Malaga oranges
5½ quarts (5.4 liters) water
18 cups sugar, warmed in a moderate oven (350°F [180°C]) for 10 minutes

Wash the oranges. Put them in a stainless steel saucepan along with the water. Put a plate on top to keep them under the surface of the water. Cover with the lid of the saucepan, simmer gently until soft; about 2 hours. Cool and drain, reserving the water. (If more convenient, leave overnight and continue next day.)

Put your cutting board on a large baking tray with sides, so you won't lose any juice. Cut the oranges in half and scoop out the soft centers. Slice the peel finely. Pop the seeds into a cheesecloth bag and put the escaped juice and sliced oranges in a large, wide, stainless steel saucepan along with the reserved marmalade liquid. Bring to a boil and add the warm sugar, stir over a brisk heat until all the sugar is dissolved. Boil fast until setting point is reached. Pour into sterilized jars and cover at once.

Note: With any marmalade, it's vital that the original liquid has reduced by half or, better still, two-thirds before the sugar is added, otherwise it takes ages to reach a set and both the flavor and color will be spoiled. A wide, low-sided, stainless steel saucepan is best for this recipe, say, 14 to 16 inches (35–40cm) wide. If you don't have one around that size, cook the marmalade in 2 batches.

Old-fashioned Seville Orange Marmalade

Makes 7 pints (3.2kg)

Seville and Malaga oranges come into the stores after Christmas and are around for 4–5 weeks.

2 lbs. (900g) Seville oranges
10 cups water
1 lemon
8 cups granulated sugar

Wash the fruit, cut in half, and squeeze out the juice. Remove the membrane with a spoon, put with the seeds, tie them in a piece of cheesecloth and soak for half an hour in cold water. Slice the peel finely or coarsely, depending on how you like your marmalade. Put the peel, orange and lemon juice, bag of seeds, and water into a non-reactive bowl or saucepan overnight.

Next day, bring everything to a boil and simmer gently for about 2 hours, until the peel is really soft and the liquid is reduced by half. Squeeze all the liquid from the bag of seeds and remove it.

Add the warmed sugar and stir until all the sugar has been dissolved. Increase the heat and bring to a full rolling boil rapidly until setting point is reached. Test for a set,

either with a sugar thermometer (it should register 225°F [110°C]), or with a saucer. Put a little marmalade on a cold saucer and cool for a few minutes. If it wrinkles when you push it with your finger, it's done. Stir well, and immediately pour into hot sterilized jars. Cover immediately and store in a cool dry place.

Note: The peel must be absolutely soft before the sugar is added, otherwise when the sugar is added the peel will become very hard and no amount of boiling will soften it.

Orange, Lemon, and Grapefruit Marmalade

Makes about 10 pints (4.5 kg)

Homemade marmalade is always a welcome present, particularly at Christmas, because quite often people

have just run out of the previous year's marmalade. This tangy 3-fruit marmalade can be made at times when Seville oranges aren't in the stores. It is made from orange, lemon, and grapefruit, so may be made at any time of year.

2 sweet oranges and 2 grapefruit, weighing 3 pound (1.3kg) altogether
4 unwaxed lemons
7½ pints (3.6 liters) water
8 cups sugar

Wash the fruit, cut each in half, and squeeze out the juice. Remove the membrane with a sharp spoon and set it aside. Cut the peel in quarters and slice the rind across rather than lengthwise. Put the juice, rind, and water in a bowl.

Put the seeds and membrane in a cheesecloth bag and add to the bowl. Leave overnight. The following day, simmer the fruits in a stainless steel saucepan along with the bag of seeds for 1½–2 hours, until the peel is really soft. Cover the pan for the first half an hour. The liquid should be reduced to between a third and a half of the original volume.

Meanwhile, warm the sugar in a moderate oven (350°F [180°C]) for about 10 minutes. Then remove the cheesecloth bag and discard. Add the warmed sugar to the soft peel and stir until the sugar has dissolved. Bring to a boil and keep concentrating it until it reaches setting point, about 8–10 minutes. Pour into sterilized jars and cover while hot.

Note: If the sugar is added before the rind is really soft, the rind will harden and no amount of boiling will soften it.

Variation
Ginger Marmalade

Follow the Master Recipe, adding 6 to 8 ounces (175–225g) of peeled and finely chopped fresh ginger to the recipe. Turbinado sugar gives a fuller flavor and darker color.

Above: Lemon Curd

Kumquat Marmalade

Fills 3 1-pound (450g) jars
In season: winter

My favorite marmalade, I first tasted this in Australia in the Regent Court off Potts Point in Sydney, one of my favorite places to stay in the world and certainly the best breakfast.

2 lbs. (900g) kumquats
6 cups water
6 cups sugar

Slice the kumquats thinly crosswise. Collect the seeds and put them in a small bowl along with one cup of the water; let stand overnight. Put the kumquats in a larger bowl along with the remaining water, cover, and let stand overnight.

Next day, strain the seeds, saving the liquid (this now contains the precious pectin, which contributes to the setting of the jam); discard the seeds.

Put the kumquat mixture into a large saucepan along with the reserved liquid from the seeds. Bring to a boil, reduce the heat, and simmer, covered, for 30 minutes or until the kumquats are very tender.

Warm the sugar for 10 minutes in a low oven. Add the warm sugar to the kumquats and stir until fully dissolved. Bring to a boil and cook rapidly with the lid off for about 15 minutes. Test for a set. Pour into hot sterilized jars.

Short-time preserves

Lemon or lime curd are what we call short-time preserves because they have a short shelf life. They are much more perishable than jam, so they should be used within a few weeks; they are best kept in the refrigerator as well. They can be made all year round, in a matter of minutes.

Master Recipe
Lemon Curd

Makes 2–3 jars

½ stick (¼ cup) butter
½ cup sugar
finely grated zest and juice of 2 large, unwaxed lemons
2 eggs and 1 egg yolk (keep white aside for meringue)

On a very low heat melt the butter, add the sugar, lemon juice, and rind, and then stir in the well-beaten eggs. Stir carefully over gentle heat until the mixture coats the back of a spoon. Remove from the heat and pour into a bowl (it will thicken as it cools).

Variation

Lime Curd

Substitute 4 limes for the lemons in the Master Recipe. You may need to add a little more sugar. It will be an odd color.

Elderflower Lemon Curd

In late spring, you can gather elderflowers – eight heads are sufficient for this quantity. Don't pick them until you are ready to make the curd, as they quickly turn brown. Use a fork to pull the creamy flowers from the stalks and add along with the sugar. This version is truly divine – an annual treat – and makes a quick dessert served with crème fraîche, meringues, and strawberries.

Chutneys

Another wonderful, age-old method of preserving vegetables and fruit. Vinegar is the most essential ingredient in chutneys and preserves because it inhibits the growth of contaminating micro-organisms. Salt and sugar are other essential preservatives. Spices add flavor.

Chutneys can be made of vegetables, fruit, or both vegetables and fruit mixed. Dried fruit such as raisins or golden raisins are frequently included. In India, mango chutney is made from the green mango; there are also a myriad different bitter pickles, which are a favorite condiment. Chutneys and pickles should not be confused with relishes, which are simply a mixture of chopped fruit and vegetables.

The fruit and vegetable for pickling must always be young and firm: nice crunchy baby onions, beets, gherkins, and cauliflower flowerets. Shredded cabbage can also be pickled as in sauerkraut. Usually, vegetables for pickles are salted or brined first to remove any excess moisture. This will enable them to absorb more vinegar, and will result in a firmer, crunchier pickle. Use plain dairy or kosher salt.

Spicy Apple Chutney

Fills 6–8 1-pound (450g) jars
In season: autumn

4 lbs. (1.8kg) cooking apples (use Bramley Seedling, Grenadier, or Granny Smith)
1 lb. (450g) onion, peeled and finely chopped (about 3½ cups)
2 cups golden raisins
4 cups granulated sugar
5 cups white malt vinegar
2 generous tablespoons salt
2 teaspoons mustard seed
1 teaspoon ground ginger
½ teaspoon curry powder
½ teaspoon cinnamon
½–1 level teaspoon ground cloves

Peel and cut the apples into quarters, remove the core, and chop finely.

Put all the ingredients into a wide stainless steel saucepan. Simmer gently until soft and pulpy, stirring frequently. Cook, uncovered, for approx. 1½–2 hours until very thick and dark brown. (It should be reduced to about a third of the original volume.)

Let it mature for about two weeks before using. Wine vinegar is less fierce but obviously more expensive.

Apple and Tomato Chutney

Fills 10 1-pound (450g) jars
In season: summer and autumn

7–8 lbs. (3.1–3.6kg) ripe tomatoes, peeled and chopped
1 lb. (450g) onions, chopped (about 3½ cups)
1 lb. (450g) eating apples, peeled and chopped (about 3–3½ cups)
6 cups sugar
4 cups white malt vinegar
2½ tablespoons salt
2 teaspoons ground ginger
1 tablespoon ground black pepper
1 tablespoon all spice
4 garlic cloves, crushed
1 level teaspoon cayenne pepper
1–1½ cups golden raisins

Prepare all the ingredients and put into a large, wide, stainless steel saucepan. Bring to a boil. Simmer steadily until reduced and slightly thick – about 1 hour (time will depend on the width of the saucepan).

Pour into sterilized hot jars and cover. Let it mature for 2 weeks before using.

Fresh Fruit and Mint "Chutney"

2 tablespoons raisins
1 orange
1 eating apple, e.g., Cox's Orange or Golden Delicious
2–3 tablespoons freshly chopped mint
½–1 fresh chile, seeded and diced (optional)
freshly squeezed juice of 1 lemon
sugar and a pinch of salt

Pour boiling water over the raisins and set aside to plump up for approximately 1 hour. Cut the peel and the pith off the orange, and dice. Remove the core from the apple and dice.

Put into a serving bowl along with the mint, add the chile and raisins. Add a little lemon juice, sugar, and salt to taste. Serve with curry or spiced dishes.

Fresh Mint Chutney

(see page 595)

Red Pepper Chutney

Makes 8–9 jars

8 ounces (225g) onions, finely chopped (about 2 cups)
5 tablespoons olive oil
1 lb. (450g) very ripe red peppers (about 3 medium peppers), seeded and chopped into small dice
1/2 teaspoon salt
1/2 teaspoon powdered ginger or grated ginger root
1/2 teaspoon allspice
1/2 teaspoon mace
1/2 teaspoon nutmeg
1 lb. (450g) very ripe tomatoes, peeled and chopped (about 2 1/2–3 cups)
1 garlic clove, chopped
1/2 cup raisins
1 cup white sugar
2/3 cup white wine vinegar

Sweat the onions in the olive oil in a tall, narrow, stainless steel saucepan until softened, and then add the peppers, salt, and spices. After 10 minutes, add the tomatoes, garlic, raisins, sugar, and vinegar. Bring to a boil and simmer very gently for about 1 1/4 hours until it looks thickish. Pour into hot, sterilized glass jars and store in a cool dry place. Good with spiced beef or cold meats or coarse pâtés.

Onion Marmalade

Makes 1 pint (450ml)

This superb recipe is especially delicious with pâtés and terrines, game and poultry. I always have some made up. It is also wonderful served warm, particularly with pan-grilled monkfish or even a lamb chop. It will keep for months.

1 1/2 lbs. (700g) white onions (about 5 cups sliced)
1 stick (1/2 cup) butter
3/4 cup sugar
1 1/2 teaspoons salt
1 1/2 teaspoons pepper, freshly ground
1/2 cup sherry vinegar
1 cup full-bodied red wine
2 tablespoons cassis

Peel and slice the onions thinly. Melt the butter in the saucepan and hold your nerve until it becomes a deep nut brown color – this will give the onions a delicious, rich flavor but be careful not to let it burn. Toss in the onions and the sugar, salt, and pepper, and stir well. Cover the saucepan and cook for 30 minutes over gentle heat, keeping an eye on the onions and stirring from time to time with a wooden spatula.

Add the sherry vinegar, red wine, and cassis. Cook for a further 30 minutes uncovered, stirring regularly. This onion jam must cook very gently (but don't let it reduce too much). When it is cold, skim off any butter that rises to the top and discard. Pour into sterilized jars as for jam.

Variation

Red Onion Marmalade

Use red onions instead of white.

Tomato and Chile Jam

Makes 3 jars

This zingy jam, inspired by Peter Gordon, is great with everything from fried eggs to cold meat. Terrific on a piece of chicken breast or fish, or spread on bruschetta with goat cheese and arugula leaves.

1 lb., 2 ounces (500g) very ripe tomatoes (about 3 cups diced)
2–4 red chiles
4 garlic cloves, peeled
about 1-inch (2.5-cm) piece fresh ginger, peeled and roughly chopped
2 tablespoons fish sauce (nam pla)
1 1/4 cups golden sugar
1/2 cup red wine vinegar

Peel the tomatoes and cut them into a 1/2-inch (1-cm) dice. Put them, along with the chiles, garlic, ginger, and fish sauce, in a blender and whizz. Put the purée, sugar, and vinegar into a stainless steel saucepan, add the tomatoes, and bring to a boil slowly, stirring occasionally. Cook gently for 30–40 minutes, stirring every now and then to prevent sticking. When cooked, pour into warmed, sterilized glass jars. Let cool. Store in the fridge.

Beet and Ginger Relish

Makes 2–3 jars

This sweet-sour relish is particularly good with cold meats and coarse country terrines.

1 lb. (450g) raw beets, peeled and grated (about 2 1/2–3 cups)
8 ounces (225g) onions, chopped (about 2 cups)
1/2 stick (1/4 cup) butter
1/4 cup sugar
salt and freshly ground pepper
2 tablespoons sherry vinegar
1/2 cup red wine
2 teaspoons fresh ginger, peeled and grated

Sweat the onions slowly in butter until they are very soft, then add the sugar and seasoning. Add the rest of the ingredients and cook gently for 30 minutes. Serve cold. This relish keeps for several weeks.

Mango Relish

(see page 92)

Pickled Kumquats with Orange Slices

Fills 1–2 1-pound (450g) jars

This delicious pickle comes from Jane Grigson's Fruit Book. Jane sweetly gave me permission to print it in Simply Delicious Christmas and we also have it here. It is delicious served with cold ham, goose, duck, or pork.

Right: Roast Turkey with Beet and Ginger Relish

1 large orange
8 ounces (225g) kumquats
1¼ cups sugar
1 cup white wine vinegar
2-inch (5-cm) piece of cinnamon stick
8 whole cloves
2 blades of mace

Scrub the orange well and rinse the kumquats. Cut a slice off the top and bottom of the orange down as far as the flesh, and discard those 2 pieces of peel. Cut the rest of the orange into slices and put them in a wide, stainless steel saucepan along with the kumquats. Cover generously with cold water. Bring to a boil, cover, and simmer until the orange slices are tender, about 20–30 minutes. The kumquats may be ready before the orange slices, so watch them if they show signs of collapsing.

Meanwhile, in a stainless steel saucepan, dissolve the sugar in the white wine vinegar, add the cinnamon, cloves, and mace, and stir until it comes to a boil. Drain all the liquid off the oranges and set aside in case you need it. Put the kumquats and oranges into the vinegar syrup and, if necessary, use some of the cooking liquid to cover the fruit. Simmer until the orange slices look transparent and slightly candied, about 10 minutes. Arrange the fruit in a wide-mouthed sterilized glass jar, pour the syrup on top, and cover tightly (not with a tin lid). Label, and let mature for 3–4 weeks before using.

Pickled Beets

Serves 5-6

Most pickled beets are far too vinegary. This is sweet and delicious but does not keep indefinitely.

1 lb. (450g) cooked beets, (see page 178)
1 cup sugar
2 cups water
1 onion, peeled and thinly sliced (optional)
1 cup white wine vinegar

Dissolve the sugar in water and bring to a boil. Add the sliced onion, if using, and simmer for 3–4 minutes. Add the vinegar and give it a stir. Pour the onion mixture over the peeled sliced beets, which should be in a glass or stainless steel bowl, and let cool. Keeps for 1-2 weeks in a fridge.

Sweet Cucumber Pickle

Serves 10–20

2 lbs. (900g) thinly sliced unpeeled cucumber
3 small onions, thinly sliced
1½ cups sugar
2 level tablespoons salt
1 cup cider vinegar

Combine the cucumber and onion slices in a large bowl. Mix the sugar, salt, and vinegar together and pour over the cucumbers. Place in a tightly covered container in the refrigerator and leave for at least 4–5 hours or overnight before using. Keeps well for up to a week in the refrigerator

Chile and Red Pepper Relish

1 ounce (25g) green chiles, seeded and chopped (about ¼ cup), or 2–3 chiles depending on size
1 red pepper, seeded and cut in ¾-inch (2cm) dice
2 x 14-ounce (400g) cans chopped tomatoes
1 clove of garlic, crushed
2 teaspoons sugar
2 teaspoons soft brown sugar
1 tablespoon plus 1 teaspoon white wine vinegar
2½ tablespoons water
salt and freshly ground pepper

Put the chiles, pepper, tomatoes, and garlic into a stainless steel saucepan along with the sugar, vinegar, and water. Season and simmer for 10 minutes until reduced by half. Store in a tightly-sealed container. Keeps for weeks in the fridge.

Ballymaloe Mincemeat

Makes about 7 pints (3.2kg)

This recipe has been passed down in Myrtle Allen's family.

2 cooking apples, such as Bramley Seedling
2 lemons
2 cups beef suet or butter, chilled and grated
3/4 cup candied peel (preferably homemade)
2 tablespoons orange marmalade
1 cup currants
2 cups raisins
1 cup golden raisins
4 1/2 cups Barbados sugar (moist, soft, dark-brown sugar)
1/4 cup Irish whiskey

Core and bake the whole apples in a moderate oven (350°F [180°C]) for about 45 minutes. Let cool. When they are soft, remove the skin and mash the flesh into pulp. Grate the rind from the lemons on the finest part of a stainless steel grater and squeeze out the juice. Add the other ingredients one by one, and as they are added, mix everything thoroughly. Put into jars, cover with jam covers, and let mature for 2 weeks before using. This mincemeat will keep for a year in a cool, airy place.

Moroccan Preserved Lemons

Tart and salty and quintessentially Moroccan – preserved lemons are easy to make at home, they keep for months, and may be added to tagines, fish stews, soups, and salad dressing.

5 unwaxed lemons
1/4 cup salt (pure dairy salt or Kosher salt)
extra freshly squeezed lemon juice to cover – about 2–3 lemons.

Quarter the lemons from the top to within a half-inch (1-cm) of the bottom, sprinkle salt on the exposed flesh, then reshape the fruit. Place about 1 tablespoon salt on the bottom of a preserving jar. Pack in the lemons and push them down, adding more salt between layers. Press the lemons down to release their juices and to make room for the remaining lemons. If the juice released from the squashed fruit does not cover them, add freshly squeezed lemon juice – not chemically produced lemon juice, and not water.

Let the lemons mature in a warm place for 30 days, shaking the jar each day to distribute the salt and juice.

To use, rinse the lemons as needed under running water, removing and discarding the pulp, if desired – and there is no need to refrigerate after opening although a layer of olive oil will keep them fresh. Preserved lemons will keep up to a year, and the pickling juice can be used two or three times over the course of a year. If you have a half a lemon left over after something else, it can be added to the pickling jar.

Crystallized Lemon or Orange Peel

We always have lots of crystallized lemon, orange, and lime peel in a jar to decorate tarts, scatter on mousses, or just to nibble.

2 unwaxed lemons or oranges
cold water to cover
1 1/4 cups Stock Syrup (see page 568)
2–4 tablespoons superfine sugar

Peel the lemons very thinly with a swivel top peeler, being careful not to include the white pith. Cut the strips into a fine julienne. Put into a saucepan with the cold water and simmer for 5 minutes. Drain, refresh in cold water, cover with fresh water, and repeat the process. Put the julienne into a saucepan along with the syrup and cook gently until it looks translucent or opaque. Remove with a slotted spoon and let cool on wax paper or a cake rack. When cold, toss in the superfine sugar and let dry in a cool place.
Can be stored in a jar or airtight container for weeks, or sometimes months.

Homemade Candied Peel

5 oranges, lemons, or grapefruit (or a mixture)
4 cups water
6 cups sugar
1 teaspoon salt

Cut the fruit in half and squeeze out the juice. Reserve the juice for another use, perhaps homemade lemonade. Put the skins into a large bowl (not aluminum, because the acid in the lemon reacts with the citrus and taints the taste), add salt, and cover with cold water. Let soak for 24 hours. Next day, throw away the soaking water, put the peel in a saucepan, and cover with fresh cold water. Bring to a boil, cover, and simmer very gently until the peel is soft, up to 3 hours. Remove the peel and discard the water. Scrape out any remaining flesh and membranes from inside the cut fruit, leaving the white pith and rind intact. (You can do the next step the following day if more convenient.)

Dissolve the sugar fully in the water, bring it to a boil, add the peel, and simmer gently until it looks translucent; this will take 30–60 minutes. Remove the peel, drain, and let it cool. Boil down the remaining liquid until it becomes thick and slightly syrupy but before it turns to a caramel. Remove from the heat and put the peel in again to soak up the syrup. Infuse for 30 minutes.

Fill the candied peel into sterilized glass jars and pour the syrup in, cover, and store in a cold place or in a fridge. Alternatively, cool the peel on a wire rack and pour any remaining syrup into the centers. Finally pack into sterilized glass jars and cover tightly. It should keep for 6–8 weeks or longer under refrigeration.

breakfast

breakfast

Every year we teach an "Irresistible Breakfast" course at the cookery school and every year the message is the same – breakfast can be the dullest of meals or a real feast; it all depends on the care with which you source your produce, right down to the freshly roasted and ground coffee, good tea made with tea leaves, or a cup of steaming rich hot chocolate.

Guests love breakfast at Ballymaloe House. It starts with freshly made breads – Brown Soda Bread, Ballymaloe Yeast Breads, Spotted Dog, breakfast scones – no sliced bread. The toast is made from Ballymaloe White Yeast Bread cut into generous slices, served still with the crusts on, a forgotten flavor. Turn to the jams and preserves chapter (see page 500) to find recipes for delicious homemade marmalades and jams. We serve honeycomb at the beginning of the new season – Michael Wolfe looks after my few beehives at the end of the orchard. Our apple blossom honey is particularly delicious, so is the heather and wild flower honey. Seek out and support a local beekeeper, and serve the honey proudly.

The Great Irish Breakfast

In Ireland the traditional breakfast is a huge fried breakfast, but whereas it used to be eaten every day, most people now save this treat for weekends and holidays. Here more than ever the quality of the raw materials can make the difference between an average meal and a sensational feast.

Despite the fact that Ireland is famous for its ham and bacon, the flavor of real bacon as we knew it as children is difficult to find, although a few passionate pioneers have started to cure and smoke bacon in the traditional way – let us hope this trend continues. Seek them out and serve their products to your family and friends. Good quality traditionally cured bacon won't ooze salt and nitrates when cooked. People love sausages but avoid those flavored with too many herbs and garlic for breakfast. Juicy sausages and good black and white pudding (blood sausage) are easier to find here as more Irish butchers make their own. Ripe tomatoes are delicious in summer (don't bother to serve them in winter). Small flat mushrooms are also delicious, and if you are fortunate enough to have a few wild mushrooms in the autumn, serve those as a special bonus. Eggs must be really fresh, from free-range hens, and better still, organic as well.

Other Options

Of course the great big fry up, though delicious when all the ingredients are good, is not the only option for breakfast.

Nothing compares with a bowl of Macroom oatmeal porridge in the winter, or some Ballymaloe strawberry muesli in the summer. The range of breakfast cereals nowadays is mesmerizing, yet I've never found one that I craved – many are unbearably sweet. Homemade crunchy granola, and nut and grain muesli are delicious, healthy, and so easy to make. Proprietary brands tend to be heavy on oatmeal and bran, and light on the more expensive grains and dried fruits.

Smoothies are also great for breakfast, just whizz up some yogurt, banana, wheat germ, maybe a mango and a few raspberries – a whole meal in a glass. You can certainly go to work on one of these. Compôtes of seasonal fruit are also a delicious part of a breakfast menu, and a winter breakfast fruit salad with lots of juicy prunes and apricots provides plenty of roughage in a delicious way. I also love thick unctuous natural yogurt made from sheep's, goat's, or cow's milk – several delicious organic yogurts are now available. Always read the label carefully, some yogurts are made from milk powder and some contain the artificial sweetener aspartame.

For a very nutritous and protein-packed breakfast, try kippers and other fish. Muffins, French toast, and croissants are other tempting alternatives, and steaming pain au chocolat with freshly brewed coffee is irresistible.

I've had some of the best breakfasts of my life in the U.S., usually in diners, not in posh hotels – great American pancakes, hash browns, huevos rancheros, oatmeal.... Then there's the memorable breakfast of congee that I ate in a neighborhood restaurant in Hong Kong, dosa and eddli appam in India, and rice noodles in Vietnam....

Fresh Fruit Juice

The term "freshly squeezed orange juice" – one of the most abused terms in the English language – should not be applied to juice that was squeezed days earlier in a huge machine and sold in plastic containers in the stores and supermarkets. Freshly squeezed juice – pure and simple – comes from a citrus fruit cut in half, juiced either manually or on a citrus fruit juicer that does not press the zest from the skin into the juice. Drink it as soon as possible to benefit from all those vitamins. Citrus fruit juices oxidize quickly when exposed to the air and it soon tastes inferior. If you absolutely must squeeze orange juice the night before, put it into a dark glass bottle, fill right to the top, seal tightly, and keep in the fridge – it will still taste very good. A single juicy orange is sufficient for one person although occasionally, if oranges are small, you may need two. Citrus fruit should feel heavy for their size – they are best and juiciest during the citrus fruit season in winter. Don't just serve orange juice ad nauseum even if it is freshly squeezed. Become a little more adventurous and serve mandarin, tangerine, pink grapefruit, blood orange, or experiment with a mixture of citrus juices. For a special brunch, mix blood orange juice with Champagne, sparkling wine, or Prosecco. For apple juice, you'll need a juice extractor, then the fun begins – all kinds of juices are possible.

Don't skip breakfast

More and more people are missing breakfast, especially during the week when they have less time. Don't be tempted to skip breakfast. Your body needs refuelling after a night's sleep, and eating breakfast will supply you with the energy you need to start the day off productively. The digestive system is also at its most efficient in the morning and eating something at this time will provide some of the fiber and essential vitamins and minerals needed to fulfil your daily quota.

Skipping breakfast because you are on a diet is equally not advisable. It might make you feel virtuous for a while, but it often results in overeating later, and increasing appetite. There's no evidence to support the idea that skipping meals will help you lose weight.

Ballymaloe Nut and Grain Muesli

Makes 12 servings

This recipe for this muesli, bursting with goodness, was given to me by my sister-in-law, Natasha Harty. It keeps in a screw-top jar for several weeks.

8 Weetabix (if unavailable, use shredded wheat instead)
2 cups oat flakes
1/3 cup bran
1/2 cup fresh wheat germ
1/4 cup raisins
1/2 cup sliced hazelnuts or a mixture of cashews and hazelnuts
1/4 cup soft brown sugar
2 tablespoons Lecithin (optional)*

Crumble the Weetabix in a bowl, add the other ingredients, and mix well. Store in an airtight container. Keeps for 2–3 weeks in a cool place. Serve with fresh fruit and fresh creamy milk.

*Available from pharmacies or health food stores, Lecithin comes from soyabeans. It is rich in phosphatidyl choline, an important nutrient in the control of dietary fat, which helps the body to convert fats into energy rather than storing them as body fat. Check that it is G.M.-free.

Grape, Pink Grapefruit, and Mint

Serves 6

3 pink grapefruit
30 green grapes
1 tablespoon mint, finely chopped
2 tablespoons superfine sugar

Garnish
4 sprigs of mint

Peel and carefully segment the grapefruit (see page 73), peel and seed the grapes and add to the grapefruit in a bowl, and sprinkle with sugar and mint. Taste, adding more sugar if necessary. Chill before serving in a pretty white bowl with a sprig of mint on top.

Note: Pomelo, sweeties, ugli fruit or ordinary grapefruit can be used instead.

Orange, Mint, and Grapefruit

Serves 4

2 oranges
2 grapefruit
1 tablespoon superfine sugar
2 tablespoons mint, freshly chopped

Garnish
4 sprigs of mint

Peel and carefully segment the oranges and grapefruit into a bowl (see page 73). Add the sugar and mint; taste, and add more sugar if necessary. Chill. Serve in pretty bowls or arrange the segments of orange and grapefruit alternately on the plate in a circle, and pour a little juice over the fruit. Garnish with fresh mint.

Melon with Raspberries and Mint

Serves 4

1 ripe melon
8 ounces (225g) fresh raspberries (about 1 1/2 cups)
2 tablespoons superfine sugar
1 tablespoon mint, freshly chopped

Cut the top off the melon; scallop the edges if you like. Discard the seeds, scoop out the melon with a melon baller and sprinkle the melon balls with the sugar and mint. Mix with the raspberries and fill into the melon shell or a pretty white bowl. Cover and chill, serving within one hour so that the fruit keeps its shape.

Melon with Sweet Cicely

Serves 4

1 very ripe melon, Ogen, canteloupe, or Galia, or better still a mixture of all three
2 tablespoons superfine sugar
juice of 1/2–1 lemon, freshly squeezed
1 tablespoon sweet cicely, freshly snipped

Cut the melons in half, discard the seeds, and cut the flesh into generous cubes. Put into a bowl and sprinkle with sugar and lemon juice. Sprinkle sweet cicely over the top and serve very well chilled.

Winter Breakfast Fruit Salad

Serves 8

This can be made ahead and kept in the fridge; we love it and often eat it as a winter dessert with a few pistachio nuts or toasted almonds added.

a heaped cup prunes
1 cup dried apricots
1 small handful of raisins
grated zest of 1/2 lemon
1–2 tablespoons honey
1 cup orange juice, freshly squeezed
3–4 bananas

Soak the prunes and apricots overnight in boiling water to cover. Next day, put them in a flameproof casserole dish or heavy pan, along with the raisins and lemon zest.

Mix the honey with 1/4 cup warm water and enough of the fruit-soaking water to cover the prunes and apricots. Bring to a boil and simmer for about 35 minutes.

Let cool and keep in the refrigerator. Just before serving, add a little fresh orange juice and some sliced bananas to each bowl. Serve with light cream. Keeps for 1–2 weeks in a screw-top jar in the fridge.

Poached Plums

Serves 4

Something amazing happens when you poach plums in a simple syrup. Plums that were dull and almost inedible are transformed into a delicious compôte. Try to use blood plums or use opal plums in season.

3/4 cup plus 2 tablespoons sugar
1 cup cold water
1 lb. (450g) fresh plums, pitted

Put the sugar and water into a saucepan and bring slowly to a boil. Add the plums; cover and simmer until the plums are soft and bursting. Turn into a bowl and serve chilled with light cream.

Variation

Poached Plums with Lemon-scented Geranium Leaves

Put 4–6 large geranium leaves into the saucepan along with the sugar and water. Continue as for Poached Plums.

Poached Apricots with Lemon-scented Geranium Leaves

Substitute apricots for plums in the recipe above. Puréed and mixed with softly whipped cream, this makes a divine fool.

Rhubarb Compôte

Serves 4

1 lb. (450g) red rhubarb (we use Timperley Early)
2 cups Stock Syrup (see page 568)

Cut the rhubarb into 1-inch (2.5-cm) pieces. Put the cold syrup into a stainless steel saucepan, add the rhubarb, cover, bring to a boil, and simmer for just one minute (no longer or it will dissolve into a mush). Turn off the heat and leave the rhubarb in the covered saucepan until cool. A few strawberries sliced into the cooked compôte make it extra delicious.

Right: Poached Blood Plums

Variation

Rhubarb and Banana Compôte

Slice 1 or 2 bananas into the cold compote.

Apple and Sweet Geranium Compôte

8 medium-sized eating apples such as Golden Delicious
3/4 cup sugar
2–3 strips of lemon rind
juice of 1 1/2 lemons
4 large sweet geranium leaves

Peel, quarter, core, and slice the apples into 1/2-inch (5-mm) segments. Put them into a stainless steel or enamel saucepan. Add the sugar, lemon rind and juice, and the sweet geranium leaves. Cover with a wax paper lid and the lid of a saucepan; cook over gentle heat until the apples are soft but not broken.

Breakfast Smoothie

Serves 2–4

This is just a guide – experiment and have fun!

1 cup milk
1 cup yogurt
2 tablespoons crushed ice (optional)
1/2–1 tablespoon honey
1 banana
2 tablespoons fresh raspberries (optional)
1 tablespoon wheat germ

Put all the ingredients into the blender and whizz. Taste, and serve immediately.

Variation

Banana Smoothie

Simply whizz a banana with a small carton of plain yogurt and sweeten to taste with honey. My favorite quick breakfast.

How to Make a Delicious Cup of Tea

First, buy best quality tea leaves; tea bags do not make such good tea, and tend to be more wasteful, particularly for single cups.

Fill the kettle with cold fresh water. When the water has come to a boil, pour a little into a teapot. Swirl the water around in the pot until the pot feels warm. Discard the water, and add the tea leaves. Traditionally, you should allow 1 teaspoon of tea per person, plus one for the pot, but add more or less depending on how strong you like your tea. Bring the water back to a boil. Pour immediately over the tea leaves, fill to the top, and cover the pot. Let the tea "draw" (steep) for 3–4 minutes before serving.

Perhaps it's my imagination but tea always seems to taste better from a china cup rather than a mug. Keep the teapot covered with a tea-cosy, if available, to retain its heat.

Proper Breakfast Kippers

Serves 2

Our neighbors, the Schwartaus, and the Woodcock Smokery in West Cork, both produce the very best kippers I have ever tasted. I like them cooked for breakfast by what I call the jug method.

2 undyed kippers
Maitre d'Hôtel Butter (see page 586)

Garnish
2 segments of lemon
2 sprigs of parsley

Put the kippers head downwards into a deep heatproof jug or pitcher. Cover them with boiling water right up to their tails. Leave for 2–3 minutes to heat through.

Lift them out carefully by the tail and serve immediately on hot plates with a pat of Maitre d'Hôtel Butter melting on top. Garnish each with a segment of lemon and a sprig of parsley.

Pan-grilled Mackerel with Mâitre d'Hôtel Butter

Serves 4

8 fillets of very fresh mackerel
seasoned flour
small pat of butter

Mâitre d'Hôtel Butter (see page 586)

Garnish
segment of lemon
parsley

First make the Mâitre d'Hôtel Butter.

Heat the grill-pan. Dip the fish fillets in flour that has been seasoned with salt and freshly ground pepper. Shake off the excess flour and then spread a little butter with a knife on the flesh side of the fish, as though you were buttering a slice of bread rather stingily.

When the grill-pan is quite hot but not smoking, place the fish fillets butter side down on the grill; the fish should sizzle as soon as they touch the pan. Turn down the heat slightly and let them cook for 4–5 minutes before turning them. Cook on the other side until crisp and golden.

Serve on a hot plate with some slices of Mâitre d'Hôtel Butter and a segment of lemon. The butter may be served directly on the fish or, if you have a pretty shell, place it at the side of the plate as a container for the butter. Garnish with parsley.

Note: Fillets of any small fish are delicious pan-grilled in this way. Fish under two pounds (900g), such as mackerel, herring, and brown trout, can also be grilled whole on the pan. Fish over two pounds (900g) can be filleted first and then cut across into portions. Large fish, 4 to 6 pounds (1.8–2.6kg), can also be grilled whole. Cook them for about 10–15 minutes on each side and then put in a hot oven for another 15 minutes or so to finish cooking.

Kedgeree

Serves 6–8

Kedgeree immediately conjures up images of country house breakfasts which were often a veritable feast.

1 lb. (450g) wild salmon, freshly cooked (see page 233), or 8 ounces (225g) salmon and 8 ounces (225g) cooked smoked haddock
1 1/3 cups white long grain rice
3 hard-boiled eggs
2/3 cup cream
3 tablespoons butter
3 tablespoons parsley, freshly chopped
1 1/2 tablespoons chives, chopped
salt and freshly ground pepper
pinch cayenne pepper

First cook the salmon and let cool.

Meanwhile, cook the rice in boiling salted water, for about 10 minutes until cooked. Hard-boil the eggs, cooking in boiling salted water for 10 minutes. Drain off the water and run under a cold faucet to stop the cooking. Peel.

Remove the bones and skin from the fish and flake into small pieces. Heat the cream and butter in a saucepan and add the parsley and chives. As soon as it bubbles, add the rice, flaked fish, and roughly chopped hard-boiled eggs. Season well with salt, freshly ground pepper, and a pinch of cayenne. Mix very gently. Taste, correct seasoning if necessary, pile into a warm dish, and serve with freshly baked bread or with hot buttered toast.

Hot Potato Cakes with Crème Fraîche and Smoked Salmon

Serves 8

2 lbs. (900g) unpeeled floury potatoes
2–4 tablespoons butter
1/2 cup flour
1 tablespoon chopped parsley, chives, and lemon thyme, mixed, (optional)
salt and freshly ground pepper
creamy milk
seasoned flour
clarified butter (see page 103) for frying
crème fraîche or, if unavailable, sour cream
4 ounces (110g) smoked salmon
2 tablespoons chives, freshly snipped

Cook the potatoes in their skins, pull off the peel, and mash right away, adding the butter, flour, and herbs. Season with lots of salt and pepper, and add a few drops of creamy milk if the mixture is altogether too stiff. Mix well. Taste and correct the seasoning. Shape into potato cakes an inch (2.5cm) thick. Dip in seasoned flour. Fry the potato cakes in clarified butter until golden on one side, then flip over and cook on the other side, for about 4-5 minutes. They should be crusty and golden. Serve on very hot plates. Put a dollop of crème fraîche on top of each potato cake. Top with slivers of smoked salmon and sprinkle with chives. Serve immediately.

Alternative Serving Suggestions

1 Use smoked mackerel or trout instead of smoked salmon.
2 Serve hot crispy bacon instead of salmon.
3 Serve smoked eel and dill instead of salmon and chives.

The Great Irish Breakfast

If you are cooking for more than 3 people, it is essential to have 2 or more pans.

Rashers (Strips of Bacon)

For me, fried rashers have the best flavor. Broiling seems to intensify the salt and harden poor quality bacon. Buy thickly-sliced bacon. Have the pan quite hot and add a tiny dash of oil. Cook the bacon until quite crisp on one side before turning. Turn down the heat slightly, if necessary. Cook until crisp on the second side. Drain on paper towels and keep warm. Pour off the bacon fat and reserve. Wash the pan before frying another batch of bacon or eggs.

Sausages

Buy good quality pork sausages and use them quickly. Oil the pan with just a few drops of oil. Cook them over medium heat, turning every few minutes until they are uniformly brown. Drain on paper towels and keep warm.

Mushrooms

Flat-capped mushrooms have the most flavor. Keep them whole or slice them. Have your pan very hot, melt a little butter, and toss in the sliced mushrooms; sprinkle with salt and freshly ground pepper and cook through, for only 2–3 minutes. The most important point here is to have a very hot pan and not to cook too many at a time. A squeeze of lemon juice will help to keep mushrooms white if that's what you want. If you cook too many mushrooms together or if you have a cool pan, the mushrooms will be soggy and wet.

Tomatoes

Choose very dark red, ripe but firm, tomatoes. Slice across in the middle and arrange, cut side up, on an ovenproof plate. Sprinkle with salt, pepper, and sugar, and put a tiny blob of butter on each. Bake in a moderate oven, 350°F (180°C), for 5-10 minutes. Alternatively, you could just fry them over a low heat turning once.

Below: The Great Irish Breakfast

Ripe tomatoes can be delicious baked whole at 350°F (180°C) for 10–15 minutes until they are soft.

Black and White Pudding (Blood Sausage)

Choose good quality puddings, preferably in natural casings, not in plastic. Cut into slices and fry for 3–4 minutes on each side in a little butter or bacon fat, over a medium heat, or cook under a broiler.

Fried Eggs

Choose very fresh eggs, preferably from free-range hens, and organic. See page 115 for frying instructions.

Kidneys

Peel the fat and membrane from the kidneys. Cut in half and remove the center core. Wash and dry well, dip in a little seasoned flour, and cook gently in a frying pan in a little melted butter. Serve hot.

Ulster Fry

An Ulster Fry also includes fried potato brad or fadge, and very delicious it is, too.

Fadge or Potato Bread

Serves 8

In Ulster, people are passionate about fadge. It can be cooked on a griddle, in a frying pan, or in the oven.

2 lbs. (900g) unpeeled floury potatoes, e.g., Golden Wonder or russett
2 tablespoons flour
1 egg, preferably from free-range hens
2–4 tablespoons butter
creamy milk
seasoned flour
salt and freshly ground pepper
bacon fat, butter, or olive oil for frying

Cook the potatoes in their skins, pull off the skins, and mash the potato right away. Add the beaten egg, butter, and flour. Season with lots of salt and freshly ground pepper, adding a few drops of creamy milk if the mixture is too stiff. Taste and correct the seasoning. Shape into a circle, an inch (2.5cm) thick, and then cut into eight wedges. Dip each section in seasoned flour. Bake in a moderate oven at 350°F (180°C) for 15–20 minutes. Alternatively, cook on a griddle over an open fire, or fry in bacon fat or melted butter on a gentle heat. After about 4–5 minutes, when the fadge is crusty and golden on one side, flip over and cook on the other side. Serve with an Ulster Fry or just on its own on hot plates with a blob of butter melting on top.

Perfect Poached Egg on Toast

Serves 1

No fancy egg poachers or molds are needed to produce a perfect result – simply a really fresh egg laid by a happy lazy hen.

1 egg
toast, freshly made

Bring a small saucepan of water to a boil, reduce the heat, swirl the water, crack the egg and slip it gently into the whirlpool in the center. For perfection, the water should not boil again but bubble very gently just below boiling point. Continue to cook for 3–4 minutes, until the white is set and the yolk still soft and runny.

Meanwhile make a slice of toast, cut off the crusts, butter it and pop it onto a hot plate. Drain the poached egg and place it on top. Serve immediately.

Note: Poached eggs are also delicious served on a bed of creamy spinach nicely flavored with nutmeg, or on top of Piperonata (see page 190).

Mushroom Omelette with Bacon

Serves 1

An omelette is the ultimate instant food but many a travesty is served in its name. The whole secret is to have the pan hot enough and to use clarified butter if at all possible.

Ordinary butter will burn if your pan is as hot as it ought to be. The omelette should be made in half the time it takes to read this recipe. Your first may not be a joy to behold but persevere, practice makes perfect !

2 eggs
2 teaspoons water or milk
salt and freshly ground pepper
2 teaspoons clarified butter (see page 103) or olive oil

Filling
2 crispy strips of bacon
Mushroom à la Crème, (see page 197)

omelette pan, preferably non stick, 9-inch (23-cm) diameter

Cook the bacon until crisp; heat the Mushroom à la Crème and keep warm. Warm a plate in the oven.

Whisk the eggs with the water or milk in a bowl using a fork or whisk, until thoroughly mixed but not too fluffy. Season with salt and pepper.

Heat the omelette pan over high heat and add the clarified butter; as soon as it sizzles, pour in the egg mixture. It will start to cook immediately, so quickly pull the edges of the omelette towards the center with a metal spoon or spatula, tilting the pan so that the uncooked egg runs to the sides.

Continue until most of the egg is set and will not run any more, then let the omelette cook for a further 10 seconds to brown the bottom. Spoon the hot mushroom mixture in a line along the center at this point.

To fold the omelette: flip the edge just below the handle of the pan into the center, then hold the pan almost perpendicular over the plate so that the omelette will flip over again, then half-roll, half-slide the omelette onto the plate so that it lands folded in three. (It should not take more than 30 seconds in all to make the omelette, perhaps 45 if you are adding a filling.)

Put the crispy bacon on top and serve immediately.

Children's Breakfast Menu

One can have lots of fun doing children's breakfast dishes and you'll be rewarded with lots of smiling faces – both parents and children! Special children's crockery and cutlery may also be used; Beatrix Potter, Bunnykins, etc.

Boiled eggs with children's name

Use either lead pencil or water-resistant markers to paint funny faces or names. Serve with sticks of toast.

Mini breakfast

Little strips of bacon, cocktail sausages, cherry tomatoes, fried bantam or quail eggs.

Toast with a face

Use scrambled egg as a base, cherry tomatoes for eyes, cocktail sausages for eyebrows and nose, and strips of bacon for the mouth.

Tiny Breakfast pancakes

Make Buttermilk Pancakes (see below) in small sizes.

Master Recipe

Buttermilk Pancakes with Crispy Bacon and Maple Syrup

Serves 10

4 cups all-purpose white flour
1 teaspoon baking soda (bread soda)
large pinch salt
2–4 tablespoons sugar
1 egg
2½ cups buttermilk
20 hot crispy strips of bacon
maple syrup or honey

Mix the dry ingredients together in a bowl, make a well in the center, and add the egg and enough buttermilk to make a batter of a dropping consistency (it usually takes the full measure).

Drop 1 large tablespoonful into a hot non-stick pan and cook for 1–2 minutes on one side before turning over; the pancakes are ready to turn when the bubbles burst. Flip over gently and cook until golden on the other side.

To serve: put one pancake on a hot plate, spread with butter, and drizzle with maple syrup or honey, and top with another buttered pancake. Put a few pieces of hot crispy bacon on top. Serve more maple syrup or honey as an accompaniment.

Variation

Buttermilk Pancakes with Sour Cream and Jam

Serve hot pancakes with jam and sour cream.

Croissants

Makes 16

Sadly, one now has to search in France to find really good buttery croissants – the quintessential French breakfast. For years I thought croissants were the most complicated thing on earth to make, particularly as the first recipe I tried came from Julia Child's wonderful book, *Mastering the Art of French Cooking*, and covered 10 pages! That dampened my spirits for a while but eventually, undaunted, I came up with this version which I find gives terrific results for the minimum amount of effort. Use the very best unsalted (sweet) butter. This recipe can be left to rise in a fridge overnight, and the uncooked croissants can also be frozen so you can bake one at a time for a real breakfast treat.

⅔ cup milk
2 tablespoons sugar
⅔ cup water
½ ounce (10g) yeast (about 1½–2 tablespoons)
4 cups white bread flour
pinch of salt
2½ sticks (1¼ cups) unsalted butter

egg wash made with 1 beaten egg

Heat the milk and dissolve the sugar in it, then add the water. Let the liquid cool to tepid before pouring it onto the yeast. Stir until dissolved.

Sift the flour into a bowl and add a pinch of salt. Rub in ¼ cup of the butter. Add the yeast liquid and mix to a dough. Knead until smooth, by hand or in a food mixer with a dough hook – about 8–10 minutes by hand or 5 minutes in a machine. Cover with plastic wrap and leave in the fridge for 2 hours.

Beat the remaining butter into a thin layer between sheets of wax paper or plastic wrap. Roll out the dough into a rectangle, put the butter on one half of the rectangle an inch (2.5cm) from the edges all around, and fold the other half over it.

Roll out the dough into another rectangle, fold in three (as for puff or flaky pastry), keeping all the sides aligned, cover, and let it rest for 30 minutes in the fridge.

With the open ends facing from your belly button, roll out the pastry again, and fold in three as before. Cover and leave in a fridge until next day; roll and fold in three once again.

Finally, roll out the pastry to 1/4-inch (5-mm) thick, 14 inches (35cm) wide, and as long as possible (usually about 22 inches [55cm]). Trim the edges and cut into half lengthwise and then into elongated triangles (the base of each should be about 6 inches [15cm] but you will have two smaller ones at either end).

Preheat the oven to 425°F (220°C).

Start at the base of each triangle and roll it as tightly as possible towards the tip. Place the croissants on a baking sheet with the tip tucked underneath. Egg wash each and put them in a warm place to rise for 30-45 minutes. When they have doubled in size, egg wash again very carefully.

Bake croissants for 10 minutes, then reduce the temperature to 350°F (180°C) for 10 minutes until the croissants are crisp, golden, and brown on the bottom. Serve with homemade jam.

Croissants may be filled with all kinds of things, from almond paste, cheese, garlic butter, and chocolate, to almost any sort of sandwich filling.

Brioche (see page 497)

Pain au Chocolat

Roll the croissant dough as above. Cut into three strips instead of two. Divide the strips into 3½ x 5-inch (9 x 12.5-cm) pieces. Arrange 2 strips of chocolate on the center of each one, about 1½ inches (4cm) apart. Cover with one piece of dough, brush the edge with water, and barely overlap with the other piece. Transfer to a baking sheet and let rise. Egg wash again. Preheat the oven to 425°F (220°C) for 10 minutes. Put in the pains au chocolat, then reduce the temperature to 350°F (180°C) for 10 minutes or until they are crisp and golden brown on the bottom. Cool on a wire rack and serve.

Note: seek out the strips of chocolate specially made for pains au chocolat.

Right: Croissants

How to make Perfect Coffee

Choose the blend of coffee beans that best appeals to your taste, low, medium, or high roast. Store in a screw-top jar or tin. Fill the kettle with cold water and bring to a boil. Meanwhile grind the coffee.

The texture will depend on the coffee-making method being used. It should be ground very fine if you are making espresso, and a little less fine for the filter method, and coarser still for the cafetière and pot methods.

The Pot Method

Bring the cold water to a boil. Pour a little into the pot to scald it. When the pot feels warm, discard the water. Add the freshly ground coffee and fill the pot with the water. The water should be **just off the boil**. Wait for 3–4 minutes, stir, cover. Serve with a strainer.

The Filter Method

Bring cold water to a boil. Meanwhile put a paper filter into the filter holder and rest over a coffee pot. Fill about halfway with finely ground coffee. When the water comes to a boil, wait for 10 seconds and then pour the water quickly over the coffee. Let it gradually drip through. (It's best to scald the pot here also.)

The Cafetière Method

Bring cold water to a boil as before. Remove the plunger. Scald the pot with some of the water and discard the water. Add the coffee. Fill the pot with just-boiled water to about 3/4 full, put the plunger into the pot. Let it sit for 3–4 minutes. Slowly push the grinds to the bottom of the pot with the plunger.

The Stovetop Espresso Method

Fill the filter container with finely ground coffee, usually high roast. Fill the base with cold water. Fit the coffee container into the base, screw on the top. Place on a burner and within a few minutes, the water will boil and the steam will saturate the coffee. Wait until it has all come through. Serve.

French Toast

Serves 4

French toast is so good that you forget how economical it is. The French don't call this French toast. They call it pain perdu or "lost bread," because it is a way to use up leftover bread you would otherwise lose – the only bread you've got on the baker's day off. French toast is actually better if the bread is a little stale, or sliced and dried out overnight.

3 eggs
2 1/2 tablespoons milk or cream
salt to taste
6 slices bread (preferably a dense homemade type; typically white, but try rye or wholewheat, too)
5 tablespoons butter
confectioners sugar

Stir the eggs, milk, and salt briskly with a fork until well blended.

Pour the mixture through a strainer into a shallow bowl in which you can easily dip a slice of bread. Dip both sides of each slice of bread in the batter and place the slices on a piece of wax paper.

Melt half of the butter in a frying pan big enough to hold 3 slices at once. Fry the bread over medium heat until very lightly browned, turning once.

Keep the cooked slices warm in an oven while frying the other three in the remaining butter. Serve warm, sprinkled with confectioners sugar.

French Toast with Bananas and Maple Syrup or Honey

Serves 1

1 egg
2 1/2 tablespoons milk
1 teaspoon sugar
1 banana
2 slices white bread
clarified butter (see page 103)

Garnish
1 banana, sliced
best-quality plain yogurt, chilled
maple syrup or honey
1 tablespoon walnuts, roughly chopped

Whisk the egg in a bowl with the milk and add the sugar. Mash the banana well with a fork and add to the mixture. Alternatively, whizz the whole lot together in a blender or food processor. Pour onto a plate and dip both sides of the bread into it.

Melt a little clarified butter in the pan, fry the bread over medium heat and, when golden on one side, turn over onto the other. Place on a hot plate, top with banana slices and a dollop of yogurt, drizzle with maple syrup or honey, and scatter with a few chopped walnuts. Serve immediately.

Marmalade Popovers

Makes about 14

1 cup all-purpose flour
1 cup milk
2 eggs, lightly beaten
1 teaspoon grated orange zest
1 tablespoon melted butter or oil
½ teaspoon salt
8–10 tablespoons homemade Orange Marmalade (see page 509)
confectioners sugar
oil or lard for greasing

Preheat the oven to 425°F (220°C). Sift the flour into a bowl. Make a well in the center and pour in the milk and eggs. Mix to a smooth batter. Stir in orange zest and whisk really hard with an egg whisk until the surface is covered with air bubbles. If possible, let stand in a cold place for about one hour, then stir in the melted butter and salt and beat again.

Grease deep muffin cups or ramekins really well with some oil or lard. Put them in the oven until they are hot. Pour in the batter, filling each cup half to two-thirds full, and put straight into the hot oven for about 10 minutes, and then reduce the heat to 350°F (180°C), and bake for about 25 minutes longer.

The popovers should be well risen, crisp, and golden brown. Put a small spoonful of marmalade into each one. Sprinkle with confectioners sugar and serve immediately.

Ginger Muffins

Makes about 10

Almost our favorite muffin recipe, this is adapted from Marion Cunningham's The Breakfast Book.

4 ounces (110g) unpeeled ginger root, cut into chunks
¾ cup superfine sugar
1 stick (½ cup) butter
zest of 2 lemons
2 eggs
1 cup buttermilk
2½ cups white flour
½ teaspoon salt
½ teaspoon baking soda (bread soda)

Preheat the oven to 400°F (200°C).

Grease one tray of muffin cups or line with non-stick paper muffin cups. Whizz up the ginger in a food processor, then put it into a saucepan along with a couple of tablespoons of sugar and place over medium heat until the sugar melts. Let cool.

Cream the butter, add the remaining sugar and the lemon zest, then add the eggs, one by one, and beat well between each addition.

Next stir in the buttermilk and ginger mixture, and blend well. Finally stir in the flour, salt, and baking soda, until just mixed. Fill the greased muffins cups with the batter, and bake for 30–40 minutes in the preheated oven. Serve warm.

Antony Worrall-Thompson's Fresh Apple Muffins

Makes about 12

1 lb. (450g) diced dessert apples, unpeeled, about ¼-inch (5-mm)
¾ cup plus 2 tablespoons sugar
4 eggs, lightly beaten
⅔ cup peanut, sunflower, or corn oil
½ teaspoon vanilla extract
2½ cups all-purpose white flour
2 teaspoons baking powder
2 teaspoons ground cinnamon
1 teaspoon salt
1 cup walnuts, coarsely chopped
a scant cup raisins

Preheat the oven to 325°F (170°C).

Grease 12 muffin cups or better still, line with paper muffin cups. Set aside three mixing bowls. Into one, mix apples and sugar, in another, the eggs, oil, and vanilla, in the third, mix together flour, baking powder, cinnamon, and salt. Add the egg mix to the apples and combine well (best using hands). Add in the flour mixture and stir just enough to combine. It should be a stiff batter. Mix in the walnuts and raisins. Spoon equal amounts into muffin cups. Bake for about 25 minutes or until a skewer comes out clean. If possible, serve warm.

Chocolate and Orange Muffins

Makes 24 muffins

The beauty of these tasty muffins lies in the fact that the batter can be kept in the fridge for 30 days, so you can bake a few muffins freshly each day. This is Dervilla Whelan's delicious version.

2 eggs
1½ cups soft brown sugar
1¾ cups milk
1 teaspoon vanilla extract

1½ cups sunflower oil
¾ cup golden raisins
a scant cup bran
3¼ cups all-purpose flour
½ teaspoon salt
2½ teaspoons baking soda (bread soda)
1 cup chocolate chips
zest of 5 oranges

Preheat the oven to 400°F (200°C).

In the bowl of an electric mixer, beat the eggs and brown sugar. Add in the milk, vanilla, sunflower oil, raisins, bran, flour, salt, and baking soda. Mix until completely blended. The mixture will be a very wet, gloopy batter but don't worry.

Take the bowl off the mixer and gently stir in the chocolate chips and the grated orange zest. Line the muffin trays with paper muffin cups and fill with the mixture, leaving about a half-inch (1cm) below the rim. Bake for approximately 30 minutes until risen and spongy to the touch.

Toby's Hot Chocolate

Serves 4

This is the hot chocolate that my son Toby makes; the flavor of "proper" hot chocolate is a revelation if you've never tried it before.

4 ounces (110g) best-quality dark chocolate (about ⅔ cup, broken up)
¼ cup water
2½ cups milk
1–2 teaspoons sugar
4 large teaspoons whipped cream
grated chocolate

Put the chocolate and water into a heavy saucepan and melt over very low heat. Meanwhile, bring the milk almost to a boil in a separate saucepan. When the chocolate has melted, pour in the milk, whisking all the time; it should be smooth and frothy. Taste, and add some sugar. Pour into warmed cups, spoon a blob of whipped cream on top, and sprinkle with a little grated chocolate.

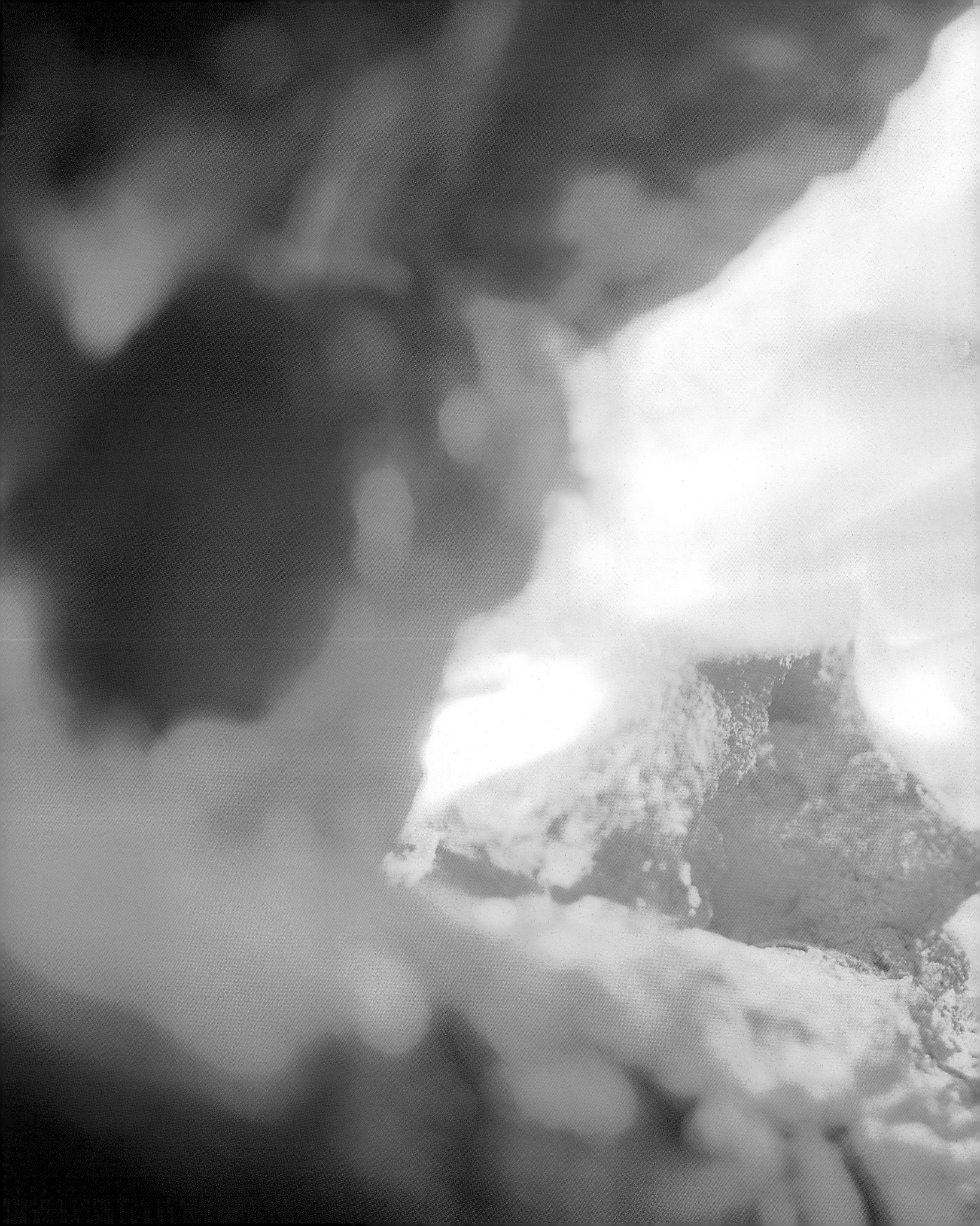

barbecues

barbecues

Cooking over an open fire is the world's oldest cooking method, somehow it seems to re-awaken our primordial instincts. Even those who wouldn't normally be caught dead in an apron feel an urge to grab the tongs when they see a barbecue! Barbecueing means less fuss, more fun, and (when one gets the hang of it) more flavor, too. It's all about easy, casual entertaining – unwinding with friends and family, while the steaks sizzle and the chicken wings crisp over glowing embers.

You certainly don't need a lot of fancy equipment to get started. I've cooked many an outdoor feast in the most basic circumstances – a circle of stones, a fire, and a wire rack will get you started. The skills one needs to learn are: how to light the fire, how to judge when the heat is right for cooking, and where to position the food in relation to the source of heat.

Choosing a Grill

Barbecueing, like any other type of cooking, is less haphazard if you understand the fundamentals and learn a few basic techniques. But first choose your grill.

The most basic type is the **foil barbecue** which comes ready-made and can be dumped in the trash after use (but do make sure that it's dampened down and totally dead first). This type is perfect for picnics and for people with a tiny garden or patio. If you want a sturdy barbecue that's still portable, **the hibachi** is hard to beat. They're cheap and easy to carry. This barbecue is perfect if you're cooking for small numbers, has the advantage of adjustable grill levels, and can even be positioned in the center of a table outdoors. One notch up, are **free-standing barbecues**. They may be wagon or kettle-grill types, with or without wheels. Some have a folding base which makes them easy to pack away and transport in the trunk of a car. The covered **Webber-type grill** comes in a range of prices and opens all sorts of new possibilities. With this type of barbecue one can cook whole cuts of meat (slow-cooked lamb, pork, chickens, ducks) or even pizza. Try barbecuing your Christmas turkey for a change – completely delicious. One can use charcoal timber, or charcoal bricks in these grills. Purists insist on wood or charcoal, but if you like to barbecue on the spur of the moment, then you should consider a **gas-powered barbecue**. Here you have push-button control, so if you don't want to get involved with charcoal and frantically fanning flames, this could be the answer. There are lots of options ranging from a simple grill to state-of-the-art models. Of course, you can also buy a kit and build a barbecue at home. It all comes down to personal preferences.

My suggestion is to get started on something really basic until you learn how to control and manage the fire.

Lighting the Barbecue and Fuel

Unless you have a gas-powered barbecue, the most important thing is to get your barbecue lit in time. This could be anything between 15 and 45 minutes before you intend to start cooking, depending on the kind of fuel you're using. There are two types of charcoal: the first will be ready to cook on within 15 minutes, but it burns off quite quickly. The second is slower-burning and has better staying power, but takes longer to reach the cooking stage. Charcoal briquets take the longest of all (up to 45 minutes), but then they last for ages and they hold their heat very well.

Charcoal is ready for cooking when it turns light gray and ashy, not before. Don't be tempted to begin cooking while there are flames still licking around the grill – this usually results in uncooked but blackened and charred food.

But don't forget about wood. I love wood barbecues. We have a great tradition of breakfast barbecues on the cliffs of Ballyandreen, and when barbecueing on the beach, collecting drift wood for the fire is all part of the experience (although I do cheat by bringing some kindling and newspaper in the back of the car, so I can get it started while others collect the wood!). Make sure there's no glue or paint on the wood, as these will release toxins when burnt.

Woodchips (apple, hickory, or oak) add different smokey flavors to the food. Soak them in cold water for a good hour or so before putting them directly onto the hot embers.

Never use firelights, kerosene, methylated spirits, gasoline, diesel, or lighter fluid to light your fire – it can be incredibly dangerous.

Cooking

Before you start barbecuing, make sure that you're organized – with your tongs, seasoning, and dishes ready. Even though these are laid-back affairs, they will only seem effortless if you've organized yourself a little first.

The fundamental principle of barbecuing is controlling the heat. On a barbecue, you do this by raising or lowering the grill. Because they cook more slowly, the larger the pieces of meat, the further from the heat source they need to be. So for thick steaks, chicken legs, and larger cuts of meat, you are better off searing over the high heat for a few minutes before transferring the meat to the edges of the grill, where the heat is lower. Searing will seal the meat, so that the juices remain inside during further cooking over a low heat. Smaller pieces of food (chicken paillarde or lamb chops) can be within 4 to 5 inches (10–12.5cm) of the coals.

It is difficult to gauge if chicken legs and wings are properly cooked through. Because of the risk of salmonella and campylobacter, it is definitely worth pre-cooking chicken drumsticks a little first – this may sound like cheating, but it's better to be safe, particularly if you are using intensively produced meat.

As you cook, fat will drip off the meat and onto the coals, producing flames. Damp these down by spraying a little water on the coals. Avoid basting with too much oil or marinade as well, as this can also cause flames to leap up. Keep turning the meat so it does not stick, burn, or dry out. Most burgers, chops, and so on should be ready within 20 minutes, but do check before serving. Fish and seafood will be much quicker.

Marinating

Marinades are fun to experiment with, and can be an excellent way to improve and strengthen the flavor of meat, but they are certainly not essential. If you start off with good quality fish and meat, you shouldn't have to do very much to it. For a simple marinade, all you need is good olive oil, sea salt or Kosher salt, a few herbs, and perhaps a little lemon or lime juice, vinegar, or red wine. You only need to marinate for 10–15 minutes, and be particularly aware not to leave meat in an acidic marinade for too long as it can be counter-productive and toughen it. A word of warning: avoid marinades with tomato or honey as they tend to burn. It's a better idea to baste the meat with sauce once it's cooked.

Food for Barbecues

Barbecues were traditionally carniverous affairs, with perhaps the odd green salad or baked potato on the side. This is far from the case now. There are some exceptionally tasty vegetarian and non-meat options to try: vegetable kabobs and wraps, stuffed flat-cap mushrooms, goat cheese wrapped in vine leaves, coal-baked potatoes, shrimp, and fish.

Remember that people's appetites increase when they eat outdoors, and of course all those lovely aromas of cooking food will make them hungrier still. Keep your guests' hunger at bay with some fingerfood – this will also ensure that they're not completely sozzled if you get your timing wrong and the cooking takes longer than expected! As a rough guide, allow per person:

3–4 portions of "main" courses, e.g., kabobs, steak, burgers, sausages, frankfurters, or fish wraps
2–3 portions of salads or vegetable dishes, e.g., baked potatoes, salads, or vegetable wraps
1–2 portions of dessert
3–4 drinks

Try to have some standby food on hand, such as extra sausages and frankfurters (which can be frozen later if they're not used) and bananas or tomatoes which can be wrapped in bacon.

Hygiene and Safety

When cooking outdoors take sensible precautions:

1 Keep all food refrigerated (or cool) until it's needed.
2 Keep cooked and uncooked meat separate and use different implements and serving dishes to avoid cross-contamination.
3 Wash your hands after touching uncooked meat.
4 Position your barbecue on a flat heat-proof surface away from overhanging trees and shrubs. Once you light it, don't move it.
5 If you are barbecuing at night, make sure there's good lighting around the cooking area.
6 Never leave the barbecue unattended.
7 Always keep a fire extinguisher at hand. A plant mister is also handy to keep flames down.
8 NEVER use a barbecue indoors.
9 Dampen down the barbecue completely before you empty out the ashes, and let it cool before moving it.

Marinades

Marinating adds flavor and acts as a tenderizer for meat. Time can be anything from 15 minutes to overnight.

Basic Marinade for Chicken and Lamb

Makes about 1¼ cups

⅔ cup olive oil
⅔ cup freshly squeezed lemon juice
3 garlic cloves, crushed
3 sprigs tarragon, thyme, or rosemary
½–1 teaspoon lemon zest, finely grated

Optional extras
1 grated onion and a good sprinkling of cinnamon

Mix all the ingredients together, taste, and correct the seasoning.

Yogurt Marinade for Chicken and Lamb

Makes 2½ cups

2 cups plain yogurt
5 tablespoons extra-virgin olive oil
2 large garlic cloves, crushed
2 tablespoons mint leaves, freshly chopped
freshly ground pepper

Optional Extras
1–2 tablespoons freshly roasted and ground cumin or 1–2 tablespoons ground coriander seeds, or a mixture of both.

Mix all the ingredients together, taste, and correct the seasoning.

Barbecue Sauce for Chicken, Lamb, Pork, or Sausages

Makes about 1 cup

¼ cup plus 1 tablespoon olive oil
2 garlic cloves, crushed
1 cup onion, finely chopped
1 x 14-ounce (400g) can chopped tomatoes
salt and freshly ground pepper
½ cup tomato paste
½ cup red or white wine vinegar
¼ cup plus 1 tablespoon pure honey
¼ cup plus 1 tablespoon Worcestershire sauce
2½ tablespoons Dijon mustard

Heat the oil in a frying pan, add the garlic and onion, and sweat gently for 4–5 minutes. Add the tomatoes and juice,
cook for a further 4 or 5 minutes, then season with salt and pepper. Purée in a blender or food processor. Pour back into a clean pan, add the remainder of the ingredients, and bring to a boil over medium heat and simmer for 4–5 minutes. Use as a basting sauce, marinade, or accompaniment.

Note: Don't marinate for longer than 15 or 20 minutes or the meat will be inclined to burn easily.

Olive Oil Marinade for all Meats and Fish

Makes about 1¼ cups (300ml)

½ cup (8 tablespoons) olive oil
4 garlic cloves, crushed
¼ cup (4 tablespoons) freshly chopped herbs, such as parsley, thyme, mint, chives, rosemary, and sage
salt and freshly ground pepper

Optional Extras
2 tablespoons orange zest, finely grated
2 tablespoons shallots, finely chopped

Combine the ingredients, and season with salt and pepper.

Olive Oil and Ginger Marinade for Pork and Chicken

Makes about ½ cup (8 tablespoons)

¼ cup (4 tablespoons) olive oil
1–2 tablespoons fresh ginger, peeled and chopped
4 garlic cloves, chopped
2 tablespoons orange rind

Combine all the ingredients and mix well.

Barbecued Chicken Breasts with Roast Pepper, Tomato, and Basil Salsa

Serves 4

1 lb. (450g) skinless chicken breasts, preferably organic
2 teaspoons honey
2 tablespoons lemon juice, freshly squeezed
1 tablespoon tomato ketchup or Hot Chile Sauce (see page 591)
½ teaspoon ground roasted cumin
½ teaspoon salt

Roast Pepper, Tomato, and Basil Salsa (see page 592)

Cut each chicken breast into 4 or 5 strips. Mix the honey, lemon juice, ketchup, and cumin in a bowl. Add the chicken and toss until all the pieces are coated, then marinate in the fridge for 1–2 hours.

Light the barbecue. Just before cooking, add the salt to the marinated chicken and toss well. When the barbecue is really good and hot, grill chicken pieces 6 inches (15cm) from the heat for 5–7 minutes each side, depending on thickness. Cook far enough from the flame, otherwise the honey will burn. The chicken must cook through but still be juicy. Serve with Roast Pepper, Tomato, and Basil Salsa.

Indonesian Chicken Satay

Serves 4–6

This delicious recipe comes from Betelnut in San Francisco.

1 lb. (450g) boneless, skinless chicken thighs, cut into 1/2-inch (1-cm) strips

Marinade
2 tablespoons shallots, chopped
3–4 tablespoons garlic cloves, crushed
1 1/2 tablespoons palm sugar, grated, or brown sugar
2 teaspoons ground fennel seeds
2 teaspoons ground cumin
2 teaspoons ground coriander
2 teaspoons lemongrass, finely chopped
2 teaspoons fresh ginger, grated
1/4 teaspoon ground turmeric
1/2 teaspoon salt

Spicy Peanut Sauce
1 tablespoon sunflower oil
2 teaspoons fresh ginger, peeled and grated
1 teaspoon garlic, finely chopped
1 teaspoon lemongrass, finely chopped
2 teaspoons shallots, chopped
1/4 teaspoon ground turmeric
2 tablespoons ground roasted peanuts
1 tablespoon hot chile sauce (sambal oelek)
1 teaspoon sugar
1 teaspoon fish sauce (nam pla)
1 tablespoon tamarind concentrate or lime juice
1/4 cup water
1/2 cup coconut milk

Garnish
salad greens
chile
cilantro leaves

First make the marinade: mix all the ingredients in a bowl and add enough water to make a smooth paste. Put the chicken strips into a bowl, add the marinade, cover, and mix well. Leave for 4 hours or overnight.

Meanwhile make the sauce: heat the oil in a small frying pan. Add the ginger, garlic, lemongrass, and shallots, and sauté for about 5 minutes or until soft but not colored. Add all the remaining ingredients plus half the coconut milk. Cover and cook over very low heat for about 20 minutes. Adjust the consistency with the remaining coconut milk.

Preheat the outdoor barbecue to hot. (Alternatively, you can use a broiler or grill-pan.) Remove the chicken from the marinade and thread onto bamboo skewers that have been soaked in water for at least 30 minutes. Barbecue or grill for a few minutes on each side until cooked through. Serve the chicken satay skewers with individual dishes of Spicy Peanut Sauce.

Chicken with Lemon and Ginger

Serves 6

6 chicken breasts

Marinade
juice of 1 freshly squeezed lemon
2 garlic cloves, crushed
1 1/2 teaspoons fresh ginger, peeled and grated
1 teaspoon lemon zest, finely grated
1/2 cup extra-virgin olive oil
salt and lots of freshly ground pepper

Mix all the marinade ingredients in a bowl, and marinate the chicken breasts in a shallow dish for half an hour. Prepare the barbecue, or heat a grill-pan to medium heat. Dry off the chicken breasts with paper towels and brush them with a very little olive oil. Grill for about 5 minutes on each side. Heat the marinade in a small pan until just simmering. Serve the chicken on very hot plates with a little of the marinade, and a green salad with arugula and cherry tomatoes.

Chicken Burgers

Serves 6

A great recipe from Bonnie Stern, well-known TV chef in Toronto. Wrap the burgers in caul fat if available; it is vital to cook the chicken burgers thoroughly but not to let them dry out – they should still be good and juicy. Serve with Teriyaki Sauce (see page 236).

1 lb. (450g) boneless, skinless chicken breasts, preferably free-range and organic
1 egg, preferably from free-range hens
1 1/3 cups fresh breadcrumbs
1 garlic clove, crushed
1 teaspoon fresh ginger, peeled and grated
2 tablespoons fresh cilantro or parsley, chopped
1 teaspoon tarragon, chopped
2 tablespoons chives or scallions, chopped
salt and freshly ground pepper
caul fat, optional
6 hamburger buns or pita breads
mixture of crisp lettuce and salad greens

Grind the chicken breasts finely; alternatively, cut them into cubes about 1/2-inch (1-cm), put them into a food processor fitted with the steel knife, and pulse until finely chopped.

Put the chicken into a bowl, add the beaten egg, breadcrumbs, garlic, ginger, cilantro, tarragon, and chives, and season with salt and pepper. Mix well.

Shape the mixture into 6 burgers. Wrap in caul fat, if using. Cover and refrigerate until ready to cook. Brush with olive oil.

Light the barbecue or preheat a grill-pan. Grill the burgers for 3 minutes each side. Keep turning and brushing with the Teriyaki Sauce every 2 minutes for about 8–10 minutes or until burgers are fully cooked through. Serve in hamburger buns or pita bread with shredded lettuce, salad greens, and tomato and cucumber slices.

Barbecue Spare Ribs

There are dozens of variations of this recipe; every Chinese chef would have his very own favorite recipe for barbecue ribs. Some call for the ribs to be par-boiled prior to being cooked, others for the ribs to be roasted in a tin foil package. This recipe, from Naranjan McCormack, is one that I have found to be very successful and simply delicious. It is, of course, a very popular appetizer in many restaurants in the West. When serving barbecued ribs as an appetizer, always provide a finger bowl as the only way to enjoy these ribs is to eat with your fingers!

2 racks of pork spareribs
1 teaspoon fresh ginger, peeled and finely grated
2 garlic cloves, crushed
1 tablespoon dry sherry
1/4 level teaspoon nutmeg, freshly ground
a pinch Chinese 5-spice powder
2–3 heaped tablespoons hoisin sauce
2 tablespoons honey

Garnish
lettuce, peppers, and slices of lemon

Using a sharp knife, slice the rack of ribs into individual pieces. If the ribs are rather small, then you would be advised to slice the ribs into twos, otherwise the meat on the ribs tends to dry out a little on barbecuing.

Place the spareribs, ginger, and garlic together into a very large bowl and add the sherry, nutmeg, and the 5-spice powder, and mix together. Then add the hoisin sauce and mix thoroughly.

Cook on the barbecue or, alternatively, line a large roasting pan with tin foil, leaving the tin foil to extend generously out over both ends. Layer the spareribs into the tin-foiled roasting pan. Fold over the tin foil, making a loose wrap, and roast the pork spareribs in a preheated oven at 400°F (200°C) for approximately one hour.

Then open out the tin foil wrap, and baste the ribs. Leave the foil open and return the ribs to the oven for about 10 minutes. Then glaze the ribs with the honey and return to the oven for another 5–10 minutes. Serve hot, garnished with lettuce, peppers, and lemon slices or wedges.

Barbecued T-Bone Steak or Rib Steak

T-bone or rib steaks, 2–2 1/2 inches (5–6-cm) thick
salt and freshly ground pepper
olive oil

toothpicks soaked in cold water

Trim the excess fat off each steak, leaving between 1/4-inch (5-mm) and 1/2-inch (1-cm). Score in several places (keep the excess pieces of fat to grease the griddle of the barbecue). If necessary, secure the tail of each steak with a toothpick that has been soaked in water.

Just before cooking, brush each steak with a very little olive oil and season generously with salt and pepper. Set the rack 4–6 inches (10–15cm) above the hot coals to preheat it, grease the griddle with some of the excess fat, and sear the steaks for 1–2 minutes on each side on the hottest part of the barbecue. Then turn onto the fat for a minute to brown it. Move the steak to a cooler part of the barbecue or raise the grill rack 1–2 inches (2.5–5cm) higher. Continue to grill until the beef is cooked to your taste. Allow a further 12-15 minutes for rare, 16–20 minutes for medium, and 25–30 minutes for well done.

This is a rough guide; it's best to judge by feel. If the meat feels soft when pressed with the tongs, it is rare; if springy, it is medium; but if it feels quite firm and stiff, it is well done.

Transfer the steak to a carving board; let rest for 10 minutes, then remove the toothpick and discard. Cut the meat off the bone and cut across the grain into 1/4-inch (5-mm) thick slices. Serve immediately on hot plates with Béarnaise Sauce, Horseradish Mayonnaise (both on page 586), or Garlic Mayonnaise (page 584).

Baked Potatoes with Dill and Yogurt Sauce

Serves 16

Of course these potatoes can equally be baked in a hot oven, but the flavor of potatoes cooked in coals is just so delicious that it is worth the bother.

16 large floury potatoes

Dill and Yogurt Sauce
2 cups sour cream or fromage blanc
2 teaspoons Dijon or grainy mustard
1 cup plain yogurt
6 tablespoons fresh dill, chopped
1/2 teaspoon salt
sugar to taste

Scrub the potatoes well, prick them in 3 or 4 places with the tip of a knife. Wrap them in tin foil and bury in the hot coals of a barbecue for 45–60 minutes. Meanwhile, mix all the ingredients together for the sauce. To serve, cut a cross in the top of each potato and spoon in some dill and yogurt sauce.

Right: Baked Potatoes with Dill and Yogurt Sauce

Butterflied Shrimp with Chili and Ginger

Serves 4

Isaac's restaurant in Cork serves these as an appetizer. Customers complain every time they try to take them off the menu!

24 scampi or tiger shrimp (uncooked)
salt and freshly ground pepper

Chili and Ginger Sauce (available in Asian stores)

Garnish
cilantro leaves
4 segments of lemon

First "butterfly" the shrimp. Remove the head from the shrimp, leaving the tails on, and split lengthwise. Remove the intestine (see page 254). Open them out flat keeping them attached at the tails. Place in a large bowl and season with salt and pepper.

Just before cooking, douse with chili and ginger sauce and toss well. Barbecue on both sides for 4–6 minutes and, when cooked, transfer to a plate and serve immediately, garnished with fresh cilantro leaves and a segment of lemon.

Barbecued Shrimp with Tartare Sauce

Serves 4

Tiger shrimp may also be used; try tossing them in sea salt and harissa first.

24 jumbo scampi, whole and uncooked
olive oil
sea salt or Kosher salt
Tartare Sauce (see page 585)

Toss the shrimp in the oil and season with sea salt. Barbecue the shrimp whole, turning from side to side until cooked through. Serve in their shells with Tartare Sauce.

Flat-capped Mushrooms with Garlic and Fresh Herbs

Makes 15–20

15–20 flat-capped mushrooms, depending on size
2/3 cup extra-virgin olive oil
2 tablespoons herbs, such as thyme, parsley, chives, and marjoram, chopped
2–4 large garlic cloves
sea salt and freshly ground black pepper

Arrange the mushrooms on a flat tray and sprinkle with the olive oil, herbs, and garlic; leave for 15–30 minutes, turning occasionally. Put gill side up on the barbecue. Season and grill for 6 minutes or until cooked through. Serve as they are, or with Garlic Butter (see page 588).

Flat-capped Mushrooms with Asian Chili Dressing

Serves 8

Another Antony Worrall-Thompson brainwave.

8 flat-capped mushrooms
1/4 cup extra-virgin olive oil
1 teaspoon sesame oil

Dressing
1/4 cup olive oil
2 teaspoons soy sauce
2 tablespoons dry white wine
1/2 red chile, seeded and chopped
2 garlic cloves, finely sliced
1 teaspoon honey
1 1/2 tablespoons mint, freshly chopped
2 tablespoons cilantro leaves, roughly chopped
1 teaspoon zest of orange (optional)
salt and freshly ground pepper

Remove the stalks from the mushrooms. Mix the olive and sesame oils, brush over the mushrooms, and season them with salt and pepper. Cook them gill side up on the barbecue for 5–6 minutes until cooked through.

Meanwhile make the dressing: put the olive oil, soy sauce, wine, chile, garlic, and honey in a small saucepan, bring to a boil and cook until reduced a little, then remove from the heat. Add the mint, cilantro, and orange zest. Season with salt and pepper. When the mushrooms are cooked, arrange them on a large serving plate and spoon the dressing over them. Serve warm or cold.

Goat Cheese in Vine Leaves

Serves 6

12 large fresh vine leaves
6 pieces of goat cheese, or use Feta, Gruyère, Emmenthal, Cheddar, or Mozzarella, cut into 2 x 1/2 inch (5 x 1cm) pieces

Blanch and refresh the vine leaves quickly and dry with paper towels.

To assemble: take a vine leaf and put a piece of cheese in the center of the "veiny" side. Fold over the edges to make a wrap, put the wrap on a second vine leaf, and wrap tightly with the seam underneath. Grill over the barbecue until the cheese starts to melt inside, about 5 minutes on each side. Unwrap and eat with crusty bread. The leaves may be eaten or discarded.

Barbecued Scallions

Serves 6

18 large scallions
3 tablespoons olive oil
sea salt or Kosher salt

Wash the scallions, trim the root ends, and cut into 6-inch (15-cm) lengths. Drizzle with oil, season with salt and pepper, and toss onto the barbecue. Cook over medium heat until golden on one side, turn and let cook on the other side.

Bananas wrapped in Bacon

bananas
thin slices of bacon

Peel the bananas and cut into chunks about 2–2½ inches (5–6cm) long (depending on the width of the bacon strips). Wrap each piece in bacon and secure with a toothpick that has been soaked in cold water. (Toss the bananas in fresh lemon juice if prepared ahead.) Cook on the barbecue 4–6 inches (10–15cm) from the coals for 5 minutes.

Master Recipe

Fruit Kabobs

Makes 16 kabobs approx.

8 peaches or nectarines
8 apricots
24 cherries
16 strawberries
4 bananas
fresh lemon juice
orange liqueur (Cointreau or Grand Marnier)
¾–1 cup superfine sugar
whipping cream

Cut the peaches or nectarines, and apricots in halves, discarding the pits, and keep the strawberries and cherries whole. Peel the bananas and cut into large chunks about ¾ inch (2cm) long and sprinkle with a little lemon juice. Mix the fruit in a bowl, sprinkle with orange liqueur, and macerate for about 15 minutes.

Thread the fruit onto skewers. Roll in superfine sugar and barbecue for 5–8 minutes or until they start to caramelize. Serve immediately with a little softly whipped cream. For real excitement, pour some of the liqueur over each, ignite them, and serve immediately. Otherwise just drink the marinade with the kabobs later on!

Variation

Cut Apple Kabobs

dessert apples cut into large chunks, or quarters, sprinkled with lemon juice

Just before cooking, toss in or paint with melted butter, sprinkle with superfine sugar, and thread onto skewers. Grill for 5–8 minutes or until golden and caramelized.

Note: The fruit can also be cooked in tin foil papillotes on the barbecue.

Black Pudding with Golden Delicious Apple Sauce

Serves 12 for canapés, 4–6 as an appetizer

12 slices best quality black pudding (blood sausage), about ½-inch (1-cm) thick
olive oil
1 tablespoon whole grain mustard
1 teaspoon honey

Golden Delicious Apple Sauce (see page 597)

First make the Apple Sauce.

Brush the slices of black pudding with olive oil. Barbecue until crisp on both sides. Mix the grainy mustard with the honey. Put a dollop on the top of each piece of black pudding and serve with Golden Delicious Apple Sauce.

Below: Fruit Kabobs

finger food

finger food

Wow! Haven't canapés come a long way. When I was little, a neighbor gave a cocktail party and I was so intrigued and exalted that I went around to help her prepare the food. I was amazed to find little chunks of cheese and grapes on cocktail sticks poking out of a melon. I thought it was the most exciting and sophisticated thing I'd ever seen.

Since those days, Lorna Wing and others have well and truly liberated us from all those predictable canapés. We can now let our imagination run riot and come up with some delicious little bites, from teeny weeny portions of fish and chips to mini poppadoms, sushi to shepherd's pie!

Canapés are most often served with drinks at cocktail parties and at occasions such as weddings and funerals. More and more people are entertaining by serving larger canapés, served one by one over a period of perhaps an hour. These may include hamburgers in buns, Thai fish cakes, wontons, spring rolls... Many canapés may be used as appetizers, too.

Presentation

Finger food is often fiddly to present and even more difficult to eat – especially if you have a glass of wine in one hand. Use your imagination to come up with creative ways of serving. Chinese porcelain spoons are an attractive solution, particularly if your canapé needs to be served with a little sauce. Delicious morsels may be threaded onto skewers or satay sticks to make perfect, easy-to-eat finger food. Sprigs of woody herbs, such as rosemary, make creative alternatives to the usual cocktail sticks and skewers.

Tiny cardboard boxes are good for crispy croquettes and raita, shot glasses for liquid canapés, tin or plastic sand buckets with crumpled paper are great for fish and chips. Oyster shells, scallop shells, and egg cups are other options. Tiny cups with saucers are perfect for serving portions of hot or cold soup.

Attractive serving platters are vitally important for presentation. One can use china, plastic, rushes, baskets, sushi and split cane mats, slate, and galvanised tin plates. Be careful that they are not too heavy or the server will be exhausted from carting them around. Balsa wood circular boxes that large bries are sold in are also terrific. Virginia creeper leaves, vine leaves, and even fig leaves are also very effective. Now that we have a banana tree in the garden, we love to serve finger food on its shiny, green leaves.

Don't forget to provide cocktail sticks, napkins, and suitable containers for your guests to discreetly deposit their used cocktail sticks, bones, and seeds into.

What to Serve, When

At a drinks party, start by serving savory canapés with your cocktails, wine, or champagne. About two-thirds of the way through the evening, you may want to switch to a good dessert wine and replace your savory selection with delicious sweet canapés such as petits fours, little lemon tartlets, and glazed strawberries.

Variety and balance are essential. If the situation allows, serve both hot and cold canapés, and balance meat dishes with vegetarian.

Choose the canapés carefully so you have a contrast of flavors and texture – some mild, some hot and spicy, some perennial favorites. You may also want to balance expensive canapés which include shrimp or lobster with a less extravagant but delicious and ever-popular favorite like Irish Cheddar Cheese Croquettes with Ballymaloe Relish.

Quantities

Fingerfood should be bite-sized, for easy eating and handling. On the whole, you will need to allow 6 or 7 canapés per person. However, if your guests are coming straight from work, they may be very hungry so allow between 7 and 9 helpings per person. You may also want to make the portions more substantial. If guests have already eaten, 5 or 6 will be adequate.

In case of emergency, you may want to keep some really good-quality cocktail sausages on hand. They are quick to prepare and are very tasty tossed with grainy mustard and honey. These can be produced if it looks like the food might run out. Ballymaloe Brown Bread (page 478) and smoked salmon is another fantastic standby. Salmon can be thinly sliced and served in a variety of quick and delicious ways (it's great with cucumber pickle).

Suggested Bases and Toppings

Here is a list of bases that we regularly make and use.

White bread or croutons, 1–1½ inches (2.5–4cm) round or square
Round, square, or diamonds of brown yeast bread or pumpernickel
White or brown cheese biscuits
Tiny pieces of Melba toast
Water biscuits
Cucumber sliced into ¼-inch (5-mm) rounds
Tiny tartlet shells
Tiny poppadoms
Tiny pitas
Savory drop scones
Crostini
Crostini cups
Round toasts and heart toasts
Corn griddle cakes
Hot potato cakes
Shrimp crisps

The bases can be combined with all sorts of toppings, so let your imagination run riot. Don't forget to season, and taste, taste, taste!

Tiny rosettes of smooth pâtes (such as Chicken Liver or Crab Pâté) can be piped onto little biscuits or pieces of Melba Toast. Tartlets can be filled with any quiche mixture, and cooked at the last minute. Potato cakes served with a little smoked salmon or warm smoked trout, garnished with dill and crème fraîche, is another canapé that will have them coming back for more.

For an Eastern flavor, spoon a little Mint Chutney or Mango Relish or Spicy Eggplant onto miniature poppadoms, or top shrimp crisps with spicy toppings or salsas.

One of the problems with canapés is that many of them need to be assembled at the last moment. If they are prepared too far in advance, they can become tired, limp, and soggy. This is particularly true when using porous bases such as shrimp crisps. Put the toppings on at the last possible minute, otherwise they will melt through. Nonetheless you can do a little preparation: arrange the bases on serving trays and have garnish ready to go.

Fingerfood Etiquette

Surprisingly, not everyone seems to realize that it is bad form to double-dip. To circumvent this, cut crudités into single bite-sized pieces.

Briouates

Makes about 25

Moroccan briouates are little stuffed wraps of paper-thin pastry deep-fried in oil. Favorite fillings are ground meat, shrimp, and chicken. If you do not like frying, you can bake them in the oven for 30 minutes at 350°F (180°C).

The pastry leaves, ouarka, are so difficult and time consuming that I substitute phyllo instead. The traditional shapes are triangles, rectangles, and cigars. This recipe comes from Claudia Roden's Mediterranean Food, which I love.

8 ounces (225g) phyllo pastry sheets
1 egg yolk, beaten
sunflower oil for deep-frying
confectioners sugar, optional
cinnamon, optional

Filling for briouates de kefta (ground meat pastries)
12 ounces (350g) lean beef (1½ cups)
½ large onion, finely chopped
small bunch of cilantro, finely chopped
small bunch of parsley, finely chopped
1 teaspoon cinnamon
pinch of ground ginger
salt
pinch of cayenne (optional)
3 tablespoons sunflower oil
4 eggs, lightly beaten

Mix together all the filling ingredients except the eggs, then transfer the mixture to a frying pan. Cook gently for a few minutes, stirring until the moisture evaporates and the meat separates. Drain off the fat, then add the eggs and stir until they set to a slightly scrambled consistency.

Cut the phyllo sheets into rectangles about 5 inches (12.5cm) wide and stack them on top of each other. Take a sheet of dough and put a heaped teaspoon of filling at one end and fold into a triangle. Stick the loose edge down with a little egg yolk. Fry in hot oil 350°F (180°C) until crisp and golden. Drain on paper towels and serve sprinkled with confectioners sugar and cinnamon, if you wish.

This combination of sweet and sour is a quintessential Moroccan flavor.

Salmon with Tomato and Ginger in Phyllo

Serves 8 as an appetizer

8 sheets phyllo pastry
¾ stick (⅓ cup) melted butter
8 x 2-ounce (50g) pieces wild Irish salmon
2½ tablespoons fresh ginger, peeled and grated
5 tablespoons tomato concassé (see page 48), seasoned with salt, freshly ground pepper, and sugar
salt and freshly ground pepper

egg wash: 1 egg beaten with a pinch of salt

Hollandaise Sauce (see page 581)

Garnish
sprigs of flat-leaf parsley or fennel
well-seasoned tomato concassé

Preheat the oven to 450°F (230°C).

Unfold the pastry dough and brush the top sheet with melted butter. Put a piece of salmon in the center of the short end of the dough and season with salt and pepper. Sprinkle with a little ginger and 2 teaspoons of tomato concassé.

Roll the pastry from the end once, then fold in the long sides and then roll over and over into a wrap. Brush with melted butter and put onto a baking tray.* Repeat with the others. Brush with egg wash just before baking. Cook in the oven for 10–12 minutes.

Meanwhile, make the Hollandaise sauce. Arrange the phyllo wraps on a hot plate with a little sauce, garnish with sprigs of flat-leaf parsley or fennel, and a little tomato concasse.

* May be prepared ahead to this point.

Phyllo Triangles

phyllo dough
melted butter

Filling of your choice
1 x Mushroom a la Crème (see page 197)
1 x Piperonata (see page 190)
scallops in Mornay Sauce (see page 252)

Preheat the oven to 450°F (230°C).

Cut a sheet of phyllo into 3-inch (7.5-cm) strips lengthwise. Put the strips on top of each other. Brush the top one with melted butter. Put 2 teaspoons of your chosen filling at the front edge. Wrap the pastry dough around and then fold over and over into a triangle; seal the edge with melted butter. Repeat with the others until all the filling is used up.

Brush with melted butter and bake in the oven for 15–20 minutes. Arrange on a warmed plate and serve immediately.

Anchovy and Mustard Sticks

Makes about 25

8 ounces (225g) Puff Pastry (see page 456)
Dijon mustard
about 24 anchovies, drained
egg wash made from 1 beaten egg
2½ tablespoons Parmesan cheese, grated

Preheat the oven to 350°F (180°C).

Roll the pastry dough into 2 rectangles, 1/8-inch (3-mm) thick. Trim the edges. Smear one piece of pastry with mustard, then arrange 4 rows of anchovies in lines lengthwise about an inch (2.5cm) apart. Put the other sheet of pastry dough on top and seal. Refrigerate just before cooking. Egg wash the pastry, sprinkle with grated Parmesan, cut into 1/2-inch (1-cm) wide strips widthwise and bake for 15–20 minutes, or until crisp and golden.

Variation

Anchovy and Sesame Seed Straws

Omit the mustard from the recipe above, and replace the Parmesan with 2 1/2 tablespoons sesame seeds.

Cheese Straws

Makes 30–40

2 cups all-purpose flour
salt and freshly ground pepper
1 stick (1/2 cup) butter
2 cups Parmesan, freshly grated
beaten egg
paprika

Preheat the oven to 400°F (200°C).

Sift the flour and seasoning into a bowl and rub in the butter to make fine breadcrumbs. Mix in the Parmesan. Stir in enough beaten egg to make a rough dough. Turn out and knead on a lightly floured surface until smooth. Roll out to 1/2-inch (1-cm) thick and cut into straws.

Put onto a greased baking sheet and cook in the oven for 8 to 10 minutes until lightly browned and quite crisp. Cool on a wire rack. While still warm, sprinkle with paprika.

Parmesan Crisps

Makes 8–12

4 cups grated Parmesan

1 sheet wax paper

Preheat the oven to 350°F (180°C).

Draw out circles about 4 inches (10cm) in diameter on the wax paper. Carefully fill the circles with the Parmesan. Spread the cheese in an even layer out to the edges of each circle. Cook in the moderate oven for 5–8 minutes, until golden and bubbly. Remove from the oven and let cool on the tray. Place gently on to a wire rack. The crisps may also be molded into shapes just before they get cold. Store in an airtight container.

Note: Be careful not to over-cook or they will taste bitter.

Cucumber Boats Stuffed with Tapenade

Makes about 20–24 pieces

Tapenade will keep for several weeks in a covered jar in the fridge, it is also wonderful served as a dip with raw vegetables.

1 English cucumber

Tapenade (see page 588)

First make the Tapenade.

Peel the cucumber, cut in half and remove the seeds with a melon baller or a teaspoon. Spoon the Tapenade into the center of each cucumber boat, cover with plastic wrap and refrigerate for about one hour, so the cucumber will be crisp and easy to slice. Cut into 1¼-inch (3-cm) pieces with a sharp knife, arrange on a plate, and serve.

Stuffed Red and Yellow Cherry Tomatoes

Delicious little red and yellow cherry tomatoes are now available almost all year round in the stores. They make perfect canapés, if you have the patience to scoop out the centers, and may be stuffed with many different fillings.

Cherry Tomatoes Stuffed With Shrimp

Makes 20

20 cherry tomatoes
20 cooked shrimp
2–3 tablespoons homemade Mayonnaise (see page 584)
1 teaspoon finely chopped chives or parsley
salt and freshly ground pepper

Cut a slice off the round end of the cherry tomatoes and scoop out the seeds with a small melon baller. Reserve the lids.

Mix the shrimp with the Mayonnaise, add a few drops of lemon juice, season, and add some chopped chives or parsley. Carefully fill the tomatoes, replace the lids, and arrange on a large plate lined with dark green salad leaves, e.g., arugula or watercress.

Alternative filling

20 black olives, pitted
10 anchovy fillets

Cut the anchovy fillets in half and wrap a piece around each black olive and pop one into every hollowed-out tomato, replace the lid. These are strong and delicious.

Other filling suggestions

Tapenade (see page 588)
Cream cheese with finely chopped mint
Cold cooked fish or shellfish, mixed with French dressing
Cold scrambled egg with chives and finely chopped smoked salmon (see page 99)
Fromage blanc with chives or dill
Crab mayonnaise

Roasted Almonds

unpeeled almonds
sea salt or Kosher salt
olive oil

Preheat the oven to 350°F (180°C).

Put dry, whole, unpeeled almonds on a baking sheet, and roast until golden and crisp, 10-15 minutes. Toss in a little olive oil and sea salt, cool.

Bacon and Banana Rolls

Makes about 12

6 large slices of bacon
6 bananas

Peel the bananas, and cut both the bananas and bacon slices in half. Wrap the pieces of bacon around the banana halves and place under the broiler. Cook for about 7 minutes, turning often, until the bananas are quite soft and the bacon slices crisp.

Note: These are great on the barbecue, too.

Crispy Potatoes with Sweet Chili Sauce & Sour Cream

Serves 4

1½ pounds (700g) potatoes
Sweet Chili Sauce (available from Asian grocers)
sour cream

Scrub the potatoes and cook in boiling salted water until tender. Drain and cool. Cut into wedges. Deep-fry in hot oil until crisp and golden. Drain on absorbent paper towels. Season with salt. Serve immediately with a bowl of sweet chili sauce and sour cream on each plate.

Note: Rustic Roast Potatoes may also be used (see page 181).

Crostini with Spiced Eggplant

Makes about 24

For this dish, I do think it makes a difference to salt the eggplants before cooking.

Topping
2 eggplants
1 teaspoon salt
1/4 cup olive oil
1 large onion, peeled and finely chopped
4 ripe tomatoes, skinned and coarsely chopped
sugar
1/2 teaspoon ground cumin
1/2 teaspoon ground allspice
pinch of cayenne pepper
2 garlic cloves, crushed
2 tablespoons raisins
1 heaped tablespoon fresh mint, chopped
1 heaped tablespoon fresh cilantro, chopped

24 crostini, 1/4-inch thick (5-mm) (see page 67)

Garnish
plain yogurt and fresh mint leaves (optional)

Cut the eggplants into 1/2-inch (1-cm) cubes. Put them in a colander and sprinkle with a little salt. Mix together with your hands and let drain for 20–30 minutes.

Meanwhile, heat 3 tablespoons of the olive oil in a pan and fry the onions until golden. Add the tomatoes, a pinch of sugar, and the spices. Stew gently for 5–10 minutes, then stir in the garlic and remove from the heat. Stir in the raisins.

Tip the eggplant into a clean dishtowel and gently squeeze them dry. Put the remaining olive oil in your largest frying pan and heat until smoking.

Add the eggplant and stir-fry briskly until thoroughly golden and cooked through. Stir in the onion and tomato mixture, and the fresh herbs. Tip into a bowl and let cool. Taste, and add more seasoning if necessary. Spoon a little spiced eggplant onto each warm crostini. Top with a little blob of yogurt and a sprig of mint, if you fancy.

Greek Salad Kabobs

Makes 20

1/2–1 crisp English cucumber, cut into cubes
20 cherry tomatoes
20 Kalamata olives
6 scallions, cut into 1-inch (2.5-cm) pieces
4–5 ounces (110g–150g) Feta or Knockalara ewe's milk cheese, cut into cubes (about 1–1 1/4 cups)

Dressing
3 tablespoons extra-virgin olive oil
1 tablespoon lemon juice, freshly squeezed
2 tablespoons annual marjoram, chopped
sprigs of flat-leaf parsley
salt, freshly cracked pepper, and sugar

20 or so satay sticks

Thread a piece of cucumber, tomato, olive, scallion, and a chunk of feta onto one end of a satay stick. Arrange on a round plate with the salad towards the center. Just before serving, whisk the dressing, sprinkle over each kabob, and serve immediately.

Olives

There are many sorts of olive; Greece is famous for its almost almond-shaped blue-black Kalamatas, and Italy has the Gaeta olives, all black and wrinkled. Spain comes in with tasty green Manzanillas and the French with Picholines and Niçoise. Olives can be cured in many ways – including dry, oil, lye, brine and water. They can be pitted and then stuffed – often with capers, anchovies, or pimientos. They can be also be seasoned with a variety of flavorings such as garlic or cumin seeds.

Green or Black Olive Purée

1 1/3 cups green or black olives, pitted
1/2 cup extra-virgin olive oil

Put the pitted olives and oil in a food processor and pulse to purée coarsely. Transfer to a sterilized jar. Pour a layer of extra-virgin olive oil over the top. The purée will keep, covered, in a fridge, for 1–2 weeks.

Note: Pouring a thin layer of olive oil over foods in jars – such as olive purée or tomato purée – makes the food last longer by excluding the air.

Marinated Olives

Serve with drinks or as part of an antipasta

2 1/2 cups black olives, Kalamata or Niçoise
1 teaspoon chili flakes
1/2–1 teaspoon cumin, freshly crushed
lemon juice, freshly squeezed
1/2 cup extra-virgin olive oil

Mix the ingredients in a bowl and let marinate for at least 15 minutes.

Marinated Black or Green Olives

Marinated olives are served in all Greek tavernas; each has its own version.

8 ounces (225g) olives (Kalamata, Vollos, Moroccon Picholine, Tunisian Salhi)
1 garlic clove, crushed
1/2 teaspoon hot paprika
1 tablespoon sherry or red wine vinegar
pinch ground cumin
2 tablespoons extra-virgin olive oil

Mix all the ingredients together and store in a jar. This way the olives will keep for several months.

Shrimp with Sage Leaves

Makes 20

10 slices of bacon
20 sage leaves
20 raw scampi, de-veined and peeled
20 button mushrooms
oil for deep frying
Rouille

Cut each slice of bacon in half crosswise and, with the back of a knife, stretch each slice.
Place 1 sage leaf on each scampi, then wrap a piece of bacon around each one.

Thread a mushroom, then a scampi onto each of 20 cocktail sticks. Heat the oil over medium heat and deep fry the skewers until the bacon is golden and the scampi are pink. Drain on paper towels and serve hot with Rouille.

Avocado, Red Onion, and Cilantro Salsa on Mini Poppadoms

Makes 25

Best made close to serving time; if you must make it ahead, omit the seasoning until just before serving.

1 avocado
3 very ripe tomatoes, seeded and diced
1 small red onion, finely diced
1/2–1 green chile, finely diced (optional)
2 tablespoons fresh cilantro, coarsely chopped
juice of 1 lime, freshly squeezed
a pinch of sugar (optional)
salt and freshly ground pepper

25 mini poppadoms (see page 492)
vegetable oil for deep-frying

Peel and pit the avocado and cut it into a dice similar in size to the tomato. Put into a bowl along with the onion, chile and cilantro, add the freshly squeezed lime juice, season with salt and pepper, and toss gently.

Taste and add a pinch of sugar, if necessary. Heat the oil to 350°F (180°C) and deep-fry the poppadoms. Drain on paper towels.

Just before serving, spoon the salsa onto the poppadoms.

Oyster Shooters

Makes 24–28

These were all the rage at drinks parties in Australia when I went to "Tasting Australia" in Adelaide.

2 1/2 cups mirin
1 3/4 cups sake
2 1/2 tablespoons Japanese rice vinegar
2 tablespoons soy sauce
2 tablespoons wasabi mustard powder
24–28 oysters

24–28 shot glasses

Put the mirin and sake into a sauté pan, bring to a boil and let it flambé. When the flames die down, turn off the heat, pour into a Pyrex measuring cup and let cool.

Add the vinegar and soy sauce, and whisk in the wasabi powder. Cover and chill in the fridge overnight.

Just before serving, open the oysters and put one into each shot glass. Cover with chilled liquid (leaving the sediment behind in the measuring cup). Serve immediately.

Rillettes of Fresh and Smoked Salmon on Cucumber Slices

Serves 15–20

The texture of this pâté should resemble that of pork rillettes, where the meat is torn into shreds rather than blended.

1 tablespoon butter
6 ounces (175g) smoked salmon
1 tablespoon water
1 1/2 sticks (3/4 cup) softened butter
6 ounces (175g) salmon, freshly cooked
salt and freshly ground pepper
pinch of nutmeg
lemon juice to taste
1 English cucumber

Garnish
sprigs of chervil, fennel, and chives

Melt the butter in a saucepan over low heat, add the smoked salmon and water. Cover and cook for 3–4 minutes or until it no longer looks opaque. Let it get quite cold.

Cream the softened butter in a bowl. With two forks, shred the fresh and smoked salmon and mix well together. Add to the softened butter, still using a fork (do not use a food processor). Season with salt, pepper, and nutmeg. Taste. Add lemon juice, as necessary.

Cut the cucumber into 1/4-inch (5-mm) thick slices. Arrange on a plate or flat basket and put a dollop of soft salmon pâté on top of each slice.

Garnish with a sprig of chervil, fennel, or some chives. Sprinkle with chive or fennel flowers too, if you have them.

Note: Chicken Liver Pâté (see page 79), Salmon Pâté and Smoked Mackerel Paté (see page 85) make great finger food, piped onto slices of cucumber or tiny pieces of Melba Toast (see page 78).

Right: Rillettes of Fresh and Smoked Salmon on Cucumber Slices

Tiny Smoked Salmon Sandwiches

Makes 24

butter
12 slices Ballymaloe Brown Yeast Bread (see page 478)
12 thin pieces of smoked salmon
freshly ground pepper
lemon

Garnish
sprigs of fennel or dill

Butter the slices of bread and make a double-decker sandwich with the smoked salmon. Season each layer with pepper and a few drops of lemon juice, then butter the top of the sandwich. Trim a slice of smoked salmon to fit the top exactly, and press down onto the butter. Then trim off the crusts and cut the sandwiches into 6 tiny squares. Garnish each with a tiny sprig of fresh fennel or dill, and serve.

Note: Good quality salami can be used instead of smoked salmon; add a little chopped parsley to the butter for the bread.

Smoked Salmon with Sweet Cucumber Pickle on Ballymaloe Brown Yeast Bread

Makes 20

20 small slices Brown Yeast Bread (see page 478)
20 thin slices smoked salmon from tail end
20 teaspoons Sweet Cucumber Pickle (see page 514)
freshly ground pepper

Garnish
chervil and wild garlic flowers

First make the Sweet Cucumber Pickle.

Cut the bread thinly and butter it. Roll each piece of salmon into a loose rosette and put a little drained Cucumber Pickle in the center.
Place on top of the bread and continue with the rest. Garnish with chervil and wild garlic flowers, if available. Serve.

Rory O'Connell's Fish Kabobs

Makes 20–30

1 red pepper, cut into ½-inch (1-cm) dice
1 green pepper, cut into ½-inch (1-cm) dice
1 medium onion, cut into ½-inch (1-cm) dice and sweated in 2 tablespoons butter
5 ounces (150g) black sole fillet, cut into ½-inch (1-cm) dice
5 ounces (150g) salmon, cut into ½-inch (1-cm) dice
olive oil for frying
1 tablespoon chopped chives
salt and freshly ground pepper

Thread cocktail sticks with the above. Just before serving, fry them gently in a little olive oil – season, and sprinkle with chopped chives. Serve immediately.

Parma Wraps

Makes about 20

10 slices Parma ham (or other prosciutto)
about 20 balls of ripe melon
20 long chives

If the slices of Parma ham are large enough, cut them in half. Put one large melon ball into the center of a piece of ham, gather up the edges to enclose the filling, and tie with chives. Cover and chill until ready to serve.

Bread Sticks with Prosciutto

Roll a half-slice of prosciutto di Parma around the end of a bread stick. Delicious.

Teeny Yorkshire Puddings with Rare Roast Beef and Horseradish Sauce

Makes about 28

Charbroil a thick sirloin steak to medium rare, rest, and thinly slice just as needed to make these delicious puds. You will need one or two muffin trays with tiny 1½-inch (4-cm) openings.

1 cup all-purpose flour
2 eggs
1¼ cups milk
1 tablespoon butter, melted

sunflower oil for greasing the muffin cups
Horseradish Sauce (see page 586)
6–8 ounces (175–225g) rare roast beef

Garnish
arugula or flat-leaf parsley leaves

Preheat the oven to 450°F (230°C).

To make the batter: sift the flour into a bowl, make a well in the center, and drop in the eggs. Using a small whisk or wooden spoon, stir continuously, gradually drawing in flour from the sides, and adding the milk in a steady stream at the same time. When all the flour has been incorporated, whisk in the remainder of the milk and the cool melted butter. Let stand for one hour.

Heat the muffin tray in the oven, grease the insides of the muffin cups with sunflower oil, and fill half-full with batter.

Bake in the preheated oven for 15 minutes or until crisp, golden, and bubbly. Remove from the tray and cool on a wire rack.

To serve: Fill each pudding with a tiny dollop of Horseradish Sauce. Top with a thin sliver of rare roast beef. Garnish with a sprig of flat-leaf parsley or an arugula leaf. Serve soon – best freshly cooked.

Thai Curry Morsels

Makes 30

1 lb. (450g) skinless and boneless chicken breasts
1/2 stick (1/4 cup) butter
1 3/4 ounces (45g) fresh root ginger, peeled and finely chopped
2 garlic cloves, crushed
1/4 teaspoon green peppercorns
1 stalk lemongrass, finely chopped
2 red chiles, finely chopped
1 teaspoon homemade Chicken Stock (see page 36)
1/2 teaspoon lime juice, freshly squeezed
1/2 teaspoon ground coriander
1 3/4 cups coconut milk (Chaokoh)
2 teaspoons cilantro leaves, freshly chopped
salt and freshly ground pepper

Cut the chicken in 30 even-sized cubes. Heat half the butter in a large frying pan and sauté the chicken pieces until lightly browned on all sides. Set aside to cool.

Melt the remaining butter in the pan, sauté the ginger, garlic, peppercorns, lemongrass, and chiles. Add the chicken stock, lime juice, and ground coriander. Gradually stir in the coconut milk, bring to a boil, then reduce the heat and simmer for 8–10 minutes.

Warm the sauce gently, stir in the cilantro leaves, and season to taste. Place a morsel of chicken on a chinese soup spoon. Spoon some sauce over the top, and garnish with cilantro leaves.

Above: Teeny Yorkshire Puddings with Rare Roast Beef and Horseradish Sauce

Alternatively, spike with cocktail sticks and arrange on a serving dish. Spoon the sauce over the chicken or serve separately as a dipping sauce. The chicken pieces may also be reheated in the sauce and served hot.

Spicy Chicken Wings

Serves 4–6, depending on whether they are served as finger food or main course

Chicken wings have become a great favorite; there are lots of delicious marinades one can use – freshly chopped herbs and olive oil are perfect also.

2 lbs. (900g) chicken wings

Marinade
1 tablespoon Szechwan peppercorns, toasted and ground
1 tablespoon garlic, crushed
3 tablespoons ginger, grated
3 tablespoons orange zest, finely grated
4 scallions, finely chopped
1 red chile, finely chopped
2 tablespoons honey
2 tablespoons soy sauce
2 cups sunflower oil
1/2 cup sesame oil
salt and freshly ground pepper

Combine all the marinade ingredients in a large bowl. Add the chicken wings and toss in the marinade until well coated. Let marinate for at least 4 hours or better still, overnight.

Preheat the oven to 350°F (180°C).

Spread the chicken wings on 1 or 2 roasting pans and cook in the oven, turning several times, for about 35 minutes. Serve just as they are or with Red Chile Mayonnaise (see page 585).

Ginger & Sesame Chicken Wings

Serves about 10

In our house, we squabble over the chicken wings; for me they are the tastiest part with perhaps the oyster pieces at the base of the legs a close runner up. Tossed in a little olive oil, freshly chopped herbs, and sea salt, and roasted until crisp and golden, they are lip-smackingly good. Alternatively, try this recipe – irresistible too, and easy to remember: 2 of everything.

2 ounces (50g) untoasted sesame seeds (1/2 cup)
2 lbs. (900g) chicken wings

Marinade
2 fluid ounces (50ml) honey (1/4 cup)
2 fluid ounces (50ml) red wine (1/4 cup)
2 fluid ounces (50ml) soy sauce (1/4 cup)
2 teaspoons ginger, peeled and freshly grated

Mix all the marinade ingredients together. Boil for 2–3 minutes in a small saucepan. Add the sesame seeds and let it get cold.

Separate the wings into joints, if attached, and discard the pinion (see page 277).

Marinate the wings for a few hours or better still, overnight. Preheat the oven to 400°F (200°C) and cook for 30–45 minutes. Serve hot or at room temperature.

Irish Cheddar Cheese Croquettes

Makes 50–60, depending on size

We get into big trouble if these crispy cheese croquettes are not on the Ballymaloe lunch buffet every Sunday. They are loved by children and grown ups, and are a particular favorite with vegetarians.

2 cups milk, infused with a few slices of carrot and onion
1 small bay leaf, 1 sprig of thyme, and 4 parsley stalks
1 cup Roux (page 580)
2 egg yolks
2 cups shredded sharp Cheddar
1 tablespoon chives, chopped (optional)
salt and freshly ground pepper

seasoned flour
beaten egg
fine dried breadcrumbs

Put the cold milk into a saucepan along with the carrot, onion, and herbs, and bring slowly to a boil. Simmer for 3–4 minutes, turn off the heat, and let infuse for about 10 minutes if you have enough time.

Strain the carrot, onion, and herbs and either discard them or, if you have a stockpot on the go, rinse them and add to the pot. Return the milk to a boil and whisk in the roux, bit by bit; it will get very thick but persevere. (The roux always seems like there's too much, but you need it all so don't decide to use less.) Season with salt and pepper. Cook for 2 minutes over gentle heat, then remove from the heat. Stir in the egg yolks, cheese, and chives. Taste and correct seasoning. Spread out on a wide plate to cool.

When the mixture is cold or at least cool enough to handle, shape it into balls about the size of a golf ball, weighing about one ounce (25g) each. First roll in seasoned flour, then in beaten egg, and then in fine breadcrumbs, and chill until firm. Bring them back to room temperature before cooking, otherwise they may burst. Just before serving, heat a deep-fat fryer to 300°F (150°C), cook the cheese croquettes until crisp and golden. Drain on paper towels and serve hot, with a green salad and perhaps a good tomato chutney.

Note: Cooked cheese croquettes can be kept warm in an oven for up to 30 minutes. They can also be frozen and reheated in an oven.

Left: Ginger & Sesame Chicken Wings

petit fours

Ballymaloe Fudge

Makes about 96

Ivan Allen, my father-in-law, could never resist Ballymaloe fudge at the end of a meal, no matter how good the dinner had been. We remember him every time we eat a piece of fudge.

2 sticks (1 cup) butter
1 x 14-ounce (410ml) can evaporated milk
a scant cup water
4½ cups light brown sugar or 4 cups granulated sugar
1 tablespoon pure vanilla extract

jelly roll pan, 9 x 13 inches (23 x 33cm)

Melt the butter in a heavy saucepan over low heat. Add the milk, water, sugar, and vanilla extract, and stir with a whisk until the sugar is dissolved. Turn up the heat to simmer, and stir constantly until it reaches the soft ball stage. To test, put a blob of the fudge into a bowl of cold water. It should be firm but malleable.

Take the saucepan off the heat, put the base of the saucepan into cold water, and stir until the fudge thickens and reaches the required consistency. Pour into a jelly roll pan and smooth out with a spatula. Let cool and then cut before completely cold.

Note: Evaporated milk is made by heating milk slowly in a strong vacuum to reduce the temperature at which it boils. Most of the water content evaporates and this thickened "milk" is then sterilized when the temperature is rapidly raised. Condensed milk is evaporated milk which has been sweetened to preserve it.

Chocolate Cups

Makes 8–10

4 ounces (110g) best-quality dark chocolate (about 2/3 cup)
20 chocolate paper cups – use fluted paper candy cups

Melt the chocolate until smooth in a very low oven or in a bowl over simmering water. Put 2 paper cups together and spread melted chocolate evenly over the inside of the paper cup, using the back of a teaspoon. Check that there are no "see through" patches when you hold them up to the light; if there are, spread a little more chocolate in that area. Stand the paper cups upright to dry. Chill until they set hard, then carefully peel the paper off the cups (it is a good idea to do a few extra cups to allow for accidents).

Note: Chocolate cups can be bought now in supermarkets. The quality of the chocolate has improved so much that they are perfectly acceptable. The paper cups or bon bon cups can be bought from a specialty kitchen shop.

Suggested Fillings

Bailey's Chocolate Cups

Fill chocolate cups with Bailey's Irish Cream liqueur – enjoy!

Sue's Hazelnut Whirls

Fill chocolate cups with 1 toasted hazelnut. Pipe a rosette of Ganache (see right) on top. Dust with unsweetened cocoa powder.

Tiramisu

Fill the cups with Tiramisu (see page 409).

Ballymaloe Chocolates

Makes 24–30

24–30 chocolate cups (see left)

Chocolate Ganache
2/3 cup cream
4 ounces (110g) best-quality dark chocolate, roughly chopped (about 2/3 cup)
1–2 teaspoons rum or orange liqueur (optional)

Decoration
Crushed Praline (see page 400) or crystallized violets or unsweetened cocoa powder

First make the Chocolate Cups (see left). Make a few extra cups to allow for accidents or thefts!

Next make the Chocolate Ganache: put the cream in a heavy, preferably stainless steel saucepan and bring it almost to a boil. Remove from the heat and add the chocolate. With a wooden spoon, stir the chocolate into the cream until it is completely melted. Transfer the chocolate cream to the bowl of a food mixer and let it cool to room temperature. Add the liqueur and whisk until it is just stiff enough to pipe. (Careful: it splits very easily if you over-whisk.)

To assemble: Using a pastry bag and a 3/8-inch (8-mm) star nozzle, pipe a rosette of the mixture into peeled Chocolate Cups. Decorate each one with a little crushed praline or a crystallized violet leaf or a dusting of unsweetened cocoa powder.

Chocolate

According to legend, it was the god, Quetzalcoatl, who first taught the Aztecs how to make chocolate from the beans of the wild cocoa tree, *Theocroma Cocao* – *Theocroma* meaning "food of the gods." When we started the Ballymaloe Cookery School in the early eighties, it was still difficult for the general public to buy good cooking chocolate and we had to buy enormous quantities at a time in order to get the top quality chocolate we wanted to use. Nowadays, many brands of good chocolate are available such as Lindt, Menier, Suchard, Lesmé, Callebaut, and Valrhona. Chocolate varies enormously in flavor. Different brands not only taste different but react differently in recipes, so experiment and choose a chocolate or chocolates to suit your taste and recipes. Working with chocolate is a fascinating art that requires skill and patience.

Melting chocolate

Chocolate needs to be melted with great care. It burns easily and is then irretrievable. Below is how we do it:
Break the chocolate into even-sized pieces. Put into a Pyrex bowl, place the bowl over a saucepan of water, and bring the water slowly to almost simmering point. Turn off the heat immediately and let the bowl sit over the saucepan of hot water. The water must not boil as the chocolate softens. Stir occasionally. Do not allow even a drop of water to get into the chocolate or the chocolate will block or seize. If this happens, no amount of stirring will remedy the situation; however, if a few drops of vegetable oil or clarified butter are added, it will loosen the mixture to the extent that it can be blended with other ingredients.

Note: If you need a large quantity of chocolate, do it in batches.
Chocolate may also be melted in the microwave in a pyrex or plastic bowl, or in a double boiler on the stove. Different brands of chocolate melt at different rates.

Types of Chocolate

Bitter or Unsweetened Chocolate
Bitter or unsweetened chocolate is just that – a cocoa mass with just a little cocoa butter added. The percentage of cocoa butter varies from brand to brand. It keeps well and gives chocolate dishes a wonderfully expensive taste. Available in specialty stores and most supermarkets, and well worth seeking out.

Dark Chocolate
Bittersweet or semisweet chocolate. This must contain at least 35% cocoa solids (cocoa mass and cocoa butter). The higher the percentage of cocoa solids, the better quality the chocolate. Check the label, many good brands of chocolate bars now have cocoa solids from 50–70%. As a general rule, the higher the amount of cocoa solids, the darker and more bitter the chocolate will be. For chocolate with a high percentage of cocoa solid, seek out Valrhona, Lindt, Menier, and Suchard.

Milk Chocolate
Made from cocoa mass and milk which is usually added in condensed or dried form. It must contain at least 10% cocoa mass and at least 12% milk solids. Both dark and milk chocolate can have fruit, nuts, ginger, coffee, and nut pastes added. Milk chocolate can be substituted for dark chocolate in most recipes, but the flavor will be different.

White Chocolate
White chocolate is not, strictly speaking, a chocolate. It contains no cocoa mass, it is merely a mixture of cocoa butter, sugar, and flavoring. Buy the best quality, otherwise it will be difficult to melt. Store in airtight containers; if it picks up moisture from the air, it will be impossible to melt properly and may crack.

Chocolate Flavored Coverings or Confectionery Coatings
A sweetened combination of vegetable fat instead of cocoa butter, flavoring, and sometimes low-fat cocoa powder and/or dry milk solids. Understandably, it does not taste as good as chocolate and is much less expensive. They also come in a variety of pastel colors.

Couverture
This is the chocolate of choice for most food professionals and pastry chefs. Couverture is a *quality* rather than a *type* of chocolate, with at least 32% cocoa butter. Quality varies from one brand to another; some have a much higher cocoa butter content and have been conched* for two or even three days. The best melt beautifully and are perfect for molding, coating, and hand dipping. Converture is sold through wholesalers and specialty kitchen shops.

Chocolate drops and chocolate chips
These are graded pieces of chocolate designed to stay whole while baking. Good for cookies, cakes, and desserts.

Tempering Chocolate
Some chocolate (e.g., couverture) needs to be "tempered" to stabilize the high cocoa butter content. Electric tempering machines are available but it can be done by hand. The chocolate is first heated to 110°F (43C°) and then cooled to 80°F (26C°), then heated once more to 90°F (40C°) before use. When chocolate is tempered it will cool with a perfect sheen.

Cocoa powder
Cocoa powder is derived from cocoa mass or cocoa liquor which has almost all the cocoa butter removed. The pressed cake is then ground into a powder called cocoa.

Dutch-Processed Cocoa
Dutch-processed cocoa has been alkalized. During manufacturing, an alkali in the form of a soluble salt, such as potassium carbonate, neutralizes the natural acidity of the cocoa bean, thereby raising the Ph level. Cocoa that has been Dutch-processed is usually darker in color than the non-alkalized or "natural" cocoa. The latter has a stronger, more chocolaty flavor.

* Conching is the final blending stage in the making of chocolate. The longer the conching, the better for chocolate.

Ballymaloe Chocolates and Cream

Serves 10

10 Chocolate Cups (see page 559)
whipped cream or pouring cream

First make the Chocolate Cups, then let them cool and set. When they are hard, carefully peel off the paper.

To serve: Arrange the chocolate cups on a plate, fill each with a rosette of whipped cream or pouring cream. Your guests can drop the cream-filled chocolate cups into their coffee and let them melt or, alternatively, they may just pour in the cream and eat the chocolate – delicious either way.

Ballymaloe Chocolates with Grapes and Kirsch

Makes about 12–14 chocolates

12–14 Chocolate Cups (see page 559)

12 small green grapes
6 tablespoons Stock Syrup (see page 568)
1 tablespoon Kirsch

First make the Chocolate Cups.

Peel the grapes and remove the seeds. Put them into a small bowl, pour the syrup and Kirsch over them, and let macerate for about 10 minutes. Put a grape into each chocolate cup and pour the syrup on top. Serve as soon as possible, certainly within 2 hours.

Note: Best quality dark chocolate should be melted very gently to avoid destabilizing the formulation and making it look whitish on the outside. It can become hard and grainy if melted too fast. Always buy the best quality chocolate you can afford.

Ballymaloe Chocolates with Banana, Walnuts, Rum, and Raisins

Makes 12

Jamaica rum is quite different in color (dark versus clear) and flavor from Bacardi rum, and should be used in all these recipes

12 Chocolate Cups (see page 559)

2 tablespoons raisins
1–2 teaspoons Jamaica rum
2 rounded tablespoons banana (diced to about the same size as raisins)
2 level tablespoons chopped walnuts

Cover the raisins with hot water and let swell for 2 hours. Drain, then mix the plumped up raisins, rum, banana, and walnuts together. Taste, fill into little chocolate cups and serve in fluted paper candy cups.

Mary Jo's Chocolates

Makes about 50

Even though these homemade chocolates are a little fiddly, believe me, when you taste them you will reckon it was worth every minute!

1¼ cups cream
8 ounces (225g) best-quality dark chocolate, roughly chopped (about 1⅓ cups)
½–1 tablespoon rum or orange liqueur

For coating the chocolates
8 ounces (225g) best quality dark chocolate
2 tablespoons tasteless oil (peanut or sunflower)

Put the cream in a heavy, preferably stainless steel saucepan and bring it almost to a boil. Remove from the heat and add the chocolate. With a wooden spoon, stir the chocolate into the cream until it is completely melted.

Transfer the chocolate cream to the bowl of a food mixer and let it cool to room temperature. Add the liqueur and whisk until it is just stiff enough to pipe. Using a pastry bag and a ⅜-inch (8-mm) plain nozzle, pipe the mixture into small blobs onto a tray lined with wax paper.

Smooth the top of the chocolates with your finger or better still, a teaspoon dipped regularly in iced water. Put the tray in the fridge to let the chocolates set.

Meanwhile, gently melt the chocolate to coat the chocolates, and stir in the oil. When the chocolates have become quite cool, with the help of 2 forks, dip them into the melted chocolate and coat them evenly. Place on a wire tray and let set. The chocolates are now ready to be served or may be decorated further by dribbling the top with more melted chocolate.

Store in a covered container in a cool place. They are best eaten on the same day but will, in fact, keep for 3 or 4 days.

Agen Chocolate Prunes

Makes 22

From Agen, a town in Aquitaine in the south of France, this is the aristocrat of prunes; soft and melting. Guaranteed to convert even the most ardent prune hater.

8 ounces (225g) best-quality dark chocolate
22 Agen prunes, pitted

Melt the chocolate gently in a Pyrex bowl over barely simmering water. Turn off the heat just as soon as the water comes to a boil; the chocolate will gradually melt in the hot bowl. Dip the prunes, one at a time, into the chocolate. Shake off excess chocolate and let set on a baking tray covered with wax paper.

Ballymaloe Chocolate Truffles

Makes 30–40

6 ounces (175g) best-quality dark chocolate
2 squares (2 ounces [50g]) unsweetened chocolate
1 tablespoon Jamaica rum
$^{3}/_{4}$ stick ($^{1}/_{3}$ cup) unsalted butter
2 tablespoons cream
3 ounces (75g) praline, finely crushed
melted chocolate and unsweetened cocoa powder for finishing

Melt the chocolate over gentle heat to a thick cream with the rum. Remove from the heat, stir in the butter bit by bit, then add the cream and praline. Put small teaspoonfuls onto wax paper. When set, have the melted chocolate ready. Put a little on the palms of the hands and lightly roll the truffles between them. Toss into a bowl of unsweetened cocoa powder. Brush off the surplus and put on racks to dry (see illustrations above).

Left: Ballymaloe Chocolate Truffles

Fruit and Nut Clusters

Makes 24

5 ounces (150g) best-quality dark chocolate
3 heaped tablespoons hazelnuts, shelled and toasted
3 heaped tablespoons raisins

Melt the chocolate in a Pyrex bowl very gently over simmering water or in a very low oven. Stir in the hazelnuts and raisins. Drop clusters onto a baking sheet with a teaspoon. Let set in a cool place. Put into dark brown fluted paper candy cups.

Chocolate-dipped Strawberries

Makes as many as are in the carton!

1–2 cartons strawberries
4 ounces each (110g) dark and white chocolate or 8 ounces (225g) dark or white chocolate

Melt each chocolate carefully in a very low oven or in separate bowls over simmering water. Hold each strawberry by the calyx and dip it into either the white or dark chocolate about three-quarters of the way up. Let drain slightly and place it on a baking tray lined with wax paper or tin foil, to set. Arrange on a white plate.

Meringue Kisses with Chocolate or Cocoa

Makes about 40

2 egg whites
1 cup confectioners sugar

Decoration
4 ounces (110g) dark chocolate or 1/4 cup unsweetened cocoa

Line several baking sheets with wax paper.

Make the Meringue mixture (see page 394). Put the mixture into a pastry bag fitted with a tiny rosette nozzle. Pipe tiny rosettes onto baking sheets. Bake in a low oven at 300°F (150°C) for 30–45 minutes, or until the meringue nests will lift easily off the paper. Turn off the oven and let them cool in the oven.

Arrange the "kisses" on a plate and dredge with unsweetened cocoa powder. You could also dip the spiky tops of the meringue in melted chocolate and let it set.

Melanie's Meringue Hearts

Makes 20–25

Adorable little heart-shaped meringues, perfect for wedding finger food or buffets.

Meringue mixture (see page 394)

whipped cream
silver dragees (balls)

Preheat the oven to 300°F (150°C). Make the meringue mixture and pipe into tiny heart shapes before baking on trays lined with wax paper.

Let cool before decorating each with a piped rosette of cream and a silver dragee.

Coconut Kisses

Makes about 40

2 egg whites
1/2 cup superfine sugar
1 3/4 cups dried coconut
40 hazelnut halves (optional)

Decoration
unsweetened cocoa (optional)
whipped cream (optional)

Preheat the oven to 300°F (150°C).

Line 2 baking sheets with wax paper. In a spotlessly clean bowl, whisk the egg whites with the sugar until very stiff, then gently fold in the dried coconut.

Drop teaspoonfuls of the mixture onto the baking sheet. Pop a hazelnut on top of each one, if you like. Cook in the preheated oven for 15–20 minutes or until crisp and dry. Let cool on the tray. Dredge some with unsweetened cocoa and leave some plain.

Glazed Fruits

Use unhulled strawberries, cherries with their stalks, grapes, segments of tangerine or clementine or physalis.

1 cup sugar
1/2 cup water

Dissolve sugar in the water in a heavy saucepan. Bring to a boil and cook to a light caramel. Carefully dip the fruits into the caramel to glaze them lightly. Put them immediately onto wax paper or onto an oiled surface where the glaze will set hard. Keep in a dry place and serve in individual fluted paper petit four cups within an hour.

Lemon Petit Fours

Preheat oven to 475°F (250°C). Fill tiny fluted paper petit four cups with a blob of Lemon Curd (see page 510), and pipe a rosette of meringue on top. Bake in the oven for 60 seconds.

Candied Peel Dipped in Sugar or Chocolate

Cut freshly made Candied Peel (see page 515) into 1/4–1/2-inch (5mm–1cm) thick slices and roll it in superfine sugar and serve with coffee. Alternatively, dip one end of Candied Orange Peel in melted dark chocolate, let set, and serve.

Caramelized Walnuts

Makes 20

40 walnut halves
3 ounces (75g) marzipan (1/3 cup)

Caramel:
a scant cup sugar
1/2 cup water

To make the caramel, combine the sugar and water in a heavy saucepan and stir over gentle heat until the sugar fully dissolves. Bring to a boil, remove the spoon, and cook until the caramel is golden brown. Do not stir or shake the pan. If sugar crystals form around the side of the pan, brush them down with cold water. When the caramel is ready, use it immediately or it will become hard and cold.

Sandwich the walnut halves together with marzipan, then coat them in caramel. Let them harden on an oiled jelly roll pan, in a dry place. Serve in fluted paper cups.

Tuiles D'Amandes

Makes about 15–20

2 tablespoons butter
1/2 cup superfine sugar
3 egg whites
1/2 cup flour
1 1/2 tablespoons almonds
few drops of vanilla extract

Preheat the oven to 425°F (220°C).

Beat the butter and sugar together. Blend in the egg white carefully. Sift the flour over the mixture and add the almonds and a few drops of vanilla. Gently mix until a smooth batter is obtained. With a teaspoon, smooth the batter into 4-inch (10-cm) circles quite thinly on a baking tray lined with wax paper.

Place in the oven and cook until golden brown, about 10 minutes. Remove immediately from the oven and, with a flexible metal spatula, transfer them to a tuile tray or lay them over a rolling pin. They will set very quickly and should be light and brittle. It is a good idea to bake just 2 tuiles first to see if the thickness and the size of the tuile is correct. If the batter proves to be too thick, it can be thinned out with a little extra egg white.

Strawberry Amandine

Serves 24

1 1/4 cups peeled almonds
3/4 cup superfine sugar
2 ounces (45g) candied angelica
1–2 egg whites
12 fresh strawberries

24 petit four paper cups

Grind the almonds in a food processor with the sugar. Cut some of the angelica into little sticks, to resemble strawberry stalks, and put aside until later. Chop the remaining angelica finely and mix it with the almonds and sugar. Moisten the mixture with enough egg white to make a paste.

Wash, hull, and dry the strawberries. Sprinkle a board with superfine sugar. Take a ball of paste for each strawberry and flatten on the board into a circle about 2 inches (5cm) across, 1/8-inch (3-mm) thick.

Place a strawberry in the middle of each, and mold the paste around. Cut in half, place the reserved angelica sticks in at one end to resemble stalks, and serve in petit four paper cups. Serve within 4 hours.

Almond Sticks

Makes about 28

8 ounces (225g) phyllo pastry sheets
3/4 stick (1/3 cup) unsalted butter, melted
2 1/2 cups ground almonds
1/2 cup superfine sugar
1/4 cup orange blossom water
confectioners sugar, for decorating

Preheat oven: 325–350°F (170–180°C).

Cut the sheets of phyllo into 4 rectangles and put them on top of each other so that they do not dry out. Brush the center of each rectangle with melted butter.

Mix the ground almonds with sugar and orange blossom water. Put 1 teaspoon of the filling at the end of each rectangle. Roll up into a cigar shape, folding the longer sides in over the filling midway. Brush with melted butter and bake in the oven for 20–30 minutes, or until slightly colored. Serve cold, sprinkled with confectioners sugar.

Note: These pastries may be deep-fried instead. The oil should not be too hot and they only need a few minutes until they are lightly colored. Phyllo pastries may be made in 2 shapes, cigars or triangles. If the pastries are filled with spinach, they are sometimes made into snail shapes but the triangular shape is also used.

Marzipan Dates

Makes 28

Use up any scraps of almond paste for these dates. The best dates, in my opinion, are Medjool dates from north Africa. They are fat and juicy with thin skin and have less fiber than many of the other dates.

28 fresh Medjool dates
4 ounces (110g) toasted almond paste or Marzipan (about a heaped 1/3 cup) (see page 443)
superfine sugar

Split one side of the date and remove the pit. Roll a little piece of marzipan into an oblong shape and fit it neatly into the opening. Smooth the top and roll the stuffed date in sugar. Repeat the procedure until all the dates and marzipan are used up. Dip in finely chopped pistachio nuts, if you like.

drinks

Every evening in Ballymaloe there's a special children's tea at 5.30pm. The children choose what they'd like to eat and this is served with lots of homemade lemonade – exactly the same lemonade that Myrtle originally devised for her children to take to school instead of fizzy drinks. Now the students make this and many variations on the theme everyday at the school. These drinks are so quick to make and refreshing. The basic syrups keep for ages in the refrigerator and can also be frozen. We also make refreshing non-alcoholic drinks from the leftover syrups of compôtes such as rhubarb and strawberry, gooseberry and elderflower, plum and apricot, by diluting them with water and lemon juice if necessary and adding lots of ice. We're also into fancy ice cubes, so we pop all sorts of things into the icetrays – herb leaves such as mint, lemon balm, and sweet cicely, as well as violas, marigold petals, pomegranate seeds, cranberries, fraises des bois, and raspberries.

Master Recipe
Stock Syrup

Makes 3½ cups

2 cups sugar
2½ cups cold water

To make the Stock Syrup: dissolve the sugar in the water over gentle heat and bring to a boil. Boil for 2 minutes, then let it cool. Store in the fridge until needed.

Flavored Syrups

These are flavored stock syrups in reality.

Rosemary

Follow the Master Recipe, adding 2 sprigs of rosemary to the pan along with the sugar and water. Strain when cool, before storing. Use this as the basis of lemonades or fruit compôtes.

Sweet Geranium

Follow the Master Recipe, adding 6–8 sweet geranium leaves to the pan along with the sugar and water. Strain when cool, before storing.

Lavender

Follow the Master Recipe, adding 1–2 tablespoons of lavender to the sugar and water in the pan. Strain when cool, before storing.

Mint

Follow the Master Recipe, adding 4–6 sprigs of fresh mint, preferably spearmint, to the sugar and water in the pan. Strain when cool, before storing.

Rose Hip Syrup

Makes 5 cups (1.2 liters)

This syrup is bursting with vitamin E. Use either wild rose hips (Rosa cavina) or the hips of Rosa rugosa. Serve with ice cream or use as the basis for a drink.

2 lbs. (900g) rose hips
a scant 3 quarts (2.6 liters) water
2 cups (450g) sugar

Bring 2 quarts (1.8 liters) of water to a boil. Meanwhile chop or mince the rose hips and immediately add them to the water. Return to a boil. Remove from the heat and let infuse for 15 minutes.

Strain through cheesecloth or a fine nylon sieve. Put the pulp back into the saucepan, add another 3¼ cups of water and return to a boil, infuse, and strain as before. Pour all the juice into a clean saucepan and reduce, uncovered, to 3½ cups. Add the sugar, stir until dissolved, and let boil for 5 minutes.

Pour the syrup into sterilized screw-cap bottles and seal tightly. It will keep for months.

Elderflower Syrup

6 heads of elderflowers
¾ cup superfine sugar
2½ cups cold water
zest and juice of 2 unwaxed lemons

Put the sugar and water into a saucepan over medium heat. Stir until the sugar dissolves, add the elderflowers, bring to a boil for 5 minutes, remove from the heat, and add the zest and juice of the lemons. Set aside to cool. Cover, and let infuse for 24 hours. Strain and bottle. Dilute as desired.

Homemade Lemonades

If you keep some chilled "stock syrup" made up in your fridge, all these fresh fruit drinks are simplicity itself to make. They contain no preservatives so they should be served within a few hours of being made. Many different types of citrus fruit may be used.

Master Recipe
Orange and Lemonade

4 lemons
2 oranges
about 2 cups Stock Syrup (see left)
about 6 cups water

Garnish
sprigs of fresh mint or lemon balm

Juice the fruit and mix with the stock syrup, adding water to taste. Pour into glasses, add an ice cube or two, garnish with sprigs of fresh mint or lemon balm, and serve.

Variation
Limeade

5 limes
1 1/4 cups Stock Syrup (see left)
3 cups water
ice cubes

Garnish
sprigs of fresh mint or lemon balm

Follow the Master Recipe, using limes. Taste, and add more water, if necessary.

Lemongrass Lemonade

Serves 6 approximately

If you want to have access to exotic ingredients in a rural area, the only solution is to grow them yourself. We've been growing lemongrass for several years and now have so much that we can afford to use it in all sorts of delicious ways. This is a refreshing and delicious drink.

Lemongrass Syrup

2 1/2 cups water
2 cups sugar
2 stems lemongrass, finely sliced

To make the syrup: put the cold water and sugar into a saucepan along with the lemongrass. Bring slowly to a boil and simmer for 2 minutes. Let get cold.

Lemongrass Lemonade

3 lemons
4 cups water
1 cup lemongrass syrup

Juice the lemons. Mix the juice, water, and the cold lemongrass syrup in a pitcher. Mix well, taste, and add more water, if necessary. Serve chilled

Limoncella (Lemon Liqueur)

Makes 3 pints (1.5 liters) of delicious dynamite!

5 ripe, unwaxed lemons
2 cups vodka
2 cups sugar
2 cups water

fine sieve or piece of cheesecloth

Remove the peel from the lemons with a swivel top peeler. Put the zest in a large glass jar or bottle, capable of holding 1 1/2 quarts (1.5 liters). Pour in the vodka, cover, and let stand in the sun for 8 days for the flavor to be extracted from the ingredients.

To make the limoncella: put the sugar and water into a saucepan. Bring to a boil, stirring to dissolve the sugar, simmer for 10 minutes, then set aside to cool.

Pour the lemon-flavored vodka through a fine sieve or cheesecloth, discard the zest, and then pour the strained liquid back into the jar. Stir in the sugar syrup. Mix well and leave for at least 10–15 days before drinking. Serve chilled as an aperitif. Better still if you can resist, keep it for several months before drinking, it will taste exquisite.

Rosemary Lemonade

Makes 4–6 glasses

A delicious, thirst-quenching lemonade inspired by The Herb Farm in Seattle.

juice of 3 lemons, freshly squeezed
1 cup Rosemary Syrup (see page 568)
4 cups water

Mix the lemon juice with the syrup and water. Add a little more syrup or water, if necessary.

Ginger and Limeade with Star Anise Ice Cubes

Makes 8–10

1/2 cup lime and/or lemon juice, freshly squeezed
1 tablespoon finely grated fresh, peeled ginger
3/4 cup sugar
2 cups water

Mix the lime juice with the ginger in a bowl. Put the sugar and water into a saucepan and bring to a boil, stirring constantly to dissolve the sugar. Let the syrup boil for 30 seconds, then let it completely cool. Add to the lime-ginger mixture. Cover, and chill thoroughly.

Serve with star anise ice cubes (see page 575) and dilute with water to taste.

Black Currant Leaf Lemonade

Serves about 6

2 large handfuls of young black currant leaves
2 1/2 cups water
1 cup granulated sugar
juice of 3 freshly squeezed lemons
3–4 cups still or sparkling water
ice cubes

Crush the black currant leaves tightly in your hand (this helps to bring out the flavor) then put them into a stainless steel saucepan along with the water and sugar. Stir to dissolve the sugar and bring to a boil slowly. Simmer for 2–3 minutes, then set aside to cool completely. When cold, add the spring or sparkling water, taste, and add more water, if necessary. Serve chilled with lots of ice.

Herb Teas and Infusions

We make fresh herb teas or infusions a lot. I've got a particular aversion to the little tea bags that are frequently used. If you have fresh herbs, all you need to do is pop a few into a pot and pour in the boiling water. Infinitely more delicious. I'm very wary about ordering herb tea in a restaurant for this reason, but one Paris restaurant I dined in recently served herb infusions in the most delightful way. The waiter came to the table with several china bowls of fresh herbs on a silver salver. With tiny silver tongs he put the guest's chosen herb into a little china teapot, poured in boiling water, and served it with flourish. Exquisite.

Bring fresh cold water to a boil. Scald a china teapot, take a generous pinch of fresh herb leaves (such as lemon verbena, rosemary, sweet geranium, lemon balm, spearmint, or peppermint), and crush them gently in your hand. The quantity will depend on the strength of the herb and how intense an infusion you enjoy. Put them into the scalded water. Pour the boiling water over the leaves, cover the teapot, and let them infuse for 3–4 minutes. Serve immediately in china cups.

Left: Ginger and Limeade with Star Anise Ice Cubes

Master Recipe
Moroccan Mint Tea

Serves 4

2 teaspoons Chinese green tea
5 tablespoons chopped mint, preferably spearmint
4 cups water
sugar, to taste

To decorate
4 lemon slices (optional)
4 small mint sprigs

Heat a teapot with boiling water, then throw out the water. Add the tea and mint to the pot. Fill it with fresh boiling water. Let it infuse and stand for 5 minutes.

Pour the tea through a strainer into warmed glasses or small cups. Add sugar to taste (remember, in Morocco, tea is supposed to be very sweet), and decorate each glass or cup with a lemon slice, if you like, and a sprig of mint.

Variation
Iced Mint Tea

Follow the Master Recipe, adding the sugar to the pot with the tea and mint. After steeping, pour the tea through a strainer over cracked ice so it cools quickly. Serve in cold glasses with ice cubes, decorated in the same way.

Sharbat (Apple Milk Drink)

For 2–4 people

2 red eating apples
2 tablespoons granulated sugar or 2 scant teaspoons rosewater or orange-flower water
2 1/4 cups cold milk
shaved ice (optional)

Peel, core, and cube the apples. Put into a blender, along with the sugar, orange-flower water, and milk. Whizz at high speed for 15 seconds. Serve, with shaved ice, if desired, in small glasses.

Homemade Ribena

This concentrated black currant cordial, packed with vitamin C, is delicious diluted with sparkling or plain water or sparkling wine – it keeps for several months in a cool place. My sister-in-law, Hazel Allen, gave me this recipe.

2 1/2 pounds (1.1kg) black currants
6 pounds (2.6kg) sugar (2 cups)
4 quarts plus 1 cup (4 liters) water
1 cup white wine vinegar

Boil the black currants and water together in a stainless steel saucepan for 15 minutes. Strain, and add the sugar to the liquid. Add the white wine vinegar. Boil for 3 minutes. Pour into sterilized bottles and seal well.

Lassi

In India we came across many different Lassi, some sweet and some salty. They can be drunk with meals or as a refreshing beverage on a hot afternoon. The yogurt is rich and wonderful in India, so don't dream of using lowfat yogurt – use the best you can find as a basis.

Salty Lassi

3/4 cup plain yogurt
1 1/2 cups ice and water
good pinch of salt
1 tablespoon fresh mint leaves (optional)

Whizz in a blender for a few seconds. Serve in chilled glasses.

Sweet Lassi

3/4 cup plain yogurt
1 1/2 cups ice and water
1–2 tablespoons superfine sugar
1/4–1/2 teaspoon rose water or kewra.

Whizz all the ingredients in a blender. Pour into chilled glasses and serve immediately.

Laxshmi's Lassi

Serves 1

Laxshmi Nair from Mumbai, whose family own the Leela Palace Hotel, where we spent a wonderful few days on a food trip, made this delicious and refreshing drink.

1/3 cup best quality plain yogurt
3/4 cup water and ice mixed
1/2 green chile, seeded and chopped
2 curry leaves
4 fresh mint leaves
pinch of salt

Put everything in a blender and whizz for a few seconds. Serve in a tall glass.

Leela's Lassi

Serves 1

Leela Palace Hotel's chefs gave me this recipe.

1 cup plain yogurt
tiny pinch saffron stamens
1 tablespoon pistachio nuts
1 teaspoon sugar
1 teaspoon mint

Put the saffron stamens in a tiny bowl with 1 tablespoon of water and soak for 10–15 minutes. Then put everything except the saffron in the blender. Pour into a tall glass and drizzle the saffron over the top.

Smoothie Classic

Serves 2

Smoothies and slushes, now all the rage, are clearly influenced by the lassi of India, and the sherbets of Morocco. This could be the granddaddy of all smoothies, which developed in America and are sweeping Europe and Australia.

1 cup range juice
1 carton fresh strawberries, hulled and quartered
2 fresh bananas, frozen and sliced
honey to taste

Pour the orange juice into a blender. Add the strawberries and bananas. Blend until smooth. Add a little honey to taste.

Hawaii Slushie

Makes 2 large drinks or 4 dessert servings

You can serve this as a dessert or a drink.

1 banana
1 peach
5 ounces (150g) strawberries, sliced (about 1 cup)
5 ounces (150g) mango, cubed (about 1 cup)
1/2 cup orange juice
1 tablespoon honey or syrup, or more to taste
1 tablespoon lemon juice

Peel the banana and cut it into chunks. Spread the banana, peach, strawberries, and mango on a baking sheet and put it into the freezer. It will take about 2 hours to freeze solid.

Place the frozen fruit in a blender. Add the orange juice, honey or syrup, and lemon juice, and whizz until smooth. Serve in a tall glass with a straw.

Tropical Smoothie

Makes 2 large drinks or 4 dessert servings

You can serve this as a dessert or a drink. Served right out of the food processor or blender, it's a delicious dessert sorbet; served in a glass with a straw, it makes a refreshing cooler (add an extra 1/2 cup juice if you are serving it as a drink right away). This recipe comes from More Heartsmart **by Bonnie Stern**

1 banana, sliced
3 ounces (75g) strawberries, sliced (about 2/3 cup)
3 ounces (75g) mango, cubed (about 2/3 cup)
1/2 cup orange juice
1 tablespoon honey, or more to taste
1 tablespoon lemon juice

Spread banana, strawberries, and mango on baking sheet and place in freezer. Freeze until solid, about 2 hours. Place frozen fruit in food processor or blender. Add orange juice, honey, and lemon juice. Purée until smooth. Serve in dessert dishes with a spoon, or in a glass with a straw.

Fruit Punch

Makes about 30 glasses

4 cups sugar
4 sweet geranium leaves (optional)
2 1/2 quarts (2.4 liters) water
4 mandarins or clementines, peeled and thinly sliced
10 oranges
6 lemons, or 4 lemons and 2 limes
4 bananas
10 ounces (275g) small seedless grapes (about 2 cups)

Right: Fruit Punch

Sea Breeze

Serves 1 or 2

1/3 cup cranberry juice
1/3 cup pink grapefruit juice
3 tablespoons vodka
lemon or lime slices

Mix the first 3 ingredients together in a pitcher and pour into tall glasses.

Serve with lots of ice and a slice of lemon or lime.

Frozen Lemon Vodka

Serves 10

1 cup lemon ice cream
1/2 bottle vodka, chilled
tonic water

Chill 10 small tumblers for at least one hour before serving. Scoop out 10 small balls of lemon ice cream and place each in the bottom of the glasses. Pour a shot of vodka over each, and top up with tonic water.

Fresh Tomato Juice

Serves 5

This is only worth making when you have very well-flavored, vine-ripened tomatoes. We make it in late summer when our tomatoes have really developed intense flavor.

1 lb. (450g) very ripe tomatoes, peeled and halved (about 5 small to medium tomatoes)
1 scallion with a little green or 1 slice onion, 2 inches (5cm) in diameter and 1/4-inch (5-mm) thick
3 large basil or mint leaves
2 teaspoons white wine vinegar
1 tablespoon olive oil
1/2 cup cold water
1 level teaspoon salt
1 teaspoon sugar
a few grinds of black pepper

Blend the ingredients together, then strain through cheesecloth or a nylon sieve. Best when fresh, and better not kept more than 8 hours. Serve, unadorned, in tall glasses.

Isaac's Ultimate Bloody Mary

Serves 10

1/4 cup Worcestershire Sauce
1 teaspoon Tabasco sauce
1 teaspoon celery salt
6 tablespoons lemon juice, freshly squeezed
1 tablespoon orange juice, freshly squeezed
1 teaspoon horseradish, grated
1 teaspoon shallot, very finely chopped
2 quarts (1.8 liters) tomato juice, fresh or canned
2 1/2 tablespoons dry sherry
1 cup vodka

Garnish
celery stalks

Blend all but the vodka in a blender. Strain the mixture through cheesecloth or a fine sieve, then stir in the vodka. Serve in glasses over ice, and garnish with a stick of celery.

Sunset Stripper

Serves 4

1/2 cup tequila
1/2 cup triple sec
1/2 cup cointreau
1/2 cup fresh lime juice
3/4 cup fresh pineapple, diced and chilled

Place all the ingredients in a blender and whizz until smooth. Serve in tall glasses.

Claudia Roden's Turkish Coffee

Serves 1

1 very heaped teaspoon pulverized coffee
1 heaped teaspoon sugar, or less to taste
1 small coffee cup water

Although it is more common to boil the water and sugar alone first, and then add the coffee, it is customary in my family to put the coffee, sugar, and water in the kanaka or pot (a small saucepan is not successful), and bring them to a boil together. By "very heaped teaspoon" of coffee I mean, in this case, so heaped that it is more than 2 teaspoons. A level teaspoon of sugar will make a "medium" coffee. Bring to a boil. When the froth begins to rise, remove from the heat, stir, and return to the heat until the froth rises again. Then remove, give the pot a little tap against the side of the stove, and repeat once again. Pour immediately into little cups, allowing a little froth (wesh) for each cup. (Froth is forced out by making your hand tremble as you serve). Serve very hot. The grounds will settle at the bottom of the cup. Do not stir them up or drink them.

Try flavoring the coffee with a few drops of orange blossom water, cardamom seeds (called heil), or a little cinnamon, adding the flavoring while the coffee is still on the stove.

Mexican Hot Chocolate

1 cup water or milk or a mixture
1 1/2 ounces (35g) Mexican chocolate, or 1 1/2 squares any unsweetened (bitter) chocolate

Put the water or milk in a saucepan, together with the chocolate, and slowly bring to a simmer over low heat. Stir continuously until the chocolate has melted, and continue to heat gently for 4–5 minutes to blend the flavors. Pour the chocolate into a pitcher and beat with a molinillo until frothy. If a molinillo is not available, use a whisk or an electric mixer. Pour the chocolate into a mug and serve at once.

Right: Mexican Hot Chocolate

sauces

A complementary sauce, judiciously made and served, can turn a simple meal into a feast. Equally, a sauce that is too abundant or luscious can make a meal seem hopelessly rich and cloying.

Many of the sauces in this chapter are what we refer to as Mother sauces. Once you have mastered the initial recipe, a myriad of daughter sauces can be made by adding some other ingredients to the basic recipe.

Mayonnaise, which is a cold emulsion sauce, can be adapted to make Aoili or Garlic Mayonnaise. Whereas classic Mayonnaise, Hollandaise, Bearnaise, and Beurre Blanc are still much loved, fresh-tasting salsa and pestos are gaining in popularity. People are becoming more adventurous with salad dressing and flavored oil and vinegars. It's well worth being able to master mayonnaise – it seems like a mystery to many people but I show students on every course how one can make homemade Mayonnaise, even by hand, in less than five minutes – it is so fast to make that one would scarcely have found one's car keys to go to the store to buy it.

Hollandaise sauce takes an even shorter time to make and can transform a piece of fresh fish into a feast – the art of sauce making is simple and is well worth mastering.

Roux

Roux is used as a thickener in flour-based sauces and occasionally in gravies. Make in small or large quantities – it's great to have some on hand. Roux can be stored in a cool place and used as needed, or it can be made up on the spot if you prefer. It will keep at least two weeks in a refrigerator.

1 stick (1/2 cup) butter
1 cup white flour

Melt the butter, add the flour, combine, and cook for 2 minutes over low heat, stirring occasionally.

Above: Roux

White Sauce

This method is a marvellously quick way to make White Sauce or Béchamel, if you already have Roux prepared.

2 1/2 cups milk (not lowfat)
1/4 cup Roux (see above)
salt and freshly ground pepper

Bring the milk to a boil, thicken with roux, and season. This simple white sauce can be the basis of a number of flavored sauces.

Mother Sauce
Béchamel Sauce

To make a classic Béchamel, one starts by making Roux in a saucepan. Then gradually add in the milk, whisking all the time to avoid lumps. However, if you already have Roux prepared, it's faster and, we think, equally good to simply whisk Roux into boiling milk to the required consistency.

1 1/4 cups milk (not lowfat)
a few slices of carrot
a few slices of onion
a small sprig of thyme
a small sprig of parsley
3 peppercorns
3 tablespoons Roux (see above)
salt and freshly ground pepper

Put the cold milk into a saucepan along with the carrot, onion, peppercorns, thyme, and parsley. Bring to a boil, simmer for 4–5 minutes, remove from the heat, and let it infuse for 10 minutes.

Strain out the vegetables and herbs, return the milk to a boil, and whisk in the roux to thicken to a light coating consistency. Let it bubble gently for 4–5 minutes. Season with salt and freshly ground pepper, taste, and correct the seasoning, if necessary.

Daughter Sauces
Parsley Sauce

Serve with boiled bacon, ham, poached fish... Follow the recipe for Béchamel or White Sauce until thickened with roux to a light coating consistency. Add 1/2–1 cup freshly chopped parsley and simmer over very low heat for 4–5 minutes. Taste, and correct the seasoning.

Mornay Sauce or Cheddar Cheese Sauce

The classic sauce for cauliflower cheese, leek gratin... Follow the recipe for Béchamel or White Sauce until thickened with roux to a light coating consistency. Add 1 cup sharp Cheddar and 1/4 teaspoon mustard, preferably Dijon. Season with salt and freshly ground pepper, taste, and correct the seasoning, if necessary.

Egg and Parsley Sauce

Serve with vegetables or smoked haddock. Add 2 roughly chopped hard-boiled eggs, plus 2 tablespoons of finely chopped parsley to 2½ cups Bechamel Sauce. You can also add ½–1 tablespoon of finely chopped chives.

Onion Sauce

Serves 8–10

Also known as Sauce Soubise, this sauce is great with roast lamb or pan-grilled lamb chops. Onion sauce is a forgotten flavor which makes a welcome change from the more usual mint jelly.

3 onions, about 1 lb. (450g) in weight, thinly sliced or finely chopped
½ stick (¼ cup) butter
½ teaspoon salt
¼ teaspoon freshly ground pepper
½ tablespoon flour
1¼ cups milk, or 1 cup plus 2 tablespoons milk and 2 tablespoons cream

Melt the butter over gentle heat, add the onions, and cook in a covered saucepan over low heat until really soft but not colored. This may take up to an hour. Season with salt and pepper. Stir in the flour, add the milk, and simmer gently for a further 5 minutes.

This sauce keeps for 3–4 days covered in the fridge and may, of course, be reheated.

Onion and Mint Sauce

Add 2–3 tablespoons freshly chopped mint to the Onion Sauce, above, before serving.

Gluten-free Bechamel Sauce

A recipe from Rosemary Kearney.

2½ cups milk
few slices of carrot and onion
3 peppercorns
sprig of thyme
4 parsley stalks
½ stick (¼ cup) butter
¼ cup cornstarch
¼ cup rice flour
salt and freshly ground black pepper

Put the cold milk into a saucepan along with the carrot, onion, thyme, peppercorns, and parsley. Bring to a boil, simmer for 4–5 minutes, remove from the heat and cool. Strain out the vegetables.

Melt the butter in a saucepan and stir in the flours over low heat. Pour in the milk, whisking continuously, and let it thicken. Season if necessary.

Mother Sauce
Velouté Sauce

This "mother sauce" can be made with veal, chicken, or fish stock. A velouté is usually enriched either with a liaison of egg yolks and cream, or with butter, just before serving. It is very good with fish, poultry, veal, vegetables, and eggs.

2½ cups well-flavored veal, chicken, or fish stock (see page 36)
Roux (see page 580)
salt and freshly ground pepper

Bring the stock to a boil, gradually whisk into the roux, then return to a boil, whisking all the time. Season with salt and freshly ground pepper. Simmer for 5–10 minutes or until the flavor and consistency are what you want.

Daughter Sauces

Sauce Supreme

Serve with chicken. Add 2 tablespoons of cream to the Master Recipe made with Chicken Stock (see page 36). Season, and whisk in ½ stick (¼ cup) butter just before serving.

Mushroom Sauce

Serve with chicken, veal, or fish. Add 1 cup sliced or finely chopped, sautéed mushrooms to a Sauce Supreme before whisking in the butter.

Sauce Aurore

Serve with fish, pork, sweetbreads, and eggs. Add 2 tablespoons of concentrated Tomato Purée (see page 49) to a basic Velouté Sauce. Season, whisk in ½ stick (¼ cup) butter just before serving.

Mother Sauce
Hollandaise Sauce

Serves 4–6; depends on what it is served with

Hollandaise is the mother of all the warm emulsion sauces. The classic version is made with a reduction but, with our superb Irish butter, we rather favor this version which is both easy and delicious. Like mayonnaise, it takes less than five minutes to make and transforms any fish into a feast. You don't need a double boiler or any special equipment, just a good heavy saucepan and a little whisk. Once the sauce is made, it must be kept warm: the temperature should not go above 180°F (350°C) or the sauce will curdle. A thermos flask can provide a simple solution on a small scale, otherwise put the sauce into a porcelain, Pyrex, or plastic bowl in a saucepan over hot but not simmering water.

Tip: Hollandaise Sauce cannot be reheated absolutely successfully. If, however, you do have a little left over, use it to enrich other sauces, enliven a fish pie, or beat it into mashed potato.

2 egg yolks, preferably organic and from free-range hens
2 teaspoons cold water
1 stick (1/2 cup) butter, diced
1 teaspoon freshly squeezed lemon juice, to taste

Put the egg yolks in a heavy stainless steel saucepan over low heat, or in a bowl over hot water. Add water and whisk thoroughly.

Add the butter bit by bit, whisking all the time. As soon as one piece melts, add the next. The mixture will gradually thicken but if it shows signs of becoming too thick or slightly scrambling, remove from the heat immediately and add a tablespoon or two of cold water. Do not leave the pan or stop whisking until the sauce is made.

Finally add the lemon juice to taste. If the sauce is slow to thicken it may be because you are excessively cautious and the heat is too low. Increase the heat slightly and continue to whisk until the sauce thickens to coating consistency.

Tip: If you are making Hollandaise Sauce in a saucepan directly over the heat, it should be possible to put your hand on the side of the saucepan at any stage. If the saucepan feels too hot for your hand, it is also too hot for the sauce. If you are making Hollandaise for the first time, keep a bowl of cold water close by so you can plunge the bottom of the saucepan into it if it becomes too hot.

Daughter Sauces

Cucumber Hollandaise

Ingredients for Hollandaise Sauce (see above)
1/4 English cucumber, peeled and cut into tiny dice
1/2 tablespoon butter
1 teaspoon finely chopped fresh fennel (herb)
salt and freshly ground pepper

Follow the Master Recipe and pour into a bowl and keep warm over hot but not boiling water. Melt the butter and toss the

cucumber in it for 1–2 minutes. Add to the sauce, along with 1 teaspoon of finely chopped fennel.

Tip: If using unsalted butter, all these sauces will need a pinch or two of salt.

Sauce Maltaise (Maltese Sauce)

This is particularly good with asparagus. Cut the zest of half a Seville orange into needle-like shreds, blanch in boiling water for 1–2 minutes, drain, and add to 1 1/4 cups Hollandaise Sauce. Add the juice of half the orange, taste for seasoning, and serve.

Sauce Mireille

Serve with eggs, asparagus, fish, artichoke hearts, Jerusalem artichokes, or variety meats. Add 1 1/2 tablespoons Tomato Purée (see page 49) and 1/2 teaspoon finely chopped basil to 1 1/4 cups Hollandaise Sauce. Taste for seasoning.

Sauce Noisette

Serve with poached eggs, broccoli, asparagus... Use *beurre noisette* rather than ordinary melted butter to make Hollandaise. First, clarify the butter and cook it over medium heat until nut brown. Then proceed as in Master Recipe.

Sauce Moutarde

Add 1–2 teaspoons Dijon mustard to 1 1/4 cups Hollandaise Sauce. Serve with eggs and fish or vegetables.

Sauce Mousseline

Serve with asparagus, fish, chicken, or sautéed sweetbreads. Add a generous 1/4 cup stiffly whipped heavy cream to 1 1/4 cups Hollandaise Sauce. Taste for seasoning.

Quick Hollandaise Sauce

There is an even faster way to make great Hollandaise. Using the same ingredients as for Hollandaise Sauce, melt the butter and heat it until it foams, then gradually pour it into the eggs, whisking all the time until it thickens to a light coating consistency. Taste for seasoning. One can use the same method using a blender or food processor.

Light Hollandaise Sauce

Whisk in 2 tablespoons of water to lighten the sauce.

Bretonne Sauce

A really delicious sauce to serve with prawns or shrimp (see page 252) or poached mackerel.

1/2 stick (1/4 cup) butter, melted
2 eggs yolks, organic, and from free-range hens
1 teaspoon Dijon mustard (we use Maille Verte aux Herbes)
2 teaspoons white wine vinegar
1 tablespoon chopped parsley, or a mixture of chervil, chives, tarragon, and fennel

Melt the butter and let it boil. Put the egg yolks into a Pyrex bowl, add the mustard, wine vinegar, and herbs, and mix well. Whisk the hot melted butter into the egg mixture little by little so that the sauce emulsifies. Keep warm, by placing the bowl in a saucepan of hot but not boiling water.

Mother Sauce

Sauce Beurre Blanc

Makes about 1 cup
Serve 2–3 tablespoons per person

This classic French butter sauce was the darling of the nouvelle cuisine era. In the restaurants of the Loire, its place of origin, it would traditionally be made with fine local butter and Muscadet wine, and served with pike from the river, but is also delectable with other poached fish. It is so versatile, many variations on the master recipe are possible, hence beurre blanc is another mother sauce. As people become more conscious of rich foods, though, this sauce is no longer a "must have" on every menu. That said, try a little with freshly poached fish – it really is exquisite.

1/4 cup dry white wine
1/4 cup white wine vinegar
1 generous tablespoon finely chopped shallots
pinch of ground white pepper
1 generous tablespoon heavy cream
1 1/2 sticks (3/4 cup) unsalted butter, diced
salt, freshly ground pepper
freshly squeezed lemon juice

Put the first four ingredients into a stainless steel saucepan over medium heat. Bring to a boil and reduce down to about a tablespoon. Add 1 generous tablespoon of cream and reduce again until the cream begins to thicken. Whisk in the chilled butter, a piece at a time, keeping the sauce just warm enough to absorb the butter. Season with salt, taste, and add a little lemon juice, if necessary. Keep warm until needed – either transfer to a Pyrex bowl over a saucepan of hot but not boiling water, or put it in a Thermos flask.

Daughter Sauces

Sauce Beurre Rouge

Substitute 1/4 cup red wine and 1/4 cup red wine vinegar for the white wine and white wine vinegar in the Master Recipe. Serve with fish or meat.

Sauce Beurre d'Anchois

Add 2 finely chopped anchovies to the Master Recipe. Serve with beef, fish, or vegetables.

Shrimp Butter Sauce

Add 1 cup peeled cooked shrimp to the Master Recipe. Serve with fish mousse or baked plaice, lemon sole, or turbot.

Lobster Butter Sauce

Add 3/4 cup diced cooked lobster to the Master Recipe. Serve with fish mousse, or poached or baked fish.

Crab Butter Sauce

Add 3/4 cup cooked crab meat to the Master Recipe. Serve as above.

Tip: Beurre blanc can curdle if the pan gets too hot. If this should happen, put 1–2 tablespoons of cream into a clean saucepan, reduce to about half, then vigorously whisk in the curdled mixture, little by little. Serve as quickly as possible. The flavor will be a little softer, so you may need a little more lemon juice to sharpen it up and cut the richness.

Oyster Butter Sauce

Serve with baked sole or fish mousse. Heat 1 tablespoon butter in a frying pan, add 8 freshly opened oysters. Cook for 2–3 minutes, just until the edges are starting to curl, then add a squeeze of lemon juice, and add to the Master Recipe.

Ginger Beurre Blanc

Add a 1-inch (2.5-cm) cube of fresh peeled ginger, cut into small dice, to the wine, vinegar, and shallots, and follow the Master Recipe. Serve as above.

Orange Beurre Blanc

Add the finely grated rind of one organic or unwaxed orange to the Master Recipe. Serve with John Dory or porgy, or whiting. If you cannot find organic oranges, scrub the skin well before using the zest.

Sauce Beurre Rouge
Orange Beurre Blanc
Sauce Beurre d'anchois
Saffron Beurre Blanc
Beurre Blanc

Saffron Beurre Blanc

Soak a good pinch of saffron in the cream. Add to the reduction and continue as in the Master Recipe. Serve with fish and shellfish.

Rosemary Butter Sauce

Add 1 tablespoon of freshly chopped rosemary to the reduction and continue as above. Serve with sole, turbot, or crab claws.

Mother Sauce
Mayonnaise

Mayonnaise is the "mother" of all the cold emulsion sauces, so once you can make a mayonnaise, you can make any of the daughter sauces by just adding some extra ingredients.

The quality of mayonnaise depends totally on the quality of the egg yolks, oil, and vinegar used. A little mustard helps the emulsion. It is perfectly possible to make a bland mayonnaise if you use poor-quality ingredients.

Many mayonnaise recipes call for olive oil, but extra-virgin olive oil will be too strong for most tastes. We use 7 parts sunflower or peanut oil and 1 part extra-virgin olive oil, or 6 to 2 for a more distinct olive flavor. If you use the best quality, you can also make it with all vegetable oil. If you would rather use all olive oil, you may want to choose pure olive oil, rather than extra-virgin.

Homemade mayonnaise does not have preservatives added like commercial brands, but will keep perfectly for at least a week, depending on the freshness of the eggs. I've happily eaten mayonnaise 3 weeks after I've made it, but then I know exactly where the eggs come from.

Serve with cold cooked meats, fowl, fish, eggs, and vegetables.

This makes 1½ cups of mayonnaise – enough for 8–10 people

2 egg yolks, organic, and from free-range hens
¼ teaspoon salt
¼ teaspoon Dijon mustard or pinch of dry English mustard
2 teaspoons white wine vinegar
1 cup oil (sunflower, peanut, or olive oil, or a mixture, 7:1 or 6:2)

Put the egg yolks into a medium-sized Pyrex bowl along with the mustard, salt, and the white wine vinegar. Put the oil into a measuring cup. Take a whisk in one hand and the oil in the other and drip the oil onto the egg yolks, drop by drop, whisking at the same time. Within a minute you will notice that the mixture is beginning to thicken. When this happens you can add the oil a little faster, but don't get too confident or it will suddenly curdle because the egg yolks can only absorb the oil at a certain pace. Taste, and add a little more seasoning and vinegar, if necessary.

If the mayonnaise curdles, it will suddenly become quite thin, and if left sitting, the oil will start to float to the top of the sauce. Should this happen, you can quite easily rectify the situation by putting another egg yolk or 1-2 tablespoons of boiling water into a clean bowl, then whisk in the curdled mayonnaise, a half teaspoon at a time, until it re-emulsifies.

Daughter Sauces
Aïoli or Garlic Mayonnaise

Add 1–4 crushed garlic cloves (depending on size) to the egg yolks just as you start to make the Mayonnaise. Add 2 teaspoons freshly chopped parsley at the end, and taste for seasoning.

Chili Basil Mayonnaise

Add a good pinch of chili powder to the egg yolks when making Garlic Mayonnaise, and omit the parsley and add basil instead. Great with salads and sandwiches.

Basil Mayonnaise

Pour boiling water over a handful of basil leaves, count to three, drain immediately, and refresh in cold water. Chop, and add to the egg yolks, and continue to make the mayonnaise in the usual way.

Tomato and Basil Mayonnaise

Add 1–2 tablespoons of concentrated Tomato Purée (see page 49) to Basil Mayonnaise.

Dill Mayonnaise

Add 2–3 tablespoons of freshly chopped dill to the Master Recipe. Particularly delicious with poached salmon or sea trout.

How to crush Garlic

Put the whole clove of garlic on a board, preferably one that is reserved for garlic and onions. Tap the clove with the flat blade of a chopping knife, to break the skin. Remove the skin and discard. Then sprinkle a few grains of salt onto the clove. Again using the flat blade of the knife, keep pressing the tip of the knife down onto the garlic to form a paste. The salt provides friction and ensures the clove won't shoot off the board.

Spicy Mayonnaise

Add 1–2 teaspoons Ballymaloe Tomato Relish and 1 teaspoon of chili sauce to a cupful of basic Mayonnaise.

Roast Red Pepper or Red Chile Mayonnaise

Add the puréed flesh of 1–2 roast red peppers, or 1 teaspoon of roasted, peeled, and diced red chile to the basic Mayonnaise or mild Aïoli (see above). Taste, and correct the seasoning. Serve with cold meat, spiced chicken, or goujons of fish.

Wasabi Mayonnaise

Add 2–4 tablespoons of Wasabi paste to the eggs, instead of the mustard.

Rémoulade Sauce

Mayonnaise
2 teaspoons Dijon mustard
1–2 tablespoons capers, chopped
1–2 tablespoons pickled gherkins, chopped
3 tablespoons freshly chopped parsley
2 teaspoons freshly chopped tarragon
4 anchovy fillets, chopped

Follow the Mayonnaise Master Recipe, then add all other ingredients. Serve with deep-fried plaice, sole, monkfish, or Fritto Misto.

Orly Sauce

Follow the Mayonnaise Master Recipe, then add concentrated homemade Tomato Purée (see page 49) to taste. Serve with deep-fried fish, for example, plaice or lemon sole.

Andalouse Sauce

Follow the Mayonnaise Master Recipe, then add concentrated homemade Tomato Purée (see page 49) and chopped sweet red peppers. Serve with chicken, salads, and fish.

Tartare Sauce

Serves 8–10

A classic tartare sauce, great with deep-fried fish, shellfish, or fish cakes. Tartare sauce will keep for 5–6 days in a fridge. Omit the parsley and chives if you wish to keep it for longer than a day or two.

2 hard-boiled egg yolks
2 raw egg yolks, preferably from free-range hens
1/4 teaspoon Dijon mustard
1 tablespoon white wine vinegar
1 1/2 cups sunflower or peanut oil, or 1 1/4 cups of either plus 1/4 cup olive oil
salt and freshly ground pepper
1 teaspoon chopped capers
1 teaspoon chopped gherkins
2 teaspoons chopped chives or chopped scallions
2 teaspoons chopped parsley
chopped white of the 2 hard-boiled eggs

Sieve the hard-boiled egg yolks into a bowl, add the raw egg yolks, mustard, and 1 tablespoon of wine vinegar. Mix well and whisk in the oil, drop by drop, increasing the volume as the mixture thickens.

When all the oil has been absorbed, add the other ingredients – capers, gherkins, chives or scallions, and parsley. Then roughly chop the hard-boiled egg white and fold in gently, season, and add a little more vinegar or a squeeze of lemon juice, if necessary.

Cheat's Tartare Sauce

A quick version can be made by adding the extra ingredients into Homemade Mayonnaise at the end.

Mustard and Dill Mayonnaise

Serves 8–10

Serve with gravlax, soused mackerel, or herring. Using sugar here may seem surprising, but it balances with the mustard and vinegar to produce a great flavor.

2 egg yolks, organic, and from free-range hens
2 tablespoons French mustard
1 tablespoon granulated sugar
2/3 cup peanut or sunflower oil
1 tablespoon white wine vinegar
1 tablespoon fresh dill, finely chopped
salt and white pepper

Whisk the egg yolks with the mustard and sugar in a medium-sized glass bowl, drip in the oil, drop by drop, whisking all the time until the mixture has emulsified, then add the vinegar and dill.

Horseradish Mayonnaise

Serve with cold rare roast beef or carpaccio. Substitute 1 heaped teaspoon of chopped parsley and 1 heaped teaspoon of chopped tarragon for the dill, and add 1 tablespoon or more of freshly grated horseradish to above recipe.

Mother Sauce

Béarnaise Sauce

One of the great classics. Use French rather than Russian tarragon if you can find it. Serve with beef, grilled food, fish, and eggs.

1/4 cup tarragon vinegar
1/4 cup dry white wine
2 teaspoons finely chopped shallots
pinch of freshly ground pepper
1 tablespoon freshly chopped French tarragon leaves
2 egg yolks, preferably from free-range hens
1–1 1/2 sticks (1/2–3/4 cup) butter approximately, salted or unsalted depending on what it is being served with

If you do not have tarragon vinegar on hand, use a wine vinegar and add some extra chopped tarragon. Boil the first four ingredients together until completely reduced and the pan is almost dry but not browned. Add 1 tablespoon of cold water immediately. Pull the pan off the heat and let cool for one or two minutes; whisk in the egg yolks and add the butter, bit by bit, over very low heat, whisking all the time. As soon as one piece melts, add the next piece; it will gradually thicken. If it shows signs of becoming too thick or slightly "scrambling," remove from the heat immediately and add a little cold water, if necessary. Do not leave the pan or stop whisking until the sauce is made. Finally add 1 tablespoon of freshly chopped French tarragon, and taste for seasoning.

If the sauce is slow to thicken, it may be because you are excessively cautious and the heat is too low. Increase the heat slightly and continue to whisk until the sauce thickens to a coating consistency. It is important to remember, however, that if you are making Bearnaise Sauce in a saucepan directly over the heat, it should be possible to put your hand on the side of the saucepan at any stage. If the saucepan feels too hot for your hand, it is also too hot for the sauce. Another good tip if you are making Béarnaise Sauce for the first time is to keep a bowl of cold water close by so that you can plunge the bottom of the saucepan into it if it becomes too hot. Keep the sauce warm in a bowl over warm water or in a thermos flask until you want to serve it.

Daughter Sauces

Sauce Choron (Tomato Béarnaise)

Add 1 1/2 tablespoons concentrated homemade Tomato Purée (see page 49) to 1 1/4 cups Béarnaise Sauce. Serve with steak, fish, eggs, or vegetables.

Sauce Foyot (Béarnaise with Meat Glaze)

Add 1 teaspoon meat glaze to 1 1/4 cups Béarnaise Sauce. The sauce should be the color of café au lait. Serve with steak.

Sauce Paloise (Mint Béarnaise)

Substitute chopped fresh mint for the tarragon. Serve this variation with lamb.

Béarnaise au Poivre Vert (Green Peppercorn Béarnaise)

Omit the chopped tarragon from the Béarnaise Sauce. Add 1 level tablespoon of drained and crushed green peppercorns to every 1 1/4 cups of sauce. Serve with steak, lamb, or salmon.

Horseradish Sauce

1 1/2–3 tablespoons horseradish root, scrubbed, peeled, and grated
1 teaspoon wine vinegar
1 teaspoon lemon juice
1/4 teaspoon mustard
1/4 teaspoon salt
freshly ground black pepper
1 teaspoon sugar
1 cup softly whipped cream

Put the grated horseradish into a bowl along with the vinegar, lemon juice, mustard, salt, pepper, and sugar. Fold in the softly whipped cream but do not overmix or it will curdle. It keeps for 2–3 days, but cover it tightly so it does not pick up other flavors in the refrigerator.

Tomato and Horseradish Sauce

Serve with cooked shrimp as a dipping sauce.

Enough for 8-10 people

1/4 cup plus 2 tablespoons best-quality tomato ketchup
1 tablespoon fish sauce (nam pla)
1 tablespoon freshly grated horseradish
sugar to taste

Mix the tomato ketchup with the horseradish and the fish sauce, then add sugar to taste.

Flavored Butters

Flavored butters are literally made in minutes. They are great to serve with pan-grilled or barbecued meat, fish, and vegetable dishes. For all the recipes below, the flavored butters can be rolled into butter pats or formed into a log, wrap in wax paper or tin foil, twisting each end closed. Refrigerate to harden. It will keep for 2–3 weeks.

Maitre d'Hôtel Butter or Parsley Butter

1 stick (1/2 cup) butter
2 tablespoons finely chopped fresh parsley
a few drops of freshly squeezed lemon juice

Cream the butter and add in the parsley and a few drops of lemon juice.

Ballymaloe

Garlic Butter

Add 3–5 crushed garlic cloves to the Parsley Butter. Serve with pan-grilled steaks and anything else you fancy.

Herb Butter

Substitute a mixture of chopped fresh herbs – parsley, chives, thyme, fennel, lemon balm... for the parsley in the recipe for Parsley Butter.

Mint or Rosemary Butter

Substitute 2 tablespoons of finely chopped mint or 1–2 tablespoons of rosemary for the parsley. Serve with roast or pan-grilled lamb.

Wild Garlic Butter

Substitute 2 tablespoons of chopped wild garlic leaves, and perhaps some flowers, for the parsley.

Nasturtium Butter

Substitute 3 tablespoons of chopped nasturtium flowers (red, yellow, and orange) for the parsley.

Lemon Butter

1 stick (½ cup) butter
finely grated rind and juice of 1 unwaxed lemon

Cream the butter, add the finely grated lemon rind, and beat in the juice very gradually.

Lemon and Parsley Butter

Add 1 tablespoon of finely chopped parsley to the above.

Mustard and Parsley Butter

Add 1 tablespoon of finely chopped parsley and 1 tablespoon Dijon mustard.

Provençale Butter

Spread this butter over cooked mussels on the half shell, dip in white breadcrumbs, and pop under the broiler for yummy garlicky Moules Provençales (see page 255). Also good slathered on mushrooms, tomatoes, or snails!

¾ stick (⅓ cup) soft butter
2 large garlic cloves
2 tablespoons freshly chopped parsley
1 tablespoon olive oil

Peel and crush the garlic and pound it in a mortar with the finely chopped parsley and olive oil. Gradually beat in the butter (this may be done either in a bowl or a food processor).

Grainy Mustard Butter

This is particularly good with pan-grilled mackerel or herring.

1 stick (½ cup) butter
1 tablespoon Dijon mustard
2 teaspoons approx. grainy mustard
1 tablespoon chopped parsley, optional

Cream the butter, then add the mustards and the parsley, if using.

Chile and Cilantro Butter

1 stick (½ cup) butter
1 red or green chile, seeded and finely chopped (we use Jalapeño or Serrano)
1 tablespoon chopped cilantro or marjoram
freshly ground pepper
a few drops of lime or lemon juice

Cream the butter, then add the chile and fresh herbs. Season with freshly ground pepper, and lime or lemon juice.

Olive and Anchovy Butter

1 stick (½ cup) butter
2–3 anchovies
6 black olives, pitted
about 2 teaspoons freshly chopped parsley

Whizz all the ingredients together in a food processor, or chop ingredients finely and mix with the butter.

Sage Butter

Serve with ravioli.

1 stick (½ cup) butter
12–16 finely chopped fresh sage leaves

Melt the butter. When it foams, add the fresh sage leaves. Let it bubble for 1–2 minutes. Toss in cooked ravioli and serve.

Tapenade

Tapenade is a paste made from olives and anchovies. Its strong gutsy flavor can be an acquired taste, but it soon becomes addictive. Serve with crudités, bruschetta, crostini, lamb, or pasta.

2 ounces (50g) anchovy fillets (about ⅓ cup)
¾ cup pitted black olives (Kalamata)
1 tablespoon capers
1 teaspoon Dijon mustard
1 teaspoon freshly squeezed lemon juice
freshly ground pepper
3–4 tablespoons extra-virgin olive oil

Whizz up the anchovy fillets in a food processor along with the olives, capers, mustard, lemon juice, and pepper. Alternatively, use a mortar and pestle. Add the olive oil as you mix to make a coarse or smooth purée, whichever you prefer.

Black and Green Tapenade

Use a mixture of black and green olives in the above recipe.

Olive and Sun-dried Tomato Tapenade

Serve on crostini, with goat cheese, with pan-grilled chicken breasts or lamb chops.

1¼ cups pitted black olives, (Niçoise or Kalamata)
2½ cups pitted green olives, try Picholine
¼ cup sun-dried tomatoes
1 tablespoon capers
1 garlic clove, crushed
2 anchovy fillets
6–8 basil leaves
1 teaspoon thyme leaves
2 teaspoons freshly chopped flat-leaf parsley
1 teaspoon marjoram
½ cup extra-virgin olive oil

Put all the ingredients except the oil into a food processor and pulse for a few seconds. Add the olive oil slowly and continue to pulse. The texture should be coarse. Store in a sterilized jar or plastic container, sealed with a layer of olive oil. Cover and store in the fridge. Keeps for 1–2 weeks.

Master Recipe

Pesto

Makes 2 jars

The best pesto is made in a mortar and pestle. However, even if you make it in a food processor it will still taste a million times better than most of what you buy. The problem is getting enough basil. If you have difficulty, use parsley, a mixture of parsley and mint, or parsley and cilantro – different but still delicious. Pesto keeps for weeks, covered with a layer of olive oil, in a jar in the fridge.

4 ounces (110g) fresh basil leaves (about 7–8 cups)
⅔ cup extra-virgin olive oil
¼ cup fresh pine nuts (taste when you buy to ensure they are not rancid)
2 large garlic cloves, peeled and crushed
1 cup freshly grated Parmesan cheese (Parmigiano Reggiano is best)
salt to taste

Whizz the basil with the olive oil, pine nuts and garlic in a food processor, or pound in a mortar and pestle. Remove to a bowl and fold in the Parmesan. Taste, and season. Pour into sterilized jars. Cover with a layer of olive oil. Screw on the lid and store in the fridge.

Pesto also freezes well but for best results, don't add the Parmesan until defrosted.

Tip: Each time you use some pesto, clean the top and sides of the jar and make sure the pesto is covered with a layer of extra-virgin olive oil before replacing in the fridge. Otherwise, the pesto will darken and go moldy where it is exposed to the air.

Variations

Pesto without Parmesan

Omit the cheese and store as above.

Mint and Parsley Pesto

Substitute 2 ounces (50g [about 3–4 cups]) fresh mint, and 2 ounces (50g [about 2–3 cups]) parsley for the basil in the main recipe.

Parsley Pesto

1 ounce (25g) freshly chopped parsley (about ½–¾ cup), leaves only
1–2 garlic cloves, peeled and crushed
¾ cup freshly grated Parmesan (Parmigiano Reggiano is best)
¼ cup pine nuts
⅓ cup extra-virgin olive oil
salt (essential to bring up the flavor)

Put all the ingredients except the oil into the food processor. Whizz for a second or two, add the oil and a little salt. Taste, and correct seasoning. Pour into a sterilized jar. Cover with oil, seal, and refrigerate.

When basil is less aromatic and scarce in winter, use parsley to make pesto. Other fresh herbs, e.g., mint and cilantro, are also delicious. Use one or a mixture of several - experiment and taste.

Rosemary and Parsley Pesto

Add 1–2 teaspoons freshly chopped rosemary with the parsley in the above variation. Serve with lamb, pan-grilled chicken breasts, portobella mushrooms, eggplant…

Roasted Red Pepper Pesto

Serve on warm olive oil-fried crostini or as a sauce for pasta with extra Parmesan.

2 large fresh red peppers
5 anchovy fillets
1 tablespoon extra-virgin olive oil
½ dried red chile or a pinch of red pepper flakes
sea salt or Kosher salt, and freshly ground pepper

Roast the peppers over a grill, under a radiant broiler, or in a hot oven. When they are well-charred, transfer to a bowl, cover with plastic wrap, and leave until cool enough to handle. The skin should peel off easily. Split the peppers and remove the seeds. DO NOT WASH THEM or you will lose the precious sweet juices. Chop the peppers roughly. Put with all the other ingredients into the bowl of a food processor. Pulse for a few seconds until the mixture has a slightly chunky texture.

Cilantro Pesto

¼ cup light olive oil or peanut oil
1 scallion, white and green parts, coarsely chopped
1 garlic clove, coarsely chopped
1 tablespoon pine nuts, toasted
1½ teaspoons freshly squeezed lemon or lime juice
1 lightly packed cup cilantro sprigs with short stems
1 lightly packed cup flat-leaf parsley sprigs, large stems removed
salt
cayenne pepper

Mix everything except the salt and pepper in the blender. Add salt and a few pinches of cayenne, purée until smooth. Taste, and correct the seasoning.

Sun-dried Tomato Pesto

3 ounces (75g) Sun-dried Tomatoes (about 3/4–1 cup) (see page 188)
1–2 garlic cloves, crushed
1 cup freshly grated Parmesan cheese (Parmigiano Reggiano is best)
1/4 cup pine nuts
1/3 cup extra-virgin olive oil
salt

Whizz all the ingredients except the oil for one to two seconds in a food processor. Add the oil and a little salt. Taste, and correct seasoning. Store in a covered sterilized jar in the fridge.

Variations

Mint and Sun-dried Tomato Pesto

Add 2 ounces (50g) fresh mint leaves (about 3–4 cups) or 1 ounce (25g) parsley (about 1–1 1/2 cups) and 1 ounce (25g) mint leaves (about 1 1/2–2 cups) to the above recipe.

Wild Garlic Pesto

Try this in early summer, when you can buy wild garlic leaves.

2 ounces (50g) wild garlic leaves (about 3–4 cups)
1/4 cup pine nuts
1 garlic clove, peeled and crushed
3/4–1 cup extra-virgin olive oil
3/4 cup freshly grated Parmesan cheese (Parmigiano Reggiano is best)
salt and sugar, to taste

Whizz the wild garlic, pine nuts, garlic, and olive oil in a food processor, or pound in a mortar and pestle. Remove to a bowl and fold in the Parmesan. Taste, and season. Store in a sterilized, covered jar in the fridge.

Pistou

Pistou is a "cousin" of the Italian pesto (it contains no pine nuts), and can be used in a similar way.

5 large garlic cloves
bunch of fresh basil leaves, approx. 30 large leaves
1 cup freshly grated Parmesan cheese (Parmigiano Reggiano is best)
1/2 cup extra-virgin olive oil

Peel and crush the garlic well, or pound in a mortar, then add the basil and continue to pound to a paste. Stir in the Parmesan, mix well, and then add in the oil, drop by drop.

Master Recipe

Tomato Sauce

Makes 2 cups

A good tomato sauce is a terrific accompaniment to all sorts of dishes besides pasta. I find it invaluable to have in the fridge or freezer as a standby. Use it on pizza, or with polenta, zucchini, or zucchini flowers. Serve hot or cold. It is wonderful with the Provençal Terrine (see page 104).

2 tablespoons butter
2 tablespoons extra-virgin olive oil
1–4 garlic cloves, according to taste, peeled and chopped
1 medium onion, finely chopped
2 lbs. (900g) very ripe tomatoes, peeled and chopped, or 2 x 14-ounce (400-g) cans Italian tomatoes, chopped
salt, freshly ground pepper, sugar, to taste

Melt the butter, add the olive oil, and toss in the chopped garlic. Cook for one to two minutes or until pale golden, then add the onion, cook for a further one to two minutes, before adding the tomatoes. Season with the salt, pepper, and a little sugar.

Cook fast for 15–20 minutes if you want a fresh-tasting sauce, or more slowly, for up to one hour, if you prefer it more concentrated. Purée through a food mill. Taste, and correct the seasoning.

Variations

Tomato Sauce with Basil or Annual Marjoram

Add 1–2 tablespoons freshly chopped basil or annual marjoram to the above.

Tomato Sauce with Balsamic Vinegar

Add 1–2 teaspoons of balsamic vinegar just before serving. It intensifies the flavor of the sauce quite magically.

Creamy Tomato Sauce

Bring the tomato sauce back to a boil (with or without herbs) and add 1/2 cup heavy cream. Let it bubble for one or two minutes, then serve at once.

Tomato and Chile Sauce

Serve with Onion Bhajis (see page 187).

1 ounce (25g) green chiles (2–3, depending on size), seeded and chopped, or 1 large red pepper, seeded and cut in 1/4-inch (5-mm) dice
1/2 x 14-ounce (400-g) can chopped tomatoes
1 garlic clove, crushed
2 teaspoons sugar
2 teaspoons soft brown sugar
1 tablespoon white wine vinegar
2 tablespoons water
salt and freshly ground pepper

First make the sauce: put the chiles or pepper, tomatoes, and garlic into a stainless steel saucepan (vinegar will react with an aluminum one), along with the sugar, vinegar, and water. Season, and simmer for 10 minutes until reduced by half.

Barbecue Sauce

Makes 1 cup approx.

Use to marinate lamb, chicken, or pork, or even sausages.

1/4 cup olive oil
2 garlic cloves, crushed
1 cup finely chopped onion
1 x 14-ounce (400g) can of tomatoes, chopped
a scant 1/2 cup Tomato Purée (see page 49)
a scant 1/2 cup red or white wine vinegar
1/4 cup pure honey
1/4 cup Worcestershire sauce
2 tablespoons Dijon mustard

Heat the oil in a frying pan, add the garlic and onion, and sweat gently for 4–5 minutes.

Add the tomatoes and juice, cook for a further four to five minutes, season with salt and freshly ground pepper. Purée in a blender or food processor, add the remainder of the ingredients, and bring to a boil; simmer for 4–5 minutes.

Hot Chile Sauce

If you want some real excitement in your life, serve this as an accompaniment to your curry. We use this as a basis for Chili con Carne as well.

4–5 fresh chiles or 6–7 small dried chiles
1 large onion, chopped
1 large red pepper
2 garlic cloves
salt

If the chiles are dried, soak for about an hour. Cut the chiles and pepper in half, and wash out the seeds.

Purée with the other ingredients in a food processor. You may need 1-2 tablespoons of cold water if the mixture is too dry. Season to taste with salt. This sauce can be stored in a covered container for a few days, or frozen for much longer.

Note: Salt brings up the flavor of chiles so don't forget to put it in.

Pixie's Peanut Sauce

1/2 cup peanut butter
1/2 cup hot water
1/4 cup light soy sauce
1/2 cup dark soy sauce
1/2 cup tahini (sesame paste)
1/2 cup dark sesame oil
2 1/2 tablespoons medium sherry

Put all ingredients except the hot water into a blender or a food processor. Whizz until smooth. Thin with the hot water to a light coating consistency. This keeps indefinitely in the refrigerator.

Salsas

Salsa is simply the Spanish word for sauce; they can be cooked or uncooked.

Tomato and Cilantro Salsa

Serves 4

This sauce is ever present on Mexican tables. Serve with nachos, quesadillas, tostadas, Mexican scrambled eggs...

4 very ripe tomatoes, chopped
1 tablespoon onion, chopped
1 clove garlic, crushed
1/2-1 chile, finely chopped (we use Serrano or Jalapeño)
1–2 tablespoons fresh cilantro, chopped
squeeze fresh lime juice
salt, freshly ground pepper, and sugar

Mix all the ingredients together. Season with salt, freshly ground pepper, and sugar, if necessary.

Tomato and Pepper Salsa

Serves 4

Now that Tomato Salsa is becoming more familiar, you can occasionally stray away from the classic Mexican version.

2 red peppers, seeded and cut into 1/4-inch (5-mm) dice
2 tomatoes, peeled and seeded, and cut into 1/4-inch (5-mm) dice
1–2 chiles, seeded and diced, optional (we use Serrano or Jalapeño)
1–2 tablespoons olive oil
salt, pepper, and sugar
2–4 teaspoons torn basil or fresh cilantro

Combine all the ingredients, taste, and correct the seasoning.

Tomato and Avocado Salsa

Serves 4

1 avocado, peeled and chopped
2 ripe tomatoes, chopped
1 tablespoon scallion, chopped
1 garlic clove, crushed
1–2 chile peppers, chopped
1/4–1/2 teaspoon lightly roasted cumin seeds, crushed
1–2 tablespoons roughly chopped fresh cilantro
salt and freshly ground pepper
freshly squeezed lime juice from 2 limes

Mix all the ingredients in a bowl, taste, and correct the seasoning.

Roast Red Pepper, Tomato, and Basil Salsa

Add peeled, seeded, and chopped roast red pepper and replace the coriander with basil.

Parsley and Chile Salsa

Serves 8

6 garlic cloves, finely chopped
2–3 large red chiles, seeded and finely chopped
2 cups flat-leaf parsley, finely chopped
extra-virgin olive oil
sea salt or Kosher salt, and freshly ground pepper

Chop the garlic and the prepared chiles together, then add the flat-leaf parsley. Put into a bowl and add lots of extra-virgin olive oil, a little sea salt, and freshly ground pepper. Serve with squid, grilled shrimp, grilled polenta, or steak. This doubles as a pasta sauce, too. Serve with a sprinkle of toasted breadcrumbs.

Cilantro, Parsley, and Chile Salsa

Use 1 cup of flat-leaf parsley and 1 cup of fresh cilantro leaves instead of 2 cups of flat-leaf parsley.

Tomatilla Salsa

Serves 6
In season: Summer and Autumn

Serve with tacos, quesadillas, and spicy sausages.

5 or 6 fresh tomatillas
1–3 chiles, chopped
1/4 cup onion, chopped
1 garlic clove, crushed
good pinch of salt
1–2 tablespoons of fresh cilantro, coarsely chopped

Remove the papery husks from the tomatillas. Wash. Put them into a small saucepan, cover with cold water, add a good pinch of salt. Cook until the fruits are soft and the skins tender – about 18-20 minutes, depending on size. Tomatillas float, so don't forget to turn them over during cooking, otherwise the tops can be undercooked. Simmer rather than boil, to prevent them from bursting.

Meanwhile grind the chiles, onions, garlic, cilantro and salt, preferably with a coarse mortar and pestle. If you don't have this, use a food processor or blender, even though purists may frown because the resulting purée is more watery.

When the tomatillas are tender, drain, but reserve the cooking liquid. Grind them with the chile base or, alternatively, blend everything together to a coarse purée. Add about 1/4 cup of the cooking water to thin the sauce to a medium consistency.

Taste, season with salt, and let stand for a half hour or so, to let the flavors develop.

Salsa Verde

Serve with pan-grilled beef, lamb, or chicken, liver, eggplant, or goat cheese.

2 bunches flat-leaf parsley
zest and juice of 1–2 lemons
3 cloves garlic, crushed
2 teaspoons freshly grated horseradish
1 1/2 tablespoons salted capers, rinsed
extra-virgin olive oil
salt and freshly ground black pepper

Put the parsley leaves, lemon zest, garlic, horseradish, and capers in a food processor. Process in an on/off method until the mixture is finely chopped. (Alternatively, chop on a wooden board with a knife or mezzaluna.) Add the freshly squeezed lemon juice and enough olive oil to make a moist salsa. Season to taste with salt and pepper.

Mother Sauce
Ballymaloe Cream Sauce

This indisputably rich sauce is one of our most requested recipes. It is truly delicious, but I'm sure I don't have to tell you to eat it sparingly. You can add freshly snipped herbs to the basic sauce, or follow one of the variations below.

1¼ sticks (⅔ cup) butter
1 cup cream
salt and freshly ground pepper

Put the cream into a small saucepan and gently reduce to about ¼ cup or until it is in danger of burning, then whisk in the butter bit by bit as though you were making a Hollandaise sauce. Thin with warm water, if necessary, and keep warm in a Pyrex bowl. Taste, and correct the seasoning, and add chosen flavoring.

Daughter Sauces
Red Pepper Sauce

Serve with poached fish, monkfish, sole, turbot, or plaice. Seed a red pepper and dice the flesh into ⅛-inch (5-mm) cubes. Sweat gently in a teaspoonful of butter in a tiny covered saucepan until soft (it's really easy to burn so turn off the heat after a few minutes and it will continue to cook in the pan). Stir into the basic sauce.

Spinach Butter Sauce

Substitute ⅓ cup cooked spinach, chopped into 1-inch (2.5-cm) pieces, for the red pepper. Thin with fish stock, if necessary. Serve with trout or salmon.

Tomato and Basil Sauce

Use 4 ripe firm tomatoes, diced and seasoned with salt, pepper, and sugar, and 10–15 freshly chopped basil leaves instead of the red pepper. Serve with pan-grilled chicken breasts or fish.

Anchoïade

Makes ¼ cup

Serve with crudités or just slathered on toast, bruschetta, or warm pita bread. Anchoïade is also great with a simple pan-grilled chicken breast.

4 ounces (110g) canned anchovy fillets (about ⅔ cup) (weight out of can)
1¼ cups olive oil
2 garlic cloves, chopped
2 teaspoons thyme leaves
1 tablespoon freshly chopped basil leaves
1 tablespoon Dijon mustard
1 tablespoon red wine vinegar
lots of freshly ground pepper

Whizz all ingredients together except the oil in a food processor. Add the oil very gradually. Taste, add a little more oil, if necessary. Store in a covered jar in the fridge.

Bread Sauce

Serves 6–8

I love Bread Sauce but if I hadn't been reared on it I might never have tried it - the recipe sounds so dull. Quatre épices is a French product made from equal amounts of ground white pepper, cloves, nutmeg, and ginger. Serve with roast turkey, chicken, or game hen.

2½ cups milk
1½–2½ cups soft white breadcrumbs
2 onions, peeled and stuck with 6 cloves each
½ stick (¼ cup) butter
salt and freshly ground pepper
2 good pinches of ground cloves or quatre épices
⅓–½ cup heavy cream

Put all the ingredients except the cream in a small, deep saucepan and bring to a boil. Season with salt and pepper.

Cover and simmer gently over very low heat or cook in a low oven 325°F (170°C) for 30 minutes. Remove the onion and add the cream just before serving.

Correct the seasoning and add a little more milk if the sauce is too thick. Serve hot.

Gravy

Gravy should be made in the roasting pan so that you utilize all the flavor of the caramelized meat juices on the bottom of the pan. The meat can be resting while you make the gravy. Be sure to use a flameproof roasting pan.

2½ cups stock (preferably homemade Beef Stock, see page 36)
Roux, optional (see page 580)
salt and freshly ground pepper to taste

Spoon the fat out of the roasting pan. Pour the stock into the remaining cooking juices and heat on the top of the stove. Boil for a few minutes, stirring and scraping well to dissolve the caramelized meat juices in the pan (I find a small metal whisk ideal for this). Thicken very slightly with a little roux, if you like (years ago flour would have been sprinkled over the fat in the pan). Taste, and add salt and pepper, if necessary. Strain and serve in a warm gravy boat.

Onion Gravy

Serves 4–6

Serve with roast beef or lamb's liver.

8 onions, about 2 lbs. (900g) in weight, thinly sliced
2 tablespoons water
2½ cups homemade Beef Stock (see page 36)

Put the sliced onions into a pan along with the water and cook very slowly, stirring every now and then. The sugar from the onions will slowly caramelize and become brown and sweet-tasting. This process can take up to an hour.
Add the stock and simmer for a further 15–20 minutes. Serve in a warmed gravy boat.

Cumberland Sauce

Serve with cold ham, turkey, chicken, guinea fowl, game, or rough pâtés.

1 orange, unwaxed
1 lemon, unwaxed
1 cup Red Currant Jelly (see page 508)
3–4 tablespoons port
a pinch of cayenne pepper
a pinch of ground ginger

With a swivel-top peeler, remove the peel very thinly from the orange and from half of the lemon (make sure there is no white pith). Shred into thin julienne strips, put in a saucepan and cover with cold water, bring to a boil, and simmer for 4–5 minutes. Strain off the water and discard it, then refresh the peel under cold water. Strain, and set aside.

Squeeze the juice from the fruit into a stainless steel saucepan and add the jelly and spices; let the jelly melt down. Then add the peel and port to the sauce. Boil it rapidly for 5-10 minutes. Test like for jam, by putting a little blob on a cold saucer. When it cools, it should wrinkle slightly.

Cumberland Sauce may be served in a bowl right away or it may be bottled and kept until needed, like jam.

Ballymaloe Mint Sauce

Serve with spring lamb.

1/2 cup finely chopped fresh mint
1 teaspoon sugar
3–4 tablespoons boiling water
1 tablespoon white wine vinegar or lemon juice

Put the sugar and freshly chopped mint into a bowl. Add the boiling water, and vinegar or lemon juice. Let it infuse for 5–10 minutes before serving.

Fresh Mint Chutney

This fresh chutney is often served in India with curries. It is good with grilled fish, or roast lamb instead of mint sauce. Surprisingly, even though it is uncooked, this chutney will keep for several days in a covered jar or plastic container in the refrigerator.

1 large cooking apple (we use Grenadier or Bramley Seedling), peeled and cored
large handful of fresh mint leaves, Spearmint or Bowles
2 ounces (50g) onion (about 1/2 a medium onion)
2–4 tablespoons superfine sugar (depending on tartness of apple)
salt and cayenne pepper

Whizz all the ingredients in a food processor, season with the salt and a little cayenne.

Tip: Serve fresh mint chutney as a really yummy dip with poppadoms before dinner as a simple appetizer.

Cucumber and Yogurt Raita

This cooling relish is good served with spicy food.

1/4 medium-sized English cucumber
1/2 tablespoon onion, chopped
1/2 rounded teaspoon salt
1/2–1 tomato, diced
1 tablespoon chopped cilantro, or 1/2 tablespoon parsley and 1/2 tablespoon mint
2/3 cup plain yogurt
1/2 teaspoon whole cumin seeds
salt and freshly ground pepper

Peel the cucumber if you prefer, then cut in half and remove the seeds. Cut into 1/4-inch (5-mm) dice. Put this into a bowl with the onion, sprinkle with salt, and let it degorge for 5–10 minutes. Drain, and add it, along with the diced tomato and chopped herbs, to the yogurt. Heat the cumin seeds, crush lightly, and add. Taste, and correct seasoning. Chill before serving.

Banana and Yogurt Raita

Serves 6

Try this with curries and spicy dishes.

2 tablespoons raisins or golden raisins
2 tablespoons blanched slivered almonds
3–4 green cardamom pods
1/2 cup yogurt
2 tablepoons cream
2 tablepoons sour cream
2 teaspoons pure honey
2 firm ripe bananas
pinch of salt

Pour boiling water over the raisins and leave for 10 minutes. Toast the almonds (watch them, as they burn really easily). Remove the cardamom seeds from their pods, crush in a mortar and pestle. Mix the yogurt with the creams and cardamom seeds, add the honey, taste, and add more honey, if needed. Add the raisins and toasted almonds. Slice the bananas, season with a pinch of salt, and add to the yogurt base. Turn into a serving bowl and scatter with toasted almonds, and chill for an hour, if possible.

Alison Henderson's Eggplant Raita

Serves 6–10

Serve with lamb, couscous, or Indian lamb dishes.

1 large eggplant
2 1/2 cups yogurt
1 large garlic clove, crushed
salt
1 teaspoon turmeric

1 tablespoon oil, plus extra for frying eggplant
2 teaspoons (1 dessertspoon) cumin seeds
1 teaspoon ground paprika

Slice the eggplant into rounds about 1/4-inch (5-mm) thick and set aside. Heat enough oil in a frying pan so that it comes halfway up the sides. When the oil is hot, put in the eggplant, a few slices at a time, frying them first on one side, then the other, so that both sides are nice and crisp. Set aside to drain on paper towels. Pour the yogurt into a bowl and stir in the crushed garlic and salt to taste. Add the slices of eggplant and sprinkle with the cumin seeds and paprika.

Minted Nuoc Cham

This recipe, given to me by ace cook Alison Henderson, who runs the café at Ballymaloe House, is an unusual combination of mint and peanuts. Serve with spicy dishes.

3 tablespoons sugar
3 tablespoons boiling water
1/3 cup fish sauce (nam pla)
juice of 1 lime, or more, to taste
3 tablespoons freshly chopped mint
1 tablespoon freshly chopped cilantro
freshly chopped hot chile, to taste
1 tablespoon crushed roasted peanuts

Combine the sugar and water in a small pan and stir until the sugar is dissolved. Let cook for 5 minutes, then add the other ingredients. Serve immediately.

Balsamic Syrup

Chefs love to drizzle this balsamic reduction around their salads and appetizers. You don't need to use very expensive vinegar.

1 cup balsamic vinegar

Put the balsamic vinegar into a small stainless steel saucepan over low heat. Let it reduce to about half its original volume – take care not to let it reduce too much. It will thicken as it cools. Store it in a bottle with a drizzle spout – it will keep for several weeks.

Vermouth Sauce with Periwinkles or Shrimp

Vermouth sauce is delicious with many types of fish, particularly turbot, sea bass, sole, brill, and plaice. It may, of course, be served without the addition of periwinkles. Cooked shelled shrimp may also be added to the sauce at the end.

1 shallot, finely chopped
2 tablespoons dry white wine
1 tablespoon dry Vermouth (Noilly Pratt)
2/3 cup homemade white fish stock (see page 37)
2/3 cup heavy cream
3/4 stick (1/3 cup) unsalted butter
fresh live periwinkles (buy a pint: you need 2–4 ounces (50–110g) of periwinkles removed from their shells)
salted water – 2/3 cup salt to every 2 1/2 quarts (2.3 liters) water

Bring the water to a boil, add the salt and the periwinkles, return the water to a boil, strain off the water, and let the periwinkles get cold. Meanwhile, sweat the shallot in two-thirds (1/2 stick) of the butter until soft. Add the wine and vermouth and reduce by half, to remove the taste of alcohol. Add the fish stock and again reduce by half. Now add the cream and reduce the sauce carefully to a light coating consistency.

Finally mount the sauce with the remaining butter, swirling the pan all the time to incorporate the butter. Check seasoning, and add a little lemon juice to sharpen the sauce.

Remove the cooled periwinkles from the shells with a pin, and add to the sauce just before serving.

Fire and Brimstone Sauce

This sauce is great to serve with pan-grilled chicken, pork, or lamb. We also use it as a dipping sauce for all kinds of fried food, especially chicken or fish goujons.

2–4 red chiles, serrano or jalapeño
4 garlic cloves, crushed
1 cup apricot jam
5 tablespoons white wine vinegar
good pinch of salt

Seed and roughly chop the chiles, then whizz all the ingredients in a food processor.

This sauce keeps for up to 2 weeks in a covered jar in the fridge.

Spicy Chicken Marinade

1 tablespoon ground cumin seeds
1 tablespoon ground paprika
1 teaspoon cayenne pepper
1 tablespoon ground turmeric

1 teaspoon freshly ground pepper
2 teaspoons salt
3 cloves garlic, crushed
5 tablespoons freshly squeezed lemon juice
2–3 tablespoons sunflower oil

Mix cumin, paprika, cayenne, turmeric, black pepper, salt, garlic, lemon juice, and oil in a bowl. Rub this mixture all over the chicken pieces. Put in a bowl, then cover; keep in a cool place for at least 3 hours.

Bramley Applesauce

Serves 10

The trick with applesauce is to cook the fruit in a covered pan over low heat with very little water. Serve with roast goose, duck, pork, and anything else you fancy.

1 lb. (450g) cooking apples, e.g., Bramley Seedling, Grenadier, Granny Smith
2–4 teaspoons water
1/4 cup sugar, depending on how tart the apples are

Peel, quarter, and core the apples. Cut the quarters in half and put in a stainless steel or cast iron saucepan along with the sugar and water. Cover, and place over a low heat. As soon as the apple has broken down, beat into a purée, stir, and taste for sweetness. Serve warm.

Note: Applesauce freezes perfectly, so make more than you need and freeze it in tiny, plastic cartons. It is also a good way to use up windfalls.

Golden Delicious Sauce

Use Golden Delicious instead of Bramleys, but you will need to reduce the sugar, as these are dessert apples. Serve with boudin noir or black pudding.

Cranberry Sauce

Serves 6 approx.

Cranberry Sauce is delicious served with roast turkey, game, and some coarse pâtés and terrines.

1 2/3 cups fresh cranberries
4 tablespoons water
1/4 cup plus 2 tablespoons granulated sugar

Put the fresh cranberries in a heavy stainless steel or cast iron saucepan with the water – don't add the sugar yet as it tends to toughen the skins. Bring them to a boil, cover, and simmer until the cranberries pop and soften – this takes about 7 minutes. Remove from the heat and stir in the sugar until dissolved.

Serve warm or cold.

Note: Cranberry Sauce will keep in your fridge for a week to 10 days.

Variations

Cranberry and Orange Sauce

Use freshly squeezed orange juice instead of water and add the grated rind of half an unwaxed orange to the above recipe.

Cranberry and Ginger Sauce

1/4 cup cider vinegar
1/2 teaspoon fresh ginger, peeled and finely grated
1/2 cup sugar
1 large garlic clove, crushed
good pinch cayenne pepper
salt and freshly ground pepper
Cranberry Sauce (see above)

Put the vinegar, sugar, ginger, garlic, and cayenne into a small saucepan and cook for 5-6 minutes, or until reduced by half. Add the Cranberry Sauce. Season, taste, and correct.

Plum or Damson Sauce

Served hot or cold, this is delicious with duck breast or wild duck, and keeps well.

1 lb. (450g) blood plums or damsons
1 cup sugar
water
1-inch (2.5-cm) piece cinnamon stick
2 cloves
2 tablespoons Red Currant Jelly (see page 508)
1/2 cup port
2 tablespoons butter

Put the fruit into a stainless steel saucepan along with the sugar, cloves, cinnamon, one tablespoon of water, and the butter and cook slowly until reduced to a pulp. Push the fruit through a fine sieve and return the purée to a clean saucepan. Add the red currant jelly and port, bring to a boil, and simmer for a few minutes.

Green Gooseberry Sauce

A delicious sauce to accompany pan-grilled mackerel, goat cheese, and roast pork with crackling.

10 ounces (275g) fresh green gooseberries (about 2½–3 cups)
Stock Syrup to cover (see page 568) (about ¾ cup
pat of butter (optional)

Top and tail the gooseberries, put into a stainless steel saucepan, barely cover with stock syrup, bring to a boil, and simmer until the fruit bursts. Taste. Stir in a small pat of butter if you like, but it is very good without it.

Tip: Red currants freeze brilliantly, so you can make this at any time of year. Put them into the freezer in a carton or a plastic bag. Once they are frozen, shake the bag and the berries will fall off their strings – much easier than painstakingly removing the stings from fresh berries

Red Currant Sauce

Serves 4–6

A simple, delicious sauce which is unbelievably quick to make. It goes well with lamb, guinea fowl, ham, and pâté de campagne.

⅔ cup sugar
½ cup water
5 ounces (150g) red currants (about 1 cup)

Remove the strings from the red currants (see tip).

Put the sugar and water into a saucepan, stir over medium heat until the sugar dissolves, then bring to a boil. Toss in the red currants, return back to a boil, cook uncovered for 4–5 minutes or until the red currants burst. Serve hot or cold.
This keeps for several weeks in a covered jar in the fridge and may be reheated gently.

Rhubarb Sauce

Serves 6

Serve warm with roast pork or with ice cream or Bread and Butter Pudding.

1 lb. (450g) red rhubarb cut into 1-inch (2.5-cm) pieces
½ cup sugar
Red Currant Jelly (see page 508), optional

Put the rhubarb into a stainless steel saucepan, add the sugar and toss around, then leave for 5–10 minutes until the juice from the rhubarb starts to melt the sugar. Cover the saucepan, put over a gentle heat and cook until soft. Taste, and add a little more sugar, if necessary. It should not be too sweet but should not cut your throat either. If you have really good red currant jelly, stir in a spoonful at the end, otherwise leave it out.

Sweet Sauces

Crème Anglaise (Custard Sauce)

This basic sauce is usually flavored with vanilla but can be made with any number of other flavorings, such as lemon or orange rind or mint. It is used in many recipes, including ice cream, though in that case the proportion of sugar is much higher than usual because unsweetened cream is added during the freezing.

2½ cups whole milk
vanilla bean or alternative flavoring
6 egg yolks
¼ cup sugar

Bring the milk almost to a boil along with the vanilla bean, if using. Beat the egg yolks with the sugar until thick and light. Whisk in half the hot milk and then whisk the mixture back into the remaining milk. Cook over very low heat, stirring constantly with a wooden spoon, until the custard thickens slightly. Your finger should leave a clear trail when drawn across the back of the spoon. Remove from the heat at once and strain. Cool, cover tightly, and chill. The custard can be kept for up to 2 days in the refrigerator.

Lemon Custard Sauce

Stir ½ cup Lemon Curd (see page 510) into 1¼ cups of Crème Anglaise.

Master Recipe

Caramel Sauce

1 cup sugar
⅓ cup cold water
1 cup hot water

Dissolve the sugar in the cold water over a gentle heat. Stir until all the sugar has dissolved, then remove the spoon and continue to simmer until the syrup caramelizes to a chestnut color. If sugar crystals form during cooking, brush down the sides of the pan with a wet brush, but do not stir. Remove from the heat, pour in the hot water, and continue to cook until the caramel dissolves and the sauce is quite smooth. Let it get cold. Delicious with ice cream.

Variation

Caramel Cream Sauce

Use 1 cup heavy cream in place of the hot water.

Irish Coffee Sauce

Serve with ice cream or parfaits.

1 cup sugar
1/3 cup water
1 cup coffee
1 tablespoon Irish whiskey

Put the sugar and water in a heavy saucepan, stir until the sugar dissolves and the water comes to a boil. Remove the spoon and do not stir again until the syrup turns a pale golden caramel. Then add the coffee and return to the heat to dissolve. Let it cool and add the whiskey.

Coffee Sauce

Omit whiskey in the above recipe and serve with coffee ice cream.

Irish Mist Sauce

Substitute Irish Mist for Irish whiskey in the recipe for Irish Coffee Sauce.

Butterscotch Sauce or Toffee Sauce

This irresistible sauce is also delicious with ice cream, but is even better with sliced bananas. It will keep for several weeks stored in a screw-top jar in the fridge.

1 stick (1/2 cup) butter
3/4 cup soft dark brown Barbados sugar
1/2 cup granulated sugar
1 1/4 cups golden syrup or, if unavailable, use 1 cup plus 2 tablespoons corn syrup and 2 tablespoons treacle or molasses
1 cup heavy cream
1/2 teaspoon vanilla extract

Put the butter, sugars, and golden syrup into a heavy saucepan and melt gently over low heat. Simmer for about 5 minutes, remove from the heat, and gradually stir in the cream and the vanilla. Return to the heat and stir for 2–3 minutes, until the sauce is absolutely smooth. Serve hot or cold.

Chocolate Sauce

Serve with ice cream, profiteroles...

2 ounces (50g) dark or semi-sweet chocolate (2 squares)
1 ounce (25g) unsweetened chocolate (1 square)
about 3/4 cup Stock Syrup (see page 568)
rum or vanilla extract

Melt the chocolate in a bowl over simmering water or in a low oven. Gradually stir in the syrup. Flavor with rum or vanilla extract.

Fresh Black Currant Sauce

Very good, served either warm or cold with vanilla or black currant ice cream or Pannacotta.

8 ounces (225g) black currants (about 1–1 1/2 cups), topped and tailed
1 cup Stock Syrup (see page 568)
1/2–2/3 cup water

Pour the syrup over the black currants and bring to a boil, cook for 3–5 minutes until the black currants burst. Blend and pour through a nylon sieve or cheesecloth. Let cool. Add the water.

Fresh Strawberry Sauce

Makes about 2 1/4 cups

Serve with ice cream or a meringue roulade or coeurs à la crème.

1 lb. (450g) fresh strawberries
3/4 cup confectioners sugar
freshly squeezed lemon juice

Clean and hull the strawberries. Purée with the sugar and strain through a nylon sieve or cheesecloth. Taste, and add freshly squeezed lemon juice, if necessary. Store in the fridge.

Fresh Loganberry Sauce

Serve with ice cream or a meringue roulade or coeurs à la crème.

8 ounces (225g) loganberries (about 1 1/2–2 cups)
Stock Syrup (see page 568), to taste
lemon juice (optional)

Make a syrup with sugar and water, cool, and add to the loganberries. Blend and strain through cheesecloth or a nylon sieve. Taste, and sharpen with lemon juice, if necessary. Store in a fridge

Fresh Raspberry Sauce

8 ounces (225g) raspberries (about 1 1/2–2 cups)
Stock Syrup (see page 568), to taste
lemon juice (optional)

Blend the raspberries with some syrup. Strain through cheesecloth or a nylon sieve, and sharpen with lemon juice, if necessary. Store in the fridge.

Fresh Mango and Passionfruit Sauce

Serve with ice cream.

1 large ripe mango
4 passionfruit
1–2 tablespoons freshly squeezed lime juice
1–2 tablespoons superfine sugar

Peel the mango, scrape the flesh from the pit, and purée in a food processor. Put into a bowl with the passionfruit seeds and juice, add the lime juice and sugar, to taste. Cover and chill.

Oven temperatures

Celsius*	Fahrenheit	Description
225°F	110°C	cool
250°F	120°C	cool
275°F	140°C	very low
300°F	150°C	low
325°F	160°C	mod. low
350°F	180°C	moderate
375°F	190°C	mod. hot
400°F	200°C	hot
425°F	220°C	hot
450°F	230°C	very hot

* *For fan-assisted ovens, reduce temperatures by 50°F (10°C)*

Volume

1 teaspoon	5ml
1 dessertspoon	10ml
1 tablespoon	15ml
1 fl. oz.	30ml
2 fl. oz.	60ml
3 fl. oz.	90ml
3½ fl. oz.	100ml
4 fl. oz. (½ cup)	120ml
5 fl. oz.	150ml
6 fl. oz.	180ml
7 fl. oz.	205ml
8 fl. oz. (1 cup)	240ml
9 fl. oz.	265ml
10 fl. oz.	300ml
12 fl. oz.	355ml
14 fl. oz.	415ml
15 fl. oz.	445ml
16 fl. oz. (1 pint)	470ml
18 fl. oz.	530ml
20 fl. oz.	590ml
24 fl. oz. (3 cups)	710ml
32 fl. oz. (1 quart)	960ml
40 fl. oz. (5 cups)	1.2 liters
48 fl. oz. (6 cups)	1.4 liters
56 fl. oz. (7 cups)	1.7 liters
64 fl. oz. (½ gallon)	1.9 liters

Weight

½ ounce	15g
¾ ounce	20g
1 ounce	30g
2 ounces	60g
2½ ounces	70g
3 ounces	85g
3½ ounces	100g
4 ounces (¼ lb.)	110g
5 ounces	140g
6 ounces	170g
7 ounces	200g
8 ounces (½ lb.)	225g
9 ounces	250g (¼kg)
10 ounces	285g
12 ounces (¾ lb.)	340g
14 ounces	400g
1 lb.	450g
18 ounces	500g (½kg)
1¼ lbs.	570g
1½ lbs.	680g
2 lbs.	900g
2¼ lbs.	1kg
2½ lbs.	1.1kg
3 lbs.	1.3kg
3 lbs. 5 oz.	1.5kg
3½ lbs.	1.6kg
4 lbs.	1.8kg
4½ lbs.	2kg
5 lbs.	2.2kg

Measurements

⅛ inch	3mm
¼ inch	5mm
½ inch	1cm
¾ inch	2cm
1 inch	2.5cm
1¼ inches	3cm
1½ inches	4cm
2 inches	5cm
2½ inches	6cm
2¾ inches	7.5cm
3½ inches	9cm
4 inches	10cm
4½ inches	11.5cm
5 inches	12.5cm
6 inches	15cm
6½ inches	17cm
7 inches	18cm
8 inches	20.5cm
9 inches	23cm
9½ inches	24cm
10 inches	25.5cm
11 inches	30.5cm

American cup measures

Butter, margarine, lard	
¼ stick	1 ounce (25g)
½ cup	4 ounce (110g)
Liquids	
1 cup	8 fluid ounces (225ml)
Golden syrup, treacle, clear honey	
1 cup	12 ounces (350g)
Sugar	
superfine and granulated	
1 cup	8 ounces (225g)
moist brown	
1 cup	7 ounces (200g)
confectioners sugar	
1 cup	4½ ounces (125g)
Breadcrumbs	
Fresh	
1 heaped cup	2 ounces (50g)
Dried	
1 cup	4 ounces (110g)
Cheese	
Shredded cheese	
1 cup	4 ounces (110g)
Diced cheddar	
1 cup	6 ounces (175g)
Parmesan, grated	
1 cup	2 ounces (50g)
Cream cheese	
1 cup	8 ounces (225g)
Dried fruits	
Currants and raisins	
1 cup	8 ounces (225g)
Apricots	
1 cup	5–6 ounces (150–175g)
Prunes	
1 cup	6 ounces (175g)
Candied cherries	
1 cup	4½ ounces (125g)
Nuts	
Almonds, whole and shelled	
1 cup	4 ounces (110g)
Almonds, slivered	
1 cup	4 ounces (110g)
Peanuts	
¾ cup	4 ounces (110g)
Hazelnuts	
1 heaped cup	5 ounces (150g)

Walnuts and pecans

1 cup	4 ounces (110g)

Chopped nuts

1 cup	4 ounces (110g)

Flour

1 cup	4 ounces (110g)

Cornstarch

1/4 cup	1 ounce (25g)

Oats

Rolled oats

1 cup	3½ ounces (100g)

Oatmeal

1 cup	6 ounces (175g)

Legumes, rice, and grains

Navy beans

1 cup	6½ ounces (190g)

Kidney beans

1 cup	7 ounces (200g)

Rice, uncooked

1 cup	7 ounces (200g)

Rice, cooked and drained

1 cup	4½ ounces (125g)

Semolina, ground rice, and couscous

1 cup	6 ounces (175g)

Split peas, lentils

1 heaped cup	8 ounces (225g)

Vegetables

Bean sprouts

1 cup	2 ounces (50g)

Cabbage, shredded

1½ cups	3 ounces (75g)

Onions, chopped

1 cup	4 ounces (110g)

Peas, shelled

1 heaped cup	5 ounces (150g)

Potatoes, peeled and diced

1 cup	5½ ounces (165g)

Potatoes, mashed

1 cup	8 ounces (225g)

Spinach, cooked purée

1 cup	7–8 ounces (200–225g)

Tomatoes, chopped

1 heaped cup	8 ounces (225g)

Fish

Fish, cooked and flaked

1 cup, packed	8 ounces (225g)

Shrimp, peeled

1 heaped cup	6 ounces (175g)

Refrigerator Storage

Meat, Poultry, and Fish

Raw meats

Cuts of meat	3 days
Bacon	7 days
Chicken	2 days
Fish	1 days
Ground meat	1 day
Variety Meats	1 day
Raw sliced meat	2 days
Sausages	3 days

Cooked Meats

Casseroles/Stews	2 days
Fish	1 day
Ham	2 days
Roasts	3 days
Sliced meat	2 days

Dairy produce

Cheese, hard	7–14 days
Cheese, soft	2–3 days
Eggs, raw	2 weeks
Eggs, hard-boiled	2 days
Milk	4–5 days

Miscellaneous

Canned foods	2 days*
Cooked vegetables	2 days
Cooked potatoes	2 days
Freshly squeezed fruit juice	1 day

* *Always transfer canned foods, once opened, into a clean, dry container with a lid.*

Freezer Storage

Meat and Poultry

Beef, lamb, pork, & veal	4–6 months
Chicken, turkey, & venison	10–12 months
Duck, goose, and rabbit	4–6 months
Cuts of ham and bacon	3–4 months
Ground beef	3–4 months
Variety Meats	3–4 months
Sausages and bulk sausage	2–3 months

Fish

Oily fish	3–4 months
Shellfish	2–3 months
White fish	6–8 months

Dairy Produce

Butter, unsalted (sweet)	6–8 months
Butter, salted	3–4 months
Cheese, hard	4-6 months
Cheese, soft	3–4 months
Cream	6–8 months
Ice cream	3–4 months
Milk, skim	3–4 months
Milk, lowfat	3–4 months

Fruit and Vegetables

Fruit juice	4–6 months
Fruit	8–10 months
Mushrooms & tomatoes	6–8 months
Most vegetables	10–12 months
Vegetable purées	6–8 months

Miscellaneous

Bread	2–3 months
Bread dough	2–3 months
Cakes	4–6 months

Highly seasoned dishes	2–3 months
Ready-prepared dishes	4–6 months

contact addresses

Mailorder firm selling Ballymaloe pickles and chutneys:
Jo Bewley
Bewley Irish Imports
1130 Greenhill Road
West Chester, PA 19380
USA
Tel: 610-696-2682
Fax: 610-344-7618
Email: jbewley@bewleyirishimports.com
Website: www.bewleyirishimports.com

Jane Murphy
Ardsallagh Goats Products Ltd.
Woodstock
Carrigtohill
County Cork
Ireland
Tel: + 353-21-488-2336
Fax: + 353-21-492545
Email: ardsallagh@hotmail.com

Bord Bia – Irish Food Board
Clanwilliam Court
Lower Mount Street
Dublin 2
Ireland
Tel: + 353-1-668-5155
Fax: + 353-1-668-7521
OR:
Tavistock Place
London
WC1H 9RA
England
Tel: + 44-20-7833-1351
Fax: + 44-20-7278-7193
Website: www.foodisland.com

The Bread Baker's Guild of America
3203 Maryland Avenue
North Versailles, PA 15137
USA
Tel: 412-322-8275
Fax: 412-322-3412
Email: bbguild@stargate.net
Website: www.bbga.org

Cáis
Irish Farmhouse Cheesemakers Association
C/o Cooleeney Farmhouse Cheese
Moyne
Thurles
County Tipperary
Ireland
Tel: + 353-504-45112
Fax: + 353-504-45450
Email: cooleeney@eircom.net

Clonakilty Black Pudding Co.
Baile an Aifreann
Clonakilty
County Cork
Ireland
Tel: + 353-23-433733
Fax: + 353-23-433664
Email: sales@clonakiltyblackpudding.ie
Website: www.clonakiltyblackpudding.ie

Dick Willems
Coolea Farmhouse Cheese
Coolea
Macroom
County Cork
Ireland
Tel: + 353-26-45204
Fax: + 353-26-45732
Email: cooleacheese@eircom.net

Euro-Toques International
(European Community of Chefs)
Website: www.euro-toques.org

Tom and Giana Ferguson
Fingal Ferguson (Bacon)
Gubbeen Farmhouse Products
Gubbeen House
Schull
County Cork
Ireland
Tel: + 353-28-28231
Fax: + 353-28-28231
Email: gubbeen@eircom.net
Website: www.westcorkweb.ie/gubbeen

Producers of Ballymaloe pickles and chutneys:
Yazi Hyde
Hyde Limited
Courtstown Industrial Estate
Little Island
County Cork
Ireland
Tel: + 353-21-4354810
Fax: + 353-21-4354811

IACP
(International Association of Culinary Professionals)
304 West Liberty Street, Suite 201
Louisville, Kentucky 40202-3011
USA
Tel: + 502-581-9786
Fax: + 502-589-3602
Email: iacp@hqtrs.com

Donal Creedon
Macroom Oatmeal Mills
Massytown
Macroom
County Cork
Ireland
Tel: + 353-26-41800
Fax: + 353-26-41800

Retail flour outlets for Odlums Flour
Mandys
830 Garrett Lane
Tooting
London
SW17 0NA
England
Tel: + 44-20-8767-9942

Mandys
161 High Road
Willesden
London
SW10 2SG
England
Tel: + 44-20-8459-2842

Bill Ramsell
Odlum Group Ltd.
Alexandra Road
Dublin 1
Ireland
Tel: + 353-1-888-7500
Fax: + 353-1-855-9295
Email: odlums@iol.ie
Website: www.odlums.ie

Slow Food
Slow Food International Office
Via della Mendicita Istruita 14
12042 Bra (CN)
Italy
Tel: + 39-172-411273
Fax: + 39-172-421293
Website: www.slowfood.com

Frank Hedderman
Smoked Foods
Belvelly Smoke House
County Cork
Ireland
Tel: + 353-21-481-1089
Fax: + 353-21-481-4323

Bill Casey
Smoked Salmon
Shanagarry
County Cork
Ireland
Tel: + 353-21-464-6955

Anthony Cresswell
Ummera Smoked Products
Inchybridge
Timoleague
County Cork
Ireland
Tel: + 353-23-46644
Fax: + 353-23-46419
Email: info@ummera.com
Website: www.ummera.com

glossary

(Br/Ir) = Britain/Ireland; (F) = France; (Ger) = Germany; (G) = Greece; (H) = Hungary; (In) = India; (I) = Italy; (R) = Russia; (S) Spain; (Sw) = Switzerland; (T) = Turkey.

Acidulated Water: Cold water with lemon juice or vinegar added to it to stop the discoloration of certain fruits and vegetables. Add 1 teaspoon of lemon juice or vinegar to every 1¼ cups water.

Agar agar: Vegetarian equivalent of gelatin, made from seaweed.

à l'anglaise (F): Served in an English style.

à la carte (F): 1. Menu from which the customer can choose dishes. 2. Dishes cooked to order.

à la crème (F): A dish accompanied by cream or cooked in a cream-based sauce.

Al dente (I): An Italian cooking term referring to perfectly cooked pasta that has a barely discernable bite.

Alla, à la (I/F): Phrase meaning "in the style of" a certain type of cooking.

Allumettes (F): Thin strips of vegetables.

Amandine (F): Cooking with or coating with almonds.

Antipasti, antipasto (I): Italian hors d'oeuvre served either hot or cold.

à point (F): Used to describe meat, medium cooked.

Arachide oil: peanut oil.

Arrowroot: Fine white starch, ground from the root of an American plant of the same name. Used to thicken sauces.
Aspic: A clear jelly made from the cooked juices of meat or fish.

Au gratin (F): Cooked food, covered with a sauce, breadcrumbs or grated cheese, and butter, then browned under the broiler.

Bain marie (F) or water bath: 1. A deep container, half-filled with hot water, in which delicate foods such as custards or fish mousses are cooked in their molds or terrines, which sit in the water bath to protect them from direct oven heat. Cooking in a bain marie in a low or moderate oven produces a gentle, steamy atmosphere which reduces the risk of curdling. 2. Container which holds several pans, used to keep food warm during restaurant service.

Barbados sugar: Soft dark brown sugar that has been treated with molasses.

Barbecue: Cooking on a grill over red hot coals, normally charcoal, or over wood. Apple or hickory chips can be added for flavor. To control the speed of cooking, food is placed either closer or further from the heat.

Barding: Wrapping meat, game, or poultry which is low in fat, with thin slices of bacon or pork fat to prevent the meat from drying out while roasting.

Basting: Spooning roasting juices over meat during cooking to moisten and add flavor.

Beating: Quickly stirring food, with either a wooden spoon, hand whisk, or electric mixer, to introduce air to make the food lighter or fluffier

Beurre noisette (F): The term for butter cooked to a hazelnut color. The foaming brown butter has a delicious nutty flavor.

Binding: The addition of eggs, cream, melted fat, or Roux, to a dry mixture to hold it together.

Blanching: Briefly boiling food 1. to loosen the skin from nuts, fruit, and vegetables; 2. to kill enzymes and set the color of food before freezing; 3. to remove strong or bitter flavors.

Blanquette (F): Poultry, veal, or rabbit stew in a creamy sauce.

Blender: An electronic mixer whose blades reduce ingredients to a smooth consistency.

Blending: Achieving a smooth consistency through the use of a spoon, beater, or blender.

Blini, Bliny (R): Buckwheat and yeast pancake traditionally served with caviar and sour cream.

Boiling: Cooking in liquid at a temperature of 212°F (100°C).

Boning: Removing the bones of meat, poultry, game, or fish.

Bouquet garni: A small bunch of fresh herbs used to flavor stews, casseroles, stocks, or soups, usually consisting of parsley stalks, a sprig of thyme, perhaps a bay leaf, and an outside stalk of celery. Remove before serving.

Bourguignonne (F): In the Burgundy style, i.e., cooked with red wine.

Braising: Browning in hot fat and then cooking slowly, in a covered pot with vegetables and some liquid.

Brine: Salt and water solution used in pickling and preserving.

Brioche (F): Slightly sweetened soft bread made of rich yeast dough.

Brochette (F): Skewer used for broiling chunks of meat, fish, and vegetables under a broiler, or over charcoal.

Broiling: Cooking food directly below (or directly above) the heat source.

Browning: Searing the outer surface of meat to seal in the juices.

Brulée (F): Describes a dish such as cream custards with a caramelized sugar glaze.

Butterfly: To slit a piece of food horizontally, almost but not quite through, so that when it is opened out it resembles butterfly wings. This technique is often applied to a leg of lamb, large shrimp, and thick fish fillets, so that they cook faster.

Canapé (F): Small tasty mouthful served as an appetizer.

Cannelloni (I): Large tubes of pasta which are then stuffed.

Capers: The unopened flower buds of a Mediterranean shrub, usually pickled and used as a garnish or flavoring.

Caponata (I): Sicilian dish of eggplants, celery, onions, tomatoes, capers, and black olives.

Carbonnade (F): Beef and beer stew.

Casserole (F): 1. Casserole dish: Cooking pot, with lid, made from ovenproof earthenware, glass, or metal. 2. Slow-cooked stew of fish, meat, or vegetables. 3. A mixture of noodles, pasta, or rice; beans, meat, or fish; bound together with a sauce and baked.

Cassoulet (F): Stew of navy beans, pork, lamb, goose or duck, sausage, vegetables, and herbs.

Chantilly (F): Whipped cream, slightly sweetened, and flavored with vanilla.

Charlotte: 1. Hot, molded fruit pudding made of buttered slices of bread, filled with fruit cooked with apricot jam. 2. Cold, molded dessert consisting of ladyfingers and filled with cream and fruit, or a cream custard set with gelatin. 3. A plain mold for Charlottes or other desserts.

Chiffonade (F): Shredded herbs or salad greens used as a garnish.

Chilling: Cooling food in a fridge, without freezing it.

Chining: The separation of ribs from the backbone to make carving a joint of meat easier.

Chinois (F): 1. In the Chinese style. 2. A conical-shaped sieve with a fine mesh.

Chorizo (S): Smoked pork sausage originally from Spain.

Clarified butter: Butter cleared of impurities and water by melting it slowly, and removing the salty skin with a spoon. The clear butter remaining is the clarified butter; discard the milky liquid at the bottom.

Clarifying: 1. Clearing fats by heating and filtering. 2. Clearing consommés and jellies with beaten egg white.

Cocotte (F): Small ovenproof dish used for baking individual egg dishes.

Coddling: Cooking slowly in simmering water, particularly of egg cookery.

Colander: Perforated metal or plastic bowl used to drain off liquids.

Compôte (F): Dessert of fresh or dried fruit, cooked in syrup and usually served cold.

Concassé (F): Roughly chopped, usually applies to the flesh of tomatoes.

Conserve: Fruit preserved by boiling with sugar, and is used like jam.

Coquille (F): 1. Scallop. 2. Shell-shaped ovenproof dish used to serve fish, poultry, or game.

Cornstarch ("Cornflour" in Br/Ir): Finely ground flour from cornmeal, used for thickening sauces or puddings.

Corn syrup: Syrup derived from maize used in baking and confectionery.

Coulis (F): A thin purée soft enough to pour, usually of vegetables or fruit.

Craisin: Dried cranberry.

Creamy milk: When one of our recipes calls for creamy milk, we mean a mixture of one-third cream to two-thirds milk, or even one quarter cream to three-quarters milk. Creamy milk is often used in soups or sauces when full cream would be too rich.

Crème (F): The term applied to fresh cream, butter, and thick creamy soups.

Crème Brulée (F): Cream custard with caramelized topping.

Crème Caramel (F): Cold molded egg custard with caramel topping, also known as "flan."

Crème Fraîche (F): Cream that has matured but not soured.

Creole: Cooked in Caribbean style.

Crêpe (F): Thin pancake.

Crêpes Suzette (F): Crêpes cooked in an orange sauce and flambéd in alcohol.

Croquettes (F): Cooked foods molded into small shapes, dipped in egg and crumbs, then deep-fried.

Croûstade (F): Small, crispy, fried or baked bread or pastry shape, filled with a savory mixture.

Croûtes (F): 1. Pastry covering meat, fish, and vegetables. 2. Slices of bread or brioche, spread with butter or sauce, then baked until crisp.

Crudités (F): Raw vegetables generally cut into bite-sized pieces or sticks, and served as an hors d'oeuvre or appetizer. One of several cold sauces or dips (e.g., aïoli, tapenade, or dukkah) are served to dip each morsel into before eating. For pinzimono, new-season vegetables are served simply with a bowl of new-season extra-virgin olive oil.

Curd: Semi-solid part of milk, produced by souring.

Curdle: The separation of different elements of a food. Cold emulsion sauces such as mayonnaise may curdle if oil is added too quickly. Acid, such as lemon juice, will curdle milk. A cake mixture can curdle if eggs are added too fast.

Cure: To preserve meat or fish by salting, smoking, or drying.

Dariole: Small, cup-shaped mold used for making jellies, puddings, and creams.

Daube (F): Stew of braised meat and vegetables.

Deep-frying: Frying food by submerging it in hot oil.

De-glaze: Adding wine, cream, or stock to dilute pan juices and make gravy.

De-gorge: Sprinkling vegetables, such as cucumber or eggplant, with salt to draw out juices or excess moisture.

De-grease: To remove grease from the surface of liquid. If possible, the liquid should be chilled so that the fat solidifies. Otherwise, skim off the fat with a large metal spoon, then trail strips of paper towel on the surface to remove the remaining globules.

Dice: Cut into small cubes.

Dough: Mixture of flour, water, milk and/or egg, sometimes enriched with fat, which is firm enough to knead, roll, and shape.

Drawing: To remove the intestines from poultry.

Dredging: Sprinkling sugar or flour over food.

Dress: To pluck, draw, and truss poultry or game.

Dressing: 1. Sauce for a salad. 2. Stuffing for meat or poultry.

Dripping: Fat that drips from meat, poultry, or game during roasting.

Dusting: Sprinkling lightly with flour, sugar, spice, or seasoning.

Éclair (F): Cigar-shaped choux pastry bun filled with whipped cream and topped with chocolate.

Egg wash: A raw egg beaten (with a pinch of salt if for savory foods) and brushed onto raw tarts, pies, buns, and biscuits, to produce a shiny, golden glaze when cooked.

Emulsion: A mixture of two insoluble liquids, e.g., oil and water.

En croûte (F): Food encased in pastry.

En papillote (F): Food wrapped, cooked, and served in oiled or buttered paper or foil, to prevent loss of flavor and to conserve moisture.

Entreé (F): Main course.

Escalope: A thin slice of meat, beaten flat and shallow-fried.

Estoufado (G): 1. Greek cooking pot 2. Greek stew typically containing chicken or rabbit, onions, and cinnamon.

Fermentation: Chemical action caused by enzymes. Intentional effervescence occurs when yeast is used to raise bread; accidental effervescence occurs in preserves or pickles that ferment when incorrectly prepared.

Fines herbes (F): A finely chopped mixture of fresh parsley, chervil, tarragon, and chives. Traditionally used in French cooking.

Flake: 1. Separating cooked fish into individual flaky slivers. 2. Grating chocolate or cheese into small slivers.

Flambé: Food flamed in a pan using burning brandy or other alcohol.

Florentine: 1. Of fish and eggs, served on a bed of buttered spinach and coated with a cheese sauce. 2. Thin petit-four biscuit made of nuts, candied fruit, and chocolate.

Foie gras (F): The preserved liver of specially fattened goose or duck.

Folding in: Using a large metal spoon or spatula to mix one ingredient or mixture into another, very gently, so as not to knock out the air.

Fondue (Sw): Melted cheese and white wine dish into which diners dunk cubes of bread. Chocolate Fondue and Fondue Bourgignonne are other versions.

Fool (Br/Ir): Cold dessert of fruit purée and whipped cream.

Freezing: Solidifying or preserving food by chilling it and storing at 0°F (-18°C).

Fricassée (F): White stew of chicken, rabbit, veal, or vegetables fried in butter, then cooked in stock and finished with cream and egg yolks.

Fromage blanc (F): A fresh cheese that has undergone lactic fermentation, i.e., made simply by separating the curds from the whey. The curds are drained and may be shaped into a mold or served simply in a bowl and flavored with fresh herbs or honey.

Fromage frais (F): Soft curd cheese with a rich taste even though it is fat-free. Its velvety texture is achieved by forcing the curds and whey through fine nozzles to homogenize the mixture and eliminate grittiness.

Frost: 1. To coat a cake with sugar icing or frosting. 2. To dip the rim of a glass in egg white and superfine sugar and then chill in a refrigerator until set.

Fumet (F): Concentrated broth or stock made from fish, meat, or vegetables.

Galette (F): 1. A flat pastry cake. 2. A flat potato cake either mashed or sliced.

Gâteau: French gâteau were originally flat, round cakes made with flour and water and gradually enriched with butter, eggs, honey, spices, cream, and, of course, sugar. Nowadays the word "gâteau" usually denotes a delicious cake embellished with lots of rich icing and often elaborate decoration.

Gelatin: Transparent protein derived from animal tissue and bones, which melts when hot and forms a jelly on cooling. *Agar agar* is the vegetarian equivalent.

Genoise (F): A rich sponge cake made from eggs, sugar, flour, and melted butter, then baked in a pan with sloping sides.

Ghee (In): Clarified butter made from the milk of the water buffalo originating in India.

Giblets: Edible internal organs of poultry and game including the liver, heart, and gizzard.

Gill: Liquid measure equivalent to a British 1/4 pint (5 fl. oz.) or roughly 2/3 US cup.

Gizzard: The muscular stomach of a bird in which their food is ground up.

Glacé: (F) Glazed, iced, or frozen.

Glacé de viande (F): 1. Meat glaze or residue in the bottom of a pan after frying or roasting meat. 2. Concentrated meat stock.

Glaze: Brushing food with milk, beaten egg, sugar syrup, or jelly after cooking to produce a glossy finish.

Gluten: A protein in flour that is developed when dough is kneaded, making it elastic.

Gnocchi (I): Small dumplings made from semolina, potatoes, or choux pastry.

Goujon (F): A term now used for little strips of fish or meat, about the size of a small fish called a gudgeon.

Goulash (H): Beef and onion stew flavored with tomato and paprika.

Granita (I): Ice made with sugar and flavoring.

Gravy: 1. Juices drained from roasted meat and poultry. 2. A sauce derived from these juices made by boiling up with either stock or wine, and often thickened with flour.

Griddle: A flat metal plate used for baking cakes and breads on top of the stove.

Grill pan: A heavy cast iron pan, with a ridged bottom, either round or rectangular. The ridges mark the food attractively while keeping the meat or fish from direct contact with the fat. A heavy pan gives a good even heat.

Grissini (I): Breadsticks.

Groats: Husked, often milled grain, especially oats.

Hanging: Suspending meat or game in a cool, dry place until it becomes tender.

Haricot vert (F): Green bean.

Hash: Dish of leftover chopped meat, potatoes, or other vegetables, fried together.

Herbs: Plants without a fibrous stem, used to add flavor when cooking.

Hors d'oeuvre (F): Hot or cold appetizer served at the beginning of a meal.

Hulling: Removing the green stems from strawberries, raspberries, etc.

Icing: Sweet coating for cakes.

Infusing: Steeping herbs, tea leaves, or coffee in water or other liquid to extract the flavor.

Irish coffee: Coffee with a shot of whiskey and a topping of thick cream.

Jaggery (Palm sugar): Brown unrefined lump sugar made from cane sugar or palm sap.

Jugged (Br/Ir): Meat dishes stewed in a covered pot, for example jugged hare.

Julienne (F): A term used when vegetables or citrus fruit rinds are cut into very fine, thin matchsticks or "needle-shreds." A recipe will sometimes indicate the size required. Generally a julienne of vegetables or citrus fruits is used as a garnish, but sometimes a much larger julienne may be used as a vegetable or as part of a salad.

Junket: Dessert made with sweetened flavored milk that's curdled with rennet and sets to a smooth consistency.

Jus (F): Juices from roasting meat used as gravy.

Kabob (T): Meat cubes marinated and grilled on a skewer with vegetables.

Kedgeree (In): Dish of cooked meat or fish, rice and eggs, often eaten for breakfast or lunch.

Kosher: Food prepared in accordance with Orthodox Jewish Law.

Ladyfingers: Thin, finger-shaped spongecake, with a sprinkling of sugar.

Langouste (F): Clawless crawfish, almost lobster size, found in warm coastal waters.

Langue de chat (F): Flat finger-shaped crisp cookies served with cold desserts, called cats' tongue cookies in the US.

Lard: Purifed pork fat used in deep-frying, roasting meats, and in pastry making.

Larding: Threading strips of fat through lean meat using a specially designed needle, to prevent meat that is naturally low in fat from drying out when roasting.

Lasagne (I): Square or rectangular sheets of fresh or dried pasta that form the base of the Italian dish of the same name.

Leavening agent: Ingredients such as yeast which cause dough to rise.

Legumes (F): 1. Vegetables. 2. Plants with a seed pod such as peas and beans.

Lentils: Seeds of a legume, soaked and used in soups, stews, and purees.

Liaison (F): Mixture used to thicken a sauce or stew, e.g., egg yolks and cream may be mixed together before being used to thicken a meat stew.

Lyonnaise (F): In the Lyons style, usually with onions.

Macaroni (I): Short hollow tubes of pasta.

Macerate: To soak fruit or vegetables in syrup or other liquid so that it will absorb flavor and/or become more tender.

Mandoline: A kitchen implement made of stainless steel or wood, with adjustable blades used for slicing vegetables into various shapes.

Marinade: Blend of oil, wine or vinegar, herbs, and spices, used to add flavor to meat.

Marinate: To steep in marinade.

Marinière (F): 1. Mussels cooked in a white wine and vinegar sauce, then served half open. 2. Fish cooked in white wine and then garnished with mussels.

Marrons glacés (F): Confections first created during the reign of Louis XIV, and made only from marrons chestnuts. They are cooked gently and slowly in syrup, packed into doileys, and can be enjoyed as a dessert, or used in ice cream, or semi-freddo.

Medallions (F): Small circular cuts of meat, fish, and pâté.

Meringue (F): Whisked egg white blended with sugar, spooned or piped on top of sweet pies or into shapes and then baked at a very low temperature until crisp.

Meunière (F): Fish cooked in butter, seasoned, and then sprinkled with parsley and lemon juice.

Milanese (I): In the Milan style, escalopes coated in egg, breadcrumbs seasoned with grated Parmesan cheese, and then fried in butter.

Mirabelle (F): 1. Small yellow plum, used in a tart filling. 2. A liqueur made from the fruit.

Mirepoix (F): Mixture of finely diced vegetables and ham which, when fried in butter, is used as a base for brown sauces or stews.

Mocha: 1. High quality coffee served after dinner. 2. A blend of coffee and chocolate.

Mouler (F): To grind soft food into a purée, or dry food into a powder.

Moules (F): Mussels.

Moussaka (G): Middle-eastern dish of eggplant, ground lamb, and tomatoes, topped with cheese sauce or savory custard.

Mousse: Light cold dish, either sweet or savory, whose ingredients may include cream, whipped egg white, and gelatin.

Muesli (Sw): Dish of uncooked rolled oats, coarsely grated apple, nuts, and dried fruit, served with milk or yoghurt. Now generally used to describe nut and grain breakfast cereal.

Navarin (F): Stew of lamb and vegetables.

Neapolitan (I): 1. In the style of Naples. 2. Ice creams and sweet cakes in colorful layers of flavor.

Niçoise (F): In the style of Nice, i.e., cooked with tomatoes, onion, garlic, and black olives.

Noodles: Flat ribbon pasta made from water, flour, and, sometimes, egg.

Normande, à la (F): In the Normandy style, i.e., cooked with cider and cream.

Nouilles (F): Noodles.

Oil glands: All young game birds have a small blind-ended passage opening on the upper side of the vent. This passage is generally known as the Bursa and is believed to play some part in disease control.

Orzo (I): A small pasta grain resembling rice in appearance, which may be used in a variety of dishes, hot and cold.

Osso buco (I): Dish of braised marrow bones prepared with tomatoes and wine.

Oyster meat: In poultry, these are the two succulent ovals of meat along both sides of the backbone, level with the thigh.

Paella (S): A traditional Spanish dish of saffron rice, chicken or shellfish, named after the traditional pan in which it is cooked.

Palette knife: A blunt knife with a rounded tip and flexible blade useful for spreading meringue etc.

Paneer (In): A fresh cheese curd.

Panettone (I): Cake-like bread containing raisins, served at Christmas.

Panko crumbs: Japanese breadcrumbs.

Paper lid: When we are sweating vegetables for the base of a soup or stew, we quite often cover them with a butter wrapper or a lid made from wax paper, which fits the saucepan exactly. This keeps in the steam and helps to sweat the vegetables.

Paprika (H): Ground, sometimes hot, sweet red pepper, either natural or smoked.

Par-boiling: Boiling for a short while to partially cook food.

Parfait (F): Frozen dessert made from whipped cream and fruit purée.

Parmentier (F): Used to describe dishes containing potatoes.

Pasteurizing: Method of sterilizing milk by heating it to 140–180°F (60–82°C) to destroy the bacteria.

Pastry: Dough made with flour, butter, and water, then baked or deep-fried until crisp.

Pastry wheel: Small, serrated metal wheel for cutting or fluting pastry.

Pasty (Br/Ir): Small pastry pie with a savory filling. Pasty is pronounced with a short "a", like the world "past".

Pâte (F): Pastry or dough.

Pâté (F): Smooth or coarse savory mixture; the latter is baked in a terrine or a pastry covering. It is occasionally served warm but usually cold.

Peanut: Groundnut, eaten roasted or plain. Can be used to make peanut butter and peanut oil (see *Arachide*).

Pearl barley (Br/Ir): Husked barley grains, used in soup.

Pectin: Gelling agent that occurs naturally in fruit and vegetables. Sets jellies and jams.

Percolator: A coffeepot in which boiling water is forced repeatedly up through a center tube and filtered through ground coffee.

Perdrix (F): Partridge.

Petits Fours (F): 1. A catch-all word for dainty little sweetmeats usually served at the end of a meal with coffee or occasionally at the end of a drinks party with dessert wine.

Petit Pois (F): Tiny young green peas.

Pickle (verb): To preserve meat or vegetables in a brine or vinegar solution.

Pilaf, pilau (T): Middle-Eastern dish of cooked rice mixed with spiced, cooked chicken, meat, or fish.

Pimiento, pimento: Green or red pepper.

Pipe: To decorate various dishes by forcing mashed potato, meringue, icing, or savory butter through a pastry bag fitted with a nozzle.

Piquant (F): Hot, pungent, and appetizing.

Pith: The white lining that attaches the rind to the fruit in citrus fruits.

Pizzaiola (I): Meat or chicken cooked in red wine and tomato sauce, and flavored with garlic.

Plastic wrap ("Cling film" in Br/Ir): Used for sealing food from the air. Use "pure" plastic wrap. Plastic wrap containing PVC is considered harmful in contact with food.

Plat du Jour (F): Dish of the day.

Pluck: To remove feathers from a dead bird.

Poaching: Cooking food in simmering liquid, just below boiling.

Polenta (I): Cornmeal, made from dried and ground corn.

Potage (F): Thick soup.

Praline (F): Candy consisting of unblanched almonds, caramelized in boiling sugar.

Preserving: Keeping food in good condition by boiling in sugar, pickling in salt, refrigerating, or using chemicals.

Pressure cooking: A method of cooking at specific levels of pressure. The higher the pressure, the higher the temperature at which water boils. Cooking food with liquid in this fashion means that the steam created by the liquid is sealed in under increasing pressure, cooking the food in less time than conventional methods of steaming.

Prosciutto (I): Raw smoked ham, served finely sliced, e.g., Parma, Serrano, Pate negra.

Provençal (F): In the style of Provence, i.e., cooked with garlic and tomatoes.

Pudding (Br/Ir): 1. Boiled or baked sweet dessert. 2. Boiled suet crust which is filled with meat, poultry, or fruit. 3. A catch-all word for desserts. 4. (US): A creamy sweet dessert, e.g., chocolate pudding.

Pulp: 1. Soft, fleshy tissue of fruit or vegetables. 2. To reduce food to a soft mass by crushing or boiling.

Purée (F): 1. Sieved raw or cooked food. 2. Thick vegetable soup blended in a blender or food processor. 3. (verb). The act of blending finely.

Quenelles: (F) Light savory dumpling, either meat or fish, used as a garnish.

Quiche (F): Open pastry tart filled with a savory mixture.

Ragoût (F): Stew of meat and vegetables.

Ramekins: Individual ovenproof dishes.

Ratafia: 1. Flavoring made from bitter almonds. 2. Liqueur made from fruit kernels. 3. Tiny maracoon.

Ratatouille (F): Mediterranean stew made from eggplant, onions, peppers, and tomatoes, cooked in olive oil.

Ravioli (I): Small savory-filled pasta pillows, boiled and served with a flavored butter, sauce, or grated cheese.

Reducing: Concentrating a liquid by boiling and evaporating excess liquid.

Refreshing: Cooling hot food quickly, often vegetables or shellfish, either by placing it under cold running water or by plunging it into iced water, thus stopping it cooking and setting the color.

Relish: Sharp or spicy sauce made with vegetables or fruit which adds a piquant flavor to other dishes, usually served as an accompaniment.

Rendering: 1. Slow cooking of meat tissues and trimmings to obtain fat.

Rennet: Extract from the stomach lining of calves used as a coagulating agent in the production of cheese curd.

Rice paper: Glossy white edible paper made from the pith of the tree grown in China.

Rigatoni (I): Ridged macaroni.

Rillettes (F): An item of French charcuterie which is normally made of pork but can also be made of duck, rabbit, or other meat.

Risotto (I): Savory rice, fried and then cooked in stock or tomato juice, then finished with cheese.

Rissole: Small roll or patty made from cooked ground meat.

Roasting: Cooking in the oven with radiant heat, or on a spit over an open flame.

Roe: 1. Milt of the male fish known as soft roe. 2. Eggs of the female fish known as hard roe. 3. Shellfish roe, known as coral because of its color when cooked.

Rôtisserie (F): Rotating spit used for roasting or grilling meat or poultry.

Roulade (F): A savory roll of meat or rolled dessert, as in rolled chocolate cake or meringue.

Roux (F): A mixture of equal parts of butter and flour, this is a basic *liaison* which is used as a thickening agent.

Saganaki (G): Small round aluminum frying pan used to fry and serve piping hot cheese.

Saignant (F): Of meat; underdone.

Salamander: Small round piece of iron on long handle. When heated it is used, for example, to caramelize sugar on crème brûlées.

Salami (I): Spiced meat sausage, sold fresh or smoked.

Sauté (F:) To fry food rapidly in hot fat.

Scald: 1. To heat milk or cream to just below boiling point. 2. To plunge fruit or vegetables in boiling water to remove their skins.

Scallion: Young onion or spring onion with an undeveloped bulb used either in salads or as a garnish. Also called "green onion."

Scallop: Edible mollusc with white flesh and orange roe or coral. The fluted, deep shell is used for serving the scallops and other foods.

Scaloppini (I): Small escalopes of veal, weighing approximately 1½ ounces (40g) and measuring about 3 inches (7.5cm) square.

Schnitzel (Ger): Veal slice; see escalope.

Scoring: 1. Cutting gashes in the surface of food. 2. Making a pattern of squares or diamonds on pie crust.

Searing: Browning meat rapidly over a high heat to seal in the juices.

Semi-freddo (I): A frozen ice cream that includes stiffly beaten egg whites. The egg white hampers the freezing process so the dessert never freezes solid. Semi-freddo often includes added ingredients such as cookies, meringue, praline, or crystallized fruits.

Sifting: Passing flour or sugar through a sifter to aerate and remove lumps.

Silver dragee: Edible silver balls used for decoration on cakes and petits fours.

Simmering: Cooking in liquid just below boiling point.

Singe: To quickly flame duck or geese to remove all traces of feathers and down after plucking.

Skewer: Metal or wooden pin that holds meat or fish together when cooking.

Skimming: Removing cream from the surface of milk, or fat or scum from jam or broth.

Smoking: Curing food, such as fish or bacon, by exposing it to warm or cold wood smoke over a period of time.

Sorbet (F): Sweet ice made with fruit juice or purée and similar to sherbet.

Soufflé (F): Baked dish consisting of a sauce or purée thickened with egg yolks, into which stiffly beaten egg whites are folded.

Soufflé dish: Straight-sided circular dish used for cooking and serving souffles.

Sousing: Pickling food in brine or vinegar.

Spaghetti (I): Solid, thin strands of pasta.

Spit: Revolving skewer on which meat, poultry, or game is roasted or grilled.

Spring-form mold: Baking pan with hinged sides that release the cake or pie when opened.

Sponge, to: A term used when working with powdered gelatin. The gelatin is sprinkled over a specified amount of liquid and left to sit for 4–5 minutes. During this period, the gelatin soaks up the water and becomes "spongy" in texture – hence the term. Gelatin is easier to dissolve if it is sponged before melting.

Starch: Carbohydrate obtained from cereal or potatoes.

Steaming: Cooking food in a tightly sealed container over boiling water.

Steeping: 1. Soaking in liquid until saturated with a soluble ingredient. 2. Soaking meat in water to remove excess salt. 3. Soaking dry ingredients in liquid until the liquid is infused with their flavor.

Sterilizing: Eliminating bacteria by heating food to a high temperature.

Stewing: Cooking food slowly in a covered pan or casserole dish.

Stir-frying: Cooking small pieces of food rapidly in very little fat, tossing constantly over high heat, usually in a wok.

Stirring: Mixing with a circular movement using a fork or spoon.

Straining: Separating liquids from solids by passing them through cheesecloth or a nylon sieve.

Strudel (A): Thin leaves of pastry dough, filled with fruit or savory mixtures, rolled and then baked.

Stuffing: A flavorful savory mixture of bread or rice, herbs, fruit or minced meat used to fill fish, meat, poultry, and vegetables.

Suet: Fat around beef or lamb kidneys.

Sumac: A coarse brick-red powder used in Mediterranean or Middle Eastern cooking to give a citrus lift to salads, flatbreads, fish, and meats.

Sweat: To cook vegetables in a little fat or oil over gentle heat in a covered saucepan, until they are almost soft but not colored.

Syrup: A sweet liquid made by boiling sugar with water or fruit juice.

Table d'hôte (F): Meal of three or more courses at a fixed price.

Tagine: 1. shallow, round, earthenware, glazed pot with a tall conical lid that traps steam during cooking and prevents stews from drying out. 2. Moroccan-style stew cooked in tagine pot.

Tagliatelle (I): Thin flat egg noodles.

Terrine (F): 1. Earthenware pot used for serving and cooking pâté. 2. Coarse pâté.

Timbale (F): 1. Cup-shaped earthenware or metal mold. 2. Dish prepared in such a mold.

Truffles: Expensive delicacies, these rare mushroom-like fungus are black or white in color and have a delicate taste.

Trussing: Tying a bird or joint of meat in a neat shape with skewers and string before cooking.

Turnover: Sweet or savory pastry made by folding a circle or square of pastry dough in half to form a semicircle or triangle.

Unleavened Bread: Bread made without a raising agent, which when baked is thin, and flattish, also referred to as flatbreads.

Unsweetened chocolate: Chocolate with no sugar added, also called bitter chocolate.

Vanilla Sugar: Sugar flavored with vanilla by storing it with a vanilla bean in a closed jar, or combining it with a vanilla bean.

Variety Meats: Edible internal organs of meat, poultry, and game.

Velouté (F): 1. Basic white sauce made with veal, chicken, or fish stock. 2. Soup of creamy consistency.

Vermicelli (I): Very thin strands of pasta.

Vinaigrette (F): Mixture of oil, vinegar, salt, and pepper, often flavored with herbs.

Vinegar: A clear acidic liquid obtained by fermenting wine, cider, or malt beer.

Vol-au-vent (F): Light flaky pastry shell of puff pastry.

Wafer: Wafer-thin cookie made of rice flour, served with ice cream.

Waffle: Batter cooked on a hot greased waffle iron until crisp.

Wax paper: A non-stick parchment paper which is widely used for lining baking trays, cake pans, etc. It may be used several times over and is particularly useful when making meringues or chocolates, because they simply peel off the paper.

Wheat germ: The living germ or "embryo" of the wheat grain. Usually extracted from the grain during milling because it is more perishable than the rest of the grain. It is high in nutritional value and may be eaten on its own or added to cereals or breads. It should be bought in small quantities and stored in the fridge.

Whey: Liquid separated from curd when milk curdles and used in cheese making.

Whisk: Looped wire utensil used for beating air into cream, eggs, or batters.

Xanthan gum: A natural product produced by fermenting sugar using a natural bacteria, Xanthamonas campestris. It is classified as a stablizer.

Yeast: Fungus cells used for producing alcoholic fermentation, or as a rising agent in dough.

Yogurt: Curdled milk that has been treated with harmless bacteria.

Zabaglione (I): Dessert made from egg yolks, white wine or marsala, and sugar, whisked together in the top of a double boiler over boiling water until thick and foamy.

Zest (F): Colored oily outer skin of citrus fruit, which can be grated with a zester to add flavor to food or liquid.

index

A

D

E

F

G

M

N

O

P

Q

R

S

U

V

W

Y

Z

Originally published in 2001 in the United Kingdom by Kyle Cathie Limited

Published by arrangement in North America by Pelican Publishing Company, Inc., 2002

Editors: Kyle Cathie, Stephanie Horner, Helen Woodhall, and Sheila Davies
Design and Art Direction: Geoff Hayes
Photography: Ray Main, assisted by Owen Gale and Sophie Munro
Copy Editor: Elaine Koster
Home Economist: Janie Suthering
Production: Lorraine Baird & Sha Huxtable
Index: Alex Corrin
Repro: Scanhouse Singapore

Printed in Singapore
Published by Pelican Publishing Company, Inc.
1000 Burmaster Street, Gretna, Louisiana 70053

Publisher's acknowledgements
Many people helped make this book. In the early stages editorially, Mary Dowey shaped the project. Grateful thanks go to Katie Joll, Esme West, Marion Dooley, Thomas ap Simon, Nicholas ap Simon and Joey ap Simon. Ray Main was assisted by Owen Gale and Sophie Munro.

We would like to thank *Le Creuset* for their generous contribution of props.